INVESTMENT MANAGEMENT

Dr. V.A. AVADHANI

M.A. Ph.D., (USA), M.A., LLB., CAIIB.

(Retired Adviser in RBI & Former Director of Training Institute in Bombay Stock Exchange, Former Adviser to HSE.)

ISO 9001:2015 CERTIFIED

First Edition : 1996
Edition : 1996
Second Revised Edition : 1997
Third Revised Edition : 1999
Fourth Revised Edition : 2000
Fifth Revised Edition : 2002
Sixth Revised Edition : 2006
Seventh Revised Edition : 2008
Edition : 2009
Eighth Revised Edition : 2011
Edition : 2014, 2017, 2018, 2019
Edition : 2022
Edition : 2025

Published by : Mrs. Meena Pandey
for **HIMALAYA PUBLISHING HOUSE PVT. LTD.,**
Ramdoot, Dr. Bhalerao Marg, Girgaon, Mumbai - 400 004
Phone: 022-23860170/23863863; **Fax:** 022-23877178
E-mail: himpub@bharatmail.co.in; **Website:** www.himpub.com

Branch Offices :

New Delhi : Pooja Apartments, 4-B, Murari Lal Street, Ansari Road, Darya Ganj, New Delhi - 110 002. Phone: 011-23270392, 23278631; Fax: 011-23256286

Nagpur : Kundanlal Chandak Industrial Estate, Ghat Road, Nagpur - 440 018. Mobile: 09325409992, 09325908881

Bengaluru : Plot No. 91-33, 2nd Main Road, Seshadripuram, Behind Nataraja Theatre, Bengaluru - 560 020. Phone: 080-41138821; Mobile: 09379847017, 09379847005

Hyderabad : No. 3-4-184, Lingampally, Besides Raghavendra Swamy Matham, Kachiguda, Hyderabad - 500 027. Phone: 040-27560041, 27550139

Chennai : No. 34/44, Motilal Street, T. Nagar, Chennai - 600 017. Mobile: 09380460419

Pune : First Floor, Laksha Apartment, No. 527, Mehunpura, Shaniwarpeth (Near Prabhat Theatre), Pune - 411 030. Phone: 020-24496323, 24496333; Mobile: 09370579333

Cuttack : Plot No. 5F-755/4, Sector-9, CDA Markat Nagar, Cuttack - 753 014, Odisha. Mobile: 09338746007

Kolkata : 3, S.M. Bose Road, Near Gate No. 5, Agarpara Railway Station, North 24 Parganas, West Bengal - 700 109. Mobile: 09674536325

DTP by : Prasad (Nagpur)

Printed at : Geetanjali Press Pvt. Ltd., Nagpur. On behalf of HPH

PREFACE TO THE EIGHTH REVISED EDITION

The theory and principles of Investment Management remain unaltered but the backdrop of the operations of investment and the practices and procedures of invesment management change from time to time. The financial markets in which most of the operations take place are a reflection of the economy and its performance. The economic and financial reforms in India are a continuing process and these affect the operations in the financial markets. The changes are to be incorporated in any revision of a book of this nature, which is being used by students of finance whether in MBA or M.com. or any other professional course. This is the rationale of the present revision, which hopefully helps the student update the information relevant to the area.

During the recent past and in the present decade from 1999 to 2009, the GDP growth was at a rate of about 8% higher than ever before, with the latest year 2006-7 showing a growth of 9.2%. Nearly 60% of this growth is due to services sector which includes the financial services like banking, insurance, stock broking etc. The financial structure and institutional framework is being stengthened and banking and e-commerce are the highlights of the recent past. Stock and capital markets are booming reflecting the strong economic fundaments and good corporate performance. Foreign funds inflow is increasing particularly during the period 2004 to 2008 when the BSE Sensex has reached a peak of 21,207 in January 2008 and after a low of 7,697 in October 2008, firmed up again to a high of 18,048 in April 2010 and is around 17,000 in May 2010. Globalization trends are perceptible in all spheres of the economy and particulary in the financial markets. These trends along with privatization of the enterprise gave a new boost to the economy and financial markets. The global recession 2008-09 had its impact along with the financial turmoil in Euro-markets due to debt crisis in Greece on the Indian markets.

The strong points in the economy are the good monsoons and rapid growth of the manufacturing sector, control of inflation and larger inflow foreign direct and portfolio investments and good buffer of forex reserves. Although the inflation rate reached a level of 10% at one stage, it is being controlled through monetary and fiscal measures. While equity market is bullish, the corporate debt market is being developed by the SEBI and the Goverment Debt market by the RBI. FDI inflows are being encouraged through the policy changes reducing the red tapism, and Govt. regulations, increase in limits for Foreign investments in selected sectors and rise in the ECB limits.

The Eleventh Plan aims at accelerating the growth of agriculture to 4% and increasing the GDP growth rate to 10% for which all necessary inputs are being planned. In the fiscal field, the fiscal deficit is being kept low; subsidies are being rationalized and fiscal prudence is being observed. In the monetary and credit field, flexibility in interest rate policy and frequent use of repo rate and CRR has curbed the growth of money supply beyond the required level. CRR was raised many times from 4.5% in 2003 to 7.75% in Jan. 2008 but it stood at 6% in April 2010. Greater autonomy is given to banks in their risk management, credit policy and interest rate policy. The RBI has been curbing the excess liquidity due to foreign inflow and foreign investment and credit creation by the banks through plastic money etc.

The call money rates are around the repo and reverse repo rates. Due to the recession in our economy, following the global recession 2009-10, The Reverse Repo was raised to 3.75% and Repo rate to 5.25%. The monetary policy was antiinflationary. While the Rupee is getting strengthened against dollar in the forex market, the RBI. is thinking of allowing the currency futures in the markets. Derivative markets in stock index and a equities are having a larger turnover than in the cash market, reflecting the larger operations of foreign FIs and MFs etc. The RBI is also allowing the rupee to find its own level but is keeping watch on the inflationary expectations.

It is in this context that the present book is revised to bring out the impact of these changes and to update the figures and data used in the text. In this task, I acknowledge with thanks the suggestions of the teaching colleages and the co-operation of the Himalaya Publishing House.

— DR. V. A. AVADHANI

PREFACE TO THE FIRST EDITION

This book on **Investment Management** is intended as a textbook for the students of M.Com. and M.B.A. Courses in Finance. Admittedly, there are many books on Finance Management and Investment Management, but what made me write this book is that it covers the syllabus of many Universities for M.Com. and M.B.A. courses, specially designed to help the students with simple presentation, practical illustrations and in the Indian background. With my experience of 32 years in the Reserve Bank of India in economic and financial research, and nearly six years of research and training experience in the Bombay Stock Exchange and Hyderabad Stock Exchange, and teaching the subjects of Finance and Investment in many management institutes, including I.I.M. Calcutta, my background is down to earth practical and my approach is teaching for job orientation. I have trained many sub-brokers to become brokers and hundreds of investors to become wise investors, which all helped me to make theory useful for practical applications.

Many professors whom I know have encouraged me to venture into this useful service to the students by presenting the subjects in a practical manner and with an Indian background. In particular, I kept the syllabus for M.Com. and M.B.A. courses of the Osmania University, Andhra University, Kakatiya University and Madras University, among others, before me when I wrote the book. Shri D.P. Pandey of the Himalaya Publishing House has been constantly helping me and giving all encouragement during the course of my writing this book. Any suggestions for improvement may be sent to him and I shall incorporate such suggestions, in the next edition.

This book is structured in a manner to be very comprehensive and sweepingly wide so as to accommodate the syllabus of almost all universities, to the extent possible. This book has the mission of serving the student community, in the areas of Commerce, Finance and Management.

This book is meant to be highly practical with Indian bias but incorporates the theoretical inputs necessary to satisfy the components of the syllabus of M.Com. and M.B.A., and the practical needs for job orientation of students, in Indian Finance and Investment Companies, Mutual Funds, Merchant Banks, Stock Broker Firms etc.

The scheme of the book is divided into six parts: *Part I* presents the Investment setting and include chapters such as Securities Markets, Savings and Investment Avenues, Tax Planning, Growth Process of the Economy and Financial System in India. *Part II* deals with Financial Markets and Institutions setting out the details of the New Issues Market, Stock Market, Money Market and Regulations, Trading and Operations in them. *Part III* sets out the Process of Investment Decision Making. It contains the sources of Information, Inflation, Security Market Analysis, Financial Analysis, Fundamental and Technical Analysis. *Part IV* discusses the Risk: Return Concepts, including Financial Arithmetic, Credit Rating, Market Indicators, Interest Rate Theories and Structure. *Part V* sets out the Valuation of Stocks and Bonds, Security Pricing, Valuation of Bonds, Stock Valuation Theorems, Valuation of Contingent Claims, Valuation of Options etc. *Part VI* deals with the Portfolio Management, Diversification, Risk and Return Analysis, Modern Portfolio Theory, Portfolio Construction, Revision, Monitoring and Evaluation and ends up with a brief treatment of the Mutual Funds and their Schemes.

I will be failing in my duty if I do not acknowledge the help of Shri D. P. Pandey in writing this book. I also owe a deep sense of gratitude to my parents who instilled in me the spirit of service to the community, in the faculty that God has given me.

— Dr. V. A. AVADHANI

BRIEF CONTENTS

PART – I

INVESTMENT SETTING

1. Securities Markets 3 - 14
2. Savings and Investment 15 - 18
3. Macro Aspects of Savings and Investments 19 - 25
4. Financial System — Intermediation 26 - 35
5. Investment Avenues 36 - 41
6. Features of Investment Avenues 42 - 52
7. Tax Planning for Investment 53 - 61

PART – II

MONEY AND CAPITAL MARKETS AND INSTITUTIONS

8. Overview of Capital Market 65 - 71
9. Institutional Structure in Capital Market 72 - 83
10. Capital Market Reforms 84 - 98
11. New Issues Market and Problems 99 - 110
12. Money Market and its Instruments 111 - 121
13. The Securities and Exchange Board of India (SEBI) 122 - 134

PART – III

SECONDARY MARKETS IN INDIA

14. Securities Trading Regulations 137 - 140
15. Instruments of Issue and Trading 141 - 153
16. Stock Markets in India 154 - 164
17. OTCEI, NSE and ICSE 165 - 182
18. Stock Market Operations and Functions 183 - 191
19. Trading in the Stock Market 192 - 203

PART – IV

SECURITY ANALYSIS

20. Sources of Investment Information 207 - 211
21. Inflation and Investments 212 - 218
22. Security Market Analysis 219 - 228

23. Investment Decision Making 229 - 234
24. Financial Analysis and Interpretation 235 - 239
25. Balance Sheet Analysis and Blue Chips 240 - 249
26. Fundamental Analysis 250 - 263
27. Technical Analysis of the Market 264 - 275
28. Efficient Market Theory 276 - 281

PART – V

RISK AND RETURN CONCEPTS AND MEASUREMENT

29. Risk and Credit Rating 285 - 295
30. Security Market Indicators 296 - 307
31. Interest Rates — Theory and Structure 308 - 321

PART – VI

VALUATION OF STOCKS AND BONDS

32. Financial Arithmetics 325 - 339
33. Security Pricing 340 - 352
34. Investment Analysis and Theory 353 - 368
35. Valuation of Bonds — Bond Market 369 - 412
36. Valuation of contingent Claims and Options 413 - 434

PART – VII

PORTFOLIO THEORY AND MANAGEMENT

37. Risk and Return in Portfolio Management 437 - 442
38. Capital Asset Pricing Model (CAPM) 443 - 468
39. Portfolio Analysis 469 - 480
40. Diversification and Techniques of Risk Reduction 481 - 489
41. Markowitz Model 490 - 508
42. Basics of Portfolio Management in India 509 - 514
43. Modern Portfolio Theory 515 - 521
44. Portfolio Management: Construction, Revision and Evaluation 522 - 548
45. Mutual Funds and their Schemes 549 - 572
46. Disinvestment Management 573 - 590
47. Securities Market Report (BSE) 591 - 607

CONTENTS

PART – I

INVESTMENT SETTING

1. SECURITIES MARKETS 3 - 14

Introduction — What is Securities Market? — What are Securities? — Mobilisation of Savings for Investment — IOUs as Securities — Characteristics of Securities — Primary Issues and Derivative Securities — Schematic Presentation of Emergence of Market — Legal Framework for Securities Markets — Companies Act — Acceptance of Fixed Deposits — Compulsory Repayment of Deposits which have Matured for Repayment — Procedure for Making Application to Company Law Board — Cases in Respect of which Applications to the Company Law Board will not Lie — Facts about Company Deposits — Care to be Exercised while Investing in Fixed Deposits — Problems in Securities Markets.

2. SAVINGS AND INVESTMENT 15 - 18

How do Savings Emerge? — Why do People Save? — Impact of Inflation — Investment Activity — What is Investment Activity? — Savings and Investments — Objectives of Investors — Investment for Consumption and Business — Investment and Speculation — Investment Opportunities — Financial Investments vs. Physical Investment — Bank Deposits.

3. MACRO ASPECTS OF SAVINGS AND INVESTMENTS 19 - 25

Structure of the Economy — What is Growth Process? — Role of Savings — Other Factors in Development — Financial Intermediation — Links of Real Economic System and Financial System — Savings Rate — Gross and Net Savings — Household Savings — Shifts within Industrial Sector — Lead and Lag Industries — Public Sector Enterprises — Paradox of High Savings and Low Growth — Role of Private Corporate Sector — Conclusions.

4. FINANCIAL SYSTEM —INTERMEDIATION 26- 35

Financial Intermediation — Ratios of Financial Intermediation — Some Financial Indicators — What Constitutes Financial Activity? — RBI and the Financial System — Money Market — Characteristics — Discount and Finance House — Operations of DFHI — Stock Market — Financial Institutions — Savings and Investment — Interest Rate Structure — Capital Market — Unorganised Financial System — Bullion Market.

5. INVESTMENT AVENUES 36 - 41

Introduction — Financial Position — Classification of Investments — What is Investment — Macro Household Savings and Investment — Modes of Investment — Cash Management — Tax Provision — Specialised Knowledge.

6. FEATURES OF INVESTMENT AVENUES 42 - 52

Objectives of Investor — Characteristics of Investment — Risk-Return Relationships — Tax Benefits — Marketability and Liquidity — Safety vs. Riskiness — Need for Tradability — Classes of Instruments — Investment Profile of Average Household — Analysis of Household Sector Savings — Non-Corporate Investments — Corporate Investments — Deposits with Banks — Instruments of Post Offices — Public Provident Fund — 10-year Social Security Certificate — Indira Vikas Patra — Kisan Vikas Patra — Public Sector Bonds — Drought Relief Bonds (Relief Patra) — Conclusion

7. TAX PLANNING FOR INVESTMENT 53 - 61

Taxation of Dividend and Interest Income — Brokerage Income and Business Profits — Tax Treatment on Investments — Interest and Dividend: Section 80 L — Tax Rebate under Section 88 — Scheme Elegible for Rebate u.s. 88 — Income Tax and Corporation Taxes — Capital Gains Taxation —Postal Investments — Wealth Tax — Gift Tax — Taxation of NRIs — Taxation of Investment Business in India — Taxation of FFIs in India — Latest Trend — Transaction Costs —Introduction — Objectives — Elements of Costing — Costs in Investment Activity — Transaction Costs — Real and Nominal Costs — Tax and Govt. Charges and Fees — Recent Changes.

PART – II

MONEY AND CAPITAL MARKETS AND INSTITUTIONS

8. OVERVIEW OF CAPITAL MARKET 65 - 71

What is Capital Market? — Structure of the Market — Players in the Market — Stock Market Intermediaries — Instruments of Issue/Trading — New Instruments — SEBI Guidelines — Indian Capital Market — Landmarks and Developments During a Decade — Recent Trends in Capital Markets — A New Order — Genesis of New Order — National Market System — Need for Larger Financial Base — SEBI Reforms of the Secondary Markets.

9. INSTITUTIONAL STRUCTURE IN CAPITAL MARKET 72 - 83

Development and Investment Institutions — UTI & Its Objectives —Activities of UTI — Investment Pattern — Schemes Offered by the UTI — IDBI — Schemes of IDBI Assistance —.Sources of Funds — ICICI — IFCI — Functions — I.R.B.I. — Functions — IIBI — Insurance Companies — Life Insurance Corporation (LIC) — General Insurance Corporation (GIC) — Public Sector Mutual Funds — SFCs/SIDCs — SHCIL (Stock Holding Corporation of India Ltd.) — Organisational Structure — Functions — Clearing Services — Depository Services — Support Services — Management Information System — Developmental Services — CRISIL (Credit Rating and Information Services of India Ltd.) — CRISIL Rating and Investor Protection — ICRA — Factors Considered — Ratings — Advantages — CARE — DPCR — FIR.

10. CAPITAL MARKET REFORMS 84 - 98

Introduction — Narasimham Committee — Free Entry to Capital Market — Liberalisation Measures — New Instruments — SEBI Guidelines — Strengthening of SEBI Powers — Stock Invest — Changes in Listing Guidelines — Guidelines for Takeovers — Relaxation of Some Restrictions — Details for Investor Protection — More Recent Changes in New Issue Market — Changes in Companies Act — Institutional Strengthening —Electronic Trading — Stock Exchange Reforms — Market Makers — BOLT System — Badla Trading — SEBI's Insider Trading Regulations — Central Depository System — Corporate Membership — Pending Reforms — SEBI norms for Book Building — SEBI Reforms on Stock Exchanges — Take over Code — Record of Take Overs — Critique of Bhagwati Committee's Report — Pending Reforms in Banking Sector — Second Generation Reforms (Budget 2000-01) — Some Recent Reforms — Banking and Financial Reforms

11. NEW ISSUES MARKET AND PROBLEMS 99 - 110

Definition — Functions — Methods of Floatation — Offer Through Prospectus — Offer of Sale — Private Placement — Right Issue — Debt versus Equity — Rights of Conversion of Debt into Equity — Preference Shares — Bonus Shares — Cost of Floatation — Underwriting Activity — Abuses in the New Issue Market — Problems of the New Issue Market — Primary Market — Problems — Public Response — Timing of New Issues — Cost of Capital Issues — Wasteful Procedures on Public Issue — Group on Primary Market Recommendations — Need for Analytical Data.

12. MONEY MARKET AND ITS INSTRUMENTS 111 - 121

Developed and Underdeveloped Markets — Integration and Specialisation — Advantages of Mature Money Market — Sub-Markets — Bill Market in India — Institutional Structure — Characteristics — Discount and Finance House of India (DFHI) — New Money Market Instruments — Classification of Money Market Instruments — Money Market Rates — Commercial Paper (C.P.) — Certificate of Deposits (C.D.) — Participation Certificates — Repos Transactions — Management in Money Market — Securities Trading Corporation of India Ltd. (STCI).

13. THE SECURITIES AND EXCHANGE BOARD OF INDIA (SEBI) 122 - 134

Introduction — Objectives — SEBI Guidelines — Reforms in the New Issues Market — Details of SEBI Guidelines — For Capital Market —SEBI Reforms on Stock Exchanges — Complaints against Members —Grievances Cell — Complaints against Companies — Customers' Protection Fund — Investors Beware — Specific Goals — Pre-requisites of Investor — Preparing to Invest — Balance Sheet Study — Choice of a Broker — Protection in the New Issues Market — Protection for Fixed Deposits — Guidelines to Investors — Legislative Protection to Investors — CRISIL Rating and Investor Protection.

PART – III

SECONDARY MARKETS IN INDIA

14. SECURITIES TRADING REGULATIONS 137 - 140

Objectives — Coverage — Recognised Stock Exchanges — Options in Contracts — Regulation of Trading — Restrictions on Transferability.

15. INSTRUMENTS OF ISSUE AND TRADING 141 - 153

Issues of Securities — Government Securities — Corporate Securities — Corporate Debentures — Other Securities — Company Deposits — Commercial Paper — Legal Provisions — Despatch of Share Certificates — Debenture Certificates — Fixed Deposits — Law regarding Dividends — New Companies Bill 1993 — SEBI Guidelines — Equity Shares — Dividend Distribution — Dividend Policy — Other Instruments — Bonus Shares — Rights Shares — Preference Shares — CCP — Government and Semi-Government Bonds — Equity Shares — Public Issue — Cost of Issue Guidelines — New Instruments — Recent Liberalisation of Policy — ADR and GDR Proceeds — Latest Foreign Investment Policy Measures — Relaxation in ECB Norms — Instruments of Foreign Borrowing.

16. STOCK MARKETS IN INDIA 154 - 164

History of Stock Exchanges — What is a Stock Exchange? — Byelaws — Regulation of Stock Exchanges — Recognition by Government — Licensed Dealers — Securities Contracts (Regulation) Rules, 1957 — Present Recognised Stock Exchanges — Qualifications for Membership — Organisation — Demutualisation of Stock Exchanges — Advantages of Demutualisation — Disadvantages — Governing Body — Functions of Stock Exchanges — Listed Paid-up Capital — Who Owns the Securities? — Bombay: Stock Exchange — Patel Committee — Regulations on Trading — Investor Protection — Measures to Promote Healthy Stock Markets — Other Reforms — Rolling Settlement System CDSL: Central Depository Services Limited — Globalisation of Stock Exchanges — Demat Form of Trading — Electronic Form of Trading — Internet Trading (e-trading) — Electronic Fund Collection — Foreign Listing.

17. OTCEI, NSE AND ICSE 165 - 182

Securities Exchanges — Structured Markets — OTC Defined — Investor Interests — Practices Abroad — OTC and New Issues Market — OTC and Stock Exchange — Advantages of OTC — Structural Weaknesses in India — Role of OTC — Over-the-Counter Exchange of India (OTCEI) — Objectives of OTCEI — Establishment of OTC — Listing on OTCEI — Investors Benefitted — Market Players — Listing Procedure — Trading on the OTCEI — Conclusion — Problems — OTCEI and Dave Committee Report — DAVE Committee Recommendations — Annexure — National Stock Exchange — National Market System — Characteristics — NSE Operations — Automated Lending and Borrowing Mechanism (ALBM) — Central Depository System — Listing of Securities — Settlement System — The National Securities Depository Limited (NSDL) — What is a Depository? — Rematerialisation — Advantages of the Depository — About the Depository Participants — NSDL's First Participants — Legal Aspects — Interconnected Stock Exchange — Objective — Computer System — Trader Work Stations — Advantages of ISE.

18. STOCK MARKET OPERATIONS AND FUNCTIONS 183 - 191

Introduction — Specified and Non-Specified Groups — Customer's Orders — Trading Ring — Block Book (or the Sauda Book) — Contract Note — Drawing Up and Bills — Cum and Ex-dividend — Settlement in Specified List — Badla Charges — Factors Influencing Badla Rates — Carry Forward Facilities — Example 1 — Example 2 — Book Closure Badla Financing (BCBF) — Settlement in Non-Specified Shares — After the Badla Day — Kinds of Delivery — Hand Delivery — Spot Delivery — Special Delivery — Delivery for Clearing — Present Position of BADLA — J.S. Varma Committee (July 1997) — Dhanuka Committee Report — Recent Reforms of Stock Exchanges.

19. TRADING IN THE STOCK MARKET 192 - 203

Pattern of Trading — 'Z' Group in Bombay Stock Exchange — Trading and Settlement — Speculative Traders vs. Genuine Investors — Types of Speculators — Activities of Brokers — Brokers' Charges — Delivery/Payment — Settlement Procedure — Auctions — Clearing Procedure — Regulation — National Market System — Characteristics — Objectives — Study Group Recommendations — Experience in Foreign Countries — National Clearance and Depository System — Present Settlement and Clearance System — National Trade Comparison and Reporting System — Internet Broking — Order Routing System (ORs) — e-Broking — SEBI's Role — Dynamics of Net Trading in Stocks — Emerging Role of Stock Exchanges.

PART – IV

SECURITY ANALYSIS

20. SOURCES OF INVESTMENT INFORMATION 207 - 211

Types of Information — Need for Information — Uses of these Data — Conclusion.

21. INFLATION AND INVESTMENTS 212 - 218

What is Inflation? — Traditional Explanation of Inflation — Demand Pull and Cost Push Inflation — Structural Factors — Inflationary Tendencies — Inflation Indicators — Causes of Inflation — Effects of Inflation — Inflation — A Fallout of Reforms — RBI's Responsibility — Inflation as a Monetary Phenomenon — Mid-term Appraisal of the VIII Plan — Impact of Govt. Measures — Role of RBI — Credit Control by RBI — Responsibility of RBI — Inflation on Investments — Inflation and Investment Decisions.

22. SECURITY MARKET ANALYSIS 219 - 228

What is Security Analysis? — Origin of Markets — Information Flows — Savings or Money Flows — Factors Influencing the Market Behaviour — Trading — Instruments — Players — Intermediaries — What is Market Analysis? — Valuation — Theoretical Framework — Schematic Presentation of Theory — Investment and Time Value of Money — Present Value Method — D.C.F. (Discounted Cash Flows).

23. INVESTMENT DECISION MAKING 229 - 234

Investment Management Involves Correct Decision Making — What is Investment Management? — Criteria for Investment Decision — Risk and Investment — What is Fundamental Analysis? — Investment Objectives — Cost-Benefit Analysis — Environmental Considerations — Chit Funds and Nidhis — Tax Planning in Investment Management — Execution of Investment Decisions.

24. FINANCIAL ANALYSIS AND INTERPRETATION 235 - 239

What is Financial Management? — Components of Financial Statements — Comparison of the Financial Statements — Ratio Analysis — Usefulness of Ratio Analysis — Fund Flow Analysis — Trend Analysis.

25. BALANCE SHEET ANALYSIS AND BLUE CHIPS 240 - 249

Annual Reports — Market Price and Corporate Performance — Ana-lysis of Financial Position — Types of Shares in the Market — Growth Shares — Cyclical Shares — Defensive Shares — Discount Shares — Net Financial Results and Profitability — Corporate Performance — How to Locate Emerging Blue Chips? — Established Blue Chips.

26. FUNDAMENTAL ANALYSIS 250 - 263

Influence of the Economy — Economy vs. Industry and Company — Industry Analysis— Example of an Industry Analysis — Petro-Chemicals — Company Analysis — Need for Forecast — Guidelines for Investment — Example of Company Analysis — How to Pick Up Growth Shares? — Pharma Industry — Profile of Pharma Industry — Future Outlook — Conclusions.

27. TECHNICAL ANALYSIS OF THE MARKET 264 - 275

Importance of Timing in Investment — Basic Tenets of Technical Analysis — Tools of Technical Analysis — Dow Theory — Major Trends — Chartist Method — Breadth of the Market — Volume of Trading — Tripod of Technical Analysis — Principles of Technical Analysis — Charts and Trend Lines — Moving Averages — Advantages of Moving Averages — Criticism of Dow Theory — Charts — Head and Shoulders — Breaking the Neckline — Resistance and Support Lines — Speculative Trading and Technical Analysis — Elliot Wave Theory — Operation of Wave Theory — Oscillators (Rate of Change or ROC).

28. EFFICIENT MARKET THEORY 276 - 281

Assumptions — Random Walk Theory — Assumptions of Random Walk Theory — Random Walk and Efficient Market Theory — Empirical Tests — Filter Tests — Serial Correlation Tests — Run Tests — Other Tests — Mutual Fund Peformance — Efficient Market Hypothesis — Semi Strong Form — Strong Form of EMH — Markets in India — Critique of EMH.

PART – V

RISK AND RETURN CONCEPTS AND MEASUREMENT

29. RISK AND CREDIT RATING 285 - 295

Introduction — Risk and Uncertainty — What Causes the Risks? — Systematic and Unsystematic Risks — Risks are Classified into Major Categories — Examples of Systematic Risks — Examples of Unsystematic Risks — Other Risks — Risks and Returns — Purchasing Power Risk — Problem — Standard Deviation and Variance — Investment Decision-Making — Risk Measurement — Range of Variation — Why Credit Rating? — Rating in USA — What is Credit Rating? — How to Understand Ratings and Rating System? — What Instruments are Rated? — Limitations to Ratings — Key Factors Considered — Risk and Credit Rating — Confidentility of Information — CRISIL — ICRA — CARE —Duff and Phelps — Fitch India Pvt. Ltd.

30. SECURITY MARKET INDICATORS 296 - 307

Introduction — Functions and Activity — Segments of the Markets — Segment of Government Securities — Yield Curve — Indicators — Corporate Securities Section — Main Indicators — Security Price Indices — RBI Index of Industrial Security Prices — BSE Sensitive Index — Scrip Selection — Methods of Compilation — Weightage — Other Adjustments — BSE Sensex Composition — BSE National Index — BSE 200 and Dollex — Daily Current Market Data — Other Indicators — Other Indices — Indexes for other Segments.

31. INTEREST RATES — THEORY AND STRUCTURE 308 - 321

Introduction — Role of Interest Income — Relative Share of Interest Income — Role of Interest Rates — Theories of Interest Rate — Structure of Interest Rates — Factors Influencing Interest Rates — Interest Rates in India — Bank Rate and Refinance Rates — Money Market Rates — Rates in Gilt-edged Market — Private and Government Bond Rates — Rates of Borrowings and Lendings by Commercial Banks — Interest Rates on Small Savings — Interest Rates on Non-resident Accounts — Export Credit — Level and Structure of Rates — Level of Interest Rates — Structure of Interest Rates — Reforms — Recent Deregulation Measures — The Yield — Current Yield — Redemption Yield — Holding Period Yield (HPY) — Real Yield — Net Yield — Maturity and Yields — Yield Curve.

PART – VI

VALUATION OF STOCKS AND BONDS

32. FINANCIAL ARITHMETICS 325 - 339

Introduction — Calculation of Returns (Yields) — Yields on Bonds/Fixed Interest Securities — Simple Yield or Interest Calculation — Yields on Equity — Time Value of Money and Securities — Time Preference for Money — Applications — Features of a Bond — Equity Valuation — Fundamentals of Valuation of Securities — Discounting — Bond Prices — Factors Influencing — Formulae — Valuation of Convertible Bonds/Debentures — Why Convertible Financing? — Valuation of Convertibles — Conversion Ratio — Conversion Premium — Valuation of 'Rights' — Example of Rights Pricing — Callable Bonds — Detachable and Non-Detachable Warrants and Loyalty Coupons — Mortgage Bonds — Time Value of Money — Problems.

33. SECURITY PRICING 340 - 352

Factors Influencing Valuation — Security Valuation — Constant Growth Model — Book Value — Liquidating Value (Breakdown Value) — Replacement Value — Instrinsic Value vs. Market Price — Equity Valuation — Single-Period Valuation Models — Example — Multi-Period Share Valuation Model — Example — Dividend Capitalisation — Earnings Capitalisation — Use of P/E Ratio — Security Pricing Models — Other Models — Graham's Approach to Valuation of Equity — Valuation of Securities in India — Example — Free Market Pricing — SEBI Guidelines — Theory of Pricing — Share Valuation Models — Granger Causality Test.

34. INVESTMENT ANALYSIS AND THEORY 353 - 368

Introduction — Flow of Funds Theory — Price Formation — Capital Assets Pricing Model — Risk and Portfolio — Efficient Market Theory — Random Walk Theory — Trend Walk Theory — Capital Asset Pricing (CAP) Theory — Modern Portfolio Theory — Concept of Beta — Fundamental School — Intrinsic Value and Market Value — Evaluation of Shares — Gordon's Hypothesis — Gordan Dividend Model — M.M. Hypothesis — Walter's Formula — Walter Model — Problems — Graham Dodd Model — Discount Model — Malkiel and Cragg Regression Model — Cootner's Price Value Interaction Model — Random Walk Theory — Random Walk Theory Assumptions — Martingale Models — Capital Market Theory — Security Market Line — CAPM — Tobin "Q" Theory.

35. VALUATION OF BONDS — BOND MARKET 369 - 412

Introduction — Bond Market In India — Special Features of Bonds — Interest Rate Structure — Properties of Bonds and Bond Value — Measures of Bond Returns — Calculation of Yield to Maturity (YTM) — Valuation of Bonds — Solved Problems — Accrued Interest — Calculation of Accrued Interest and Value — Discrete Models — Bond Price Theorems — Malkiel Bond Theorems — Risk Premium on Bonds — Yield Curves — Term Structure — Types of Bond Management — Active Strategies — Yield Curve Study — Objectives of Raising Incremental Return — Need for Tax Planning — Sequence of Steps for Bond Issues — Steps in Management of the Issue — General Benchmarks in Making Issues — Valuation of Bonds — Price Risk — Riding the Yield Curve — Duration Measure — Risks to be Covered — Duration and Immunisation — What is Duration? — Use of Duration as a Concept — Macaulay's Duration (MD) — Duration (Example) — Theorems Emerging from MD — Advantages of M.D. — Uses of Duration — Interest Rate Elasticity and Risk — Modified Duration (by Hicks) — Short Cut Formula for Duration — Immunisation — What is Immunisation? — Immunisation Process — Immunisation Operations — How Immunisation is Effected? — Problems of Immunisation — Bond Holding Strategies — Immunisation —Cash Matching (Dedicated Portfolio) — Price Elasticity — Illustration — Volatility of Bond Prices — Immunisation — Immunisation — (A) Present Value of Bonds: (Total PV = 62.05) — (B) Face Value of Bonds: (Yield is 11%) — Macauly' Duration — Problems in Bonds.

36. VALUATION OF CONTINGENT CLAIMS AND OPTIONS 413 - 434

Introduction — What is Contingent Claim? — Pricing of Such Claims — Free Market Pricing — What is a Convertible Security? — Valuation of Rights Shares — Preference Shares — CCP — Legal Provisions — Norms for N.C.D. of Non-Convertible Portion of P.C.D. — Conversion Value — Conversion Premium — Pricing of Convertibles — Valuation of Convertibles — Graphical Presentation — Role of Interest Rate — Graphical Depiction — Brigham's Model on Convertible Bonds — Valuation of Options — Factors Affecting the Option Value — Call and Put Options — Hedge Ratio (Black-Scholes Model) — Hedge Ratio Data — Black-Scholes Formula — What is Black-Scholes Formula? — Implications — Solved Problem (B/S Model)

PART – VII

PORTFOLIO THEORY AND MANAGEMENT

37. RISK AND RETURN IN PORTFOLIO MANAGEMENT **437 - 442**

What is the Objective? — What is Risk? — How to Minimise the Risks? — What is Beta? — Risk Return Analysis — Degree of Risk and Risk Free Return — Capital Market Instruments — Money Market Instruments — What is a Portfolio? — Definition of Portfolio? — Speculative Instinct — Precautions for Investment — Decomposition of Return.

38. CAPITAL ASSET PRICING MODEL (CAPM) **443 - 468**

CAPM-Assumptions — CML — Security Market Line (SML) —CAPM Analysis — Market Model — Uses and Limitations — Capital Asset Pricing Model — Limitation of CAPM — SML Security Market Line — CAPM — Diversification — Why Diversification — Example on Measurement of Risk — Calculation of Standard Deviation —Example Escorts — Example of Simple Diversification — Markowitz Diversification — CML — SML — CAPM — Asset Pricing Implication of SML — Equilibrium price: (SLM) — Problem on CAPM — Problem on SML.

39. PORTFOLIO ANALYSIS **469 - 480**

Return on Portfolio — Risk on a Portfolio — Example of Standard Deviation — Regression Equation — Alpha — Beta — Rho or Correlation Coefficient (covariance) — An Example for Covariance and Correlation — Expected Returns — Calculation of Beta — Calculation of Alpha — Calculation of Residual Variance — Calculation of Residual Variance — Method of Calculation of (r) — Variance of IBM — Variance of BSE Index — Covariance of Returns — Correlation Coefficient.

40. DIVERSIFICATION AND TECHNIQUES OF RISK REDUCTION **481 - 489**

What is Diversification?— Principles — Random Diversification — International Diversification — Why International Diversification? — Risks in Foreign Investments — FFI's Investment in India — NRI Investment in India — A. Personal Investments Scheme — B. Direct Investment Scheme — (C) Portfolio Investment Scheme — Passive International Investment Strategy — Active International Investment Strategy — Return Forecasts — International Investing — Problem — Advantages of Diversification — Naive Diversification — Evans & Archers' Study.

41. MARKOWITZ MODEL **490 - 508**

Assumptions of Markowitz Theory — Markowitz Diversification — Parameters of Markowitz Diversification — Criteria of Dominance — Markowitz Model — Measurement of Risk (Example) — Portfolio Risk — Equation for Portfolio Return — Equation for Portfolio Variance — Arbitrage Pricing Theory — Introduction — Asset Selection in the Above Model — Components of Expected Returns — Empirical Testing of APT Model — Arbitrage Pricing Theory — Problem — Sharpe Model — Optimal Portfolio of Sharpe — Basis for Cut-off Rate — Distribution of Investments.

42. BASICS OF PORTFOLIO MANAGEMENT IN INDIA **509 - 514**

Some Aspects of Portfolio Management — Investment Strategy — Objectives of Investors — Risk and Beta — Modern Portfolio Theory (MPT) — Time Value of Money — Compounding — Discounting — Perpetuity — Annuity — Application to Portfolio Management — Portfolio Construction, Revision and Evaluation — MPT and Dominance Concept — Diversification Process — SEBI Guidelines for Portfolio Managers — Portfolio Management Service — Method of Operation — SEBI Norms — Who can be a Portfolio Manager?

43. MODERN PORTFOLIO THEORY 515 - 521

What is Modern Portfolio Theory (MPT) — Basis of Modern Portfolio Theory — B. Cap Theory and Concept of Dominance (Capital assets pricing model) — Dominance Concept — C. Role of Beta — Portfolio Investment Strategy — Asset Allocation — Risk Management Strategy — Duration — Beta — Target Return — Borrowing for Investment — Problems — Portfolio Return Equation is — Portfolio Risk = Standard Deviation of Portfolio.

44. PORTFOLIO MANAGEMENT: CONSTRUCTION, REVISION AND EVALUATION 522 - 548

Fact Sheet — Clients' Data Base — Objectives of Investors — Motives for Investment — Tax Provisions — Capital Gains — Portfolio Construction — Risk-Return Analysis — Time Horizon of Strategy — Types of Risk — Efficient Portfolio — Market Efficiency Theorem — Diversification — Portfolio Management — Elements of Portfolio Management — Execution of Strategy — Monitoring — Building of the Portfolio — Portfolio Revision — Security Pricing and Portfolio Management — Markowitz Model of Portfolio Theory — Risk Analysis — Evaluation of Portfolio Performance — Criteria for Evaluation of Portfolio — Example of Sharpe's Measure — Treynor's Measure Evaluation Problem — Comparison — Jensen's Measure — Jensen's Model — Evaluation Criteria for Portfolios — Portfolio Performance Evaluation — Jensen's Performance Measure: (JP) — Returns and Performance Evaluation — Problems — Take Home Problems.

45. MUTUAL FUNDS AND THEIR SCHEMES 549 - 572

Introduction — Definition — Types of Funds — Unit Trust of India — UTI Schemes for Resident Indians — Off shore Funds — SBI Mutual Fund — India Magnum Fund N.V. — Other Funds — Overall Progress in India — Investment Policy — Steps to Popularise Mutual Funds — Response of NRIs — For All MFs Common Rules — Advantages of Mutual Funds — Progress in Nineties — Regulation of Mutual Funds — Authorisation of Existing Mutual Funds — Money Market Mutual Funds (MMFs) — MMMF's Regulation — Authorisation of New Mutual Funds — Mutual Funds Present Status — Taxation and M.Fs — Wealth Tax — Gift Tax — Tax Benefit under 1999-2000 — Saga of Fortunes of MFs — Stocklending by Mutual Funds — Latest Trends — Annexure I - RBI Guidelines on Mutual Funds — Annexure II -SEBI.

46. DISINVESTMENT MANAGEMENT 573 - 590

Introduction — What is Disinvestment? — Why Disinvestment? — Role of Disinvestment — Disinvestment Under Adverse Conditions — Disinvestment Motivated by Market Conditions — Types of Disinvestment — Factors Influencing Disinvestment — Role of Fundamental Factors — How to Make Disinvestment Decision? — Objectives — Investment Avenues — Stock Market Disinvestment — Fundamental Analysis — FIIs and the Art of Contrariness — FII Investments in India — Role of Technical Factors — Timing of Disinvestment (Through Technical Analysis) — R.S.I (Relative Strength Index) — Moving Average Convergence and Divergence (MACD) — Disinvestment by Government Sector — Problems of PSU Disinvestment — NAVARATNAS — Central Public Sector Undertakings — Divestment Methods of Government — Open Bidding Process of Divestment — A Proposal on Mutual Fund Route — Banks' Divestment Scheme

47. SECURITIES MARKET REPORT (BSE) 591 - 607

Introduction — Global Comparison — Overview of BSE Market Report — Globalisation Trend — Daily Report Analysis — Sensex Shows 5% Fall on FII Selling — Price Index Snapshots of the Market — Trade Turnover — Advance/Decline Line — Role of Institutional Agencies — Trading Cycle — Record Dates and Book Closure — Circuit Band Hitters — Speculative Positions — Surveillance System — Index Details — BSE Stock Tables — Main Indicators — Face Value — Market Macro Indicators — Badla Statistics — Derivatives Trading.

PART — I
Investment Setting

Chapter 1: Securities Markets
Chapter 2: Savings and Investment
Chapter 3: Macro Aspects of Savings and Investments
Chapter 4: Financial System – Intermediation
Chapter 5: Investment Avenues
Chapter 6: Features of Investment Avenues
Chapter 7: Tax Planning for Investment

CHAPTER 1 Securities Markets

Introduction

The issue of securities by corporate units in India is as old as the introduction of joint-stock enterprises by the British Government. The 18th and 19th centuries saw the emergence of cotton and jute textiles, tea and other plantation industries in India. Many companies were set up as joint-stock enterprises with liability limited by shares. A vast number of businessmen in major cities purchased these shares and trading started in them early in the 19th century, thanks to their enterprising spirit. In those days, although many of these companies were financed by the issue of shares to the public, they mainly depended on the joint-stock British banks in India and borrowals from abroad. British enterprise and the British Government have thus helped the emergence of the securities markets in India. The corporate securities have come to have a market first. So far as the Government securities are concerned, the British India Government borrowed mostly in London by issue of Sterling consols. Only later in the 19th century the Government issued treasury bills and Government securities in rupees. This led to the emergence of the Government securities market also in India.

What is Securities Market?

Securities markets are markets in financial assets or instruments and these are represented as I.O.Us (I owe you) in financial form. These are issued by business organisations, corporate units and the Governments, Central or State. Public sector undertakings also issue these securities. These securities are used to finance their investment and current expenditure. These are thus sources of funds to the issuers.

There are different types of business organisations in India, namely, partnership firms, co-operative societies, private and public limited companies and joint and public sector organisations etc. The more frequently organised method is the company, registered under the Indian Companies Act 1956. Under this Act, there are three types of companies: *(a)* companies limited by guarantee; *(b)* companies which are private limited companies — limited by shares paid up; and *(c)* companies which are public limited companies — limited by shares paid up and companies limited by guarantee cannot enter the market. The private limited companies can have 50 members and their shares are not transferable freely. These companies reserve the right to refuse any transfer of shares and as such trading in them is restricted. Due to these inhibitive features, private limited companies do not have easy access to the securities markets. Only public limited companies are largely popular as they can raise funds from the public through the issue of shares. The methods of raising funds used by the corporate sector are to issue securities, either ownership instruments or debt instruments.

What are Securities?

Securities are claims on money and are like promissory notes or I.O.U. Securities are a source of funds for companies, Governments and Semi-Government bodies. There are two types of sources of funds namely internal and external and securities emerge when funds are raised from external sources.

The external sources of funds of the companies are as follows:

(A) *Long-term Funds*

(i) Ownership Capital — equity and preference capital, and Non-voting Shares.

(ii) Debt Capital — debentures and long-term borrowings in the form of deposits from public or credit limits or term loans or advances from banks and financial institutions, etc.

(B) *Short-term Funds*

(i) Borrowings from banks, and other corporates.

(ii) Trade credits and suppliers' credits, etc.

Of the above sources, the most popular are those which are tradable and transferable. They have a market and their liquidity is ensured, as in the case of equity shares, preference shares, debentures and bonds. Of these the ownership instruments, particularly the equity shares, are generally the most liquid as they are not only tradable in the securities markets but also enjoy the prospects of capital appreciation, in addition to dividends. The market for these has thus grown much faster than for others.

Mobilisation of Savings for Investment

The issue of securities can be looked at from various angles. These may be set out as follows:

(i) From the point of view of issuers, these are the sources of finance for long-term capital investment and for working capital. They can thus invest more than their resources;

(ii) From the point of view of investors, these are IOUs or promissory notes, giving an income or a return to their investment. They provide a channel to their savings and cater to the asset preferences of the public with varying characteristics of risk, income, maturity, etc.;

(iii) From the point of view of the nation, these issues mobilise the savings for investment and capital formation in the country. They promote the growth of output and income by a multiplier leading to a rise in the output by a multiple of the original investment over a period of time;

(iv) From the point of view of the financial intermediaries like banks, financial institutions, etc., these issues are a source of income to them for the management of these issues placing them with the public, providing liquidity and marketability to them and by activating idle funds.

Thus, the securities markets comprise all the above players, namely, issuers, savers, investors, intermediaries, etc. and the major activity is the moblisation of funds from saving and their channelisation into investment.

IOUs as Securities

In the securities markets, the securities dealt with are equity shares, preference shares, debentures and bonds. These securities being financial claims are issued as I.O.U.s or Promissory Notes. In the primary market, the issues are made to the primary or original savers. The other forms of holding debt or borrowings such as public deposits or bank owned IOUs are not securitised and hence not tradable. In certain cases like the P.O. Certificates, bank deposits, LIC policy certificates etc., they are not transferable by endorsement, but they have a primary market as these primary issues are I.O.U.s, used to mobilise the savings of the public. The market for such primary securities is limited to one stage and there is no secondary market for them. The UTI units and the instruments of many mutual funds in India belong to a hybrid category, as these are not securities according to the strict definition of the term under the Indian Companies Act. But as they can be sold back to the issuing institution or sold in the market if they are quoted on the Stock Exchange, they enjoy liquidity. Thus UTI units under the 1964 scheme for example can be repurchased by the UTI, which provides liquidity to these instruments. The master shares of UTI and the stocks of some mutual funds can also be traded as they are quoted on the Stock Exchanges and they are close ended schemes.

The securities markets emerge out of the two characteristics of financial instruments: *(a)* mobilising primary savings from the public to serve as sources of funds for the issuing authority; and *(b)* providing liquidity to these instruments through regular quotations in the financial markets and thus traded. The primary markets exist only if the first condition is satisfied. The secondary market also operates if both the conditions are satisfied.

The pattern of corporate financing and the extent of their dependence on the external sources of funds, as opposed to the internally generated cash flows, would thus determine the creation of new securities. The retained earnings are the internally generated funds which have an opportunity cost but whose issue costs are zero. These can be converted into securities by issue of bonus shares to existing share holders. There are, however, issue costs for equity and preference shares, convertible and non-convertible debentures etc. The capital market and stock market do provide the facilities for new issues and conversion of issues into money and *vice versa,* so that investors are assured of liquidity for their investments so as to induce them to enter these markets.

Characteristics of Securities

The major characteristics of securities are their transferability and marketability. These help the process of trading and investment in them.

Under the Indian Companies Act, Sections 82 and 111 deal with the transfer of shares. In the case of public limited companies, the objective of the Companies Act as also of the Listing Agreement with the Stock Exchanges is to ensure free and unfettered transfer of shares. Under Section 82 of the Companies Act, shares are treated as any movable property. As any right to property, these are freely transferable. By one amendment in 1985, Section 22(A) of the Securities Contracts (Regulation) Act has denied the right to refuse to transfer shares by a public limited company except on technical grounds. The other grounds on which the transfer can be refused are specifically laid down under the Act and the company has to specify the reasons for such refusal to transfer and reference has to be made to the Company Law Board whose decision to refuse or not to refuse the transfer of shares will be final. Thus the essential characteristic of transferability of shares is well preserved which gives them the market which in turn extends liquidity to these shares. This has led to the emergence of securities markets in India.

Primary Issues and Derivative Securities

Primary issues are those issued to the public by the companies, Governments and financial institutions. Derivative issues are those which are based on the original primary issues. There are a number of derivative instruments which are used to generate a market for the primary issues. Thus in many developed markets abroad, there are warrants, options, futures, index linked instruments etc. which have well-established markets and they are based on some primary instruments. In India, options are now permitted and some form of futures trading exists in Group A securities on the stock exchanges as they are permitted to be carried forward from settlement to settlement without taking delivery of shares. Since January 1995, options and futures have been permitted by change in law by the Government and they are now developing under strict control of SEBI, since 2000.

More recently, new instruments have been developed in India, namely, warrants, Zero coupon bonds, conversion options, rights options etc. But in many cases these are not well developed and secondary markets for these instruments are under developed and trading does not take place as in the case of listed shares and particularly those on the specified group (Group A) of stock exchanges.

Reference is made in the subsequent chapters to many new instruments which are introduced both in the capital market and the money market in India. Besides, the RBI has also recently permitted the securitisation of book debts of banks and financial institutions in the sense that the debit balances on companies' accounts can be transferred to other banks and financial institutions which are willing to discount them or purchase them at a price but the market in many new instruments is yet to be developed in India.

Derivatives Markets in India

In India, options and futures were allowed as securities to be traded in stock exchanges by necessary changes in the S. C. (R) Act 1956, in the year 1996-97. But actual trading in them did not take place until 2000-2001, due to the need for preparing the members for this new system and for setting up the necessary architecture and infrastructure for trading in derivatives.

In June 2000, Index futures and in November 2001, stock futures were started, on NSE and BSE. But the index options were initiated in June 2001 and stock options in July 2001. More importantly interest rate futures were introduced only in June 2003 on the NSE. But the process in interest rate futures and currency futures are yet to take off.

The volume of turnover has grown faster on the NSE than on BSE. Secondly, turnover in derivative markets has grown faster than in the cash markets, although the former were started only a decade ago.

Schematic Presentation of Emergence of Market

A schematic presentation of the emergence of markets through the flow of cash, credit and savings of the public is made in Charts 1.1 to 1.5. It will be seen from Chart 1.1 that money flows lead to claims on financial assets and physical assets and financial assets in turn when issued as securities result in trading in markets. The money and capital markets are shown separately as short-term and long-term wings of the markets. The components of capital market are shown as primary and secondary markets whose details are explained in terms of instruments traded, institutions involved and operations undertaken in Charts 1.3 and 1.4 respectively. Chart 1.2 explains the savings flows of the household sector into financial assets invested by the household sector, namely, currency, deposits of banks, etc. Chart 1.5 presents the inter-relations of the various institutions and markets, namely, the stock exchange, brokers, banks, financial institutions, etc. Finally, the investor clients and corporate clients and the various services rendered to them by these markets are briefly depicted in this chart as constituting the totality of the markets. The further details of these charts are explained in later chapters.

Chart 1.1

Broad Contours of Money Flows

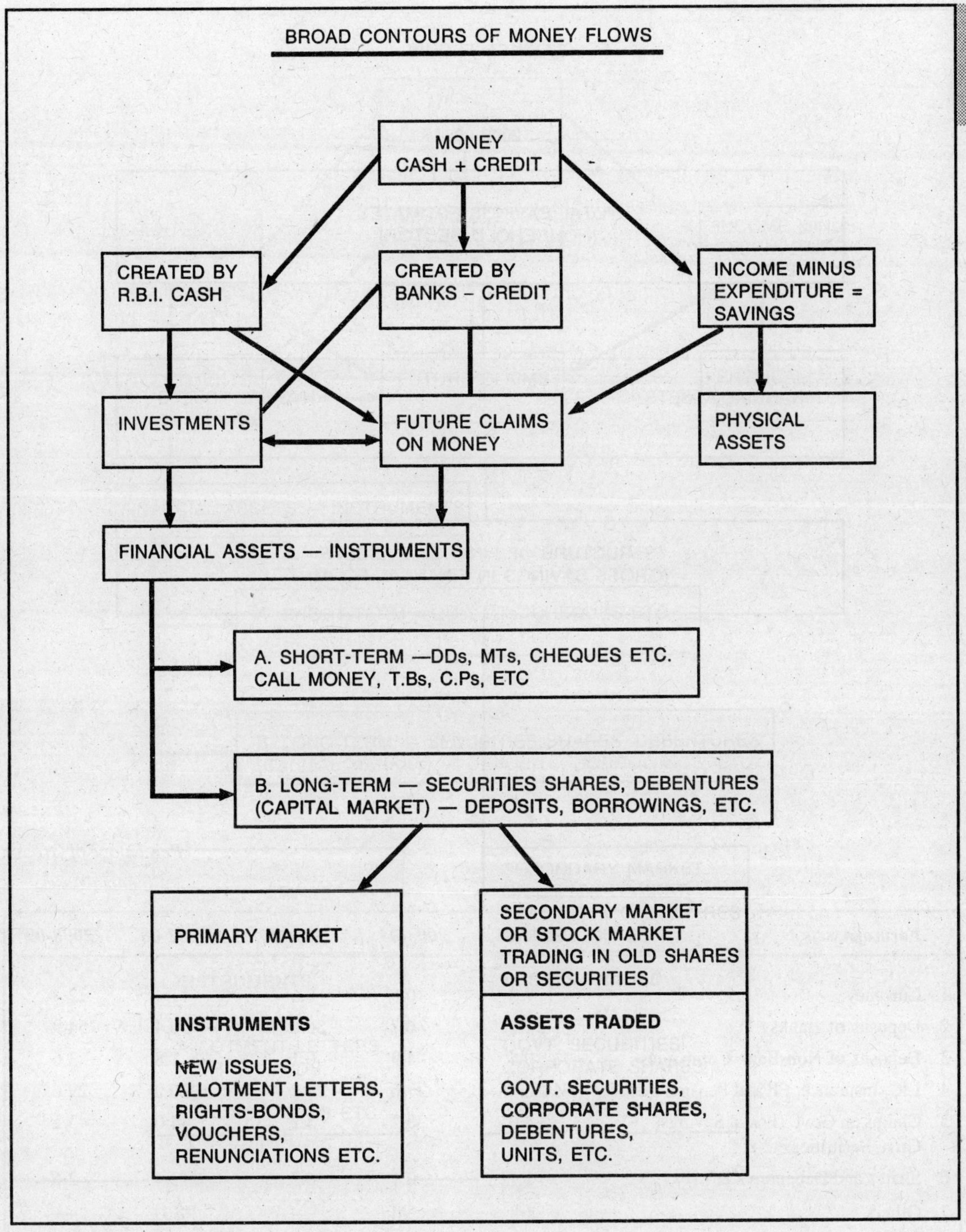

Chart 1.2

Saving Profile of Macro Household

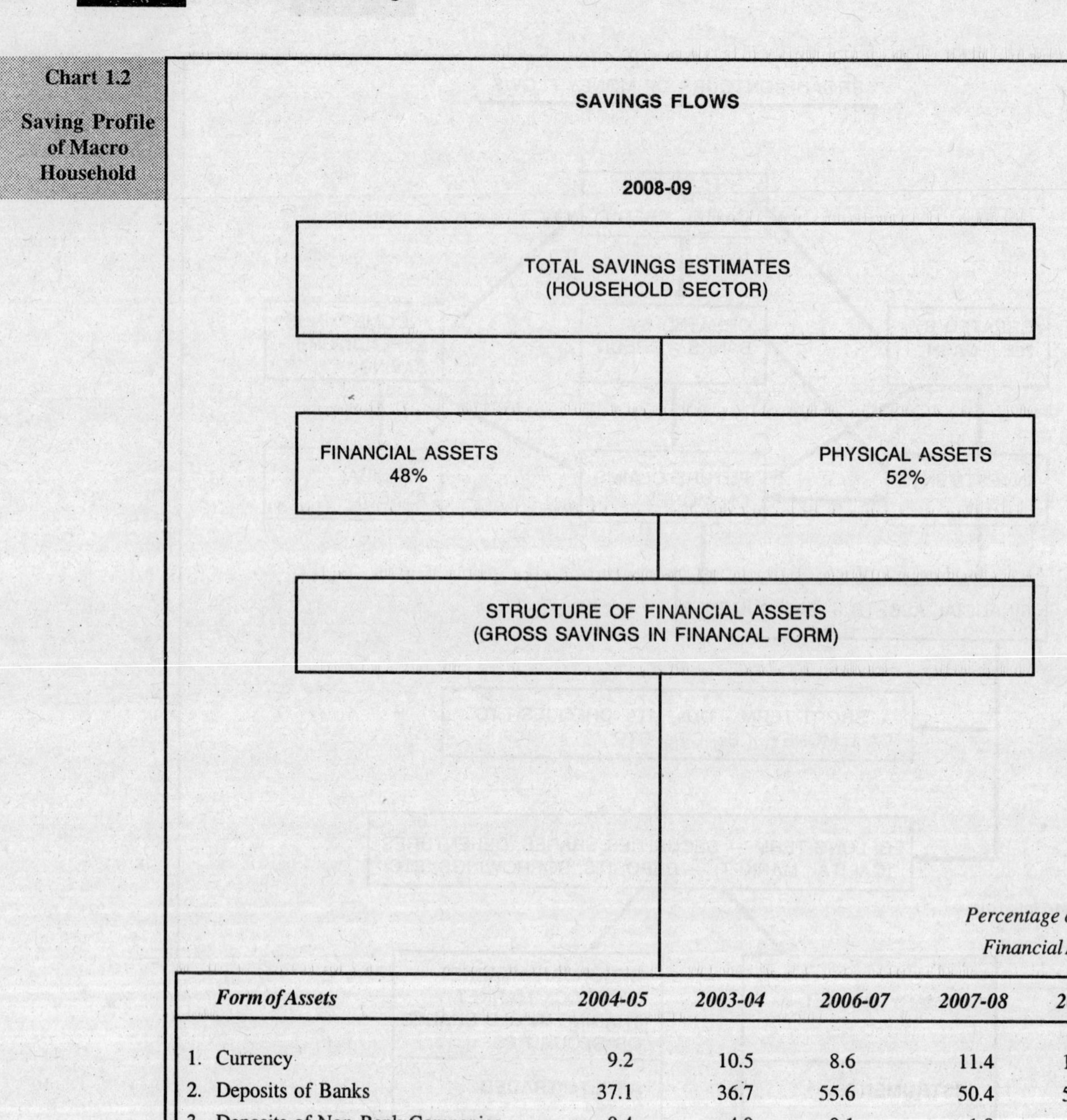

Percentage of Gross Financial Assets

Form of Assets	*2004-05*	*2003-04*	*2006-07*	*2007-08*	*2008-09*
1. Currency	9.2	10.5	8.6	11.4	12.4
2. Deposits of Banks	37.1	36.7	55.6	50.4	54.9
3. Deposits of Non-Bank Companies	0.4	4.9	0.1	1.8	3.6
4. LIC, Insurance, PF and Pension Funds	26.4	27.6	24.2	20.0	29.6
5. Claims on Govt. (Postal Savings, Govt. Securities etc.)	24.0	20.2	5.2	–4.0	–3.1
6. Shares and Debentures & MFs	1.1	0.1	6.3	12.4	2.6
7. Others	1.8	Nil	—	8.0	—
Total	100	100	100	100	100

Source: **Latest RBI Annual Reports**

Chart 1.3
Primary Market

INSTRUMENTS — PRIMARY MARKET

CORPORATE SHARES, DEBENTURES, RIGHTS, ETC., ARE THE INSTRUMENTS

BASIS:

1. ENABLING LEGISLATION, PRACTICES, PROCEDURES
2. PATTERN OF CORPORATE FINANCING - STRUCTURE

A. INTERNAL FINANCE, RETAINED INCOME

B. EXTERNAL SOURCES — METHODS

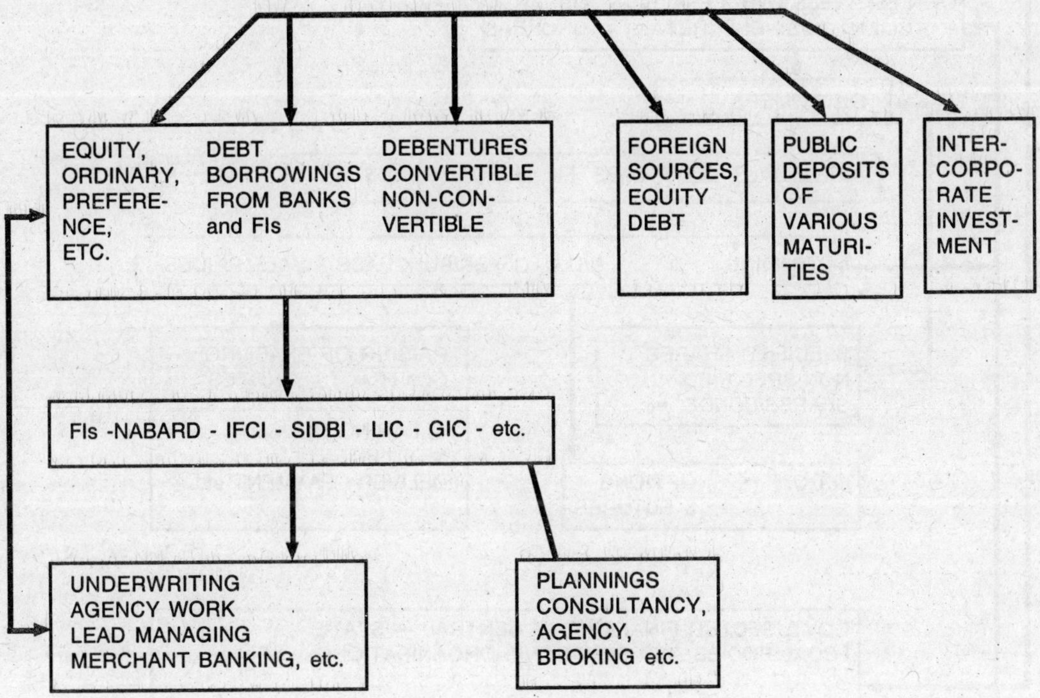

EQUITY, ORDINARY, PREFERE-NCE, ETC.

DEBT BORROWINGS FROM BANKS and FIs

DEBENTURES CONVERTIBLE NON-CON-VERTIBLE

FOREIGN SOURCES, EQUITY DEBT

PUBLIC DEPOSITS OF VARIOUS MATURI-TIES

INTER-CORPO-RATE INVEST-MENT

FIs -NABARD - IFCI - SIDBI - LIC - GIC - etc.

UNDERWRITING AGENCY WORK LEAD MANAGING MERCHANT BANKING, etc.

PLANNINGS CONSULTANCY, AGENCY, BROKING etc.

3. PRIMARY MARKET OPERATIONS

PROJECT PLANNING, FINANCE PLANNING, CONSULTANCY, FINANCIAL MANAGEMENT, TAX PLANNING, GOVT. REGULATIONS, DEALINGS IN THE PRIMARY MARKET-ISSUES TO THE HOUSEHOLDS, etc. PROSPECTUS, ALLOTMENT, LISTING, etc.

Chart 1.4
Secondary Market

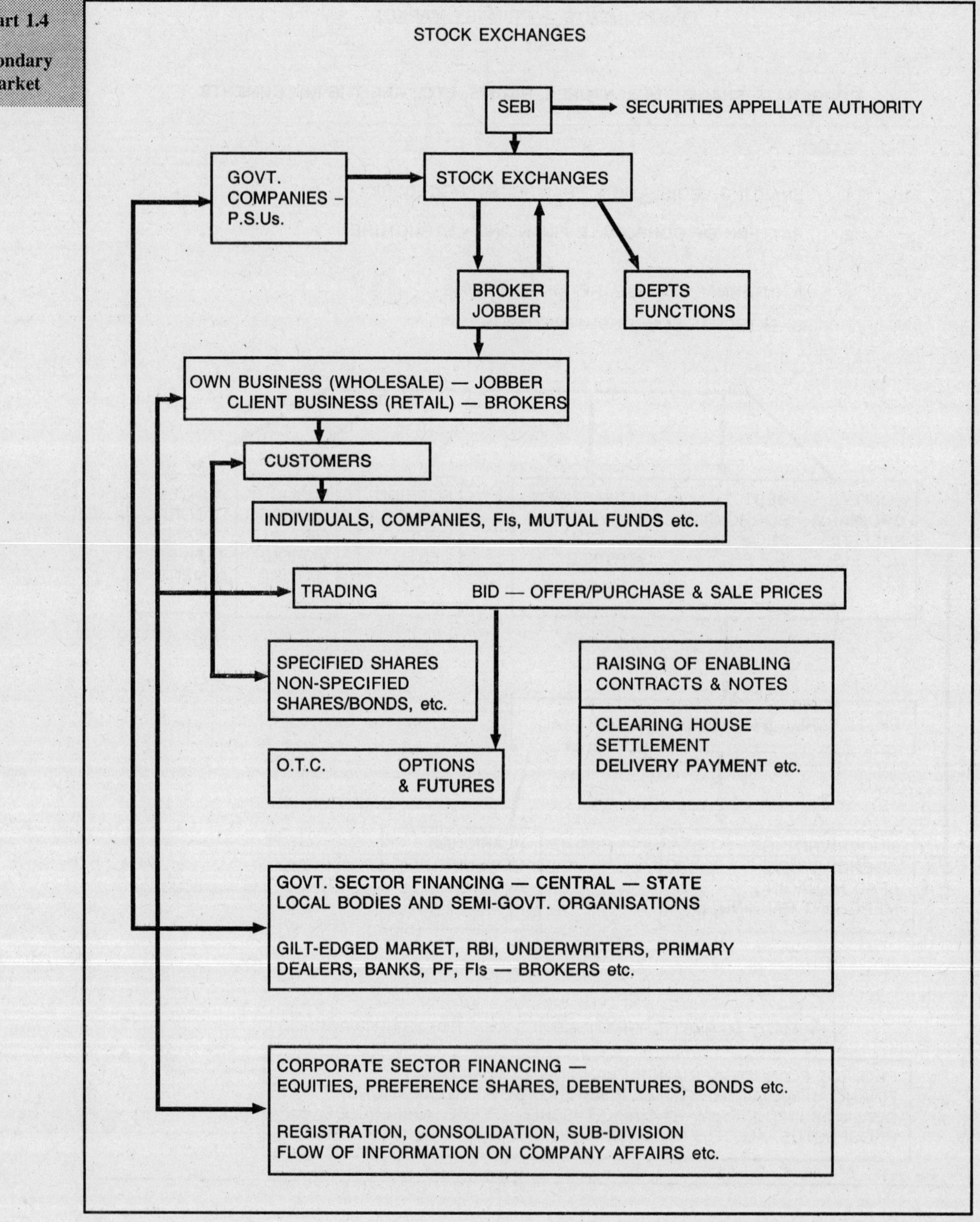

Chart 1.5
Inter-relations

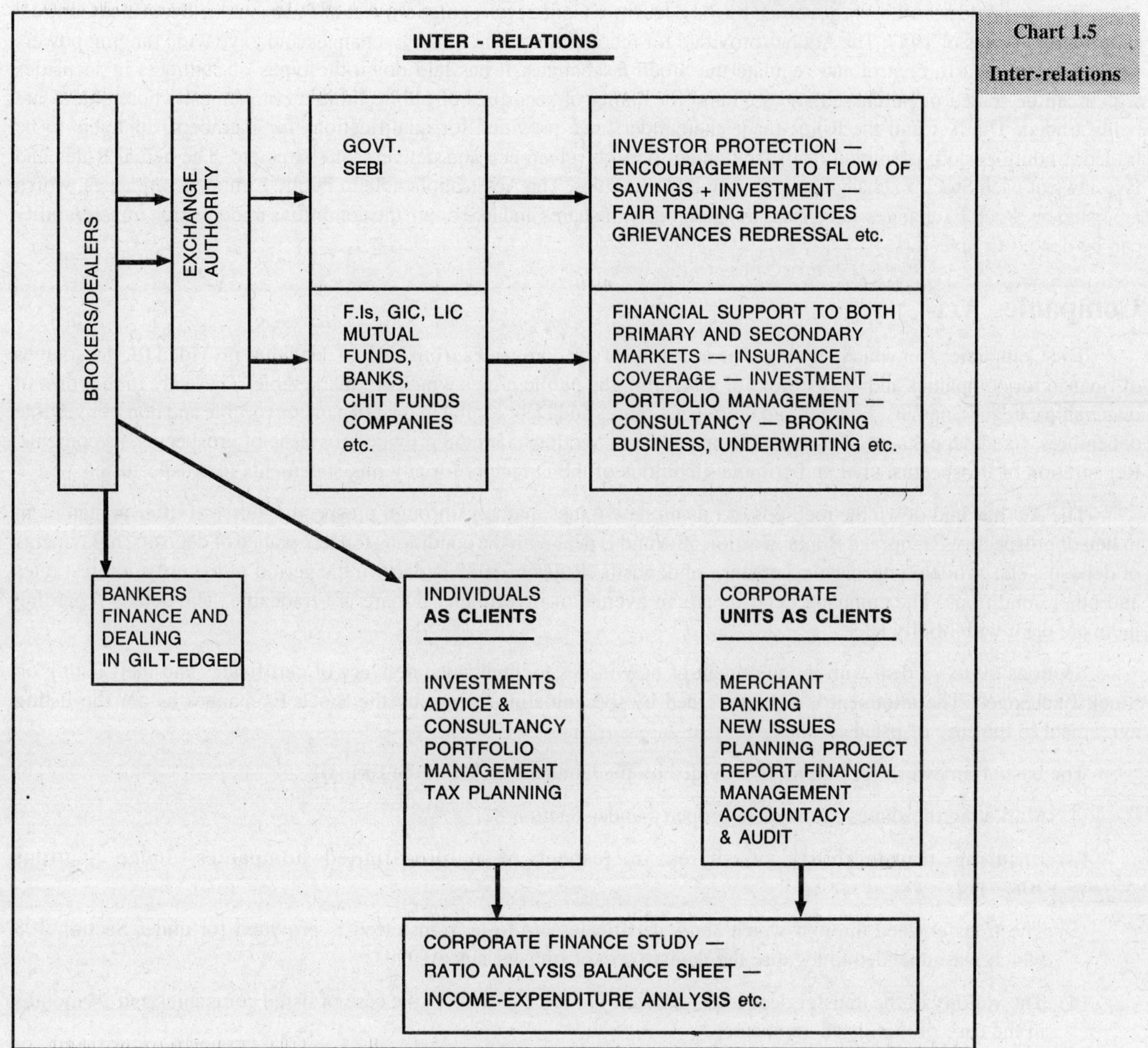

LEGAL FRAMEWORK FOR SECURITIES MARKETS

New Issues Market and Stock Exchange are a part of the Capital Market where the shares, debentures, bonds and other securities of companies and Government are traded. The Stock Exchange provides facilities for exchange of shares into money and *vice versa.* New Issues Market is the Primary market where the issuers can sell securities, but cannot buy. Stock Exchange is defined as an Association of Member Brokers who assist, facilitate and regulate trading in securities. One can buy and sell in the Stock Exchange or Secondary market.

These securities are issued by the Companies under the Companies Act and by the Government under the Indian Public Debt Act, since replaced by the Government Securities Act in 1999. Since the public are not interested in Government Securities due to lower level of interest rates on them, the public awareness of this market is little or negligible. This market is mainly confined to banks, financial institutions etc.

The capital market comprises of two components, namely, New Issues Market where companies issue directly securities to the public and the Stock Market or the Secondary Market where the existing securities are bought and sold.

Trading in old securities is governed by the Securities Contract (Regulation) Act of 1956 and the Securities Contract (Regulation) Rules of 1957. The Act has provided for recognition to the Stock Exchanges and gave wide ranging powers to the Government to control and regulate the Stock Exchanges. It has laid down the types of contracts in securities which can be traded or purchased and sold and for listing of securities of public limited companies, whose shares are being traded. The Act and the Rules made thereunder have provided for qualifications for members, contracts to be traded, trading period, permitted deals, settlement periods, clearance and delivery of shares etc. The actual Rules and Bye-laws of each Stock Exchange have enshrined these rules. The Act is applicable to Public Limited Companies, which are listed on Stock Exchanges and ensure transferability of shares and laid down the conditions under which transferability can be denied to investors.

Companies Act

The Companies Act which regulates the activities of the companies from birth to death has provided for the sources of finance for companies and the methods of marketing the public issues which are marketable. These are in the form of ownership category, namely, Equities and Preference shares and Debt capital in the form of convertible and non-convertible debentures, fixed deposits etc. Under the Companies Act, Sections 55 to 68 provided for issue of prospectus, its contents, Registration of Prospectus, civil and criminal liabilities of the Directors for any mis-statements in prospectus etc.

The Act has laid down the methods of raising new issues, namely, through prospectus, letter of offer or statement in lieu of prospectus, Rights and Bonus. Section 58 A and B deal with the conditions for acceptance of deposits, repayments of deposits, etc., while companies (acceptance of deposits) Rules of 1975 laid down the period of maturity, interest rates and other conditions. The company deposits are an avenue of investment, but are not tradeable. The details regarding them are dealt with briefly later.

Sections 69 to 73 deal with the allotment of new issues to applicants, delivery of certificates and their listing on Stock Exchanges. The allotment is also governed by the guidelines given by the Stock Exchanges as per the listing agreement in the case of listed companies.

The basic framework for trading is provided by the Companies Act in the form of:

(1) Marketing the shares as movable property under Section 82.

(2) Ensuring transferability of shares in respect of public limited companies under Sections 108 - 112.

(3) The transfer deed through which share certificates are to be transferred is provided for under Section 108 which was amended to legalise the demat form of transfer since 1999.

(4) The validity of the transfer deed under Section 111 is 12 months in the case of listed companies and 24 months in the case of non-listed companies.

(5) Section 114 provides for issue of share warrants.

So far as investors are concerned, it is desirable that they know the main provisions of the Companies Act, because the issue of prospectus, the contents of it, allotment of new issues, despatch of certificates, transferability etc., are all laid down in it. The rights of shareholders and debentureholders, and different categories of creditors and debtors of companies are set out. The book closure for accounts, presentation of Balance Sheet and Income-Expenditure accounts, payments of dividends etc., are all provided for in this Act. In Particular, Section 82 provides for transferability of shares and Section 73 lays down the conditions for listing of Public Limited Companies. While these sections ensure the marketability of shares of listed public limited companies, trading in them is made possible by the Securities Contracts Regulation Act and the Rules made thereunder.

In view of the fact that purchase and sale of shares through recognised Stock Exchanges and through licensed Stock Brokers are only legal, and those are governed by the SC(R) Act, the investors have to be familiar with this Act and the Rules made thereunder. The relations between the Brokers and Investors and in particular, the disputes if any, between them are governed by the Rules and Bye-laws of the Stock Exchanges which are formulated under this Act.

Acceptance of Fixed Deposits

A company cannot accept deposits in excess of 35% of the paid up capital and free reserves. Of this, 25% deposits can be accepted from the public and the rest 10% from shareholders of the company. The minimum period of acceptance of deposits is one year and the maximum period is limited to 3 years. The company is under an obligation to maintain an amount not less than 15% of the company's deposit liability maturing during the course of the year, in liquid investments such as Government securities, units, deposits with banks etc. The maximum rate of interest that can be offered on deposits is fixed at 11% to 14%. A ceiling on brokerage payable on deposits has been fixed at 1%. The interest earned on fixed deposits of companies does not enjoy any exemption from income tax. Neither does the amount of deposit qualify for any exemption under wealth tax. Under the existing provisions of the Income Tax Act, tax on interest paid/payable is deducted at source if the interest payment exceeds Rs. 2,500 in a financial year unless suitable declaration is furnished by the depositor in regard to the total income of the depositor not exceeding the minimum liable to tax in a financial year. (Form 15(H) under I.T. Act)

The acceptance of deposits by non-bank non-financial companies is governed by the Companies (acceptance of deposits) Rules 1975 as amended from time to time. Along with the prescribed application form the terms and conditions of acceptance of deposits are required to be furnished by companies, to the RBI in the case of non-bank finance companies and a copy in case of non-bank non-finance companies.

A careful study of either the financial data in the advertisement or the prescribed particulars as available within the application form would generally reveal the working results and the financial position of the company.

Compulsory Repayment of Deposits which have Matured for Repayment

The Companies Act, 1956 has been amended by the Companies (Amendement) Act, 1988 with effect from 1.9.1989 so as to provide for compulsory repayment of deposits which have matured for repayment (Section 58(9)]. Under the amended provisions, the Company Law Board has been empowered to take cognizance of non-repayment of any deposit on maturity and to direct repayment of such deposits on such conditions as may be specified by the Company Law Board in its Order. This will help and ensure repayment of public deposits and will create confidence amongst the public.

Procedure for Making Application to Company Law Board

The person holding a matured fixed deposit which he has not renewed and which the company has failed to repay, has to make an application in triplicate in Form No.11. The application has to be accompanied by a fee payable by way of bank draft in favour of the Pay & Accounts Officer, Dept. of Company Affairs, New Delhi/Mumbai/Kolkata/Chennai.

The Company Law Board has four Regional Benches. The aggrieved depositors may make an application to the Bench of the Company Law Board having jurisdiction according to the Registered Office of the company. The Company Law Board would, after giving a reasonable opportunity of hearing to the company and other persons interested in the matter, make suitable orders for repayment of such deposits. Non-compliance of the order of the Company Law Board is a punishable offence attracting penalty by way of imprisonment upto 3 years and fine of not less than Rs. 50 for every day till such non-compliance continues.

Where the deposit which has fallen due for payment remains unpaid the depositor can seek remedy in a civil court, or can file an application for winding up of the company to the court after serving on the company written demand requiring the company to repay the deposit (Section 433, 434 and 439 of the Companies Act may be referred to for the purpose). The SEBI is not permitting such companies to make public issues.

Cases in Respect of which Applications to the Company Law Board will not Lie

It is essential to know that under Section 58A of the Companies Act, the power to order repayment of matured deposits can be exercised by the CLB only in respect of deposits accepted Under the Companies (Acceptance of Deposit) Rules 1975 as amended from time to time. In other words, an application to the Company Law Board of repayment of matured deposits shall not lie in the following cases:

(*i*) Deposits made for booking purchases of scooter, car etc.

(*ii*) Deposits accepted by financial companies like, hire-purchase finance company, a housing finance company, an investment company, a loan/mutual benefit financial company, a chit fund company, which are governed by the rules made by the RBI.

(*iii*) Deposits accepted by companies which have been notified as 'relief undertakings' under special laws enacted by various State Governments. Court rulings point to the fact that the monetary liabilities of relief undertakings during the notified period stand suspended and any proceedings including the proceedings for compulsory repayment of deposits under Section 58A(9) shall accordingly remain stayed.

(*iv*) Deposits accepted by a sick industrial company covered by the Sick Industrial Companies (Special Provisions) Act, 1985 in respect of which, the Board for Industrial and Financial Reconstruction has specifically, by order suspended the operations of any contract, agreement, settlement, etc. under Section 22(3) of the Act.

Facts about Company Deposits

The deposits accepted by a company are not repayable before the date of maturity. It is left to the discretion of a company to allow premature repayment of a deposit. If and when the deposits are prematurely repaid the depositors are entitled to a lower rate of interest than the contracted rate. Most importantly, the company deposits are unsecured and rank *pari passu* with other unsecured liabilities. Hence, the investor has no recourse to any asset of the company in case of default by a company to repay the deposit on maturity.

Care to be Exercised while Investing in Fixed Deposits

Invitation to deposits from public for various schemes of deposits is invariably published in newspapers in the form of a statutory advertisement giving the following details:

(*i*) Terms of acceptance of deposits, rate of interest on different maturities, minimum amount of deposits, cumulative or non-cumulative nature of the deposit, etc.

(*ii*) Brief details of the name of the company, date of its incorporation, business carried on by it, places where the company has offices and names and address of directors.

(*iii*) Details of profits and dividends for the last three years.

(*iv*) Summarised financial position to the company (i.e., assets and liabilities) as appearing in the two latest audited balance sheets, alongwith details of contingent liabilities not provided for.

(*v*) Details regarding maximum amount of deposits which a company can accept.

(*vi*) A specific declaration that deposits accepted are unsecured and would rank *pari passu* with other unsecured liabilities.

(*vii*) A statement of deposits remaining unpaid.

Problems in Securities Markets

Securities markets are highly sensitive to any socio-economic and political factors. As such, the stock market is said to be the window of the economy. A large element of speculation is rampant in these markets and a right dose of regulation is a necessary evil. The sensitivity of external factors has increased after 1992 economic and financial reforms, when liberalisation and globalisation trends began to be perceptible.

Lack of professionalisation and broker-banks nexus has led to a number of scams. Even big banks got involved in Scams, in 1991-92 and 2000-01. Corruption and malpractices including mismanagement led to many bank failures, involving the U.T.I. as well. The trust and confidence reposed in the markets by investors were rudely shaken by the failure of U.S. 64 Scheme of UTI, urban corporative banks' failures and non-refund of deposits by many financial and non-financial companies. The laxity in regulation and in supervision by C.L.B., SEBI and RBI is one obvious reason for increased malpractices in the financial system, shaking the confidence of savers and investors. The failure of global Trust Bank, and scam of Satyam Computers are examples of laxity in supervision.

How do Savings Emerge?

Savings are excess of income over expenditure for any economic unit. Thus S = Y – E where S is savings, Y is income and E is expenditure. Secondly, excess funds or surplus in profits or capital gains are also available for investment. Thus, $S = W_2 - W_1$ where W_2 is wealth in period 2 and W_1 is wealth in period 1 and the difference between them is capital gains or losses. Thirdly, investment is also made by many companies and individuals by borrowing, from others. Thus the Corporate Sector and Govt. Sector are always net borrowers, as they invest more than their savings. Thus, S = B – L where "B" is borrowings and "L" is lendings. Savings can be positive or negative.

Why do People Save?

Saving is abstaining from present consumption for a future use. Savings are sometimes autonomous coming from households as a matter of habit. But bulk of the savings come for specific objectives, like interest income, future needs, contingencies, precautionary purposes, or growth in future wealth, leading to rise in the standard of living, etc.

Impact of Inflation

All investments lose in value due to inflation or rise in prices leading to depreciation of the rupee. When the rate of inflation is about 10%, the real value of money is lost by 10% every year. The investors have therefore to protect themselves from this loss of real values of their assets by proper Investment planning and by securing returns, higher than the inflation rate.

Some investments give income like bank deposits, P.O. Certificates, Company deposits etc. Some assets show capital appreciation if they are shares in companies or bullion, land and buildings. Some are safe and liquid, like the investments in Govt. securities, bonds of P.S.Us, etc. A few investments like those Blue Chips are easily transferable and marketable. So also the shares and securities, listed and traded on the Stock Exchanges. But all the above investments may not satisfy all the needs and objectives of investors, referred to later, including securing a hedge against inflation.

All objectives of income, capital appreciation, safety, marketability and liquidity as also hedge against inflation can be secured only by proper selected investments in *corporate securities*. The table below shows the real rates of return on all investments. In the long-run, investment in capital market gives a higher real return. But at macro level, only 5-6% of household savings in financial form are invested in instruments, giving real positive rates of return.

Investor's Cash Planning

Cash versus Other Alternative Assets (Data for March 2009)

Asset Class	*Proportion Held By Average Household* *	*Nominal Return*	*Real Return*
Cash	12.5	0 %	- 0 %
Bank Deposits	55.0	S.B. 3.5 %	0 to –2 %
	F.D. 4.5% to 7.5%		
Insurance (life etc.,) Pension funds, P.F.s etc., (LIC, GIC, HDFC etc.)	29.6	Estimated at 3 to 5% **	0 to -3%
Company Deposits	3.6	11%-14%	3% to 6%
Company Shares & Debentures	4.3	Around 10 - 15%	2 to 7%
Claims on Government Post-Office Deposits Postal Certificates etc.	1.4	Maximum rate of 8%	0%
MF Schemes	(–) negative	12%-15%	2%-7%

* as percentage of total financial savings. Inflation rate is assumed at 8% which is average rate for Nineties. Totals do not tally due to rounding up, and exclusion of "others" category.

Investment Activity

At the outset any study on Investment Activity should start with the question of what is investment. It means many things to many persons. If one person has advanced some money to another, it may be his loan which may be considered his investment for a return. If a person has purchased one kg of gold for the purpose of price appreciation or a consumer durable like washing machine for the flow of services, it is his investment. If he purchases an insurance plan or a pension plan, it is an investment. Thus there are various types of investments, for various persons.

For the individual, it is the exchange of the money or cash for a future claim on money or the purchase of a security of a promise to pay at a later date along with a regular income as in the case of a share, bond, debenture, etc. For the issuer of security it is the use of money for fixed capital equipments, working capital or any other productive and unproductive activity. Sometimes, it is also a service like consultancy, construction, hotel or hospital and services in future, as in the case of consumer durables.

What is Investment Activity?

Investment activity includes buying and selling or trading in the above claims on money and/or promissory notes. An investment for one may be disinvestment of another as in the case of stock market trading or may be a fresh investment in a new issue. In the New Issue Market, one can only buy securities. Investments can also be made in non-marketable securities or instruments or other avenues discussed in another chapter.

All purchases of securities are thus investment although for the economy as a whole, some investments are offset by corresponding disinvestments. There are two terms which are relevant in this context, namely, Gross and Net Investments. Gross are total investments made from all sources by an economy or a single economic unit. Net investments are those which are Gross investments, minus disinvestments for an economic unit. Gross Assets and Investments minus Depreciation for the economy or a company or Corporate Sector or Govt. Sector, is net Investment, which is termed also as Capital formation.

Savings and Investments

Investors are savers but all savers cannot be good investors, as investment is a science and an art. Savings are sometimes autonomous and sometimes induced by the incentives like fiscal concessions or income or capital appreciation. The number of investors was estimated at about 100 million out of population of more than one billion in India. In the nineties and later, savers came from all classes except in the case of the population who were below the poverty line. The growth of urbanisation and literacy have activated the cult of investment. More recently, since the nineties the investment activity has become more popular with the change in the Govt. policies towards liberalisation and financial deregulation. The process of liberalisation and privatisation was accelerated by the Govt. policy changes towards a market oriented economy, through economic and financial reforms started in July 1991.

Savings and Investments Rates in Asia

The 11th Five Year Plan has projected a savings growth rate of 38% and investment growth rate of 40%. Already the savings and investment rates in 2008-09 were placed at 37.7% and 39.1% respectively as per C.S.O. estimates. The gap between the savings and investment is met by foreign savings, which is the same thing as current account balance.

In many Asian countries, the general trend, in the present decade is to have current account surpluses, due to growing exports of services sector, as in the case of Japan, China and India counter-balanced by sharp increases in the current account deficits in the U.S.A., and E.U.

In Asia, the savings habit is far surpassing that of developed countries. But even so, the investment rate is higher due to growing investment in infrastructure, oil, gas and roads, etc., in the coming years. Even if the global oil demand may push up the oil import bills, as in the case of India, it has comfortable forex reserves covering financing upto 13 - 14 months of imports, which will cushion up the inflationary trends, in the economy.

In Asia, the highest savings rate is in Singapore, followed by China, Malaysia and India. Except in Singapore, where the investment rate is lower than the savings rate, the other, Asian countries including India, show a higher investment rate than the saving rate.

Objectives of Investors

(a) Income

(b) Appreciation of Capital

(c) Safety

(d) Liquidity

(e) Hedge against inflation.

(f) A method of tax planning

The mix of these objectives may also depend on the time frame of his investment.

(a) Short-term/day-to-day trading gains.

(b) Short-term capital appreciation upto one year (short-term capital gains).

(c) Long-term appreciation of more than 1 to 3 years (long-term capital gains).

Investment preferences of public may be set out in terms of their savings for:

(a) Transactions purpose (for daily needs or regular payments).

(b) Precautionary purposes (for contingencies or special needs).

(c) Speculative or asset purposes (for Capital gains and building of assets).

Investment for Consumption and Business

The income is divided into two components, namely, consumption and investment. The amounts not consumed are saved and invested. But investments are also useful for present and future consumption in the case of consumer durables, cars, gold and silver etc. But investments generally promote larger consumption in future as they lead to more income and larger capital appreciation in the years to come.

Some investments in business are used in trade and transport and other services. Thus, doctors, lawyers, traders etc., spend money for making investments for their business, which lead to further consumption or income.

Investment and Speculation

Purchase of assets like shares and securities can be for either investment or speculation or for both. Investment is long-term in nature while speculation is short-term. Investment aims at income and normal long-term capital growth while speculation aims only at short-term trade-gains through buying and selling. Investment is less risky and speculation is more risky.

Basically, both aim at income and capital appreciation. But the difference is in motives and objectives. All investments are risky to some extent but speculation is most risky as it involves short-term trading, buying and selling which may lead to profits sometimes and losses at other times.

Investment Opportunities

Investment avenues are multifold and each has it own risk-return characteristics. Riskless investments in the common parlance are bank deposits, Govt. securities, bonds of Govt. and semi Govt. bodies, post office savings schemes, P.O. deposits etc., Provident funds and pension fund schemes, Insurance for life, endownment, accident, etc. The details are discussed in another chapter.

Financial Investments vs. Physical Investment

Many savers will have their first preference for physical investments which are less productive and rarely income earning. Such investments are in consumer goods — non-durables or durables, gold, silver, cars and antiques and 'Curios.' These are satisfying the immediate consumer needs, for comfort, luxuries, social status, ego satisfaction, etc. Some investments of physical nature are more in real estate, land, buildings etc. Some of them if rented out to others give income and sometimes capital appreciation also, if the location is at good places or commercial areas. Similarly, gold, silver and other metals, diamonds, and antiques may present capital appreciation, without giving any regular income. Some investments are for social status and prestige as gold, diamonds, jewellery etc.

Bank Deposits

Commercial and cooperative banks accept deposits from public in the form of current account which bears no interest, savings Accounts which bear interest at 3.5% per annum, and fixed deposits of varying maturities from 15 days to 3 years. The interest rates will vary from bank to bank but the ceiling rates are fixed by the RBI upto one year deposits at present. These deposits are also insured with the Deposit Insurance and Credit Guarantee Corporation. Besides the operation of the banks, being regulated and inspected by RBI, the deposits kept with them are supposed to be safer and risk free. Although the returns are lower, the risk is also lower and risk averse investors will prefer investments in these avenues.

Next to keeping in cash most savings generally flow into some form of the bank deposits. The average households in India keep about 10% of their savings in financial form in cash and nearly 50% in bank deposits of various forms. But these avenues of investment give a return which is zero in the case of cash or a return less than or equal to the inflation rate of about 8% per cent per annum which is the average annual rate of inflation in the recent past.

CHAPTER 3

Macro Aspects of Savings and Investments

Savings and Investment which are promoted by the capital market are the basis of capital formation and economic growth in the country. As such it is necessary to present at the outset the inter-relation between savings and investment and growth in relation to the financial system in the process, in the macro sense.

Structure of the Economy

The Indian Economy has undergone vast changes since planned development was initiated in 1951. Early in the fifties total domestic savings as a percentage of GDP was hardly 5% and rate of growth of GDP was around 3%.

The structure of Indian Economy in 1951-52 showed that the shares of the primary sector, secondary sector and tertiary sector were 56%, 17%, and 27% respectively. The primary sector consists of Agriculture, Forestry, Fishing, Mining and Quarrying. The secondary sector comprises Manufacturing, Construction, Electricity etc. The tertiary sector encompasses the rest of the economy, *viz.*, Transport, Communication, Trade, Finance, Real Estate, and Other Services. By the end of the year 2009 after five decades of planning, agriculture accounted for 17% and manufacture and construction sector for 19% and the tertiary sector accounted for the rest (64%). At the beginning of new Millennium 2000, primary Sector accounted for 27%, secondary sector for 22% and tertiary sector for 51%. The share of agriculture is shrinking, while that of the tertiary or service sector is growing.

It would thus be seen that the importance of agriculture has gone down from 56% to 27% while the significance of manufacturing and services has gone up significantly over the planned period mainly due to shifts of resources from the primary sector to other sectors of the economy and in particular the services sector. The saving rate continued to be 22 to 24% of the GDP during the eighties and nineties while the same in fifties was only 10%. Now, savings rate is around 37% and investment rate around 39%.

What is Growth Process?

The economic performance is reflected in the growth of income or GDP and growth refers to a rise in output and incomes. The rate of growth of income and the distribution of income are the factors which influence the savings and are a function of the growth process. As the economy develops, production of goods and services would increase, leading to a rise in their consumption and the standard of living of the people. The growth of the economy involves a rise in incomes of the people, but development is a wider term, which includes both growth and qualitative improvement in the standard of living of the people and a better distribution of incomes. Development thus involves a rise in the level of income and better standard of living in general through growth plus socio-economic changes. This is what, in the present day parlance is terned as Inclusive Growth.

Role of Savings

Growth is a function of savings and investment in the economy, which along with the capital-output ratio determines the level of income. By increasing investment in fixed assets, plant, machinery, etc., capital formation rises which results in a rise in output depending on the capital-output ratio. The latter is a ratio of output to capital employed in any industry or productive activity. The total capital-output ratio for the economy, speaking in macro terms, and the total volume of investment in the economy would determine the growth of output and incomes. Thus, output (O) is a function of investment (I) and capital-output ratio (K); $O = f(I,K)$. Thus, $\Delta O = f(\Delta I, \Delta K)$ where Δs are incrementals and ΔK is marginal capital-output ratio, defined as $\Delta O/\Delta I$, namely, a rise in output resulting from a given incremental capital used in the productive process. The average capital-output ratio and incremental capital-output ratio are the two ratios to be looked into for the multiplier process to work from investment to income or output. Crudely expressed, if investment rises by 12% and capital-output ratio is 4:1, then the income would rise by 3% ($12 \div 4$). These ratios vary from industry to industry, sector to sector and activity to activity. Similarly, the savings ratio and investment ratio also vary in each of the industries and units, and among the various sectors.

In India, the net savers are the household sector whose savings are higher than their investment, leading to their positive contribution of savings in the economy. On the other hand, business and government sectors are negative savers in that their investment is higher than the savings leading to a net negative contribution to the economy. The foreign sector also contributes to net savings due to a larger inflow of funds through commercial borrowings and other forms of capital inflows.

Other Factors in Development

Another factor which influences the standard of living of the people is the rate of inflation which is measured by the rate of rise of prices, namely, wholesale prices or consumer prices (WPI or CPI for industrial workers). A rise in prices leads to the lowering of the value of money and its purchasing power, which in turn leads to the lowering of consumption basket of goods and services. This results in a lower standard of living of the people, other things remaining the same. The distribution effects of inflation are also adverse to the development process. Some income groups gain at the expense of others and the saving capacity may go down for the bulk of the population which are marginal savers.

Savings and investment not only depend upon income, but on its distribution among the population. The level of income in real terms is what matters for the standard of living of the people and this in turn depends on the distribution of income and the rate of inflation in the economy. So investment and income are to be looked into from the point of view of the inflation rate in the economy, namely, in real terms rather than in nominal terms. The other factor is the poverty ratio, which connotes the number of population below a level of minimum subsistence. The lower the poverty ratio, namely, if the proportion of those below the minimum subsistence level of income is lower, the better is the performance of the economy, as it shows a rising standard of living of the people.

The rate of savings also depends on the structure of the economy. As noticed above, agriculture used to dominate the Indian economy with a share of 56% of total national income in terms of output and nearly 70-80% of employment in terms of population. The saving potential of these people is low as agriculture used to be mainly for subsistence rather than for commercial and marketing purposes. This proportion of agriculture to GDP declined to around 35% at the end of the eighties by expansion of the industry and services sectors. In the early 21st century agriculture accounted for about 27% of total income of the people, although about 60% of the population still depend on agriculture either directly or indirectly. The contribution of agriculture to GDP fell to 17% by 2009. This shows that there has been a considerable widening of the base of economic activity into industry and services. Growth process leads to shifts in the structure of the economy from the primitive agriculture to modern capitalistic production in industry and services sectors. The savings have also increased enormously and that investment has also accelerated.

Financial Intermediation

The development process involves a larger role of financial intermediation and shifting of savings away from investment in physical assets to investment in financial assets. The financial intermediation not only promotes savings *per se* but leads to the process of shifting resources from less productive activities or underproductive activities to more productive activities. Not only the total quantum but the distribution of investment in the economy as between the various activities and sectors is relevant to the growth process. These factors can be effectively influenced by the financial institutions, namely, banks, UTI, LIC, FIs like IFC, SIDBI, NHC, NABARD etc., through their lending operations. The degree to which these institutions can influence the investment and productive activity depends on the depth and sophistication of the financial system and its structure. Thus the variety of instruments available for investment and trading, the specialisation among institutions and the range of their services and a host of other factors influence the productive activity and growth process. The sophistication in the financial structure depends on the degree of financial intermediation. In India, the financial system has been developing rapidly in the last two decades and the proportion of financial savings has been growing. Thus, savings in financial form of the household sector has increased from around 30% of the total in the fifties to 45% to 55% in recent years. As a proportion of GDP total savings of household sector in financial form is about 12% of GDP during 2000 to 2008.

Links of Real Economic System and Financial System

There is a continuous interaction between the financial system and the real economic system. The flows of funds in the form of savings and investment emanate from the financial system and promote production of goods and services in the real sector, leading to a rise in output and incomes of the people. The role of the financial system is thus to promote savings and investment in the economy and to enlarge these resources flowing into the financial assets, which are more productive than the physical assets. Even among financial assets, some are more productive than others and a proper financial intermediation and sophistication in financial services would promote larger production of goods and services in the economy. The financial system thus has an important role to play in the productive process and in the mobilisation of savings and their distribution among the various productive activities. The stock and capital markets have thus a significant role to play in this context because they are part of the financial system. They promote *inter alia* a larger mobilisation of savings by facilitating investment in financial assets such as shares, debentures, securities, etc., and a greater degree of liquidity is imparted to the existing investments by facilitating the purchase and sale of existing securities through the secondary market (*viz.*, stock market). They also provide encouragement to the listing of the shares of companies which facilitates their trading and the valuation of their assets by virtue of a quotation on the stock exchange, and help them to raise further resources, if need be. These institutions promote the expansion of the new issues and in the raising of larger resources in the capital market through widening the base of trading, increase in the number of instruments for savings and investment and through widening the base of trading, increase in the number of instruments for savings and investment and through widening the network of saving moblisation efforts. The recent increase in the financial institutions such as leasing and hire purchase and Housing Finance companies, merchant banks and mutual funds also helped to increase the degree of specialisation in the financial structure. New instruments of trading such as participation certificates, certificates of deposits, commercial paper are being developed in the money and capital markets which have widened the scope of financial services and sophistication in India.

Savings Rate

The Central Statistical Organisation (CSO) has defined savings as the excess of current expenditure over income at macro level and is a balancing item on the income and outlay accounts of producing enterprises and households, government administration and other final consumers. In simple words, savings are the excess of income over expenditure of the economic units. For the purpose of estimating domestic savings, the economy in a closed set up has been divided into three sectors: household sector, private corporate sector and public sector. The savings at household sector, which account for the bulk of savings, are measured by the total of financial savings and savings in physical assets. The savings in financial form include savings in currency, bank deposits, non-bank deposits, life insurance funds, provident and pension funds, claims on government, shares and debentures, units of UTI and trade debts. Of these, currency and deposits are voluntary savings and motivated by transactions and precautionary motives and are governed by interest income and other incentives. The savings in life insurance, provident and pension funds are contractual savings governed by precautionary and contingency motives. The claims on government include P.O. Savings media compulsory deposits, tax credits and investments in government bonds, etc. The savings in the form of units, shares and debentures etc. are all voluntary savings and are used for investment in the business sector, directly or indirectly. The above are the gross savings against which should be set off the financial liabilities such as borrowings by them from the government, business sector and other sectors of the economy. The flow of *net* savings in financial form is a relevant variable for influencing the growth process in the economy. The foreign sector is the fourth sector in an open economy contributing net savings.

The gross savings of the household sector constituted around in 22% of the GDP in recent years. Of these more than 45% is in physical assets and 55% in financial form. The savings in physical form include agricultural implements, tools, tractors, consumer durables, gold, silver etc. among the rural households, and such items as real estate, buildings, durable goods, gold, silver etc. among all households. The savings in physical form are less productive, while savings in financial form are more productive in various degrees depending on the efficiency of their use.

Gross and Net Savings

The gross domestic savings were at around 30% of GDP during 2000 to 2008. Of these, around 23% of GDP was accounted for by the household sector, 5% in the private corporate sector and 1 to 2% in the public sector. For illustration in 1994-95 total net domestic savings stood at 16% and gross domestic savings rate was 24.4% of GDP. The difference was accounted for by the high degree of obsolescence and capital depreciation in India at that time.

The investment in gross domestic capital formation is at a slightly higher rate of 39% in 2008-09 as against the gross savings rate of 37%. The difference between the domestic savings and investment is made good by foreign capital inflows, which constitute the saving in the foreign sector. Savings and investment rates have slowed down during 1998-99 and 2000-01, due to recession in the Economy. During 2001 to 2008, the savings rate stood around 30 to 34%.

Household Savings

The savings of the economy are mostly concentrated in the household sector in more recent years. For example, more than 100% of the domestic savings have originated from the household sector in 1988-89 due to negative savings in the public sector and insignificant savings in the private corporate sector in terms of percentages to the GDP. During 1997-98 and 1998-99, the same proportion has come down due to better performance of public sector and of the corporate sector. In 2007-2009, the savings rate was 8.1% of GDP in the case of Private Corporate Sector and in the case of public sector, it had a contribution of less than four per cent, during nineties and has now a contribution of 4.5%.

The savings in the household sector are mobilised directly in the form of units of the Unit Trust, premiums to the LIC and other insurance companies, contribution to pension funds, provident funds, etc., which are contractual forms of savings. Savings in the form of currency and deposits with commercial and cooperative banks are direct voluntary savings in financial form. Indirect investments from the household sector are investments in the secondary markets through purchases of shares and debentures, etc. by banks and financial institutions. The investments through provident fund and pension fund, UTI, etc., of household sector are also indirect investments. Investments in the new issues market are direct investments in the corporate sector by the households. At present, the direct investment in the corporate sector in the form of shares and debentures including UTI and mutual funds hardly accounts for less than 5% of the total financial savings of the household sector in the years 2001-2008, but come down to 1-2% of the total financial savings in the early years of the 21st century and now stood of 5.2% in 2006-07 and less than 1% in 2008-09. Some forms of holding savings particularly in the form of currency are barren and unproductive while some are less productive, such as those in real estate or buildings, in the sense that there will be no further production of goods and services. There is a large scope in our economy not only to raise savings in financial form but also to increase the investment in shares and debentures through shifts of assets held by the household sector and investments to more productive forms available to savers.

Shifts within Industrial Sector

Growth process involves structural shifts in the economy as between agriculture and industry and in favour of the latter, which was reported earlier. More importantly, within the industrial sector, there have been shifts over the long run in favour of the organised manufacturing activity and from consumer goods to capital goods and durable goods. The base of industrial structure has been widened and many new industries have been added in India after the initiation of the planned process. Among the various industries, production in mining, telecom., oil exploration and gas products, etc. has been increased significantly both in quantitative terms and relative terms in India. The unregistered manufacturing sector, particularly small-scale sector accounted for about 8% of the NDP while registered manufacturing activity constituted 13% of the NDP. It is no doubt true that the growth of modern large-scale industry under the planned process has reduced the importance of the unorganised small sector. But even so, the unorganised small sector now accounted for around one-third of the total industrial production. This shows that this sector still occupies an important position in the Indian Industry.

The other main features in the structure of the Indian economy are a larger rise in the shares of service sector, transport, communications, energy, banks and insurance, which shows that the role of infrastructural industries in the economy has increased significantly. Besides, the share of public administration and defence has also grown over the past few decades, partly due to the increase in the role of the public sector in the economy and partly due to the expansion of the government activities in providing infrastructure and other services. I.T. and BPO activities have further increased the role of service sector during the last decade.

Lead and Lag Industries

Among the industries, there are some as lead sectors and others as lag sectors. The savings and investment flowing into the lead sectors result in accelerated growth while those in the lag sectors may have less dynamic effects. Some of the lead sectors also called "sun-rise industries" are electronics, computers, chemicals, communications and high-technolgy industries. The future growth prospects of the economy depend on these industries, some of which have high capital-output ratios. The secondary market trends, the share prices and market capitalisation would depend more upon these industries in future, in addition to service sectors.

Public Sector Enterprises

The various five-year plans laid emphasis on capital-intensive industries *vis-a-vis* wage goods industries. The result is that there was scarcity of many consumer items while utilisation of capacities in capital-intensive industries like steel, coal, electricity, etc. was poor and capital was used most inefficiently. Large capital investment in the public sector has taken place over the past few years with the result the underproduction and underutilisation of capacities exist in these industries. There was continued low productivity and low profitability of a majority of the public sector undertakings like coal, steel, electricity, and Railways.

In the business sector, many public undertakings have negative savings due to the high capital intensity, high borrowing costs, and low earning potential. The managements in many of these public sector undertakings are inefficient and less dynamic and their contribution to the total profits and retained earnings are so small that they cannot meet their capital expenditure from their own resources. The budget allocation for investment has been withdrawn recently with the result that they have to depend on public borrowing. This is particularly true in the case of Railways, Food Corporation of India and a number of State Electricity Undertakings. Capital formation in these undertakings is poor, in view of their low profits and poor internal accruals.

Paradox of High Savings and Low Growth

In India, we have the paradox of a high savings rate and a low growth rate in the economy. With a savings rate of 22-24% and investment at 24%-26% the economic growth has averaged at around 4-5% during the eighties and nineties. This is explained by a high capital-output ratio in the Indian economy at around 4.5:1. The Seventh Plan projections were based upon a capital-output ratio of around 4.5 and savings rate of around 21-23%. The capital-output ratio was only 3.2:1 in the First Plan period, which has gone up to a high of 5.7:1 during the Fourth Plan but has since declined to 4.3-4.5 in the Seventh Plan period as per the estimates of the Planning Commission. The recent Tenth Plan has assumed a capital-output ratio of 4.1:1. This has given an average rate of growth of economy of around 8% in the Tenth Plan. This may be later scaled up or down. In the 9th Plan the average rate of growth was placed at around 5-6%. This was lower than the rate of 6-7% achieved during the Eighth Plan (1992-97).

The Seventh Plan gave an average rate of growth of around 5% and the Eighth Plan has placed it at a rate of growth of around 5.5%. A rate of growth of this order is necessary to increase the standard of living of people because there is a continuous growth in the population at a rate of about 2% per annum. In the fifties and sixties, for example, when the average rate of growth of incomes was around 3.5% and the population growth at more than 2%, there was hardly enough growth in the *per capita* incomes of the people (namely, at 1.5%). During the period 1951-1990 the annual rate of increase in *per capita* income at this level of 1.5% compares very badly with the most advanced countries. This should be attributed to inadequate savings potential of the public sector undertakings and poor capital formation in the private corporate sector.

Some Macro-parameters for the Recent Plans

RATES/RATIOS	SEVENTH PLAN (1985-90)	EIGHTH PLAN (1992-97)	TENTH PLAN 2002-07	ELEVENTH PLAN 2007-12
GDP Growth Rate	5.8%	5.6%	8%	9%
Domestic Savings Rate	20.4%	21.6%	29.8%	34%
Investment Rate	22.7%	23.2%	32.6%	36%
Current Account Deficit	2.4%	1.6%	2.8%	2.5%
Incremental Capital - Output Ratio	3.9	4.1	4.08	4
Growth Rate of Exports	8.1	13.6	27.6	—
Growth Rate of Imports	10.1	8.4	29.5	—

Some Macro-parameters for the recent plans achieved or projected are presented in the above table.

In the Eleventh Plan, the plan priorities are as follows:

(1) Generation of employment, and inclusive growth

(2) Reforms leading to globalisation and privatisation.

(3) Complete elimination of illiteracy and emphasis on elementory education for all.

(4) Drinking water, primary health, education, sanitation and health to be given primacy in objectives.

(5) Emphasis on agricultural and rural development.

(6) Strengthening of infrastructure.

Public sector investment was brought down from 45.7% in 7th Plan period to 43.2% of total investment in 8th Plan period. Draft on foreign savings is estimated at 1.4% of GDP. The Public Sector Financing method is also changed in the latest plan period: 70% of it has to come from capital market or household saving, 20% from own savings and 10% from foreign sources.

Role of Private Corporate Sector

It was seen earlier that the performance of the private corporate sector and public sector in generating savings was poor. The reasons for poor performance of the public sector have been explained above. The performance of the private corporate sector has also been disappointing in so far as its contribution to raising the Indian savings rate is concerned. In spite of five decades of development and a significant rise in manufacturing output, the contribution of savings of the private corporate sector to total net domestic savings was about 5% over the last few years. This compares very badly with the performance in developed countries where the corporate sector's retained earnings constitute a significant proportion of the total savings in the economy.

The reasons for poor savings by the corporate sector in India are many. Firstly, they place undue reliance on the loan capital due to the low level of owned resources. Besides, the share of profits in factory incomes has declined or did not rise as fast as the incomes out of interest. Secondly, a significant portion of the business in India is done by the unincorporated enterprises and partnership concerns, whose profits are reflected in income and savings of the household sector and not in the corporate sector.

Thirdly, the taxation policy in the corporate sector encourages the use of loan capital by companies and the dividend policy does not encourage the accumulation of retained earnings.

Conclusions

As referred to earlier the savings rate of the household sector at around 20-22% of GDP over the last few years has been stagnant mainly due to increased inflation rates and a tapering off of the level of growth of savings. This stage of growth is called "low level equilibrium trap." Even so, the average rate of growth of around 6% over the last two decades should be considered as a good achievement by the Indian planners. Besides, the other achievements of planning in India are rapid growth in the public sector and a mixed economy with a contribution of public sector of around one-fourth of the total production. The basic and capital goods industries which were well developed since the Second Five Year Plan have led India into one of the leading industrial producers in the world with a diversified industrial base and structure. It should also be noted that India has developed a high level of infrastructural facilities such as transport, communications, irrigation, railways etc. and entered into a number of high-technology industries like computers, I.T., satellite communication and non-conventional energy. The commendable performance of these industries, particularly transport, communications, energy, etc. have helped the industrialisation process in India. During the second half of Nineties the growth of infrastructure industries was stagnant. These achievements are in no way insignificant and can be attributed mainly to the growing role of financial intermediation in India during eighties and nineties. In recent years, more varieties of financial institutions have come up like Venture Capital Fund, factoring agencies, securities firms etc. The new economy of the new millennium is characterised by growth of knowledge based industries, e-commerce, I.T., multi-media, bio-tech industries, etc. Poverty ratio was brought down to 26% of the population due to a number of poverty alleviation programmes. India became a leader in I.T. software and knowledge based services. India has built up huge foreign exchange reserves and enough foodstocks. These achievements cannot be set aside as small and insignificant, at the time of the beginning of Eleventh Plan in (2007-08). But later on, The Globle recession of 2008 and 2009 has affected the Indian economic growth and increaset the inflation rate to a two digit figure at one stage.

Financial System – Intermediation

As opposed to Financial Activity, the real system deals with the production, distribution and consumption of goods and services. The introduction of money as a medium of exchange for goods and services, measure of value of the goods and services in the real system and as a store of value led to the Financial system. Financial System refers to the activity relating to the provision of the above services in terms of money and facilitates activity in real system. When we have the growth of financial system, providing inputs to productive activity, we have the growth of savings and investment and economic development. Financial Sector provides inputs in the form of cash credit and assets in financial form necessary for production in real system. Finance is the lubricating mechanism for economic activity to run its cycles.

Financial sector provides *inter alia,* the following essential services for the real system to function and grow:

(1) Economic growth and development depends on savings and investment which is the role of the Financial System to mobilise and channel savings into investment and capital formation.

(2) Capital formation is the basis for economic growth and under the capitalistic system of production, this plays a major role.

(3) Financial system promotes the liquidity in the system and allocation and reallocation of savings and investment into various avenues of economic activity is facilitated.

(4) Financial system serves a most crucial function of intermediation, between savers and investors and among various avenues of investment and between real activity in physical form and financial activity in the form of providing a means and a medium of exchange.

(5) As a store of value, the command on future goods and services is secured by financial assets such as Bank deposits, company deposits, and corporate and Govt. securities. Money as a store of value leads to financial assets and wealth and according to Friedman school of thought, money is held in the form of financial assets and constitutes the Asset Motive for money. The first and most vital function of money is to serve as a medium of exchange and a measure of value. Here the objective is to use Money for transactions and precautionary purposes. The second and equally important function of money is the store of value function, as per Keynes' Analysis. But Milton Friedman and his followers have converted this store of value function into asset function. The speculative motive of holding money in terms of Keynes' motives of holding money will now be analysed in terms of asset motive as money is a form of wealth and holding money in one's portfolio increases the wealthiness of the individual.

The above analysis conclusively proves the crucial role that financial system plays in functioning of real economy and for the growth of the economic activity. The sophistication and growth of intermediation role of financial system and the growth of financial assets in the economy are the sine-qua-non for the smooth functioning of the economy and growth of economy through rise in GDP and the rate of growth of GDP and of per capita incomes measuring the standard of living of people.

Financial Intermediation

The role of financial institutions is to provide intermediation between financial and real sectors and between savers and investors and promote capital formation and economic growth. The study of the national balance sheet shows that over any period, how the ratio of financial assets to total assets has been growing. This ratio is one of the indicators of economic growth. Over the planned period in India, this indicator has been rising, as reflected in the ratio of financial assets to total domestic assets excluding land. This was mainly due to rapid rise in financial assets, attributed to expanded role of public sector during 1950 to 2000 and large capital investments in capital intensive projects. But more importantly there was more active financial intermediation and widening and deepening of the financial system in terms of range of financial arehetect are and instruments and magnitude of funds raised., since the economic and financial reforms started in 1991-92.

Ratios of Financial Intermediation

The ratio between direct debt issued by non-financial institutions and indirect debt issued by financial institutions is called financial intermediation ratio. But the ratio of total debt to total investment activity is the financial inter-relations ratio. These ratios indicate the extent of the role played by financial institutions in the economy, in terms of the services they render. The specialisation in savings and investment activity is indicated by the growth of financial inter-relations ratio, namely, total financial issues to total physical asset formation (investment).

The following are the indicators which are more frequently used to assess the role of financial institutions and their services for the growth of economy.

Some Financial Indicators

(1) Indirect issues of financial institutions to non-financial sector

(2) Issues of non-financial sector

(3) Issues of rest of the world

(4) Total Issues = (1) + (2) + (3)

(5) Total physical assets formation (investment)

(6) Financial inter-relation ratio = (4) ÷ (5)

(7) Investment financed by the financial institutions = (1) ÷ (5)

(8) Financial intermediation ratio = (1) ÷ (2)

(9) New issues ratio = (2) ÷ (4).

Savings mobilisation and promotion of investment are functions of the stock and capital markets which are a part of the organised financial system in India. The objective of all economic activity is to promote the well-being and standard of living of the people, which depends on the income and distribution of income in terms of real goods and services in the economy. The production of output, which is vital to the growth process in the economy, is a function of the many inputs used in the productive process. These inputs are material inputs (in the form of physical materials, viz., raw materials, plant, machinery, etc.), human inputs (in the form of labour and enterprise) and financial inputs (in the form of capital, cash and credit). The easy availability of financial inputs promotes the growth process through proper co-ordination between human and material inputs.

The financial inputs emanate from the financial system, while real goods and services are part of the real system. The interaction between the real system (goods and services) and the financial system (money and capital) is necessary for the productive process. Trading in money and monetary assets constitute the activity in the financial markets and are referred to as the financial system.

What Constitutes Financial Activity?

The term "liquidity" is used to refer to cash, money and nearness to cash. Money and monetary assets are traded in the financial system. Thus, provision of liquidity and trading in liquidity are the major functions of the financial system. While cash creation is the function of the RBI, credit creation is done by banks and claims on money or monetary assets are dealt in by financial institutions including the RBI, banks and term-lending institutions. These institutions are all a part of the financial system. The Financial institutions activate the idle balances of money and thus influches available money in the economy.

Besides, the financial system is also geared to the mobilisation of savings and channelisation of these savings into productive activity. Through appropriate differentials in the rate of return and other incentives, funds flow from less productive to more productive activities. These flows of funds are facilitated by the efficient functioning of the financial system.

Sector-wise, government and business sectors are the major borrowers whose investment is always greater than savings. On the other hand, in India the household and foreign sectors are the net savers, with savings exceeding investment. The financial system provides the intermediation between savers and investors and helps the process of specialisation and sophistication in the financial infrastructure, leading to greater financial development which is a pre-requisite for faster economic development.

RBI and the Financial System

The original source of liquidity in the economy is the Reserve Bank of India. As a controller of currency and credit and creator of currency, the Reserve Bank is the central piece of the financial system. As a banker to the banks, the Reserve Bank controls the credit and banking system including the financial institutions. These are together called the organised sector of the financial system.

The functions of RBI with respect to the financial system are: *(i)* provision of finance and refinance; *(ii)* regulation of banking and financial institutions for protecting the interest of the public and for monetary and foreign exchange stability; and *(iii)* development of sound financial system by strengthening the institutional structure and by promoting saving and investment in the economy and *(iv)* Protection of domestic and external value of the currency namely the Rupee.

Money Market

An important segment of the financial system is the money market which refers to all transactions in near money such as short-term claims on banks, financial institutions and corporate sector. It is a market for short-term monetary assets or claims on money. The duration should normally be less than one year. These include transactions in inter-bank call money (Call money market) and treasury bills issued by the government and commercial bills issued by the private corporate sector (Bills Discount market). The money market is the short-term wing of the financial system dealing in claims on money of a short-term nature, say, of a few days to a few months. Next to the currency, the most liquid assets are the short-term claims or call money of a duration of up to 14 days. The bills, both of the government and the private corporate sector, may run for three to six months. But all these instruments would generally be of a few days to one year and fall into the category of short-term monetary instruments. The intercorporate funds market is also a part of this market which conducts the borrowing and lending operations among the corporate units in the private sector. The banks, financial institutions and companies operate in these markets and effect purchase and sale transactions in these near-money assets.

The commercial paper (CP) issued by companies for raising short-term working capital is being developed in India. The participation certificates (PC) issued by banks and financial institutions, the deposit certificates (CD) issued by banks and factorisation bills are the other instruments. The institutions operating in these markets are banks, development finance companies like the LIC, UTI, GIC, etc. and other financial institutions. In the inter-bank money market, however, only the LIC and UTI have been permitted to operate in addition to banks. In 1990, the GIC, IDBI, NABARD, Mutual Funds and other financial institutions have also been permitted to operate. In April 1991, the RBI allowed the entry of any mutual fund and any entity with bulk lendable resources of Rs. 20 crores and above as also the Money Market Mutual Funds to enter the call money market. This market is being developed in India by the establishment of Discount and Finance House by the Reserve Bank in April 1988, in collaboration with the financial institutions.

The money market is developing at present. The qualities of a developed money market such as cohesion, integration of sub-markets, specialisation in various categories of business and openness to foreign forces are absent in India. There is no developed secondary market for many instruments like Treasury Bills, Commercial Bills, CPs and CDs, etc. Recently, schemes for the development of secondary market in commercial paper and for trading in certificates of deposits and participation certificates have been initiated by the RBI.

Characteristics

The money market establishes the link between the RBI and banks and the policy of RBI is felt in this market first before it percolates to other markets. The inter-bank market matches the deficits and surplus of banks; SBI and foreign banks are the major players in this market. This market provides an important area or venue for central bank intervention in the economy. It is also a place to secure the short-term requirements of banks and FIs. This provides a link between the cash and near-money assets and to long-term wing of the capital market. Operations in this market extend to dealings in UTI units, PSU Bonds, and short-term bonds of semi-government and government sector etc.

Discount and Finance House

The Discount and Finance House of India (DFHI) was set up in April 1988, in accordance with the recommendations of the Working Group on Money Market under the chairmanship of Shri N. Vaghul. The paid-up capital of Rs. 100 crores was contributed jointly by the RBI (Rs. 51 crores), public sector banks (Rs. 33 crores) and financial institutions (Rs. 16 crores). The aim of DFHI is to deal in short-term money market instruments with the primary objective of imparting improved liquidity to such instruments.

The functions of DFHI are as follows:

1. Discount/purchase etc., of 91 day Treasury bills and 364 day Treasury bills;
2. Discounting and rediscounting of short-term commercial bills for banks and financial institutions; and
3. Participation in the inter-bank call money market, both as lender and borrower, subject to the regulations of Indian Banks Association and the RBI.

The sources of finance are as follows:

1. Paid-up capital of Rs. 100 crores;
2. Credit limits of Rs. 200 crores with public sector banks; and
3. Back up refinance lines from the RBI.

Operations of DFHI

The DFHI purchases and sells Treasury Bills of 91 days, and 364 days. Continuous bid and offer rates are maintained. The yields to investors varied from 9 to 14% depending on the conditions in the market. It is the vehicle of operations of RBI in the money market. For some time, it has operated in the Govt. securities market also particularly before the STCI was set up.

The DFHI rediscounts from the banks commercial bills at the going market rates; also purchases and sales are carried out and bid and offer rates are quoted. It also operates in the inter-bank call money market, both as lender and borrower.

Stock Market

In the stock and capital markets, there are various types of term-lending institutions, all-India and state financial corporations and finance companies and development corporations, which deal in money and debt claims. The trading in debt claims of a medium and long-term nature can be classified into those of the government sector and of the private sector. The securities of government are traded in the stock market as a separate component, called gilt-edged market. The securities of the government sector include those of the Central and State Governments, local bodies, semi-government bodies and those guaranteed by the government. These securities may have a maturity running up to 25 years. In this market, there are again three types of securities — short, medium and long-dated government securities, depending upon the maturity period.

Another component of the stock exchange deals with trading in corporate shares, equities, and preference shares which are forms of raising funds of an ownership category. When these equities are floated to the public for the first time by the companies as shares, they constitute the new issues market, which is a component of the capital market. Besides, there are also further issues which are floated by the existing companies for additional capital for expansion, modernisation, etc. The new issues and further issues are the claims of the public on the corporate sector. The claims on the private corporate sector can also take the form of preference shares which are also of ownership category. There are also securities of a debt nature such as bonds/debentures and the companies may borrow from the public directly by raising deposits. This constitutes the debt segment of the capital and stock markets. These are of various maturities extending up to 3-5 years in the case of company deposits and 5 to 7 years in the case of debentures. Debentures may be convertible or non-convertible, depending on the availability of option for conversion into equity. Similarly, preference shares may be cumulative or non-cumulative depending on the provision for accumulation of dividends or not. More recently, convertible preference shares and debentures are also permitted, which can be converted into equity shares at a later stage. An instrument permitted by the Government since 1985 but which has not become popular is the cumulative convertible preference share (CCP) which is not only cumulative with respect to payment of arrears of dividends but also convertible into equity after 3 to 5 years. These shares carry a fixed rate of dividend of 10% until conversion. A number of new instruments have also been introduced and referred to later.

The latest component added to the Stock Exchange is Options and Futures trading, which are discussed later in the book under the caption of Derivatives.

Financial Institutions

The various financial institutions which trade in these stock and capital markets are all-India financial institutions like IFC, SIDBI and NHC and various SFCs, for which the apex institution is the RBI. Institutions which issue primary securities to collect the savings from the public directly are MFs, GIC, LIC, etc. They collect savings of the public directly in the form of units or premiums. These are called investment institutions. More recently, some public sector banks such as SBI, Indian Bank, Bank of India, Canara Bank, etc. have started their mutual funds, as also the LIC and GIC. These are also part of the stock and capital markets. These institutions trade and invest in these markets. The securities traded by them may be the claims of the government or of the private corporate sector. The all-India institutions and state financial institutions like the ICICI, IFC or SFCs, etc., raise resources directly from the public in the form of deposits or by issues of bonds/debentures. They may also borrow from the banks and other financial institutions as also from the RBI. These are called Development Corporations. The uses of their funds are investments in corporate shares, securities and bonds/debentures and loans and advances to corporate units. More recently, a number of new finance companies have cropped up, namely, lease finance, housing finance, merchant banks etc. The range of instruments offered to the public has accordingly widened and the capital market has been deepened and broadened enormously in recent years.

Savings and Investment

The household sector is the major saver in India and contributes to the bulk of the total savings that flow into financial assets which may take any of the forms of currency, deposits with banks and companies, PF, insurance and corporate shares, bonds, etc.

In addition to providing liquidity to investments, the stock and capital markets promote mobilisation of savings and channelise them into investment. As already referred to, the major borrowers are government and business sectors in the economy, which invest more than they save. The net savings flow from the household and foreign sectors. The financial system helps the process of institutionalisation of these savings for promoting investment and production in the economy. The financial intermediaries play a crucial role in the process in the stock and capital markets in India. The importance of underwriting of shares and stock-broking activities of brokers and dealers is to be appreciated in this context, as brokers are financial intermediaries like banks and financial institutions.

Interest Rate Structure

The interest rates paid on these various securities are fixed by the government and the RBI. The bank rate and other interest rates as applicable to the banks are fixed by the Reserve Bank and the others by the government in consultation with the RBI. In India, the interest rates are partly administered and the rates in the organised financial system are controlled. The peculiar feature of the structure is that interest rates do not reflect the free market forces nor do they reflect the scarcity value of capital in the economy. Most of these rates are determined on an *ad hoc* basis, in tune with the exigencies of monetary and credit policy or fiscal policy. Normally, interest is a reward for risk and return for abstaining from present consumption. In India, certain priority sectors like borrowings by the government and operations of agriculture, exports and other priority sectors are financed at concessional rates on considerations other than risk/ return. Since 1992, there has been some deregulation of the financial system and many interest rates have been freed from controls. These and other details are discussed in later chapters.

The Interest rates on company bonds are now freed which were earlier fixed by the Govt. Certain returns like those in National Saving Certificates of the government also carry fixed interest rates in addition to certain tax exemptions and other fiscal benefits. The criteria of fixing these rates differ from their nature and from instrument to instrument. The interest rates on 14 days, 91 days and 364 days Treasury bills introduced in the reforms since 1986-87 are determined by auctions and expected to reflect the free market forces. The coupon rates on government loans were already revised upwards in the early years of the nineties to be more realistic and market-oriented. Although almost all the interest rates in India are fixed, the interest rate policy is operated in a flexible manner so as to reflect the emerging conditions in the economy.

Reference may be made here to the relevant recommendations of the Chakravarthy Committee to review the working of the monetary policy (RBI, 1985). This Report highlighted the need to bring the interest rates nearer to the free market rates and to fix them at levels of positive return in real terms adjusted for inflation. Debentures are the corporate debt just as deposits are, but while debentures are mostly secured, deposits are not. Some of the debentures are convertible into equity shares, called convertible debentures. The interest rates offered on them are lower than on non-convertible debentures. The interest rates on debentures are allowed to be fixed by the companies depending on the free market forces and their credit Rerting. The inter-bank call rate had a ceiling of 10%, which was removed in May 1989. The short-term deposit rates of banks vary and the maximum rate payable by banks on deposits is now freed for deposits of above one year.

Under the ownership category of capital, there are equity and preference shares. The interest rate on preference shares is fixed by the government at 14% while the returns on equity depend on the dividends declared by the company and the operational performance of the corporate sector. All these categories of securities are of a long-term nature and are basically the claims of the public on the government and the corporate sector.

Some of these are quoted and traded in the market while others are not. Of those quoted, a few are more actively traded than others. The trading on the stock exchanges is called the secondary market, while the primary market refers to the issue of new securities to the original savers, viz., the households, trusts, charities, corporate entities, non-corporate enterprises, government etc.

Capital Market

As referred to earlier, in the category of financial institutions, there are some which issue primary securities. Besides the corporate sector which issues primary securities in the form of new issues and further issues, there are also financial institutions like LIC and GIC, which sell insurance certificates for collecting the savings from public directly. They also collect the premiums and mobilise savings of the public. These funds are mobilised for channelling them ultimately into the stock and capital markets.

The public sector units and the government are in fact the largest borrowers in the primary market. Many public sector undertakings like Railways, SAIL, FCI etc., are now directly issuing bonds to the public. Similarly, UTI also issues certificates and other unit schemes leading to mobilisation of savings directly from the public. The units of UTI as well as the certificates of LIC, GIC, etc., are all part of the capital market transactions of mobilising savings directly from the public. The Mutual Funds floated by some public sector banks and more recently by Private sector also raise funds directly from households and invest them in turn in the primary and secondary market in shares, debentures, bonds, deposits etc. of the companies or in government securities floated from time to time. The financial institutions like NHC, NABARD IFC, etc., also issue bonds in the market to raise funds for their operations. In the case of primary market, the institutions may underwrite or make direct subscription to the new issues or further issues of the corporate sector. The brokers, banks and the financial institutions referred to above are all intermediaries operating in the primary and secondary markets.

In the primary market, the brokers act as underwriters, managers, Registrars and even merchant bankers to the new issues. In the secondary market, the claims of a long-term nature of one year and above are traded both on spot or forward basis. This trading imparts liquidity to investments and thus promotes savings and investment. These financial institutions can only change the velocity of circulation of money (cash and credit), while dealing in the primary and secondary markets, but the banks can influence both creation of money and its velocity.

The RBI has linkages with banks and other financial institutions through its control and finance functions and provision of cash and currency. Besides, the money market trades in claims on money of varying maturities of a few days to a few years. The trading in the money claims is what constitutes the financial system, controlled by the RBI and is called the organised financial system. Banks have linkages with both brokers and dealers in securities through the credit limits granted to them and through their operations in the primary and secondary markets.

Unorganised Financial System

In India, we have an unorganised financial system which is not amenable to control by the Reserve Bank directly. In this system, there are a number of moneylenders, traders, landlords, who lend money to the public and indigenous banks who also accept deposits from them. There are also private finance companies, Nidhis, chit funds and host of other unincorporated bodies whose activities are not amenable to the financial discipline of RBI. But some activities like deposit taking activities, the maturity and interest rates on their deposits etc. are controlled by the RBI and the government. In this system, claims on money are traded, bills of exchange are discounted, monies lent, advances made and a host of other transactions take place in money and near money assets. The rates of interest may vary from 20% to even 100%, depending upon the stringency in the market. There are links between the organised system and unorganised system in the form of credit limit sanctioned to the moneylenders, brokers and finance companies by the commercial and co-operative banks. In this process, both commercial and co-operative banks play an important role as the links between these two segments of the financial system. The RBI, however, controls the acceptance of deposits and interest rates thereof of financial companies, while those of other companies are controlled and regulated by Company Law Board (CLB) and Department of Company Affairs of Government of India. Some like chit funds, money lenders etc., are also controlled by the respective State Governments under their state laws.

Bullion Market

In the last resort, gold, silver, bullion and even real estate can also be considered as monetary assets in the long spectrum of liquidity as people prefer to hold them as alternatives for company deposits, debentures, etc., in the organised sector. It would thus appear that the spectrum of liquidity is very wide spreading from cash/currency of the Reserve Bank to long-term securities, shares, etc., which are not easily realisable and even to monetary metals like gold and silver. The bullion market is thus an adjunct of the capital market in the sense that funds which could not be deployed in the capital or stock market may sometimes flow into the bullion market and *vice versa.* In the overall financial system, the money market, capital market and bullion market are closely linked and the flow of funds in either direction is possible as between them.

Charts 4.1 to 4.7 depict a schematic presentation of the financial system in India.

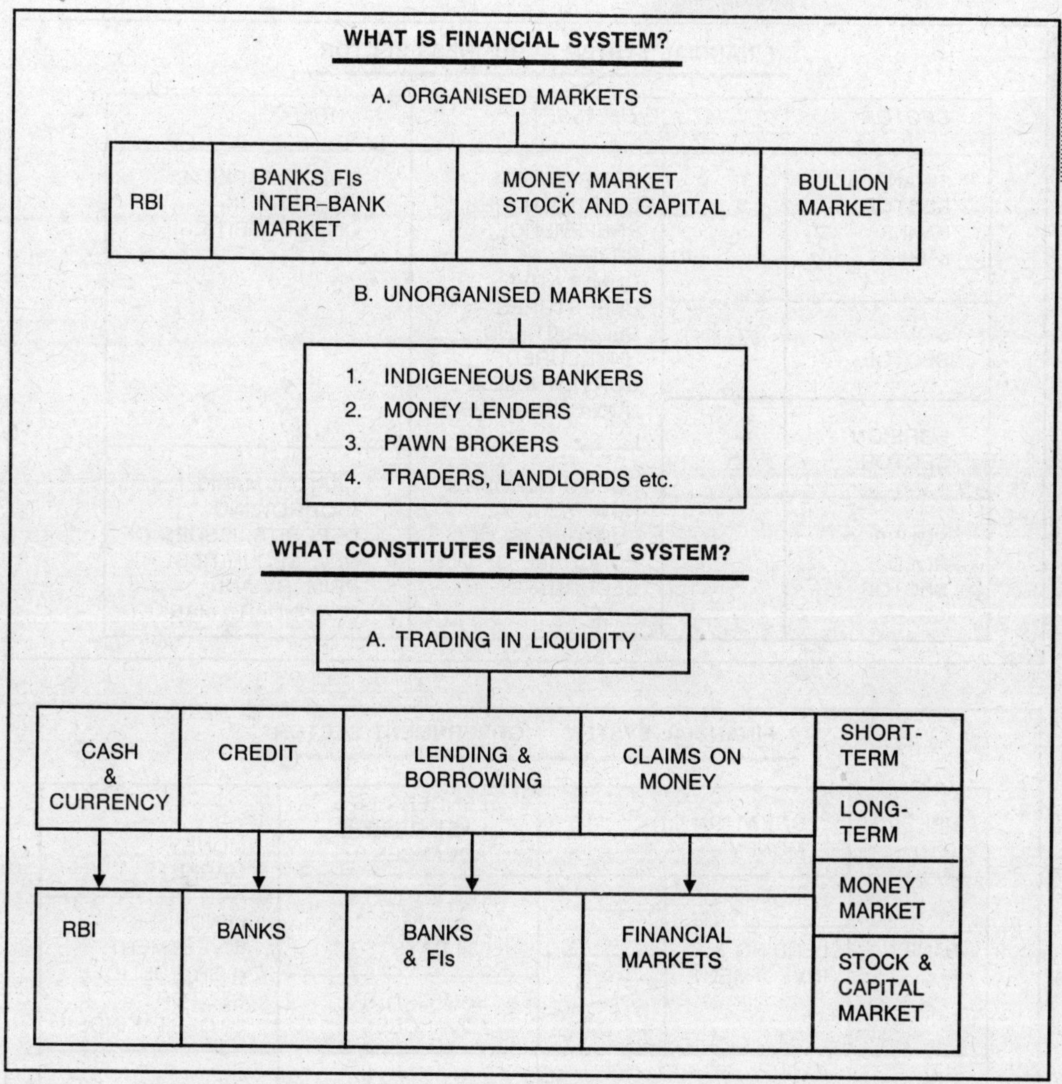

Chart 4.1
Schematic Presentation of the Financial System in India.

Chart 4.2

B. MOBILISATION OF SAVINGS AND PROMOTION OF INVESTMENT

	SECTORS	*S/I*	*MARKETS*
NATIONAL SAVINGS & FLOW OF INVESTMENT	HOUSEHOLD SECTOR	S > I	PRIMARY MARKETS
	FOREIGN SECTOR	S > I	ALL MARKETS — NEW ISSUES & CAPITAL MARKET & FOREX MARKET
	BUSINESS SECTOR	I > S	PRIMARY AND SECONDARY MARKETS
	GOVT. SECTOR	I > S	CAPITAL MARKETS — GILT-EDGED MARKETS

S: Savings I: Investment

Chart 4.3

FINANCIAL SYSTEM — BUSINESS SECTOR

SECTOR	*NATURE OF ASSETS*	*MARKETS*
FINANCIAL SECTOR BANKS & FIs GOVT. SECTOR FOREIGN SECTOR HOUSE-HOLD SECTOR	BORROWINGS EQUITY SHARES PREFERENCE SHARES CUMULATIVE DEBENTURES — SECURED AND UNSECURED CONVERTIBLE & NON-CONVERTIBLE	STOCK MARKETS (TRADING IN OLD SECURITIES)
	PUBLIC DEPOSITS NEW ISSUES FURTHER ISSUES, PURCHASE OF OLD SECURITIES	CAPITAL MARKET (BORROWING DEPOSITS, ISSUES OF NEW SECURITIES) PRIMARY AND SECONDARY MARKET

Chart 4.4

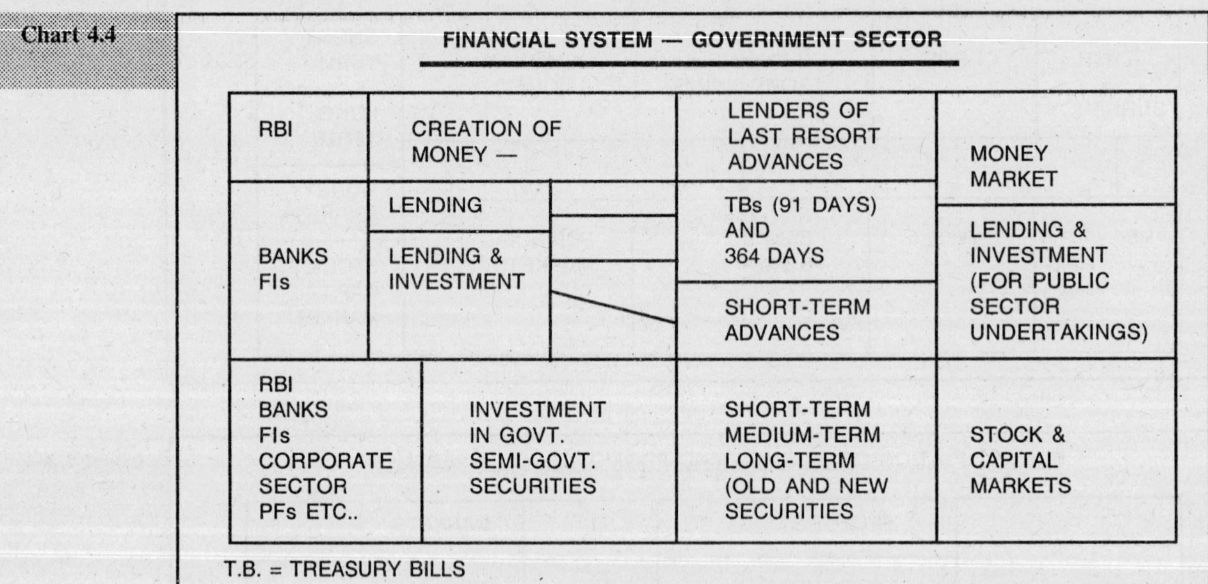

Chart 4.5

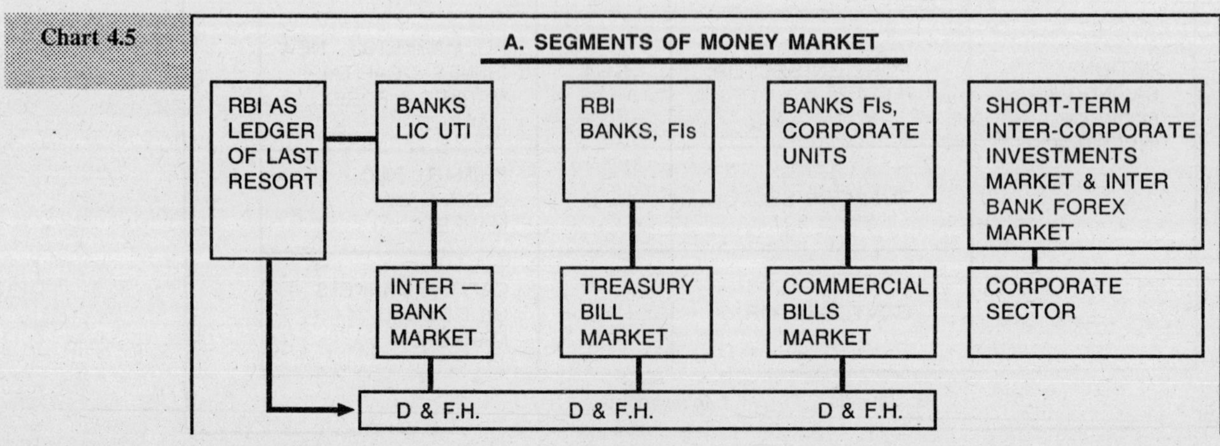

B. SEGMENTS OF CAPITAL MARKET

APEX BODY	INSTITUTIONS		OPERATING MARKETS	
SEBI	IFCI BANKs SFCs DEVELOPMENT AGENCIES PFs	LIC UTI GIC FINANCE COMPANIES INVESTMENT COMPANIES BROKERS	NEW ISSUE MARKET — SECURITIES MARKET — DIRECT BORROWING — FROM BANKS — FROM PUBLIC DEPOSITS — OTHERS	INITIAL ISSUES FURTHER TRADING —

Chart 4.6

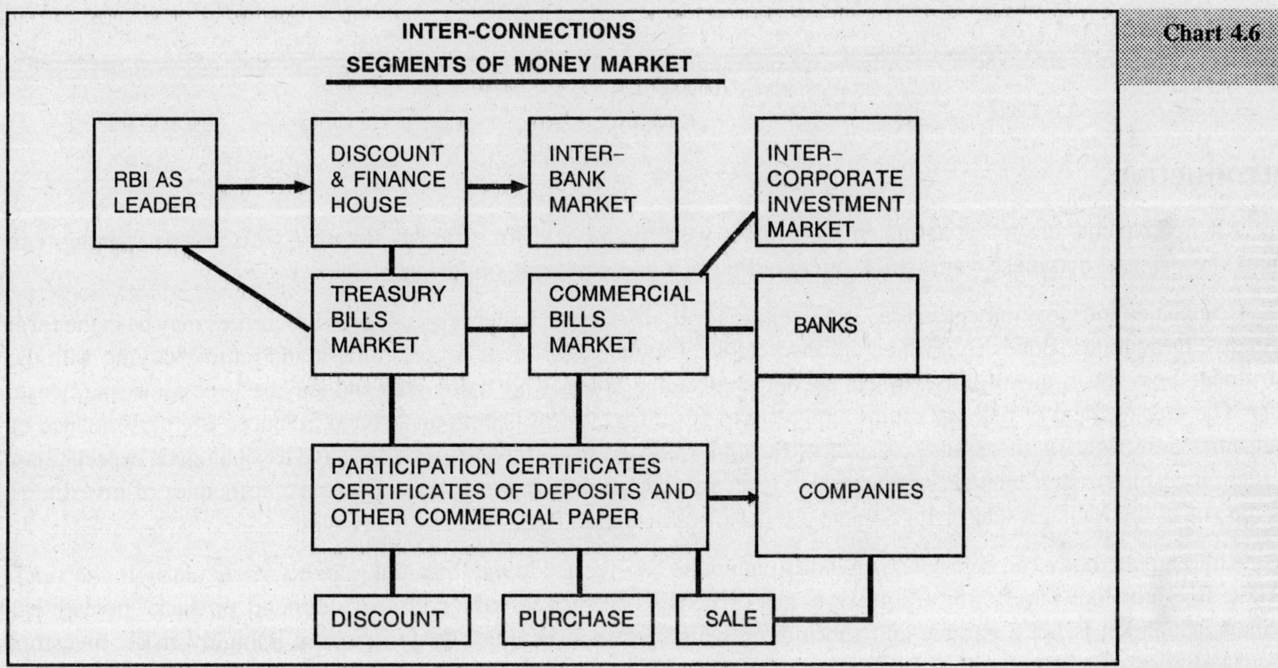

Chart 4.7

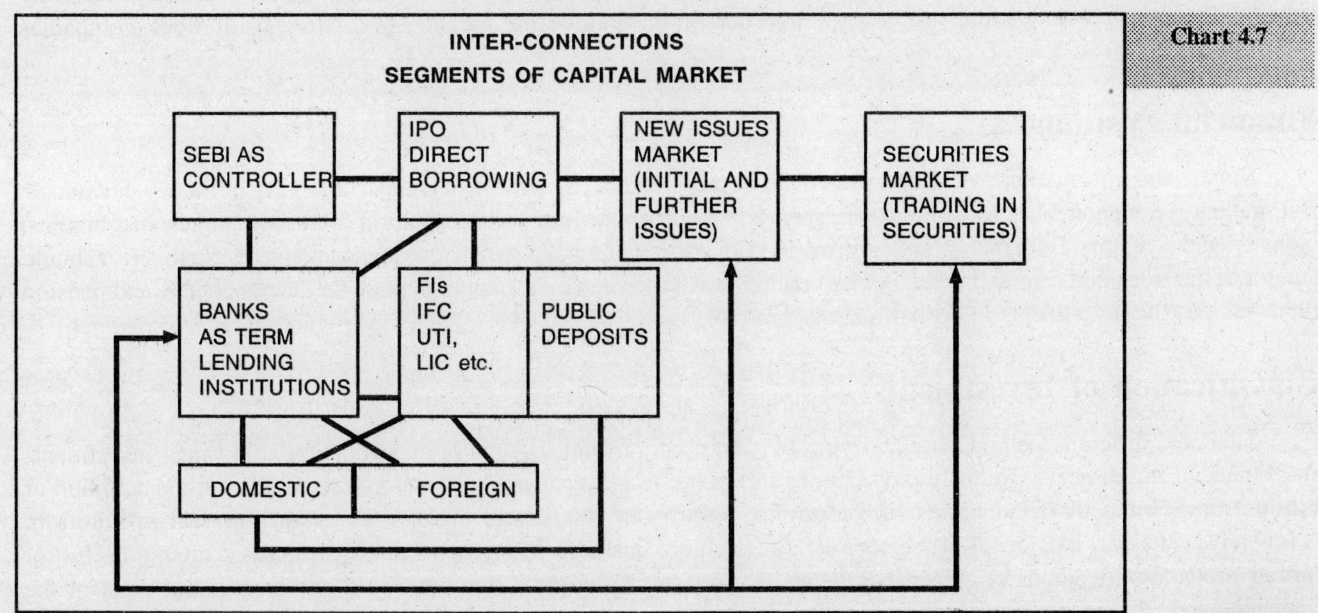

CHAPTER 5

Investment Avenues

Introduction

All Investments are risky, as the Investor parts with his money. An efficient Investor with proper training, can reduce the risk and maximise returns. He can avoid pitfalls and protect his interests.

Companies and Government sell securities, either for equity Capital or debt capital. These securities may be in the form of Shares, Debentures, Bonds etc., which are marketable. They have different degrees of risk and return, varying with the Instrument. Some instruments of investment are non-marketable and they are more risky and may become sometimes waste paper. The management of risk and return requires expertise. Investment is both an Art and Science. The performance of Companies and changes in share prices are all based on some fundamental principles, sentiment and psychological expectations. As such, investor has to use his discretion, which is an art to acquire by learning and experience. Principles of Investment and the Art of the Management of Investment are basic requirements for a successful Investor.

Although anybody can be a saver, anybody cannot be an investor in the financial markets, particularly in the stock market. It is not like purchasing a lottery ticket or betting on horses, which mostly depend on luck. Investment in financial market is not a gamble and speculation which some investors indulge in and it is highly risky. Investors should be those who invest with the objective of receiving some income, share in the prosperity of the company and gain capital appreciation in a longer time span. Investors in the wider sense include speculators, institutions, companies and even banks.

Financial Position

Money and Information are the basis and the first requirement of investment is the availability of money or savings. But, money is not enough, as investments are generally made on the basis of information of the companies, instruments, industry, and economy. Both money and information flow do help in making investment management. No investor should enter into the stock and capital market, before making provisions and investments in housing insurance, P.F. and pension funds etc., as the investments in capital markets are most risky.

Classification of Investments

There are different methods of classifying the investment avenues. A major classification is Physical Investments and Financial Investments. They are physical, if savings are used to acquire physical assets, useful for consumption or production. Some physical assets like ploughs, tractors or harvesters are useful in agricultural production. A few physical assets like lorries, cars, jeeps etc. are useful in business. Many items of physical assets are not useful for further production of goods or create income as in the case of consumer durables, gold, silver, etc. But most of the financial assets, barring cash are used for production or consumption, or further creation of assets, useful for production of goods and services.

Among different types of investments, some are marketable and transferable and others are not. Examples of marketable assets are shares and debentures of public limited companies, particularly the listed companies on Stock Exchanges, bonds of P. S. Us, Govt. securities, etc. Non-marketable securities or investments are bank deposits, provident and pension funds, Insurance certificates, Post Office deposits, National Savings Certificates, company deposits, private limited Companies' shares etc. These three types of assets are detailed in the chart below.

What is Investment?

As referred to earlier investment refers to acquisition of some assets. It also means the conversion of money into claims on money and use of funds for productive and income earning assets. In essence, it means the use of funds for productive purposes, for securing some objectives like income, appreciation of capital or capital gains, or for further production of goods and services with the objective of securing profits.

Investment Activity involves the use of funds or savings for further creation of assets or acquisition of existing assets.

Investment Activity

INVESTMENT ACTIVITY
(ACQUISITION OF ASSETS)

I. FINANCIAL ASSETS

CASH

BANKS' DEPOSITS

P.F., L.I.C. SCHEMES

PENSION SCHEME

P.O. CERTIFICATES AND DEPOSITS

SAVER

BECOMES

INVESTOR

BY ACQUIRING THE ASSETS

II. PHYSICAL ASSETS

1 HOUSE, LAND, BUILDINGS, FLATS

2 GOLD, SILVER AND OTHER METALS

3 CONSUMER DURABLES

III. MARKETABLE ASSETS

SHARES, BONDS, GOVT. SECURITIES, etc.
M.F. SCHEMES, UTI UNITS, etc.

STOCK AND CAPITAL MARKETS

NEW ISSUES

STOCK MARKET

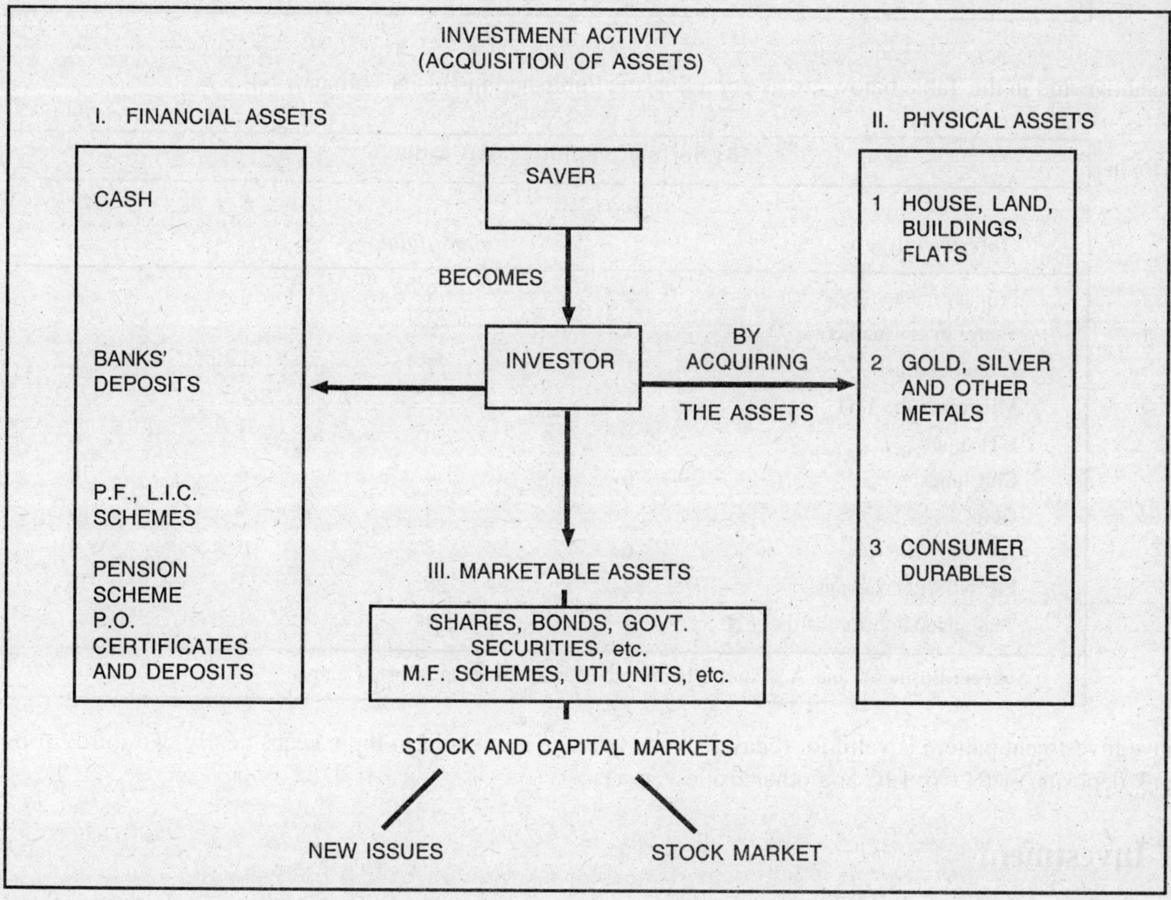

Macro-Household Savings and Investment

As per the RBI data, published from time to time total financial savings and physical assets held by households are available for discussion. For recent years the data shows that the net investment in financial assets and physical assets are 48% and 52%, respectively.

The Structure of Financial Assets is shown in chapter 1.

The Tables and Chart below presents the data on the proportion of investment in various forms held by the public. As the Indian public are risk averse, bulk of their investment is in LIC/P.O./bank deposits. (A + B in the chart below)

Average Proportion in Various Investment Types

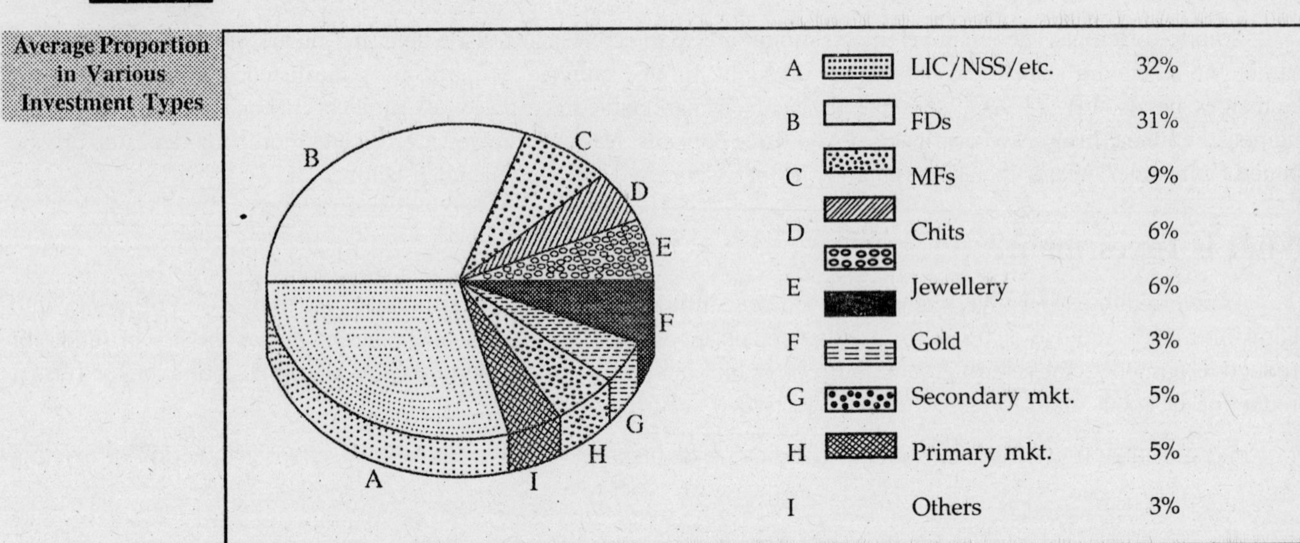

The data above and in the Table below are as per a Survey, Published in Business line.

Current Portfolio

	By Socio-economic Classification			
	Total	*A*	*B*	*C/D*
Investment type		*% of portfolio*		
Primary market inv.	5	9	5	2
Shares in sec. market	5	9	5	1
Fixed deposits	31	27	31	38
MFs other the UTI	1	2	1	1
UTI units	8	9	7	6
Chit funds	6	4	6	10
Gold	3	4	4	3
Jewellery	6	8	6	4
LIC/NSS/P.O. Savings	32	28	33	35
Teak plantations/orchards	1	1	1	1

Source: Business Line. A, B and C/D refer to Metro, Urban and Rural Centres.

The above investment pattern is valid for today also and average household in India keeps nearly two-thirds of its savings in bank deposits, or P.O. or LIC and other riskless assets.

Modes of Investment

In continuation of the discussion of the Investment Avenues it is attempted below to give specifically all modes of investment.

There are different types of securities conferring different sets of rights on the investors and different sets of conditions under which these rights can be exercised. The various avenues for investment, ranging from risk-less to high risk investment opportunities consist of both security and non-security forms of investment. All securitised forms given below are marketable.

A. Security Forms of Investment

1. Corporate Bonds*/Debentures
   (*a*) Convertible
   (*b*) Non-convertible
2. Public Sector Bonds
   (*a*) Taxable
   (*b*) Tax Free
3. Preference Shares
4. Equity Shares
   (*a*) New Issue
   (*b*) Rights Issue
   (*c*) Bonus Issue

B. Non-Security Forms of Investment (non-marketable)

1. National Savings Scheme
2. National Savings Certificates
3. Provident Funds
   (*a*) Statutory Provident Fund
   (*b*) Recognised Provident Fund
   (*c*) Unrecognised Provident Fund
   (*d*) Public Provident Fund
4. Corporate Fixed Deposits
   (*a*) Public Sector
   (*b*) Private Sector
5. Life Insurance Policies
   (*a*) Whole Life Policies
   (*b*) Limited-payment Life Policy
   (*c*) Convertible Whole Life Assurance Policy
   (*d*) Endowment Assurance Policy
   (*e*) Jeevan Mitra
   (*f*) The Special Endowment Plan with Profits
   (*g*) Jeevan Saathi
   (*h*) The New Money Back Plan
   (*i*) Marriage Endowment/Educational Annuity Plan with Profits

* Innovations in the traditional instruments include, among others
(*a*) Zero Coupon Bonds (ZCBs)
(*b*) ZCBs with option to convert interest earned to equity on maturity
(*c*) Bonds with detachable warrants.

(*j*) Bima Sandesh Premium Back Term Insurance Plan

(*k*) New Children's Deferred Assurance Plan

(*l*) Jeevan Dhara

(*m*) New Jana Raksha Plan with Profits

(*n*) Jeevan Akshay Plan

(*o*) Jeevan Balya Plan

(*p*) Jeevan Kishor

(*q*) Jeevan Griha

(*r*) Jeevan Sarita and others like market plus and wealth plus etc.

6. Unit Schemes of Unit Trust of India (Some are marketable among these)

(*a*) Unit Scheme, 1964

(*b*) Re-investment Plan, 1966

(*c*) Unit Linked Insurance Plan, 1971

(*d*) Capital Gains Unit Scheme, 1983

(*e*) Children's Gift Growth Funds, 1986

(*f*) Parents' Gift Growth Funds, 1987

(*g*) Monthly Income Unit Scheme with extra bonus plus growth

(*h*) Mastershares

(*i*) Mastergains

(*j*) Equity Linked Savings Scheme

(*k*) Growing Monthly Income Unit Scheme

(*l*) Mastershare Plus and Many More

There are many other UTI schemes on similar lines and a number of commercial banks and financial institutions have set up Mutual Funds. Various schemes for equity investment, Debt and Balanced investments or some specialised portfolio schemes have been launched by many public sector and private sector Mutual Funds, some of which have foreign partners. The open ended Funds, which are not listed on stock exchange, have arrangements for repurchse based on their NAV.

7. Post Office Savings Bank Account

(*a*) Recurring Deposits

(*b*) Time Deposits

(*c*) Monthly Income Scheme

(*d*) National Savings Certificates

8. Others

(*a*) Rahat Patras or Relief Bonds

(*b*) Senior Citizens' Deposits

(*c*) Kisan Vikas Patras

9 Deposits in Banks, Commercial and Coop.

(i) Recurring Deposits

(ii) Time Deposits etc.

(iii) Savings and Current Account Deposits

Cash Management

Investment management involves proper cash management and asset management. Some amount of minimum cash and bank balances are to be kept necessarily for meeting the daily expenditures and contingencies despite the fact that they yield no real return or even negative real return after adjustment for inflation rate. Next in importance is the provision for Housing, Insurance, pension etc. which are referred to earlier and it is only after the above requirements are met, that the investment in risky assets, both marketable and non-marketable has to be planned.

Tax Provision

Many investors are tax paying individuals. The income tax rates vary from 10% to 30% with a surcharge of 3% to 15% for all income brackets. The tax rate on capital gains of a long-term was 10% to 20%, but the short-term capital gains are taxable at normal I.T., rates. What is long-term and short-term depends on the nature of investments. If the investment is in corporate shares and securities, the holding for more than 12 months will make them long-term in nature, while for others holding for less than 36 months will be of short-term nature. In the case of these other investments such as house, land, gold, etc., the minimum holding period is 36 months to be eligible to be considered as long-term for calculation of capital gains.

Specialised Knowledge

In management of investments, there is need for a sort of expertise, because investment is both a science and an art. As investments are risky of some degree or other and the returns are higher, the higher is the risk taken, the investor should know the degree of risk on each of his investments, expected returns and the time frame of investments. Time is an important element both for tax purposes and for risk taken. Thus, the effective and proper management of investment involves — (1) efficient use of cash and proper distribution of money among different investments. (2) Proper analysis of risk and return for each of these investments. (3) Expertise in analysing information for proper investment decision, based on a study of fundamentals, expectations and mood of the markets (Technical Analysis and security analysis).

Thus, the investment management involves various elements for getting the best returns (1) Study of tax implications (2) Time duration and proper stategy for reducing taxes, increasing the after tax returns and (3) Expert knowledge for understanding the markets.

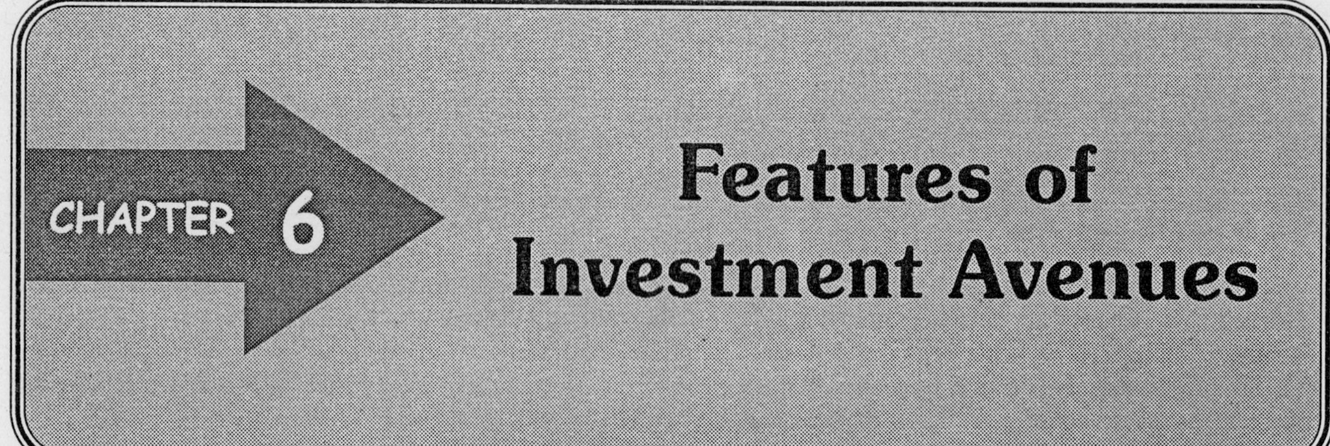

Objectives of Investor

The investor has various alternative avenues of investment for his savings to flow in accordance with his preferences. Savings flow into investment for a return, but savings kept as cash are barren and do not earn anything. Savings are invested in assets depending on their risk and return characteristics. But a minimum amount of cash is always kept in hand for transactions and contingencies. Any rational investor knows that money is losing its value by the extent of the rise in prices. If money lent cannot earn as much as rise in prices or inflation, the real rate of return is negative. Thus, if inflation is at an average annual rate of 10%, then the return should be 10% or above to induce savings to flow into investment. Thus, if an investment is made in short-term deposits with banks or in securities of Government, then the rate of interest is around 8% to 10%. As the risk of loss of money is almost negligible in such cases, this rate can be called a risk-free return. All investments involve some risk or uncertainty. The objective of the investor is to minimise the risk involved in investment and maximise the return.

Characteristics of Investment

A. Risk: The risk depends on the following factors:

1. The longer the maturity period, the larger is the risk. Thus, deposits of two years carry a higher rate than one-year deposits.
2. The more the creditworthiness of the borrower or agency issuing securities, the less is the risk. Thus, the risk of loss of interest and principal is less with the Government or semi-Government bodies than with the private corporate units.
3. The nature of instrument, namely, the debt instrument or fixed deposit or ownership instrument like equity or preference share, also determines risk. The risk of loss of money is less in the case of debt instruments like debentures, as these are secured and fixed interest is payable on them. In the case of ownership instruments, the risk of loss is more due to their unsecured nature and variability of their return and ownership character which burdens them with all the risks connected with the enterprise.
4. The risk of variability of returns is more in the case of ownership capital as the return varies with the net profits after all commitments are met. As such, equity and preference shares of companies are more risky than debentures or bonds. Among the ownership instruments, equity is more risky than preference shares or other forms of ownership instruments such as partly or fully convertible debentures, convertible and cumulative preference shares, as equity holders are residual owners of the firm.
5. The nature of tax liability on the instruments — the tax provisions would influence the return as the net effective return for a tax-payer would be higher for tax-free instruments as in the case of NSS, NSC, (VI or VII Series) or those whose interest income is tax-free up to a limit as in the case of UTI dividends, RBI Relief Bonds

or interest on P.O. deposits. The net return on such instruments is higher by different degrees to the tax-payers, depending upon the income tax brackets into which they fall.[1] Thus, tax implications of investment are an important factor in considering the retun on investment. Besides risk, investment decisions are based upon return, safety, liquidity, marketability, etc., which are examined below.

B. Return: A major factor influencing the pattern of investment is its return, which is the income plus capital appreciation, if any. The difference between the purchase price and the sale price is capital appreciation and the yield is the interest or dividend divided by its purchase price. Thus, if Rs. 25 is the dividend on a share of the face value of Rs. 100 but purchased at Rs. 150, then the return is 25/150 = 16.6%. Suppose, there is capital appreciation also in a year, say, Rs. 10 on the purchase price of Rs. 150, then the total return is (25+10)/150, which is 23.3% per annum.

C. Safety: The safety of capital is the certainty of return on capital without loss of money or time involved. In all cases of money lent, some transaction costs and time are involved in getting the funds back. But leaving aside such general costs like stamp duty, postal charges, etc., the time involved is also an important factor. If money is returnable not on the same day but after a lapse of time, then the loss of liquidity is involved and if the time of return of funds is not certain and if costs of selling or realisation of proceeds are involved, then the safety of funds is also not perfect. Thus, if safety of capital is to be assured, then riskless return as in the case of Government bonds is to be chosen. If the return is higher, as in the case of private securities, then the degree of safety is less.

D. Liquidity: If a capital asset is easily realisable, saleable or marketable, then it is said to be liquid. If an investment can be encashed with a time lag as in the case of equity shares or with loss of money as in the case of corporate deposits, then they are less liquid. If, on the other hand, there is a good market for the capital asset and no risk of loss of money or capital and no uncertainty of time involved, then the liquidity of the asset is good. If liquidity is high, then the return may be low as in the case of bank saving deposits or MF units.

An investor generally prefers liquidity for his investments, safety of his funds, a good return with a minimum risk or minimisation of risk and maximisation of return (dividend plus capital appreciation).

E. Marketability: This refers to transferability or saleability of an asset. Those listed on a stock market are more easily marketable than those that are not listed. Public limited companies will have their shares more easily transferable than those of private limited companies.

Risk-Return Relationships

1. Risk: Risk is inherent in any investment. This risk may relate to loss or delay in repayment of the principal capital or loss or non-payment of interest or variability of returns. While some investments are almost riskless like Government securities or bank deposits, others are more risky. There are differences in risk as between instruments, which can be represented as a spectrum of risk, as in Fig. 6.1.

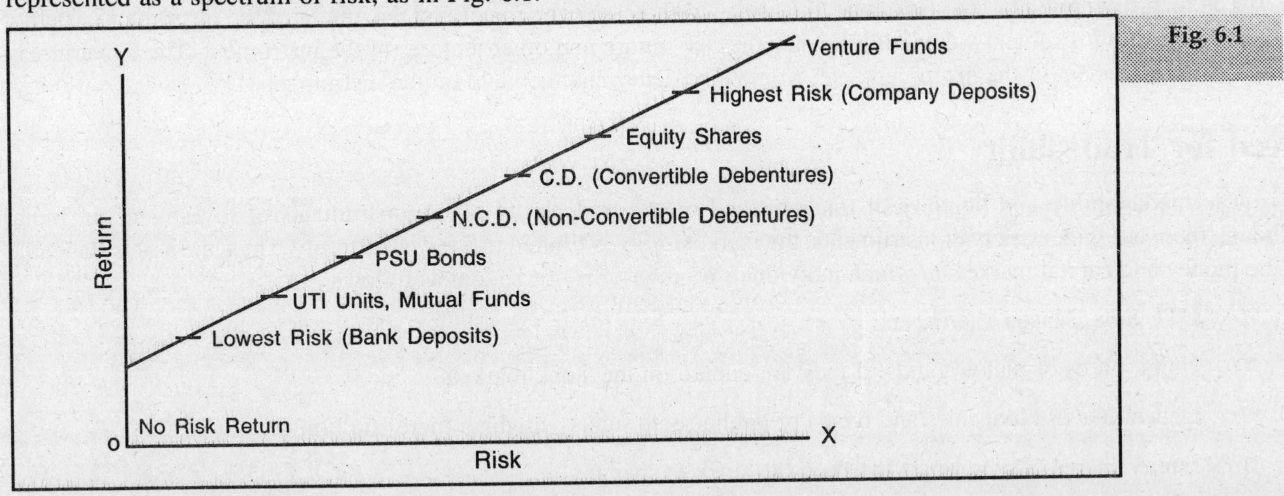

Fig. 6.1

1. Another factor influencing the average investor is whether interest and dividend on the investment is paid without any tax deduction at source. Thus, in the case of P.O. deposits and certificates, etc., there was no tax deduction at source. The investor is interested in the return net of his tax liability and tax deduction. Income from mutual funds and interest on bank deposits is also subject to TDS from 1995-96. In 1999-2000, all incomes from equity linked mutual funds and UTI are made exempt from all taxes and TDS.

2. *Return:* Yield or return differs from the nature of the instruments, maturity period and the creditor or debtor nature of the instrument and a host of other factors. The most important factor influencing return is risk. Normally, the higher the risk, the higher is the return. The return is the income plus capital appreciation in the case of ownership instruments and only yield or interest in the case of debt instruments like debentures or bonds.

Tax Benefits

Some instruments floated by the Government and semi-Government bodies enjoy tax benefits and hence their net return is higher. Thus in India, P.O. deposits, bank deposits, Government securities, etc., are exempt from income tax either in part or in full. Under Section 80L of IT Act, the income emanating from certain investments like bank deposits, NSC, P.O. deposits, etc. and in respect of income from UTI units is exempt as in the case of dividend income of mutual funds upto a limit. The income tax rebates were all removed except on exemption of investment in selected avenues upto Rs. 1 lakh in the year 2005-06, under Section 80C of I.T. Act. The other forms of tax benefits are the exemption or rebate with respect to wealth tax or capital gains tax. The investments made in specified instruments of Government and semi-Government securities, NSS, PPF, equity shares, bonds or debentures, etc., are fully exempt from wealth tax. Exemption of original investment as also the income from it is granted in the case of PPF and NSS, subject to certain conditions.

Marketability and Liquidity

Some Instruments are not marketable like company and bank deposits, P.O. deposits, NSC, NSS, etc. Only advances can be secured against bank deposits and NSC subject to margins from banks. Some instruments like preference shares and debentures are marketable but there are no buyers in many cases and hence liquidity is negligible in respect of these instruments. Liquidity arises from the availability of marketing and trading facilities as also buyers and sellers. Thus, even when there is marketability, it is possible that there is no liquidity.

Safety *vs.* Riskiness

Safety is another feature which the investor desires for investments. Normally, savers invest only in safe or risk-free investments. Only a few opt for risky investments for which the returns would also be higher. Thus, a higher return of 15% is available for three-year deposits of companies which are most risky and which was later fixed at 11%. Besides, there are debentures of companies whose yield may be more than 15%, if they are purchased at a discount in the market. But debentures and bonds carry a coupon rate of 11 to 14% or even more as there is no ceiling on this rate. Some of the equity shares might give a better return but the general average yield rate on equities is lower than on other types of securities available for investment. But equities are chosen more for their capital appreciation rather than dividend yield.

The maturity period of the instrument, the creditworthiness of the issuer and the nature of the instrument, whether debt or ownership instrument would all influence the risk, return and other features of the instrument. The Government policy or tax treatment of the instrument, etc. would also determine the yield on the instruments.

Need for Tradeability

The marketability and liquidity of funds depend on the tradeability of the instruments of investment. In India, although there is a wide variety of instruments, the marketability is limited to a few assets only. Thus, the assets tradeable in the money and capital markets in which individuals do invest may be set out as follows:

(a) UTI units, Master shares, etc.

(b) Units/shares of mutual funds, if they are quoted on the stock markets.

(c) Debentures of companies and bonds of public sector units, in which there is a limited market.

(d) Equity shares of companies listed on the stock exchanges.

(e) Government securities, capital investment bonds, rural investment bonds, shares of P.S.Us etc.

There are a host of other investments made by individuals and households, which are not easily marketable. These are not quoted on the stock markets as in the case of those issued by private limited companies. In the case of Government securities, PSU bonds and debentures of companies, the public interest is less but quoted on the stock markets, and they are traded by banks, financial institutions, etc.

The assets not quoted and are not marketable are not securities, namely,

(a) Bank deposits; *(b)* Company deposits; *(c)* P.O. deposits, NSC, etc.; *(d)* PF and pension funds; *(e)* Insurance policies of LIC, GIC, etc.

Some of the above assets can be used for securing loans from banks, if liquidity is required. The investments in PF, pension, insurance, etc. are contractual forms of saving and not regular tradable assets as such. Thus, nearly a third of the household sector savings in the financial form is flowing into the contractual forms of investment. They are meant to protect the future contingencies, retirement, accident and other unexpected possibilities. These contractual savings are thus not voluntary investment avenues and have to be treated on a separate footing. They are not the usual investment assets, either marketable or tradable. The assets which are voluntary in nature but not tradable are deposits with banks and PO, NSCs and instruments of savings with banks and POs and investments in chit funds, investment/finance companies, etc.

Classes of Instruments

Instruments traded can be classified on the following criteria:

1. By ownership or debt nature of instruments.
2. By term period to maturity — short-term, medium-term and long-term.
3. By the issuer's creditworthiness, say, Government securities or private securities or PO certificates, etc.

Ownership category instruments are equity, preference shares, deferred shares, non-cumulative preferred shares, cumulative preferred shares, etc. Debt category assets are debentures, bonds, deposits with banks and companies, etc.

The term period of a security or the maturity period also varies from security to security and with the time of purchase. Barring the equity shares, other securities have some maturity period and redemption. Thus, the debentures may be up to 7 years and preference shares up to 12 years. Fixed deposits may vary from 1 to 5 years. Almost all the debt instruments have a maturity period.

The creditworthiness of the issuer of securities will determine the risk involved in the payment of interest and repayment of principal. If the issuer is the Government the risk is the least as the Government does not default. There is no uncertainty in respect of these instruments.

The data in Table 6.1 presented below show that the various instruments can be classified by risk-return characteristics and that the returns are variable on these instruments as also the tax treatment given by the Government in respect of these instruments. In January 2000, the interest rates on Savings media of the Govt. were lowered to reduce the cost of borrowing by the Govt. The interest rates in general were sought to be brought down to be in tune with lower inflation rates. In October 2001, Bank rate was lowered to the level of 6.5% and further to 6% by stages in 2003. The deposit and lending rates also fell accordingly in respect of banks.

Table 6.1 Selected Investment Avenues (2007)

	Name of Security (1)	Rate of Interest per Annum (2)	Income-tax Concession (3)
1.	Post Office Saving Bank accounts	3.5%	Exempt under Sec. 10(15)(ii)
2.	Saving deposits of banks	3.5%	— do —
3.	Public Provident Fund Accounts (PPF)	8.0%	Exempt under Sec. 10 and 88 upto Rs. 60,000 P.A.
4.	Post Office Time Deposit Accounts	6.25 to 7.5%	—
5.	Bank Fixed Deposits	6.25 to 8%	—
6.	Post Office Recurring Deposit Accounts	8%	—
7.	National Savings Scheme (NSS), 1992	8.0%	Investment and income completely exempt (Section 88 and 80L), Since withdrawn
8.	6-year Post Office Monthly Income Scheme	8.0% (Payable monthly)	Qualifying for deduction under Sec. 80L within limit of Rs. 12,000, since repealed
9.	Indira Vikas Patra@ (period 7.25 years)	@	No
10.	Kisan Vikas Patra (period of 8 years & 7 months)	8.41% (Compounded)	No
11.	NSC VIII Issue	8.0%	Eligible under Section 80C
12.	Units of UTI/schemes of mutual funds	Variable	Taxable
13.	Equity shares of companies	Variable	1. Dividend in the hands of investors is tax-free 2. Provision for a tax rebate at 20% on any investment in eligible equity linked schemes of Rs. 10,000 maximum – a rebate of Rs. 2,000
14.	Convertible Debentures	Variable	Taxable
15.	Non-convertible Debentures	— Do —	Taxable
16.	Fixed deposits of companies	11 to 14%	Taxable
17.	Preference Shares (Redeemable or cumulative)	14% — 15%	Dividend exempted under Sec. 80L withdrawn in 2005-06
18.	Cumulative Convertible Preference Shares (CCP)	0%	— do —
19.	Bonds of Public Sector Companies (PSU)	(i) 9% — 10.5%	Taxable
20.	Senior Citizens Saving Scheme	(ii) 9%	Taxable

@ This scheme was discontinued in July 2000. Rates on savings schemes of P.O. were lowered by one-half percent from March 2002, and lowered again in 2003.

Gross Domestic Investment and Savings

The Household Sector Savings rate was 15.7% during the eighties and increased to 19.1% during 1992-93 to 1996-97 and stood at 19% in 1997-98 and the average rate for 2000 to 2008 was 23% of GDP. (not shown in the Table below).

Table 6.2

Savings and Investment (as percentage of GDP)

	1997-98	1999-2000	2003-04	2005-2006	2007-08
I. Gross Domestic Saving					
1. Household Sector	19.0	19.8	24.3	22.3	24.3
2. Private Corporate Sector	4.3	3.8	4.1	8.1	5.8
3. Public Sector of which	1.4	—	–0.3	—	—
— Public Authorities	(–) 2.1	(–) 1.2	—	2.0	—
— Non-Dept. Enterprises	3.5	—	—	—	0.9
4. Total	24.7	22.3	28.1	32.4	29.7
II. Net Capital Inflow	2.6	1.0	–1.8	1.3	0.2
III. Gross Domestic INVESTMENT	26.2	23.3	26.3	33.8	29.9

The rise on this account was mainly due to a large increase in the Household sector savings in financial form in the form of bank deposits; P.F. and Small savings due to financial reforms.

Similarly, there was sharp rise in the savings and investment in the private corporate sector from below 2% during the Eighties to 4.3% in 1997-98 and stood at 8.8% in 2007-08. The investment rate was 4.4% in the Eighties and savings rate was less than 2%. In the Nineties, the investment rate rose to of 7.4% and during 2000 to 2008, it was 9.5%

The public sector savings rate was low both in the Eighties and Nineties. The rate of public savings declined from 2.8% during the Eighties to 1% during 1991-92 to 1996-97, but stood at in 2000 to 2008. The public sector investment rate similarly declined from 10.3% in the Eighties to 8.4% to 7.5% during 1993-94 to 1997-98. It stood at 7.2% in the period 2000 to 2008.

Gross Domestic Investment as a percentage of GDP was 24.8% during 1993-94 to 1997-98 and stood at 26.2% in 1997-98 and 39% in 2007-08. The savings and investment rate declined in 1999-2000, as seen from the attached Table, despite the rise in GDP at constant prices from 4% in 2002-03 to 7.5% in 2004-05 and 9.7% in 2006-07 as compared to 5% in 1997-98 and around 7.2% in 2000 to 2008.

Investment Profile of Average Household

The asset preferences of an average Indian household can be analysed from the data on the savings estimates of CSO and RBI. The data of RBI provide in particular the pattern of assets in financial form of the household sector in India.

If an average Indian saves Rs. 100 (as net savings), nearly Rs. 52 is set apart for investment in physical assets like consumer durables, housing, real estate, gold, silver, etc. The remaining Rs. 48 flows into various forms of financial assets.

Taking savings in the financial form, the preferences of the Indian household are such that the investor keeps 12.5% of it in cash and currency and 55% in bank deposits, which are both riskless assets but with nil return or low returns (0—6 per cent). There is also a category of contractual savings in the form of insurance. PF and pension funds, whose return is also small or moderate, but are based on the requirements of insurance coverage, contingency and precautionary requirements of individual savers. The investment in this category is 30% of total financial savings in recent year.

The relatively less risky but voluntary investments relate to UTI units and mutual fund schemes whose return is about 8 to 10%. The investment in this category is around 5 to 8% of the financial savings of the household sector and these stood at a negative typer in 2008-09 due to global freedem.

Another category of less risky return with tax concessions is that of investment in Government securities, P.O. savings media, PSU bonds, etc. The return on these investments vary widely from 6-9% depending on income-tax concessions. Among the category of most risky investments is that of deposits with companies (2%) and of shares and debentures (4.3%).

If all the above investments are arranged in the order of riskiness to get a picture of the risk aversion of the average Indian investor, we notice that only about 10% of savings are attracted by the high return/high risk profiles, 30% flow in the form of contractual savings and 50% as currency and bank deposits. Moderately risky or less risky investments like P.O. instruments, Government bonds, UTI units, etc., attract less than 5% of the total savings in financial form (as their returns vary around 6 to 8%).

If investment in public securities and private securities are taken to represent respectively, the less risky and more risky investments, the proportion of financial savings in the form of the former is as high as 80%, and the latter 10%, which clearly evidences the risk aversion of average household in India. Besides, a proportion of about 10% of savings is held in the form of currency. This is an over all average picture of houshold sector profile in India.

The pattern of household sector investments is shown graphically below:

Fig. 6.2

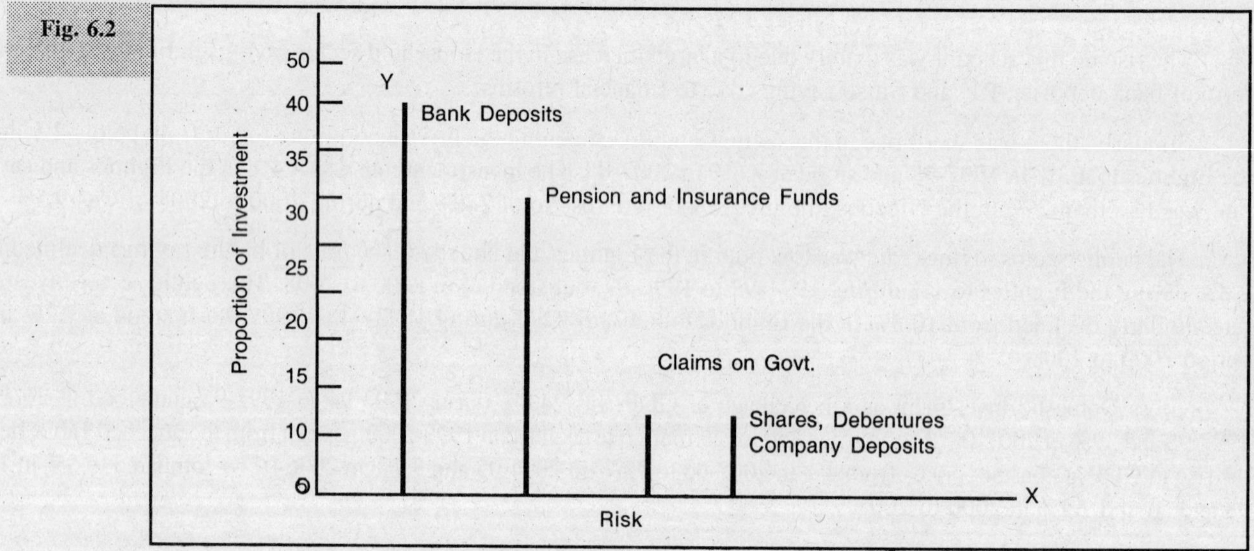

Including the currency holdings, all the financial assets held by the household sector are shown in the Table. 6.3. Bulk of the investments in the public sector is indirect investment. Thus, Bank deposits, UTI units, PF and pension funds, etc. all find their way into investments in private and public securities. Leaving aside a proportion of statutory investments in Government, semi-Government and Trustee securities, the rest is invested in new issues of companies, shares and debentures of existing companies, deposits with companies, etc. Thus, although only less than 10% of the direct investments of the households flow into shares, debentures and company deposits, etc. as shown in Table. 6.3, there is a large component of indirect investments by the households in the private corporate sector through their bank deposits, PF, insurance, pension funds, UTI units, Mutual Funds, etc.

Analysis of Household Sector Savings

The savings of the Household Sector represent the macro saving habits of the public. The Table below presents the data on Savings of the Household Sector in financial form.

Table 6.3 Savings of Households in Financial Assets

(Percentage Distribution of Total)

	1990-91	95-96	97-98	99-2000	2004-05	2006-07	2008-09
I. Currency	10.6	13.2	7.2	8.9	9.2	8.6	12.5
II. Bank Deposits	31.9	32.0	44.5	33.6	37.1	55.6	54.9
III. Non-Banking Deposits	2.2	10.6	4.4.	3.6	0.3	0.1	1.8
IV. Life Insurance	9.5	11.1	10.9	12.1	13.2	14.6	19.5
V. Provident and Pension Fund	18.9	17.8	18.4	23.1	13.2	9.6	9.5
VI. Claims on Government	13.4	7.7	12.4	12.2	24.0	5.2	–3.1
VII. Shares and Debentures	8.4	7.1	2.1	6.3	1.1	1.5	4.3
VIII. Units of UTI	5.8	0.2	0.3	0.4	– 0.1	4.8	–1.4
IX. Trade Debt (net)	– 0.8	0.3	– 0.2	– 0.1	0.0	0.0	1.8

Source: RBI Annual Reports

Note: Totals do not tally due to others, nor included here.

The Household Sector Savings in both physical and financial form constitute about 24% of GDP. The savings in financial form are about the same as in physical form, indicating the role of intermediation and the deepening and widening of the Financial System. The savings in financial form rose from 7% of GDP in eighties to 12% of GDP in 2007-08. The savings of Household Sector in physical form was only 12% of GDP. The Gross domestic savings rate of all sectors is around 30%-37% in recent years, bulk of which is coming from the Household Sector.

The pattern of distribution of financial assets of the Household Sector is seen from the above Table. The precautionary investment is in contractual form of savings in Insurance, PF, pension etc. which account for about 30% of total in financial form. The motive in transactions is seen in the currency and bank deposits, held by households at around 64%. These two forms of investment for transactions and precautionary purposes account for about 95% of the total financial savings. The most risky forms of investment indicating the risk taking by households are in shares, debentures and non-banking deposits with companies, which account for only about 2% to 4% of financial savings of household sector in India. This indicates the degree of risk aversion of average Indian households.

Non-Corporate Investments

In addition to securities of the corporate sector into which savings of the households flow to a minor extent, there are a number of other avenues for investment such as deposits with commercial and cooperative banks, post office savings banks, National Savings Certificates, Provident fund and pension fund contributions, insurance, deposits with companies, purchase of real estate, gold and silver etc. There are other lines of investment, more frequently resorted to by companies, financial institutions etc. such as securities of the Government and semi-Government bodies, *viz.*, Treasury bills, Government bonds, Public sector bonds, Government securities, etc. These investments are of many types and can be classified as follows:

1. Marketable and non-marketable: Real estate, gold, silver, etc. are marketable and are most popular among the households. Treasury bills, bonds and Government securities are also marketable but are popular only with financial institutions and banks. Some of these like UTI units, tax-free bonds, etc. which enjoy a number of tax benefits are also popular with companies and institutions. The investments in the nature of deposits with banks, companies, National Savings Certificates, etc. are not marketable as they are not transferable by endorsement.

2. Interest payable regularly or reinvested: Some investment media like bank deposits pay interest quarterly or half-yearly. Some investments will have annual interest or dividends paid as in the case of UTI units or half yearly on P.O. savings certificates. Some media will have the interest reinvested as in P.O. cumulative time deposits etc. Repayments can also take the form of annuity, that is, to say, a payment combining interest with principal.

3. Payment linked to an event: In the case of life insurance, payment is at the event of death, accident-insurance, at the occurrence of an accident, provident fund at the time of retirement etc. Payment out of pension funds, or out of annuities, will be spread over a number of years.

4. Regular savings media of investment vs. lumpsum investment at a time: Some investment media like LIC insurance premium or contributions to PF and insurance are regular monthly savings either voluntarily or compulsorily. Similarly, contributions to the recurring deposit schemes of banks and post offices are regular monthly savings media. On the other hand, purchase of NSC or a fixed deposit with a notice period or for a fixed period of time are examples of the lumpsum investments at a time.

Corporate Investments

The major avenues of investment among corporate securities are equity shares and preference shares, which are of ownership category and debentures and fixed deposits from the public, which are of debt category. Of these, preference shares debentures and deposits are having a fixed interest while equity shares are of variable dividend. The risk is high in the case of fixed deposits of companies as they are unsecured, while equity shares are of high risk and high return profile.

Deposits with Banks

Among the non-corporate investments, the most popular are deposits with banks such as current accounts, savings accounts and fixed deposits. On current account deposits, no interest is paid as these are meant for regular transactions by businessmen and companies. Savings deposits are those on which interest is paid at 3.5%, which is the lowest among the various categories of investments. There is also the category of fixed deposits, which has varying characteristics. Thus, fixed deposits may be recurring deposits wherein savings are deposited at regular intervals or fixed deposits of varying maturities or with varying notice periods such as 7 days, 15 days, or one to 5 years etc. The interest rates on these deposits vary depending upon the maturity period, from 4.5 to 9% at present. Banks are permitted to offer higher rates for large amounts from October 1, 1995. The banks also provide other varieties of schemes for savings and for raising deposits from the public. The rates on them are now free from RBI control. The amount of interest on these deposits is payable half-yearly or quaterly calculated on the basis of simple interest. The method of payment on interest on savings accounts was directed by the RBI to be changed to be calculated on the basis of the daily average balances kept in the account. Some of the banks have reinvestment plans wherein the interest is reinvested as is accrued and paid at the end of the fixed period, say, of 1 to 5 years. The principal and the accumulated interest are paid to the investor on maturity.

Instruments of Post Offices

The investment avenues provided by the post offices are generally non-marketable, as they are the savings media. The only exception is Indira Vikas Patra, which are bearer bonds transferable by delivery and they are discontinued now. The major instruments of P.O. enjoy tax concessions such as exemption of investment contribution from tax or interest income from tax or both up to certain limits.

1. Saving Deposits: These are savings deposited by public up to a maximum of Rs. 50,000 in individual account and Rs. 1 lakh in joint account. They carry interest at 3.5% which is tax-free totally. Just as the savings deposits of commercial and co-operative banks, these accounts are operated subject to certain conditions.

2. Fixed Deposits: These accounts are open to individuals either separately or jointly for varying fixed periods of time, say upto 5 years. The interest rates vary from 6.25% for one year deposits to 7.5% for 5-year deposits. The interest is payable half-yearly and interest income is tax exempt up to a limit of Rs. 12,000 per annum. There is no TDS for P.O. Saving avenues.

3. Recurring Deposits Upto 5 Years: This is an instrument of regular monthly savings. The account-holder has to save and deposit every month a fixed amount of Rs. 5 or in multiples of Rs. 5 upto say 60 months. This account carries a rate 8% on the balance to the account, compounded quarterly and payable at maturity at the end of 5 years. It has its own rules of nomination, withdrawal, income and wealth tax exemption etc.

4. Fixed Investment with Monthly Income: Under this scheme, an individual can invest from a minimum of Rs. 5,000 to Rs. 1 lakh lumpsum for a period of six years. Interest at 8% is payable monthly and bonus of 10% at the end of maturity. Income up to Rs. 12,000 per annum is tax-free.

5. Six-Year National Savings Certificates (Savings Certificate VI and VII issues): There are various series of this issue with slight changes with regard to payment of interest rate. These investments, as in the case of some other instruments, are exempt from income accrued up to a limit under Section 80L. The interest payable is 8% compounded half-yearly. The interest along with the principal is payable at the time of maturity; interest accrued is deemed to have been reinvested in the case of VI series, while the same is paid half-yearly in the case of VII series. These are now discontinued.

6. Six-year National Savings Certificates (VIII Series): This is slightly different from other NSCs. The rate of interest payable is 8% compounded half yearly payable at maturity. Accrued interest is reinvested but is eligible for tax rebate under Section 80C of I.T. Act.

There are a number of other avenues of savings with POs which are tax havens such as PPF and NSS, whose details vary from scheme to scheme. Early in 21st century the interest rates on small savings schemes were lowered.

Public Provident Fund

The PPF deposits can be made in monthly instalments with a minimum of Rs. 100 and a maximum of Rs. 60,000 per annum. These deposits carry cumulative interest of 8% credited to the account. The account has a maturity period of 15 years. It is not transferable, but has nomination facility. One withdrawal per financial year can be made any time after 5 years from the end of the year in which the subscription is made. Withdrawal is limited to 50% of the balance at the end of the fourth year. All subscriptions to PPF are completely tax-free and the balances in PPF are not taken into account for wealth tax purposes.

NSS

Deposits made in NSS were completely tax exempt under Section 80CCA of I.T Act but income, however, is taxable at the time of withdrawal. Interest is credited to the account at the end of each month at the rate of 10% per annum. Now the number of deposits that can be made are only 12 in a year and the deposits have to be in multiples of Rs. 100 and not exceeding Rs. 40,000 per annum. Only one withdrawal can be made in a year up to the maximum of the balance outstanding at the end of the fourth preceding financial year. The account can also be closed at the end of three years from the end of the year in which the last deposit is made. A passbook is given with a nomination facility. The scheme was withdrawn in 1992-93 Budget and a new NSS 1992 was introduced with some variations.

10-Year Social Security Certificate

These certificates are in denominations of Rs. 500 and Rs. 1,000 and mature at the end of 10 years. The maturity value of the certificate is triple the face value, giving a compound rate of interest of 10.3%. A special feature of this is life insurance coverage. In the event of death by accident or natural cause after two years from the date of purchase, the nominee or legal heirs receive the full maturity value immediately. This certificate can be purchased by individuals between 18 and 45 years of age only. These are now discontinued.

Kisan Vikas Patra

These are certificates in denomination of Rs. 1,000, Rs. 5,000, Rs. 10,000 and Rs, 50,000, which will double in 8 years and seven months. These can be encashed after 2-1/2 years for specified amounts of money. This has nomination facility but is not transferable.

Public Sector Bonds

There are twos categories of these bonds, namely, tax-free and taxable. The tax-free bonds are 9 or 10% bonds issued for Rs. 1,000; interest compounded half-yearly and payable half-yearly. They have a maturity period of 7 to 10 years with the facility for buy-back sometimes provided to small investors upto certain limits. Taxable bonds have normally a face value of Rs. 1,000 and have buy-back facilities similar to taxable bonds, and carry a better rate of interest.

Drought Relief Bonds (Relief Patra)

These are completely tax-free bonds. These carry 8.0% interest compounded annually with a face value of Rs. 1,000 and maturity period of 5 years. These investments are completely tax-free, both for wealth and income tax purposes. Interest income, either payable or reinvestible, is also tax free. This has also nomination facility. A new series of tax-free bonds with 10% return was announced by the Govt. in 1995. There are also 10.5% tax-free PSU bonds for investment by public. Some of these were withdrawn early in the 21st century.

Senior Citizens Savings Scheme

The Senior Citizens Savings Scheme with 9% return was announced in 2004. Senior Citizens about the age of 60 can invest upto a maximum of 15 lakhs as deposits with the P.O. or some nationalised banks. They have a lock-in period of 5 years with 9% interest, payable quarterly, with a nomination facility. This can be a single or joint account with wife/husband as the case may be. The interest incomes of these deposits are however taxable and there is a TDS on such income.

Conclusion

There are a large number of investment avenues for savers in India. Some of them are marketable and liquid while others are more risky and less safe. Risk and return are the major characteristics which an investor has to face and handle.

The investment avenues can be broadly categorised under the following heads:

(1) Corporate Shares, Debentures, etc.

(2) Bank Deposits and Corporate Deposits.

(3) UTI and Mutual Fund Schemes.

(4) P.O. Deposits/Certificates, etc.

(5) Government and Semi-government Bonds/Securities.

The investor has to choose proper avenues from among them depending on his preferences, needs and abilities to take the minimum risk and maximise the returns. To enable investors to know the degree of risk on debt instruments, credit rating is now made compulsory for them.

The investors are interested in real rates of return net of taxes. It is therefore necessary for investors to know the tax provisions relating to securities. The present tax system provides some benefits to tax paying investors, although many of them were deleted in the recent Budgets for reasons of simplification of the tax system. Investors need to make tax planning which is not the same thing as tax avoidance. It means adopting a strategy for reducing the tax liabilities by proper planning. The basic objective is to have a net of tax return, which is higher than the inflation rate and provides a proper risk premium.

The tax provisions are subject to frequent changes in the Annual Budgets and in between the Budgets. So the present discussion on tax planning is to emphasise the need and rationale of tax planning and is based on the existing rates of taxation. The readers have to update the information to gain most from the tax planning, which is relevant for both companies and individuals for their investment management.

Taxation of Dividend and Interest Income

The dividend and interest incomes including the returns from mutual funds, bank deposits etc. used to enjoy a tax rebate upto Rs. 12,000 per annum, under Section 80L of I.T.Act. Some investment incomes like those on PPF, Tax free bonds, Rahit Patra, etc., were free from income tax. There is a tax deduction at source (TDS) if the incomes from dividends or interest exceed Rs. 2,500 per annum. The rate of taxation is 10% for interest income and 20% plus a surcharge for dividend income. The return from mutual funds exceeding Rs. 10,000 P.A. is subject to TDS at 15% for individuals and 20% for companies. The TDS rate for interest income from banks, exceeding Rs. 5,000 P.A. is 10% for individuals plus surcharge. There is also a service charge on brokerage income at 5% of their brokerage, which is now collected from investing clients. Venture capital funds are now treated like mutual funds for all tax purposes, in respect of dividends, capital gains, etc.

Dividends Received are Eligible for Following Deductions for Tax Purposes

Sums incurred for collection or commission for realisation, any interest paid on borrowed capital, for being invested and eligible for dividend. Dividend incomes from companies are exempt from taxation in the hands of investors but taxed at 10% from the companies only from 1997-98 onwards. From 1999 April, all dividend income from Mutual Funds is exempt from Income Tax, but income by way of interest from M.F.s. is subject to a tax of 10%.

Brokerage Income and Business Profits

All firms dealing in securities will have to pay a tax on brokerage income at normal income tax rates. Their business profits or trading profits are subject to normal tax rates, on short-term capital gains and speculative losses can be carried forward to be offset by only short-term speculative gains, later.

Tax Treatment on Investments

Investments in approved categories, as in PF, LIC, ULIP, NSS., etc. are eligible for direct deductions for income tax purposes upto 20% of a total investment of Rs. 60,000 P.A., of this, an investment upto Rs. 10,000 is separately set apart for approved equity linked mutual fund schemes with a tax rebate of direct deduction of 20%. Thus, under Section 88 and 88A, of I.T. Act, a total investment of Rs. 60,000 will enjoy a tax rebate upto 12,000 P.A. which was raised to Rs. 70,000 in 1997-98 with a rebate upto Rs. 14,000 by inclusion of investment in Infrastructure bonds upto Rs. 10,000. FI bonds dedicated to Infrastructure, or units of MFs meant for Infrastructure or investments in Infrastructure companies are also eligible for this tax rebate upto 20% on investments upto Rs. 10,000 in each of them. All these tax rebates were consolidated into one total exemption upto Rs. 1 lakh for investment in approved and listed categories like NSC with effect from 2005-06 financial year, under Section 80(C)

Interest and Dividend : Sec. 80L

Aggregate earnings from some specified sources are eligible for deduction upto of Rs. 15,000 from the taxable income out of which Rs. 3,000 was specially earmarked for government securities and UTI/MFs. However, now that UTI/MF income has become tax-free and since individuals do not normally go in for government securities, this special limit often goes unutilised. The schemes are:

* Deposits with *(a)* Banking Company or Co-operative Banks *(b)* Approved financial corporations or public companies to provide long-term finance for industrial or agricultural development or for construction or purchase of residential houses; (the 'Home Loan Account Scheme' of National Housing Bank is not covered by Sec. 80L but it enjoys the benefit of tax rebate u/s 88) *(c)* Industrial Development Bank of India and *(d)* Housing Boards.

* Small Savings Schemes *(a)* National Savings Certificates VIIIth issue *(b)* Post Office Time and Recurring Deposits *(c)* National Savings Scheme, 1992 and *(d)* Post Office Monthly Income Scheme.

Tax Rebate under Section 88

Contributions out of income chargeable to income tax by an individual or HUF to some specific schemes (see Table) qualify for deductions from tax payable at a flat rate of 20% of the contributions made. This reduction was made 10% in 2002-03 Budget. The aggregate contribution to all these schemes qualifying for deduction is subject to a ceiling of Rs. 60,000, and raised to Rs. 70,000 by including investment in infrastructure bonds.(Valid upto 2004-2005).

Schemes Eligible for Rebate U/S 88

	Saving Schemes	*Maximum Limit*
1.	Life Insurance Premiums	No limit
2.	Recognised Provident Fund	No limit
3.	Family Pension Scheme	Within prescribed limits
4.	15-yr Public Provident Fund	Rs. 60,000 p.a.
5.	10/15-yr Dhanaraksha	
6.	National Savings Certificate - VIII	No limit
7.	National Savings Scheme-92	No limit
8.	Jeevan Dhara/Jeevan Akshay of LIC	No limit
9.	Equity-Linked Tax-Saving Schemes	Rs. 10,000
10.	Retirement Benefit Plan of UTI	No limit
11.	Instruments of Infrastructure Companies and Units of MFs Dedicated to Infrastructure or Infrastructure Bonds	Each of these schemes attract an extra ceiling of Rs. 10,000

For an individual who is an author, playwright, artist, musician, actor, sportsman or athlete, the qualifying ceiling is higher at Rs. 70,000 and so is the rate of tax rebate at 25%. The only condition for applicability of the extra concession is that the income from profession should be more than 25% of his total income. Here, capital gain is taken as a part and parcel of the total income inspite of treating it as a separate block of income.

All exemptions for investments were withdrawn in 2005-06, except for one consolidated investment upto Rs.1 lakh in approved securities, as under Section 80C. Other Sections like 88 and 80L were all deleted.

Income Tax and Corporation Taxes

For income tax, individuals, now enjoy a threshold exemption limit of Rs. 1.60 lakh and there is no standard deduction for salaried incomes. The tax rates now range from 10% to 30% for individuals. The surcharge of 12% levied on incomes above Rs. 1,000,000 was withdrawn, but reintroduced at 15% in 2000-1. Standard Deduction on salaried income was removed in 2005-06.

Corporate taxation was simplified with only one Tax rate of 30% for domestic companies and for foreign companies, which are also subject to a surcharge The earlier distinctions of trading and manufacturing companies and of closely held and widely held companies were dispensed with. There is however a surcharge of 10% on income for domestic companies in addition to a Minimum Alternate Tax (MAT) on some companies. The MAT rate was raised from 15% to 18% in 2010-11.

When incomes like lease rentals are received by a company, and it is operational lease, deductions for repairs, maintenance etc. are deductible. Depreciations made on such leased assets are also eligible for exemption.

Capital Gains Taxation

For securities, capital gains will become long-term, if held for not less than 12 months. For holding securities for less than 12 months, there will be short-term capital gains, which are chargeable under normal income tax slabs. If it is long-term capital gains, the tax rate is only 10% to 20%. For investments other than securities like gold, real estate etc. they have to be held for 36 months to be considered as long-term capital gains. FFIs and NRIs are given further tax benefit of paying only 10% on such long-term capital gains. The rate of short-term capital gains taxation for companies and individuals is now at 10% as against 40% before 1994-95.

For arriving at Capital gains of short-term nature, the costs of acquisition, cost of improvements and cost of transfer are allowed to be deducted. For long-term capital gains, the indexed cost of acquisition (with Base year 1981-82=100 and index for 1993-94 Rs. 244, and so on), the indexed costs of improvement and costs of transfer are allowed to be deducted. That means the costs of acquisition and improvements can be inflated by appropriate index numbers, given for each year by the government from 1981-82 as 100, onwards. Under same Section such as 54(7) if long-term capital gains are invested in approved securities of govt., UTI, and HDFC bonds or deposits they are exempted from capital gains taxation.

Postal Investments

Original investment in PF and PPF enjoy tax advantages. Incomes from NSS, NSC etc. are having tax rebate along with other eligible avenues of investment under Section 80L of I.T. Act. This section was replaced by Section 80C since 2004-05.

Besides, there are 9% tax free Relief bonds and 7% Capital Investment Bonds which enjoy non-Taxable incomes. Investment in NSS and NSC enjoy some tax rebate under Section 88 of I.T. Act as referred to earlier. Unaccounted money can be invested in Vikas Patra, but income from them is not tax free from 1995-96. Such unaccounted money wherever invested is liable for tax payable at 60% of total income.

Wealth Tax

All investments in productive assets like shares, debentures of companies, PPF, NSS, Capital Investment Bonds, National Defence Bonds, Postal Deposits, etc. are all exempted from wealth tax. But other categories of assets like gold, jewellery, house and real estate, etc. are subject to wealth tax, beyond an exemption limit of Rs. 15 lakhs.

Gift Tax

The gift tax exemption, whether given in shares/debentures/or other forms/is available upto Rs. 30,000/-. In case of marriage of dependents, a gift of Rs. one lakh is exempt from gift tax. Under the latest tax provisions since 1998 gift tax is abolished and gifts are all treated as incomes in the hands of donees.

Taxation of NRIs

Since the launching of economic reforms in July 1991, the rates of taxation on NRIs, were reduced and the tax procedures for them were simplified. The investment income in the form of dividends and interest is now being taxed at a uniform rate of 20% whether they are individuals or institutions or corporate bodies. Besides the NRIs would not lose their NRI status, even when they stay upto 181 days in India at present.

Taxation of Investment Business in India

(1) Brokerage income at normal rates of income tax as applicable to individuals, HUF or Companies.

(2) Jobbing/Trading gains — treated as Business Profits and taxed as applicable to business profits.

(3) Badla interest income — taxable at normal income tax rates as applicable to different tax brackets.

(4) Capital gains from securities — short-term gains are taxed at normal tax rate of 10% and long-term capital gains are exempt. This is a phisicable to NRIs only brokers converting into corporate units are exempt from capital gains, if any arising during the process.

Interest on FDs, debentures, etc. are taxed in the year in which they fall due, while dividend income is taxable in the year in which dividends are declared, whether received or not in that year.

Taxation of FFIs in India

The income through interest and dividends is taxable at the rate of 20%. Income through long-term capital gains is taxed at 10% and on short-term capital gains at 30%. Transactions done outside India are not taxable in India.

Latest Trends

In the field of personal income taxation, the goverment in 2002-03 introduced many changes. The tax exemption under Section 88 has been brought down to 10% from 20% earlier upto a total investment of Rs. 80,000. The corporate dividends and mutual Funds income is taxable at rates applicable to individuals in their respective tax brackets, which were earlier tax free in the hands of investors. The tax payable earlier by mutual funds on their income distribution at 10% was withdrawn in 2002. There is now a withholding tax on income distribution by them.

The interest rates on Postal Savings media are brought down by stages during 2001 to 2003 and linked to market rate of yields on Govt. securities. The interest rates will continue to be flexible and subject to changes, depending on market conditions.

Domestic companies pay tax at a rate of 30% plus surcharge of 10% and individuals pay an Education Cess of 3% of the tax payable.

Latest Changes

Exemption from capital gains taxation under Section 54 EC is extended to investment in SIDBI and NHB Bonds. In the Budget 2003, long-term capital gains or investments made after March 1, 2003 are also exempt from tax. The changes made in the later Budgets are as follows:

In the central budget for 2005-06, the rates of direct Taxes were kept intact, but the Surcharge on individual income tax was removed while that on corporate tax reduced to 2.5% and there was an education cess of 2%. The maximum basic rates continued to be 30% for individuals and for corporates. For investors, there will be no tax on dividends in their hands from companies and mutual funds. But the companies and M.Fs have to pay a distribution tax of $12\frac{1}{2}$%, on the amount distributed, it they are debt oriented funds.

But the service tax on all taxed services, including brokerage was raised from 5% to 8%, which will increase the transaction costs. This tax is generally passed on to the investors. The Section 80L exemptions under I.T. Act was raised from Rs. 9,000 to Rs. 12,000 for income of dividends and interest, with a additional exemption of Rs. 3,000 for income from investment on Govt. securities in 2003. The Standard deduction for salaried income was raised to Rs. 30,000 for incomes upto Rs. 5 lakhs and to Rs. 20,000 for incomes above that limit. They will now be eligible for tax rebate of Rs. 12,000 per child for education upto two children and for tax free leave Travel allowance and for medical expenses upto a limit. The fiscal reforms were continued in 2005-06. In the central budget for 2005-06, the securities transactions tax was retained, as in the case of capital gains taxation. But the standard deductions and other tax rebates under Section 80L, and 88 were withdrawn, but gave a fixed amount of Rs. one lakh exemption for investment in approved securities in a consolidated manner under section rote of the IT Act. The corporates have to pay Fringe Benefits Tax on their perquisites given to employes at varying rates. The MAT was retained and even loss making companies have to pay some taxes.

As in 2005-06, the corporate and personal income taxes were simplified, but there are deterring taxes, like fringe benefits tax and cash withdrawal taxes on bank deposits in India. Even the STT (Securities Transactions Tax) is not welcome to the capital and stock markets imposed since 2004-05. Taxation influences directly or indirectly the FII and FDI inflows into Economy of any country. It will be seen from the later chapters that the Price Indexes of Stock markets in India are directly correlated with the FII inflows into the markets. As the Indian capital and stock markets are open markets, there is a large component of foreign investment in these markets. The FFI and FII investment is again influenced by the tax system, rigour and depth of the tax impact on their operations and the take home profits of their operations. Thus, taxation is also an important factor for tax planning by FFIs and FIIs operating in the Indian markets, although there are many other factors also influencing them.

In a recent study by Ernst and Young, for FORBES Global (Refer to ET of 27 June, 2005) on the comparative picture of the tax misery in various countries in the world, it was found that Indian taxation does not fare as badly as that of its competitors in Asia like China or even developed countries like UK. Its ranking is 45th which is better than of UK and China but worse than in Singapore, UAE and even Hong Kong.

The comparative better picture of India is due to continuous fiscal and tax reforms undertaken here since 1992 an lowering the peak rates in both direct and indirect taxes and rationalisation of administrative procedures and reduction in red tape in administration. This picture has to be read with caution as there is still a large scope for improvement in red tape and corruption in India. This is referred to here due to a large influence that foreign inflows play in the Indian capital and stock markets and other financial markets. Despite this, the FDI in China is much more than in India, because of better investment climate which is another factor influencing foreign capital inflow. So far as the tax system is concerned, there is definitely scope for better administration which is now being attempted.

TRANSACTION COSTS

Introduction

Costs are expenses incurred in rendering any service or activity or in producing a product or service. Costing involves time and money, some quantifiable and others not quantifiable. Proper costing helps to improve the operational efficiency of any activity. In the area of any service activity, operating cost concept is very useful and more so the case of investment service, or activity. As the pricing of a service is generally *cost plus* basis which means costs actually incurred plus a reasonable margin of profits, the historical costing is used to determine the cost of any service, rendered in the past. This method is to be supplemented by concurrent costing method, so that costs of each element involved in rendering the service is recorded as the activity goes on, until it is completed. Then the present costs can be compared with the historical costs, so as to assess the improvement or deterioration in the performance efficiency. Some use the concept of standard costs to compare the present operational costs of a unit with the standard costs on that line of activity, say an industry or service.

Thus these are three basic methods of determining costs among others; *(i)* Historical Costs, *(ii)* Standard Costs, and *(iii)* Concurrent Costs.

Objectives

The objectives of cost accounting are the following: *(i)* to economise on costs and improve efficiency, *(ii)* to make it a basis for rendering any service and pricing it, and *(iii)* to fix the price on the basis of cost plus a margin of profit for any product or service.

Cost accounting aims at a systematic record of all expenses in each line of activity in the provision of any service or manufacture of any product in any organisation, so as to ascertain the total cost of manufacture or rendering of any service. Ultimately, these costs will be the basis of fixing the price for it and maximise the profit through *(i)* reducing the costs and *(ii)* increasing the profit margin in the price fixed. This costing also helps in planning, budgeting and forecasting, as a tool of analysis. Efficiency can be improved by reducing or avoidance of wasteful expenditure or unnecessary expenditure and reducing the costs by economising in some units of inputs or labour used.

Elements of Costing

Two major elements of costs in services are the Direct Costs and Indirect Costs corresponding to the concept of variable costs and fixed costs in manufacture. The Direct Costs are materials used, labour and other incidental expenses. These are the elements of cost, which generally appear but some activities differ from others depending on the nature of the activity. The other direct elements are payments of some royalty for technology or any process used and expenses for water or electricity used in rendering the service, in question.

Indirect expenses are works overheads like the rent on land, factory overheads, office or administrative heads and the selling and distribution expenses. The total of direct and indirect costs is the total costs of production or for rendering a service. This cost plus a margin of profit is the basis for fixing the price. In some cases, there will be other methods like the rent on rented office premises, other than the manufacturing premises, interest paid on capital borrowed, taxes paid to the govt. on any inputs or outputs, etc.

Taxes and costs go together and these costs include payments to all factors, namely, land, buildings, factory and office premises, capital borrowed, personnel or employees, used for the production of the goods or service. These costs can be actual costs or estimated costs and price includes an element of profit so as to induce the enterprise to continue to provide the service or manufacture the goods.

Marginal costing system in to estimate costs of receiving an additional service or producing an additional item of output. This is the addition to the cost-due to an additional unit produced.

In the case of manufacturing activity the price is fixed on the basis of average costs or marginal costs of producing them. In the case of a service activity, marginal costing is generally not possible and it has to be based on historical costs, estimated costs or concurrent costs; as referred to earlier.

Costs in Investment Activity

In the field of investment, there are a number of implicit costs, like the use of mental ability for investment decision making, time involved in the collection and analysis of information and data, opportunity costs of time and money used in this process etc. There are some overheads also in this activity, such as money spent on an establishment premises, necessary equipment like a calculator, typing machine or even a computer, investment made in the office furniture and premises in the books and Journals or Dailies for collection of information, etc. These are fixed costs for the type of activity. Besides, the equipments may include a Telephone, Telex, Photocopier (Xerox Machine), depending on the type of services or activity, involved and the breadth or width of the activity undertaken. The scale of operations will decide the equipments, furnitures, etc. needed, which differ from case to case.

In a service activity like investment, the overheads will depend on the scale of activity and the extent of services rendered. As investment is both a Science and an Art, the investment Analyst and consultant should have incurred some overheads in acquiring the needed expertise, like a doctor or a lawyer. They would not only acquire some professional degrees or qualifications but spend considerable time or even years in apprenticeship for gaining experience. Such expenses in the case of medical profession are definitely larger compared to Chartered Accountant or Auditor or Lawyer.

Investment consultant comes also under these categories of professionals and the overheads spent by him in acquiring the professional degrees and expertise in the field, so as to possess the necessary skills of both a science and an art and to render efficient service in the field, will be the overheads for his profession.

Transaction Costs

After the overheads are accounted for through proper costing method, then each transaction of investment can be similarly accounted for. The cost of each transaction will be different from others as these are not standardised, or uniform in any manner.

Transaction costs in Investment include:

(1) Direct Material costs and expenses in Monetary terms.

(2) Indirect costs of time and expert analysis involved in the purpose of making the transaction.

(3) Some intangible or qualitative elements, which are not quantifiable. Direct material costs are of various items like the costs of taking a draft from a banker for payment; charges of brokerage to the broker, his service charge, service tax, Demat charges or payments for the Transfer deed, registering the letters to be sent to the company, or the Transfer deed and Share certificates to be posted to the company for Transfer of Shares into one's name etc. These can be classified as:

(i) Costs for stationery/typing, and clerical costs.

(ii) Costs incurred for payments to brokers, sub-brokers, bankers, etc. (intermediaries).

(iii) Cost incurred for mailing and stamps.

(iv) Payments to consultant if any or for purchase of any literature for taking the investment decision.

Except for the Second and Third items others are not capable of specification. They vary from transaction to transaction and there is no standard measure for them. But for the item of payments of brokers, this charge varies from 1 to 2% of the total value of shares, debentures, bonds, etc., purchased or sold. Besides the broker also charges 5% of the brokerage income as a service tax which the broker passes on to the client as a charge that he pays to the govt. collected from the client. The client also spends money on putting the stamps necessary on the Transfer deed to be stamped. In the case of equity Share Transfer, the stamps should be of a value equivalent to 0.5% of the value of the consideration for such transaction, as on the date of the deal (market price, at which the share is purchased). In the case of debt instruments, like the bonds and debentures the stamp duty is higher varying from Rs. 0.75 to Rs. 3 per Rs. 100 of value of the consideration. This varies from state to state, as it is a state subject, under the State Stamp Act. Stamp duty is not payable for transfers under Demat form, but there are charges to be paid for opening an account with charges for making physical shares into Demat form and there are also transaction costs for purchase and sale effected.

The company does not charge anything for effecting transfers, splits or consolidation of shares, as any listed company is obliged to do so free under the listing agreement signed with the Stock Exchange, where it is listed. But transfers involve costs if the T.D. is invalidated, for revalidation or for witnessing the signature by a magistrate, in some cases of signature differences or bad deliveries, or for following the required formalities in case of lost certificates or for inheriting the property under shares by the legal heirs of the deceased, in whose name the shares are held at the time of his death. This is called transmission which involves some legal formalities.

Costs of any Transaction also include all incidental and consequential costs, of getting the shares delivered or taking delivery or for converting the bad delivery into a good delivery, costs of making the payments through drafts, T.T. or pay orders of banks, to the seller or his broker.

The indirect costs of each transaction are not amenable to any reasonable estimate as these are for making the investment decisions, expertise involved in the analysis made or information secured for analysis etc.

Each transaction has alternatives and the opportunities lost by this transaction are called the opportunity costs. The information costs, costs of analysis and expert advice are not amenable to any cost estimates as referred to already. There are many overheads in each transaction and there are opportunity costs for each transaction, which are also not possible to quantify. These are qualitative factors or intangible factors.

From the above discussion, it is evident that investment transaction cost is a vague term and includes many tangible and intangible elements, some of which are not quantifiable. Conceptually they can be identified, but in actual practice, the only costs which are identifiable are *(i)* brokerage costs, *(ii)* transfer costs, *(iii)* incidental and consequential costs, which may vary from transaction to transaction, *(iv)* stamp duties, taxes to govt. and other fees and charges.

Real and Nominal Costs

Real costs are those opportunity costs for the money spent and time wasted in each transaction. This should also include Money Costs adjusted for qualitative factors, which are not quantifiable. Nominal costs are those which are payable and incurred in monetary terms in each transaction. Money costs are the only tangible costs which are amenable for cost accounting in respect of each transaction. These are the actual costs incurred in current money terms in the transaction.

Tax and Govt. Charges and Fees

For all dealings in shares, debentures, bonds, and promissory notes, investment in them and income therefrom are subject to some taxes which are payable as also the fees or duties etc. to the central, state and local bodies. The fees are to be paid by an individual investor or çorporate investor. Examples are income and corporate taxes, excise or sales tax (on turnover for investment consultant, brokers etc.), stamp duties, share transfer stamps, revenue stamps, brokers' service charges, registration charges, mailing charges and so on including the latest STT imposed in 2004-05.

These charges are common, whether they are clients or customers or professionals of investment consultants, in the business of investment. Taxes and charges are an important part of Transaction Costs.

In 1996-97 budget, all investments in approved debentures or equity issues of private companies, meant for infrastructure creation are made eligible for tax rebate. The corporate income tax surcharge was reduced from 15% to 7.5% in the same budget, but later abolished to boost the sagging investment climate in the capital market, in 1997-98. The surcharge on personal Income Tax was raised to 15%. As per the provisions early in 2000, there was no wealth tax and gift tax was abolished. The tax on profits distributed by companies was raised from 10 to 20% in the Budget for 2000-01. The income tax rate on debt oriented mutual funds in respect of their income distributed was raised from 10% to 20% in the same Budget. However, the corporate dividends in the hands of investors and the dividends paid to investors by equity oriented funds [M.F. dividends] are tax free.

Recent Changes

In the Budget for 2000-01, the direct tax system was changed in many ways. In the field of personal income taxation, thee is a surcharge for incomes more than Rs. 0.6 lakh at the rate of 10% in 1999-2000. This was raised to 15% for the category of above Rs. 1.5 lakhs in the year 2000-01 making the highest tax rate at 34.5% instead of 33%, while retaining the surcharge of 10% on income between Rs. 60,000 to 1,50,000. Senior citizens will get a rebate of Rs. 15,000, as against Rs. 10,000 before. Women tax payers will get additional rebate of Rs. 5,000. The income from Mutual Funds (of equity based) schemes will be free from income tax in the hands of investors. In 2002-03 Budget, this income in the hands of investors has become taxable. Besides, the companies and MFs are directed to withhold tax at a 10% before income distribution on interest income. Exemption for U.S. 64 and open ended schemes would continue. The Tax on interest income from M.F.s including the UTI was kept at 10%.

In the field of corporate income taxation the tax paid under Section 115 on dividend distributed has been doubled to 20% plus a surcharge of 10% (in effect to 22%). The foreign branches and subsidiaries of foreign companies pay a corporate tax of 30% plus surecharge. Indian companies paying at 38.5% of corporate income plus a dividend tax of 20% alongwith a surcharge of 2% (total of 22%) will make the effective rate for the Indian companies at par with the foreign companies. Besides those companies coming with in the MAT (Minimum Alternate Tax) will now pay at a flat rate of 18%, instead of 15% hitherto on book profits. Tax exemption on export earnings is to be phased out over five years with the result that 80% of income of export earner will be exempt from tax in 2000-01 to be followed in further reductions at the rate of 20% per annum in the subsequent years. For the year 2000-2001, surcharge on corporate income was raised to 15% (as against 10% before). In 2002, the reforms were carried further. In 2010-11, the surcharge on corporate tax was reduced from 10% to 7.5%

The tax holiday for new units in the industrially backward states and districts was extended and existing tax benefits for SSI units were also extended upto March 31, 2002. Companies resulting from splitting of statutory bodies enjoy demerger breaks subjet to certain conditions.

The interest tax on banks and FIs which was existing for the last few years was abolished. The exemption granted for capital gains tax under section 54 EA and 54 EB is given up. Now relief from capital gains taxation is available if only capital gains are invested in NABARD and NHAI bonds to be used for agriculture and rural development and roads. Non-agricultural incomes of the farm houses was brought under the income tax net. Besides by applying any one of Six criteria (such as phone, house, car, club membership, foreign travel, credit card) the number of income tax assesses was increased from one crore to two crore. It is expected to be increased further by applying this scheme to more cities and towns with population of more than 2 lakhs.

The exemption of profits from exports was extended beyond corporates to individuals in 1999-2000. This benefit for both corporates and individuals will be reduced by 20% each year to be completely removed over a period of 5 years. This benefit is available to media industry, film and Documentaries, etc. Long-term capital gains benefit under Sec. 54F is extended to assessees already owning a house.

The Budget for 2002-03 imposed a 5% surcharge, instead of 2% imposed earlier. The Section 88 tax rebate of 20% on approved investments was brought down to 10% in 2002. The corporate dividends and Mutual Fund income distribution to investors has become taxable in the hands of investors at the rates applicable to them, as per the rules. In 2004-05, a securities transactions tax was imposed on trading in Stock Exchanges. Debt oriented MFs have to pay 10% on long-term capital gains and 30% on short-term capital gains. Buyers of MF units have to pay STT. Equity oriented investment of MFs, companies and others are exempt fom tax on long-term capital gains but pay a tax of 10% on short-term capital gains.

In 2005-06, the government introduced many tax changes relevant to investment. Thus, tax rebates on many investments under Section 80L and Section 88 of I.T. Act were withdrawn. But a total of investment in approved categories like NSC, PPF, insurance etc., is exempt upto Rs. one lakh from the assessment year 2006-07. The STT on certain categories of investment was raised, but long-term capital gains continue to be exempt from tax. The short-term capital gains are subject to a tax rate of 10%. The changes in personal income taxation are raising of exemption limit to Rs. 1 lakh with special limits for women and senior citizens. The changes in corporate taxation are to keep the rate on domestic companies at 30% and the same rate on foreign companies at 30% and no surcharge on companies with a taxable income of Rs one crore or less. The personal Income tax provision like exemption and surcharges changes year after year. The nates of taxation were kept unchaged at 10% to 30% Govt. the state at which they were appriciable varied from year to year.

The Union Budget 2007-08 proposed to limit exemption given to venture capital funds to investments in a limited number of avenues, mainly relating to I.T. industry. The Fringe Benefits Tax was expanded to cover the Esops given to employees. The MAT base was also expanded to include profit of Technology parks, EOUs, etc., later on.

The rate of Dividend Distribution Tax on companies was raised from 12.5% to 15% and to 25% in respect of money market mutual funds and Liquid Mutual Funds.

The Education surcharge was raised from 2% to 3% of the tax paid by companies and individuals.

PART — II

Money and Capital Markets and Institutions

Chapter 8: Overview of Capital Market

Chapter 9: Institutional Structure in Capital Market

Chapter 10: Capital Market Reforms

Chapter 11: New Issues Market and Problems

Chapter 12: Money Market and its Instruments

Chapter 13: The Securities and Exchange Board of India (SEBI)

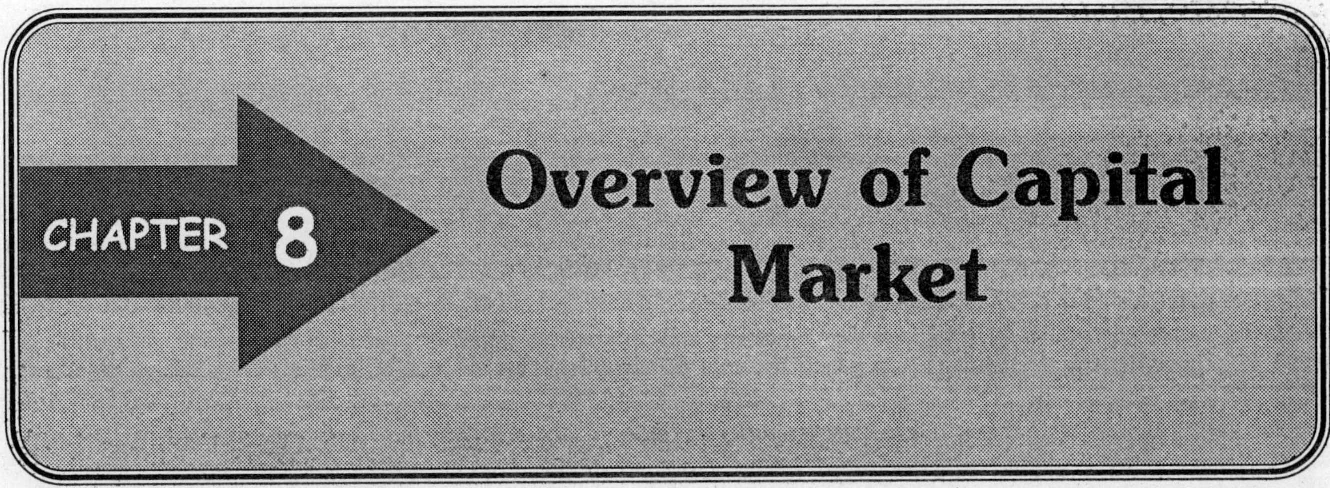

What is Capital Market?

Capital Market is a wide term used to comprise all operations in the New issues and stock market. New issues made by the companies or governments constitute the primary market, while trading in the existing securities relates to the secondary market. While we can only buy in the primary market, we can buy and sell securities in the secondary market.The term capital market encompasses all operations of F.I.s, Banks, etc., at the long-end of spectrum of maturities. The demand and supply for long-term funds are reflected in the capital market which is a market for borrowing and lendings of funds of more than one year.

Structure of the Market

There are various sub-markets in the capital market in India. The structure has undergone vast changes in recent years. New instruments and new institutions have emerged on the scene.

The sub-markets are as follows:

1. Market for corporate securities — for new issues and old securities.
2. Market for Government securities — Primary and Secondary markets.
3. Market for Debt instruments — debentures and bonds of private corporate sector, bonds of public sector undertakings, public financial institutions, etc.
4. Mutual fund schemes and UTI schemes, etc.

So far as the individual investors are concerned, the market for corporate securities and Mutual funds schemes are more relevant. They satisfy the requirements of investors, namely income, appreciation of capital, safety, liquidity, and hedge against inflation. In respect of corporate securities, leaving aside new issues market, the structure of the secondary market has undergone some changes which are depicted in the chart below:

Secondary Market Structure

Regular Stock Exchanges (21)	*Over the Counter Exchange of India (1)*	*National Stock Exchange (1)*
For big companies with paid up capital above Rs. 5-10 crores — Trading ring and physical operations includes principal exchanges like Mumbai, Kolkata, Delhi, etc., and regional exchanges like Cochin, Indore, etc. — Computerised trading in all exchanges.	Computerised trading for smaller companies with paid up capital of Rs. 30 lakhs to Rs. 25 crores. No trading ring — started operations in Oct. '92. The upper limit is now removed.	Recognised in April '93 and started operations later, only in Govt. securities and money market instruments. Equity Trading started in Nov. 1994. Two Segments – Equity and Debt markets.

Note: The Inter-connected Stock Exchange was set up and recognised in 1998 but started trading electronically in 1999. It was promoted by 15 Regional Stock Exchanges.

Players in the Market

The players in the New Issues market are many and the most important of them are the following:

1. ***Merchant bankers*** — their functions and working are crucial to new issue market. They are the issue managers, lead managers, co-managers and are responsible to the company and SEBI. They take all policy decisions for and behalf of the company regarding the new issues and coordinate the various agencies and give "Due Diligence" certificate to the SEBI regarding the true disclosurers as required by law and SEBI guidelines.
2. ***Registrars*** — their functions are next to merchant bankers in importance. They collect the applications for new issues, their cheques, stock invests etc., classify and computerise them. They also make allotments in consultation with the regional stock exchange regarding norms in the event of oversubscription and before a public representative. They have to despatch the letters of allotments, refund orders and share certificates within the time schedules stipulated under the Companies Act and observe the guidelines of SEBI and the Govt. and RBI. Besides they have also to satisfy the listing requirements and get them listed on one or more of the stock exchanges.
3. ***Collecting and co-ordinating bankers*** — collecting and co-ordinating bankers may be the same or different. While the former collects the subscriptions in cash, cheques, stock invests etc., the latter collates the information on subscriptions and co-ordinates the collection work and monitors the same to the registrars and merchant bankers, who in turn keep the company informed.
4. ***Underwriters and brokers*** — underwriters may be financial institutions, banks, mutual funds, brokers etc., and undertake to mobilise the subscriptions upto some limits. Failing to secure subscriptions as agreed to, they have to make good the shortfalls by their own subscriptions. Brokers along with their network of sub-brokers market the new issues by their own circulars, sending the application forms and follow up recommendations.
5. ***Printers, advertising agencies, and mailing agencies*** are the other organisations involved in the new issue market operations.

   Persides the soliatore and Auditors also play a note in the preimary issues market.

Stock Market Intermediaries

The players in the market are the issuers of securities, namely, companies, intermediaries like brokers, sub-brokers etc., and the investors who bring in their savings and funds into the market.

The stock brokers are of various categories, namely:

1. ***Client brokers*** — doing simple brokering between buyers and sellers and earning only brokerage for their services from the clients.
2. ***Floor brokers*** — authorised clerks and sub-brokers who enter the trading floor and execute orders for the clients or for members, and also called trading brokers.
3. ***Jobbers*** — those members who are ready to buy and sell simultaneously in selected scrips, offering bid and offer rates for the brokers and sub-brokers on the trading floor and earning profit through the margin between buying and selling rates. This category includes market makers for some scrips.
4. ***Arbitraguers*** — those who do inter market deals for a profit through differences in prices as between markets say buy in Kolkata and sell in Mumbai and *vice versa.*
5. ***Badla financiers***[@] — those members who finance carry forward deals in specified group (A Group) for a return in the form of interest, called badla rate. They lend money or shares for the brokers who are overbought or oversold respectively at the time of settlement.

@ A system of borrowing and lending of securities for trading and settlement is now practiced on N.S.E. and B.S.E. Badla was replaced by ALBs (Automatic Lending & Borrowings).

Instruments of Issue/Trading

The sources of funds that the companies can resort to has been laid down in the Companies Act. More recently, new financial products are being issued by the companies. Traditionally, equity shares and preference shares are issued as ownership capital and debentures and bonds are issued as debt capital. A few variants of ownership capital such as convertible preference shares, cumulative convertible preference shares have been tried but not with much success. But in the area of debt capital, convertible into equity, there has been significant success, as in the case of convertible debentures — fully convertible or partly convertible (FCD or PCD). The regular debt portion is non-convertible portion (Khokas) of the convertible debentures and NCDs. As per the SEBI guidelines, the portion convertible into equity within 18 months is treated as equity for purposes of debt-equity ratio. Loyalty coupons and warrants are other examples of debt which are convertible into equity at a specified future date.

New Instruments

Secured premium notes are those which do not bear interest but will be redeemed at a premium at a specified future date, giving only capital gains but not income. Discount bonds and Deep Discount bonds are issued at a discount initially but will be redeemed at par at a specified future date, involving again capital growth only. Zero coupon bonds are also similar to discount bonds as they do not bear any coupon interest rate, but are sold at a discount initially based on an appropriate interest rate. Non-voting equity shares and floating interest rate bonds and host of other new financial instruments are being issued.

Companies are also allowed to issue securities abroad in the form of GDRs or IDRs (Global or International Depository receipts), Euro dollar Notes, Offshore Mutual Funds, Foreign Currency Covertible Bonds etc. Foreign equity is allowed in Indian companies upto 51% of the paid up capital.

SEBI Guidelines

SEBI guidelines encompass all activities of capital market like new issues, stock trading, settlement, buy back of shares, acquisition and mergers, raids, insider trading, corporate governance and host of other activities of listed companies, stock exchanges and members of Stock Exchanges.

The more important guidelines of SEBI affecting the New Issues market are set out here. To start with it is necessary to note that all companies are free to raise capital from the market and that they can price their shares freely with a proper justification of the premia fixed. The draft prospectus is to be approved by the SEBI before issue to the public. Since October 1996, this responsibility was passed on to the merchant bankers. The SEBI guidelines contain provisions regarding which companies can issue at premium and which cannot.

Promoters' quota and quotas of associates and friends etc., are not transferable for 5 years respectively and investors should not buy any non-transferable shares in private placements. Similarly quotas of employees, NRIs, etc. were also non-transferable for specific periods earlier and made transferable since Oct. 1995.

Underwriting is now optional, but if despite such underwriting, even 90% of the public issue is not subscribed, within the time limits, such subscriptions are to be returned to the public within 120 days of the last subscription date. Letters of allotment or refund orders are to be despatched within 30 days and are to be listed in the stock exchange for a quotation.

In the event of oversubscription, proportional allotment is to be given to the applicants. This allotment is to be done in consultation with the regional stock exchange. The company making the public issue and getting their shares listed has to place a deposit of 1% with the stock exchange which will be forfeited if the conditions of listing and the time schedule for listing are not observed.

Stock Invest is an instrument for applying for new issues which is being encouraged by the SEBI. The companies do not discriminate any applications with stock invest. They are expected to report to SEBI the applications made with stock invest and the amounts involved and the successful applicants with stock invest and the amounts accepted. Later, stock invest was banned when the Demat form allotment and trading were started and time limit for allotment was reduced. The allotment of shares in Demat form and reduction of allotment time from 30 days to 15 days have also been implemented, which made stock invest redundent.

INDIAN CAPITAL MARKET

LANDMARKS AND DEVELOPMENTS

1. Amendment to Banking Regulation Act in 1983 permitted banks to undertake non-banking functions like merchant banks and Mutual funds which started operations in the Capital market through their subsidiaries.
2. Entry of Public sector banks through their Mutual funds in a big way since 1987 for channelling small savings into the Capital market.
3. Setting up of the SEBI by the Govt. in 1988 to oversee capital market.
4. Establishment of SHCIL by All India Financial Institutions (FIs) and banks introducing a new concept of depository functions and book-keeping for stock market dealings of the sponsoring institutions.
5. Setting of credit rating agencies, namely, CRISIL, IICRA, CARE etc. from 1988 onwards popularising the credit rating function by Companies issuing debt instruments.
6. Introducing a new tier to the Capital Market Structure, OTCEI was set up in 1989 — started operations in 1992.
7. Issue of public sector bonds since 1985 and disinvestment of equity shares to the public since 1991 by the P.S.Us.
8. SEBI got the legal status by the passing of the SEBI Act in April 1992.
9. Abolition of the CIC Act and the Controller of Capital Issues resulting in a free entry into the Capital market and free pricing of shares by the Companies since May 1992.
10. Offshore Funds are allowed to be floated by banks and FIs abroad from 1985 onwards.
11. Indian companies are allowed to raise capital abroad on commercial lines, from 1993 onwards.
12. FFIs and FIIs are allowed to operate in Indian capital market after registration with the SEBI (including the OCBs), and with the permission of the RBI.
13. More liberal investment entry for NRIs and foreign investment in Indian companies allowed upto 51% after 1991 economic reforms.
14. Mutual funds are allowed to be set up in the private sector (1992-93) and a large number of them have already entered the fray.
15. National Stock Exchange was set up and recognised by Govt. in 1993 and started operations of trading in 1994 — electronic trading, settlement and clearance.
16. Dematerialisation of physical certificates into book entry form — Demat form of allotment and trading
17. Introduction of Futures and options trading on major Stock Exchanges.
18. Adoption of Rolling Settlement involving daily settlement of trades on compulsory basis.

RECENT TRENDS IN CAPITAL MARKETS

A New Order

A new era in capital markets in India was ushered in July, 1991, with the starting of a process of financial and economic deregulation. Beginning with the devaluation of rupee by about 20% in July 1991, industrial policy was totally reshaped to dispense with licensing of all industries except the 18 scheduled industrial groups. Further, removal of MRTP limit on assets of companies, dilution of FERA and foreign trade liberalisation etc., were some of the other reforms. Fiscal policy was rationalisd to reduce the Central Budget deficit and public sector undertakings were freed from government controls by professionalising their managements, giving greater autonomy to them and by disinvestment of their shares in favour of the public.

Greater role is visualised for the private sector in the future investment growth. Liberalisation of controls and financial deregulation allowed a freer role to the market forces. The economy is expected to shift to a market-oriented competitive environment. Freer entry and exit to foreign financial and corporate units from abroad would encourage freer competition, cost effectiveness and improved productivity in the Indian Economy. These would improve the growth of the economy, role of private corporate sector and of the capital market. The dependence of the government, semi government bodies, P.S.Us and of corporate sector on the capital market is bound to expand in the years to come. The potential of the Indian Capital Market to growth is vast.

Genesis of New Order

The beginning of liberalised policies dates back to 1985 when the Seventh Five Year Plan was started. The Banking companies Amendment Act of 1983 gave new avenues of activities to banks in the form of participation in non-funded activities and financial services such as leasing, hire-purchase, merchant banking, etc. The public sector banks have started setting up subsidiaries for merchant banking, lease financing, mutual funds etc., since that time. After 1992 even private sector is allowed to enter into these financial services, including banking, mutual funds, etc. By 1987, many public sector banks have set up Mutual Funds.

The SEBI was set up in April 1988 to oversea and control the capital market and it has been given legal powers since April 1992 by an Act. A number of new institutions like CRISIL for credit rating and SHCIL for clearance and share depository services have been set up. A new structured securities market was initiated by setting up of an over the Counter Exchange of India (OTCEI) for computerised trading of small and ill-traded companies. This Exchange was the 22nd Exchange to be given recognition under the SC(R) Act, in 1989.

NSE

Following the Pherwani Committee recommendations, the government have initiated steps for NMS and recognised the NSE in 1993 for setting of National market system, in which the electronic trading, and settlement is possible throughout the country on the basis of standard prices and a fixed margin of service charges or commission for the broker. NSE was the 23rd Stock Exchange to be recognised under SC(R) Act, and set up in 1993.

With increasing regulation by SEBI on Exchanges the future role of Exchanges will be radically different from the present, as their developmental role will be increasing much faster than their regulatory role. Not only the Stock Exchange but all the players in the market, namely, companies, brokers, intermediaries and investors have come under the supervision and control of SEBI. Along with increasing self regulation and a stricter enforcement of a code of conduct on the members, the Stock Exchanges will have to emerge as Public Service Institutions catering to increasing demands of investors in the country. Listed companies have also a role in this process to collaborate and extend all help for more efficient functioning of Exchanges. To improve the quality and efficiency of service, trained and professional category of intermediaries and brokers is also necessary. Education, training and research would be the hallmark of future Stock Brokers and other intermediaries, in the markets.

National Market System

The Pherwani Committee recommended the setting up of the national market system based on the new Stock Exchange which was already set up in Mumbai. To make the national market system effective, the committee recommended several support agencies to provide high quality trading, settlement and depository services. In this context, it has recommended that there should be three tiers, namely, National Stock Exchanges at Mumbai, Kolkata etc., regional Stock Exchanges like those in major State Capitals and additional trading floors sponsored or managed by Principal or Regional Stock Exchanges. The structure of Securities markets was on the following lines:

1. Regular Stock Markets which are 21 in number at present.
2. National Market System with a separate set of licensed brokers all over the country mostly like Banks and Corporate units, attached to NSE, which was recognised in 1993.

3. Retail Broking through a series of registered sub-brokers attached to the Regular Stock Markets or to NMS.
4. Additional Trading floors licensed for trading in securities on the basis of a Regional Stock Exchange quotations. This concept of ATF did not get acceptance from the investors and brokers but the on-line electronic trading from BSE and NSE became popular.
5. OTCEI for risky and venturesome companies and companies which cannot satisfy the listing requirements of regular Stock Exchanges, such as small companies. Most of those recommendations have already been implemented, but OTCEI has not become popular.

Need for Larger Financial Base

Although Pherwani Committee on stock market reforms recommended the opening of four more Stock Exchanges in addition to the existing 21 Exchanges, the trading floors recognised by SEBI can operate in those places linked to a main-regional Exchange. Because, the Stock Exchanges in the future cannot function without better infrastructure, computerisation, etc, this recommendation is not implemented. But in Sept. 1996, Visakhapatnam Stock Exchange is recognised for electronic trading. For brokers also, capital adequacy norms have been laid down by the SEBI but not yet implemented.

Not only there is need for better infrastructure in the form of space, Telecommunications, electronic network connecting all broker firms but also the broker firms shall themselves need a better capital base.

SEBI Reforms of the Secondary Markets

As soon as the SEBI Act was passed in April 1992, the SEBI has swung into action for regulating the intermediaries in the stock market. Before the legal powers were given to the SEBI, it had already started regulating the merchant bankers and mutual funds by registering and licensing them and later through a code of conduct to be observed by them. With the legal powers bestowed on it, later on it had asked all the existing stock brokers and sub-brokers of Exchange to register with the SEBI. Despite initial opposition, this task of registration was completed in 1992 only.

The other reforms initiated are as follows:

1. Changes in the composition of Board of Directors: Stock exchange so far were governed by their own board of Directors, which comprised mostly exchange member - brokers, with one/two representatives from Govt. and public. But the SEBI guidelines impose a condition that 50% of the Board members should be non-broking public or Govt. representatives. This was accepted by the stock exchanges and is being implemented.
2. Transparency in trading and accounting practices: The brokers were asked to show their prices and brokerage separately in the contract notes and their accounts. This is also being implemented by the brokers. The service tax which brokers have to pay is collected from clients and is shown in the contract note separately.
3. Stock exchanges were asked to subject the broker accounts to better inspection and audit. The stock exchanges are themselves inspected by the SEBI officers from time to time. Sometimes the SEBI itself is organising inspection of broker firms and their accounts. Penalties and suspension are imposed on the brokers for violation of the Rules and regulations and the guidelines of the SEBI.
4. As referred to earlier, Brokers are expected to maintain a minimum capital of Rs. 5 lakhs in major exchanges and Rs. 2 lakhs in minor exchanges. Besides, a minimum networth of 8% of the annual turnover is recommended to be kept by brokers.
5. Better investor services by the brokers and the exchanges: Norms have been laid down for broker client relations and for collection of margins from clients. Stock exchanges are to provide funds for investor claims, through Customer Protection Funds, set up for the purpose. They have to submit periodic reports on their activities, trading, brokers and sub-brokers.
6. The inter-connected Stock Exchange linking electronically some 15 Regional Stock Exchanges for a national market system was recognised by SEBI in 1998.

7. Insider Trading Regulations were imposed for illegal and unethical practices in trading.
8. Rules for corporate governance, Book Building, buy back of shares, mergers and acquisitions, take over, etc., have been laid down.
9. Regulations for Margin trading for brokers lending and borrowing of shares by brokers for trading and settlement, Rolling Settlement etc. have been set out and implemented.
10. Futures and options trading on stock Indexes was permitted in July 2000 and on individual stocks chosen selectively since November 2001, and derivative trading is encouraged.
11. Book Building is now being replaced by the Auction System in the sale of shares, as IPOs.
12. Demutuation of stock exchanges was insisted upon and those which could not do this, in the permitted time period, are to be derecognised.

CHAPTER 9

Institutional Structure in Capital Market

Development and Investment Institutions

Functionally, there are two types of financial institutions in the Indian capital market, namely, developmental institutions and investment institutions. In the former category, there are institutions of all-India stature, namely, IDBI, IFCI, ICICI and IRBI, now called IIBI and of State-level stature, namely, State Finance and Development Corporations. As in 2009-10, in the all India category, only IDBI, ICICI have become universal banks. IRBI was converted into IIBI which is being wound up for its non-viable character. Now, the all India development and finance bodies are only IFCI, NABARD, NHB, SIDBI etc., In the category of investment institutions, there are all India bodies like UTI, LIC, GIC, etc. and State-level bodies like the State Industrial Development Corpns. (SIDCs) and State Industrial Investment Corpns. (SIICs) and State Infrastructural Development Corpns. There are some specialised financial institutions like IVCF, ICICI Venture and IFCI Venture Funds. The all-India bodies provide finance, entrepreneurial guidance, training and technical guidance, etc., to the all-India projects and regional projects of medium and large size. They lend at concessional terms for the development of no-industry districts and backward regions. Among the all-India bodies, IDBI is the leader of financial institutions. But in 1988, the SEBI was set up as the developmental and regulatory body of the securities industry in India.

The state-level bodies provide finance and entrepreneurial guidance to state-level small and medium entrepreneurs and undertake developmental and investment activities to promote infrastructure and industrial growth in the respective states. Some of them have set up industrial estates and undertook joint ventures with the private sector to promote industries in their respective states.

These are the main players in the market, either in the primary market or in the secondary market. Besides giving loans and advances to industrial units, they invest in their debentures and equity shares, provide the seed capital for new and small entrepreneurs, underwrite stock, shares, debentures and various other instruments in the capital market or subscribe to new issues or buy or sell these instruments in the secondary market, etc. A number of mutual funds have also become players in the market since 1987.

The SEBI as the regulatory authority deserves our first attention as this book is concerned with the security markets. This was discussed in a separate chapter.

The UTI and other Mutual Funds are the major players in the capital market. With $ 88 Billion assests Indian MF industry ranks 24th in the world.

Of the major players in the market, namely, the investment institutions like LIC, GIC and UTI, the bulk of the activity is generated by the UTI by its mobilisation of savings from the public through its various schemes, referred below. It has investible funds to the tune of about Rs. 72,487 crores at the beginning of new millennium and it actively participates in trading in the market and in subscribing to new issues of shares, debentures, etc. A detailed write-up of the activities and functions of UTI is provided below.

UTI & its Objectives

The Unit Trust of India (UTI) was set up in 1964 with a major contribution from the RBI under the Unit Trust of India Act, 1964. Subsequently, with the passing of ownership of UTI to government in 1976, the IDBI became its shareholder along with the LIC, SBI and other financial institutions. Its activities, namely, the schemes it operates to mobilise saving and its investments, are all governed by the Act. It had originally a paid-up capital of Rs. 5 crores and it was the only Unit Trust or Mutual Fund in the public sector allowed to operate in India. It was accorded special treatment for tax assessment and tax deductions. Not only is its investment income-tax free but its dividend payments are also tax-exempt up to certain limits in the hands of the investors.

Its main objectives are to mobilise savings, particularly from the low and middle income groups, to channelise these savings into productive investment and to provide an assured income to savers. It provides the savers with expert investment service, portfolio management and assured income. The risk-averting savers would not normally invest in stock and capital market. They are afraid to do so due to lack of expertise and easy access. The UTI provides expert management of their funds, steady income and liquidity for their investment through repurchase facility. The UTI mobilises the savings through the sale of its units and operates a number of schemes with varied characteristics to suit the requirements of savers and investors. These characteristics include income, capital appreciation, liquidity through repurchase, an element of insurance, etc.

Activities of UTI

The activities of UTI include a wide variety of services to the corporate world as well as investors. It can underwrite new issues, make direct subscription to public issues or private placements, keep deposits with banks and companies and operate in the money market by subscribing to Treasury bills, commercial bills, etc. It can also partake in the inter-bank market as a lender or borrower of short-term funds. It can borrow from the RBI or the Government in case of need.

The units of UTI are in denominations of Rs. 10 or 100, through which it mobilises funds from the household and business sectors. It can also sell units to foreign individuals and institutions. For example, NRIs are eligible to invest in the units without prior permission of the RBI on a non-repatriation basis. The UTI has a network of agents all over India to sell units and service the unit-holders. It has arrangements with some banks to operate its schemes, but since 1996 UTI Bank is itself acting as one of its main bankers.

Investment Pattern

The normal pattern of investment of its funds is broadly as follows although it may vary from year to year, and from scheme to scheme.

	% of total investment
Equity and Preference Shares	55.1
Debentures/Bonds	30.9
Advance deposits for underwritten shares/debentures	—
Term loans	3.1
Government Securities	8.3
Money Market Instruments	2.3
Deposits with companies and Banks	0.3
Total	100.00

It will be seen from the above that the bulk of its funds flow into the corporate sector in the form of loans, deposits, debentures, equity, etc. Barring about 14% with banks and in Government securities, and Money Market Instruments, the rest is invested in high-yielding corporate instruments.

Two unit schemes, viz., India Fund and India Growth Fund, were floated in foreign countries to mobilise foreign funds for investment in India. These two offshore funds were operated since 1986. The first one was India Fund floated in July 1986 in association with the Merrill Lynch and collected $ 75 million. These shares were quoted in London.

The second fund, namely, India Growth Fund, was launched in July 1988 and mobilised $ 60 million. These shares were quoted in New York. These two Funds have been doing well in their performance with the result that a number of other offshore funds were floated by the Grindlays Bank, SBI Caps, CanBank and others.

Besides, the UTI has also launched two Venture Capital Funds in 1989 and 1990 respectively for the promotion of green-field companies and new ventures having a high-risk component.

Schemes Offered by the UTI

1. *Unit Scheme 1964:* It is a perpetual scheme, each unit with a face value of Rs. 10, transferable and repurchased by the UTI. Dividend income from the UTI qualifies for deduction of income tax under Section 80L of the Income-Tax Act and eligible for Wealth Tax exemption. Reinvestment facility as an alternative to dividend distribution is available. This scheme was abandoned in 2001, when the U.T.I. was involved in gross mismanagement.

2. *Unit-linked Insurance Plan (ULIP) 1971:* Schemes of 10-year and 15-year periods are available both with life insurance and accident insurance. The target amount is a maximum of Rs. 60,000 and the age limit is 55 years. The life coverage is secured from the LIC by the contributions of UTI. The contributions of the insured are payable yearly or half-yearly.

3. *Capital Gains Unit Scheme (CGUS):* Investment in part or in full of the capital gains due to sale of any long-term capital assets in the Capital Gains Units Scheme would qualify for exemption from capital gains tax under Section 54A of the Income-tax Act. This investment is to be made within six months of the date of the sale of capital assets and there is no maximum limit. This is to be held for a minimum period of three years. Dividend income along with others is exempt under Section 80L of Income-tax Act upto Rs. 12,000 and from the wealth tax up to Rs. 5 lakhs.

4. *Children's Gift Growth Plan:* Units with a face value of Rs. 10 are gifted to a minor child under this scheme, maturing at the age of 21 by the child. Gifts up to Rs. 20,000 or Rs. 30,000 were exempted from gift tax, and gift tax was itself abolished since 1998-99.

5. *Various Close-ended Schemes:* Such schemes as monthly income unit scheme, growing income unit scheme, etc. were started in various years since 1982 for meeting the varying needs of investors.

6. *Master Shares Floated for Indian Investors and Indian Fund and India Growth Fund etc. for Foreign Investors:* The Mutual Fund Subsidiary Unit Scheme (Master Shares) 1986 are quoted on the stock exchanges and are treated as shares. A third offshore fund was initiated in 1989-90 with the help of a Japanese securities firm and ADB, in addition to the two, referred to above. UTI operates more than sixty schemes with an outstanding amount of Rs. 44,607 crores as at end June 1997. As at end July 2001, UTI had total investible funds of Rs. 54,223 crores at market value, of which about Rs. 24,704 crores was in the form of equities.

UTI has also set up its own Bank (UTI Bank) and some other subsidiaries to serve its investors.

The first three schemes are the most popular of all and account for 70 per cent of the total investible funds of the UTI. The second venture capital fund which is managed by the Technology Development and Information Company of India Ltd. was set up in March 1990 with a contribution of Rs. 35 crores from the UTI and contributions from other financial institutions. This fund like the earlier one, helps the financing of greenfield ventures from new entrepreneurs to promote industrial growth.

IDBI

The Industrial Development Bank of India (IDBI) was the leader in the Indian capital market. It has both regulatory and developmental functions. The IDBI was established in July 1964 as a wholly-owned subsidiary of the Reserve Bank but was transferred to the ownership of Central Government, under the Public Financial Institutions Laws (Amendment) Act, 1975. By an Amendment Act of 2004, it was made a corporate unit and later become a universal Bank.

The role of IDBI in the market is to promote and develop industries as per the planned projections of the Government, to provide technical and administrative assistance for the expansion and modernisation of industry and for rediscount and refinance facilities to financial institutions. The IDBI operated a number of schemes for the benefit of promoting enterprises and concessional finance facilities were also provided for industries in backward areas.

The IDBI, as the leader in the market, coordinated and monitored the credit facilities by all-India and state-level financial institutions and development corporations. The IDBI also undertook the responsibility for promoting and financing the small and cottage industries and also the import-export trade of the country until separate bodies were set up for them. Thus, the Exim Bank was set up in 1981 for assisting the export-import trade sector and in particular for promoting exports. The Small Industries Development Bank of India (SIDBI) was set up in 1989 to help small and cottage industries.

The paid-up capital of the IDBI was Rs. 100 crores up to 1980 and stood at Rs. 653 crores in March 2005 and has vast reserves and after 2005, IDBI was converted into an universal bank. The main sources of funds for the IDBI were borrowings from Government, RBI and from the market by issue of bonds, both internal and external, to the public.

Schemes of IDBI Assistance

The major schemes, performance-wise, were as follows:

(i) Textile Modernisation Fund Scheme for the purpose of promoting modernisation of jute and cotton textile industries;

(ii) Venture Capital Fund Scheme for the purpose of developing new ventures and promoting risky ventures by new technicians and new entrepreneurs;

(iii) Technology Upgradation Scheme for the purpose of upgrading technology in selected capital goods industries;

(iv) Energy Conservation Scheme for the purpose of financing of energy-saving proposals of industries; and

(v) Seed Capital Scheme for the purpose of providing initial seed capital in the form of promoters' contribution to new ventures.

The IDBI operated direct assistance schemes whereby project appraisal and financing for medium and large-scale projects was undertaken. It coordinated its activities with all-India institutions like IFCI, ICICI, etc. It was the leader and provided guidance and coordination of services for long-term financial institutions.

It provided refinancing under the Industrial Loans Scheme for the loans extended by commercial and cooperative banks and SFCs. This refinance is for assisting SSIs, transport operators and units in the backward areas, etc.

The IDBI undertook a number of promotional activities like provision of finance out of the Technical Assistance Fund for techno-economic surveys, preparation of project report, undertaking industrial potential survey, promoting market research, training and conducting entrepreneurial development programmes, etc.

The IDBI has also sponsored a number of technical consultancy organisations in different parts of the country to help the new entrepreneurs with identification of projects, preparation of project reports, market studies, setting up of science and technology parks and promoting research and development in the areas of capital market. The promotional role is also noticed in its operation of the Seed Capital Assistance Scheme referred to earlier. Under this scheme, SFCs provide special share capital to SSIs out of the funds provided by the IDBI for this purpose. The IDBI has also its own scheme to help middle-sized projects up to Rs. 1 crore with Seed Capital through the SIDCs and SIICs. Besides, the IDBI also contributes to the share capital and bonds of SFCs and other financial institutions. It has set up a Development Assistance Fund for the purpose of providing assistance to projects approved by the Central Government, which may not be financed by banks and FIs. It operates a Bills Rediscounting Scheme under which banks and financial institutions can get rediscount of bills and promissory notes arising out of the sale of machinery and capital goods on a deferred payment basis.

Sources of Funds

The IDBI also borrows abroad and secures funds under arrangements with foreign financial institutions, foreign banks and foreign governments and operates foreign lines of credit, secured by the Government. The foreign funds are used for financing of the foreign currency component of the project finance, for providing foreign currency loans and financing of imports and to make payments to foreign suppliers of capital goods, plant and machinery in foreign countries. It can borrow from the Government and the RBI, but it has been borrowing from the capital market since 1994, through bonds and debentures.

ICICI

The Industrial Credit and Investment Corporation of India (ICICI) was set up in 1955 in the Private Sector to meet the private sector financial needs and to channel the World Bank assistance to the private corporate units. The objectives of this corporation were to encourage industrial investment in the private sector and to promote participation of private capital, both internal and external, with a view to widening the base of industrial development and of capital market in India. It has been providing full merchant banking services, Venture capital financing and allied financial services.

The ICICI has been assisting both private and joint-sector enterprises with rupee and foreign currency loans and advances, underwriting, guaranteeing of loans from other agencies, equity participation and other forms of assistance particularly to the new enterprises. Its outstanding loans and advances stood at Rs. 46,279 crores at end March 2001, in Indian Rupees and foreign currencies. Afterwards, it got itself into an universal Bank.

The sources of funds of ICICI were its paid-up capital, borrowing from the Government, IDBI, RBI, etc. It can also raise funds from the capital market by issue of bonds or equity and borrow from abroad with the permission of the Government.

It has contributed to the development of backward areas through industrial growth, promotion of investment priorities of the Government and for the growth of private corporate sector.

It has set up Venture Capital Funds for the promotion of green field companies and risk capital investment and joined the other financial institutions in setting up SHCI, CRISIL and OTC Exchange of India Ltd. It has recently set up its own bank and a mutual fund, like the UTI. In 2001, ICICI has entered a new phase of universal banking by consolidation and merger of all its subsidiaries including ICICI Bank. ICICI and IDBI have now become universal banks.

IFCI

The Industrial Finance Corporation of India was set up by the government in 1948 by the IFC Act, 1948 for the purpose of assisting the medium and long-term projects for capital expenditure on projects, expansion, modernisation and technological upgradation, etc. It has also a promotional and developmental role, particularly in relation to the small and medium-scale entrepreneurs.

It has a paid-up capital of Rs. 1,108 crores in 2009 of which 50% is held by the IDBI and the rest by the scheduled commercial and co-operative banks and other financial institutions. The IFCI can also borrow from the Government, RBI and the market by the issue of bonds.

Functions

Its operations extend to both rupee loans and foreign currency loans. The foreign loans are through foreign credit lines from foreign banks and foreign governments, etc. It can also provide underwriting and guaranteeing facilities to the industrial concerns. It can provide term loans or contribute to the debentures or equity. It has outstanding loans and advances of Rs. 17,281 crores in March 2000, which fell to Rs. 7,020 crores by March 2009.

Under the IFC Act, it can provide financial assistance to limited companies either in the private, public or joint sectors and cooperative societies engaged in the following activities: (1) Manufacturing, preservation and processing of goods; (2) Shipping; (3) Mining, (4) Hotel Industry; (5) Electricity generation and distribution, etc.

The IFCI collaborates with other FIs in financing all big projects of Rs. 10 crores and above. It concentrates mostly on medium and large-scale projects, as in the case of ICICI and IDBI. By an agreement with other FIs and IDBI, the IFC specialises in financing of certain industries like jute, cement, sugar, etc.

IRBI

The Industrial Reconstruction Bank of India was set up in 1985 by reorganising the earlier IRCI to provide assistance to sick but potentially viable units and extend finance for their modernisations, expansion or diversification.

Its paid-up capital and reserves are Rs. 176 crores at the time of conversion into IIBI in 1997 and other sources of funds are the borrowings from the Government and the RBI, IDBI and others. It can also raise funds by the issue of bonds to the public and market borrowings. These are used for term loans, hire-purchase, leasing finance, etc. for industrial reconstruction and rehabilitation. Its outstanding loans and advances stood at Rs. 1,350 crores at end March 1997.

Functions

The IRBI has its Head Office at Kolkata, while the rest of the institutions of all-India nature referred to above have their head offices either in Mumbai or Delhi. The IRBI mainly assisted the sick jute and cotton textile industries and the sick units in other industries. The potential viability of these units at a future date and their national importance in terms of employment and output are also taken into account by the IRBI.

Its sources of funds are the Government, borrowing from the IDBI, RBI, etc. It can also issue debentures or bonds to the public or raise deposits from the public. These funds are advanced to the assisted units in the form of term loans, working capital term loans, investments and other forms of assistance.

IIBI

In 1997, the IRBI has been completely restructured, when it has become sick by itself due to financing of sick industrial units. The NPAs of sick industries were wiped out and the paid up capital of IIBI stood at Rs. 446 crores at end March 2006. It has converted itself into a limited company under the Companies Act and operates now under the new name Industrial Investment Bank of India. It has shed off its work of financing sick units and emerged as an Industrial Investment Bank devoted to growth, expansion and diversification of existing and new industrial undertakings and not sick units as before. It has become a Development Financial Institution (DFI) with a five year tax holiday in addition to completely restructured capital structure and new procedures and systems. But due to non-viability of this company with increased NPAs, it is now in the process of voluntary winding up.

INSURANCE COMPANIES

Life Insurance Corporation (LIC)

The provision of life insurance in India is the monopoly of the Life Insurance Corporation of India (LIC). It provides cover of risk of life, retirement, disability, etc. Since 1956, when it was set up as a nationalised public body, it was acting as a major financial institution in the capital market for mobilising savings through premiums for life and endowment insurance and using these funds for investment in government and corporate securities for economic growth. The LIC operates in both the money and capital markets although it is a long-term financial institution.

Its sources of funds are the paid-up capital, premium collections, borrowings from government and the RBI and presently, the mobilisation of savings by insurance companies accounts for 10 to 15% of the financial savings of the household sector.

Under the Insurance Act, as applied to the LIC, the pattern of investment is laid down. The proportion of funds to be deployed at their discretion was hardly 25% of the total investible funds, while the rest are earmarked for specified government and semi-government securities (50%) and for lending for socially-desirable projects like housing finance loans, mortgage loans, loans to approved bodies for electricity, housing, water, etc. (25%).

The LIC invests in shares/debentures of companies, provides rupee loans to companies, makes initial subscription and underwriting of new issues of shares and debentures, etc. It has control over a huge volume of funds namely Rs. 7.62 lakh crores at end March 2009 and has an important role in the stock market and capital market operations. Investments by the LIC are of gigantic proportion as in the case of U.T.I.

It has set up in 1989 a Mutual Fund for operating various schemes for mobilisation of savings from the public, particularly from the rural and urban areas and channel these funds to the stock and capital market. The LIC has considerable expertise in investment management by virtue of its earlier operations of funds.

In addition to all these activities the LIC makes direct lending to industry, subscription to initial and further issues of shares and debentures of companies, financial institutions of the Centre and States etc. Out of the total disbursements of all financial institutions to all sectors, LIC's contribution comes to around 50-55%.

Insurance Sector is now opened upto private sector with a limit of ownership to foreign companies at 26%. An Insurance Regulatory Authority was set up with powers to regulate all their activities.

General Insurance Corporation (GIC)

The General Insurance Corporation (GIC) was set up by the Government in 1971 by taking over the then existing GIC and merged all the then existing general insurance companies into four subsidiaries in 1974 (National, New India, Oriental and United India).

The objectives of the GIC are to carry on the general insurance business other than life, such as vehicle, insurance, accident, fire insurance, etc. to aid and advise the subsidiaries to conduct the insurance business and to help the conduct of investment strategy of the subsidiaries in an efficient and productive manner.

Its sources of funds are paid-up capital, reserves, profits and premium income. It can also like the LIC, operate in the money and capital markets, earn on underwriting and making of long-term loans and investments. Its investment policy is governed by the Insurance Act like the LIC and its investments are accordingly spread in specified proportions in Central and State Government securities, semi-Government bonds, debentures, preference shares and equity shares of companies, deposits with companies and other loans and advances.

Public Sector Mutual Funds

As referred to earlier, the UTI had the monopoly of Mutual Fund movement until 1986, when for the first time public sector banks were allowed to set up mutual funds with the prior approval of the RBI and the Government. This was made possible under the Government's scheme of financial liberalisation and the passage of the Banking Laws Amendement Act 1983. The SBI Caps and CanBank Financial Services were the first to set up mutual funds to mobilise savings for investment. Subsequently, the Indian Bank, Bank of India, Punjab National Bank, Bank of Baroda, etc. have set up their own Mutual Funds. The schemes floated by them have varying characteristics as regards income, growth, maturity etc., To give examples, SBI Magnums, Canara Bank's CanStock, Canshare, CanGrowth and CanGilt, etc., are a few such schemes. The LIC and GIC have also set up Mutual Funds on the same lines as the banks in 1989-90. In 2008-09, public sector bank sponsored mutual funds raised less than 20% of the total funds mobilised by all M.F.s. Only PSB and FI mutual funds had positive resource mobilisation.

The schemes of LIC Mutual Fund have some special characteristics, in that they include an insurance element also. Examples are Dhana Raksha and Dhana Vriddhi. Both these schemes have an insurance cover and proportion of investment is set apart for this. Proof of age and certificate of good health are necessary for insurance cover.

SFCs/SIDCs

The State Financial Corporations have been set up after the passage of the State Financial Corporations Act in 1951 by the Government of India. These are development finance bodies designed to provide the short and medium-size enterprises with term finance and promote the growth of industrialisation in the states. There are 26 SFCs at present, including the Tamilnadu Industrial Investment Corpn., set up by various State Governments.

Their sources of funds are issue of bonds and debentures in the market, fixed deposits from the public, borrowings from RBI, IDBI, State Governments, etc. These funds are deployed mostly as loans and advances to the various medium and small enterprises, investments in Government securities, corporate shares, debentures, etc. These bodies are to assist in particular small-scale industries, units in backward areas, new entrepreneurs, etc. Some State Governments have set up Industrial Development Corporations, Industrial Investment Corporations and state-level Infrastructural Development Corporations for the promotion of industrial enterprises in the states through equity participation and through loans and advances, including entrepreneurial assistance, seed capital to new enterprises, etc.

These are set up by the State Governments for promotional activity, infrastructural development, financial, managerial and entrepreneurial guidance to the industrialists, provision of industrial sheds/plots for setting up of small units, etc. They help in backward area development and promotion of industrialisation in the states in particular.

Besides, there is the National Small Industries Corporation (NSIC) and National Industrial Development Corporation (NIDC) in the country. The former helps the SSIs with the promotional and extension services, hire-purchase finance, supply of marketing network, raw materials, etc., while the latter provides the consultancy services, designing project planning and project preparation, etc. Thus, many of these institutions in the capital market are developmental and promotional in nature.

SHCIL (Stock Holding Corporation of India Ltd.)

One of the important institutions set up more recently for toning up of the stock and capital markets in India is the Stock Holding Corporation of India Ltd. (SHCIL). It was intended to facilitate quicker share transfer among financial institutions, *inter se*, and their transfers with other investors, members of Stock Exchanges etc. It provides infrastructural facilities for post-trading services, such as clearing, depository and other support services. Its services were later extended to banks, Mutual Funds etc. It now deals with all dematerialised securities of FIs banks, etc.

Organisational Structure

The SHCIL was set up in October 1987 by seven all-India financial institutions, *viz.*, IDBI, IFCI, ICICI, LIC, GIC, UTI and IRBI. It has a paid-up capital of Rs. 7 crores subscribed by the sponsoring FIs. SHCIL is Board-managed and has a whole time President in charge of day-to-day management. Besides its Office at Mumbai, SHCIL has branches at other important cities where stock exchanges are functioning. It is a member of major stock exchanges. SHCIL is operating on commercial lines and will levy fees/charges for its various services so as to cover its costs and earn a sufficient surplus for expanding its activities and for giving a reasonable return on its equity.

Functions

In the first instance, SHCIL was offering its services to its own seven promoter institutions. It acted on the basis of Letter of Authority/Power of Attorney issued by the financial institutions and rendered the following services:

(a) Clearing services.

(b) Depository services.

(c) Support services.

(d) Management/information services.

(e) Development services.

The SHCIL is eliminating paper work which clogs the post-trading activities. It does so by replacing the physical transfer of shares by passing the necessary receipts and keeping the shares with itself as a depository for the sponsoring financial institutions. In other words, SHCIL will ultimately emerge as a bank for securities. The book entry transfer system will eliminate needless paper work and speed up the transfer of securities and the related payments and receipts. Unlike under the present system which generally involves considerable delays in the actual transfer of shares to the buyer after he has paid for them and the actual receipt of the price consideration by seller after he has handed over the scrips to his broker, under the computerised book entry transfer system, the transfers and the related payments can be effected within a couple of days. The inefficiency of the then share transfer system, where speculative transactions play a dominant role could be reduced by this system of paperless transfers, if this can be extended also to all investors. It was already extended to the members of the BSE by the setting up of BOI Holdings, referred to later and to trading in most shares through Dematerialisation of physical certificates.

Clearing Services

SHCIL is a member of the Clearing House of the major Stock Exchanges. It provides the post-trading agency work for the FIs. It receives and/or delivers the securities on behalf of the institutions after each settlement of the Stock Exchange. The SHCIL monitors the execution of the purchase/sale orders of the institutions by the brokers. It lodges securities and transfer deeds to Share Departments. The SHCIL ensures that the securities are duly and in time transferred to the names of the institutions. It holds all shares and securities in Demat form and acts as a Depository participant and as a major holder of securities, it is now permitted to do securities lending to the market participants.

Depository Services

SHCIL has provided a custodial service for securities and related services to the institutions while the securities are in its custody. Those services related to the collection of dividend warrants, and interest cheques; it attends to the necessary consolidation or splitting of shares, redemption and collection of bonus and rights and other privileges attached to shares, debentures and other instruments.

Support Services

The SHCIL arranges to monitor interest/dividend payments due to the institutions and ensures that the warrants are received from the companies and are deposited in the banks to the credit of the institutions without delay.

Management Information System

The SHCIL also provides various management information services to the institutions such as trade monitoring system, safe custody, book closure or record dates announced by the companies, details of interest/dividend due and details of redemption/conversion/rights, etc.

Developmental Services

The SHCIL after streamlining the existing procedures has introduced new technologies to upgrade its own capability to handle on a fully automated basis, growing volumes of transactions emanating not only from its own sponsoring institutions but also from others. The developmental services include the geographical spread of its services, extension of its services to newer clients and analysis and dissemination of market information.

CRISIL (Credit Rating and Information Services of India Ltd.)

The CRISIL was set up in 1988 jointly by the ICICI, UTI, LIC, GIC, SBI and ADB along with a number of other financial institutions. The objective of this institution is to rate the debt obligations of Indian companies on a voluntary basis with a view to providing the investors a guide as to the risk of timely payment of interest and principal by the company. The rating is at present confined only to fixed deposits, bonds, debentures, preference shares and short-term instruments like commercial paper. The CRISIL does not rate equity shares or the performance of the company as a whole. The ratings are specifically meant for the instruments referred to above.

CRISIL Rating and Investor Protection

Investors should also be familiar with the ratings given by the Credit Rating and Information Services of India Ltd. (CRISIL) for protecting their interests. The CRISIL ratings are given only for debt instruments of companies, namely, Commercial Papers (CP), debentures, bonds and fixed deposits. Since early 1992, the ratings of Investment Information and Credit Rating Agency (ICRA) are also used by companies. These are given on a voluntary basis and may be publicised or not, depending upon the company's own perception of the impact of these on the investors. The ratings in use by the companies are published by the CRISIL in their "CRISIL Rating Scan." The companies use them only when the ratings are favourable to them and when they are making any public offer for deposits or debentures, etc. The investors should examine these symbols with regard to their benefits and their implication. Since a rating given can be revised upwards or downwards, the investors should keep a watch on any such revisions. Now, the CRISIL itself would publicise them for the benefit of the investors although it is a private and autonomous organisation but is required to do so by the SEBI. The SEBI guidelines now insist that all companies should get these ratings and publicise them compulsorily, if they are borrowing through issue of debentures. Many companies accepting fixed deposits are also using these CRISIL ratings. Rating of company deposits is made Compulsory under the New Companies Bill 1993.

The implications of the rating used are as follows:

For Debentures, simple 'A' and 'B' are used; for preference shares, "Pf" is prefixed. For fixed deposits and short-term instruments, "F" and "P" are prefixed.

Debenture Ratings		***Implication***
Triple A — (AAA)	—	Highest Safety
Double A — (AA)	—	High Safety
Single A — (A)	—	Adequate Safety
Triple B — (BBB)	—	Moderate Safety
Double B — (BB)	—	Inadequate Safety
B, C & D	—	High risk and default-prone
Fixed Deposits Ratings,		
F Triple A — (FAAA)	—	Highest Safety
F Double A — (FAA)	—	High Safety
F Single A — (FA)	—	Adequate Safety

FB, FC and FD are inadequate, high-risk and default-prone instruments.

ICRA

Another Credit Rating Agency was set up later, namely, The Investment Information and Credit Rating Agency of India Limited, registered in 1991, sponsored by the IFCI and a number of other financial institutions. It has its headquarters at Delhi, while the CRISIL has its headquarters in Mumbai.

Credit Rating is now mandatory for all debt instruments issued by the companies both short-term and long-term. The debentures of both convertible and non-convertible nature require credit rating, if they are not convertible within 18 months.

Those convertible or repayable within 18 months are also directed to be rated by the SEBI, as the position stands at present.

As investments have a risk, investor should know the extent of the risk he is taking. For this, risk rating is necessary, particularly now when interest rates on debentures are freed. Debentures, bonds, preference shares and fixed deposits are eligible to be rated. The rating is instrument wise but not for the whole company. The ratings given by the credit rating agency like ICRA are indicators of the correct opinion of the relative capability of timely servicing of debts and obligations by the company.

The ratings given are AAA, AA or A for safety, BBB, BB or B for less safe investments C and D indicate no safety and default prone respectively. But as equities are essentially risky and investor is willingly entering the risky investment of equity, credit rating for equity is neither possible nor necessary. Only in respect of debt instruments, investor wants to avoid risk and so he should know the extent of the risk, he is taking. Equity holder is the owner and takes risk voluntarily while the debentureholder is creditor and he does not want to take risk in respect of interest or in payment of the principal. Even so, equity issues are also now open for Rating Agencies.

Factors Considered

In evaluating the instruments in question, CRISIL takes into account the various risks involved in servicing of instruments. They undertake business analysis, financial analysis, management evaluation and fundamental analysis. They also take into account the regulatory and competitive environment faced by the company and other relevant factors.

In business analysis, the CRISIL takes into account the legal position in terms of prospectus, memorandum, articles of association, etc., industry risk, demand and supply position for the company's products, market share of the company and its operational efficiency. In financial analysis, the CRISIL evaluates the accounting quality of the company, its inventory norms, depreciation policy and its accounting and audit methods. The financial flexibility is shown in the capital structure, methods of raising funds, adequacy of working capital funds, cash flows and earnings protection, etc.

The CRISIL also evaluates the management risk as judged by the track record of the management, planning and control system, managerial expertise, tax planning and expansion plans of the company. In general, the goals and objectives of the company, its sales and assets growth, capacity to overcome adverse economic and market conditions, etc., will be assessed by the CRISIL.

Under fundamental analysis, evaluation is carried out for the equity earnings per share, book value, capital and sales turnover, management, debt-equity ratio, current assets to liabilities ratio, contingent liabilities, etc. Besides, the asset quality will be judged by the risk element of various assets and interest and tax sensitivity of the company and its profitability position in general.

Any Credit Rating Agency follows the same principles, although, they may vary in methods and procedures and the weightage given to various factors considered.

Ratings

All the above types of analysis will be done by experts after discussions with the company executives, its suppliers, customers and market competitors. The information is gathered on a confidential basis and assessed with a view to examine the capacity of the company to service the instruments issued to the public.

Broadly, there are three categories of ratings:

(a) Long-term Instruments

(Debentures and Preference Shares) Triple A to triple B

(b) Medium-term Instruments

(Fixed Deposits) FAAA to FA

(c) Short-term Instruments

(C.P., etc.) P_1 + to P_3

The rating indicates the degree of risk and the highest safety possible is under the rating of AAA or FAAA or P_1. The creditworthiness is indicated in the ratings and reflects the capacity of the company to service them adequately with a view to ensure the timely payment of interest and principal.

Advantages

For the company a good rating from CRISIL will help raise funds in the capital market. Although many companies have got their instruments evaluated by CRISIL to get an independent view of their credit standing, a few only have publicised them. For the investors these rating help them in making a decision of their investment in various instruments. Besides such ratings have a demonstration effect and improve competitiveness of the companies to outperform each other. The services of CRISIL are charged to the company and the use of the rating is left to the choice of the company. If it chooses not to use it, it is free do so. This rating is also updated from time to time by the CRISIL whenever additional information is available and compulsorily every year. The lay public and the investors would benefit from such information about the performance of the company and their servicing capacity. This will in turn help to improve the climate of investment and the tone of the capital market. Under the latest guidelines rating is compulsory for all issues of debentures, either convertible or non-convertible if they are issued to public. It was made compulsory for deposits raised from the public, under New Companies Bill 1993. As per SEBI guidelines tration has to be publicased for issues made to the puthe.

CARE

A new credit rating agency was set up in April 1993 in the Private Sector and many more may come up in the future, as credit rating became compulsory for all debt instruments. The new institution is called the Credit Analysis and Research Limited for its activity of credit analysis and rating. The objects and functions of CARE are the same as those of CRISIL and ICRA. Companies will now have a better choice in entrusting the work of rating of their debt instruments issued to the public. The choice will be based on the efficiency and cost effective service given by the various credit rating agencies. CARE has started operations in November 1993 and their operations increased faster than that of ICRA.

DPCR

Duff Phelps Credit Rating India Pvt. Ltd. is another Credit Rating Agency set up in Private Sector in 1996. It has already rated a number of companies. Many others are in the pipeline. But SEBI has started giving guidelines to them with a view to regulate them as one of the capital market institutions.

FRIL

Fitch Ratings India Ltd. is another rating agency, set up recently in India by the Fitch, the world's third largest rating agency. It has become a 100% owned subsidiary of Fitch, with Rs. 5 crores of net worth to be eligible for registration with SEBI. It has a dual focus on structured financial products and bank ratings and help Indian companies wanting to raise funds off shore.

Another rating agency, set up later on was the SME Rating Agency, which also does credit rating of private corporates' issues of bonds or public deposits or commercial paper.

Introduction

The capital market reforms were initiated in 1991, as part of the Structural Reforms comprising industrial deregulation, privatisation, globalisation, and financial reforms through liberalisation of domestic economic policies and foreign exchange policies. Foreign direct investment is permitted upto 51% of equity in 34 select areas and automatic approvals are granted upto the permitted levels and in selected industrial sectors for foreign technology and foreign investments by the Secretariat For Industrial Approvals and the Foreign Investment Promotion Board.

Trade policy was also liberalised to allow freely exports and imports subject to a small negative list. All quantitative restrictions were abolished and discretionary controls and most of the licensing requirements were dispensed with in the EXIM policy in periods the Eighth, Nineth and Tenth Plan periods.

Rupee was made convertible on trade account in March 1993 and on current account in March 1994. There was a further liberalisation of the FERA regulations since 1992 with the result that free inflow of funds by FIIs and FFIs etc., was allowed for investment in the capital market and Rupee was allowed to float with the RBI fixing the reference rate for its deals in Dollar *vs.* Rupee.

Narasimham Committee

A high level committee on the financial system with Shri M. Narasimham as the Chairman was set up in 1991, which made far-reaching recommendations for banking sector and non-banking financial sector to improve the flexibility and operational efficiency of the markets and the institutions, namely, banks and financial institutions. The major recommendations are being implemented in the direction of deregulation, and liberalisation of policies.

In the area of capital market reforms, the Narasimham Committee emphasised the need for strengthening the SEBI powers, vesting of CCI powers in the SEBI and freeing of operations in the capital market with the SEBI as the Supervisory and Regulatory authority.

As per the recommendations, the SEBI Act was passed in March 1992 vesting legal powers on SEBI to act as regulatory authority on the stock and capital markets in India and also for all the intermediaries such as Merchant bankers, Registrars, brokers, underwriters etc. Mutual funds are brought under the control of the SEBI first in 1992 and venture capital funds later in 1995. All these funds are kept open to the foreign sector and the private sector since 1992 and not necessarily to the public financial institutions, as before.

Free Entry to Capital Market

In May 1992, the Capital Issues Control Act was abolished and the functions of Capital Issues Controller were entrusted to SEBI. But with freedom to enter capital market to raise any amount they want from the public by the corporates and free pricing of securities issued to the public, a new era of free capital market was ushered in. Now, any company is free to enter the capital market anytime to raise any amount they want and at any price that they can justify to the SEBI and investors. The SEBI powers in this regard are to oversee and vett the draft prospectus, with a view to ensuring investor protection. Slowly these powers of vetting and ensuring the transparency and full disclosures in the prospectus came to be delegated to the Merchant bankers, in respect of right issues and debt issues. Only statements and copies of prospectus are lodged with the SEBI in respect of these issues. Even in respect of equity issues, the SEBI has delegated the responsibility to the merchant bankers in the later years. But the final powers of control and penalisation of SEBI would deter the companies and the merchant bankers for any lapses. The grading of draft prospectus and penalty points awarded for any lapses to the merchant bankers would be the methods of control of the latter.

Liberalisation Measures

Interest rates on debentures and on P.S.U. bonds were freed in August 1991 with the result that they can now offer any rate to the public depending on their credit rating. All debt instruments are to be compulsorily credit rated by a credit rating agency. There are at present six credit rating agencies, which are awarding credit rating to the Money Market instruments, and debt instruments of debentures, deposits, etc. in the capital market. These agencies are:

CRISIL: Credit Rating Information Services of India Limited, *IICRA:* Investment Information and Credit Rating Agency and *CARE:* Credit Analysis and Research Ltd. Duff Phelps Credit Rating India Ltd., Fitch Rating's India Ltd., and SME Rating Agency Ltd.

As referred to earlier, the business of mutual funds, venture capital funds and credit rating and even banking have been kept open to the private sector and foreign enterprise. Accordingly, many private and joint sector mutual funds, venture funds, and private banks have started their operating since 1993-94.

The interest rates on deposits of NBFCs as much as of banks are still controlled by the RBI through the fixation of the minimum and/or maximum rates. In October 1995, the maximum rate on bank deposits of maturity above 2 years and later in 1996 those above 1 year were also removed so that banks are now free to fix their own rates, consistent with their cost structure.

The ceiling rate of interest on lending by financial institutions was replaced by a minimum lending rate of 15%. Since August 1991, Companies with good standing and credit rating were permitted to borrow through commercial paper in India and through GDR and FCCBs abroad. The FFIs and FIIs are permitted to operate in the Indian Capital market and some foreign security firms were also registered with SEBI for acting as intermediaries. In the stock and capital market, banks and PSUs are permitted to borrow directly from the public in the capital market. Even public financial institutions including IDBI have been allowed to access funds directly from the public.

Quantum of Funds: The result of these reforms is that the quantum of funds raised from the capital rose phenomenally in the Nineties. The amount of equity raised rose faster. Many new companies have become public to raise funds in the capital market and many public companies have sought listing on the stock exchanges. New capital issues raised in 1990-91 was Rs. 4,312 crores by 364 issues made, which rose to Rs. 26,456 crores by 1685 new issues in 1994-95. These amounts relate to those raised by Non-government public limited companies, in the form of equity and preference shares plus debentures, convertible or non-convertible either as rights or public issues.

During the 12 months of 1996-97 (April 1996 to March. 1997) there were 1428 public issues, aggregating Rs. 10,457 crores, as compared to 1677 issues for Rs. 16,172 crores in 1995-96. The quality of the issues is poorer and the public response was reported to be lukewarm, and discretionary later on. The response picked up in 1998-99 to Rs. 5,013 crores from a low of Rs. 3,138 crores in 1997-98. This stood at Rs. 21,115 crores in 2005-06 and Rs. 63,637 crore in 2007-08 which declined to Rs. 14,670 crore in 2008-09. These figures relate to non-Government public limited companies. If the figures of Banks, FIs, PSUs etc. are also considered including these sold by private placement, the amount stood at Rs. 34,755 crores in 1997-98 which sprurted upto Rs. 1,35,551 crores in 2006-07, and stood Rs. 2,745 crore in 2008-09.

New Instruments

Qualitative changes include a larger number of equity issues relative to debt. Among debt instruments, convertible debentures either partly or fully convertible have become popular. A number of new financial instruments have come into vogue after 1992. Innovative financial instruments are introduced like convertible preference shares, secured premium notes, warrants, Zero coupon bonds, Deep Discount bonds, discount bonds, Flexibonds, loyalty coupons, etc.

In the foreign capital markets, the Indian Companies have issued global depository receipts, listed and traded abroad, foreign currency bonds, convertible bonds, foreign currency notes, Eurocurrency bonds etc. Both private sector companies and public sector undertakings raised funds abroad for varying periods of time, say 5 to 9 years.

The depth and width of the capital market in India has expanded, as judged by the

(a) Quantum of funds raised in general.

(b) Quantum of funds raised by PSUs and public financial institutions.

(c) Premium at which they raised these funds.

(d) The variety of instruments, through which these funds are raised.

(e) The number of issuers of securities, the intermediaries and the final investors which have all gone up phenomenally during the quinquennium of 1990-91 to 1995-96 and there was set back in the latter half of Nineties.

(f) The number of investors are estimated to have risen to 40-50 million from hardly 10-15 million before the Reforms were started in 1991. This number must have doubled by 2010.

(g) The FFIs, FIIs, NRIs, OCBs etc. have all been permitted to operate in the Indian Capital market, both under direct investment and portfolio investment.

SEBI Guidelines

The SEBI set up originally in April 1988, became a legal entity in March 1992 and has since acquired larger and sweeping powers early in 1995. The SEBI has first started with issuing guidelines for merchant bankers, mutual funds, Portfolio Managers and then extended its regulations to all intermediaries in the market, like brokers, sub-brokers, underwriters, Registrars, collecting bankers, debenture Trustees, etc.

SEBI has issued Regulations for controlling Insider Trading, frauds and malpractices, for Takeovers and Acquisitions, central depositories and practices of brokers in particular of all Stock Exchanges. A code of conduct to be followed by all registered intermediaries in the market has been laid down by the SEBI, separately for each.

The SEBI guidelines have also provided for market makers who will specialise in buying and selling of securities by offering two way quotes. To ensure that market makers would be in a position to impart liquidity to scrips and reduce volatile movements in share prices bank finance is made available to them as per the RBI guidelines of August 1993. Banks have been permitted to grant limits to market makers on commercial considerations and working capital requirements for them may be met by banks. The existing minimum margin of 50% of loans to individuals against shares/debentures/bonds would not be applicable to bank advances to market makers as also the prudential limits of Rs. 5 lakhs for each against shares.

Regulations of underwriters of capital issues and capital adequacy norms for the stock brokers in the recognised Stock Exchanges were announced in October 1993. At the same time, the SEBI issued guidelines for disclosures in prospectus for investor protection. Allotment of new issues was made on a proportionate basis and minimum application amount was made for Rs. 5,000/- later reduced to 200 shares. Reservations for various categories like Indian FIs (20%) Indian Mutual Funds (20%) FFIs (24%) and Associate Companies (10%) and employees (10%) were allowed subject to a maximum reservations of 75% (including the promoters' contributions of 20% in the case of paid up Capital of more than Rs. 100 crores and 25% in the case of paid up capital of less than Rs. 100 crores). In all cases of public issue with a view to securing listing on recognised stock exchange, the minimum public issue was fixed at 25%, in 1993 instead of 60% minimum prevailing earlier. These reservations were all scrapped in October 1995, except those of minimum public issue of 25%, promotors' quota of 20% or 25% and employees' quota of 10%. Merchant bankers are allowed a quota of 5% of post issue equity since October 1995. In 1996, promoter's quota was reduced to 20% in some cases and promoter's lock in period was reduced to 3 years and no lock in for rights issues.

SEBI issued separate guidelines for Development financial Institutions, debenture Trustees MFs and Asset Management Companies and for the various instruments of issue like FCD, PCD, NCD and bonus issues. As these guidelines are changed so frequently that they cannot be enumerated here.

Underwriting, which was compulsory earlier was made optional in October 1994. Preferential allotments have to be made at market related prices or at the net asset value basis in the case of unlisted companies.

Strengthening of SEBI Powers

By a gradual process the powers of the Government under the Securities Contracts (Regulation) Act 1956 to control the Stock Exchanges and their members were delegated to the SEBI; with final appellate power however resting with the Ministry of Finance. Besides, by an amendment to the SEBI Act in 1995, the SEBI has been entrusted with penal powers and more extensive coverage of their jurisdiction. Options and futures which were earlier illegal are permitted to be introduced subject to the SEBI's approval. Control on provisions of listing agreement with the companies and penal powers for violations of the listing agreement now rest with the SEBI. Even companies are brought under the SEBI powers in respect of their capital market operations. Powers to grant recognition to Stock Exchanges, inspection and audit of Stock Exchanges and Stock brokers' membership and other matters relating to Stock Exchanges, including the recognition to Attached Trading Floors have been given to the SEBI.

Venture capital funds are brought under the control of SEBI and similar to guidelines given by SEBI for Mutual funds, guidelines are also given for venture capital funds in February 1996. Under the Amendment to SEBI Act, 1995, many more powers on controlling the intermediaries investors and all players in the stock and capital markets including penal powers — both civil and criminal are now vested in SEBI.

Stock Invest

The stock invest is a method of making applications for new issues in lieu of cash or DD or cheque. This instrument provides protection for investors against loss of interest and delay in allotments. In March 1992, the SEBI in consultation with RBI has designed this instrument to be issued by banks like the pay order or DD but with a difference that the money kept is now on lien with the Bank until the allotment or non-allotment but earning interest for the investor during this period. The money will be credited to the company only on allotment and not before. The instrument is valid for 4 months before which the company has to make allotment, or advise refund of the instrument due to non-allotment. At the end of 4 months, the investor has to get back the funds in the event of non-allotment or partial allotment. On giving the indemnity to the bank the investor can make the bank vacate the lien on the deposit and thereafter use the funds for himself in the event of non-allotment or default of giving advice by the company after 4 months from the issue date. As the instrument is issued against a deposit of money in savings or fixed deposit with the bank, the money is kept on lien with the banks during the period of 4 months earning interest on Savings Account or fixed deposit at the current interest rates.

In September 1994, the RBI has directed that the use of Stock invest should not be misused and that it should be confined to mutual funds and individual investors. The RBI has also removed the lock in period of one year for NRIs and OCBs for transfer under the portfolio investment scheme. Lock in periods were also removed for all categories except for promoters. With the reduction of allotment time from 70 to 30 days in 1996 and the use of demat form of share allotment and trading later on the need and use of stock invest has disappeared.

Changes in Listing Guidelines

The listing agreement has been amended in many directions since the reforms were started. Firstly, the unabridged balance sheets have to be given to the shareholders. Secondly, the company has to submit statement on an yearly basis to the Stock Exchange showing the variations between utilisation of funds and projections given the prospectus or letter of offer. Thirdly, the minimum paid up capital has to be Rs. 10 crores for getting itself listed on the B.S.E. as in the case of N.S.E. In the case of other Stock Exchanges the minimum paid up Capital for listing was raised from Rs. 3 crores to Rs. 5 crores only. Besides the Companies should have a track record of two years of commercial production and three years of dividend payment or profitability before listing. The Exchange can reject listing for violation of the requirements. The listed companies have to effect transfers and splits and consolidation etc. within one month of the receipt of request.

In the event of signature differences, the company has to send to the seller to get his signature authenticated by a registered stock broker which should be taken as final for effecting transfers. This measure announced by the B.S.E. should help the process of quickening the transfers and reduction of delays in bad deliveries.

Guidelines for Takeovers

The SEBI has issued guidelines for takeovers and substantial acquisitions to supplement the provisions of the listing agreement in this regard — Clause 40 A and 40 B. In November 1994, the SEBI issued the regulations for "substantial acquisition of shares and takeovers." These Regulations provide for disclosures within 4 days, when acquirer's shareholding exceeds 5% of the paid up capital of the listed company and requires half yearly disclosures. If the holding exceeds beyond 10% it is necessary for the acquirer to offer to other shareholders, the right to sale shares as in case of takeovers. It contains separate provisions for bail-out takeovers and negotiated acquisition of shares. SEBI has power to investigate any violations of these regulations. These are discussed in detail later.

In March 1995, SEBI permitted listing of investment and finance companies, leasing and hire purchase companies and amusement parks on the OTCEI. Those were prohibited earlier to be listed on the OTCEI. Even in the case of regular Stock Exchanges, the listing requirements for Finance and Investment Companies are more rigorous and need a three year track record of profitability, before getting listed, in addition to a paid up capital of more than 5 crores and the company should have been registered with the RBI as the NBFC.

Relaxation of Some Restrictions

During the year 1995, many of the provisions were relaxed as in the case of removal of reservations, exemption from vetting by SEBI in respect of rights issues and debt issues etc. The proportional allotment system is continued with an amendment in May 1995 giving a minimum of 50% quota of the total offer made to the public out of the public issue reserved for the individuals applying for less than 1000 shares in each case. For listing requirements the minimum public offer continues to be 25% and out of that, 50% is reserved for small investors. Even now some reservations are imposed for small and retail investors.

Details for Investor Protection

The prospectuses and abridged prospectuses would have to contain some additional details on accounts as per the requirements of the Institute of Chartered Accountants of India. Following the acceptance of the Malegam Committee Report in October 1995 the SEBI has further clarified the required disclosure guidelines in March 1996, which were made applicable from May 1996. The offer documents should contain more details as shown below:

The accounts should show the adjusted data if footnotes or auditor's statement contain any qualifications, such as, incorrect accounting practices, or changes made in such practices; changes in the activities of the company such as change in suppliers, distribution agency or loss of market share; significant accounting policies, accounting ratios and financial statements properly audited; other ventures or companies promoted by the same promoters and information on them; the details of the public or rights issues made in the preceding three years and a comparison of the actuals with the projection made in those offer documents; details of tax implications say the book depreciation and tax provision and their profits; accounting ratios to be given are EPS, RONW and NAV, and a profit forecast for the year immediately before and the equity and debt equity ratio the issue date and capitalisation details of debt.

More Recent Changes in New Issue Market

In January 1996, the SEBI has dispensed with the requirement of a minimum promoters' contribution and lock in for listed companies with a three year dividend track record in the past five years. The lock in period for employees in their stock option schemes was also withdrawn, preferential issue guidelines, published by SEBI will continue to operate and lock in will still apply to any preferential allotment made to promoters, but pricing of such issue would be based on the market prices. The lock in for promoters and Directors has since the beginning of the scheme been exempt for *inter se* transfers among the directors and promoters.

Since July 1995, the letters of offer for pure rights issue, unaccompanied by public issue are required to be filed with the SEBI but no vetting of the same is done by the SEBI and no acknowledgement card is necessary for rights issues. In January 1996, the SEBI announced that it has stopped vetting all pure debt issues also, if unaccompanied by conversion facility into equity and if such issues are credit rated for adequate safety. Such rights and debt issues would be vetted and finalised by the merchant bankers themselves. Later in 1996 even equity issues were directed to be vetted by merchant bankers.

The regulations for custodians were finalised by the SEBI in January 1996 containing all the details about registration, annual fees, code of conduct, segregation of activities of each client, annual systems audit books of accounts, records etc. to be kept for inspection etc. The custodians would not be allowed to delegate work except to other registered custodians. The reports to be submitted to SEBI by the custodians have all been incorporated in these regulations.

The minimum public offer of 25% of paid up capital for primary issues was relaxed in the case of I.T. Companies for going public and for listing purposes. Companies have also been allowed to buy back their own shares upto 25% of paid up capital and reserves for the purposes of capital restructuring of existing companies. Private placement market has grown faster since 1996 due to poor response to public issues.

The uniform face value of Rs. 10 for all new issues was removed and now shares can be issued with any face value of Rs. 1 to 10. All new public issues have to be allotted in Demat form. New public issues can be made through auction and book building process.

Changes in Companies Act

Companies (Amendment) Bill, 1996 provided for issuance of non-voting shares. Rules have been laid down for postal ballot and scrutiny of their voting rights, differential voting or non-voting rights. Companies (Amendment) Act 2000 covered issuance of shares with differential voting rights, postal ballot and corporate governance among others.

The rules made in March 2001, prescribed some conditions for issuing shares with differential voting rights. Firstly, they can be issued by companies with a record of three years of profitability. Secondly, they can be issued upto 25% of total share capital, including preference share capital, after issue. Thirdly, there should be no default in meeting investors' grievances, authorisation by the Articles of Association for such issue, and there should be no default in filing annual accounts and returns, or in repayment of deposits, debentures and dividends etc. and non-conviction of any offence under SEBI, FEMA and Securities Contracts Regulation Act.

In October 2001, an ordinance was passed for easing the conditions of buy back of shares of companies: The Board of Directors can decide to buy back shares upto 10% of share capital and reserves and by special resolution of the general body upto 25%. This makes acquisition of shares easier.

Institutional Strengthening

The Reforms, included the setting up of OTCEI in August 1989, which started operations in October 1992. The National Stock Exchange (NSE) was recognised by the government in 1993 and it started operations in 1994. Both the Exchanges, namely, the over the Counter Exchange of India and the National Stock Exchange have computerised structure of trading systems and have unique features like shorter settlement periods (T + 7) and quicker payments and deliveries within a period of 7 to 14 days. While the OTCEI is for smaller companies and venturesome and risky companies, the NSE is for bigger companies with a wide network of shareholders.

NSE has two major components, namely, debt market, which started operations early in July 1994 and equity market which was launched in November 1994. In the debt segment, Money market instruments, PSU bonds, and government securities are traded, while in the equity segment there are presently about 1,432 companies with a trading value of Rs. 27 lakh or more per annum on an average. These are all big companies already listed on other Stock Exchanges. Trading on the NSE is over the counter, through the Telex, Telephone and through electronic media. The RBI has given directive to all operators in Money Market and Government securities market to channel this trade through NSE which has considerably strengthened its trading. Similarly, the government patronage and encouragement is also there for the NSE to grow rapidly.

Electronic Trading

The OTCEI has started a new tier in the Stock trading operations, through the electronic media. It is meant for smaller companies of Rs. 30 lakhs to Rs. 25 crores of paid up capital and companies, which are venturesome and risky, due to new entrepreneurs and new products. Long gestation projects etc. are eligible to be listed here. It has more than 80 companies, and average value of transactions *per month* is only Rs. 25 to 30 crores. It has about 100 members and 250 dealers and about 3 lakhs investors with it. Although it has many advantages like transparency, quick delivery, market making with no speculative fervour, it is not popular and has very low volumes.

NSE on the other hand, has become popular with larger volumes with bigger companies listed on it. Only those with a paid up of Rs. 10 crores and market capitalisation of Rs. 50 crores are listed on this exchange. Its growth was faster both in the number of listed companies and volume of trading due to its growing network centres all over the country.

With the introduction of BOLT, and its becoming operational in May 1995, by the BSE, and subsequent expansion to other centres with terminals, a new era of electronic trading started, with NSE and BSE competing to set up on-line trading terminals throughout the country. Other stock exchanges are also in the process of changing over to on-line trading and inter-exchange trading can also take place in future leading to a national market system and an inter-market trading system. These are already operating in many developed countries like the USA and UK.

Stock Exchange Reforms

Starting with the licensing and registration of Stock brokers and sub brokers, many far reaching reforms were effected in the operations of the Stock markets, since May 1992. It has made regular inspections of Stock Exchanges and their member brokers as and when necessary. Their accounts and books are subject to special inspection and audits. Capital adequacy norms were laid down for brokers depending on the Stock Exchange and its activity and the members' turnover. The books of accounts are to be kept in a manner that the clients' accounts are separated from those of broker's own accounts, starting with a separate bank account for clients. Contract notes are to show transparency in deals with price, brokerage and Service tax shown separately. The contract notes and bills are to be passed duly on time, failing which brokers are liable to penalties, depending on the days of default.

The composition of the Board of Directors is to be changed to comprise of 50% of the total directors to be from elected members and the other 50% from non-elected public members including three from the SEBI nominated persons and/or of the Government. The surveillance Depts. of the exchanges are to be strengthened and rigorous application of Margins and other regulations on trade are expected from the Stock Exchange authorities.

The SEBI has issued Regulations on Unfair Trade Practices, frauds etc. in November 1995 with penal powers for punishing any party including investors for indulging in malpractices in the market.

All the brokers and sub-brokers and other players will be liable for action for any price manipulation, or misstatements, misleading information and any other fraudulent practices.

The Regional Stock Exchanges have started their own subsidiaries to become members of NSE/BSE, so that their members can trade in on them.

Market Makers

The SEBI has notified norms for market makers, in October 1995. The Companies seeking listing, with paid up capital ranging between Rs. 3 crores and Rs. 5 crores and without a track record of commercial production of atleast two years, shall have to appoint market makers compulsorily. They have to be appointed on the exchanges, where the shares of such companies are to be listed. Each such market maker has to undertake an obligation to offer two way quotes for a minimum period of 18 months. Besides there should be on additional market maker for each such company to undertake the obligation for atleast 12 months from the date of allotment of shares. Such quotes offered by them shall be for 3 marketable lots, and the spread between the Bid and offer rates should not exceed 10% at any time. For enabling them to do this, the market maker should have an inventory of a minimum of 5% of the post issue capital of the company, allotted to him by the company at the time of issue. The bank finance for such inventory holding and RBI guidelines in this regard were already referred to. The same guidelines will apply whether the company is listed on OTCEI or on regular stock exchanges.

Listing of companies with paid up capital of not less than Rs. 5 crores was not allowed on the regular stock exchanges, as per the SEBI guidelines, given in October 1995, following the recommendations of Malegam Committee for raising the threshold limit for listing to Rs. 10 crores of paid up capital.

BOLT System

BSE went over to electronic trading system in January 1995, called BOLT, similar to that of NSE and this became fully operational in May 1995. Besides BSE moved to a weekly settlement system in specified shares and in another B1. category of cash scrips with about 200 of them, during Feb. 1996. The BSE has also raised the minimum paid up capital for listing of companies to Rs. 10 crores at the same time. If a company is already listed on a stock exchange and requires listing on BSE, it should have a paid up equity of at least Rs. 5 crores and net worth of Rs. 10 crores and minimum market capitalisation of 15 crores. For all companies which have got acknowledgement card on or before February 26th, 1996 the limit of paid up capital of Rs. 5 crores will apply and for those securing SEBI approval after February 26, the limit of 10 crores will apply. The trading and settlement cycles are also brought on par with NSE. The Trading cycle on BSE will be from Monday to Friday while that on NSE will be from Wednesday to Tuesday. Besides carry forward is allowed on BSE, but not on the NSE. Settlement is through the clearing House for both BSE and NSE. The pay out will be after 12 days on BSE and 10 days on NSE. The auctions will also be quicker on BSE, for each settlement, as in the case of NSE, at present. BSE is quickly following whatever NSE is doing to achieve quicker settlement and delivery and to attract more volumes. With this objective, BSE raised the threshold limit for listing to Rs. 10 crores, moved on to a weekly settlement system and quicker auctions for each settlement. The BSE has also allowed expansion of on-line trading system (BOLT) to members of other Stock Exchanges and have terminals in other cities since August 1995, to counter the move of the countrywise network of terminals by the NSE. The neck to neck competition between NSE and BSE has almost drowned the operations of smaller exchanges and their volumes have shrunk. Late in 1998 both NSE and BSE have agreed to have common trading and settlement cycles.

Badla Trading

Badla was banned in March 1994 and has reintroduced again, following the G.S. Patel Committee recommendations in March 1995. After five months of prolonged deliberations, the SEBI came out in July 1995 with a modified Badla proposal which was not the same as recommended by the G.S. Patel Committee. This proposal of July 1995 was turned down by the stock exchanges and brokers. Later, again a compromise proposal was put up in October in 1995 which was adopted finally by the BSE in Jan. 1996. Even this modified badla was accepted only by 50% of the brokers and confined to a few scrips in 'A' Group shares which have come to have a weekly settlement since March 1996. This modified Badla will have stiffer margins, transparency and daily reporting with a maximum period of 90 days by which, the position has to be squared up or delivery given or taken. Badla was replaced by automatic lending and borrowing system (ALBS) and has lost its relevance since 2001 due to introduction of derivatives trading.

SEBI'S INSIDER TRADING REGULATIONS

The SEBI has got legal powers in January 1995 to enforce these regulations and penalise the culprits. As per these Insider Regulations, an insider means any person who is or was connected with the company or is deemed to be so connected and who is reasonably expected to have access, by virtue of such connection to unpublished price sensitive information, in respect of securities of such company. A person is deemed to be a connected person, if such person is a group company, or any subsidiary, an official of the Stock Exchange or stock brokers, merchant banker or any intermediary in the market, or a director or an official of any of these companies or agencies or of the financial institutions financing that company or banker of the company or any related person or relative to any of the above categories of persons. If such persons have access to the unpublished price sensitive information and is proved to have used it for personal gain or profits or price manipulation, they are liable to be penalised under these regulations. Such price sensitive information should be unpublished and confidential and if published, it should materially affect the price of security of the concerned company. Such information relates to dividends, bonus, Rights, financial results, likely issue of shares, expansion plans, amalgamations, mergers and takeovers contemplated, disposal of any of its assets, acquisition of another company or its subsidiaries, and any other information bearing on financial policies, financial results or earnings, etc.

Central Depository System

In Sept. 1995, the Govt. have accepted in principle the proposed law for setting up of depositories and of a central depository for immobilisation of physical certificates. The central depository is set up as a Trust to hold the physical custody of shares and effect transfers by book entries without the need to deal and transfer the physical certificates between parties. This is sponsored by public financial institutions and banks and will have a minimum net worth of Rs. 100 crores, as proposed by the SEBI. This central depository can be connected to a number of share depositories for effecting transfers in book entries. The foreign financial institutions, foreign institutional agencies, NRIs and OCBs have for long required the depository of this type for facilitating their trade in the Indian Stock markets. The foreign security firms who were licensed by the SEBI, are operating in India, but physical custody of the Indian securities has to be handled by Indian Custodian such as a bank which can now be converted into the depositories to be licensed by the SEBI. Above all these depositories there will be a central depository which will coordinate these depositories and the modus operandi of these operations were worked out by the SEBI. The guidelines and regulations in respect of the operations of depositories will help smooth *inter se* operations among depositories and their operations with the central depository.

Corporate Membership

The applicant company must be a company registered and satisfy the requirements of Section 12 of the Companies Act and meet with the financial networth criteria as laid down by SEBI from time to time. There should be two experienced directors who are eligible to be members of a Stock Exchange as per SC (R) Rules and Rules and Byelaws of the Stock Exchange. For NSE requirements the minimum networth should be Rs. one crore and minimum paid up capital Rs. 30 lakhs and an undertaking that they would have an arrangement or office in Mumbai. Two experienced directors should be whole time persons and hold atleast 5% each of the paid up capital of the company and the identified dominant shareholders of the applicant company should hold atleast 51% of the paid up capital, along with other family members. In Nov. 1994 the Rules were amended by the Government for non-Indians and NRIs to become directors of stock broking companies.

The networth requirements for the Corporate members change from Stock Exchange to Stock Exchange. Two directors in the firm should possess atleast two years of experience in dealing in securities or portfolio managers, investment consultants etc. The company can have any number of shareholders. The liability of members is limited and they can acquire membership of more than one exchange provided they satisfy the financial requirements of each separately. The Company should only confine to stock broking and related financial services like underwriting, Market making, portfolio management, investment consultancy, merchant banking and related services.

Pending Reforms

SEBI desired that all the stock exchanges should go for on line electronic trading latest by June 1996. Already BSE and DSE have gone for electronic trading and it is followed by Kolkata and Ahmedabad Stock Exchanges. The smaller exchanges being shrouded into sideline, by the enlarging network of N.S.E. and B.S.E. on-line trading into various cities, are hastening to strengthen themselves by trying for inter-exchange trading or joint trading for a group of smaller exchanges or regional groupings. An inter-connected Stock Exchange was set up in 1997 and become operational in 1999.

Among the reforms which also took effect is the launching of Depository system and immobilisation of physical transfer of shares, on-line electronic trading for all exchanges, registration of all subbrokers throughout the country to be eligible for client order booking and enforcement of capital adequacy norms and change in the composition of the Board of Directors of all Exchanges. Many of these reforms were effected in 1997 and 1998. Book Building process is yet to take off as the equity limit of Rs.100 crores for this, fixed in 1995 is too high for many companies. Book building helps the private placement of big premium issues by inviting a syndicate of big merchant bankers and underwriters to give their quantities and prices at which they are prepared to subscribe. The lead manager will be the book-runner, who then fixes the premium on the basis of these bids. The limit of Rs. 100 crores referred to above was removed in 1996.

SEBI Norms for Book Building

Building process includes the syndicate of members appointed by the Book runners; either of them should be present at the electronically linked computer terminal at all bidding centres.

The issue size shall be fully underwritten by the syndicate members/book runners. Book Building should be for the portion other than that for promoters and permanent employees. The issue company has to compulsorily offer and additional 10% to individual investors not participating in the bidding process. Also, about 15% of the issue for which resources are being raised though book Building should be reserved for allocation to individual investors applying upto 10 tradeable lots.

These guidelines are effective from September 1997. These guidelines make it compulsorily linked to transparent facilities for the bidding process to determine the price and the demand for the securities. The guidelines will apply to all issues following the 100% book building route to raise finance from the public. It was only since 1999 that some companies started book building route of making new issues. Now many new issues are made through book builidng process through banks, FIs, etc. subject to SEBI guidelines.

SEBI Reforms on Stock Exchanges

The SEBI regulation of stock exchanges and their members had started as early as February 1992 and the reforms later introduced have been on a continuous basis. It was started with the licensing and registration of brokers and sub-brokers in the recognised stock exchanges. This was later extended to underwriters, portfolio managers and other categories of players in the stock market including foreign securities firms, FFIs, Debenture Trustees, Collecting bankers, etc.

The other reforms are briefly summarised below:

(1) Compulsory audit and inspection of stock exchanges and their member brokers and their accounts.

(2) Transperancy in the prices and brokerage charged by brokers by showing them in their contract notes.

(3) Broker accounts and client accounts are to be kept separate and clients' money are to be separately maintained in bank's accounts and the same to be reported to the stock exchanges.

(4) Board of Directors of stock exchanges has to be reconstituted so as to include non-brokers, public representatives, and Government representatives to the extent of 50% of the total number of members.

(5) Capital adequacy norms have been laid down for members of various stock exchanges separately depending on their turnover of trade and other factors.

(6) Guidelines have been laid down for dealings of FFIs and Foreign broker firms in the Indian stock exchanges through Indian brokers.

(7) Badla and carry forward business which was banned on major exchanges early in 1995 was reintroduced in October 1996 and renewal business was also subject to close scrutiny, for cash shares.

(8) New guidelines for corporate members have been laid down with limited liability of directors and opening up of their membership to more than one stock exchange without the limiting requirement of experience of five years in one exchange, as imposed earlier.

(9) Demat form of trading was introduced since 1996.

(10) Roll over settlement on a daily basis in selected scrips.

(11) Introduction of options and futures on Index and on individual scrips in 2000 and 2001.

(12) Adoption of a system of lending and borrowing of shares by brokers and for brokers.

Take Over Code

The SEBI has finalised the code for Take overs, based on the Report of Justice P.N.Bhagwati (August 1996). Take overs will not be free for all any more. Only genuine take overs will have to use the mechanism of SEBI Code.

Take over is the acquisition by any interested party, individuals, corporate bodies etc; of the shares of an existing company. It is mandatory to make a public offer to buy shares of the company, if the acquirer is acquiring more than 10% of the shares of the target company. SEBI has got powers to control the acquisition of shares for any change in control of Management. Preferential allotments are exempt from the requirement of a public offer. In public offer, the minimum offer price is to be the highest of either the negotiated price, the six month average of highs and lows, or the price paid by the acquirer for buying of shares in the target company in the last one year.

The acquirer, making a public offer, has to deposit 10% of the total offer amount in an Escrow account, which can be forfeited in the event of default. As against the earlier limit of 14 days, competitive bids have to be kept open for 21 days. Directors of the target company have a right to make their own recommendations on the offer to shareholders. Competitive bids have to be made within 21 days of public offer announcement and the original bidder has to revise the offer within 14 days of the competitive bid or withdraw from the offer.

Public offer can be revised upwards in the price and quantity also, within the time limits. The grounds for withdrawal from the offer are clearly specified by the SEBI.

The SEBI has permitted vetting of these offers by the merchant bankers and not by SEBI itself. The merchant banker has to file the offer documents with the SEBI within 14 days of the public announcement. The acquisitions of the existing managements which do not attract public offer norms are as follows:

Acquirer holding 10 to 25% of the equity can acquire additional shares at the rate of 2% per year. Those holding 25-50% of the equity can acquire shares at the rate of 5% per year, without triggering the take over code. Take over code does not apply to unlisted companies.

Healthy take overs are now more easy with the result that the earlier family run concerns can be targeted to be acquired by other managements also. If mergers are promoted by such take overs and acquisitions, the capital market can become healthier.

The take over code provides for orderly take overs, transparency of terms, fairness to existing shareholders. If the acquirer wants to acquire by an agreement with the existing management, he has to make a public offer to buy from existing share holders another 20% of the target company and keep 10% of this offer amount in an escrow account with a bank.

The code has also defined take over and the word control. Control shall include right or power to appoint or remove a majority of directors or M.D. or change or formulate policy decisions exercisable by a person or persons, directly or indirectly.

There are however clear guidelines to follow for the hostile take overs. The role of financial institutions and the foreign Investment Promotion Board is also being defined in the new code. Both the foreign and Indian Collaborator would be asked to make a public offer for such number of shares as it has agreed to take up, at the price at which the preferential allotment would be made to him. If they could not get from the public (the required number of shares), then the course of preferential allotment to them could be adopted by the company. Justice Bhagwati was also in favour of applying the code to preferential allottees and to allotment of primary issues in the new issue market as that route can also be used for secret take overs. But primary market purchases are kept out of this take over code.

The existing promoters and directors will no longer be able to manipulate to make a company sick and avoid take overs. The Buy Back arrangement allowed in the New Companies Bill 2000 will also ward off take over of healthy companies. The code is designed to facilitate healthy take overs, even if they are hostile to the existing management. But these regulations apply to listed companies. An unlisted company can take over a listed company to get its shares listed on the Stock Exchanges. The take over code applies to all acquirers and raiders whether they are Indians, NRIs, OCBs or FFIs etc.

Record of Take Overs

The SEBI Take Over Code became effective in 1997. During the first three years (1997-99), 181 open offers were made, involving a take over value of Rs. 2,052 crores, worth of shares. Of this amount, 24% were made for change in management control, 49% were for consolidation of holdings and the rest 27% were for substantial acquisitions in target companies.

Of the total amount of Rs. 11,600 crores actually taken over, during the three financial years, 1997-98, to 1999-2000, those that come under the Take over code and acquired through open offers amounted to Rs. 2,050 crores, while the acquisition of shares through exemption from the take over code route were worth Rs. 9,550 crores. As many as about 700 companies have made acquisitions of shares, either through public offers or through the route of exemption from the code (510 companies).

In terms of value of shares acquired, about 74% of these acquisitions were through preferential offer route. *Inter-se* transfer of shares accounted for 24% and these are all exempt from take over code. It is found that companies preferred acquisitions falling outside the code of take overs. As the Table below shows, acquisitions for Management change predominated; 49% of the firms accounting for 24% of the total worth of shares was for Management change. But only 24% of firms accounting for 49% of the total worth of shares was for consolidation of stakes. Nearly 27% of firms accounting for 27% of total worth of shares are for substantial acquisition. Of the total public offers, those accepted accounted for 67.8% in 1997-98, which declined to 34.8% in 1999-00. This means that the investor response for open public offers was declining over the years. The foreign companies did not show adequate interest and this declined from 27.5% in 1997-98 to 12% in 1999-00. In 2003-04, the total number of acquisitions were 828 involving an amount of Rs. 34,813 crores, against which mergers were only 289 showing the importance of acquisition in the corporate sector. In 2005-06, there were reported acquisitions of 874 involving an amount of Rs. 1,00,612 crores while the mergers were only in respect of 394 units.In 2006-07, the acquisitions were 924, involving an amount of Rs. 2,04,597, crores, while the mergers were only 358, in number.

Objectives of Open Offers	Year-By-Year Number 97-98	98-99	99-00	Total	No.Of *Firms	Take-Over *Value
Management Change	18	29	42	89	49	24
Stake Consolidation	10	25	9	44	24	49
Substantial Acquisition	12	12	24	48	27	27

*As Percentage of-3-Year Total number and value.

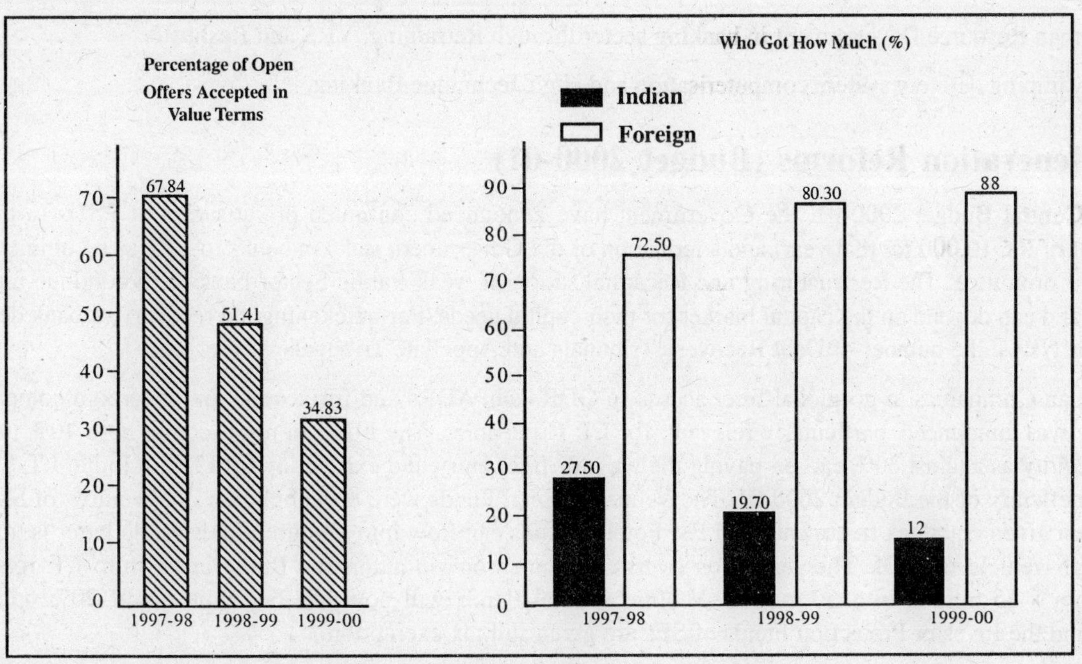

Critique of Bhagwati Committee's Report

(1) Exempting acquisition of shares though the preferential offer route is not fair. If a public offer is made, and he is not able to acquire the entire quantity required from the public, then only preferential allotment may be justified at the minimum price as governed by SEBI guidelines.

(2) It is not fair to the non-management shareholders to limit the offer to 20% of their holdings. It should be 100% of their holdings, as they may like to get out of the company, if the management is changing.

(3) Managements with a 51% stake can consolidate their holdings without also attracting the provisions of the guidelines, as the code has made some provisions for them.

(4) Regulation (3) says that nothing contained in regulations 10, 11 & 12 shall apply to requisition of shares in companies, whose shares are not listed on any stock exchange.

(5) Persons acting in concert, have excluded developmental institutions (FIs) which might lead to some loopholes.

(6) Regulation (12) states that even if there is a change in control without acquisition of shares or voting rights, a public offer has to be made. The code has provided for such change in control without acquisition of shares.

(7) Major loopholes are in terms of encouraging the take overs by cash rich companies and by NRIs and foreigners.

(8) Acquisitions in small quantities and through rights and new issue route would still be possible.

These are some of the limitations of take over code:

Pending Reforms in Banking Sector

The RBI Governor Dr. Bimal Jalan said early in February 2000 that the pending reforms in banking sector which will be continued under the phase of second generation Reforms are the following:

(1) To increase the interest rate flexibility or freer rates.

(2) Development of Debt Market.

(3) Reduction of NPAs.

(4) Restructuring of weak banks without recapitalisation by Government in the case of P.S.Bs.

(5) Legal reforms and consolidation of Law as applicable to the Financial Sector.

(6) Human Resource Development in banking sector through Retraining, VRS and Reshuffle.

(7) Revamping delivery system computerisation and High Technique Banking.

Second Generation Reforms (Budget 2000-01)

In the Central Budget 2000-01, the Government have announced continued privatisation of PSUs (a target of disinvestment of Rs. 10,000 for that year) and a reduction of the Government stake in banks to 33% as recommended by Narasimham Committee. The Restructuring and Recapitalisation of weak Public Sector banks will continue until they look healthy and can depend on the capital market for their capital needs. For quickening the recovery of bank debts and lowering their NPAs, the number of Debt Recovery Tribunals and Appellate Tribunals was increased.

For Indian Companies to go global freer access to GDRs and ADRs and for acquisition of foreign companies, a liberal policy was announced, particularly relevant, for I.T. Companies. The FIIs can now acquire upto 40% in Indian company's equity as against 30% earlier, paving the way for freer entry and exit policy for FDI, in India. I.T. Sector is the major beneficiary of the Budget 2000-01. The Venture Capital Funds were brought under one window of SEBI and they have been given equal tax treatment as M.F.s. Foreign funds can flow into Venture Funds as the latter is treated as a pass through vehicle for FDI. The ceiling on overseas acquisition via automatic Route apart from I.T. route, was enhanced from $ 15 million to $ 50 million. Venture Capital Funds will now pay one time tax of 20% on income distribution and the Investor Protection Funds of SEs are given full tax exemption.

New Millennium Reforms

In 1999 October, when Vajpayee Government was installed at the Centre, Yaswant Sinha, the then Finance Minister promised a series of second generation reforms in economic and financial sphere. Accordingly in the new millennium year of 2000, many reforms were initiated.

To start with, Insurance Bill was passed and Insurance Regulatory Development Act became a reality. This Act has provided for privatisation of insurance and entry of foreign investment upto 26% of equity of Insurance Companies and opening up of the insurance sector to competition and free market forces. Besides, several legislative measures were initiated in conformity with the Government Policy of globalisation and economic liberalisation. Like the IRDA in insurance sector, Securities Laws (Amendment) Act was passed to promote Demat form of Securities trading, internet broking and derivatives trading on the Stock Exchanges. FEMA was passed in place of FERA to regulate and to promote in a liberalised way the foreign exchange market and transactions in foreign currencies. Trade Marks Act, Patents Act and Copyright Amendment Act, 1999 are the other examples of legislation to promote and safeguard intellectual property rights and for protection of innovation and knowledge based technology and for freer trade and investment.

In the banking and finance area, the new policy of lower interest rates on small savings media was announced. Banks are given greater freedom and way to recapitalise without Government support and reduce their NPAs. There would be no closure of loss making banks, but banks are advised to restructure their policies, strengthen their operations and reduce their costs and improve their profitability. New guidelines were given by RBI in respect of NBFCs for their registration, minimum capital, and prudential norms etc. Many public representatives on the Boards of Banks were removed with a view to infuse new blood into the Boards.

Reforms in the power sector, privatisation of selected international airports in the country, passing of the Information Technology Bill, Providing legal recognition to e-commerce, opening up of a new Ministry of Information Technology, and setting up of a Rs. 100 crores National Venture Capital Fund to provide funding to the I.T. industry, further liberalisations for promotion of I.T. industry in India and setting up of Foreign Investment Implementation Authority and for freer access to foreign borrowings (ADRs and GDRs) for equity of Indian corporates etc. are some of the other measures announced under the second generation reforms, initiated in new millennium ,

In the fiscal sphere, Centre and States have decided to implement uniform floor rates for sales tax from Jan.1, 2000 and VAT from 1st April 2005. The subsidies element in the Budget are being curtailed and fiscal deficit is sought to be contained. The Centre's borrowing from the RBI has come down due to excess liquidity in the banking system. The Fiscal Responsibility Act, thrust a responsibility and accountability on the centre with a view to limiting the fiscal deficit to as low as needed for the fiscal stability.

A series of reforms were undertaken in the Telecom Sector and a New Telecom Policy was announced. A group on Telecom and I.T. convergence headed by Finance Minister was constituted to formulate new policies.

Banking and Financial Reforms

As part of second generation reforms, measures have been initiated for privatisation of Indian Airlines to the extent of 51%, with Government keeping 49% of equity. Of the 51% of equity to be divested 26% will be sold to a strategic partner, who will have control on management and the balance will go to employees, financial institutions and public. Airlines was opened upto 74% under the latest policy; disinvestment is limited to a few non-viable and loss-making PSUs in 2005. There are about 240 PSUs which are in the line for the divestment of which about 58 are being actively considered for divestment at the earliest depending on the market conditions.

So far as the financial sector is concerned, in tune with the recommendations of Narasimham Committee (II) on Banking Sector Reforms, in addition to capital adequacy (CRCAR) norm of 10%, prudential norms for income recognition and provisioning for bad and doubtful debts were provided for. Disclosures and Transparency were insisted upon by the RBI.

In order to bring in better internal controls extensive use of Information Technology in banks is recommended. It is laid down by the Central Vigilance Commission that banks should do 70% of their business by computerisation by Jan.1, 2001. There is need for infrastructural upgradation, better asset liability management, and adopt improved risk management and evaluation techniques. The RBI has issued guidelines for banks to adopt international standards of covering risks. In tune with the B.I.S. core principles, banks have to adopt principles of risk management of not only credit risk, but of all types of market risks, like liquidity, interest rate, forex as well as legal and reputational risks.

The banks and F.Is have to adopt the concept of universal banking, and follow the international standards of accounting and audit, take advantage of international markets by adopting the practices and procedures of global banking, observe the risk management techniques and follow the capital adequacy and prudential norms suitable for global banking. Computerisation and adoption of ECS and latest technology in clearing and settlement are some of the reforms effected by banking sector.

The reforms should be viewed from the point of view of how much freedom is given to individual banks but more importantly by how much benefit does it bring to the public, by way of lower costs, better service and greater efficiency. The role of Government will continue and the public character of banks will be maintained with however, no fresh financial commitment from Government and no administrative interference. The real criteria is how much the reforms have helped the development in the country.

Competitive environment in banks has improved. Cost consciousness and quality of service and the use of I.T. in banking have become the landmarks. The problem of NPAs and the role of correct appraisal, monitoring and internal controls have been emphasised by Narasimham Committee and Verma (M.S.) Committee on Banks. They have looked at the problems of weak banks and the need for better recovery practices, recapitalisation of banks from market sources and not from Government and even closure of weak banks have been recommended. The adoption of VRS and HRD and financial restructuring etc. have been already adopted by banks.

The end result of these reforms has been the growing integration of various segments of the financial system, greater role for market forces, opening up, liberalisation and globalisation of markets and closer convergence of the Indian financial system with the practices prevailing in International financial markets and wider variety of financial institutions and instruments available for trading, greater access to international markets and larger volumes of trading due to increased depth and width of the markets and adoption of electronic and computer services and the I.T. techniques. Greater role for ALM and Risk management techniques is however the need of the hour.

Financial Sector is reported to have acquired greater efficiency as seen from the trends of globalisation, competition, spread of width and depth of the markets, integration of markets, greater transparency and flexible use of monetary tools etc. There was strengthening of institutional structure and greater freedom of operations to banks and FIs and openness of the markets to foreign forces. The economic and financial reforms have thus succeeded in leading the financial markets to greater efficiency. Even so, there are still many scams and economic offences which have to be dealt with on a firm basis and regulation has to be more selective and efficient.

Strengthening of the Banking System

Legal Reforms and a suitable legal framework are a pre-requisite to strengthening the financial sector and banking system. The IDBI Act was repealed and the IDBI (Transfer of undertaking and Repeal) Act was passed in Dec. 2005, as a result of which the IDBI was converted into a company registered under the Companies Act and became a Universal Bank by merging itself with its subsidiary IDBI Bank.

Early in 2004, the BIFR and Appellate Authority for Industrial and Financial Restruction were dissolved and proceedings before them abated. This gave greater freedom to both private and public sector banking companies to reorganise or resort to mergers or privatisation.

The Government Securities Act was passed in 2004 to replace the public Debt Act of 1944, which helped the promotion and development of gilt edged market in India. Dematerialisation and electronic clearing and settlement system further strengthened this market. Branch networking and inter bank networking was made functional by INFINET. The Board for Payment and settlement system would supervise at national level the settlement system between domestic and cross border systems. The Board for financial supervision has aimed at strengthening the supervisory role with respect to internal controls in banks, better disclosures, ratings etc. Introduction of Risk based supervision and audit, better corporate governance and specific reporting of suspected frauds etc., are encouraged.

During 2001 to 2005, various measures were effected to improve operational efficiency of banks. These included reduction of NPAs better transparency, setting up of the Asset Reconstruction Companies (ARCs), to take over the NPAs of banks and FIs, better dissemination of credit information through Information Bureau, set up in March 2003, etc.

Measures were taken to improve the instruments and operations of Financial Markets operations in CDs, CPs, government securities, etc., and practices in Forex Market were rationalised and strengthened by better supervision and liberalisation. Financial architecture was fine tuned to strengthen the institutional structure, better integration of sub-markets, better disclosures and reporting and achieve the needed market discipline.

New Issues Market and Problems

Definition

The New Issue Market deals with the raising of fresh capital either for cash or for consideration other than cash by companies, Govt. and Semi Govt. bodies, PSUs, etc. and encompasses all institutions dealing in the issue of fresh claims on money. The forms in which these claims are incurred by corporates are equity shares, preference shares, debentures, rights, bonus, deposits, miscellaneous loans, etc. All the financial institutions in the capital market which contribute, underwrite or directly subscribe are part of the New Issue market. Thus, development corporations like IDBI, IFCI, ICICI and investment corporations like LIC, GIC, UTI and other financial institutions contribute to the bulk of the underwriting activity and direct investment. Banks and brokers have also been participating in underwriting of capital issues in a larger measure. Some of the banks have already started merchant banking divisions to help floatation of issues by companies. Brokers have been underwriting limited amounts of new issues on the strength of their own or borrowed funds. These brokers may be individuals, partnership firms or private limited companies formed as Investment and Consultancy Firms. They also undertake management of the share issue, act as lead managers, advisers and consultants etc. or do liaison work for getting loans from banks, after getting clearance from the SEBI.

Normally, the whole amount of public issue is underwritten by one institution or by a group of institutions jointly. The underwriting institutions including banks would consult among themselves before they accept joint underwriting. Sub-underwritting is common in India among brokers and consultancy firms. Some brokers do sub-underwriting along with banks or other financial institutions. Sub-underwriters sometimes include institutional investors, investment trusts, provident funds, etc. Underwriting is now optional for smaller issues, as per the latest SEBI guidelines. The underwriting commission is about 2-1/2% and brokerage 1 to 1-1/2% for the issue of shares and debentures.

In case the issue is fully subscribed, the underwriters will get their commission or brokerage but if the issue is undersubscribed, the underwriters have to shoulder the responsibility of direct subscription pro-rata on the basis of their commitments and to the extent of their underwriting responsibility.

Functions

The government and the corporate sector are the main borrowers from the capital market and are the issuers of securities. The methods of raising funds in the case of corporate sector are retained earnings out of profits and external borrowings. These borrowings may take any of the following forms, which are in addition to the original issue of share capital in the form of equity and preferences shares (including CCPs) (Fig. 11.1).

Fig. 11.1

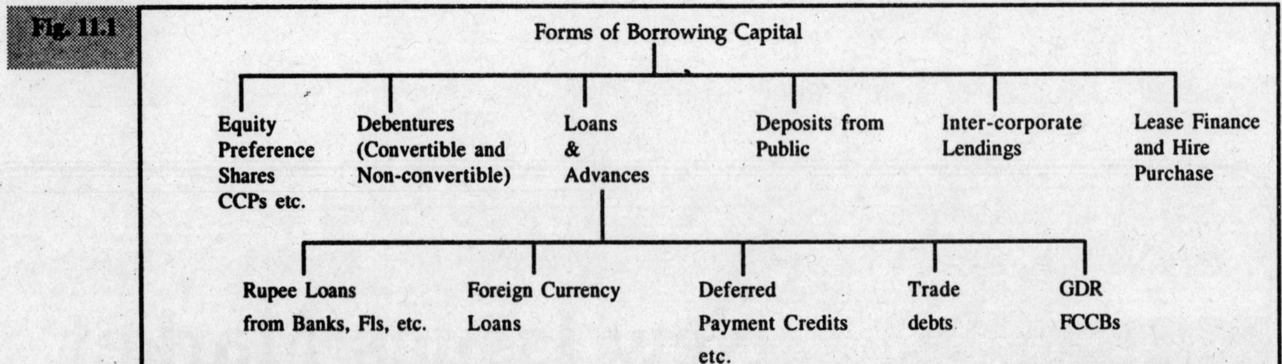

The objectives for which funds are raised may be for setting up new projects, expansion, diversification, modernisation of existing projects, mergers and takeovers, etc. The proportion in which funds are raised in various forms as own capital (equity) and debt capital (borrowings and debentures, etc.) indicate the capital structure of the company and measures the leverage in the form of ratio of borrowed funds to owned capital and the servicing commitments of the company on borrowed funds.

Methods of Floatation

Initial issues are those floated by new companies for the first time, while further issues are subsequent issues floated by the existing companies. Issues can also be classified as those given for cash, for exchange of technical know-how, exchange of shares of another company or exchange for any other services rendered by the agencies or promoters.

The placement of the issues may be through *(i)* prospectus, *(ii)* offer of sale, *(iii)* private placement, and *(iv)* rights issue. These are discussed in brief below.

Offer Through Prospectus

Public issue with prospectus is the most popular method of raising funds by the public limited companies. This involves inviting subscription from the public through issue of prospectus. This method of raising funds accounts for the bulk of capital raised and is necessary for listing of shares on the exchanges. The price at which the securities are offered for sale is at the face value of the share in the case of new companies and may be at a premium or discount in the case of old companies. The prospectus is a document which is a notice or circular or advertisement inviting offers for subscription or purchase of any shares or debentures from the public. The prospectus should contain authentic data and should be delivered to the Registrar of Companies for registration. The prospectus would contain details with regard to the name of the company, address, activities, board of directors, location of industry, authorised, subscribed and paid-up capital, dates of opening and closing of the subscription list, names of brokers and underwriters, etc. The draft of the prospectus should be approved by the Board, solicitors, lending financial institutions, and the stock exchanges in which they are to be listed.

Offer of Sale

The method of "offer or sale" consists of outright sale by the company instead of offering shares to the public or through intermediaries such as issuing houses or sharebrokers. In this case, the company sells shares *en bloc* at an agreed price to brokers or merchant bankers who in turn resell them to the investing public. The issuing houses may act as agents of the company in such cases. Offer of sale of shares takes place in the case of existing shareholders purchasing *en bloc* and then reselling them to the public. Similarly, foreign collaborators or promoters may sell their shares to the Indian public through offer of sale which may be either through brokers or through prospectus.

Private Placement

The third method of issue of shares is private placing which is defined as sale by the issuing house or broker to his own clients of securities previously purchased by him. Under this method the issuing houses or financial intermediaries buy them outright with the intention of placing them with their clients afterwards. Here the brokers act as almost wholesalers selling them in retail to the public. These brokers would make their profit in the process of reselling to the public. This method of private placing is used to a limited extent in India but is very popular abroad. Before the issues are placed in the market by the promoters, they sell to their own friends and well-wishers as the Govt. guidelines require a minimum contribution from the promoters and their friends. Private placement increased rapidly after 1996 when the primary market was in a state of depression. Private placing is also made by bargaining with the financial institutions for their share of contribution. The OTCEI (Over the Counter Exchange of India) has accepted this method for the companies to be listed on it. Companies can themselves sell their shares by private placement method through brokers or merchant bankers.

Rights Issue

Another important method of placing shares to the public is, the right issue which is next in importance to the placing of shares through prospectus. The rights issue is an offer with a preemption right to the shareholder of existing companies to contribute to the share capital or its debt capital in the form of debentures. An existing company can issue rights to augment its equity base, if necessary. These are offered to the existing shareholders in a particular proportion to their existing shareownership. The ratio in which the new shares or debentures are offered to the existing shareholders of the company would depend on their requirements of capital. The rights are themselves transferable and saleable in the market. No new company can issue rights shares. Under the Companies Act, where a company increases its subscribed capital by the issue of new shares either after two years of its formation or after one year of the first issue of shares whichever is earlier, these have to be first offered to the existing shareholders with the right to reserve them in favour of a nominee.

A company issuing rights is required to send a circular to all existing shareholders. This circular letter should provide information on how the additional funds would be used and their effect on the earning capacity of the capital. The company should normally give a time limit of at least one month to two months to shareholders to exercise their right before it is offered to the public. Rights may also be offered through underwriters. If a company is doing well, rights will be received well by the shareholders and the need for underwriting may not be felt.

One of the conditions for issue of rights is that the shareholders be given an opportunity to apply for additional shares. Besides, if the rights are not fully taken up, the balance is to be equitably distributed among the applicants for additional shares. Any balance still left over after making such allotment is required to be disposed of by the company in the market at the ruling price or the issue price.

Debt vs. Equity

The capital structure of a company depends on its requirements of fixed assets and a proportion of working capital. Equity and preference capital being in the nature of permanent capital, owned funds should cover the bulk of the fixed assets and would also be the basis on which long-term debt capital can be raised by the company. These requirements vary from company to company, as some industries and units are more capital intensive than others.

Equity by itself may not be adequate or economical as debt capital is cheaper than equity and provides a leverage for raising the level of profits to equity holders. On the other hand, availability of debt itself depends on the existing equity base as that would determine the state of the company as servicing of debt depends on the equity base and the net earnings of the company through efficient use of capital. These twin considerations are kept in mind to assess the requirements of both equity and debt in the capital structure.

Debt may be short-term or long-term and includes bonds, debentures, loans and advances. The considerations influencing the two are different. While short-term finance influences the liquidity of the company, long-term finance affects the capital structure, and is an alternative to equity. The reliance on debt has increased in India due to tax treatment of interest on debt as an expenditure item of the company. Debt includes all fixed interest-bearing securities, loans, deferred payments and preference shares with a redemption period of less than 12 years. Debt may be from government, other companies or financial institutions. Debt from government is confined to mostly public sector enterprises and a few private sector enterprises of public importance. Loans from other companies are governed by section 370 of the Indian Companies Act designed to limit the inter-corporate lending, particularly those under the same management. The ceiling on such lending is now fixed at 30 per cent of the share capital of the investing companies, which has been removed in 1999.

Short-term debt is mainly provided by trade credits and borrowing from banks. Companies are generally opposed to too much short-term debt due to the adverse effect of it on the subjective valuation of shares by outsiders. Too much of short-term debt *vis-a-vis* equity implies that the company has not even adequate capital base to support operations and in periods of financial stress, such a firm might be forced into liquidation.

The Indian Companies Act and the Govt. guidelines place some limits on borrowed funds. The upper limit is an amount equal to the paid-up capital and reserves without prior approval of the shareholders in a general meeting. Guidelines would not normally allow debt more than twice the paid-up capital and free reserves.

Rights of Conversion of Debt into Equity

As per the policy of the government since June 1971, the public financial institutions retain the right of conversion of a part of rupee loans granted by them to any firm into equity, if the assistance exceeds a limit of Rs. 50 lakhs. Such a right is left optional to the financial institution if the loan is between Rs. 25 lakhs and Rs. 50 lakhs. The exercise of this right implies a larger role to the joint sector and the participation of the financial institutions in the future prosperity of companies. This right is now exercised by all-India financial institutions after a period of 5 years from the date of issue of loan. The extent and terms of conversion depend upon the agreement, negotiated between the company and the financial institutions. The conversion in the case of new companies is at par and for old companies, it may be at a premium or discount. This right of conversion of loan into equity was withdrawn by Govt. in the latest financial reforms except when the repayment instalments are in arrears.

Advantages of the debt are as follows:

1. It provides for larger increase in profits due to larger trading made possible by debt finance, without a need for additional equity.
2. It improves the earnings of equityholders due to larger earnings at a lower cost of debt than of equity finance.
3. There is no interference in management matters which takes place by the issue of new equity capital.
4. There are tax advantages for debt which are not available for equity. Debt carrying capacity would, however, depend upon the level of gross profits and equity base.

As against these, there are a number of advantages of equity:

1. Debt is to be repaid while equity would remain with the company.
2. Equity increases the interest of the promoters and their stake in the company and thus reduce the investor risk in the company.
3. It improves the credit standing of the company for future borrowing and acts as a buffer for future fluctuations in the fortunes of the company.
4. It provides greater leeway for the company to adjust to the changing economic climate and investment conditions.

Debentures are issued by the old companies normally while new companies depend on loans from financial institutions. A special category of debentures which have become popular in the eighties is convertible debentures. Debentureholders of this category are permitted to exercise the option of conversion into equity of the company after a period of time. Some companies have provided for compulsory conversion, instead of giving option. Such debentures are very attractive to the investing public if the company is doing well, as they give a future right to participate in the profits and prosperity of the company. The company in turn would benefit by not only attracting funds as debenture capital at present but also by widening the equity capital base in future. This type of issue is particularly suitable for expanding and diversifying companies.

Share capital includes equity shares and preference shares with a period of redemption of 12 years or more. A share is a form of transferable right representing the interest of the owner in the company, either of equity or preference capital. For a new company, some minimum equity base is necessary to prove the stake of promoters and their willingness of risk-taking. What is the extent of the minimum would depend upon the project cost, the state of the capital market, national importance of such a project, the financial institutions' interest in it and the general level of interest rates, the background of company, the cost of capital for the company from various sources, etc. The SEBI guidelines impose a limit of 20-25% of paid up capital for promoters to get the shares of that company to be listed on a Stock Exchange.

Preference Shares

Preference shares are a category of shares having a preferential right in respect of payment of dividend and repayment of principal. The Companies Act authorises the issue of preference shares and the fact that various companies have issued preference shares indicates that they have a role to play in the capital structure of the companies. Preference shares are of various categories, namely, redeemable preference shares, cumulative and non-cumulative preference shares and participating preference shares.

Redeemable preference shares are to be redeemed out of profits or capital specially raised for the purpose. Under the Companies Act as recently amended, redemption of the preference shares is now compulsory after 9-12 years. No such shares will be redeemed except when they are fully paid-up and provision is made for a special reserve fund called capital redemption account created for the purpose of redemption.

Cumulative preference shares have a right to be paid dividends in arrears in a cumulative manner, once the company makes profits. In 1985, the government have introduced a new instrument of cumulative convertible preference shares (CCP) issued at 10% fixed dividend. These are convertible into equity after 3 to 5 years. Non-cumulative shares have no right of accumulation of arrears. Participating preference shares have a right to participate in residual profits after all the claims of creditors and owners are met along with equityholders.

Preference shares stand in between debentureholders and equity-holders in the matter of rights. While a debentureholder is a creditor who is to be paid irrespective of the profits made, the equityholder gets the residual as owner of the company. Preference shares are a hybrid category standing in between these — neither a complete creditor nor owner of the company. Preference shareholders have priority of repayment of principal over equity shareholders in the event of winding up of the company. They have also the right to participate in the left-over assets or capital after the equityholders are paid in full.

Voting rights of the preference shareholders are exercised in the event of arrears of dividends for more than two years and in matters relating to the interests of the preference sharesholders. In practice, these voting rights are highly circumscribed by the overwhelming power of the equityholders who are a majority. In almost all companies, preference shareholding constitute roughly one-third or less of the total equity holdings. A norm of preference to equity ratio of 1:3 is generally insisted by the Govt.

So long as the company is doing well, the preference shareholders have nothing to grumble and they are paid their due dividends. They are treated as good as creditors in such circumstances, but in times of adverse conditions, profits are not adequate to pay dividends to the preference shareholders and they are not treated as creditors but as owners, though their interests may not be identical with the equityholders. They are, however, bound by the decisions of the majority equityholders. The creditors of the company, viz., financial institutions, banks, etc., have a greater say so far as their dues are concerned than that of preference shareholders. If institutions are preference shareholders themselves, then the situation is somewhat better as they can bargain for better terms. Whatever is the category of holders, these shareholders would suffer from capital depreciation once the shares are quoted and traded on the exchanges, due to a rise in interest rates in the market.

Preference shareholders are generally at the mercy of the equityholders particularly in adverse years. They would neither be able to get away from the company nor improve the lot of the company by management changes and active interference. It is in this sense that preference shareholders are in perpetual bondage to the company.

Preference shares are in demand despite such disadvantages, particularly with the financial institutions. The investors' preference for these can be explained by the following features of preference shares: *(i)* less risk, *(ii)* fixed income and *(iii)* special attractions like cumulative dividends or redeemable shares.

From the point of view of the company, preference shares are chosen for the following reasons: *(i)* it would be cheaper to issue preference shares than equity although costlier than the issue of debentures; *(ii)* equityshareholders gain by the gearing ratio provided by the preference capital in the capital structure of the company as it is a fixed interest security; *(iii)* the companies can cater to the needs of investment trusts, UTI, LIC, etc., who require fixed interest securities in their portfolios and preference share capital neither dilutes the equity nor interferes with management by equityholders.

From the point of view of the company, it is costlier to issue preference shares than debentures as the company would have to earn more to maintain a given return on preference capital than that of debentures. Thus to earn Rs. 14 to pay a dividend of 14 per cent to preference shareholders, the company would have to make profits of almost double that, whereas to pay Rs. 14 to debentureholders, the company needs to earn only Rs. 14. For the purpose of taxation, the interest paid on debt or debentures is treated as part of the expenses and commitment on gross profits whereas the dividend paid on preference shares is taxable. The grossed-up rate is the rate which the company has to earn in order to pay a dividend to the preference shareholders and would depend upon the rate of taxation on the company and the coupon rate on the preference share. The higher the tax rate the higher should be the gross profits of the company in order to maintain a given rate of distribution to preference shareholders.

Bonus Shares

There are certain regulations regarding the issues of bonus shares enforced by the Govt. The Companies Act, however, takes no notice of bonus shares except for a passing reference that share premium may be applied by a company for issuing fully-paid bonus shares to the members. The issue of bonus shares is a normal practice adopted by the companies to bring the paid-up capital in line with the market value of the shares. Companies, are not required to get the consent of the Govt. under the latest guidelines. Bonus issues are permitted subject to the following conditions:

(1) They are made out of free reserves (free and unencumbered from any commitments or charges).

(2) They may be issued out of general reserves or capital profits or reserves not including reserves out of revaluation of assets and not based upon cash accruals, or out of development rebate reserves or development allowances reserves, capital redemption reserve and share premium received in cash.

(3) Total amount permitted to be capitalised for bonus share issue should not exceed the total paid-up equity of the company (except in certain cases such as dilution of foreign companies).

(4) Residual reserves after issue of bonus shares should be at least 40% of the increased paid-up capital.

(5) After the declaration of bonus shares, one-third of the pre-tax profits of the company should be able to meet the requirements of at least 10% dividend on the increased capital of the company.

(6) Bonus shares are permitted only if all the existing shares are fully paid-up and are not in lieu of a dividend.

(7) The time lag between two such bonus issues should be at least 12 months.

(8) A resolution for the proposed capitalisation should be approved by the General Body of the shareholders provided the Memorandum and Articles of Association permits such an issue of bonus shares. After the issue of the bonus shares, the paid-up capital should not exceed the authorised capital of the company.

The issue of bonus shares would not require any Govt. clearance under the latest guidelines.

Bonus issue is permitted before conversion of a private limited company into a public limited company provided the interests of the participating public are protected to the extent of the equity interest of the existing shareholders. The issue of preference shares as bonus shares is generally not favoured except when the proposed preference shares are redeemable and the ratio between the equity and the preference capital does not exceed 3:1.

Free reserves out of which bonus shares are to be issued are accumulated retained earnings, capital and current reserves and general reserves not specifically earmarked for any purpose, and sinking fund reserve for debentures (after the debentures are redeemed), development rebate reserve or allowance reserve, capital redemption reserve and share premium account received in cash.

Cost of Floatation

The cost of raising equity is generally lower than the cost of raising preference shares and debentures. The fixed cost of floatation include underwriting commission, brokerage, etc., and are generally expressed as a percentage of the capital floated. The variable cost relates to those expenses such as administration fees, etc. Expenses vary from issue to issue depending upon the nature of the company, the amount of issue, structure of the capital (equity, preference etc.). Although brokerage and underwriting commission are generally fixed at 1-1/2% and 2-1/2% respectively giving a total of about 4% of the total floatation, the other expenses vary between 3 and 5% of the total amount floated. The managing merchant bankers to the issue who do the secretarial work and coordination are given commission of 1/2% for managing the issue. The variable cost element varies with the nature and size of the company, the amount of issue and is different for new and old companies. Besides, the cost of floatation of new companies is generally higher than for existing companies, in view of the economies of scale under "other" expenses for the latter companies as they do not have to undergo all the formalities of bringing out the issue.

As per the study on "Capital Issues and Public Response" published in the RBI Bulletin of October 1989, the cost of new issues as a percentage of the amount floated has risen from 8-9% in 1981-83 to 11.5% in 1984 and fell to 9.3% in 1985. In respect of a few companies, the variable costs are as high as 20% while the average variable costs are about 5% of the new capital issued. These costs should have risen substantially at present; the rates paid to Registrars and merchant bankers are, however, variable and amenable to bargaining.

Registrars are paid at a rate of Rs. 3 to 5 handling charges in respect of each successful application.

The amount of funds, raised in the new issues market is referred to later in this chapter. There is another indicator of the magnitude of funds channelled into the corporate sector in the capital market, namely, the assistance sanctioned and disbursed by the development corporations of all India and State-level nature and investment corporation like UTI, LIC and GIC, etc. The disbursement made by them in total had been increasing at a rapid rate. Similarly, the capital issues and capital raised have also increased substantially. The bulk of the rise was on account of debentures.

Underwriting Activity

In the new issues market, the major activity relates to underwriting and marketing of new issues. In India all financial institutions and brokers undertake this business. Banks have entered this market in a big way by starting their own divisions of merchant banking or their subsidiaries. Insurance and investment companies are also an important category of underwriters. While banks and financial institutions account for the bulk of underwriting, UTI, insurance and consultancy companies and brokers account for the rest.

Underwriters and financial institutions subscribed more for preference shares and debentures than for equity shares as the latter are more attractive to the investing public and thus devolve less on the underwriters. The amount subscribed by them is higher in debentures as part of their policy of investment in corporate sector in high yielding and fixed income securities.

Brokers help in the floatation of new issues not only through underwriting or as managing brokers but also as financial consultants, advising on the proper capital structure, methods of raising capital and requirements of the Companies Act and the Securities Contracts (Regulation) Act, and listing requirements etc.

Abuses in the New Issue Market

Government has been attempting to regulate the abuses in the New Issue market in collaboration with the stock exchange authorities. The SEBI has taken over this responsibility of regulating and developing the new issues market since 1992. These abuses relate to the following categories. Firstly, the companies were publishing projected figures of turnover, profits, dividend, etc. of future years which are not warranted. Secondly, companies have been making exaggerated claims about prospects to the public in press conferences and privately circulated brochures.

Thirdly, advertisements about over-subscription were used to be made falsely, which the Government prohibited if not accompanied by documentary evidence. Fourthly, trading in new issues prior to the formal listing of such issues is also prevalent. Besides rigging up of prices before floating of new issues, arranging and manipulation of high premiums on new issues are also rampant. Lastly, delays in refunding the application money, issuing of allotment letters, posting of share certificates, etc. are quite common.

Problems of the New Issue Market

It will be pertinent to summarise briefly the main problems of the new issue market here. Firstly, the new issue market could not mobilise adequate savings from the public as less than 5% financial savings of the household sector are mobilised for investment in shares and debentures. A large portion of the capital requirements of companies is placed on the market privately or with financial institutions, in more recent years.

Secondly, the new issues market suffers from functional and institutional gaps, particularly in terms of the new instruments to appeal to the investing public. Thus, a wholesale market for new issues is yet to develop in India and merchant banking is in its infancy. The merchant banks are presently not playing a developmental role. In technical, managerial and entrepreneurial aspects, particulars in project preparation and technical aspects, adequate attention has not been given so far. This would be the responsibility of merchant banks and is not at present performed by them with the result that small investors are duped by the companies. Merchant bankers are now asked by the SEBI to do this. Thirdly, with a risk aversion in the new issue market, funds are diverted from the risky market to less risky debentures as well as deposits with the companies. Companies have themselves shifted away in the eighties from equity financing to debt financing and to larger reliance on debentures of convertible nature in more recent years. The costs of floatation have also been found to be abnormally high, particularly for new and small-sized companies. There is much scope for rationalising and economising the administrative costs of floatation of new issues in which banks can play an important role through merchant banking divisions.

In semi-urban and rural areas if the investor has to send application forms to centres where banks are authorised to accept them, he has to spend on securing a bank draft, postal charges for sending, and suffer loss of interest and collection charges for refund orders. There are inordinate delays in allotment of shares, refunding of application money, posting of share certificates and effecting transfer of shares etc. These are to be despatched by registered post, or by certificate of posting in some cases, which is not done by many companies at present and they do not pay any interest for the delayed period as required by law.

All these problems would amount to considerable hardship to the small investors in the countryside. Similarly, dividend warrants, refund orders, interest payment not being encashable at par in all centres, the investors again lose. As the time taken for allotment is often two to three months or even more, there is considerable loss of interest on money to investors. The time limit for allotment was reduced to 30 days in 1996. These hardships are more in rural and semi-urban areas and do great injustice to them *vis-a-vis* those in metropolitan centres.

Another feature of the market is that existing companies with a good track record received good response for new issues as compared with new companies. The underwriting support and devolution on underwriters was more in the case of new companies due to the cautious response of investors to these companies. There was also evidence to show that investors do prefer debentures to equities and more so, if they are convertible debentures. Recently, new regulations are imposed by SEBI on merchant banks, which may improve the climate of investment in the new issue market. The merchant banks have to give due diligence certificate: they have to certify the bonafides of the information contained in the prospectus, justify the price fixed for the share and take the full responsibility for vetting and scrutiny in the case of rights issues. Their code of conduct is enforced by their own Association — Association of Merchant Bankers (AMBs).

Primary Market — Problems

The experiment in free pricing, being new in India created some problems of undue over pricing initially by some companies. Soon within a few months, investors became more discrete in making investments in new issues with hefty premiums. Many new issues have become flops in raising subscriptions, if their premiums are unreasonably high. It is now obvious that the experiment of free pricing will survive the criticism of the public particularly due to stricter norms by SEBI for better disclosures and more rational justification of the premium fixed by merchant bankers.

Accompanying the demand for control on premium is the pressure of the public to regulate the timing of the entry of companies in the new issues market and on the quantum of their issue. These steps being retrograde steps for the ongoing reforms, it is left to merchant bankers and the companies to decide on the basis of their experience and expertise. The demand for such controls emerged due to unrestricted entry of companies and the bunching of new issues at the same time and high premiums confusing the investors as to what to contribute with their limited funds.

The problem of timing and bunching of new issues will also lead to investor problems in the form of scramble for limited resources and inadequate appraisal of the projects. This may result in poor response to some new issues.

Public Response

As against the oversubscription of more than 10 times in respect of 51% of the issues in 1991-92, the public response to new issues in 1992-93 was poor. As per the 'PRIME' Data, 86 Companies (16%) have to extend the subscription date till the last closing date, and 67 Companies (13%) have to extend the closing date by 1 to 6 days and even so the undersubscription was many times covered up by institutional backup and discount sales to Mutual Funds and Financial Institutions.

One thing seems certain that the amount of premium collected was by far the highest in 1992-1994 and secondly the proportion of funds raised in the form of equity went up, while the same in the form of debt has come down as seen from the following table. This trend noticed upto 1995-96 was reversed since 1998-99. Later the proportion of equity and premium came down and that of debt increased. More importantly the funds raised in the form of rights were only Rs. 3,851 crores in 1991-92 while the same were Rs. 12,792 crores in 1992-93. Total rights issue amount was at a high of Rs. 15,661 crores in 2007-08 but came down to Rs. 11,907 crores in 2008-09. The emerging trends are clear and striking and debt became more prominent during 92-93 to 2003-04. Premium issues came down from 1995 onwards, and went up again in 2003 to 2009. Equity was encouraged during recent years. Premium was very high in the year 2006 to 2007, due to boom in stock market.

Table 11.1
Shares of Equity/ Premium Percentages

	1991-92	*1992-93*	*1994-95*	*1995-96*	*2000-01*	*2003-04*	*2006-07*	*2007-08*	*2008-09*
Equity	47.4	27	34	44	28	22	32	3	12
Premium	25.0	24	32	31	25	39	65	86	88
Debt	27.6	49	34	25	47	39	3	11	0

Source: B.S.E./Prime and RBI Reports.

Note: In 1993-94, the total funds raised barring public issues and rights amounted to around Rs. 29,649 crores and in 1994-95, they were Rs. 31,014 crores. During 1993 and 1994 the Premiums barring a few stray cases have also come down. During 1995 to 2001 the new issue market was mostly subdued following malpractices by companies. Private placement began to grow from 1996 when markets were depressed. There were only 15 issues raising an amount of only Rs. 392 crores in 2001. The Prime data shows a free fall in the number of new issues and the amounts raised in primary market, after 1996.

Timing of New Issues

Crowding of new issues, sometimes as many as 6 to 10 new issues opening in one week, would be hazardous to both the companies and investors. It would be impossible for investors to come to any right conclusion of issues which are good in their view. This also leads to their subscription for only 200 shares which is the minimum shares to be applied for and spreading their funds in as many issues as possible. Here again the investors have to learn to cope with the alternative avenues of investment and proper education of investors is necessary to enlighten them to be selective in investments by use of tools of research and analysis and for deciding for themselves the extent of risk taking and whether to invest in new issues or mutual funds schemes and to what extent they invest in alternative avenues.

Added to the above complaints the SEBI's raising of the limit of minimum subscription to 500 shares or shares worth Rs. 5,000 in 1994 from the level of 100 shares has been criticised as retrograde for the growth of investment cult. But it is justifiable both from the point of companies and better services for the investors. Those who apply for 100 shares have been putting in multiple applications and have been found to be applying to as many new issues as possible as if it is lottery unaware of what issues will be allotted to them and how much. Such gambling should not be encouraged on the part of investors. As per our sample survey of investors nearly 52% of respondents are applicants for only 100 shares, who apply for about 5 issues at the same time, to take a chance for allotment, as if it is lottery and such practices are to be discouraged. Now such category is eliminated by SEBI. In October 1996, this limit is again reduced to 200 shares to attract investors back to the market.

Cost of Capital Issues

One of the burning problems in capital structuring of companies is the cost of capital used by the company. Broadly capital can be owner capital and Debt capital. The normal understanding is that debt capital is cheaper due to tax advantage it enjoys and leverage extended by it to equity capital. The equity capital is considered cheap but if alternative use of capital and opportunity cost is taken into account it is not the cheap source.

The concept of cost of capital is relative to the stage of the growth of the company, the nature of its product, its available alternative sources of funds, etc. Thus, a brand new company has to perforce depend on the share capital and particularly from promoters, FIs and the public issue of equity. If it is an old company and is also a capital intensive company, it has to depend heavily on debt capital relative to equity capital on term loans, debentures, public deposits etc. If it is an existing profit making company, besides share capital and cash accruals, it has to depend on the public issues and rights issues of equity and debentures.

The approximate cost of borrowed funds to the company, is shown below. But these estimates are rough and ready proximate numbers and will vary from company to company and from time to time. The cost of raising funds from each of the methods will depend on the rate of interest/return and the accompanying costs of raising the funds.

Table 11.2 Funding Methods (2009)

	Normal Margins	*Rate Per Annum (including costs)*
(a) Bank Term Loans (or FI Term Loans)	20-25%	14%
(b) Bank Working Capital	25%	11 - 12% at PLR
(c) Public Debentures/Bonds		
(i) Convertible	—	11 to 13%
(ii) Non-Convertible	—	11 to 14%
(d) Public Deposits	—	12%
(e) Deferred Credits } Suppliers Credits	25-40%	Free (not fixed)
(f) Hire Purchase/Lease etc. } and other private sources	25%	20% free

It will be seen from the above that the minimum rate is 10% while the maximum rate is around 20% if it is from organised sector and this includes the cost of raising funds.

Corporate Studies have shown that nearly one-fourth to one-third of the fund requirements are met from internal accruals or retained earnings. The rest are raised from the capital market through new issues or from borrowings from financial institutions and public through loans, advances and deposits.

Whether a company goes for public issue, right issue, or for borrowing from institutions will depend on a number of factors, such as cost and available limits with Banks, FIs and for raising public deposits, as they are all related to equity share capital and free reserves and earning potential to service these forms of raising funds to the company. The reliance on new issues market is thus one of the alternatives available to the companies and if new issue is the method chosen, it can be internal or domestic markets or foreign markets or it can be either for equity or rights, debt, etc. The costs on all these types of raising funds vary and the cheapest method is borrowing abroad but it is open to very high rated and creditworthy companies only, with foreign exchange earnings.

Wasteful Procedures on Public Issue

As referred to earlier, the investors in New Issues Market had some difficulties in that a vast majority of them read the Form 2-A (Memorandum of Prospectus) but complain of the difficulty of reading due to small print. Many depend upon the opinion of Brokers/Sub-Brokers, due to difficulty of reading the prospectus or due to lack of time or lack of expertise in reading the prospectus intelligently. As per our sample study, the majority of investors depend on what daily Newspapers write on the new issues (34%) and on Journals (17%) and on friends/brokers/relatives etc. (47%). It will be thus seen that only a small proportion of investors seem to be educated enough in the capital market analysis. So education is the prime need of the hour.

Many application forms are not used at all or misused as waste paper and the selected investors receive the same forms from more than one source. There is thus wasteful expenditure on application forms. Another wasteful expenditure is on too many intermediaries — two or more co-managers in addition to lead manager, too many brokers/banks and too many collection centres. Compulsory underwriting also adds to the cost, as underwriting is a matter of investor protection and forced on company as per SEBI guidelines and presently it is optional.

Although nearly 90% of the small investors applied for less than 500 shares and about 52% applied only for 100 shares, the SEBI has raised the minimum subscription as Rs. 5000/- or 500 shares. Innumerable applications mainly from small investors applying for 100 shares sometimes in multiple applications and in fictitious names may lead to larger work load and wasteful expenditure to the company. The same may lead to larger investor complaints. So the minimum subscription limit was already raised. This was again brought down to 200 shares in 1996 to boost sagging investor interest in the market.

On the same lines of argument, for smaller issues of Rs. 50 crores or less, it may be left to the company to reduce the number of managers to the issue, brokers and underwriters and the number of collection centres. Some regional issues may prefer concentrating on selected centres, if they are confident of raising their subscription. Underwriting may raise costs but may be necessary for confidence of investors, provided stricter enforcement is made of their underwriting obligations, which hopefully SEBI's new code for underwriters would achieve. Underwriting is dispensed with now in many cases. The vetting of draft prospectus for all issues by SEBI has been dispensed with and merchant bankers are given the responsibility. The minimum collection centres were reduced first from 57 to 30 in 1993 and then to 4 in Sept. 1995.

Another problem of investors which our Survey has highlighted is the limited use of "stock-invest", despite its many advantages.

The reasons are as follows:

1. Procedural formalities in the bank branch for issue of stock invest, which are now simplified.
2. The charges made by banks for issuing the stock invest, while a cheque or cash involves no cost, and this practice of charging was later dispensed with.
3. The fear of discrimination by the company in the allotment for those who apply through stock invest. The SEBI has allayed these fears to a large extent.
4. The inefficiency in service in many banks leading to waste of time and the torture of extended formalities. With the reduction of allotment period to 30 days, the need for stock invest has disappeared since 1996.

The investors are not obviously convinced of the superior advantage of stock invest over the Cheque/Draft which inhibits the use of stock invest. Firstly it is a matter of education and secondly it is a matter of improved services by bank branches, which is not under the control of SEBI. It is in this context advantageous to encourage big companies to have their own collection centres, superceding the banking system. The quality of services may be better in the private sector banks which are coming up, or the companies can have their own arrangements. With the reduction of allotment time to 30 days and even 15 days in some cases, the advantage of stock invest is lost to investors.

Another wasteful expenditure is in the hands of the Company. With the prime objective of making the issue a success, the companies compete among themselves to throw Dinners/Lunches at Press Conferences, Brokers' Conferences and Investors' Conferences etc. The SEBI guidelines have come out prohibiting such Five Star Lunches/Dinners as it may tantamount to bribing/or discounting/or extending incentives.

Group on Primary Market — Recommendations

An informal group on Primary Market under the Chairmanship of Shankar N. Acharya suggested stringent listing requirements, stricter enforcement of disclosure norms, standardistation of accounting norms in line with Generally Accepted Accounting Principles (GAAP), introduction of safety net/exit route to small investors and transparency in corporate goverance. Banks and Insurance Companies are recommended to participate more in primary issues. GDR issues may be asked to offer a part of their equity in domestic market.

A company going for public issue should not have any outstanding warrants or preference shares. The cost of equity issues shiould be brought down by popularising book building, reduction in mandatory collection centres, the offer of new issues in 'demat' form through the depositories and printing of application forms in Newspaper. New instruments like puttable equity and equity commitment notes should be allowed. The facility of private placement is recommended to be confined to not more than 99 qualified institutional investors and traded on the OTCEI. Banks FIs etc. who participate in private placement should regularly furnish the information to SEBI and RBI.

The group emphasised more responsibility to Chartered Accountants and capital market intermediaries and the need for promoting the market making activity to encourage secondary market and creation of low cost form of transfers by creation of a Domestic Depository Receipt market and a derivative trading system and Demat form of holding shares, which were implementted.

Need for Analytical Data

Another complaint of investors is that information contained in the Form - 2 A (Memorandum on Prospectus) is too formal and trivial. Many companies do not provide analytical data and results of research and qualitative information on a true and factual basis which are truly educative and informative to investors. In this context, the Investor Service Fund which the companies are asked to set up under the new companies Bill 1993 may be used for investor education on new issues through voluntary non-profit associations, such as Rotary Clubs, Investor Associations etc. Investment Analysis should be made through them to get all issues analysed and qualitative information is provided to the investors through such forums. At present some Investor Associations are active in such education. But no Stock Exchange barring B.S.E. is doing this work of educating the investors on a regular basis, although they have been asked to set apart some funds out of listing fees for investor services cell and some for customer protection fund. The SEBI can enforce on the Stock Exchanges to use such funds for spread of investor education and information by themselves or through accredited agencies or through non-profit making bodies in the local areas. The new Companies Bill 2008 has proposed some measures in this direction.

At present, majority of Stock Exchanges have not reorganised their Boards to bring in 50% for public representation on their boards. Very few have their Training Centres and Investor Education Programmes. It is hoped that SEBI will insist immediately on the Stock Exchanges to change their Bylaws, in this regard which is done.

Table 11.3 presents the data on the magnitude of new issue mobilisation from the primary market, for illustrative purposes.

Table 11.3 New Issue Mobilisation of Resources from Primary Market

(Rs. crores)

	1996-97		*2000-01*		*2006-07*		*2007-08*		*2008-09*	
	No.	*Amount*	*No.*	*Amount*	*No.*	*Amount*	*No.*	*Amount*	*No.*	*Amount*
By Prospectus and Rights										
1. Private Sector	842	10,424.1	145	4,849	118	31,600	115	63,638	45	14,671
2. P.S.U. Bonds	—	50.0								
3. Govt. Companies	3	650.0	—	—	—	—	2	2,516	—	—
4. Banks F.I.s	6	4,352.0	5	14,770	1	782	2	17,553	—	—
Sub-total	852	15,476.1	150	12,421	119	32,382	119	83,707	45	14,671
By Private Placement										
1. Private Sector	—	2,493.0	387	24,399	1,539	84,387	1616	1,29,677	1053	93,036
2. Public Sector	—	12,573.0	200	43,101	139	61,184	199	83,048	228	1,09,709
Sub-total	—	15,066.0	587	67,500	1,678	145,571	1815	2,12,725	1281	2,02,745
Total	—	30,542.1	737	79,921	1797	177,953				

Source: R.B.I. Annual Reports.

Note: Totals do not tally with sub-totals or constituents due to offers of sale data. The amounts raised by private placement were most of the times higher by 3 to 5 times the amounts raised through prospectus and rights. This indicates the poor market conditions or fears of poor public response or due to lower costs of issue in the case of private placement.

CHAPTER 12 Money Market and its Instruments

In this Chapter, discussion is centred on the money market and its components in India. Although short-term Government Securities UTI units, PSU bonds, etc., are also a part of the money market these are not discussed in this Chapter, as they are covered in other chapters.

Money Market has no geographical constraints and relates to all dealings in money or monetary assets. J.S.G. Wilson@ defined the money market as a "centre in which financial institutions congregate for the purpose of dealing impersonally in monetary assets." This is giving too literal an interpretation of money market. In fact, 'money market' is a wide term and encompasses a variety of transactions, instruments and institutions involving only short term funds. Money market is a centre where borrowers and lenders of money and near money assets are put together. It may comprise a group of such markets for various types of money assets characterised by relative liquidity or nearness to money. Such assets may be called call money, treasury bills or bills of exchange etc. Secondly, although there are various centres of money market such as Mumbai, Kolkata, Chennai, etc., they are not separate independent markets but are inter-linked and related. Thirdly, in a true sense of free and perfect competition, there should be only one price for each category of money assets, which would result from dealing of purchase and sale made on a purely impersonal basis and through blind economic forces. The financial institutions dealing in these assets may be spread over so wide a geographical area that it would be impossible to specify the geographical limits of the market. The fact that there are some geographical centres does not limit the operations to these centres.

Developed and Underdeveloped Markets*

Indian Money Market is not well developed. Following the Vaghul Committee recommendations (1989), a number of new instruments have been introduced to develop the market. The essential characteristics of a developed money market such as the ones in London or New York are integrated structures between sub-markets, free flow of funds as between sub-markets or segments of the same sub-market, a high degree of specialisation with regard to dealings in instruments by various institutions and a single price for each of the instruments traded.

An important aspect of the Indian money market is the seasonality in the demand for funds following the agricultural operations. The busy season for funds extends from November to April and the slack season from May to October.

Besides, the Indian money market is also characterised by insulation from the foreign money markets due to the operation of exchange controls in the economy despite some liberalisation recently and freeing of the rupee. Another important aspect of the money market is the dichotomy between the organised and unorganised markets which will be referred to again later. Unlike a developed money market, the Indian market is not characterised by a high degree of integration and cohesion.

@ J.S.G.Wilson: *Monetary Policy and Development of Money Market.*

* E. Nevin: *Capital Funds in Underdeveloped Countries.*

The essential pre-requisites for integration are that there must be links between the several sub-markets and their relative prices for each of the assets traded and continuous contacts and relationship of borrowings and lending are maintained through the spillover flow of funds from one sub-market to another. Although the degree of risk and uncertainty varies from segment to segment and there are various frictions and hurdles to shiftability of funds such as costs of brokerage commission, taxes, etc., which might explain to some degree the difference in prices between the sub-markets, there should be an essential unity of purpose in securing the highest return for funds and a general free flow of funds and information in the market. The integration may not be possible if there are special groups of institutions with separate standing and methods of operation and customers are attached to these institutions, each such group tending to be isolated from the others. This is the case particularly with the indigenous banking system in India. Capital should be priced at the true scarcity value of it in the country.

Integration of this market with other sub-markets helps the siphoning off of the excess or short-fall in this market to others such as Treasury bills or government securities market. Integration also aids the more economical use of cash by banks who are the major institutions in the market.

Integration and Specialisation

A well developed market would satisfy both the criteria of integration and specialisation. If the market is well integrated, the flow of funds between sub-markets will be free and quicker, increasing thereby the value of transactions. Specialisation is a natural result of the growth of the market, as the specialist is bound to emerge as soon as a sufficient demand develops for his services. In India, the market is not specialised to the degree present in Western developed countries, as we do not have discount houses, acceptance houses etc. The need for such institutions has not been felt and the volume of business did not warrant the emergence of such specialist houses.

Modern discount houses have developed on the basis of the growth of bill business as in the U.K. The merchants who were acting as intermediaries for those who wished to invest in bills began to evolve as dealers in bills themselves acting as wholesalers for the banks to buy and sell in retail.

Another example of the specialist institution is the acceptance banker who developed into acceptance houses doing the business of accepting a bill of exchange by lending its name for a client known or recommended to them, thereby facilitating negotiations. Acceptance business is very prominent in the London market by virtue of its acting as a financial centre for various parts of the world.

The trend towards specialisation is seen in the USA also in the development of firms for Government securities dealings, houses specialising in placement of private commercial bills and those concentrating on handling bankers' acceptances and federal funds, etc.

Advantages of Mature Money Market

The advantages of a mature money market are multifold. The gaps between the separate sub-markets can be bridged by operators through arbitrage which lead to a single price for each category of assets. Secondly, it facilitates the profitable deployment of surplus funds of banking institutions. Thirdly, where money market is compact and integrated the control by the central bank would be easier. The central bank action would percolate quickly from one segment to another of the market and be more effective. The central money market may be developed alright but not properly linked with the periphery markets in the unorganised sector as in India. Alternatively, as in Thailand and a few other less developed countries, even the central money market is not well developed and the central bank's action may have to be direct and the traditional indirect instruments may not work. Fourthly, a developed money market helps promote certain attitudes and practices by bankers regarding the maintenance of minimum reserves and cash. Healthier practices by banks in this regard help control by the central bank and develop stronger banking system. In addition, the central bank may exert its influence by consultation directly with the respective groups of interests in the market such as Discount Houses Association, Accepting Houses Association or Foreign Exchange Dealers Association and this also facilitates operation of the instrument of moral suasion by the central bank. In 1994 Securities Trading Corporation was set up to deal in Govt. Securities on behalf of the RBI, to promote gilt-edged market. Earlier in 1988, Discount and Finance House of India was set up to develop the money market in India.

Sub-Markets[@]

The call money market in India and Pakistan and federal funds market in the U.S.A. are examples of a sub-market dealing with near cash or overnight money. The demand comes from banks who fall short of reserves overnight or a few days and the supply comes from those who have got excess reserves with them. In India, this is called the inter-bank call market wherein funds are borrowed overnight for book adjustments by banks who fall short of the statutory cash reserves requirements. Brokers put through these transactions between banks or the banks may choose to deal directly among themselves. In London and Paris, the discount houses who deal with bills wholesale require such funds for holding the bills. In New York such funds may emanate from Government security dealers. Both in U.K. and U.S.A. as in India, the dealers in the market act as intermediaries for these dealings in inter-bank funds. Not infrequently the banks put through their transactions by themselves. In U.S. banking, the need for such market is more than in India and the U.K., where branch banking predominates and branch adjustments for excess funds can always take place. The federal funds market in U.S. provides a mechanism for meeting shortage of funds. In some countries, where exchange control does not restrict their dealings abroad, the banks may depend more upon correspondents abroad for excess or shortfall of funds than in India.

In the inter-bank market in India, in addition to all banks, foreign and Indian, GIC, UTI and LIC which are non-bank institutions also operate, mostly as lenders. RBI is the apex body for these institutions and acts as the lender of last resort to the market. In the inter-bank market, foreign banks are the main borrowers because by the nature of their operations they finance trade and operate in the market mostly with a narrow cash base. This sub-market is the most sensitive to changes in liquidity, as the stringency or surfeit of funds with the banks and the impact of the credit control operations of the RBI are felt here. After 1994 Mutual Funds, other Institutions and Companies with excess funds of above Rs. 20 crores are allowed to operate in this market, as lenders.

In the ultimate analysis, it is the readiness of the central bank to act as a lender of last resort to the market that sets standards of liquidity to be kept by banks and their readiness to lend in turn. The integration of sub-markets also depends on the central bank acting as a lender of last resort. In a country like India with a seasonal ebb and flow of demand for banks funds either the banks keep excess reserves (which was true upto sixties in India) or have a ready recourse to the central bank. In the latter event, the central bank may impose discipline on the banks' operations. Generally, banks loathe the hegemony of central banks and hence prefer to keep excess reserves as far as possible. When some banks keep excess reserves, others can always borrow from them and thus the interbank market began to develop and thrive. The rate depends on the excess funds of the banking system as a whole and is regulated by the inter-bank agreement through the Indian Banks Association. The rate varies from day-to-day and transaction to transaction. The inter-bank agreement specified the maximum rate of 10 per cent in this sub-market, which was withdrawn in May 1989. Now, the rate may fluctuate freely depending on the market forces.

In India there is a good bill market in which all banks, and particularly the big banks, discount approved inland and foreign bills. There is, however, no true market in bills as there are no further dealings in them, except when they are rediscounted with the Reserve Bank or IDBI on Exim Bank.

Treasury bills constitute a separate segment of the market. These are of *three months* duration (91 days), issued on tap by RBI on behalf of the Government for financing Government investment and other expenditure. In addition, there are Treasury Bills of six, and twelve months duration. At present, the RBI sells Treasury Bills on behalf of Govt. both on auction basis and fixed rate basis of 14 days and 91 days and 364 days. Mostly banks, UTI, LIC etc. Contribute to these bills in addition to government departments or agencies with surplus funds. These Bills are now sold on auction basis, and interest rates are freed.

In the structure of money market in India, mention may be made of the role of stock brokers. They are a part of the money market as they borrow finance for carrying out stock market transactions and carry-over business called Badla. Some of the badla financiers borrow from commercial and co-operative banks for supplementing their own resources for stock market operations. Limits are sanctioned to these operators and brokers by the commercial banks.

[@] V.A. Avadhani: *Studies in Indian Financial System*, JAICO, 1978.

Bill Market in India

A Bill of Exchange is an instrument in writing containing an unconditional order by the maker directing a specified person to pay a sum of money to the order or to the bearer of the bill. Such bills augment the instruments of financial transaction, supplementing the available resources in times of seasonal stringencies for the purpose of refinance from the Reserve Bank.

The Reserve Bank of India Act has provided for refinance to commercial banks through buying or rediscounting of bills of exchange or other commercial paper eligible for rediscount under the Act. This provision under Section 17 of the RBI Act was meant to relieve the seasonal stringency in the absence of a properly organised bill market. The factors which affected adversely the growth of a bill market in India are the lack of uniformity in drawing bills, varying borrowing practices in different parts of the country with respect to bills, absence of distinction between trade bill and finance bill, high stamp duty, and popularity of cash credit and overdraft and arrangements as a means of borrowing from commercial banks. In India there is a traditional attachment to cash transaction and neglect of credit transactions, which has also hindered the growth of a bill market.

INSTITUTIONAL STRUCTURE

At the head of the structure of the Money Market is the RBI which controls and regulates this market through DFHI. The control extends to all those operating in the Call Money Market mostly Financial Institutions, Banks and Mutual Funds. More recently companies and individual units have also been operating in the Money Market.

The commercial paper (CP) issued by companies for raising short-term working capital is being developed in India. The participation certificates (PC) issued by banks and financial institutions, the deposit certificates (CD) issued by banks and factorisation bills are the other instruments that are being developed in this market. The institutions operating in these markets are banks, development finance institutions like IFC, ICICI and IDBI, investment finance companies like the LIC, UTI, GIC, etc. and other financial institutions. In the inter-bank money market, however, only the LIC and UTI have been permitted to operate in addition to banks. In 1990, the GIC, IDBI, NABARD, Mutual Funds and other financial institutions have also been permitted to operate. In April 1994, the RBI allowed the entry of any entity with bulk lendable resources of Rs. 20 crores and above as also the Money Market Mutual Funds to enter the call money market. This market is being developed in India by the establishment of Discount and Finance House by the Reserve Bank in April 1988, in collaboration with the financial institutions.

The money market is being Developed at present. The qualities of a developed money market such as cohesion, integration of sub-markets, specialisation in various categories of business and openness to foreign forces are absent in India. There is no secondary market for many instruments like Treasury Bills, Commercial Bills, CPs and CDs, etc. Recently, schemes for the development of secondary market in commercial paper and for trading in certificates of deposits and participation certificates and forfaiting bills etc. have been initiated by the RBI.

Characteristics

The money market establishes the link between the RBI and banks and the policy of RBI is felt in this market first before it percolates to other markets. The inter-bank market matches the deficits and surplus of banks; SBI and foreign banks are the major players in this market. This market provides an important area or venue for central bank intervention in the economy. It is also a venue to secure the short-term requirements of banks and FIs. For long, the inter-bank market is kept confined to banks and FIs to control liquidity better. This provides a link between the cash and near-money assets and to various sub-markets in the money market and to long-term wing of the capital market. Operations in this market extend to dealings in UTI units, Bonds of PSU, short-term bonds of semi-government and government sector etc.

DISCOUNT AND FINANCE HOUSE OF INDIA (DFHI)

The RBI is the leader and controller of Money Market and to perform these functions on her behalf, the DFHI was designed and set up by the RBI in April 1988 with a paid up Capital of Rs.100 crores. This was supposed to oversee and supervise the Money Market Operations. It can operate and intervene through the Bid and offer rates in the interbank market, treasury bill market, rediscount or discount treasury bills, short-term commercial bills, commercial paper and other money market instruments. Of the paid up capital, Rs. 51 crores was contributed by the RBI, Rs. 33 crores by Public Sector Banks and Rs. 16 crores by Public Financial Institutions. Thus, DFHI is a public sector institution for the purpose of stabilising the money market through purchase and sale operations in the instruments of trading and develop secondary market in them.

Its sources of funds are the following:

(a) Paid up capital of Rs. 100 crores.

(b) Credit limits of Rs. 200 crores with Public Sector Banks.

(c) Back up refinance lines with the RBI.

Its functions at present are as follows:

1. Operations in inter bank call money market.
2. Purchases and Sales (through bid and offer rates) of Treasury Bills of 91 days, 182 days and 364 days respectively.
3. Discount and Rediscount of Commercial Bills, Certificates of Deposit and Commercial Paper etc.
4. Buying and Selling of government securities with banks and Financial Institutions.

For the Treasury Bills, Commercial Bills etc., it gives Bid and offer Discount rates, say 364 days, T.Bs 9.90% (Bid) and 9.50% (Offer) and for Commercial paper it gives only one discount rate, say 10.75%. For government securities it quotes both buying and selling prices, at which it does business on a daily basis. The work of Govt. securities trading was entrusted to the Securities Trading Cooperation set up in May 1994.

Relative Rates of Return at year end March

(Per cent per annum)

	1991	*1995*	*1996*	*2001*	*2005*	*2007*	*2009*
Call Money Rate Average	21.5	15.63	16.28	7.15	5.30	7.22	7.06
91 day Treasury Bills (Auction)	—	11.99	12.97	6.83	5.21	6.64	3.2
182/364 day Treasury Bills (Auction)	10.08	11.94	13.20	7.16	5.51	7.01	4.5
Certificate of Deposits	12.44	12.50	17.13	8-10	4 - 7	10.77	9.31
Commercial Paper	15.10	14.50	20.15	9-10	5 - 6.50	13.35	10.54
Bank Maximum Deposit rate	10.00	12.00	12.00	9.5-10	6.25	9.50	9%
Bank Minimum Lending rate	16.00	15 to 17%	16.50	10.5-11	10.25 - 10.75	12.50	11 -12%

Source: RBI Annual Reports; Monthly Bulletins.

DFHI is buying and selling sometimes, while at other times, it only buys. The operations are not dictated by commercial considerations but by the requirements of money market conditions and the R.B.I. policy.

It was only in 1992, that the DFHI has started operation in the Government securities market in addition to its operations in the Money market. While the discount or rediscount rates are given in the case of money market instruments, actual purchase and sale prices as offered by the DFHI in the Government securities market are published by the Press, as released by the DFHI. Since June 1994, STCI has begun its operations in Govt securities.

It should also be noted that DFHI is operating in crores of rupees in a variety of instruments both in money market and the Govt. securities market. Bulk of these operations are in response to the market conditions and to absorb the excesses of supply and demand.

NEW MONEY MARKET INSTRUMENTS

The excess cash balances of corporate units, banks and financial institutions flow into money market. But the money market has for long remained primitive and underdeveloped, confined to inter bank call market and 91 day Treasury Bills. It was only since the publication of Chakravorthy Committee Report on the Monetary System (1985) that reforms started. Beginning with freeing of some interest rates and raising the coupon rates on govt. securities, a new institution of DFHI was set up and new instruments of trading were introduced as referred to earlier. Thus, Treasury Bills on auction basis were initiated for 14 days, 91 days, 182 days and 364 days, respectively. The rates on them are determined by market forces. These come under government sector instruments. The 182 day Treasury bills were discontinued since May 2001, as also the 14 day Treasury bills.

The 14 day Intermediate Treasury bills was introduced in April 1997, following the decision to discontinue tap T. Bs of 91 days. The auction T.Bs of 14 days were started in June 1997. This may lead to a more comprehensive yield curve and promotes better cash management by the Govt. These will have comparable rates as those on ways and means advances.

For encouragement of bill finance by banks and to promote a Secondary Market in bills, the RBI has permitted the issue of negotiable usance promissory notes against trade bills discounted by banks. The govt. has waived the stamp duty payable on trade bills so as to encourage the Secondary Market in them.

The following new instruments are introduced in the Banking Sector and in the Private Corporate Sector:

(a) 91 day participation certificates, involving non-transfer of underlying asset risk to the borrower but subject to a ceiling rate of 12% (ceiling rate removed in 1993).

(b) 91 to 180 days p.cs., bearing the full risk of underlying asset but subject to a floor rate of 14% (ceiling since removed).

(c) *Commercial paper:* The companies with good credit rating say P_2 are allowed to borrow through issue of commercial paper of 91 to 182 days with market determined rate of interest.

(d) Certificates of deposit of 6 months to 12 months, representing the deposits of the Private Sector in the Banking System which are negotiable and tradeable.

(e) *Factorisation Bills*: Involving the Bills receivable and supply Bills payable to companies and banks converted into factorisation bills with or without recourse. These factoring and allied services are being provided by subsidiaries setup by banks, namely, SBI, Canara Bank, PNB etc. These bills are purchased by the subsidiaries mentioned above from the creditors and the funds are collected in due course from the debtors. These bills can be either with risk or without risk, involved in all debt collection.

Recent Evolution of Money Market

The present day money market started evolving with the recommendation of Vaghul Committee in the late 1980s. The administered interest rate regime was dismentled. The ceiling on the call money rate was removed. The auction system of sale of Treasury Bills was started to have free market forces determining the rates. The DFHI was started to operate in the Money Market on behalf of the RBI, in 1988 to develop the secondary market in money market instruments. This was followed by a system of primary dealers to act as wholesalers and underwriters of the government borrowing programmes, since 1996.

The commercial paper segment was started in 1990, Repos (Repurchase Agreements) with RBI in 1992, Market Repos, Forward Rate Agreements (FRAs), Interest Rate Swaps (IRS) and Ledger Adjustment facility from RBI were all started in the late Nineties. The collateralised borrowing and lending obligation was initiated in 2003.

The other developments were the strengthening of payment system infrastructure through the formation of Clearing Corporation of India Ltd. (CCIL) in April 2002, introduction of Negotiated Dealing System (NDS) in February 2002 and the introduction of Real Time Gross Settlement System (RTGS) from 2004.

The gradual phasing out of non banks from the call money market and lowering of the CRR requirements on banks and the development of the Repo market to operate along with the Call Money Market have integrated the money market segment and increasing cohesion and sophistication were noticed in more recent years of the 21st century.

Classification of Money Market Instruments

The instruments of Money Market fall under the broad heads as shown below:

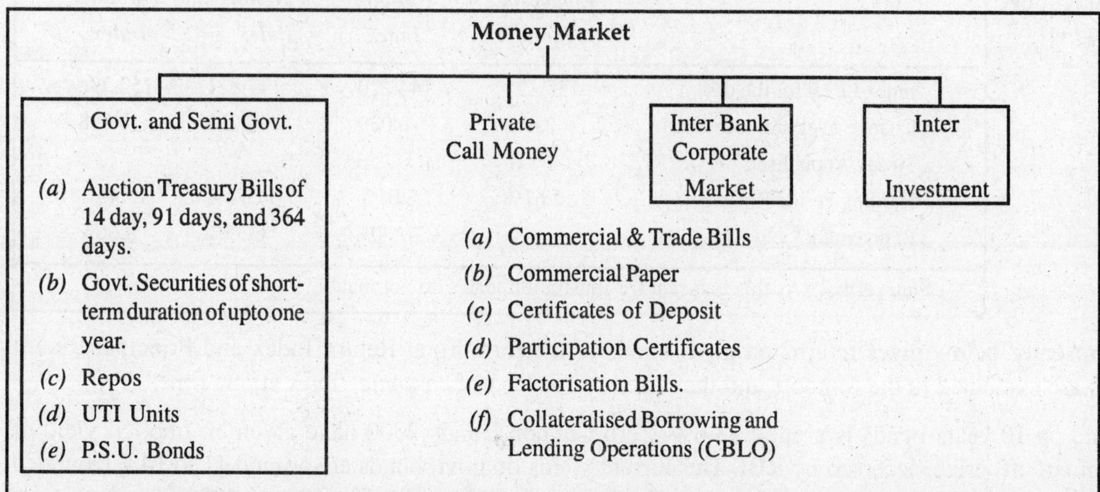

Among the instruments more recently initiated, no beginning worth the name was made in respect of participation certificates and factorisation Bills. Although some headway was made in respect of commercial paper and certificates of deposit, there is no Secondary Market in these instruments, as visualised by the R.B.I. The reason for this is that the holders of these bills keep them in their portfolio until maturity for two reasons. Firstly, many banks and financial institutions lack the technical expertise of proper portfolio management and secondly there was no well developed market for many segments of the money market. Thirdly, payment of stamp duty is a hurdle to the trading in secondary market. Till recently, there were no worthwhile avenues of investment open to the operators in the money market. Only over last few years, new instruments were brought into the money market and a secondary market is being developed in them along with financial deregulation and liberalisation of procedures in the market. The market is now open for a larger number of players and the volume of funds flowing into the market has since increased enormously. These developments were the result of recommendations of Vaghul Committee on Money Market Reforms and recommendations of Narasimham Committee on Financial Reforms.

Money Market Rates

The most liquid of the money market instruments, namely, call money has a rate which fluctuates widely from 1% onwards, as it depends upon the liquidity position of banks. It also depends on the Repo rate, all of which are related to demand and supply for overnight money. The highest rate is probably on the L.C. Bills of 90 days and Non L.C. Bills which may go upto 18-20%. The RBI Bulletin gives various instruments of money market and their rates of return, yields to maturity and other details of duration etc. The main instruments traded in this market which can be seen from the accompanying tables are Treasury bills, Clean and L.C. Bills, commercial paper and certificates of deposits etc. The expertise of management lies in selecting the right mix of assets consistent with his fund position and market conditions, to suit his liabilities mix.

TREASURY BILL INDEX (OF J.P. MORGAN INDIA)

In the money market, the most actively traded and dealt with is the Treasury Bill. It has various maturities and yields vary on daily basis from transaction to transaction.

The Index level compiled on a daily basis by J.P. Morgan India reflects the present value of Rs. 100 invested on April 1, 1996. The indices were compiled for 1 month 3 months and 6 months and they also published a composite Index, which tracks returns on Treasury Bills of all maturities combined. The 30 day annualised holding period return was also compiled by them on a rolling basis daily for 30 days hence. The bench mark yield was published for 1 month, 3 months and 6 months, compiled by linear interpolation of traded Treasury Bill. The above data are useful for investors in Treasury Bills and for yield comparisons and for trading in Treasury Bills for all operators in Money Market.

Base, April 1, 1996 = 100

Treasury Bills Index (for illustration) for April 27, 2000

	Composite Index	*1 Month Index*	*3 Months Index*	*6 Months Index*
Index Level for the day	150.195	144.220	147.821	152.796
Change over previous day	0.048	-0.039	0.018	0.098
30 day Annualised Holding Period Return	12.61%	8.01%	11.74%	15.45%
Bench mark yield	–	7.97%	8.35%	8.66%

Source: E.T., As this is meant for illustration, dates do not matter.

Bond Index, presented below gives returns on govt. bonds in the form Total Return Index and Principal Return Index. These Indices are explained in the footnote and they used to appear in *Economic Times* at one time.

The coupon rate on 10 years bonds is around 13.6%. Zero Coupon Bonds 2000 have given an Implicit yield of 13.1% on the basis of cut off price, accepted by RBI. The current yields on govt. bonds are around 11 to 14% (rounded off) in 1995 and 9 to 13.6% in 1996 and around 10% in 2001, and 8% in 2007 and 7.20 to 8% in 2009.

i-SEC Bond Index (i-BEX)

	Total Return Index	*Change*	*Principal Return Index*	*Change*
24.04.00	2035.31	0.76	1103.85	-0.26
22.04.00	2034.55	—	1104.11	—
01.08.94	1000.00	1035.31	1000.00	103.85

Source: E.T.

Total Return Index: This index tracks the total returns available in the market, it captures both interest payment — accrued and capital gains/losses. An index level of 1049 implies that an investment of Rs. 1000 on base date August 1, 1994 is now worth Rs. 1049 including accrued interest and capital changes.

Principal Return Index: It is the movement of net prices in the market that is, prices quoted in the market exclusive of accrued interest. This could be seen as the mirror image of yield movements. A principal return index of 966 implies a drop of 3.4% in prices (capital losses) since base date."

These are discontinued now. Secondary money market rates for call money, Repo, 91 days T.Bs, short-term gilt edged rates etc., are published, by the RBI.

Commercial Paper (C.P.)

C.P. is a short-term instrument of raising funds by a company. Originally C.P. is carved out of the bank Cash Credit limits and there was surety that on maturity, it would be repaid out of bank credit limit. This link was cut off in Oct. 1994, with the result that the C.P. stands on credit worthiness of the company.

The Commercial Paper is a new money market instrument introduced by the RBI. A company with a net worth of more than Rs. 10 crores (later reduced to Rs. 4 crores) can issue a commercial paper. Its maximum permissible bank finance (MPBF) for working capital requirements should not be less than Rs. 25 crores (later reduced to Rs. 4 crores). It should have a current ratio of 1.33: 1 and a credit rating of excellent (PI) (plus) should be secured from the CRISIL (later relaxed to P_2 only). A company should be listed on one or more of the stock exchanges and can be a FERA company or Indian company@. The maturity period should be 3-6 months and the issue should be for a minimum of Rs. 1 crore (later reduced to Rs. 25 lakhs) and in multiples of Rs. 25 lakhs (later reduced to Rs. 5 lakhs). The effective discount rate for March 2009 was in the range of 6.4 to 12.5% for commercial paper.

The secondary market transactions may be for an amount of Rs. 5 lakhs and multiples. The RBI's prior permission is required for each issue and the general permission is required for each company to enter this market which was later delegated to the banks. The C.P. should be raised only for working capital purposes and should be less than 75% of the cash credit limit of bank's finance to the company. This was made 100% in cases the bank finance limits are more than Rs. 20 crores. In 1996, it was completely delinked from cash credit limits of banks. The banks are authorised to decide on the terms and amount of the C.P. issued by the company. The company will have to bear the expenses of issue, commitment charges, stamp duty, etc. These are not permitted to be underwritten. The NRIs are permitted to invest on a non-repatriation basis. A company may enter into stand by facilities with the bankers to ensure the meeting of the C.P. liabilities of the company. The brokers can enter only in the secondary market trading as the issue is not permitted to be underwritten.

Certificate of Deposits (C.D.)

Only banks can issue the CDs. It is a document of title to a time deposit. It is a bearer certificate and is negotiable in the market. The minimum C.D. should be for Rs. 1 crore, later lowered to Rs. 50 lakhs and in multiples of Rs. 25 lakhs, later lowered to Rs. 10 lakhs.

It is issued by banks against deposits kept by individuals, companies and institutions and is marketable after 45 days and since April 2000 after 15 days only. It can have a tenure of 15 days to 1 year. Banks are to observe CRR and SLR rules. These are permitted up to 1% of average aggregate deposits, later raised to 10% of average aggregate deposits. They are issued on discounting basis. No loans and no buy-backs are permitted and no duplicates are to be issued by banks. Banks cannot discount them or negotiate them.

Certificates of Deposits are permitted to be issued during 1991-92 by the All India Financial Institutions like IDBI, ICICI, IFC, etc. The maturity period for them may range from 1 year to 3 years and the RBI may fix an aggregate limits for them. There is no ceiling interest rate on them. But the effective discount rate for C.Ds in March 2009 was in the range of 6-11.5%.

Participation Certificates

As in the case of certificates of deposit, participation certificates are also issued by banks for periods ranging from 3 months to 6 months or upto a maximum period of one year. All these instruments are as per the recommendations of Vaghul Committee Report on Money Market for the development of Money Market Instruments for participating in the advances by a bank in need of funds by other lender banks and FIs. Two types of such certificates are being developed.

1. 91 day p.cs involving no transfer of the underlying asset risk to the borrower but subject to a ceiling rate of 12.5%.
2. 91 to 180 days p.cs bearing full risk on the underlying asset but not requiring statutory reserves unlike in the above case and subject to a floor rate of 14% (Floor and ceiling rates on all were removed in 1994).

The first one is unsecured debt, but securitised for the purpose of negotiation and development of Secondary Market. The second one which may extend upto one year is more risky and carry a higher return.

Repos Transactions

A major development in the govt. securities market is the introduction of a repurchase facility. This instrument of repurchase Agreement (Repos) is between the RBI and the Primary dealers and commercial banks, started since December 1992.

@ Since withdrawn during the financial reforms in 1992.

This is an asset for short-term liquidity management of banks. The period of Repos has stabilised at 14 days since August 1993. The rates on Repos depend on the market conditions and varied from 5% to 11.5% in 1993-94 and from 14 to 25% in 1995-96 and around 6% in 2001 and 6.34% in 2007. The auction Repo rate for March 2009 was 5% and Reverse Repo rate was 3.5%

The Repos can also be effected between banks and financial institutions and among banks themselves. The instrument has since become popular with banks. The RBI stipulated that it should be for a minimum period of 3 days since Spetember 1995 so that it is not used for call money purposes.

A new line to reverse Repo facility was opened to the DFHI and STCI (Securities Trading Corporation of India) by way of liquidity support from the RBI. This enabled RBI to intervene in the market to arrest the excesses. This was started in 1994-95, in the form of repos and Reverse repos.

MANAGEMENT IN MONEY MARKET

Conversion of cash into short-term instruments of Money Market, utilise the surpluses of cash for earning positive return and conversion back into cash to meet liquidity needs is the main objective of Money Market operations. The management of such activities of investment has to balance between the opposing objectives of liquidity needs on the one hand and income earnings on the other. This requires expertise and experience. Besides the selection of proper instruments among Treasury Bills, Commercial Bills, Intercorporate Investments, commercial paper etc., involves a critical choice, as that should enable the manager to maximise returns without sacrificing the needs of liquidity. Should he use his funds in bill discounting, investment in commercial paper or other avenues of Money Market and in what proportion? In this selection process, he should have a clear direction of the period for which he can spare the funds, risk he can take and the return he can expect or aim at. The bankers manage their CRR and daily cash balances by resort to Money Market, call money or Repos etc, as the need arises.

In the process of management of funds, the Finance Manager thus has to have a perspective of

1. Return aimed at
2. Risk prepared to take and
3. Time duration of investment.

Money Market provides a buffer between cash or liquidity and long-term high return investments in the Stock and Capital Market. The Cash inflows due to maturing Money Market instruments are to be adjusted to synchronise with outflows, as projected by the funds Manager.

SECURITIES TRADING CORPORATION OF INDIA LTD. (STCI)

The RBI has set up the STCI in May 1994, with an authorised capital of Rs. 500 crores. Its objective is to promote a secondary market in Govt. securities. So far this work was partially attended to by DFHI, but to give full fillup to Govt. securities market, the STCI was set up, while the DFHI would continue to operate in Money Market. STCI is referred to here as it is on an adjunct to DFHI.

The STCI started operations in June 1994 with a paid up capital of Rs. 125 crores. During 1994-95, the first year of its operations, its operation extended to Govt. dated securities in Treasury bills, in borrowing and lending in Call and Notice Money. DFHI also operates in call funds, Treasury bills, in addition to commercial paper, commercial bills, C.D.s, and term deposits etc.

PORTFOLIO MANAGEMENT

In Portfolio Management also, the manager has to keep a proportion of his funds in Money Market Instruments. This proportion depends on the objectives of the fund, growth versus regular income or various combinations of these objectives. Once the proportion allotted to Money Market Instruments is chosen, next, the major task is the allocation of the allotted funds into various instruments within Money Market depending upon their risk-return characteristics.

The basic principles of management would apply in respect of investment in Money Market also. Cost effectiveness and maximisation of returns are the objectives that the management aims at. These objectives can be achieved by a proper choice of the instruments bearing in mind their characteristics.

The Money Market Instruments are classified under the category of government instruments, of maturity upto one year, inter-bank call money, corporate instruments, P.S.U. bonds and UTI Units etc. The risk on Govt. and semi Govt. instruments is lower, but their return is also low compared with the investments in the Corporate Sector. Thus, Investment Managers aiming at higher returns concentrate on bill discounting, commercial paper, certificate of deposits and inter-corporate investment. But a judicious combination of investment in call money for higher returns and in the Treasury Bills for quick liquidity would be necessary for a balanced investment. Besides he has to balance the maturities of asset instruments with the liabilities falling due and secure a proper asset liability mix for the company.

CHAPTER 13

The Securities and Exchange Board of India (SEBI)

Introduction

The Government has set up the Securities & Exchange Board of India (SEBI) in April, 1988. For more than there years, it had no statutary powers. Its interim functions during the period were *(i)* To collect information and advice the Government on matters relating to Stock and Capital Markets *(ii)* Licensing and regulation of merchant banks, mutual funds etc. *(iii)* To prepare the legal drafts for regulatory and development role of SEBI and *(iv)* To perform any other functions as may be entrusted to it by the Government.

The need for setting up independent Govt. agency to regulate and develop the Stock and Capital Market in India as in many developed countries was recognised since the Sixth Five Year Plan was launched (1985) when some major industrial policy changes like opening up of the economy to outside world and greater role to the Private Sector were initiated. The rampant malpractices noticed in the Stock and Capital Market stood in the way of infusing confidence of investors which is necessary for mobilisation of larger quantity of funds from the public and help the growth of the industry.

The malpractices were noticed in the case of companies, merchants bankers and brokers who are all operating in the Capital Market. The need to curb these malpractices and to promote healthy Capital Market in India was felt. The security industry in India has to develop on the right lines for which a competent Govt. agency as in U.K. (SIB) or in U.S.A. (SEC) is needed.

As referred to earlier, malpractices have been reported in both the primary market and secondary market. A few examples of malpractices in the primary market are as follows:

(*a*) Too many self styled Investment Advisers and Consultants.

(*b*) Grey Market or unofficial premiums on the new issues.

(*c*) Manipulation of market prices before new issues are floated.

(*d*) Delay in allotment letters or refund orders or in despatch of share certificates or in Demat form of allotment now.

(*e*) Delay in listing and commencement of trading in shares.

A few examples of malpractices in the Secondary Market are as follows:

(*a*) Lack of transperancy in the trading operations and prices charged to clients.

(*b*) Poor services due to delay in passing contract notes or not passing contract notes, at all.

(*c*) Delay in making payments to clients or in giving delivery of shares.

(*d*) Persistence of odd lots and refusal of companies to stop this practice of allotting shares in odd lots, which was obviated by Demat form of allotment.

(*e*) Insider trading by agents of companies or brokers rigging and manipulating prices, and collusion of brokers and bankers etc.

(*f*) Take over bids to destabilise management.

Objectives

The SEBI has been entrusted with both the regulatory and developmental functions. The objectives of SEBI are as follows:

(*a*) Investor protection, so that there is a steady flow of savings into the Capital Market.

(*b*) Ensuring the fair practices by the issuers of securities, namely, companies so that they can raise resources at least cost.

(*c*) Promotion of efficient services by brokers, merchant bankers and other intermediaries so that they become competitive and professional.

Pending the legislative sanction to SEBI it carried out the functions of supervisory and advisory body of the Govt. It has initiated the basis for control and regulation of the market, arranged for the licensing of merchant banks, mutual funds etc. and performed the advisory functions to the Govt.

The legislation giving powers to SEBI was passed on 4th April 1992 in the form of the Securities and Exchange Board of India Act to protect the interests of investors in securities and to promote the development of and to regulate the securities market and for matters connected therewith or incidental thereto.

Leaving aside Chapter I of the Act dealing with preliminaries and definitions, Chapter II deals with establishment, incorporation, administration and management of the Boards of Directors etc. Chapter III provides for the transfer of assets and liabilities of the existing Boards to the new Board, under the Act.

Investor protection is the major responsibility of the SEBI. For this purpose, the draft prospectus of the companies is scrutinised for full and fair disclosures and guidelines have been given in the form of a code of conduct for all the players in the capital market. Merchant bankers are held responsible for fair disclosures of the companies in the new issues market. Prospectus is graded and penal points are awarded for any lapses of the merchant banks. Similarly, licensing and registration of all intermediaries in the capital market including underwriters, registrars, portfolio managers, etc. was also completed. In particular registration and regulation of all brokers and sub-brokers of stock market, control of insider trading, inspection and audit of stock exchanges and their members were taken up in full swing. The SEBI had spread out its powers of regulation to all corners of the primary and secondary markets.

The substantive part of the powers and functions of the Board is however, incorporated in Chapter IV. Thus, Section 11 of the Act specifies the functions as follows:

Regulatory	Developmental
(*a*) Registration of brokers and sub-brokers and other players in the market.	(*a*) Investor education.
(*b*) Registration of collective Investment Schemes and Mutual Funds.	(*b*) Training of Intermediaries.
(*c*) Regulation of stock exchanges and other S.R.O.s, merchant banks, Portfolio Managers etc.	(*c*) Promotion of fair practices and a code of conduct for all S.R.O.s.
(*d*) Prohibition of all fraudulent and unfair trade practices.	(*d*) Conducting Research and Publishing information useful to all market participants.
(*e*) Controlling Insider Trading and take over bids and imposing penalties for such practices.	

Chapter V deals with registration of Stock brokers, sub-brokers, Transfer agents etc. on which action was already taken by the SEBI, since May 1992. The members of recognised Stock Exchanges and their authorised sub-brokers operating as on 21st Feb. 1992 were already registered with the SEBI. The SEBI has got powers under the Act to collect information, call for special audit and impose fines, penalties etc. The activities of SEBI are financed by grants from the Govt. in addition of fees, charges etc. made by SEBI. The fund called the SEBI General Fund, is set up to which all grants, fees, charges etc. are credited. This fund is used to meet the expenses of the Board and to pay salaries of staff and remuneration to officers, members of the Board etc.

In Chapter VII of the Act, the Central Govt. has taken powers to issue directions to the SEBI Board, to supercede the Board if necessary and to call for returns and reports etc., as and when necessary. The final powers over SEBI rests with the Govt., as can be seen from Sections 20 and 28. An appeal lies with the Central Govt. from any decision of the SEBI by the aggrieved party under Section 20. The Section 28 gives the power to the Central Government to exempt any person or class of persons from the operation of sub-Section (1) of Section 12, dealing with the registration of intermediaries. The Central Government has also powers to give any guidelines or to make regulations and rules for SEBI and its operations. The Securities Appellate Board was set up as an authority for appeals against the decisions of SEBI.

SEBI has spread its network of control to all intermediaries in the market. Many more powers under SC(R) Act were delegated by the Govt. to the SEBI. Legislation on Amendments to SEBI Act and on Insider Trading was effected. In September, 1994, SEBI has been delegated concurrent powers with the government under many provisions of SC(R) Act such as recognition and derecognition of Stock Exchanges. By an ordinance passed in January, 1995, SEBI got more powers on companies, intermediaries and Stock Exchanges and their members. SEBI can now impose penalties and file suits for insider trading, violation of listing agreement and failure to redress the investor grievances and takeover bids and violations of its guidelines.

SEBI Guidelines

SEBI has issued guidelines from time to time which run into volumes and have been published as handouts separately. Such guidelines are issued separately for New Issues market, Stock market, Mutual Funds, Merchant banks, Registrars and transfer agents, Underwriters, Brokers, sub-brokers, Portfolio Managers, etc. Thus, the SEBI guidelines encompass all the intermediaries in the Capital Market, and a code of conduct is also laid down for each category separately. The guidelines and the code of conduct are to be observed under the ken of SEBI and lapses are subject to penal points. In fact all the intermediaries have to seek first the licence and registration for operating in the capital market. The criteria and eligibility requirements for each category are separately set out by the SEBI. During 1994 even FFIs and Foreign Broker firms were licensed by SEBI to operate in Indian capital market. In view of the voluminous material involved in these regulations of SEBI, a brief outline is attempted in respect of major reforms involved.

Reforms in the New Issues Market

(1) Free entry and free pricing of new issues in the capital market subject to observance of some guidelines.

(2) Minimum public offer of 25% of paid up capital to be eligible for listing on stock exchanges out of which half is reserved for investors applying for Rs. 10,000 and less.

(3) Minimum subscription by Promoters and Directors at 25% for issues less than Rs. 100 crores and 20% for paid up capital of more than Rs. 100 crores.

(4) Preferential allotment to OCBs and FFIs is subject to a ceiling of 30% later reduced to 20% and a lock in period of 5 years which was removed in 1996.

(5) FFIs and foreign security firms are allowed to operate both in the new issue market and stock market but through Indian brokers.

(6) Reservation of quotas under public subscription can be had up to 20% for FIs and Mutual Funds, 24% for FFIs and OCBs which were withdrawn in 1996 and 10% for employees. Merchant bankers are given now a quota of 5% in the issues that they manage.

(7) Stock Invest was introduced as a mode of making payments replacing cash and cheque for applying for shares and debentures. This would save loss of interest for investors from the time of applications to the time of allotment.

(8) Private placement of non-transferable shares of promoters and directors was prohibited as also the sale of shares under discount to institutions and mutual funds etc.

(9) Minimum number of shares to be applied for was raised to 500 from 100 shares earlier, so as to reduce the workload of the companies with large number of applications for smaller lots, although this would hit the small investors with a few hundreds, for investment. This minimum was lowered to 200 shares in 1996 as against 500 shares earlier.

(10) Allotment on a proportional basis was introduced in the event of oversubscription so as to reduce the evil of multiple applications. No amount of oversubscription can be retained by the companies. The SEBI representative will be present at the time allotment to prevent any malpractices by companies. In the event of undersubscription of less than 90% of the public issue, the full application amounts have to be returned within 120 days from the opening date of subscription.

Details of SEBI Guidelines — for Capital Market

(1) SEBI guidelines were issued after the repeal of the CIC Act whereby the CCI guidelines became out of date. New guidelines by SEBI were issued starting from the month of June, 1992. Some CCI guidelines were still retained, as in the case of those for premium fixation.

(2) *Guidelines for New Issues Made by New Companies:* They have to be issued at par. Free pricing is permitted only if the new company is promoted by the existing company with not less than 50% of equity.

(3) New issues made by Private Limited Companies and Closely held companies can be made by free pricing, for listing purposes if such companies have had three years of track record of consistent profitability out of last 5 years. Not less than 20% of equity is to be offered to the public, in such cases.

(4) Public issues by existing listed companies can be made through free pricing, if they are further issues and if they are disclosed in the prospectus. The NAV and the market price have to be considered for the last 3 years. The companies with foreign holding wishing to enhance the limit upto 51% will have to get the prices approved in the general body meeting by a special resolution under Sec. 81(A) of the Companies Act, and subject to RBI approval.

(5) *Listing of Shares on the O.T.C.:* If the new issues are made through OTC, normal guidelines will apply if the sponsor is not taking any share. If the shares are taken by the sponsor, subsequent offer to the public may be made at such a price as the sponsor may deem fit. The promoters should retain 25% quota with a lock in period of 5 years, the sponsor should act as market maker for a period of atleast 3 years and also find another market maker for compulsory market making. This condition was relaxed later to encourage OTC Listing.

(6) Underwriting is optional if the issue is made to the public and should not include reserved or preferencial quota or employees' quota. If the subscription is not up to 90% of the total issue from the public including contribution of underwriters, the public should be refunded of their subscription within 120 days from the date of opening the issue. The compulsory underwriting provision was also waived for smaller issues.

(7) *Composite Issues:* Issues to the public by existing company can be priced differently as compared to the rights issued to shareholders.

(8) *F.C.D. & P.C.D.:* The issues of F.C.D.s with a conversion period of more than 36 months will not be permissible unless conversion is optional. In case F.C.D.s are convertible after 18 months, credit rating is compulsory; credit rating is now made compulsory for all issues made to public, other than equity; the D.R.R. has to be created in such issues with a maturity of more than 18 months. In case, the non-convertible portion of the P.C.D. is to be rolled over, non-maturing debenture holders should have option to withdraw from the scheme.

(9) *New Financial Instruments:* The terms and conditions of the new instruments such as Deep Discount Bonds, debentures with warrants and secured premium notes etc. should be disclosed clearly so that the investor can assess the risk and return scenario of the instrument.

(10) *Reservation in Issues:* The unreserved portion offered to public should not be less than the minimum required for listing purposes. Preferential allotment can be made to promoters, Companies, shareholders of those companies, NRIs, Employees and Associate Companies of the same group. The allotment shall be subject to a lock in period of three years, if it is made on firm basis, outside public issue.

(11) *Deployment of Issue Proceeds:* Where the total proceeds exceed Rs. 250 crores, the company will voluntarily disclose the arrangements made to utilise proceeds. When the total issue proceeds exceed Rs. 500 crores, there is need for making compulsory disclosure and for the financial institutions to monitor the deployment of funds, to the stock exchanges.

(12) *Minimum Interval between Two Issues:* 12 months should elapse between the public or rights issue and Bonus issue. The promoters should bring in their share of the capital before the public issue.

(13) *Employees' Stock Option Scheme:* The reservation for employees should not be more than 10% at present and this quota is non-transferable for 3 years and subject to a maximum allotment of 200 shares per employee, and the lock in was removed later.

(14) *Lock in Period:* The Lock in period for Promoters' quota is 5 years and the lock in period for preferencial allotment for associates and friends is 3 years.

(15) *Bonus Shares:* Bonus issues are to be made out of free reserves, the share premium collected in cash, Development Rebate Reserves and Investment Allowance Reserve. Contingent liabilities disclosed in the audited accounts should be deducted from net profits for calculation of residual reserves. Residual reserves after the bonus issue should be atleast 40% of the increased paid-up capital. 30% of the average profits before tax for the previous 3 years should yield a rate of dividend of 10% on the expanded capital base. Reserves out of revaluation should not be used for bonus payment. Bonus issue cannot be made in lieu of dividends and if there are partly paid up shares, no bonus issue is permitted. Expanded paid-up capital after bonus issue should not exceed authorised share capital. When a company has P.C.D. or F.C.D., pending conversion, no bonus issue can be made unless this right is kept open to the holders of F.C.D. and P.C.D. falling due for conversion within 12 months.

(16) *Debenture Issues:* All debentures which have a life of more than 18 months should have a D.R.R. created by company out of profits. D.R.R. should be created only for non-convertible portion of the debentures. Contribution to D.R.R. should commence from the date of commercial production and when there are profits after tax, interest and depreciation. The D.R.R. will be considered as a part of the general reserves for payment of the bonus issues. D.R.R. should be created and maintained at 50% of the amount of the debentures before repayment starts. Some liability should have already been redeemed by the company. D.R.R. and the creation of Debenture Trust are necessary only if the debentures have a maturity period exceeding 18 months. The Lead Institution for each issue should monitor the use of debenture funds either from the working capital or from the project finance. The SEBI now insists on prior licensing of debenture Trustees; Trust deed should be ready within 6 months from the date of allotment.

(17) By a recent amendment to Listing Agreement, the Companies have been asked to provide unabridged Balance Sheet to shareholders. The companies have to give the disposition of the funds raised in public issues and compare the actuals with targets every six months, when they present balance sheet to investors.

(18) By another amendment through listing clause 49, good corporate governance of most listed companies was made compulsory.

SEBI Reforms on Stock Exchanges

The SEBI regulation of stock exchanges and their members had started as early as February 1992 and the reforms later introduced have been on a continuous basis. It was started with the licensing and registration of brokers and sub-brokers in the recognised stock exchanges. This was later extended to underwriters, portfolio managers and other categories of players in the stock market including foreign securities firms, FIIs, OCBs, FFIs, Debenture Trustees, Collecting bankers, etc.

The other reforms are briefly summarised below:

(1) Compulsory audit and inspection of stock exchanges and their member brokers and their accounts.

(2) Transperancy in the prices and brokerage charged by brokers by showing them in their contract notes.

(3) Broker accounts and client accounts are to be kept separate and clients' money are to be separately maintained in bank's accounts and the same to be reported to the stock exchanges.

(4) Board of Directors of stock exchanges has to be reconstituted so as to include non-brokers, public representatives, and Govt. respresentatives to the extent of 50% of the total number of members.

(5) Capital adequacy norms have been laid down for members of various stock exchanges separately and depending on their turnover of trade and other factors.

(6) Guidelines have been laid down for dealings of FFIs and Foreign broker firms in the Indian stock exchanges through Indian brokers.

(7) Badla and carry forward business which was banned on major exchanges early in 1995 was reintroduced in October 1996 and renewal business was also subject to close scrutiny, for cash shares.

(8) New guidelines for corporate members have been laid down with limited liability of directors and opening up of their membership to more than one stock exchange without the limiting requirement of experience of five years in one exchange, as imposed earlier.

The term "Investor Protection" is a wide term encompassing various measures designed to protect the investors from malpractices of companies, brokers, merchant bankers, issue managers, Registrars of new issues, etc. "Investors Beware" should be the watchword of all programmes for mobilisation of savings for investment. As all investments have some risk element, this risk factor should be borne in mind by the investors and they should take all precautions to protect their interests in the first place. If caution is thrown to the winds and they invest in any venture without a proper assessment of the risk, they have only to blame themselves. But if there are malpractices by companies, brokers, etc., they have every reason to complain. Such grievances have been increasing in number in more recent years.

The complaints of investors come from two major sources:

(*i*) against member broker of Stock Exchanges;

(*ii*) against companies listed for trading on the Stock Exchanges.

Besides, there can be complaints against sub-brokers, agents, merchant bankers, issue managers, etc., which cannot be entertained by the stock exchanges as per their rules. These are now entertained by SEBI, which has been given power to penalise and take legal action, where needed.

Complaints against Members

Investors have complaints against brokers regarding the price, quantity etc. at which transactions are put through, defective delivery or delayed delivery, delayed payment or non-payment etc., non-settlement of vyaj badla dues, non-payment of agreed brokerage to authorised assistants, etc. In the event of default of a member broker, the dues of clients are also to be looked into.

There is a Grievance Cell in all Stock Exchanges which attends to investor complaints. Of the total, nearly 95% are against companies and they are more difficult to settle, as many companies do not attend to the complaints promptly despite reminders and warnings by the stock exchange, in view of the fact that penal powers of the Exchange are limited.

The grievance procedure in respect of complaints against members is as follows:

(*a*) Joint meeting of members *vis-a-vis* the clients for an amicable settlement.

(*b*) Arbitration proceedings by the committee under the bye-laws.

(*c*) Special committee appointed by the Executive Director for settlement.

(*d*) Disciplinary proceedings including warnings, fines, penalties, etc. particularly in cases of fraud, cheating, etc. by the members.

Grievances Cell

Complaints against members were in the nature of non-payment of sale proceeds, non-settlement of accounts etc. Of the total complaints against members, about 85% settled during the year, itself.

Complaints against Companies

The complaints against companies are in the nature of non-receipt of allotment letters, refund orders, non-receipt of dividends, interest etc., delay in transfer of shares and in splitting and consolidation. The clearance of these complaints is also attended to by the Cell by writing to the companies, follow-up telexes, etc. and finally by warning to delist the companies concerned. But the clearance of these complaints is slow due to the non-compliance or slow compliance by the companies to the references made by the Cell. The powers of the Stock Exchange are limited to warnings and delisting of shares and as such compliance by the companies was poor. SEBI has now powers to penalise companies violating the listing norms.

Investors' Protection Fund

The Investors Profection Fund is constituted by the Stock Exchanges to safeguard the interests of the investor clients from defaults of the stock brokers. The Fund is financed by way of a levy on the turnover of members and from out of the listing fees, earmarked by the Exchanges.

The Fund is being administered by the Stock Exchange for the benefit of the clients of the member brokers, in case of a default of a member. The compensation of any single client is, however, limited to Rs. 2 lakhs in BSE which varies from exchange to exchange. When a member is declared a defaulter, the net assets in the hands of the Defaulter's Committee after defraying costs, charges, expenses, etc., relating to the realisation of the assets will be used to meet the claims of the Exchange, clearing house and then the admitted claims of the members of the Exchange against the defaulter. After meeting all these claims, if anything is left over, the claims of the clients of the defaulting member will be satisfied. If nothing is left over, the genuine claims of clients can be met from the Customer's Protection Fund. This is the same procedure adopted by other Exchanges also where this Fund was set up.

Investors Beware

Investors in stock and capital markets need a word of caution. Firstly, these investments are more risky, returns are uncertain and share values are subject to wide fluctuations. Secondly, such investments require an art and expertise to pick up the right stocks, failing which the investors would burn their fingers. Thirdly, the players in the market, namely, brokers and issuers of securities, namely, companies, are not rated high for their honesty with the result that investor complaints against stockbrokers and companies have been increasing over the years. It would, therefore, be necessary for investors to prepare themselves well before entering this market.

Specific Goals

The investor should be clear in his objectives of income, capital appreciation, short-term gains or long-term gains, etc. He should have made already enough investment in housing and for a regular income to meet his minimum needs and comforts of life. Even if all the stock market investments are wiped out due to a market crash continued bearishness as in 1997 and 1998, the investor should not be a pauper on the streets. Besides, if the investor spends sleepless nights on the fall of share prices, he cannot be a good stock market investor. Nor can he gloat over a sporadic success and be a spendthrift.

Pre-requisites of Investor

The investor should have abundant common sense and a strong heart to withstand the vicissitudes of fortune. He need not be a holder of high academic degrees like an MBA from Harvard or a finance graduation from the Wharton School. Nor does he need to have hereditary characteristics or family tradition of investment. The only requirement he should have is abundant logic and common sense and strong nerves and develop the art of investment on a scientific basis.

Although Peter Lynch[1] calls it an art and is skeptical of the application of academic scientific theories, the fact remains that he attributes the success of investors to personal preparation, hard work involved in the collection of relevant information, knowledge and research and analysis. This shows that it is expertise combined with intuition that plays a vital role in this game on the Dalal Street. Unlike a chess game which requires intelligence or a football game which needs physical prowess, the stock market game requires both an art and a scientific technique.

1. Peter Lynch, "One up on Wall Street" Penguin Books, 1990.

Preparing to Invest

Investors desiring to invest in stocks require a lot of preparation. The weak-hearted and risk-averter should first make an entry by buying only debentures, particularly convertible debentures of good companies, or subscribe to new issues of promising and well-established companies. After sufficient study and preparation, the investor should act like rag-pickers in the market, picking up scrips on a selective basis. That means selected companies from promising and growing industries should be picked up after collection of all relevant information and data on the companies and a scientific analysis of their fundamentals. The undervalued scrips should be purchased at the right time with the help of technical analysis. Rumours and advice of so-called consultants have to be carefully scrutinized. As the market investment is both a science and an art, it requires both expertise and intuition. There is need for prior preparation and a lot of home work before investments are undertaken. A high degree of caution and planning is necessary but the scientific basis and knowledge are to be acquired by a proper study.

Balance Sheet Study

Investors entering the stock market should also get into the habit of detailed and careful study of the balance sheets of companies in which they wish to invest. Similarly, they should examine carefully the detailed prospectus before subscribing to the new issues of companies. The habit of relying on rumours, or advice of brokers or friends should be replaced by the habit of self study of balance sheets and prospectuses of companies. The factors which should be looked into and ratios that should be analysed and the aspects that should be examined are set out under fundamental analysis.

Choice of a Broker

Investors should as far as possible deal only with registered members of recognised stock exchanges. In places where there are no stock exchanges, they may deal with those sub-brokers who have connections with registered brokers. An honest and dependable broker is to be chosen through proper introduction and orders should be placed with him in a proper manner with limits on prices at which sales or purchases can be made. As and when a transaction is completed, he should insist on a contract note in due time.

Protection in the New Issues Market

The main source of information on which investors depend in the new issues market is the prospectus, which should contain correct statements of facts. Any false statements, fraud, etc. are punishable under the Companies Act. Under Section 56 of the Companies Act, the Directors are subject to civil liability for any misstatement of facts or untrue statements.

Under Sections 63 and 68 of the Companies Act, the Directors are also liable criminally for any fraud of false statements in the prospectus. Companies' liability for misstatements arises from untrue statements and statements which are material for investors and particulars on which investors depend to make investments. The directors or promoters of the company are thus subject to both criminal and civil liability under the Act for any misstatements in the prospectus. Even so, the small investors cannot afford to go to court and, should therefore, carefully read and examine the prospectus for viability of the project and marketability of the product and for the integrity and dependability of the promoters. The investors have also a responsibility to assess the prospects and the risk involved in the project before making any investment.

Protection for Fixed Deposits

Section 58A of the Companies Act deals with the subject of Fixed Deposits. There are some rules which apply to non-banking companies, private and public limited companies, who wish to raise deposits from the public. The Stock Exchange and SEBI have however no Jurisdiction on the company deposits.

No deposits can be invited from investors or the public unless the companies follow the rules and guidelines made by the Department of Company Affairs in consultation with the RBI. Interest rates, maturity period of deposits, and the amount permissible to be raised by the companies are all given in the form of guidelines by the Department of Company Affairs. The companies have to follow these guidelines while accepting deposits from the public. Renewal and repayment are also regulated by the Companies Act and the rules framed by the Department of Company Affairs. When a company fails to repay the deposit, the depositor can complain to the Company Law Board (CLB) in the specified form duly filled in, together with the fees for non-payment of interest or non-repayment of deposit. The order of the CLB is final and binding on the company and the company has to comply with it. Any non-compliance with the order of the CLB or violation of the provisions of the company law would invite penalty of imprisonment and fine. This provision however, does not apply to sick companies. The business of NBFCs is now being controlled by RBI after they are registered with the RBI, since Jan. 1999.

Guidelines to Investors

1. Deal with a registered member of the stock exchange. If you are dealing with a sub-broker, make sure that all bills and contracts are made in the name of a registered broker.
2. Insist that all your deals are done in the trading ring, or electronically recorded.
3. Give specific orders to buy or sell within the fixed price limits and/or time periods within which orders have to be executed.
4. Insist on contract notes to be passed on to you on the dates, when the orders are executed.
5. Make sure that your deal is registered with the stock exchange in a souda Block Book or recorded electronically. In the case of a dispute, this will help trace the details of the deal easily.
6. Collect a settlement table from the stock exchange mentioning the pay-in and pay-out days. Each stock exchange has its own trading periods which are called settlements. All transactions done within this period are settled at the end of it. All payments for shares bought and their deliveries take place on the pay-in day. An awareness of pay-in and pay-out days is useful when a broker tries to make excuses.
7. Keep separate records of dealings in specified shares (Group A) and non-specified shares (Group B_1, and B_2). The settlement for each is on different days.
8. Execute periodic settlements of dues and delivery of shares to avoid accumulation of transactions.
9. Insist on delivery. If the company returns your papers and shares with objections, contact your broker immediately.
10. Ensure that shares bought are transferred in your name before the company's book closure date. This is necessary to make sure that you receive benefits like dividend, interest and bonus shares. All companies have a book closure date on which the list of shareholders in the company is finalised.
11. Complain if the broker does not deliver the shares bought in your name. Proceed to contact another broker with the bill/contract given to you by the earlier broker, and the Exchange authorities and the latter will purchase the shares on your behalf. In such an event, the first broker will have to pay the difference in price.
12. Do not sell shares that are not transferred in your name after the book closure as these are not valid in the market.
13. Do not sell/deal in shares where any one of the holders has passed away. In cases where the holder has died, a succession certificate is necessary. In cases where one of the joint shareholders passes away, the surviving holder should send the shares along with the death certificate to the company. Only after the name of the deceased has been deleted from the shares, can they be transferred.
14. Do not expect the money for shares to come immediately. It will take at least a fortnight at present from the date of transaction.
15. Unless you have a special arrangement with the broker, do not expect the adjustment of purchases and sales against one another. One pays first and receives later.
16. Do not take delays or harassment lying down. You have to complain to the Grievance Cell of the stock exchange or the Securities and Exchange Board of India (SEBI) in case of delay or harassment.

Legislative Protection to Investors

The Companies Act and the Listing Agreement of the Stock Exchanges provide certain safeguards to investors. The normal complaints against companies and the protection available are listed below:

Complaints	Legislative Provision	Relief Provided
1. Delay in refund of excess application money or allotment letters	Section 73 of the Companies Act as amended by Amendment Act of 1988	Payment of interest for the delayed period beyond 30 days from the closure of subscription list at the rate of 15%.
2. Delay in transfer of shares	Section 111 of the Companies Act	A time limit of two months provided in the Act for effecting transfer. As per the Listing Agreement, the time limit is only one month from the lodgment of shares.
3. Refusal to transfer shares	Section 22(A) of SC(R) Act. This section lists the reasons for which transfer of shares can be refused	Transfer can be refused only for specific and valid reasons given in the Act and not otherwise.
4. Problem of odd lots	Listing Agreement provides for issue of certificates in marketable lots and avoidance of odd lots. Demat form of trading and transfer gets over the odd lot problem.	Need for consolidation of odd lots and ensuring the issue of shares only in marketable lots through conversion of debentures or rights issue, provision of an odd lot trading session and listing out brokers willing to trade in odd lots.
5. Takeover bids	New Clauses of 40(A) and 40(B) of Listing Agreement SEBI Rules on take over Bids	Purchases or acquisition of shares beyond 5% to be notified to the stock exchange. Acquisition beyond 10% puts an obligation on the transferor and transferee and intermediary to notify the Stock Exchange and the public and offer to the other shareholders of the company to buy at their price or the highest market price during the preceding six months.
6. Insider trading, rigging and other malpractices	SEBI (Insider Trading) Regulation 1992	The investors have to guard themselves regarding the price and their investment.
7. Delay and non-payment of interest/fixed deposits by companies	Section 58(A) of the Companies Act	Complain to the Company Law Board.
8. Delay and non-payment of dues or non-delivery of shares, etc. by brokers	Rules, Bye-laws, etc. of the Stock Exchange	Complain to the Grievance Cell of the concerned Stock Exchange and to SEBI.

CRISIL Rating and Investor Protection

Investor should also be familiar with the ratings given by the Credit Rating Agencies for protecting their interests. The CRISIL ratings are given only for debt instruments of companies, namely, Commercial Papers (CP), debentures, bonds and fixed deposits. Since early 1992, the ratings of Investment Information and Credit Rating Agency (ICRA) are also used by companies. CARE is another agency in the credit rating business, operating since 1993. Duff & Phelps is another private agency set up in 1996 for rating purposes and the latest addition to credit rating agencies is Fitch Ratings India Ltd. These are given on a voluntary basis and may be publicised or not, depending upon the company's own perception of the impact of these on the investors. The ratings in use by the companies are published by the CRISIL in their "CRISIL Rating Scan." The companies use them only when the ratings are favourable to them and when they are making only public offer for deposits or debentures, etc. The investors should examine these symbols with regard to their benefits and their implication. Since a rating given can be revised upwards or downwards, the investors should keep a watch on any such revisions. Unfortunately, the CRISIL itself would not publicise them for the benefit of the investors as it is a private and autonomous organisation and is under no obligation to do so. The SEBI guidelines now insist that all companies should get these ratings and publicise them compulsorily, if they are borrowing through issue of debentures. Many companies accepting fixed deposits are also using these CRISIL ratings. Rating of company deposits is made compulsory under the New Companies Bill 1993 and by RBI in the case of NBFCs. The SEBI had brought these agencies under its control through giving Directives and a Code of Conduct.

The implications of the ratings used are as follows:

For Debentures, simple 'A' and 'B' are used; for preference shares, "Pf" is prefixed. For fixed deposits and short-term instruments, "F" and "P" are prefixed.

Debenture Ratings		*Implication*
Triple A — (AAA)	—	Highest Safety
Double A — (AA)	—	High Safety
Single A — (A)	—	Adequate Safety
Triple B — (BBB)	—	Moderate Safety
Double B — (BB)	—	Inadequate Safety
B, C & D	—	High risk and default-prone
Fixed Deposits Ratings		
F Triple A — (FAAA)	—	Highest Safety
F Double A — (FAA)	—	High Safety
F Single A — (FA)	—	Adequate Safety

FB, FC and FD are inadequate, high-risk and default-prone instruments.

SEBI ON IPOs

The SEBI has announced in Sept. 1999 that I.T. companies are subject to a minimum public offer of only 10% of the issued capital instead of 25% for other companies. But I.T. companies have to offer atleast Rs. 50 crores or give out atleast 20 lakh shares. This relaxtion is not applicable to Telecom and Multimedia sectors as they already enjoy some concessions under Infrastructure industries. Thus, Infrastructure Companies get exemption from minimum public offer of 25% of the Issued Capital. It is not mandatory for them to secure 90% of minimum subscription before closing the issue and allotment of shares.

The requirement of 5 shareholders for every Rs. 1 lakh of offer is waived for them. But all their public issues should be an Demat form.

The number of Mandatory collection centres for public issues of above Rs. 10 crores was reduced to 4 metro centres in addition to the places where the Regional Stock Exchange is situated. This is the minimum requirement and companies can have as many collection centres as they want. Besides, the threshold limit for issues that can be sold through book building route is reduced to Rs. 25 crores from Rs. 100 crores fixed earlier. This was intended to encourage the use of this route by the merchant bankers and reduce the cost of issues. The fixed par value of Rs. 10 per share is now dropped and companies can have any value of share.

The SEBI has earmarked companies whose shares have to be traded and settled in electronic book entry form from 4th January 2000. The demat form of issue of initial public offers of new issues is made compulsory (from the date to be fixed by the SEBI). This is made compulsory for all companies, so as to encourage demat form of trading through electronic book entry system.

To develop the debt market, in collaboration with the RBI, a committee was appointed, as per the SEBI announcement early in Feb. 2000. The SEBI also announced that Registrars of new issues under I.P.O could also undertake the depository functions for those issues.

Some of the Reforms in the primary market were referred to earlier in this book. The major reforms relate to registration and enforcement of a code of conduct on all the intermediaries in the market, extension of regulation to UTI along with all mutual funds in the private and public sectors and to Money Market Mutual Funds which were so far regulated by the RBI and enforcement of all regulations on venture capital funds on par with all mutual funds and on FIIs and FFIs along with the powers exercised by the RBI under the FEMA. Even credit rating Agencies are brought under the Guidelines of the SEBI.

New issues under IPOs are brought compulsorily under the fold of Demat form of allotment in some cases. The SEBI has successfully reduced the time gap for allotment of new issues to 30 days and enforced stricter surveillance on end use of funds raised through public offer, reduced the mal practices in the new issue market, such as price rigging and insider trading etc. The problems of bad delivery, and delays in transfer of shares and odd lots etc. were solved by making the trading as well as transfers in demat form of electronic book entry.

SEBI IN THE NEW MILLENNIUM

By beginning of the new millennium in 2000 SEBI has strengthened and established itself as an all powerful regulatory body for the capital market, all intermediaries in it, SROs, stock Exchanges, listed companies, Venture Funds, Mutual Funds including M.M.F.s, etc. Already it has been regulating the FFIs and FIIs and other foreign bodies in respect of their operations in the capital market. A code of conduct has been laid down for each of the category of players in the capital market.

Early in January 2000, the SEBI has come out with a series of measures to enhance transparency and deepen the capital market. These measures include permission for e-broking, share trading via net with orders to be routed through the websites of brokers, acceptance of Kumarmangalan Birla Report on Corporate Governance and of K.B. Chandrashekhar Panel Report on Venture Funds. The SEBI has given directives to the listed companies and to the top 150 companies in particular to observe the code of corporate governance by March end 2001. The SEBI has relaxed the entry norms for IPOs of Venture Funds, I.T. Companies and knowledge based companies for listing purposes and entry and exit norms were relaxed for high networth foreign individuals and companies to operate in the capital market as in the case of FIIs and FFIs.

It is understood that, SEBI has set a creditable record of regulation for growth of capital market on healthy lines during the decade of 1995-2005. In the coming years the tasks set for itself are the following in particular.

(1) Strengthening the Rolling settlement system which has already been initiated.

(2) Pursuit of healthy corporate Governance Regulations by listed companies.

(3) Development of Internet trading practices by brokers on their websites.

(4) Promotion of trading in debt market and in securitised debt instruments.

(5) Introduction and development of trading in derivative instruments.

In Feb. 2000, the SEBI has asked the Stock Exchanges to amend their listing Agreement with companies by adding clause 49 providing for observance of the Rules of corporate governance mandatory for companies, seeking listing for the first time. For the existing listed companies, the observance of corporate governance Rules was subject to a time schedule, as shown below:

	Time Limit
(1) Group A Companies and those included in B.S.E. sensex and in Nifty Index of NSE	March 31, 2001
(2) All Listed Companies with paid-up Capital of above Rs. 10, crores or Net Worth of above Rs. 25 crores	March 31, 2002
(3) Other Listed Companies with paid up Capital of Rs. 3 crores and above	March 31, 2003

The SEBI has set up a committee to streamline existing Risk containment Measures on Stock Exchanges, such as Margin system, circuit breakers etc., with a view to streamline and simplify the systems and procedures in this regard. The SEBI has directed all listed companies to reduce the nc delivery period to one week in respect of their Demat Shares.

The SEBI has approved the Y.H. Malegaon Committee Report on accounting standards and issued guidelines in this regard in Jan. 2000. The disclosure norms were widened and relevant accounting standards upgraded to those of internationally accepted standards. Additional disclosures in the unaudited quartely statements are required to be given to make them more meaningful and transparent. All listed companies are now obliged to observe compulsorily the clauses of listing Agreement and SEBI is given powers to enforce them through the Stock Exchanges. All announcements of companies have to be made after the trading hours.

The SEBI has allowed the domestic Mutual Funds to invest in foreign listed securities and to manage foreign funds and foreign portfolios. The Mutual Funds and Venture Funds are now put on par for regulation. The MMFs, so far regulated by RBI have been brought under the control of SEBI. The Mutual Funds are now required to send a complete statement of their portfolios to all unitholders within one month of the close of half year. In order to deter the Mutual Funds from delay in despatch of redemption warrants, SEBI has directed Mutual Funds to provide for payment of interest to unit holders for this delayed period, whenever applicable.

All FIIs together can invest upto 24% or 30% of a company's paid up capital, if it is approved by the company's general body. This limit of 30% was raised to 40% in the Central Budget for 2000-01. There was also an individual limit of 5% for foreign individuals and foreign corporates investing in Indian Companies.

In 2001, SEBI introduced Compulsory Rolling Settlement System in selected scrips, with a view to reducing the price manipulation by brokers and companies. Following Ketan Parekh Scam involving Madhavpur Co-operative Urban Bank and Global Trust Bank, Control on Banks' involvement in lending against shares and in the capital market operations was streamlined. Trading in futures and options against individual scrips, in addition to Stock Index was also permitted. Margin trading was allowed on a selective basis, to help boost the market sentiment in a sagging market.

SEBI reforms are a continuing process. During 2003 to 2009 book building Process and Buy back of shares were streamlined, particularly for unlisted companies making IPOs. Green shore option was added to the provisions under IPOs, through book building mechanism, to help stabilise the post listing prices of its shares. Private placement system was rationalised for better disclosures.

Interest Rate Derivatives were allowed to be traded and it was opened to banks for hedging purposes. More attention was paid to streamline trading in derivatives and to margin trading by brokers for their clients. The SEBI has specified the Risk Containment measures and exposure limits for derivative trading by FIIs and NRIs.

A Central Listing Authority was established to bring about uniformity in due diligence process for scrutinising the new listing application. The settlement cycle was reduced to T + 1 in 2003 and straight through process (STP) was made compulsory for all insitutional trades. Corporate goverance norms were strengthened by making compliance compulsory for all companies, in all aspects of it.

The rulings of the SEBI can be challenged before the Securities Appellate Authority, if the aggrieved party is not satisfied. Even so, the SEBI has been enforcing its regulations and control with penal powers more strictly than before. The SEBI has powers of dragging any defaulting member of the exchanges or any intermediary in the capital market to the competent courts of law for persistent fraud, inaction or criminal malpractice.

PART — III
Secondary Markets in India

Chapter 14: Securities Trading Regulations
Chapter 15: Instruments of Issue and Trading
Chapter 16: Stock Markets in India
Chapter 17: OTCEI, NSE and ICSE
Chapter 18: Stock Market Operations and Functions
Chapter 19: Trading in the Stock Market

Securities Trading Regulations

The Securities Contracts (Regulation) Act, 1956 (the SCR Act) is the basis for regulation of Securities Contracts and the Stock Exchanges in India. It was enacted in 1956 and came into force on February 20, 1957. It regulates the business of trading on the stock exchanges and options trading and provides for recognition of stock exchanges and related matters like listing of securities, transfer of securities, etc. The regulation of trading is also governed by the Rules and Byelaws of the Stock Exchange.

Objectives

The Preamble to the Act says: "An Act to prevent undesirable transactions in securities by regulating the business of dealing therein, by prohibiting options and by providing for certain other matters connected therewith."

The Act defines what is a security. The Act also lays down what transactions in securities are legal and what are void and illegal.

A reading of the Preamble itself indicates that the key word is "securities" which has been defined in Section 2(h) of the SCR Act. The definition is inclusive in nature and includes shares, scrips, stocks, bonds, debentures, debenture-stock or other marketable securities of a like nature in or of any incorporated company or other body corporate. It also covers government securities and rights or interests in securities. But it does not include securities of private companies as they are not capable of being dealt in on a stock exchange and are not marketable securities due to the possible restrictions on transfer. The shares of public limited companies which are closely held and which are not dealt in on a stock exchange are also outside the purview of the said Act, as their transferability may also be limited.

Coverage

Section 28 of the SCR Act also empowers the Central Government in the interest of trade and commerce or the economic development of the country to issue a notification in the *Official Gazette* and specify any class of contracts as contracts to which the SCR Act will not apply. In pursuance of this power, the Central Government has issued a Notification dated 27th June 1961 specifying contracts for pre-emption or similar rights contained in the promotion or collaboration agreements or in the Articles of Association of limited companies as contracts to which the SCR Act shall not apply. By another notification dated 13th May 1966, the Central Government has declared that contracts pertaining to sale or purchase of shares of Government companies (as defined in Section 617 of the Companies Act 1956), which are not listed on any recognised stock exchanges, shall not be subject to the constraints of the SCR Act.

Recognised Stock Exchanges

Besides the Act, the Securities Contracts (Regulation) Rules were made in 1957 to regulate certain matters relating to the stock exchanges. Section 3 of the SCR Act lays down that a stock exchange is required to apply to the Central Government for recognition. In terms of Rule 3 of the Securities Contracts (Regulation) Rules, 1957 (the SCR Rules), this application has to be made in the prescribed Form A. The application for recognition in Form A has to be accompanied by a copy of the byelaws of the stock exchange and also a copy of the rules of the stock exchange.

On receiving such application, the Central Government, in terms of Section 4 of the SCR Act read with Rule 5A of the SCR Rules, makes an inquiry as to whether the rules and byelaws are in conformity with the prescribed conditions and whether it would be in the interest of the trade and public to grant recognition to the applicant stock exchange.

After making such an enquiry and if the Central Government is satisfied that the prescribed conditions have been met, it grants recognition to the stock exchange. Such recognition is granted in Form B as prescribed under Rule 6 of the SCR Rules, and it may be for a temporary period or on a permanent basis. The Bombay Stock Exchange was the only Exchange which was recognised on a permanent basis from the beginning of the operation of the Act.

Mention may be made here to the provisions under Rule 9 of the SCR Rules which lays down that all contracts between the members of a recognised stock exchange have to be confirmed in writing and are to be enforced in accordance with the rules and byelaws of the stock exchange.

Options in Contracts

The word "contract" has been defined in Section 2(a) of the SCR Act to mean a contract for or relating to the purchase of securities, or sale of Securities.

The expression "option in securities" means a contract for the purchase or sale of *a right to buy or sell* securities in future and a contract for the purchase or sale of *a right to buy and sell* securities in future. By an Amendment to SC(R) Act in 1995, options are made valid and legal.

The expression "spot delivery contract" means a contract which provides for the actual delivery of securities and the payment of a price thereof either on the same day as the date of the contract or on the next day.

The difference between a "spot delivery contract" and an "option in securities" is that the latter is a contract in future of an intangible right to buy or sell the securities, while the former provides for the actual purchase and delivery of securities.

Section 13 of the SCR Act empowers the Central Government having regard to the nature or volume of transactions in securities, to issue a Notification in the *Official Gazette* declaring that a "contract" entered into in a notified state or area otherwise than:

(i) between members of a recognised stock exchange in such state or area; or

(ii) through or with such member shall be illegal.

Under the SCR Act and the Rules, Byelaws of the Stock Exchange, monopoly to stock exchanges recognised by the Government is given thereby barring the unrecognised stock exchanges to operate in such areas.

Section 20 of the SCR Act prohibits "option in securities." By this Section, options in securities are not only made illegal but are also void. The more important effects of this Act are that:

(i) options in securities are illegal and void but made legal by an ordinance of Jan. 1995.

(ii) only spot delivery contracts or contracts for cash or hand delivery can be entered into with those other than members of the stock exchanges;

(iii) contracts other than spot delivery contracts (such as contracts for cash or hand delivery) can be entered only between members of the Stock Exchange or through or with such members, in places where a recognised Stock exists.

The other Provisions of the Act give wide ranging powers on the Stock Exchanges and their members to the Central Govt. which are now delegated to SEBI.

Regulation of Trading

Securities are claims on money and trading in them involves passing of contracts or entering into agreements. The contracts of general nature are regulated by the Indian Contracts Act but contracts in securities are governed by the special Act, namely, Securities Contracts (Regulation) Act. This special Act supercedes the general Act but where there is no provision in the Special Act as in the case of Principal and agent relationship or bailer to bailee relationship, the Indian Contracts Act will apply. The SC(R) Act is supplemented by the Rules framed thereunder and the Rules and Byelaws of the Stock Exchange which are approved by the Government and adopted by the Stock Exchanges.

Under the Rules and Byelaws of the Exchange, all trading activities and post trading issues are governed by a set of rules. The Byelaws provide for Business days, hours of trading, trading floor and authorised Clerks and Remissiers who can put through the deals etc.

The trading floor is supervised by the Exchange authorities; only brokers and their authorised clerks can enter the floor and make deals. The Rules provide for quotations for bid/offer rates for all listed securities and permitted securities for deals and trading lots etc. The rules of the game involve the records of the purchase and sales transactions in the Sauda block books, comparison of Saudas, taking delivery are all important aspects of regulation of trading. In case of disputes in the trading floor or in their recording of deals etc., the Rules and Byelaws have provided for arbitration and settlement of disputes and dispensation of justice in various tiers of judicature as in the case of courts of law.

Trading is regulated by the Stock Exchange authorities as per the Rules and Byelaws of the Exchange supervised by the SEBI and the Government. As per the Rules, the admission to trading, the method of recording of deals, the price quotations, types of bargains to be struck, rules governing each category, margins to control trade, restriction on prices and quantity of trade etc. are all regulated by the Exchange. Provisions for inspecting the accounts of brokers, control on their cornering of shares, closing out and buying-in are provided for. The Exchange regulates trade through:

(1) Fixation of daily margins on purchases and sales.

(2) Fixation of adhoc margins on excessive speculation.

(3) Carry forward margins on outstanding purchases and sales at the settlement.

(4) Fixation of ceiling and floor prices for any volatile scrip.

(5) Penalties on violation of rules.

(6) Fees and charges for any services rendered by the Exchange.

(7) Arbitration and Settlement of disputes among members and between members and their clients.

As part of the regulation of trading, arrangements are also made by each Stock Exchange for settlement and clearance with the help of a bank. The giving and taking delivery of shares, settlement through net payment or receipt by each member through a clearing bank, arrangement of auction for effecting deliveries in case of failure to deliver by any member. Where there are securities for clearing with facility for carry forward from one settlement to another, the Exchange provides facility for badla financing and carry forward of net outstanding position.

Restrictions on Transferability

Section 22A was introduced in the SCR Act by an amendment and has come into force effective from 17th January 1986. The net effect of this section is that a public limited company whose securities are listed on a recognised stock exchange cannot refuse to transfer shares lodged with it for transfer, unless the case for refusal falls under the specific provisions laid down in Section 22A. This section has been introduced to ensure that public companies whose shares are listed on a recognised stock exchange do not act in an arbitrary or capricious manner in dealing with a transfer application lodged with it. Thus, a public limited company whose shares are listed on a recognised stock exchange can refuse an application for transfer only for the first of following grounds. For the rest of the grounds (ii) to (iv) the company has to make a reference to CLB.

(i) that the instrument of transfer is not proper or has not been duly stamped and executed or that the certificate relating to the security has not been delivered to the company, or that any other requirement under the law relating to registration of such transfer has not been complied with;

(ii) that the transfer is in contravention of any law;

(iii) that the transfer is likely to result in such change in the composition of the board of directors as would be prejudicial to the interests of the company or to the public interest; and

(iv) that the transfer is prohibited by any order of any court, tribunal or other authority under any law for the time being in force.

The above Section 22A is a very welcome change made in the SCR Act and ensures that transferability of listed securities is not denied on frivolous grounds by the company. If a transfer is refused, it has to be done within the specified period of two months and the reasons for refusal have to be intimated to the transferor and transferee.

Section 22A applies only to listed companies. This right to refuse registration of shares without adequate reason has been taken away only for listed companies.

The transfer of shares fall within the purview of the Companies Act. Section 82 describes the nature of shares and declares them as movable property. Since shares are a movable property, ordinarily a simple delivery should be enough to complete the transfer. Section 82, however, leaves it to the companies to lay down in the Articles of Association the manner in which the transfer should be effected. It is a general practice in India that the Articles of a Company invariably empower the Board of Directors to refuse the registration to transfer of its securities.

It is Section 111 which recognises the right of companies to refuse registration of transfer of shares and has been substituted by a new one by the Companies (Amendment) Act, 1988. The recasting of Section 111 has been made in pursuance of the recommendations of the Sachar Committee. The Committee considered that, while it might be necessary

the company, this right should be hedged in with adequate safeguards. Specially, under Section 111, as it stood prior to the amendment in 1988, the company was not required to give reasons for refusal to register transfers and it was the right of the adjudicating body only to require the company to disclose reasons at the appellate stage. It has now been made a compulsory requirement for companies to disclose the reasons for refusal to register any transfer at the initial stage itself, that is, at the time of refusal and convey the same to the transferor and the transferee.

Under Section 22A of SCR Act as presently under Section 111 of the Companies Act, corporate managements can easily stall the takeover bids. The assumed contravention of some or the other law, viz., MRTP, Industrial licensing, FERA, Benami law to mention some, would come handy to counter the takeover bid.

In terms of this provision, the Board of Directors gets two months (period reckoned from the day the instrument of transfer along with the share certificates is lodged with the company) within which to form an opinion and in case it proposes to refuse registration, to make a reference to the CLB and forward the copies of such reference to that transferor and transferee. Thus Section 22A, as at present, promotes the interest of the company as also of the transferor and transferee.

CHAPTER 15

Instruments of Issue and Trading

The major instruments of trading on the stock market are equity shares of companies followed in that order by debentures, preference shares, public sector bonds and government securities. Trading in government securities is over the counter as between brokers, banks, financial institutions, etc. The system of auction trading with bid and offer rates to arrive at a competitive price is mainly with respect to the equity shares.

Issues of Securities

There are various alternative issuers of primary securities, which all compete for the savings of the public. Classified by the sectors of the economy and the nature of their activities, these issuers may be set out as follows:

(a) Central and State Governments.

(b) Quasi-government bodies and PSUs.

(c) Financial and Investment Corporations.

(d) Private corporate sector.

Government Securities

The government is the major borrower in India. The instruments issued are stock certificates, promissory notes, bonds, etc. Besides, the government also raises funds through National Savings Certificates and other instruments of savings sold by the Post Offices.

The Central Government borrowed from the market in recent years nearly Rs. 2.42 lakh crores and State Governments another Rs. one lakh crores per annum on a net basis. The quasi-government bodies and public sector undertakings also borrowed a major chunk on Central and State Government guarantees, as per the RBI data. As the financial institutions are mostly in the public sector, the borrowing by the government and the public sector constitute the major component of the total issue of securities. But the secondary market in these securities is nil or negligible. But trading in government securities and PSU bonds takes place and is confined to a few institutions and banks as they are the major holders.

Although the P.O. savings instruments are held by the non-bank public and households, there is no secondary market in them as they are not marketable. The bonds and securities issued by the financial institutions and co-operatives are not attractive to the public to hold as their returns are low and they are not easily marketable. Thus, the secondary market trading is mainly confined to the securities of the private corporate sector.

Corporate Securities

The reason for wider public interest and trading in corporate securities is the attractive returns on them, free transferability, and marketability. Although the interest rates on various financial instruments are fixed by the government, namely, those on preference shares at 14% and fixed deposits with companies at 10%-12% the returns or yields on equities are attractive and freer transferability of these securities attracts wider trading in them. The ceiling rate on debentures was removed in 1991 with the result that the companies can offer any rate that their creditworthiness permits. It is to be admitted that some tax saving instruments of government and post offices carry a higher net return after tax as in the case of NSS, NSCs, CTD and annuity deposits but they are not transferable and not tradable. The private corporate sector borrowed more than Rs. 26,416 crores in 1994-95 and an amount of Rs. 63,638 crores in 2007-08 from the capital market, most of which will be available for trading, as they are quoted on the stock exchanges, and they do not include figures of private placement which are substantial in recent years. The capital raised from the capital market fell to Rs. 14,671 crores in 2008-09, due to depressed market conditions and economic recession in 2009.

Corporate Debentures

Debentures are securities of creditor nature and represent the loans taken by a company from the public. Debentures are mostly secured either by a fixed charge or a floating charge on the assets of the company. Rarely unsecured debentures, called naked debentures, are issued but are not permitted by the Government.

There are various types of debentures, namely, registered and unregistered debentures, convertible and non-convertible debentures, redeemable and non-redeemable debentures, etc.

Registered holders of debentures are those whose names appear in the registers of companies. These debentures are transferable like equity shares by the execution of transfer deeds and registration of transfer in the books of the company. These transfer deeds may not be date-stamped as in the case of equities and there is no special form for these securities. The rates of stamp duty payable on debentures vary from state to state and are different from those paid on equity shares (which is 50 paise per Rs. 100 of value of the contract).

The unregistered debentures are bearer bonds, which can be freely transferred by endorsement and physical delivery, without registration with the company. Besides, there is no need for execution of a transfer deed. These securities are like bearer bonds issued by the government or public sector undertakings, government or semi-government bodies. Presently, these are not popular and are not issued by the companies due to the difficulties of establishment of ownership at the time of repayment of principal and the fear of loss of certificates, etc. Interest is paid to the holder on the production of the attached warrants in their case.

Redeemable debentures are those which are repaid after a fixed period of time, normally 7 years, as per the terms of issue. The principal amount is repaid in one or more instalments as the case may be. Irredeemable debentures are those which are not repayable at any fixed date, but can be redeemed at the will of the company or may be perpetual debentures to be repaid on liquidation of the company only. Such irredeemable debentures are not permitted to be issued.

More recently, convertible debentures have become attractive to the public and are issued by many companies. These are convertible into equity in part or full or in instalments spread over a number of years. Partly convertible debentures have two components: of ownership capital (convertible portion) and creditor capital (non-convertible part). These enjoy the benefits of both riskless return on the non-convertible portion and variable risky return of equity along with capital appreciation at a future date. The conversion is sometimes optional and sometimes compulsory. Those which are not convertible are also tradable and transferable like other debentures. They may also be redeemable at a specified fixed date of 7 to 9 years.

The private corporate sector is not permitted to issue non-re-deemable debentures and bearer bonds. These are not attractive to the investing public. The companies find it easy to attract the public with convertible debentures, which are either partly or fully convertible into equity and convertible in one or more instalments depending on the company's own cash flow and profitability projections for the years ahead. During recent years, a good chunk of the capital raised was in the form of convertible debentures. Equity was popular during 1992 to 1994, when the new issue market was in boom conditions but debt was resorted to later during 1995 to 2003, when the market was sluggish and private placement increased vastly during recent years 2005 to 2009.

Other Securities

Leaving aside government securities and private corporate securities referred to earlier, the broker firms also deal in UTI units, Master Shares, investments in Mutual Funds of public sector banks, etc. The more important category of intermediation done by the brokers is in the mobilisation of public deposits with companies and arranging inter-corporate deposits, inter-corporate investments, etc. They also deal in P.S.U. bonds and shares of P.S.U. who have recently started disinvesting in favour of the public.

As per the norms laid down in the Companies Act, corporate units can lend their surplus or borrow the deficits to meet their short-term requirements for periods of one to six months. The limit on such investments is 25% of their total assets which was removed in 1999. These deposits being unsecured are high-risk instruments. The interest rates are also accordingly high as shown below and may vary with the market conditions, and have come down during 2001-04 due to downward move of the interest rate structure in the country. They are now free to vary with market conditions.

Deposits up to one month	...	9½	—	to	—	11½%
Deposits of three months	...	11	—	to	—	13%
Deposits of six months to one year	...	13	—	to	—	15%

The role of brokers here is to act as intermediaries between the lenders and the borrowers and bring them together. For this brokers need to have contacts with the top executives of companies and know in advance their requirements and surplus and deficit positions. This activity of brokers goes in conjunction with their deposit mobilisation for companies.

Company Deposits

Another investment avenue for savers and additional source of funds to the corporate sector is the fixed deposits of various maturities. Companies of non-financial nature are allowed to accept deposits from the public for one to three years and the rates of interest allowed to be offered are 10 to 13% depending upon the maturity and size of the company. Here the brokers act as middlemen on a brokerage varying from 0.5 to 2% of the funds mobilised.

The regulations governing the mobilisation of deposits by non-government public limited companies are different from those of finance companies and chit funds. The latter are regulated by the RBI and the former by the Department of Company Affairs and Registrar of Companies. The finance and leasing companies are permitted to accept deposits of 2 to 5 years but the maximum rate permissible is only 14% as in the case of non-finance companies.

There are two types of deposits, namely, cumulative and non-cumulative. In the case of the former, interest is reinvested and paid in a cumulative manner at the time of maturity. In the case of the latter, interest is paid monthly, quarterly or half-yearly.

Commercial Paper

Another instrument for raising finance by companies is the commercial paper. The issue of commercial paper by established companies has been permitted by the RBI since January 1990. These are unsecured promissory notes issued by companies, with a net worth equivalent to Rs. 4 crores and a maximum permissible bank finance of Rs. 10 crores. The company should have a credit rating of P_2 from the CRISIL and a status Health Code No. 1 from bankers. The company should have a current ratio of 1.33 :1 and should have been listed on a stock exchange.

The tenor of these instruments should be 3 to 6 months issued with a minimum size of Rs. 25 lakhs in denominations of Rs. 5 lakhs each. The ceiling amount of such issue should be 75% of the cash credit limit with banks. The trading unit should be of Rs. 5 lakhs. Many of these restrictions are removed and greater autonomy was given to banks to decide on terms. The CP is delinked from bank finance

The issue which should be in the form of usance promissory notes should not be underwritten but should be privately placed. In this process, brokers have a role for placement and sale of this issue. The initial investor would pay the discounted value of the CP with a given tenor of 3 to 12 months and this determines the discount rate. The investor could be individuals, banks, companies or unincorporated bodies.

The stamp duty and other charges like issue expenses, commitment charges, credit rating charges, etc. are all payable by the company. The interest rate on these instruments is determined by its discounted value. Thus, if the paper of 6 months' tenor for Rs. 100 is discounted for Rs. 93, this gives an interest rate of 14% per annum, viz,

$$\frac{(100-93)\times 12}{6} = 14$$

The CP is an instrument which is unsecured and hence the interest rate would be higher than that on the inter-bank rate or the bill discounting rate. This rate should be comparable to the rate on inter-corporate investments.

As the brokers are already operating in the inter-corporate market as also in company deposits, it is expected that they also play a role in the marketing of commercial paper. A time may come when the secondary market can also be developed in them. Although these instruments fall more aptly in the short-term money market, the brokers are eligible and are operating in this market as much as in the new issues market or the long-term capital market.

Legal Provisions

Under the Companies Act, 1956, the public limited company may raise resources from the public through issue of equity shares, preference shares, bonds or debentures or warrants coupons etc. The Government and semi-government bodies or PSUs may issue securities, bonds, etc.

Allotment to applicants has to be made within 70 days from the last date of subscription, now reduced to 30 days by SEBI. In the case of over subscription, allotment is to be made in consultation with the Stock Exchange, in the case of public limited companies listed on a Stock Exchange.

Allotment letters are themselves transferable but delay in allotment often takes place beyond permitted 30 days. If the allotment letters or refund orders are not posted within 8 days after the time limit, the company is liable to pay penalty at a rate of 4 to 15% depending on the total delay period, under Section 73 of the Act.

The allotment letters are expected to be sent by Registered post. Any complaints in this regard have to sent to the Registrar of companies, in addition to the Stock Exchange in respect of listed companies.

Despatch of Share Certificates

As per the Section 113 of the Act, the investor is entitled to receive the Share Certificate within three months after allotment. This section also provides relief to the investor in case of default; the investor must first serve notice on the company. If ten days after receipt of this notice, the company fails to deliver the share certificates, then the investor can make a reference to the Company Law Board (CLB). The officers of the company responsible for the default are punishable with fine as per the Act.

Debenture Certificates

There is no provision in the Companies Act in case of any default in respect of debentures, either in respect of payment of interest or repayment of principal. However, in respect of non-receipt or delay in receipt of debenture certificate, the investor can proceed against the company under Section 113 of the Act as in the case of equity or preference share certificates.

Under Section 118 of the Act, the investor can ask for a copy of the Trust deed and avail of the rights as provided in it. He can ask the Trustees for redressal of his grievance under Section 119. If he fails to get the redressal, he can even send a notice under Section 434, after which he can also file a suit for winding up of the company under Section 433. Under the latest law, all debentures should have a time span of not more than 7 to 9 years and they should be compulsorily redeemed after that and in the case of preference shares after a period of 12 years.

Fixed Deposits

Companies raise funds through deposits from public upto a limit. But these are not securities and not transferable. The acceptance of fixed deposits by companies is governed by Section 58(A) of the Companies Act and the Companies (Acceptance of Deposits) Rules, 1975, issued by the Dept. of the company affairs. The periods of maturity, interest rates, the limits to the amounts to be accepted are all set out in these Rules, which are formulated by the Dept. of Company Affairs. The Act has made it compulsory for companies to repay these deposits on maturity. If there are any grievances of non-receipt of interest or principal in this regard, the investor can apply to the company Law Board for redressal of grievance, on a specified proforma along with a fee for it. The ruling of the CLB is binding on all the parties.

Law Regarding Dividends

Under Section 207 of the Act, the company declaring dividend is obliged to pay it to the investor within 42 days from the date of declaration. For non-payment or default in this regard, Section 207 has provided for the imposition of penalties on the concerned officers. The investor can also take recourse to Section 621 and file criminal proceedings against the officers for default. In case of wrong payments of dividends also, such as payment to transferor when the transferee is entitled to it under the rules, the company is liable for default.

New Companies Bill 1993

The new bill has provided for the simplification of procedures, reduction in the number of returns to be submitted and a number of other far-reaching reforms. This has sought to empower the C.L.B. to take up cases of companies defaulting in payment of principal or interest in respect of debentures, prohibits companies from accepting deposits in the event of a default on principal or interest on earlier deposits and provided for the nomination facility for the depositor, shareholder, debentureholder etc. It has exempted the requirement of endorsement on the share transfer deed for transactions of nominal value, and arranged for the setting up of an Investors' Protection Fund for the benefit of the investors.

Among the important provisions in the new Bill, mention may be made of the following:

(1) Compulsory rating for creditworthiness of all debt instruments, including fixed deposits.

(2) Issue of new instruments like non-voting equity shares.

(3) Provision for buy back of shares, if necessary.

The Company Act has been amended later in 1996, 2000 and 2001 to plug in loopholes and to improve corporate governance and transparency.

New Companies Bill of 2008

The more important provisions of this Bill to replace the existing Companies Act of 1956 are briefly set out here:

This Bill gave greater prominence to better Investor protection, transparency, good corporate governance, and permissible use of the electronic documents for evidence, etc.

The single person company got legal sanction and it was laid down that a single entrepreneur can start a company with his own invention or strategy or technology to work with. Similarly a partnership has been redefined as a firm with 100 partners instead of 20 persons earlier. There should be greater disclosures of the results or plans or the minutes of the Board meetings, etc.

The key persons in a company are defined as the Company Secretary, CEO or Chief Executive Officer., Financial Officer, who are held responsible to the investors or the shareholders of the company. The interference or enquiry of the government is now replaced by the shareholders' interference or queries. The shareholder has a right to claim the dividend even after 7 years lapse instead of barring him after 7 years as before. Investor Education and Protection Fund of a company is to be administered by a Statutory authority in future instead of the company itself. The Bill sought to give greater importance to the investor or shareholder of a company as the owner of the company.

Provision for issue of shares at a discount to promoters was removed and now no company can issue shares at a discount to the promoters as it is prohibited. Restrictions were also imposed on listed companies to raise public deposits, without proper authorization from the CLB or the Government.

Now it is laid down that one third of the Board members should be from outside independent persons to act as directors on the Boards of the companies.

The companies are now forced to appoint company secretaries compulsorily and annual, or quarterly reports and financial statements have to be signed by him. These reports are to be submitted to the stock exchanges where their shares are listed within the time limits, as stipulated by the listing agreement.

SEBI Guidelines

Under the latest SEBI guidelines, companies, including PSUs, and Development Financial Institutions are allowed to issue any type of new instruments. They are also free to price them or fix any interest rates or coupon rates, depending on their credit rating. But the terms and conditions of the new instruments should be clearly stated in the beginning itself so that investors can have a chance to decide whether to invest in them or not.

Equity Shares

Equity shares constitute the ownership capital of a company and the equity holder has the right of voting and sharing in profits and assets in proportion to his holding in the total net assets of the company. He is entitled to all rights and obligations of the owners and to residual profits and assets of the company after all the claims of creditors are met. As he is entitled to residual profits, the dividend distributed to him may be uncertain, variable and fluctuating. The equityholder gets his return in the form of dividends distributed plus capital appreciation on his shares.

The dividends distributed depend upon the net earnings of the company after meeting the interest on loans and debentures, depreciation, taxation and any dividends declared on preference shares. The earnings of a company vary from year to year depending upon the profits of the company as return on capital employed. Earnings per share are calculated by dividing net earnings of the company (after all the commitments are met such as interest, depreciation and taxation) by the number of equity shares. Thus, assume that the net earnings of the company are Rs. 2 crores and there are equity shares of one crore for Rs. 10 each, then the earnings per share can be worked out as Rs. 2. This would influence the share prices in the market which will lead to fluctuations in prices and capital appreciation.

The earnings per share of a company depend on a host of factors like the amount of debt per equity share, the ratio of current assets to current liabilities and gross profit to net worth. The price of a share is expressed as a multiple of the earnings per share, if the ratio of price (P) to earnings per share (EPS) is taken. For example, the earnings per share of the Tisco is Rs. 8.8 in 2000-01 and the Tisco's share was quoted at an average price of Rs. 165 during the year. The multiple is 19 times. This multiple depends on many factors such as the outlook for profits, the quality of the management, dividend and bonus policy of the company and investors' expectations regarding the performance of the company.

The companies follow different practices regarding distribution of profits and retention for expansion and diversification. The future earnings depend on the retention policy and expansion plans. The market price in turn depends on the dividend distribution, earnings capacity, expansion and diversification programme and growth prospects. Generally, companies with growth prospects will have a large capital appreciation and share prices show a substantial rise from the Book value. They have a good dividend record and are called blue chips. Thus, Tisco share price is around Rs. 165 with a face value of Rs. 10. Although the dividend distributed is as high as 40%, still the yield is less than 2.5 per cent. The average yield on equities in the market is around 3-5% which is relatively low compared to the yields on other securities, but if capital appreciation is also considered, then the return on equity may be much higher than other securities like debentures or preference shares.

Dividend Distribution

The dividend payments are regulated by the Central Government under Section 205 and 205A of the Companies Act. According to the Company Transfer of Profits to Reserves Rules framed under the above sections in 1975, an amount representing at least 2.5%, 5%, 7.5% and 10% respectively of the current profits has to be transferred to reserves if the dividend declared in any year is between 10-12.5%, 12.5-15%, 15-20% and above 20% respectively of the paid-up capital. A company can transfer a higher percentage of profits to reserves, provided the shareholders are given dividends at a rate of not less than the average of the last three years with an adjustment for the bonus issues. According to the company's Declaration of Dividends out of Reserves Rules framed under the above sections in 1975, a company can draw on the reserves to pay the dividend subject to the following conditions:

(1) The rate of dividend paid is that for the last 5 years or 10% whichever is lower.

(2) The total amount withdrawn from the reserves should not exceed 1/10 of the net worth (Equity Capital + Reserves).

(3) The balance in the reserves after withdrawal should not fall below 15% of the paid-up capital.

Dividend Policy

Dividend policies of companies are the offshoot of a number of factors such as the expansion programmes of the company, choice of capital financing methods, cost of external capital and the government policy, etc. Some companies distribute all the earnings as dividends and they have no expansion or modernisation plans. At the other extreme, some companies retain a large proportion of their earnings for future growth. Some maintain a consistent dividend of, say, 12% or 15% and plough back the rest into reserves. Different companies distribute different proportions of their net earnings. The interests of the shareholders are kept in mind as dividend income is the main income of some investors. If, however, larger earnings are retained, these reserves could be used later for the issue of bonus shares, while using these funds for expansion and diversification. Thus, whether profits are distributed or not, these are shareholders' funds. They are given either as dividends or as bonus shares at a future date.

The dividend distribution is sometimes manipulated to the advantage of the promoters. This is particularly true in closely-held companies and private limited companies. If the personal tax liabilities of promoters dictate lower distribution of dividends for the purpose of tax planning, the company itself decides to declare lower dividends and increase the retentions. Then the policy is of lower dividend distribution. In the case of companies having fluctuating profits, a prudent management may also declare lower dividends and retain larger profits. Besides, some unscrupulous promoters may desire to disinvest in a company when they may choose not to retain any profits but to declare all as dividends. Sometimes, dividend distribution is also dictated by the promoters' concern to manipulate the share prices. Since the distribution policy of a company affects its prices, such manipulations will be in the interests of a few and to the detriment of the majority of shareholders.

The Companies Act provided against such contingencies and to foster financial discipline among the companies and to protect the interest of investors. With these objectives, the government have announced some guidelines in 1975 for controlling the transfer of profits to reserves and the use of reserves to declare dividends.

If the minimum average of the dividend rates in the last 3 years is maintained, then it is possible for a company to transfer more than 10% of the company profits to reserves. If the distributable profits are about 20% lower than the average distributable profits of the last 2 years, then the above rules regarding minimum distribution of dividends do not apply. The rules formulated by the Government have the objective of securing a compromise between excessive distribution and excessive retention so that the interests of both the company and the investors are protected.

Sections 104 and 105 of the IT Act require that the statutory percentage of distributable income will be distributed as dividend, which varies from 45% in the case of consultancy companies to 90% for an investment company. When dividend distribution is less than the statutory percentage, then the company is liable to pay income tax at higher rates.

Other Instruments

Among the other categories of ownership capital, mention may be made of preferred ordinary shares and deferred ordinary shares. Preferred ordinary shares carry dividend and capital repayment rights ahead of the ordinary shareholders but only after the claims of the preference shareholders are met. The deferred shareholders are a category whose claims on dividends and assets of a company are ranked after the demands of ordinary shareholders are met. These deferred shares are also called founder shares enjoying the voting rights in more than proportionate terms as compared to ordinary shares. But these are no longer existing as the voting powers have been equated among all ordinary shareholders, including promoters and founders. Those categories of shareholders falling under ownership capital now enjoy equal rights in respect of equity shares whose dividends are variable and hence called variable dividend industrial securities.

Bonus Shares

Retained earnings of a company are kept as reserves in various reserve accounts. These are shareholders' funds and are used for purposes of capital expenditure or current expenditure of the company. When they reach a level of accumulation, they are distributed as bonus shares to the present equityholders in a certain ratio to their existing holdings.

Bonus shares can be issued without the consent of the Government or SEBI subject to their guidelines on Bonus Issues:

(1) Bonus shares can be issued out of free reserves comprising general reserves, development rebate reserve, share premium received in cash, capital redemption reserve and balances held in the debentures redemption, sinking fund and in profit and loss account. Under free reserves, all reserves except reserves built on revaluation of assets involving no cash accruals are included.

(2) The issue of bonus shares cannot be in lieu of dividend.

(3) The residual reserves after the proposed capitalisation should be at least 40% of the increased paid-up capital.

(4) 30% of the average amount of profits before tax of the company in the last three years should yield at least 10% of the increased capital of the company. This ensures that profitability of the company is adequate to service the increased capital base.

But a company which has defaulted in respect of statutory dues to the employees such as PF, Gratuity, etc. is not permitted to issue bonus shares. Similarly, a company which has defaulted in its liabilities on fixed deposits or debentures cannot issue bonus shares. The other details are given under the SEBI guidelines. Bonus shares are now valued at zero for taxation purposes and for calculation of capital gain.

Rights Shares

Companies can also issue rights shares which are a right to buy the equity shares of the company given at par or a premium to the existing shareholders in a particular proportion to their holdings. Under Section 81 of Companies Act, companies issuing further capital after two years of the formation of the company or after one year of the first allotment of the shares have to offer the same as rights to the existing shareholders.

The premium used to be fixed on the basis of the average book value of the company and post-tax earning capacity of the shares normally capitalised at 15% and even at 10% if the market price is substantially higher than the fair price. The average of the two prices worked out on the basis of book value and the earning capitalisation model is accepted. If earnings for share is Rs. 3 and capitalisation rate is 15%, then the fair price is $3/15 \times 100 = 20$ according to the earnings capitalisation formula. The price on the basis of book value is, say, Rs. 30[1]. Then the average of these two prices Rs. 20 and Rs. 30, namely, Rs. 25 is taken as the fair price for fixing the premium (namely, Rs. 15 on a share with the face value of Rs. 10)[2].

The rights are quoted in the market. The price of the rights will depend on the ratio on which they are issued. If the ratio is 1:3 and the market price is Rs. 50, then valuation of rights is done as follows:

Let the premium be Rs. 15, then,

$$\frac{50 \times 3 + 25}{4} = \frac{175}{4} = 44$$

1. Book value is net worth of the company divided by the number of equity shares.
2. The method of premium fixation adopted by the erstwhile CCI is given in another chapter.

The value of one right is Rs. 44 – 25 = 19 which is got for three shares (Rs. 6.33 for one existing share).

Rights can be issued only if authorised by a special resolution of the company. The company making the rights has to inform the existing shareholders as to the use to which the additional funds are put, the future earning capacity of the company and other financial indicators such as sales, estimated gross profit or loss, etc. This information would enable the shareholders to decide to opt for the rights or not.

Chart 1 The Existing Instruments Issued in the Capital Market

Marketable Instruments	*Type by Issuer*	*Ownership Rights*	*Yield/Return*	*Trading or Marketability*	*Tax Status*	*Redemption if any & Remarks*
Equity shares (Rights & Bonus)	Companies	Ownership Capital	Average 3 to 4% (variable return) Expected return Risk free return (12%) plus risk premium (15 to 20%)	Group A & Group B good trading	Income upto Rs. 12,000 tax exempt, among others Investment in new issues exempt upto limits under 88A	Nil
Preference shares Convertible Non-convertible Re-deemable Non-redeemable Participating Non-participating Cumulative Non-cumulative	Companies	Both Owner-ship & Debt Both Owner-ship & Debt	*14%*	No trading	Exempt from Income tax under Section 80 L Replaced by section 80 (c)	Redeemable in 7 to 10 years
Cumulative Convertible Preference Shares (C.C.P.)	Companies	Both Owner-ship & Debt	*10%*	No trading	Taxable	Convertible into equity in 3 to 5 years
Debentures Convertible Non-convertible Registered Non-registered Secured Non-secured Redeemable Non-redeemable	Companies	Debt Capital	Rates Freed	Limited trading	Taxable	Redeemable in 5 to 7 years
P.S.U. Bonds	Public Sector units.	Debt Capital	9% to 10.5% tax free 13% to 14% taxable	Limited trading	Both taxable and tax free	Redeemable in 5 to 7 years
P.S.U. Shares	Public Sector units	Equity Capital		for trading listed	Taxable	Nil

Note: Tax status has since changed and is changing in many cases and can best be updated through Financial Press. A number of exemptions and tax rebates were withdrawn and Section 80 C has replaced Section 88 and 80 L, etc.

Preference Shares

Preference shares are of a hybrid category having ownership rights like equity and also a fixed income like creditor capital. They have preferred rights for payment of dividend, along with arrears, if any, if such provision is made in the Articles of Association. They are paid their fixed dividend before any dividend is declared to the equityholders. Besides they have also similar preferential right over equity to payment of capital and their share of assets in the event of winding up of the company. This right is, however, subject to the claims of creditors.

This instrument is suitable to some investors who would like to take some risk but not as much as equityholders but more than debenture-owners. They get an income which may, however, fluctuate depending upon the profits of the company but fixed, if profits are adequate to service all preference and equityholders. They may also get back their capital after a fixed period like debentures as per the present law.

The return on preference shares is fixed by the Government at 14% since April 1987. The preference shareholders do not enjoy any voting rights except in respect of resolution affecting their rights or when their dividends due are in arrears for the past two financial years.

There are various types of preference shares like redeemable and non-redeemable, cumulative and non-cumulative, participating and non-participating and convertible and non-convertible.

Preference shares are redeemable generally after 12 years and for this purpose, the company is required to provide for transfer out of profits a sum to the reserves called Capital Redemption Reserve. If there is no provision to redeem these shares, they are non-redeemable. As these non-redeemable shares were not popular, they were abolished by the Companies Amendment Act of 1988.

Preference shares which have a right to receive dividends in a cumulative fashion are called cumulative preference shares. These enjoy the right to receive dividends in all the years in which the dividends are skipped, as profits were inadequate in those years. The fixed dividend on preference shares should be paid later in a cumulative way when profits are adequate before any dividends are declared for equityholders. Those which have no such right are called non-cumulative preference shares.

Preference shares are convertible, if there is a provision for their conversion into equity after a specified period in a particular ratio to the existing shares. Preference shares may not be convertible if no such provision is made. Preference shares are participating, if they can share in profits in excess of a guaranteed fixed return, if such a provision is made in the Articles of the company and specify the level of profitability such as an equity dividend of 20%. If these are not so participative, they are called non-participating.

C.C.P.S.

A new instrument called Cumulative Convertible Preference Shares was introduced by the Government in 1985, the features of which are as follows:

(1) The CCPs can be issued by any public limited company to raise finance for new projects, expansion and diversification, etc.

(2) The amount of issue of CCP will be to the extent of the equity issue to the public for subscription.

(3) The dividend payable is fixed at 10%.

(4) The entire issue of CCP would be convertible into equity shares between three and five years.

These issues have not proved popular with the companies as the dividend on their shares is not a tax deductible item as in the case of interest on debentures. Besides, the dividend of 10% for the first 3 to 5 years has not proved attractive to investors.

But preference shares as a class are attractive to institutions and individuals in the high income brackets as the dividend income on them is tax exempt under Section 80L unlike interest income on debentures and company deposits. But companies themselves do not find these preference shares as an attractive alternative to raise funds, except in the special conditions when the company is unable to raise funds from fresh equities from the public or in the form of rights.

The existing instruments of issue and their features are set out in the chart attached. These are presently traded and other new instruments are dealt with later. The Chart 1 gives the marketable instruments which are traded by type of issuer, ownership rights, yield, return, extent of trading, tax status etc.

Government and Semi-Government Bonds

In the Capital Market the major issuers of securities are companies, Government, P.S.U. and U.T.I. and Mutual Funds. The Government securities are no doubt less risky and more creditworthy due to Government's credibility, but the public interest in these securities is poor due to lower rates of interest on these securities and lack of capital appreciation. The instruments issued by Government are the Stock Certificates, Promissory notes, Bonds etc. Besides the Government raises funds through issue of Treasury bills of 14 days to 364 days for short-term requirements of funds for their expenditure. There are also instruments of Post Offices, which are another source of raising funds for the Government. These instruments are NSC, NSS deposits, Time deposits, Indira and Kisan Vikas Patras etc. But these Postal savings instruments are not transferable and marketable. The Government — Central and State securities and the bonds issued by the semi-Government undertakings are popular with banks, FIs, Companies etc. The Public Sector undertakings also issue bonds, shares and borrow through deposits from public. These bonds and shares are however transferable and marketable. Bonds are either taxable or tax free and interest rates vary accordingly. Bearer bonds are not allowed to be issued at present.

Equity Shares — Public Issue

SEBI Guidelines cover the public issue through Prospectus rights, private placement or offer of sale. In these cases the draft prospectus is to be approved by the SEBI which is now delegated to lead managers.

Debt equity norm is 1:2, which is relaxable for capital intensive projects. Equity preference ratio should be 3:1. Current ratio should be again 1:2 for issues to finance working capital. Underwriting is normally mandatory but is left optional to companies more recently. Cost of public issue is governed by the guidelines as follows:

Cost of Issue Guidelines

Equity and Convertible debentures upto Rs. 5 crores should have a mandatory cost plus 5%. For issues above Rs. 5 crores, the mandatory costs plus 2% is permitted. For NCDs, the corresponding limits are the mandatory costs plus 2% and mandatory costs + 1% respectively. The mandatory costs include expenditure on bankers, underwriters, listing fees and other payments to solicitors, auditors etc. The non-mandatory costs include all the others like those of stationery, printing, advertisement etc.

New Instruments

(1) *Secured Premium Notes*: These are the instruments, issued by companies for raising debt which can be converted into equity or redeemed at a premium after 3 to 5 years. No Coupon rate is fixed.

(2) *Discount Bonds and Deep Discount Bonds*: These are sold at a discount today to secure a face value of Rs. 100 or Rs. 1000 after 5 to 30 years. The discount rate depends on the amount of discount and the number of years of waiting.

(3) *Warrants*: These are entitlements to buy an equity at a concessional price after a period of 2 to 3 years. These are debt at present, but can be converted into equity.

(4) *Loyalty Coupons*: These are entitlements to the holder of debt for 2 to 3 years to exchange into equity shares at discount prices. These are to be held by the original subscriber for the entitlement.

(5) *Zero Coupon Bonds*: These are debt instruments with a Zero rate of interest and redeemed at a premium securing capital gains to the holder.

(6) *Non-Voting Equity Shares*: Somewhat equal to preference shares for which terms have not been finalised and companies have not yet issued to public. These shares are not entitled to voting right, but to dividend, bonus etc.

Some more instruments which have been recently issued for raising funds by financial institutions are the following:

1. Floating Rate Bonds: SBI has issued Floating Rate Bonds in 1993. Although no coupon rate is fixed, the rate of interest payable half yearly is adjusted at two percentage points above the Bank's deposit rate of say, 12%. If the Bank deposit rate is changed, the interest rate payable on these Bonds will also change. In the case of borrowing abroad in foreign currencies, the floating rate notes are issued with a clause that interest rate is above 1 per cent or 2 per cent above the LIBOR (London Inter Bank Offer Rate). These are loans or debt instruments of short duration of 6 months to one year, but renewable on the same terms or different terms, for longer periods.

2. Zero Coupon Convertible Bonds: These were issued at one time by L & T and they do not carry any interest until conversion. When conversion is given into equity, at the end of one year to three years, the terms are favourable and the equity shares will be at par, when the market price is much above. The loss of interest for one to three years is compensated by the favourable conversion of debt into equity. There are attractive to those belonging to high income tax brackets, who can postpone payment of tax for a period.

Recent Liberalisation of Policy

In the field of Foreign borrowing, there was further liberalisation of policy early in 2000. Indian companies are given free access to ADRs and GDRs without the need for permission, if the foreign borrowing is for equity issues in overseas markets. This move has spurred more companies, particularly in I.T. field to reach out for global markets and for global valuation of their stocks. All the procedural formalities and administrative red tape are done away with at one stroke. After issue companies have to inform the Finance Ministry and the RBI within 30 days. This automatic route is only for equity and for expanding capital base but is not available for debt or partly or fully convertible bonds.

Employee stock option by software and I.T. companies will also be automatic. But the automatic GDR/ADR issue would be subject to the sectoral ceilings of Foreign investment as in the case of 49% in the Telecom Sector. Approvals under FDI Policy, Companies Act, Limits on overseas investments. FERA/FEMA provisions etc. would still apply. Similarly, the Rules for retention of Funds abroad, repatriation, and end-use etc. would still be applicable.

Indian corporates mobilised through ADR/GDR route US $ 460 million in 1999, as against a peak of U.S. $ 3,031 million in 1994. In 2000-01, thirteen issues were made for an amount of Rs. 4,197 crores, as against six issues for an amount of Rs. 3,487 crores in the preceding year.

In the year 2005-06, the amount raised through ADR/GDR was U.S. $ 2.5 billion which rose to $ 4 billion in 2006-07. In terms of rupees, in 2005-06, 48 Euro issues for an amount of Rs. 11.352 crores were made, while in 2006-07, 40 issues for an amount of Rs. 17,005 crores were made.

In 2007-08, 28 issues for an amount of Rs. 26,556 crore and in 2008-09, 13 issues for an amount of Rs. 4,788 crore were issued.

ADR AND GDR PROCEEDS

The new guidelines on ADR and GDR would allow the proceeds to be used entirely for acquisitions abroad by the Indian corporates, if they want to invest abroad for J.Vs outside India. The Indian corporates and I.T. Companies in particular are expected to be free to use the entire proceeds of ADR/GDR as they like, instead of being tied up with the previous limit of 50% of the proceeds to be used for investment abroad. This liberalisation is expected to help the I.T. companies in India.

Latest Foreign Investment Policy Measures

Reforms in the field of foreign investment since October 1999, when new Government was formed at the centre, include removal of barriers to the flow of foreign investment and should reduce red tapism at the administrative level and FIPB, and raise the level of foreign investment to 74%, instead of 51% in the case of Pharmaceuticals, their preparations and formulations. The Government have done away with dividend balancing curb for foreign companies from January 1, 2000, by which they are no longer forced to export to the extent of the dollars taken out as dividend earnings. This would mean that dividend pay outs to foreign investors would no longer be based on exports, that they make. They are free to take out dividends as they like, subject to the RBI guidelines and free to export as they like and both are delinked. After 2004, foreign equilty investment and direct investment is encouraged more than portfolio investment. The Government slowed down the process of raising limits to foreign investment and for increasing the pace of privatisations due to political compulsious.

Relaxation in ECB Norms

With a view to delegate move powers to RBI the Government have authorised it to clear ECB permits upto $ 20 million during 2000-2001. For easing the procedures, companies are now allowed to seek ECB clearances from the Regional offices of RBI. These liberalisations relate to automatic clearance window of the RBI.

Liberalisation is also effected for the Discretionary window of the Ministry of Finance. Under the new norms, companies would be able to get clearances in three stages, instead of four stages. The visits to RBI and Ministry of Finance are brought down to three stages, namely two times to the Ministry at the time of filing the application and the time of signing the loan agreement and once to the RBI at the end, when both the FERA clearances would be granted and the draw down of the loan would be permitted. After 2004, foreign equity investment and direct investment is encouraged more then portfolio and direct investment. The government slowed down the process of raising limits to foreign investment and for increasing the pace of privatisation, due to political compulsions.

Finally, when the RBI is ready to take over the work of all clearances of ECB, the Ministry of Finance has decided to delegate all powers of this work to the RBI.

Instruments of Foreign Borrowing

GDRs — equity shares of Indian Companies, Converted from rupees into foreign currencies for investment by foreigners — Euro-currency bonds or Foreign currency convertible bonds, or non-convertible bonds.

Euro Bonds — debt instruments in foreign currencies issued by Indian companies. Offshore Funds — Funds raised in dollars or sterling by public FIs for investment abroad upto 80% and for investment in India upto 20% of the Fund. These instruments are traded and quoted in foreign markets.

Warrants are either detachable or not. The Warrare holder at the time of conversion is entitled to that right. Warrants are tradeable like the rights entitlements, but the loyalty coupons are not tradeable.

ADRs — equity shares of Indian Companies converted into foreign currencies, namely Dollar — Bonds, quoted and traded, in foreign markets.

The conditions under which they are permitted by Indian Corporates, changed from time to time, but many companies have already issued ADRs and GDRs and they are being traded abroad.

CHAPTER 16

Stock Markets in India

Stock exchanges are the most perfect type of market for securities whether of government and semi-government bodies or other public bodies as also for shares and debentures issued by the joint-stock companies. In the stock market, purchases and sales of shares are made in conditions of free competition. Government securities are traded outside the trading ring in the form of over-the-counter sales or purchases. The bargains that are struck in the trading ring by the members of the stock exchanges are at the fairest prices determined by the basic laws of supply and demand.

History of Stock Exchanges

The only stock exchanges operating in the 19th century were those of Mumbai set up in 1875 and Ahmedabad set up in 1894. These were organised as voluntary non-profit-making associations of brokers to regulate and protect their interests. Before the control on securities trading became a central subject under the Constitution in 1950, it was a state subject and the Bombay Securities Contracts (Control) Act of 1925 used to regulate trading in securities. Under this Act, the Bombay Stock Exchange was recognised in 1927 and Ahmedabad in 1937. During the war boom, a number of stock exchanges were organised even in Mumbai, Ahmedabad and other centres, but they were not recognised. Soon after it became a Central subject, Central legislation was proposed and a Committee headed by A.D. Gorwala went into the Bill for securities regulation. On the basis of the committee's recommendations and public discussion, the Securities Contracts (Regulation) Act became law in 1956.

What is a Stock Exchange?

"Stock Exchange means any body or individuals whether incorporated or not, constituted for the purpose of assisting, regulating or controlling the business of buying, selling or dealing in securities." It is an association of member brokers for the purpose of self-regulation and protecting the interests of its members. When the stock exchanges became corporate bodies with demutualisation, the control and ownership are in different hands. The above definition will change accordingly.

It can operate only if it is recognised by the Government under the Securities Contracts (Regulation) Act, 1956. The recognition is granted under Section 3 of the Act by the Central Government, Ministry of Finance.

The powers of the Central Government under the Act are far-reaching and include the following in particular:

(1) Grant and withdrawal of recognition, approval or change of byelaws.

(2) Call for periodical returns from the Stock Exchange.

(3) Direct enquiries on the members or on the Stock Exchange.

(4) Liability of the Exchange to submit annual reports.

(5) Directing the Stock Exchange to make certain rules.

(6) Supersede the Governing Board of the Exchange.

(7) Suspend the Governing Board of the Exchange.

(8) Impose any other conditions or regulations for trading.

Byelaws

Besides the above Act, the Securities Contracts (Regulation) Rules were also made in 1957 to regulate certain matters relating to trading on the Stock Exchanges. There are also byelaws of the Exchanges, which are concerned with the following subjects:

Opening/Closing of the stock exchanges, administration timing of trading, regulation of blank transfers, regulation of badla or carryover business, control of the settlement and other activities of the Stock Exchange, fixation of margins, fixation of market prices or making up prices (Havala rates), regulation of taravani business (jobbing), etc., regulation of brokers' trading, brokerage charges, trading rules on the Exchange, arbitration and settlement of disputes, settlement and clearing of the trading etc.

Regulation of Stock Exchanges

The Securities Contracts (Regulation) Act is the basis for operations of the stock exchanges in India. No exchange can operate legally without the government permission or recognition. Stock exchanges are given monopoly in certain areas under Section 19 of the above Act to ensure that the control and regulation are facilitated. Recognition can be granted to a stock exchange provided certain conditions are satisfied and the necessary information is supplied to the government. Recognition can also be withdrawn, if necessary. Where there are no stock exchanges, the government can license some of the brokers (licensed dealers) to perform the functions of a stock exchange in its absence.

Recognition by Government

As referred to earlier, a Stock Exchange is recognised only after the government is satisfied that its Rules and Byelaws conform to the conditions prescribed for ensuring fair dealings and protection to investors. Government has also to be satisfied that it would be in the interest of the trade and public interest to grant such recognition. Mumbai, Kolkata, Delhi, Chennai, Ahmedabad, Hyderabad, Bangalore Indore etc. have so far been granted permanent recognition. Others are granted temporary recognition from time to time.

The rules of a recognised stock exchange relating in general to the constitution of the Exchange, the powers of management of its governing body and its constitution (including the appointment thereon of not more than three government nominees), the admission of members, the qualifications for membership, the expulsion, suspension and readmission of members, the registration of partnerships and the appointment of authorised representatives and clerks must be duly approved by Government. These rules can be amended, varied or rescinded only with the previous approval of government. Likewise, the byelaws of the recognised exchanges providing in detail for the regulation and control of contracts in securities and for every aspect of the trading activities of members must also be sanctioned by government and any amendments or modifications must be similarly approved. Government's authority extends much further to make or amend *suo motto* any rules or byelaws of a recognised stock exchange, if it so considers desirable in the interest of trade and in public interest.

The Act empowered the government with even more drastic powers — the power to make enquiries into the affairs of a recognised stock exchange and its members, to supersede the governing body and take over the property of a recognised exchange, to suspend its business, and lastly, to withdraw the recognition granted to an exchange should such steps be deemed indispensable in the interest of trade and in public interest. Government has thus complete control over the recognised stock exchanges.

Licensed Dealers

The recognised stock exchanges are the media through which government regulation of the stock market is made effective. Where there are no stock exchanges, the Securities Contracts (Regulation) Act, 1956 empowers government to license dealers in securities and prescribe the conditions subject to which they can carry on the business of dealing in securities. These licensed dealers are now operating for OTCEI and NSE.

Securities Contracts (Regulation) Rules, 1957

Under the Act, government has promulgated the Securities Contracts (Regulation) Rules, 1957 for carrying into effect the objects of the legislation. These rules provide, among other things, for the procedure to be followed for recognition of stock exchanges; submission of periodical returns and annual reports by recognised stock exchanges; inquiry into the affairs of recognised stock exchanges and their members; and requirements for listing of securities. The rules are statutory and they constitute a code of standardised regulations uniformly applicable to all the recognised stock exchanges.

Present Recognised Stock Exchanges

At present, there are 21 stock exchanges recognised under the Securities Contracts (Regulation) Act, 1956. The other two are NSE, OTCEI, in addition to I.C.S.E.I. They are located at Mumbai, Kolkata, Chennai, Delhi, Ahmedabad, Hyderabad, Indore, Bhuvaneshwar, Mangalore, Patna, Bengaluru, Rajkot, Guwahati, Jaipur, Kanpur, Ludhiana, Baroda, Cochin and Pune. The recently recognised stock exchanges are at Coimbatore and Meerut. Visakhapatnam Stock Exchange was recognised in 1996 for electronic trading. A stock exchange has also been set up at Gangtok, Sikkim early in 1986. No recognition has been sought for this body as the jurisdiction of the Securities Contracts (Regulation) Act, 1956 has not so far been extended to the areas covered by the State. A decade ago, there were hardly 8 stock exchanges in the country. There is no trading, however, in Meerut and Vishakhapatnam Stock Exchanges.

The stock exchanges operate under the rules, byelaws and regulations duly approved by government and constitute an organised market for securities. They offer the most perfect type of market for various reasons. There is an active bidding and in the case of shares and debentures a two-way auction trading, so that purchases and sales are made in conditions of free and perfect competition. The bargains that are struck by members of the exchanges are the fairest price determined by the basic laws of supply and demand. In consequence, though gilt-edged securities represent ownership of public debt and shares and debentures of joint-stock companies represent interest in industrial property — mills and factories, plant, machinery and equipment — they become the most liquid of assets and capable of being easily negotiated.

Qualifications for Membership

The members of recognised stock exchanges should have the following qualifications:

- Age 21, Indian Citizen, not bankrupt.
- Not compounded with the creditors.
- Not convicted for fraud or dishonesty.
- Not engaged in any other business except as agent or broker.
- Educational Qualifications should be graduate.
- Not connected with a company or corporation.
- Not a defaulter of any other stock exchange.

Companies and financial institutions are not members as per the earlier rules. But the government has permitted change in the byelaws of the exchanges to permit corporate and institutional members and also grant permission for a member of any stock exchange to be a member of another stock exchange in 1993.

Members are prohibited from entering into contracts with persons other than members or from dealing with clients as principals. Spot delivery transactions are exempt from the provisions of the Act. Contracts can be passed only by the members in the notified areas where the stock exchange exists. The sub-brokers can also pass valid contract notes or confirmation Notes, if they are registered with SEBI.

Organisation

The recognised stock exchanges at Mumbai, Ahmedabad, Indore are voluntary non-profit-making associations, while the Kolkata, Delhi, Bangalore, Cochin, Kanpur, Ludhiana, Guwahati and Kanara Stock Exchanges are joint-stock companies limited by shares and the Chennai, Hyderabad and Pune stock exchanges are companies limited by guarantee. Since the Rules or Articles of Association defining the constitution of the recognised stock exchanges are approved by the Central Government, there is a broad uniformity in their organisation. In fact, the Madras Stock Exchange was reconstituted and the Calcutta Stock Exchange had to undergo a major reorganisation as a condition precedent to their recognition by the Government of India.

Demutualisation of Stock Exchanges

What is Demutualisation? It is dissociation of ownership from control and Regulation of Stock Market operations. The Stock Exchanges are self Regulatory organisations, owned and regulated by the member brokers themselves. Traditionally, the control and ownership rested with the same member brokers. But in India, the first attempt at Demutualisation was made by OTCEI set up in 1992 and NSE in 1994. Both are owned by banks, FIs and other agencies other than member brokers. BSE has chosen to become a corporate unit with its shares listed for trading and it was effected in August 2005.

Advantages of Demutualisation

Firstly, the interests of public and investors can be better taken care of by the vesting of control and regulation in a separate agency other than the trading members. Secondly, professionalism in Management is possible when it is owned by non-trading public. Thirdly, the derivative markets can be better controlled and regulated by professionals and experts. Fourthly, the larger funds needed by the Stock Exchanges for infrastructure development and electronic trading can be better accessed from the Capital Market and the public.

Disadvantages

Firstly, if it is owned by the public, profit motive and the return on investment become paramount concerns which is not good for regulation. Secondly, it dilutes the regulatory authority given to Stock Exchanges, which are SROs, under Article 226 of the constitution. Sometimes, the volumes go down and the capacity utilisation of the Stock Exchange infrastructure will be poor leading to poor return on investment. Lastly, in India demutualisation may not be needed as the competition from the ATS and ECNs (Alternative trading system and Electronic trading) would not be there as the matching of Buy and sell orders in the broker firms is not allowed by SEBI.

Governing Body

The governing body of a recognised stock exchange has wide governmental and administrative powers and is the decision-making body. It has the power, subject to governmental approval, to make, amend and suspend the operation of the rules, byelaws and regulations of the exchanges. It also has complete jurisdiction over all members and in practice, its power of management and control is almost absolute.

Under the constitution, the governing body has the power to admit and expel members, to warn, censure, fine and suspend members and their partners, attorneys, remisiers, authorised clerks and employees, to approve the formation and dissolution of partnerships and appointment of attorneys, remisiers and authorised clerks, to enforce attendance and information, adjudicate disputes and impose penalties, to determine the mode and conditions of stock exchange business and regulate stock exchange trading in all its aspects and generally to supervise, direct and control all matters and activities affecting the stock exchange. The organisation of Bombay Stock Exchange is typical. The members on roll elect 16 members to be Directors on the Governing Board, who in turn elect a President, Vice-President and Treasurer. The Executive Director is appointed by the government on the recommendation of the Governing Board to be the Chief Administrator of the Exchange. There are also three representatives from the Government, three from the public and one from the RBI on the Board to represent their interests. As per the SEBI guidelines, the Exchanges have agreed to have 50% representation to non-members on the Governing Board.

Functions of Stock Exchanges

Stock exchanges provide liquidity to the listed companies. By giving quotations to the listed companies, they help trading and raise funds from the market. Savings of investors flow into public loans and to joint-stock enterprises because of this ready marketability and unequalled facility for transfer of ownership of stocks, shares and securities provided by the recognised stock exchanges. As a result, over the hundred and twenty years during which the stock exchanges have existed in this country and through their medium, the Central and State Government have raised crores of rupees by floating public loans; Municipal Corporations, Improvement Trusts, Local Bodies and State Finance Corporations have obtained from the public their financial requirements, and industry, trade and commerce — the backbone of the country's economy — have secured capital of crores of rupees through the issue of stocks, shares and debentures for financing their day-to-day activities, organising new ventures and completing projects of expansion, diversification and modernisation. By obtaining the listing and trading facilities, public investment is increased and companies were able to raise more funds. The quoted companies with wide public interest have enjoyed some benefits and asset valuation has become easier for tax and other purposes.

In tune with the growth in the new issues market during the eighties, the secondary market also expanded fast during this period. The number of stock exchanges has increased from 8 in 1980 to a total 23 in 1993 and Vishakhapatnam Stock Exchange was recognised for electronic trading in 1996. The membership of the stock exchanges has also increased substantially to around 8,000 now from about 1,200 a decade ago. The listed companies of all stock exchanges were at around 9,000 now. The market capitalisation has also shown a substantial increase in the eighties and nineties and stood at Rs. 17 lakh crores at end March 2005 and Rs. 34 lakh crores at end of March 2009. The volume of daily turnover of trade has also increased more than ten-fold over the decade. The turnover of trading put through was as high as Rs. 11 lakh crores during 2008-09 on the BSE and 28 lakh crores on NSE.

Listed Paid-up Capital

The paid-up share capital of listed companies in 1946 was Rs. 270 crores while in 1997, the figure was more than Rs. 1.07 lakh crores. The market value of the capital of these listed companies stood at around Rs. 5 lakh crores in 1997 which has gone down to around Rs. 3.5 lakh crores due to sharp fall in prices during 1998 and zoomed up during the boom period of 2007-08 to Rs. 51 lakh crores and above, on the BSE. Both the market capitalisation and the turnover were lower in 2008-09, due to depressed market conditions and global recession.

Who Owns the Securities?

The gilt-edged securities are officially listed on the recognised stock exchanges as soon as they are issued by the authorities concerned. These securities constitute the largest amount of debt traded on the stock exchanges as the government sector is the major borrower in the economy.

Almost the entire outstanding rupee debt is owned by the commercial banks, the Life Insurance Corpn., Provident Funds and charitable trusts. Less than one per cent is owned directly by individuals. But anyone who has a bank account or is a policyholder or a beneficiary of a public or private trust is basically involved in the ownership of gilt-edged securities. Therefore, an increasingly large number of persons is being interested indirectly in Government securities. Their number will grow as savings increase and development under the Five-Year Plans is financed by public borrowing on a more extensive scale. This evidences the influence of the gilt-edged market and its vital significance in the economic life of the country.

The growth and present position of stocks and shares of joint stock companies listed on the recognised stock exchanges indicate a substantial increase in the public stake in listed stocks over the past. A study of the ownership pattern of the companies listed on the BSE in 1989 by the author showed that individuals continue to be the major category of holders although their share declined from 56.4% in 1984 to 45.9% in 1989. The shares of corporate bodies and financial institutions have stood at around 28.4% and 11.2% respectively in 1989. The share of corporate bodies has increased from 17.8% in 1984 to 28.4% in 1989. This trend got accentuated due to proportional allotment system imposed by SEBI, and the share of individuals fell further, during Nineties.

Bombay Stock Exchange

The Bombay Stock Exchange is the premier stock exchange in India. It was the first to be recognised on a permanent basis in 1957. The capital listed in Mumbai accounted for about 40% of the overall capital listed on all the stock exchanges whereas its share of the market capitalisation amounted to around 50%. In terms of the total number of companies and total number of stock issues listed also, Mumbai ranked first. It has 4929 listed companies, while the same on NSE was only 1432 companies.

The Bombay Stock Exchange regularly publishes statistics on market turnover of securities though similar figures for the other exchanges are now available with the SEBI. It is, however, roughly estimated that the turnover of Bombay Stock Exchange is about 40% of the overall turnover of all the stock exchanges in the country and NSE accounts for more than 50% of the total all India figure, in recent years.

The total turnover at BSE during 2008-09 was Rs. 11 lakh crores as against Rs. 28 lakh crores on the NSE. The BSE market capitalisation was however, higher Rs. 31 lakh crore as aganist Rs. 29 lakh crore on NSE in 2008-09.

Patel Committee

A high-powered committee under the chairmanship of Shri G. S. Patel, former Chairman of the Unit Trust of India, was set up by the Union Government in May 1984 to make a comprehensive review of the functioning of the stock exchanges and make recommendations.

The terms of reference of the Committee included *inter alia,* the following:

— to examine the general functioning of the stock exchanges as an integral part of the financial system;

— to suggest measures to improve the overall service to investors by the members of stock exchanges and to encourage small investors particularly in semi-urban and rural areas to invest in industrial securities;

— to look into the existing system of organisation and management of stock exchanges with a view to broadbase it so as to make it representative of all concerned interests and to suggest a uniform model of organisation, etc.

After deliberations which lasted more than a year, the Committee submitted its Report to the Union Finance Ministry in December 1985. In the light of the recommendations made by the Committee in their interim Report, the government issued several guidelines and directives to the stock exchanges relating to matters of securities on the stock exchange, creation of a Customers' Protection Fund and insurance cover for members of stock exchanges, etc.

Regulations on Trading

As regards the regulations on trading in the ring of the Exchange, the Stock Exchange authorities operate a variety of regulations in the following ways:

Firstly, only authorised clerks of the members are permitted to enter the trading ring with their badges. Sauda Block Books or confirmation Memos are provided by the Stock Exchange. Entry into the Trading Ring is restricted to members and their authorised clerks. The inspectors of the Stock Exchange visit the ring and check the presence of unauthorised persons, any indiscipline or violence or other malafide acts. Persons involved in such acts could be removed from the trading ring, suspended or punished otherwise. The security guards provide physical help to the inspectors.

Secondly, the Monitoring Dept. or Surveillance Dept. of the Exchange keeps a watch on the price movements and the trading volume of the members and take such action as is necessary to control excessive trading and speculative fervour. It may impose *ad hoc* margins, suspend trading and enquire into any special developments.

Thirdly, in the case of any disputes on the trading floor as between members or their authorised assistants, the floor committee can officially intervene and give their judgment on the dispute, whether relating to the price or quantity or the scrip or there can be administrative intervention by inspectors. Trading Ring has lost its importance with the use of electronic type of trading and matching of purchase and sale transactions through the Exchange. The inspection of trading operations is also done electronically.

Fourthly, the Operations Department of the Stock Exchange will supervise the operations, make any announcements at the time of trading, suspension of trading or collection of quotations, giving of company information, etc. The fixation of different types of margins, making up prices (Havala rates) and supervision of trading etc. are the responsibility of the Executive Director. The auctions of shares and related matters connected with settlement are looked into by the Operations Department.

The types of margins imposed are as follows:

(1) Daily margins on purchases or sales of members at varying rates or on the total outstanding position in each scrip.

(2) Carry-over margins at the time of settlement on each of the scrips at varying rates up to 50% or more depending upon whether they are purchases or sales.

(3) Limits imposed on total trade by each of the members in all scrips together to keep a control on overtrading by members.

(4) *Ad hoc* margins, imposed specially on any scrip or scrips subject to high speculative attacks.

(5) Suspension of trading in any scrip for any period of time, shifting of a scrip from group A to group B and *vice versa,* etc. depending on conditions of trading in the scrip.

(6) Fixation of minimum or maximum prices for any of the scrips called filter levels. Circuit breakers are now used for rise or fall in prices of scrips beyond a stipulated level of 10% or 15% on any trading day.

To give examples of how margins operate on trading, let us take the following cases:

Member A has purchased 500 and sold 200 with a net purchase position of 300 scrips. The price of the TISCO scrip is Rs. 115. The margin on purchase is at a rate of Rs. 5 per scrip. Then the purchase price becomes Rs. 115 – 5 = 110. An amount of 500 × Rs. 5 = Rs. 2,500 is deposited with the Stock Exchange to the credit of the member. This is a margin on the gross purchases.

Member B has purchased 800, sold 1,000 with a net sale position of 200 scrips. The price of the Century scrip is Rs. 3,400. The imposed margin is Rs. 400 per scrip. Then the sale price becomes Rs. 3400 + 400 = Rs. 3,800. An amount of 200 × Rs. 400 = Rs. 80,000 is kept with the Stock Exchange to the credit of the member, which is a margin on net sales.

These margins will apply in the same manner whether it is a daily gross or net position or carry-over net position. But they vary depending on the scrip, its price and speculative position in the market. These rates are different for purchases and sales. The net price after adjustment of margins is used for the purpose of carry-over.

Investor Protection

Certain measures of investor protection adopted by the Exchanges deserve special mention here. Firstly, the Exchanges have set up a Customer Protection Fund, in tune with guidelines issued by the Ministry of Finance. The objective of the fund is to compensate the investor clients of member brokers who have defaulted. In all genuine cases of claims, the clients are compensated upto a maximum which varies from Exchange to Exchange. This Fund is financed by a levy on the turnover of members collected at the rate of one rupee for every Rs. 10 lakhs of turnover and by contributions from the listing fees, collected at the rate of 2% from the companies.

Another service provided was through Investor Complaints Cell set up a decade ago, but rechristened as Investor Service Cell in some exchanges. The service was strengthened to render expeditious service to the investors and to attend to their grievances. As many as thousands of complaints are received per month, of which 90-95% are against the companies and the rest against the brokers. The nature of complaints is non-receipt of refund order, allotment letters, dividends, brokerage, underwriting commission, etc. Of the complaints received, about 50% are attended satisfactorily.

Another service provided by major exchanges is to arrange an insurance policy to broker-members through the New India Assurance Co. This policy covers the perils of forgery, fabrication of securities and transfer deeds and receipts, identity of the transferer, loss of securities in transit, etc., which the brokers are subject to during their transactions with clients for delivery of shares for transfer. In view of this protection, the brokers can attest the signatures of transferers which will help quicken the process of share transfer.

To expedite the process of delivery of shares in the settlement and clearing procedure of the Stock Exchange, the BOI Shareholdings Ltd. was set up jointly by the Bank of India and the Stock Exchange, Mumbai in November 1989. This new organisation takes over the clearing and delivery of shares for both 'A' and 'B' Group shares on the Stock Exchange. The actual delivery of shares as between the member brokers is now replaced by Delivery Slips, passed or credited and debited with BOI Holdings. No physical transfer of shares takes place and hence it saves a lot of time involved in delivery after clearing. This is comparable to the present day demat form of trading.

Many Stock Exchanges have also provided a service to investors in the form of fixing up an odd lot trading session on every alternate Saturday and shortlisting a group of brokers who agreed to deal in odd lots for the benefit of purchase/sale/consolidation etc. of odd lots. The investors can get quotations for odd lots in major scrips and deal in them more freely than before. The service of purchase from investors of odd lots was later extended by the UTI, GIC and Canbank and others as an over-the-counter facility. This odd lot trading has lost its significance with the dematerialisation of physical shares into book entries.

Measures to Promote Healthy Stock Markets

With a view to reduce delays in listing arising out of conversion, the Govt has issued a circular authorising the stock exchanges to take action and monitor the issues of over Rs. 10 crores and if the delay is deliberate without adequate reasons, the Exchange should report the matter to the Registrar of Companies, SEBI, etc., and also take suitable action. The Government has amended the SCR rules in December 1988 to permit multiple membership of stock exchanges and to enable the granting of membership to financial and corporate institutions.

In October 1988, the Bhansali Committee's recommendation on share transfer procedures was implemented whereby the newly-allotted shares have to be treated on par with the old shares for delivery purpose, subject to the adjustment of the dividend depending on the time of allotment. The minimum capital for listing has been raised to Rs. 3 crores of which Rs. 1.8 crores should have been issued to the public effective February 1989. This was further raised to Rs. 5 crores or Rs. 10 crores depending on the Stock Exchange from October 1995. The guidelines for listing have also been amended, particularly with regard to book closure and record dates and to give more powers to the stock exchanges to monitor the allotment of new issues and to curb insider trading or takeover bids. Banks have been permitted to lend up to 90% of the value of shares to be acquired by the employees out of their quota of new issue subject to a ceiling.

The government has approved the creation of Over-the-Counter Exchange of India (OTC) which would help the introduction of a multi-tiered market for securities. Stock exchanges have been directed to transfer the scrip of company from the specified section to the spot section if the company intends to come out with the rights issues. The Employees' Option Scheme was partially modified restricting the allotment of the unavailed portion of the public/rights issues earmarked for employees only to financial or investment institutions or mutual funds.

As it has been found that the various stock exchanges are following different methods of calculating the amount of dividend to be deducted while trading in the new shares, which are on a *pari passu* basis, the government has clarified in June 1990 that all stock exchanges should follow the same practice and the new shares should be traded and delivered along with old shares provided the new shares are traded and delivered at least one day in the relevant settlement period. The dividend can be deducted from the price for the new shares at not more than the amount of dividend for one year.

Clause 40 of the listing agreement has been replaced by 40A and 40B. Under clause 40A, when any person acquires 5% or more of the shares of a company in terms of its nominal value, the stock exchange should be notified within two days of such acquisition or agreement to purchase by the company, by the intermediary or by the acquirer. Under clause 40B, if there is a take-over offer, a public announcement of the offer should be made both by the offeree and offerer. This requirement is necessary when any person acquires shares carrying 10% or more of the total voting rights of the company through their shareholdings or to secure control over the management of the company. The offer should be made public and by a public announcement and notification to the stock exchange and SEBI with regard to the terms of offer, identity of offeror and other terms and conditions and such information should be made available to all the shareholders of the offeree and offeror companies. Clause 41 was added recently to the listing Agreement to enforce half-yearly publication of results of the working of the company. This was made quarterly publication of Results by the listed companies during 1999.

The government has also notified certain guidelines for institutional transactions in shares. For any sale of over 1% of paid up capital of the company, the information regarding such transactions should be reported to the SEBI and the concerned stock exchanges and to the public within a day of the transaction through a press release. The Board of each financial institution should lay down the criteria for such transactions. The guidelines also state that all purchases or sales should be for delivery and they should be made through approved brokers at market prices. Besides no sale should be made at a negotiated price to non-institutional buyers. If, in the case of a sick company, the management changes, and such negotiated sale takes place, that should be disclosed to the public through a press release and also to the SEBI and the concerned stock exchange.

Clause 16 of the listing agreement has also been amended to require companies to fix the date of book closing and record dates either on the 1st or the 16th of any month and to give a notice to the Exchange of at least 42 days in advance. The company should also ensure that the time gap between the book closures and record dates should be 90 days. The company is also required to undertake that the securities delivered for transfer will be transferred and despatched within a period of two months from the date of receipt under the Law and within one month as per the Listing agreement.

As regards the capital issues, under-subscribed in the rights or public issues, the companies have been instructed to refund all the application monies within 120 days of the opening of issue if a minimum of 90% subscription is not secured. If the refund orders are not passed even on the expiry of 10 days after a period of 120 days, interest at the rate of 15% is payable. The subscription amount would be kept in a specific bank account and companies will have no access to the funds unless the concerned stock exchange has permitted the allotment. This allotment will not be permitted until the 90% limit of subscription is achieved. It is also essential for the promoters to make their subscriptions in advance before the public issue opens and give a certificate to this effect to the concerned Exchange. If the level of 90% is not reached by the public subscription, the underwriters will have to make the subscriptions up to their limits of underwriting to achieve the minimum level of 90% subscription. The stock exchanges and in particular the regional stock exchanges are thus given a crucial role in the allotment and listing of new issues.

OTHER REFORMS

Among other reforms mention may be made of broad basing the boards, better surveillance over companies and brokers, stricter enforcement of the trading regulations and listing norms and better disclosures for transperency. Weekly settlement system was enforced on all Stock Exchanges uniformly which was followed by Daily Rollover System in Selected Scrips from 1999. Trade guarantee fund and Investor Protection Funds were maintained in many Stock Exchanges. Enforcement of a code of corporate governance, quarterly publication of results and better disclosures were insisted upon the listed companies. Uniform settlement cycle of Monday to Friday on all Stock Exchanges was also recommended by the SEBI and uniform listing procedures were adopted and coordinated by an All India Listing Authority since 2004.

BOLT system was enlarged and more centres in India got connected for internet trading. NSE has also planned for overseas centres for trading purposes. Badla system was streamlined and strengthened with better surveillance in selected scrips. Volumes of trading and liquidity had increased due to electronic trading. This trend was facilitated by Demat form of holding shares, quicker weekly settlements and clearing supported by a powerful regulatory system, operated by SEBI.

Rolling Settlement System

The recent reforms of SEBI with regard to stock market include *inter alia,* the strengthening of the Rolling Settlement System which was done during 2000-2001. Bulk of the reforms during 1996 to 2000 encompass the electronic trading system, clearance and settlement systems. Uniform trading cycle, clearance and settlement through Demat system, without the need for physical certificates, weekly settlements and T + 2 settlement, setting up of Trade Guarantee Funds for ensuring settlements, Customer Protection Funds, quicker Settlements, Internet trading, Broker Website Trading etc. are some of the examples of the recent Stock Market reforms, effected by SEBI.

The SEBI had announced early in Feb. 2000 that Stock Markets would move towards a rolling Settlement System for selected Scrips in 'B' group and trading for them in a Demat form. Some 153 companies were earmarked for a Demat form of trading and compulsory Rolling settlement system. During March to June 2000, these selected companies must have signed an agreement with Central Depository Services Limited and NSDL for compulsory dematerialisation of their stocks for trading in Demat form for all investors and their trading on the stock markets will be compulsorily done on rolling settlement basis. Such companies which have recently changed their names to represent their software business and some NBFCs which have been delicensed by the RBI would be on compulsory Demat form and on rolling settlement basis. Similarly, some companies which exhibited high volatility have been earmarked by the SEBI for trading on Rolling Settlement basis before June end 2000. Shares of companies which have gone recently for initial public offering but are not yet listed will be traded only in a Demat form, although investors not trading can continue to keep their stock in physical form. Demat form of trading was imposed on all scrips, gilted securities etc, after 2000.

CDSL: CENTRAL DEPOSITORY SERVICES LIMITED

The CDSL is promoted by Bombay Stock Exchange. The SEBI has mandated that the major Stock Exchanges like NSE, Delhi, Ahmedabad and Calcutta should be connected to CDSL. The clearing members of these Exchanges should open accounts with CDSL to facilitate settlement of trade in Demat form. This is in addition to existing NSDL, set up mainly by NSE.

The rolling settlement was introduced from Jan. 10, 2000 in selected scrips and later extended to most of the traded scrips. The clearing members have to compulsorily open a clearing account with a Depository participant. All pay in and payout operations are to be settled in a Demat form.

GLOBALISATION OF STOCK EXCHANGES

Demat Form of Trading

Majority of Scrips are put in Demat form for trading in the last few months during 1999 to 2004. Earlier compulsory Demat form was introduced to most of the "A" group scrips and some leading "B" group scrips. This will increase volumes in trading and there will be consequent increase in liquidity. Nearly 90% of trade is already in Demat form, with nearly 600 scrips in compulsory Demat trading as at end May 2000. By 2005, all scrips which are traded are in Demat form of trading with T + 1 settlement.

Electronic Form of Trading

Globalisation of Stock Exchanges is now on way. The electronic age has come to the stock market. Nearly 100% of all transactions are executed through electronic media on line trading system. The number of cities covered by NSE and BSE electronic network would have crossed 1000 mark, by end 2000. More and more brokers and sub-brokers are getting into the internet trading system.

Internet Trading (e-trading)

The SEBI have allowed e-trading and brokers would rush to the web-sites and trading through web sites would increase. On the internet, one would be able to trade instantly and transparently from any part of the world. Trade is confirmed via the internet in no time and by this method, the investor comes to know immediately the trade, member, time, rate at which the trade took place. There will also be quicker settlements and collections.

Electronic Fund Collection

Under this system, the brokers get their funds directly credited to their accounts and the clients can in-turn get their accounts credited or debited for the net funds to flow across the country. This facilitates quicker payments, improves the liquidity position of brokers and gets funds one day after the pay out day to obviate possible defaults or cash-out positions of brokers and sub-brokers.

The web-site on the basis of investor's portfolio can give the investor information on company results, report cards, company analysis and the performance of the company.

There will be a number of improvements in the process as well as the products. So far as the process is concerned, there will be settlements on a daily basis and on a rolling basis, electronic settlement and clearance, e-mail for transmission of funds, badla trading on a daily basis, internet based trading etc. So far as product improvements are concerned, portfolio of investors may include a number of new products such as derivatives and synthetics.

The other facilities include Basket trading, trading in Index Funds, Voting and Non-voting shares, Tracker shares and complex derivatives. Tracker shares refer to the separate divisional shares of a company such I.T. Divisions of Wipro or Tatas. Portfolio Tracker for valuation on web-site, company analysis and M.I.S. on the companies in one's portfolio are presented through the web-site. There will be automatic borrowing and lending facilities, institutionalised security lending, Automatic financing or margin buying and a host of other facilities on the Stock Exchanges.

Foreign Listing

As the country opened upto foreign operations many more Indian Companies got listed on Foreign Stock Markets of London, New York, Nasdaq etc. Internet and on line trading facility is created in selected foreign centres. The regional stock exchanges and local trading became gradually redundant in the context of global trading. Slowly foreign companies would be listed on the Indian Exchanges and trading would take place in such foreign shares in India.

Indian capital account controls are slowly getting dismantled and liberalised. Freer flow of FDI funds into India and liberal borrowing facilities for Indian Companies abroad tended to globalise Indian markets. Indian Mutual Funds are allowed to invest in Foreign Securities upto a limit. The GDRs and ADRs of Indian Companies are well received in foreign markets and are traded freely in foreign stock markets.

OTCEI, NSE and ICSE

Securities Exchanges

A well-developed securities market ensures easy and quick marketability to the securities which imparts liquidity to them. If this objective of liquidity is to be ensured, all the securities, good or bad, have to have a market for trading and dealings. This market can be fostered and developed by proper marketing strategies and provision of infrastructure for the purpose. One such strategy is to have a multi-tier market to suit the various types of securities.

The companies may be in various stages of growth, young and newborn, growing, mature and decaying, etc. All cannot have equal status in terms of liquidity, safety, marketability, etc. Similarly, all cannot satisfy the same standards of performance in terms of return, risk, service to investors, etc. So, in order to meet the objectives of the market, and to meet the varying types of companies, there is a method of differentiation of the market segments by creating some tiers of exchanges with varying requirements of standards. These meet the different characteristics of the companies and at the same time, ensure product differentiation for investors to have more than one method of trading and investment. It is with these motives that a multi-tier structure of exchanges is established and promoted by many countries.

Structured Markets

In many developed countries as in the USA, there is a well-structured market for securities. There, the secondary market trading in securities can be classified as under:

First Market: Trading on the floor of the Exchange of the listed companies.

Second Market: Trading over the counter for OTC issues.

Third Market: Trading off the Exchange floor of listed securities of the Exchange with the aid of brokers.

Fourth Market: Trading of the listed securities of the Exchange off the floor without the aid of brokers as between buyers and sellers.

The OTC market as seen above is one such tier of the structure and generally comprises:

(1) Inactive issues and less liquid shares, not eligible for listing in the regular exchange.

(2) Thinner issues with limited public holding but command some national trading interests.

(3) Actively-traded issues listed on the OTC.

OTC Defined

Over-the-Counter Market is a market where buyers seek out sellers and *vice versa* and then attempt to arrange terms and conditions for purchase/sale acceptable to both parties. It is a negotiated market place that exists anywhere as opposed to the auction market place, represented by activity on the Securities Exchanges.

Thus, in the OTC, trading takes place by putting buy and sell orders by telephone, telex, letter, oral message, etc. There is no particular market place in the geographical sense.

The OTC relates to a type of security trading in which the market caters to some basic objectives, like

(a) quicker liquidity;

(b) fixed and fair price;

(c) liquidity for a less traded security or that of smaller company;

(d) simplified process of buying and selling;

(e) creation of public interest in risky but viable ventures; and

(f) easy and cheaper means of making public sale of new issues.

Investor Interests

As companies differ in their size and performance, there is need for different tiers for their listing. Besides, there is another reason why a well-structured market is necessary for future growth of the capital market in India. The uninitiated individual investors are at present left to the mercy of the professional traders and speculators on the regular exchanges. These individual investors have different investment profiles of risk-return combinations and other perceptions of income, safety and liquidity which are completely different from the professional investors, institutional investors, mutual funds, financial institutions, etc. For such category, a different and simpler type of market is needed, which the OTC provides. The rules of fair practice, charging fair and reasonable prices in relation to market conditions, a maximum mark-up policy of, say, 5% as in the NASDAQ are some examples of standardisation of rules and regulations, which will protect the uninitiated investors from being cheated by brokers, players, etc. in the market. Such rules are also adopted in India. In the USA, for example, the byelaws and rules imposed by SEC on their OTC, namely, NASDAQ, will protect the investors and they have also a right to complain about any unethical practices of members with respect to prices or margins etc. These rules are of four distinct categories in the USA:

(a) Uniform practice code in their dealings among the member firms.

(b) Code of procedure for violations of these rules and dealing with complaints.

(c) Rules of fair practice, specifying the rules governing the members *vis-a-vis* the investing public.

(d) Code of Arbitration laid down the procedure for arbitration of disputes between brokers and investing members of the public.

Practices Abroad

In OTC, the broker can act as an agent or principal. He acts as agent when he puts through the transaction with a market-maker or some other broker. He then charges a commission. But if he acts as a principal, he is a market-maker himself, quotes both bid and offer rates and executes the order at his quoted price but does not charge commission as his profit lies in the spread between bid and ask prices. Dealing with the market-makers helps the investors save on the commission paid to the agent broker and to be assured that he is charged a fair price as the market-maker is supposed to know the position of the company and its performance to fix a fair price.

Although there is no trading place and no apparent visibility of the bargaining process as in the trading ring of the exchanges, the OTC rules would impose strict norms of fair margins and competitive bidding by the market-makers. As trading is computer based there is transparency of all deals and prices. Besides, to check on the brokers' quotations, the investor can enquire with the market-makers for the bid and offer rates for any scrip.

OTC and New Issues Market

As per the practices in the USA, OTC dealers can operate both in the primary and secondary markets, while on the Stock Exchange, market-makers or specialists can only operate in the secondary market. Besides, the OTC market keeps its doors open to all types of new issues, namely, those that are not eligible to be listed on the regular stock exchanges, and those that are eligible. The advantage of being on the OTC is the lower cost of raising new issues, the lower expenses of servicing and maintaining the existing investors in its registers, etc.

The cost of raising fresh issues has to be kept low, so that new entrepreneurs and fresh entrants into the market can raise funds at lower rates than the existing ones as well as the bigger companies. The loading to share prices, that the speculative elements will lead to, may overburden the regular and the smaller investors. Correct pricing of shares, keeping the cost of trading and of raising of new issues to the minimum are some of the objectives of the OTC.

OTC and Stock Exchange

Besides introducing structural changes, the OTC can correct some of the drawbacks of the existing market mechanism on the stock exchanges like illiquidity of a number of scrips, speculative manoeuvring, rigged-up prices, delays in the realisation of the proceeds of sale or delivery of scrips and high volatility of prices, etc. are referred to below. The major problem so far as the public is concerned is that this should help new and small investors to come into the corporate folders and, for the companies to raise the necessary capital at the lowest possible cost. Besides, the share valuation defy any laws or reasons. In the case of new issues of new companies, there is no acceptable method of valuation. There are also innumerable difficulties in the valuation of even the existing shares. Only highly qualified experts among the merchant bankers can provide a guide for correct valuation. Regular stock exchanges may or may not reflect the correct values.

Advantages of OTC

Briefly, specific advantages of OTC as it operates abroad can be set out as follows:

(1) Advantages to smaller companies and less liquid companies to be listed as they are not eligible for listing on the regular exchange.

(2) Lower costs of new issues and lower expenses of servicing the investors.

(3) Family concerns and companies closely held can go public through OTC.

(4) Competition as between the dealers exists better than on the regular stock exchange and the larger the number of dealers, the better is the market.

(5) Dealers can operate both in new issues and secondary markets at their option.

(6) Greater freedom to choose stocks by dealers for market-making in both the primary and secondary markets.

(7) Information flows are freer and more direct from market-makers to customers due to close contacts between firms and market-makers.

(8) Regulatory measures are adopted and a strict code of conduct exists for members.

Structural Weaknesses in India

In India, there are many structural weaknesses in the securities market. To start with, there is a mushroom growth of companies without proper assessment of their viability, with the result that the number of listed companies grew to more than 8,000 of which hardly 300 companies are well-traded. In nearly 90% of the companies, there is no liquidity as the market is not developed in them. In a study made by Shri Paul Joseph on thinly-traded shares, it was shown that leaving aside a large number of shares in which there is either no trading or there is no information on their trading, nearly two-thirds of the companies for which information is available are not traded well in the sense that they are traded only for less than 50% of trading days. Nearly, one-half of these companies are traded only in less than 10% of the trading days. This clearly brings out the woeful lack of liquidity, despite the common belief that the stock exchanges provide liquidity to investors. (Thesis of Shri Paul Joseph submitted to the University of Hull, U.K., 1990).

Secondly, there are a large number of small companies which are closely held and in which public holding is small and hence no market exists for them. The study of Shri Paul Joseph has also shown that nearly 75% of the inadequately traded companies have a paid-up capital less than Rs. 3 cores and their public holding is poor. Nearly 80% of the thinly-traded companies have public holding of less than 60% of the paid-up equity. In the bulk of these companies, there are less than 10,000 shareholders on their registers which can hardly lead to any public interest. In most of such companies, the holding of promoters and financial institutions is so heavy that no public interest exists and trading cannot take place. Thus, the main factors which explain the lack of proper trading are the size of equity paid-up and the share of public holdings. For such companies, OTC can be expected to provide a market through an open sale to public.

Thirdly, there is inadequate supply of good scrips leading to supply and demand imbalances in them for two reasons. This is mainly due to the fact that financial institutions are holding large chunks of these scrips which they do not part with. They have become major investors rather than mere financiers which may really be objectionable from the point of view of making the issues widely held by the public. Besides, management in India are jealously guarding themselves against possible takeovers, outside interference and threat to their family interests. They generally do not part with their shares due to the fear of possible management interference or takeover which can be mitigated only by the OTC.

Fourthly, the existing market mechanism does not permit the public to know the correct share values both in the primary and secondary markets due to manipulation of premium in the new issues market and rigging and speculation in the secondary market. The free market forces do not operate and the control of SEBI and the stock exchanges is inadequate. The correct share pricing can be ensured by market-makers in the OTC if they are guided and regulated properly.

Fifthly, there is a major complaint of neglect of genuine investors, small and less educated investors and rural and semi-urban public. These categories do not have enough knowledge of the market operations and are cheated by the so-called sub-brokers. To begin with, the prices they pay may not be fair prices as they are manipulated by speculative forces and the knowledge of fair prices is not spread and understood by the investors. Besides, they are overcharged due to brokerages and commissions etc. They are misguided by the investment magazines, companies, brokers and sub-brokers about the prospects of the companies. The problem of these investors are manifold and they are growing both in the new issues market and secondary market. These problems can be reduced to some extent if the OTC can operate in a way that fair prices are fixed and advertised by the market-makers and the cult of investment through OTC is spread to rural and semi-urban areas and to less educated investors. Of course, the small investors can also be served better if mutual funds become popular with them.

Sixthly, delivery of shares to buyers and payment of money to sellers is at present taking an unduly long time on the major stock exchanges. Many investors have suffered due to the funds being tied up in application money in new issues and in the sale of shares on the stock exchanges. Sometimes, funds could not be realised for more than three to six months. Similarly, companies do not send the shares or allotment letters for long periods of time with the result that shares could not be sold and money realised. There are innumerable such complaints by the public against companies and brokers. Many of these problems can be reduced if trading is shifted to OTC where the methods of operations are such that the scope for manipulation, speculation and malpractices is less. The time gap in many of these operations would also be less and liquidity requirements can be met quickly and easily.

Yet another problem is price volatility of shares on the regular stock exchanges. The daily fluctuations of prices are sometimes so wide that genuine investors suffer, if they are not wary. The speculative pressures are responsible for these wide fluctuations and it is reported that jobbers' spread is also wide in many scrips. These problems lead to some complaints from genuine investors who are not interested in speculative gains. Their calculations may go wrong and price changes as between the placing of order and its execution may lead to an adverse position to the parties. Such problems may not exist in the OTC.

Role of OTC

In the above context of prevailing structural weaknesses in the securities markets in India and the malpractices rampant in both the primary and secondary markets, drastic reforms are long overdue. Firstly, there is urgent need for legislative reforms by amendments to existing laws, whereby the legal loopholes can be plugged and corporate behaviour can be improved. Many malpractices and defaults of companies can be corrected by penal powers given to the SEBI, and stock exchanges, which has been done.

Secondly, control and supervision of the activities of the merchant bankers, advisers, investment consultants, etc. are necessary to reduce the malpractices and improve the climate of new issues market. The SEBI has initiated steps in this direction and laid down guidelines for merchant bankers.

Thirdly, certain malpractices adopted by the Registrars to new issues, banks, companies, etc. involved in allotment of new issues to the public, despatch of refund orders, share allotment letters, etc. have all been brought under the net of penal provisions for protecting the interests of investors and public, by the SEBI. The introduction of Demat form of allotment and trading reduced these malpractices.

Fourthly, as the major culprits in primary and secondary markets are the companies themselves, the provisions relating to the new issues, transfer of shares, issue of dividend warrants and services to investors in all forms should be brought into the ambit of heavy penalties imposed on companies for all investor complaints. The motto that the investor is the king has to be enshrined in the legislative framework of the Amendments to Companies Act, Securities Contracts (Regulation) Act and the SEBI Act.

So far as the secondary market is concerned, a multi-tier exchange system for trading as in New York and London, has to be developed in India. A beginning in this direction is made through the OTC Exchange of India and by SEBI reforms. Secondly, a large number of companies in which there was no trading and which were only listed on the stock exchanges for the purpose of quotation and for the tax benefits should be delisted if there is no public interest in such companies. Another exchange can thus be permitted for trading in the delisted companies and if the companies are really interested in promoting public interest, trading will take place in such an exchange for those companies which are viable.

Companies with a capital base of not less than Rs. 5 crores of paid-up equity and a public issue of Rs. 1.25 crores can be listed on the regular stock exchanges. Such companies should have a track record of two years after commercial production was started. The type of companies not eligible to be listed on the regular exchange now enter the OTC Exchange.

There are two other categories of companies which deserve special attention in India, namely, sick companies and the public sector companies, which the government would like to privatise. In respect of these two categories, acquisition and takeovers can be encouraged and/or a slow process of public participation in their issues can be promoted. The public sector companies, which require revitalisation to improve efficiency, may be shifted to the joint sector with a gradual increase in participation by the private sector. The shares allotted to the public in this respect can also be traded in the stock exchange whereby their performance can be assessed from time to time.

In India, more recently public sector financial institutions have set up venture capital funds for promoting risky enterprises by the new entrepreneurs. The promotion of these companies and their popularisation with the public should be their responsibility. The OTC can take care of them, so that these venture capital greenfield companies can have a better future in the Indian markets. The financial institutions which have set up the OTC Exchange may also think of a separate counter for sale of shares of existing companies, which are good in their track record and whose shares are in demand with the public. Normally, institutions do not sell their holdings but only acquire from the public and individuals. Thus, there is a great imbalance in supply and demand for the blue chip companies and debentures of good companies with triple "A" rating are not easily available. This institutional counter should buy and sell at fair prices rather than at the market prices, as the latter include a large component of speculative burden loaded to the fair price to the great disadvantage of the small investors, retired persons, widows, etc. and for this OTCEI can be a venue.

There are many such potential reforms possible in the Indian capital market. The OTC Exchange of India is perhaps the most important reform which can take over trading in a number of companies under the above categories but it should be admitted that OTC is only a beginning of the reforms in the direction of multi-tier structure of exchanges in India. The advantages of the OTC referred to above can be realised depending upon the role that it assumes in future.

Over-the-Counter Exchange of India (OTCEI)

Although the Indian stock exchanges had a hoary antiquity and history of more than 100 years, they are still in their adolescent stage. The markets suffer from many weaknesses, despite diverse regulatory and reformatory measures taken by the government. This is because these measures were half-hearted and *ad hoc*.

Despite a large number of companies of more than 8,000 listed on these markets, hardly 20-30% of these enjoy any worthwhile liquidity and marketability. In fact, only 200 to 300 companies are well traded and have an assured market, on any day.

Secondly, the stock exchanges have no effective powers to control the malpractices of companies listed despite the enabling provisions laid down in the Listing Agreements as these cannot be enforced by them in the absence of penal powers.

Thirdly, the supply of shares of good companies is limited due to a large component of them being concentrated in the hands of the financial institutions and mutual funds. The public holdings of many of these companies is limited to 20-30% of their total paid-up capital on an average.

Fourthly, even when there is liquidity and marketability shares, the time taken to realise cash from sales is unduly long, ranging from two to three months, due to settlement and clearance procedures of the exchanges which has been reduced drastically by SEBI through its reforms. Lastly, the cost of raising funds through new issues has increased sharply and many small companies find it difficult to raise funds under these conditions. Besides, there are many malpractices both in the new issues market and the secondary market, in the form of delay of refund and allotment orders, rigging up of prices before listing, delay in effecting transfer of shares of more than 2 to 3 months and insider trading, overcharging and other malpractices in the secondary market. Besides, excessive speculative activity has marred the prospects of correct valuation of shares with the result that the real investors suffer and some are duped by manipulators in both new issues and secondary markets. The market being single tier, there is no effective competition.

In this type of monolithic structure of the securities market, there is a great need for reforms. A properly tiered structure with companies of various sizes of paid-up capital and liquidity is to be developed in India. A market of multi-tier structure exists in many developed countries, as over- the-counter market, cash counter, 24-hour trading, options, futures trading and trading in index derivatives, etc.

In India, an attempt has just been made in the direction of developing a multi-tier market with the opening of the OTC Exchange of India, in 1992.

Objectives of OTCEI

The formal approval of the government for the setting up of the Over-the-Counter Exchange of India was granted in August 1989 under the Securities Contracts (Regulation) Act, 1956, but the actual operations started only in October 1992. It was an event of far-reaching consequence for the Indian capital market as it introduces another tier to the structure of the securities market. It provides a less expensive method of getting shares listed for trading and for raising capital from the market. The OTC market will initially prove a boon to the small investors as it provides easier liquidity and quicker transactions and ultimately help in the formation of "national market."

Shares could be bought and sold over the counters with licensed dealers and across the country. Initially, the OTC market will permit trading in the shares of "greenfield companies" nurtured by the mutual funds and venture capital funds. But eventually, the OTC market will create a market-place for all tradable securities listed as well as convertible and non-convertible debentures. The objective is to impart liquidity to every existing instrument and more particularly to those for which small investors are unable to get a fair price. The OTC market will cover all places where there are stock exchanges initially after experimenting in Mumbai and later on extend its ambit to the remote areas as well. The investor is protected against manipulation by brokers and companies and has a better chance of security as no speculative effect or rigging is possible in the market.

The small investors invariably complain of lack of reliable advice due to manipulated market information and too much delay in transaction and harassment. They have no easy method of finding out fair prices. These investors are taken for a ride by unscrupulous promoters of new companies who present a rosy picture of their non-starting projects, obtain huge subscriptions from gullible investors and then vanish from the scene or divert the funds to other purposes. The OTC market will protect small investors from the malpractices of brokers as well as promoters by quoting reasonable prices as judged by the fundamentals and at competitive spread. Investment and disinvestment are made easier and quicker and better liquidity is provided.

Establishment of OTC

The OTC Exchange was promoted jointly by the Industrial Credit & Investment Corpn. of India (ICICI), the Unit Trust of India (UTI), IFCI, IDBI, SBI Capital Markets Ltd., Canbank Financial Services Ltd., the General Insurance Corpn. (GIC) and the Life Insurance Corpn. (LIC). To start with, it was set up with a paid-up capital of Rs. 5 crores in Oct. 1990. The above institutions will be the sponsor members of the OTC Exchange, and their main responsibility is to sponsor the assisted companies' shares in the market. In other words, any company which wants to list its shares on the OTC Exchange will have to be sponsored by an OTC member. The sponsors will have also to perform the market-making function, apart from appointing a second market-maker and licensed dealers.

Market-makers are like jobbers, who offer over the telephone two-way quotes every day for the securities of these companies. The bid and offer prices depend on the value that the market places on the scrip and may even be below par. The appointment of market-makers and dealers, supervision of their work and disciplinary action, if needed, are the responsibilities of the OTC Exchange Authorities.

Listing on OTCEI

Any company, new or existing, intending to sell its securities through the OTC market, must offer at least Rs. 20 lakhs to the public and have a paid-up capital of atleast Rs. 30 lakhs. Even in the case of a new company, the sponsors offer securities to the public which are privately placed with them by the company. The companies save in issue expenses as the OTC will negotiate the issue price and make placement of these shares. It provides a method of raising funds in the market and does not interfere with the management stability. The companies which would list in this exchange are small companies with a paid-up capital of less than Rs. 3 crores, but with Rs. 30 lakhs or more, closely-held companies going public and venture capital funds. Companies listed already on a stock exchange have also been listed on the OTC. Companies with paid-up capital of more than Rs. 3 crores, but less than Rs. 25 crores can get listed on OTC if they are not listed on regular Stock Exchange.

Investors Benefited

Although the basic framework of the OTC Exchange is that of a *national market, yet there is no physical location, no counters, no trading ring, no stock exchange building and no hustle and bustle scenes as at the conventional stock exchanges.* The buyers and sellers living apart from each other trade in corporate securities over the telephone. The system cuts across urban and rural areas, extending the frontiers of the stock market to the entire country. The market-maker who may be the sponsor initiates trading by quoting two-way prices (bid and offer rates) for the security for which he wants to create a market. The other important person involved is the "licensed dealer" who has been licensed to trade in securities by the OTC Exchange Board. The deals in securities are negotiated through telephone or in person at convenient locations. The licensed dealers can buy and sell at prices exhibited by market makers through the electronic network or telephones. They in turn quote their prices to the public for investment and disinvestment.

The role of the OTC market envisaged in India is similar to that in the U.S., U.K. and Japan. These OTC markets are fully automated exchanges where transactions are completed through a network of telephones/tellers/computers right from the first centre to the last centre. In addition, only professional people are authorised to render financial services. In India too, these infrastructural facilities and professional services are being used for the success of the OTC market. It is necessary to ensure a dependable and efficient telecommunication system and information network to provide accurate on-line data and prices for this type of trading. Greenfield companies and venture capital activities will get a boost by the OTC. Besides, the private limited companies and closely-held companies can be helped to go public and raise capital from the capital market. It has trading outlets in 42 cities across the country, and connected through satellite telecommunication.

Market Players

These market players are set out in the accompanying Chart I. The members are sponsors who buy wholesale and make the market through a network of licensed dealers. The final buyers and sellers are investors dealing in retail. The other players are the companies whose shares are listed, custodians and registrars for the company's shares. The OTC provides facilities for purchase on the spot by payment of cash/cheque or selling with an arrangement for payment

Chart - I

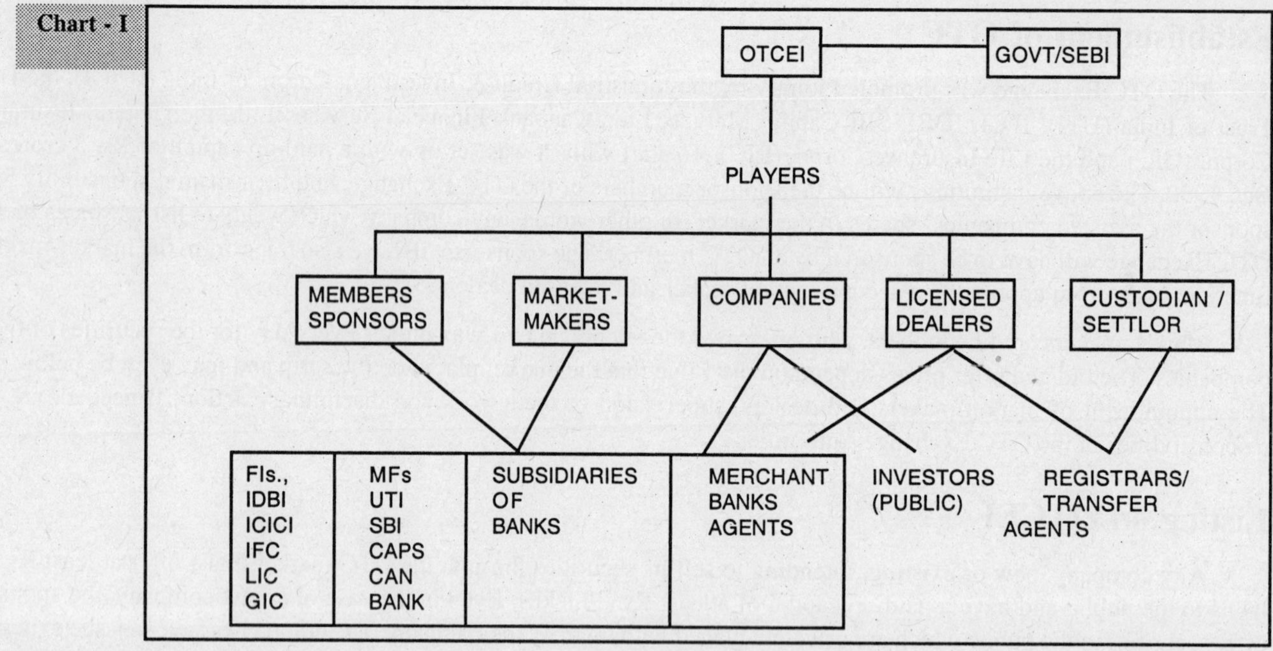

within, say, six days or less. The transfer of shares from one name to another can be done by the OTC members without reference to the company up to a limit. In fact, shares can be replaced by counter receipts issued by the market-makers/ sponsors. Ringless trading and transactions at any place are possible in this system.

Listing Procedure

The company to be listed should appoint a member of OTCEI as its sponsor, who appraises the project as to its viability and underwrites and arranges for the public issue after fixing its price.

The proposals have to be approved by the SEBI before public issues, in addition to the other formalities to be observed by the company under the Companies Act. The sponsor would certify to OTCEI as to the fairness of price, full and fair allotment of all shares to the public and guarantee to its full subscription and make market until it is listed and cannot withdraw during the first three years of market making. An additional market maker may be arranged by the sponsor, if necessary or required by the company. These requirements of compulsory market making were relaxed later on.

The sponsor has to arrange for appointment of Transfer agents and to effect share transfers within 15-18 days. The actual counter receipts would serve as share certificates which along with the transfer deed will be presented to the transfer agents for transfer. These counter receipts will be issued by dealers on the basis of the deal that they had reported to OTCEI. The standard share price is Rs. 10 and traded in minimum lots of 100 or its multiples. The investor has also to register with OTCEI before he does any business with the dealer.

The OTCEI will have to approve the draft prospectus and other agreements of the company in addition to the SEBI's approval. The letter of offer and listing formalities are to be observed before a listing agreement is actually entered into with the company.

There are about a hundred companies listed on OTCEI as end 2000, as against 49 at end March 1995. There are also many permitted securities traded on OTCEI, which include debentures. Now, even Govt. Securities can be traded on the OTCEI and RBI had recognised OTCEI members as authorised members for brokering in government securities. But later, both the companies and investors have lost interest in this market due to lack of capital appreciation and limited trading.

Trading on the OTCEI

All other rules and regulations of the OTCEI will apply and requirements of the Companies Act and SEBI Act have to be fulfilled, before listing and trading. After initial public offer (IPO), OTC counter receipts (CR) are issued to the investor. This CR will have 3 copies — one for investor, one for the counter and one for the custodian and settlor. The CR will give the details of the company, name of the settlor, price and brokerage, total value of transaction, time and date of transaction, investor's signature, his bank A/c No., and unique transaction code and dealer's code etc. Any investor in OTC has to give these details in a proforma to the dealer. In case of transfer, Application Acknowledgement Slip (AAS) is also generated in three copies and investor also gives to the counter the stamped and attested transfer deed. At the end of the day, all transfer deeds alongwith relevant CR and AAS will be sent to the settlor or custodian.

If the investor wants to sell, he produces the CR, sent to him by the settlor. The seller signs on the TD and hands over the CR and TD to the counter for sale. After the sale, the counter gives sale confirmation slip (SCS) to the investor. Three copies of the SCS will be prepared — one for investor, one for the counter and one for the custodian. At the end of each day, all the CRs and SCS along with the TDs will be sent to the custodian. Each counter will report by telex all CRs and SCS, issued by it to the OTCEI along with a consolidated statement showing company wise transactions. The volume of turnover in 1994-95 was Rs. 365 crores but afterward's the volumes fell steeply and investor interest in this Exchange failed, due to lack of speculative gains.

The counter will send to the Registrar the TDs filled by the seller along with the buyer's CR and signature of the transferee, if the share transfer is to be effected. Automatic transfer to the buyer's name will take place within seven days, if the transactions involve less than a specified size of holding say 0.5% of the company's equity. Thus, the time taken for delivery of share certificate or payment of sale proceeds will not take more than 10-15 days. There will be no speculative manipulation of prices and investor is protected from these malpractices on the OTCEI.

It will be seen from the above that the setting up of the OTC in India is the first step in the right direction. It will be the beginning of a multi-tiered structure for the securities market in India. It will mitigate some of the evils and malpractices of both the primary and secondary markets. It can reduce if not eliminate some of the investor complaints. It can hopefully promote a wider base of investor interest in the countryside and a healthier capital market in future. The raising of resources from the capital market, particularly by small entrepreneurs and venture enterprises, will be made easier and cheaper. The OTC has thus, an important role to play in India for the future of the capital market.

Problems

Companies and investors began losing interest in the Exchange after the NSE started operating in 1994 which soon picked up the volumes. The small number of companies listed, their small size and the uncertain nature of their performance dissuaded investors from trading in this Exchange. Besides, the lack of trading cycle and speculative element in it have reduced the scope for speculative gain or capital appreciation. Companies themselves did not favour this exchange, if they are eligible to be listed on other regular exchanges. There was diversion of trade and fall in the volumes during 1995 to 1997. It was in this context that Dave Committee (1996) on Revitalising the OTCEI submitted its report as per SEBI's directive in this regard.

OTCEI and Dave Committee Report

As already referred, the performance of OTCEI in terms of companies listed, their paid up capital and trading value was poor, more so during 1995 and 1996. This was mainly due to the nature of companies listed, systems, practices and procedures, related to the trading on this Exchange. To study these weaknesses and suggest remedies, the SEBI has appointed a committee under the Chairmanship of Dr. S.A. Dave, who reported in September 1996.

Many of the recommendations of the committee which are set out below have been accepted by SEBI and are being implemented. The OTCEI has liberalised conditions of listing and removed the ceiling of Rs. 25 crores of the paid up capital. It has included a number of companies listed on other exchanges to be permitted securities on OTCEI and provided them with a trading cycle of T + 7, as in the case of other Exchanges. Besides, the debt segment is strengthened by including not only corporate debt but government debt for trading purposes. The RBI has announced that dealings of Government bonds can also be channelised through the OTCEI, as in the case of NSE and OTC members are made eligible to deal in Government securities. The number of companies listed has also increased following the liberalisation of conditions imposed on sponsors, like compulsory market making, holding of a minimum of 5% of company's stock, as investor confidence booster and facilitate market making by the sponsor or additional market maker appointed by the sponsor. As a result of such measures, the volumes on the OTCEI have also picked up late in 1997.

DAVE Committee Recommendations

(1) All those companies which are ineligible for listing on the regular Stock Exchanges should be provided listing on OTCEI.

(2) The companies which do not satisfy the requirements for listing on other Exchanges such as three years of dividend paying record, out of the last 5 years and appraisal by an Indian F.I. may get listing facility on OTCEI, provided they get the sponsorship and market making facility.

(3) Companies with a paid up capital of less than Rs. 10 crores should be listed on OTCEI, as it has screen based trading and market makers (2 in number) to provide liquidity - (the same recommended by Malegam Committee).

(4) The upper limit of Rs. 25 crores for listing on OTCEI should be removed and OTCEI should be put on par with other Exchanges for listing purposes.

(5) The companies which do not have the share holding pattern, as required by SEBI, for the purpose of listing namely 5 members for every Rs. 1 lakh, in case of public issue and 10 members per Rs. 1 lakh of issue in case of offer of sale, should be allowed on OTCEI.

(6) All Bought out deals (BODs), which do not satisfy the requirement of 3 year dividend paying record or the appraisal by on FI should be allowed to be listed only on OTCEI.

(7) Trading in the equity of all unlisted companies can be channelised through OTCEI, as Mutual Funds, FIs and FFIs do trade in them.

(8) Companies delisted on other Exchanges and those with an offer on Tap system should be allowed to be listed only on the OTCEI.

(9) OTCEI should be allowed to develop markets in futures, options, forward contracts on stocks and other forms of forward transactions.

(10) The committee recommended a shift from T + 3, prevailing then, to T + 7 which is operating on other regular exchanges, for the purposes of settlement. This is particularly relevant in respect of permitted securities which are traded on other Exchanges on a T + 7 basis. The OTCEI should be given a free hand to increase the number of permitted securities and permitted debenture segment.

(11) The promoters should play a more active role in increasing the number of companies listed and traded.

(12) The market making requirements on the sponsors should be liberalised. The Committee recommends that only issues with a paid up capital below Rs. 10 crores should attract compulsory market making, with an inventory of 5% of the total issues. Companies with a market capitalisation between Rs. 5 crores and Rs.10 crores will require on initial market making inventory of only 2%. The committee recommended that market making inventory may be varied from 1% to 5% of the issue depending on its paid up capital. The higher the paid up capital the lower is the need for holding inventory by the market makers.

(13) The market making tenure for compulsory and additional market makers of such companies would continue to be 18 months and 12 months respectively, which is prevailing at present.

(14) All efforts should be made to increase volumes on the OTCEI and make it a viable alternative to other Exchanges and should not be allowed to wither away. The OTCEI and NSE, being set up by almost the same financial institutions should work together to complement and promote each other.

ANNEXURE

GOVERNMENT GUIDELINES ON OTCEI

It has been decided by the Government that the issue of securities by companies and their listing on the OTCEI will be governed by the following guidelines:

(i) the minimum issued equity share capital of a company for eligibility for listing on the OTCEI will be Rs. 30 lakhs, subject to a minimum public offer of equity shares worth Rs. 20 lakhs in face value;

(ii) for companies with an issued equity capital of more than Rs. 300 lakhs, the minimum public offer should be 40% of the issued capital or Rs. 20 lakhs worth of shares in face value, whichever is higher, in relaxation of Rule 19(2)(b) of the Securities Contracts (Regulation) Rules, 1957;

(iii) companies with an issued equity capital of more than Rs. 300 lakhs seeking listing on the OTCEI will have to comply with the listing requirements and guidelines as are applicable to such companies for enlistment on other recognised Stock-Exchanges;

(iv) companies covered under the MRTP Act/FERA may be listed on the OTCEI only if they satisfy the guidelines for listing on other recognised Stock Exchange, such as minimum issued equity capital of Rs. 500 lakhs or such other limit as may be prescribed from time to time;

(v) a company with an issued equity share capital of more than Rs. 25 crores will not be eligible for listing on the OTCEI;

(vi) companies which are engaged in investments, leasing, finance, hire-purchase, amusement parks etc. shall not be eligible for listing on the OTCEI; these are now permitted to be listed on OTCEI since March 1995;

(vii) a company which is listed on any other recognised Stock Exchange in India would not simultaneously be eligible for listing on the OTCEI;

(viii) the minimum number of centres for collection of application forms in respect of issue of securities by companies under the OTCEI shall be four, one each from the Northern, Western, Southern and Eastern regions of the country. However, OTCEI shall have power to increase the number for the issue of securities made by a company;

(ix) whenever securities are issued to the public, the price will be determined by the merchant banker in consultation with the company;

(x) company shall not issue securities at par in case the securities are eligible to be issued at a premium.

The OTCEI shall make it clear to the companies, their shareholders and investors that tax concessions, if any, in respect of companies listed on it and investments in their shares will be as per the tax laws and/or the decisions of the Department of Revenue, Ministry of Finance. It is also clarified that the functioning and operations of the OTCEI shall be subject to the provisions of the Securities Contracts (Regulation) Act, 1956, the Companies Act, 1956 and other relevant laws which are applicable to the corporate sector and the investors.

Issue of Shares through OTC — SEBI Guidelines

Where a direct public issue is made through OTC without the sponsor taking any shares, the normal guidelines for disclosure and investor protection shall apply.

Where the shares of a company has been taken by the sponsor, such shares may be offered to the public at a later date at such price as the sponsor may deem fit in accordance with the regulations of OTC subject to the following conditions:

(i) the promoters after such offer retain atleast 25% of the total issued capital with lock-in period of five years from the date of the sponsor taking up the shares;

(ii) the sponsor agrees to act as market maker for the shares atleast for a period of three years on a compulsory basis and also finds an additional market maker for such compulsory market making; and

(iii) the sponsor compulsorily gives two-way quotes based on minimum or maximum trading prices as may be stipulated by OTC in respect of the scrip.

NATIONAL STOCK EXCHANGE

The National Stock Exchange was set up by IDBI and other all India Financial Institutions in Mumbai in November 1992 with a paid up equity of Rs. 25 crores. It was recognised by the Government in the same year and the Exchange started operations in wholesale Debt market in June 1994 and in equity trading in Nov. 1994. The wholesale debt market or the money market segments would cater to banks, FIs, etc. to encourage high value transactions in PSU bonds, UTI Units, Treasury Bills, Government securities and call money. There is no trading floor of the exchange. Trading is in large volumes and over the telephone, telex etc. Trading is done on computer with the help for PC Terminals in broker offices. The Capital market segment is also done similarly on computer based trading. The settlement is on T + 7 basis for equity trading.

Benefits accrue to both issuers of securities and investors. As this is screen based trading with a national network, transparency and cost effectiveness are ensured. Besides, the investment counters can be spread wide in the country under the NSE electronic network.

About 1432 companies were already listed on NSE at end March 2009. Trading in them is continuing simultaneously with those in the principal and regional Stock Exchanges. As the Central Depositories are set up in 1998, book entry of deals and immobilisation of certificates is taking place. At present the volume of daily trade is around Rs. 3,000 to 4,000 crores, on the NSE going upto Rs. 7,000 crores on some days during the boom period. The market capitalisation of listed companies is Rs. 29 lakh crores in 2009. There are also more than 320 permitted securities for trading on the NSE, as at end March 2009. The trading turnover was Rs. 28 lakh crores in cash segment and Rs. 110 lakh crores in derivative segment in 2008-09.

National Market System

A high powered study Group on the Establishment of New Stock Exchanges under the Chairmanship of Shri M. J. Pherwani has submitted its Report in June 1991. This Study Group has recommended some criteria for setting up of new Stock Exchanges and favoured the licensing of additional trading floors (ATF) instead of multiplying the number of Stock Exchanges in the country.

The Study Group has also recommended the setting up of a model National Stock Exchange at Navi Mumbai (NSE) which will develop the National Market System in the country. Any infrastructure in terms of space, Tele-communications, Computerisation, on-line processing system, Library, Research facilities, Publicity Dept, etc., are all recommended for the "National Market" to be set up by NSE.

The market will have two types of members, viz., participating trading members, who can only trade on their behalf and intermediary trading members (dealers) who can deal on behalf of their clients. Trading members will have computer terminals connecting to the other trading members (PTM) and to the central computer system at the NSE. Trading orders to buy and sell securities or to borrow and lend are entered into the computer system and stocked in its memory in an order book. Trading being order driven, it will be matched with a matching counter order. If matched, both the buyer and seller are informed by the NSE computer system. By the end of the trading day, the Exchange System will give out rates and a list of completed transactions for each trading member.

Characteristics

The characteristics of National Market System are as follows:

(1) Completely automated system in terms of both trading and settlement procedures to be provided through the Securities Facilities Support Corporation.

(2) Compulsory market makers/jobbers to provide liquidity and ready market (in the form of Principal Trading Members, i.e., PTM).

(3) The members are large Corporate and Institutional members and professionals, drawn from various parts of the country and to represent the professionals on an All India Basis.

(4) Only large and medium sized companies and PSUs are listed on this Exchange and it will complement the existing Exchanges.

(5) The NSE would have a separate trading facility and time allotted for debt instruments in order to have the beneficial effect of creating an active secondary market in debt instruments particularly of Government debt.

NSE Operations

The above recommendations were accepted by the Government and accordingly NSE was set up and recognised by the Government. As reported earlier, it has started trading in money market instruments, Government securities and other debt instruments on OTC basis. In the Capital market segment, corporate equity shares are traded on a weekly settlement basis since November 1994. It has no trading floor. Each trading member will have a computer in his office, anywhere in India which will be connected to the Central Computer System of NSE through leased lines or VSATs (Very Small Aparture Terminals) for an interim period, to be followed by a satellite link. The members for Debt market will be different from the Equity market and the same members cannot operate for both markets, as originally visualised. NSE terminals are located at many centres in the country with about 850 brokers connected through more than 2000 VSATS, with users of thousand of investors.

The NSE will operate two segments, namely, Debt market (Money market) and equity market (Capital market) and operations in both are separately maintained. Post trade services are also automated. For confirmed trades, the settling bank will arrange for payment and clearance and depository for effecting transfers by electronic book entry system. The clearing house facility is provided by Canara Bank and many banks are providing the depository facility for NSE.

Automated Lending and Borrowing Mechanism (ALBM)

ALBM is a new product developed by NSE to meet a felt need of lending and borrowing of securities by short sellers. This does not involve borrowing and lending of money, as in the case of Badla trade. This is a flexible instrument, to be pressed into service for smooth trading and settlement and clearance.

In the segment of Rolling Settlement market, ALBM is well suited to ensure that settlement took place daily. The securities borrowing and lending market in U.S.A. is estimated at $ 100 billion per annum. Some institutions like S H C I specialise in lending of securities and short sellers need to borrow securities. The instrument does not have anything to do with carry forward or Badla nor does it finance purchases or long buyers.

Central Depository System

The Government has accepted the system of multiple depositories and SEBI was asked to frame guidelines for their operations in 1996. These Depositories will keep physical custody of share certificates leading to immobilisation of shares to be followed later by dematerialisation and complete book entry system of trading achieved now.

This means that the statement given by the Depository is evidence of the ownership of the shares. This method was operated for the FIs and FFIs and banks and mutual funds, in the beginning and was extended to corporates and individuals later on. The depository will transfer the securities between the participants through electronic book entry, while the settling bank will effect the transfer of funds.

Listing of Securities

All medium and large sized companies with paid up equity Rs. 10 crores and above eligible to be listed on regular Stock Exchanges can be listed on NSE. Some of them may be listed and traded on regular Stock Exchanges also. The same formalities of listing are observed by NSE and a listing agreement is entered into with the company, as on a regular exchange and as approved by the SEBI.

Settlement System

Trading period on any day will vary for the debt segment and equity segment. For capital market operations the trading is done in equities, convertible and non-convertible debentures. Trading network can be spread all over the country, depending on the electronic link though the Satellite. A rolling settlement system operates in NSE with settlement period of T + 7. Thus, a rolling T + 7 period means that transactions on a given day (T) will be settled seven days later (T + 7). On that day, funds and securities are exchanged by passing electronically proper debit and credit entries.

The National Securities Depository Limited (NSDL)

This is an organisation promoted by the Industrial Development Bank of India, the Unit Trust of India and the National Stock Exchange of India Limited to provide electronic depository facilities for stock traded in the equity and the debt market.

The National Securities Depository Limited has been registered with the Securities Exchange Board of India and launched on Nov. 7, 1996 as India's first depository to facilitate trading and settlement of securities in dematerialised form. Settlement of securities in dematerialised form will eliminate problems that are normally associated with settlement through physical certificates, like tearing/mutilation of share certificates due to careless handling, loss of certificates by postal authorities or delays with registrars and investors', problems of bad delivery of shares. Cases of forgery of certificates will be eliminated in an electronic environment. Settlement of trades will bc faster and hassle-free leading to shorter settlement cycles.

What is a Depository?

A Depository is an organisation where the securities of a share holder are held in the electronic form at the request of the share holder through the medium of a depository participant.

A depository can be compared to a bank for securities. If an investor wants to utilise the services offered by a depository, the investor has to open an account with the depository through a depository participant — this is very similar to the opening of an account with any of the branches of a bank in order to utilise the services of that bank, as a Depository Participant (D.P.).

The depository can legally transfer beneficial ownership which a custodian cannot. The main objective of a depository is to minimise the paper work involved with the ownership, trading and transfer of securities.

Facilities offered by NSDL:

1. Enable surrender and withdrawal of securities to and from the depository (i.e., dematerialisation and rematerialisation).
2. Maintain investor holdings in the electronic form.
3. Effect settlement of securities traded on the exchanges.
4. Carry out settlement of trades not done on the stock exchanges (i.e., off-market traders).

Rematerialisation

If anybody wishes to get back his securities in the physical form all he has to do is to request his Depository participant for the rematerialisation of the same.

Advantages of the Depository

There are a number of reasons why Investor should opt for the electronic form of holding securities. Depositing Investor's securities with NSDL will give freedom from the worries of loss of share certificates through theft, mutilation, fire, etc.

The process of opening an account with a depository participant is similar to the opening of a bank account. The investor can get a list of depository participants from NSDL. The depository participants may also advertise the services offered by them once they are registered. The Investor can approach any DP of his choice and fill up an account opening form.

The depository participant will give a pass book or a statement of holdings. The statement of holdings will be despatched to the Holder periodically by the Depository participant; however, the statement of holdings can be sent to Holders, as and when requested for a fee.

The depository has not prescribed any minimum balance. In fact, the holder can even have zero balance in his account. However, the depository participants may fix some minimum limits. Many FFIs, FIIs and Indian FIs and banks have joined the Depository System, as it is very suitable for their trade in large volumes.

About the Depository Participants

Similar to the brokers who trade on behalf of the customers in and outside the stock exchanges, a Depository Participant is the representative (agent) in the depository system. The Depository Participant will maintain the securities account balances and intimate to the Holder about their holdings from time to time. According to SEBI guidelines, financial institutions, banks, custodians, stock brokers, etc. can become participants in the depository.

There are absolutely no restrictions to the number of DPs that the Investor can open accounts with. Opening an account with a depository participant is very similar to opening a bank account. Just as a person can have savings or current accounts with more than one bank, the person can open accounts with more than one depository participant.

The person can exercise the option such as a rights issue or optional conversion of debentures to shares. The holders do have a choice of either physical or electronic mode of holdings. However, corporate entitlements such as bonus will be made in the same form as the original holdings. Compulsory demat form of trading was enforced by SEBI in most of the well-traded stocks, soon after.

The depository will also establish a help desk which will direct the holder to the appropriate agency. When the depository is ready to start functioning, it will advertise the help, desk, telephone lines, etc.

NSDL'S FIRST PARTICIPANTS

SHCIL

ILFS

IIT TRUST CORP. SERVICES

GLOBAL TRUST BANK

HDFC BANK

CITI BANK CUSTODIAL SERVICES

MORGAN STANLEY CUSTODIAL SERVICES

RELIANCE SHARE & STOCK BROCKING

JANTA SAHAKARI BANK

INDUSTRIAL DEV. BANK OF INDIA

STATE BANK OF INDIA

STANDARD CHARTERED

NATIONAL SEC. CLEARING CORP.

DEUTSCHE BANK

Legal Aspects

NSDL was set up by passing the Depositories Act, 1996 but with retrospective effect from Sept. 1995. Companies Act and SCR Act were amended to the extent necessary. Section 22A of SCR Act dealing with restrictions on transfer of shares was deleted. Sections 108 and 111 of the Companies Act were amended to dispense with transfer form and other formalities relating to the physical transfer of shares. The Depository's statement is a valid documents of title, under law and transfers are effected by book entries in the pass-books of D.P.s. The exemption from stamp duty was also granted for transactions in Demat form.

Inter-connected Stock Exchange (ICSE)

The Inter-connected Stock Exchange of India Ltd. was promoted by 15 regional Stock Exchanges and Federation of Indian Stock Exchanges. It was incorporated as a public limited company under Section 12 of the Companies Act in January 1998. Its registered location is at International Infotech Park, 7th Tower, 5th Floor, Vashi Railway Complex, Sector 30A, Vashi, Navi Mumbai-400 705.

Its paid up capital or the project cost is Rs. 15 crores, which is covered by the contribution of Rs. 1 crores form each of the participating member in the form of admission fee of Rs. 5 lakhs and Infrastructure fee of Rs. 95 lakhs. The following participating exchanges paid the Initial Capital:

(1) Bangalore Stock Exchange

(2) Bhuvaneshwar Stock Exchange

(3) Cochin Stock Exchange

(4) Coimbatore Stock Exchange

(5) Guwahati Stock Exchange

(6) Hyderabad Stock Exchange

(7) Jaipur Stock Exchange

(8) Ludhiana Stock Exchange

(9) Madhya Pradesh (Indore) Stock Exchange

(10) Madras Stock Exchange

(11) Magadh (Patna) Stock Exchange

(12) Mangalore Stock Exchange

(13) Saurashtra Kutch (Rajkot) Stock Exchange

(14) Uttar Pradesh (Kanpur) Stock Exchange

(15) Vadodara Stock Exchange

All these 15 Stock Exchanges have a total membership of 4613, which account for 51% of total membership of all exchanges in India in 1998. The total number of listed companies in these participating exchanges is 3,467, which accounts for 35% of total listed on all Stock Exchanges in India (9,833 in 1998). But in terms of turnover of trade, the ISE participating Stock Exchanges account for Rs. 45,226 crores in 1997-98, which constitutes about 4% of the total turnover of all the Stock Exchanges in India.

ISE has got the SEBI approval under Section 4 of S.C. (R) Act in November 1998. The SEBI laid down the conditions of a minimum Base Capital of Rs. 2 lakhs to begin with by members to be raised to Rs. 4 lakhs by the end of one year. The participating exchanges will have a uniform trading and settlement cycle of Thursday to Wednesday, which is the actual cycle adopted by the ISE. Besides, the ISE has set up a settlement guarantee fund to guarantee payouts. Additionally every participating exchange is required to maintain with ISE, a Settlement Stabilisation Fund of Rs. 10 lakhs to meet any temporary exigencies at the time of pay in so that there is no delay in declaration of payout.

ISE provides a national market system where in a trading member of one Stock Exchange can deal with a trading member of another exchange from his local Trader Work Station (TWS). Through the Inter-connected market system, ISE provides for trading, clearing and settlement alongwith surveillance and Risk Management to the inter-connected trading system.

It has got SEBI's clearance to start trading in Nov. 1998 but it has started training of members and stock trading sessions in the early months of 1999.

Objective

The basic aim of the Inter-connected Market System (ICMS), which ISE sets up is to consolidate the small fragmented and less liquid markets into a national level market, with the state of art infrastructure and systems support. It will create a level playing ground for all participating exchanges, reduce transactions costs, promote liquidity and volumes, necessary for survival of regional Stock Exchanges.

Its functions are to provide trading among the inter-connected exchanges in their listed securities by using the Electronic Securities Architecture Software and decentralised clearing and Settlement at all participating Exchange centres. The central clearing bank of ISE namely ABN AMRO-Vysya Bank Consortium provides for exclusive funds transfer, electronically and sharing the relevant information on margins settlements and capital adequacy positions by opening of extension counters at the premises of participating Stock Exchanges.

The ISE hires the services of the Elbee Couriers to ensure timely movement of securities across the Exchanges for smooth settlement of deliveries, payouts and Auction payouts. The ISE has a Settlement Guarantee. Fund (SGF) to guarantee settlement of all trades validly executed in the ISE system. A real time risk management and surveillance system would ensure instant information on gross exposures, intra-day trading exposure and cumulative loss positions of member brokers etc. with a view to prevent gross irregularities undue price fluctuations and impose margins on members of various types, for the purpose of stopping overtrading by members and their consequent defaults and failures.

The listed securities on the ISE are divided into three groups: Group A, which consists of 50 most popular scrips; Group B which has about 500 actively well traded shares and Group C which has all the rest of the listed scrips which are generally thinly traded.

Risk Management and Surveillance System: The ISE has established a Risk Management and Surveillance system that is a system driven to monitor the position of traders and dealers on a real time basis. The risks are controlled by the following methods:

(a) Intra-day trading limits: trades allowed upto 33.33 times their Base Minimum Capital (BMC) and 25 times their additional capital, if any. Traders are warned by the system when they reach the trading limits of 60%, 70% and 90% and then as the limit reaches 100% of permitted level, the trader and dealer will be disabled to access the ICMS.

(b) Gross exposure limits: The trader can have maximum gross exposure of 12.5 times of capital deposited by the trader. The gross exposure is the sum of net purchases and sales and includes the exposure form the previous settlement waiting pay in.

(c) Cumulative loss margins: The system will not allow the cumulative loss of a trader to cross the capital adequacy amount. The loss is computed by marking to the market values the net purchases and sales and carry forwards. The traders will have to deposit the loss margin, if the loss goes beyond the cash component of his capital adequacy amount.

Accordingly, the traders and dealers would be required to pay on a T + 1 basis the daily Mark to Market Margins on the loss suffered by them on their outstanding positions. Losses on any scrip would not be allowed to be set off against profits on others and a basic exemption limit of 25% of the capital adequacy amount is given to the trader while computing the margin liability. The extra losses would have to be covered by extra margin deposits.

Daily circuit filters: The system would also operate daily and settlement circuit limits to scrip prices, which set the limit to fluctuations of prices, unduly rising or falling. The filter is the point fixed by the ISE on the basis of previous day's closing or settlement closing price or base price.

Suspension of securities and traders: The ISE has powers to suspend any security or trades if they are for any reason suspended on the participating regional Stock Exchange.

Computer System

For interconnected market system, there is a computer system provided by the Indigo Technologies with a Central Computer at Vashi, Navi Mumbai and Compaq N.T. Server Machines at the Regional Stock Exchanges. Similarly, there will be another computer system for trading set up by Tandem Computers, a subsidiary of Compaq company, while Compaq N.T. servers and work stations will be used for clearing and settlement and for Risk Management and Surveillance.

The electronic Securities Architecture Software uses a modular architecture consisting of expandable set of business modules such as:

Automated traded

Manual trading module

Market control

System administration

Market information and dissemination

Trader Work Stations

In each Regional Stock Exchange, there can be multiple work stations for trading. Trader work stations comprise Member Server Application (MSA) and a Trader Workstation Application (TWS). The MSA will be responsible for maintaining local data base and submits requests to the central system through the TWS. The trader work stations provide for order management through submission, modification and withdrawal of market orders and limit orders and allows the market view of the 10 best bids and offers, depth of the market and market statistics brokers can set up their own hierarchy and a system of scrutiny and control through setting up of trading limits.

Advantages of ISE

Volumes of trade can increase and there will be greater liquidity to scrips. More than 4,000 scrips are kept under permitted category. The cost of each transaction will be lower, on an average. The cost of acquiring membership rights on ISE is only Rs. 5,000 per annum to the member brokers of Regional Stock Exchanges, which gives a cost advantage to traders on ISE.

The additional facilities which the ISE may provide include trading in Demat form through a tie up with the CDSL, set up by the B.S.E. Besides, the RSE can have established ATFs and ATCs, for the purposes of facilitating trading in centres where the Stock Exchange is not available within the jurisdiction of R.S.E.

The ISE has also proposed to set up a modified carry forward system, subject to the permission of SEBI and extend the trading rights as dealers to institutions like subsidiaries of banks, mutual funds, FIIs, etc.

Advantages to Members of RSEs are:

(1) Increase in the business and earnings.

(2) Increase in liquidity in shares that they trade in.

(3) Appreciation in the value of membership at the particpating exchange.

(4) Greater Safeguards against defaults, bad deliveries, and frauds, etc.

(5) Long-term strategy to survive in the face of competition from the big National Exchanges like NSE and BSE.

(6) Creation of efficient and orderly market.

(7) Establish transparency in dealings and improves the price discovery process.

(8) Creates a level playing ground for all the participating exchanges and provides a larger ground to play to member brokers of RSEs.

(9) The possibility of expansion to remote rural and semi-urban areas and expansion of retail investor business.

Introduction

On any Stock Exchange, there are members who deal with client orders, institutional orders and in line business (arbitrage operations). Some brokers specialise in the new issues market and some in badla financing. Some act as Jobbers and market makers making two-way offers to buy and sell in selected shares. All members are permitted to trade in the Trading Ring or electronically with the mainframe computer. Each member is permitted to have authorised assistants up to a maximum number as fixed by the Stock Exchange. The members do trading on their own behalf or on behalf of their clients. If the member acts as a broker, he is doing retail business or purchase and sale transactions for the customers. If a member is doing wholesale business, offering both purchase and sale prices (bid and offer) to the other member brokers then he is called a jobber. Both brokers and jobbers or market makers are an essential part of the stock market operations.

The purchase and sale transactions in the market relate to dealings in securities listed on the Stock Exchange, namely, Equity Shares, Preference Shares, Debentures (both convertible and non-convertible), Gilt-edged Securities and semi-Government bonds. Listing of securities of the corporate sector is done in accordance with the regulations embodied in the Securities Contracts (Regulation) Act, 1956 and the Securities Contracts (Regulation) Rules, 1957 and the Byelaws of the Stock Exchange. The securities of the Centre, State and semi-Government bodies are listed for trading automatically after they are issued to the public without any listing fees and procedure.

Specified and Non-Specified Groups

The listed securities of the companies are classified into a specified group and non-specified group (cash list) on the basis of certain criteria. Those included in the specified list should be fully paid-up equity shares listed already on the Exchange for at least three years on the cash list and the company's paid-up equity capital should be above Rs. 10 crores. The shares should have been actively traded while on the cash list. The equity shares should be widely disbursed and a large volume of shares is available with the public for trading. The company should have a record of good earnings and dividends over the past few years before inclusion in the specified list. Speculation is permitted only in the specified list. Trading is genuine, if delivery is taken or given and speculative if no delivery is involved. Those which are first listed will be kept in Non-specified or Cash group. In addition to specified (A group) Non-specified groups (B group) was split into B_1 and B_2 groups, based on the volume of trade turn over and the good fundamentals of the company. There is a category of permitted securities. These are not listed on that exchange but listed on some other exchange and permitted to be traded here. There is, however, no such permitted list on BSE.

Customer's Orders

The investor can place an order by telegram, telephone, letter or in person. The order may be for the purchase or sale of a specified number of shares of a company at a specified rate or range of prices. The member broker is a custodian for the shares/securities of his client till they are sold or delivered. The order to buy or sell may be given for a fixed price or at a maximum or minimum price range which is also called a limit order. Some orders are 'At Best' or 'At the Market price.' The member broker has to execute the order at the best obtainable price in the market on a specified date. Some orders may be 'Immediate' or 'Cancelled', which signifies that the broker has to buy or sell at the specified price immediately such as sell 100 Colgate at Rs. 430 and if the price in the market is unfavourable, the order is cancelled. Some orders are open orders, which can be executed at any time within a range of prices while others are discretionary leaving the discretion to the broker.

After receiving the orders, the member enters these orders in his books and then purchase and sale orders are distributed among his authorised assistants to handle them separately in the specified list, non-specified list and as odd lots. The member would have three alternatives in executing the orders. He may go to the trading ring to buy or sell the required shares. Alternatively, the member can set off matching orders of purchase and sale of different clients of his own or purchase or sales from out of his own stock of portfolio held by him. But all these orders have to be executed at the prevailing market prices on that day. In electronic trading, these orders are fed to the computer and order matching is done electronically and confirmation or rejection comes automatically.

Trading Ring

Trading on the Stock Exchange used to be officially done in the trading ring for three hours from 11.30 a.m. to 2.30 p.m. or 12 noon to 3 p.m. Under electronic trading, hours are extended from 10 a.m. to 4 p.m. from Monday to Friday. From January 2010, the trading time was changed to 9 a.m. to 4 p.m. on week days. Trading before or after official hours is called kerb trading. In the trading ring, space is provided separately for specified and non-specified sections. The members or their authorised assistants have to wear a badge or carry with them identity cards given by the Exchange to enter the trading ring. They carry a sauda block book, or confirmation memos, duly authorised by the Exchange and carry a pen with them. On the trading ring, there are jobbers in some exchanges who do wholesale business of purchase and sale, giving two-way quotations of bid and offer for each share. The jobber may specialise in some scrips and stand at a specified place in the ring indicating the share or shares that he is trading in. The authorised assistant approaches one or more jobbers specialising in the scrips that he wishes to buy or sell and make the best possible bargain with the jobbers. When the deal is struck, both jobber and broker make a note in their sauda block books of the transaction, or enter into confirmation memos. In Exchanges where electronic trading takes place, as in OTCEI or NSE, as also in BSE there is no need for trading ring.

Some members are both jobbers and brokers. Each jobber tries to purchase and sell those shares he is specialising in such quantities that he can match as far as possible the purchases and sales in each share by the end of the day. According to the supply and demand position of the shares, the prices of purchase and sale would vary in the market and the jobber would do his best to match his purchases and sales and the margin between the purchase and sale prices would be his profit.

Block Book (or the Sauda Book)

After each order is executed, suitable entries are made in the concerned member's Block Book (or pass confirmation memos). This is a book of transactions executed on the floor and appropriate entries are made after every deal to record the number of shares traded, the prices of the purchase/sale, and the name or code number of the other member through whom the deal was finalised. Each page of the sauda book or the block book taken to the floor of the Stock Exchange should be duly authorised by the Stock Exchange authorities. Under electronic trading the computer software is designed to give all the returns to be submitted to Stock Exchange and the accounts to be maintained by the broker himself.

It is mandatory to submit a copy of the Sauda Sheets or computerised sheets (separate for specified and non-specified) after 4.00 p.m. every evening to the Stock Exchange. If the Stock Exchange authorities find untallied transactions (i.e., if some details do not match with what the counter-member has recorded), they will issue a memo and the member is required to attend to it immediately and clear the objections raised therein and return the memo.

Contract Note

From the sauda block book (where the transactions are sketchily written up), the details are transferred to the sauda book (which gives complete details). From the sauda book the contract notes are drawn up. It is important to ensure that the contract note is written up on the day of the deal and posted to the client. This is a proof that the contract was executed on that day and not on any other day since prices fluctuate every day. Besides, under Article 43(b) or (bb) of Schedule 1 of the Indian Stamp Act, the broker must affix a revenue stamp (based on the value of the contracted transaction or face value whichever is higher).

Drawing Up and Bills

For A Group: Both sale and purchase bills are prepared along with the contract note and it is posted on the same day or the next day.

For B Group: Bills are prepared only after receipt of delivery order/payment order.

Thus, in a purchase transaction, once the shares are delivered to the client after the client effects payment for the purchase and pays the stamp fees for transfer; a bill is made out giving the total cost of purchase, including other expenses incurred by the broker in the price itself. Now all these have to be shown separately from brokerage and price.

Cum and Ex-dividend

Sometimes, shares are purchased cum-dividend (or sold cum-dividend) but delivery is made/given ex-dividend. This means that though the buyer is entitled to the dividend, he gets the shares only after book closure for dividend payment. The dividend thus goes to the seller while it rightly belongs to the buyer. The price paid to the seller is adjusted for full dividend. Thus, when the bill is made out, the broker has to credit the buyer for the dividend and debit him only with charges for stamp fees and other expenses net of dividend. Similar situations arise in the case of shares bought cum-bonus/cum-rights and where the delivery is effected ex-bonus/ex-rights. Further, for tax purposes, the document that the ITO relies on is not the contract note but the bill which gives the total consideration of the transaction.

Settlement in Specified List

Settlement for scrips purchased and sold in the specified list is different from those of the non-specified list because in the case of the former, speculative transactions are allowed to be carried forward to the next period. Stock Exchanges allow speculative trading in shares listed in the forward list, allowing thereby for short-selling and long-buying of shares.

All transactions on the specified list are taken stock on the badla day, once a week, being every Friday which is now on a weekly basis. The mechanics of these badla transactions are quite intricate, though pretty logical. In any settlement period — a fortnight, now a week — (effectively 5 trading days), there would have been a certain amount of genuine buying/selling as well as speculative buying/selling. The day on which such transactions are posted for settlement or carry forward is called the "Badla Day."

All those contracts which are not to be carried over are settled between the members by effecting deliveries and payment before the next badla day.

Two things may happen on the badla day as far as speculative transactions are concerned:

1. They are carried forward from one settlement period to the next by drawing up a fresh set of contract notes to give effect to the carry forward.
2. Either an interest called Seedha Badla is paid to the seller by the buyer or charges as Undha Badla is paid by the seller to the buyer depending on the net overbought or oversold position in any scrip.

To effect steps (1) and (2) stated above, the Stock Exchange authorities fix the HAVALA RATE and, the CARRY FORWARD MARGIN and the BADLA CHARGES are determined by the market forces. Havala Rate is the price at which each scrip in the specified list can be carried forward, also called the Standard Rate or the Making-up price. The rate is normally based on the closing price of the scrip on the day prior to the badla day, i.e., based on the closing prices on the last trading day. If the Stock Exchange authorities wish to impound a part of the profit by bulls or bears (i.e., the price difference between the contracted rate and the havala rate) as a result of excessive speculative activity in the scrip between the two settlement periods, they can decide to fix a havala rate which in their opinion is the most representative.

The Carry-Forward Margin: This margin is fixed by the Stock Exchange authorities on all scrips, with a right to levy heavy margins on those which are subject to heavy speculative activity. Different charges are payable by the buyers and the sellers. The Havala Sheet, which is published by the Stock Exchange, lists the MARGIN requirements to be paid by the bulls/bears on each scrip, as also the carry-forward rates for both (after adjusting the margin with the havala rate).

The Badla Charges (also known as Vyaj Badla): The carry forward charges or interest is to be paid by the buyer or seller in each scrip depending on whether the net position in that scrip is overbrought or oversold. Long buyers are normally more than short sellers. Short-selling without having shares is highly speculative but is rewarded by badla charges paid to him by the long buyers for squaring up their position. But SEBI ordered the withdrawal of badla payment to short-sellers in April 2000. In fact most of the above descriptions were applicable for the period before 1996 and not after computerised trading was started with compulsory Rolling settlement and Demat form of trading was operated.

Badla Charges

Undha Badla charges are payable when there is more "speculative selling" than "speculative buying" in any scrip, i.e., when the scrip is oversold. In effect, this means that there are more buyers willing to take delivery than there are shares available for delivery.

It is generally found that there is always more "speculative buying" than "speculative selling" in the Stock Exchanges based on human psychology. Two possible reasons could be given for this situation. First, it is more difficult for a person to comprehend that he can first sell what he does not own and buy it back at a lower rate later and make a profit than to comprehend that he can buy something today and sell it later at a profit.

The second reason is that if the floating stock in a scrip is limited and there is excessive short-selling, then the bull operators can capitalise on this technical position and demand delivery or demand extortionate interest charges at the settlement. The bear operator is then caught as there is no floating stock to deliver and he then has to purchase scrips from the market or borrow them from a financier to deliver. He may then have to pay a heavy price for these scrips. This proves a deterrent to excessive short-selling. In this case, it is possible that shares due for delivery can be auctioned in the market and delivery secured and the amount involved is debited to the member due to deliver but failed to do so.

On the other hand, a bull operator who is long or overbought can always borrow money or take delivery of scrips if he finds that the badla financier is charging exorbitant interest rates. Money is easier to obtain than shares. Badla paid for purchases carried forward is called Seedha Badla. In lieu of Badla, the NSE has introduced Automatic lending and borrowing mechanism in respect of shares to facilitate short selling and yet give and take deliveries at the time of settlement. (ALBM)

Though the badla rates are fixed by the market forces of demand and supply of funds and scrips, the Stock Exchange has the authority to intervene if they think that the rates are unreasonable, and could as a result destabilise the market.

Factors Influencing Badla Rates

The badla charges or the amount of interest charges (also called Vyaj Badla) that are contracted to be paid as a result of carrying forward a transaction are based on several factors, namely:

(a) The total amount of badla finance available in the market.

(b) The technical position of the market, i.e., the extent to which it is overheated in terms of speculative buying, and hence the total volume and value of shares overall which have to be financed.

(c) The total amount of badla finance available for a particular scrip — some scrips are not favoured by the financiers due to their poor liquidity — and for several other reasons.

(d) The overall money market interest rates.

(e) The psychological state of the market.

Carry Forward Facilities

If the buyers/sellers wish to carry forward their transactions from one settlement period to the next settlement period, they draw up a fresh set of contract notes to give effect to the carry forward of the purchase/sale at rates which reflect the havala rate, the margin and the badla charges.

Example 1

Assume that a broker has transacted a sale order at the rate of Rs. 700 per share and that the standard rate for the share is fixed at Rs. 730, the carry forward margin payable is Rs. 40 per share for the seller, and that the badla charge is fixed at Rs. 4 per share.

So, a contract note would already have been drawn up, stating — Sold N number of shares at Rs. 700 (minus brokerage) per share.

The seller then has a choice of either giving delivery or carrying the transaction forward to the next settlement period.

(i) If he wants to give delivery, then the settlement will be made at the rate agreed upon, being Rs. 700 (less brokerage) per share.

(ii) If he carries it forward:

(a) A new contract will be drawn up as having purchased shares at Rs. 770 (Havala Rate Rs. 730 + Margin Rs. 40 + brokerage) per share.

(b) A new contract will then be made on the same day as having sold N shares at Rs. 774 (the rate on the purchase contract Rs. 770 + badla charges receivable Rs. 4) per share.

Note: If the Havala Rate is less than the selling rate of Rs. 700, say, Rs. 680, then the rates on the contract in (a) will be Rs. 720 (Rs. 680 + Rs. 40) and the rate on the contract in (b) will be Rs. 724.

Example 2

Suppose a broker has executed a purchase order of N number of shares at Rs. 700 and the carry forward margin on the buyer is also Rs. 40 and all others are as in the above example. Therefore, a contract note effecting this purchase would have already been drawn up as having bought at Rs. 700 (plus brokerage). The buyer then has a choice of either taking delivery or carrying it forward:

(i) If he wants to take delivery, then the settlement will be made at Rs. 700 (plus brokerage) per share.

(ii) If he wants to carry it forward:

(a) A new contract is drawn up as having sold N shares at Rs. 690 (Standard rate Rs. 730 – Margin payable Rs. 40) adjusted for Brokerage per share.

(b) A new contract will then be made on the first day of the next settlement period as having bought N shares at Rs. 694 (the rate of the sale above Rs. 690 + badla payable Rs. 4).

Note: As in the above note, if the Standard Rate is (say) Rs. 680, then the rates in the above contracts will be Rs. 640 and Rs. 644 respectively.

Therefore, for carrying forward a contract to the next settlement, the following steps have to be taken on the Badla day:

1. Draw up a contract squaring up the position. The price in this contract note will be the respective carry forward rates specified in the Havala Sheet.
2. Draw up a fresh contract maintaining the position which was to be carried forward, the rate being the one indicated in (i) above + the badla charges or as in (ii) above minus the margin payable in the case of purchase order.

Book Closure Badla Financing (BCBF)

Such financing differs from the normal fortnightly financing, as financiers take interest for a month as against for a fortnight or a week in the normal badla financing.

BCBF is for a one-month period (unless otherwise stated), because it takes 14 days to get delivery of scrips purchased from the clearing house and the buyer is given a further 14 days to lodge the shares for transfer.

The share becomes ex-right one month before the book closure day, i.e., on the book closure badla day. When the company announces the book closure date, the Stock Exchange accordingly fixes a suitable badla day, which is about a month prior to this date, as the book closure badla day.

BCBF occurs at the time of book closure for dividends, bonus issues, right issues etc.

BCBF money costs more due to the following reasons:

1. The longer holding period (and hence the greater the risk) and the fact that the shares have to be lodged for transfer. Besides, financiers also charge for stamp fees on transfer and the cost of materials and registered post charges.
2. The financier who takes delivery of the shares on behalf of the buyer has to lodge the shares for transfer to his name, and hence the identity of the new owner becomes known. This creates a psychological fear in the mind of the financier, and thus such financing can be done with only the "tax paid" money.

Settlement in Non-Specified Shares

All business transacted in any week, between a Monday and Friday of the week, is settled on the next Saturday (not the one immediately following). The price at which they are actually bought or sold is considered for the settlement. Delivery is made on the following Monday.

If for some reason the settlement is not made within three settlement periods, then the difference in the price can be claimed by the buyer. Here the buyer has an advantage in that if the price were to go up within this stipulated time and settlement has not been made (i.e., he has not received delivery), then he can claim the excess amount, or he can demand delivery of the shares.

Settlement and delivery in respect of specified shares take place as between the members and through the clearing house. Both delivery of shares and payment or receipt of money would be through the clearing. But in the case of non-specified shares, delivery of shares is done directly as between the members while payments and receipts are effected through the clearing.

After the Badla Day

All deliveries of shares/payments arising out of the badla day adjustments have to be SETTLED with respective deliveries and payments before the next badla day.

The transactions contracted by the member in respect of specified shares are entered into the "Settlement Register." The transactions executed during the settlement period with the clients/other members are balanced in this register and the outstanding transactions are adjusted at the "Carry Forward" or the "Havala" rates on the badla day.

Thereafter, the balances in the client's accounts are posted to the clients' ledger. In the case of non-specified shares, transactions are directly entered in the clients' ledger from the Sauda Book.

Kinds of Delivery

A contract which has been executed on behalf of a client or on the member's own account, culminates in the delivery/receipt of payment for shares.

Deliveries of securities can be effected in four ways:

1. Hand Delivery
2. Spot Delivery
3. Special Delivery
4. Delivery for clearing

Hand Delivery

Delivery and payment should be completed on the date stipulated when entering into the bargain, which shall not be more than 14 days following the date of the contract.

Spot Delivery

These transactions are to be settled by delivery and payment on the date of the contract or on the next day. For completion of the contract, the actual period for the despatch of the securities or remittance of money through post is excluded in the computation when the parties to the contract reside at different places.

Special Delivery

Delivery and payment made any time exceeding 14 days, but not exceeding 2 months, following the date of the contract as may be stipulated when entering into the bargain and permitted by the Governing Board or the President.

The three types of transactions described above, namely, spot delivery, hand delivery and special delivery, are called "spot" or "ready transactions." They must be settled by delivery and payment and cannot be carried forward.

Delivery for Clearing

All transactions in securities in the specified list are effected only through the clearing house. The securities for delivery will be delivered to the buyer within a week and the seller receives all member dues within the same time from the clearing house on the respective "pay-in" and "pay-out" days.

The function of the clearing house is confined to the receipt and delivery of securities and receiving payments from members for their sales. In the event of a member defaulting on his liability to the clearing house, the responsibility for recovering the amount due from the member on account of his purchases, devolves on the other member with whom the transaction was entered into. The clearing house does not come into the picture. This custom forces each member to examine the financial soundness and integrity of the other member before concluding a transaction. In the case of 'B' Group Shares, delivery of shares is effected directly between members.

Present Position of BADLA

The badla trade was banned in March 1994. Subsequently, trade volumes declined and liquidity was impaired. The Government had second thoughts and a Committee on Review of Badla System was appointed in Feb. 1995, under the Chairmanship of G.S. Patel.

After the G.S. Patel Committee submitted its report in March 1995, there was a long delay in the acceptance of their recommendations. The SEBI gave some proposals and the Stock Exchanges gave counter proposals but finally on October 5, 1995, the SEBI has announced the acceptance of the Committee's recommendations in full.

The recommendations accepted are as follows:

(i) Carry forward of deals are permitted subject to more rigorous scrutiny and Transparency.

(ii) A flat margin of 15% will be recovered from brokers for carry forward deals and on a marked to market basis every week. Margins will depend on the market prices from time to time, adjusted on a weekly basis.

(iii) A capital adequancy norm of 3% for individual brokers and 6% for corporates has been stipulated. Brokers are allowed self certification, in place of audit, regarding their deals carried forward. The Stock Exchange or SEBI would however check on those self certified statements.

(iv) Mandatory squaring up is imposed for all transactions carried forward with in 90 days.

(v) The Stock Exchanges will strengthen their monitoring system and review the position of capital adequacy norms of brokers in badla deals, so as to protect the investor interests. The stipulation of publishing the carry forward position broker wise, scrip wise, before the start of each badla session was retracted. This leads to total acceptance of G. S. Patel Committee recommendation and the system was implemented.

J.S. Varma Committee (July 1997)

This Committee recommended the Modified Carry Forward System (MCFS), which consists of the following features:

(1) elimination of the limit of 90 days for carry forward system

(2) elimination of settlement only by delivery after 75 days

(3) removal of the limit of Rs. 10 crores on the financier funding.

(4) the clearing house should have an insurance policy, covering the aggregate value of shares lying with them.

(5) abolition of the twin track system of seggregating carry forward trades and delivery trades.

(6) a uniform margin of 10% of the gross position (instead of 15% as before) with a daily marking to market prices.

(7) in case of Vyaj Badla, the financier should be allowed to take custody of the shares with safeguards. The shares lent by badla financiers will continue to be deposited with the clearing house.

(8) capital adequacy and other prudential safeguards should be strictly enforced.

(9) scrips chosen for carry forward should have sufficient floating stock.

(10) exchanges should strengthen the maintenance and surveillance system to enforce the rules on the carry forward trading.

Dhanuka Committee Report

This Committee set up by SEBI to review the securities related Acts and Regulations reported in October 1997. The committee recommended that all SROs like AMBI, AMFI etc. should register with the SEBI. All market players and intermediaries should have their own respective Associations which are registered and controlled by SEBI. The schemes of M.F., promoted by UTI were brought with in the purview of SEBI. The SEBI Act was extended to UTI, and will prevail over any provisions in UTI Act which was amended in 2001. The committee also recommended that SEBI should be allowed to confiscate and impound all ill-gotten gains of any players and intermediaries in the stock and capital markets.

RECENT REFORMS OF STOCK EXCHANGES

Disclosures and Transparency of listed companies and their code of corporate governance are enforced by Stock Exchange which have undergone major structural reforms. Their surveillance systems have improved and their Boards are now broad based. The trading cycle is made uniformly for 5 days. 23 Stock Exchanges have approximately 8,000 electronic trading terminals all over the country. The Stock Exchanges have set up Trade guarantee funds to ensure smooth trading and reduce counter party risk. Their regulation of members has improved as also of trading, settlement and clearing. Demat form of trading electronically has increased volumes and shortened the settlement and clearance period. Compulsory rolling settlement has replaced badla trading in the case of most stocks. These are to be settled on the same day T + 1 basis but the other scrips are on T + 2 day settlement period. Reforms continued on a regular basis both in IPOs and Stock Exchanges. For IPOs, conditions were made more conducive for public issues for retail investor. The qualified institutional buyers (QIBs) were controlled by not allowing them discretionary allotment but forced to deposit margin money of 10% of their bids.Listing and Corporate governance rules are more strictly enforced. Insider trading regulations and other malpractices are subject to greater scrutiny by Stock Exchanges and SEBI.

A centralised listing authority was set up to bring about uniformity and comman practices and procedures in the listing of securities of the corporates. Electronic clearing and settlement system was put into practice which quickened the flow of funds and transfers and settlement of trades. For listed companies, the SEBI has directed the Stock Exchanges in the middle of 2010, to enforce 25% of paid up capital to be under public holding compulsorily.

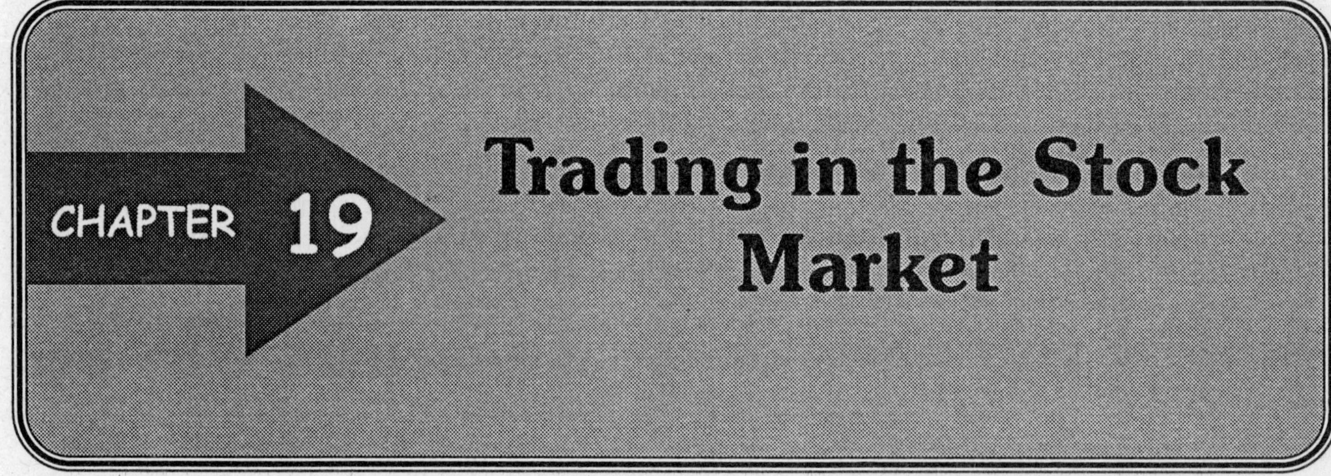

Pattern of Trading

Trading in the stock market takes place under three sections (Bombay Stock Exchange):

(i) Group (A) —Specified shares.

(ii) Group B_1 and B_2 — Non-specified shares or Cash Shares.

(iii) Group (Z)[@] — Companies violating listing norms

Under Group (A), only those actively traded (around 150 on the BSE) are included. The criteria for listing in specified group has been dealt with in an earlier chapter. The rest of the listed securities are placed in Group (B) of which those well traded are put in group B_1. There are 8,000 scrips in total and 6,000 companies quoted on the BSE of which 90% are equities. Out of these equity shares, only about 300 companies are well traded on a daily basis. The trading in the rest is nil or negligible. The standard face value of Rs. 10 was given up in favour of any face value of Rs. 1 and above in 1999-00. The permitted securities are those that are not listed on the Exchange, but are permitted to be traded on this Exchange, also called foreign securities as they are listed on other stock exchanges in India. On BSE, there are no permitted securities, under their Byelaws 25 & 26 of Rules & Byelaws.

The securities traded may be corporate securities, semi-government securities or public sector bonds. The latter are not traded on the trading floor but over the counter through telephone, telex, etc., as between brokers, RBI, etc.

The instruments of trading are equity shares, preference shares, debentures, CCPs, PSU bonds and government securities.

The two main stock market indicators are price and quantity of shares traded. The indirect market indicators are the velocity of price changes or spread of market prices (volatility) and the intensity of trading per hour, and the number of advances and declines in prices etc.

Barring the equity which have a variable dividend, the other securities have a return fixed and trading in them is restricted. In fact, there is not much trading in preference shares and PSU bonds. Only in respect of equity shares and that too of major companies, there is trading of any worthwhile magnitude. The equity shares are ownership capital enjoying tax exemption for dividend income in the hands of individual investor from 1997-98 and have a good marketability. There is also an exemption up to a limit in respect of investment in new issues of specified companies. Investment in shares, securities etc., is also exempt from wealth tax. The market, therefore, provides good liquidity to only equity shares and that too of a limited number of companies. Trading in debt instruments is more concentrated on NSE.

@ Group 'Z' now renamed as "others" — companies of 'T', 'S' 'TS' and so called 'Z' categories. These terms are explained later in the book.

One indicator of the market trading is the turnover of shares in volume and value. In 1996, the monthly market turnover is around Rs. 11,080 crores with average daily turnover of around Rs. 500 - 800 crores on the BSE which spurted upto Rs. 1,300 crores per day due to on line trading system on BSE and NSE in 1998-99 and further to Rs. 4,000 crores per day in 2007. This rise in turnover is made possible due to expansion of BOLT (on line trading) to 500 cities by June 2000. Nearly 80% of trading is confined to the specified group. (A Group). The daily turnover on the NSE was much higher at around Rs. 10,000 crores in 2008-09.

'Z' Group in Bombay Stock Exchange

In July 1999, the B.S.E. has introduced a new class of scrips, namely 'Z' group, which Comprises of companies, not complying with clauses of the listing agreement and are not redressing the grievances of investors. This is a kind of black listed companies which are erring presistently in following the Rules and Regulations of the listing agreement or not paying the listing fees, not calling for meetings and delay in annoucements and in complying with investor complaints. If the pending complaints are increasing and the company is not responding, the BSE authorities have been shifting such companies from B_2 group to 'Z' group in order to caution the prospective investors, against such companies. Before shifting such companies to 'Z' group, the Exchange sends them notices advising remedial action by the companies and if they refused to comply and not respond to such notices, they are shifted to 'Z' group.

More than 300 companies were in 'Z' group at that time in 1999-2000 and the companies in this group are increased from time to time depending upon the complaints against such erring companies. Unfortunately, this measure did not help to correct the erring companies, nor did it shift away the investor interest in them. Many investors are placing orders for scrips in this group, despite such warning signals, from The Stock Exchange authorities. The 'Z' group is thus a group of black listed erring companies which should give a red signal to any investor who wants to invest in them. Afterwards, this list was dropped as some of them were delisted and some have remedied the situation.

Another indicator of the market trading is the price in terms of individual scrips and for groups of securities in the form of indices. The BSE publishes two types of series — Sensitive series of 30 most actively traded scrips and secondly, National series of 100 actively traded scrips on the major stock exchanges of Mumbai, Ahmedabad, Delhi, Kolkata and Chennai. Fig. 19.1 shows the price trends in terms of B.S.E. Sensex over a period of 10 years. The graph shows that over the period 1991 to 2000 the price rise has shown an increase nearly 8 times indicating the degree of appreciation of capital in the market. Sensex reached a peak again in Sept. 2005, having had a boom period during 2004 and 2005. The appreciation reflects the corporate performance, on the one hand, and increase in liquidity in the economy, on the other.[1] The rise in prices of shares has provided a hedge against inflation, if these prices are considered for a longer period of 5 to 10 years. Thus, the market is providing liquidity in major shares and also acting as a hedge against inflation. Another important function provided by the market is the increase in the capital raised from the public in terms of new issues and the volume of securities to be traded in the market. About Rs. 26,500 crores are raised from the capital market in 1994-95 as against the Eighth Plan projection for an amount of Rs. 13,000 per annum over the period 1992-97. The fresh capital listed on the stock exchanges has also increased accordingly. The amount raised through all methods, including private placement by Private and Public Sectors was Rs. 2,02,745 crores in 2008-09 (RBI Annual Report).

1. V. A. Avadhani, "Monetarist Approach to Share Prices in India," *BSE Stock Exchange Review*, May 1991.

Fig. 19.1

BSE Sensitive Series Index.

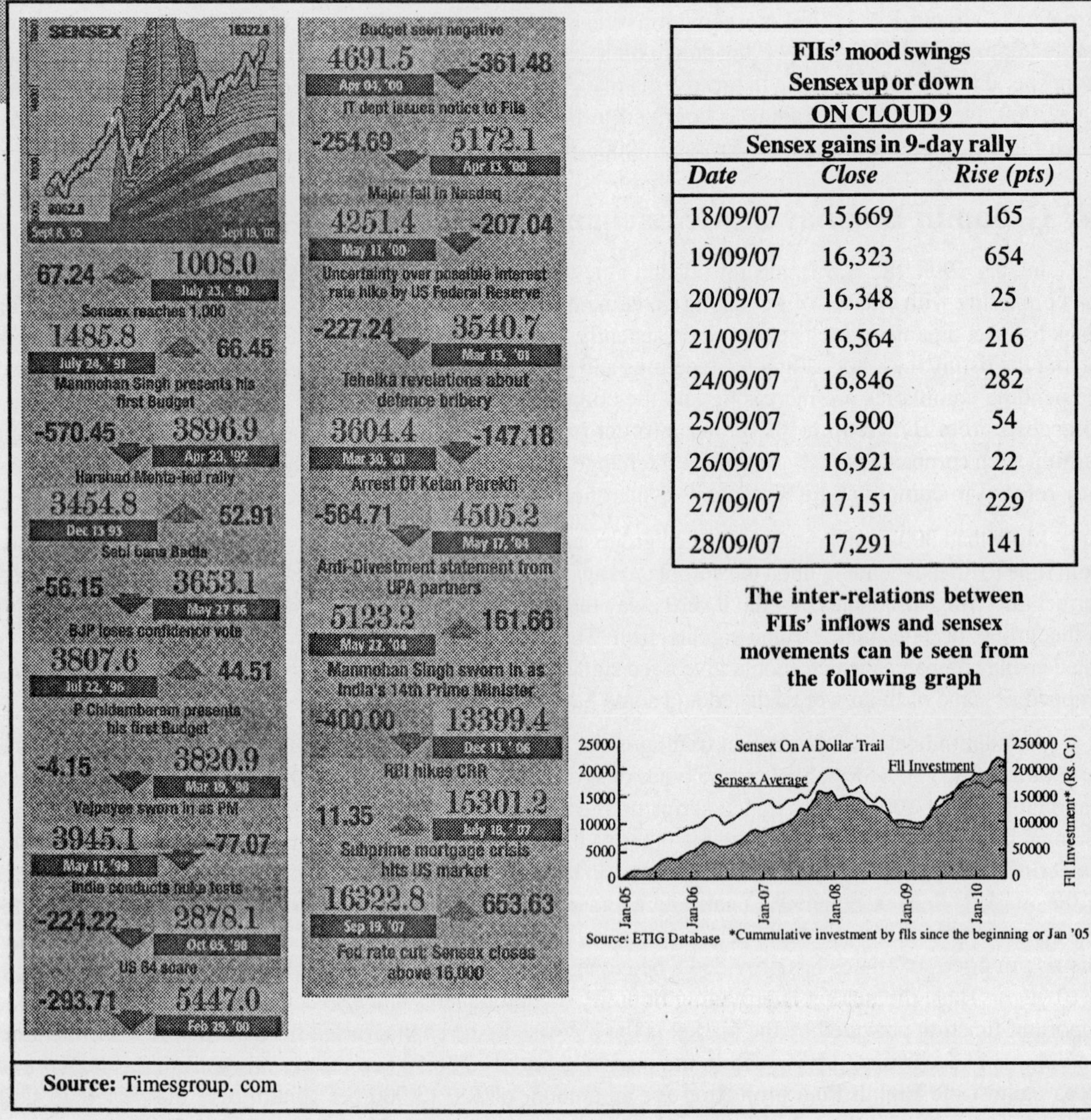

FIIs' mood swings		
Sensex up or down		
ON CLOUD 9		
Sensex gains in 9-day rally		
Date	*Close*	*Rise (pts)*
18/09/07	15,669	165
19/09/07	16,323	654
20/09/07	16,348	25
21/09/07	16,564	216
24/09/07	16,846	282
25/09/07	16,900	54
26/09/07	16,921	22
27/09/07	17,151	229
28/09/07	17,291	141

The inter-relations between FIIs' inflows and sensex movements can be seen from the following graph

Source: Timesgroup. com

The ups and downs and major swings in the sensex can be seen from the above charts. When the Economic Reforms started, it was about 1, 486 (July 24, 1991) it rose to around 5,000 by the time that new millennium started in April 2000. Between April 2000 to May 2004, it was around 5,000 only. But since May 2004 to July 2007, it has zoomed up by three times to around 15,000 and crossed 16,000 by mid Sept. and 18,000 by end Oct. 2007. It has reached a 3-year high of 21,207 in Jan. 2008 but Feb. to a low of 7,697 in Oct. 2008. After reaching a peak of 21,207 in January 2008, in fell. to a low of 7,697 in October 2008, The sensex reached a level of 18,047 in April 2010 and by end May it stood at 16,944. It crossed the level of 20,000 in October, 2010.

Note: After a spate of depression in the markets during 2001 to 2003 there was an upsurge again reaching all time high going beyond 8000 in Sensex in Sept., 2005. The boom in the market was seen during 2004 and 2007, reaching more than 14,000 in BSE Sensex in February 2007 and more than 18,000 in October 2007.

TRADING AND SETTLEMENT

Speculative Traders vs. Genuine Investors

The investors in the stock market can be classified as genuine investors and speculative investors. The former take delivery of shares and give delivery with no intention to deal in carry-forward business. The latter, however, do not give or take delivery of shares but only deal in differences in purchase and sale prices. Even if they take delivery, their intention is to make gain on differences between purchase and sale prices. Short-term gains are the motive of the genuine investors. Any genuine investor can have short-term gains of a few months when he buys and sells along with delivery. The essential difference between these two classes lies in the intention to take and give delivery of shares or to just carry forward and to gain in differences.

Types of Speculators

On the stock markets, there are various classes of brokers, depending on their activities and specialisation. Essentially, a broker is an intermediary between buyers and sellers of securities. His clients may be individuals, institutions like companies, trusts, charities, etc., banks and financial institutions (including mutual funds). Some of these clients may be speculators also doing business of carry forward and dealing in differences in prices. Secondly, there are jobbers or *Taravaniwallas* who are wholesalers doing both buying and selling in selected scrips. They give both bid and offer prices for the scrips they trade in. They are like market-makers in foreign markets. Thirdly, there are *badliwallas* financing the carry-forward transactions and lending securities when necessary. Such carry-forward or *badli* transactions are facilitated by blank transfer of T.D.s. with shares. These blank transfers are transfers without any insertion on them, the names of the transferees and without any need for payment of stamp duty, etc.

On the stock exchange, there are two main categories of speculators, namely, bulls and bears. Bulls are *Tejiwallas* who buy shares in expectation of selling at higher prices. Bears are known as *Mandiwallas* who sell securities in expectation of a fall in prices and buying at a later date. *Stags* are those members who neither buy nor sell but apply for subscription to new issues expecting to sell them at a higher price later when these issues are quoted on the stock exchange.

Activities of Brokers

In addition to the above classes of brokers who are members of the stock exchange, there are a few who act as arbitrageurs as between two or more stock exchanges. Thus, these members buy in one market and sell in another market to take advantage of the price differences in the same scrip as between different markets.

Some brokers specialise in dealing in the specified Group (A) which are speculative scrips and have carry forward facility (badla). There are others who only deal in non-sepcified Group (B) where delivery of shares is given and taken. There are a few dealers who used to specialise in odd lots which are not in the marketable lots so as to facilitate buying and selling in them for investors. Some Stock Exchanges used to hold separate trading sessions for odd lots on specific days when the brokers put through their transactions. Marketable lots are shares of 100 or 50, when the share's face value is Rs. 10; and 5 when the shares are of face value of Rs. 100 and Rs. 50. Since 1999, SEBI has allowed issues without fixed face value such as Rs. 10 or Rs. 100. The relevance of odd lots has disappeared when physical certificates are replaced by Demat form of them.

There is a separate category of brokers dealing only in new issues, underwriting, marketing, lead management and even merchant banking etc. Besides, many brokers also undertake the business of mobilising fixed deposits for companies. Some activities akin to money market operations are undertaken by brokers like arranging inter-corporate investments, discounting of commercial bills of exchange or trading in UTI units or PSU Bonds etc. Some brokers specialise in government securities market, which is a part of the stock market operations. The government and semi-government securities and government guaranteed bonds are quoted on the stock exchanges. Their trading does not take place in the trading ring but over the counter of the brokers *vis-a-vis* the investing banks, financial institutions or other brokers.

As referred to earlier, many brokers undertake activities in the primary market in addition to the secondary market. These two markets are complementary and brokers having activities in both the markets are at an advantage in that they can secure contacts with companies, lead banks, financial institutions, etc. They can secure shares of these companies underwritten or marketed by them for keeping as their inventories. In this market, the brokers act mainly as marketing agents sometimes as underwriters, issue managers, lead managers, merchant bankers, consultants and even as registrars. The most common activity undertaken by brokers in this respect is consultancy and advice to investors, be they individual clients or institutional clients. As a follow-up of this, they also provide the services of portfolio management to big clients, institutions and NRIs. The investment consultancy firms established by brokers specialise in this portfolio management.

Thus, the activities of brokers can be set out as follows:

In the Primary Market: To act as underwriter-broker for new issue marketing — lead manager — issue manager — merchant banker — portfolio manager — adviser/consultant etc.

In the Secondary Market: To act as dealer, broker, jobber, etc. in the trading ring, badla financier for carry forward business — arbitrageur buying and selling as between the different markets, as in Mumbai and Delhi — dealer in government securities, bonds, etc. adviser, consultant and portfolio manager, etc.

Allied Services: Investor services like home delivery of shares, arranging for transfer of shares, safe custody of shares, etc. dealing in inter-corporate investment to act as broker for fixed deposits of companies, to operate in the money market, PSU bonds, UTI units, Mutual Fund Schemes, etc.

Brokers' Charges

Except to the charitable trusts, the broker charges brokerage to all clients, after effecting the purchase or sale and at the time of passing the contract note. The brokerage, which may range from 0.5 to 2.5%, is included in the price charged but not separately shown. The SEBI has now insisted on their showing the brokerage separately. Even a smaller brokerage may be charged depending on the volume of business and frequency of dealings put through for the client. Generally, the prices charged by the broker are higher than those officially quoted in the quotation list. This is because the broker includes the brokerage in the price and in the price band prevailing in the market on any day, the higher price is used for sale to the client and lower one for purchase as he has to buy from and sell to the jobber, who quotes in the reverse order, namely, buy low and sell high. This is the general practice of brokers, and this can be mistaken by the clients as if the broker is overcharging them. Brokers are also collecting from clients the service tax of 5% on the brokerage income which they pay to Government and which is shown separately in the Contract Note.

Delivery/Payment

The broker takes the cheque for purchase first and delivers the shares later in a purchase deal. He pays by cheque later but takes delivery of shares first for a sale transaction. This is explained by the settlement procedure of the stock exchanges, which has fixed the pay-in day and delivery dates first. All the members have to pay money or deliver shares first to the clearing house. On a later day fixed for payout, the clearing house pays by cheque and delivers the shares to the members. These transactions of members with the clearing house can be effected only when their clients in turn first pay in and send the cheques or deliver shares and later get the cheques from them or shares delivered later after the pay-out day.

If the shares are not available with the selling brokers as there were short sales and the buyer insists on the delivery, the buyer member can ask the stock exchange for auction of those shares and get them from any member for delivery. This process takes a few more days and leads to delays in the settlement and clearing process. It is, therefore, possible that the buyer can get shares only after 40 to 50 days in the case of Group A shares and 15 to 30 days in the case of Group B shares. Similarly, the seller receives his cheque for payment after 45 to 60 days after the sale is put through in the case of Group A and 30 to 40 days in the case of Group B, on the B.S.E. With the introduction of on-line trading called BOLT in May 1995 the above periods were brought down drastically, and time taken was cut down to a few days, say a week or ten days.

Settlement Procedure

The settlement procedure of the stock exchange is to be understood to comprehend why such delays take place. The Settlement Committee of the Exchange fixes the schedules of trading and settlement for each group separately (A, B_1 and B_2 Groups). In these schedules, for each settlement, there will be 5 to 15 trading days (Saturdays, Sundays, and holidays excluded) after which three days would be set apart for effecting squaring up and carry forward (Badla). There will be one or two days for correcting errors and omissions and secure a final settlement of each member's position *vis-a-vis* others in respect of all scrips. Taking both sales and purchases scrip-wise, the net position is arrived and payment to be made or received is determined accordingly. Then a pay-in-day is fixed for delivering cheques or shares to the clearing house by those who are due to give. There will be a first pay-in day and after a couple of days, a final pay-in day to help clear up all payments due. Then finally pay-out day is fixed with a gap of a day or two for the clearing house to make all payments out or delivery for shares to members.

Auctions

Auctions are arranged for scrips which could not be delivered even on the final day. These auctions are tenders for sale of the desired scrips in the quantities purchased but not delivered so that delivery can be effected to the buyers. Auction in group A is automatic when the seller fails to deliver on the appointed day and at the request of the buyer in the case of group B. Auctions are arranged by the stock exchange by inviting bids from members to buy the shares on behalf of the member who could not deliver the shares.

Clearing Procedure

Daily after trading is completed, members submit to the exchange their saudas (memos of purchases and sales scrip-wise). On the next day, if there are any objections or corrections, they are submitted in the form of wandha memos. This process goes on daily for all the 5 trading days. These memos are fed to the computer and the daily net position is arrived at. If the stock exchange authorities impose any margins, they are collected from members and deposited in the clearing house. At the end of the settlement, the overall net position of a member is arrived at after taking into account the dealings, squared up and those to be carried forward. On the three days, set apart for badla settlement, members' squaring up position and carry forward position is known. Any objections or errors are recorded and corrections carried out. Then the final corrected position of members is arrived at. At this stage, the carry over margins, if imposed, are collected. This forms the basis for asking the members to pay in or deliver the shares on the pay-in day. The entire process involves time varying from 30 day to 40 days, mainly due to the large trading volume and secondly, due to the large component of speculative trading and carry forward transactions on the BSE. All this procedure and time taken is brought down drastically due to electronic form of trading now and dematerialisation of shares. On the NSE, the deliveries and auctions take place within a shorter period of 7 to 10 days. On the BSE also, after the on-line trading was introduced all the above process was replaced by computer generated notes and reports.

Regulation

The regulation of trading on the stock exchange takes various forms. The objective is to curb excesses and to ensure a stable market. Over-trading and possible defaults can be avoided by these measures. Normally, the fixation of trading hours, methods of trading, clearing and settlement, etc. are all done as per the Rules and Byelaws of the Exchange. The methods of regulation of trading are as follows:

1. Fixation of daily margins on both purchases and sales which are to be paid by buyers and sellers on their daily position.
2. Fixation of carry-over margins to be paid on purchases and sales carried forward to the next settlement.
3. *Ad hoc* margins on any scrip or a group shares, if trading exceeds some limits.
4. Fixation of limits to trading in each scrip and/or for each member.
5. Fixation of maximum and minimum prices or a band of prices for shares in times of extreme volatility of the market. (Volatility Margins)
6. Suspension of trading in a few or all scrips or banning carry forward business, through circuit breakers.*
7. Shifting scrips from Group A to Group B and *vice versa* to reduce carry-over business.
8. Reduce the trading hours and/or confine trading to hand delivery basis or cash basis, etc.

* Circuit breaker is stoppage of trading if price of any scrip rises or falls beyond 8 to 12%.

NATIONAL MARKET SYSTEM

A high powered Study Group on the Establishment of New Stock Exchanges under the chairmanship of Shri M. J. Pherwani has submitted its Report in June 1991. This Study Group has

recommended some criteria for setting up of new Stock Exchanges and favoured the licensing of additional trading floors (ATF), instead of multiplying the number of Stock Exchanges in the country.

The Study Group has also recommended the setting up of a model National Stock Exchange at New Mumbai (NSE) which will develop the National Market System in the country. Any Stock Exchange should have the minimum level of infrastructure in terms of Space, Tele-communications, Computerisation, On-line processing system, Library, Research facilities, Publicity Dept. etc. All these were recommended for the "National Market" to be set up by NSE.

Characteristics

The characteristics of National Market System are as follows:

1. Completely automated system in terms of both trading and settlement procedures to be provided through the Securities Facilities Support Corporation.
2. Compulsory market makers/jobbers to provide liquidity and ready market.
3. The members would be as large as 1000 and Corporate and Institutional members would also be there drawn from various parts of the country and to represent the professionals on an All India basis.
4. Only medium and large sized companies and PSUs are expected to be listed on this Exchange and it will complement the existing Exchanges.
5. The NSE would have a separate trading time allotted for debt instruments in order to have the beneficial effect of creating an active secondary market in debt instruments.

Objectives

The objectives of this NMS are as follows:

1. To help thc privatisation of Public Sector Units through listing of their shares on this Exchange.
2. To spread the investment habit and cult to savers in the rural and semi-urban areas as well.
3. To professionalise the members with a view to improve the investor services.
4. To create more employment opportunities in the service sector within the orbit of the Capital Market.
5. To promote the market for debt instruments.

Study Group Recommendations

As per the recommendation of the Study Group, the present system of Stock Exchanges has failed to cater to the needs of the genuine investors. The debt market or debenture and bond trading was neglected and speculation and manipulation of the markets became the order of the day. The Study Group has therefore recommended the setting up of a new National Stock Exchange at New Mumbai and National Market System, based on the New Bombay Stock Exchange transactions.

The NMS was to be developed on a three tier basis for uniform and high quality trading, settlement, clearing and depository services for the nation as a whole. The three tier Stock Market structure is as follows:

1. Principal Stock Exchanges comprising the five major Exchanges at Mumbai, Delhi, Kolkata, Chennai and Ahmedabad.
2. Regional Stock Exchanges comprising of other Exchanges in the country.
3. Additional Trading Floors, sponsored and managed by the principal or a Regional Stock Exchange, as the case may be.

Experience in Foreign Countries

In the U.S., the Securities Act Amendments of 1975 directed to SEC to work towards setting up of a NMS. The SEC has left the initiative to the security industry. In 1977 the New York Stock Exchange has linked itself to Philadelphia Stock Exchange to create an Inter-market Trading System (ITS). By 1981 almost all the Stock Exchanges were linked to New York Exchange. The ITS arranges for concurrent display electronically of the current quotes of eligible shares. The broker has a choice to put his deal either in the Exchange where he is physically present or in any other Exchange. If he decides to deal in another Exchange he has to put his order or commitment to trade in the electronic system, this is valid for a fixed period at that specified price. If it is accepted by anybody in that Exchange, the deal is put through, otherwise it is rejected.

The companies under NASDAQ (National Association of Security Dealers Automated Quoted system), have also joined the NMS as a next stage in 1982. Such companies satisfying some financial criteria were designated as Tier I companies and are designated as part of NMS. Some other companies have also been permitted to be on NMS on Tier II on a voluntary basis. More than 1000 companies of NASDAQ are traded on the NMS and constitute an important component of the NMS in the U.S.

In the U.K., London is the market around which all other markets revolve and before the London market the other Stock Exchanges fade away into insignificance. The NMS in the U.K. is developed on the basis of London quotes and other markets are more or less trading floors only.

The Inter-market Trading System in U.K. connects all Stock markets in U.K. to London and the trading pattern revolves around the London Quotes although the other Stock Markets have maintained their individualities in theory. The electronic display on the Quotes around the whole of U.K. of all scrips quoted in London, facilitates the Inter market Trading System.

The eight national Stock Exchanges in FDR of Germany were linked in 1989 into a single screen based trading system, wherein Frankfurt became the centre piece of the trading and others were trading on the basis of Frankfurt Quotes. But in none of the other developed or developing countries, a new Stock Exchange was set-up to develop the NMS, as proposed by Pherwani Committee.

The Bombay Stock Exchange which accounts for 2/3rds of total trading in India has claimed that it can act as the Centre piece of NMS as New York in USA and London in UK and that there is no need for setting up a separate New Bombay Stock Exchange (NSE), as suggested by Pherwani Committee. But the Government has accepted the Committee's recommendations and entrusted to the Stock Holding Corporation of India (SHCI), the task of setting up the Central Depository System to immobilise the Paper Certificates, a National Clearing and Settlement Corporation to administer a National Settlement System as between the Stock Exchanges and a Securities Facilities Support Corporation to establish and maintain an electronic network for this purpose. The National Stock Exchange was set up accordingly in 1992, as referred to earlier.

NATIONAL CLEARANCE AND DEPOSITORY SYSTEM

The new system which the Stock Holding Corporation of India is assigned to set up by the Ministry of Finance for clearance and depository functions of the Stock Exchanges at the national level is called the National Clearance Settlement and Depository System. It comprises of (a) National Depository System (b) National Trade Comparison and Reporting System and (c) National Clearance System.

From the world wide experience, there does not appear to be any single system which can be transplanted on Indian soil as it is. There is a complexity of legal hurdles, procedures and habit problems to face in India for a change of this type.

Present Settlement and Clearance System

The growth of equity cult in India in eighties has put the present system of settlement and clearance to serious strain. Besides the work load on the Clearing Agencies and Share Transfer Agencies has increased multifold. These led to many problems to investors arising out of systematic risks like counter party risk, credit risk, bad deliveries, long delayed deliveries, counterfeit scrips, forged scrips, etc. These have increased to alarming levels in the Nineties. The Indian investors may not themselves tolerate these developments not to speak of International investment Groups or Funds, interested in Indian markets.

Our present system had outlived its usefulness and since it is not possible to have a revolutionary change in the system, it is better to evolve a system of settlement based on dematerialisation of physical certificates and transfer of shares on the basis of book entries.

The new system will have to be based on a change in legal system, changes in banking practices, settlement and clearance system. To start with, a book entry system for transfers as between broker members can be arranged as is done by the Bombay Stock Exchange with the Bank of India Holdings, set up separately for this purpose. At the national level, the National Depository was set up along with many participant depositories. The Central depository system was accepted by the government and SEBI Guidelines were issued for the depositories and the Central Depository.

National Trade Comparison and Reporting System

Its function is to establish the forms and conditions of contracts after trade execution in the securities markets. First the trade execution and then reporting of these for matching of the terms of the contracts and trade comparison will lead to the output of National Trade Reporting Systems as matched transactions. This will be the input for the National Clearing System.

National Clearing System ensures that clearing as between brokers of different Stock Exchanges should be through book entries. This would mean that clearing can take place nationally on a standard basis to prepare the matched transactions for a depository settlement.

The Central Depository System aims at immobilisation of physical certificates. This is done by means of book entries with Central Depository who keeps custody of all physical certificates as a first step. As a next step, new issues will be made as book entries only and not as physical certificates. Book entry transfers will lead to quicker transfers and at lower costs. It can meet the increasing work load of investment activity and dealings leading to increasing volume of transfer work.

To put into practice the above system, a number of hurdles have to be overcome and changes have to be effected in the legal system, inheritance rights, pledges and hypothecation and practices of banks in this regard and practices of companies with regard to share transfers etc. The legal system should recognise the transfer of ownership by the necessary book entries. The rights of beneficial ownership are to be vested on the basis of the records with the Depository. The practices of banks and other financial institutions have to be changed also to permit pledge and release of pledge on the basis of hypothecation of National Depository System on behalf of the investors and not by physical scrips, as before. Companies and transfer agents have to recognise the book entry transfer system. Similarly, the need for transfer deed and collection of stamp tax for transfers have to be modified to suit the book entry system of transfers. Most of these changes are already implemented in the transfer mechanism adopted by NSE and BSE. The legal hurdles were removed and the new practices are implemented.

INTERNET BROKING

The SEBI has approved internet trading in a limited form towards the end of 1999. The SEBI Committee on internet based trading and services has allowed internet to be used as an Order Routing System (ORS) through registered stock brokers on behalf of clients for execution of trades. Internet broking refers to the use of the Net as a medium for communicating client orders to the Stock Exchanges through the Broker websites. These sites may serve a variety of functions from allowing full trading through the website to features like on line stock quotes, information and analysis, etc.

Order Routing System (ORS)

The broker offering internet trading facility provides an electronic space for the customer to enter the name of the security, buy and sell orders, quantity and price specifications. Records are kept by the broker of all such customer orders for execution. Once the broker system receives the client order, it is checked electronically against the customer's account and routed out by the broker to the appropriate exchange for execution. This constitutes what is called order routing system and the customer receives a message confirming the order. Once the transaction is completed the client's portfolio ledger account is updated to reflect the transaction.

This internet facility has both advantages and disadvantages. It provides transparency, and best quotes possible at any time. An investor will have control over the information and quotes and will be able to hit a quote on an on-line basis. Doubts about the broker's capacity and integrity will be non-issues. The problems with internet broking are the risk of safety and confidentiality. There are possibilities of someone hacking into the system and possible malpractices. These are controlled by SEBI through the Stock Exchanges. For an individual broker a networth of Rs. 50 lakhs is laid down and Stock Exchanges can insist a adequate networth, limits to trading and collect margins and ensure Trade guarantees. Presently e-broking on internet constitutes about 25% of total trade on NSE.

E-BROKING

SEBI's Role

SEBI has asked the Stock Exchanges to ensure that the broker has enough verifiable information about clients and asked brokers to have clearly set exposures and turn over limits for each client. A model broker client agreement form set out by SEBI spells out the obligations and rights of each side to the agreement. The broker web sites should contain information on Investor Protection Rules, Arbitration Rules and display all Stock Exchange Rules and Regulations. Brokers cannot offset transactions of clients but have to go through the Exchange.

Among security features demanded by SEBI include unique user identification number and passwords which can be changed from time to time to prevent hacking by outsiders. SEBI has laid down that the system should have security reliability and confidentiality of data through the use of encryption technology. The Exchanges must also ensure that records are maintained in electronic form by the broker and that they are not susceptible to manipulation and that adequate back up and storage facilities are available.

The NSE Members planned to provide internet trading facilities in 22 countries outside India, including U.S.A., and South Asian Countries. NSE has 300 centres within the country with the facility to execute a deal on the NSE from anywhere in the country within two seconds. As a result, a non-resident investor will be at the same level as a resident investor in terms of facility for trading.

In India, SSKI, KBS Cap, Motilal Oswal, Khandwala Securities, I-sec, IL & F Securities are some of the brokerages which has got into internet broking shortly after it was set to operate. Now many more security firms have joined the bandwagon.

Dynamics of Net Trading in Stocks

Net broking is now permitted by SEBI, subject to the following guidelines:

(1) SEBI registered brokers must apply to their respective Stock Exchanges for formal permission.

(2) Brokers must have a minimum net worth of Rs. 50 lakhs.

(3) SEs must ensure that the system used by brokers has the provision for security, reliability and confidentiality.

(4) The brokers must have sufficient verifiable information on clients, their creditworthiness, etc.

(5) Brokers must enter into agreements with such clients who want to use net trading, setting out the rights and obligations, including fees, service standards, etc.

(6) S.Es have to monitor complaints and to ensure minimum service levels by brokers.

(7) Contract Notes to be passed to clients within 24 hours of trade execution.

(8) All orders of clients have to pass through the Exchange and no cross trading is permitted.

The mechanics of Net trading is as follows:

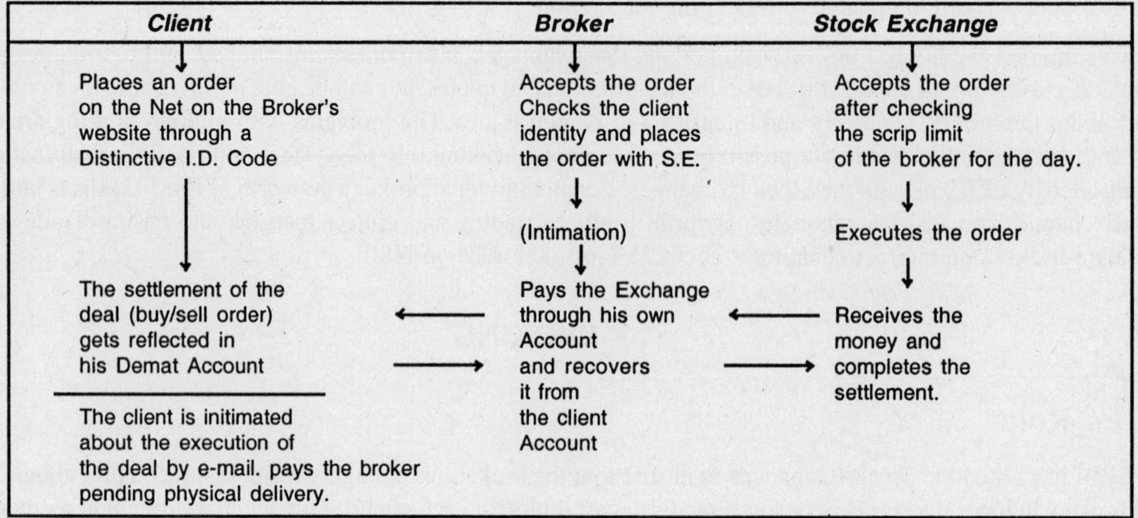

EMERGING ROLE OF STOCK EXCHANGES

1. As per the existing Law, the Stock Exchange is an association of member brokers for the purpose of facilitating and regulating trading in securities. It is thus a self regulatory organisation (SRO). The traditional emphasis was on regulation by the SRO in the interests of members. Now demutualisation of Stock Exchanges has separated the ownership from regulation of exchanges.

2. The world wide trend is now towards greater self regulation by the SROs along with the co-ordinating and supervisory role of the Government. At the same time, the role of SROs including those of Merchant Bankers and Mutual Funds has increased in the direction of stricter enforcement of a code of conduct and the rules of the game in the conduct of their business. The SEBI is however moving in the direction of more regulation.

3. In the evolution of the role of the stock exchanges, the trend is moving more in the direction of the public interest. The investor population has increased and their interests have become paramount both in the eyes of the government and the SROs for reasons of promoting the Capital Market. This has led to a greater emphasis on the developmental role of Stock Exchanges. The representation of public on the Board of Directors, the facilities provided to redress their grievances through the Grievances Cell of the Stock Exchanges have all proved to be in this direction.

4. The Stock Exchanges have been growing as Public Service Institutions by providing a variety of services to the investors. To give examples of such services, mention may be made of the following:

(a) Provision of Directory of Corporate information useful for a scientific assessment of the fundamentals of the companies before making investment.

(b) Publication of share prices at which trade took place daily in various scrips traded — open, high, low and closing along with the volume.

(c) Publication and supply to public of useful handouts/handbooks/pamphlets giving out information on the Stock Exchanges — the operations and developments in the Capital Market etc.

(d) Investor education and training programmes for investors.

(e) Settlement of disputes between member broker and their clients and investors.

(f) Attending to the investor complaints against registered members and listed companies.

5. The future role of Stock Exchanges will be radically different from the present, as their developmental role will be increasing much faster than their regulatory role. Along with increasing self regulation and a stricter enforcement of a code of conduct on the members, the Stock Exchange will emerge as Public Service Institutions catering to increasing demands of investors in the country. Of the developmental activities, education, training and research will dominate in the years to come bringing the Stock Exchanges and the public nearer and together. This is conspicuous by its absence now.

6. With the increasing emphasis on the National Market System and the growth of automation, the new trend would be integration and interlinking of Stock Exchanges at the regional and national level. This trend would be beneficial to investors, in that they would enjoy a better market and fair play. Quicker services and better price realization at lower costs could be achieved by the new system. The Stock exchanges would thus move in the direction of a National Market system through mutual co-operation, co-ordination and electronic linkages of the trading floors through the satellite telecommunication system and quicker display of information. The BSE has introduced the BOLT on line electronic trading. The BOLT of BSE is now kept open to members of other Stock Exchanges, which may open up a National Market System[@] in India. An Inter-connected Stock Exchange is already set up with a few regional Stock Exchanges like Hyderabad, Cochin, Bangalore, Vadodara, etc. as members. The members of these regional Exchange can also deal in I.C.S.E.

7. Where there are no Stock Exchanges, trading floors would be provided and electronic display of the prices of shares in the national market would help trade in the local trading floors. In the Computer-aided Trading System, there is no need even for the trading floor; it is more economical with electronic trading than setting up of separate Stock Exchanges at innumerable centres.

8. With the setting up of the Central Depository System and the National clearing and settlement system, there was dematerialisation and immobilisation of physical paper certificates and the trading and settlement would take place on the book entry system. The method of pass book entries in the banks would be the order of the day for the Stock Exchanges. The National Securities Depository Ltd. is the Central Depository for the operations in a Demat form of the various Stock Exchanges in the country. Most of the scrips are now in compulsory demat trading.

9. NSDL is helping the operations of the Rolling Settlement System in 10 scrips at the start of the new millennium in 2000, which was extended to all scrips in the later years. There were about 96 scrips in Compulsory Rolling Settlement System, in 2000-01, which was increased further to all in the latter years.

10. e-broking and e-transfer of funds and e-trading etc. is tending to make our stock exchanges on line with major international Exchanges like New York or London. Many of our company shares are listed in foreign exchanges and traded. The trend to globalisation is growing faster due to the operation of many FIIs and FFIs in the Indian Capital market.

11. Derivative segment is growing fast particularly since 2001, when trading in options and futures in individual scrips was allowed. Bulk of the trading in derivatives is concentrated in Mumbai, followed by Delhi and Kolkata.

12. Most of the scrips are traded in demat form. The Rolling Settlement System covers almost all specified scrips. The other scrips are on T + 2 settlement system. Thus by end 2009, all the scrips are on T + 1 or T + 2 settlement basis, with the help of electronic clearing and the same day transfer of funds.

@ BOLT stands for B.S.E. On Line Trading System

PART — IV
Security Analysis

Chapter 20: Sources of Investment Information

Chapter 21: Inflation and Investments

Chapter 22: Security Market Analysis

Chapter 23: Investment Decision Making

Chapter 24: Financial Analysis and Interpretation

Chapter 25: Balance Sheet Analysis and Blue Chips

Chapter 26: Fundamental Analysis

Chapter 27: Technical Analysis of the Market

Chapter 28: Efficient Market Theory

CHAPTER 20

Sources of Investment Information

Security Analysis requires as a first step the sources of information, on the basis of which analysis is made. The Securities market is a perfect auction market where demand/supply pressures determine the price. These demand/supply pressures depend upon the available money and the flow of information. It is in this context that sources of information become relevant. Besides the market analysis and estimate of the intrinsic value around which the market price revolves, would also need an analysis of the flow of information.

Types of Information

The types of information, which are relevant for our purposes are of the following categories:

(i) *World Affairs*: International factors, which influence domestic income, output and employment and for investment in the domestic market by F.F.I.s, O.C.B.s, etc. Also foreign political affairs, wars, crude oil prices and the state of foreign markets affect our markets.

(ii) *Domestic Economic and Political Factors*: Gross domestic products, agricultural output, monsoon, money supply, inflation, Govt. policies, taxation, etc., affect our markets.

(iii) *Industry Information*: Market demand, installed capacity, competing units, capacity utilisation, market share of the major units, market leaders, prospects of the industry, international demand for exports, inputs and capital goods abroad, import competing products, labour problems and Govt. policy towards the industry are all relevant factors to be considered in investment decision making.

(iv) *Company Information:* Corporate data, annual reports, Stock Exchange publications, Dept. of company affairs and their circulars, press releases on corporate affairs by Govt., industry chambers or associations of industries etc. are also relevant for security prices analysis.

(v) *Security Market Information:* The Credit rating of companies, data on market trends, security market analysis and market reports, equity research reports, trade and settlement data, listing of companies and delisting, record dates and book closures etc., BETA factors, etc. are the needed information for investment management.

(vi) *Security Price Quotations:* Price indices, price and volume data, breadth, daily volatility, range and rate of changes of these variables are also needed for technical analysis.

(vii) *Data on Related Markets:* Such as Govt. securities, money market, forex market, commodities markets etc. are useful for deciding on alternative avenues of investment.

(viii) *Data on Mutual Funds:* Their schemes and their performance, N A V and repurchase prices etc. are needed as they are also investment avenues.

(ix) Data on Primary Markets/New Issues, etc.

Need for Information

Investors and Market Analysts depend on the timely and correct information for making investment decisions. In the absence of such information, their decisions will depend on hearsay and hunches. In order to enable the correct investment decisions to be made, investors need to know the sources of information. In the fast expansion of the markets, and increasing complexity of economies, the amount of information is also fast growing. The collection of information and its analysis is time consuming and expensive. Besides analysis of the information also requires expertise which all investors may not have. The available books on the subject deal with the theoretical aspects and not much practical analysis and down to earth operational aspects. Here, as elsewhere, knowledge is power. As such the investors are left to make decisions by hunches and intuition and not on scientific analysis of the data. Those who have better information use it to make extra mileage on such information. It is also possible that insiders who have the information before it becomes public take advantage of it called Insider trading. At present the SEBI has acquired powers to control insider trading, malpractices and rigging up of prices in the secondary markets in India, and penalise the offenders.

1. *World Affairs*: The day-to-day developments abroad are published in Financial Journals like *Economic Times, Financial Express, Business Line,* etc. Some foreign Journals, like wall street journal, *London Economist, Far East Economic Review* and Indian Journals like, *Business India, Fortune India* etc., also contain developments of economic and financial nature in India and abroad. IMF News Survey, World Bank and IMF Quarterly Journal, (namely, *Finance and Development*) News Letters of Foreign Banks like those of Grindlays, Standard, etc., contain all the needed information on world developments.

2. *National Economic Affairs*: The daily news papers particularly financial papers referred to above contain all the national information; Besides Journals like *Economic and Political Weekly, Business India, Dataline Business, Business Today, Fortune India* contain the material on economic developments. RBI's Annual Reports, Reports on currency and finance and RBI monthly Bulletins and CMIE reports all contain a wealth of information on the economy and the country. The Economic Survey of the govt. of India and reports of C.S.O., D.G.T.D. and Dept. of companies, etc. do provide the information on, economy, industry, trade sectors of the country. The reports of the Planning Commission and annual reports of various ministries also contain a lot of information. The website of RBI, SEBI, BSE and NSE etc., contain the information and data on the respective organisations.

3. *Industry Information*: There are various Associations — Chambers of Commerce, Merchants' Chamber and other agencies who publish Industry data. The reports of Planning Commission, govt. of India, publications from Industry and Commerce Ministries also contain a lot of information. The CMIE publishes various volumes and update them from time to time containing data on various sectors of the economy and industries, and the subscribers get these volumes and reports.

Directory of Information published by the B.S.E. also contains information on industries and companies and this is updated from time to time. Many Daily financial papers bring out regularly studies on various Industries and their prospects. Industry data at micro level is available in Govt. publications, industry-wise, but in view of a large time lag involved in their reports, the monthly reports of various Associations of Industries give more uptodate and timely information.

4. *Company Information*: The information on various Companies listed on Stock Exchanges is readily available in daily financial papers. Besides the Fortnightly Journals of *Capital Market, Dalal Street, Business India* contain a lot of information on the industries and companies, listed on stock exchanges. Results of equity and Market Research are also published in these Journals. As referred to earlier the B.S.E. (Bombay Stock Exchange) publishes Directory of Information on Industries and Companies, which are listed on Stock Exchanges, and the Journals of *Capital Market* and *Dalal Street* also publish these data. Computer software on these data are available with a number of software companies. The B.S.E. also publishes weekly Reviews, monthly Reviews giving data on various aspects of listed companies and financial information on them.

The Annual Reports of companies and their half yearly unaudited results are another source of information on the companies. The financial journals give write ups on various companies after interviewing their executives and these are published in *Economic Times* and other financial Dailies, like *Business Line & Financial Express.*

5. *Security Market Information*: A number of big Broker Firms who have equity research are sending newsletters on Market Information with Fundamental and Technical analysis, combined in those reports to their clients. *The Invest Guide, Dalal Street, Business India* and few other Stock Market Journals like *Fortune India,* contain the information on

security markets. The ICFAI also publishes a monthly called *Chartered Financial Analyst,* which contains economic data, company information, and market information, Security analysis, Beta factors and a host of other items, useful for security analysis. The data on Trade cycles and settlements, record dates, book closures etc., are contained in financial papers like *Economic Times, Business Line, Financial Express* etc., after they are released by stock exchanges and companies. While the newsletter of Merchant Bankers, brokers' firms, Investment Analysts, are available to subscribers or their own clients, others are available for all at stipulated prices. Data on FII, FIs and MFs purchases and sales etc., on a daily basis are available with SEBI and published in the Financial Press.

6. *Security Price Quotations*: The daily quotations on various Stock Exchanges OTCEI and NSE are published in the daily papers. Each Stock Exchange is publishing its own daily quotations list, giving out opening, high, low and closing quotations of all traded securities. They also publish volume of trade for individual securities and also the total for all securities traded on a daily basis, in terms of shares and value of trades.

The Price indices, for all securities, industry-wise, region-wise etc., are published by the RBI, B.S.E. and major Stock Exchanges, in the country. Besides each financial Daily has its own Index published in its paper. All these indices, daily volumes, highs, lows, advances, declines etc., of well traded Companies, Gainers and Losers and such similar information, useful for both technical and fundamental analysis is available from all Stock Exchanges and published in financial Dailies and Journals. *The Capital Market* and *Dalal Street* journals also give Company information regarding their fundamentals, P/E, EPS, GPM, etc., along with the price data. Daily highs and lows, can be seen as against yearly highs/lows for each of the securities in financial Dailies.

The pattern of share holding, distribution schedule, floating stock, past price data are available in all softwares and B.S.E Directory. B.S.E. publishes all the data useful for technical analysis and these data are compiled by the computer specialists and floppies are available on official Daily quotations and Technical charts of each of the major companies listed on Stock Exchanges. The computer software data are also sold by software companies for those who have computer facility. For others, these data can be collected from daily papers, weekly and fortnightly Journals on Stock Markets, like *Financial Express, Economic Times, Dalal Street* and *Capital Market.,* etc.

7. *Data on Related Markets*: Data on Money Market, Govt. Securities Market are available in the publications of RBI and Indian Banks Association, Securities Trading Corporation and banks and NSE. These data are published on a daily basis on the financial Dailies and journals. The publications who deal with these markets are however fewer in number compared to those on stock and capital markets. The information on Forex Market is available in RBI publications, Foreign Exchange Dealers Association (FEDAI) and foreign banks. These data are published in the form of exchange rates and cross Currency rates and Forex reserves in Financial Dailies regularly. The developments in these markets are reviewed in the Dailies or weekly and fortnightly Journals.

The data on Bullion market and rates for gold and silver are available on a Daily basis in the financial press. These data are published in RBI Bulletins and are also available in CMIE reports. Many of these data on Forex Markets in countries abroad can be obtained from *London Economist, Far Eastern Economic Review,* and *Wall Street Journal.*

8. *Data on Mutual Funds, UTI etc.*: These are published in the Daily financial papers — atleast once in a week in the *Investment Weekly* or *Investors' Guide.* They give the Current Schemes, NAV of each scheme if quoted as against the Market price, if traded, repurchase price, redemption rate, etc. in respect of close ended funds and daily purchase and sale prices for open ended funds. Besides, however all the journals, magazines and reports on Stock Markets also contain the relevant information on Mutual funds, as many of their schemes are quoted and traded on the Stock Exchanges. Thus, the Capital Market, Dalal Street and Business India also contain information on Mutual Funds. Since 1999, the data on mutual funds — their sales and Repurchases, NAV of schemes etc. are available from the Association of Mutual Funds (AMFI).

9. *Data on Primary Market*: New Issues in the Pipeline are first known to the SEBI as they get the Draft Prospectus for vetting and even before that, they would come to know of them from Merchant bankers' reports. But consolidation and publications of this information is done by a Magazine called "PRIME" publication. Prime publishes all information of new issues in the pipe line — industry-wise and size-wise analysis and public over subscription and undersubscription etc. The performances of companies, Merchant bankers, underwriters and brokers etc., in the New Issue Market are also analysed by them. Geographical and centrewise collection of new issues and other relevant company information are given by them.

Following them a number of Magazines, merchant bankers, Registrars and Brokers like Karvys are publishing them. Financial journalists are giving a write up on the forthcoming new issues as also some cable operators. The RBI and Dept. of Company Affairs in addition to SEBI collect and publish these data from time to time in their reports once in a quarter, half yearly and yearly.

Uses of these Data

The Broker firms, Investment consultancy firms, Portfolio Managers require all the investment information on Companies, industry and Economy, for their analysis and research.

Their tasks in this connection can be set out as follows:

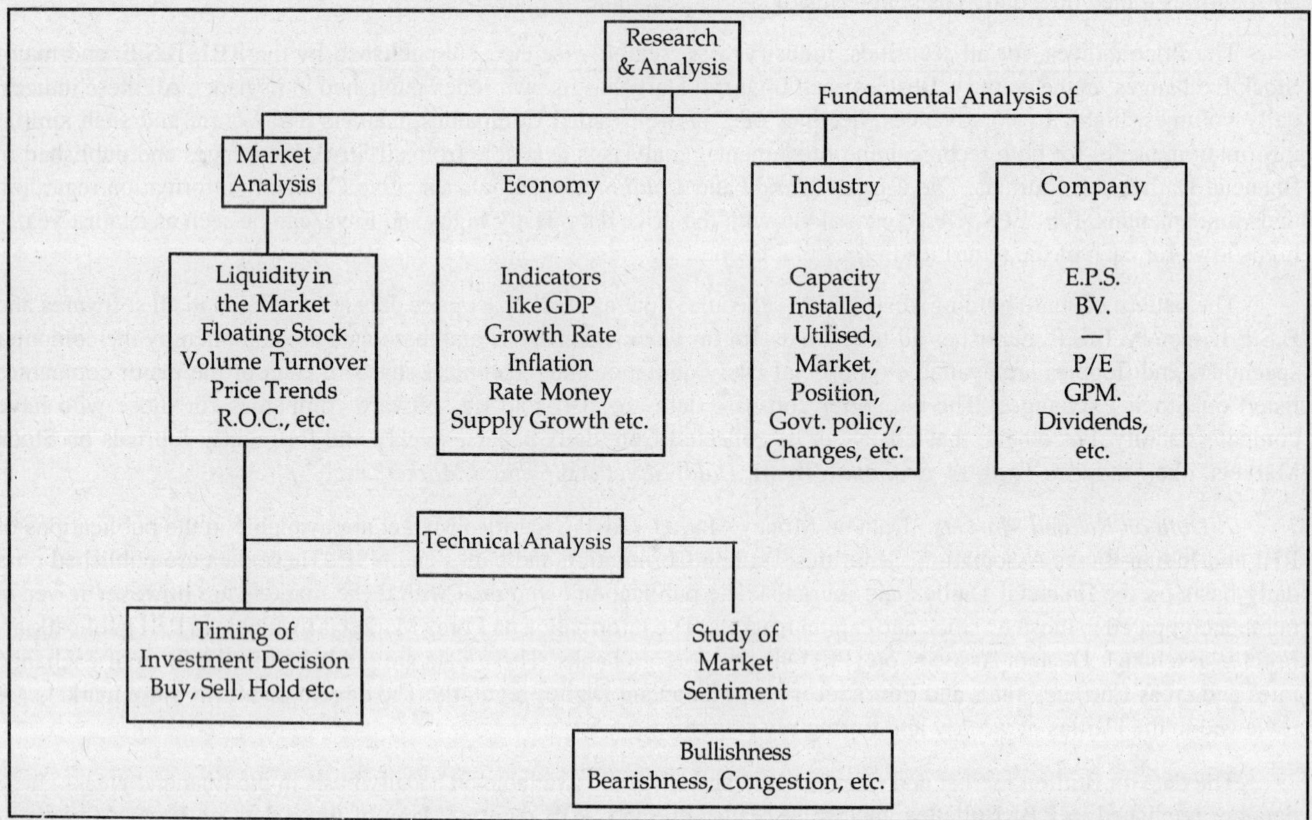

ROC is rate of change of prices and volumes. Research Methods are very varied starting from Deskwork to plant visits.

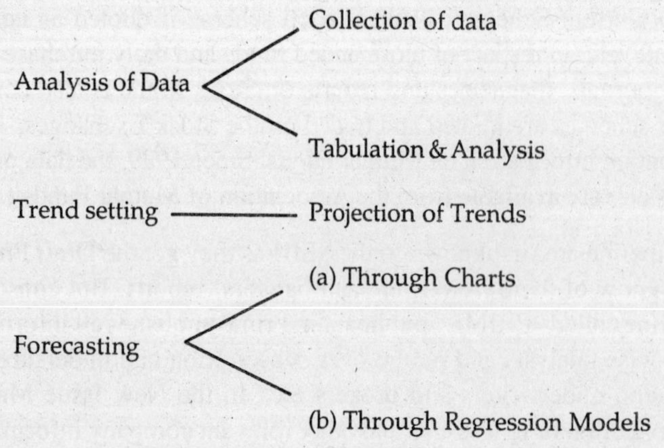

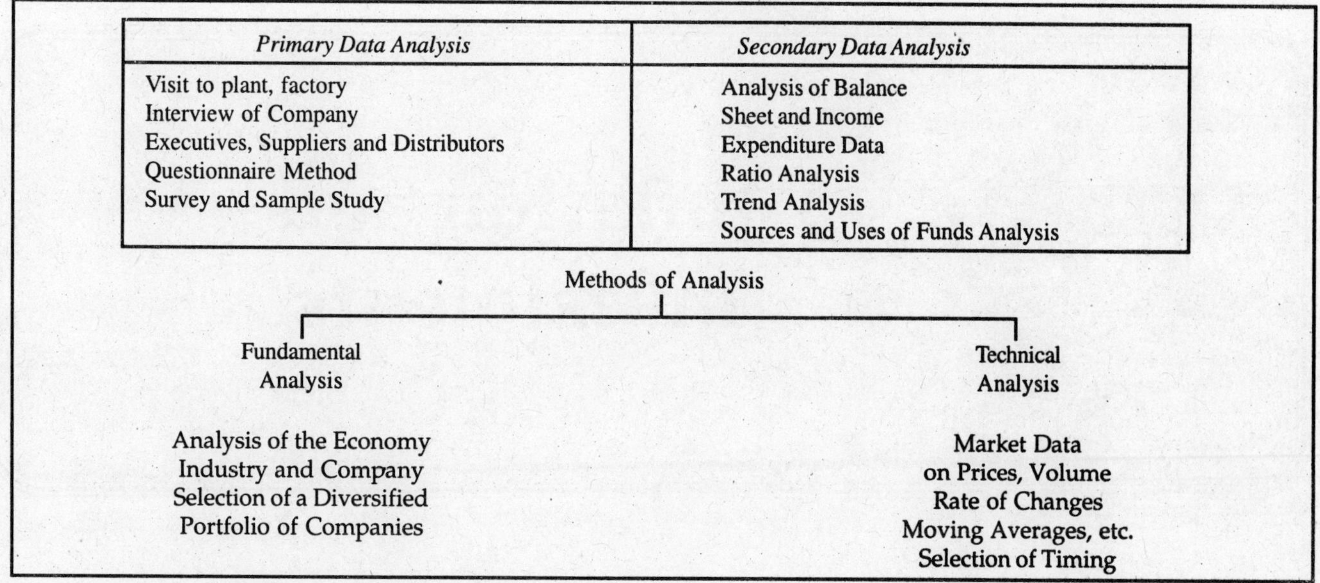

Steps to be followed —

(*a*) Pattern of ownership of shares

(*b*) Proportion of public holding

(*c*) Floating stock for trading

(*d*) High/Low prices for the year

(*e*) Daily volatility of prices

— Opening, High, Low asnd Closing

(*f*) Breadth of the Market

(*g*) No. of shares traded and their volumes *vis-a-vis* the total volume for all companies

(*h*) Declines/Advances among scrips

(*i*) Chart of Daily price trends, moving average trends — to get signals of buy/sell etc.

(*j*) Trace out the intrinsic value of the share by Fundamental Analysis — Adjust for the expectations and sentiment in the Market to take a decision whether the price in the market is fair price or not.

Study of the company through financial variables (BV, EPS, P/E, etc.), visit the plant and interview the chief executives of the company for knowing the expectations, as also of the merchant bankers and financial institutions, are the further steps.

Scrips chosen on all these counts are properly timed through Technical Analysis for a proper investment decision making. An analysis of risk in terms of variability of returns (standard deviation) of each company *vis-a-vis* the Market, use of Beta factor for risk which is systematic and diversification of investments into various industries and companies to reduce the unsystematic risks are the further steps in portfolio management.

Conclusion

It will thus be seen that the sources of information for investment purposes is only the first step. Collection and collation and analysis of the data are the more important next steps. The direction of analysis may be fundamental analysis or technical analysis and the emerging investment decisions are referred to in another Chapter. The data and information, set out in this Chapter are necessary for not only proper investment decision, but for Portfolio Management, revision and evaluation. Equity research and Market analysis, so necessary for stock broking investment consultancy and portfolio Management are also based on the information collection and data processing for which the sources of information referred to in this Chapter are vitally important.

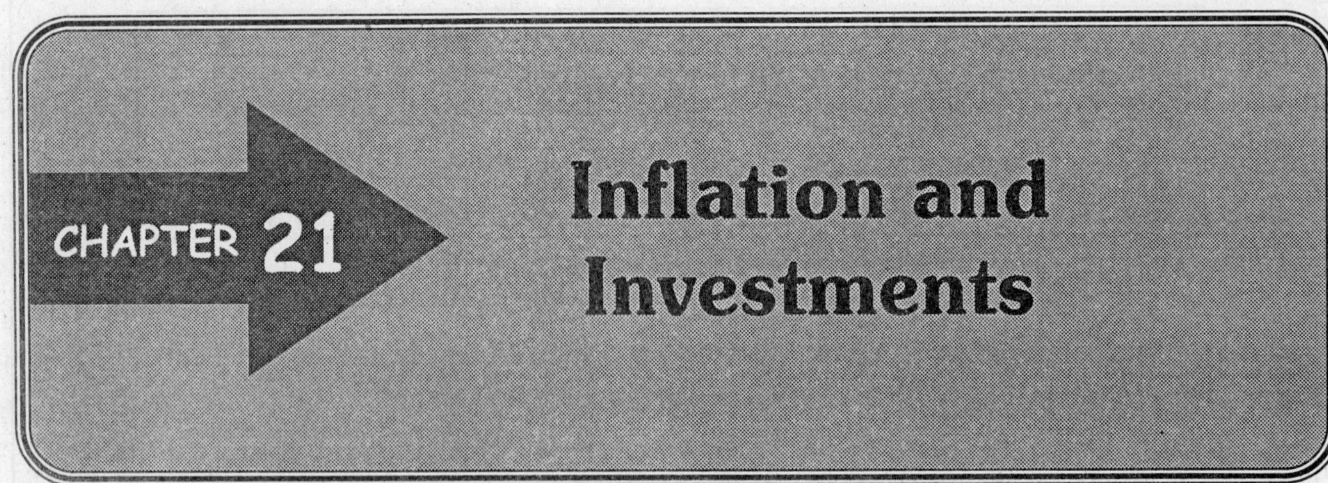

Inflation and Investments

As security analysis aims at valuation of securities, real values are derived after adjusting the nominal values for actual or expected inflation rate.

What is Inflation?

Inflation refers to the rise in prices. It can be defined as a "state in which the value of money is falling as prices are rising" (Crowther). With the rise in prices, the real value of money in terms of number of goods or the amount of goods and services that can be purchased by one unit of currency or money will fall. Thus, if sugar price has increased over the last few years from Rs. 6 to Rs. 15 the same currency note of Rs. 100 can now buy about 6 kg of sugar, instead 16 kg of sugar before. Here is the real loss to the consumer in terms of lowering of his purchasing power and his standard of living or consumption.

Traditional Explanation of Inflation

Under Keynes theory, price rise is explained as follows in macro terms.

If the resources are fully employed but the demand continues to grow, then prices will start rising. Price is a function of demand and supply and so long as there is capacity to increase supply and output to meet the demand, prices need not rise.

Quantity theory of Money explains inflation in terms of the increase in the quantity of money. Following Fisher's equation of Exchange: $P = M \frac{V}{T}$ where P is price, M is money supply, V is the velocity of money supply and T, is total transactions. Thus, P will rise if Money Supply (M) or its velocity (V) will increase, with T' remaining constant or not growing at the same rate. Thus the modern Monetarist Theory also explains the phenomena of inflation in terms of the quantity of money supply (Quantity Theorists).

Demand Pull and Cost Push Inflation

Demand pull factors arise when the total monetary demand for goods and services exceeds the available supply. This situation is caused by expanding demand, when total money supply exceeds required quantity. The excess demand situation for goods is the reason for Inflation, under this theory.

The cost push factors emerge due to rise in costs of production due to wage increase or rise in profit margins. The private sector and Govt. sector may push up prices due to rise in input costs, namely, electricity, raw materials or wages for labour. Business and Industry may increase prices due to semi-monopoly conditions to exploit the rise in costs of production following wage increases. Trade union activities and recurrent wage increases have been attributed as reasons for the price rise, under this theory.

The above factors explain the rise in prices except when the goods are under Govt. controls or with administered prices or if there are monopolistic or semimonopolistic conditions in the production of those goods.

The Govt. administered prices in respect of coal, petrol, electricity etc. have been attributed as reasons for funnelling the rise in prices of other goods. If the products are supplied by Multinational Corporations (MNCs), their prices are based on the principle of "what the market can bear" and not necessarily on the costs of production. Under these conditions, among others, prices of goods and services rise in a fashion of vicious circle — some price rises leading to others.

Structural Factors

In India, inflation is caused by many factors mainly due to structural factors as it is a developing economy, without full employment. There is no possibility of inflation after full employment in such an economy. Inflation occurs even before full employment is reached as in the case of India due to lack of some inputs or parts, rise in their prices, inadequate supplies of some materials rising import inputs, labour problems and a host of other reasons.

Inflationary Tendencies

The reasons for inflationary tendencies in India are briefly set out below:

(1) Monsoon failures and inadequate agricultural products and raw materials. Cyclones and natural calamities also produce shortages leading to rise in prices

(2) Trade union activities leading to rise in their wages beyond the rise in the rise in productivity.

(3) Inadequate power supply and rise in costs of coal, power and petroleum.

(4) Govt. budget deficits leading to creation of money by RBI rising the demand pressures and leading to inflationary expectations.

Inflation Indicators

Inflation is measured by the percentage rise in prices. But these prices are measured by index numbers with a base year, which will have price index equal to 100 in 1993-94 = from April 2000.

These index numbers of prices measuring inflation are the following:

(1) Index of wholesale prices, Base 1981-82 = 100 1993-94 = 100 from April 2000

(2) Consumer price Index for Industrial workers, Base year 2001 = 100 from Jan; 2006

(3) Consumer price Index for urban Non-manual Employees, Base year 1984-85 = 100

(4) Consumer price Index for Agricultural labourers, Base year 1986-87 = 100

(5) Consumer Price Index Number for Rural Labourers, Base 1986-87 = 100.

All these are published on a weekly, monthly and yearly basis by the Govt. and the RBI in their reports and their publications.

Causes of Inflation

(1) Rise in the administered prices of commodities under Govt. control, namely, Railway freight charges, electricity, coal etc.

(2) Deficit financing due to rise in Govt. expenditure and fall in Govt.revenues leading to creation of currency beyond the requirements of trade and industry.

(3) Expansion of Money supply and rise in bank credit to Govt. and to the private sector beyond the reasonable limits justified by rise in production.

(4) Supply shortages due to natural calamities, inadequate imports due to foreign exchange problems and bottleneck problems, etc.

(5) Wage increases due to trade union activity, unjustified by their productivity trends.

(6) Rise in import prices due to rise in customs duties or higher international prices leading to higher domestic prices.

(7) Black marketing and hoarding by unsocial elements, traders and speculators to push up the prices and make quick profits.

(8) Bottleneck in transport, strikes and lockouts can also create supply shortages leading to rise in prices.

(9) Psychological expectations of inflation may lead to rise in wage demand and to rise in wages, which in turn lead to rise in prices.

(10) Increase in foreign inflow of funds or rise in foreign reserves leading to rise in domestic money supply.

Effects of Inflation

(1) Inflation erodes the value of money and is invisible tax, imposed by the Govt. on the public. The profligacy and unproductive expenditures of the Govt. lead to additional burden of lower purchasing power on the public and tax payers.

(2) It leads to social evils of hoarding, profiteering and black money.

(3) Fixed income people lose in real standard of living while businessmen and producers may gain.

(4) Social discontent and income inequalities will increase and the poor people will be more adversely affected than others by these trends.

(5) If inflation is mild, it is favourable to producers to have expectations of profit and to increased production.

(6) If inflation is high and is galloping then investment will be affected due to rise in costs leading to cost over-runs and delay in productive process.

(7) Whether inflation is mild or galloping, consumers will suffer due to fall in their real purchasing power. The quality of life will fall and saving potential will decrease.

(8) The inflationary effects in income distribution will be unfair and discriminatory. Businessmen and traders gain more by super profits while fixed income classes, wage earners, pensioners will all suffer by fall in their real income and their standard of living.

Inflation — A Fallout of Reforms

Inflation is the worst form of taxing the common man. The rise in prices of goods and services consumed by him leads to a fall in the real value of his income, and his effective purchasing power will come down. Very few will realise that the currency note printed this year is not of the same value as the one printed last year. One hundred rupee note kept in a safe for a year will find itself worth only Rs. 90 or less, due to inflation of 10 per cent per annum or more. Who gains and how? The government is gaining at the expense of the common man. It is an inevitable tax on currency held by the public.

The effects are very adverse to the economy and the public. As a tax, it is not progressive but regressive as it affects more the poorer than the richer. The creditors gain by borrowing. Fixed income groups are adversely affected while the rich, black marketeers, profiteers and speculators gain in the process. Income distribution becomes skewed, with the rich becoming richer and poor becoming poorer. The impact of inflation varies inversely with the wealth. The less fortunate poorer classes are the worst affected by the erosion of money value.

Who is responsible for this great social injustice? It is the Reserve Bank of India which is entrusted with the task of creation of currency and the government which borrows this money. The excess creation of money chases the few goods and services available and leads to rise in prices. The RBI is abettor in this process created by the government through its excess expenditure over income and its borrowing from the RBI.

RBI's Role

In India, there is no statutory limit to the creation of currency by the RBI. As per Section 33 of the RBI Act, the rules for note issue require only the RBI holding of government debt as the source of money creation. The RBI was given the monopoly power of note issue under Section 22 of the Act and Section 26 also gives the legal tender status to these notes with the result that the RBI alone is the judge of how much currency to create and RBI Act makes it impossible for anybody to sue the RBI for this act of excess creation of currency and the resultant miseries of common man. As per the above provisions of the RBI Act, the connivance of the RBI with the government can make it possible for the RBI to create any amount of currency and credit and lead to an economic crisis due to unbridled inflation and still go scot free legally. It is really an odd situation and the only solution to the common man is to defeat in elections the party in power and elect only such party which will set a limit to the creation of currency at, say, two times the projected rate of growth of output and income in the economy (based on present money velocity). If say, the economy is growing at a rate of five per cent per annum, the growth of money supply cannot be more than 10 per cent.

This extra rise of another five per cent will take care of increasing monetisation in the economy and facilitate trade and business. If such currency creation is falling short of the requirements in any year, there will be greater use of credit cards, and velocity of circulation of money will increase, and trade and business will not be affected by it. On the other hand, it protects the economy and the public from excess currency and false play on the common man, due to rise in prices caused by the RBI. The connivance between the RBI and the government who owns the RBI is always possible and the public can be cheated by both acting together. The best protection for them is therefore, to elect a Parliament which will set a limit to creation of currency by the RBI at, say, two times the projected rate of growth in output in any year.

The RBI targets not the inflation rate as such, but the inflationary expectations which vitally effect investment and output — planned and realised. The RBI monetary and credit policy therefore aims at curbing the inflationary expectations of business and industry through its measures.

Inflation as a Monetary Phenomenon

The RBI will argue that inflation is not caused by their creation of currency but many other factors such as structural imbalances, hoarding, poor distribution, bottlenecks, and a host of other non-monetary factors. By such arguments, people think that inflation in India is a non-monetary phenomenon as India is a developing country, with a large component of currency held by rural people. If, therefore, currency creation is curtailed by the RBI, a majority of the rural population will suffer as 60 per cent of the population live in villages. Such arguments of textbooks are taken for protection by the RBI and the government for their actions. The same arguments are given for centuries before or at least since the RBI was set up in 1934 and no controls on the creation of currency by the RBI were allowed.

The RBI blames the government and the government blames the underdeveloped nature of the economy and growing credit needs of socially backward classes, and backward regions. Such outmoded arguments have been still current and the common man in India is caught in this vicious circle. It is high time to break this vicious circle.

In fact, the recent gimmicks of inflation rates going up and down are reported in bold by the press, as the government strategy is to show to the public that government has controlled the inflation rate to a single-digit figure and to less than 5%. It is right time to put an end to the outmoded ideas of allowing the money supply growth uncontrolled by the RBI. The arguments that extra currency is required for a developing economy for monetising non-monetised sector should also be given a burial. The monetary growth should only be related to output growth and nothing else. The RBI should not be a party for cheating the common man by inflation.

Populist Measures

The Planning Commission has highlighted the failures of the government on the economic front, namely, increasing unemployment, poverty, none-too-encouraging industrial growth and lukewarm response from foreign direct investment. The high rates of inflation added fuel to the fire. The government's so-called economic and financial reforms have made the rich richer and the poor poorer. This explained why there were so many populist measures in the Central and state Budgets, which will further add to inflationary pressures, namely, increase in non-planned expenditure, increase in subsidies and growth in revenue and fiscal deficits of the government and socio-political measures like free mid-day meals, rural housing and bank credit for backward classes and social insurance for rural poor, etc. But employment creation is a better way of helping the poor rather than distribution of doles. The Tenth Plan (2002-2007) has been finalised with an ambitious growth rate of 8%, infrastructure development, rural and agricultural growth etc.

Impact of Govt. Measures

The impact of the policy measures of the government on the RBI credit is to increase it to a peak of Rs. 20,925 crores as on August 1995 against the norms of Rs. 9,000 crores agreed to earlier between the government and the RBI. This is caused by increasing revenue and fiscal deficits of the government. The fiscal deficit was later sought to be kept to at lesss than 4% of GDP by the Fiscal Responsibility Act.

During 1991-96, inflation rate on an average was 10 per cent; even though inflation rate was brought down to 6.5% in 1996-97 and 8% in 1997-98 which was mainly due to low growth rate of output (GDP) in real terms at an average rate of 5 per cent, while the money supply growth rate was at a simple average rate of 18 per cent. How can the RBI allow a rise in money supply at around 18 per cent while the real output was rising hardly by 5 per cent. The real GDP growth of 10 per cent warrants only a growth of money supply of 10 per cent and the extra 8 per cent growth leads to inflation. It is simple arithmetic for a common man to understand how the RBI is responsible for inflation, despite its disclaimer to the contrary. In fact, the rise in currency, which is the immediate cause of inflation due to RBI credit to government was at an average rate of 17 per cent to 18 per cent in the past. During the second half of nineties, the rate of inflation was lower at around 5 per cent as judged by WPI and 8 per cent as judged by C.P.I.

The conclusion is that inflation, which is the main cause of poverty for the common man, is the result of government policies supported by RBI credit, and the so-called economic reforms have not benefited the poor in India.

Govt's Reliance on Deficits

RBI as the Central bank of the country has a monopoly in creation of currency. It is banker to the Govt. and to the banks. It controls and administers foreign exchange dealings. It finances the Govts' Budget deficit.

As a Govt. banker, it gives credit to the Govt. particularly the Central Govt. who owns the Reserve Bank. In the process, it accommodates the Govt. financially, when their expenditure is more than their income. It manages the borrowings of the Govt. and their public debt.

But RBI is also a monetary authority and is bound to act in public interest and in the interests of business and trade as per the RBI Act. In the process, it has double obligation, namely, to help the Govt. and banks with financial accommodations and at the same time maintain the monetary stability and price stability.

The main reason for inflation in developed countries in the monetary and fiscal policy — monetary policy of the Central Bank and fiscal policy of the Govt. Both are interlinked in that fiscal deficits lead to monetary impact, raise borrowings and lead to larger money creation and inflation. In developing countries like India, structural bottlenecks supply inelasticities, hoardings, smuggling etc. also play an important part. RBI's control on money supply is also dependent upon the foreign exchange inflows, which will add to money supply domestically. With the massive inflows of foreign funds during 1992 to 1994 when the rupee was made convertible on trade account followed convertibility on current account in March 1994, the problem of controlling the money supply by neutralising these foreign inflows has become a major issue for controlling inflation. Even so the RBI has kept the growth rate of money supply at reasonable levels of 15 — 16% per annum during latter half of Nineties and even 14% early in the 21st century.

From the above discussion of RBIs Role and its credit controls, it is obvious that the growth of inflation in India is also due to other factors like supply constraints, unproductive expenditure of Govt. and wage increases and freer role of corruption, hoarding and black economy. This does not mean that RBI's monetary policy is well managed and that it is not responsible along with the Govt. for fast rising inflationary expectations and inflation rates.

Credit Control by RBI

As seen from the above analysis RBI Control on money supply is only partial and requires the Govt. support to control money supply in tune with the requirements of the economy and to offset all inflationary tendencies. The RBI has entered into a memorandum of understanding (MoU) to limit the Government's reliance on RBI credit and to control the creation of *ad hoc* Treasury bills to Rs. 9,000 crores in 1995-96 and bring it down to nil by 1998. But this agreement is honoured by violation with the result that money supply expansion has gone beyond the requirements of the economy which led to inflation. The growth rate of money during the last five years 2004-05 to 2008-09 was 18% on average, while the, GDP growth rate was only 8% on average during the same period.

The other important category of RBI controls is credit to private sector and to banks. More recently, with the financial liberalisation and deregulation of lending rates and lending norms, RBI has left banks to operate in the commercial interests. The credit control measures still operate to a limited extent on the bank credit to the private sector. Thus, this factor influencing inflation has become less important for price rise.

But since the economic and financial reforms were started, corporate sector, PSUs and even Govt. bodies began to rely more on capital market and public borrowing directly rather than from banks.

Responsibility of RBI

Under the RBI Act, it has been entrusted with a duty to maintain price and monetary stability. In the process of acting as Govt. bank and as an authority for currency creation, it can control the creation of Reserve money (Currency with public plus cash balances with banks and other deposits with RBI) which in turn can influence Money Supply.

Although the RBI is the controller of currency and credit, the major factors influencing the changes in money supply or rise in money beyond the requirements of production are the following:

(1) Uncontrolled rise in credit to Govt. by the RBI as the RBI is owned by the Govt.

(2) Changes in credit to banks and the private sector. These are controlled through credit controls, cash reserve ratio and statutory liquidity ratio and other monetary tools of the RBI.

(3) Charges in Net foreign exchange assets of the RBI which can also be controlled through its foreign exchange policy, exchange controls or intervention in the foreign exchange market and Govt. controls on foreign investments and other foreign flows.

Of the above factors, the main culprit for inflation is the *RBI's Credit to Govt.* which is many times uncontrolled by the RBI as socio-political factors play a role in the creation of money and Bank credit to Govt. Sector in India.

Inflation and Savings

The impact of inflation is felt on the economy through savings and investment. With rising inflation rates, real value of savings with fall and the savings are thereby discouraged. The rate of investment and allocation of investment will also change due to changes in savings and investment. In India, the savings are affected by not only inflation, but by the interest rate policy of the RBI and taxation policy of the government. Not only interest rates on savings accounts are lowered in the recent period 2001-2007, but the interest income on deposits with banks are subject to taxation, which has adversely affected the savings and investment potential of the common people. The poor or those below the poverty line are not savers at all among the Household Sector, which constitutes the net savers in the Indian economy. But the middle and higher income households are net savers. Of these, savings accounts are mostly held by the middle class who are the backbone of the economy and they are adversely affected by the government's interest rate policy and taxation policy.

The total amount of savings accounts with all commercial banks constitute about 1/3rd of aggregate bank deposits and they are paid only $3^1/_2$% interest on their money, while the average inflation rate in the quinquennium 2001-06 is about 5%. Even some fixed deposits of banks are paid less than 5%, which erodes the value of their money. It not only violates all cannons of justice and equity, but defies all principles of economic growth through increasing levels of savings and investment. It is inflation adjusted savings and investment which has to be taken into account for any exercise in investment management either by individuals, or by corporates and the institutions. It is in this sense, that inflation is an important factor in Investmet Management.

Inflation on Investments

Investment management has to take into account the impact of inflation on the following factors:

(1) Real rates of return on investments after adjustment for inflation have to be taken into account.

(2) Adjustments for cost over-runs and project failures have to be considered before making investments in new projects.

(3) Projects dependent on inputs or imports whose prices are rising will have adverse effects on their profitability. Projects are to be judged through inflation adjusted returns.

(4) Inflation accounting of the Balance Sheets of companies, their cash flows inventories and their earnings and projects will have to be done by investors before making investment decisions.

(5) In fast rising inflationary situations, companies will be discouraged to make large scale investments due to uncertainty of cost factors and high risk factors. But mild inflation is conducive to growth of investment on good profit expectations.

(6) Investors do have risk-return calculations, after adjusting for inflation rates and inflationary expectations in the economy.

Inflation and Investment Decisions

Investment decisions are affected by inflation as investors are interested in real returns after adjusting for inflation. The adjustment is to be done by taking the returns, dividends and capital gains and deflate them by an appropriate price index — wholesale price index or retail price index (consumer price index numbers). The deflation can also be done by the calculated inflation rate and arrive at the real rate of return. Such real rates are to be compared for various attractive investments, before making investment decision.

Original and projected cash flows can be adjusted for inflation, actual or projected. These adjusted future flows can be discounted to the present date to arrive at the Net Present Value (NPV) by using a discount factor. The normal discount factor is the risk free return (8%), which is the yield rate on government bonds, or expected rate of return (15-20%). The NAV of two proposed projects or Investments are generally compared before an investment decision is made on the basis of inflation adjusted returns and, if possible, net of tax rates.

Security Market Analysis

What is Security Analysis?

Security analysis refers to the analysis of trading securities from the point of view of their prices, returns and risks. All Investments are risky and the expected return is related to the risk. Their analysis will help in understanding the behaviour of security prices and the market and in decision-making for investment. If it is an analysis of only one scrip, it is called micro-analysis of a company. If it is an analysis of market of securities, it is referred to as a macro-picture of the behaviour of the market.

Origin of Markets

The security market emerges out of the new issues made by companies, government, local bodies and public undertakings. These issuers of securities borrow in the form of ownership capital or debt capital for financing their operations. They issue IOUs or promissory notes with a promise to pay the funds at later date. All securities are in this form of IOUs except those of ownership shares. Securities of more than one year came into the categories of capital and stock markets. The shares of ownership category are transferable and tradable which will impart liquidity to these instruments, but they are not repurchased by the company, under the present law. The Govt. have announced their guidelines for allowing buy back facility in October 1998.

Information Flows

Markets are influenced by information flows, on the one hand, and money flows, on the other. If the information flows are perfect and free, and the markets adjust to these flows quickly and effectively, the markets are said to be perfect. If the information is imperfect or partial, the markets will be imperfect and the price formation will be unpredictable, haphazard and volatile.

The information whether perfect or imperfect has to be analysed to know its impact on the market prices and forecast trades. For this purpose, analytical tools and forecasting ability are necessary. If information is not perfect, a few with inside information would gain at the expense of others. If information is free and unbiased, the markets behave rationally and nobody can gain extra profits and normal returns are available to all whenever they enter the market.

Savings or Money Flows

The markets are also influenced by the flows of savings or money. The micro level flows would depend on the following objectives: income, capital appreciation, hedge against inflation, liquidity and safety to investors, etc. These are the criteria by which individual savers would enter the market for investment.

At the macro level, savings flows determine the level of investment in the corporate sector and in the economy and lead to capital formation and growth of fixed assets. The introduction of technology would also depend on these investment flows. The fixed capital formation would promote growth of output and income by a multiplier process. This leads to the theory of savings and investment of Keynes and also to Modern Monetarist Theory linking money flows to the growth of output and income in the economy.

Factors Influencing the Market Behaviour

Many of these factors relate to the economy, industry and company, which constitute the fundamental factors.

1. Factors external to the company like environmental factors, economic and political developments.
2. Internal factors of the company or of the market. These relate to the physical and financial performance of the company or companies.
3. Size of paid-up capital and pattern of distribution of shareholding among the public and size and growth of Gross Block.
4. Investment habits and trading habits of the people.

A host of other factors, psychological and emotional, also play a role in the market operations.

Trading

The market in securities is influenced by the forces of supply and demand which in turn are influenced by the above factors. These forces of supply and demand determine the volume of trading-turnover and also the prices. These two indicators, namely, volume and price of the market, are macro-indicators for studying the market behaviour used in the technical analysis.

The volume of trading is reflected in the number of deals per day or hour, number of days in a year in which the company's share is traded or the number of shares traded in a day or a year. Our empirical studies show that the liquidity of shares, which depends on trading, is confined to a few scrips on the stock exchange, namely, 20-30% of the total. The liquidity is closely related to the spread of shareholding, size of capital and pattern of holding of share capital. It is also related to the intrinsic worth of the company and other financial indicators like P/E ratio. Nearly 50% of the performance of the share price is explained by the internal factors of the company like its earnings, per share debt servicing, book value, etc. The rest of the factors are external to the company such as demand conditions, government policy, environmental factors, etc.

The *main constituents* of and players in the markets are as follows:

(1) Instruments traded.

(2) Institutions and individuals as investors.

(3) Intermediaries.

The main *indicators* of the market operations are as follows:

(1) Quantity raised from the new issues market and quantity traded in the secondary market.

(2) Prices of instruments.

(3) Velocity of price changes.

(4) Intensity of trading and turnover of trading.

Instruments

The instruments traded and their characteristics are set out in an earlier chapter. There are equity and preference shares in the category of ownership capital and debentures, bonds and P.S.U. Bonds, and Government securities in the category of debt capital. In the hybrid variety, there are convertible debentures and cumulative convertible preference shares which although have the characteristic of debt capital would eventually be ownership capital. A number of new instruments like warrants, Zero Coupon Bonds etc. are also being issued at present.

Players

The institutions or players in the market are the issuers of capital, namely, corporate units, government and semi-government bodies and public sector undertakings which are the major borrowers, the investors and intermediaries such as banks, financial institutions and brokers. More recently, a number of Mutual Funds, FFIs, NRIs, OCBs have also started as players in the markets.

Intermediaries

As referred to earlier the intermediaries are the brokers, merchant bankers, financial institutions, financial and investment consultancy firms etc. These are active in both the primary and secondary markets. The investments by FIIs, OCBs, etc., are subject to regulations depending on the economic condition of the country and aimed at controlling the inflows and outflows and the direction of these flows.

What is Market Analysis?

The security market analysis refers to the analysis of markets and securities traded there in terms of the risk-return, quantities raised or traded, price trends and other indicators of the market referred to above. The market analysis is made in terms of fundamental macro factors and technical factors like price and volume trends in the market. As regards the risk-return factors as the expected return varies, so is the risk attached to the instruments. Some instruments like government securities, P.S.U. Bonds or UTI units are least risky but have a cost in realisation. The cost of conversion or realisation of funds is zero in the case of bank deposits. The relationship between the risk and return in respect of various assets can be set out in macro terms as in Fig. 22.1.

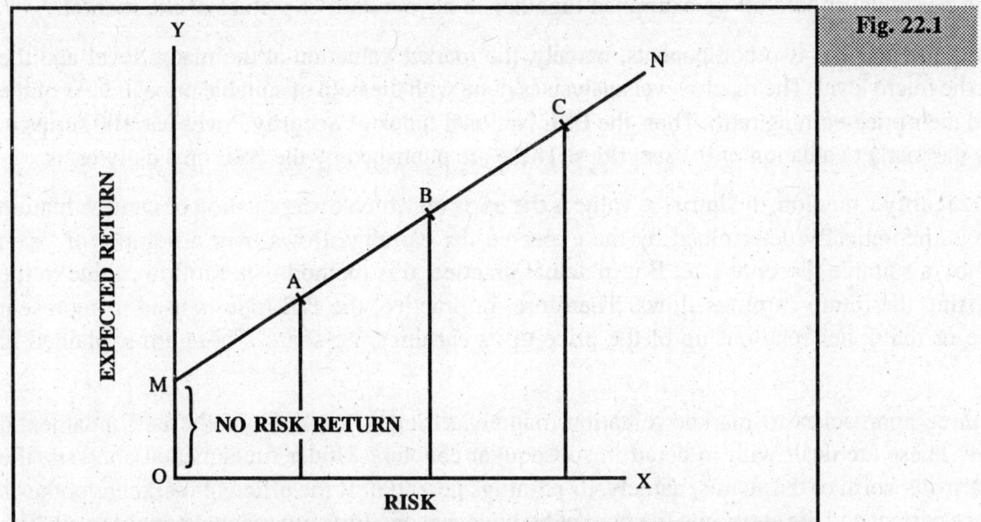

Fig. 22.1

A, B, C, etc., are denoted to represent the various instruments with different combinations of risk-return characteristics. OM is the risk free return on bank deposits.

In respect of individual scrips in the market, the security is valued in terms of the returns or earnings it fetches. The valuation is, therefore, an important aspect of security analysis. The market price depends on the supply and demand forces but basically veers around its intrinsic value, which in turn depends on the financial performance and fundamental factors of the company. These inter-relations can be represented as follows in Fig. 22.2.

Fig. 22.2

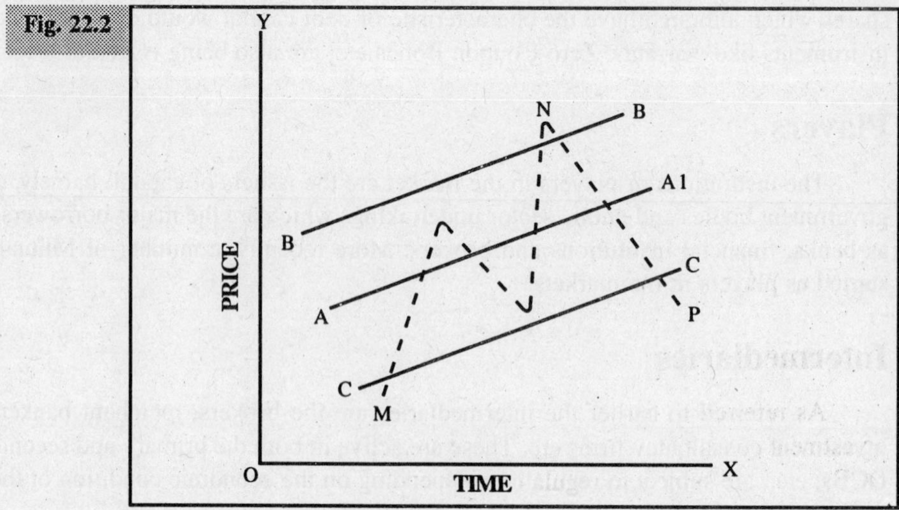

AA^1 = Instrinsic Value. B and C provide the range of error around the instrinsic value. MNP is the actual price curve in the market. The market price hovers around the intrinsic value namely AA^1.

Valuation

The basic objective of market analysis is to know the fair valuation of shares for buying and selling. The market comprises hundreds of securities whose prices change from day-to-day and from time to time. The investors should have information of fair prices for making their decisions of buying and selling. It is, therefore, necessary to make security valuation an important part of market-analysis. Besides, the trends of prices and volume of trading are inter-connected. Therefore, the market indicators of price, volume of trading, velocity of price changes and intensity of trading, etc. (volume of trading per hour) should all be examined together to have a correct picture of the market.

The valuation analysis in particular has two components, namely, the market valuation at the macro level and the individual security valuation at the micro level. The macro level analysis is done with the help of suitable price indices of the leading scrips in the market and their price-earning ratio. Thus, the BSE National Index of Security Prices has 100 scrips in it and their P/E ratio represents the market valuation of the securities. These are published by the BSE on a daily basis.

As regards the individual security valuation, the intrinsic value is the basis on which overvaluation or undervaluation is judged. The intrinsic value is theoretically determined by the expected net earnings flows over a number of years discounted to the present time by a suitable discount rate. But in actual practice, this method is not followed due to the practical difficulties of forecasting the future earnings flows. Therefore, in practice, the P/E ratio is used to represent the pay back period of a share or multiplier relationship of the price to its earnings per share. These are explained in detail later.

There are theoretically three approaches to market valuation, namely, efficient market hypothesis, fundamental analysis and technical analysis. These are dealt with in detail in subsequent chapters. Under fundamental analysis, the share value depends on the instrinsic worth of the shares, namely, its earnings potential. If the efficient market hypothesis is used, then the market becomes perfect and the entry into the market by buyers at any time gives equal benefit to all. The prices are determined in a random manner by competitive forces and perfect information flow and are independent of the past prices. This information is not only free and perfect, but it is absorbed fully and immediately by the market. But in actual practice, the information flow is not free and perfect and markets are not, therefore, efficient. Where the efficient market hypothesis does not hold, technical analysis is applicable. Under technical analysis, the prices move in a predictable manner and in waves and trends. The present prices are the result of past trends and can accordingly be predicted. Thus, by the use of analytical tools of charts and curves, the price trends can be studied and future trends can be predicted to decide on when to buy and sell.

In Fig. 22.3 the schematic presentation of valuation approaches and the three major methods of valuation of shares are depicted. The methods of valuation which are explained in detail later also are: (i) Discounted value of future income streams or dividends (ii) No. of years of payback period. (P/E ratio) in Table 22.1

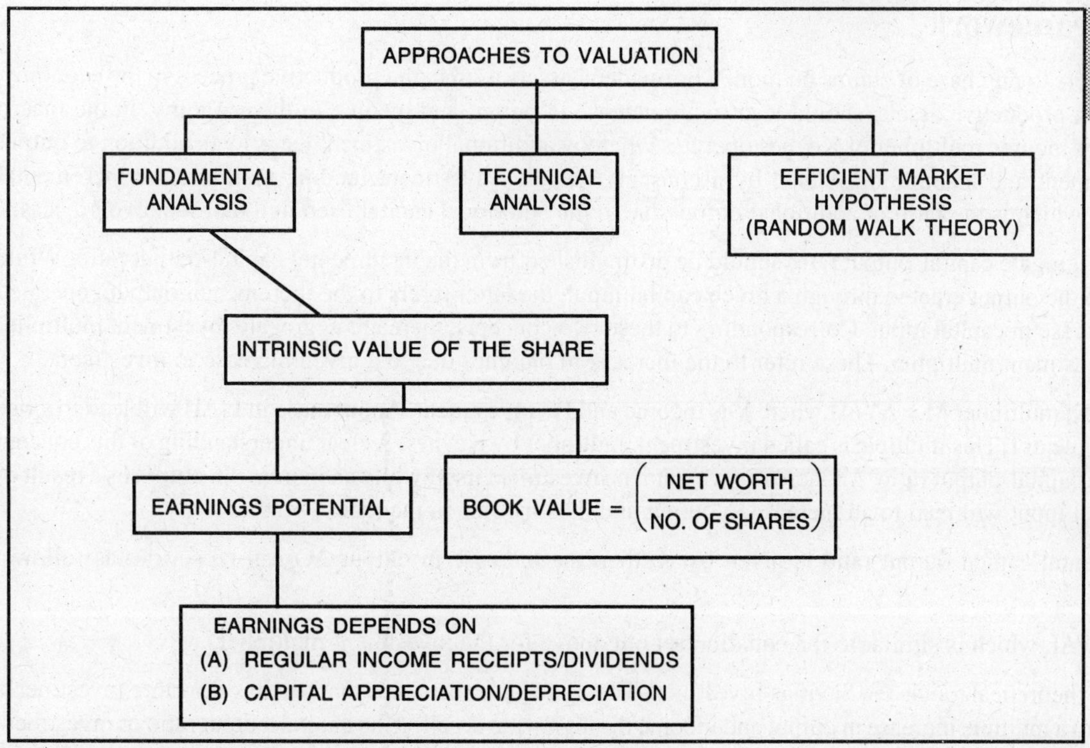

Fig. 22.3 Approaches to valuation.

TABLE 22.1 Method of Valuation (Simple examples)

A. Discounted Value of Future Income Streams Compounding

Take 5% interest rate and capital of Re. 1.

Compounding

In one year, it becomes Rs. $(1 + 0.5) = 1.05$

In two years, it becomes Rs. $(1 + 0.5)^2 = 1.1025$

In three years, it becomes Rs. $(1 + 0.5)^3 = 1.1576$

This method is called compounding.

The reverse of the above is called discounting.

Discounting

If we receive Rs. 116 at the end of three years, and if it is discounted to the present day at 5%, it will be equal to Rs. 100 at present.

The present value of the principal of Rs. 100 at the time of maturity of 5 years at 8% return will be Rs. $100/(1+0.08)^5$ = Rs. 68.

The present value of Rs. 100, ten years hence, will be 39 at a discount rate of 10%.

The above principle will apply to bond valuation and debenture valuation.

B. No. of Years of Payback Period

(Capitalisation or Multiplier approach to valuation)

For valuation of equity shares, the payback method is used in the form of P/E ratio.

Earning per share (dividend) covers the price paid for a share in, say 5 years. For example, earning is Rs. 20 and the price Rs. 100. P/E Ratio is 5. Then the earnings multiplier is 5. The payback period is 5 years. The smaller is the period, the higher the return.

C. NPV of future flows or Bookvalue per share also represents true intrinsic value of a share

Theoretical Framework

Investment refers to purchase of claims on money or financial assets used in the productive process in the economy. Investment, if it is in productive assets, should lead to an increase in output and income in the economy. In the macro sense, the investment income multiplier of Keynes operates whereby additional investment leads to an addition to output and income. Investment and income are related by a constant, namely, investment income multiplier or incremental capital-output ratio, which is the ratio of additional output due to the additional capital used in the productive process.

Besides, the aggregate capital-output ratio should be distinguished from the incremental capital-output ratio. While the former relates to the output created through a given capital input, the latter refers to the incremental output generated through a given increase in capital input. Corresponding to these two concepts, there are aggregate investment multiplier and incremental investment multiplier. These refer to the increase in incomes due to a given increase in investment.

Mathematically, multiplier $M = \Delta Y/\Delta I$ where Y is income and I is investment. An increase in I (ΔI) will lead to a rise in Y (ΔY), as a multiple of I. This multiple is called investment multiplier by Keynes. A clear understanding of this concept will also explain the capital-output ratio. An increase in capital is investment itself while an increase in output as a result of an increase in capital input will lead to an increase in output and thus income in the macro sense.

If the incremental capital-output ratio is given by K, then the increase in output ΔO can be set out as follows: $\Delta O = K \times \Delta I$.

Thus, $K = \Delta O/\Delta I$, which is similar to the equation set out above for the investment multiplier.

Thus, the first theoretical tool is the Savings Investment Theory, which postulates that savings flow into investments which in turn leads to a multiple increase in output and income through what is called the capital-output ratio or investment multiplier. Thus, savings promote capital formation and economic growth through increase in output and incomes of the country. The mobilisation of savings for capital formation is through the capital market comprising the new issues market and the stock market. The role of capital market is thus primarily to promote economic growth. The instruments through which this process is carried out is through the sale of corporate securities, which are claims on financial assets. These instruments are issued by the corporate sector to raise capital through such securities, as equities, preference shares, debentures, etc. The purchase and sale of these securities is carried on in the stock and capital markets, which impart liquidity to these investment instruments and thus promote the flow of public savings into these financial markets.

Secondly, the market behaviour also depends on the players and their role in trading. An analysis of the market price behaviour is thus possible through the number of buyers and sellers available and the free flow of correct and unbiased information into the market. The Capital Market Efficiency Theory, Random Walk Theory and many other theories explain how prices behave in the market in the macro sense. Competitive market conditions with a large number of buyers and sellers and with free and perfect flow of information will result in correct price formation in which prices tend to move near to their true intrinsic values of shares. In the absence of the above conditions, the share price movements may be erratic and biased; they may be overvalued or undervalued at any point of time. The inside information, rumours, cornering of shares and semi-monopoly conditions would all lead to imperfections in the market and price formation would be unrelated to the prevailing fundamentals of the company and its shares. The theoretical analysis of the market for its price behaviour would enable the investor to understand the market and make the right investment decisions regarding corporate securities.

The third theoretical tool in investment analysis is the fundamental analysis which explains why prices are what they are. This is an analysis of fundamental factors affecting the market in the macro sense, namely, economic, industry and company analysis. In the micro sense, the price of a share can be analysed through security valuation to find out the intrinsic value of a share and to examine whether a share is overvalued or undervalued. In the security valuation the most important tool is the ratio analysis or examination of the balance sheet and profit and loss accounts of the company, whose share is being examined. The examination of these fundamentals will enable us to locate the undervalued shares and overvalued shares and to decide what shares to buy and what shares to sell.

The next question is when to buy and when to sell. This leads to the fourth theoretical tool, namely, technical analysis, which is an analysis of the price behaviour of the aggregate market and of individual shares with the help of charts on price, trading volume and moving averages. An analysis of the price behaviour of the individual scrip historically in the background of the market price index behaviour will help to locate the turning signals indicating the likely changes in trends and suggesting the buy and sell points in the charts. The Dow theory and Elliot Wave theory are some of the theories in this analysis, which explain the price behaviour in the past and help us forecast the likely behaviour in the immediate future.

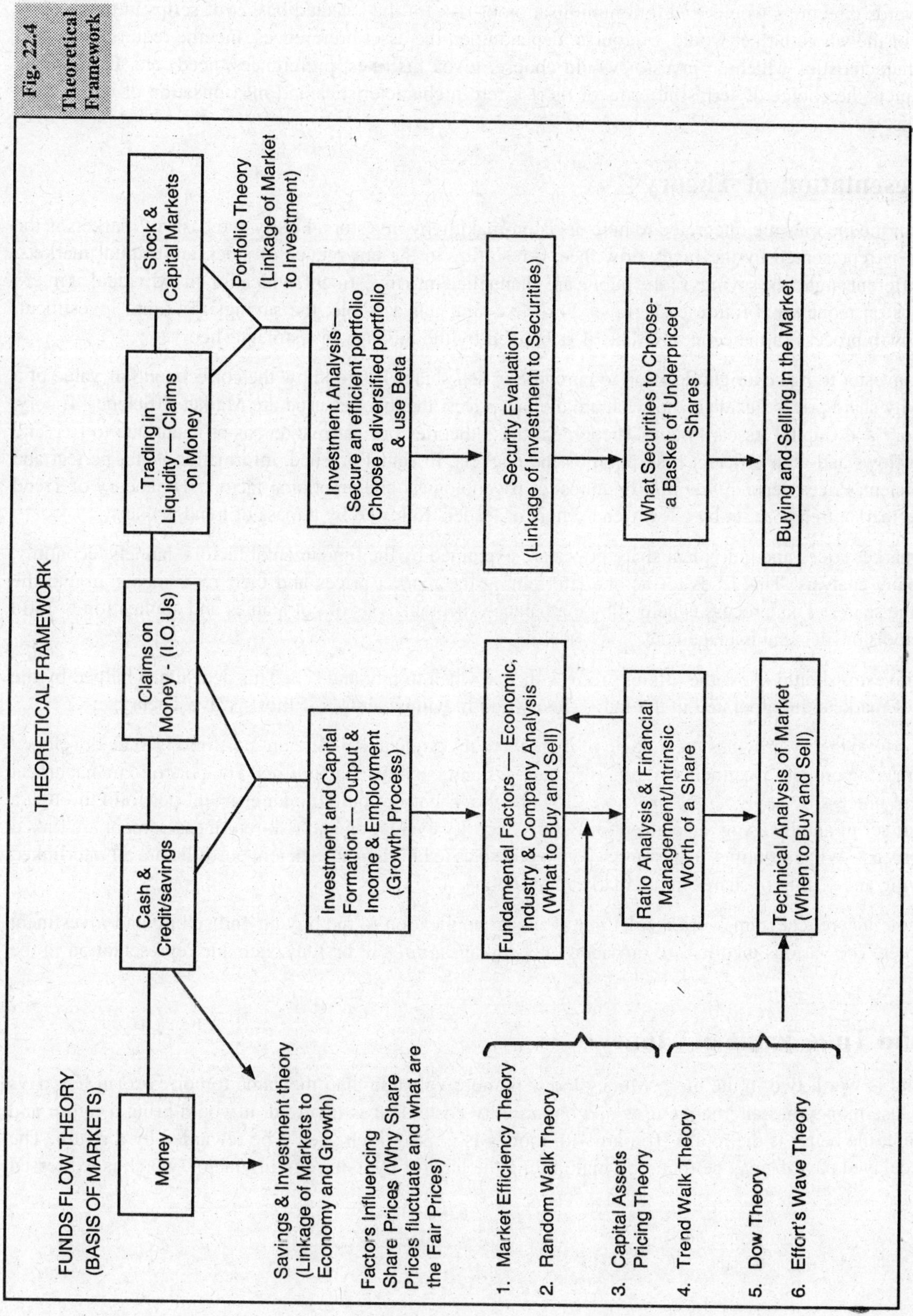

Fig. 22.4 Theoretical Framework

Yet another type of analysis is the analysis of risk and return which are the two major characteristics of any investment. This is sought to be achieved by the use of portfolio theory and portfolio management. In the analysis, the choice of scrips is decided by an analysis of risks involved in relation to the return in the background of the market risks and market return. A diversified portfolio of scrips is decided by an analysis of risk involved in relation to the return in the background of the market risks and market return. A diversified portfolio of scrips with varying degrees of risks in the upward and downwards directions would lead to a minimisation of risk for the selected basket of scrips in the market. The degree of risk of the whole basket would, of course, depend upon the asset preferences, income requirements and other investment characteristics which an investor would choose, given his likes, preferences, needs etc. Broadly the portfolio theory depicts the choice of scrips in terms of its risk-return characteristics and maximisation of returns and minimisation of risks.

Schematic Presentation of Theory

In Fig. 22.4, all the theories are integrated to help decision-making by investors. Firstly, the basis of markets is the money flow, which is represented by the funds flow theory, resulting in the emergence of stock and capital markets. Looked at from a different angle, the savings of the public are channelled into investment, which for an individual at micro level leads to claims on money and future cash flows. For the country as a whole, the savings flow into investment, which helps the growth process in the economy. This is explained by the Savings Investment Theory.

Secondly, an investor to make a right decision to purchase or sell shares has to know the correct and fair value of a share. To explain why share prices fluctuate and what are the fair prices, the theories used are Market Efficiency Theory, Random Walk Theory and Capital Assets Pricing Theory. All these theories present markets as efficient due to free and perfect information flows and their efficient absorption by the markets. In actual practice, information is not perfect and markets are not efficient. Prices depend *inter alia* on a host of psychological and emotional factors. The theory of Trend Walkers explain the market trends as set by a few trend setters or leaders followed by a mass of trend walkers.

Thirdly, the market prices and individual share prices are explained by the fundamental factors, namely, economy, industry and company analysis. This leads to factors determining the market prices and their movements around the intrinsic worth of the shares. This process is helped by the balance sheet analysis of companies and application of ratio analysis and other tools of financial management.

Fourthly, an investor should know the timing of investments, when to buy and sell. This decision is helped by the technical analysis of markets, incorporated in the Dow Theory and moving averages, Elliot's Wave Theory, etc.

Lastly, the portfolio theory provides the linkage of markets to investment. An efficient portfolio is to be developed by the investor by making proper investments to minimise the risks and maximise the returns. The portfolio management helps the investment process by applying the principles of Portfolio Theory to build up an efficient portfolio through a diversified basket of scrips and by using the concept of Beta.[@] Security evaluation and risk return assessment are linked to the investment process. What securities to buy and when to buy so as to build up an efficient portfolio are all interlinked to result in the buying and selling of shares in the market and trading.

Thus, the whole theoretical framework results in a practical application to the buying and selling and investment process in the market. The various theories are provided inter-linkages, *inter se* by the schematic representation in the Fig. 22.4.

Investment and Time Value of Money

A bird in hand is worth two in the bush. Money today is more valuable than the same tomorrow or a few days hence. This is because money has alternative uses and opportunity costs. If it is invested, it would bring a return and better the investment, the better is the return. To part with money is a risk which should be rewarded by a return. The present value of a delayed pay off may be found by multiplying the pay off by a discounting factor, which is expressed

@ Beta Concept is explained in a later chapter.

as the reciprocal of 1 plus a rate of return. Thus the discounting factor = $\frac{1}{1+r}$, where r is the rate of return that investor thinks adequate for his parting with money. Money has also a psychological satisfaction and value and to part with money is to part with a value which can only be compensated by a return.

Present Value Method

Thus the present value (PV) = $\frac{1}{1+r}$ X C, where C is the expected cash flow or pay off in the period. If there are more than one period, then

$$PV = \frac{C_1}{(1+r)} + \frac{C_2}{(1+r)^2} + \frac{C_3}{(1+r)^3} = \Sigma \frac{C_t}{(1+r)^t}$$

where, C_1, C_2 etc. are returns in periods 1 and 2 etc. and r remains as the same rate of return during all these periods. If r is the required rate of return or reward for the risk of parting with money and it remains the same throughout all the periods considered, and if C_1, C_2, C_3 etc. are the same cash receipts in all the periods, then PV = C/r or PV × r = C. Thus, given the required rate of return, the needed cash flow can be derived.

In the above equation, r refers to the nominal return. The real return is the nominal return divided by the rate of inflation or rise in prices. Money is losing its value by the degree of inflation, year after year. In the eighties, the average rate of inflation per annum was around 8%, the real return is negative if it is less than 8% and if r is 8%, then the real return is zero. Only if it is more than 8%, then the real return becomes positive.

Thus the return r, required to compensate the lender or investor of money, should give a minimum of inflation rate (or riskless return) plus a reward for risk for parting with liquidity. This reward for risk element varies from instrument, maturity period, the creditworthiness of the issuer of the instrument and a host of other factors.

In India, the Bank rate (6.0%) or the long-term rate of government securities (around 8%) could be considered the risk-free return and anything above this is the return for risk. Thus, the rate of preference shares and fixed deposits is kept by the Government fixed at 11% - 14% and the rate of PSU bonds (taxable) at 10% - 12%. The yield on equities should be definitely more than these rates as they are subject to higher risks. The debenture rates are left free to market forces now.

D.C.F. (Discounted Cash Flows)

The present value of future flows should thus yield a return which includes a riskless return (for the degree of inflation) plus a return for the risk shouldered in the investment. The same can be understood as discounted cash flows of the future periods to the present period. Thus, cash flows (C_1, C_2, C_3, etc.) in periods 1,2,3 etc. should be discounted to the present period by the required rate of return (r) as shown below:

$$\frac{C_1}{(1+r)} + \frac{C_2}{(1+r)^2} + \frac{C_3}{(1+r)^3} \text{ etc.}$$

Assuming the cash flow of C_1, C_2, C_3, etc. as constant (C) and the rate of returns is the same throughout the periods when these returns come, the present value can be set out as having a pay-off period of [PV/C], say, 6 to 10 years, depending upon the return of 15% to 10%. If the rate of return is 20%, then the pay-off period is 5 years. This concept of pay-off period shows how many years one has to wait to get back the present value of investment at the required rate of return. The shorter the period of waiting, the better is the investment. It is obvious that alternative investments have to be weighed before deciding on any investment. Thus, any two investments can be compared in terms of:

1. Actual rate of return above the risk-free return as compared to return on other similar assets;
2. Pay-off period;
3. Net present value which is equal to the present value of cash flows in future minus the actual investment in the present period (NPV).

After making Security Market Analysis, as discussed above, both in micro and macro senses, one can take any rational investment decision. The process of Investment Decision making is an offshoot of this and is discussed in the next chapter.

Investment Management Involves Correct Decision Making

As referred to earlier any investment is risky and as such investment decision is difficult to make. Investment decision is based on availability of money and information on the economy, industry and company and the share prices ruling and expectations of the market and of the companies in question.

What is Investment Management?

In the Stock Market parlance, investment decision refers to making a decision regarding the buy and sell orders. As referred to already, these decisions are influenced by availability of money and flow of information. What to buy and sell will also depend on the fair value of a share and the extent of overvaluation and undervaluation and more important, expectations regarding them. For making such a decision the common investors may have to depend more upon a study of fundamentals rather than technicals, although technicals are also important. If investment is for short-term and for speculation, technicals are more important. Besides, even genuine investors have to guard themselves against wrong timing regarding both buy and sell decisions. Otherwise, they will burn their fingers as happened in 1992 following the Harshad Mehta Scam and in 2001 following Ketan Parekh Scam. For this purpose, a study of company's performance, past record and expected future performance are to be looked into. It is necessary for a common investor to study the Balance Sheet and Annual Report of the company or analyse the quarterly and half yearly results of the company and decide on whether to buy that company's shares or not. This is called fundamental analyis. The decision of what to buy is easier, and if investors are tuned to making fundamental analysis, then decision-making becomes scientific and rational. The likelihood of high risk scenario will come down to a low risk scenario and long-term investors will not lose.

Criteria for Investment Decision

Firstly, investment decision depends on the mood of the market. As per the empirical studies, share prices depend on the fundaments of the company only to the extent of 50% and the rest is decided by the mood of the market and the expectations of the company's performance and its share price. These expectations depend on the analyst's ability to foresee and forecast the future performance of the company. For, price paid for a share at present depends on the flow of returns in future, expected from the company.

Secondly and following from the above, decision to invest will be based on the past performance, present working and the future expectations of the company's performance, both operationally and financially. These in turn will influence the share prices.

Thirdly, investment decision depends on the investor's perception on whether the present share price is fair, overvalued or under valued. If the share price is fair he will hold it (Hold Decision), if it is overvalued, he will sell it (Sell Decision) and if it is undervalued, he will buy it (Buy Decision). These are general rules, but exceptions may be there.

Thus, even when prices are rising, some investors may buy as their expectations of further rise may outweigh their conception of overvaluation. That means, the concepts of overvaluation or under valuation are relative to time, space and man. What may be over valued a little while ago has become undervalued following later developments; information or sentiment and mood may change the whole market scenario and of the valuation of shares. There are two more Decisions, namely, Average Up and Average Down of prices.*

The investment decision may also depend on the investor's preferences, moods, or fancies. Thus an investor may go on a spending spree and invest in cats and dogs of companies, if he has taken a fancy or he is flooded with money from lottery or prizes. A rational investor would however make investment decisions on scientific study of the fundamentals of the company and in a planned manner.

At present, investors mostly depend on hearsay and advice of friends, relatives, sub-brokers, etc. for the investment decision, but not on any Scientific study of the company's fundamentals. In view of the increasing mushroom growth of companies and lack of any track record of many promoters, investment decision-making became more difficult now. Even otherwise, risk will increase in case of all investments made on hunches, hearsay etc.

Risk and Investment

Stock Market investment is risky and there are different types of investments, namely equity, fixed deposits, debentures etc. Company specific risk also called unsystematic risk can be reduced by diversifying investments into 10 to 15 companies. But the systematic risk relating to the market cannot be reduced but can be managed by choosing companies with that much risk (high or low) that the investor can bear. For example, some investors can take high risk and they may invest in new ventures, turnaround companies, even when they are incurring losses, and some speculative companies like Reliance and G.E shipping etc. But risk-averse investors will choose only Blue Chip Companies with a good track record like Colgate, ICICI, Telco, Hindustan Lever etc. It is therefore, necessary for investors to be selective and discrete and analyse the risk along with return for each investment. Companies are Blue Chips, some are emerging Blue Chips etc. and some are risky ventures. Their evaluation can be done through fundamental analysis of companies, quoted on the Exchanges.

What is Fundamental Analysis?

This relates to an examination of the intrinsic worth of the company, to find out whether the current market price is fair, overpriced or underpriced. This is done by studying the various aspects of the company (Company Analysis) in the background of the performance of industry to which the company belongs and the general economic and socio-political scenario of the country. Thus, the fundamental analysis of the share price involves three major steps.

(a) Economic Factors and their Analysis.

(b) Industry Analysis.

(c) Company Analysis.

The logic of this three tier analysis is that the company performance depends not only on its own efforts and working but on the general industry and economic factors, which influence its performance. No company can work in vacuum. It is a part of the industry and the economy and its performance depends on these forces which are external to the company. As referred to earlier, studies have shown that a company's share price depends on the intrinsic or internal factors only to the extent of about one-half of the total forces and the rest is contributed by the external forces, namely, psychological and expectational factors regarding the company, relative to others in the industry and the sentiment in the market, which depends on the socio-economic and political forces operating on the market. This reflects the dictum that Stock Market is window of the economy and the totality of forces operating on the economy would influence the Stock market. Details of fundamental Analysis are given in a separate Chapter.

* It is average down decision if we buy as prices fall to bring down the average price of our shares held. Average up is for selling in small doses to bring up the average price of all sales.

In the economy, some industries are expanding while others are stagnant and some contracting, depending on the demand and market conditions. The investor has to choose the growth industry and in that industry, choose the scrips undervalued as judged by his study and analysis.

Investment Objectives

The first basic objective of investment is the return on it or yields. The yields are higher, the higher is the risk taken by investors. The riskless return is the bank saving deposit rate of $3^1/_2$% at present or Bank rate of 6.0% (Sept., 2007). Here the risk is least as funds are safe and returns are certain.

Secondly, each investor has his own asset preferences and choice of investments. Thus some risk averse operators put their funds in bank or post office deposits or deposits/certificates with co-operatives and PSUs. Some invest in real estate, land and buildings while others invest mostly in gold, silver and other precious stones, diamonds etc.

Thirdly, every investor aims at providing for minimum comforts of a house furniture, vehicles, consumer durables and other household requirements. After satisfying these minimum needs, he plans for his income, saving in insurance (LIC and GIC etc.), pension and provident funds etc. In the choice of these, the return is subordinated to the needs of the investor.

Lastly, after satisfying all the needs and requirements, the rest of the savings would be invested in financial assets which will give him future incomes and capital appreciation, so as to improve his future standard of living. These may be in stock/capital market investments.

Cost-Benefit Analysis

In making investments of the last category, namely, in financial assets of deposits, bonds, debentures, shares, etc., investment management involves a cost-benefit analysis.

The major costs are the risk involved and major benefits are the returns involved.

Risk is measured by the variability of the returns. But the risk is of various types — non-payment of dividend/ interest, delay or non-payment of principal, variability of return or market value of investments.

These risks can be classified as follows:

(a) Company Risk

(b) Market Risk

(c) Business Risk

(d) Commodity/Product Risk

(e) Financial Risk

(f) Economy Risk of the Nation

(g) International Factors

Among examples of International factors imports and exports and international prices of inputs of domestic goods, etc., can be cited. Among economy risk, Govt. Policy, Inflation, Monetary and fiscal policies etc., can be given as examples.

The other risks particularly the risk of Business is relative to trade/business of the Company, Product, Inputs/ Outputs etc. Interest Rate, Labour Problem, Inflation effect may lead to financial and market risks. Company risk is unique to the company, about its own management and operations.

There are many other risks such as socio-economic factors, political and commercial problems etc. The costs are the expenses to be incurred in acquiring the assets, say registration, brokerage charges etc. In addition there will be uncertainties and risks, involved due to possible non-payment of interest or dividends or capital losses etc.

There are corresponding benefits to be assessed in terms of regular incomes (interest and dividends) — regularity and certainty of them — capital appreciation, safety and security of funds, marketability and liquidity of investments and a host of other factors. The investor has to assess the costs and benefits of each investment, in the process of investment Management.

Environmental Considerations

Many times, investor has to take into account the environmental factors in investment management. His past background, family requirements, the assets of neighbours or of colleagues and other external factors may influence his investment decisions.

People in rural and semi-urban areas are influenced by their immediate environment and access to avenues. The agriculturists invest in ploughs, tractors and other requirements, needed for his occupation and environment. Beyond these, he invests in gold and silver or real estate due to the influence of environment as people are assessed in those places by the amount of gold and real estate, they hold and possess.

On the other hand, the environment in urban and metropolitan centres is different. The alternatives available to them are more varied. The funds are invested in vehicles, consumer durables, mutual funds, corporate securities and various other instruments. In many semi-urban and urban areas, housing finance companies, finance and investment companies and chit funds attract the public funds with attractive returns and incentives.

Chit Funds and Nidhis

Among the categories of investments popular with semi-urban and rural areas, there are various types of deposits kept with non-bank finance companies like hire-purchase, investment and finance companies, housing finance companies, mutual benefit funds, chit funds and nidhis. These are mostly governed by State Acts and partly controlled by the RBI in respect of their deposit raising activities.

Chit funds are of various categories, prize chits, normal and conventional chits, lottery chits, etc. They collect regularly the savings of investors on a monthly basis and lend, if necessary to members and give a lump sum money once in a year depending on the results of lottery or any other mechanism.

Mutual benefit funds and nidhis are also saving mobilisation agencies, for the benefit of members, who are saving households. These are normally registered as trusts or friendly societies and operate in mobilisation of savings and lending for the benefit of members. So long as the promoters are honest and dependable, the funds are safe and members benefit from these activities. But there are many reports, about unscrupulous elements among these promoters, fly-by-night operators who collect the funds and misuse them for trading and speculation or disappear from the scene after working for sometime. Although there are laws and rules to regulate them, the subject being a state subject, the regulation and control on them is lax and hence funds may not always be safe.

Investors have to weigh the pros and cons of making investments in such agencies. Similarly, all deposits with companies private limited or public limited are unsecured debt and hence the investors should be careful in taking this risk of investment in deposits in the chits, nidhis and even companies.

Tax Planning in Investment Management

As Investment management aims at the highest return possible, reduction in tax liability can increase returns. Tax planning is done to reduce tax liability by proper investment strategy. The elements of tax planning are as follows: Reference may also be made to chapter 7 of this Book.

Personal Income Tax: Interest income and dividend income upto Rs. 2,500 is not subject to tax deduction at sources. Income from dividends and Mutual funds schemes, bank deposits etc. is exempt from tax upto Rs. 12,000 P.A., under Section 80L of Income Tax Act which was widened to encompass the contributions to N.S.S, P.F. etc., to be eligible for tax exemption. The maximum tax rate is 30% plus 2% education cess. The 80L Section and other rebates were replaced by a new Section 80C giving a total exemption of Rs. one lakh for approved categories of investment, from 2005-2006.

Wealth Tax: Investment in shares and debentures are totally exempt from wealth tax without limit. The other investments in real estate, gold, housing, cars etc. are subject to wealth tax beyond Rs. 15 lakhs with some exemptions for specific purposes.

Corporate Taxation: From 1994-95, there is a single rate of corporate tax of 40% for all whether widely held or closely held companies. There is also a surcharge of 15% for corporate income above Rs. 1,00,000 which was withdrawn in 1997-98 Budget. Foreign companies will pay at a tax rate of 55% as against earlier rate of 65% with effect from 1994-95. In 2000-01 the maximum corporate tax rate was 35% for domestic companies which was raised to 36.5% in 2002-03 and 48% for foreign companies, with a surcharge of 10%, which was lowered to 40% plus 5% surcharge in 2002-03. Since 2005-06, domestic and foreign companies pay at the same rate of 30% plus surcharge.

TDS: The current rate of tax deduction at source is 10% for interest income and 20% for dividend income. Mutual funds and banks were exempt from making tax deduction at source for such income payments, but since July 1995, TDS is enforced on them also.*

Tax rebates were gradually reduced on many categories. Thus, investments in approved Securities or P.O. certificates, are exempt from income tax, if it is upto Rs. 60,000 and the rebate is upto 20% of investment. In approved mutual fund equity linked schemes, investment upto Rs. 10,000, enjoy a rebate upto Rs. 2,000 in income tax payable for the year. This exemption or rebate for investment upto Rs. 10,000 is within the above limit of Rs. 60,000 under Section 88 of IT Act. Another Rs. 20,000 is granted from 2000-01 for same tax treatment if invested in bonds for infrastructure development or in any schemes approved by the Govt. for this purpose, such as NHAI and NABARD Bonds. All exemptions under 80L and 88 of IT Act were replaced by Section 80C, since 2005-06.

Capital Gains Tax: Long-term capital gains are taxable at 20% for individuals and 30% for corporate Units. Short-term capital gains are taxable at the same rates as applicable to individual income tax payers and corporate tax payers. Long-term capital gains are those realised after 12 months in the case of shares, UTI and Mutual Fund schemes. But they should be held for more than 36 months to be considered long-term capital gains in the case of other assets like real estate etc. In 2005-06, short-term capital gains tax was kept at 10%while removing any tax on long-term capital gains.

Gift Tax: Gifts made by NRIs to resident relatives and friends are completely exempt from gift tax. Gifts made by residents to other residents are exempt up to a limit of Rs. 30,000 P.A. Exemption limits of gifts on marriage of dependent relatives are raised from Rs. 30,000 to Rs. one lakh in the Budget for 1994-95. In 1997-98 gift tax was abolished and gifts are included in income for tax purposes, in the hands of the Donee.

Execution of Investment Decisions

If investment is made in corporate securities and having chosen the scrips, to buy or sell, investor gives his orders to the broker. As per the Rules and Byelaws of the exchange, the stock broker and if sub-broker is dealing with clients, the sub-broker should accept orders in the form of entries in their inward Registers. These orders can be oral, written or by Telex or Telephone etc. or on website of a broker in the case of e-broking. The broker has to pass the contract note to the client on the same day or next day after the order is executed. If the order is executed by buying or selling on his own account *vis-a-vis* the client, then the consent of the client is necessary and the deal should be put through at the market rate, as if it is done in the Trading Ring. But this is not allowed in e-broking and the orders have to pass through the Exchange.

The sub-broker cannot pass contract notes; but based on the contract note of broker to sub-broker, he can pass the confirmation notes to the client. The client has to check the price noted in the contract note or confirmation note with that as reported in the papers. But some variations are permissible as the broker purchases or sells at one price while market price fluctuates within a range from minute to minute. If the Stock Exchange gives the daily highs and lows and the price charged by the broker falls within that range with some margin for the broker's and sub-broker's commissions then the deal should be considered to be fair. Otherwise, complaint can be made with the Exchange.

* Mutual funds have to deduct tax at source for income above Rs. 10,000 p.a. at a rate of 10% for individuals and 20% plus surcharge in the case of companies, which was withdrawn later.

As per the latest directives of the SEBI, the contract note should show separately the price of the scrip and the brokerage charged and service tax payable to brokers on their brokerages income which they pay to Govt. This ensures transparency and the client should insist on this. At present, SEBI registered sub-brokers can also pass contract notes to the clients and investors should deal with them only and insist on contract notes to be passed.

The client has to pay on or before the pay-in-day if he is a buyer and receive the Certificates on the pay out day. If the client is a seller, he should deliver the shares before the pay in or settlement date and receive the money on or after the pay out day. These pay-in and pay-out dates are fixed well in advance and the brokers know these dates and the clients should insist on this information, from the brokers and sub-brokers. Every Stock Exchange has a Trading Cycle of 5 days for each settlement. The SEBI directed all the Stock Exchanges to have uniform period of 5 days for all. Many Exchanges follow Trading Cycle of 5 days if they have only cash scrips or 'B' group shares and pay-in-day comes after about 10 to 15 days from the first day of trading. After a couple of days from the pay-in-day, the pay-out-day is fixed. Thus, the client has to wait for about 15 to 20 days from the date of transaction to realise the proceeds of his sale or get delivery of shares. Some banks lend against shares if investors need funds. Now all scrips are put on rolling settlement basis, except those which are on T + 2 settlement basis.

The client has to make a note of these days and insist from the sub-broker or broker for cheques or shares, as the case may be, on the due dates. The awareness of these dates and the amounts due to them will help the clients in their transactions with brokers. Similarly, knowledge of the Rules of the Stock Exchange and practices of brokers will help them to protect their interests. In the event of non-payment of cheque or non-delivery of shares on due dates, clients have to promptly take up with brokers and if they do not respond, complaints have to be made to the Stock Exchange.

CHAPTER 24

Financial Analysis and Interpretation

Financial Analysis Comprises of Financial Statement Analysis and Balance Sheet Analysis, which are two side of the same coin. Financial Statement Analysis is attempted in this chapter while Balance Sheet Analysis is set but in the next chapter.

Share price depends partly on its intrinsic worth for which financial analysis of a company is necessary to help the investor to decide whether to buy or not the shares of that company. The soundness and intrinsic worth of a company is known only by such analysis. The market price of a share depends, among others on the sound fundamentals of the company, the financial and operational efficiency and the profitability of that company. These factors can be examined by a study of the financial management of the company. An investor needs to know the performance of the company, its intrinsic worth as indicated by some parameters like book value, EPS, P/E multiple etc., and come to a conclusion whether the share is rightly priced for purchase or not. This, in short is the importance of financial analysis of a company to the investor.

What is Financial Management?

The financial management of a company is concerned with management of its funds which reflects how efficiently the company is managing its funds. The overall objective of all business is to secure funds at low cost and their effective utilisation in the business for a profit. The funds so utilised must generate an income higher than the cost of procuring them. Here it is to be noted that all companies need both long-term and short-term capital. The finance manager must therefore keep in view the needs of both long-term debt and working capital and ensure that the business enjoys an optimum level of working capital and that it does not keep too many funds blocked in inventories, book-debts, cash, etc. The capital structuring and average cost of capital for the company should also be examined.

Financial analysis is analysis of financial statements of a company to assess is financial health and soundness of its management. "Financial Statement analysis" involves a study of the financial statements of a company to ascertain its prevailing state of affairs and the reasons therefore. Such a study would enable the public and investors to ascertain whether one company is more profitable than the other, and also to state the causes and factors that are probably responsible for this.

Components of Financial Statements

The term 'financial statements' as used in modern business refers to the balance sheet, or the statement of financial position of the company at a point of time and income and expenditure statement, or the profit and loss statement over a period. To this is added, the profit allocation statement which reconciles the balance in this account at the end of the period with that at the beginning. Thus, the financial statements provide a summary of the accounts of a company over a period of one year, and the balance sheet reflecting the assets, liabilities and capital as at a point of time say at the end of the year.

Analysis and Interpretation: With a view to interpret the financial statements, it is necessary to analyse them with the object of formation of an opinion with respect to the financial condition of that company.

This Analysis involves the following steps:

(a) Comparison of the financial statements, over two to five years.

(b) Ratio analysis, for two to three years.

(c) Funds Flow analysis, over a short period.

(d) Trend analysis, over a period of 5 to 10 years.

The salient features of each of the above steps are discussed briefly in this chapter.

Comparison of the Financial Statements

Comparison is the pre-condition for a meaningful interpretation. It may be of:

(a) figures of one year with that of another year;

(b) inter-firm comparison of figures, within the same industry;

(c) comparison of one product figures with that of another product; and

(d) comparison of budgeted figures with the actual figures.

For the purpose of analysis, the figures in the balance sheet and the income statements are to be arranged properly which will facilitate the work. The statements are prepared in single (vertical) column form as shown below for this purpose.

Balance Sheet as at	
Fixed Assets	
Investments	
Working Capital:	
Current assets *Less:*	
Current Liabilities	
Capital Employed Total	
Less:	
Funded Debts	
(Debentures and Long-term liabilities)	
Shareholders' Fund	
Represented by:	
Equity Share Capital	
Preference Share Capital	
Reserves and Surplus *Less:*	
Preliminary Expenses	

Profit and Loss Account for the year ended

Sales (Net)

Less:

Cost of goods sold

Gross operating Profit:

Less: Operating Expenses (Office, selling and distribution expenses)

Net operating profit:

Earning Before Interest and Tax (EBIDT)

Minus Interest, Depreciation and Taxation

Profit After Tax (PAT)

Meaningful analysis can be achieved by comparing the financial data and ratios of one firm with that of another. This process is called inter-firm comparison. When the performance in various departments of a single firm is compared, the term used is intra-firm comparison.

For inter-firm comparisons the financial statements must be made as far as practicable, comparable so as to derive reliable conclusions on analysing. The stated amounts of the two enterprises must be on the same price levels, and the accounting methods used by them must be similar.

Ratio Analysis

The ratio is a statistical yardstick that provides a measure of relationship between any two variables. It can be effectively used as a tool of management along with Fund Flow Statements and Trend Analysis for interpretation of the financial statements. As ratios are simple to calculate and easy to understand, there is a tendency to employ them profusely.

The ratios are conveniently classified as follows:

(i) Balance Sheet Ratios which deal with the relationships between two items or groups of items which are both in the Balance Sheet, e.g., the ratio of current assets to current liabilities (Current Ratio).

(ii) Revenue Statement Ratios which deal with the relationship between two items or groups of items which are both in the Revenue Statement, e.g., ratio of gross profit to sales or gross profit margin.

(iii) Composite Ratios: Balance Sheet and Revenue Statement Ratios which deal with real relationships between items from the Revenue Statement and items from the Balance Sheet, e.g., ratio of net profit to own Funds (Composite Ratios).

(a) Revenue Statement Ratios:

(i) Gross Profit Ratio

(ii) Operating Ratio

(iii) Expense Ratio

(iv) Net Profit Ratio

(v) Stock Turnover or Turnover of Inventory

(b) Balance Sheet Ratios:

(i) Current Ratio

(ii) Liquidity Ratio or Quick Ratio

(iii) Debt to Equity Ratio

(iv) Asset to Equity Ratio

(c) Composite Ratios:

(i) Return on Total Resources

(ii) Return on Own Funds

(iii) Turnover of Fixed Assets

(iv) Turnover of Debtors

Usefulness of Ratio Analysis

Ratio Analysis should be based on some common standards such as comparison between two companies in the same industry and within the same assets group. Since the performance of companies varies from industry to industry and from location to location, the ratios are not comparable exactly.

What is proper for Hotel Industry which is seasonal in nature may not be true for cement and steel industry which belong to infrastructure sector.

The use of Ratio Analysis depends on the object in mind. The question to be put to oneself is what do I want to know of the company? Let us say its capital efficiency is to be examined. Then ratio such as Gross Block to equity or Fixed Assets to Share Capital or Net Profit to Capital employed are to be used. Thus, there are different ratios for different purposes.

Ratio Analysis will be meaningful to establish relationship regarding financial performance, operational efficiency and profit margins with respect to companies over a period of time and as between companies within the same industry group. Comparison over a period of time shows the improvement or deterioration in the performance of the company.

In addition to the Ratio Analysis, financial analysis involves fund flow Analysis and the Trend Analysis. Fund Flow Analysis involves the examination of sources and uses of funds. Thus inflow of funds is due to sale, and other income, whereas uses are increases in investment or purchase of assets or for regular wage and other payments etc. Cash accruals and how they are utilised will be studied in this process.

Fund Flow Analysis

The Balance Sheet of a Company reveals its financial status at a point of time. The financial executive must know the flows of funds underlying the balance sheet changes. The operation of business involves the conversion of cash into non-cash assets which are recovered back into cash form. The statement showing sources and uses of funds is properly known as "Fund Flow Statements." It shows the ebb and flow of funds into and out of a business. It covers all movements that invoices an actual exchange of assets and only transactions representing book-keeping adjustments are not reported. Thus, Funds Flow Statement is a useful tool in the kit of financial management and is a report of the financial operations of a company. The term funds should not be interpreted as literal cash, but it extends the concept to include assets or financial resources which do not effect cash or working capital. Examples are the purchase of property in exchange for issue of shares and bonds. The broader approach provides a more complete and informative presentation.

The changes representing the "sources of funds" in the business may be issue of debentures, increase in net worth, addition to funds, reserves and surplus, retention of earnings.

Changes showing the "uses of funds" include:

(a) Additions to assets — fixed and current

(b) Addition to investments.

(c) Decrease in liabilities by paying off loans and creditors.

(d) Decrease in net worth by incurring of losses, withdrawal of funds from business and payment of dividends. If the net profit for a particular accounting year is a source of funds, a net loss as shown by an income statement is an application of funds. This is so because where a loss has been incurred, funds have gone out of the business.

The changes in net working capital take place either by the decrease in current assets or increase in the liabilities as sources of funds and the reduction in current liabilities. These changes in net working capital are available from the comparative balance sheet. An increase in net working capital in this manner represents a net application of funds. A statement of source and application of funds can be prepared from the two comparative balance sheets with an accompanying increase-decrease column. From the stand-point of the balance sheet, funds may come from three sources: an increase in liabilities, a decrease in assets and an increase in net worth. The increase in net worth is used to represent two sources of funds, namely, net profits and contribution of funds. Likewise, applications represent three uses of funds, decrease in liabilities, increase in assets and decrease in net worth. Here again, the decrease in the net worth represents the uses, namely, net losses and decrease in capital funds.

The fund flow statement helps in guiding the destiny of a business by enabling the executive to visualise the movement of funds that constantly take place. A failure to detect pattern of change can perpetuate undesirable trends and lead to financial difficulties. An extended reliance on external sources can create a top heavy capital structure. This statement helps in detecting the sources for financing the heavy accumulation of inventory and book-debts. It is also helpful in forecasting the flow of funds. It is used for projecting working capital requirements. It also highlights future need for funds and plays an important role in the evaluation of trade credit. It points out any asset liability mismatch in terms of maturity, quantum etc. and its impact on liquidity and solvency of the company.

Trend Analysis

Trend Analysis refers to comparison of some important ratios and rates of growth over a time period of a few years. These trends in the case of GPM or Sales Turnover are useful to indicate the extent of improvement or deterioration over a period of time in the aspects considered. The trends in dividends, E.P.S., asset growth or sales growth are some examples of the trends used to study the operational performance of the companies. Any temporary rise in inventories to sales would indicate sluggish demand for the products of the company.

Thus the trends of the results, rather than the actual ratios and percentages, are important. Structural relationships taken from the financial statements of one year only are of limited value and the trends of these structural relationship established from statements over a number of years may be more significant than absolute ratios. Investor wants to know how well the business is operating in comparison with planned performance and if actual results are not good enough, what should the future indicate for the company. The financial results of all businesses are affected by general economic condition, by competition, and local factors relating to company.

It should be particularly emphasised that one particular ratio used without reference to other ratios may be very misleading. In other words, the combined effect of the various ratios must be considered in arriving at a correct diagnosis which will be of assistance in interpreting the financial condition and earning performance of the business. Each ratio plays its part in this interpretation.

Finally, it should be realised that ratios are only preliminary step in interpretation and must be supplemented by rigorous investigation into all aspects of operations of company before safe conclusions can be drawn from them. Trend analysis should supplement the ratio analysis to assess the good and bad aspects of working of a company.

More importantly not only the objective factual data should be analysed from Balance Sheet and Income-Expenditure Statements of the company, but a scrutiny of subjective factors indicated in the Directors' and Auditor's Reports should also be made with particular reference to any mention in footnotes to contingent liabilities, unpaid taxes, doubtful debts etc. Besides research into practical day-to-day operations of the company can be done only by a plant visit and study on the spot the prospects of the company in the coming year or two.

CHAPTER 25

Balance Sheet Analysis and Blue Chips

Balance Sheet Analysis in Stock market studies involves the use of the Financial Data available in Balance Sheet and Income and Expenditure statements of a Company. The objective of this analysis is to know the overvaluation or undervaluation of a share as judged by its intrinsic worth and compare it with its market price and that of the similar companies within the same industry. The Company's performance in terms of its physical operations is reflected in its Balance Sheet and Income and Expenditure Statements in terms of financial data.

Annual Reports

The main components of the Annual Reports of Companies, containing Balance Sheet and Income and Expenditure data are as follows:

1. *Chairman's Speech to its Investors:* This would bring out the management views of the Company's performance, in the backdrop of the economy and industrial growth, its plans for expansion or diversification if any, difficulties or problems faced by the Company and their plan of action to meet these challenges and the immediate future prospects of the Company etc.

2. *Director's Report:* This is a factual account of the operations of the Company during the past year and the Financial results of these operations, profits or losses, the allocation of profits for depreciation, interest, taxes, dividends etc. After allocating these sums, the residual profits are ploughed back to the reserves or losses are written off. The input availability, market for the outputs, labour problems, Government policy changes with regard to them, if any, exports or imports made by the Company etc., are all presented in this report for the benefit of its shareholders.@

3. *Balance Sheet and Income and Expenditure Accounts:* These are accompanied by the profit allocation statement and the detailed schedules for each of the items in the accounts. The method of presenting these data varies from company to company although the contents are almost the same. These data would reflect the Prima facie position of the company's operations and the financial results of these operations over a period say six months or a year.

4. *Auditor's Report:* This is a statutory report testifying the correctness of the accounts and giving their own comments on the accounting practices and procedures of the company. The real position of the company's operations is known from the footnotes to the accounts and the comments of the Auditors. They indicate the contingent liabilities, bad debts, changes in accounting practices adopted to camouflage the poor financial performance, method of providing for depreciation, provision for D R R fund and other statutory obligations, revaluation of assets if any, dividends not paid, advance calls, etc. In fact, the most vital information to be provided to Investors as per the Companies Act is contained in the footnotes. As such the analysts should examine carefully these notes and Auditors' Report to make any correct assessment of the valuation of a share.

@ The company has to disclose information on conservation of energy, technology absorption, R & D Expenditure and benefits from it, foreign exchange earnings and outgo etc., which are also useful for investment analysis.

Market Price and Corporate Performance

The market price of a share depends primarily on the Company's performance, reflected in the earnings per share or cash earning per share, dividend record and bonus payments made by the company. Empirical studies have shown that stock price also depends on the gross block and its gorwth. Besides, share prices also depend on the goodwill factors which are subjective in nature such as management reputation, expansion plans, Tax planning, technological set-up, reputation of collaborators and locational advantages. The management rating is subjective and is a factor contributing to the goodwill of the company. This goodwill also depends on the Government attitude to the management, of the company Government policy with regard to exports and imports and the company performance on export front.

Honesty, integrity and consistency of management gives good rating for the company. The price of a share also depends on subjective factors like sentiment of the market, phase of the market such as gloom, fear, indecision, optimism and euphoria etc.

To sum up, the market price of share depends on some fundamental factors like Intrinsic value of the share, subjective and goodwill factors and sentimental factors depending on the phase of the market. The intrinsic worth of the company is judged by the net present value, derived by discounting future returns of shares to the present, book value of the share, earnings per share etc.

ANALYSIS OF FINANCIAL POSITION

The following financial parameters are looked into for judging the company's performance, as an illustration:

Financial Ratios	Significance
Equity to Networth	Strength of owned funds
Equity to capital employed/Equity to GB	Efficiency of Capital use
Equity to sales	Equity Turnover
Right & Bonus	Expansion Prospects
MP to book value	Over/Under valuation
MP to EPS	Over/Under valuation
P/E Multiple	Comparison with Industry Average
G P M & N P M	Profitability
Dividend	Distribution of Profits

The above are some of the quantifiable factors derived from the Annual Accounts. But the non-quantifiable factors like goodwill and sentiment cannot be judged from the Balance Sheet data except in an indirect manner. Thus the management policy, expansion and Tax planning schemes can be known from the Chairman's speeches, financial press and Directors' Report.

Future prospects of the Company can be assessed indirectly from the hints given by the Chairman in his speech to the Investors in the General Body meeting or in the Press conferences. Similarly, the genuineness and dependability of the accounting practices and true and factual disclosures as shown in the Auditors' report will reflect on the management integrity, honesty and their reputation. The Balance Sheet analysis is thus an important subject in the direction of fundamental analysis of a share price which the Analysts and Investors should undertake as part of their research for indentifying the shares to buy and the shares to sell.

Types of Shares in the Market

At any stage in the economy, there are different types of Industries, some start up Companies, some mature and grown, some expanding into growth Industries and some showing decline in their prosperity and popularity. Some industries are seasonal, some in key or core sectors, some in export sector etc.

Similarly, in each Industry there are different types of companies, some growing, some stagnant and some declining. There are thus different types of companies within the same Industry and different types of Industries within the Economy. A genuine investor should try to identify the potentialities of each of these groups and concentrate on growth oriented Industries or emerging Blue Chips and established Blue Chips. Within each Industry, there are some companies which are turn-around companies showing signs of emerging into Blue Chip Companies. Company characteristics also vary, viz., innovative unique product companies, leaders, single product and multiproduct companies, captive demand companies, etc.

Blue Chip Companies are in simple language, Growth Oriented Companies showing signs of expansion, diversification, modernisation of Technology and reputation for consistent profitability and profit margins to sustain the consistent dividend distribution, growing profits and expanding net worth.

The management of these companies have got a dynamic and growth oriented policy and have a reputation for a vision for future growth and expansion and maintain a sustained growth in assets, sales turn-over and profits. Emerging Blue Chip companies are those which are turn-around companies and exhibit potentiality to grow and expand in gross block, sales and net profit. The actual Blue Chip Companies like Colgate, Hindustan Lever, SPIC, L & T etc., have a consistent record of dividend pay outs, growth in dividends, expansion and bonus from time to time. The main characteristics of the Blue Chip Companies may be set out as follows: Reliance, I.T.C., Infosys etc. are examples.

1. These companies belong to the Industry groups which are in general expanding and growing.
2. They are market leaders as in the case of Indian hotels in the Hotel Industry, ACC in Cement Industry, Hero Honda in Scooter Industry and Colgate in Tooth Paste Industry.
3. These Companies show capacity to diversify and grow and generate larger gross block, higher sales turnover and growing profit margins. They continuously expand the capital base in terms of debt or equity or rights etc.
4. They have purposeful tax planning and consistent modernisation and expansion plans. They have the capacity to meet the emerging challenges like input or labour problems.
5. The Management outlook is dynamic and their vision is ambitious expansionism. They are highly aggressive leaders in the Industry.
6. They have also commitments to research and development and are quick to adopt new Technologies and lower costs and rise profits. They have reputed foreign collaborators to back them up.

Growth Shares

Such companies are very attractive to the long-term Investors as the return to the equity shareholders in such companies are continuously expanding due to dividends, growth in dividends, networth, bonus and rights etc. Besides in view of the consistent good performance, detailed monitoring by Investors of such companies may not be necessary. They are a good hedge against inflation and rising costs. The Investor is also benefitted by capital appreciation or capital gains and by multiplying his original investment in a short period of time. The Investor has only to identify such scrips and make long-term investment in them which will ensure steady return on their investment, safety, marketability and continued capital appreciation, regular dividends, rights, bonus shares etc.

The examples of such growth shares which should be included in the portfolio of every investor are Bajaj Auto and Telco in automobiles, Tisco in Steel Industry, East India Hotels in Hotel Industry, CEAT Tyres and Apollo Tyres in Tyre Industry, Brooke Bond and Tata Tea in Tea Industry, Britannia in Food Industry etc.

Cyclical Shares

Other categories of shares are Cyclical shares whose fortunes may depend upon the business cycle and trading like shipping, fertilisers, tea and machine tools etc. They make sometime huge profits and sometimes poor profits depending on the Cycles of business and trade.

Defensive Shares

Another category of companies is defensive shares whose prices are stable and do not fluctuate widely. Normally they pay regular dividends within a narrow range and have standard practices of Ploughing back profits and declaration of modest dividends. These are defensive shares whose dividends are stable and profits and profitability are expanding but at a consistent and slow rate. Many plantations and cotton Textiles come in this category.

Discount Shares

Besides there is a a category of discount shares whose prices are depressed due to low profits but with a hope of higher profitability in the immediate future due to the change in the management or in Government Policies or due to new technological changes. Among the Companies in this group, there may be many undervalued groups whose potentialities for growth are high and therefore they are called Turn-around Companies, or emerging Blue Chips. The category of Blue Chips emerge out of corporate performance and can be attributed to rich parentage arising from foreign collaborators or foreign technicians, ambitious and driving promoters, unique products, special technologies, marketing strategies, management reputation, etc. Pasupati Acrylon and Amar Raja Batteries, Hotel Leela etc., are some examples, which can show signs of growth.

NET FINANCIAL RESULTS AND PROFITABILITY

The Company's Balance Sheet reflects the Financial position of a company at a point of time, while its Income-Expenditure Account presents the picture of its physical operations over a period of say one year. So the Balance Sheet and its Income Expenditure Statement are related closely and the combined net position of the latter is transferred to the Balance Sheet in the form of residual profits or losses shown in liabilities or assets of the company.

A study of the corporate performance over a period of time is thus possible through the Balance Sheet Analysis. The assets and liabilities in Balance Sheet and of Income and Expenditure Statement are to be studied together.

It will be seen from the proforma table on Income and Expenditure that Gross Operating Profit reflects the Financial results of the Physical Operations. The Net Profits are the true residual profits to be passed on to the Balance Sheet after meeting the required payments of interest and taxes and providing for depreciation. But cash profits or net cash earnings include the net profit plus depreciation as the depreciation provision keeps the funds with the company only and it is only a book entry.

INCOME AND EXPENDITURE STATEMENT (For the Year Ended ....)	
Income	*Expenditure*
Sales	Materials consumed
Other Income	+ Excise Duty
Total	+ Manufacturing Expenses
	+ Other Factory Expenses Like Factory Wages
	Total Factory Cost
Sales - Factory Cost = Gross Operating Profit	
Gross Operating Profit	Salaries & Wages of Staff
	+ Administrative Expenses
	+ Selling and Distribution Expenses
	Total Non-Factory Cost or Selling Expenses

Gross Operating Profit - Non-Factory Costs =	Earnings Before Interest, Depreciation and Taxes (EBIDT) = Gross Profit
Gross Profits (EBIDT)	= Profits after meeting Factory Cost and Non-Factory Expenses
Net Profit (PAT)	= EBIDT - Interest, Depreciation and Taxes.

Corporate Performance

The long-term Investors prefer mostly companies with a solid past performance and continued good performance in future. Such companies are called growth companies, or Blue Chip Companies. Of the factors which influence the share prices, the most important one is corporate fundamentals, namely, company's intrinsic worth, net asset value or book value. The corporate performance is thus the single largest force, influencing share price. This is studied by the ratio analysis referred to below, funds flow analysis — namely sources and use of funds — and trend analysis of growth rates of important parameters like sales, gross block etc.

Corporate performance depends on a number of variables, both internal and external to the company. The major internal factors are: *(i)* efficiency of capital use *(ii)* productivity of total capital employed *(iii)* Growth of Gross Block and its capacity utilisation *(iv)* Sales turnover and operational efficiency *(v)* Profitability of the operations *(vi)* return on capital employed *(vii)* expansion plans and internal reserves built up and *(viii)* Tax planning and accounting practices etc.

All the above factors are reflected and measured in Financial Ratios, referred to below — growth rates of major assets and liabilities and operational ratios measuring the profitability and profit allocation.

Selected Ratios	Their Use
1. *Capital Cost Ratios* Ex: Cost of Debt Capital/Cost of Equity Capital	For Capital Structure Analysis — methods of Financing the project.
2. *Leverage Ratios* Ex: Debt/Equity ratio, or Borrowed Capital/ Total Capital employed.	Long-term stability of the company — leverage enjoyed by owned Capital through borrowed funds.
3. *Solvency Ratios* Ex: Total long-term debt to total owned funds, Total liabilities to total shareholders' equity.	Long-term solvency and Company's Financial ability to fulfill the obligations of repayments and expenses involved.
4. *Liquidity Ratios* Ex: Current Ratio, Acid Test Ratio — Current Asset to Current Liabilities.	Company's Financial position in the short run and the capacity to meet short run obligations.
5. *Turnover Ratios* Ex: Fixed Assets to Sales Sundry Debtors to Sales Inventory Turnover Ratio (cost of goods sold to total Inventory).	Efficiency of the use of Capital and operational efficiency in keeping high sales relative to fixed capital and management efficiency in collecting debts and keep low inventory to sales.
6. *Profitability Ratios* Gross profits to sales operating profits to sales Net profits to Equity Capital/ or to total owned funds.	Measures the profitability relative to sales, and relative to capital invested indicates the efficiency of management to generate profits against sales, or capital employed.

7. *Capital Efficiency Ratios* Gross Block/Equity Sales/Equity or Sales/ Capital employed.	Measures the efficient use of owned funds or all Capital employed.
8. *Debt Servicing Ratios* Interest payments to total net earnings Total debt servicing to total gross earnings.	Measures the efficiency on the use of Capital, particularly debt Capital, capacity to service Capital borrowed through earnings.
9. *Profit Allocation Ratios* Equity dividends to Net Profits All dividends to Net Profits — Tax and depreciation as % age of Gross Profits.	Profitability of operations – not profits and their use – Management policy of dividend distribution, expansion plans, consistency in dividend distribution, bonus payments, Retention Policy etc.

10. *Overall Performance of Company*

$$\frac{\text{Gross Block}}{\text{Equity}} \times \frac{\text{Sales}}{\text{Gross Block}} \times \frac{\text{Net Profits}}{\text{Sales}} = \frac{\text{Net Profits}}{\text{Equity}}$$

(Capital use) (Turnover Efficiency) (Profitability) = (Return on Investment)

11. Comparison of Growth Rates of Gross Block, Sales, Gross Profits, etc., so as to know the efficient use of Capital and the Growth of Capital relative to sales reflecting the optimal use of capacity and profitability of operations.
12. *Investor Valuation of Company*

    Earnings per share, Book value per share, Net Asset value per share, Break down value of Equity Share, P/E Ratio, or payback period of Investments.
13. *Management Rating*

    Measured by their honesty, integrity, keeping up to schedules of project construction or fulfilling the sales target or Gross Profit margin, Consistency in dividend distribution, bonus payments, expansion plans and Tax Planning.

How to Locate Emerging Blue Chips?

Research on the Companies' operations and their financial result is necessary for locating Emerging Blue Chips. This can be done through fundamental analysis which helps us to decide what to buy and what to sell. This research has to be both on the desk and on the field. On the desk, the financial results and Balance Sheets have to be examined to locate the potentiality of companies to emerge as turnaround companies. *Prima facie,* such companies, have been in losses for a year or two but due to some expected management changes leading to higher capacity utilisation or due to new projects in the last phase of completion, these Companies show the potentiality for turning into profitable projects in the coming year or two. Research on the field is to interview the officers of the Companies, visit to the plant and secure the opinions of the experts, suppliers, stockists, etc. This fundamental analysis is to be supplemented by Technical analysis to decide on when to buy and when to sell.

Some Companies may be building up Gross Block due to expansion and diversification but sales are not rising fast enough due to low capacity utilisation. Then the Company may not be making adequate profits to service investors temporarily. A few companies may have both gross block and sales rising but Gross Profit margin is low due to high costs of manufacture or sale and due to inefficiency of management. Any changes in policy to improve efficiency or improvements in Technology may be expected to increase the profits and the company may be in the process of growth as a Blue Chip Company. Here are some examples of turnaround companies, or emerging Blue Chip Companies: Amar Raja Battery, Hotel Leela Venture etc., are some examples of turn-around companies which have come out to be growth companies.

The expertise of the analyst lies in locating the emerging Blue Chips. Shri N.J. Yasaswy has in book "Emerging Blue Chips", identified 177 highfliers for the year 1992-93. But these Blue Chips of yesteryears are no longer the Blue Chips of today. Similarly, there is no guarantee that the Blue Chips of today will be the Blue Chips of tomorrow. Thus for long in the eighties, Scrips like Reliance, Orkay, Century etc., were the Blue Chips. In the nineties, the Essar Gujarat, Videocon, Finolex etc. took over the lead, and so on.

Established Blue Chips

For a conservative investor, established growth Stocks with an assured return are attractive. These companies are leaders in the Industry, like Reliance and Raymonds in the Textiles and TISCO in Steel etc. They have a strong capital base net worth, well established financial position, organised and professionalised management. They reward the investor with uninterrupted dividends, steady rise in Capital values and bonus from time to time or rights or other privileges. Such Companies are worth holding for long and are recommended in all the portfolios of Investors. The risk of holding such scrips is low and their Betas are generally around the market Betas and their rewards are generally above average performance of the market. Investors in such Blue Chips as TISCO, Colgate, Glaxo etc., have benefitted by regular dividends and bonus shares.

The characteristics of established Blue Chips are as follows:

1. *Management Rating:* Highly professionalised and efficient management. Reputed for honesty and integrity. Financial practices and accounting are consistent and dependable.

2. *Gross Profit Margin* and Sales turnover are high and the company captured a substantial chunk of market demand. The quality and after sales service are the strong points of the company and they are one of the leaders in the Industry.

3. *Dividend Record*: The company has been making continuous profits of which a resonable dividend is declared. A prudent policy of ploughing back profits for expansion and diversification is also pursued.

4. The company's net worth is high relative to equity and is expanding year after year. The leverage enjoyed by equity through long-term borrowings (debt) is also high. Their long-term solvency is rated high.

5. The current liability position is also strong. Their current assets cover their current liabilities including contingent liabilities by more than twice, and their sales management is such that inventory holding is always optimal. Their sales and distribution strategies are sound and cash efficient.

6. The Company has expansion and diversification plans for future growth as reflected in the rise in net worth and gross block. Such expansion plans are accompanied by Tax planning so as to conserve resources for growth. Alternatively the company is already diversified and has still expansion plans.

7. The management has a vision for the future of the company and their policy is ambitious expansion and growth. The policies adopted are result-oriented and efficiently executed.

8. The company's net worth is growing due to ploughed back profits and funds are available for bonus payments to satisfy the Investors from time to time.

9. The market price of such shares is rising consistently and steadily and any possible fall in price is small and temporary. The price fluctuations are narrow and the long-term trend of its price is upwards.

10. The company has earned a reputation for fair practices and their servicing of Investors through dividends, bonus allotments, share transfer etc., is generally rated good.

In the category of Blue Chips, mention may be made of Colgate, L & T, Tata Tea, Glaxo and TISCO whose selected financial ratios are to be studied. Those for Tisco and Rehiance are presented here.

A case study of a company which is not a blue chip, namely Finolex is given at the end of the chapter.

An example in respect of TISCO is given below:

FINANCIAL RATIO ANALYSIS

Name of Company: Tata Iron & Steel Co. Ltd. (March end)

Sr. No.	Particulars	1990	1991	1992	1993	1994	1995	1996	1999	2005	2007	2009
1.	Equity (Rs. crores)	229.43	229.89	230.12	2780.45	335.21	336.87	367.23	368	366	380	6203
2.	Networth (Rs. crores)	1332.54	1424.11	1545.00	1986.39	2524.74	2688.04	3742.4	4131	7081	14474	30,176
3.	Earning per share (Rupees)	6.15	6.95	6.55	4.57	5.39	8.34	16.2	7.67	8.6	7.3	8.3
4.	P/E Ratio	19.06	24.46	55.00	64.47	57.64	39.65	13.0	20.6	6.0	7.9	57.8
5.	Book Value per share (Rupees)	57.93	61.89	70.96	71.34	75.32	79.79	102.0	112.0	192.0	249	46.7
6.	Dividend (%)	30%	31%	35%	25%	30%	35%	45%	40%	130%	155%	155%

Face value was changed from Rs. 100 to Rs. 10 in 1990.

Reliance Industries Ltd. (RIL) is an excellant example of growth oriented Blue Chip Company, with a good weightage in the Sensex BSE Price Index. The key financial indicators of this company are presented below for illustration.

Particulars	1985	1995-96	2000-01	2004-05	2005-06	2008-09
Equity (Rs. in crores)	52	458	1,053	1,393	1,393	1,574
Net Worth (Rs. in crores)	311	8,405	14,765	40,403	49,804	1,26,373
Book Value Per Share (in Rs.)	29.5	89.5	140.1	289.9	357.4	798
EPS (in Rs.)	6.9	14.0	25.1	54.2	67.4	98.8
P/E Ratio	17.4	21.4	39.1	54.6	55.0	13.7
Dividend %	50	60	42.5	75.0	100	130%
Debt Equity Ratio	1.66:1	0.49:1	0.72:1	0.46:1	0.44:1	0.63:1

Source: Balance Sheets and Profit and Loss Accounts of the Respective Companies.

The consistency of growth and strength is evident from the data and similar studies on other companies are encouraged for the purpose of analysis by readers.

Case Study on Share Valuation of a Company

Example: **Finolex Industries Ltd.**

This is a listed company, listed in the "others" group of B_1 and B_2 categories and has been in operations for the last 26 years. It is neither a growth company nor a Blue Chip, but stable profit making company, with manufacture of PVC Resin and PVC pipes and fittings. This is chosen to represent an average company.

Its Financials are briefly set out below: *year 2006-07*

	Rs. Crores			*Rs. Crores*	*2007-08*
Equity	124	Income	1072		1435
Net worth	529	Expenditure	970		1333
Book value	Rs. 42.6	Gross Profit	102		102
Current ratio	1 : 1.5	Net Profit		**68**	71
Debt Equity ratio	1 : 3.8	**Selected Ratios**			
Debt	479	Profitability Ratio			
Net Profits	70	(PAT) = $\frac{N.P.}{Sales} = \frac{68}{1072}$		**6.3%**	5%
Sales	1072	Capital turnover			
Net Profit to Sales	6.5%	$\frac{GB}{Equity} = \frac{659}{124} =$		**5.3**	
Market Price H/L	103/65	Sales turnover			
(Average MP) =	84	$\frac{Sales}{G.B} = \frac{1071}{659} =$		**1.6**	2.2
EPS	5.6				6
P/E ratio	14.6				9.3
Dividend	30%				30%

The Market P/E ratio is 20 - 21, while market price is 4 to 5 times higher than Book value for the last three years, in general.

While we are looking at the share price valuation, we have to keep an eye on the future of the company performance. Short-term solvency represented by current ratio is good at 1 : 1.55, but it could be better say 1 : 2.

The long-term solvency as reflected by debt equity ratio 1 : 3.8, which is high risk scenario but taking the debt versus the owned funds of shareholders, then the ratio improves to 1 : 1.1, which shows good solvency. It's profit margin is however low at 5 to 6%.

The company's market price is Rs. 84 which is around twice the book value. But the market's comparable ratio is higher at five times in 2007. Besides, the company's P/E multiple is only 14.6, while the market potential is about 21 times. By all these criteria, the M.P. of the share is undervalued at Rs. 84. But this is justified by its relatively low profitability, despite strong fundamentals in terms of owned funds, gross block and divident performances.

Its gross block is nearly 5 times its equity, but is equal to the owned funds or slightly more than the owned funds. It's reliance on debt is also moderate, but not heavy. It has built up reserves which is nearly four times the equity. Its sales to gross block is 1 : 1.62 indicating that sales are high but not too high. Its sales turnover not very high, but the capital turnover is high. As seen above, the profit margin being moderate to low, the company's share price could not go up beyond twice the book value. Out of the factors to be considered, the negative factors of the future are more than the positive factors, which might have kept the market price of the share at a reasonably low figure. This company's performance has to be viewed against the industry background, PVC pipes and fittings which have no high growth prospects.

Despite its good fundamentals, the Finolex company does not seem to have good future, as reflected by the past performance. For the year 2008-09, The company had a loss of Rs. 59 crores as against net profits of Rs. 71 crore in 2007-08. It has also deferred tax liabilities of Rs. 22 crore. Its market price fell to Rs. 56 as in Febraury 2010, as against Rs. 84 in 2007. The present performance and the prospects for the future are bleak and hence it does not seem to be a good company to hold or to buy.

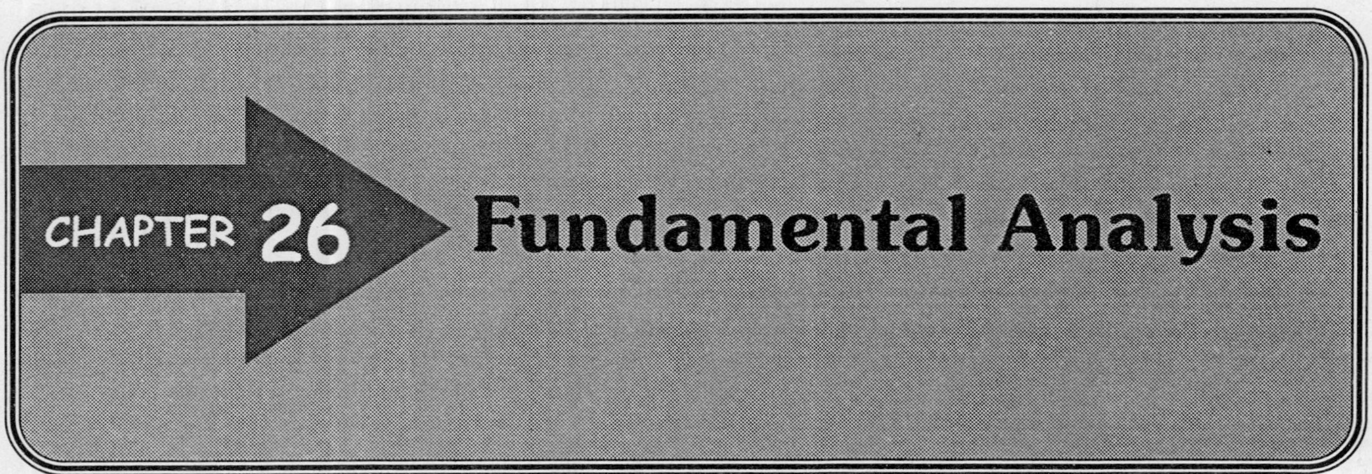

Fundamental Analysis

Influence of the Economy

Companies are a part of the industrial and business sector, which in turn is a part of the overall economy. Thus, the performance of a company depends on the performance of the economy in the first place. If the economy is in recession or stagnation, *ceteris paribus,* the performance of companies will be bad in general, with some exceptions however. On the other hand, if the economy is booming, incomes are rising and the demand is good, then the industries and the companies in general may be prosperous, with some exceptions however.

In the Indian economy, the matters to be considered in the first place are the behaviour of the monsoon and the performance of agriculture. As agriculture is the mainstay of the 60% of the population and contributes nearly 17% of the output of the economy, it is important for the assessment and forecast of industrial performance. If the monsoon is good and agricultural incomes rise, the demand for industrial products and services will be good and industry prospers.

Secondly, India has a mixed economy, where the public sector plays a vital role. The Government being the biggest investor and spender, the trends in public investment and expenditure would indicate the likely performance of the Indian economy. Concomitant with this, the government budget policy, tax levies and government borrowing programme along with the extent of deficit financing will have a major influence on the performance of the Indian economy, as these influence the demand and incomes of the people. The changes in excise and customs duties, corporate taxes, etc. are all relevant to assess the trends in the economy as they have an impact on the industry and the companies.

Thirdly, the monetary policy and trends in money supply which mainly depend on the government's budget policy, its borrowing from the public and credit from the banks and the RBI, have a major impact on the industrial growth through the cost and availability of credit, the profit margins of the companies etc. The monetary situation along with the budgetary policy influences the movement in price level (inflation) and interest rates. The tight money position, increasing budget deficits and RBI creation of currency lead to an inflationary spiral. Although some interest rates in the organised financial system are now freed, the bazaar rates in the unorganised market do reflect the availability of funds in the free markets. So interest rates in the free markets and the degree of inflation do have a major influence on the economy and the performance of the industries. Although a mild inflation is good for business psychology, higher degrees of inflation, particularly in two digits, will defeat all business planning, lead to cost escalations and squeeze on profit margins. These will adversely affect the performance of industry and companies.

Fourthly, the general business conditions in the form of business cycles or the level of business activity do influence the demand for industrial products and the performance of the industry. In India, there are no business cycles but outputs do fluctuate depending upon the state of the economy, performance of agriculture, availability of power and other infrastructural products including oil, etc., imported inputs and a host of other factors. These factors do influence the costs and profit margins of companies from both demand and supply sides. The business earnings and profits are affected by such changes in business conditions.

Fifthly, the economic and political stability in the form of stable and long-term economic polices and a stable political system with no uncertainty would also be necessary for a good performance of the economy in general and of companies in particular. The Government regulations being all-pervasive in India, the government policy has to be known in advance in all its aspects and there should be no uncertainty about the political system as economic and political factors are interlinked. Political uncertainties and adverse changes in government policy do adversely affect industrial growth. Government policy relating to projects, clearance for foreign collaboration and foreign investment, price and distribution controls, and listing requirements on stock exchanges and a host of other matters like import restrictions do affect the performance of companies. The foreign exchange position and the balance of payments situation at any time would also indicate the rigours of government policy with regard to imports, exports, foreign investment and related matters.

All the above factors of the economy influence the corporate performance and the industry in general. In any investment analysis, a broad picture of these factors and a forecast of the growth of the economy and of industry would be necessary to decide when to invest and what to invest in. The performance of the economy is noticed in the Economic Survey of the Goverment of India, CMIE estimates and RBI Reports, etc. Industry Reports are available with Industry Associations, Chambers of Commerce, CII Reports and The Ministries of Industries and Commerce, Govt. of India, in their Annual Reports.

Economy vs. Industry and Company

At any stage in the economy, there are some industries which are growing while others are declining. The performance of companies will depend among other things upon the state of the industry as a whole and the economy. If the industry is prosperous, the companies, within the industries may also be prosperous although a few may be in a bad shape. The performance of a company is thus a function not only of the industry and of the economy, but more importantly, on its own performance. The share price of the company is empirically found to depend up to 50% on the performance of the industry and economy. The economic and political situation in the country has thus a bearing on the prospects of the company.

There are different phases in the economy such as boom, depression, recession, etc. The performance of the economy in India is not cyclical as in the case of developed countries exhibiting business cycles, as the Indian economy depends basically on the monsoon and the growth rate of agriculture. Besides, with a huge public sector in our mixed economy, the performance of the five-year plan, yearly public investment, government expenditure and a host of other factors influence the economy, industry and company. Thus one important factor is the fiscal policy which incorporates government expenditure and taxation, borrowing, deficit financing, etc. and which influences both the public and private sectors in the economy. The industrial growth in general and of infrastructural industries in particular influence the corporate performance.

As referred to earlier at any stage in the economy, there are some industries growing fast while others are declining. The performance of companies will depend among other things upon the state of the industry as a whole. If the industry is prosperous, the companies, within the industries may also be prosperous, if the economy is also doing well. The performance of a company is thus a function of the industry and of the economy, in addition to its own performance. (Fig. 26.1)

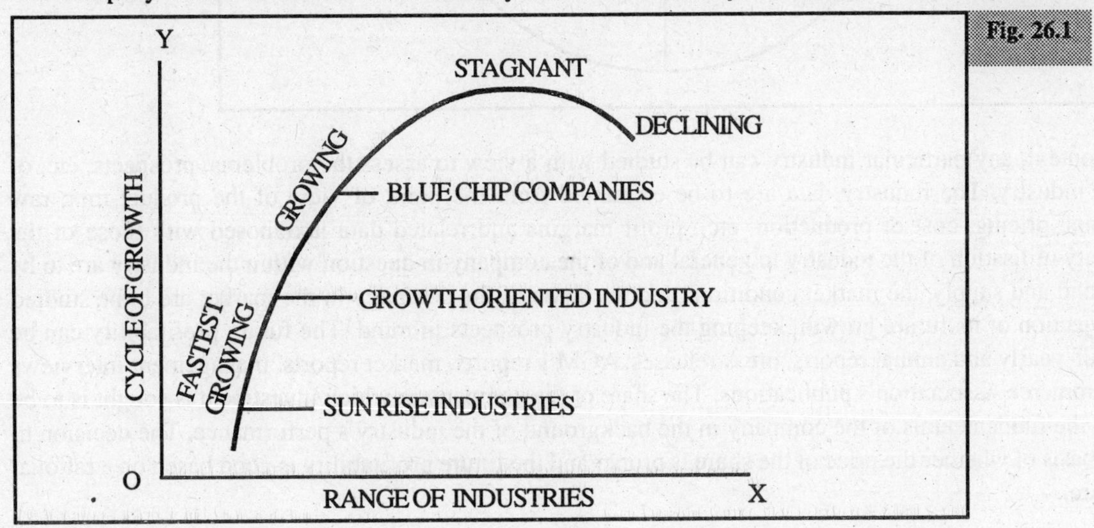

Fig. 26.1

As referred to earlier, the share price of the company is empirically found to depend upto 50% on the performance of the industry and economy. The economic and political situation in the country has thus a bearing on the prospects of the company. The industries in different stages of growth are shown below: (Fig. 26.2)

Fig. 26.2

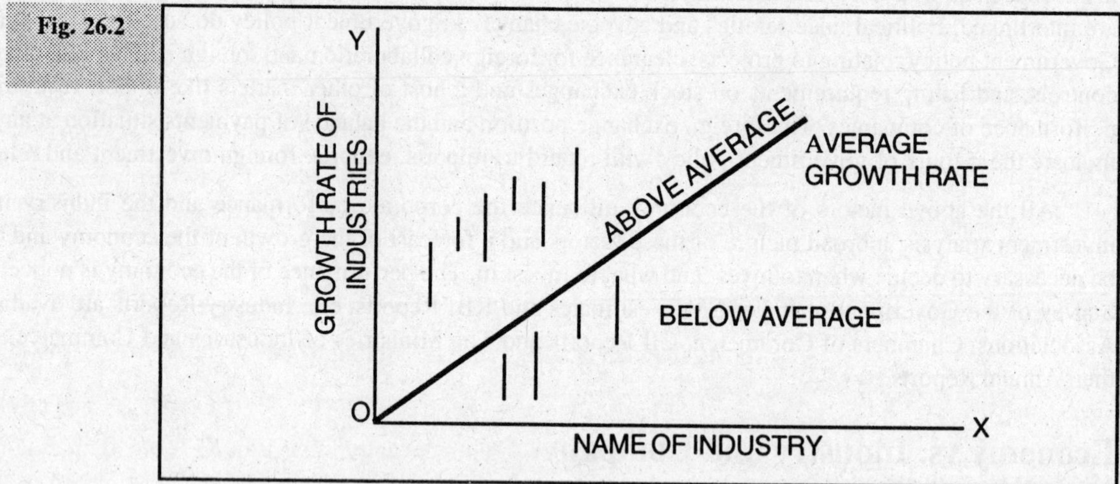

Even in industries of above average growth, there may be some companies of poor growth or no growth at all. The fundamentals of the company will explain this. The Market Price of any company's share is a function of intrinsic factors to the extent of about ½ of it and the rest is accounted by the expectations, psychological and sentimental factors, as shown below.

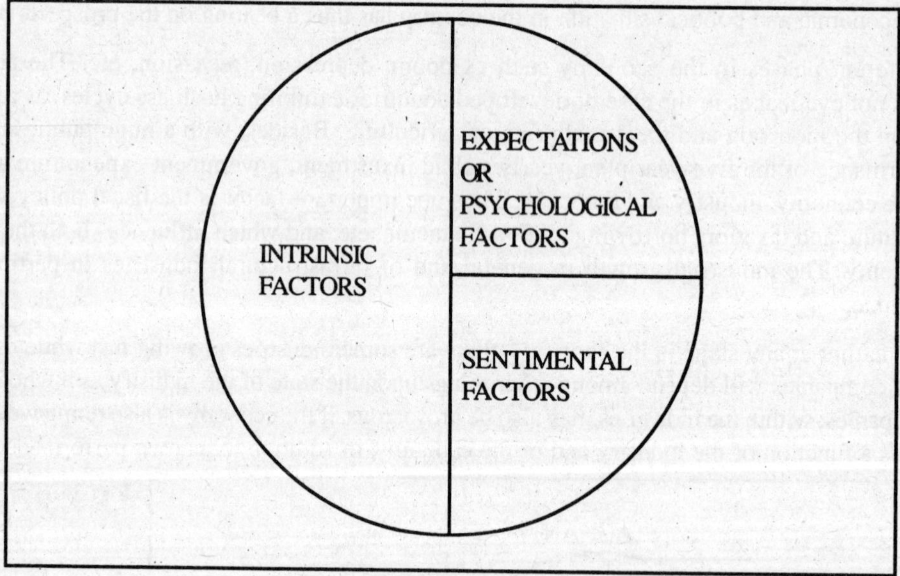

In the above context, any particular industry can be studied with a view to assess the problems, prospects, etc. of the company in the industry. The industry data are to be examined from the point of view of the product-mix, raw materials, components, pricing, cost of production, etc., profit margins and related data juxtaposed with those of the company. The capacity utilisation of the industry in general and of the company in question within the industry are to be compared. The demand and supply, the market conditions and the share of the company in the market are to be studied before making a projection of its future growth, keeping the industry prospects in mind. The future profitability can be assessed from the half-yearly and annual reports, press releases, AGM's reports, market reports, management interviews and Industry and Commerce Association's publications. The share of the company in which investment is sought is to be analysed in terms of the fundamentals of the company in the background of the industry's performance. The decision to buy has to be on the basis of whether the price of the share is proper and the future profitability is good based on a rational forecast for the future.

We have to consider the quantifiable factors and qualitative factors of the company. Among the quantifiable factors we have to consider the capital efficiency and the sales turnover and the profitability margins. The quantifiable data are based on financial statement Analysis, referred to in an earlier chapter.

The qualitative factors are:

(a) Management efficiency,

(b) Rating of promoters,

(c) Rating of collaborators,

(d) Uniqueness of the product,

(e) Location, government policy and patronage, etc.

The industrial position not only depends upon the economic growth but on the nature of the industry itself. Within the industry, the factors which have to be taken into account are the product-mix, the various outputs, nature of the products, inputs and raw materials, installed capacity of the industry — utilisation of capacity — the market nature of the inputs, their domestic availability and the problems of the industry in general. The pricing and the Government controls on prices, distribution, etc., controls on imports and tax policy, excise and customs duties, etc. would influence the cost of production and the profit margins of the industry, as also the prospects of growth. In the area of market, the demand for the products produced and the prospects for exports, protection or tariff preferences, etc. influence the prospects of the industry. In many industries, the raw materials and other inputs and their availability domestically, particularly of electricity, have a major influence on the market from the point of view of supply. Labour conditions in the industry should also be looked into and have a bearing on growth prospects.

In the company analysis, the financial highlights of the companies, which are influenced by the industry and the economy are the capacity utilisation, demand, cost and profit margins. The state of the capital market and the capacity to raise capital from the market not only depend on the performance of the companies but of the economy and the industry as well. The fundamentals of the company are to be analysed in terms of its financial structure, leverage, liquidity and profitability, financial viability, etc. The information for this purpose is to be secured from the annual reports of the company, balance sheets, press reports, AGM's reports, management's press releases and the publications of the Industry and Commerce Associations.

The most important variable influencing the company's performance is management, namely, the quality, capability, popularity and integrity of the management. Generally, the rating of the promoters and management has to be looked into through their plans, financial management, growth orientation, expansion plans, tax planning, R & D, technology, etc. The popularity of the management is known from their track record, retention policy, distribution of dividends and bonus, etc. The honesty and integrity of the management can be seen from the shareholding pattern and the availability of floating stock and the liquidity of shares of the company. In the area of financial management, companies' financial structure, retention policy, dividend record, bonus policy and liquidity ratios, etc. are to be looked into. The market capitalisation of a share is to be compared with the book value and the intrinsic worth of the company. The share has to be examined to know whether it is properly priced and reflects its true intrinsic value. The P/E ratio and earnings per share, book value, etc. are to be looked into in this context. Only shares which are underpriced are to be generally purchased, provided they have the potential for growth and capital appreciation.

In the above context, any particular industry can be studied with a view to assess the problems, prospects, etc. of the company in the industry. The industry data are to be examined from the point of view of the installed capacity and its utilisation, raw materials, components, pricing, cost of production, etc., profit margins and related data juxtaposed with those of the company. The capacity utilisation of the industry in general and of the company in question within the industry are to be compared. The demand and supply, the market conditions and the share of the company in the market are to be studied before making a projection of its future growth, keeping the industry prospects in mind. The future profitability can be assessed from the half-yearly and annual reports, press releases, AGM's reports, market reports, management interviews and Industry and Commerce Association's publications. The stock of the company in which investment is sought is to be analysed in terms of the fundamentals of the company in the background of the industry's performance. The decision to buy has to be on the basis of whether the price of the share is proper and the future profitability is good based on a rational forecast for the future.

To examine the financial highlights, we have to consider among other things, the capital efficiency and the sales turnover and the profitability margins. For this purpose, the following components may be taken into account:

$$\underset{\text{(Capital turnover)}}{\frac{\text{GB}}{\text{Equity}}} \times \underset{\text{(Sales turnover)}}{\frac{\text{Sales}}{\text{GB}}} \times \underset{\text{(Profitability)}}{\frac{\text{GP}}{\text{Sales}}} = \frac{\text{GP}}{\text{Equity}}$$

Normally, a company uses capital efficiently by having a high turnover of equity. Similarly, the use of capital is efficient if there is a high sales turnover to gross block. The company may have only a small profit margin but if the sales turnover is high, the profits will also be high. Gross profts-to-sales ratio measures the profit margins. In this context, the growth of gross block, sales, equity, and gross profits are to be analysed in respect of each company within the industry. On this basis, these ratios of companies within the industry are to be compared with the industry's overall operating performance in respect of the variables referred to earlier. The gross profit (GP) is also to be examined in relation to the market capitalisation. The riskless return is 12% and a reasonable return is 15%. Depreciation, taxes, etc. may account for another 15%. A total return in the form of gross profit of not less than 30% is, therefore, to be expected from any company to start with. If a company in any industry is less profitable than that, it is not worth the purchase. Similarly, gross profit to gross block and the dividend policy, earning per share and bonus payouts are all to be examined from the point of view of the future prospects of the company in the background of industry performance and possible capital appreciation of the shares.

Industry Analysis

At any point of time, there may be industries which are on the upswing of the cycle called sunshine industries and those which are on the decline called sunset industries. In India, there are some growth industries like electronics and communications which are the key industries. The engineering, petro-chemicals and capital goods industries are in the core sector. A few industries like diamonds, engineering, etc. are in the export sector. Jute and cotton textiles are the decadent industries. At present, Tele Communications, Computer Software, energy etc. are some examples of Sunrise Industries.

As referred to earlier, performance of a company has been found to depend broadly up to 50% on the external factors of the economy and industry. These externalities depend on the availability of inputs, like proper labour, water, power and inter-relations between the economy and industry and the company. It is, in this context, that a well-diversified company performs better than a single product company, because while the demand for some products may be declining, that for others may be increasing. Similarly, the input prices and cost factors would vary from product line to product line, leading to different margins and a diversified company is a better bet for investor.

The industry analysis should take into account the following factors among others as influencing the performance of the company, whose shares are to be analysed:

1. *Product Line:* The position of the industry in the life cycle of its growth — initial stages, high growth stages and maturing stages are to be noted. It is also necessary to know the industries with a high growth potential like computers, electronics, chemicals, diamonds, etc. and whether the industry is in the priority sector or the key industry group or capital goods or consumer goods groups. The importance attached by the government in their policy and of the Planning Commission in their assessment of these industries is to be studied. Product may be new one or an import substitution product which has good future.

2. *Raw Material and Inputs:* Under this head, we have to look into industries depending on imports of scarce raw materials, competition from other companies and industries, and the barriers to entry of a new company, protection from foreign competition, import and export restrictions, etc. An industry which has a limited supply of materials domestically and where imports are restricted, for example, will have dim growth prospects. Labour is also an input and industries with labour problems may have difficulties of growth.

3. *Capacity Installed and Utilised:* The demand for industrial products in the economy is estimated by the Planning Commission and the government, and the units are given licensed capacity on the basis of these estimates. If the demand

is rising as expected and the market is good for the products, the utilisation of capacity will be higher. If, however, the quality of the product is poor, competition is high and there are other constraints to the availability of inputs and there are labour problems, then the capacity utilisation will be low and profitability will be poor.

4. *Industry Characteristics:* Whether the industry is cyclical, fluctuating or stable, has to be looked into first, as the prospects for growth will depend on this to an extent. If the demand is seasonal as in the case of fertilisers, pesticides, etc., their problems may mar the growth prospects. If it is consumer product and the demand is all over India, freight charges are an important component of the cost of production. The scale of production and the width of the market would also determine the selling and advertisement costs. The nature of the industry would thus be an important factor for determining the scale of operations and profitability. The growth prospects would depend on raw materials, easy access to inputs, particularly power, transport and other infrastructual facilities.

5. *Demand and Market:* The demand for the product should be expanding and its price should not be controlled by the government, if the industry is to have good prospects of profitability. If the demand is income-elastic and price-elastic, the supplier should be able to sell the goods at a going rate and the prospects of growth are good. It is also important that the prices of raw materials and other input costs like freight, electricity, etc. should not be controlled by the government. The demand should also be growing and there should be export demand for the product. If the nature of the product is such as drugs, fertilisers or other consumer goods, whose price and distribution are controlled by the government, the growth prospects would be less. Thus, decontrol of cement recently has helped the cement industry to grow and expand.

6. *Government Policy with Regard to Industry:* The government policy is announced in the Industrial Policy Resolutions and subsequent announcements from time to time by the government. The policy can also be seen from the strategy as laid down in the five-year plans and importance given to the industry by the Planning Commission and the expected demand in the economy. The Plan priorities for the industry, the physical and financial targets of investment and foreign collaboration in that industry are important variables affecting its fortunes. The government has powers of control over industry in terms of output, price and distribution of the product and a number of other aspects. The government policy with regard to granting of clearances, installed capacity and reservation of the products for small industry, etc. are also factors to be considered for industrial analysis. The recent delicensing of the TV, VCR and consumer durables have boosted the prospects of these industries.

7. *Labour and other Industrial Problems:* The industry, whether it is capital-intensive or labour-intensive, has to use labour of different categories and expertise. The productivity of labour as much as the capital efficiency would determine the progress of the industry. If there are problems of labour, strikes, lockouts and poor productivity, that industry should be unwelcome for the investors. The best example is banking, where labour productivity has been improving recently after deregulation.

There are some decaying industries, like jute and cotton textiles, whose shares are to be avoided by the investors unless such companies are diversified into other lines as in the case of Birla Jute. Certain industries with problems of marketing like high storage costs, high transport costs, dependence on foreign markets etc. as in the case of fertilisers, tea, etc. may have poor growth potential and investors have to be careful when investing in such companies.

8. *Management*: An industry with many problems may be well-managed, if the promoters and the management are efficient and capable of steering the company through difficult days. Such management like Tatas, Birlas, Ambanis etc. who have a reputation, built up their companies on strong foundations. The management has to be assessed in terms of their capabilities, popularity, honesty and integrity. In the case of new industries and new managements, there will be no track record and the investors have to carefully assess the project reports and the assessment of financial institutions in this regard. The capabilities of management will depend upon tax planning, innovation of technology, modernisation, expansion of R & D, etc. A management with a broad vision will plan for the expansion and diversification, make tax planning, increase the retained earnings with a consistent dividend policy so that the future expansion plans are put on a sound basis. A good management will also ensure that their shares are well distributed and liquidity of shares is assured and trading is fair and just in the market with no malpractices like cornering of shares or insider trading.

9. *Future Prospects:* Many of the factors of operation in industry are interlinked such as capacity utilisation, demand and markets, government policy, availability of inputs, infrastructure, etc. It is, therefore, necessary to have an overall picture of the industry and to study these problems and prospects. After a study of the past, the future prospects of the

industry are to be assessed. For this purpose, the projected demand, input availabilities, unutilised capacities, the alternative growth strategies, methods of reducing of cost, economies of scale and the position of competitors in the market are to be probed into. A company has to be assessed in terms of its strategies to meet the challenges as they emerge and its future prospects should be assessed before an investment is made.

Industry Policy Changes

During the recent years (2001-07), a greater thrust was given to FDI inflow into industries and services. An Investment Commission was set up to promote investment in industrial sector and encourage universal access in Telecommunication, I.T., media, bio-technology and other growth oriented sectors. Privatisation was allowed in Airports, Airways and insurance. Greater inflow of FII was encouraged into banks, FIs, etc.

The National Manufacturing Competitiveness Council was set up in 2004-05, to help sustaining the growth in manufacture through better competitiveness and improved productivity. Many task forces were set up as in I.T., power, communications etc., to recommend measures to promote these sectors and their recommendations were being implemented. For the same purpose, customs, excise and other taxes were reduced to the bear minimum on the industrial inputs and capital goods to promote growth of infrastructural industries and growth of exports.

In fundamental analysis, intrinsic worth as reflected by BV or EPS or GPM, etc. is expected to indicate the market price. But in actual practice it is not so. Take the Tyres/Tubes Industry for example. The table below shows how the market prices of similar companies in the same industry do not bear any perceptible relationship to BV, EPS or GPM.

Tyres/Tubes Industry

(In Rupees)

Name of the Company	*Book Value (BV)*	*Market Price (MP)*
Apollo	50.41	150
Govind Rubber	50.13	90
Modi Rubber	63.87	50
Dunlop Rubber	45.83	65
Name of the Company	*EPS*	*MP*
Ceat	10.17	78
J K Industry	10.24	128
Dewan Rubber	11.41	55
Apollo Tyres	11.84	150
Vikrant Tyres	11.86	40
Name of the Company	*GPM*	*MP*
Premier Tyres	7.8	300
Falcon Tyres	7.7	15
Dewan Rubber	7.9	55
Ceat	7.1	78
MRF Tyres	6.9	625

Note: Data relate to 1993, but date is immaterial for illustration.

EXAMPLE OF AN INDUSTRY ANALYSIS

Petro-Chemicals

Product Nature: Petro-chemicals are derived from petroleum and natural gas. The product groups are aromatics, plastics, surfactants, etc.

Raw Materials: Coal tar, intermediates, etc., calcium carbide, alcohol, etc.

Market (Users): Food processing, clothing, housing, health care, automboiles, etc.

Demand Scenario: The first enterprise in the public sector was Indian Petrochemicals Corpn. Ltd. (IPCL) set up in 1979. Demand was poor until 1983. After the pioneering work of IPCL to promote uses, the demand picked up. As per the demand projections of the government, demand and supply gap has persisted and necessitated imports costing more than Rs. 1,000 crores per annum.

Policy of Government: The government has placed petro-chemicals under the core sector as being vital to the national economy. The Planning Commission's study group headed by Abid Hussain has estimated the need for an investment of Rs. 22,000 crores to achieve self-sufficiency by 2000 A.D. The government has sanctioned a number of new projects which were set up such as those of Hindustan Lever, Nirma Chemicals, etc. Already RIL and TNP have set-up projects and there are others also on stream.

Problems of the Industry: (1) Long delays in government clearances and project cost escalations;

(2) Projects established were not of economic size in many cases;

(3) High prices of main feed stock, namely, Naptha;

(4) Need for R & D and introduction of new technologies which are most cost effective; and

(5) High excise duties on Naptha.

Competition: What is the share of the company in question in the total market demand? Soon after IPCL, ABS Plastics began production whose capacity is currently 2000 tonnes p.a. and is expected to be raised to 5000 t.p.a. The main competitors are Polychem with a 30% share in the market. There are others such as Indo-Nippon, Bansali Engineering, etc. The companies in this line with strong fundamentals are ABS Plastics, Gujarat Petrosyl, PIL, NOCIL, Polychem, etc.

Cost Comparisons: The cost per tonne of the Bansali Engineering is three times that of ABS Plastics. ABS and Polychem are leaders in cost-effectiveness. The industry is asking for protection from foreign competition. The ban on exports of petrochemicals may help some units.

Process Comparisons: Mysore Petrochemicals uses Oxelene Oxidation route; Tirumalai Chemicals adopts the benzene route; Rama Petrochemicals uses the alcohol as feed stock, while competitors are using propylene.

Company Analysis

In the case of company analysis, the balance sheet data should be first analysed for:

(1) efficient use of capital;

(2) leverage enjoyed in the use of capital;

(3) return on net worth; and

(4) return on equity.

The capital structure and the cost of different types of capital and the problems of servicing the borrowed funds are to be taken into account. For this purpose, the interest burden, tax and depreciation provision are to be examined. The cash profits and profit after depreciation should be considered in relation to equity and net worth.

The sales turnover is an important indicator of the activity of the company and an assessment of gross profits in relation to sales is to be made. Sales to equity would be high to indicate a good turnover of sales for equity (or NW) employed in the business. The profit margins, earnings per share and P/E ratios will indicate the earning potential of the company for the equityholders.

A fair return on capital employed can be assumed to be 10-15% as the government and public sector bonds give a return of around 13%. A provision for tax and depreciation has to be made at around 15%. These together would account for about 30% as gross profit for a company to be eligible for investment. The gross profits as well as net profits are to be related to the market capitalisation for each company. Besides, the performance of the company analysed has to be compared with that of its competitors in the industry under the following heads:

(1) Cost per unit;

(2) Profit margins;

(3) Earnings per share and P/E ratio;

(4) Bonus payments;

(5) Dividend distribution policy; etc.

The variables to be studied for each company and the relative ratios are set out below:

1. Capital Efficiency = $\frac{GB}{Equity}$ and $\frac{Sales}{GB}$ (GB = Gross Block)

2. Leverage Employed = $\frac{Debt}{Equity}$; $\frac{\text{Borrowed Capital}}{\text{Net Worth}}$

$\frac{\text{Total Borrowed Capital}}{\text{Total Capital Employed}}$

3. Size for the Company — The expansion and growth of the company has to be judged by the growth of sales, assets, gross block and net block.

The growth of the company can also be judged by the rate of growth of any of the above variables while the size of the company has to be judged in terms of its sales, installed capacity utilisation with a view to see that the company is of an economic size.

The profitability of the company is to be judged by the net profits (PAT) or cash profits in relation to sales, equity or net worth, dividend distributed, etc.

The following variables are also to be analysed for a company analysis:

1. Company's share in industry — its capacity utilisation *vis-a-vis* the utilisation in the whole industry.

2. Modernisation and expansion plans — reflected in tax planning, retention policy, bonus policy, etc.

3. Turnover of capital: $\frac{Sales}{GB}$ or $\frac{Sales}{\text{Trading Assets}}$

4. Leverage = $\frac{GB}{NW} = \frac{\text{TotalAssets}}{\text{NWorEquity}}$ or $\frac{Debt}{Equity}$

5. Profitability: $\frac{PAT}{GB}$; $\frac{PAT}{Sales}$

6. Earnings per share, cash earnings per share and P/E ratios.

Need for Forecast

The disadvantage of the above type of analysis is that it is based on the past performance and that it may not be an indicator of future performance. So a forecast is necessary for the coming six months or one year for making an investment. Such a forecast can be made on the basis of some assumptions of costs, prices and demand for its products. The earnings, gross and net profits, the EPS, etc. can be worked out and an assessment can be made whether the scrip is worthwhile purchasing judged by its prospects a year hence.

For making a forecast, some subjective weights may be given to management (50%), expansion and growth (25%), prospects of bonus (15%) and other subjective factors like Government patronage or changes in market conditions (10%). These give a total weight of 100%. Companies in the same industry group can be studied by using the above weights to decide on which scrips to purchase depending on their rating. These weights and consequent judgement will be subjective and the result would depend on the ability and expertise of the analyst.

Guidelines for Investment

A company which has a high intrinsic worth is not necessarily the best stock to buy. It may have no growth prospects or it may be overpriced. Similarly, a company that performs well during any one year may not be the best to buy. On the contrary, a company which has been doing badly for some time might have turned the corner and it may be the best buy, as its shares may be underpriced and it has good prospects of growth. So an analyst should not be guided by one or a few indicators but has to consider the performance of the whole company, and over a period of time, say, 5 years. Besides a company is to be judged in the background of the industry's performance, product nature, prospects of the industry, etc. A study of the industry factors constitutes the industry analysis. Next to economy's performance, industry's performance is vital for an assessment of a company's prospects and growth.

Case Study: Asian Paints

Paint industry growth was at a rate of 12% during the past few years. The industry as a whole will continue its grow at not less than 8-10% rate in the coming years. Asian Paints is the leader in decorative paints, controlling 45% of market segment of the total of Rs. 1,800 crore paints and varnishes industry. In industrial paints, it is the largest player with a market share of 14%.

With a low per capita consumption of paints in our country, it has good future prospects. The prospects for exports are good with an actual export growth of more than 10%. The users in industrial sector, namely, automobiles and its accessories, household appliances and consumer durables etc. are showing prospects of rapid growth. Thus, the potential for the industry both in the domestic and export sector is good.

Asian Paints which is a leader in this industry has an installed capacity of 1.08 lakh T.P.A. of Paints enamels and varnishes. Its gross block grew from Rs. 123 crores in 1993-94 to Rs. 187 crores in 1995-96, due to continuous expansion of capacity. The sales turnover recorded a compound growth rate of 13.5% p.a. during the past five years, while its net profit grew faster by 27.5% during the same period.

This company has many plus factors: (1) Good Collaborator, namely, Chemische Werke HHals A.G Germany for manufacture of Vinyl Pyridine Latex and PPG Industries Inc. USA, for electro deposition coating on automobiles. (2) Product differentiation and brand image is secured by Asian Paints by spending only 1.5% of revenue on advertisements to testing the quality, availability and dependability. (3) Plants well distributed geographically. (4) Six joint collaborations in foreign countries and good export growth. (5) Good stress on R & D for absorption of foreign technologies and their upgradation.

Asian Paints is one of the three winners of the ET — Harvard Business School Association of India awards for its performance in 1994-95. The measures used by them are as follows:

Financial Ratios of the Company	
Gross Profits/Total assets	21.36%
Retained Profits/Net worth	18.24%
Net Profit/Net Worth	25.96%
Growth in Market Cap/Growth in Net worth (over 5 years)	1.60
Cash Flow to Gross Assets	20.64
Source: Balance Sheets.	

Example of Company Analysis

It is necessary to analyse the financial data of the company in the background of the industry performance as shown below:

Company	Debt equity ratio (D/E)	Gross profit to sales (GPM)	Profit after tax to net worth	Book value	Rate of Divi-dend-%	EPS (Rs.)	P/E Ratio	Market Price
Industry	—	10.6	32.3	—	—	—	10.4	—
ABS Plastics	1.82	12.74	45.45	21.0	21%	9.5	8.5	81
Cochin Refineries	0.89	5.25	54.45	275.0	36%	120	6.8	810
NOCIL	0.78	16.14	27.16	405.0	40%	89	13.8	1255
Reliance Petro	7.84	25.56	4.62	10.1	15%	0.5	53	25

The data relates to 1996, but that may not matter as it is for illustration. Only selected companies are studied above. The debt-equity ratio representing leverage is good for NOCIL and Cochin Refineries. But PAT to NW is higher and the actual market price is covered by book value three times in the case of Cochin Refineries. As compared to the industry averages, although the gross profit margin is lower, capital efficiency is higher, and P/E ratio is lowest indicating that a multiple of 7 of price to earnings exhibits some potential for capital appreciation in the case of Cochin Refineries. Besides, examine the data of Gross Block, NW, Sales, Gross and Net Profits and their growth rates over a period of 5 years. Then assess whether the company's EPS and P/E ratios are better than the average industry performance and whether the scrip is underpriced or overpriced and buy only if it is underpriced with growth prospects or is fairly priced for its fundamentals. In the above example, Cochin Refineries is the best buy at its price.

How to Pick Up Growth Shares?

The growth companies are also called blue chip companies. The blue chips of yesteryears are not necessarily the blue chips of today. The investor has to review and assess the companies from time to time to locate the blue chips, based on fundamental analysis.

In order to enable one to identify these blue chips of tomorrow, one should know the nature and characteristics of these companies. A few guidelines in this regard are set out below.

Firstly, the management should be experienced and efficient; they should have the honesty, integrity and vision for expansion and growth. Such is the case with Ambanis, Tatas and Birlas.

Secondly, the market share of the company should be substantial and at least more than one-third. The larger the share, the better the prospects of controlling the market and profit margins and expanding the operations. Bajaj Auto has a share of two-thirds in the two-wheeler and three-wheeler market. So is the case with Asian Paints, Laxmi Machine Works etc.

Thirdly, the company must be well-diversified into areas of growth potential. The growth potential changes from time to time. At present, industries with a growth potential are cement, paper, petrochemicals, etc. Thus a company with a good diversification into such growth areas would do well in sales, profits, and earnings. Some of the consumer product industries producing soaps, cosmetics, toothpaste and powders etc. would generally record a consistent growth. A well-diversified company like L & T, Hindustan Lever, or Century Textiles is a good buy at any reasonable price.

Fourthly, the company's policy of expansion should be consistent and has a long-term perspective. Its assets growth should be reasonably good, reflecting its expansion goals. Growth helps the industry to stabilise its earnings from undue fluctuations and help the diversification process. The companies with a good asset growth are Reliance, L & T, GSFC etc.

Fifthly, the company should have a consistent and stable distribution policy with good profit margins. The company should distribute a reasonable proportion of its profits as dividends, bonus etc. Such companies like Ponds, Colgate, Glaxo etc., would be in good demand, as investors prefer regular dividend-paying companies.

Sixthly, such a company services the investors well with bonus or rights issue or convertible debentures, from time to time in addition to increasing dividend payments. The financial structure and utilisation of capital are efficient. The profit margins are growing and the company is gaining in financial strength.

Lastly, the industry or industries in which the company is operating should have good growth prospects like that of Pharmaceuticals, Biotech or multimedia. The products should be in continuous demand like food products, paper soaps, etc. or consumer non-durable goods. The future outlook of the company and prospects of the industry are interlinked. The prospects would depend also on the government policy and whether it is subject to price and distribution control or any restrictions or regulations. The prospects of the industry in which the company is operating should be assessed from all points of view.

Thus, in the choice of blue chips, the investor has to examine the fundamentals of the companies through balance sheet analysis for a period of at least five years before finally selecting the shares. The time of purchase should be decided on the basis of technical analysis referred to later. But for a layman, the purchase time should be in the bearish phase of the market, when an all-round decline in prices is recorded. At such times, the companies with strong fundamentals should be picked up at low prices for long-term investment if they can be classified as blue chips as per the above guidelines.

Pharma Industry

One of the Sunshine industries in India which has grown rapidly in the past and which has still potentiality to grow is the Pharma Industry. It has grown at a compound rate of 17% during the last decade and is expected to grow at a rate of 19% as estimated in 2009-10. Still the per capita consumption of medicines in India at $ 3 is one of the lowest in the world, despite a high rate of incidence of disease, compared with the world averages.

The pharma market in India is one of the fastest growing sectors with new product launches, growth of product patents, financial and business restructuring to strengthen the hold of existing MNCs, etc. The favourable factors for the growth of this industry are reduction of price controls, huge potentiality for the growth of this industry acceptance of patented drugs from outside into India through MNCs, and non-cyclical and non-seasonal nature of the industry. The foreign MNCs with a huge R & D support, lower costs and global markets are able to out perform the Indian counterparts. But Indian drug manufacturers like Dr. Reddy's Labs, SOL Pharma and Cheminar Drugs etc. have a distinct cost advantage due to low labour cost and lower overheads compared to the foreign MNCs.

Profile of Pharma Industry

The pharmaceutical industry comprises of formulations and bulk drug with formulated sales at Rs. 9,125 crores and bulk drug sales of Rs. 1,822 crores in 1996-97. Although there are 77 therapetical segments, according to disease profile the largest ten segments such as Antibiotics, Vitamins, Anti-T.B, Anti-parasitic, Anti-Rheumatic etc. comprise 61% of total formulations market. Further, the top largest four companies alone account for a significant market share of each of the therapeutic group. Thus, in Anti-Biotics, 24% share of the market is held by Ranbaxy, Cipla & Glaxo, while in the case of Anti-T.B. drugs, 65% of the market share is controlled by Lupin, H. Ciba and Cadilla.

Further, the top 25 pharma companies control over 54% of the entire retail formulations market. While these companies have a wide product range, most of their income is generated by only 2 or 3 segments contributing to more than 50% of total sales. The same is the case with the bulk drug segment. While there are over 23,000 units, producing bulk drugs the top ten drug manufacturers namely, Ranbaxy, Lupin, Kipron, IPCA Morepen, Natco, Dr. Reddys, Orchids, Cheminar and German Remedies account for about 84% of production and exports.

The health indicators point to a larger reliance on drugs in future. Those above the age of 65 will increase and birth rate will be higher and death rate be lower, which leads to greater demand for drugs. India accounts for 15% of world population but consume a mere one per cent of the global pharma sales. The growing middle and upper classes in India, with rising disposable income higher literacy and increased medical awareness will increase the demand for drugs. Besides, poor sanitation, pollution, accidents and other health hazards will improve the usage of drugs.

The price controls on as much as 350 items in 1979 have been brought down to a small number by 2007. The reduction of controls on the drug industry, the favourable inflow of R & D results in India and low cost and high margin scenario would expectedly lead to a widening and deepening of the drug industry in India and the future of this industry is bright. Among the existing producers the foreign MNCs stand to gain more than the Indian MNCs, who in turn may reap better returns than the all industry average or the average for many industry groups.

Future Outlook

The future outlook for this industry is bright. It is expected to grow at not less than 19% per annum in terms of sales, as against the growth rate of GDP of 7-8%, in the short-run and its prospects are much brighter in the long-run. This industry is undergoing many changes to strengthen itself and improve its profitability. The following are some of these trends:

1. FERA was diluted and foreign MNC can increase their stake upto 51% in the subsidiaries.

2. DPCO eliminated the need for compulsory bulk drug manufacture in India upto a minimum amount, thereby enabling them to close down some uneconomical units/divisions.

3. Corporate tax rate is brought down to 30% and import duty on chemicals was cut from 110% to 30% as at end of 2009.

4. The acceptance of GATT and WTO by India has paved the way for recognition of product patents.

5. Reorganisation and restructuring is going on among foreign MNCs and Indian MNCs to strengthen themselves by brand acquisitions, permitted take overs, and voluntary merges.

6. Encouragement to product launches, particularly if export oriented.

7. Possible 100% investment by Foreign MNCs due to FDI liberalisation and freer Royalty out flow permitted by FERA liberalisation.

8. Growing global generic market changing mind set, more R & D investment and unlocking of unproductive assets, shedding off the excess fat by VRS for employees and selling off uneconomical capital wasting divisions. R & D is being encouraged through tax incentives.

A few case studies of pharma companies are presented below for an example of analysis.

(in Rs. Crores)

Pharma Industry	DABUR			SUN PHARMA		
	For the year	2006-07	2008-09	For the year	2006-07	2009-10
	Net Sales	1795	2805	Sales	2301	4702
	Gross Profit	318	513	Gross Profit	584	1453
	Interest	4	23	Interest	−103	+114
	Depreciation	28	45	Depreciation	46	153
	Taxation	32	54	Taxation	12	68
	PAT. (Net Profit)	254	391	PAT. (Net Profit)	629	1346
	Equity	86	86	Equity	97	104
	Reserves	317	732	Reserves	2351	7725
	Net worth	403	818	Net worth	2448	7829
	B.V. (N.W/Equity)	Rs. 4.7	Rs. 9.5	B.V. (N.W/Equity)	126	372
	F.V.	Rs. 1	1	F.V.	5	5
	M.P. (Average)	Rs. 102	Rs. 128	M.P. (Average)	950	1070
	EPS (PAT/Equity)	2.9	4.5	EPS (PAT/Equity)	33	65
	P/E Ratio	32.9	28.5	P/E Ratio	28.8	16.5
	Dividend	175%	175%	Dividend	135%	135%
	Actual Market Price		Rs. 184 as on June 1st 2010.	Actual Market Price		Rs. 1680 as on June 1st 2010.
				@ P/E ratio as per ETD only was 25.8		

CIPLA			
For the year	2006-07	2008-09	2009-2010
Net Sales	3114	4960	5358
Gross Profit	802	1105	1543
Interest	11	34	24
Depreciation	80	170	189
Taxation	102	125	248
PAT. (Net Profit)	609	776	1082
Equity	60	155	160
Reserves	1914	4186	4186
Net worth	1974	4341	4346
B.V. (N.W/Equity)	65	56	54
F.V.	Rs. 2	2	2
M.P. (Average)	290	224	324
EPS (PAT/Equity)	20.3	10	14
P/E ratio	14.3	22.4	23.2
Dividend	100%	100%	100%

Source: Annual Reports – Financial statements of the companies

Conclusions

The above Tabular Presentation of three pharma companies is for illustration of their fundamentals. The data for the latest available date in their web-sites are presented here. This is only the starting for further research with data for 5 to 10 years. Barring Sun Pharma, the others are modestly priced and the small and medium sized companies are picked up for study. During the period for which the data are presented, the market was bullish, with sensex rising from a low of three years at 4,723, (in 2004-05) to a high of 14,723 (in Feb 2007) and ruling at around 16,500 in July 2010. During the peried of 2007-10 for which data are available for corporate information, the sensex fluctuated between 7,697 in October 2008 and 21,207 in January 2008. The sensex reached a level of 18,000, in April 2010.

An analysis of the three pharma companies and of the pharma industry in general reveals that their future prospects are good. They have become multinationals, by mergers and acquistions (M&A) and promotion of R & D segment. This is particularly true of the major pharma companies like Dr. Reddys, and Ranbaxy (not shown here).

All the above companies are running in profits with the profitability ratio of NP to sales ranging from 14% to 27%. The Sun Pharma has EPS at Rs. 33.5 and priced at an average of Rs. 950 in 2006 – 07. Its market price is 3.5 times the Book value, while the total market ratio of BV to MP is around 5 times; its profitability is also high.

In the case of three companies studied, their intrinsic worth, in terms of book value and EPS are low but they are also priced moderately as compared to the giants of Dr. Reddys and Ranbaxy Among the companies of Cipla, and Dabur, the data show that Dabur is doing relatively better and its profits and profitability are good, with a dividend declared for 2008-09 at 175%. At the market price of Rs. 128, it is a good buy among all the three companies studied. The market price of Dabur is higher in June 2010 at Rs. 185 indicating its strong fundamentals.

The market price as in June 2010, in the case of Cipla was Rs. 324 and in the case of Sun Pharma was Rs. 1,680 and in the case of Dabur, Rs. 185. In the case of Cipla the market price is 6 times the Book Value. For Sun Pharma the market price is 3 times the Book Value. And for Dabur the market price is about 12 times. One can assess the ranking of these shares on the basis of criteria of Book Value to price ratio and P/E multiple.

The above analysis, which is illustrative, is relevant only for the year 2007 to 2010 and the reader has to make similar studies for any point of time, as the market sentiment and external and internal factors of the company change from time to time. The limitation of the illustration is that they are not fully reflecting the growth prospects of the pharma industry in general and the study is confined only for one or two years. Research on the above lines for a longer period of all representative companies in any industry is necessary.

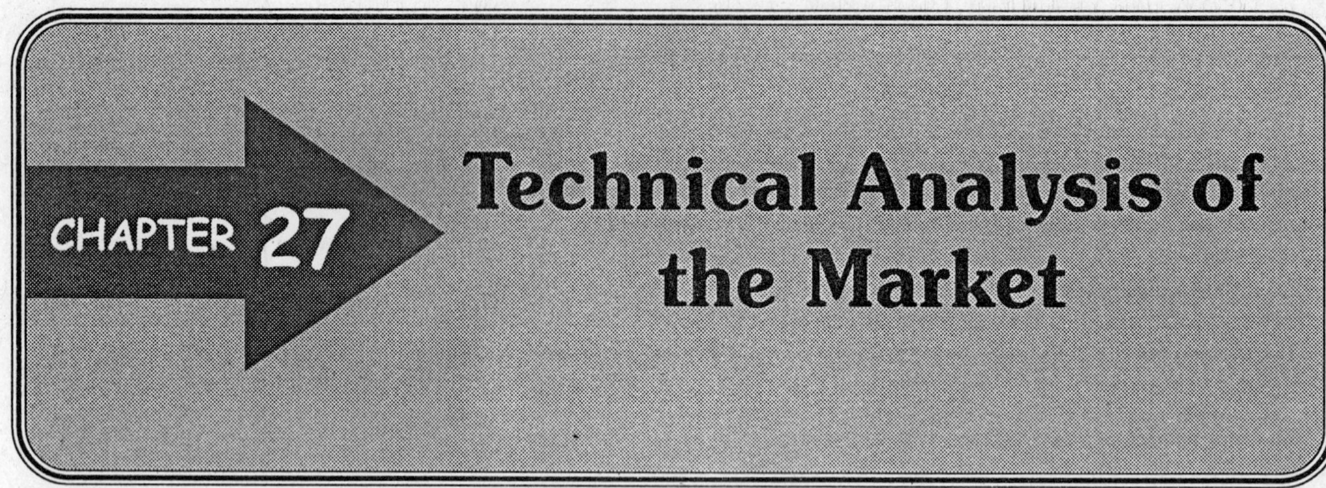

Importance of Timing in Investment

While fundamental analysis and security evaluation explain why share prices fluctuate, how they are determined and what to buy or sell, the technical analysis will help the decision when to buy and sell. The traditional theory of capital market efficiency postulates that entry into the market at any time would lead to the same average return as that of the market. But in the real world of imperfections, there are investors who have burnt their fingers by entering the market at the wrong time. Investment timing is, therefore, crucial as the market is continuously jolted by waves of buying and selling and prices are moving in trends and cycles and are never stable. The Stock market is different from other markets, as there is a continuous buying and selling and bid and offer rates as under a system of auctions. The resultant prices, led by the sheer force of the market, may fluctuate either way and may exhibit waves or trends. Entry and exit in the market will, therefore, make all the difference to the spread between buying and selling prices and the profits or losses. Timing of investment is, therefore, of vital importance for trading in the stock market. Broadly, one can say that fundamental analysis is necessary for investment and technical analysis helps trading in the stock market.

Basic Tenets of Technical Analysis

Technical analysis of the market is based on some basic tenets, namely, that all fundamental factors are discounted by the market and are reflected in prices. Secondly, these prices move in trends or waves which can be both upward or downward depending on the sentiment, psychology and emotions of operators or traders. Thirdly, the present trends are influenced by the past trends, and the projection of future trends is possible by an analysis of past price trends. Analysis of historical trends confirmed the above principles and the Random Walk Theory explaining the randomness of price changes has been found to be not applicable by the technical analysts in practice.

Tools of Technical Analysis

1. *Daily Fluctuation or Volatility:* Open, High, Low and Close are quoted. Changes between Open and Close or High and Low can be taken in absolute points or in percentages to reflect the daily volatility. Such fluctuation can be worked out on weekly, monthly or yearly basis also to reflect the general volatility of the market. The use of this indicator is to caution the investor against high volatility in any scrip. But a stable uptrend or downtrend can be discerned from these changes for the investor to interpret the market.

A Bar chart as given below can be used to depict the daily variations:

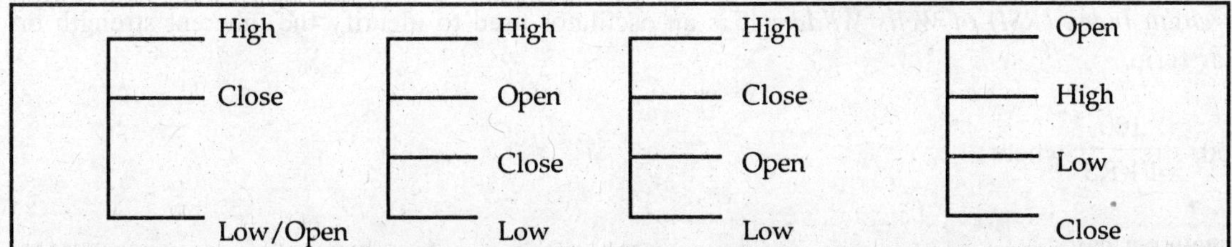

An yearly High-Low indicates the possible levels within a range that the price may move which helps to locate entry and exit points.

2. *Floating Stock and Volume of Trade:* Floating stock is the total number of shares available for trading with the public and volume of trade is any part of that floating stock. The higher this proportion, the higher is the liquidity of a share which is to be purchased or sold. Volume trends are also a supporting indicator to the price trends to interpret the market.

3. *Price Trends and Volume Trends:* The Chartist method and Moving average method can be used to depict these trends

4. *Rate of Change of Prices and Volumes or the ROC Method:* This is useful like the moving average method to indicate more clearly the buy and sell signals. The Chartist method is useful to indicate the directions and the trend reversals. ROC is calculated by dividing the today's price by the price five days back or few days back. It can be expressed as percentage or positive or negative change. Thus they can be moving around 100, in the case of percentages or zero line, in the case of positive and negative percentage changes.

5. *Japanese Candlestick Method:* There are three main types of Candlesticks with each day's trade being shown in the form of candlesticks. Each stick has the body of the candle and a shadow. The body shows the open and close prices while the shadow shows the high and low prices. The three main types are as follows:

(a) Closing price is higher than open price (White candlestick).

(b) Closing price is lower than the open price (Black stick).

(c) Open and Close are at the same level (Doji candlestick).

This method will indicate any likely changes in trends in the short-run.

6. *Dow Theory:* There are three major trends in this theory. Minor, inter-mediate and major trends representing daily or weekly, monthly and yearly trends in prices respectively, comparing the price trends to waves. tides and ripples.

7. *Elliot Wave Theory:* The market is unfolded by a basic rhythm or pattern of 5 waves up to be corrected by three waves down with a total of 8 waves - a philosophy of price trends.

8. *Theory of Gaps*: Gaps in price between any two days causing a discontinuity is called a gap. The high of one day may be lower than the low of the previous day when prices are falling. Gaps indicate the likely acceleration of the trend or reversal.

Gaps are of different categories, namely:

(a) Common gaps — When prices move in a narrow range, a gap can occur in prices.

(b) Break out gaps — When price trend is likely to change, a gap can occur in either direction. This gives a break to congestion in any direction.

(c) Runaway gaps — These gaps occur continuously in a downward phase or an upward phase, accelerating or decelerating the trends.

(d) Exhaustion gaps — These occur when the rally is getting exhausted. When the runaway gap is coming to an end, there can be exhaustion gap to indicate the likely completion of the uptrend.

9. *Advance Decline Line or Spread of the Market:* The ratio between advances to declines will indicate the relative strength of upward or downward phases. When the advances are increasing over declines it is an upward phase and the reverse indicates the downward phase.

10. *Relative Strength Index (RSI) of Wells Wilder:* It is an oscillator used to identify the inherent strength or weakness of particular scrip.

$$\text{Thus, RSI} = 100 - \frac{100}{1+\text{RS}} \text{ where}$$

$$\text{RS} = \frac{\text{Average gain per day}}{\text{Average loss per day}}$$

R.S.I. is calculated for one scrip while RSC or the relative strength comparative, is the ratio of two prices of two different scrips, used for comparison of two or more scrips. RSI can be calculated for any number of days say 5 or 10 etc. to indicate the strength of price trend.

Dow Theory

The Dow Theory postulates that prices of industrial securities tend to move in tune with business cycles of the boom, depression etc. in the economy. As the corporate performance depends on the industrial growth and the tone of the economy, prices of shares should broadly reflect the overall trends in the economy, which in developed countries are dependent on the business cycles and business expectations. If the business conditions are good, demand increasing, industrial performance will be good and the corporate share prices will be on the upswing. The reverse is true in times of recession and depression in the economy. The trends in the economy are reflected in the market average prices of shares. All fundamental factors are thus discounted by the market, and get reflected in average prices. It will thus be seen that factors affecting these supply and demand conditions in the market are summed up in the average prices in the market. A study of these average market prices is what is attempted in technical analysis and its trends are in the form of peaks, troughs and cycles.

Major Trends

The trends in stock prices are divided under three heads — primary, secondary and minor. The primary trend is a long-term trend of a year or more reflecting the basic mood of the market showing upward or downward movement. The secondary or intermediate trend represents the correction to the primary trend and is of a short duration of a few weeks to a few months. The minor trends may be in either direction on a daily or weekly basis, but pointing to the underlying primary trend either upward or downward. These three trends are comparable to the tides, waves and ripples of the sea respectively. If the successive waves move further inland towards the beach than the preceding ones, then the tide would reflect the upward trend through higher peaks and troughs. On the reverse side, if the tide is moving inwards into the sea, then the trend is downwards and prices tend to decline on average. Each successive minor trend and intermediate trend result in a net downward movement and support the primary market trend in the downward direction.

In the Dow Theory, the major trends, namely, bullish or bearish trends, have three phases. In the first phase of bullish trend, called the accumulation phase, only a select elite of investors who perceive the coming things first start buying shares. In the second phase, the followers of trend notice a distinct uptrend and begin to participate in the buying and then the mass buying starts. The third phase is the end of the uptrend when the first elite group who initiated the first phase should dislodge their shares for profit-taking. Then there will be a reversal of the trend. The fall in the prices in a bull phase is a technical reaction and a rise in prices in a bear phase is a technical rally. The concentration in the hands of bulls is called accumulation, which when sold off gets distributed and there will be a decline in prices.

So far as the volume of trade is concerned, it should expand in the direction of the major trend. During the uptrend period, the volume would expand when prices rise and decrease when prices decline. During the down-trend, there will be a reversal of the trend and the volume will expand when prices drop and contract when they start rising.

The only problem which is a grey area in the Dow Theory is the signal for reversal of the trend. The first symptom of a change would call for "buy or sell" decision and those who perceive the change first would gain in speculation. As the primary trend continues, the gain from speculation decreases. The fact of the matter is that it is not easy, except for the expert eyes, to detect a change in direction in the existing trend and the first leg of the new trend in the opposite direction. For knowing the reversal point, a lot of experience and expertise is necessary in this line.

The reversal pattern is explained below. A, B, C are the successive peaks during the upswing, but M is a point of trough which is lower than the earlier troughs of D and E. The point S_1 is the point of sell signal. This is called the failure swing diagram (Fig. 27.1).

Fig. 27.1

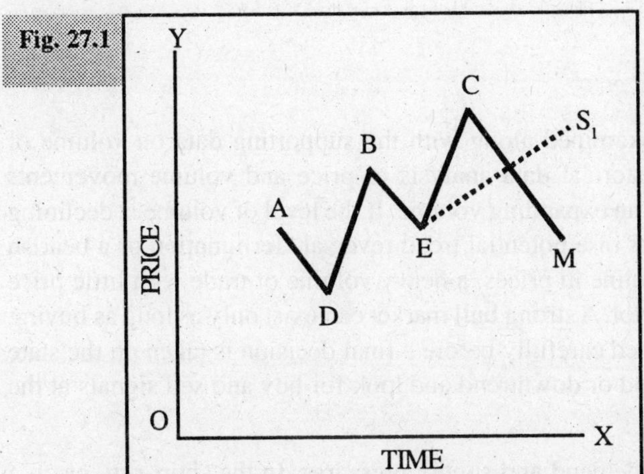

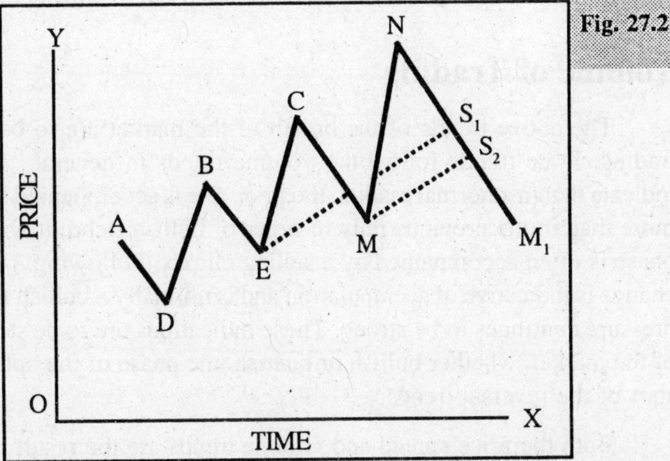

Fig. 27.2

In the non-failure swing diagram, E is below M but the peak C is still above peak B. So it is not certain whether the point S_1, or S_2 should be the sell signal. Whether the point of reversal has set in or not is not clear from the diagram. Such occasions arise in both upswing and downswing diagrams (Fig. 27.2).

Chartist Method

As referred to earlier, technical analysis is a study of the market data in terms of factors affecting supply and demand schedules, namely, prices, volume of trading, etc. A study of the historical trends of market behaviour shows the cycles and trends in prices which may repeat as the present is a reflection of the past and the future of the present. This is the basis for forecasting the future trends which are used for deciding on the basis of the buy or sell signals. For forecasting, analysts use charts and diagrams to depict the past trends and project the future. But these methods are rough and ready methods and there are no foolproof methods of forecasting the stock prices. The technical analysis only helps to improve the knowledge of the probabilities of price behaviour (upswing or downswing) and help the investment process. The technical analysis does not claim 100% chance of success in predictions that are made for investment.

In view of the limitations inherent in the technical analysis, this analysis is generally juxtaposed with fundamental analysis of the market and the scrips. It was the past experience that the receipt of information and the actual price absorption of the information would not coincide and there is a time lag between them. As a result, the current price changes would give a clue to the subsequent price changes, if properly analysed and interpreted.

In the market analysis, the variables to be taken into account are the breadth of the market, volume of trading etc. Market breadth is the dispersion of the general price rise or decline, which means daily cumulation of a net number of advancing or declining issues. Breadth analysis focuses on change rather than level in prices. Breadth of price changes in terms of the number of gainers or losers among the scrips is analysed to know the width of rise or fall in prices.

Breadth of the Market

The breadth of the market analysis is based on the nature of stock market cycles. Bull markets are viewed as long-drawn-out affairs, during which individual stocks reach peaks gradually with the number of individual peaks accelerating as the market averages rise to the turning point. Thus the turning point for a bull phase is at that point where a larger number of stocks are falling when the averages are still rising. In the bear market, there is a large number of stocks falling in a period of time. The end of the bear market is near when there is a selling climax and a large number of sellers rush to sell all at once. The breadth is measured by the number of scrips rising or falling to the total number. In a bull phase there will be a large number of net rises and in a bear phase, a large number of net falls.

Normally, the breadth and the market average (BSE Index) lines move in tandem. In a bull phase, if the breadth line declines to successive new lows, while the market average is going up, it means that a larger number of scrips are declining although blue chips included in the BSE Index continue to rise, but the suggestion is that there is an approaching peak in the averages and a major downtrend is in the offing later.

Volume of Trading

The above trends of the breath of the market are to be examined along with the supporting data on volume of trading. Price trends follow the volume trends in general.[1] Historical data analysis of price and volume movements indicate that in a normal market, the price rise is accompanied by an expanding volume. If the level of volume is declining more than in the previous rally in times of bullish trend, it warns of a potential trend reversal. Termination of a bearish phase is often accompanied by a selling climax. Following a decline in prices, a heavy volume of trade with little price change is indicative of accumulation and is normally a bullish factor. A strong bull market can exist only as long as buying pressure continues to be strong. These indications are to be studied carefully before a final decision is taken on the state of the market, whether bullish or bearish, the phase of the uptrend or downtrend and look for buy and sell signals at the start of the reversal trends.

Both the price spread and volume trends are the result of demand and supply pressures. In the short-run, or on a day-to-day basis, the demand and supply for each scrip is based on a host of fundamental, technical and other factors. Trading in futures, options and arbitrage activity would distort the pure demand and supply analysis. The money flow analysis of the market generally adopted by the analysts is also distorted by the dynamics of insider trading, short sales, "buying on weakness" and "selling on strength", etc.

Tripod of Technical Analysis

1. Market prices are determined by a host of fundamental, technical and other factors which are both rational and irrational. It is possible that the market prices may be overvalued or undervalued always.
2. Average market price discounts all developments and is a reflection of the sum total of all forces operating on the market.
3. History or past trends have a role in the shaping of the future and as such an analysis of the past helps the projection for the future.

The above tripod leads to a science of recording in a graphic form, the price trends. The actual history of trading on the stock market is recorded in terms of price changes, moving averages of prices, velocity of price changes, namely, oscillators, and the volume of transactions in any scrip together. Based on the past behaviour, the future trends are predicted and investment suggestions are made based on such predictions of trend changes. The timing of an investment when to buy or sell is facilitated by a study of these charts and graphs. These are no doubt subjective factors based upon the behaviour and psychological aspects of human beings which influence the market. As opposed to fundamental factors, which are statistical, incorporating the financial and physical variables of corporate units and economy, the market is also influenced by the non-statistical information such as behaviour aspects, emotions, etc.; for the latter factors, technical analysis assumes importance in the investment strategy. In particular the decision to buy or sell is a fundamental decision, but the decision when to buy or sell is a decision arising out of technical analysis of the market.

Principles of Technical Analysis

The principles involved in technical analysis and in particular in the Dow Theory analysis, can be summarised as follows:

(1) Principle of wave motion and trends leads to different types of price trends.

(2) Action and reaction resulting from buying and selling pressures lead to corrections and rallies to the major uptrends and downtrends respectively.

1. "If you can predict volume, you can predict the movement of the Stock Market" (in *Investment Analysis and Portfolio Management* by Cohen, Zinbarg and Zeikel, p. 257).

(3) Principle of congestion involving support and resistance lines results in a phase of activity, in which the market is undecided, hesitant and the trend undermined. The prices move within a band of resistance and support lines, and the trends involve up and down movements in a more or less horizontal path, until the prices are driven up or down.

In congestion, the continuous pressures of buyers are met equally. But when the buyers exceed the sellers, both in volume and value of deals, then the price emerges from the bottom of the range and there will be an up breakout. When the sellers predominate, there will be a down breakout in the price level, the resistance and support lines are broken in either case. When buyers are increasing their purchases and the volume increases, then there is said to be accumulation. When sellers are increasing their sales and the volume rises, then there is said to be distribution. When buying exceeds selling and persists, then there is a breakout of prices from the congestion into a bull phase. On the other hand, when selling exceeds buying and continues to persist, the congestion is broken out into a bear phase.

Charts and Trend Lines

The use of charts for analysis of prices in technical analysis was referred to. Fitting a trend line for price changes on a daily basis is the first step in the analysis of charts. These changes may be pointing upwards or downwards or stable over a horizontal one. The movements are such that there are both peaks and troughs in these price changes — peaks showing an upward trend troughs or reactions to the uptrend, viz., line joining the lowest points or troughs pointing up. If this line is pointing downwards, then it is a bearish phase (Fig. 27.4). If the movements are downwards generally, then there will be rallies moving up the prices. These upper peaks, if they are joined, give the trend line as much as the lowest troughs. The bull phase depicts the rising peaks successively (Fig. 27.3), while the bear phase shows the falling peaks successively (Fig. 27.4).

When the share prices are rising or falling, there will be a resistance level above which the prices may not pierce in the upward direction or a support level, below which the price may not fall.

These support lines and resistance lines are clearly noticed when the prices are moving in a narrow band for some time. When the price pierces the resistance line, this is the first indication of the reversal of the trend in the upward direction. So also in a bull phase when the price line falls below the support line, a reversal of the trend is indicated.

Various configurations of price movements like stable pattern, M and W patterns, head and shoulders etc. are formed. It is possible that various triangles, flags, pendants, etc. can be described by the price trends. The basic analysis involves the deciphering of the trend identifying of the reversal and fixing up of buy and sell signals in these price movements. The stable price pattern is ideal for genuine investors to enter the market.

Fig. 27.3

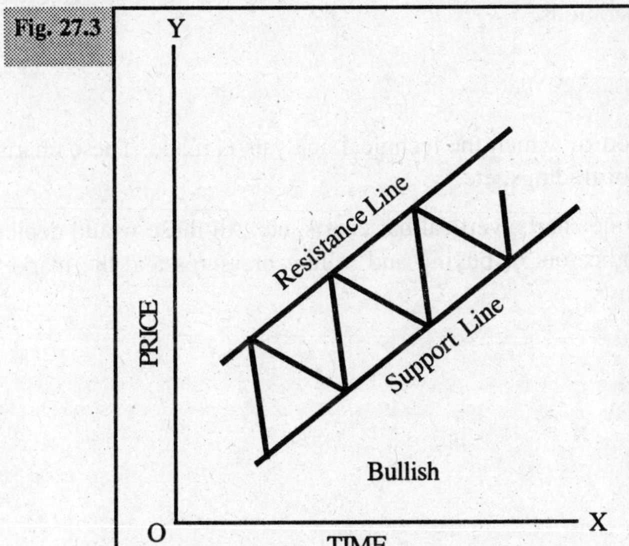

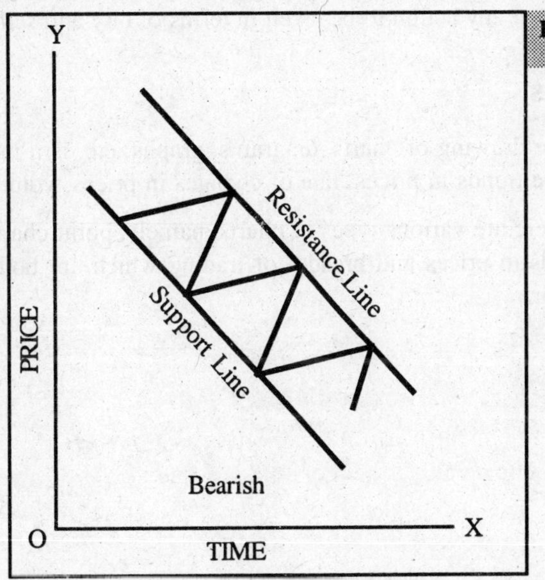

Fig. 27.4

Moving Averages

The analysis of the moving averages of the prices of scrips is another method in technical analysis. Generally, 7-day, 10-day and 15-day moving averages are worked out in respect of scrips studied and depicted on a graph along with similar moving averages of the market index like BSE Sensitive Index. There will then be two graphs to be compared and when the trends are similar, the scrip and BSE market index will show comparable average risks.

The theory of moving averages also lays down the following guidelines for identifying the buy and sell signals. Whenever the moving average price line cuts the actual price line of the scrip or of the market index from the bottom, it is a signal to sell shares. Conversely, when the moving average line cuts the actual price line from above, it is the right time to buy shares. Here the comparison can be made separately for the BSE market index moving average with its actual price index and the moving average price of any scrip with its actual price.

Advantages of Moving Averages

Since the price fluctuations are wide and frequent, reflecting the volatility of the market and the scrips, some amount of smoothing can be achieved by taking the moving averages of the prices. Generally, the closing prices of these scrips are taken for the moving averages. The usefulness of this will also depend on the number of days (7 days, 10 days, 20 days, etc.) for which these averages are worked out. These averages can be represented in a graphical form to help identification of buy and sell signals. The first indication is that when the actual scrip price crosses the short-term moving average line (or, say, 7 or 10 days). This is to be supported by other evidence of a reversal of the trend to justify the buy signal. The short-term moving average of 7 or 10 days should cross the longer-term moving average of 15 or 20 days, which in turn should cross the further long-term moving averages (of, say, 60 or 120 days) to finally confirm the buy signal. In other words, the buy signal is to be given when the moving average line cuts the actual price line from above. If it cuts from below, then the signal is to sell. This signal of moving averages can also be confirmed by further analysis of other technical factors like the trend reversal shown in the chart-graphs referred to in (Fig. 27.5).

Criticism of Dow Theory

The Dow Theory is subject to various limitations in actual practice. Dow has developed this theory to depict the general trend of the market but not with the intention of projecting the future trends or to diagnose the buy and sell signals in the market. These applications of the Dow Theory have come to light in analytical studies of financial analysts. This theory is criticised on the ground that it is too subjective and based on historical interpretation; it is not infallible as it depends on the interpretative ability of the analyst. The results of this theory do not also give meaningful and conclusive evidence of any action to be taken in terms of buy and sell operations.

Charts

The drawing of charts, diagrams, graphs, etc. is a method by which the technical analysis is made. These charts depict the trends in prices, rate of changes in prices, volume of tradings, etc.

There are various types of charts, namely, point charts, line charts, vertical bar charts, etc. All these would depict the trends in prices and breadth of trading which are both indicators of buying and selling pressures and the market behaviour.

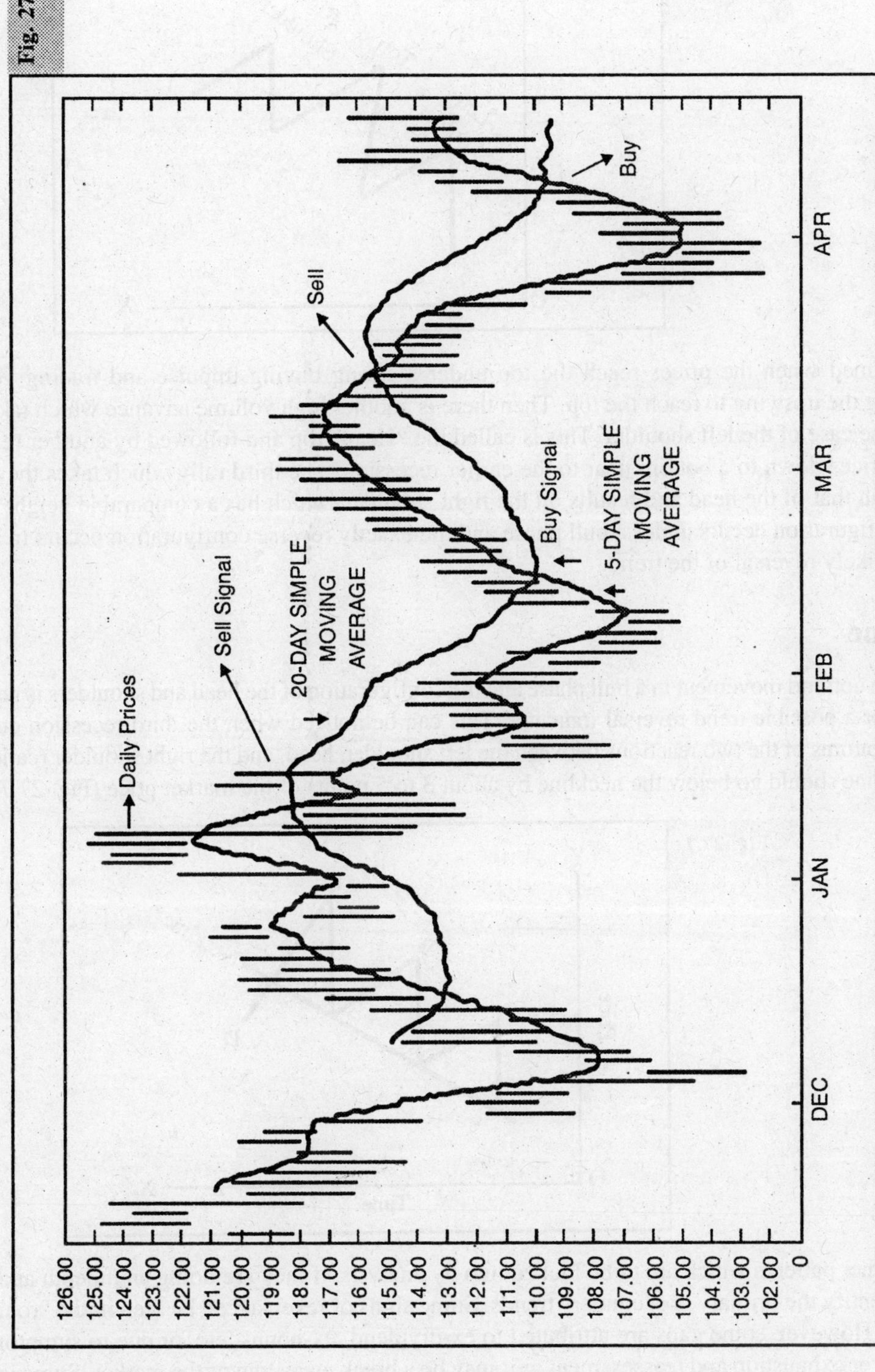

Fig. 27.5 Daily actual prices are dashed lines. When the daily price line cuts the moving average of 5 days and the line of 5 days cuts the line of 20 days, from above, there are sell signals. The buy signals are when the actual prices cut the moving average lines from below.

Head and Shoulders

The configurations emerging from the charts show different patterns. Of these, the most important is the "Head and Shoulders." It depicts a top and a reversal pattern in either the bull phase or the bear phase (Fig. 27.6).

Fig. 27.6

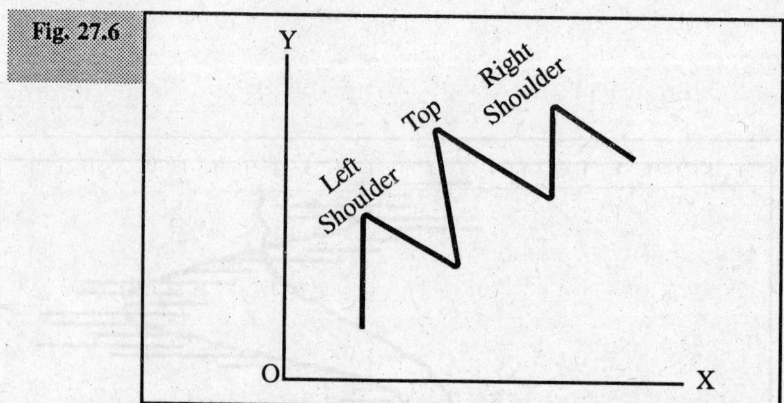

The left shoulder is formed when the prices reach the top under a strong buying impulse and trading volume becomes less than it did during the upswing to reach the top. Then there is another high volume advance which takes the price to a higher top than in the case of the left shoulder. This is called the "Head" top and followed by another reaction on less volume which takes prices down to a bottom near to the earlier recession. The third rally which takes the prices up reaches a height of less than that of the head and results on the right shoulder, which has a comparable height as the left shoulder. This type of configuration occurs under a bull phase and the exactly reverse configuration occurs in a bear phase. This is indicative of a likely reversal of the trend.

Breaking the Neckline

If the prices are having an uptrend movement in a bull phase and the configuration of the head and shoulders is noticed, then the analyst has to look for a possible trend reversal indicator. This can be noticed when the third recession cuts the support line down across the bottoms of the two reactions between the left shoulder, head, and the right shoulder (called the neckline) and the actual price line should go below the neckline by about 3 to 5 points of the market price (Fig. 27.7).

Fig. 27.7

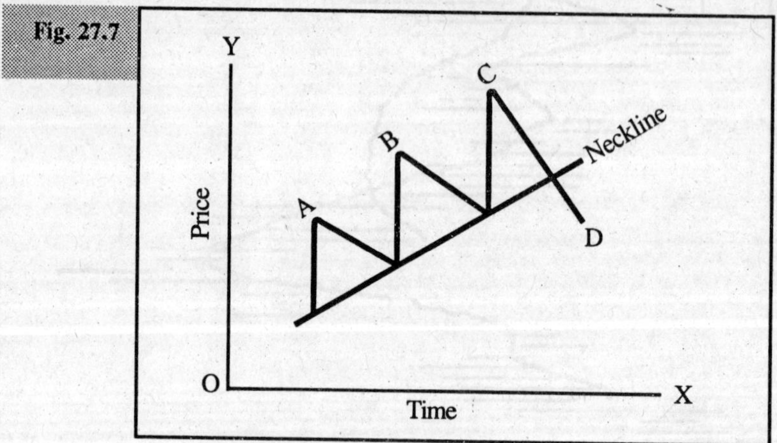

There are a number of other patterns which are to be looked into by analysts, if they are doing an indepth analysis. These patterns are useful to identify the primary or secondary trends. Some signs of reversal can be seen in the "rounding turns" and triangles and gaps. However, some gaps are attributed to ex-dividend, ex-bonus, etc. or due to symptoms of consolidation and acceleration or exhaustion and reassessment or it may be a break away gap of the market. Some insight into the future movement of prices can be had by a close study of the pattern that prices are making. Thus forecasting is a practical use to which the charts in general and these configurations in particular can be put to.

The bull market indicators are as follows. The bear market has been in progress for a long time. The peaks of advancing points are still sloping upwards. The number of advancing points is substantially higher than the number of declining points. Then if the stock establishes certain levels of accumulation and consolidation over a number of days or weeks and if the volume of trading slows down, then it is certain that distribution is taking place and it will meet with the resistance level soon. So, as a rule, it is safe to buy at the top or three points below or around the old bottom.

The bear market indications may be set out as follows. A bull market has been in progress for a long time. The recovery is occurring on low volume and the number of advancing points is only slightly higher than the number of declining points. The line connecting the peaks of declining point is sloping upwards but the price line may cross the support level soon due to exhaustion of the market pressure. It is better to sell at the previous high to peak or 3 points around that high.

Resistance and Support Lines

The point and figure charts should clearly indicate the bull or bear phases. But some configuration do not clearly indicate the definite signals such as in the case of a symmetrical triangle. While the ascending triangle and descending triangle indicate the upward and downward phases respectively (Figs. 27.8 and 27.9), the symmetrical triangle drawn below does not clearly indicate anything (Fig. 27.10).

Fig. 27.8

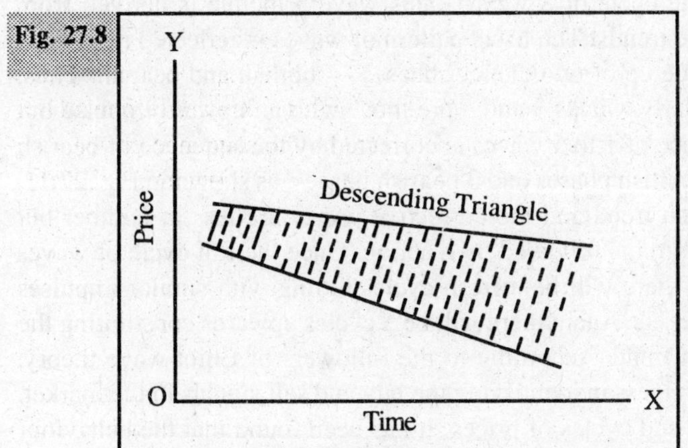

Fig. 27.9

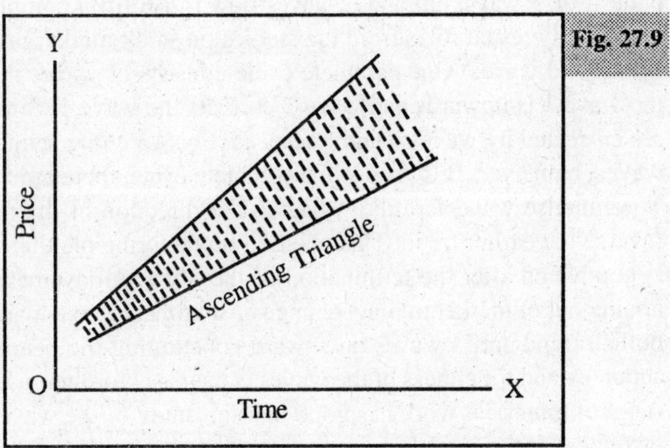

Consolidation refers to time interval in which the price of a share does not break through in either direction. Then the price movements are in a narrow band with both the resistance and support lines moving horizontally.

Fig. 27.10

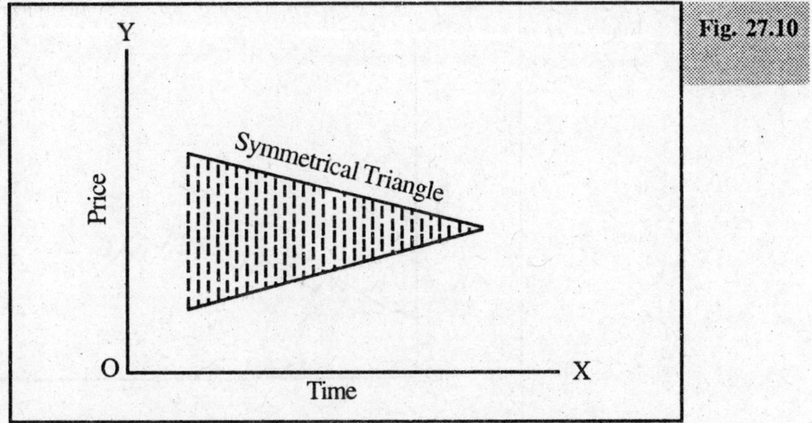

Speculative Trading and Technical Analysis

Timing of purchase and sale is very important particularly for speculative trading. The basic rule is to follow the daily chart of highs/lows or tops/bottoms. When the long-term trend is bullish and price trend is pointing up, the advance line must make higher tops and higher bottoms. One can enter the market any time so long as the uptrend is continuing as indicated by the higher tops and bottoms. The best buy point is when the prices decline by 50% of the higher ever peak achieved or at a level of 50% between the extreme low and extreme high. The best points to sell are when prices rise to the old top levels or near to those levels or when the prices start advancing after being below the 50% point between the extreme high and extreme low. There is no sanctity of these levels, as they are set by experience and observation. Experience and analysis are the best guides in these matters.

Before taking the buy and sell decisions, one has to observe the rules of the game:

(i) Put stop loss order at, say, 10% of one's capital at any time. This will protect the extent of losses possible in speculation.

(ii) Draw the daily, weekly, monthly charts separately and observe the highs and lows and the mid-points and turning points carefully.

(iii) The buy and sell signals can be located at 3 points below the highs or 3 points above the lows, etc.

Elliot Wave Theory

There are a number of theories which seek to explain the behaviour of the market. In the area of technical analysis, one such theory is that of Ralph Elliot. According to this theory, the market is unfolded through the basic rhythm or pattern of 5 waves up and 3 waves down to form a complete cycle of 8 waves. This wave principle is derived from empirically tested rules from the studies on stock market price trends. The basic pattern of waves is reflected in various cycles and waves. One complete cycle consists of waves made up of two distinct phases — bullish and bearish. Thus, the wave 1 is upwards and wave 2 corrects the wave 1. Similarly, waves 3 and 5 are those with an upward impulse but are corrected by waves 4 and 6 respectively. An entire sequence of 1 to 5 waves is corrected by the sequence of bearish waves, namely, A,B,C. Thus, in a complete cycle, there are 5 bullish phases and 3 bearish phases, as shown in Fig. 27.11. The impulse waves are the waves in the direction of the main trend and the corrective waves are less in number but reverse the earlier trend. This is based on the principle that action is followed by reaction. Once the full cycle of waves is completed after the termination of the 8-wave movement, there will be a fresh cycle starting with similar impulses arising out of market trading, change of sentiment in the market etc. Again there will be 5 cycles upwards constituting the bullish trend and 3 waves downward constituting the bearish trend. According to the followers of Elliot wave theory, accuracy and timeliness of the waves is the basis for their usefulness in identifying the buy and sell signals in the market. A lot of empirical work has gone into the study of the waves and cycles of prices. It has been found that the behaviour of prices on the stock markets conforms to the cycles and waves and it is possible to use these data for predicting the price change and deciding on the buy and sell signals. The fact that there are more upward cycles than downward cycles proves the fact that in the long run, the market prices show a rise and there may be capital appreciation or rise in market capitalisation.

Fig. 27.11

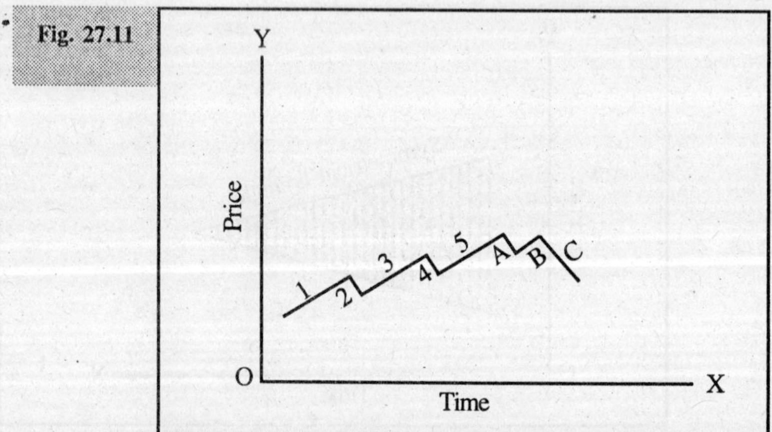

Operation of Wave Theory[2]

The wave is a movement of the market price from one change in the direction to the next change in the direction. The waves are result of buying and selling impulses emerging from the demand and supply pressures on the market. If the demand exceeds supply, there is pressure of overbought position leading to a rise in prices. If the supply exceeds demand, there is an oversold position in the market leading to a downward trend in the prices. Depending on the pressure of the oversold and overbought position, the waves are generated in the prices.

2. R.R. Prechter Jr. (Ed.): *The Major Works of R.N. Elliot.*

The stock market has been found to behave in a consistent manner giving rise to a basic rhythm and a wave movement in prices. The basic rhythm is reflected in 3 impulses in one direction followed by 2 waves of corrective nature with a total of 5 in the wave phase and 3 cycles in a reverse phase. These 3 waves correct the entire movements of 5 major upward movements.

The personality of each wave is an integral part of the reflection of mass psychology that it embodies. Although sometimes these wave counts are not clear, the shape and length may vary depending on the buying and selling pressures. But the analysts who have the experience and expertise can discern the waves in both upward and downward directions and also the impulse waves and corrective waves. These will help the analyst to learn what the chart tells regarding the phase and turning points. The wave principle offers the tools of identifying the market turns and their approach. As a limitation, however, it should be noted that the wave theory is not perfect and there are many limitations in its practical use. the rhythm as well as the count number of the waves may not be consistent and it may not be possible to clearly discern the turning points and take proper decision on buy and sell. But on the whole, it should be accepted as one of the tools of technical analysis for the investor and trader to decide on the timing of investment.

Oscillators (Rate of Change or ROC)

Oscillators refer to the velocity of price changes reflecting the market momentum which is measured by the rate of change of prices. This rate of change may be over the short period of 5 to 10 days or a longer period of 3 to 6 months. These oscillators may also be based upon the daily market prices when the volatility of the market spread is measured on a daily basis. Most oscillators would move in the same direction, either positive or negative, depending on the trends of the market. A positive reading reflects on overbought market and negative reading reflects oversold market. These oscillators in the form of velocity of price changes are plotted around a zero line to reflect both positive and negative values of the graph. The shape of the oscillator will depend on the period for which it is calculated say 5, 10, or 20 days. If the oscillator is for a longer period, it will become a smoother curve and if it is compiled on a daily basis, it will be widely fluctuating.

Usefulness of the oscillator graph depends on a proper reading of the graph. As a general rule, if the oscillator reaches the extreme lower end, it is suggested to buy and if it is at the upper end, then the suggestion is to sell. The crossing of the zero line may also be understood as the first indication of buy and sell signals.

The crossing of the zero line is an important indicator of the price trends and its direction. The market is said to be overbrought when the oscillator is at the upper extreme and is oversold when the oscillator is in the lower extreme. These points provide the signals of buy and sell to the investor. Generally, the peaks and troughs in the actual price chart also reflect the peaks and troughs of the oscillator graph. A study of oscillators is thus useful to confirm the conclusions arrived by the basic trend analysis and the use of charts. (Fig. 27.12)

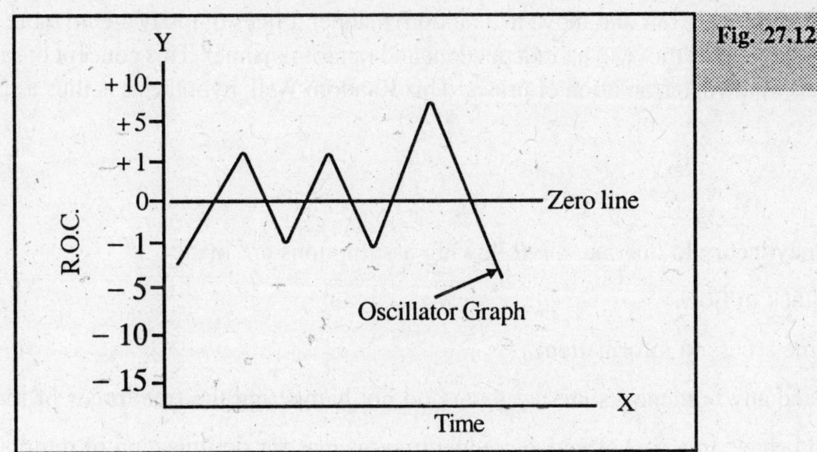

Fig. 27.12

CHAPTER 28

Efficient Market Theory

Financial Markets are influenced by money flows and information flows. In free and highly competitive markets, demand and supply pressures determine the prices or interest rates. In a theoretical sense, markets are said to be efficient, if there is a free flow of information and market absorbs this information fully and quickly. James Lorie has defined the efficient security market as follows:[@]

"Efficiency... means the ability of the capital market to function, so that prices of securities react rapidly to new information. Such efficiency will produce prices that are appropriate in terms of current knowledge, and investors will be less likely to make unwise investments."

In the above context, what will happen is that market making mechanism is free and unfettered. There are no pockets withholding information or interested parties making undue gains by insider information by manipulation of supply and demand forces. There will be no monopoly elements and malpractices or corruption etc. are not prevalent. Information flow is free and costless. In the normal course, capital or money flows into areas which are most profitable which in turn depends on their efficiency and competitiveness. Money flows also from less profitable to more profitable avenues if information flow is free, fast and costless. In such market scenario, all investors will have the same information, which is immediately reflected in the stock prices and nobody can gain extra profits. All instruments in the market will be correctly priced, as all the available information is perfectly absorbed and any investor entering the market any time will have the same advantage or returns. No excess profits are possible in this scenario. As the demand and supply forces are playing their role freely, the emerging prices are fair and move in a random manner. Prices of today are no more a function of the prices in the past as the day-to-day forces move in an independent and random manner. This concept of randomness has led to the theory of Random Walk in the determination of prices. This Random Walk hypothesis is thus a special case of the Efficient Market Theory.

Assumptions

For the capital market efficiency theory to operate, the following assumptions are made

(1) Information is free and quick to flow.

(2) All investors have the same access to information.

(3) Transaction costs, taxes and any bottlenecks are not there and not hampering the free forces of market.

(4) Investors are rational and behave in a cost effective competitive manner for optimisation of returns.

@ James H. Lorie: "Public Policy for American Capital Markets," Dept. of Treasury, USA.

(5) Every investor has access to lending and borrowing at the same rate.

(6) Market prices are not sticky and absorbs the market information quickly and the market responds to new technology, new trends, changes in tastes, habits of consumers etc., efficiently and quickly.

Random Walk Theory - Definition

As per this theory, changes in stock prices are independent of each other. The prices of today are independent of the past trends. The present price is randomly determined and only information flow can influence prices. As information is free and independent, the resulting prices are free and independent. A word of caution is necessary here. This Random walk hypothesis was postulated by researchers on the basis of empirical work on the market price behaviour. It does not therefore tantamount to the same theory as the capital market efficiency theory. Only market efficiency promotes randomness and is therefore not a necessary condition. The fact that prices move independently has been found empirically and the analysts found an explanation for this in the efficient functioning of the markets and the market absorption of the information quickly and efficiently. The equilibrium price of a stock is determined by demand and supply forces, based on the available information. Quickly as the fresh information becomes available, a new equilibrium point is reached and the resultant price is thus independent of the past.

This Random walk hypothesis contradicts the Chartist and Technical School which believes that the present prices are the result of the past trends and that averages discount all fluctuations and that the average trends move in a predictable manner as the history of trends repeats itself. On the other hand, fundamental school postulates that the prices are a function of the intrinsic value of the stock and prices result from changes in the intrinsic value and information relating to fundamental factors influence the equilibrium prices. Random walk hypothesis is an offshoot or a phase of the capital market efficiency theorem. The market efficiency theory postulates that prices are the result of free flow of information which the market absorbs quickly and efficiently.

Assumption of Random Walk Theory

(1) Market is supreme and no individual investor or group can influence it.

(2) Stock prices discount all information quickly.

(3) Markets are efficient and that the flow of information is free and unbiassed.

(4) All investors have free access to the same information and nobody has superior knowledge or expertise.

(5) Market quickly adjusts itself to any deviation from equilibrium level due to the operation of free forces of demand and supply.

(6) Market prices change only on information relating to the fundamentals, when the equilibrium level itself may shift.

(7) These prices move in an independent fashion, without undue pressures or manipulation.

(8) Nobody has better knowledge or insider information.

(9) Investors behave in a rational manner and demand and supply forces are the result of rational investment decisions.

(10) Institutional investors or any major fund managers have to follow the market and market cannot be influenced by them.

(11) A large number of buyers & sellers and perfect market conditions of competition will prevail;

Random Walk and Efficient Market Theory

Random Walk hypothesis is considered as restatement or a form of Efficient Market Theory by some Analysts. The EM - (Efficient Market Hypothesis) is based on the flow of free and correct information and the market absorption of it. This information flow and its absorption by the market are the critical elements of this theory. There are three types of information affecting the market, namely, past *Prices* and trends, other *public information* and *inside information.* If all these types are not absorbed perfectly by the market, there is a possibility of some gaining above average returns, from the investments.

Based on the above three types of information, the analysts have placed the market absorption and the related theory under three heads; namely:

(a) Weak Form of EMH, which absorbs only market price information, *(b)* Semistrong Form which absorbs price information and also all other public information and *(c)* Strong Form which absorbs all types of information including insider information.

Weak form of EMH is closely related to the Random Walk Hypothesis, as the past prices are already absorbed by the market and the present prices move therefore independently of the past, which is the same as the Random walk hypothesis. The present trends are thus random variables, and past data cannot be used to predict the future. All the information on the past data on price trends and volumes was already absorbed earlier.

As prices have no memory of the past, yesterday prices have nothing to do with today's prices. To give an example from BSE quotation Dr. Reddy Labs has yearly low of Rs. 190 and a high of Rs. 333; its price at close on Oct. 15, 1996 was Rs. 215, but it opened on Oct. 16, at Rs. 212 and closed at Rs. 210. A day later it opened again at a higher price, independent of the last closing. It is a futile exercise that the present day price can be derived by any past data, at least in short run.

If that is proved empirically, then prices move in a random fashion like the walk of a Drunkard, each move independent of the other. It is anybody's guess or the result of a toss of coin of what will be the price of TISCO today or Dr. Reddy Labs tomorrow. Thus, the Random Walk hypothesis states that prices move in random manner, independent of the past prices.

In the real world, the weak form of market efficiency may exist, as prices do move in an independent manner which the empirical evidence has shown as the past prices are already absorbed by the market. However, it is to be conceded that market imperfections, costs of information and blocks to the free flow of information may stand in the way of free play of market forces. Speculators and groups of interested parties or even brokers may manipulate the prices through cornering of shares and reducing the floating stock of the market. There are also costs, and obstructions to the full absorption of information due to trade restrictions like margins, fees, etc.

Both the Random walk hypothesis and weak form of EMH, state almost the same thing, namely, that knowledge of the past stock price does not aid the investors to gain any improved performance. The prices move independent of the other; although they may move in a random manner they move around a trend line decided by the anticipated real earnings of the company and its fundamentals. Both EMH in weak form and the Random Walk Theory, thus postulate that analysing the past does not improve the forecasting ability of stock prices and new information and prices that result from them cannot be predicted.

Empirical Tests

There were several empirical tests on the Random Walk Theory. The question tested was whether the security prices follow a "Random Walk", or whether today's prices are in any way a function of the past prices. Similarly weak form of Market efficiency also states that no investor can use the price information of the past to earn superior return on investments. Investors who analysed the past fundamentals involving price behaviour of the past did pick up good blue chips in their portfolio, but that did not give them superior portfolio performance.

Empirical tests were conducted both in the past and the present and in India and abroad on the validity of Random Walk hypothesis. These tests to some extent support the hypothesis that price changes of today are independent of the past price changes. But the evidence is not conclusive and results varied with the time periods chosen and the data used. Cowles (1934) and Jones (1937) and Kendall (1953) etc. have shown in their research that security prices moved in a random fashion.

Filter Tests

Filter tests are based on the principle of fixing a filter level varying from 0.5% to 5%, and then examine how well price changes pick up both trends and reversals. Thus, if a stock moves up a filter point say 5%; then buy it and hold it long; when it reverses by the same filter point, 5%, sell it and take a short position in it. A short position is one where one sells even without holding shares to deliver. When the stock price reverses again at the filter point, cover the short position by buying the shares in the market. By this process, the contention of chartists that prices and volume data of the past are supposed to tell the entire story and our approach is to forecast the trends and reversals only. Filtering is the screening of the important information affecting the prices from unimportant ones and see how well the price changes pick up the trends and reversals.

The results of tests conducted by Fama, Blume and Alexander on the basis of filter points also did not give conclusive proofs. If the filter level is low, the market swings capture these levels, but if the filter level is taken to be large, then results did not prove the hypothesis. Even in case of smaller filters, if transaction costs and other charges are taken into account the investors did not profit by using the filter tests. In sum, the results of filter tests did not prove the chartist school's validity. Stock prices do not move in a predictable fashion of movement and reversals and one cannot make return in excess of the results warranted by the risks assumed by the investors. These results prove that the weak form of market efficiency holds good as it is not possible to gain more from the price information of the market.

Serial Correlation Tests

Mr. Moore tested the movement of stock prices through serial correlation tests. Serial correlation is used to measure the extent of association of one series of security prices with a series in the past. Moore measures the correlation coefficient of price changes of one week with the price changes a week later and so on down the line. Its results showed that the correlation coefficient is very low indicating that a price rise did not show the tendency to the price fall and *vice versa* in any predictable manner. The price changes of this week do not therefore depend on the past price changes to any significant extent.

Fama did the same correlation tests on daily price changes in 1965. He studied the companies included in the Dow Jones Industrial average for five years. His research showed low correlation and this proved that there is no significant relation between price changes in successive periods. Serial correlation or auto correlation of price data of different time periods did not show significant positive results. This proves that prices move in an independent fashion to a large extent.

Run Tests

A run is a set of consecutive price changes in the same direction. The time series data on price changes of stocks are used to test whether there are dependencies among these series in terms of signs and reversal of signs. Fama made Run Tests to examine whether the price changes were likely to be followed by further price changes in the same direction. Run tests are conducted by the following method:

Example Elecon Engi: Suppose the price changes are as follows:

Rs. 40, 40.5, 41.50, 41.5, 45.0, 44.0, 44.0, 44.5, 46.0, 45.0 - 10 observations for ten days, then count the number of consecutive signs in the same direction which will have (+) sign. Then count the number of signs with no change with a zero sign and those with consecutive price declines (with Minus sign). In the above example we have two positive, two zero sign and then one positive, one negative sign, two with zero sign and two again with positive sign and the last with a negative sign. These data, show that there are no price dependencies. Yesterday's prices neither tell us of today's price nor today's price of to-morrow's price. There is no consistency in the price changes. This conclusion also gives support to Random Walk hypothesis. Hagerman and Richmond made a similar study for price changes observed on securities traded on O.T.C. (Over the Counter). The efficiency of options Market was tested by Black and Scholles. Their research showed that the market was not perfect and that the transactions costs are so high that those trading in the market could not make abnormal returns. Granger and Morgenstern used a method known as Spectral Analysis in 1963 to test the Random nature of the stock prices. They did not notice any worthwhile relationship between the returns of security in one period and the returns in the previous periods. Most of these research results proved that security prices moved in a random manner and are not amenable to any precise forecast.

Other Tests

Brownian motion in physics is a kind of Random Walk. The research conducted by Osborne showed that stock prices moved in a Brownian fashion. This means that simulation tests conducted by some authors showed that the mechanism of Random Walk generated variables which are similar to movement of stock prices. Robert's research in simulation tests in particular confirmed that price changes in the present period are independent of the past trends.

Research conducted by Levy in 1967 and by Jensen and Bennington in 1970 and many others did not find any significant abnormal returns due to a study of past price and volume data used in portfolio selection.

Mutual Fund Performance

Similarly, mutual fund performance based on insider information is also not found to bear any superior returns. Friend in 1972, Sharpe in 1966 and Jensen in 1969 studied relative performance of mutual funds. It was found that their results are no better. The hypothesis tested and found void is that mutual funds could earn extra ordinary returns and constantly achieve a higher average performance, because they have better access to insider information. Research studies made by Blume, Williamson and others in this line proved that the mutual fund performance was not extraordinary or superior to average market performance. They have probably no insider information or their expertise is not superior or their administrative costs are higher than for individuals.

Efficient Market Hypothesis

As referred to earlier, there are three forms of the Hypothesis, namely, weak form of EMH discussed under Random Walk Theory, semi strong form and strong form. In the words of Fama, efficient market is defined as the market where there are a large number of rational profit maximisers actively competing with each trying to predict the future market and where the current information is almost freely and equally available to all participants.

Analysis of the Research studies done so far confirm partly the weak form of EMH. But the other two forms of the Theory are found not realistic in the Practical Market Scene.

Semi-Strong Form

This form of EMH postulates that the market absorbs quickly and efficiently not only the price information but all publicly available information. Examples of this public information are found in the Financial reports, Balance Sheets and Profit and Loss Accounts, Earnings and Dividend Reports, financial results etc. In addition to financial data, any material information affecting the financial position, such as financial structure, liquidity, solvency etc., is also found relevant and absorbed by the market in the price formation. Some data and information may be contradictory and biased information, rumours etc. would also flow in as news affecting the market. Revision of data or changes in conditions of the company also affect the price. Studies on the time lag involved in the impact of any change of fundamentals on the company share price showed varied time lags, some being discounted even before the event is announced and some before the event took place. Such matters like earnings reports, bonus, rights affect the market even in anticipation before the formal announcement.

The studies on the semi strong form of market efficiency related to the effect of any public information released, on the share price. The tests are invariably based on pricing models, as under the CAPM or some econometric models. These studies showed that the absorption of this information on share prices was inefficient and varied from scrip to scrip, and the time period studied. The inefficiency in the market mechanism absorbing this data is found to be corrected over a time period as investors take time to analyse and conclude the effect of any public information.

Thus, the semi-strong form is empirically not well supported, but in many foreign markets, the semi-strong form is found to be applicable and markets quickly absorb all published information. This is possible in those markets due to strict law enforcement, by the market authorities, instantaneous display of all market information through electronic media and investor awareness of their impact and their quick absorption of the data. The revolution in informatics and communication technologies has made it possible for the application of the semi-strong form of the EMH to these markets in developed countries.

Strong Form of EMH

Under this hypothesis markets are so perfect that all information including private information, insider information and unpublished data, affecting the market are absorbed in the stock prices. Any investor can then gain the same average returns, whenever he enters the market. The information of all types is flashed to all investors simultaneously and all players have the same information at the same time. This means that only superior analysis and interpretation can give better market returns. This is possible for inside traders, floor brokers and institutional investors who have highly efficient market research component. The acumen with which price movements can be forecast can only result in superior return and not otherwise. Studies made in developed markets have showed that strong form of efficient market does not exist there also. Investors have not shown consistently higher returns even with all the information available to them. It was also found that average investor could do better by picking up securities in a random fashion.

Markets in India

It will thus be seen that the EMH in its strong form is not realistic in the actual markets. In India, in particular, despite all best efforts of SEBI, market prices are rigged up, and it is common to notice various price behavioural patterns and manipulation of prices. Information is costly and time consuming. No unqualified empirical support is found for efficient market hypothesis, even in its weakest form in India. In the case of institutional investors, equity market research is a tool used for forecasting prices and identification of undervalued scrips through fundamental analysis and determining the timings for purchase and sale by technical analysis. Although the followers of Technicals or Chartist methods are very few in India, the major component of market research revolves around both fundamental and technical factors. In practice, therefore many of these Theories, including the random walk theory are inapplicable to Indian conditions. Speculation is as high as 70-80% in Indian markets and markets are not perfect and the absorption of all types of information is also not timely and efficient. The investors in India go by research into fundamentals and select the scrips on the basis of their assessment of the extent of overvaluation and under valuation. Investment analysis therefore only involves the market research, fundamental analysis to a great extent and technical analysis to lesser extent with a view to select the undervalued scrips in the context of market conditions, reflected in the sentiment and psychology of the market.

Critique of EMH

Opinion is divided as to the validity of the EMH particularly in the strong form. In weak form Random Walk hypothesis holds good, as per some studies. The semi-strong form has found less support from the empirical studies. The perfect markets do not exist, as the stocks as a rule do not sell at the best price based on intrinsic values. Many times, speculative fervour sentiment and expectations play a greater role on the stock prices than the fundamental factors.

Similarly, news does not spread evenly among all segments of the market and among all investors. Institutional investors gain through market equity research and through economies of scale and better expertise. But individual investors do not gain by speedy spread of information and the absorption of the same by market. To gain, superior advantage, there was no adequate evidence from any of the empirical studies, based on past prices or information. There is thus a controversy on the validity of Efficient Market Theory. In real market operations, this theory did not find support, as portfolio managers did not perform better based on the results of this theory.

This theory posed a challenge to both the chartist school and the fundamentalist school. If Random Walk or Weak Market Efficiency holds good, chartist school finds its tools are not of real value to gain superior returns. Similarly, if random walk holds good, following the study of fundamentals will not secure better returns, unless additional information and insights into the company or better insider knowledge are available to investors.

PART — V

Risk and Return Concepts and Measurement

Chapter 29: Risk and Credit Rating

Chapter 30: Security Market Indicators

Chapter 31: Interest Retes – Theory and Structure

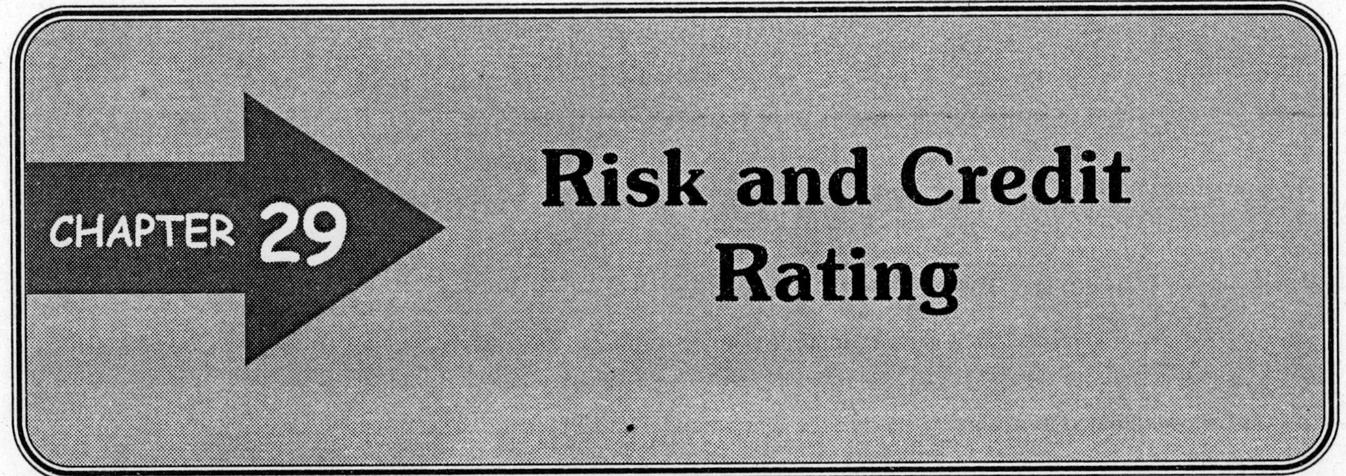

Risk and Credit Rating

RISK-CONCEPT

Introduction

All investments are risky, whether in stock and capital market or in banking and financial sector, real estate, bullion, gold, etc. The degree of risk however varies on the basis of the features of the assets, investment instrument, the mode of investment, or the issuer of the security etc. Even the so called riskless assets like bank deposits carry some cost and time in realisation of proceeds or in conversion into cash.

Risk and Uncertainty

Risk and uncertainty go together. Risk suggests that the decision maker knows that there is some possible consequence of an investment decision, but uncertainty involves a situation, where the outcome is not known to the decision maker. But basically, whether the outcome is known or not, the investments involve both risk and uncertainty. For our discussion, the word "Risk" is used to comprise all elements of variability of return, uncertainty of the outcome, etc.

Some risks can be controlled by the investors and some by the issuers of securities by planning. Others cannot be so controlled and they are to be borne compulsorily by the Investor.

What Causes the Risks?

These Risks are caused by the following factors:

(1) Wrong decision of what to invest in.

(2) Wrong timing of investments.

(3) Nature of the instruments invested say, the category of assets like corporate shares or bonds. Chit funds, Nidhis, Benefit funds etc. are highly risky, as they are in the unorganised sector. Some instruments as bank deposits or P.O. Certificates are less risky, due to their certainty of payment of principal and interest.

(4) Creditworthiness of the Issuer: The securities of Govt. and semi Govt. bodies are more creditworthy than those issued by the corporate sector and much less secure are those in the unorganised sector like indigenous bankers, shroffs, chit funds, or Private Ltd. Companies.

(5) Maturity Period or the length of investment: The larger the period, the more risky is the investment normally.

(6) Amount of Investment: The higher the amount invested in any security the larger is the risk, while a judicious mix of investments in small quantities may be less risky.

(7) Method of investment, namely, secured by collateral or not.

(8) Terms of lending such as periodicity of servicing, redemption periods, etc.

(9) Nature of the Industry or business in which the company is operating.

(10) National and International factors, acts of God, etc.

SYSTEMATIC AND UNSYSTEMATIC RISKS

Risks are Classified into Major Categories

(1) Systematic Risks are out of external and uncontrollable factors, arising out of the market, nature of the industry and the state of the economy and a host of other factors.

(2) Unsystematic Risks emerge out of the known and controllable factors, internal to the issuer of the securities or companies.

Examples of Systematic Risks

(i) Market Risk: This arises out of changes in Demand and Supply pressures in the markets, following the changing flow of information or expectations. The totality of investor perception and subjective factors influence the events in the Market which are unpredictable and give rise to risk, which is not controllable.

(ii) Interest Rate Risk: The return on an investment depends on the interest rate promised on it and changes in market rates of interest from time to time. The cost of funds borrowed by companies or stockbrokers depend on interest rates. The market activity and investor perceptions change with the changes in interest rates. These interest rates depend on nature of instruments, stocks, bonds, loans etc., maturity of the periods and the creditworthiness of the issuer of securities. But basically the monetary and credit policy which is not controllable by the investor affects the riskiness of investments due to their effects on returns, expectations, and the total principal amount due to be refunded.

(iii) Purchasing Power Risk: Inflation or rise in prices lead to rise in costs of production, lower margins, wage rises and profit squeezing etc. The return expected by investors will change due to change in real value of returns. Cost push inflation is caused by rise in the costs, due to wage rise or rise in input prices. Demand pull forces operate to increase prices due to inadequate supplies and rising demand. The increase in demand may be caused by changing expectation of future interest rates and inflation or due to increase in Money supply or creation of currency to finance the deficits of the govt. This element of purchasing Power Risk is inherent in all investments and cannot be controlled by him.

Examples of Unsystematic Risks

(i) Business Risk: This relates to the variability of the business, sales, income, profits etc. which in turn depend on the market conditions for the product mix, input supplies, strength of competitors, etc. This business Risk is sometimes external to the company due to changes in govt. policy or strategies of competitors or unforeseen market conditions. They may be internal due to fall in production, labour problems, raw material problems or inadequate supply of electricity etc. The Internal Business Risk leads to fall in revenues and in profit of the company, but can be corrected by certain changes in the company's policies.

(ii) Financial Risk: This relates to the method of financing, adopted by the company, high leverage leading to larger debt servicing problems or short-term liquidity problems due to bad debts, delayed receivables and fall in current assets or rise in current liabilities. These Problems could no doubt be solved, but they may lead to fluctuations in earnings, profits and dividends to shareholders. Sometimes, if the company runs into losses or reduced profits, these may lead to fall in returns to investors or negative returns. Proper financial planning and other financial adjustments can be used to correct this risk and as such it is controllable.

(iii) Default or Insolvency Risk: The borrower or issuer of securities may become insolvent or may default, or delay the payments due, such as interest instalments or principal repayments. The borrower's credit rating might have

fallen suddenly and he became default prone and in its extreme form it may lead to insolvency or bankruptcies. In such cases, the investor may get no return or negative returns. An investment in a healthy company's share might turn out to be a waste paper, if within a short span, by the deliberate mistakes of Management or acts of God, the Company became sick and its share price tumbled below its face value.

Other Risks

In addition to the above major risks, both in controllable and uncontrollable categories, there are many more risks, which can be listed, but in actual practice, they may vary in form, size and effect.

Some of such identifiable risks are the *Political Risks,* following the changes in the govt., or its policy shown in fiscal or budgetary aspects, etc., through changes in tax rates, imposition of controls or administrative regulations etc.; *Management Risks*, due to errors or inefficiencies of management, causing losses to the company; *Marketability Risks* involving loss of liquidity or loss of value in conversions from one asset to another say, from stocks to bonds, or *vice versa.* Such risks may arise due to some features of securities, such as callability; or lack of sinking fund or Debenture Redemption Reserve fund, for repayment of principal or due to conversion terms, attached to the security, which may go adverse to the investor.

All the above types of risks are of varying degrees, resulting in uncertainty or variability of return, loss of income, and capital losses, or erosion of real value of income and wealth of the investor. Normally, the higher the risk taken, the higher is the return. But sometimes the risk is caused by acts of God and there may be no return at all.

These other risks in any investment may be summarised here:

(1) Economic risk

(2) Political and Social risk

(3) International risk, such as currency risk

(4) Management risk

(5) Liquidity and solvency risk

(6) Callability risk

(7) Convertibility risk

(8) Acts of God like, earthquakes, etc.

Purchasing Power Risk — Problem

A problem in purchasing power risk can be set out as follows:

X invested Rs. 1,00,000 in one year bond at a coupon rate of 8%. The expected inflation rate is 5% during that year. Tax rate applicable is 30%.

Real rate of return = $\frac{1.0+r}{1.0+q} - 1$ where r is the nominal rate and q is the inflation rate.

Answer

$$\text{rr (real rate)} = \frac{1.0+0.08}{1.0+0.05} - 1$$

$$= \frac{1.08}{1.05} - 1 = 0.0285$$

If the tax rate is considered.

After tax nominal return $= 8\ (1 - \text{tax rate})$

$= 8\ (1 - 0.3)$

$= 5.6\%$

Setting this in the above equation

We have $\dfrac{1+0.056}{1+0.05} - 1 = \dfrac{1.056}{1.05} - 1 = 0.0056$

This gives a real after tax return of .6 of 1%

In general, the risk is measured by the variability of returns. Suppose there are two investments whose returns show variances over the mean as shown below which one is more risky? It is definitely Investment "B", which is more risky than "A". The reason is that it has more variability. This variability is measured by variance and standard deviation of the given series of observations.

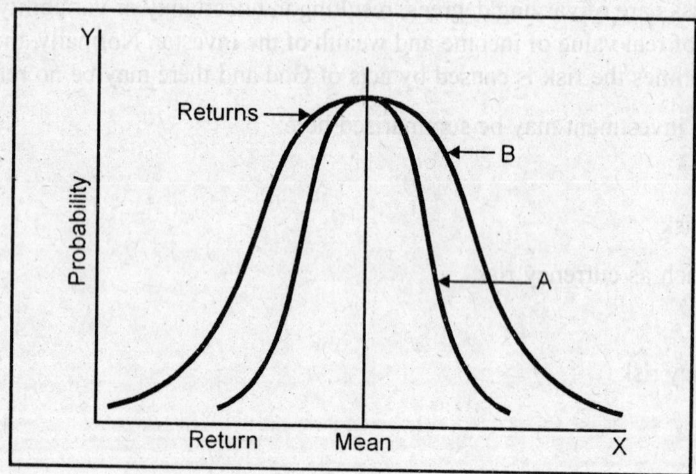

Standard Deviation and Variance

For the given data of the *X* company, calculate the SD and variance

Year	Return %
1	20
2	−6
3	14
4	−5
5	10

Formula for S.D. (σ)

$$\delta = \sqrt{\sigma^2} = \sqrt{\text{Variance}}$$

Calculation of variance:

$$\sigma^2 = \frac{\sum (r_i - \bar{r})^2}{T}$$

Where $\bar{r} = \dfrac{\sum r_t}{T} = \dfrac{33}{5} = 6.6\%$ ($\bar{r}$ is mean of observations)

$$\sigma^2 = \frac{(20-6.6)^2 + (-6-6.6)^2 + (14-6.6)^2 + (-5-6.6)^2 + (10-6.6)^2}{5}$$

$$\sigma^2 = \frac{539.2}{5} = 107.84 \text{ which is variance}$$

$$\sigma = \sqrt{107.84} = 10.38\% \text{ which is standard deviation .}$$

RISKS AND RETURNS

Investment Decision-Making

Investment decision is vital for Portfolio Management.

What to Buy and Sell are the first decisions to be made and at what price? The decision to buy or sell depends on the expectations or estimations of the fair intrinsic value of the shares, overvaluation/undervaluation of the share and a number of other factors.

The objectives of investors are income, capital appreciation, liquidity, marketability, safety and hedge against inflation. Alternative Investment Avenues with Risk-Return relationship are set out here:

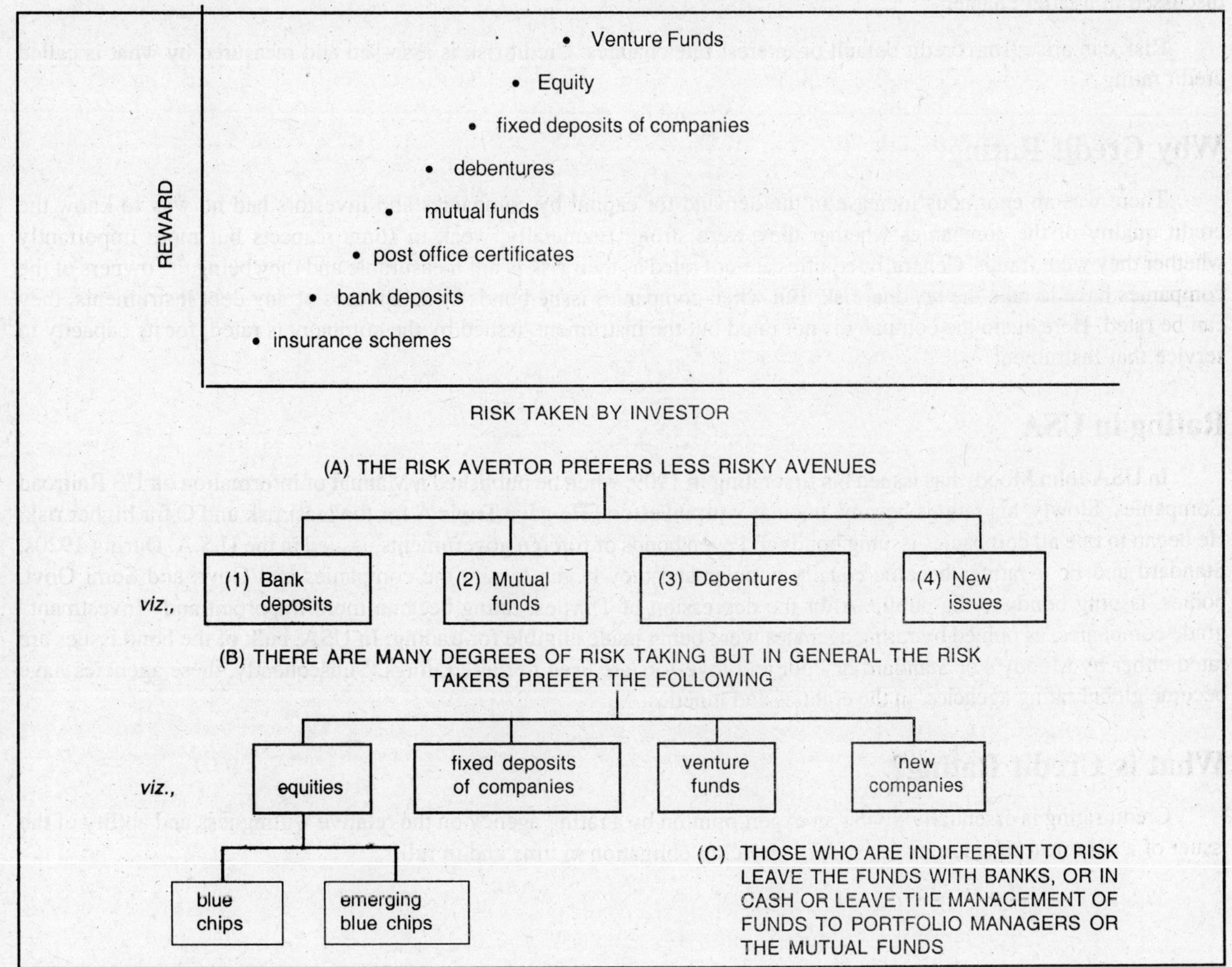

Risk Measurement

Total Risk of any investment is total variance or volatility of returns on that investment. This can be represented by spread or range of variations or fluctuation, creating uncertainty of the return and its amount. Range is the spread or breath of variations. The concepts of variance, standard deviation, dispersion over the mean covariance and beta coefficients etc. are also used to explain the measure of risk. In the context of portfolio of assets, or investment in any assets, risk is inherent in all such dealings. This risk primarily arises first out of parting of your funds or loss of liquidity. Money lent or parted is always having an element of risk. This element is the same as the concept of total risk.

Some investments in bank deposits and post office deposits or certificates or insurance, PF, etc. are less risky, but they are also not devoid of any risk. Risk may take the form of loss of time, cost involved in realisation of cash or theft of certificates etc. These are very elementary forms of risk, attached to any investment.

Range of Variation

One measure of risk is the variability or range of variability of return. If the returns for example fluctuate from zero to 20%, it is a high risk investment, which might arise due to wrong choice of companies or securities invested in. On the other hand, if the returns fluctuate from zero to 8 then it is less risky. The degree of variability is measured by dispersion or variance. The default prone bonds, or equity shares of some sick or sick prone companies may show such a wide range of fluctuation in returns. Generally, equity investments are subject to such variability of returns, within a wide range and hence called most risky investments. The range is a relative term and can be expressed as a percentage change. Risks in relation to porfolios are different from risk of individual securities. Risk in relation to portfolio is discussed in a latter chapter.

Risk can arise from credit default or interest rate changes. Credit risk is assessed and measured by what is called credit rating.

Why Credit Rating?

There was an enormous increase in the demand for capital by companies and investors had no way to know the credit quality of the companies whether they were strong financially, weak in some respects but more importantly whether they were frauds. Generally, equities are not rated as their risk is not measurable and they being the owners of the companies have to take the residual risk. But when companies issue bonds or debentures or any debt instruments, they can be rated. Here again the company is not rated but the instrument, issued by the company is rated, for its capacity to service that instrument.

Rating in USA

In USA John Moody has issued his first rating in 1909, when he published a Manual of information on US Railroad Companies. Slowly, his ratings became popular with investors. He gave Triple A for the least risk and C for higher risk. He began to rate all companies issuing bonds and even bonds of foreign governments, issued in the U.S.A. During 1920s, Standard and Poor ratings became equally popular and they began to rate the companies and Govt. and Semi Govt. bodies, issuing bonds to the public. After the depression of Thirties, rating became more important and "Investment" grade companies, as opined by rating agencies were being made eligible for trading. In USA, bulk of the bond issues are rated either by Moody's or Standard or Poor and investors are used to these ratings. Subsequently, these agencies have become global rating agencies, in the eighties and nineties.

What is Credit Rating?

Credit rating is essentially giving an expert opinion by a rating agency on the relative willingness and ability of the issuer of a debt instrument to meet the debt servicing obligation in time and in full.

How to Understand Ratings and Rating System?

These rating grades are quite common with Triple *AAA*, as least risky. *AA* less risky, *A* more risky, *B* just adequate to service and *C*, inadequate to service and highly risky and *D* is default prone. The agency rating will add their own prefix or suffix to those grades to indicate their stamp of rating. Thus in India, at present there are six rating agencies, such as, CRISIL, ICRA, CARE, Duff Phelps, Fitch and SME Ratings Ltd. It is now made compulsory that companies issuing debt instruments not convertible within 18 months to get the ratings and publish them. If a company is not satisfied with a rating of an agency, it can go to another agency.

What Instruments are Rated?

Among debt instruments in capital markets bonds, debentures not converted into equity within 18 months, preference shares and different categories of debt instruments and deposits are to be rated. Besides, among the money market instruments, commercial paper and short-term instruments of less than one year and fixed deposits of one to three years are also rated. When rating is done analysis of the company's financial and operational aspects is carried out on the basis of the data available at that time. Even debentures, convertible into equity within 18 months have been forced to be rated by SEBI.

Limitations to Ratings

These ratings are no doubt important to the investment activity in the capital market. But they have their own limitations.

(1) They do not give ratings of equity, as equityholders are supposed to take risk.

(2) Ratings of bonds, debentures and other types of instruments of debt are rated, only as indicators of risk.

(3) Ratings are only matters of opinion but coming from bodies which are experts in the field, they carry some weight.

(4) Ratings become out of date soon and hence they are to be updated, atleast every quarter or six months and any fresh information or developments may change the grade of rating.

(5) Ratings play a useful role to investors when the regulatory authority takes no responsibility for those who raise funds, and investors are left to fend themselves.

(6) Credit ratings become necessary when many default prone companies are entering the market, for which there is no regulatory provision.

(7) Credit rating agencies should maintain expert professional staff with qualifications and competence of lawyers, CAs, CS, MBA, finance and marketing and bankers etc. Besides their staff should be permanent and not too frequently changing. If these conditions are not satisfied ratings become undependable.

Key Factors Considered

Rating process involves detailed exercises involving analysis of financial statements, visits to the factory and offices of the company holding of discussions with auditors, bankers or creditors etc. Detailed desk work, outdoor work and work of specialists like those of bankers, CAs etc. are to be dovetailed and various factors are to be examined. The types of analysis attempted in this process are the following:

(i) Business Analysis: Under this head, the risks involved in operations of the companies are examined, namely, *industry risk*, with competition from others, market factors, demand and supply position, govt. policies, etc. *Marketing Risk* with competitive advantages or disadvantages, market share, selling and distribution network. Quality of customer service, *operating efficiency* involved in locational advantages, labour cooperation, cost efficiency and operating margins and lastly *legal* position, as reflected in security offered, Trust Deed and Trustee's reputation, etc.

(ii) Financial Analysis: Under this head, the rating agency examines the *accounting* quality under methods of depreciation, income recognition, treatment of bad debts, contingent liabilities, etc., *Earnings protection,* under projection of future earnings, EPS, profitability ratios, proportion of interest to G.P. and N.P. etc., *Adequacy of cash flows*, reflected in working capital management, current ratio, inventory to sales, etc. and *financial flexibility,* examined in terms of capital financing plans, flexibility in financing through alternative methods, planning methods and their flexibility.

(iii) Management Evaluation: This is examined in relation to track record of promoters, managers and top executives, their qualifications and experience, planning and control systems, capacity to adjust with flexibility, foresight to meet adverse situations, goal setting, monitoring and evaluation with a view to achieve goals, foresight for expansion and diversification etc.

(iv) Regulatory and Competitive Environment: This is assessed in terms of the structure and regulatory framework of the financial system, the efficiency of operations of the regulatory authorities, trends in regulation or deregulation and the reactions of the competitors to regulations, etc.

(v) Fundamental Analysis: Under this head, the rating agency considers the company's *liquidity management*, capital structure, debt leverage, long-term solvency, short-term solvency, matching of cash inflows to outflows and ratio analysis of the company. It will also consider assets quality, in terms of credit risk management, receivables to current assets, systems of monitoring the sector credit, individual customer risk and management of problem credits. The company's *profitability* and financial position is also analysed, through study of historical profits, spread on funds deployment, revenues on non-fund based services, accretion to reserves, profit margins etc. Besides, the impact of *Interest and Tax Rate* changes on company's net profits is analysed. The interest as a proportion of cash inflows or of gross profits is also used to examine the interest burden and potential for future earnings and the impact of debt burden on them is analysed. These and many more of such fundamental factors of the company are also analysed.

Risk and Credit Rating

All investments are risky and debt instruments carry a risk less than that of equity. Besides risk on debt instruments is easier to assess, but the residual risk of equityholders is unlimited. The debt instruments only are thus credit rated. The risk on these instruments can be known to investors before investing in these instruments, as they want to reduce risks or manage risk facing to a desirable extent.

Confidentiality of Information

The information supplied to the credit trading agency is confidential and many times during discussions, they come to know a lot more information than the public know. Under these conditions, rating agency is under an oath of secrecy. The Agency only gives the grading to the company and does not publicise it without the permission of the company, while the company itself free to use it or not. If not satisfied with one rating agency, it may go to another. The SEBI has made it compulsory to publish credit ratings.

Subjective Factors in Assessment: The agency rating has no fixed formula and it has to encounter a number of subjective elements like management quality, asset quality, auditor's quality, accounting accuracy etc. Despite the highly competent and experienced staff the credit rating agency can give only an indication and cannot claim any foolproof and 100% reliability of its assessment.

The rating work in India is in its infancy and it has drawn heavily on the experience of USA and UK. With the setting up of CARE in the private sector, it has now opened up competition among rating agencies and efficiency and cost effectiveness will be taken into account. The Govt. policy is to make rating compulsory for all debt instruments including deposits and other instruments of raising both short-term and long-term debt.

CRISIL (Credit Rating and Information Services of India Ltd.)

The CRISIL was set up in 1988 jointly by the ICICI, UTI, LIC, GIC, SBI and ADB along with a number of other financial institutions. The objective of this institution is to rate the debt obligations of Indian companies on a voluntary basis with a view to providing the investors a guide as to the risk of timely payment of interest and principal by the company. The rating is at present confined only to fixed deposits, debentures, preference shares and short-term instruments like commercial paper. The CRISIL does not rate equity shares or the performance of the company as a whole. The ratings are specifically meant for the instruments referred to above.

CRISIL Rating and Investor Protection

Investors should also be familiar with the ratings given by the Credit Rating and Information Services of India Ltd. (CRISIL) for protecting their interests. The CRISIL ratings are given only for debt instruments of companies, namely, Commercial Papers (CP), debentures, bonds and fixed deposits. Since early 1992, the ratings of Investment Information and Credit Rating Agency (ICRA) are also used by companies. These are given on a voluntary basis and may be publicised or not, depending upon the company's own perception of the impact of these on the investors. The ratings in use by the companies are published by the CRISIL in their "CRISIL Rating Scan." The companies use them only when the ratings are favourable to them and when they are making any public offer for deposits or debentures, etc. The investors should examine these symbols with regard to their benefits and their implication. Since a rating given can be revised upwards or downwards, the investors should keep a watch on any such revisions. Unfortunately, the CRISIL itself would not publicise them for the benefit of the investors as it is a private and autonomous organisation and is under no obligation to do so. The SEBI guidelines now insist that all companies should get these ratings and publicise them compulsorily, if they are borrowing through issue of debentures to the public. Many companies accepting fixed deposits are also using these CRISIL ratings. Rating of company deposits is made Compulsory under the new companies Bill 1993. The RBI made it compulsory for all N.B.F.Cs registered with it to get themselves rated, before they borrow from public in any form.

The implications of the rating used are as follows:

For Debentures, simple 'A' and 'B' are used; for preference shares, "Pf" is prefixed. For fixed deposits and short-term instruments, "F" and "P" are prefixed, respectively.

Debenture Ratings	*Implication*
Triple A — (AAA)	— Highest Safety
Double A — (AA)	— High Safety
Single A — (A)	— Adequate Safety
Triple B — (BBB)	— Moderate Safety
Double B — (BB)	— Inadequate Safety
B, C & D	— High risk and default-prone
Fixed Deposits Ratings,	
F Triple A — (FAAA)	— Highest Safety
F Double A — (FAA)	— High Safety
F Single A — (FA)	— Adequate Safety

FB, FC and FD are inadequate, high-risk and default-prone instruments.

ICRA

Another Credit Rating Agency was set up later, namely, The Investment Information and Credit Rating Agency of India Limited, registered in 1991, sponsored by the IFCI and a number of other financial institutions. It has its headquarters at Delhi, while the CRISIL has its headquarters in Mumbai.

As investments have a risk, investor should know the extent of the risk he is taking. For this, risk rating is necessary, particularly now when interest rates on debentures are freed. Debentures, bonds, preference shares and fixed deposits are eligible to be rated. The rating is instrument wise but not for the whole company. The ratings given by the credit rating agency like ICRA are indicators of the correct opinion of the relative capability of timely servicing of debts and obligations by the company.

The ratings given are AAA, AA or A for safety, BBB, BB or B for less safe investments C and D indicate no safety and default respectively. But as equities are essentially risky and investor is willingly entering the risky investment of equity, credit rating for equity is possible but not compulsory. ICRA has started rating equity also. Only in respect of debt instruments, investor wants to avoid risk and so he should know the extent of the risk, he is taking. Equity holder is the owner and takes risk voluntarily while the debentureholder is creditor and he does not want to take risk in respect of interest or in payment of the principal.

Factors Considered

In evaluating the instruments in question, CRISIL takes into account the various risks involved in servicing of instruments. They undertake business analysis, financial analysis, management evaluation and fundamental analysis. They also take into account the regulatory and competitive environment faced by the company and other relevant factors.

In business analysis, the CRISIL takes into account the legal position in terms of prospectus, memorandum, articles of association, etc., industry risk, demand and supply position for the company's products, market share of the company and its operational efficiency. In financial analysis, the CRISIL evaluates the accounting quality of the company, its inventory norms, depreciation policy and its accounting and audit methods. The financial flexibility is shown in the capital structure, methods of raising funds, adequacy of working capital funds, cash flows and earnings protection, etc.

The CRISIL also evaluates the management risk as judged by the track record of the management, planning and control system, managerial expertise, tax planning and expansion plans of the company. In general, the goals and objectives of the company, its sales and assets growth, capacity to overcome adverse economic and market conditions, etc. will be assessed by the CRISIL.

Under fundamental analysis, evaluation is carried out for the equity earnings per share, book value, capital and sales turnover, management, debt-equity ratio, current assets to liabilities ratio, contingent liabilities, etc. Besides, the asset quality will be judged by the risk element of various assets and interest and tax sensitivity of the company and its profitability position in general.

What is discussed above with regard to CRISIL holds good for any credit rating Agency in India. All of them are now brought under the ken of the regulation by SEBI.

Ratings

All the above types of analysis will be done by experts after discussions with the company executives, its suppliers, customers and market competitors. The information is gathered on a confidential basis and assessed with a view to examine the capacity of the company to service the instruments issued to the public.

Broadly, there are three categories of ratings:

(a) Long-term Instruments (Debentures and Preference Shares)	Triple A to triple B
(b) Medium-term Instruments (Fixed Deposits)	FAAA to FA
(c) Short-term Instruments (C.P., etc.)	P_1 to P_3

The rating indicates the degree of risk and the highest safety possible is under the rating of AAA or FAAA or P_1. The creditworthiness is indicated in the ratings and reflects the capacity of the company to service them adequately with a view to ensure the timely payment of interest and principal.

Advantages

For the company a good rating from CRISIL or any other Rating Agency will help raise funds in the capital market. Although many companies have got their instruments evaluated by CRISIL to get an independent view of their credit standing, a few only have publicised them. For the investors these rating help them in making a decision of their investment in various instruments. Besides such ratings have a demonstration effect and improve competitiveness of the companies to outperform each other. The services of CRISIL are charged to the company and the use of the rating is left to the choice of the company. If it chooses not to use it, it is free do so. This rating is also updated from time to time by the

CRISIL whenever additional information is available and compulsorily every year. The lay public and the investors would benefit from such information about the performance of the company and their servicing capacity. This will in turn help to improve the climate of investment and the tone of the capital market. Under the latest guidelines rating is compulsory for all issues of debentures, either convertible or non-convertible whatever is their maturity. It is made compulsory for deposits raised from the public, by all registered NBFCs.

CARE

A new credit rating agency was set up in April 1993 in the Private Sector and many more may come up in the future, when credit rating becomes compulsory for all debt instruments. The new institution is called the Credit Analysis and Research Limited for its activity of credit analysis and rating. The objects and functions of CARE are the same as those of CRISIL and ICRA. Companies will now have a better choice in entrusting the work of rating of their debt instruments issued to the public. The choice will be based on the efficiency and cost effective service given by the various credit rating agencies. CARE has started operations in November 1993 and their operations increased faster than that of ICRA.

Duff and Phelps

This is a private sector credit rating agency with foreign collaboration set up in 1995-96. It has made rating exercises to many companies and provided a competitive environment for rating agencies.

The rating agencies are now prepared to rate equity in both the primary and secondary markets. All ratings are expected to be publicised and updated on a quarterly basis.

Fitch

Fitch Ratings India Limited is another credit rating agency, set up as a subsidiary of the Foreign Company in India.

SME Ratings Ltd., is the latest agency set up in 2005, for rating of risk of companies and the instruments floated by them.

CHAPTER 30

Security Market Indicators

Introduction

Security markets are those financial markets in which securities, like shares, bonds, debentures, etc. are issued and traded. The constituents in these markets include broker firms, financial institutions, banks, investment companies and many others including mutual funds which actively participate in the market as dealers, traders or as intermediaries. The demand emanates from investors while the supply comes from the issuers of securities.These issuers may be government, semi-government bodies, public undertakings, private corporate sector, financial institutions etc. In the case of old securities, demand and supply may emanate from the buyers and sellers. In the case of new issues, these are issued direct to savers including households, companies, institutions, PFs, etc.

Different types of securities and financial instruments are traded, purchased and sold in these markets. These instruments may be of ownership nature like equities and preference shares or of debt nature like debentures, bonds, etc. Bulk of the trading in the stock market is in these corporate securities which are traded in the trading ring or on electronic system. However, there are some instruments issued by the Government, Central or State, or by government bodies, municipalities, local bodies, etc. in which case they are called government and government-guaranteed bonds or semi-government bonds. The section of the market in which these are traded is also a part of the stock market and is called gilt-edged market.

Functions and Activity

These markets perform some basic functions and activity in the markets reflects these functions. The activity in turn is represented and measured by some leading indicators. Therein lies the importance of these indicators. These indicators would throw light on the degree and extent of the activity and trends in the market and reveal the importance of the market.

Basically, the functions of these markets are:

1. Provision for securitisation of the debt or capital issued, which promotes savings mobilisation through new capital issues.
2. Extending facilities for trading (buying and selling) in these securities so as to impart liquidity to these instruments so that investors can disinvest while new savers can invest and enter the market. This will facilitate the reallocation of funds as between securities or companies.
3. Making a quotation for a share available to the investors and companies so that their net asset values are known and they can be used for tax purposes.

4. This market also enables the companies to raise more capital from the capital market than is possible without these facilities for disinvestment, trading and liquidity.
5. For the economy as a whole, these markets help mobilisation of savings for financing of corporate and government investment in order that economic growth and rise in incomes of the people can take place on a continuing basis.

These markets have thus a vital role to play for investors at the micro level and for the economy at the macro level. For investors, it provides a venue for use of their savings for earning an income, capital appreciation and returns. For the economy, it facilitates savings mobilisation for capital formation which is necessary for economic growth.

The constituents of the markets are:

(1) issuers of securities like Companies and Government;

(2) investors or traders who buy and sell securities; and

(3) intermediaries like brokers, merchant bankers etc., who mediate between issuers and investors and as between buyers and sellers.

Segments of the Markets

Fig. 30.1 describes the segments of the security markets.

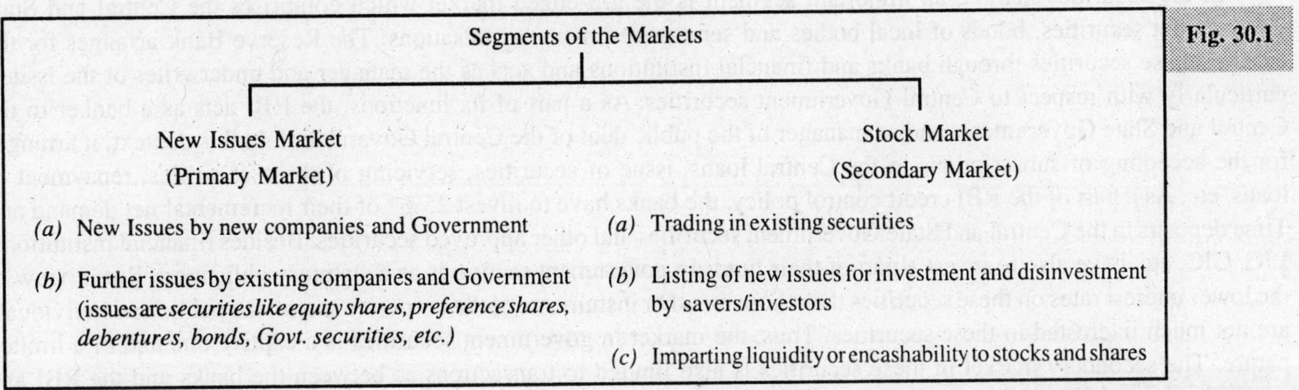

Fig. 30.1

The investors in the primary issues or new issues would be only buying in the primary market but cannot sell there. They will be dealing in buying and selling in the secondary market only. Investors or institutions and buyers and sellers would deal in the secondary market through the intermediaries or brokers. The issuers of securities are the corporate units, Government and semi-Government bodies and public sector undertakings. The public, savers, investors and institutions, etc. can invest in both the primay and secondary markets. Their investments would be the sources of funds for the issuers of securities.

The primary market is called new issues market or the capital market while the secondary market is called the stock market. In the primary market, the government and the public sector undertakings as well as corporate units borrow funds or issue capital in the form of securities, shares, bonds, etc. The activity here refers to raising capital of ownership or debt nature. In this market, the primary savers or investors can keep their funds for a return. In the secondary market, they can both buy and sell existing securities, invest and disinvest or rechannel funds from one company into another or one type of security into another.

The secondary market is thus an important adjunct of the primary market. The activity in these two markets is inter-linked and the indicators are also related although separate in themselves and the starting link is listing of issues on the Stock Markets.

The new issues, which are floated in the primary market, are permitted to be issued to the public by a nod of SEBI at price which is at par (face value) in the case of new companies or at a premium or par in the case of existing companies. The Capital Issues Controller as the authority to regulate was abolished. But in the secondary market the

SEBI, the Ministry of Finance, and the Stock Exchange Division control and regulate the stock markets and the stock exchange authorities. The stock markets are directly regulated by their own board of directors, namely, the Stock Exchange authorities, with the consent and approval of the government. The stock exchanges are recognised bodies to trade and deal in securities through their members who are brokers. The Stock Exchange authorities are self-regulatory bodies under the overall supervision of the SEBI and Stock Exchange Division of the Government.

The new issues of companies are in the form of shares — equity and preference shares — debentures, etc. The securities issued by the companies and government are listed on the stock markets after they are floated and issued to the public. So far as the government and the semi-government securities are concerned, they are automatically listed for trading without any conditions or fees but in the case of corporate securities, the companies have to approach the respective stock exchanges where their registered office is located for the purpose of listing. A listing agreement is entered into containing all the rules and regulations governing the conduct of the companies in respect of shares listed and the relations between the stock exchange and listed companies. The listed shares can be bought and sold and traded which will lead to price formation for shares. The resultant price may be at par or face value or at a premium or discount of the face value depending upon the demand for and supply of these shares. These demand and supply forces may in turn depend on the physical and financial performance of the companies in question and their future prospects, etc. Trading before listing is called the grey market, which is not controlled.

Segment of Government Securities

In the securities market, an important segment is the gilt-edged market which comprises the Central and State Government securities, bonds of local bodies and semi-government organisations. The Reserve Bank arranges for the issue of these securities through banks and financial institutions and acts as the manager and underwriter of the issues, particularly with respect to Central Government securities. As a part of its functions, the RBI acts as a banker to the Central and State Governments and as manager of the public debt of the Central Government. In this context, it arranges for the accepting of subscriptions to the Central loans, issue of securities, servicing of these securities, repayment of loans, etc. As a part of the RBI credit control policy, the banks have to invest 25%* of their incremental net demand and Time deposits in the Central and State Government securities and other approved securities. Besides financial institutions, LIC, GIC, etc. have also to invest a part of their funds in government securities as a statutory obligation. But in view of the lower interest rates on these securities than those on other instuments of the corporate sector, the public and individuals are not much interested in these securities. Thus, the market in government securities is a captive one and of a limited nature. The secondary market in these securities is also limited to transactions as between the banks and the RBI and among banks and financial institutions.

The market in these securities is over the counter (OTC), through telephones, personal contact, telex etc. and hence the data on prices and yields etc. are not properly reported to the stock exchange where they are quoted. But as the manager of the public debt of the Government and through the operations undertaken in the open market (called open market operations), the RBI collects some information on prices and compiles data on yields. The prices and yields on government securities are thus compiled and published by the RBI regularly in their monthly and annual publications.

* Effective from October 1994, the S.L.R. on aggregate deposits was reduced to 31.5%, and further to 25% in October 1997. As from November 2008, the SLR stood at 24% of NDTL.

Fig. 30.2

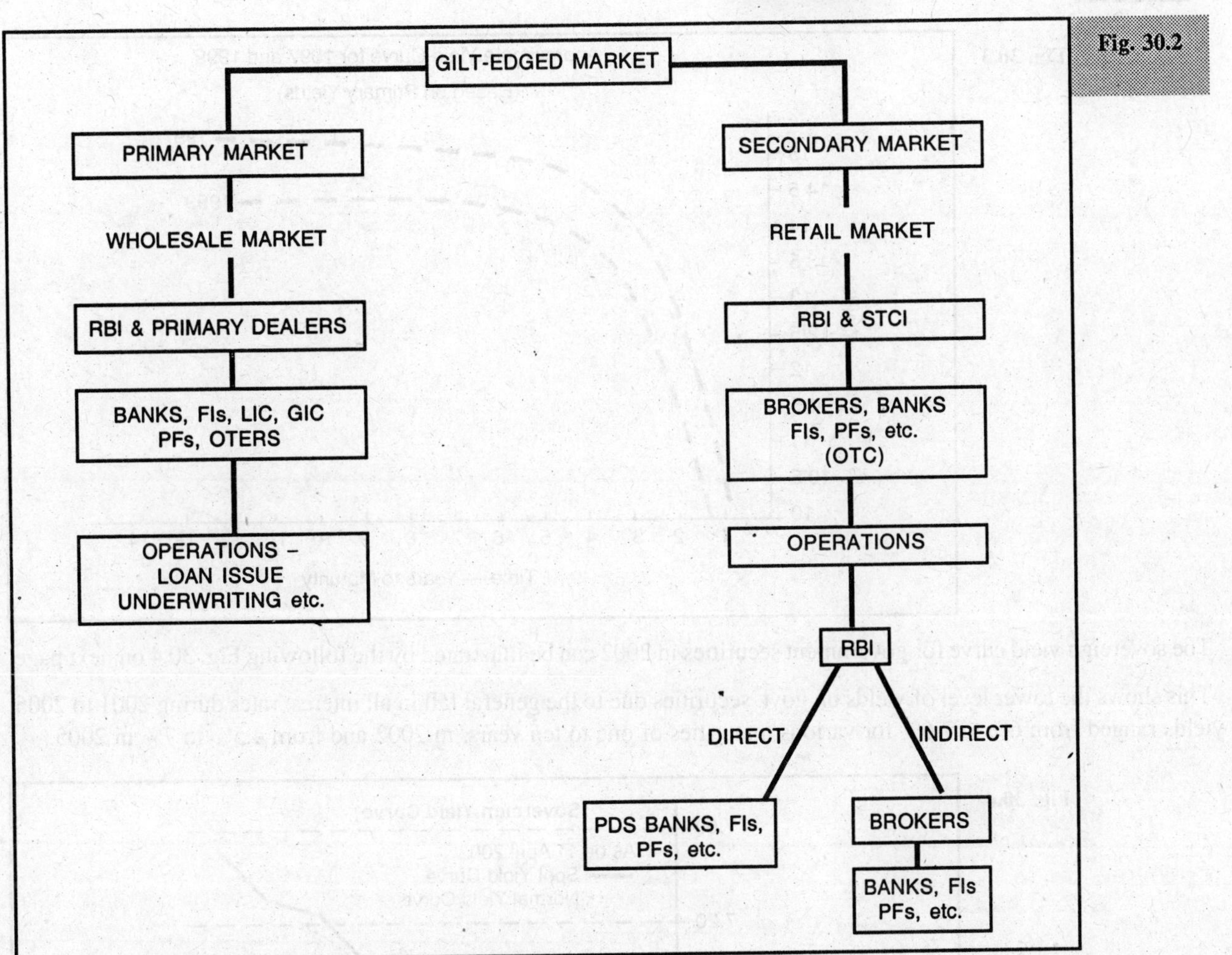

Fig. 30.2 presents a picture of sections within the gilt-edged market, namely, primary and seconday sections, representing the issue of government securities, wholesale and trading in retail respectively. The players in the market are RBI, STCI Primary Dealers, banks, FIs and brokers. The RBI is the main lead manager and underwriter with respect to Central Government securities and a major holder of these securities. The banks and financial institutions, PFs and companies deal in these securities with or without the help of brokers.@ The RBI conducts open market operations of purchase and sale directly with banks and financial institutions or with the help of brokers. New securities are now sold through auctions, as well as through offer of sale.

Yield Curve

To give an example of the use of yields, Fig. 30.3 presents the yield curve of the Central Government securities of various maturities. The securities are loans carrying coupon rates such as C.G. 9.90%-2005 and 10.70%-2020. (Here C.G. stands for Central Government). The figure shows that the yields vary from about 10 to 14% which came down recently depending upon the maturity period of the loan, demand and supply factors, attractiveness of loans in terms of rate of interest payment and date of redemption etc. These yields are worked out on a daily basis and are used for making decisions by banks and FIs for purchases and sale deals and reshuffling of their portfolios of government and semi-government securities with the objective of maximising returns and booking capital gains or losses for tax purposes. The yield curve has gone down further in 2001 to 2005 to a range of 4.5 to 7% for Govt. and Semi-Govt. Securities.

@ The RBI has announced a scheme of licensing primary market dealers in Govt. securities in March 1995. They act as market makers and help placement of these securities develop secondary market and act as conduit for open market operations of RBI.

Fig. 30.3

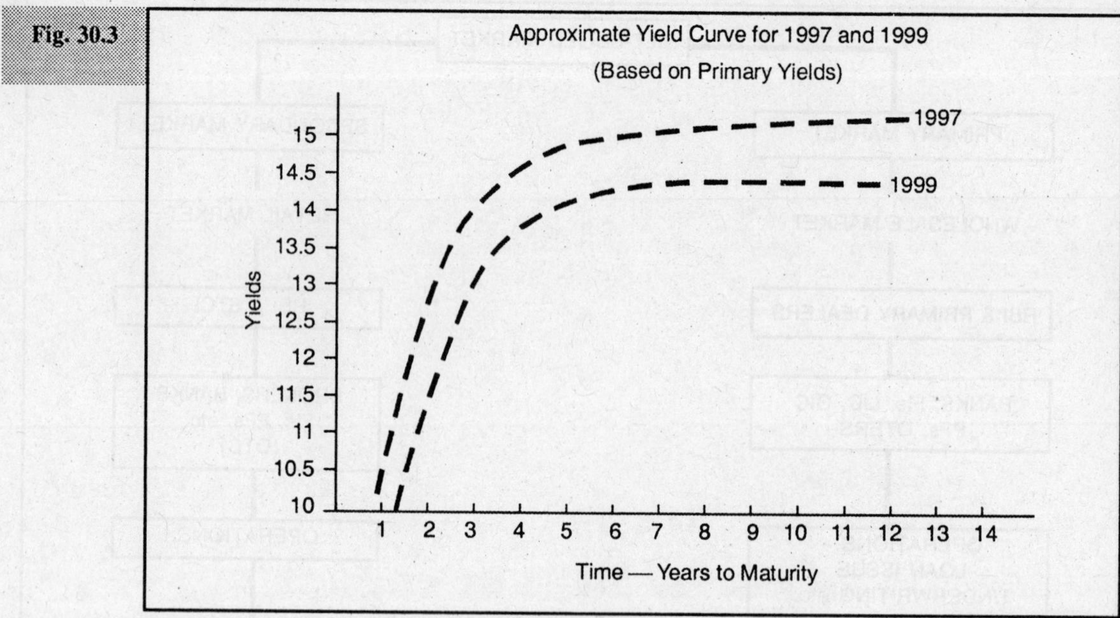

The sovereign yield curve for government securities in 2002 can be illustrated by the following Fig. 30.4 on next page.

This shows the lower level of yields on govt. securities due to the general fall in all interest rates during 2001 to 2005. The yields ranged from 6% to 7.6% for various maturities of one to ten years, in 2002 and from 4.5% to 7% in 2005.

Fig. 30.4

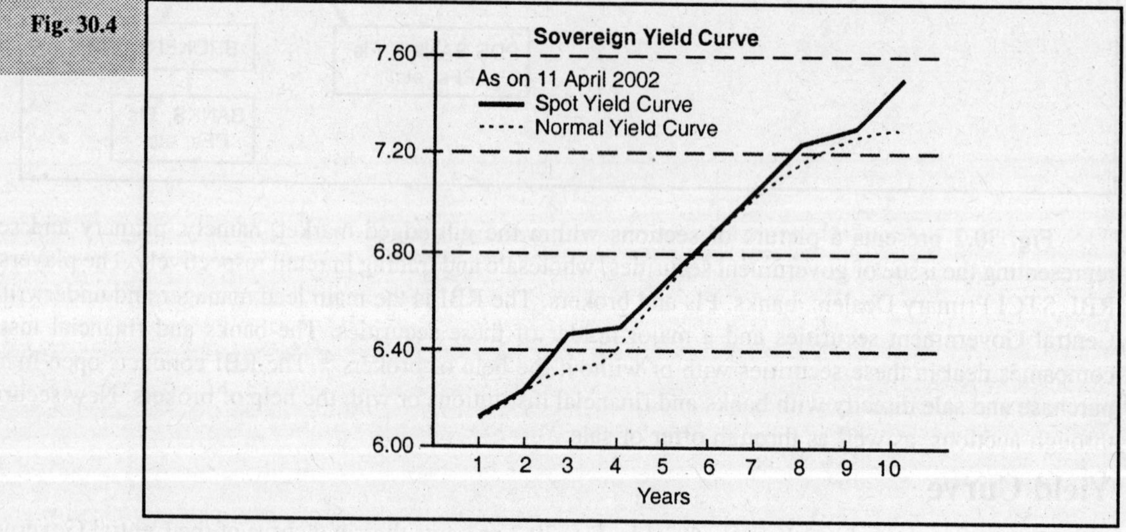

The yield curve as in 2006 - 07 is given in Chapter 35. The yields ranged from 7.25% to 8.21% for maturities of 5 years and ten years respectively in 2006-07, which are almost similar in 2008-09.

Indicators

The main indicators in the section of government securities are:

1. Volume of turnover, on which data are collected or published by RBI and NSE.
2. Prices of these securities which are collected by the RBI and reported to the Stock Exchange by the brokers from time to time.
3. Yields on these securities — current yields and redemption yields[1] complied and published by the RBI and the stock exchanges on which they are quoted.

1. These concepts have been explained in another chapter.

RBI publishes data on a monthly basis on Turnover in Government Securities (Face Value) at Mumbai, Secondary market outright transactions in dated Government Securities maturity wise, and RBI open market operations.

The NSE publishes on a daily basis data security-wise traded value and weighted yields with weights proportional to trade value.

The available indicators in this segment of the market are thus only the prices, yields and turnover. The data on the total volume of trade turnover are now available but there is no good reporting system on a daily basis as the market is over the counter and on prices and yields in respect of various government and semi-government bonds/securities are, however, reported to the stock exchanges and the RBI publishes, collects these data, as they are also directly involved in this market under open market operations, under which they buy and sell Central Government securities to stabilise the market and to influence the structure of yields.

The data on prices and yields are reported and published by the RBI under three heads as shown below, in the form of indices:

(a) Central Government Security price indices.

(b) State Government Security price indices.

(c) Semi-Government Security price indices.

These data used to be published region-wise and on all-India basis in the publications of the RBI. but now discontinued. The regions covered were the five major centres of Mumbai, Kolkata, Delhi, Chennai and Ahmedabad, where the major stock exchanges are located. The security price indices reflect the pressures of demand and supply for the securities. The yields are the returns on these investments expressed in terms of income as a percentage of purchase price. Yields are compiled mainly in respect of fixed interest securities. As the purchase prices of these securities vary depending on the supply and demand pressures but interest rates (or coupon rates) on them are fixed in terms of the face value (Rs. 100), the yields vary from the coupon rates depending upon how much purchase price varies from the face value. Yields thus reflect the return on these instruments and influence the demand and supply forces.

Corporate Securities Section

The other important section in the securities market is the trading in securities issued by the corporate sector in the form of equity shares, preference shares and debentures. In this section, the most actively traded securities are equities in respect of which prices (or price indices), volume of trading (or turnover), yields and spread of fluctuations in prices, etc. are all available in respect of major stock exchanges like BSE and NSE. In respect of debentures and preference shares, trading is less active for two reasons. One is that they are held mostly by financial institutions and public participation is poor. Secondly, these are not attractive enough for investors who want capital appreciation, as these are only fixed income securities. In respect of these securities, only prices and yields are available. The price indices and yields in respect of equity (variable dividend industrial securities), are published by the RBI in their monthly and annual publications (Monthly Bulletin and Handbook of statistics on Indian Economy of the RBI). In respect of equity shares, a number of market indicators are available. The price indices of various types and other indicators are available on a daily, weekly and monthly basis from many sources, as referred to later.

Main Indicators

In addition to the prices, the other main indicators of securities markets may be set out as follows:

1. No. of companies quoted of which —

(a) Those most actively traded daily and placed in Group A or specified group (eligible for carry forward business);

(b) Those less actively and less frequently traded and placed on a cash list (not allowed to be carried forward but for delivery only) called Group B_1 and B_2.

(c) Trading volume and value in permitted Securities on Exchanges other than BSE.

2. No. of issues/scrips available for trading in
   (a) Equity issues; *(b)* Preference shares; *(c)* Debentures.
3. Paid-up capital of companies listed in Equity issues.
4. Market value of companies (or market capitalisation) listed in respect of:

   Equity issues.
5. Value and volume of trading or turnover daily (or number of shares or transactions and their value) indicating the extent of activity in the market.
6. Volatility of price changes daily, weekly or monthly (indicating the stability of price behaviour or the range of spread of prices in the market).
7. Breadth of the market, namely, daily gainers or losers among scrips indicating the extent of bullishness or bearishness in the market (No. of scrips rising in price and falling in price) Advances and Declines.
8. Market price as a ratio to earning per share of each scrip or for all traded scrips in the market also called P/E ratio, indicating the relationship of market behaviour to the performance of companies.
9. Velocity of price changes or rate of change of prices of each scrip or for the market index, indicating how fast or quickly the price, representing the price behaviour and likely reversal of the trend or acceleration or deceleration of market activity.
10. Yields or returns on investments at the current market prices and at the time of maturity if the securities are bonds, debentures or preference shares (also called fixed income securities).
11. Badla rates for carry forward of shares in the specified shares (Group A) which tell about the technical position in the market, whether the market is overbought or oversold in a scrip and the extent of overheating in the market and the availability of finance for badla and the money market conditions. These badla rates are now irrelevant after the starting of the Rolling Settlement System on the BSE and NSE.

SECURITY PRICE INDICES

RBI Index of Industrial Security Prices

As noted earlier, the RBI has been compiling since 1949 indices of security prices under the following heads. These are revised from time to time by shifting the base year and enlarging the coverage, *until they are all discontinued in 1999.*

1. Government and semi-government securities.
2. Debentures of joint-stock companies.
3. Ordinary shares.

The discontinued RBI series is with base 1980-81 = 100. The price indices are compiled on a weekly basis and the average of weeks for months/years etc. These are presented on an all-India basis and on a regional basis for the five regions, namely, Mumbai, Kolkata, Chennai, Ahmedabad and Delhi. However, the compilation of index numbers of prices for debentures and preference shares was discontinued with effect from December 1979, for the reason that these were not actively traded and their price quotations were not up-to-date.

Among the ordinary shares, only 338 are included in this series with the following regional distribution: Mumbai 32%, Kolkata 26%, Chennai 17%, Ahmedabad 10%, Delhi 15%. The selection of individual scrips in each industry group was made on the basis of —

1. size of the average market value of the share capital of the company during the base year; (Market Capitalisation) and
2. the activity of the scrip as indicated by the number of price changes during the base year (turnovers).

The number of sample scrips selected at each centre has been so fixed taking into account the total number listed and their paid-up capital and taking care to see that the sample scrips accounted for 60-70% of the aggregate market value of scrips in each centre.

The weights given to each company and to each industry group are proportional to their share in the aggregate average market value of share capital of total companies quoted on each stock exchange. The regional market weights for group and sub-group indices of ordinary shares are proportional to the aggregate average market value of share capital of all the scrips belonging to the group or sub-group and quoted on the respective stock exchanges as on the base date, namely, March 31, 1981. The all-India weights in respect of various group/sub-group indices are proportional to their respective shares of their average market value to total market value of all scrips in the concerned groups/sub-groups quoted at all centres, counting only once the average market value of scrips quoted at more than one centre. The all-India index is thus secured from the regional groups.

The method of compilation is such that the weekly average price of each sample is obtained as the arithmetical average of daily closing quotations in the week. The price relative for a scrip during a particular week is worked out as the ratio of the average price for the current week to the base year average price of that scrip. The price relative to a sub-group at each region is obtained as the unweighted geometric mean of price relatives of scrips selected in that sub-group.

BSE Sensitive Index

The Stock Exchange, Mumbai, has started its own price index since January 1, 1986, called the BSE Sensitive Index of Equity Prices. It has 30 scrips which are actively traded, many of which are in Group A (specified group) and a few in Group B (non-specified group). It has a base year 1978-79 = 100 and represents all the major industries quoted on the Exchange. These indices are published on a daily, monthly and yearly basis since April 1979. These are available in the daily papers and in the publications of the BSE.

The selection of the base year is made only on the basis of its price stability and its proximity to the current period. The year 1978-79 was selected for this purpose as it has shown relative price stability and proximity to the latest years.

Scrip Selection

The selection of scrips has been made on the basis of market activity in these scrips and for giving representation to all major industrial groups. All the 30 scrips chosen are actively traded on a daily basis on the BSE. A revision of the scrips included in the sensex was undertaken in August 1996 and again in 1998 and 2001 but the total number is retained at 30.

Methods of Compilation

The index for a day is calculated as the percentage of the aggregate market value of the equity shares of all companies in the sample on that day to the average market value of the equity shares of the same companies during the base period. This method of compilation enables the necessary flexibility to adjust for arbitrary and non-market related price changes caused by the issue of rights and bonus shares.

Weightage

The weightage given to each scrip is according to the number of shares outstanding in that scrip. The current market value for any share in the list is obtained by multiplying the price of the share by the number of shares outstanding, so that it would influence the index of price in proportion to the market importance of each scrip.

Other Adjustments

When bonus or rights issues are made or when consolidation or splittting of shares takes place or mergers are efffected or when convertible debentures are converted into equity, necessary adjustments are made and a new weighting factor is arrived at after taking the number of shares outstanding, its face value and its market value after the event has occurred. If by the issue of right share or merger, the total paid-up capital is changed, necessary changes are made in both the base year and current year. When the bonus issue is made, the number of shares will increase but not the net worth. When rights are issued, the number of shares and paid-up capital will change. In such cases, base year weights are changed accordingly to make them comparable to the current period.

BSE Sensex Composition

At end of 1998, the composition of the BSE Sensitive Index was changed drastically after a similar change in August 1996. Many Banking and Finance Sector Companies and the representation to Services Sector were found in the new Index. Only 30 scrips were retained by deleting equal number of old scrips and inclusion of the same number of new scrips. In April 2000, again the composition of sensex was changed to include New Economy Scrips. Satyam Computers, Zee Telefilms, Infosys and Dr. Reddy's Labs were included, alongwith Reliance Petroleum. The weightage given to the New Economy Stocks namely Infosys, Satyam, Zee Telefilms and NIIT is about 50% of the revised Index. The scrips which have been replaced include Indian Hotels, IDBI, Tata Chemicals and Tata Power.

In 1998, Infosys NIIT, Castrol and Navortis were inducted by deleting Arvind Mills, G.E. Shipping, SAIL, and IPCL. In 2000, Satyam, Zee Telefilms, Dr. Reddy's Labs and Reliance Petroleum were brought in, by dropping Indian Hotels, IDBI, Tata Chemicals and Tata Power.

The revised Market Cap of the 30 Scrips in the Sensex worked out to 39% of the total Market cap of BSE. The earlier 30 scrips had only a market cap of 29% of the total market cap.

BSE National Index

This series of BSE National Index has been started by the Bombay Stock Exchange in 1988-89 with the base year 1983-84 = 100. This series has 100 scrips, including also the 30 scrips belonging to the BSE Sensitive Series. These 100 scrips have been chosen from almost all industrial groups which represent the listing on the major stock exchanges, namely, Mumbai, Kolkata, Chennai, Delhi and Ahmedabad. The method of compilation and other details are almost similar to the compilation of BSE Sensitive Series. Adjustments are also made from time to time for the bonus issues, right issues, conversion of debentures, etc.

Of these 100 scrips, 22 are quoted in Mumbai only while 72 scrips are quoted on the BSE besides other stock exchanges, while the remaining six scrips are quoted only on the other stock exchanges. Thus, nearly 95% of the issues covered are quoted and traded on the BSE.

The National Series is compiled from April 1984 while the Sensitive Series has been available from April 1979. A comparison of these two series shows that the National Index is more broad-based and has been showing a relatively more stable picture of price trends as compared with the BSE Sensitive Series. Although percentage changes in prices over a long period correspond to each other in both the series, the sensitive series is more fluctuating and more sensitive to changes in prices of a few scrips, which are highly speculative. These two series are, therefore, complementary and are compiled and published on a daily basis by the Bombay Stock Exchange.

The choice of the base year 1983-84 is due to its price stability and relative proximity. The weightage pattern and method of compilation are similar to those adopted in the case of BSE Sensitive series. The price of each component share in the index is weighted by the number of shares outstanding so that it will influence the index in proportion to its respective market importance. The current market value for any share is obtained by multiplying the price of the share by the number of shares outstanding. The index for a day is calculated as the percentage of the aggregate market value of the equity shares of all the companies in the sample on that day to the average market value of the equity shares of the same companies during the base period.

As in the case of Sensitive Series, adjustments are made for bonus issues, rights issues, conversion of debentures into equity or loans into equity by financial institutions, mergers, etc., where necessary as in the case of rights or debenture conversion. When paid-up capital will change, the base year average is suitably adjusted on the basis of ex-right or ex-conversion price of the equity share.

Base year changes are in effect proportional adjustments in the base year average market value to offset price changes in the market values upon which the index is based. The formula is:

$$\text{New Base Year Average} = \text{Old Base Year Average} \times \frac{\text{New Market Value}}{\text{Old Market Value}}$$

For example, a company issues rights to raise capital by Rs. 100 crores. Its base year average is, say, Rs. 2,450 crores, its old market value is Rs. 4781 crores and by the addition of rights, its new market value is Rs. 4,781 + 100 = Rs. 4,881.

$$\text{The new base year average} = \frac{2450 \times 4881}{4781} = 2501.24$$

The figure of 2501.24 will be used on the base year average for calculating the index number from then onwards till the next base change becomes necessary.

BSE 200 and Dollex

Two more indexes were compiled by B.S.E. since 1993, with base year, 1989-90 = 100. Both include very actively traded scrips from Group A and Group B, accounting for about 73% of total market capitalisation. BSE 200 is in rupee terms while the Dollex is dollar terms.

Daily Current Market Data

The main indicators published in daily press surround around the price indices, volume or turnover of trade, (or number of shares traded) P/E Ratio, opening, High, low and close of Stock Price and 52 week peak and trough. Besides data on FII activity in the form of purchases and sales and net on a daily basis, and data on Mutual Fund activity in the form of purchases and sales are also published in some dailies. Data on the major markets which account for 90% of total value of trade turnover on the Indian Stock Exchanges, namely the BSE and NSE are separately published in the Daily Press.

For example, ET daily publishes the above data in the following Format:

(1) Major Price Indices of ET -

ET Mindex, ET Lifex and ET - 100 ET - Construction ET - Brandex, ET Mid-cap and ET small-cap

(2) BSE price Indices -

BSE Sensex, BSE National (100), BSE 200, Dollex in dollar terms.

BSE — Mid-cap

BSE — Small-cap

BSE — I.T.

BSE — PSU

BSE — Bankex, etc.

(3) NSE Price Indices - NSE - S & P, C N X Nifty 50, S & P, C N X 500.

(4) Global Indices for France, U.K., Germany etc.

(5) Turnover on BSE and NSE

— Turnover in Rs. crores (Value)

— Turnover in number of shares (lakhs)

(6) Advances and Declines in terms of number of scrips quoted on the Exchange.

(7) High and lows, FII and MF Activity

(8) Latest Day's, open, High, low, close, 52 week High and low, three year High and low, etc.

Other Indicators

Table 30.1 presents the data on major stock market indicators, other than those of prices. Although over the last few years, the number of stock exchanges has increased by only 8, listed companies and their paid-up shares quoted on these markets had increased sharply. Market capitalisation shot up many times and trade turnover has also zoomed in the year 2000 and again in 2005-06. The market capitalisation refers to the market price of a share multiplied by the number of shares in that company and these values are aggregated for all the companies quoted on the stock exchange. The trade turnover relates to the value of deals or number of transactions put through in the market during the official hours during all the trading days of the year. The width of activity and intensity of trading have increased substantially in these markets, reflecting the growing investment habits of the public and the expansion of the capital market in India, particularly during the last few years. This growth is also due to increasing role played by FIIs and FFIs, OCBs etc.

TABLE 30.1 Stock Market Indicators (BSE)

Year Ended March	*No. of Stock Exchanges (BSE)*	*No. of Listed Companies (Rs. Crores)*	*Paid-up Capital of Listed Companies Crores) (at the end)*	*Market Capitalisation (Rs. Crores)*	*Yearly Trade Turnover (Rs.*	*$\frac{P}{E}$ Ratio (SENSEX)*
1989	19	6,250	29,000	65,238	28,032	19.81
1992	22	6,480	31,495	3,23,363	45,696	25.88
1995	23	9,077	90,176	4,68,837	67,748	41.24
1996	23	9,730	1,37,959	5,63,748	50,064	19.92
1997	24	9,890	1,44,832	5,05,137	1,24,284	15.35
1998	23	6,998	1,66,574	6,30,221	2,07,644	14.51
1999	24	9,877	N.A.	5,74,064	10,23,382	12.86
2001	24	5,955	N.A.	5,71,553	10,00,031	23.90
2005	24	4,731	N.A.	16,98,428	5,18,717	16.6
2007	24	4,821	N.A	35,45,041	10,15,192	20.3
2008	24	4887	N.A.	51,38,015	15,78,858	20.1
2009	24	4929	N.A.	30,86,076	11,00,074	13.7

Source : R.B.I. Annual Reports.

The annual trade turnover used to work out to about 20-40 per cent of the market capitalisation increased to more 100% in the year 2000 and which is a good performance in trading as compared with many markets in the developing world in Asia and Far East. In fact, India compares very well with even developed countries in the number of companies listed and the per hour intensity of trading. The Indian markets are linked to U.S. Markets and other World Markets more recently reflecting the globalisation trends.

Other Indices

NSE has been compiling since November 1995 (with the base year 1995 = 100) the indices on a daily basis for well traded scrips, numbering 50 called S & P CNX NIFTY out of total listed scrips of 970 and total traded scrips of 1300 (including permitted securities). Many other Stock Exchanges including OTCEI, DSE, CSE, MSE, etc. have their own price indices. Besides, the Crisil 500 and Midcap 200 (both with 1994 = 100) are published on a daily basis. The Skindia GDR (with 1995 = 100) gives the price indices of GDRs, quoted and traded abroad, reflecting the daily performance of Indian shares abroad.

ET publishes Mindex, ET, LIFEX, ET, Brandex, etc; so also other Financial Dailies. The BSE I.T. and BSE PSU are the indices published by BSE, in addition to its National Index 100 and Sensex 30. The more recent emphasis is on TMT stocks, namely Technology, Media and Telecom Stock which are the leading sectors in the New Economy and are heavily weighted in E.T. Mindex and the latest revised BSE Sensex. The ET daily stopped publishing now of E.T. indices.

INDEXES FOR OTHER SEGMENTS

There are no Index numbers for bonds debentures and Mutual Fund activity, whose importance has increased since 1998. With the plethora of indices for Stock Markets, an investor is generally confused as to which one to depend on. There are no standard criteria adopted in the existing Indices either in the base year or in the pattern of weightage. Each Index has to be considered unique and the investor has to follow whatever is considered suitable. But the most popular index followed by the majority of investors is the sensex on the B.S.E. and Nifty on the N.S.E. (See Table below)

During 1998 and 1999 some index numbers were developed and published for Government bonds namely ISEC Bond Index (I-Bex) with base 1-8-1994 = 1000. Similarly, J.P. Morgan Indian Treasury Bill Index is being published for trading in Treasury bills on the NSE with the base data as April 1, 1996 = 100.

The following Table presents the market Indicators on the N.S.E.

	1997-98	*2000-01*	*2004-05*	*2006-07*	*2007-08*	*2008-09*
1. S & P - CNX Nifty Index -						
Average	1088.0	133.48	1,805	3,572	4,897	3,731
End of the year	1116.9	1148.20	2,036	3,822	4,735	3,021
2. Turnover (in Rs. crores)	3,70,193	13,39,511	11,40,071	19,45,285	35,58,038	27,52,023
3. Listed Companies	612	785	970	1228	1,381	1432
4. Market Capitalisation (in Rs. crores)	3,08,520	5,43,575	15,85,585	33,67,350	48,58,122	28,96,194

Source: RBI, Annual Reports.

Besides, the RBI publishes every year, the market indicators of BSE and NSE in their Annual Report, and in the monthly Bulletin, the indices of BSE and NSE and the volume of corporate debt traded on the NSE. In respect of Govt. Securities Market, the RBI Monthly Bulletin provides RBI open market operations, Secondary market transactions in dated Govt. securities and in Treasury Bills, in addition to yields on them.

CHAPTER 31

Interest Rates – Theory and Structure

Introduction

The object of this chapter is to examine the conceptual and operational aspects of interest rate policy in India. The importance of this policy can be better appreciated in the background of a conceptual discussion on the mechanism of its operations and its significance to the economy. It would thus be apt to start with the role of interest rates in India, and they also influence the financial markets and investment decisions.

Role of Interest Income

Conceptually, interest is a return to the capital as a factor of production. According to the traditional theory, interest is paid for abstaining from present consumption leading to savings. Savings is the basis of investment and capital formation. At the macro level, capital is a major factor of production to which interest is a reward or income just as wages, profits, rents, etc., are rewards to the other factors of production.

Inter-alia, investment is a function of interest rate, and the quantum and directional flow of investment determine income. More scientifically, the impact of interest rate is both on savings and investments in the economy. In other words, the borrowings as well as lendings are influenced by the interest rates. The costs of production which depend upon the production function also include the credit costs, as credit is an input in the productive process.

In the macro sense, interest rate and interest income have a vital role in the economy, as capital, for which it is a reward, plays a significant part in the growth dynamics of the economy. Capital formation and capital accumulation are very much dependent upon the level and rate of savings and investment in the economy. Thus, interest is not a simple monetary phenomenon; it is the product of interaction of the monetary system with the real system.

The savings and investment in the economy which are influenced by the interest rates are the real economic variables. The incomes and expenditures of the various sectors of the economy result in excess savings or excess investment in each of the sectors. The sectors having excess savings provide them to those with excess investment. It is these savings and investment activities of the real sector which are influenced and facilitated by the flow of funds from the financial system. Here both domestic as well as international forces operate if the economies are open. We, however, assume in our study that the economy is closed as we are studying the domestic savings rate in relation to domestic interest rates.

Relative Share of Interest Income

The importance of interest income as a factor reward has been growing in India over the last few decades. Dr. V.K.R.V. Rao has observed thus: "There is a clear indication of the increasing role of loan capital in financing the development of non-self-employed economic activity. Credit has thus played a crucial role in India's economic development" (India's National Income 1950-80, Publication of 1983, page 119).

The factor income shares in the Indian economy are available from the C.S.O., published in their National Accounts Statistics for various periods. The relative importance of interest income is revealed here. At the macro level, the share of interest income in the total national income at current prices has shown a consistent rise over the past three decades. Sector-wise the largest rise of the interest income took place in the secondary sector comprising mining and manufacturing activity. This is attributed to the increasing use of loan capital in these activities.

Role of Interest Rates

Interest rate has diverse roles in the economy such as a reward to capital which is a factor of production, a return to saving and a cost to investment and an instrument of monetary policy for credit control. The role of interest rate mechanism in India has been the subject of controversy. In fact, even in theory, there has been a controversy from the days of Lord Keynes about the role of interest rates in the economy. In this background, it is relevant to examine the role of interest rates in India. Do interest rates influence mobilisation of savings? Do they have an allocative role in the distribution of savings as between different instruments? How far the interest rates influence deposits of banks and shifts as between deposits of various maturities? These and other aspects of interest rates are relevant for policy makers.

At the macro level, interest is a reward to the capital which is a factor of production. In the developing economy, capital formation and capital accumulation are of vital importance to economic development. Interest rates influence both savings and investment in the economy and serve a vital role for the mobilisation of savings. Besides, interest rate has a role in the allocation of investment funds as between different uses. Thus, in addition to influencing their cost, and availability of funds from the supply side, interest rates also influence the quantum of investments from the demand side and thus determine the income and employment in the economy.

Despite the common belief that savings in India are interest-insensitive, our study has shown that while the overall household sector savings are mildly influenced by interest rates, household sector savings in the form of bank deposits are highly sensitive to interest rates. It would, therefore, appear that investment rates have a positive role in the savings mobilisation, particularly with regard to savings in the form of bank deposits. In addition to interest rates, personal disposable income, *per capita* income, the ratio of non-agricultural income to agricultural income and the population coverage per bank office have been found to be significantly influencing household savings in bank deposits.

Interest rates have also a significant role in the investment process in India. Our empirical tests have shown that domestic capital formation in India is a function of GDP, MEC@ and the cost of capital.

The costs of borrowing from banks to the corporate sector are not high, constituting as they do only about 5 per cent of the total value of production in respect of large and medium public limited companies, as revealed by the Company Finance Studies of the RBI.

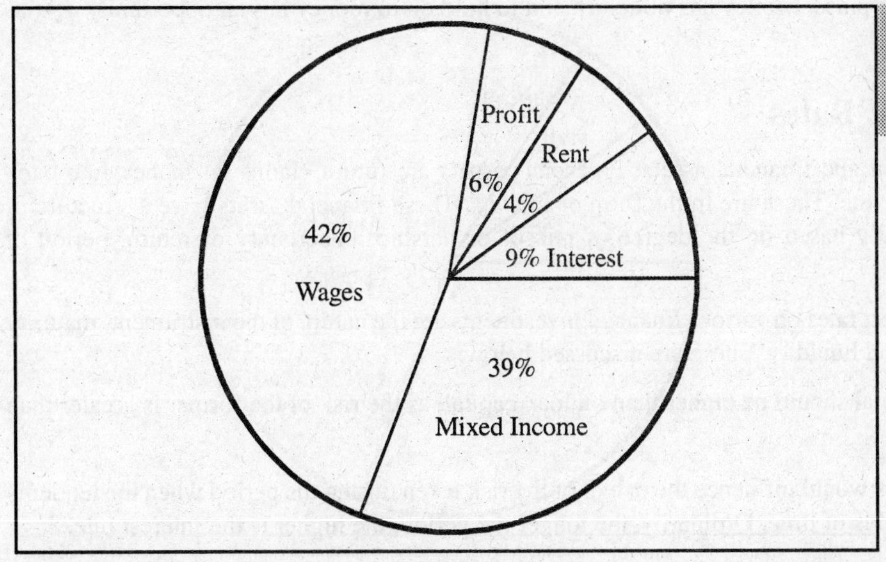

Fig. 31.1

National Income — Share of Interest

@ Marginal efficiency of capital represented by Return on Investment (ROI).

The share of interest income in comparison with the shares of wages, rent and profits in the Indian economy is presented in the Fig. 31.1. It is seen that interest income constitutes about 9% of the total income and is tending to rise over the years due to the preference of the corporate sector for debt capital *vis-a-vis* ownership capital and increasing borrowings of the government for financing public investment and their expenditure. A part of mixed income may also be a return to capital.

Theories of Interest Rate

The classical view of interest rate can be expressed as the loanable funds theory which postulates that interest rate is determined by the supply of and demand for loanable funds. These loanable funds are in the present-day parlance the I.O.U.s of financial institutions. The demand for and supply of these funds will determine the interest rate.

When Keynes considered the interest rate as a monetary phenomenon, he took money as an asset with an opportunity cost, namely, the return on short-term bonds. Under the partial equilibrium approach, one can assume that the forces in the real economic system remain constant and analyse the financial factors which explain the interest rates. Under this theory, interest rate is determined by the relative supply of and demand for liquidity or money in the economy which is a function of the financial system. Keynes' motives for the demand for liquidity are well known, namely, the transactions, precautionary and speculative motives. The last motive has been renamed as an asset motive by the neo-classical economists.

The nominal interest rates according to the neo-classical theories depended also on the expectations of the public and the rate of inflation in the economy. According to Irving Fisher, for example, interest rate is also a function of inflation as the nominal rate is affected by the expected rate of inflation. The Gibson-Wicksell proposition that interest rates and wholesale prices move together in the long run has been found to be empirically valid but the linkage co-efficient is less than unity in India; this is so if only the organised financial sector is considered. During periods of inflation, the gap between the rates in the organised financial system and those in the unorganised system widen sharply although the linkages are weak. Funds flow from the organised to the unorganised sector and *vice versa* which influence rates in both the sectors.

Structure of Interest Rates

The maturity pattern of debt is an important factor for interest rate determination. The maturity pattern is particularly relevant in the gilt-edged market, small savings schemes and deposit and lending rates of banks. The longer the maturity, the larger is the risk and hence the risk premium. The prime criterion to be looked into is the extent of liquidity premium that public is prepared to pay on money *vis-a-vis* near-money assets. The public are concerned with the real rate of return as the nominal interest paid can be eroded by the degree of inflation. The flow of savings and availability of funds would depend on positive real rates in the first place. Money has no return and to hold on to money has an opportunity cost as the alternatives to money have returns.

Factors Influencing Interest Rates

Saving flow into various physical and financial assets. Financial assets are future claims on money like bank deposits, UTI units, shares, debentures, etc. These are in the form of I.O.U.s. These financial assets have a structure of interest rates which should be rationally based on the degree of risk of ownership, uncertainty of return, period of maturity and a host of other factors.

The factors which influence interest rates on various financial investments are the nature of the instrument, maturity period, risk, tax status, marketability and liquidity. These are discussed below:

(1) The return on ownership capital should be higher than on loan capital, as the risk of the former is greater than that of the latter.

(2) Difference in maturity periods would influence the extent of the risk taken during the period when the lender is out of funds for varying periods of time. Ordinarily, the longer the period, the higher is the interest rate.

(3) The degree of default risks or uncertainty of return would also determine the interest rates. Such risks are nil or negligible in the case of government bonds while they are higher in the case of private debt or private ownership securities or company deposits. The rate is to be higher on those which have a higher risk.

(4) The tax provisions on the financial instruments or incentives or disincentives in the form of taxes on interest income or tax concessions would also influence the demand for different types of financial assets. Thus, the effective rates on some postal certificates are higher due to tax concessions which would increase the effective take home rates.

(5) Another factor is the marketability of financial instruments with facilities for discounting or re-discounting and/ or ready saleability which thus imparts liquidity and/or ready saleability which thus imparts liquidity to instruments. Liquidity means convertibility of assets into cash as and when required without loss of time or money.

(6) Safety of funds is another factor and is reflected in the creditworthiness of the borrower and expected return flow of principal and interest money.

The normal pattern of yields is that the short-term rates are lower than the long-term rates and under normal expectations, the yields on ownership capital (risk-taking ventures) would be higher than on loan capital. Besides the interest rates on government bonds which are less risky would also be lower than those on private securities of similar maturity. It is also true that the interest rates on some securities subject to special incentives or tax concessions may be lower than on comparable other instruments. Similarly, the financial instruments which have a good marketability like units of the Unit Trust of India or the shares quoted on the stock exchange may have lower rates than those which are not so marketable and not quoted on the stock exchanges. It would thus be seen that a number of cognisable factors operate on the determination of interest rates. In India even now the rates are partly fixed by the government and the Reserve Bank of India, but the above basic principles of interest rate determination hold good. The existing term structure in India is a by-product of administrative fiat and exigencies of monetary and credit policies.

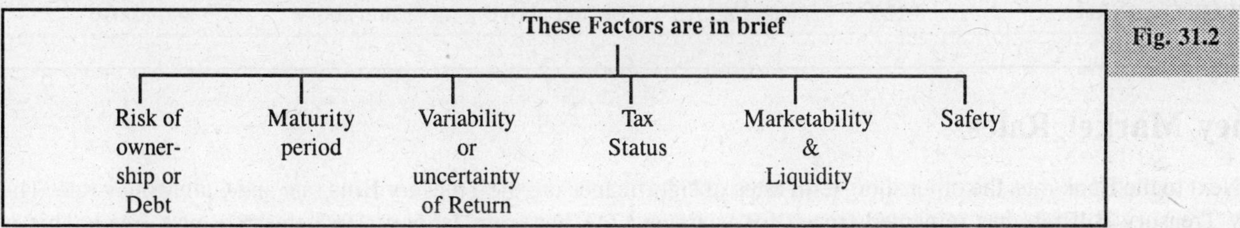

Fig. 31.2

There are drawbacks inherent in any system of partially controlled market forces with some rates fixed by the government, some rates by the Reserve Bank and a few left to the market forces. The multiplicity of controls and the agencies controlling have made the interest rate system in India complicated and distorted. This complex system prevailing even in the organised markets is made more difficult to comprehend by the generally uncontrollable interest rates charged in the unorganised and primitive markets in India. The deficiencies and anamolies in the present system of partially administered rates in India are ably brought out by the Sukhamoy Chakravarthy Committee (RBI, 1985).

Interest Rates in India

Most of the interest rates in India are controlled and administratively fixed. It would, therefore, be difficult to isolate the free market forces which influence the interest rates in India. So far, interest rate policy has been used as a support to other instruments of monetary policy in India. Even under these controlled conditions, the basic postulates that interest rates are influenced by the money, liquidity and the rates of inflation etc. hold good particularly in uncontrolled unorganised market. But where there exists some correspondence, the linkages are weak statistically. But these linkages became stronger in the nineties and interest rates became free and flexible, due to various financial reforms introduced since 1992.

Bank Rate and Refinance Rates

In the organised sector of the financial system for which data are available, interest rate policy is set by the actions of the Central Bank as its discount rate (viz., Bank rate is the leader of interest rates). In India, the bank rate is the discount rate at which the central bank of the country makes advances to the commercial and co-operative banks against eligible assets. Section 49 of the RBI Act defines Bank Rate as the standard rate at which the Bank is prepared to buy and discount bills of exchange or other commercial paper eligible for purchase under the Act. In view of the limited role of the money market and bill market in India, the Bank rate is not the real leader among the interest rates. Under Section 17 of the RBI Act, the Reserve Bank provides refinance through various windows at different rates. It is these refinance rates which are the discount rates of the central bank in India. But Bank rate is made active indicator of cost of bank funds since 1997.

The weighted average rate of interest on these various types of refinance would be the effective rate of discount by the RBI. This is different from the Bank rate. The multiplicity of rates is necessitated by the social obligations of the banking system and the nature of our financial system.

Over the seventies, the Bank rate was raised twice to keep it adjusted to the general level of interest rates in the economy, viz., from 7% to 9% in July 1974 and further to 10% in July 1981. The Bank rate has been raised to 11% in July, 1991 and to 12% in October 1991 and the rate was lowered to 10% in 1997 and 8% in March 1999. But the cost of funds provided by the RBI would be influenced by its refinance policy. The rates are as follows:

(March) in per cent per annum

	1999	*2002*	*2005*	*2007*	*2009*
RBI Bank Rate	8%	6.5%	6%	6%	6%
Banks' Prime lending Rate	12.0%	10-12%	10..25-10.75%	12.25-16.50	11-12%
For food credit provided by banks	8%-10%	8½-10½%	8.25-10.25%	(PLR-2.5)	(PLR-2.5)
For export credit provided by banks	8%-10%	9-10%	8-10%	(PLR-2.5)	(PLR-2.5)
Term loans of banks	14% (free)	free (10%)	free	free	free
RBI Refinance Rates (General/Penal)	8-12%	6.5% and above	6% and above	6% and above	6% and above

Money Market Rates

Next to the Bank rate, the other short-term rates of significance are the Treasury Bills rate and Call Money rate. The 91-day Treasury Bill rate has remained frozen for years at 4.6% but from January 1993 this rate was freed. This is because there was no market for Treasury Bills in India and the instrument is used for the purpose of financing government expenditure. As such this rate has no significance for the general structure of interest rates. Treasury bills of 182 days sold on auction basis since 1987 bear higher rates which are more realistic and market-oriented. In 2009, Auction rates on 91 days T.Bs is 6.96%, 182 days T.Bs is 7.41% and 364 T.Bs rate is 7.19% (weighted average)

As regards call money rate, it has no doubt some relevance to the money market conditions, as the stringency or otherwise of the banks' funds is reflected in this market. The ceiling rate was fixed at 10% in April 1980 but was removed in May 1989. Since then the rates fluctuated daily depending on the demand and supply conditions. The other money market rates are those on C.P.; C.D; P.C., etc. The average call rate for 2008-09 is 7.06%

Rates in Gilt-edged Market

In the government securities market, interest rates are set by the government in the form of coupon rates and are freely determined through auctions since the reforms were started. The yields on these securities are also influenced by the RBI through their purchase and sale operations in the market. In India, there is a captive market in the government securities as the banks are required to invest a proportion of their funds in government securities and other approved trustee securities as fixed by the statutory liquidity ratio (SLR). Similarly, the non-bank financial institutions, provident funds, trusts etc. are also required to invest a proportion of their funds by law in the government securities. From the point of view of risk, these securities are least risky and if the return is to be positive in real terms, the yield has to be higher than the actual inflation rate in the economy. The yields are also related to the maturity period and a differential is maintained as between the Centre and States and government-guaranteed bonds. As part of reforms in gilt-edged markets their rates of interest are decided through auction system.

The auctioning system of 182 days of Treasury bills was extended to Treasury bills of 364 days since April 1992. This has become an additional money market instrument between 91 day Treasury bill and dated Government security. The Discount and Finance House of India Ltd. was allowed to operate in Government securities since April 1992, in addition to their operations in Money Market instruments like Treasury bills and Commercial paper and in the inter-bank call market.

Private and Government Bond Rates

Earlier there used to be a gap between the return on public debt *vis-a-vis* the return on the private debt. The interest rates on debentures and company deposits and preference shares are substantially higher at around 14-15 per cent before reforms started in 1992 as against the yield of 7 to 8 per cent which one might get on government debt. This anomaly dissuades investors from entering the government securities market. So there is need for two types of adjustments is gilt-edged market; firstly, the long end of the spectrum is to be made more attractive, consistent with the expected rate of inflation. Secondly, the yields on government securities should be attractive *vis-a-vis* yields on private securities, which is reflected in gaps and reverse gaps. A gap is positive if the risk is rewarded. If it is a reverse gap, there is risk aversion in the economy which has to be corrected.

These adjustments were started in the decade of the eighties with the result that the gap between them is narrower at around 2 percentage points. The coupon rates offered in the gilt-edged market during the last few years have been jacked up to bring them to realistic levels of the market rates and expected rate of inflation. Besides, this has improved the earnings of banks and made them more attractive to banks and non-bank investors.

Rates of Borrowings and Lendings by Commercial Banks

In view of the limited role of the interest rate policy in India and the weak linkages as between the various segments in the market, it has become necessary for the RBI to resort to direct controls on banks' lending and borrowing rates. Minimum lending rates of scheduled commercial banks were first fixed in 1960 and the maximum lending rates in 1964. Similarly, interest rates on deposits have been fixed by the Reserve Bank of India since September 1969. The control encompasses almost all categories of borrowers and different maturities of deposits.

The Reserve Bank of India derives its authority to fix interest rates of banks under Sections 21 and 35(A) of the Banking Regulation Act. These provisions have been used by the Reserve Bank in a flexible manner since 1960.

The rationale of direct controls on interest rates may be briefly set out here. Firstly, in view of the weak linkages between the Bank rate and/or refinance rate of the RBI with other money market rates, the effectiveness of monetary and credit policy can only be ensured by the direct fixation of various categories of interest rates. Secondly, the banking structure of India is such that there is uneven competition amongst the banks, namely, as between the weaker and smaller banks and dominant bigger banks. It is, therefore, necessary that competition in matters of interest rates has to be regulated by the Reserve Bank. Thirdly, with the acceptance of social obligations by the Banking system following the nationalisation of banks in 1969, the multiplicity of lending rates has become necessary to encourage lending to priority sectors, neglected segments of the economy and backward classes of people. The geographical and sectoral credit gaps have to be filled in through price and non-price incentives. Lastly, the developmental needs of the country have to be met at the lowest possible costs by the banking system through bank credit to government borrowings through bonds, treasury bills, etc. This has also necessitated the differential interest rate system in India.

The Sukhmoy Chakrabarty Committee has opined that the administered interest rate system has adverse effects on the financial system and the economy due to the complexity introduced by it. The number of administered rates were brought down since then.

The same policy of fixing the interest rates was followed for the co-operative banks as well. However, in respect of co-operative credit societies, the RBI has permitted the payment of additional interest of 1/4 to 1 per cent per annum on deposits over and above those allowed for commercial banks. Similarly, the RBI stipulations on lending rates were also made applicable to co-operative banks.

The data on interest rates prevailing on term credit by banks and the IDBI show that they are generally kept lower to facilitate long-term investment in capital assets by borrowers and promote capital formation in the corporate sector. The bank lending rates were freed from control of RBI in October 1990. There is no minimum lending rates for limits above Rs. 2 lakhs. Each bank is expected to declare its prime lending rate for its high credit rated companies. The controls on deposit rates are also reduced, following the recommendations of Narasimham Committee on financial reforms. (1989-91)

Interest Rates on Small Savings

Interest rates on saving deposits, cumulative time desposits and other categories of deposits in post offices are fixed from time to time by the government in consultation with the Reserve Bank. These rates are marginally higher than those offered by commercial and co-operative banks in order to attract the small savers and to encourage the flow of savings into the government sector. Similarly, interest rates on various categories of national savings certificates, social security certificates etc., are fixed higher, as they are for lumpsum investments and meant for small savers, some are given tax incentives. In Jan. 2000, the rates on small savings instruments were brought down by one percentage point to lower the interest rate structure; which is part of the strategy of the Govt. to follow a flexible interest rate policy. The interest ratees on small savings were brought down again in March 2002 and in 2003.

Interest Rates on Non-resident Accounts

Since 1975, the Government of India has been encouraging the inflow of foreign currency funds and Non-resident Deposit Accounts. The FCNR deposits scheme was introduced in November 1975 for non-resident Indians to keep their accounts in time deposits of one to five year duration in US $ and Pound Sterling[1] with remittances from abroad. Till March 1982, interest rates under FCNR deposits were the same as those applicable to domestic deposits. However, from March 1982, the deposits under Non-resident External (NRE) Rupee Accounts were offered at 2% higher interest rates than those on domestic deposits.

Interest rates under FCNR Accounts continued to be higher than those offered in international currency markets on European deposits but there is no cover for exchange fluctuations. This incentive of additional interest has attracted the non-resident funds to India judged by the net inflow in the past, although it is no longer true now, due to fluctuating rupee rate; the rates offered on FCNR and NRNR accounts are now freed by RBI and are fixed by banks, in tune with international rates for similar maturities. These rated are related to LIBOR - higher or lower than LIBOR depending on the Indian market conditions and govt. policy directives.

Export Credit

Interest rates on export credits have been subject to a ceiling with a view to encouraging exports from India. These rates have been uniformly lower than those applicable to domestic creditors. Term credits and those on deferred payments arrangements are kept still further lower. The ceiling rates on export credit stood at a range of 9.5% to 13% in 2001 depending upon the nature of goods and period of credit. While the interest rate on credit under deferred payments is at present 8.6%, the credits by Exim Bank are given at 8.5%. Banks have been asked to provide at least 12% of their total advances to exports and to reduce the interest rate by one percentage point, but the philosophy of subsidised credit to exports was given up. Early in 2002, when the Bank rate was 6.5%, interest rates on export credit varied from 9.5 to 10.5%, and then stood lower at 8 to 10% in 2005 with Bank rate at 6%, and it is linked to PLR, such that export credit rate is 2.5 percentage points lower than Bank's Benchmark rate or PLR. If the PLR is 12.5% as in March 2010 the rate on expert credit will be 10% (less by 2.5% over the PLR).

1. Later extended to Japanese yen and Deutsche mark.

Level and Structure of Rates

Table 31.1 shows that interest rates are adjusted by the government and RBI from time to time in tune with the requirements of the economy. The table compares the rates in 2001 and 2009 with those in 1980. There are some which were raised while others were lowered and freed. The ceiling of 10% on call money rate was removed in May 1989. Similarly, in October 1990, the banks were given freedom to charge rates for lending at their own discretion in respect of non-priority sector advances. The government policy of lending at concessional rates to priority sectors like agriculture, SSIs, weaker sections of society etc., however, continued to be operative; but the slabs are brought down from 4 to 3.

New treasury bills of 182 days were sold on an auction basis since 1986-87 and their interest rates are determined by the free market forces. The short-term deposit rates varied from 9 to 12% and were brought down further after 2000 and 2003. The yields on government securities were raised over the period in a significant way so as to make them attractive to investors and to bring them nearer to the free market rates. The recent liberalisation of interest rate policy in respect of banks' lending rates is also in tune with the policy of financial deregulation followed by the government and recommended by the Committee, to review the working of Monetary Policy (Chakrabarty Committee1985). The term-lending rate was for the purpose of encouraging long-term investment and raised to 15.5% only while the other rates were raised more. This was lowered to 14% in 1997 and further lowered in 1999. Later the term lending rate was kept at 2.5 percentage points lower than the PLR. But the rate of rise was neither consistent throughout nor was it offsetting the fall in the value of money through inflation. In fact, the rate payable on company deposits was lowered to 14% over the decade along with a similar cut in the rate on debt capital of debentures and on ownership capital of preference shares. The only significant rise in interest rates is seen in the case of those on government securities as they were kept at artificially lower rates for a long time and hence the need for readjustment in an upward direction. The rate on company deposits was 15%-16% as of June 1996 and was lowered to 14% in 2000 and the rate on debentures was freed from controls since 1992.

The level and structure of interest rates in India is thus a product of *ad hoc* policies pursued from time to time. The rates do not reflect the true value of capital, risk element and the maturity period of the instrument. The free market forces are not operating in India. Only in limited spheres is the liberalisation process implemented and that too on an *ad hoc* basis. While some controlled rates still continue some free market rates are now available. Similarly, the changes in rates are affected to suit the changing conditions in the economy and in tune with the monetary policy.

Thus, in India, the structure of interest rates is complicated and administered by the government although there is some liberalisation in this policy in recent years. The process of unfixing the interests rates started with the reform process and the policy in the new millennium is to make them more flexible and market determined.

Level of Interest Rates

Leaving aside the basic postulate that there are many factors influencing interest rates in general as referred to above, we have to note that in some countries like India, the interest rates are fixed by the government or by the Central bank of the country (RBI). In such cases, the level and structure of interest rates will be determined by the policy of the government and the RBI and not by the market forces of supply and demand.

Talking of the economy in macro terms, according to the traditional theory, the level of interest rate is determined by the supply and demand for money or loanable funds. The larger the available funds for lending, the lower is the interest rate. Similarly, the larger the demand for funds, higher is the interest rate. The level of interest rate, therefore, depends on the demand and supply pressures in the market. Looked at from a different angle, if there are more borrowers than lenders, interest rates would be high. On the other hand, if there are more lenders than borrowers, interest rates will be lower.

Assuming free market forces where demand and supply presures determine the interest rates, the level of interest rates can be depicted as shown in the following diagram. If MN is the available supply of money or funds, then the amount of demand for funds will determine the level of interest rates. Thus when D_1 - D_1, is the demand curve for funds, the interest rate will be R_1 and if the demand increases to D_2 - D_2, the interest rate will rise to R_2. Similarly, if the demand falls to D_0 - D_0, the interest rate will also fall to R_0 as shown in Fig. 31.3.

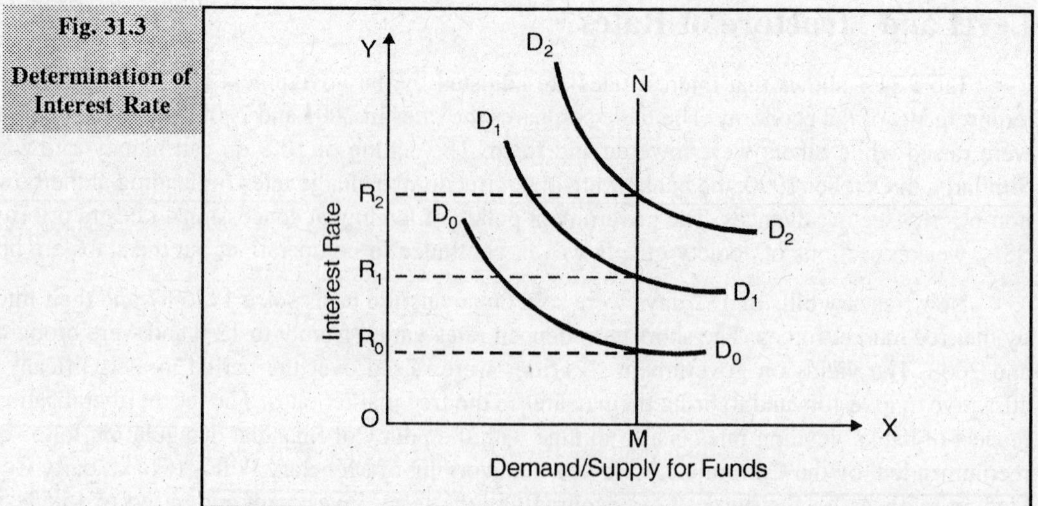

Fig. 31.3
Determination of Interest Rate

Structure of Interest Rates

Leaving aside the time factor, the increase in risk in respect of banks' lending rates and the longer period involved in such lending have been reflected in the higher level of interest rates on them. As compared with the call money rates or treasury bill rates, which are for short periods, the interest rates on debentures, PSU bonds and term-lending rates by banks are higher due to the higher risk involved. Thus risk, maturity period, the safety and certainty of funds, etc. would influence the relative levels of interest rates and the structure of rates as seen from Table 31.1 which also, represents the data on the structure of rates. There are various types of instruments with varying rates of interest rates in India. These rates will depend on the characteristics of these instruments like ownership risk, variability of return, maturity period, safety, marketability, etc. The data clearly brings out the upward and downward shifts in the structure of rates depending upon the level of risk, time period of maturity and other features of the financial instruments involved.

The change in the level of interest rates as between 1980 and 2009 can also be seen from Table 31.1. The Bank rate and other rates fell, as also the banks' borrowing and lending rates and yields on government securities, etc. But the rate on company deposits stood at around 14%. The term lending rate of banks and FIs is left free to be decided by the respective bodies.

TABLE 31.1 Structure of Interest Rates in India

(in percentages)

Sr. No.	Types of Interest Rate	1980	1996	End 1999	End 2001	2005	2007	2009
1.	Bank Rate of RBI	9	12	8	6.5	6.0	6.0	6%
2.	Auction Treasury Bill Rate (91 days) Average	Not applicable	12.93-12.94	9.45	6.93	5.17	6.8	6.96%
3.	Auction Treasury Bill Rate (364 days) Average	Not applicable	12.71-13.03	10.27	6.96	5.63	7.0%	7.19%
4.	Call Money Rate	7.12	16.28	7.35	7-9.0	5.0	Avg. 7.22	7.06%
5.	Banks' Deposit Rate — Maximum @	10	@ 12 & above	10.5	9.0	6.25	9.50	7.75%
6.	Banks' Lending Rate — Minimum	13.50	17-18	12.5	11.0	10.75	12.50	11-12%
7.	Term Lending Rate of FIs	14.00	15.50	-	free	free	14.0	14% free
8.	Rate of Preference Shares	11.00	14.00	14.00	14.0	14.0	free	14%
9.	Rate on Debentures	13.50	16 - 18	-	free	free	free	free
			(free rate)	free	free	free		
10.	Company Deposit rate — Maximum	15.50	15.00		11.0	free	free	free
11.	Yields on Govt. Securities — Maximum	6.44-7.49	10.00-14.00 }	-	7-10	5-68	7.78	6.53 to 10.03%

@ Banks are allowed to pay more than 12% for deposits above 2 years since October 1995, and more than 11% for deposits above one year from July 1996 and 10% from October 1996. In 2004-05, banks have themselves fixed the rate at around 6.25%, which was raised to 8% to 9.5%, depending on the bank later on.

The structure of interest rates has changed over time as between, say 1980 and 2001. Generally, the level of gilt-edged rates has increased over time to reflect the increased cost of raising funds and degree of inflation which erodes the value of money. The policy in 1997 to 2001 was of reducing the interest rates, in tune with the lower inflation rate and recession in the economy.

In India, as seen above, some of these interest rates are fixed by the government. The banks' deposits and lending rates and those of financial institutions are fixed by the RBI, while the rates on P.O. instruments, PSU bonds and those on government securities are all fixed by the Government in consultation with the RBI. Some are left to be decided by banks between 2005 and 2009; the rates are more or less stable.

The rationale of regulating interest rates in India is as follows:

(i) It keeps the interest cost low for the government borrowings and their investment.

(ii) It promotes the socio-economic objectives of providing cheaper finance to weaker sections and priority sectors of the economy.

TABLE 31.2
Secondary Money Market Round-Up
(Ranges)

Rates (% per annum)

Last Week	***April 2002***	***April 2005***	***April 2007***	***April 2010***
Call money	6.10 - 6.60	4.55 - 5.01	4 - 15.0	2.25 - 5.75
Repos	5.60 - 8.00	3.70 - 5.58	6 - 7.75	5.0
364 Day T-Bill	5.79 - 6.78	5.22 - 5.64	7.74	5.15
91 Day T-Bill	5.46 - 6.30	4.80 - 5.26	7.35	4.38
CP	7.60 - 8.35	5.40 - 6.60	10 - 14	5.30 - 9.0%
CD	7.85	4.10 = 6.60	9.40 - 11.50	4% to 7.30%
GOI Securities	5.06 - 11.89	5.20 - 7.30	8.07 - 8.69	7.55 - 8.64%
State Government	6.79 - 10.92	7.30 - 7.50	7.27 - 8.31	7.84 - 8.90%

Source: RBI, Monthly Bulletins

Most Traded Government Paper

Instrument	***Volume (Rs Cr)***	***% of tatol***	***Price Range (Rs)***	***Yield Range (%)***
7.49% 2017	2,507.31	35.55	95.25 - 99.72	7.53 - 8.20
8.33% 2036	1,028.13	14.59	98.03 - 99.87	8.34 - 8.51
6.65% 2009	660.00	9.37	98.39 - 99.75	6.80 - 7.64
7.38% 2015	643.85	9.14	95.81 - 96.76	7.92 - 8.09
7.99% 2017	574.68	8.16	100.00 - 100.27	7.95 - 7.99

Note: Volume in Rs crore, Yields mentioned are as calculated by RBI-NDS Data

Table 31.2 presents the interest rates in the Money Market at a point of time for illustration. The rates are all comprehensive for all instruments, short and long-term traded in the Secondary Money Market, as at end of April 2005 and in April 2010. The Table on most Traded Government Paper presents the data on price range and yields on selected Central Govt. bonds.

Reforms

Certain adjustments may be necessary to remove the deficiencies in the interest rate structure. Firstly, interest rates in the Indian economy are to be positive in real terms so as to promote real savings in the economy. This point has been emphasised by the Sukhmoy Chakrabarty Committee. The implementation of this suggestion involves a projection of the expected rate of inflation and ensuring that the basic or the minimum rates are marginally above the average inflation rate. Secondly, the short-term money markets, namely, bill market, discount market and call money market, are to be further developed and broadbased. Thirdly, in the gilt-edged market the government and the public sector bodies should be provided finance in the forms of treasury bills or of government securities and/or loans and advances at positive real rates. This would ensure that the government gets its funds at the scarcity value of capital and curtail the Reserve Bank credit to the government to the minimum.

It was felt necessary to rationalise call money rates to reflect the scarcity of inter-bank funds or stringency in the resources of the banks. Thus, the then existing ceiling of 10% was removed in May 1989. The need for a ceiling was eliminated when the supply of funds was augmented by allowing non-bank financial institutions, mutual funds and even corporates also to operate in this market.

In the government securities market, the interest rate reforms were already started earlier and coupon rates were adjusted in an upward direction to reflect the scarcity value of the capital in India and to improve the attractiveness of the government bonds with the primary savers and financial intermediaries. These reforms are to be carried forward to rationalise the term structure of the interest rates. The short-term debt which is of a low proportion is being increased and long-term debt is being reduced. The gaps between these short and long-term yields and the gap on government debt *vis-a-vis* the private debt should be rational. Between the venture (ownership) yield and debt yields, there is a reverse gap discouraging the flow of funds to the equity market.

The then existing framework of controls on bank lending and borrowing operations has been based on some justification. The reforms were in the form of reducing the various tiers of interest rate to a minimum of three or less both at the lending and borrowing ends. Interest rates on special categories like term credit, export credit, etc., are to be kept out of this normal spectrum of interest rates by funding the concessionalities on them either by the government or the Reserve Bank. The fiscal and tax benefits should be kept out of the purview of these savings instruments.

Recent Deregulation Measures

Following the recommendations of the High Level Committee on Financial System (of Shri M. Narasimham, November 1991), some measures of deregulation were initiated in the banking and monetary system. The S L R on an incremental basis stood at 25% in 1995 and the incremental CRR of 10% was discontinued. The Committee's recommendations on capital adequacy norms, prudential norms of income recognition and provisioning for bad debts are also being implemented in stages. The recommendations aimed at improving the functional autonomy of banks and financial institutions and enhance competition, efficiency and profitability.

Interest rates are being increasingly left to market forces. In August 1991, interest rates on debentures and P.S.U. Bonds were freed from all restrictions. The system of ceiling rates for term lending institutions was replaced by a system of minimum rate. The ceiling rate on fixed deposits of companies was raised to 15% in January, 1992, but was lowered to 14% in 2000.

The banks have been given greater autonomy in their lending operations and rates of interest charged subjected to a ceiling on deposit rates at 11% in 1997. The deposit and lending rates of banks were freed from controls in the new millennium after 2001 and were lowered in 2001 and 2003 and were kept flexible after 2003 to change from time to time, depending on the monetary and credit policy of RBI. New financial instruments such as Participation Certificates, Commercial Paper, Certificates of Deposits, Money Market Mutual Funds and Non-Resident (Non-repartiable) Rupee Deposit Scheme are being promoted at the market related interest rates, since 2005.

New guidelines were issued in Jan., 1998 for Non-bank financial institutions. The maximum interest rate payable is 11% at monthly interests, on a compounding basis. As in the case of shares, deposits can be accepted in joint names, not exceeding three with or without either or survivor etc. These guidelines were applied to the registered NBFCs accepting public deposits.

Premature repayment is permitted without penalty in the event of death of the depositor to surviving holder or the legal heirs of the deceased.

In respect of Hire Purchase and Equipment leasing companies which enjoy separate limits and conditions, it has been decided that if a company is engaged in hire purchase finance and equipment leasing activities, its business in both these lines will be taken together in determining its classification.

THE YIELD

Current Yield

The concept of yield relates to return on investment made in any security or financial instrument and is related to interest rates. Yields may be classified into different types depending on the securities. In the case of equities, the yield refers to the current yield, which means the return on investment made at the present juncture. The yield is derived by dividing the Dividend + Capital appreciation by the purchase price of share. In the case of debentures and government securities, they are having coupon rates. Normally, the coupon rate is the rate of interest payable on a face value of Rs. 100. It is not related to the market price or the purchase price. The current yield in the case of these fixed income securities is annual interest divided by current price or purchase price of the security. Thus, if 6% 2009 government loan was purchased at Rs. 95, the current yield is = 6/95 × 100, which gives 6.3% as current yield.

Redemption Yield

Redemption yield refers to yield to maturity. It is the average rate of return involving the return in the form of interest as well as appreciation or depreciation of capital over the period remaining to maturity. Thus, for working out the redemption yield for a government bond or a debenture, the following steps are to be taken:

1. Compute the capital gain (or loss) if it is held up to the maturity date. If the purchase price is Rs. 95 and its face value is Rs. 100, the amount realised will be Rs. 100 involving a capital appreciation of Rs. 5 at the time of maturity.
2. Allocate a capital gain for the remaining part of the maturity or life of the security. Thus, if the security has five-year maturity, an appreciation of Rs. 5 is to be distributed equally among all the 5 years, which means that there will be an appreciation of one rupee per year.
3. This annual appreciation is to be added to the annual interest rate paid on the security. If the coupon rate is 6%, an income distribution of Rs. 6 per annum is available and this is to be added to rupee one per annum as capital appreciation.
4. As a next step, add the redemption proceeds at the time of maturity and the purchase price and divide it by 2 which gives the average cost of holding the security.
5. Then divide the total return of investment, namely, (6+1) by the average holding cost, arrived at as above. In the example, the average cost of holding (100+ 95) divided by 2 is equal to Rs. 97.5. Then the redemption yield is arrived at by dividing the total return by the average cost of holding, namely, Rs. 7/97.5 = 7.2%.

It will thus be seen that the redemption yield is slightly different from other concepts. The redemption yield gives the actual return on investment in the form of Interest or Dividend + Capital Appreciation or – Depreciation. The formula for deriving redemption yield is as follows:

$$V = \sum_{n=1}^{n} \frac{I_n}{(1+i)^n} + \frac{P_N}{(1+i)^N}$$

where *V* is the value of the bond, *I* is the interest amount paid in absolute terms, "i" is the rate of interest or yield required to be derived, P_N, is the face value at maturity and *N* is the number of years to maturity.

Holding Period Yield (HPY)

Where redemption yield is not relevant, holding period yield (HPY) is used. Holding period yield brings out the possibility of purchase and sale of a security during the period of its maturity without waiting until the maturity. Thus, one can buy a 13.5% debenture of Reliance Petro at Rs. 80 against its face value of Rs. 100. It could be sold at Rs. 85 after a year, without waiting up to the time of maturity, say, after 5 years. In this case, the holding period yield is relevant. The investor has purchased at Rs. 80 and sold at Rs. 85 after a year. The holding period is one year and the yield is interest at 13.5% that he receives during the year + an appreciation of Rs. 5 for holding it over the year, which gives a total of 18.5%. The formula for the holding period yield is as follows: The return (18.5) is divided by the purchase price (Rs. 80) which gives the holding period yield (23.1%).

$$\text{The formula is HPY} = \frac{(P_t - P_o) + I}{P_o}$$

where I is interest payment, P_o is price at the beginning of the holding period and P_t is price at the end of the holding period.

Real Yield

Real yield is a different concept which takes into account the depreciation in the value of money. Thus, as opposed to nominal yield, which is the coupon rate as, for example, 6%, the real yield is adjusted for depreciation in the value of the rupee, namely, an increase in the prices of goods and services. If the price increase is represented by Wholesale Price Index (WPI), then the nominal yield is deflated by the rise in WPI over the period considered. Thus, the nominal yield of 6% if deflated by the rise in prices of, say 4% will give a positive real yield of 2%. Thus, the concept of real yield presents the picture of the real return in terms of goods and services and purchasing power of the return.

Net Yield

The above concepts of yields present the picture of general yields common to any investor, irrespective of his status such as tax status or type such as an individual or institution, etc. As such, they are gross yields — yields prior to tax payment. The net yield is that after payment of tax. As tax liability varies from individual to individual or company to company, the general tax deduction rate can be applied, say 10% or 20% of the gross yield to arrive at the net yield. Interest and dividend incomes are paid without deduction of tax at source for amounts up to Rs. 2,500 per annum. These tax factors become relevant for net incomes. Banks and mutual funds were to deduct tax at source for the interest payment, on their income distributed.

Maturity and Yields

Yields vary depending not only on the type of security and interest rate, coupon rate but on the maturity of the security. Thus, the yields are higher, if the maturity is longer. This is particularly true of government securities, which are issued with varying maturities.

Yield Curve for Each Maturity

If yields on any security are available on a Gross basis, a yield curve can be drawn to serve for comparative purposes or for indicating the trends and for forecasting purposes. The yield curve is mainly useful in the government securities market where yields differ mainly on the basis of maturity. It depicts the relationship of time periods to yields, referred to earlier. The relative sovereigh yield curve was depicted in Chapter 30. (Fig. 30.4).

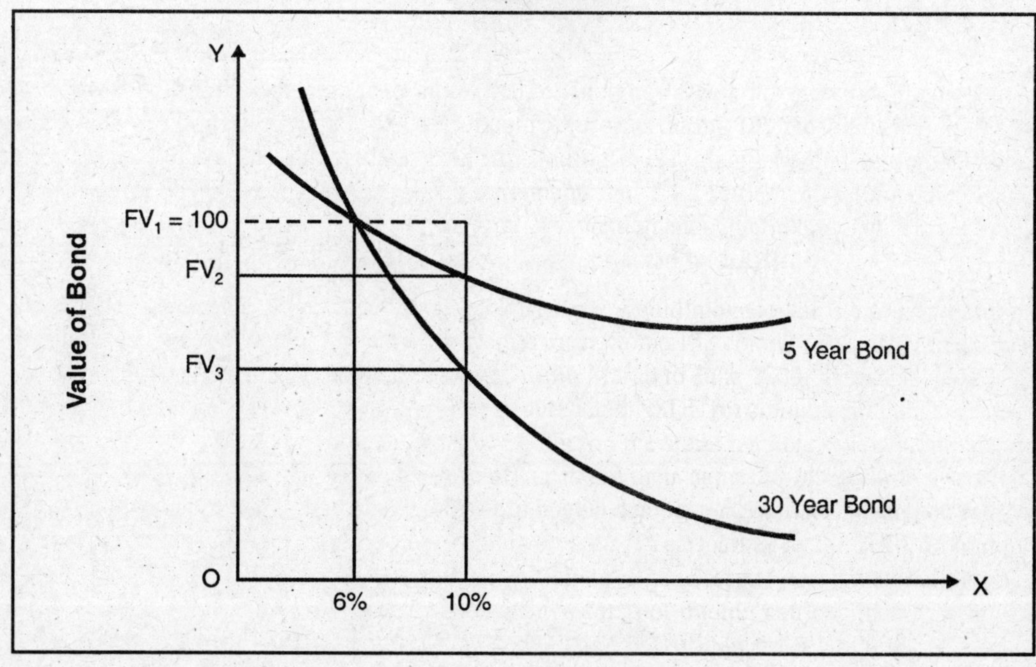

The effect of interest rate changes on value of bonds is shown below.

Example: Take one bond of 5 year maturity and another of 30 year maturity — both with a coupon rate of 6%.

If the Required Rates of Return (r) goes up to 10%, the fall in value of 30 year bond is steeper than a 5 year bond (that is FV_1 to FV_3, as against FV_1 to FV_2), as shown in the Chart above.

PART — VI
Valuation of Stocks and Bonds

Chapter 32: Financial Arithmetics
Chapter 33: Security Pricing
Chapter 34: Investment Analysis and Theory
Chapter 35: Valuation of Bonds – Bond Market
Chapter 36: Valuation of Contingent Claims and Options

Introduction

Investment decision is made on the basis of sound financial arithmetics. Investment involves parting with money and taking some risks. Money has many alternative uses and the returns vary with the risk taken. Thus investment in risk free assets like bank deposit requires a minimum return, called risk free return. This is the compensation for saving by foregoing present consumption and for parting with liquidity (nearness to cash or actual cash). The risk free return is thus the minimum return for investment, required, if that investment is to be made. This minimum rate is the bank rate, or the Govt. Bond yield of one year maturity.

Calculation of Returns (Yields)

Lending of money is for a return in the form of interest. The rates of interest vary with the purpose and maturity and a host of other factors. Thus, advances made by banks and financial institutions are at varying rates of interest and Reserve Bank has allowed freedom to banks to fix their prime lending rates, which are the rates charged for high credit-worthy borrowers and the minimum basic rate for lending.

If the individuals and institutions make an investment in any asset they base their decision to invest on the basis of some financial arithmetic which takes into account the following factors, among others:

(a) Creditworthiness of the party.

(b) Time period of lending or investment.

(c) Risk of the activity of investments.

(d) Expected returns over the time period chosen.

(e) Safety and marketability of investments.

YIELDS ON BONDS/FIXED INTEREST SECURITIES

Normally, if we purchase an asset like a bond or debt instrument or debenture or lent money for any purpose the return is calculated by the formula

$$\text{Rate} = \frac{\text{Total return}}{\text{Principal invested}} \times 100\text{; which is also called yield}$$

If we invest an amount of Rs. 900 on a 12% bond with a face value of 100 by purchasing 10 bonds at Rs. 90 each, then the coupon rate of bond is 12% and face value is Rs. 100, but the market price is Rs. 90. Hence an investment of Rs. 900 got for the investor 10 bonds.

What is his yield per annum? In an investment of Rs. 90 per bond of face value of Rs. 100, he gets an annual interest of Rs. 12 being the coupon rate which is the interest rate promised for each bond of Rs. 100. Thus, if Rs. 90 can secure Rs. 12 the rate of yield for the investor is $\frac{12}{90} \times 100 = 13.3\%$.

The above is called current yield. The yield is the return on an investment as a percentage per annum.

Simple Yield or Interest Calculation

The formula is:

Principal	×	Interest rate	×	No. of periods
(s)	×	(i)	×	(n)

where principle is 100 and interest rate is 12%, and number of years is 3, then simple interest on Rs. 100 is Rs. 36 (12 × 3)

The formula for compound interest is $p = s \times (1 + i)^n$. With data in the above example, $100\ (1 + 0.12)^3 = 140.49$

Present value factors and future value factors are available in the published tables (given at the end of the chapter) readily and can be referred to them.

To exemplify the calculation	Rs.	100
+ First year Interest of		12
		112
+ Second year Interest on 112		13.44
		125.44
+ Third year Interest on 125.44		15.05
Total		140.49

The same is derived through the formula given above.

This is called compounding and the reverse is disounting. If 140.49 is to be received in 3 years, what is its present value? The formula is:

$S = Px \frac{1}{(1+i)^n}$; where P = 140.49 and S = NPV and "i" is interest rate of 12%.

Using the above data, S = 100

After discounting the future flows to the present (NPV). then comparison of any two investments can be made and a decision about desirable investment can be finalised.

Yields on Equity

If the investment is in equity shares of a company, the return is in the form of dividend per annum plus capital appreciation or minus depreciation of the original investment due to fluctuations in market prices of shares. Thus, for example, an investor purchased Tata Steel at Rs. 260 per share and the company declared a dividend of 30%. But the market price of the share increased over the year to Rs. 290 involving a capital gain of Rs. 30 per annum. Thus, an investment of Rs. 260 yielded a return of Rs. 30 as dividend and another Rs. 30 as capital appreciation. The total return is Rs. 60 on an investment of Rs. 260.

The rate of return is $\frac{60}{260} \times 100 = 23\%$ P.A.

The yield on equity is generally lower if only dividends are considered. But an investor in equity shares desires not the yield only, but possible capital appreciation.

Yields are more relevant on all fixed interest yielding investments or instruments like, debentures, bonds, loans, deposits etc., with banks, companies and Govt.

TIME VALUE OF MONEY AND SECURITIES

Time Preference for Money

We prefer today's money to that of tomorrow due to our pressing needs for consumption and cost of abstinence from the present consumption, fall in the value of money of tomorrow due to inflation and possible use of money when exchanged for tomorrow's money. Thus, when we lend money, we forego all the advantages of liquidity, ready usability, pressing needs, safety, etc. We abstain from present consumption when lent to somebody, or invested. All these will lead to what is called the time preference for money. To compensate for that, future money will have to be discounted to the present time, because both are not the same. Future money has to be more say 120, if the present money is Rs. 100, taking a discount factor of 20%, for one year.

Tomorrow's money or money a year hence has to be discounted to the present day by discount rate suitable as a reward for the above sacrifices. This is called discounting, used for cash flows or dividends to be received in future and to be calculated for the present.

Similarly an investment of today, if it is to be returned after a year or so, today's money has to be compounded by a discount rate to equate to the future funds likely to be available in return. This is called compounding. Compounding and discounting are thus two major methods of analysing the time value of money.

Applications

In purchase or sale of a share, bond, or debenture, the price we pay has to be compared to the value of future flows in terms of dividends, or interest and future price realised. The principle of buy low and sell high has to be applied after an analysis of the present value of future flows of dividends, bonus, possible rights etc., as compared to the present price paid for it.

Future Value of a Single Cash Flow

Year	*Principal at the beginning*	*Interest 10%*	*Principal at the end*
1	1000	100	1100
2	1100	110	1210
3	1210	121	1331

$FV = PV (1 + r)^n$; FV = Future value; PV = Present value; r = rate of interest; n = number of years

Future Value of an Annuity @ 10%

1	2	3	4	5	
1000	1100	1210	1331	1464	$(1+r)^4$
	1000	1100	1210	1331	$(1+r)^3$
		1000	1100	1210	$(1+r)^2$
			1000	1100	$(1+r)^1$
				1000	$(1+r)^0$
				6105	

$$FV = A\,[(1+r)^{n-1} + (1+r)^{n-2}\ (1+r)^{n-3} + (1+r)^{n-4} + \text{—} + (1+r)^{n-n}]$$

$$= A\left[\frac{(1+r)^{n-1}}{r}\right]$$

Sinking Fund Factor

$$F = A\left[\frac{(1+r)^{n-1}}{r}\right]$$

$$A = F\left[\frac{r}{(1+r)^{n-1}}\right]$$

$$= F \times \frac{1}{\text{FVIFA}\,(r,n)}$$

Present Value of an Annuity @ 10%

0	1	2	3	
909.1	1000			$\frac{1000}{(1+0.1)^1}$
826.4	909.1	1000		$\frac{1000}{(1+0.1)^2}$
751.3	826.4	909.1	1000	$\frac{1000}{(1+0.1)^3}$
2478.8				

$$PVA = A\left[\frac{(1+r)^{n-1}}{r(1+r)^n}\right]$$

$$FVA = A\left[\frac{(1+r)^{n-1}}{r}\right]$$

$$PV = FV\,\frac{1}{(1+r)^n}$$

$$PVA = A$$

DOUBLING PERIOD

Rule of 72 $\frac{72}{\text{Interest Rate}}$ for rough estimate

Rule of 69; $0.35 + \frac{69}{\text{Interest Rate}}$ for exact estimate

With 12% rate of interest

Doubling period Using Rule of 72; $\frac{72}{12} = 6$ Years

Using Rule of 69; $0.35 + \frac{69}{12} = 6.10$ Years

Shorter Compounding Period

If interest is credited quarterly @ 12% per annum

Quarter	*Balance at the Beginning* *Rs.*	*Interest* *Rs.*	*Bal. at the end* *Rs.*
1	1000	30	1030
2	1030	30.90	1060.90
3	1060.90	31.827	1092.727
4	1092.727	32.782	1125.509

Effective rate of interest = 12.551%

$$r = \left(1+\frac{k}{m}\right)^{m-1}$$

$$FV = PV\left(1+\frac{k}{m}\right)^{m\times n}$$

where k = Nominal rate of interest

m = Number of times compounding is done during a year

n = Number of years for which compounding is done

Bond Valuation

Features of a Bond

1. Par Value
2. Coupon rate of Interest
3. Maturity Period

Par value	Rs. 1000
Coupon rate	12%
Maturity Period	5 years
Required Rate of Return	10% 12% 15%

At 12%

Rs. 120 × PVIFA (12%, 5) + 1000 × PVIF (12%, 5)

= Rs. 1000

At 10%

Rs. 120 × 3.791 + Rs. 100 × 0.621

Rs. 1075.92

(Values of PVI FA, PVIF, FVIFA and FVIF are given in Tables at the end)

At 15%

Rs. 120 × 3.352 + Rs. 1000 × 0.497

Rs. 899.24

If the Maturity Period is 3 Years

At 12% Rs. 120 × 2.402 + Rs. 1,000 × 0.712 = Rs. 1,000

At 10% Rs. 120 × 2.487 + Rs. 1,000 × 0.751 = Rs. 1,049.44

At 15% Rs. 120 × 2.283 + Rs. 1,000 × 0.658 = Rs. 931.96

Yield to Maturity

$$\text{Ytm} = \frac{\text{Interest} + (\text{Par Value} - \text{Present Price} / n)}{(\text{par Value} + \text{Present Price}) / 2}$$

Equity Valuation

Dividend Capitalisation Approach

Present value of the dividends expected

\+ Present value of the resale price expected

= Value of an Equity share

Basic Assumptions

1. Dividends are paid annually.
2. The first dividend is paid one year after the equity share is bought.

Single Period Valuation Model

$$P_o = \frac{D_1}{(1+k)} + \frac{P_1}{(1+k)}$$

If the price is expected to grow at rate 'g'

$P_1 = P_o (1 + g)$

$$P_o = \frac{D_1}{(1+k)} + \frac{P_o (1+g)}{(1+k)}$$

$$P_o = \frac{D_1}{k - g}$$

where K = Rate of interest

P_o = Present Price

P_1 = Price in Period 1

D_1 = Dividend for Period 1

Tables for PVIF, PVIFA, FVIF, FVIFA etc. are readily available.

Fundamentals of Valuation of Securities

If we need to estimate the present value of future flows, then the Discounting Method is used. If we want the future value of present investment, we have the Compounding Method. Both help the decision making process in investment in securities.

Discounting

If the final value of the present investment is Rs. 116 at the end of 3 years and if it is discounted to the present day at 5%, then it will be equal to Rs. 100 at present.

The formula for PV (present value)

$$PV = \sum_{t=1}^{T} \frac{C_t}{(1+r)^t}$$

C_t represents the cash flows, t for period of years and r is the discount rate or is called internal rate of return in the exercises of capital budgetting.

Take an example: — r = 8%, payable once a year and t is 5 years and the factor value — summation of cash flows is Rs. 100.

$$\text{Then, } PV = \frac{100}{(1+0.08)^5} = \text{Rs. } 68 \text{ (use Log Tables)}$$

This Formula also applies to one period return of Rs. 100 at the end of 5 years, the present value of which is Rs. 68 at a rate of return of 8%.

Compounding

If the interest rate is 5% and PV is Rs. 100, the future value for one year will be Rs. 105, by using the formula of $= 100\ (1+ 0.5)^1 = 105$.

In two years, it becomes $100\ (1+0.5)^2 = 110.25$

In three years it becomes $100\ (1+0.5)^3 = 115.76$ and so on.

In the case of discounting, it is the reverse of the above formula namely,

$$PV = 100\left(\frac{1}{1+r}\right) + 100\left(\frac{1}{(1+r)^2}\right) + 100\left(\frac{1}{1+r)^3}\right) \text{ etc.}$$

For the same three year period, at the end of 3 years, the future value should be Rs. 100 for investing Rs. 86.4 at present, when r = 0.5

These formulae are based on some critical assumptions of constant flow of cash every period, the same reinvestment rate and the period is fixed.

Bond Prices — Factors Influencing

Bond prices fluctuate with market interest rate *vis-a-vis* the coupon rate, inflation rate, tax factors, security provided, maturity period, callable feature of the bond, credit rating of the company, etc. Some bonds, are attached with call or put options. Call means that the company can repay before maturity, if interest rates have fallen. Put means that the investor can exercise the option for selling the low yielding bond to the high yielding bond of the same characteristics as before.

Formulae

Future value of a single cash flow formula is $FV_n = PV_n \times (1+k)^n$

This is the same thing as compounding, referred to above:

$$14 + \frac{105 - 95}{6} = \frac{14 + 1.67}{100} = 15.67$$

Dividing both sides by $(1+k)^n$ we get $PV_n = FV_n \left(\frac{1}{1+k)^n}\right)$ this formula $\left(\frac{1}{1+k)}\right)$ is called discounting factor or the present value interest factor (PVIF, kn)

There is also similarly a future value interest factor (FVIF, kn) for compounding.

Yield to Maturity (Ytm)

Example (Short-cut Method)

$FV_n = 105$ k = 14% (I) Interest rate

PV = 95 N = number of years 6

$$Ytm = \frac{1 + \left(\frac{F - P}{n}\right)}{\frac{F + P}{2}}$$; Putting the above values in the formula,

we have

$$Ytm = 14 + \frac{105 - 95}{6} = \frac{14 + 1.67}{100} = 15.67$$

15.67 becomes 15.67%

Ytm is thus 15.67% in the above example.

Valuation of Convertible Bonds/Debentures

Convertibles enjoy the benefits of both debt (initially) and equity (later). The terms of conversion will decide the pricing of these convertibles, which is left to free market forces in India, now. It is the company's perception what they can sell to investors and at what price.

As per SEBI guidelines, fully convertible debentures (FCDs) and partly convertible bonds (PCBs) have special features and are not governed by guidelines for non-covertible bonds/debentures (NCDs). Their pricing methods, are different from bonds.

Why Convertible Financing?

(1) It will delay the issue of equity and hence dilution of earnings per share is delayed.

(2) It will give breathing time for the company for increasing its earnings, when it will be in a position to expand equity base and service them.

(3) Initial bond financing will earn leverage for the company as interest expense on debt is not taxable and the cost of debt financing is lower than that of equity for some companies.

(4) Companies in initial stages of expansion or project financing, or with low credit rating but with the potential for larger earnings in a couple of years prefer convertibles.

(5) Investors are attracted to convertibles, due to the sweeteners like premium on conversion and dividends and capital appreciation later.

Valuation of Convertibles

Whether it is FCD or PCD, the pricing of the convertible portion is complicated by the mixture of debt and equity elements. The coupon rate on debt portion will be lower than the market rate of NCD of the same duration, because of the benefits enjoyed on conversion later on.

If conversion is within 18 months, they are as good as equity for debt-equity ratio and if they are convertible within coming 12 months, they will be eligible to rights after conversion or bonus declared during the preceding 12 months.

The specification of pricing is difficult, except that the company follows the principles of what "the market can bear." What is the proportion of convertible portion to the total and the time period of waiting? The terms of offer also depend on the credit rating of the company.

Assume the conversion period is 12 months when the PCD will be converted into equity upto 50% and the rest will be NCD. Then if the expected gain on conversion is say, 2% to 5%, then the debenture will be offered at a coupon rate of 12% to 13% if the normal market rate is 14% to 15%. Coupon rate will be lower, the higher the premium permitted on conversion into equity.

Conversion Ratio

Conversion ratio is set out as so many equity shares for Rs. 100 of debenture. If the conversion price is set at Rs. 50, then the market price may be already ruling at Rs. 60 or Rs. 70 and one debenture will be converted into two equity shares. *Conversion value* is the conversion price multiplied by the number of shares given for each debenture. If conversion value is Rs. 50 and market price is say, Rs. 60, the conversion premium is Rs. 10 per share and Rs. 20 is gained by holding a debenture of Rs. 100 for one year. The debentureholder gets only say 12% as interest. The return on this investment is in fact 12% + 20% = 32%, Where 12% is interest on debt and 20% is conversion premium for two equity shares for the convertible portion.

Conversion Premium

The company may offer a lesser premium, for one year and a larger premium for 18 months to 36 months. After 36 months, any conversion offer is subject to call and put options as per SEBI guidelines.

A call gives the right to buy from the company the share at the offer price if it is lower than the market price. A put option gives the Right to sell the share eligibility to the company (and then buy the shares *in the market)* when the offer price is higher than the market price. A call option is exercised if the market price is higher and put option is exercised, if the market price is lower, at the time of conversion.

Valuation of 'Rights'

Right issue is a method of selling equity or debt securities to existing shareholders at concessional rates. Rights issues in India are governed by Section 81(A) of the Companies Act. As these rights will give incentives or discounts on market prices or market rates, they are attractive to investors and they are given to those shareholders who are on the registers of the company at a point of time called the Record date fixed by the Board of Directors. But the terms of rights issue, if made open to the public will be different from those when they are offered only to the existing shareholders.

Example of Rights Pricing

To illustrate the pricing of rights entitlements, an example is given below:

Existing paid up capital (PUC) = Rs. 3 crores; present issue of Rights = Rs. 2 crores.

Ratio of rights issue is 3:2. That means if the investor holds 3 shares, he is entitled to 2 rights shares at a discount.

Let the Market Price (MP) = Rs. 40 and Rights offer based on their book value is let us say, Rs. 30.

The market price quoted Cum-Rights is Rs. 40. If you buy three shares it will be Rs. 120 which when registered with the company will entitle you to 2 shares at a price of Rs. 30 (two shares will cost Rs. 60). The total cost for five shares is 120 + 60 = Rs. 180. The cost of one share is $\frac{180}{5}$ = Rs. 36.

The price of one right share thus becomes Rs. 36, while the market price is Rs. 40. The difference is only Rs. 4 per entitlement but this price of Rs. 4 will be available subject to the last date of renunciation of rights by the rightholders. When the quotation becomes exrights, then the market price would accordingly adjust to Rs. 36, wiping out the benefit of Rs. 4. Here the assumption is that company is a well rated company and its shares are in demand which means that there is a market for renunciations. Besides, we have not considered the brokerage costs and other incidentals involved in acquiring the rights and then selling them off.

Callable Bonds

The company sometimes reserves the right to redeem earlier than the stipulated period, if the interest rates are falling. Such bonds are priced lower and discount will be more on the face value. Some bonds are redeemed in instalments, spread over 3 to 5 years. This will also be subject to Risk of interest rate changes and are accordingly priced lower. Default prone bonds and junk bonds of companies with poor and falling credit rating will be substantially discounted ranging upto 50% on the face value of even short maturities.

Detachable and Non-detachable Warrants and Loyalty Coupons

These are sweeteners attached to the debt instruments. Keeping the coupon rate at the then prevailing market rate (say, 12.5%) the company can attract investors by giving them a warrant, which will entitle the holder to buy the equity share at a discount over the market price but not lower than the intrinsic value as judged by Book value or EPS.

Loyalty coupons or non-detachable warrants require the minimum holding period of say, 3 to 5 years to be eligible to this right of purchasing equity shares at face value or book value, which are much lower than the market price.

Such non-marketable warrants, attached to debt instruments are called latent warrants, which are entitled to conversion at the fixed maturity period of 3 to 5 years, while the debt portion remaining with the investor is sold in the market at a discount. However, the premium gained at conversion into equity is much more than the discount lost in the NCD portion. Some companies provide the safety net of purchasing back through their financial institutions, the NCD portion at the face value after a period of 1 to 3 years, or immediately after allotment depending on the terms.

Mortgage Bonds

Non-callable and Non-convertible bonds are to be secured by collaterals if they are to be attractive to investors and carry the market interest rates with or without clause of adjustment to floating interest rates. The bond prices in such cases depend on the equity prices and the company's performance. They are not default prone, if the company is performing well, fundamentals are strong and the share market price is rising. Such bonds are normally near to the market prices. In fact, the rates expected on various bonds depend on their ratings by rating agencies, such as Standard and Poor, in USA. In India, compulsory Credit rating is imposed for NCDs given by companies and interest/coupon rates are decided accordingly on the basis of credit rating.

Time Value of Money — Problems

Q. — Tom retires at 60 and he is now 30. He wants to have Rs. 20 lakhs at retirement and gets 10% on the Recurring deposit account. How much should he save per year.

Answer — Here Pt = 20,00,000 i = 10%

t = 30 years. The equation for Pt is

$$Pt = A \sum_{t=1}^{T} (1+r)^{t-1}$$

$$20{,}00{,}000 = A = \sum_{t=1}^{30} (1.10)^{30-t}$$

The future value factor for 30 years, at the rate of 10% is 164.494.

Thus 20,00,000 = A × 164.494

$$A = \frac{20{,}00{,}000}{164.494} = 12158.498$$

A is annuity to be paid every year to get Rs. 20,00,000 at the end of 30 years, by Tom. Thus, A is **12,158.50.**

Q. — Given the annuity paid as Rs. 1,000 per year and the interest rate at 5%. What is his future value at the end of 30 years.

Answer — Here A = Rs. 1,000, interest rate i = 5% t = 30 years

$$Pt = A \sum_{t=1}^{30} (1.05)^{30-t}$$

$$= 1000\ (1.05)^{30-t}$$

$$= 1000 \times 66.439$$

= Rs. **66,439**

(From the Future Value factor Tables, the value of it at 5%, for 30 years, is 66.439).

(PVIF)

Period	1%	2%	3%	4%	5%	6	7%	8%	9%	10%	12%	14%	15%	16%	18%	20%	24%	28%	32%	36%
1	.9901	.9804	.9709	.9615	.9524	.9434	.9346	.9259	.9174	.9091	.8929	.8772	.8696	.8621	.8475	.8333	.8065	.7813	.7576	.7353
2	.9803	.9612	.9426	.9246	.9070	.8900	.8734	.8573	.8417	.8264	.7972	.7695	.7561	.7432	.7182	.6944	.6504	.6104	.5739	.5407
3.	9706	.9423	.9151	.8890	.8638	.8396	.8163	.7938	.7722	.7513	.7118	.6750	.6575	.6407	.6086	.5787	.5245	.4768	.4348	.3975
4.	.9610	.9238	.8885	.8548	.8227	.7921	.7629	.7350	.7084	.6830	.6355	.5921	.5718	.5523	.5158	.4823	.4230	.3725	.3294	.2923
5.	.9515	.9057	.8626	.8219	.7835	.7473	.7130	.6806	.6499	.6209	.5674	.5194	.4972	.4761	.4371	.4019	.3411	.2910	.2495	.2149
6.	.9420	.8880	.8375	.7903	.7462	.7050	.6663	.6302	.5963	.5645	.5066	.4556	.4323	.4104	.3704	.3349	.2751	.2274	.1890	.1580
7.	.9327	.8706	.8131	.7599	.7107	.6651	.6227	.5835	.5470	.5132	.4523	.3996	.3759	.3538	.3139	.2791	.2218	.1776	.1432	.1162
8.	.9235	.8535	.7894	.7307	.6768	.6274	.5820	.5403	.5019	.4665	.4039	.3506	.3269	.3050	.2660	.2326	.1789	.1388	.1085	.0854
9.	.9143	.8368	.7664	.7026	.6446	.5919	.5439	.5002	.4604	.4241	.3606	.3075	.2843	.2630	.2255	.1938	.1443	.1084	.0822	.0628
10.	.9053	.8203	.7441	.6756	.6139	.5584	.5083	.4632	.4224	.3855	.3220	.2697	.2472	.2267	.1911	.1615	.1164	.0847	.0623	.0462
11.	.8963	.8043	.7224	.6496	.5847	.5268	.4751	.4289	.3875	.3505	.2875	.2366	.2149	.1954	.1619	.1346	.0938	.0662	.0472	.0340
12.	.8874	.7885	.7014	.6246	.5568	.4970	.4440	.3971	.3555	.3186	.2567	.2076	.1869	.1685	.1372	.1122	.0757	.0517	.0357	.0250
13.	.8787	.7330	.6810	.6006	.5303	.4688	.4150	.3677	.3262	.2897	.2292	.1821	.1625	.1452	.1163	.0935	.0610	.0404	.0271	.0184
14.	.8700	.7579	.6611	.5775	.5051	.4423	.3878	.3405	.2992	.2633	.2046	.1597	.1413	.1252	.0985	.0779	.0492	.0316	.0205	.0135
15.	.8613	.7430	.6419	.5553	.4810	.4173	.3624	.3152	.2745	.2394	.1827	.1401	.1229	.1079	.0835	.0649	.0397	.0247	.0155	.0099
16.	.8528	.7284	.6232	.5339	.4581	.3936	.3387	.2919	.2519	.2176	.1631	.1229	.1069	.0930	.0708	.0541	.0320	.0193	.0118	.0073
17.	.8444	.7142	.6050	.5134	.4363	.3714	.3166	.2703	.2311	.1978	.1456	.1078	.0929	.0802	.0600	.0451	.0258	.0150	.0089	.0054
18.	.8360	.7002	.5874	.4936	.4155	.3503	.2959	.2502	.2120	.1799	.1300	.0946	.0808	.0691	.0508	.0376	.0208	.0118	.0068	.0038
19.	.8277	.6864	.5703	.4746	.3957	3305	.2765	.2317	.1945	.1635	.1161	.0829	.0703	.0596	.0431	.0313	.0168	.0092	.0051	.0029
20.	.8195	.6730	.5537	.4564	.3769	3118	.2584	.2145	.1784	.1486	.1037	.0728	.0611	.0514	.0365	.0261	.0135	.0072	.0039	.0021
25.	.7798	.6095	.4776	.3751	.2953	.2330	.1842	.1460	.1160	.0923	.0588	.0378	.0304	.0245	.0160	.0105	.0046	.0021	.0010	.0005
30.	.7419	.5521	.4120	.3083	.2314	.1741	.1314	.0994	.0754	.0573	.0334	.0196	.0151	.0116	.0070	.0042	.0016	.0006	.0002	.0001
40.	.6717	.4529	.3066	.2083	.1420	.0972	.0668	.0460	.0318	.0221	.0107	.0053	.0037	.0026	.0013	.0007	.0002	.0001	*	*
50.	.6080	.3715	.2281	.1407	.0872	.0543	.0339	.0213	.0132	.0085	.0035	.0014	.0009	.0006	.0003	.0001	*	*	*	*
60.	.5504	.3048	.1697	.0951	.0535	.0303	.0173	.0099	.0057	.0033	.0011	.0004	.0002	.0001	*	*	*	*	*	*

* The factor is zero to four decimal points

Future Value of $ 1

Period	1%	2%	3%	4%	5%	6%	7%	8%	9%	10%	12%	14%	15%	16%	18%	20%	24%	28%	32%	36%
1.	1.0100	1.0200	1.0300	1.0400	1.0500	1.0600	1.0700	1.0800	1.0900	1.1000	1.1200	1.1400	1.1500	1.1600	1.1800	1.2000	1.2400	1.2800	1.3200	1.3600
2.	1.0201	1.0404	1.0609	1.0816	1.1025	1.1236	1.1449	1.3664	1.1881	1.2100	1.2544	1.2996	1.3225	1.3456	1.3924	1.4400	1.5376	1.6384	1.7424	1.8496
3.	1.0303	1.0612	1.0927	1.1249	1.1576	1.1910	1.2250	1.2597	1.2950	1.3310	1.4049	1.4815	1.5209	1.5609	1.6430	1.7280	1.9066	2.0972	2.3000	2.5155
4.	1.0406	1.0824	1.1255	1.1699	1.2155	1.2625	1.3108	1.3605	1.4116	1.4641	1.5735	1.6890	1.7490	1.8106	1.9388	2.0736	2.3642	2.6844	3.0360	3.4210
5.	1.0510	1.1041	1.1593	1.2167	1.2763	1.3382	1.4026	1.4693	1.5386	1.6105	1.7623	1.9254	2.0114	2.1003	2.2878	2.4883	2.9316	3.4360	4.0075	4.6526
6.	1.0615	1.1262	1.1941	1.2653	1.3401	1.4185	1.5007	1.5869	1.6771	1.7716	1.9738	2.1950	2.3131	2.4364	2.6996	2.9860	3.6352	4.3980	5.2899	6.3275
7.	1.0721	1.1487	1.2299	1.3159	1.4071	1.5036	1.6058	1.7138	1.8280	1.9487	2.2107	2.5023	2.6600	2.8262	3.1855	3.5832	4.5077	5.2295	6.9826	8.6054
8.	1.0829	1.1717	1.2668	1.3686	1.4775	1.5938	1.7182	1.8509	1.9926	2.1436	2.4760	2.2826	3.0590	3.2784	3.7589	4.2998	5.5895	7.2058	9.2170	11.703
9.	1.0937	1.1951	1.3048	1.4233	1.5513	1.6895	1.8385	1.9990	2.1719	3.3579	2.7731	2.2519	3.5179	3.8030	4.4355	5.1598	6.9310	9.2234	12.166	15.916
10.	1.1046	1.2190	1.3439	1.4802	1.6289	1.7908	1.9672	2.1589	2.3674	2.5937	3.1058	3.7072	4.0456	4.4114	5.2338	6.1917	8.5944	11.805	16.059	21.646
11.	1.1157	1.2434	1.3842	1.5395	1.7103	1.8993	2.1049	2.3316	2.5804	2.8531	3.4785	4.2262	4.6524	5.1173	6.1759	7.4301	10.657	15.111	21.198	29.439
12.	1.1268	1.2682	1.4258	1.6010	1.7959	2.0122	2.2522	2.5182	2.8127	3.1384	3.8960	4.8179	5.3502	5.9360	7.2876	8.9161	13.214	19.342	27.982	40.037
13.	1.1381	1.2936	1.4685	1.6651	1.8856	2.1329	2.4098	2.7196	3.0658	3.4523	4.3635	5.4924	6.1528	6.8858	8.5994	10.699	16.386	24.748	36.937	54.451
14.	1.1495	1.3195	1.5126	1.7317	1.9799	2.2609	2.5785	2.9372	3.3417	3.7975	4.8871	6.2613	7.0757	7.9875	10.147	12.839	20.319	31.691	48.756	74.053
15.	1.1610	1.3459	1.5580	1.8009	2.0789	2.3966	2.7590	3.1722	3.6425	4.1772	5.4736	7.1379	8.1371	9.2655	11.973	15.407	25.195	40.564	53.358	100.71
16.	1.1726	1.3728	1.6047	1.8730	2.1829	2.5404	2.9522	3.4259	3.9703	4.5950	6.1304	8.1372	9.3576	10.748	14.129	18.488	31.242	51.923	84.953	136.96
17.	1.1843	1.4002	1.6528	1.9479	2.2920	2.6928	3.1588	3.7000	4.3276	5.0545	6.8660	9.2765	10.761	12.467	16.672	22.186	38.740	66.461	112.13	186.27
18.	1.1961	1.4282	1.7024	2.0258	2.4066	2.8543	3.3799	3.9960	4.7171	5.5599	7.6900	10.575	12.375	14.462	19.673	26.623	48.038	85.070	148.02	253.33
19.	1.2081	1.4568	1.7535	2.1068	2.5270	3.0256	3.6165	4.3157	5.1417	6.1159	8.6129	12.055	14.231	16.776	23.214	31.948	59.567	108.89	195.39	344.53
20.	1.2202	1.4859	1.8061	2.1911	2.6533	3.2071	3.8697	4.6610	5.6044	6.7235	9.6463	13.743	16.366	19.460	27.393	38.377	73.864	139.37	257.91	468.57
21.	1.2324	1.5157	1.8603	2.2788	2.7860	3.3996	4.1406	5.0398	6.1088	7.4002	10.803	15.667	18.821	22.574	32.323	46.005	91.591	178.40	340.44	637.26
22.	1.2447	1.5460	1.9161	2.3699	2.9253	3.6035	4.4304	5.4365	6.6586	8.1403	12.100	17.861	21.644	26.186	38.142	55.206	113.57	228.35	449.39	866.67
23.	1.2572	1.5769	1.9736	2.4647	3.0715	3.8197	4.7405	5.8715	7.2579	8.9543	13.552	20.361	24.891	30.376	45.007	66.247	140.83	292.30	593.19	1178.6
24.	1.2697	1.6084	2.0328	2.5633	3.2251	4.0489	5.0724	6.3412	7.7911	9.8497	15.178	23.212	28.625	35.236	53.108	79.496	174.63	374.14	781.02	1602.9
25.	1.2824	1.6406	2.0938	2.6658	3.3864	4.2919	5.4274	6.8485	8.6231	10.834	17.000	26.461	32.918	40.874	62.668	95.396	216.54	478.90	1033.5	2180.0
26.	1.2953	1.6734	2.1566	2.7725	3.5557	4.5494	5.8074	7.3964	9.3992	11.918	19.040	30.166	37.856	47.414	73.948	114.47	268.51	612.99	1364.3	2964.9
27.	1.3082	1.7069	2.2213	2.8834	3.7335	4.8223	6.2139	7.9881	10.245	13.110	21.324	34.389	43.535	55.000	87.259	137.37	332.95	784.63	1800.9	4032.2
28.	1.3213	1.7410	2.2879	2.9987	3.9201	5.1117	6.6488	8.6271	11.167	14.421	23.883	39.204	50.065	63.800	102.96	164.84	412.86	1004.3	2377.2	5483.8
29.	1.3356	1.7758	2.3566	3.1187	4.1161	5.4184	7.1143	9.3173	12.172	15.863	23.749	44.693	57.575	74.008	121.50	197.81	511.95	1285.5	3137.9	7458.0
30.	1.3478	1.8114	2.4273	3.2434	4.3219	5.7415	7.6123	10.062	13.267	17.449	29.959	50.950	66.211	85.849	143.37	237.37	634.81	1645.5	4142.0	10143
40.	1.4889	2.2080	3.2620	4.8010	7.0400	10.285	14.974	21.724	31.409	45.259	93.050	188.88	267.86	378.72	750.37	1469.7	5455.9	19126	66520	*
50.	1.6446	2.6916	4.3839	7.1067	11.467	18.420	29.457	46.901	74.357	117.39	289.00	700.23	1083.6	1670.7	3927.3	9100.4	46890	*	*	*
60.	1.8167	3.2810	5.8916	10.519	18.679	32.987	57.946	101.25	176.03	304.48	897.59	2595.9	4383.9	7370.1	20555	56347	*	*	*	*

(PVIFA) Present Value of an Annuity of $1

Number of Payments	1%	2%	3%	4%	5%	6%	7%	8%	9%	10%	12%	14%	15%	16%	18%	20%	24%	28%	32%
1.	0.9901	0.9804	0.9709	0.9615	0.9524	0.9434	0.9346	0.9259	0.9174	0.9091	0.8929	0.8772	0.8696	0.8821	0.8475	0.8333	0.8065	0.7813	0.7576
2.	1.9704	1.9415	1.9135	1.8861	1.8594	1.8334	1.8080	1.7833	1.7591	1.7355	1.6901	1.6467	1.6257	1.6052	1.5656	1.5278	1.4568	1.3916	1.3315
3.	2.9410	2.8839	2.8286	2.7751	2.7232	2.7630	2.6243	2.5771	2.5313	2.4869	2.4018	2.3216	2.2812	2.2459	2.1743	2.1065	1.9813	1.8684	1.7663
4.	3.9020	3.8077	3.7171	3.6299	3.5460	3.4651	3.3872	3.3121	3.2397	3.1699	3.0373	2.9137	2.8550	2.7982	2.6901	2.5887	2.4043	2.2410	2.0957
5.	4.8534	4.7135	4.5797	4.4518	4.3295	4.2124	4.1002	3.9927	3.8897	3.7908	3.6048	3.4331	3.3522	3.2743	3.1272	2.9906	2.7454	2.5230	2.3452
6.	5.7955	5.6014	5.4172	5.2421	5.0757	4.9173	4.7665	4.6229	4.4859	4.3553	4.1114	3.8887	3.7845	3.6847	3.4976	3.3255	3.0205	2.7594	2.5342
7.	6.7282	6.4720	6.2303	6.0021	5.7864	5.5824	5.3893	5.2064	5.0330	4.8684	4.5638	4.2883	4.1604	4.0386	3.8115	3.6046	3.2423	2.9370	2.6775
8.	7.6517	7.3255	7.0197	6.7327	6.4632	6.2098	5.9713	5.7466	5.5348	5.3349	4.9676	4.6389	4.4873	4.3436	4.0776	3.8372	3.4212	3.0758	2.7860
9.	8.5660	8.1622	7.7861	7.4353	7.1078	6.8017	6.5152	6.2469	5.9952	5.7590	5.3282	4.9464	4.7716	4.6065	4.3030	4.0310	3.5655	3.1842	2.8681
10.	9.4713	8.9826	8.5302	8.1109	7.7217	7.3601	7.0236	6.7101	6.4177	6.1446	5.6502	5.2161	5.0188	4.8332	4.4941	4.1925	3.6819	3.2689	2.9304
11.	10.3676	9.7858	9.2526	8.7605	8.3064	7.8869	7.4987	7.1390	6.8052	6.4951	5.9377	5.4527	5.2337	5.0286	4.6560	4.3271	3.7757	3.3351	2.9776
12.	11.2551	10.5753	9.9540	9.3851	8.8633	8.3838	7.9427	7.5361	7.1607	6.8137	6.1944	5.6603	5.4206	5.1971	4.7932	4.4392	3.8514	3.3868	3.0133
13.	12.1337	11.3484	10.6350	9.9856	9.9396	8.8527	8.3577	7.9038	7.4889	7.1034	6.4235	5.8424	5.5831	5.3423	4.9095	4.5327	3.9124	3.3472	3.0404
14.	13.0037	12.1062	11.2961	10.5631	9.8986	9.2950	8.7455	8.2442	7.7862	7.3667	6.6282	6.0021	5.7245	5.4675	5.0081	4.6106	3.9616	3.4587	3.0609
15.	13.8651	12.8493	11.9379	11.1184	10.3797	9.7122	9:1079	8.5595	8.0607	7.6061	6.8109	6.1422	5.8474	5.5755	5.0916	4.6755	4.0013	3.4834	3.0764
16.	14.7179	13.5777	12.5611	11.6523	10.8378	10.1059	9.4466	8.8514	8.3126	7.8237	6.9740	6.2651	5.9542	5.6685	5.1724	4.7296	4.0333	3.5026	3.0882
17.	15.5623	14.2919	13.1661	12.1657	11.2741	10.4773	9.7632	9.1216	8.5436	8.0216	7.1196	6.3729	6.0472	5.7487	5.2223	4.7746	4.0591	3.5177	3.0971
18.	16.3983	14.9920	13.7535	12.6593	11.6896	10.8276	10.0591	9.3719	8.7556	8.2014	7.2497	6.4674	6.1280	5.8178	5.2732	4.8122	4.0799	3.5294	3.1039
19.	17.2260	15.6785	14.3238	13.1339	12.0853	11.1581	10.3356	9.6036	8.9501	8.3649	7,3658	6.5504	6.1982	5.8775	5.3162	4.8435	4.0967	3.5386	3.1000
20.	18.0456	16.3514	14.8775	13.5903	12.4622	11.4699	10.5940	9.8181	9.1285	8.5436	7.4694	6.6231	6.2593	5.9288	5.3527	4.8696	4.1103	3.5458	3.1129
25.	22.0232	19.5235	17.4131	15.6221	14.0939	12.7834	11.6536	10.6748	9.8226	9.0770	7.8431	6.8729	6.4641	6.0971	5.4669	4.9476	4.1474	3.5640	3.1220
30.	25.8077	22.3965	19.6004	17.2920	15.3725	13.7648	12.4090	11.2578	10.2737	9.4269	8.0552	7.0072	6.5660	6.1772	5.5168	4.9789	4.1601	3.5693	1.1242
40.	32.8347	27.3555	23.1148	19.7928	17.1591	15.0463	13.3317	11.9246	10.7574	9.7791	8.2438	7.1050	6.6418	6.2335	5.5482	4.9966	4.1659	3.5712	3.1250
50.	39.1961	31.4236	25.7298	21.4822	18.2559	15.7619	13.8007	12.2335	10.9617	9.9148	8.3045	7.1327	6.6605	6.2463	5.5541	4.9995	4.1666	3.5714	3.1250
60.	44.9550	34.7609	27.8756	22.6235	18.9293	16.1614	14.0392	12.3766	11.0480	9,9672	8.3240	7.1401	6.6651	6.2492	5.5553	4.9999	4.1667	3.5714	3.1250

Future Value Factors

Number of Periods	1%	2%	3%	4%	5%	6%	7%	8%	9%	10%	12%	14%	15%	16%	18%	20%	24%	28%	32%	36%
1.	1.0000	1.0000	1.0000	1.0000	1.0000	1.0000	1.0000	1.0000	1.0000	1.0000	1.0000	1.0000	1.0000	1.0000	1.0000	1.0000	1.0000	1.0000	1.0000	1.0000
2.	2.0100	2.0200	2.0300	2.0400	2.0500	2.0600	2.0700	2.0800	2.0900	2.1000	2.1200	2.1400	2.1500	2.1600	2.1800	2.2000	2.2400	2.2800	2.3200	2.3600
3.	3.0301	3.0604	3.0909	3.1216	3.1525	3.1836	3.2149	3.2464	3.2781	3.3100	3.3744	3.4396	3.4725	3.5056	3.5724	3.6400	3.7776	3.9184	4.0624	4.2096
4.	4.0604	4.1216	4.1836	4.2465	4.3101	4.3746	4.4399	4.5061	4.5731	4.6410	4.7793	4.9211	4.9934	5.0665	5.2154	5.3680	5.6842	6.0156	6.3624	6.7251
5.	5.1010	5.2040	5.3091	5.4163	5.5256	5.6371	5.7507	5.8666	5.9847	6.1051	6.3528	6.6101	6.7424	6.8771	7.1542	7.4416	8.0484	8.6999	9.3983	10.146
6.	6.1520	6.3081	6.4684	6.6330	6.8019	6.9753	7.1533	7.3359	7.5233	7.7156	8.1152	8.5355	8.7537	8.9775	9.4420	9.9299	10.980	12.135	13.405	14.798
7.	7.2135	7.4343	7.6625	7.8983	8.1420	8.3938	8.6540	8.9228	9.2004	9.4872	10.089	10.730	11.086	11.413	12.141	12.915	14.615	16.533	18.695	21.126
8.	8.2857	8.5830	8.8923	9.2142	9.5491	9.8975	10.259	10.636	11.028	11.435	12.299	13.232	13.726	14.240	15.327	16.499	19.122	22.163	25.678	29.731
9.	9.3685	9.7546	10.159	10.582	11.026	11.491	11.978	12.487	13.021	13.579	14.775	16.085	16.785	17.518	19.085	20.798	24.712	29.369	34.895	41.435
10.	10.462	10.949	11.463	12.006	12.577	13.180	13.816	14.486	15.192	15.937	17.548	19.337	20.303	21.321	23.521	25.958	31.643	38.592	47.061	57.351
11.	11.566	12.168	12.807	13.486	14.206	14.971	16.781	16.645	17.560	18.531	20.654	23.044	24.349	25.732	28.755	32.180	40.237	50.398	63.121	78.998
12.	12.682	13.412	14.192	15.025	15.917	16.869	17.888	18.977	20.140	21.384	24.133	27.270	29.001	30.850	34.931	39.580	50.894	65.510	84.320	108.43
13.	13.809	14.680	15.617	16.626	17.713	18.882	20.140	21.495	22.953	24.522	26.029	32.088	34.351	36.786	42.218	48.496	64.109	84.852	112.30	148.47
14.	14.947	15.973	17.086	18.291	19.598	21.015	22.550	24.214	26.019	27.975	32.392	37.581	40.504	43.672	50.818	50.195	80.496	109.61	149.23	202.92
15.	16.096	17.293	18.598	20.023	21.578	23.276	25.129	27.152	29.360	31.772	37.279	43.842	47.580	51.659	60.965	72.035	100.81	141.30	197.99	276.97
16.	17.257	18.639	20.156	21.824	23.657	25.672	27.888	30.324	33.003	35.949	42.753	50.980	55.717	60.925	72.939	87.442	126.01	181.86	262.35	377.69
17.	18.430	20.012	21.761	23.697	25.840	28.212	30.840	33.750	36.973	40.544	48.883	59.117	65.075	71.673	87.068	105.93	157.25	233.79	347.30	514.66
18.	19.614	21.412	23.414	25.645	28.132	30.905	33.999	37.450	41.301	45.599	55.749	68.394	75.836	84.140	103.74	128.11	195.99	300.25	459.44	700.93
19.	20.810	22.840	25.116	27.761	30.539	33.760	37.379	41.446	46.018	51.159	63.439	78.969	88.211	98.603	123.41	154.74	244.03	385.32	607.47	954.27
20.	22.019	24.297	26.870	29.778	33.066	36.785	40.995	45.762	51.160	57.275	72.052	91.024	102.44	115.37	146.62	186.68	303.60	494.21	802.86	1298.8
21.	23.239	25.783	28.676	31.969	35.719	39.992	44.865	50.442	56.764	64.002	81.698	104.76	118.81	134.84	174.02	225.02	377.46	633.59	1060.7	1767.3
22.	24.471	27.299	30.536	34.248	36.505	43.392	49.005	55.456	62.873	71.402	92.502	120.43	137.63	157.41	206.34	271.03	469.05	1040.3	1850.6	3271.3
23.	25.716	28.845	32.452	36.617	41.430	46.995	53.436	60.893	69.531	79.543	104.60	138.29	159.27	183.60	244.48	326.23	582.62	1040.3	1850.6	3271.3
24.	26.973	30.421	34.426	39.082	44.502	50.815	58.176	66.764	76.789	88.497	118.15	158.65	184.16	213.97	289.49	392.48	723.46	1332.6	2443.8	4449.9
25.	28.243	32.030	36.459	41.645	47.727	54.864	63.249	73.105	84.700	98.347	133.33	181.87	212.79	249.21	342.60	471.98	898.09	1706.8	3226.8	6052.9
26.	29.525	33.670	38.553	44.311	51.113	59.156	68.676	79.954	91.323	109.18	150.33	208.33	245.71	290.08	405.27	567.37	1114.6	2185.7	4260.4	8233.0
27.	30.820	35.344	40.709	47.084	54.669	63.705	74.483	87.350	102.72	121.09	169.37	238.49	283.56	337.50	479.22	681.85	1383.1	2798.7	5624.7	11197.0
28.	32.129	37.051	42.930	49.967	58.402	68.528	80.697	95.338	112.96	134.20	190.69	272.88	327.10	392.50	566.48	819.22	1716.0	3583.3	7425.6	15230.2
29.	32.450	36.792	45.218	52.966	62.322	73.790	87.346	101.96	124.13	148.63	214.58	312.09	377.16	456.30	669.44	984.06	2128.9	4587.6	9802.9	20714.1
30.	34.784	40.568	47.576	56.084	66.438	79.058	94.460	113.28	136.30	164.49	241.33	356.78	434.74	530.31	790.94	1181.8	2640.9	5873.2	12940	28172.2
40.	48.886	60.402	75.401	95.025	120.79	154.76	199.53	259.05	337.88	442.59	767.09	1342.0	1779.0	2360.7	4163.2	7343.8	22728	63977	*	*
50.	66.463	84.579	112.79	152.66	209.34	290.33	406.52	573.76	815.08	1163.9	2400.0	4994.5	7217.7	10435	21813	45497	*	*	*	*
60.	81.669	114.05	163.05	237.90	353.58	523.12	813.52	1253.2	1944.7	3034.8	7471.6	18535	29219	46057	*	*	*	*	*	*

CHAPTER 33

Security Pricing

Security evaluation is important to decide for the portfolio of an investor. All investment decisions are to be made on a scientific analysis of the right price of a share. Hence an understanding of the valuation of securities is essential. Investors should buy underpriced shares and sell overpriced shares. Share pricing is thus an important aspect of trading. Conceptually, four types of valuation models are discernible. They are: *(i)* Book value, *(ii)* Liquidating value, *(iii)* Intrinsic value, *(iv)* Replacement value *vis-a-vis* Market price.

Factors Influencing Valuation

Security price depends on a host of factors like earnings per share, prospects of expansion, future earnings potential, possible issue of bonus or rights shares, etc. Some demand for a particular stock may give pleasure of power as a shareholder or prestige and control on management. Satisfaction and pleasure in the non-monetary sense cannot be considered in any practical and quantifiable sense. Many psychological and emotional factors influence the demand for a share.

In money terms, the return to a security on which its value depends consists of two components: *(i)* regular dividends or interest and *(ii)* capital gains or losses in the form of changes in the capital value of the asset. If the risk is high, return should also be high. Risk here refers to uncertainty of receipt of principal and interest or dividend and variability of this return.

The above returns are in terms of money received over a period of years. But money of Re. 1 received today is not the same as money of Re. 1 received a year hence or two years hence etc. Money has time value, which suggests that earlier receipts are more desirable and valuable than later receipts. One reason for this is that earlier receipts can be reinvested and more receipts can be got than before. Here the principle operating is compound interest.

Thus, if Vn is the terminal value at the period n, P is the initial value, g is rate of compounding or return, n is the number of compounding periods, then $Vn = P(1 + g)^n$.

If we reverse the process, the present value (P) can be thought of as reversing the compounding of values. This is discounting of the future values to the present day, represented by the formula:

$P = Vn/(1 + g)^n$, where the meaning of the terms used is the same as indicated above.

Security Valuation

The major factor which influences security prices is the return on expected return on equity capital to the investor. This return may be in the form of dividends or net earnings of the company. Thus, the value of a share is a function of the company's dividend paying capacity or its earnings capacity. The dividends may be different from the earnings depending on the amount of profits retained by the company for the requirements of liquidity, expansion, modernisation, etc.

Normally, the value of a share is its book value or net asset value, if the shares are not quoted on the market. On the other hand, the market price of shares quoted will differ from the book value based on investors' perception of the future earning potential of the company, growth prospects and the industry prospects, quality of management, the goodwill or the intangibles of the company.

If the security is a bond or debenture and has a fixed return like 14% per annum, its market price depends upon investor's perception of the capitalisation rate which may be assumed to be 15%. In this case,

$$\text{Market Price (MP)} = \frac{\text{Earnings}}{\text{Discount rate}} = \frac{14 \times 100}{15} = \text{Rs. } 93$$

If the security is an equity share, its return is Dividend + Capital appreciation. Then the future dividends may not be constant or fixed as also the degree of capital appreciation.

Constant Growth Model

For equity securities, the market price depends upon the discounted future dividends or earnings flows. Thus,

P = Value = D/K - g

D = Expected dividend

K = Discount rate

g = Rate of growth of earnings power.

In this simplified model, dividend flows are assumed to be constant and the rate of growth of earnings fixed.

The discount rate in the above model is subjective and is assumed to be a specific rate such as risk-free market rate or the long-term yield rate on government bonds. A few analysts[1] use the implied discount rate or internal rate of return, which is derived by equating the present value of the projected dividend stream with the current market price.

The actual selection of the discount rate as the fair rate of return on capital is a concept which is to be defined by the analysts and used as a subjective factor. Many people use a crude discounting model whereby the dividend stream is constant and the discount rate is also fixed as the internal rate of return on the project. In actual fact, the discount rate is a rate on fixed income securities, which is risk-free like government bonds. The yield on govt. bonds at 7% - 8% is taken normally as the risk-free rate in India. But some use the bank rate of 6% as a risk-free return.

Book Value

Book value of a security is an accounting concept. The book value of an equity share is equal to the net worth of the firm divided by the number of equity shares, where the net worth is equal to equity capital plus free reserves. The market value may fluctuate around the book value but be higher if the future prospects are good. The market price to Book value ratio for BSE sensex stock was 5.10 in March 2006 as against 5.6 in March 1995. It was 5.2 in March 2008 and 2.7 in March 2009.

Liquidating Value (Breakdown Value)

If the assets are valued at their breakdown value in the market and take net fixed assets plus current assets minus current liabilities as if the company is liquidated, then divide this by the number of shares, the resultant value is the liquidating value per share. This is also an accounting concept.

Replacement Value

When the company is liquidated and its assets are to be replaced by new ones, their prices being higher, the replacement value of a share, will be different from the Breakdown value. Some analysts take this replacement value to compare with the market price. The replacement value of all assets, divided by the number of equity shares gives the replacement value of a share.

1. E. J. Elton & M. J. Gruben, *Modern Portfolio Theory and Investment Analysis.*

Intrinsic Value vs. Market Price

Market value of a security is the price at which the security is traded in the market and it is generally hovering around its intrinsic value. There are different schools of thought regarding the relationship of intrinsic value to the market price. Market prices are those which rule in the market, resulting from the demand and supply forces. Intrinsic price is the true value of the share, which depends on its earning capacity and its true worth. According to the fundamentalist approach to security valuation, the value of the security must be equal to the discounted value of the future income stream. The investor buys the securities when the market price is below this value. He buys for the future returns.

Thus, for fundamentalists, earnings and dividends are the essential ingredients in determining the market value of a security. The discount rate used in such present value calculations is known as the required rate or return. Using this discount rate all future earnings are discounted back to the present to determine the intrinsic value. This has been referred to earlier.

According to the technical school, the price of a security is determined by the market demand and supply and it has very little to do with intrinsic values. The price movements follow certain trends for varying periods of time. Changes in trend represent the shifts in demand and supply which are predictable. The present trends are the offshoot of the past and history repeats itself according to this school.

According to efficient market hypothesis, in a fairly large security market where competitive conditions prevail, market prices are good proxies for intrinsic values. The security prices are determined after absorbing all the information available to market participants. A share is thus generally worth whatever it is selling for in the market.

Generally, fundamental school is the basis for security valuation and many models are in use based on these tenets.

Equity Valuation

The intrinsic value of an equity share depends on the dividends declared by the company. These models can be broadly classified for simplicity's sake into:

(i) Single-period valuation models; and

(ii) Multi-period valuation models.

In these models, the infinite stream of future dividends are valued for the present time as price-dividend ratio. If the net earnings are assumed to be the same as dividends and no retained earnings, then the price-dividend ratio contracts to price-earnings ratio.

Single-Period Valuation Models

Assume that *(i)* the dividends are paid annually; *(ii)* the first dividend is received after one year and *(iii)* the resale occurs at the end of the year. Then, the price of the share is $P_o = \frac{D_1}{(1+i)} + \frac{P_1}{(1+i)}$ where Po is the current price, P_1 is the price after an year, D_1 is the dividend after a year and i is the required rate of return.

Example

A company's equity share is expected to bring a dividend of Rs. 2 and fetch a price of Rs. 18 after an year. If the investor buys at Rs. 18, there is no capital appreciation. Assuming the required rate of return to be equal to 12%,

$$P_o = \frac{2.0}{(1.12)} + \frac{18.00}{(1.12)} = \frac{20}{(1.12)} = 17.86$$

If the investor purchase at Rs. 18, he incurs a loss of Rs. 0.14 on every share.

Multi-Period Share Valuation Model

An investor would hold the security for more than one period. In this case, the price of the share is given by the formula

$$P_o = \sum_{t=1}^{n} \frac{D_t}{(1+i)^t} + \frac{P_n}{(1+i)^n}$$

Where D_i is the dividend in period i and P_n is the selling price. In case the dividends grow at a constant rate of g, the equation reduces to $P_o = \frac{D_i}{1-g}$

In the special case of g = 0

the equation is $P_o = \frac{D_i}{i}$

Example

The expected earnings per share is Rs. 3 and dividend Rs. 2 respectively. If the required rate of return is 15%, what should be the share price assuming g = 0%, 5% and 10%.

Therefore, when g = O, $P = \frac{2}{0.15} = 13.33$ When the company shows no growth

when g = 0.05, $P = \frac{2}{0.15-0.05} = 20$ in period 2, it shows a growth rate of 5%

when g = 0.10, $P = \frac{2}{0.15-0.1} = 40$ in period 3, it shows a growth rate of 10%

The above example shows how the share price appreciates very high, if the company evinces growth prospects and declares rising dividends.

Dividend Capitalisation

Sometimes, the firms do not declare dividends so as to finance their future programmes. In such cases, the dividends are non-existent, but the market prices may be high. In these cases, it is seen that the investors use earnings as a proxy for dividends in the above models. The dividend capitalisation model and the earnings capitalisation model yield the same result only when all the earnings are paid out as dividends. Then there is no growth. $P = \frac{E_i}{i}$, where the earnings (E_1) (or dividends) and i is the required discount rate. Where the earning or dividend grow at a constant rate (g) then the formula is $P = E_1/i\text{-}g$.

When a portion of the earnings is retained, the dividend capitalisation model is to be used. When growth in the expected future dividends is taken as a function of retained earnings that are reinvested in profitable projects, it is double counting to include both the earnings and the future growth rate of dividends in the same model as the latter depend upon the former also, in part.

Earnings Capitalisation

It is to be noted that higher future dividends are an *alternative* to present dividends and are *not an addition* to the present dividend stream. If E = D, the firm cannot grow. Thus the investors who use the price-earnings ratio tend to overstate the market price due to the double counting problem.

In reality, the earnings do not grow at a constant rate nor do the dividends. For theoretical nicety, these assumptions are made. But as limitations, it should be noted that the desired rate of return and the actual rate may not coincide and there is an element of subjectivity in the desired rate of return. Besides, the use of price-earnings ratio following the dividend capitalisation model, suffers from the fact that earnings data are historical but price is the present price, which already takes into account the past dividends, and the future dividend flow may not depend on the past earnings, and price is paid for the future returns.

Use of P/E Ratio

Many practising analysts use the simple multiplier technique of P/E ratio, but not the present value models referred to above.

The ratio P/E = Current Market Price/Earnings per share.

By an analysis of the company's performance, the analysts computes the P/E multiplier (the times P is higher than the earnings per share). In this case, he forecasts the future earnings per share for the next six months or one year and uses this historical multiplier of the same company or of the industry average multiplier to arrive at the market price. The resulting market price is compared with the actual market price to find out whether it is overpriced or underpriced. If it is overpriced, it is to be sold as per the principles of trading operations based on fundamental analysis.

The valuation technique based on discounting is cumbersome and serious forecasting problems arise in the process. The discount rate to be used is a subjective factor and a number of assumptions are required to be made regarding the dividend flows in the present value models. Therefore, analysts and investors use only the P/E ratio for security valuation in practice.

To sum up, the models more commonly used for security pricing are the Dividend Discounting method/Earnings Discounting method and the P/E ratio model. These models are dealt with in detail below.

Security Pricing Models

The Dividend Discounting Method: The expected future dividend payments by the company are discounted to the present day by the use of an appropriate discount rate, which is supposed to reflect the magnitude of risk-free return. The risk premium of stocks may have some risk element and many additional uncertainties. In this model, each of the future year's dividend up to, say, for 'n' years (10 years) is discounted with the appropriate discount rate to the present and summed up to arrive at the worth of the stock today. Dividends are expected to remain constant and the discount rate is assumed to remain unchanged. In this simplified model, no provision is made for changes in dividend or for a variable growth of dividend/earnings. The formula is D/K - g, where D is the dividend, k is the discount rate and g is the constant growth rate of dividends. In this model, the discount rate is a matter of individual perception and is subjective. It is based on the expected depreciation of the rupee and one's own time premium of the present over the future. Thus today one rupee may be worth Rs. 1.10 in the next year (a premium of 10 per cent inclusive of inflation).

P/E Ratio Model: The present value of the stock is also arrived at through the assumed relationship between the earnings per share and market price of the share (P/E ratio) of a company and that of the average of the whole industry in which the company is. If the company's P/E ratio and the industry P/E ratio have relationship, these can be related to derive the industry relative, which can be applied to the company's earnings per share to arrive at its price. Thus, if P/E for electronics has a P/E relative at 15, then for the company in electronics, data on earnings per share can be multiplied by 15 to arrive at its price. If this price is higher than the market price, the security is undervalued and *vice versa*. P/E is relative to time and scrip and varies widely. P/E multiple based on BSE sensex scrips is 12.86 in March 1999 and 16.6 in March 2005 as against 41.2 in March 1995. It was 20% in 2008 and 13.7 in 2009 (March).

Other Models

Some writers speak of two supplementary guides to valuation which came into fairly wide use, namely, price-to-asset ratio and price-to-sales ratio (ref. p. 365, *Investment Analysis and Portfolio Management* by Cohen, Zinbarg and Zeikel). According to the first, the stocks of a company are evaluated by reference to the true net asset values using various capital goods and inventory price indices to adjust reported book values. A number of analysts define this as the replacement cost of book value of the company. Some take it as the net working capital per share measured by current assets minus current liabilities minus long-term debt and preferred stock minus intangible assets divided by the number of shares. This is something like the breakdown value of the company's assets.

According to the second, the average price-to-sales ratio of the industry group is applied to the company price to sales or P/S ratio to judge whether it is overpriced or underpriced. A low P/S ratio indicates a low probability of bankruptcy and hence a good buy, if other conditions are satisfied for choosing the company.

Graham's Approach to Valuation of Equity

In their book on Security Analysis (1934) Benjamin Graham, and David Dodd, argued that future earnings power was the most important determinant of the value of stock. The original approach of identifying the undervalued stock is to find out the present value of forecasted dividends, and if the current market price is lower, it is undervalued. Alternatively, the analyst could determine the discount rate that makes the present value of the forecasted dividends equal to the current market price of the stock. If that rate (I.R.R. or discount rate) is more than the required rate for stocks of similar risks, then the stock is underpriced.

Graham and Dodd had argued that each dollor of dividends is worth four times as much as one dollar of retained earnings (in their original Book); by subsequent studies of data showed no justification for this. Graham and Rea have given some questions on Rewards and risks for financial data analysts to answer yes or no and on the basis of these ready to answer questions, they decided to locate undervalued stocks to buy and overvalued stocks to sell.

Such readymade formulas or questions are now out of favour due to various empirical studies which showed that earnings models are as good as or better than dividend models and that a number of factors are ably studied for common stock valuation and no unique formula or answer is justifiable.

THEORETICAL APPROACHES

The major theoretical approaches to the question of valuation of stock are set out briefly here:

Classical Theory

The Classical Theory and the traditional view is that debt is cheaper than equity and that firms can increase the shareholder's value by reducing the cost of capital through debt route. By raising the proportion of debt to equity, upto a limit atleast, the level of gearing to equity can be increased. Tax considerations of treating debt servicing as an expense item by the firm also confirms the view that debt is a cheaper alternative to equity, as dividends paid to equity are taxable. However, there is a trade off between the benefits of leverage to the company and the larger risk that it leads to for the company for a possible state of illiquidity due to the servicing needs of debts. This Theory thus postualtes that there is an optimum level of debt for a firm at any point of time depending on the average cost of debt and average return on capital.

Neo-Classical Theory

Modigliani and Miller (1958)[@] questioned this traditional view as it is based on unrealistic assumptions, such as free and perfect markets and free competition and free flow of information. M & M laid down the foundations for Modern Theory of valuation of firms. They showed that valuation of the firm is independent of the capital structure. The financing decision is made independent of investment decision. Both external and internal sources of finance are substitutes and profits retained or dividends paid make no difference, so long as the return on capital is higher than the cost of capital. As sources of finance, it does not matter which source is tapped. M & M Theory also called neo-classical Theory of

@ Modigliani F. and Miller M.: - "The Cost of Capital etc. .." AER. 48, (1958) p. 261.

Investment has thus showed that the firm is indifferent between internal and external sources of capital. The only requirement is that the return on investment should be higher than the cost of capital.

Modern Theories

Modern Theories are based on the cash flows generated by an Investment. The "pecking order" Theory of financing states that capital market imperfections raise the cost of external financing whereby firms first finance the new investments by resort to internal sources, to be followed by low cost debt and then finally by resort to external equity from public.

There are two approaches to cash flow theories:

(i) Managerial approach; and

(ii) Information — Theoretic approach.

(i) Managerial Approach

Under this theory, Managers are the maximisers of the size of the firm and its profits and do not necessarily aim at the maximisation of the shareholders' wealth. This theory separates ownership from control and differentiates the interests of shareholders from those of Professional Managers. This theory postulates that the firm relies more on internal finance as the resort to external sources leads to the firm subjecting itself to the discipline of the capital market, which managers try to avoid.

(ii) Information — Theoretic Approach

This theory is based on the asymmetric information model where in the Managers have the private information about the firm's return streams, and Investment opportunities. Myers and Majiluf (1984) @ have showed that if the capital market is less informed than the insiders about the value of firm's assets, equity may be mispriced and low quality equity gets mixed up with high quality equity. The firm's preference is of internal funds, riskless and less costly debt, followed by exernal sources in that order.

What is missed in the above approaches is the concept of return versus risk. Cash flows and Investment are closely related and hence net present value of cash flows should be the major method of valuation of the firm. Dividend capitalisation Model and Earnings capitalisation Model have thus become more acceptable among modern theories. They are more frequently used in the valuation of the firm in the modern literature.

Valuation of Securities in India

In India, the valuation of securities used to be done by the CCI for the purpose of fixing up the premium on new issues of existing companies. These guidelines used by CCI were applicable upto May 1992, when the CCI was abolished. Although the present market price will be taken into account a more rational price used to be worked out by the CCI on certain criteria.

Thus, the CCI used the concept of net asset value (NAV) and profit-earning capacity value (PECV) as the basis for fixing up the premium on shares. The NAV is calculated by dividing the net worth by the number of equity shares. The net worth includes equity capital plus free reserves and surplus less contingent liabilities. The PECV is estimated by multiplying the earnings per share by a capitalisation rate of 15% for manufacturing companies, 20% for trading companies and 17.5% in the case of intermediate companies. Earnings per share (EPS) is calculated by dividing the three-year average post-tax profits by the total number of equity shares. Thus, if EPS is Rs. 5 and if the price earnings multiplier is 15, the price of share, which is reflected by the PECV, should be Rs. 5 × 15 = 75 (if it is a manufacturing company).

To be more specific,

The net asset value of a company (NAV) = Total assets less liabilities, borrowings, debts, preference capital and contingent liabilities which is to be divided by the number of equity shares.

@ Myers S. & Majiluf. N. - "Corporate Financing --- etc. ---- " in Journal of Financial Economics - 13, p. 187.

The profit-earning capacity value (PECV) is obtained by capitalising the average profits after tax (over the past three years) by a rate varying from 15% to 20% depending on the nature of the activity of the company as already noted.

The fair value of the share is the average of the NAV and PECV. This fair value (FV) is taken into account for comparison with the average market price over the preceding three years and the average market price should be less than the fair value by at least 20%. If the average market price is 20% to 50% of the FV, the capitalisation rate to be used is 12%. If it is 50% to 75% of the FV, the capitalisation rate is 10% and if it is more than 75% of FV, the capitalisation rate is 8%.

Example

The following example will make the above exercise clear.

Take a manufacturing company (TISCO)

Average Market Price over the last three years = Rs. 123

Net Asset Value (NAV) computed as shown above = Rs. 68

Profit-earning capacity value (PECV) = Earnings per share Rs. 5.4 capitalised by 15% for manufacturing company

$$= \frac{5.4 \times 100}{15} = \text{Rs. } 36.$$

Average of NAV and PECV is (68 + 36)/2 = Rs. 52 which is the fair value.

The market price (Rs. 123) is more than 75% of the Fair Value (Rs. 52). Hence the captialisation rate of 8% is to be applied as referred to above to the earnings per share.

Earnings per share is Rs. 5.4.

At the capitalisation rate of 8%, the PECV = Rs. 67.50.

Book value per share or NAV is Rs. 68.

The average of the two above is Rs. 67.75.

For a share of Rs. 10 of face value, the premium is thus Rs. 57.75.

Since May 1992, with the repeal of C.I.C. Act, free market pricing of shares has been permitted. The price of new issue can be decided by the company and its Merchant banker. As per the existing guidelines of SEBI, the merchant banker has to submit the proposals regarding the share price, premium, if any, etc. of new issues to the SEBI for vetting, along with the justification for the same. A margin of 20% on either side is permitted to change the actual premium from the premium submitted to SEBI for approval, as the time of public offer may be different from the time of submission of proposal and market condition may change.

FREE MARKET PRICING

During May 1992, the Capital Issues Control Act 1947 was repealed by a Presidential ordinance, whereby the Government control on issue of capital to public was withdrawn and free pricing of shares for issue to public as per market conditions is allowed. On June 11th, 1992 the SEBI has come out with the guidelines for pricing of shares and for public issues, by different types of companies. The letter of offer to the public should have been vetted by the SEBI before issue. Full and fair disclosures alongwith the risk involved in the project are to be made public. The SEBI has set out guidelines separately for public issue, rights, bonus, debentures etc. and also for issues made by development financial institutions.

Until May 1992, whatever conditions were imposed with regard to pricing of shares or premium fixation for public issue or right issue etc. by the Controller of Capital Issues (CCI) were made applicable to the respective companies. Later, the SEBI has replaced the CCI in its functions in the new issue market and the new guidelines of SEBI were made applicable since then. In principle, the responsibility for proper pricing of shares now rests with the merchant bankers, who have to give convincing reasons to the SEBI and the public investors for the prices fixed for shares to be issued. The governing factors considered and the method of estimation or calculation have to be provided to the SEBI. Besides the merchant banker should be convinced that all the disclosures of facts were made by the company and he should certify to that effect to the SEBI.

SEBI Guidelines for New Issues

(a) First issue of new companies: A new company is one which has not completed 12 months since commercial production started and its operative results are not available. Such companies have to issue shares at par and they are not listed at that time on any Exchange. In Sept. 1995, no new company without two years of track record of commercial production can be listed on an Exchange, and from April 1996, only companies with a 3 year dividend paying record in the last 5 years and those projects appraised and funded by FIs can get their shares listed. Later, this condition was relaxed in respect of I.T. Companies.

(b) New companies set up by well established old companies: If existing old company has atleast 5 years track record of profits and hold at least 50% of share capital of new company, then the shares of new company can be freely priced. But the criteria for pricing have to be disclosed in the prospectus and SEBI should be satisfied with the same. Guidelines were also issued for existing private limited company going public and for already listed company, which are referred to below.

(c) First issue by existing privately and closely held companies: Such companies if they have atleast three years of track record, can freely price the shares issued to the public. They should disclose the reasons for such pricing, giving the net asset value of the company. They have to offer atleast 20% of the total issue to the public.

(d) Fresh issue or further issues by existing listed companies: They can price the shares freely in consultation with the lead managers. The prospectus need not be vetted by the SEBI since Oct. 1996 but should contain the disclosure of N.A.V. and high and low price data as quoted on the Exchange and proper justification for the pricing of the share.

(e) Composite issues of equity alongwith FCD or PCD or Rights Issues: Such issues can be priced differently, if they are offered to the public, as against right shareholders. Similarly pricing of composite issues may have different basis to take into account the attractiveness or otherwise of the offers on the alternative instruments issued to public.

SEBI Guidelines for Development Financial Institutions

The SEBI has issued separate guidelines on September 30th 1992, for the Development Financial Institutions in the public sector, as opposed to Investment and Finance companies in the private sector. The guidelines issued on June 11th 1992 do not cover such institutions which are set up by statute.

The DFIs may raise fresh capital from public by freely pricing their issues, provided they fulfill the following conditions:

(1) The D.F.I. has a track record of profitability over a three years period out of the past five years, with profits during the last two years prior to the issue. These profits are net profits after providing for interest, depreciation and tax.

(2) The D.F.I. may determine the issue price in consultation with the lead manager, provided the price is approved by the shareholders and the Board as the case may be.

(a) In fixing the price, consideration is to be given to a fair capitalisation rate and projected earnings for the next three years and the reasons for making such estimates.

(b) Past performance with regard to net earnings per share, book value for the past five years.

(c) Stock market data covering the average high and low prices for the last three years

The principles observed abroad by merchant bankers are the following:

(a) Charge what the market can bear.

(b) Make the price comparable to the similar companies in the same industry.

(*c*) There should not be much of overvaluation or undervaluation.

(*d*) Estimate the net asset value or the earning capacity of the company.

The highs and lows of prices in the market should be taken into account in the last two or three years for listed companies going to public for raising capital.

THEORY OF PRICING

Theoretically the major factor which influences the security price is the intrinsic value of the share. This is estimated by discounting the future flow of earning to the present day. The discount rate chosen by each individual may differ from others depending on his perception of what is the desired rate of return on investment. In theory, price is determined by the free play of supply and demand conditions. Supply of and demand for shares depend not only on intrinsic worth but on the expansion plans, management reputation and future prospects. To avoid theoretical niceties and subjective factors, the analysts take an accounting concept and estimate the intrinsic value as net worth divided by the number of shares which is the same thing as book value. Some writers take the liquidating or breakdown value of a share which is the value of a share if all the assets are liquidated to meet the liabilities. This is equal to fixed assets plus current assets minus current liabilities divided by the number of shares.

Some analysts of security valuation use P/E multiple to estimate the price. Thus the average market price over the last three years divided by the average earnings per share (EPS) for the last three years gives a multiple by which price is related to earnings per share. Then the future earnings flows for an year or two can be estimated and earnings per share (EPS) can be worked out. This EPS is multiplied by the past multiple derived as an average for the last three years to arrive at the price for the investors prepared to pay now. All the above methods are relevant for share valuation of existing companies. But in the case of a new company, there are no reserves, no book value or a past record of earnings per share. The only solution in such cases is to estimate the future flow of earnings or net profits after interest and tax in the coming three years on the assumption of some rate of capacity utilisation and discount the future flows of cash earnings to the present day by using an appropriate discount rate or a required rate of return of say 20%. This will give the present value of the share at which the public offer is to be made. In this case, the earnings capitalisation model is used, as shown below. In practice, new companies issue shares at par (Rs. 10).

Assume Ei is earnings (Rs. 2) per share in period i and required rate of return per share is r (20%) and the face value of share to be fixed is P_o then

$P_o = E_i/r = 2/0.20 =$ Rs. 10/-

If we assume that these earnings will grow at a rate of 10% per annum, then the present share price P_o should be

$P_o = D_1/(r–g) = 2/0.20–0.10 = 2/0.10 =$ Rs. 20

The simple formula is $Po = D_i/r–g$

The above formula is one of the various models that can be used for price fixation.

Further discussion on share valuation models is set out in next chapter.

Share Valuation Models

Theoretically the share valuation models may be set out as dividend capitalisation model or earnings capitalisation model. In a company with all earnings used for distribution of dividends for simplicity, in a multi-period model, the dividend capitalisation model giving the present value as Po may be set out as

$$P_o = \sum_{t=1}^{n} \frac{D_1}{(1+i)^t} + \frac{P_n}{(1+i)^n}$$

Where D_i is dividend in period i and P_n is the selling price in period (n).

In case the dividends grow at a constant rate of g, the equation is

$P_o = D_i/(i-g)$

Where g = 0, then equation reduces to D_i/i

If the dividend declared is Rs. 2/- and the desired rate of return is 15% then the share price should be

$P_o = 2/0.15 = 13.3$

If the expected growth rate 'g' is 10%

P_o then is 2/0.15 – 0.10 = Rs. 40

The difference in the two prices of nearly Rs. 27 is due to expected growth rate of the company. Thus, there is a lot of difference in the estimated price due to any change in assumptions. The more realistic the assumptions, the better is the emerging picture.

Therefore, the merchant bankers have to make realistic assumptions of the projected earnings in the next three to five years to get a correct share price valuation.

Over-valuation is possible, if replacement value of plant and machinery per unit of production is taken into account. Thus, to produce one tonne of cement may require, say for example Rs. 10 crores at present, while it costed only Rs. 2 crores ten years back. If old assets are revalued at the replacement cost and profitability is calculated, it may lead to huge share premium, unrelated to the existing potential for earnings. Similarly, share prices can be boosted by unrealistic assumptions of costs based on past low input costs or unrealistic tax benefits.

Problems

(1) Hotel Bharat paid a dividend of Rs. 4 per share. Dividends have been growing on annual rate of 8% and this growth rate is expected to continue. What is the present value of stock if the required rate of return is 14%.

Ans: $D_o = 4$, g = 8, k = 14.

the equation for price of common stock is $P_o = \frac{D_o(1+g)}{K-g}$

Applying thus formula

$$P_o = \frac{4(1+0.08)}{0.14-0.08} = \frac{4(1.08)}{0.06} = \frac{4.32}{0.06}$$

$$= \text{Rs. } 72$$

(2) DPL Co. is a sick company. Its net earnings, are declining at a rate of 6% per year. Its present dividend is Rs. 3% per share and Dividends decline proportionate to earnings. Its required rate of return is 14.5%. What is the present value of stock. It is now quoting at Rs. 18. Is it overvalued or undervalued.

Ans. $D_o = 3$, g = –6, K = 14.5%

$$P_o = \frac{D_o(1+g)}{K-g}$$

$$= \frac{3(1-0.06)}{0.145-(-0.06)} = \frac{3(0.94)}{0.205}$$

$$= \frac{2.82}{0.205} = \text{Rs. } 13.75$$

The present value of stock should be Rs. 13.75 and if it is quoting at Rs. 18 it is over valued.

(3) TCL is now showing a dividend growth rate of 20%. After 5 years, its expected to slowdown and come to normal growth rate of 6%. Its required rate of return is 15% and its present dividend is Rs. 0.50 per share. What is the current value of its stock.

Ans: D_o 0.50, $g_1 = 20$, $g_2 = 6$ K = 15, N 5

Its formula for two stage growth model is

$$P_o \sum \frac{D_o\ (1+g_1)^t}{(1+k)^t} + \frac{DN\ (1+g_2)}{(k-g)\ (1+K)^N}$$

$$= \sum \frac{0.50\,(1.20)^5}{(1+0.15)^5} + \frac{0.50\,(1.20)^5 \times 1.06}{(0.15-0.06)\,(1.15)^5}$$, and expanding this,

$$= \frac{0.50\,(1.20)}{1.15} + \frac{0.50\,(1.20)^2}{(1.15)^2} + \frac{0.50\,(1.20)^3}{(1.15)^3}$$

$$+ \frac{0.50(1.20)^4}{(1.15)^4} + \frac{0.50(1.20)^5}{(1.15)^5} + \frac{0.50(1.20)^5(1.06)}{(0.9)(2.01\ 1)}$$

$= 0.522 + 0.544 + 0.568 + 0.593 + 0.619 + 7.290$

$= 10.136$

= Rs. 10.14

the current value of this stock should be Rs. 10.14

Solve the following Problems

Questions

(1) ABC has issued a dividend of Rs. 2 last year. The dividend is expected to grow at 5% per year in the next 3 years; the price of stock three years hence is say Rs. 34.72 which means P_3 = Rs. 34.72 discounted at 12% rate. Calculate the present value of dividend stream and the expected future price, given above.

(2) XYZ has issued a series of 3.4% — 30 year bonds with annual interest payment in the year 1995, at a par value of Rs. 1,000. Ten years later the price fell to Rs. 650. What is the YTM of bond in 2005. Assuming that interest rates fell again later to 2.4% by 2010, what is the price of bond in the year 2010?

(3) Mark Ltd., is paying a dividend of Rs. 3.5, which is expected to grow at 15% for the next four years and then it levels off at 8%. If the capitalisation rate is 12%, what is the market value of equity share.

(4) Orient Co. Ltd., is paying a dividend of Rs. 5 per share. The market expects the dividend to grow at 10% in the next three years and then at 5%. The market capitalisation rate is 13% for earnings of similar companies, calculate the share value of this company.

(5) Pluto Ltd., has a sales turnover of Rs. 25 crores. In the coming two years, sales are expected to grow at 20% and 10% respectivley. The company is expected to maintain a profit margin of 8% and the Dividend payout at 50%. The number of equity shares is 10 lakhs. It is expected that the share will trade at a multiplier of 15 at the end of two years. What is the intrinsic value of stock, if the investors required rate of return is 8%.

(6) Shankar sells short 200 shares of Saturn Ltd., at a price of Rs. 42. Thereafter the company declares a dividend of Rs. 1.5 per share. Later, Saturn's Stock declines to Rs. 35 and at that point, the short seller covers the position. Calculate the gain or loss as percentage of his total transaction, if the transaction costs amount to 1% of the transaction.

APPENDIX

Granger Causality Test

Granger Test refers to the relationship between primary market and secondary market in the capital market, as they are the two segments of the same. The argument that they are closely related is based on economic and financial logic. If the primary market is booming there will be more new issues to be listed in the secondary market for trading. The listed paid up capital and volume of trading will increase. With this there can be rise in the Index of Stock Prices. Looked at from another angle, stock prices movements influences the firm's decision to approach the public or not for fresh funds. The stock prices are reflecting the public opinion and hence the public response to new issues will depend on stock price trend.

Besides, the pricing of shares in new issues will depend upon the present and past trends of the share price, in addition to other criteria. The market price of share, therefore, influences the firm's financing decision to shift of funds from stock market to new issues market and not *vice versa.* Generally, funds meant for new issues are not diverted to stock market, as sentiment will be dull at that time in the stock market which plays a major role on the trading volumes as bulk of trading (namely 70-80% of it) is only speculative in Indian markets. The economic and financial logic, would thus suggest either relationship one way to the other or a two way relationship.

By using "F" statistic, which indicates the direction of the causation, one can examine the relationship between the above segments. They can be reflected in the monthly or yearly new capital issues to the public and the share prices of the market, as reflected in the B.S.E. Sensex or National Index.

One RBI study published in their Annual Report 1995-96 presented the data and results of Granger Causality Test based on "F" statistic; for primary market monthly data on new capital issues is used and for secondary market sensex of B.S.E. is used. The time series monthly data are taken from April 1986 to March 1996. The results show that there is a two way causality in the Indian Capital Market.

Investment Analysis and Theory

Introduction

The stock exchange provides facilities for listing of shares of companies, viz., equities, preference shares, bonds, debentures, etc. These listed shares are traded which gives the price for each share. Trading imparts liquidity to the shares, so that investment is promoted and savings flow into investment. Besides, the stock market provides for free and fair trade in shares, as the demand and supply forces play a free role to determine the prices of shares. It is like an auction system, where the quotes of bid and offer determine the prices. The Stock Exchange authority is a regulatory body for ensuring fair trading practices and protecting the interests of its member brokers and investors. Besides, the stock market reflects the economic and financial developments in the country and industry and is, therefore, a watchdog of the economy. It also protects the investor's interest and ensures the safety and liquidity of their funds.

The market is influenced by the flow of information and money flows. Various other environmental forces also operate. All these factors in the stock market determine the prices. These various factors are called the fundamental factors, technical factors and psychological factors. The information which conveys the fundamental factors has a vital role in the pattern of trading. These fundamental factors refer to the forces emanating from the economy (economic factors), those emanating from the industry (industry factors) and those emanating from the company (company factors). All these factors influence the share prices daily and in the long run.

It will thus be seen that the stock prices are a function of a number of factors, some of which are subjective, while others are quantifiable. Some of these factors emanate from human behaviour and preferences. The three major identifiable factors may be set out as follows:

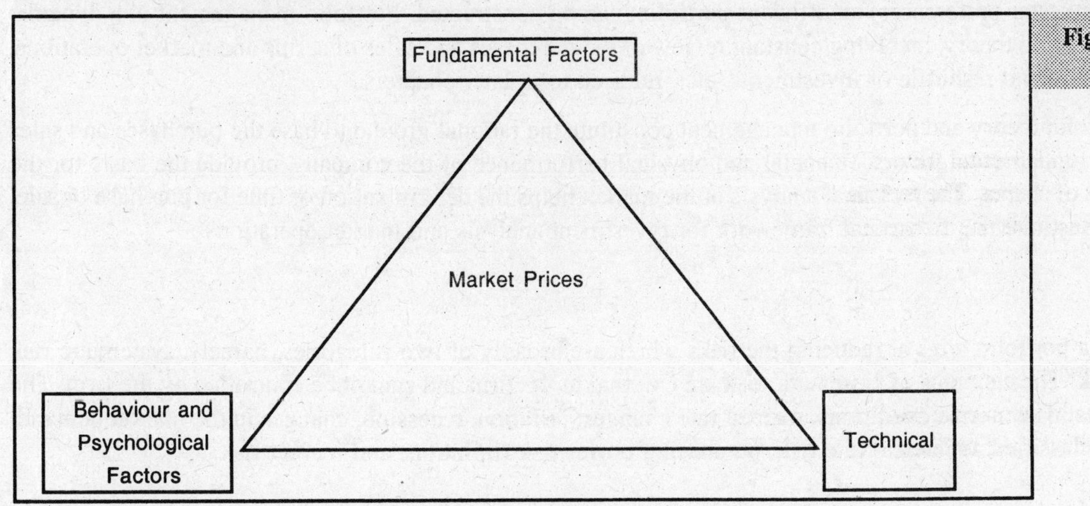

Fig. 34.1

The theoretical framework for operations (buying and selling) in the stock market has been presented in the preceding chapter.

Flow of Funds Theory

To start with, the economy and the financial system are interlinked through the lubricating role of money. Money flows in the form of cash and credit and savings are the basis of investments, which take the form of claims on money. Trading in these claims constitute the financial markets such as stock and capital markets. At the macro level, investment leads to capital formation and is the basis of production of goods and services and income, which results in economic growth. At the micro level, the savings flow into investment based on a scientific analysis of the forces operating on the markets — fundamental analysis — economic, industry and company forces — financial and physical performance of companies analysed through financial ratios (financial management and management accounting) and technical analysis of the market trends based on past market behaviour.

Price Formation

The theory of Market Efficiency and Random Walk Theory explain the price formation through the absorption of information in a perfect manner and postulate that prices move in a random fashion independent of past trends. The market is said to be efficient, if price is determined by competitive forces of supply and demand based on the free flow of correct and full information. In the real world, information is not free and complete. There are trends in which prices move and technical analysis is the answer and the Dow Theory is applicable here. If the market absorption and information flows are not perfect, market prices move around the intrinsic worth of the shares but may not reach them. The actual pricing of shares is to be evaluated in terms of its earnings potential (EPS), dividend distribution, P/E ratio and a host of other financial ratios and a forecast of the prices is to be made to assess whether the share is overpriced or underpriced. Then the principle of buying underpriced shares and selling overpriced shares is adopted by the investor. If the random walk theory is disproved, then the markets are not efficient.

Capital Assets Pricing Model

According to the capital assets pricing model, there is an efficiency frontier for each investor and following the Markowitz model, the capital market line and efficiency frontier line can be drawn to arrive at efficient portfolios for each investor. The efficient portfolio minimises the risk for a given level of return or maximises the return for a given level of risk. The risk-return analysis under portfolio theory helps the construction of an efficient portfolio.

In modern portfolio theory, the risk is represented by the concept of Beta in substitution of the standard deviation of expected returns in CAPM. This Beta relates the specific risk of a company to market risk and is represented by the slope of the capital market line. The scrips with a high Beta are aggressive such as ACC and Reliance. They are more risky and give a higher return than the market average. The scrips with a low Beta are defensive and have lower returns but are less risky than the market average like ITC or Hindustan Lever. If the specific risk of a company is the same as that of the market risk, the company's risk premium (Beta = 1) is equal to the risk premium of the market. By using a proper Beta, consistent with the investor preferences, an efficient portfolio, can be constructed. Portfolio management is a dynamic process, based on portfolio theory, involving constant review of the purchases and sales of scrips and market operations, revision of the portfolio and reshuffle of investments, etc., referred to in later chapters.

Thus, the portfolio theory and portfolio management constitute the rational ground to base the purchases and sales of the investor. The fundamental factors, financial and physical performance of the company, provide the basis for the forecast of the prices of shares. The technical analysis of the market helps the determination of time for purchase or sale. All those together constitute the theoretical framework for investment analysis and market operations.

Risk Analysis

The choice of a portfolio aims at reducing the risks which are broadly of two categories, namely, systematic risk and unsystematic risk. The elements of systematic risk are external to the firm and cannot be controlled by the firm. The examples are changes in economic conditions, interest rate changes, inflation, recession, changes in the market demand, etc. These risks are classified as interest rate risk, purchasing power risk (inflation) and market risk.

The unsystematic risk is the controllable variation in earnings due to the peculiar characteristics of the industry, management efficiency, consumer preferences, labour problems, raw material problems, etc. These are classified as market related risks business risks, financial risks, etc. The total risk is defined as the total variability of returns, which is the summation of systematic and unsystematic risks referred to above.

For a scientific basis for investment, the analyst or investor has to make a rational analysis of the market and the scrips in which he would like to invest. For this purpose, he should be familiar with factors that influence the market prices and the rationale of price formation. One should ask, what determines the prices? Why is the present price of a scrip of TISCO at Rs. 486. Why is Reliance scrip quoted at Rs. 1011 today? Is it overpriced or underpriced? Is it worth buying at this level or not? These and other questions should be analysed and understood by the investor and trader. The theoretical basis for this price formation is, therefore, important. These are briefly explained below in a simple non-technical language.

Efficient Market Theory

This theory states that the market is capable of adjusting quickly and efficiently to the new information generated from the economy, industry and company. Under this theory, the prices are determined by market forces which are in turn influenced by perfect and free flow of correct, unbiased and costless information. These conditions are obtained under an ideal set up and not in the real world. This is discussed in detail in another chapter.

Random Walk Theory

This theory holds that no one can predict the prices of shares based on the past or historical trends. As the market is assumed to be efficient, all information is quickly absorbed in the prices, which move in a random manner and history does not repeat itself. The prices today do not depend upon the prices of yesterday. The prices have the equal capability of going up or down and it is, therefore, impossible for an average investor to earn more than the average profits except by chance. The prices move in a random manner depending upon the flow of information and any combination of shares is as good as any other combination to secure fair returns.

Trend Walk Theory

As opposed to the Random Walk Theory, the Trend Walk Theory postulates that the investor goes by the past trends and buys those which others are also buying. The trend is set by the so-called trend-setters and the investor follows the trends and is called the trend-walker. He goes by what he thinks is the trend set by the majority in the market. This behaviour is rational and justified by the logic that the market is determined by the past trends. The present is the offshoot of the past and the market absorbs the information imperfectly and as such random movements are not logical and consistent with reality. The market pattern is set by the majority and the trend-walkers follow the market trends on a day-to-day basis. In contrast to the Random Walk Theory, this theory is more realistic as the information flows are often incorrect and biased and the market absorption is imperfect. The early risers or the trend-setters who are the first to realise the changes or are better informed would start the trends in the market and generally they are the gainers. The trend-walkers are the average investors who may sometimes get beaten up in the market when the trends change suddenly against them.

Capital Asset Pricing (CAP) Theory

Under this theory, the return on each security is related to the total risk inherent in that security. This risk is made up of systematic risk related to the market and unsystematic risk related to the company. If the risk is spread over a number of securities in the market, then the company-related risks are covered, reduced or eliminated. In a diversified portfolio, the unsystematic risk is eliminated but only the market-related systematic risk remains. In this model, the return is the same on different portfolios, if they are diversified in the sense that the risk is reduced. The earlier theory that the higher the risk, higher the return is not always true under this theory. The reward is related to risk and high risk scrips provide high returns under normal conditions.

In the Capital Asset Pricing Theory, the company risk is eliminated and only the market risk remains. The market should be a free market with a large number of players who are influenced fairly and accurately by the demand and supply forces generated by the free flow of correct and perfect information. This information is digested by the market from time to time and the resultant prices are fair and competitive prices. Thus, the price of a share is determined as in an auction system and the market is the best performer and no individual can outperform the market.

This model postulates that the company stock risk and the market risk are related by a variable called "Beta." The following equation for security valuation presents the concept of "Beta":

$$(Ri - Rf) = Bi\ (RM - Rf)$$

where Ri is the rate of price appreciation on the scrip i (return on it).

Rf = Risk-free rate or return.

RM is the market risk or average market rate of return and Bi is the constant, which relates the premium of the market rate over the risk-free rate to the company's risk premium (Ri – Rf). While (Ri – Rf) is the risk premium of the i scrip, (RM – Rf) is the risk premium of the market and these concepts are related by the multiplier named "Beta", which is thus a measure of the company's risk relative to the market risk.

Modern Portfolio Theory

This theory is closely related to the above CAP Theory. Under this theory, the companies have different types of risks. These risks cannot be eliminated completely in any investment in shares on the stock market. But the investors are generally risk averse. They would like to choose a portfolio, which is least risky but with high returns. In the portfolio theory, the risk is reduced or eliminated by choosing companies in the portfolio whose covariance is negative, which means that they are not dependent upon the same economic variables. Thus, companies manufacturing autos should be combined with companies manufacturing its competitive products like scooters, cycles, etc. In this context, it is necessary that one should classify the companies into those with positive covariance (complementary) and negative covariance (competitive). Industries and companies, which move differently to the same economic variables, should be chosen in a portfolio in order to reduce the risk.

As referred to earlier, the risk is of two types, namely, systematic risk (market related) and specific risk (company related). Systematic risk reflects the behaviour of individual scrip to the market sequence. Some shares move along the market more closely than others. This relative measure of volatility by individual scrip to the market behaviour is given by "Beta."

Concept of Beta

This concept of Beta as a measure of systematic risk is useful in portfolio management. The Beta measures the movement of one scrip in relation to the market trend*. Thus, Beta can be positive or negative depending on whether the individual scrip moves in the same direction as the market or in the opposite direction and the extent of variance of one scrip *vis-a-vis* the market is being measured by Beta. The Beta is negative, if the share price moves contrary to the general

* The calculation of "Beta" is explained below:

The concept of B is defined commonly as that part of the variability of the return of a scrip which is relative to the overall variability of the market return.

The formula is $Rj = a + Bj\ RM + u$

Where Rj is the return on security j, RM is the return on market index, Bj is a measure of the risk, a is the intercept term and u is the error term introduced to estimate this regression equation. This model is commonly known as market model and Beta can be derived from the equation. For example, if the risk-free rate is 10%, the expected market return is 15% and B is 1.5, the expected return on the security should be worked out as follows:

Risk free rate + B [expected return on market Portfolio – Risk free rate] = 10 + 1.5 (15 – 10)= 10 + 7.5 = 17.5%.

While the market rate is 15%, the rate on the security considered gives a larger return of 17.5%, as it is more risky than the market average.

trend and positive if it moves in the same direction. The scrips which are having a high Beta of more than 1 are called aggressive, and those with a low Beta of less than 1 are called defensive. The portfolios with aggressive scrips will outperform the market. It is, therefore, necessary to calculate Betas for all scrips and choose those with high Betas for a portfolio of high returns. But aggressive scrips are also risky as they outperform the market in uptrend as well as downtrend and fluctuations are wide. If the B is 1.5, this security is more risky by 50% than the market portfolio. If B is 1, the risk of the security is the same as that of the market.

Fundamental School

The fundamental school believes in the behaviour of shares on the basis of the companies' performance and indirectly through the forces operating from industry and the economy. This approach depends on an assessment of the past behaviour of the company for projecting its future price behaviour. Besides, this school believes that the share price generally converges towards its intrinsic value. Any company will have its shares valued by its intrinsic worth, which in turn depends upon the estimate of its future earning potential and future growth of the company. The school proceeds to assess the value of a share in terms of its intrinsic worth which depends on the operation of the market forces and other fundamental factors influencing the company. These factors may emanate from the economy, industry and company. If the information flows are perfect and correct, the market price veers around the intrinsic value of the share. But if there are imperfections in the market and information flows are false, biased and inadequate, then there will be divergence between the market price and the instrinsic value of the share. At any time, the intrinsic value is the individual investor's perception of the price of the scrip depending upon his forecast of the company's earning potential. The intrinsic value of a scrip, which was explained earlier, is the discounted value to the present of future earnings of the company, which will be distributed as dividends to the sharesholders. In reality, the market price diverges from the intrinsic worth very frequently. The factors of sentiment and emotional nature cannot be captured by the approach of fundamental school. Hence, there is need for technical analysis also.

Intrinsic Value and Market Value

In any fundamental analysis, the objective of the analyst would be to find out the securities which are undervalued or low-priced in the market in comparison with the intrinsic value. Graham & Dodd (Securities Analysis) have defined the intrinsic value "as that value which is justified by the facts of assets, earnings, dividends." These facts are reflected in the earning potential of the company. The analyst has to project the future earnings per share and value them for the present time by summing up the discounted future dividends or earnings. This means that all future earnings are discounted to the present value, which gives its intrinsic value at present. Another method is to take the earnings rate and multiply it by the industry average P/E ratio. For example, if the earnings per share is Rs. 5, as in the case of ABS Plastics, and its capitalisation rate or multiplier is assumed to be 11, which is the industry average P/E ratio, then the market price should be around Rs. 55 (11 × 5). The present market price at about Rs. 80 is, therefore, an indication of overvaluation, which may partly reflect the investors' perception of capital appreciation and the premium they place on the share of the company for psychological and behavioural reasons.

The relationship of intrinsic value and market price may be set out as in Fig. 34.2.

Fig. 34.2

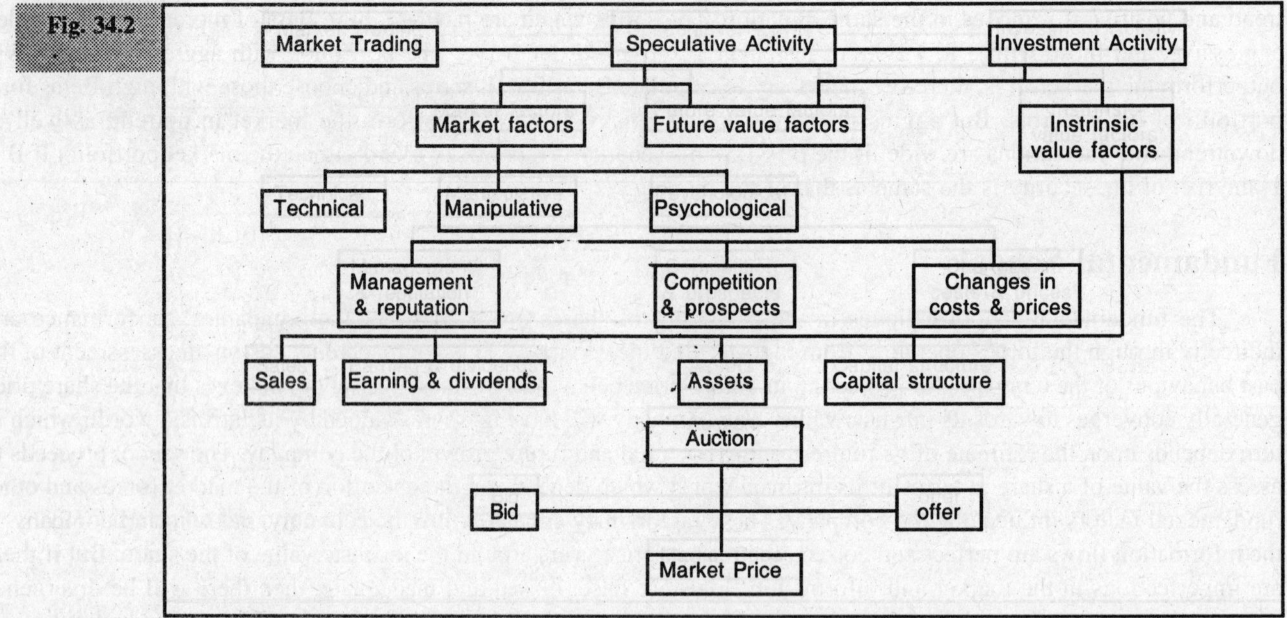

Evaluation of Shares

At any time, the investor likes to choose the scrips which are undervalued with a view to buy them and make a profit later when the value is high. Therefore, an evaluation of securities is very important for an investor to choose the portfolio. The scrips which are undervalued may be growth-oriented chips or blue chips or income stock or cyclical or defensive stocks. Generally, people prefer growth stocks or blue chip stocks, which have expansion plans and have unbroken records of earnings and dividend payments and issue of bonus. Some of the blue chip stocks may also be growth stocks, which are expanding and diversifying and their growth rates are higher than the market averages. Many investors, who are particularly averse to risk, prefer income stocks. These stocks are expected to give consistent dividends and with a good record of income distribution. Such companies which earn good dividends are mutual funds, unit trusts, public limited companies with a good record. A careful evaluation is, however, necessary to decide what undervalued scrips are to be bought.

Crudely expressed a share is undervalued, if its risk is lower than the market risk, but the return is higher than the market reward. The market price can also be compared to book value of the share or its P/E ratio can be compared to similar ratios of companies in the same industry or the industry average, to know whether the share price is undervalued.

Empirical Tests

In the real world, imperfections are there; transactions costs and information costs may lead to non-availability of information to all participants equally and at the same time which may lead to pockets of better absorption and poor absorption. These may lead to less than or more than the equilibrium profits, namely, excess profits or losses. Thus, the efficient market theory has been found to have some limitations in application to the real world. The results have been almost unanimous in supporting the weak form of *Efficient Market Hypothesis.* If so, the Random walk hypothesis holds good in the real world.

If markets are truly efficient, then the fundamentalist will be successful only when he has insider information, or he has the superior ability to analyse publicly available information and gain insight into the future of the firm or he uses the above insider information or his superior ability to reach long-term buy, sell and hold investment decisions.

Gordon's Hypothesis

M. J. Gordon has postulated a hypothesis called *Bird — in the Hand Model*, in which dividend policy becomes relevant, in the real world, as dividends today are more valuable than dividends in future. That means that internal rate of return = r and appropriate discount rate = k may or may not be equal. If r = k, the introduction of risk in the model, makes

$K_t > K_{t-1}$ and K cannot be held constant. If this factor is also taken into account, namely, today's dividends are taken as more valuable than tomorrow's, then two possibilities occur: r > k or r < k rates of return r, on each successive investment goes upto a point and then declines, due to operation of Laws of Returns.

Gordon Dividend Model

Question

Coxton Co. has its dividend growing at a constant rate of 7%. Its current Dividend rate is Rs. 3 per share. Assume that its expected return is 15%. What is its current price. Thus, k = 0.15 and g = 0.07.

Answer

Constant growth Gordon Model is

$$P_o = \frac{D_o(1+g)}{(k-g)} = \frac{3(1.07)}{0.15-0.07}$$

$$P_o = \frac{3 \times 1.07}{0.08} = \frac{3.21}{0.08} = \text{Rs. } 40.12$$

Question

Under the two stage growth model — required rate of return = 16% and growth rate upto 10 years 15% and thereafter 10%. Last year dividend is Rs. 0.71 per share. Calculate the present price of stock.

Answer

PV of first ten year dividends is as follows:

$$\sum_{t=1}^{10} \frac{do(1+gs)^t}{(1+rs)^t} = \frac{0.71(1+0.15)^t}{(1+0.16)^t} = \text{Rs. } 6.82 \text{ (Working not shown)}$$

Present value of the stock at the end of 10 years

$$P_{10} = \left(\frac{dt+1}{r-gn}\right) = \frac{2.88\ (1.10)}{0.16-0.10} = \text{Rs.} 52.80 \quad \text{(where } 0.71(1.15)^{10} = 2.88)$$

Discount P_{10} down to the present day

$$Pv = P_{10}\left(\frac{1}{1+rs}\right)^{10} = 52.80\,(.226) = \text{Rs.} 11.93 \quad \text{(where PVIF } = \frac{1}{1.16} \text{ for 10 years} = 0.226)$$

Sum of the total value of the stock.

6.82 + 11.93 = Rs. 18.75

The value of a share according to Gordon depends on the dividends policy of the firm. The market value of a share is equal to the present value of the expected future dividends. The current earnings (yo), dividend rate (b) internal rate of return (r) and cost of capital (k) are the variables which influence the firm's share value under this model. If r = k, the dividend policy becomes irrelevant. Miller and Modigliani Thesis holds good here in that dividend pay outs are irrelevant, in this limited case. So long as r = k, it does not matter whether retained earnings are used or borrowed capital is used for expansion. The investors are indifferent as between debt and equity with respect to leverage as the real cost of debt is the same as that of equity.

According to Gordon (M.J. Gordon: Optimum Investment and Financing Policy, Journal of Finance, May 1963), the value of the share continuously drops with the decrease in dividends pay out ratio. When the internal rate of return is less than cost of capital, shareholders would not like the company to retain profits because the shareholders can use the funds elsewhere with better returns. The retention of funds or increase in retention would thus reduce the value of the firm.

The Gordon's hypothesis seems to hold good in India, where shareholders prefer current dividends to future dividends and empirical results showed that dividend payout would influence the share price significantly. But the assumption of his hypothesis of constancy in r and k, no taxes and no debt leverage and no outside finance, are not realistic.

K is itself changing due to the principle that dividends today are more valuable than those in future due to the introduction of risk.

M. M. Hypothesis

Miller & Modigliani Hypothesis postulates that dividend payout has no effect on share prices. What is relevant for share valuation is its earnings capacity. Whether earnings, cash flows and/or dividends are taken the result is the same for the above purpose. If dividends are not paid they are used in the firm for investment and total return on capital employed is more relevant for valuation of the firm than what is paid as dividend for the shareholder. But this hypothesis is based on some assumptions.

(a) Perfect markets, and no uncertainty

(b) No taxes and no transactions costs

(c) Fixed Investment policy of the firm

(d) Return on capital employed is the same as the cost of capital acquired from outside say $r = k$, which means that internal rate of return is the same as the cost of capital.

Under the above assumptions arbitrage process operates in a way that it is the same for the company (or for investor) if they use the retained earnings or external funds for investment. This approach is cost of capital approach.

Equation for M & M model is

$$V_o = \frac{D_o}{K - g}$$

Where D stands for dividends or earnings and k for required rate of return and g is the rate of growth of dividends.

Walter's Formula

The Model of Walter is based on the hypothesis that dividends affect the share price.The reasoning is that the firm's internal rate of return (r) and its cost of capital (k) may be different. If it is cheaper to raise funds from external sources, then it is better to pay out dividends and raise resources from outside. If the return on investments (r) exceeds cost of capital (k) then the firm should payout the earnings as dividend. Since these two sources of funds have different returns, dividend payouts do matter and the value of the firm is affected by dividend payout policy. Investor prefers to invest funds from outside the company, if $r > k$.

Walter's equation can be set as follows:

$$P_o = \left[D + \left(\frac{r}{ke} \right) (E - D \right] Ke$$

E = earnings, D = dividends per share r = internal rate of return

Ke = market discount rate or required rate of return or normal capitalisation rate.

Walter took into account both dividends and earnings, as they both affect the share prices. An example will make it clear.

* F. Modigliani & M.H. Miller, *The Cost of Capital* .... AER, 1958.

Walter Model — Problems

Problem 1:

Scot & Co. had a dividend payout ratio of 40%, earnings per share Rs. 10. Its Internal rate of return is 25% and the normal capitalisation rate or cost of capital is 20%. What is the price of share?

Answer:

Using the formula

$$P = \left[D + \frac{r}{ke}(E - D\right]Ke$$

$$= \left[4 + \frac{25}{20}(10 - 4)\right]20$$

$$= [4 + 1.25 \times 6]20 = 11.5 \times 20$$

Market price is thus = Rs. 230

Problem 2:

The market capitalisation rate of an equity is 12% and IRR of the firm is 18. Its EPS is Rs. 15 and its Dividend payout is 30% using the Walter's model, calculate the market value of the share.

Answer:

Using the Walter's formula,

$$P = \left[3n + n\frac{18}{12}n\,(15n - n3)\right] \times 12$$

$$P = [3 + 18]\,12 = \text{Rs. } 252$$

Market Price is Rs. 252

Earnings Model

The market value of a share is determined by the present value of all anticipated future earnings flows.

$$pt = \sum_{t=1}^{n} \frac{E_t - I_t}{(1+K)^t}$$

Et is earnings per share during various periods. I_t is investment per share during the period and the other variables are the same as above.

Graham Dodd Model

According to Graham & Dodd, the dividends of a firm determine its share value, the equation can be set out as:

$$P = M\left(D + \frac{E}{3}\right) + A$$

M = Total earnings of firm

E = Earnings per share

A = Adjustment for Asset Values (say Book value per share)

D = Dividend per share

Stock Valuation

$\frac{P}{E}$ Ratio and its Determinants:

$\frac{P}{E}$ ratio is the market price divided by the earnings per share. $\frac{P}{E}$ ratio is one of the models used for comparing prices of shares, like the Dividend discount model or earnings model.

Discount Model

Consider the Dividend Discount Model which is given as:

$$P_o = \frac{D_1}{r - g}$$

Dividend D can be written as Eb, where E is earnings and b is payout ratio, then

$$P_o = \frac{Eb}{r - g}$$, and rearranging, we have

$$\frac{P}{E} = \frac{b}{r - g}$$

Then $\frac{P}{E}$ ratio can be taken as a function of three variables — *pay-out ratio, Discount rate* and *growth rate* of earnings.

The *Whitbeck and Kisor Model* has calculated the undervalued and overvalued portfolios for 1960-61, quarterwise. As per their study (V.S. Whitbeck and M. Kisor — "New Tool in Investment Decision-Making," *Financial Analyst Journal,* May-June 1963) one method of "beating the market" is to estimate the undervalued portfolios compared with the market portfolio as given by Standard & Poor 500 Index and choose such companies in the portfolio. The undervalued portfolio is calculated on the basis of P/E ratios, estimated and the actuals. The performance of each portfolio is compared with that of the Standard & Poor market index. Undervalued portfolio gives the above market return, called "Beating the Market."

Malkiel and Cragg Regression Model@

Malkiel and Cragg used the regression model to suggest that the cross sectional regression models explain a good deal of the cross sectional variance in P/E ratios at any particular point of time. The dependent variable in the regression equation is P/E, the three independent variables were *expected earnings growth rate (g), expected payout ratio (b) and the risk measure (β).*

The regression equations for 5 years, studied by him are shown below:

@ B. G. Malkiel and J. G. Cragg: *Expectations and The Structure of Share Prices,* A.E.R., Sept. 1970.

R. J. Fuller and J. C. Farrell : *Modern Investments and Security Analysis,* McGraw-Hill (International) Book Co.

Table 34.1

Year	Equation	R^2
1961	$\frac{P}{E} = 4.73 + 3.28g + 2.05\,b - .85\beta$	.70
1962	$\frac{P}{E} = 11.06 + 1.75g + 0.78\,b - 1.61\beta$	.70
1963	$\frac{P}{E} = 2.94 + 2.55g + 7.62\,b - .27\beta$	.75
1964	$\frac{P}{E} = 6.71 + 2.50g + 5.23\,b - .89\beta$	.75
1965	$\frac{P}{E} = 0.96 + 2.74g + 5.01\,b - .35\beta$	.85

As for each year, the R^2 ranged between 0.70 to 0.85. The authors have concluded that there is a good relation between P/E and the independent variables g, b and b. Similarly, one can use ROE and other variables like ROA (ROE is return on equity and ROA is return on assets, etc.).

Cootner's Price-Value Interaction Model

Stock valuation Models take into account future cash flows discounted to the present time. The Standard Model can be represented by the following equation:

$$\text{Present Value} = \frac{\text{Income}_1}{(1+i)^1} + \frac{\text{Income}_2}{(1+i)^2}$$

$$+ \frac{\text{Income}_3}{(1+i)^3} \text{ ... and so on}$$

where t = 1,2,3...etc. periods

i = Discount rate expected

If these incomes or cash flows vary in every period, then Cf_1, Cf_2, Cf_3... etc. will be discounted to the present time.

Paul Cootner[@] had suggested that security prices can be viewed as series of constrained random fluctuations around their intrinsic value. There are two classes of investors. Of these, the more important *professional investors* who have better avenues to get information and analyse them, make estimates of intrinsic value and if its market price goes very much off the intrinsic value, they start buying or selling. The second class of investors, whom he calls *Naive Investors* follow the 'hot tips' or the mass media and buy and sell following the path set by the professionals.

Actual prices in the market move around the intrinsic value, for which the trend is set by the professionals and naiye investors follow them. Buying and selling pressures emenate from the mass of the naive investors but the professionals snatch the cream of the gains, as they have the better information to foresee to changes in intrinsic value and book profits when necessary. This market is then called the intrinsic value random walk market.

Random Walk Theory

Reference was made earlier to this theory many times. According to Random Walk Theory, security's intrinsic values change and market prices move randomly around these intrinsic values. The new information affecting the market arrives at random intervals. This new information will force the analyst to reestimate the intrinsic value and again the stock prices move randomly around the new intrinsic value.

@ P.H. Cootner: "Stock Prices — Random Versus Systematic Changes", *Industrial Management Review*, 1962.

This Theory thus states that security prices move randomly in a continuous fashion to set new equilibriums. There may be upward or downward movements and changes take place in a random manner. If the trade barriers are imposed, then there may be lower reflecting barriers (support lines) or upper reflecting barriers (resistance lines) etc. The movements in share prices thus move generally within a narrow band, in a random fashion and these trends are changed from time to time with the flow of new information. These random steps are based on the market absorption of the information. With perfect absorption, there will be continuous moves to equilibrium and this is what Samuelson had in continuous equilibrium model, under perfectly efficient market conditions leading to perfectly efficient prices. This is based on the assumption of continuous flow of market information, which will change the stock prices, following the changes in the estimates of intrinsic value of the company's shares.

Random Walk Theory — Assumptions

The price movements under Random Walk Theory are randomly distributed, in such a way that the present steps are independent of past steps and in view of such random movements entry into the market any time gives same returns for the same risk to the investors.

This theory is based on the following assumptions:

(1) Market is perfect and free without any restrictions.

(2) Market absorbs all the information quickly and efficiently.

(3) Information is free and costless and is quickly available to all at the same time.

(4) Information is unbiased and correct.

(5) Market players can analyse the information quickly and the information is absorbed in the market through buy and sell signals.

(6) Demand and supply pressures are absorbed in the market through price changes. Such absorption leads to quick and prompt movements in prices which are random in fashion.

Martingale Models

Under Random Walk, prices move independently and are identically distributed. In view of such movements and the past trends being no indications of the future trends, these movements are of no use for investment. As these distributions are not stable over time, they have no predictive value. For, not only the distributions change, but they will shift upwards and to the right due to the long-term upward trend of share prices.

Empirical studies, taking absolute prices and price changes have shown that these distributions varied with time and in dissimilar fashion. But the rates of changes of daily, weekly, monthly and quarterly price changes tend to conform to a stable relative frequency distribution. This is particularly found to be true empirically, when the price changes are drawn for atleast one complete business cycle. Distributions of returns of the vast majority of firms are fairly stable. Thus, a stable random walk model may be construed for rates of return or rates of price changes.

Martingale Models are those which follow the Martingale Process, which is a mathematical process in which the conditional expectation of the (n+1) th value equals the nth value in some set of data. A Martingale does not require that successive numbers of the series be either independent or be identically distributed.

Symbolically, the rates of return, follow a Martingale model, if the following equation is not violated.

$$E\,({}_J\gamma_{t+1} / {}_J\gamma^r_t \ldots {}_J\gamma_{t-n}) = {}_J\gamma_t$$

Where ${}_J\gamma_t$ is the return for security J at period t.

This equation is a symbolic representation of the weekly efficient market hypothesis which says that knowledge of all historical returns of some securities suggests only that the next period's return is expected to equal the last period's return.

A stronger form of the Martingale exists if the following equation is not violated:

$$E\,({}_J\gamma_{t+1} / Nt) = {}_J\gamma_t$$

Where Nt is all the public news and information which existed at period 't.' This is the semi-strongly efficient market hypothesis, implying that all available news is already reflected in the prices. The above equations imply that future returns are independent of past data, but they do not imply complete independence of the entire series of returns.

Security prices are a sub-Martingale process, since they drift upwards over time. The following equation defines the sub-Martingale process:

$$E\,[({}_JP_{t+1}/{}_JP_t, {}_JP_{(t-1)} \cdots {}_JP_{t-n}) > {}_JP_t$$

${}_JP_t$ is the price of security J at period t.

Capital Market Theory

Capital market theory is a major extension of the portfolio theory of Markowitz. The portfolio theory explains how rational investors should build efficient portfolio based on their risk-return preferences. Capital Market Asset Pricing Model (CAPM) is a relationship, explaining how assets should be priced in the capital market.

Assumptions of Capital Market Theory are:

(1) Investors make decisions based solely on risk-return assessments (expected returns and standard deviation measures).

(2) The purchase and sale transactions can be undertaken in infinitely divisible units.

(3) Investors can sell short any amount of shares without limit.

(4) There is perfect competition and no single investor can influence prices.

(5) There are no transactions costs.

(6) Personal income taxation is assumed to be Zero.

(7) Investors can borrow/lend, the desired amount at riskless rates.

(8) Investors have identical expectations, identical planning horizons, decision periods, and identical reactions to given risk.

The above assumptions, although some of them are unrealistic provide a basis for an efficient frontier line common to all. Different expectations lead to different frontier lines. If borrowing and lending is introduced the efficient frontier line can be thought of as a straight line. Lending is like investing in a riskless security say of Rf in the graph below:

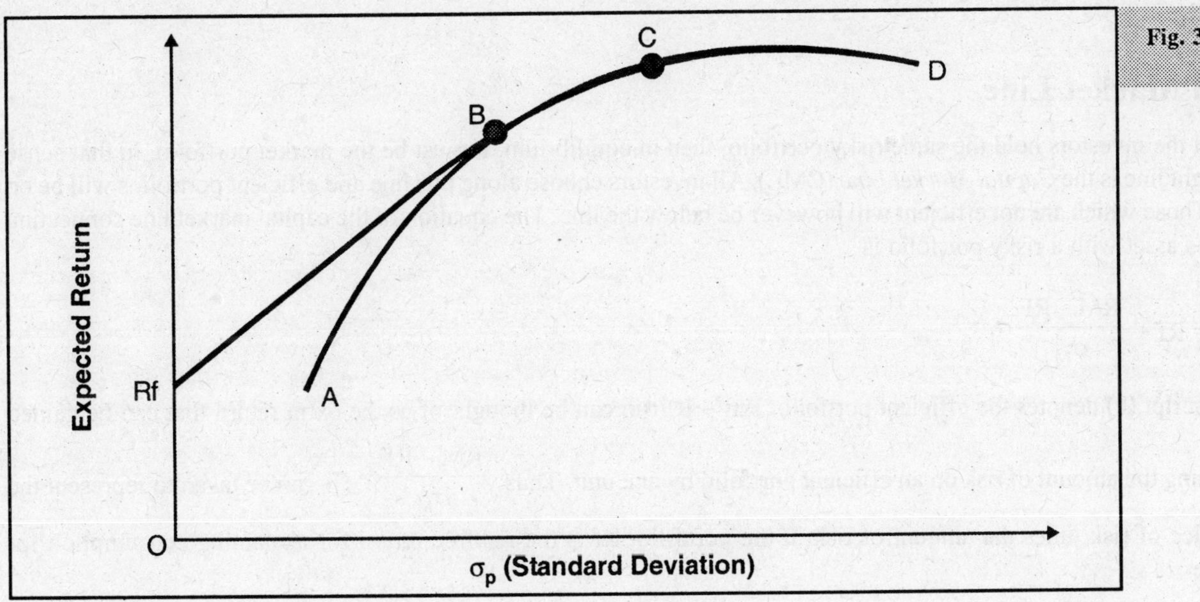

Fig. 34.3

Rf = Risk free investment. If he places part of his funds in Risk free assets (Rf) and part of his funds in risky securities (B) along the efficient frontier, he would generate portfolios along the straight line segment R_fB. (Fig. 34.3)

Rp	$= xR_m + (1 - x)$ Rf
where Rp	= expected return on portfolio
x	= percentage of funds invested in risky portfolio
(1 – x)	= percentage of funds invested in riskless asset
Rm	= expected return on risky portfolio
Rf	= expected return on riskless asset
and	$\sigma p = x\ \sigma m$
σp	= expected standard deviation of the portfolio
σ_M	= expected standard deviation on risky portfolio

Fig. 34.4

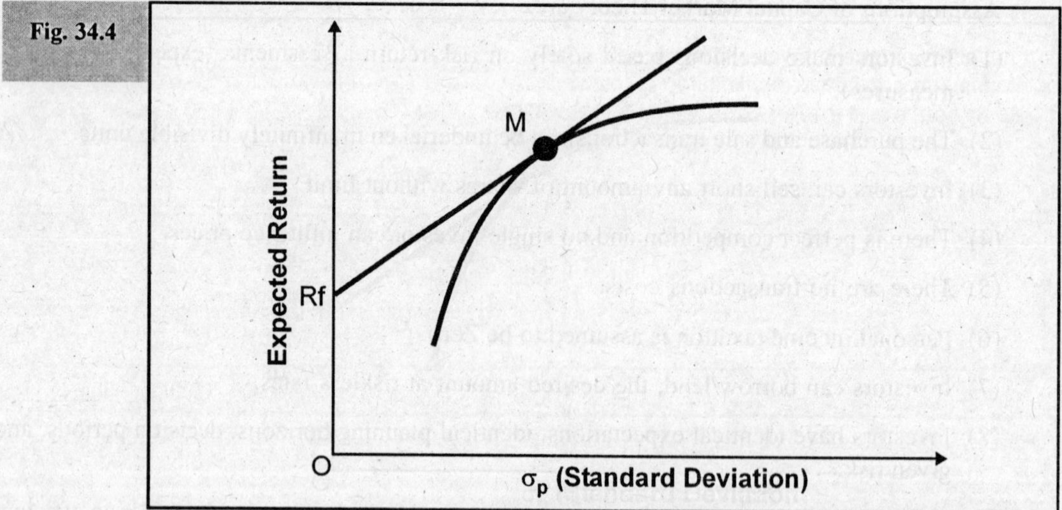

Introduction of both borrowing and lending has given us an efficient frontier that is a straight line throughout as shown in the graph above. M is the optimal portfolio of risky investments. The decision to purchase at M is the investment decision and the decision to buy some riskless asset (lend) or to borrow (leverage the portfolio) is the financing decision. (Fig. 34.4)

Capital Market Line

If all the investors hold the same risky portfolio, then in equilibrium, it must be the market portfolio. In that sense RfM straight line is the *Capital Market Line* (CML). All investors choose along this line and efficient portfolios will be on this line. Those which are not efficient will however be below the line. The equation of the capital market line connecting the riskless asset with a risky portfolio is

$$Re = Rf + \frac{RM - RF}{\sigma_M}\sigma_t$$

Subscript (e) denotes the efficient portfolio. Rm – Rf/σm can be thought of as the extra return that can be gained by increasing the amount of risk on an efficient portfolio by one unit. Thus, $\frac{RM - RF}{\sigma_M} \times \sigma_t$ can be taken to represent the market price of risk times the amount of risk in the portfolio. Rf is the riskfree return for abstaining consumption for period one.

Security Market Line

In case of portfolios involving complete diversification, where the unsystematic risk tends to go to zero, there is only systematic risk measured by Beta (β) the only dimensions of a security, which concerns us are expected return and Beta. We have seen earlier that all portfolios of investments lie along a straight line in the return to Beta space. To determine this line we need to connect the Intercept (where Beta is zero as it is riskless security), and the market portfolio (Beta of one and return of R_M). These points are Rf and M in the graph below. The equation of that straight line is Security Market Line (SML):

$R_i = \alpha + b\,\beta_i$

$R_F = \alpha$ as $b\,\beta_i$ becomes zero for riskless asset ($\beta = 0$)

where $\beta = 1$

$R_M = \alpha + b\,(1)$ or $R_M - \alpha = b$

Since $R_F = \alpha$, then $R_M - R_F = b$

Combining the above two results, we have

$R_i = R_F + \beta_i\,(R_M - R_F)$

This is the key equation for Security Market Line and can be rewritten as $R_i - R_F = \beta i\,(R_M - R_F)$, which was discussed earlier.

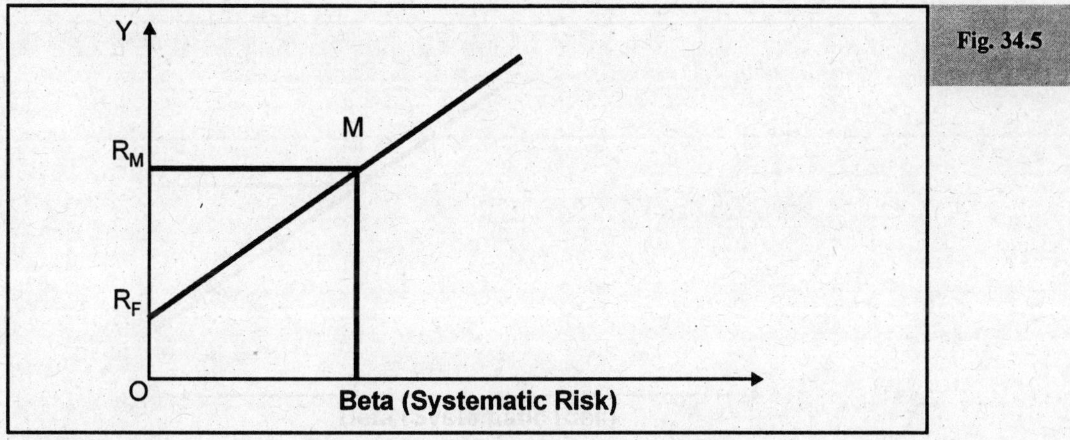

Fig. 34.5

CAPM

As Betas differ according to the market proxy, that they are measured against, then in effect, CAPM, has not been and cannot be tested. We may recall that CAPM states that

Return = Risk free rate + Beta (Market Return – Risk free rate)

A security with a zero Beta should give a risk free return. In actual results these zero beta returns are higher than the risk free return indicating that there are some non-Beta risk factors or some left over unsystematic risk.

Besides, although, in the long run, high Beta portfolios have provided larger returns than low-risk ones, in the short-run, CAPM Theory and the empirical evidence diverge strikingly and sometimes the relationship between risk and return may turn out to be negative which is contrary to CAPM Theory.

It can thus be concluded that CAPM Theory is a neat Theoretical exposition. The CML and SML are the lines reflecting the *total risk* and *systematic risk* elements in the portfolio analysis, respectively. But in actual world, the CAPM is not in conformity with the real world risk-return trends and empirical results have not always supported the Theory atleast in the short-run. More details can be found in Part-VII dealing with Portfolio Theory and Management.

TOBIN "Q" Theory

This theory states that the rate of investment of a firm is determined by the market valuation of firm's stock to its replacement cost. As per CAPM, stock market value of firm's stock depends on earning and the profits and dividend payment ratios. This means that the a company's investment growth (Gross Block) is related to the stock prices. This relationship was contested by Fisher, S and Morton R.C. (Macro economics and financing. The Role of Stock Market — Carnegie Rochestear Conference Series, on Public Policy Vol. XXI, 1984). Firms' investment plans may not truly be reflected in stock prices. On the other hand stock prices may influence the firms investment plans, inducing them to invest more in stock boom period.

An RBI Study published in their Annual Report 1995-96 showed a significantt relation between stock prices and corporate investment in the Indian Context. The study is for a period of 30 years ending in 1994-95 and the relation is lagged (with r = 0.36).

CHAPTER 35

Valuation of Bonds – Bond Market

Introduction

Bond is an unsecured debt of the issuer, either in the Government sector or corporate sector. Bonds with special features, of zero interest or floating interest rate (as against a fixed coupon rate, normally issued) are also issued in India. Some of the bonds are however secured by collaterals, while unsecured bonds are the common feature. The Indian Companies Act does not provide for bonds, but only for debentures and warrants of various categories. Basically and in practice, both bonds and debentures are the same, and are fixed income securities like the preference shares.

Bond market in India is undeveloped and only banks, FIs and a few institutional investors trade in them for meeting with the legal requirements, such as S.L.R. The National Stock Exchange is developing this bond market in India, particularly of PSUs and Government and Semi-Government bonds.

The debentures are confined to the corporate sector and have varying features such as redeemability at a fixed date or over a period of 3 to 5 years, convertibility into equity at different time periods, etc. As per the Act, only secured and redeemable debentures can be issued in India through public offer and the registers of bondholders should be kept for effecting transfers of debentures by the investors.

Investors, mostly in the category of banks FIs, companies, PF, mutual funds, etc., hold the bonds and debentures, in India. The secondary market in these instruments is poor and underdeveloped. The normal strategy of investors in this category is passive, holding them for income and wealth purposes and not for maximisation of wealth.

BOND MARKET IN INDIA

The wholesale debt market on NSE comprises Bank bonds, certificates of deposit, commercial paper, Corporate bonds, Government and Semi-Government bonds, and Institutional bonds, including those of IDBI, UTI, etc.

Bonds are issued by some Companies, public sector financial institutions, PSUs and semi-Government bodies in India. The secondary market in bonds is not well developed. Since 1985, PSUs have been issuing bonds and after the start of the financial reforms, and the trend of privatisation of PSUs by the Government the PSUs, public financial institutions, etc., are all encouraged to borrow directly from the public. It is in this context, that a bond market has emerged in India. Some of these are tax free and some taxable. The rates of interest are allowed to be fixed by the Government at varying levels.

The corporate sector has been issuing Non-Convertible Debentures (NCD) or Bonds (NCB). These are to be rated, if they are issued to the public and the coupon rates fixed on them vary with this rating. The details of coupon rates, face value, interest payment dates, redemption dates current yields and Yields to Maturity (YTM) vary depending on the issuer, instrument and conditions in the market.

Special Features of Bonds

(1) They are fixed income earners with a coupon rate or without a coupon rate, as in the case of Discount Bonds or Premium Notes, giving a fixed premium at the end of maturity.

(2) Their prices move inversely with yields. Thus, if the issue price (face value) is Rs. 100 with a fixed coupon rate of 14%, then the bond may be quoting in the market at a discount if the expected market rate is, say 16% depending on the market perception of its risk and return in the market for similar risks, say Rs. 90.

(3) The longer is the maturity period of the Bond, the greater is the risk and larger is the percentage change in its price, relative to interest rate changes.

(4) The risks involved in Bonds to the investor are the following:

(a) *Purchasing Power Risk* with rising inflation rates, the bond redemption price being fixed, at the end of maturity of say 10 to 12 years, the real value of the redemption price will be completely wiped out by an inflation rate 10%. The only way to protect from inflation is to have accounting for real rates or yields for calculating the present bond price or to have yields, which will give risk free return plus inflation adjusted return for the risk premium. Thus, if risk free return is 6% (bank rate in India) plus the risk premium which may be around 8-10% the total yields may vary from 14-16%, in nominal terms. Slightly higher is the rate that the equity holders of good blue chips would aim at, which will of course include dividends and capital appreciation.

(b) *Default Risk* is another risk, related to the company or agency, issuing the bonds. This is the risk of non-payment or delayed payments of interest and redemption value. For managing the default risk, the investor has to use the techniques of analysis of the financial statements of the company (including the past ratios of debt to equity, finance charge, relative gross profits, debt leverage ratios, and current liquidity ratios). The investor has to refer to the rating given to the company by a reputed credit rating agency like CRISIL, or ICRA. Now, it is compulsory for companies issuing non-convertible debentures or bonds, with or without convertibility within 18 months, to get the credit rating for these issues, of NCDs, in particular.

(c) *Interest Rate Changes:* If the bond has a coupon price, the risk of change in interest rates is high, the higher the maturity period, and lower the coupon rate. The volatility of bond price increases in response to interest rate changes, if the maturity is longer than when it is shorter, and if the coupon rate is lower and the present level of bond yields is low.

Interest Rate Structure

These theories of interest rates are discussed in separate chapter. The required rate of return on a bond depends on the time preference for consumption, measured by risk free return, expected rate of inflation and risk associated with investment. Thus, the required rate of return (γ)

$$\gamma = \left(\frac{\text{risk free}}{\text{real rate}}\right) + \left(\frac{\text{expected}}{\text{inflation}}\right) + \left(\frac{\text{risk}}{\text{premium}}\right)$$

If the interest rates fall relative to coupon rate then, the bond price rises and the company may even call for repayment of high rate bonds with a view to issue low interest bonds. If the interest rates rise relative to coupon rate then bond price falls.

The theories that explain interest rates are many and the major ones are set out below:

(1) *Expectation Theory:* This explains why the future level of interest rate depends on the average expectation of what future spot rate should be. The implicit forward rates reflect the market's consensus of expected future spot rates.

(2) *Availability of Funds:* (Loanable Funds Theory): The supply of funds for lending will determine the interest rates, which will lead to changes in bond prices. Demand and supply pressures are expected to decide the interest rates on funds, and the supply is dependent on the money supply creation and Government fiscal deficits. The expectation of interest rates as well as the present rates depend on the business activity, prices, employment, inflation, money supply,

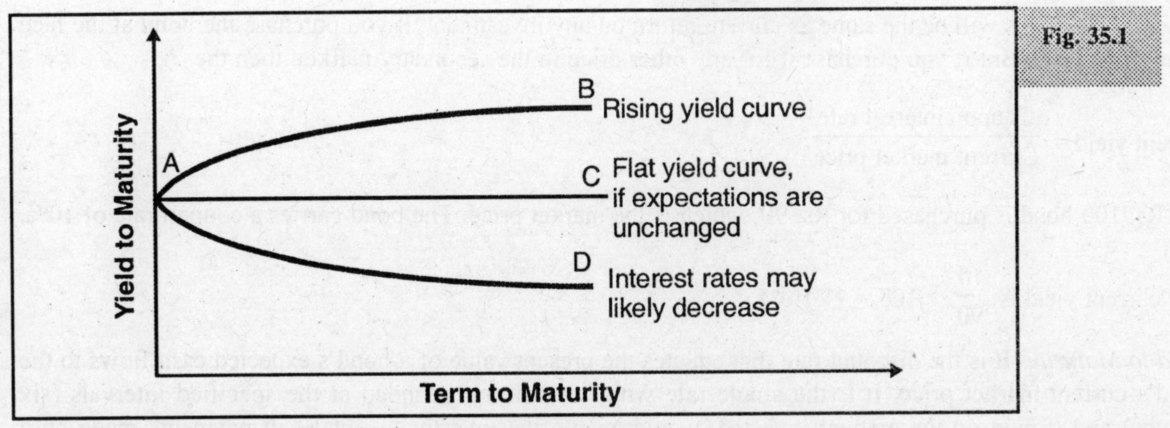

Fig. 35.1

fiscal factors and a host of other factors. Fig. 35.1 presents the yield curves for different types of expectation of interest rates. If expectations of future short-term rates are upward, the AB curve depicts the rising yield curve. If expectations of future short-term rate are downward, AD curve depicts the falling yield curve.

Properties of Bonds and Bond Value

In India, bonds have a maturity period and companies, semi-Government and Government bodies are not issuing irredeemable bonds. They are redeemable in 5 to 9 years in respect of bonds and 12 years for preference shares.

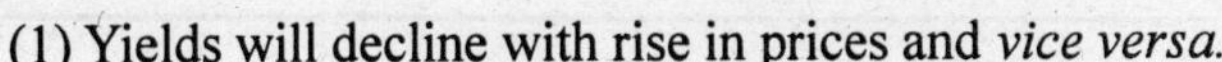

The properties of bonds can be described through the following graph (Fig. 35.2). The price and yield relationship is revealed in the curve AB which is convex to the origin. 'X' axis measures the yield and 'Y' axis the price of Bond. The relationship of yields to price and to maturity periods can be set out in the following axioms:

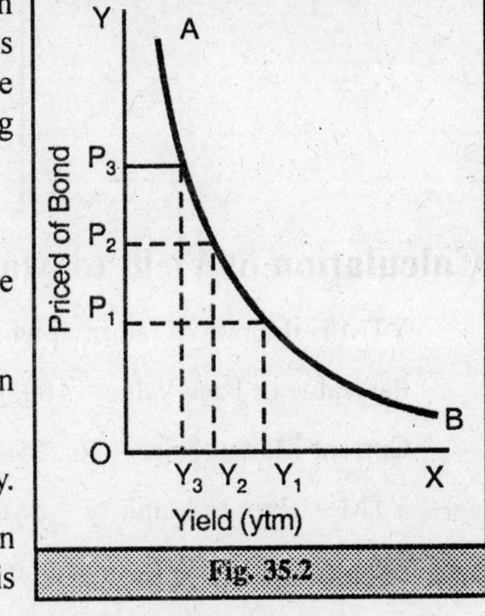

Fig. 35.2

(1) Yields will decline with rise in prices and *vice versa.*

(2) If required rate of return is the same as the coupon rate, bond price is the par value.

(3) If required return is lower than the coupon rate, bond price is higher than face value and reverse is true.

(4) Discount or premium on face value will fall as the bond approaches maturity.

(5) Interest Rate Elasticity Sensitivity of bond price changes to a given change in interest rates will be high, if the bond is of longer maturity, and the coupon rate is lower.

(6) As the YTM increases, the percentage change in price increases at a diminishing rate. The capital gains/losses on bonds will emerge on account of changes in price due to interest rate changes.

Measures of Bond Returns

Yield is the measure of return on a bond. There are many variants in this measure:

(1) *Coupon Rate:* It is the nominal rate fixed and printed on bond certificate. It is the rate of interest fixed as say, 10% on a bond of Rs. 100, as face value.

(2) *Holding Period Yield or one Period Rate of Return:* For one period of holding, the return will depend on the coupon rate due or accrued plus or minus the capital gains or losses. The same can be presented in a formula.

$$\gamma i = \frac{\text{Capital gains or loss} + \text{coupon rate}}{\text{Purchase price of bond}}$$

(3) *Current Yield:* This will be the same as current return on any investment, if you purchase the bond at the face value of Rs. 100. But if you purchase it for any other price in the secondary market, then the

$$\text{Current yield} = \frac{\text{Coupon interest rate}}{\text{Current market price}}$$

one Rs. 100 bond is purchased for Rs. 90, which is the market price. The bond carries a coupon rate of 10%.

The current yield is $\frac{10}{90} \times 100 = 11.1.0\%$.

(4) *Yield to Maturity:* It is the discount rate that equates the present value of a bond's expected cash flows to the bond's current market price. It is the single rate with interest compounded at the specified intervals (six months) and if paid on the amount invested, would enable the investor to obtain all payments made on a security, in question.

Fig. 35.3

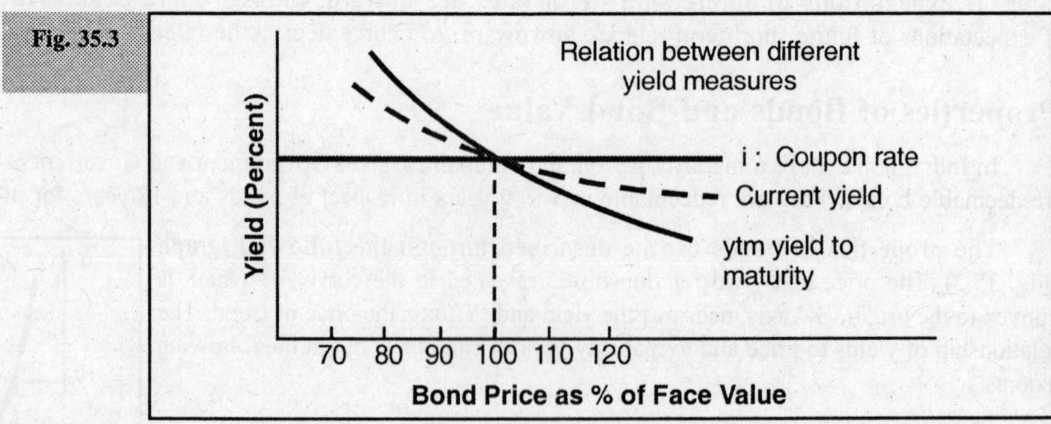

Calculation of Yield to Maturity (YTM)

YTM is the rate of return at which NPV of a bond is equal to zero (use the AYTM method).

Par Value or Face Value = 100 (coupon rate 14% paid annually)

Current Market Price = Rs. 95

YTM = Term to Maturity = 6 years Maturity value 105

*Rs. 95 = 14 × PVIFA (Ytm, 6 years) + 105 × PVIF (Ytm, 6 years)

Assum ytm = 17%; Calculate the approximate rate

Po = 14 × 3.589 + 105 × 0.390 = Rs. 91.20

Assume ytm = 15%

Po = 14 × 3.784 + 105 × 0.432 = Rs. 98.34

$$\text{Using Linear Interpolator} = \text{ytm} = 15 + 2\left(\frac{98.34 - 95}{98.34 - 91.20}\right)$$

$$= 15 + 2\left(\frac{3.34}{7.14}\right)$$

Note: These concepts are referred to in our earlier chapter.

* As the bond is below the face value at Rs. 95, ytm should be above 14%, assume 15% or 17%. See Tables at the end of the chapter for values of PVIFA and PVIF.

$$= 15.93\%$$

$$\text{ytm} = 17 - 2\left(\frac{95 - 91.20}{98.34 - 91.20}\right)$$

$$= 17 - 2\left(\frac{3.80}{7.14}\right) = 15.94\%$$

Present Market Price is Rs. 95; with ytm estimated at 17%, 98.34 and estimated at 15%, 91.20 by Interpolation, ytm works out to 15.94%.

Valuation of Bonds

The value of a Bond is simply the present value of the security's future cash flows. The buy and sell decision depend on the estimated value of the bond as also other features of the bond. But basically, market price and expected yields are the major determinants of the bond value.

The static present value model is illustrated in the para below. This indicates the intrinsic economic value of the market asset, namely, the bond or and fixed income security.

The present value of all income flows in future during its life of maturity is called the intrinsic worth of the bond. Thus, the Present Bond Value

$$\text{is expressed} = \sum_{T=1}^{T} \frac{\text{income}}{(1+K)^t}$$

where, k is the appropriate market discount rate.

More specifically the present value of a bond can be set out in the following formula as a continuous model:

$$\text{Present value} = \frac{\text{Coupon 1}}{(1+\text{interest rate})^1} + \frac{\text{Coupon 2}}{(1+\text{interest rate})^2}$$

$$+ \frac{\text{Coupon 3}}{(1+\text{interest rate})^3} \cdots\cdots \frac{\text{Coupon T} + \text{Face Value}}{(1+\text{Interest rate})^T}$$

Expressed Symobolically,

$$Po = \frac{K_1}{(1+r)^1} + \frac{K_2}{(1+r)^2} + \frac{K_3}{(1+r)^3} + \ldots\ldots\ldots + \frac{K_T + P_T}{(1+r)^T}$$

Where, Po = Present value and P_T is the maturity value and T is the maturity period.

$K_{1 \text{ to } T}$ are coupon rates of interest paid, semi-annually or annually, by the bond issuer, r is the required rate of return, may also depend on his expectations of the future yields. This element of subjectivity or the analyst's perception of the future rates may be the cause of the different valuations of the same bond.

Solved Problems

(1) What is the present value of a Bond with (Fv) Face value Rs. 1000, coupon rate 8% and maturity period of 3 years and yTM = 10%

Present value (pv) =

$$Pv = \frac{Coupon_1}{(1+ytm)_1}.........+\frac{Coupon_r + P_T}{(1+ytm)^T}$$

$$Pv = \frac{80}{(1+0.10)^1}+\frac{80}{(1+0.10)^2}+\frac{80+1000}{(1+0.10)^3}$$

$$= \frac{80}{1.10}+\frac{80}{1.21}+\frac{1080}{1.331}=$$

72.72 + 66.12 + 811.42 = 950.26

Pv = Rs. 950.26

(2) Determine the price of ZCB with a face value of Rs. 1000, yTM of 16% and maturity period of 10 years.

$$Price = \frac{Face\ value}{(1+yTM)^t}=\frac{1000}{(1+0.16)^{10}}=\frac{1000}{4.411}$$

= 226.68 (using the calculator)

The present price of ZCB is Rs. 226.68

(3) Given Face Value of Rs. 1000, yTM = 6%, and Coupon rate 3.5%, what is its present value if its maturity period in 10 years. Interest paid annually, cash flow is Rs. 35 per year.

$$\text{Present value Pv} \sum_{t=1}^{10} \frac{35}{(1+0.06)^{10}}+\frac{1000}{(1+0.06)^{10}}$$

$$PV = \sum_{t=1}^{10} \frac{35}{(1+0.06)^{10}}+\frac{1000}{(1+0.06)^{10}}$$

= Rs. 816 (using the calculator)

The present value of the bond is Rs. 816

Accrued Interest

If the bond is purchased in between the semi-annual interest payment dates the seller will receive the accrued interest from the buyer for the period he was holding since the last interest payment. Interest at the coupon rate for the number of days he held is calculated in the following formula:

$$\text{Accrued interest} = \frac{\text{Days since last interest payment}}{\text{days between the coupon payment}} \times \frac{\text{Interest amount}}{\text{Semi-Annual last and next}}$$

For example, interest at coupon rate is 10% on Rs. 1000 — payable on March 31 and September 30 — Rs. 50 each time; if the seller sold the bond on June 30,

then Accrued interest is $\frac{90}{180} \times 50 = \text{Rs. } 25$

The bond price will be adjusted for the accrued interest as the buyer, the coupon holder is entitled to the interest due on the above dates.

Calculation of Accrued Interest and Value

1. Calculate the bond value using normal bond valuation model as of the next coupon date.
2. Add the coupon payment received on the next coupon payment date.
3. Discount this sum back to current date.
4. From this subtract the accrued interest.

To give an example, let us take these data:

Par value of the bond = Rs. 100

Coupon rate = 14%; half-yearly 7%

Coupon payment is half-yearly (30/6 and 31/12)

Maturity date is 31-12-2010

Maturity value = Rs. 105

Computation of bond value on 21-3-2006, assuming a ytm of 18% p.a. is as follows: (9% for half-year)

Step. 1: The value of bond on 30/6/2006 will be

= 7 × PVIFA (9%, 9) + 105 [PVIF(9%, 9)] (from the tables at the end)

= 7 × 5.996 + 105 × 0.460 = Rs. 90.27

Step. 2: Add the next coupon payment, i.e., 30/6/2006

Rs. 90.27 + 7.00 = Rs. 97.27

Step 3: Discount this to current date (Assume half year as 180 days)

∴ the value on 21/3/2006 = $97.27/(1.09)^{100/180}$ = Rs. 92.72

Step 4: Subtract the accrued interest for 80 days (from 1-1-06 to 21-3-06),[@] i.e., an amount of Rs. 7 × 80/180 = Rs. 3.11

Hence, ex-interest value on 21/3/06
= Rs. 92.72 – 3.11 = Rs. 89.61.

In continuous models, the discount factor used is the ytm (yield to Maturity) and it is used to calculate the reinvestment of coupon interest amounts. This type of model is useful only for academic interest, as in reality, the bondholder normally invests and disinvests many times before the maturity period, to take advantage of higher return, capital gains or for adjustment of duration. The immunisation process also involves frequent changes in the bonds held in a portfolio with a view to insulate the portfolio from the risks of interest rate changes and take advantage of higher reinvestment rates.

But the continuous model is useful for calculating the intrinsic value of the bond, in terms of the required rate of return. If the required rate is the same as the coupon rate, then the present value is the same as face value. There are *Bond Tables* which give the ytm for any given price and maturity. As referred to earlier the ytm for a bond is the discount rate which equates the present value of all net cash flows to the cost of the investment.

If riskless bonds are to be valued then the discount factor, to be used is the risk free return, namely, the bank rate of 6% or Government bond yield of 8%.

@ for simplicity, these dates are chosen in the example.

- - -

Discrete Models

Bond valuation in the above discussion is based on certain assumptions:

(1) The bond is held until maturity rather than selling it at a price different from the face value before its maturity expires.

(2) All cash flows, received from coupon payments are reinvested at the same yield to maturity (ytm), promised.

(3) The coupon payments are made regularly and the principal in full at the scheduled times.

If any of the above assumptions do not hold good, then the valuation model given above becomes inapplicable. Under the conditions of limited holding periods or trading in bonds under portfolio management, the valuation of a bond has to be discrete and relevant to the current market interest rates or expected returns of the investor. In such cases, the required rate of return or the market rate for the same maturity, at the present time will be taken into account in calculating the value of bond.

Then the formula is

$Po = \sum_{T=1}^{T} \frac{ct}{(1+k)t}$ where Po is the present value, ct are the cash flows for the holding period of say, 1 to 3 years (t) and k is the required rate of return for reinvestment based on the present market/interest rate structure. This price will be different from the face value and varies with the values given to 'K' and 't.'

Bond Price Theorems

BP Theorem 1: Bond Face Value may be different from the Bond price in the market, if the coupon rate on bond is different from market rate.

BP Theorem 2: Bond market price fluctuations depend on the interest elasticity of the Bond price, duration, term to maturity and other bond characteristics such as callability, tax benefits, creation of Debenture Redemption Fund, security or collateral provided and a number of other factors.

BP Theorem 3: Call and put options for debentures which are convertible after 36 months, are compulsory for them as per SEBI guidelines. If the Debenture is convertible within 18 months, it is as good as equity for purposes of debt-equity ratio. This was dropped in March 1998.

BP Theorem 4: Bonds issued to the public should be compulsorily credit rated and interest rates are free to be fixed, as per market conditions and credit rating of the company, except when they are issued by public financial institutions or Government organisations.

BP Theorem 5: The percentage price change on a bond price increases at a diminishing rate as the maturity term is larger.

BP Theorem 6: The higher the coupon rate on a bond, the smaller is the percentage price change for any given change in yields.

BP Theorem 7: Bond price in the market is relative to the coupon rate, and its maturity period. Bonds of longer maturity involve larger capital losses than those of short-term maturities, if the bond is sold.

BP Theorem 8: Bond prices fluctuate more widely in times of freely fluctuating interest rates and quick changes in interest rate policy.

Malkiel Bond Theorems

Many Theorems were derived by B. G. Malkiel from his study "Expectations, Bond Prices and the Term Structure of Interest Rates." Quarterly Journal of Economics, May 1962. These theorems are summarised below:

(1) Theorem 1: Bond Prices (or the present value of anything) move inversely to the yield to maturity (that is, the discount rate used).

(2) Theorem 2: For any given difference between the coupon rate of interest and the yield to maturity of a bond, the associated price change will be greater, the longer the time, bond has to maturity.

(3) Theorem 3: The percentage price changes described in Theorem 2, increases at a diminishing rate as term to maturity increases.

(4) Theorem 4: For any given maturity, a decrease in yields, causes a capital gain which is larger than the capital loss resulting from an equal increase in yields.

(5) Theorem 5: The higher the coupon rate on a bond, the smaller is the percentage change of price for any given change in yields (except for one year and perpetual bonds).

Risk Premium on Bonds

Risk premium is higher for two economic reasons: The unemployment and fear of job loss and risk aversion are more in recession. So risk premiums are higher during recessions of the business cycle. Secondly, corporations which issue bonds may be experiencing reduced sales and lower profits and hence their bonds are more risky and this requires more premium.

The non-cyclical factors, which influence risk premiums may be set out here.

Fears of future inflation, domestic political factors, fears of war or riots, foreign political factors and uncertain government policies.

Yield Curves — Term Structure

The term structure of interest rates is the one major factor influencing the yields. For a given bond issuer, the structure of yields for bonds with different terms to maturity (but no other differences) is called the term structure of interest rates. *Ceteris paribus,* the term to maturity of a bond will affect its yield.

The market interest rate of the 'i' th bond at the 't' th time period is affected by varying the bond issue term to maturity.

Market interest rate for 'i' at 't'	=	real rate of return	+	Risk premium for 'i' at 't'	+	Expected rate of inflation at 't'	+	Term structure of interest rate for 'i' at 't'

The term structure of interest rates is also called the yield curve and is defined as the relationship of yields to maturities of bonds.

The following graph of yield curve can be given as an example:

Fig. 35.4

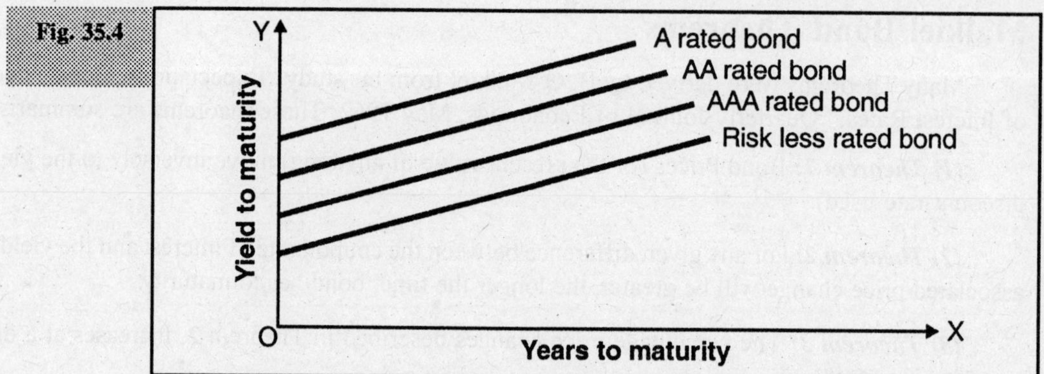

The above chart shows that higher the risk the higher is the return. The longer the maturity, the higher is the return.

Types of Bond Management

Investors in bonds may adopt either the passive bond management strategy or active bond management strategy; both have their own advantages and disadvantages.

Under passive management, one can have Buy and Hold strategy or Bond Ladder strategy. These are dealt with here separately.

(1) Buy and Hold Strategy: The investor ignores the expectations of future interest rate changes but selects bonds for given income with minimum risk and default free. These investors desire a fixed income and are a category by themselves, examples of which can be found among banks, P.F.s insurance companies, retired persons and even Pension Funds in India. By holding the securities to maturity, but reinvesting income at prevailing market rates, in similar securities, the portfolio manager maximises his income. Income Funds and Index tied funds basically follow this strategy to provide diversification, lower costs and maximise income with the least research base and costs.

(2) Bond Ladder Strategy: The investor under this strategy buys some bonds every year with a given amount, with a view to hold different maturities, say one to ten years; the laddering means that bonds of each group of maturity are rungs of the investment maturity ladder in which investments are made in a well diversified manner. By such regular investments market fluctuation in prices and yields can be evened out and a diversified portfolio is secured. If interest rates rise, he will invest in the higher yield bonds from the amount invested in that year. Similarly, if interest rates fall, he will have already some bonds of long maturity to provide capital appreciation.

In the Indian context, public financial institutions PSUs and government and semi-government bodies are issuing bonds with different features and maturities. The bond investor has to diversify into these securities under both Buy and Hold strategy and Bond Laddering strategy. Under the former, it is a random purchase of all default free bonds which by law of averages may contain all maturities and incorporate bonds of all features. Here no expectations nor active buying and selling are involved. In the case of laddering strategy also, a fixed amount is used to purchase bonds of fixed income, every year, involving deliberately all maturities and diversification into all types of bonds available in the market, which are default free and with minimum of risk. In the ladder strategy, there is less randomness and some discretion, but is also automatic like the former.

(3) Semi-Active Management Strategy: If the investor has time horizon, with in which investment has to fructify to give an amount of wealth to meet his obligations or liabilities, he has to follow at least a semi-active management strategy. This is necessary because in the actual market, interest rates do change frequently and reinvestment of income from interest will yield lower or higher amounts than expected and capital gain or loss will also arise due to interest rate changes. Interest Risk has two components namely price risk and coupon reinvestment risk, which move in opposite directions. If interest rates decline for example, the market price of bond will go up at the time of repayment, but the interim cash flows through coupon interest receipts will be reinvested at lower rates, which will lead to lower wealth for the investor. The reverse is what happens if interest rates rise in the interim period before maturity. Thus, investor may or may not achieve the desired wealth position at the end period due to these opposing forces. Elimination of these effects, on the Bond portfolio is called Immunisation discussed later in the chapter.

(4) Active Bond Management: Increased volatility of interest rates and disappointing returns in the equity market and growing bond market, relative to equity market forced managers of portfolios to involve themselves in active Bond Management. If the major emphasis is to capture the capital gains through bond price changes, as in the case of equity, then the portfolio has to be essentially short-term from a few days to a few months, upto say one year. Active bond management is through trading in bonds, as we do in equities. This requires major strategy decisions of the type of bonds, maturity and other terms of bonds, their yields, term structure of yields and expected shape of the yield curve, etc. As a result of active management, returns can be increased by changes in the maturity structure, coupons, and asset quality, to take advantage of changes in bond prices in the daily market and yield pattern. Shifting of bonds of low yield and high risk to high yield and low risk, from taxable bonds to tax free bonds, low quality to high quality bonds etc., is done through outright purchase or sale, swaps and Repos in the market.

Active Strategies

(a) Sector and Asset Substitution among bonds say from Central Government securities to higher yielding semi-government bonds or from Government to corporate bonds.

(b) Maturity Adjustments by shortening the maturities when interest rates are expected to rise and lengthening the maturities when interest rates are expected to fall.

(c) Quality Diversification into various grades of risk, through expected or actual ratings of bonds by Rating agencies.

(d) Coupon Adjustments or Yield Substitutions: Bonds of lower coupons are preferred when speculative capital gains or losses are aimed at. High coupon bonds are preferred to reduce the price fluctuations for higher incomes, and if expectations are for rising interest rates, the investor may prefer long-term bonds with high coupon rates. High coupon bonds, quoting above their redemption price are called cushion bonds, as they provide a cushion against sharp price declines in times of rising interest rates. To give an example in the Indian context, the Central Government resorted to short maturity bonds of three to ten years during 1994-96, with coupon rates ranging from 12½ to 14%, because of the uncertainty of future market rates, and with the intention of lowering the maturity structure of central government debt, which is heavily weighted in favour of long maturities of above 10 years.

YIELD CURVE STUDY

A study of the yield curve on a daily basis is needed for quick decisions for making active Bond Management Strategy effective. Swaps, switches, and active trading in bonds and their futures are necessary to take full advantage of yield differentials, as they emerge. Besides capital gains can be booked and capital losses can be reduced or avoided, if the investor's expectation come out to be correct.

Yield curve expectations and changes in the interest rates, short, medium and long-term play an important role in the active debt management. Mapping of expected returns, based on the expected volatility, maturity and coupon changes and likely changes in interest rates, is also necessary.

Expected return = Coupon income (C) + Amortisation of premium/discount (A) + Replacement or roll over of low yielding by high yielding bonds (R)

$= C + A + R$

As $C + A =$ yield,

Yield plus replacement benefit (R) will give the return expected.

Objectives of Raising Incremental Return

The component of 'R' is the one involved in active debt management. If the anticipation of yields can be made correctly or changes in interest rates are properly anticipated, R component can be positive and maximum. 'R' is the incremental return.

The strategies or tactics to be adopted for maximising the 'R' component are swapping or bond substitution and switches from one type of bond to another and Repo sale with buy back arrangements for adjusting the maturities or yields. Incremental return, reflected through 'R' component involved in active bond management can be maximised by trading in secondary market, participation in the primary market and capturing all yield advantages as they emerge in these markets. Repos and Switches are undertaken in India in government bonds by banks and FIs to adjust the liquidity or CRR requirements or for securing required maturities of bonds in the portfolio. These can be done with the RBI to a limited extent or with STCI or DFHI or with other banks and financial institutions in the market.

Need for Tax Planning

Some switches are undertaken to book losses or gains for income tax purposes not having any bearing on yield or maturity considerations. Such deals are called Washed sales, undertaken by banks and financial institutions. All these ingredients of active bond management involve expertise and large research base and it is necessary keep in touch with the market by actively trading and interacting with other market participants. Expectations of yields and interest rates are to be effectively correct to secure better results.

Sequence of Steps for Bond Issues@

Decide on the Rate of Issue or/and Maturity: T.B. Rate, Government bond rate, libor related rates, floating rate or fixed rate, frequency of interest rate payments, quarterly, half yearly, etc.

Repayment Schedule: Bullet repayment, instalment schedules, bonds on perpetuity not issued, in India — short-term notes, medium-term note issuance facilities, long-term bonds.

Steps in Management of the Issue

(a) Privately placed issues — Banks and investment and securities firms

(b) Publicly placed issues — Registration with SEC. (USA) or Government or SEBI in India.

General Benchmarks in Making Issues

1. Appointment of group managers or lead managers etc.
2. Appointment of underwriters.
3. Entering into written agreements with managers and underwriters.
4. Completion of regulatory requirements, with SEBI, stock exchange, etc.
5. Pricing of the issue.
6. The actual issue.
7. A tombstone i.e., an advertisement recording the issue of the bonds.
8. Complying with the requirements of the Government, SEBI, Central Bank, etc.

Valuation of Bonds

Bond YTM varies inversely with the price. The price depends on a number of factors like.

Term to maturity

Coupon rate

@ The markets which are free for capital market borrowings are: U.S.A., U.K., Germany and Japan. Controls are most in Japan and less in U.K. and U.S.A. borrowing is most in U.S. Dollars (30-38%) followed by Yen (11%) and D.M. (7-8%).

Controls in Euro Markets are less than in domestic markets. No controls on interest rates, no reserve requirements and no Government interference in the operations, completely free market and competition prevails.

Rate of return required by the investor

Credit rating of the bond

Call features of the bond, callable or not

Secured or unsecured

Part or full conversion or incentives like warrants, etc.

YTM assumes a reinvestment rate of return on intermediate cash flows equivalent to YTM. There is no default risk in respect of payment of coupon rate and the maturity value and its repayment. The bond should be held until maturity, for calculation of YTM.

Risks in Bond Holding (as it is Fixed Income Security)

Purchasing power risk: (Inflation or loss in Value of money) (Expected inflation Uncertainty of inflation rate in the years ahead)	Interest rate risk (Changes in rate of interest or required rate of return will change the bond value)	Reinvestment rate risk (When interest rate changes, the rate of reinvestment also changes which leads to Bond value changes)

Price Risk

1. The lower the coupon rate the greater is price volatility.
2. The higher the yield level from which fluctuation in yields starts the greater will be the price volatility.
3. The longer the maturity the greater will be the bond price volatility. As the maturity lengthens, volatility increases but at a diminishing rate.

Graph on convex shape of the price and yield relationship.

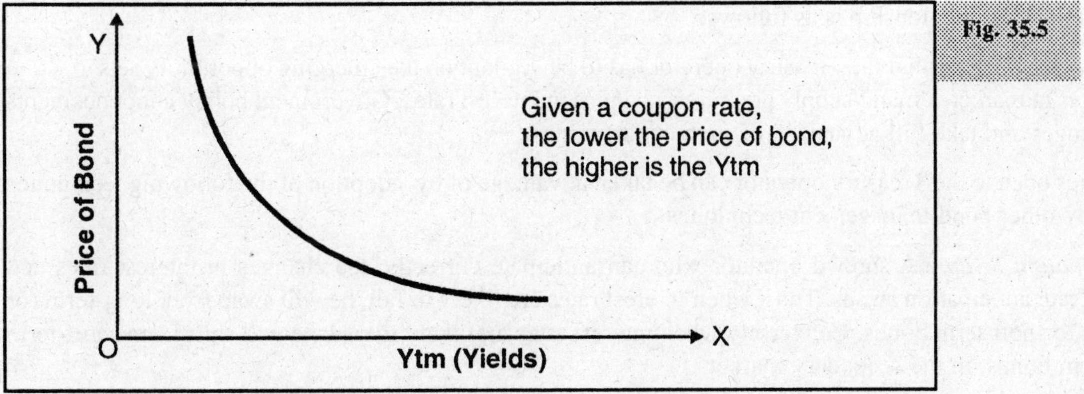

Fig. 35.5

RIDING THE YIELD CURVE

Any Treasury operator in a bank or FI has to pay attention to the yield curve in order to operate in the gilt edged market, effectively. The yield curve at any point of time is drawn, based on the relationship of yields to the maturity periods. The yields may be as reflected in the primary market (new issues of gilts) or in the secondary market. The yields may be or short-term Treasury bills or medium and long dated Government securities. Towards the close of 1996, the yields, based on the primary market were as follows. Subsequently yields fell during 1998 to 2005, went up to 2007 and fell later on during 2008 to 2010.

Table 35.1

	Mar. 1996		Mar. 1999		2001-02	Mar. 05	Mar. 07	Mar. 10
3 Months maturity @	Yield	8.5%	Yeild	7.80	7.91	5.32	7.68	4.38
6 " "@@	"	10.5%	"	9.88	8.42	5.43	7.98	4.62
12 " "	"	12.5%	"	10.07	9.40	5.61	7.90	5.14
1 year "	"	13.5%	"	10.65	9.70	5.73	7.90	5.23
5 to 10 years "	"	14.0	"	11.5 to 12.0	11.70	6.21	8.11	7.81

@ 14 day Treasury bill was introduced in June 1997.

@@ 182 day T.B.S. were reintroduced in May 1999.

Source: RBI Bulletins

The Table above shows how yields have fallen over the decade ending in March 2010 and particularly more in the long end of the spectrum:

Fig. 35.6

Government Securities Yield Curve

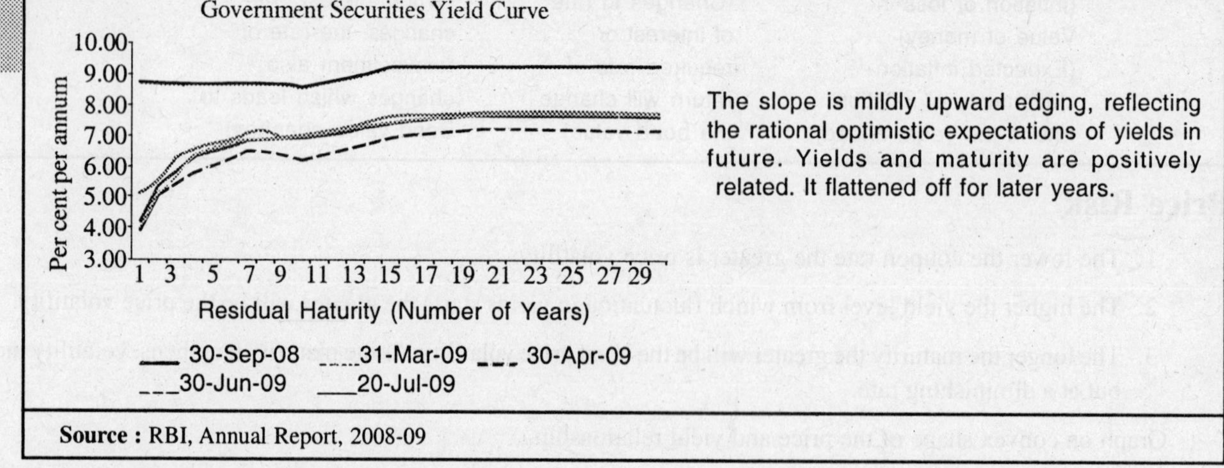

Source : RBI, Annual Report, 2008-09

The curve depicting that relationship is as follows:

Riding the yield curve means that the Treasury operator has to be vigilant on the emerging opportunity sets, open to him due to any changes in market demand/supply pressures, changes in interest rates, Government policy announcements and credit policy changes and take full advantage of such opportunities.

The opportunities open to the Treasury operator can be taken advantage of by adoption of the following techniques of bond swaps, or any other bond management techniques.

(a) *Rate Anticipation Swaps:* A shrewd operator who can anticipate correctly, the changes in interest rates and yields, can enter into rate anticipation swaps. Thus, when interest rates are likely to fall, he will swap from long-term (or medium-term) bonds to short-term bonds. Conversely when interest rates are likely to rise, he will shift from short-term bonds to medium-term bonds, in the secondary market.

(b) *Inter Market Swaps:* Swap from money market instruments to gilted securities and *vice-versa* is an example. Similarly, swift from semi-Government bond to a P.S.U. bond is another example of inter-market swaps. This is to take advantage of price/yield changes.

(c) *Substitution Swaps:* One security, if exchanged for a similar security of the same maturity is called substitution swap. This is a perfect substitute for price advantage but future anticipations may be different for these two bonds. The one fitting with the preferences of the investor is chosen for swap; the intention is a future gain in yields.

(d) *Pure Yield Pick up Swaps:* This is swapping of a low yield bond to a high yield bond, if such differences in yields are noticed in the secondary market due to changes in demand and supply conditions.

In the above context, price change is split up into time effect + yield change effect; correct anticipation of yield change is critical for quick operations of advantage.

Some of Bond Value Theorems are as follows:

1. Interest rate sensitivity is high for bonds of long maturities.
2. Interest rate sensitivity is high for bonds of low coupon rates.
3. The percentage change in price increases at a diminishing rate as the YTM is increased.
4. Given the YTM, the capital gains due to fall in yield are higher than the capital losses resulting from an increase in yield.
5. Required rate of return is the same as the coupon rate, if the value of bond is at par.
6. If the required rate of return is higher than the coupon rate, the value of the bond is lower than the par value and *vice versa.*
7. If the bonds are callable their values are generally lower and they depend on the call terms.
8. As the bond approaches the maturity, the premium or discount will fall and finally disappear on the date of maturity.
9. Some bonds have both call and put options and their pricing depend on the terms of the call and put.
10. Term structure influences the yield curve and the prices of bonds.
11. Short-term rates fluctuate more violently than long-term rates.
12. Long-term bond prices fluctuate more than short-term bond prices.
13. The normal yield curve first slopes upwards, then flattens and finally slopes downwards, representing the interest rate expectations, recession, recovery and boom phases of the economy.
14. Long-term interest rates are the average expected values of the future short rates in the economy.

DURATION MEASURE

Risks to be Covered

1. Term to maturity
2. Weighted average maturity
3. Weighted average cash flow is given by

$$= \sum_{t=1}^{n} \frac{Cft}{TCF} \quad \text{where Cft is cash flow in time period 't' and TCF is total cash flow}$$

Duration is measured by the weighted average maturity of a bond's cash flows and present values of these flows are used as weights. Duration is a measure of average time prior to receipt of payment.

$$\text{Duration (years)} = \sum_{t=1}^{n} \frac{PV\,(Cft) \times t}{TPV}$$

where Cf is Cash Flows, PV is Present Value, 't' is the time period or the number of years from the present TPV is maturity value, or the total present value of the bond or its price.

$$\text{Duration is} = f\left(\frac{1}{ytm}\right)$$

The details on duration are referred to below.

DURATION AND IMMUNISATION

What is Duration?

Duration is a concept, which means the weighted average measure of time period of bond's life. This is valuable in understanding how bond's prices change in response to interest rate changes. Bonds with the same duration respond similarly, *inter alia* to given changes in interest rates. If the bond has no coupon rate as in the case of zero coupon bonds, duration is equal to the maturity period, or Po = PV (Ct) for only one cash flow.

The formula for a bond's duration (D) is as follows:

$$D = \sum \frac{pv(ct) \times t}{Po}$$

pv (ct) is the present value of cash flow to be received at time t, that is cash flow discounted by a discount factor of yield to maturity (ytm), Po denotes the current market price and 't' denotes the remaining life to maturity.

The above equation can be rewritten as

$$D = \frac{\sum_{t=1}^{T} pv\,(ct) \times t}{\sum_{t=1}^{T} pv(ct)}$$

To explain this verbally, the present value of each flow [pv(ct)] is expressed as a proportion of the market price (Po). These proportions are then multiplied by the respective amount of term until the cash flows are received. Lastly, these figures are added, with the sum equal to the duration.

To give an example of calculation of duration the table below presents the data. (7% Bond of Rs. 1,000 Face value and 3 years to maturity).

Table 35.2
Calculation of Duration

Time Until Receipt of Cash Flow (1)	*Amount of Cash Flow Interest or Interest Plus Principal* (2)	*Present Value Factor at 7% of Rs. 1* (3)	*Present Value of Cash Flow = 2 x 3* (4)	*Present Value of Cash Flow X Time* (5)
1	70	0.9346	65.42	0.065
2	70	0.8734	61.14	0.122
3	1070	0.8163	873.44	2.619
			1000	2.806

To use the formula:

$$D = \frac{1\left(\frac{70}{(1.07)}\right) + 2\left(\frac{70}{(1.07)^2}\right) + 3\left(\frac{1070}{(1.07)^3}\right)}{\frac{70}{(1.07)^1} + \frac{70}{(1.07)^2} + \frac{1070}{(1.07)^3}} = 2.81$$

Use of Duration as a Concept

This calculation of duration is necessary for a study of the effect of changes in interest rates on bond prices and yields. This concept is also useful to make proper investment decision on bonds. The technique of Bond Portfolio Management (called Immunisation) involves the use of Immunisation process. Prices and duration move in the same direction, and larger the coupon rate, the smaller is the duration. Duration declines as maturity approaches and duration for a perpetual bond is equal to $\frac{1+r}{r}$, where "r" is ytm. For coupon paying bonds, duration is less than the term to maturity. Limiting value of the duration is, $\frac{1+ytm}{ytm}$ calculation of the duration helps in investment decision-making, revision of portfolio of bonds etc.

Macaulay's Duration (MD)

Macaulay's Duration is defined as the weighted average number of years, until the cash flows occur, where the relative present values of each cash payment are used as the weights. The formula for MD is as follows:

$$MD = \frac{\sum_{t=1}^{T} \frac{Ct}{(1+Ytm)^t} + \frac{Ft}{(1+Ytm)^T}}{Vo}$$

$$\begin{bmatrix} \text{Weighted} \\ \text{Average} \\ \text{Maturity} \end{bmatrix} = \begin{bmatrix} \text{Maturities of} \\ \text{various time} \\ \text{periods of} \\ \text{payment, and T} \end{bmatrix} \times \begin{bmatrix} \text{Proportion of} \\ \text{Bond' s value} \\ \text{accounted for} \\ \text{by the payments} \\ \text{in square brackets} \end{bmatrix}$$

To give an example, let the Face value F_T = Rs. 1,000

ytm = 6%, coupon rate C = 7.0%,

Annual coupon payments = C_t = 0.07 × 1,000 = 70 = ct

No. of years to Maturity = T = 3 years

Market price = Po = 1,026.73

Premium over face value = 26.73 = (1,026.73 – 1,000)

Market price or present value is calculated by the formula

$$\text{Vo or Po} = \sum_{1}^{T} \frac{ct}{(1+ytm)^t} \text{ [put the above values]}$$

Year, (Na) (1)	*Cash Flow (ct)* (2)	*1 / (ytm)ᵗ* (3)		*4 = 2 × 3 Vo = Present Values of Cash Flows* (4)
1	70	$\frac{1}{(1.06)^1}$	= 0.9434	66.04
2	70	$\frac{1}{(1.06)^2}$	= 0.893	62.30
3	1070	$\frac{1}{(1.06)^3}$	= 0.839	898.39
				1,026.73 = Vo

[Calculation of MD]

Year (1)	*Present Value of Cash Flow Vo* (2)	*Present Value as Proportion of Vo,* (3)	*Columns 3 × 1 =* (4)
1	66.04	0.0643	0.0643
2	62.30	0.0607	0.1214
3	898.39	0.8750	2.6250
	1026.73	1.00	MD 2.8107

Duration (Example)

Q. An investor wants to purchase a Bond with maturity 3 years, coupon 11% and par value Rs. 100

(*a*) If the investor requires YTM 15% of equivalent risk and maturity, what is the price he should pay.

$$P = \frac{11}{1+0.15} + \frac{11}{(1.015)^2} + \frac{111}{(1+0.15)^3} = 90.86$$

(*b*) If the bond is selling at a price of Rs. 97.59 what is its YTM.

YTM is to be estimated by Trial and Error method. Consider 12% as YTM Then

$$\frac{11}{(1+0.12)} + \frac{11}{(1.012)^2} + \frac{111}{(1+0.12)^3} = 97.59$$

Hence, YTM is 12%.

(*c*) What is the duration of this Bond, if the YTM is 12% and expected return is 10.06%.

Duration	*Value =*	*% age Value*	*Weighted Duration*
1 year	$9.82 = \frac{11}{1.12}$	10.06%	0.1006 = 1 × .1006
2 year	$8.77 = \frac{11}{(1.12)^2}$	8.99%	0.1798 = 2 × .0899
3 year	$79.01 = \frac{11}{(1.12)^3}$	80.95%	2.4285 = 3 × .8095
Total	97.60	100.00	2.7087

In the case of above bond of YTM of 12% and expected return 10.06%; the weighted duration of the portfolio is 2.70.

THEOREMS EMERGING FROM MD

These theorems describe the relationship of Bond's term to maturity and M.D.

M.D. Theorem 1: A bond's duration equals its term to maturity, only if it is zero coupon bond.

Theorem 2: The maturity of coupon bond of more than one year maturity has a duration less than its term to maturity.

Theorem 3: The duration of perpetual bonds which are not permitted in India is equal to $\left(1.0+\frac{1}{\text{ytm}}\right)$ irrespective of its coupon rate.

Theorem 4: The duration of a coupon bearing bond selling at a market price below its face value reaches a maximum before its maturity date reaches infinity and then recedes to the limit of $\left(1.0+\frac{1}{\text{ytm}}\right)$.

Theorem 5: The duration of a coupon bearing bond selling at or above its face value increases monotonically with its term to maturity and approaches the quantity $\left(1.0+\frac{1}{\text{ytm}}\right)$ as its term to maturity approaches infinity.

Theorem 6: The duration of a coupon bearing bond selling below its par value reaches the maximum value when T reaches the value indicated in the following formula:

$$T=\frac{1.0}{\log(1.0+\text{ytm})}+\frac{1.0-\text{ytm}}{(\text{ytm}-i)}+\frac{\text{ytm}-1}{i\,(1.0+\text{ytm})\,T\log(1.0+\text{ytm})}$$

Theorem 7: The duration of a coupon bearing bond, selling below par reaches its maximum at a maturity which is directly related to the bond's coupon rate and inversely related to the bond's yield to maturity.

Theorem 8: The longer a coupon paying bond term to maturity the greater is the difference between its terms to maturity and its duration.

Advantages of M.D.

The above Theorems reflect the advantages of MD over normal measure of duration or term to maturity. Duration can be compiled for a single bond as also for a basket of bonds or fixed interest bearing securities, included in a portfolio. A bond's years of duration are considered to be a better measure of the time structure of an investment cash flow than its years to maturity T, because the duration reflects the amount and timing of every cash flow rather than merely the length of time until the final payment occurs. Further, the MD is a measure of bond's interest rate risk.

Elasticity of interest rate to the bond's price is the ratio between the change of price of bond and the change in the ytm. Bond's Price elasticity to interest rate changes is given by the formula

$$I\,\Sigma_{ii}=\frac{\text{Percentage change in price for the bond i in period t}}{\text{Percentage change in Yield to maturity for bond i}}$$

The bond's interest rate risk and bond's price movements are explained separately.

The graph below shows the duration and term to maturity for premium and discount.

Fig. 35.7

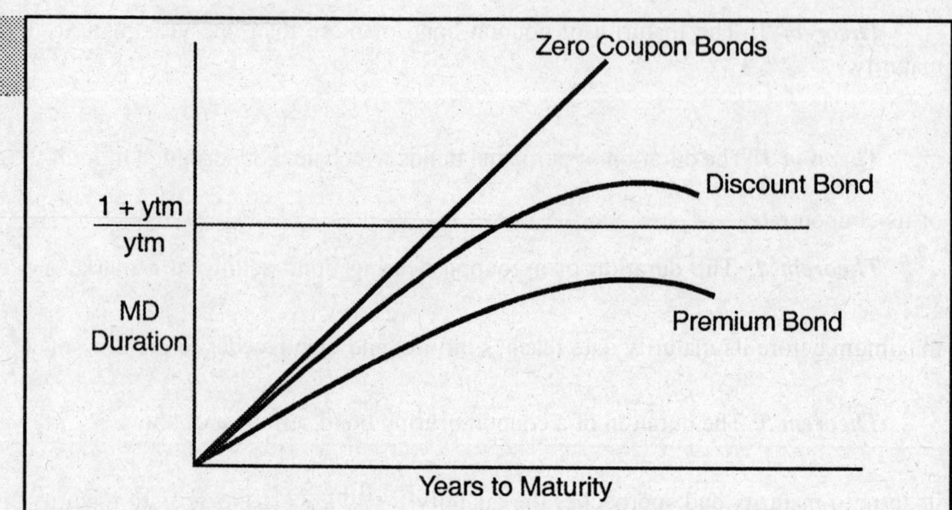

Uses of Duration

(a) It can be used as a measure of the responsiveness of bond price to changes in market yields.

(b) It is used to immunise a bond from interest rate risk by setting the investment horizon equal to bond's duration.

Interest Rate Elasticity and Risk

$IE_{it} = \frac{\Delta Po}{Po} / \frac{\Delta ytm}{ytm}$ and it is Interest Rate Elasticity and always negative.

$\frac{\Delta Po}{Po} = IE_{it} \times \frac{ytm}{\Delta ytm}$ it is the interest rate risk.

Modified Duration (by Hicks)

Dmod = where D is Macaulay's Duration.

y is ytm in decimal points.

f is discounting periods per year.

Percentage price volatility using D mod is:

$\frac{\Delta P}{P} \times 100 = \text{Dmod.}\ \Delta Y$

The following example will help understand the above formulas.

P = Rs. 100, C = 10%/p.a., r = 10%, n = 10 years.

For a change in r to 11%,

New Po = 10 (PVIFA 11, 10) + 100 × (PVIF 11, 10)

Po = 10 × (5.889) + 100 (0.352) = 58.9 + 35.2 = 94.1 (From the Tables at the end of the Chapter)

$\text{I.E.} \left(\frac{5.9}{100}\right) \times \left(\frac{.01}{.10}\right) = \frac{0.59}{100}$ namely –.0059

$$\frac{\Delta Po}{Po} = (.0059) \times \frac{.10}{.01} = .059 \text{ or } 5.9\%, \text{ which is interest elasticity.}$$

$D = PVIFA_{10,10} \times (1 + 0.10) = 6.76$ years.

[6.145 × 1.10 = 6.76]

$$\text{Interest rate risk} = \frac{0.591 \times 0.01}{0.10} = 0.0591 \text{ or } 5.91\%.$$

$$\text{Dmod} = \frac{6.76}{1 + 0.10/1} = 6.15 \text{ years.}$$

Short Cut Formula for Duration

$$D = \frac{rc}{rd} \times PVIFA_{\gamma d,n} \times (1 + rd) + \left(1 - \frac{rc}{rd}\right)^n$$

where,

rc = Current yield (= coupon interest/bond price)

rd = YTM

n = Term to maturity

(In case of a bond selling at par) rc = rd and

$D = PVIFA_{rd}\ n \times (1 + rd)$; then the formula is

$$D = \frac{i(1+r)\ PVIFA_{r,n} + (r - i)PVIF_{r,n}}{i + (r - i)PVIF_{r,n}}$$

Where,

i = Coupon rate

n = Term to maturity

r = ytm

(It should be noted that the short cut formula can be applied only in case of bonds redeemable at maturity. Duration of callable bonds and bonds redeemable in instalments should not be computed by this method).

IMMUNISATION

What is Immunisation?

A bondholder faces the interest rate risk and fluctuations in rates will lead to changes in bond returns. A bond which is of longer period faces larger fluctuations with a given change in interest rate than a short duration bond. Bond investor faces the interest rate risk between the time of investment and the future holding period. Interest rate risk is composed of two risks:

Price Risk and *Coupon Reinvestment Risk*: If interest rates rise in the meantime, the bond price will fall and there will be capital depreciation. Second risk is the coupon reinvestment risk, as the yield to maturity computation implicitly assumes that the coupon flows will be reinvested. Thus, if the interest income is reinvested at a higher rate, then the total end sum may be above than that expected.

The above two effects are opposed to each other. While one increases the total bond return, the other decreases it, in the case of fall in interest rate. The reverse is true in the case of rise in interest rates. *The elimination of these risks is called bond immunisation.* If the realized return on investment in bonds is sure to be atleast as large as the appropriately computed yield to the time horizon, then the investment is immunised.

The maximisation is achieved by making the duration of the portfolio as equal to the desired holding period. Duration is the time period at which price risk and coupon reinvestment risk of a bond portfolio are of equal magnitude and opposite in direction.

Immunisation Process

What is Immunisation has been referred to earlier. It is a process by which the effects of changes in interest rates can be offset in a portfolio of Bonds. A change in interest rates has two effects: (1) Price effect, which is negative (as the interest rates rise, the bond prices fall). (2) Reinvestment effect, which is positive (interest rates reinvested at higher rates lead to larger return). Immunisation attempts to offset the effects of the above on the bond portfolio — protecting the return from interest rate changes.

Immunisation Operations

It is accomplished by simply calculating the duration of the promised outflows and then investing in bonds which have identical duration. This duration of a portfolio of bonds is equal to the weighted average of the durations of individual bonds in the portfolio.

If the rate of interest rises from 9% to 11% capital loss occurs and this loss has to be made good by reinvesting, the Coupon income at higher rate of 11%. In order to earn the original target return of 9%; the duration has to be 6.79% as shown in the Table below (Table 35.3)

Table 35.3
(9% Ten Year Bond)

Income Source	*Interest Rate at Time of Reinvestment*	*Holding Periods in Years*			
		1	*3*	*6.79@@*	*10*
Coupon Income	7%	90	270	611	900
Capital Gain/Loss	—	132	109	56	0
Interest on Interest		2	25	149	355
Total Return		224	404	816	1255
Total Yield		22%	12%	9%	8.5%
Coupon Income	9%	90	270	611	900
Capital Gain/Loss	—	—	—	—	—
Interest on Interest		2	32	205	495
Total Return		92	302	816	1395
Total Yield		9%	9%	9%	9%
Coupon Income	11%	90	270	611	900
Capital Gain/Loss		112	95	56	0
Interest on Interest		2	40	26	647
Total Return		20	215	816	1547
Total Yield	2%	6.7%	9%	9.8%	

@@ Duration of 9% Bond purchased at par-10 years hence due is shown here as 6.79 years

Source: D. E. Fischer & R.J. Jordon: Security Analysis & Portfolio Management (Chapter 11)

Bond of Rs. 1,000/-

To explain the items in the Table take the illustration of how the data of 3 years holding with 7% rate are arrived:

Coupon Income is $90 \times 3 = 270$

Viz. 90 is one year interest

Coupon income plus interest on interest	45 is half year interest $45 \times 6.55 = 295$ = Where 6.55 is taken from Annuity Tables for the future value of annuity for 6 periods at a rate of 3.5% per period.

$295 - 270 = 25$ is interest on interest

Coupon Income = 270

Interest on interest = 25

Capital gain = Price of 9% Bond due in 7 years with a 7% market return = 1109 (take from Bond Tables).

Capital gain = Market Value – Face Value

$1109 - 1000 = 109$

Total Return = $270 + 25 + 109 = 404$

An example for effecting immunisation by matching the holding period with the duration period of a bond is given in Table 35.4. It is a case of holding period of 8 years, and present yield to maturity for 8 year bonds is 8%. The end period wealth required by investor is $1.8509 = [(1.08)^8]$. If the amount required at the end of 8 year is Rs. 18,500, and the present amount with them is Rs. 10,000, the immunised portfolio can be set up for 8 year period and assume a single change in interest rate (8 to 6%).

Table 35.4 (Maturity Strategy vs. Duration Strategy)

	Maturity Strategy			*Duration Strategy*		
Year	*Cash Flow*	*Reinvestment Rate*	*Accu-End Value*	*Cash Flow*	*Reinvestment Rate*	*Accu-End Value*
1	80	.08	80	80	.08	80
2	80	.08	166.40	80	.08	166.40
3	80	.08	259.71	80	.08	259.71
4	80	.08	360.49	80	.08	360.49
5	80	.06	462.12	80	.06	462.12
6	80	.06	596.85	80	.06	596.85
7	80	.06	684.04	80	.06	684.04
8	1080	.06	1805.08	80	.06	1845.72

Source: *Ibid.*

Interest Rate fell from 8% to 6% at end of 4th year; 8% Ten year Bond, Face value Rs. 1,000 — can be sold at Rs. 1,040.64 at the end of 8 years.

Expected Wealth Ratio: 1.8509

With the Duration strategy the target is achieved and uncertainty is removed for the given assumptions. Duration strategy can be used both actively and passively — actively when it is used to capitalise on interest rate change and passively to neutralise interest rate risk.

How is Immunisation Effected?[@]

Immunisation is a protection against interest rate changes and corresponding changes in yields. If yields rise, then the portfolio's losses due to selling the three year bond at a discount after two years will be exactly offset by the gains from reinvesting the maturing one year bonds along with the coupons on the three year bonds at a higher rate. If on the other hand, the yields fell, then the loss from reinvesting the maturing one year bonds and the first year coupons on three year bonds would be exactly offset by having to sell the three year bonds, after two years at a premium. The process tries to protect from the effects of interest rate changes on prices of bonds and due to reinvestment of coupons.

If immunisation is to be used, then the solution can be found by solving simultaneously a set of two equations, involving two unknowns.

$$W_1 + W_3 = 1$$

$$(W_1 \times 1) + (W_3 \times 2.78) = 2$$

Here we take a bond of 4 year maturity with a duration of 2.78 years as an example. W_1 and W_3 are the weights in which proportion the portfolio funds of Rs. 1,000 are to be invested in bonds with maturities of one and three years. The second equation states that the weighted averages of the bonds in the portfolio must equal the duration of the cash out flow which is two years. But bonds carry 10% coupon rate. The solution to the two above equations can be worked out as follows:

$W_1 = 1 - W_3$, substituting this, in the second equation, we have

$[(1-W_3) \times 1] + (W_3 \times 2.78) = 2$

$1.78\ W_3 = 1$ and $W_3 = \dfrac{1}{1.78} = 0.562$

$$\begin{aligned} \text{Then } W_1 &= 0.438 \\ \text{plus } W_3 &= 0.562 \\ \hline W_1 + W_3 &= 1.000 \end{aligned}$$

The investment in this example is for two years and for a target of 10%. Then the portfolio Manager needs

$\dfrac{1{,}000}{(1.10)^2}$ = Rs. 826.0, which is distributed as Rs. 363 to buy one year bonds and Rs. 463 to buy three year bonds. This will give an immunised portfolio with duration of 2 years and target amount of Rs. 1,000. In this example, one year bonds are selling at Rs. 972 and three year bonds at Rs. 950 (approx.). The above exercise proves that the portfolio's losses due to selling 3 year bonds after 2 years will be exactly offset by the gains from reinvesting the maturing one year bonds at a higher rate.

Problems of Immunisation

The immunisation exercise is based on some assumptions: (1) Bond will not be called back by the Company. (2) There is no default risk. (3) Yield curves move horizontally and any shift in it will be parallel. In reality, the shifts in the curves may not be parallel. If the one year and three year bonds will have initial yields of 10% and 10.5%, respectively, it is possible that the yields on them will fall by 1% and 0.8% respectively after one year, which means that falls are not of the same magnitude.

Remedies are suggested for such non-parallel shifts in yield curvers, namely:

(1) *Cash Matching:* It involves the purchase of bonds, so that the cash received during each period from the bonds is identical in size to the promised cash outflow for that period.

@ W. F. Sharpe & G.J Alexander *Investments*, p. 387 (Prentice-Hall).

(2) *Dedicated Portfolio:* In the cash matching portfolio of bonds, there is no need for reinvestment of cash inflows in the future as cash outflows and inflows are matched exactly. Such a portfolio is called dedicated portfolio, which avoids the reinvestment rate risk and no interest rate risk either as the bonds do not have to be sold before Maturity.

Immunisation requires continuous and active management as some rebalancing may be required always due to changes overtime of yields, durations at different rates and emergence of non-horizontal movement of yield curves and a host of other factors.

(3) *"Bullet" or Focussed Portfolio:* It is portfolio which has less stochastic process risk than any other. Such a portfolio is one where the bonds in it have durations, most closely matching the duration of the promised outflows.

Alternatively, the portfolio manager may adopt both passive and active elements involving contingent immunisation.

This means that portfolio is actively managed as long as favourable returns are obtained and if unfavourable result starts falling, he will resort to the process of immunisation.

(4) *Bond Swaps:* Swap is an exchange of one type of bond for another category. Bond swapping is to manage a portfolio actively by exchanging bonds of one category to another to take advantage of superior ability to predict the yields and prices. Substitution swap is an exchange of one bond for another of the same category to take advantage of temporary price differential due to mismatch of supply and demand factors. There are a number of other types of swaps adopted by Portfolio Managers, namely, rate anticipation swaps, inter-market spread swap or pure high yielding pick-up swap, which all aim at improving the over all yields or return on the Bond Portfolios. Some swaps will benefit tax payments and some swaps increase yields while others secure the required maturity.

Bond Portfolio Management Strategies

1. Buy and Hold Strategy.
2. Bond Ladder Strategy.
3. Semi-Active Management Strategy.

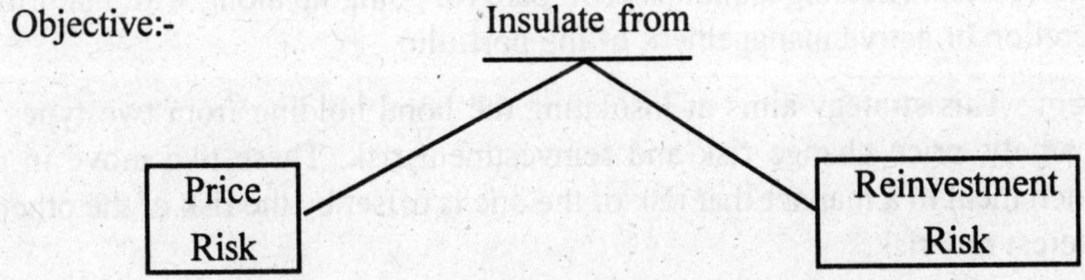

First Calculate Duration. Then use Technique of Immunisation

Example: How to Calculate Duration (D)

Data

$$D = \frac{\sum Pv(ct) \times t}{Po}$$

Par Value Rs. 1,000

Market Price Rs. 50.25

Po = Present Value of all future Cash Flows

ytm = 10%

8% Coupon Rate

Annual Coupon Payment – Rs. 80

Maturity 3 years (T)

Period	Cash Flow Amounts	Present Value Factors at 10%	Present Value of Cash Flows PV (CT)	Present Value of Cash Flows × Time (t)
1	80	.9091	72.73	72.73
2	80	.8264	66.12	132.23
3	1080	.7513	811.40	2434.21
			950.25	2639.17

$D = \frac{2639.17}{950.25} = 2.78$; $\frac{\sum Pv(ct) \times t}{Po}$ is the formula used.

Modified duration MD = D/1 + $\frac{r}{p}$; where r = ytm and p is number of times interest is paid.

$\frac{\Delta P}{P} = -D\frac{\Delta ytm}{1 + ytm}$. We can use D or MD in the equation.

Bond Holding Strategies

Some of the strategies are already referred to

1. *Passive Buy and Hold Strategy:* This is what is adopted by many Indian Banks. This is based on Index linked investments, such as standard and poor Bond Index. These investments yield a continuous flow of fixed incomes, stable and known in advance. It needs very little planning.

2. *Bond Ladder Strategy:* In this strategy investments are made in bonds of different maturities, in a well planned manner, so as to constitute a ladder of maturities, reflecting a similar yield pattern, going up along with maturities. This follows a set pattern, without much discretion or active management of the portfolio.

3. *Semi-Active Management Strategy:* This strategy aims at insulating the bond holding from two types of risks emanating from interest rate changes namely, price change risk and reinvestment risk. These two move in opposite directions. The Bond Manager has to match them in a manner that risk of the one is offset by the risk of the other and the portfolio is then immunised from the interest rate risk.

Immunisation

Immunisation is a process, referred to earlier, whereby, the realised rate of return on investment in bonds is as large as expected and computed yield for a given time horizon, namely, the duration. Duration is the weighted average measure of bond's life, where the various time periods of it are weighted by size of the present value of cash flows from it.

Cash Matching (Dedicated Portfolio)

Liability matching cash flows can be generated by proper Bond Management Strategies. In a dedicated portfolio, referred to earlier, there will be exact synchronising of all cash payments or out flows by matching inflows. It should be an optimal portfolio which releases cash inflows from the coupon receipts and or principal repayment plus accrued interest from a prior balance, just sufficient to meet the next liability falling due.

This following illustration makes this matching concept clear.

Take the following data:

Table 35.5

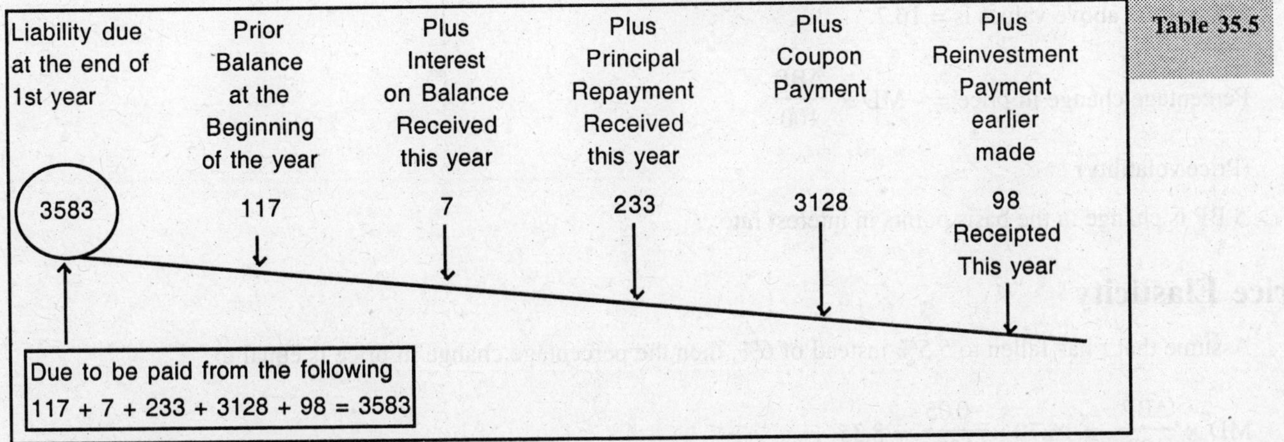

This involves many steps.

The stream of liability payments is anticipated correctly. The cash inflows due to cash expected from various sources, like coupon payments this year interest on invested portion, received this year, principal repayments, capital gains booked, if any, etc. are also to be properly planned. Then only through proper planning of duration of the Bond Portfolio can the manager achieve the dedicated portfolio.

What is Duration? This is explained by the following formula.

$$D = \frac{\sum_{N=1}^{N} (n)\,(Cn)\,/\,(1+i)^n}{\sum_{N=1}^{N} \frac{Cn}{(1+i)^n}}$$

Numerator = sum of the weighted present values of cash flows, weighted by the time period of each of the flows.

Denomintor = Sum of the present values of future cash flows or present and current market price.

where i = ytm. N = number of period of time.

Cn are cash flows.

Duration of the bond is bounded by

$\frac{r+P}{rp}$, where r is ytm, p is number of times in a year that interest is paid on the bond.

If r = 6%, p is 2 times and the application of the above formula is shown by plugging in the above figures

$$\frac{0.06+2}{0.06\times 2} = \frac{2.06}{0.12} = 17.2 \text{ years}$$

It is the duration of the bond for the above values of r and p.

Modified Duration (Md)

$$MD = D/1+\frac{r}{p} = \left(\frac{17.2}{1+\frac{0.06}{2}}\right) = \frac{17.2}{1.03}$$

MD for the above values is = 16.7

$$\text{Percentage change in price} = -\text{MD} \times \frac{\Delta BP}{100}$$

(Price volatility)

Δ BP is change in the basis points in interest rate.

Price Elasticity

Assume that r has fallen to 5.5% instead of 6%, then the percentage change in price is equal to

$$\text{MD} \times \frac{\Delta BP}{100} = 16.70 \times \frac{-0.05}{100} = 8.35$$

is the formula referred to above as the Interest Elasticity.

For a fall of 50 basis points, the Bond should have risen by 8.35%, which reflects the interest rate sensitivity of the Bond.

We have already noted that there is a direct relationship between duration and interest rate risk.

Price volatility can arise due to maturity of the bond, interest rate changes, yield charges and due to reinvestment price. Time element is reflected in the duration.

Immunisation referred to earlier will help the offsetting of the interest rate risk on the Bond portfolio. A bond portfolio is said to be immunised, against interest rate risk, if the duration of the portfolio is equal to be desired holding period.

Illustration

Volatility of Bond Prices

I. Volatility due to maturity (6% coupon rate, face value Rs. 100)

Required Yield	Number of years to maturity						
in %	1 year	10 years		20 years		30 years	
4	102	116	(13.7)	127	(9.5)	135	(6.3)
5	101	108	(6.9)	112	(3.7)	115	(2.7)
6	100	100	—	100	—	100	—
7	99	93	(–6.0)	89	(–4.3)	88	(–1.1)
8	98	86	(–12.2)	80	(–7.0)	77	(–3.7)

Note: Figures in brackets refer to % changes over the previous column.

II. Volatility due to interest rate changes (fixed 20 year maturity)

Coupon Value	Interest Rate Rise			Interest Rate Fall		
in %	7%	8%	% Change	7%	8%	% Change
4	68	60	– 11.3	68	87	27.9
5	78	70	– 10.3	78	100	28.2
6	89	80	– 10.1	89	112	25.8
7	100	90	– 10.0	100	125	25.0
8	110	100	– 9.1	110	137	24.5

III. Volatility due to yield changes (Level of rates)

6% 20 year Bond; Basis point change of 10% from original yield.

Original Yield in %	***Interest Rate Rise***				***Interest Rate Fall***			
	Price	***New Yield***	***New Price***	***% Change***	***Price***	***New Yield***	***New Price***	***% Change***
4	127	4.4	121	– 4.8	127	3.6	134	5.5
5	112	5.5	106	– 5.4	112	4.5	120	7.1
6	100	6.6	93	– 7.0	100	5.4	107	7.0
7	89	7.7	83	– 6.0	89	6.3	96	7.8
8	80	8.8	74	– 7.5	80	7.2	87	8.8

IV. Reinvestment Risk

Total realised compound yield over the life of 8% Bond due 20 years purchased at par (Rs. 100) under varying assumptions relative to the coupon reinvestment rate: Coupon rate is 8% and reinvestment rate is 8% then the normal return is the same as the realised say 8%.

Reinvestment Rate in %	***Total Realised Compound Yield***
4	4.84
6	6.64
8	8.00
10	9.01

Immunisation

They company is required to pay Rs. 36,560.78 in 7 years. Show that this liability will be immunised with Rs. 20,000 of 10-year maturity 9 per cent coupon par value bonds, even if interest rates were to change immediately to — *(i)* 8%, *(ii)* 10%, *(iii)* remains at 9%, and stay at these assumed levels for 7 years.

Answer:

(1) Future value of Rs. 20,000 investment to be determined at all assumed levels of interest for 7 years.

(2) The future value of an ordinary annuity (FVA) is used to determine (1).

(a) If interest rate falls to 8 per cent

F.V. of Interest payments = Total Interest pay × FVIFA (8%.7)

$$= (0.09)\ (20{,}000) \times 8.9228$$

$$= 1{,}800 \times 8.9228 = 16{,}061.04$$

Bond prices (end of years 7), Interest rate of 8%

$$= \frac{1{,}800}{(1.08)^1} + \frac{1{,}800}{(1.08)^2} + \frac{1{,}800 + 20{,}000}{(1.08)^3}$$

$$= 1666.7 + 1543.4 + 17301.5$$

$$= 20{,}511.6$$

$$\text{Total} = 16061.04 + 20{,}511.6 = 36572.6$$

(b) If interest rate rises to 10 per cent

PV of interest payments = Total interest pay × FVIFA (10%,7)

$$= (0.09) \times (20{,}000) \times 9.4872$$

$$= 1800 \times 9.4872 = 17{,}076.96$$

Bond price for end of 7 years

$$= \frac{1,800}{(1.10)^1} + \frac{1,800}{(1.10)^2} + \frac{1,800 + 20,000}{(1.10)^3}$$

$$= 1,636.36 + 1,487.60 + 16,378.66 = 19,502.62$$

$$\text{Total} = 17,076.96 + 19,502.62 = 36,579.58$$

$$= 36,579.58$$

(c) If interest rate remains at 9 per cent:

FV of interest payments = total interest pay × FVA (9%,7)

$$= (0.09)\ (20,000) \times 9.2004$$

$$= 1800 \times 9.2004 = 16,560.72$$

Bond prices (end of year 7)

$$= \frac{1,800}{(1.09)^1} + \frac{1,800}{(1.09)^2} + \frac{1,800 + 20,000}{(1.09)^3}$$

$$= 1,651.38 + 1,515.15 + 16,833.97$$

$$= 20,000$$

$$\text{Total} = 16,560.72 + 20,000 = 36,560.72$$

Note that with the rates of 8 per cent and 10 per cent, there is a small surplus. Duration is only exact for every small changes in interest rates. When interest rates change, so do the bond's M.D., making the duration making strategy an approximated immunisation.

Immunisation

Question:

Suppose that X corporation must make a Rs. 20 lakhs pension fund payment each year for the next 4 years. Determine the average Macaulay duration (MD) for this four year payment liability. Suppose that X corporation decided to immunise the payments by currently investing in zero coupon bond with 2 years and 5 years maturities. What per cent should X allocate to each zero coupon bond? What will be the accumulated face value of the bonds? Assume the yield curve is flat at 11 per cent?

Answer:

The duration of the payments can be determined for treating each payment like a zero coupon bond with a maturity date equal to the maturity date of the payment.

Year	*Payment*	*P.V. of 11%*	*Per cent of Total*	*Payments M.D. (1 × 4)*
1	2	3	4	5
1	Rs. 20 lakhs	18.02	.29	.29
2	Rs. 20 lakhs	16.24	.26	.52
3	Rs. 20 lakhs	14.62	.24	.72
4	Rs. 20 lakhs	13.17	.21	.84
	Total	62.05	1.00	2.37 = MD

[PVIF = (20 ×.9009); (20 × .812); (20 × .731); (20 × .659); (column 3 above)

To determine the immunizing asset allocation, we let *'X'* equal the per cent of the 2 year bonds that are needed. This implies that *(1 – x)* will be the per cent of 5 year bonds because the two weights must sum to 1.

(MD of 2 year bonds) (x) + (MD of 5 year bonds) (1 – x) = 2.37

= (2 years) (x) + (5 years) (1 – x) = 2.37

2x + 5 – 5x = 2.37; 3x = 2.63

$$X = \frac{2.63}{3} = .88 = 88\%;\ 1 - x = 100 - 88 = 12\%$$

∴ 88 per cent of the portfolio will be 2 year bonds and 12 per cent will be 5 year bonds. The duration for a zero coupon bond is equal to its time to maturity.

(A) Present value of bonds: (Total PV = 62.05)

(a) 2 years bonds

0.88 × 62.05 = 54.60

(b) 5 year bonds

0.12 × 62 .05 = 7.45

Total 62.05

(B) Face value of bonds: (yield is 11%)

(a) 2 year bonds is

$54.6 \times (1.11)^2 = 54.6 \times 1.2321 = 67.27$

(*b*) 5 year bond is

$7.45 \times (1.11)^5 = 7.45 \times 1.6851 = 12.54$

Macaulay's Duration

Question:

Determine Macaulay's duration of a bond which has a face value of Rs. 1000 and 8 per cent annual coupon rate, and 4 years to go for maturity. The bonds YTM is 10 per cent?

Answer:

$[C, t/(1 + YTM)^t] + F^T/(1 + YTM)^T$

$= V_o$

C, is the coupon to be received in time t

F_T, is the face value of the bond

V_o, is the present/market value of the bond.

$[80\ t/(1 + .10)] + 1000\ T/(1\ .10)^4$

$= V_o$

The value of Vo is equal to

Year	Cash flow	1/ (1 + YTM) t	(2 × 3)
1	2	3	4
1	80	$.9091 = 1/(1.10)^1$	72.73
2	80	$.8264 = 1/(1.10)^2$	66.11
3	80	$.7513 = 1/(1.10)^3$	60.10
4	80 + 1000	$.6830 = 1/(1.10)^4$	737.64
			V_o = 936.58

Year	pv of C.F.	pv of Cf as proportion	3 × 1= D
1	2	3	4
1	72.73	.0777	.0777
2	66.11	.0705	.1412
3	60.10	.0642	.1926
4	737.64	.7876	3.1504
	936.58	1.00	3.5619

Duration 3.56 years

The Modified Duration for this bond is

$$\text{MMD} = \frac{\text{MD}}{1+\text{Ytm}} = \frac{3.56}{1+0.10} = \frac{3.56}{1.10} = 3.23 \text{ years}$$

Problems in Bonds

The term structure of Interest rates is also called yield curve. This reflects the relationship at a point of time between YTMs of homogeneous Bonds and years to maturity for the bonds. According to Expectations Hypothesis, long-term interest rates are the geometric mean of expected forward or future short-term interest rates. The equation for this can be set out as follows:

$$\text{YTMn} = [(1+\text{YTM}_1)(1+F_{1.2,})(1+F_{2.3})....] - 1$$

putting it in a generalised form

$$\text{Ft, t+n} = \sqrt[n]{\frac{(1+\text{yTM}_{T+N})t+n}{1+\text{yTmt}}} - 1$$

(1) To give an example. Take the following problem: the YTM on a 7 year Bond is 9% and YTM on 10 year Bond is 10.5%. What is the implied average forward rate for a 3 year Bond, starting in 8th year.

Answer:

Using the above equation

$$F_{7,10} = \sqrt[3]{\frac{(1.105)^{10}}{(1.09)^7}} - 1$$

$$= \sqrt[3]{\frac{(2.714)}{(1.828)}} - 1$$

$= \sqrt[3]{1.487} - 1$

$= 1.408 - 1 = 0.1408$

$= 14.1\%$

This is the average for three years namely 8th, 9th and 10th years.

(2) You are given two bonds to choose from namely ZCB of 5 years and 20 years and your target duration is 10 years. How much do you allocate to each Bond to achieve your target duration:

Answer:

ZCB or Zero Coupon Bonds have their duration equal to their maturity.

Assume that you invest X per cent in 5 year Bonds and (1 – x) per cent in 20 year bonds, then the total weight is one.

$5x + 20(1 - x) = 10$

$5x + 20 - 20x = 10$

$15x = 10$

$x = \frac{10}{15} = 0.67\ (67\%)$

$1 - x = 0.33\ (33\%)$

(3) ICL Co. must pay Rs. 25 lakhs at the end of each of next 2 years. Bonds are currently yielding 12%; what is the MD of this liability?

Answer:

Put the data in the following Tabular Form

Year 1	*Liability* 2	*Present value of (2) at 12%* 3	*(3) as % age* 4	*MD (1) × (4)* 5
1st year	Rs. 25 lakhs	$25 \times \frac{1}{1+0.12} =$	22.32 = 53%	0.53 × 1 = 0.53
2nd year	Rs. 25 lakhs	$25 \times \frac{1}{(1+0.12)^3} =$	19.93 = 47%	0.47 × 2 = 0.94
			42.25 = 100	1.47 years

M.D. of this liability is 1.47 years.

In order to immunise the above portfolio a 12% ZCB with a maturity of 1.47 years (or one year 5 months and 19 days roughly) has to be purchased by the ICL Co.

(4) VSTCO has to make the following payments in the next 5 years.

Year 1 - Rs. 10 lakhs, Year 2 - Rs. 9 lakhs,

Year 3 - Rs. 8 lakhs, Year 4 - Rs. 8 lakhs, Year 5 - Rs. 7 lakhs

If the market interest rates are 9% for these maturities, determine the duration of the above liabilities.

Answer:

Assume that all the payments could be tunded by investing in ZCBs with face value equal to the deserved payments. The duration of ZCB is equal to its maturity period.

By putting the data in a Tabular format

Year of payment = 1	*Payment liability = 2*	*Present value of (2) at 9%= 3 (from the tables)*	*(3) as per cent of total = = 4*	*M.D. 1 × 4 = = 5*
1.	10	0.917 = 9.17	0.28	0.28
2.	9	0.842 = 7.58	0.23	0.46
3.	8	0.772 = 6.18	0.18	0.54
4.	8	0.708 = 5.67	0.17	0.68
5.	7	0.650 = 4.55	0.14	0.70
		33.15	1.00	2.66

Weighted average MD is 2.66 years.

If you want to immumise the payments with two ZCBs of 2 years and 3 years maturities, the percentages to be invested in each is as follows: let x be invested in 2 year Bonds and (1 – x) in 3 year Bonds. Then,

$2x + 3(1 - x) = 2.67$

$2x + 3 - 3x = 2.67$

$x = 0.33$; 1/3 rd in 2 year Bonds

$1 - x = 0.67$ 2/3 rd in 3 year Bonds

Bonds Valuation — Problems

Problem

(1) The Company x issued in 1998 bonds of 12% at face value of Rs. 1,000 for a thirty year maturity calculate its YTM.

Answer:

As the bonds are issued at par, the original YTM is the same as coupon rate of 12%.

(2) If the interest rate fell to 10% from 12% by 2003 AD five years hence, what is the price of bond then 30 year bond has coupon payments twice a year and it has 25 years to run.

Answer:

$$V = \sum_{t=1}^{50} \frac{120/2}{\left(1+\frac{0.10}{2}\right)^{50}} + \frac{1000}{\left(1+\frac{0.10}{2}\right)^{50}}$$

$= 60$ (PVIFA 5%, 50,) + 1000 (PVIF 5% 50)

From Tables (PVIFA 5% 50) = 18.2559

(PVIF 5% 50) = .0872

Inserting the values given above

V = 60 (18.256) + 1000 (0.0872)

V = 1095 + 87 = Rs. 1182

(3) Find out the current yield and capital gains on the bond as in 2003 AD, from the data given above.

Answer:

$$\text{Current yield} = \frac{\text{Annual Coupon Payment}}{\text{Price}}$$

$$= \frac{120}{1182} = 10.15\%$$

(4) With a currency of only 10 years more the company x's bonds are sold at Rs. 896.64. What is the YTM at that time?

Answer:

Using the formula

$$896.64 = \frac{60}{(1+ytm/2)^{19}} + \frac{1000}{(1+ytm/2)^{19}}$$

Take the Approximate yield formula for YTM from the Author of this formula namely R.J. Rodriquez.

$$\text{viz., YTM} = \frac{1+\dfrac{M-V}{n}}{(M+2v)/3}$$

$$= \frac{60+(1000-896.64)/19}{(1000+1793.28)\div 3}$$

$$= \frac{65.44}{931.09} = 7.03\% \text{ for Semi-Annual period.}$$

Therefore, the YTM per annum is 14.06% or roughly 14% P.A.

Now let us apply this rate of 14%

V = I (PVIFA 7% 19) + M (PVIF 7% 19)

896.64 = 60 (10.336) + 1000 (0.2765)

From the Tables PVIFA (7% 19) = 10.336 and PVIF (7% 19) = 0.2765

896.64 = 620.14 + 276.50

= 896.64

This confirms that YTM as at end of 2018 - with only 10 years to run is 14%.

Bonds

Question 1

1. If the cash flow each year is Rs. 100 and the principal repayment at the end of 5 years is Rs. 1,000 and current market price is Rs. 960 what is its current yield and what is its YTM?

Question 2

2. If a bond has semi-annual coupon payments of Rs. 50 and the principal payment of Rs. 1,000 in 8 years and a price of Rs. 1,000, what is the duration of the bond, if the yield curve is a flat 10%?

Question 3

3. Given the following data on the three bonds and their duration, construct three different portfolios of these three bonds, each with a duration of 9 years.

Bond	*Duration*
A	5
B	10
C	12

Yields and Macaulay's Duration

Question 1

Determine Macaulays' duration of a bond that has a par value of Rs. 1000 with a coupon rate of 8%. While the remaining period to maturity is 4 years, the YTM is 10%. Determine the modified duration also.

Question 2

Modi Rubber issued a Bond of Rs. 1,000 at a coupon rate of 12%. Interest is payable at annual intervals over a period of 20 years. What is the price of bond if the market rate of interest is 14%. What is the Modified Macaulay's Duration, using the continuous discounting model.

Question 3

A bond with maturity of 10 years has a YTM and coupon rate of 10%. Calculate Macaulay's Duration, using the continuous discounting model.

Question 4

A bond with a par value of Rs. 1,000 and a coupon rate of 8% is sold at Rs. 944.63. If the term to maturity is 4 years, calculate the current yield and YTM.

APPENDIX

Table A.1

Future Value Interest Factor (FVIF)

$FVIF(k,n) = (1+k)^n$

Period n	1%	2%	3%	4%	5%	6%	7%	8%	9%	10%	11%	12%	13%
0	1.000	1.000	1.000	1.000	1.000	1.000	1.000	1.000	1.000	1.000	1.000	1.000	1.000
1	1.010	1.020	1.030	1.040	1.050	1.060	1.070	1.080	1.090	1.100	1.110	1.120	1.130
2	1.020	1.040	1.061	1.082	1.102	1.124	1.145	1.166	1.188	1.210	1.232	1.254	1.277
3	1.030	1.061	1.093	1.125	1.158	1.191	1.225	1.260	1.295	1.331	1.358	1.405	1.433
4	1.041	1.082	1.126	1.170	1.216	1.262	1.311	1.360	1.412	1.464	1.518	1.574	1.630
5	1.051	1.104	1.159	1.217	1.276	1.338	1.403	1.469	1.539	1.611	1.685	1.762	1.842
6	1.062	1.126	1.194	1.265	1.340	1.419	1.501	1.587	1.677	1.772	1.870	1.974	2.082
7	1.072	1.149	1.230	1.316	1.407	1.504	1.606	1.714	1.828	1.949	2.076	2.211	2.353
8	1.083	1.172	1.267	1.369	1.477	1.594	1.718	1.851	1.993	2.144	2.305	2.476	2.658
9	1.094	1.195	1.305	1.423	1.551	1.689	1.838	1.999	2.172	2.358	2.558	2.773	3.004
10	1.105	1.219	1.344	1.480	1.629	1.791	1.967	2.159	2.367	2.594	2.839	3.106	3.395
11	1.116	1.243	1.384	1.539	1.710	1.898	2.105	2.332	2.580	2.853	3.152	3.479	3.836
12	1.127	1.268	1.426	1.601	1.796	2.012	2.252	2.518	2.813	3.138	3.498	3.896	4.335
13	1.138	1.294	1.469	1.665	1.886	2.133	2.410	2.720	3.066	3.452	3.883	4.363	4.898
14	1.149	1.319	1.513	1.732	1.980	2.261	2.579	2.937	3.342	3.797	4.310	4.887	5.535
15	1.161	1.346	1.558	1.801	2.079	2.397	2.759	3.172	3.642	4.177	4.785	5.474	6.254
16	1.173	1.373	1.605	1.873	2.183	2.540	2.952	3.426	3.970	4.595	5.311	6.130	7.067
17	1.184	1.400	1.653	1.948	2.292	2.693	3.159	3.700	4.328	5.054	5.895	6.866	7.986
18	1.196	1.428	1.702	2.026	2.407	2.854	3.380	3.996	4.717	5.560	6.544	7.690	9.024
19	1.208	1.457	1.754	2.107	2.527	3.026	3.617	4.136	5.142	6.116	7.263	8.613	10.197
20	1.220	1.486	1.806	2.191	2.653	3.207	3.870	4.661	5.604	6.728	8,062	9.646	11.523
25	1.282	1.641	2.094	2.666	3.386	4.292	5.427	6.848	8.623	10.835	13.585	17.000	21.231
30	1.348	1.811	2.427	3.243	4.322	5.743	7.612	10.063	13.268	17.449	22.892	29.960	39.116

APPENDIX

Table A.1 (Continued)

Future Value Interest Factor (FVIF)

$FVIF(k,n) = (l+k)^n$

Period n	14%	15%	16%	17%	18%	19%	20%	24%	28%	32%	36%	40%
0	1.000	1.000	1.000	1.000	1.000	1.000	1.000	1.000	1.000	1.000	1.000	1.000
1	1.140	1150	1.160	1.170	1.180	1.190	1.200	1.240	1.280	1.320	1.360	1.400
2	1.300	1.322	1.346	1.369	1.392	1.416	1.440	1.538	1.638	1.742	1.850	1.960
3	1.482	1.521	1.561	1.602	1.643	1.685	1.728	1.907	2.097	2.300	2.515	2.744
4	1.689	1.749	1.811	1.874	1.939	2.005	2.074	2.364	2.684	3.036	3.421	3.842
5	1.925	2.011	2.100	2.192	2.288	2.386	2.488	2.392	3.436	4.007	4.653	5.373
6	2.195	2.313	2.436	2.565	2.700	2.840	2.986	3.635	4.398	5.290	6.328	7.530
7	2.502	2.560	2.826	3.001	3.185	3.379	3.583	4.508	5.629	6.983	8.605	10.541
8	2.853	3.059	3.278	3.511	3.759	4.021	4.300	5.590	7.206	9.217	11.703	14.758
9	3.252	3.518	3.803	4.108	4.435	4.785	5.160	6.931	9.223	12.166	15.917	20.661
10	3.707	4.046	4.411	4.807	5.234	5.695	6.192	8.594	11.806	16.060	21.647	28.925
11	4.226	4.652	5.117	5.624	6.176	6.777	7.430	10.657	15.112	21.199	29.439	40.496
12	4.818	5.350	5.936	6.580	7.288	8.064	8.916	13.215	19.343	27.983	40.037	56.694
13	5.492	6.153	6.886	7.699	8.599	9.596	10.699	16.386	24.759	36.937	54.451	79.372
14	6.261	7.076	7.988	9.007	10.147	11.420	12.839	20.319	31.961	48.757	74.053	111.120
15	7.138	8.137	9.266	10.539	11.974	13.590	15.407	25.196	40.565	64.359	100.712	155.568
16	8.137	9.358	10.748	12.330	14.129	16.172	18.488	31.243	51.923	84.954	136.969	217.795
17	9.276	10.761	12.468	14.426	16.622	19.244	22.186	38.741	66.461	112.139	186.278	30.914
18	10.575	12.375	14.463	16.879	19.673	22.901	26.623	48.039	85.071	148.023	253.338	426.879
19	12.056	14.232	16.777	19.748	23.214	27.252	31.948	59.568	108.890	195.391	344.540	597.630
20	13.743	16.367	19.461	23.106	27.393	32.429	38.338	73.864	139.380	257.916	468.574	836.683
25	26.462	32.919	40.874	50.658	62.669	27.388	95.396	216.542	478.905	1033.590	2180.081	4499.880
30	50.950	66.212	85.850	111.065	143.371	184.675	237.376	634.820	1645.504	4142.075	10143.019	24201.432

Table A.2

Future Value Interest Factor for an Annuity

$$FVIFA\ (k,n) = \frac{(l+K)^{n-l}}{k}$$

Period n	1%	2%	3%	4%	5%	6%	7%	8%	9%	10%	11%	12%	13%
1	1.000	1.000	1.000	1.000	1.000	1.000	1.000	1.000	1.000	1.000	1.000	1.000	1.000
2	2.010	2.020	2.030	2.040	2.050	2.060	2.070	2.080	2.090	2.100	2.110	2.120	2.130
3	3.030	3.060	3.091	3.122	3.152	3.184	3.215	3.246	3.278	3.310	3.342	3.374	3.407
4	4.060	4.122	4.184	4.246	4.310	4.375	4.440	4.506	4.573	4.641	4.710	4.779	4.850
5	5.101	5.204	5.309	5.416	5.526	5.637	5.751	5.867	5.985	6.105	6.228	6.353	6.480
6	6.102	6.308	6.468	6.633	6.802	6.975	7.153	7.336	7.523	7.716	7.913	8.115	8.323
7	7.214	7.434	7.662	7.898	8.142	8.394	8.654	8.923	9.200	9.487	9.783	10.089	10.405
8	8.286	8.583	8.892	9.214	9.549	9.897	10.260	10.637	11.028	11.436	11.859	12.300	12.757
9	9.369	9.755	10.159	10.583	11.027	11.491	11.978	12.488	13.021	13.579	14.164	14.776	15.416
10	10.462	10.950	11.464	12.006	12.578	13.181	13.816	14.487	15.193	15.937	16.722	17.549	18.420
11	11.567	12.169	12.808	13.486	14.207	14.972	15.784	16.645	17.560	18.531	19.561	20.655	21.814
12	12.683	13.412	14.192	15.206	15.917	16.870	17.888	18.977	20.141	21.384	22.713	24.133	25.650
13	13.809	14.680	15.618	16.627	17.713	18.882	20.141	21.495	22.953	24.523	26.212	28.029	29.985
14	14.947	15.974	17.086	18.292	19.599	21.015	22.550	24.215	26.019	27.975	30.095	32.393	34.883
15	16.097	17.293	18.599	20.024	21.579	23.276	25.129	27.152	29.361	31.772	34.405	37.280	40.417
16	17.258	18.639	20.157	21.825	23.657	25.673	27.888	30.324	33.003	35.950	39.190	42.753	46.672
17	18.430	20.012	21.762	23.698	25.840	28.213	30.840	33.750	36.974	40.545	44.501	48.884	53.739
18	19.615	21.412	23.414	25.645	28.132	30.906	33.999	37.450	41.301	45.599	50.396	55.750	61.725
19	20.811	22.841	25.117	27.671	30.539	33.760	37.379	41.446	46.018	51.159	56.939	63.440	70.749
20	22.019	24.297	26.870	29.778	33.066	36.786	40.995	45.762	51.160	57.275	64.203	72.052	80.947
25	28.243	32.030	36.459	41.646	47.727	54.865	63.249	73.106	84.701	98.347	114.413	133.334	155.620
30	34.785	40.568	47.575	56.805	66.439	79.058	94.461	113.283	136.308	164.494	199.021	241.333	293.199

(Continued)

Period n	14%	15%	16%	17%	18%	19%	20%	24%	28%	32%	36%	40%
1	1.000	1.000	1.000	1.000	1.000	1.000	1.000	1.000	1.000	1.000	1.000	1.000
2	2.140	2.150	2.160	2.170	2.180	2.190	2.200	2.240	2.280	2.320	2.360	2.400
3	3.440	3.473	3.506	3.539	3.572	3.606	3.640	3.778	3.918	4.062	4.210	4.360
4	4.921	4.993	5.066	5.141	5.215	5.291	5.368	5.684	6.016	6.362	6.725	7.104
5	6.610	6.742	6.877	7.014	7.154	7.297	7.442	8.048	8.700	9.398	10.146	10.946
6	8.536	8.754	8.977	9.207	9442	9.683	9.930	10.980	12.136	13.406	14.799	16.324
7	10.730	11.067	11.414	11.772	12.142	12.523	12.916	14.615	16.534	18.696	21.126	23.853
8	13.233	13.727	14.240	14.773	15.327	15.902	16.499	19.123	22.163	25.678	29.732	34.395
9	16.085	16.786	17.518	18.285	19.086	19.923	20.799	24.712	29.360	34.895	41.435	49.153
10	19.337	20.304	21.321	22.393	23.521	24.709	25.959	31.643	38.592	47.062	57.352	69.814
11	23.044	24.349	25.733	27.200	28.755	30.404	32.150	40.238	50.399	63.122	78.998	98.739
12	27.271	29.002	30.850	32.824	34.931	37.180	39.580	50.985	65.510	84.320	108.437	139.235
13	32.089	34.352	36.786	39.404	42.219	45.244	48.497	64.110	84.853	112.303	148.475	195.929
14	37.581	40.505	43.672	47.103	50.818	54.841	59.196	80.496	109.612	149.240	202.926	275.300
15	43.842	47.580	51.660	56.110	60.965	66.261	72.035	100.815	141.303	197.997	276.979	386.420
16	50.980	55.717	60.925	66.649	72.939	79.850	87.442	126.011	181.868	262.356	377.692	541.988
17	59.118	65.075	71.673	78.979	87.068	96.022	105.931	157.253	233.791	347.310	514.661	759.784
18	68.394	75.836	84.141	93.406	103.740	115.266	128.117	195.994	300.252	459.449	700.939	1064.697
19	78.969	88.212	98.603	110.285	123.414	138.166	154.740	244.033	385.323	607.472	954.277	1491.576
20	91.025	102.44	115.380	130.033	146.628	165.418	186.688	303.601	494.213	802.863	1298.817	2089.206
25	18.371	212.793	249.214	292.105	342.603	402.042	471.981	898.092	1706.803	3226.844	6053.004	11247.199
30	356.787	434.745	530.321	647.439	790.948	966.712	1181.882	2640.916	5873.231	12940.859	28172.276	60501.081

Table A.3

Present Value Interest Factor

PVIF (k,n) = (l + k)

Period n	1%	2%	3%	4%	5%	6%	7%	8%	9%	10%	11%	12%	13%
0	1.000	1.000	1.000	1.000	1.000	1.000	1.000	1.000	1.000	1.000	1.000	1.000	1.000
1	0.990	0.980	0.971	0.962	0.952	0.943	0.935	0.926	0.917	0.909	0.901	0.893	0.885
2	0.980	0.961	0.943	0.925	0.907	0.890	0.873	0.857	0.842	0.826	0.812	0.797	0.783
3	0.971	0.942	0.915	0.889	0.864	0.840	0.816	0.794	0.772	0.751	0.731	0.712	0.693
4	0.961	0.924	0.889	0.855	0.823	0.792	0.763	0.735	0.708	0.683	0.659	0.636	0.613
5	0.951	0.906	0.863	0.822	0.784	0.747	0.713	0.681	0.650	0.621	0.593	0.567	0.543
6	0.942	0.888	0.838	0.790	0.746	0.705	0.666	0.630	0.596	0.564	0.535	0.507	0.480
7	0.933	0.871	0.813	0.760	0.711	0.665	0.623	0.583	0.547	0.513	0.482	0.452	0.425
8	0.923	0.853	0.789	0.731	0.677	0.627	0.582	0.540	0.502	0.467	0.434	0.404	0.376
9	0.914	0.837	0.766	0.703	0.645	0.592	0.544	0.500	0.460	0.424	0.391	0.361	0.333
10	0.905	0.820	0.744	0.676	0.614	0.558	0.508	0.463	0.422	0.386	0.352	0.322	0.295
11	0.896	0.804	0.722	0.650	0.585	0.527	0.475	0.429	0.388	0.350	0.317	0.287	0.261
12	0.887	0.788	0.701	0.625	0.557	0.497	0.444	0.397	0.356	0.319	0.286	0.257	0.231
13	0.879	0.773	0.681	0.601	0.530	0.469	0.415	0.368	0.326	0.290	0.258	0.229	0.204
14	0.870	0.750	0.661	0.577	0.505	0.442	0.388	0.340	0.299	0.263	0.232	0.205	0.181
15	0.861	0.743	0.642	0.555	0.481	0.417	0.362	0.315	0.275	0.239	0.209	0.183	0.160
16	0.853	0.728	0.623	0.534	0.458	0.394	0.339	0.292	0.252	0.218	0.188	0.163	0.141
17	0.844	0.714	0.605	0.513	0.436	0.371	0.317	0.270	0.231	0.198	0.170	0.146	0.125
18	0.836	0.700	0.587	0.494	0.416	0.350	0.296	0.250	0.212	0.180	0.153	0.130	0.111
19	0.828	0.686	0.570	0.475	0.396	0.331	0.276	0.232	0.194	0.164	0138	0.116	0.098
20	0.820	0.673	0.554	0.456	0.377	0.312	0.258	0.215	0.178	0.149	0.124	0.104	0.087
25	0.780	0.610	0.478	0.375	0.295	0.233	0.184	0.146	0.116	0.092	0.074	0.059	0.047
30	0.742	0.552	0.412	0.308	0.231	0.174	0.131	0.099	0.075	0.057	0.044	0.033	0.026

(Continued)

Period n	14%	15%	16%	17%	18%	19%	20%	24%	28%	32%	36%	40%
0	1.000	1.000	1.000	1.000	1.000	1.000	1.000	1.000	1.000	1.000	1.000	1.000
1	0.877	0.870	0.862	0.855	0.847	0.840	0.833	0.806	0.781	0.758	0.735	0.714
2	0.769	0.756	0.743	0.731	0.718	0.706	0.694	0.650	0.610	0.574	0.541	0.510
3	0.675	0.658	0.641	0.624	0.609	0.593	0.579	0.524	0.477	0.435	0.398	0.364
4	0.592	0.572	0.552	0.534	0.516	0.499	0.482	0.423	0.373	0.329	0.292	0.260
5	0.519	0.497	0.476	0.456	0.437	0.419	0.402	0.341	0.291	0.250	0.215	0.186
6	0.456	0.432	0.410	0.390	0.370	0.352	0.335	0.275	0.277	0.189	0.158	0.133
7	0.400	0.376	0.354	0.333	0.314	0.296	0.279	0.222	0.178	0.143	0.116	0.095
8	0.351	0.327	0.305	0.285	0.266	0.249	0.233	0.179	0.139	0.108	0.085	0.068
9	0.308	0.284	0.263	0.243	0.226	0.209	0.194	0.144	0.108	0.085	0.063	0.048
10	0.270	0.247	0.277	0.208	0.191	0.176	0.162	0.116	0.085	0.062	0.046	0.035
11	0.237	0.215	0.195	0.178	0.162	0.148	0.135	0.094	0.066	0.047	0.034	0.025
12	0.208	0.187	0.168	0.152	0.137	0.124	0.112	0.076	0.052	0.036	0.025	0.018
13	0.182	0.163	0.145	0.130	0.116	0.104	0.093	0.061	0.040	0.027	0.018	0.013
14	0.160	0.141	0.125	0.111	0.099	0.088	0.078	0.049	0.032	0.021	0.014	0.009
15	0.140	0.123	0.108	0.095	0.084	0.074	0.065	0.040	0.025	0.016	0.010	0.006
16	0.123	0.107	0.093	0.081	0.071	0.062	0.054	0.032	0.019	0.012	0.007	0.005
17	0.108	0.093	0.080	0.069	0.060	0.052	0.045	0.026	0.015	0.009	0.005	0.003
18	0.095	0.081	0.069	0.059	0.051	0.044	0.038	0.021	0.012	0.007	0.004	0.002
19	0.083	0.070	0.060	0.051	0.043	0.037	0.031	0.017	0.009	0.005	0.003	0.002
20	0.073	0.061	0.051	0.043	0.037	0.031	0.026	0.014	0.007	0.004	0.002	0.001
25	0.038	0.030	0.024	0.020	0.016	0.013	0.010	0.005	0.002	0.001	0.000	0.000
30	0.020	0.015	0.012	0.009	0.007	0.005	0.004	0.002	0.001	0.000	0.000	0.000

Table A.4

Present Value Interest Factor for an Annuity

$$PVIFA\ (k,n) = \frac{1 - \frac{1}{(l+k)^4}}{k}$$

Period n	1%	2%	3%	4%	5%	6%	7%	8%	9%	10%	11%	12%	13%
0	1.000	1.000	1.000	1.000	1.000	1.000	1.000	1.000	1.000	1.000	1.000	1.000	1.000
1	0.990	0.980	0.971	0.962	0.952	0.943	0.935	0.926	0.917	0.909	0.901	0.893	0.885
2	1.970	1.942	1.913	1.886	1.859	1.833	1.808	1.783	1.759	1.736	1.713	1.690	1.666
3	2.941	2.884	2.829	2.775	2.723	2.673	2.624	2.577	2.531	2.487	2.444	2.402	2.361
4	3.902	3.808	3.717	3.630	3.546	3.465	3.387	3.312	3.240	3.170	3.102	3.037	2.974
5	4.853	4.713	4.580	4.452	4.329	4.212	4.100	3.993	3.890	3.791	3.696	3.605	3.517
6	5.795	5.601	5.417	5.242	5.076	4.917	4.765	4.623	4.486	4.355	4.231	4.111	3.998
7	6.728	6.472	6.230	6.002	5.786	5.582	5.389	5.206	5.033	4.868	4.712	4.564	4.423
8	7.652	7.235	7.020	6.733	6.463	6.010	5.971	5.747	5.535	5.335	5.146	4.968	4.799
9	8.566	8.162	7.786	7.435	7.108	6.802	6.515	6.247	5.995	5.759	5.537	5.328	5.132
10	9.471	8.983	8.530	8.111	7.722	7.360	7.024	6.710	6.418	6.145	5.889	5.650	5.426
11	10.368	9.787	9.253	8.760	8.306	7.887	7.499	7.139	6.805	6.495	6.207	5.938	5.687
12	11.255	10.575	9.954	9.385	8.863	8.384	7.943	7.536	7.161	6.814	6.492	6.194	5.919
13	12.134	11.348	10.635	9.986	9.394	8.855	8.358	7.904	7.487	7.103	6.750	6.424	6.122
14	13.004	12.106	11.296	10.563	9.899	9.295	8.745	8.244	7.786	7.367	6.982	6.628	6.302
15	13.865	12.849	11.938	11.118	10.380	9.712	9.108	8.559	8.060	7.606	7.191	6.811	6.462
16	14.718	13.578	12.561	11.652	10.838	10.106	9.447	8.851	8.312	7.824	7.379	6.971	6.604
17	15.562	14.292	13.166	12.166	11.274	10.477	9.763	9.122	8.544	7.022	7.549	7.120	6.729
18	16.398	14.992	13.754	12.659	11.690	10.828	10.059	9.372	8.756	8.201	7.702	7.250	6.840
19	17.230	13.678	14.324	13.134	12.085	11.158	10.336	9.604	8.950	8.365	7.839	7.366	6.938
20	18.050	16.351	14.877	13.590	12.462	11.470	10.594	9.818	9.128	8.514	7.963	7.469	7.025
25	22.023	19.523	17.413	15.622	14.094	12.783	11.654	10.675	9.823	9.077	8.422	7.843	7.330
30	25.808	22.397	19.600	17.292	15.373	13.765	12.409	11.258	10.274	9.427	8.694	8.055	7.496

(Continued)

Period *n*	*14%*	*15%*	*16%*	*17%*	*18%*	*19%*	*20%*	*24%*	*28%*	*32%*	*36%*
0	1.000	1.000	1.000	1.000	1.000	1.000	1.000	1.000	1.000	1.000	1.000
1	0.877	0.870	0.862	0.855	0.847	0.840	0.833	0.806	0.781	0.758	0.735
2	1.647	1.626	1.605	1.585	1.566	1.547	1.528	1.457	1.392	1.332	1.276
3	2.322	2.283	2.246	2.210	2.174	2.140	2.106	1.981	1.868	1.766	1.674
4	2.914	2.855	2.798	2.743	2.690	2.639	2.589	2.404	2.241	2.096	1.966
5	3.433	3.352	3.274	3.199	3.127	3.058	2.991	2.745	2.532	2.345	2.181
6	3.889	3.784	3.685	3.589	3.498	3.410	3.326	3.020	2.759	2.534	2.339
7	4.288	4.160	4.039	3.922	3.812	3.706	3.605	3.242	2.937	2.678	2.423
8	4.639	4.487	4.344	4.207	4.708	3.954	3.837	3.421	3.076	2.786	2.540
9	4.946	4.772	4.607	4.451	4.303	4.163	4.031	3.566	3.184	2.868	2.603
10	5.216	5.019	4.883	4.659	4.494	4.339	4.193	3.682	3.269	2.930	2.650
11	5.453	5.234	5.029	4.836	4.656	4.486	4.327	3.776	3.335	2.978	2.683
12	5.660	5.197	5.197	4.988	4.793	4.611	4.439	3.851	3.387	3.013	2.708
13	5.842	5.583	5.342	5.118	4.910	4.715	4.533	3.912	3.427	3.040	2.727
14	6.002	5.724	5.468	5.229	5.008	4.802	4.611	3.962	3.459	3.061	2.740
15	6.142	5.847	5.575	5.324	5.092	4.876	4.675	4.001	3.483	3.076	2.750
16	6.265	5.954	5.669	5.405	5.162	4.938	4.730	4.033	3.503	3.088	2.758
17	6.373	6.047	5.749	5.475	5.222	4.990	4.775	4.059	3.518	3.097	2.763
18	6.647	6.128	5.818	5.534	5.273	5.033	4.812	4.080	3.529	3.104	2.767
19	6.650	6.198	5.877	5.584	5.316	5.070	4.844	4.097	3.539	1.109	2.770
20	6.623	6.259	5.929	5.628	5.353	5.101	4.870	4.110	3.546	3.113	2.772
25	6.873	6.464	6.097	5.766	5.467	5.195	4.948	4.147	3.564	3.122	2.776
30	7.003	6.566	6.177	5.829	5.517	5.235	4.979	4.640	3.569	3.124	2.778

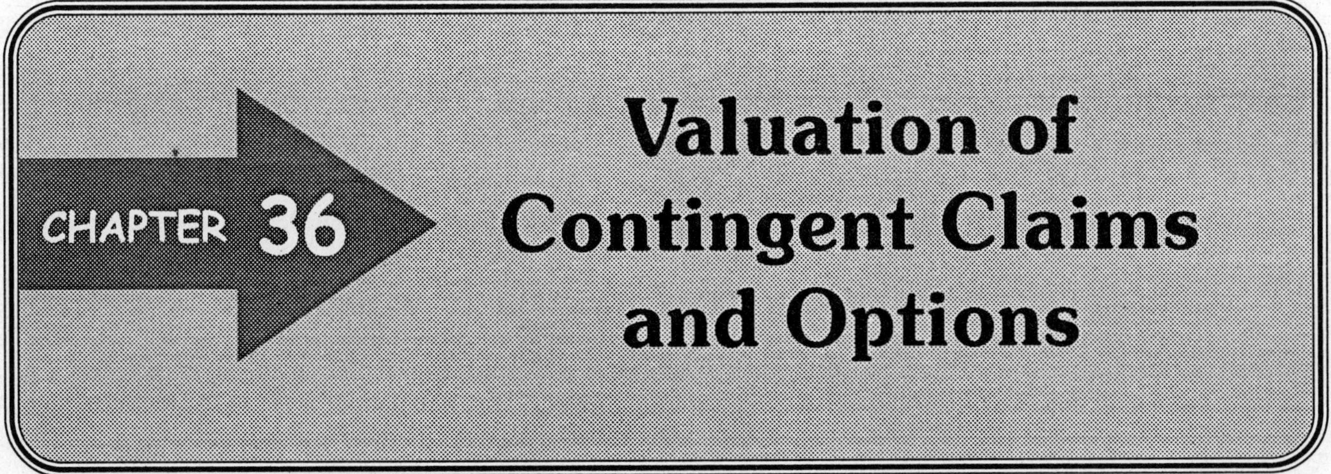

Introduction

Normally, any Company follows the accounting norms in valuation of all the assets and liabilities, as laid down by the Institute of Chartered Accountants. Subject to these guidelines, the accounting practices vary from company to company. When a company is due to pay interest or repay the principal, these become contingent liabilities, due at specified future dates. They are paid out of current revenues if it is interest and out of profits or Debenture Redemption Reserves fund, created for this purpose if it is repayment of principal of debt.

If the contingent liabilities are some dues to be paid to the excise, customs or income tax authorities, or other claims pending, they are shown in the Balance Sheet under Notes or Auditor's Comments. These have to be met as they fall due for payment, and sometimes provisions are made, for them in advance by prudent companies and kept in special accounts. Normally, a company is healthy and liquid if its current assets are two times the current liabilities so that if the current assets are sold as they are, atleast 50% of the book value or market value of current assets can be realised and liabilities can be met in full. Then in the investors' perception, the company is rated as fully solvent for current purposes.

What is Contingent Claim?

Contingent claims due to options, warrants, convertible debentures and similar instruments are different from the ones referred to earlier. These claims arise in the event of the holders of debt instruments opting for equity — a right or option given to them in the above instruments by the company. Then the claim of debtor is to become owner with the following implications:

(1) Tax benefits for interest income as a deductible expense will disappear for the company with its impact on net profits.

(2) The leverage enjoyed through the debt for equity capital may also vanish to the extent that the return on total capital employed is higher than the interest burden on debt and that privilege to trade on borrowed funds will not exist.

(3) Conversion of debt into equity will increase equity base and larger profits have to be earned for servicing this larger equity base.

(4) The cost of servicing equity is higher than servicing debt with the result that the company will have to earn larger profits through larger sales and/better profit margins.

The above factors lead to changes in capital structure, average cost of capital and profitability. On the other hand, a company with larger equity and less debt has the following advantages: (1) Dividends or equity need not be paid if profits are not adequate but interest to creditors has to be paid, (2) The riskiness of the venture will come down due to reduction of debt burden and credit rating will improve for the company, (3) With a larger equity base, the potential for borrowing from banks and financial institutions and even from public at any future date will increase and company can expand and diversify better than before. There are the both plus and minus points in the case of contingent claims.

Pricing of Such Claims

There is no standard method of pricing of such contingent claims. But the erstwhile CCI used some guidelines for fixing the pricing of securities, particularly for equity shares. But in the case of debentures, bonds and debt instruments, they are issued at par, with a face value of Rs. 100, normally except in the cases of discount bonds or Premium Notes.

It is also laid down that if conversion facility is offered the company has to justify the premium or the price fixed to the SEBI before they are issued to the public, but no formulas are presented by the SEBI.

If such claims are partly or fully convertible into equity shares as warrants and loyalty coupons, etc., then the issue of their pricing becomes relevant. The non-convertible part of pure debt instruments is taken at par, while the convertible part is priced as per the normal pricing mechanism of equity shares. This in essence involves first a decision on the part to be converted or the terms of the warrants such as period of time etc. The pricing of warrants and the convertible part of bonds are freely decided by the company and SEBI does not interfere, except for seeking disclosures and justifications for the premium or price fixed.

Free Market Pricing

This is dealt with in a separate chapter but under the current policy of Government free market pricing is permitted for any category of ownership funds. But the norms used by companies or merchant bankers can be set out as follows:

(1) SEBI has permitted differential pricing if the company is going for rights cum public issue, with separate prices for rights to the existing shareholders from that offered under public issue.

(2) In case of FCD, PCD etc., with convertibles or warrants pricing for convertible portion is again freely decided by the company, subject to their confidence of acceptability by the public and justification to the SEBI. The principle adopted, as in foreign markets, is what the market can bear, or what investors perceive as reasonable for investment.

(3) In practice, the price fixation is based on the past price record of the share and its future projection based on some bench marks like EPS and P/E multiple.

(4) The average of the market prices for the last three years is one criteria if it is already listed and traded.

(5) The book value and earnings per share (EPS) and projection of its future price based on P/E multiple for the industry or for comparable companies are also sometimes taken into account.

What is a Convertible Security?

A convertible security is a bond or debenture or preferred stock that can be converted into equity of a company. The original security is a debt instrument, which can be converted into an ownership instrument, after a time. The period of holding necessary for conversion, the ratio of conversion and other terms including the price are to be laid down in the beginning itself. Once the conversion terms are stated, they cannot be altered by the company unilaterally.

The SEBI guidelines cover all the categories of convertible instruments and new financial products like warrants, loyalty coupons etc. As per these guidelines, a company can issue three types of debentures as debt instruments, viz.:

(*a*) *Fully Convertible Debentures:* These are fully convertible into equity in phases at predetermined times, say 6 months or 12 or 18 months etc., and the terms of conversion including the conversion price are to be spelt out in the beginning itself including the compulsory nature of conversion. The company decides the periods and prices, at which they will be converted into equity. They may be converted in instalments or all at one instalment. Thus, fully convertible debentures can be converted in two instalments of 50% for 6 months hence and the other 50% at the end of 12 months or in three or more instalments such as 25% of the total each time.

If the conversion period is within 18 months, these amounts will be treated as good as equity, as per the SEBI guidelines, for the purposes of debt equity Ratio and other legal and procedural requirements since withdrawn in March 1998. They do not have to follow the guidelines applicable to debt, namely, bonds or debentures, which are not convertible. FCDs with a conversion period of more than 36 months are not permissible to be issued except under special terms. Instruments of less than 18 months have to be treated as debt for the purpose of rating by Credit Rating Agencies.

(*b*) *Partly Convertible Bonds:* These are the second category of debt which are convertible in part while the rest is non-convertible. Thus, a debt instrument can have a face value of Rs. 100 of which Rs. 60 is convertible at the end of 12 months at a specified price and in specific convertible ratio such as two equity shares for Rs. 60, each of Rs. 30, (for a share of face value of Rs. 10 and with a premium of Rs. 20). As the market price may be ruling higher than Rs. 30 per equity share, the conversion facility will appear attractive to the investors. During the first year, the bondholder gets interest at a fixed rate of say 14% and after that Rs. 60 out of Rs. 100 (for each bond) will become two equity shares on which dividend will be paid, if declared out of profits at the end of second year. Thus, it has the advantage of both debt and equity.

The rest of 40% will remain as debt only and will continue to get interest at the specified coupon rate of 14% for the rest of its life, until redemption. As per the Companies Act and the Rules made thereunder all debt instruments say, bonds or debentures can have a maturity period of 5 to 7 years, extendable upto nine years in some cases, after which redemption becomes compulsory. Any such non-convertible bonds can be renewed, if the company wants after maturity at the specific written consent of the investors only.

(*c*) *Non-Convertible Bonds (NCDs):* The third category of debt instruments is the non-convertible debentures called N.C.D. (also called khokhas for the non-convertable portion). This category will have to be held until the maturity or redemption date after 5 to 9 years. It is entitled to only interest per annum, payable half yearly or once in a year. This category is pure debt while the first category of fully convertible debentures is as good as equity and the second category is partly debt and partly ownership capital. All the above categories are to have specific terms, spelt out in the beginning itself before investors decide to put in their funds. No debt instrument or bond can be issued in India without redemption, under the law.

Valuation of Rights Shares

Companies can also issue rights shares which are a right to buy the equity shares of the company given at par or a premium to the existing shareholders in a particular proportion to their holdings. Under Section 81 of Companies Act, companies issuing further capital after two years of the formation of the company or after one year of the first allotment of the shares have to offer the same as rights to the existing shareholders.

The premium used to be fixed on the basis of the average book value of the company and post-tax earning capacity of the shares normally capitalised at 15% and even at 8% if the market price is substantially higher than the fair price. The average of the two prices worked out on the basis of book value and the earning capitalisation model is accepted. If earnings for share is Rs. 3 and capitalisation rate is 15%, then the fair price is 3/15 × 100 = 20 according to the earnings capitalisation formula. The price on the basis of book value is, say, Rs. 30.[1] Then the average of these two prices Rs. 20 and Rs. 30, namely, Rs. 25 is taken as the fair price for fixing the premium (namely, Rs. 15 on a share with the face value of Rs. 10).[2]

The rights are quoted in the market. The price of the rights will depend on the ratio on which they are issued. If the ratio is 1:3 and the market price is Rs. 50, then valuation of rights is done as follows:

Let the premium be Rs. 15, then,

$$\frac{150 + 25}{4} = \frac{175}{4} = 44$$

The value of one right is Rs. 44 – 25 = 19 which is got for three shares (Rs. 6.33 for one existing share).

Rights can be issued only if authorised by a special resolution of the company. The company making the rights has to inform the existing shareholders as to the use to which the additional funds are put, the future earning capacity of the company and other financial indicators such as sales, estimated gross profit or loss, etc. This information would enable the shareholders to decide to opt for the rights or not.

1. Book value is networth of the company divided by the number of equity shares.
2. The method of premium fixation adopted by the erstwhile CCI is given already.

Preference Shares

Preference shares are of a hybrid category having ownership rights like equity and also a fixed income like creditor capital. They have preferred rights for payment of dividend, along with arrears, if any, if such provision is made in the Articles of Association. They are paid their fixed dividend before any dividend is declared to the equityholders. Besides they have also similar preferential right over equity to payment of capital and their share of assets in the event of winding up of the company. This right is, however, subject to the claims of creditors.

This instrument is suitable to some investors who would like to take some risk but not as much as equityholders but more than debenture-owners. They get an income which may, however, fluctuate depending upon the profits of the company but fixed, if profits are adequate to service all preference and equityholders. They may also get back their capital after a fixed period like debentures as per the present law.

The return on preference shares is fixed by the Government at 14% since April 1987 although some companies offer a higher or lower rate with the permission of the government. The preference shareholders do not enjoy any voting rights except in respect of resolution affecting their rights or when their dividends due are in arrears for the past two financial years.

There are various types of preference shares like redeemable and non-redeemable, cumulative and non-cumulative, participating and non-participating and convertible and non-convertible.

Preference shares are redeemable generally after 12 years and for this purpose, the company is required to provide for transfer out of profits a sum to the reserves called Capital Redemption Reserve. If there is no provision to redeem these shares, they are non-redeemable. As these non-redeemable shares were not popular, they were abolished by the Companies Amendment Act of 1988.

Preference shares which have a right to receive dividends in a cumulative fashion are called cumulative preference shares. These enjoy the right to receive dividends in all the years in which the dividends are skipped, as profits were inadequate in those years. The fixed dividend on preference shares should be paid later in a cumulative way when profits are adequate before any dividends are declared for equityholders. Those which have no such right are called non-cumulative preference shares.

Preference shares are convertible, if there is a provision for their conversion into equity after a specified period in a particular ratio to the existing equity shares. Preference shares may not be convertible if no such provision is made. Preference shares are participating, if they can share in profits in excess of a guaranteed fixed return, if such a provision is made in the Articles of the company and specify the level of profitability such as an equity dividend of 20%. If these are not so participative, they are called non-participating.

C.C.Ps

A new instrument called Cumulative Convertible Preference Shares was introduced by the Government in 1985, the features of which are as follows:

(1) The CCPs can be issued by any public limited company to raise finance for new projects, expansion and diversification, etc.

(2) The amount of issue of CCP will be to the extent of the equity issue to the public for subscription.

(3) The dividend payable is fixed at 10%.

(4) The entire issue of CCP would be convertible into equity shares between three and five years.

These issues have not proved popular with the companies as the dividend on their shares is not a tax deductible item as in the case of interest on debentures. Besides, the dividend of 10% for the first 3 to 5 years has not proved attractive to investors.

But preference shares as a class are attractive to institutions and individuals in the high income brackets as the dividend income on them is tax exempt under Section 80L unlike interest income on debentures and company deposits. But companies themselves do not find these preference shares as an attractive alternative to raise funds, except in the special conditions when the company is unable to raise funds from fresh equities from the public or in the form of rights.

Legal Provisions

The Companies Act provides for issue of debentures, warrants and other bearer certificates, under Sections 114 to 120. These instruments may provide for an entitlement to the holder a specified number of equity shares. If these debentures or bonds are not convertible into equity or are not converted, the debenture or bondholder has no voting rights in the company and does not become an owner. But debenture holders are represented by the debenture Trustee in the meetings of equityholders (AGM or EGM). They are entitled under the Act, for asking for transfers and for Copies of Annual Reports. In respect of registers to be maintained under Sections 15 and 152 of the Companies Act, the debenture holders are treated alike as shareholders. The closure of registers, the procedure for transfers of debentures are all similar to those of equity shares.

The SEBI has also laid down that in the event of declaration of bonus by a company with convertible debentures or bonds, due for conversion within 12 months, provision has to be made to protect the rights of such holders to equity and subsequently to bonus, declared during the year. Convertible bonds thus enjoy some specific privileges and incentives.

Norms for N.C.D. and Non-Convertible Portion of P.C.D.

These are pure debt instruments and are governed by norms of issue laid by SEBI. Briefly all debentures are to be credit rated for risk element involved and the capacity of the company to redeem the principal and service the creditors with interest etc.

These debt instruments can be issued subject to the following conditions:

(a) They are to be compulsorily redeemed. Debentures issued for working capital should not exceed 20% of total current Assets.

(b) Debt to equity ratio should normally be 2:1 ratio, except for some capital-intensive projects.

(c) They are creditors of the company and cannot therefore attend the AGMs of the company. But their interests are protected under a debenture Trust Deed.

(d) All debt or debenture issues should be covered by a Trust Deed and a debenture Trustee is appointed to operate under the Trust deed, which governs the relations of the company and debentureholders. The Trust deed and debenture Trustee have to be approved by the SEBI.

(e) The company has to complete the above formalities within 6 months from the date of allotment of debentures and/or despatch of debenture certificates.

(f) The company has to create a Debenture Redemption Reserve Fund (DRR), out of the profits of the company, after the commercial production started. These reserves should reach a stage of 50% of the total debenture amount, before it can be used to redeem the debentures. Besides, their use can be started for repayment purposes, after the company has already redeemed at least 10% of the outstanding amount due from out of the current profits.

Conversion Value

Conversion value of a convertible security is the conversion ratio[@] of the security, times the market price, per share. Conversion price is the price at which the debenture will be converted into equity. If it is a convertible debenture, it has to be compulsorily converted at the specific price and time which should have been specified in the terms of issue.

If the present market price of Satyam Comp is Rs. 260 and the conversion price is fixed at Rs. 250, the premium on conversion is Rs. 10 (260 – 250). The minimum period of holding or conversion time is fixed at the beginning of issue and normally converted on allotment, six months hence etc. If the actual price is Rs. 280 in the market, the investor gains a premium of Rs. 280 – 250 = Rs. 30 per share. If the debenture amount is Rs. 500 and is to be converted into equity shares at Rs. 250 each, two equity shares will be allotted to him and his total premium is Rs. 60 per debenture.

@ Conversion ratio of 1 : 2 means that a holder of one debenture is given two equity shares. Then market price of equity shares is to be multiplied by two to arrive at Conversion Value.

If the debenture is a convertible one, the right to call before conversion by the company is not given, but the call provision may be incorporated in case of N.C.D. or bonds.

In the case of NCD, or non-convertible bond, the company is allowed to offer a premium upto 5%, on the face value, at the time of redemption, as an incentive for holding the debenture until maturity.

Conversion Premium

As already referred, convertibles enjoy the benefit of a premium on conversion. If market price is say Rs. 280 and conversion price is Rs. 250, the premium enjoyed is Rs. 30. If suppose the market price has fallen to Rs. 220, there is no incentive to holders of convertibles on conversion. To offset such contingencies SEBI has permitted conversion only at an incentive price and not at a disincentive. Thus, whatever the market price, a company can offer conversion at the book value/face value or at a discount of Rs. 20 or so on market price.

In some cases, the option of Call and Put is given to the holders of convertibles, if the period of conversion is after 36 months. Compulsion of conversion is only provided for, if it is made immediately on allotment, so that the market price and intrinsic value of share are all known and the premium on conversion is ensured. For all conversions, after the allotments, substantial discounts are provided for in the conversion terms. If the debenture is NCD, provision for buy back at face value through a financial institution or a lead bank is made, so that investors do not lose in the capital value of bond due to fall in its price, after allotment.

PRICING OF CONVERTIBLES

Valuation of Convertibles

Whether it is a bond or debenture with an option of convertibility or compulsory conversion at the end of a perid of time, the value of that bond or debenture is related firstly to the value of *equity* into which it can be converted and secondly to the value of residual non-convertible portion of the debenture instrument, which remains as debt instrument.

Both the above components vary with the market conditions, time to expiry of the bond, prevailing interest rates or yields, etc. Let us take the first component of convertible bond convertible into equity (say C_1). This C_1 depends on the number of equity shares into which that convertible portion can be converted. The face value of bond say Rs. 75, convertible into 5 equity shares at Rs. 15 each. The bond face value is, normally Rs. 100 of which Rs. 75 is convertible at the end of three years into 5 equity shares at Rs. 15 per share, the residual Rs. 25 will remain as bond and carry coupon rate of 12%, payable annually (here denoted as C_2). Thus, Bond face value Rs. 100 consists of two components namely $C_1 + C_2$.

For the First Three Years Rs. 100, the face value of the Bond carries with it an interest return of 12% per bond. At the end of three years, Rs. 75 is converted into 5 equity shares. If the market price is Rs. 20 and exercise price for conversion is Rs. 15, then the convertible portion gains by Rs. 5 per share, say a total gain of 25 (5 X 5). Besides for the next two years, equity shares may show capital gains or losses plus dividends, if any declared for the rest of the period to maturity. The non-convertible portion of the Bond earns 12% per year namely, Rs. 4 on Rs. 25 of the Bond of Rs.100.

Graphical Presentation

The price of the convertible bond and the conversion value of the bond are related by the equation $C_1 = \frac{F}{Pc} \times Ps$, where, F is the principal vlaue of the Convertible Bond; Pc conversion price into equity. Ps Market price of equity.

Upto Rs. 15, the exercise price or the conversion price is the same as the market price. Thus, Pc = Ps; then $C_1 = F$, and the value convertible bond is the same as the market price.

If Ps is greater than Pc, that is, if market price is more than conversion price, then C_1 is greater than F. If Pc > Ps, that is, if conversion price of 15 is more than the market price (say Rs. 10), then the $C_1 < F$. In the graph below, conversion value is shown on the Y-axis and price of equity share is represented on the X-axis.

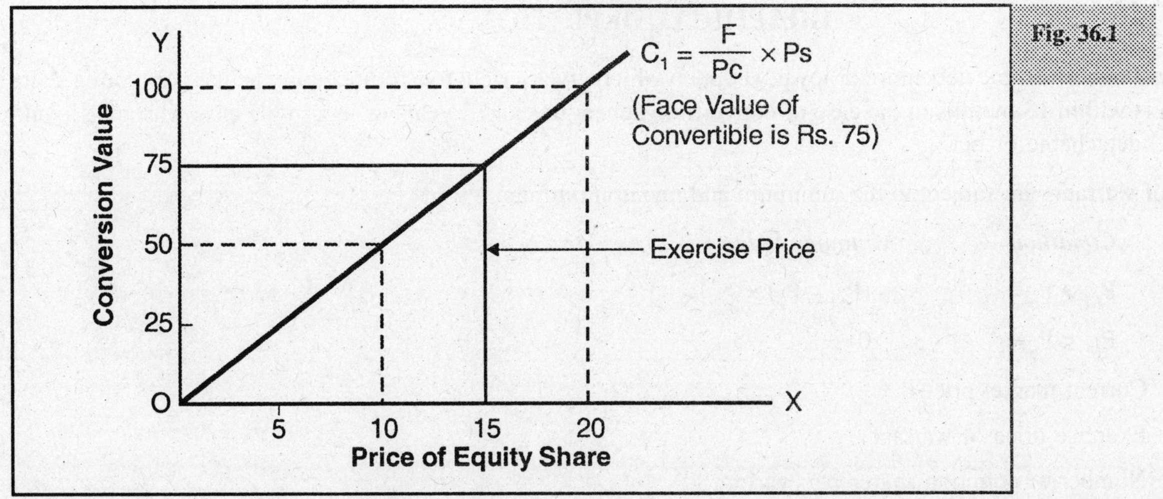

Fig. 36.1

If the price of equity in the market is Rs. 20, then the conversion value is Rs. 100 as against the face value of Rs. 75. During the first three years, when conversion has not become exercisable, it is as good as debt but the conversion value of the convertible bond will go up and down over the face value of Rs. 75 and after that, it depends on the market price of equity for 5 equity shares.

Suppose the conversion portion of the Bond is Rs. 75 and the non-conversible bond is Rs. 25; if total bond value is Rs. 125, as against face value of bond of Rs. 100. The conversion value of convertible debenture sets the minimum market price of the convertible bond. If actual market price is higher, then arbitraguers operate and buy equity shares and short sell the convertible bond. If the actual market price of the bond is less than its value as equity, the Arbitraguers will purchase the bond and sell short the equity and the shares later purchased through the bond would cover the short sale of equity.

To give an example, the convertible bond may be selling at Rs. 60, when the equity based price is Rs. 75 based on Rs. 15 as exercise price for 5 equity shares, then arbitraguers will buy the convertible bond at Rs. 60 and exercise the option to get 5 equity shares at Rs. 15. The short position taken by the buyer will be covered by conversion option in which he makes a profit of Rs. 15.

The supply and demand factors operate to determine the price of the convertible bond, but is basically dependent on the conversion value of the convertible bond. Normally, the convertible has also a debt component, namely Rs. 25 and hence its actual price will be Rs. 60 + 25 = Rs. 85 and at the exercise price of Rs. 15, the bondholder gets Rs. 75 + 25 = 100. Then the conversion bond quotes at a premium over its face value, if the conversion value of the bond is less than the market price of corresponding equity shares.

Role of Interest Rate

As regards the convertible bond, the coupon rate offered on it is generally lower than the market rate offered on non-convertible bonds of comparable maturity. The reason is that such bonds are quoted at a premium due to the value added incentive following from the conversion facility. The value of bond as debt, is lower than that of the convertible bond which includes partly equity component and partly debt component. Since interest paid on convertible debenture is fixed, the value of this bond varies inversely with interest rate. The higher is the interest rate, with coupon rate fixed at say 12½%, the lower is the value of the convertible bond, for the same degree of risk and maturity. The market operators would buy convertible bond to attain the higher yield, if its price is lower than that floor. The operators can not force down the price any more beyond the floor price of the non-convertible debt, even if the value of the equity into which the convertible portion is to be converted were to decline. The reason is that at the floor point the whole Bond value is treated as equal to debt which sets the floor, but at the peak level, the limit is set by the market price of equity and conversion value of the convertible bond plus the face value of the non-convertible portion of the convertible bond. There is thus insurance at the floor level but with opportunity of gain the upper end of the bond price.

GRAPHICAL DEPICTION

A warrant or convertible debenture or loyalty coupon which gives a right to a future equity is like non-voting share, if conversion is within 18 months in the case of convertible debentures and 3 years or less in the case warrants, loyalty coupons, etc., detachable or not.

Prices of warrants are subject to the minimum and maximum limits.

Condition	*Minimum Value*
$P_M > P_e =$	$(P_M - P_e) \times N$
$P_M < P_e =$	0

P_M = Current market price

P_e = Exercise price of warrant

N = Number of common shares per warrant

Minimum value of warrant is zero, if market price is less than or equal to the exercise price. The maximum value is $P_M \times N$. The discussion assumes that there is a market for the warrants and they are detachable. The minimum exercise price may be the book value or something based on intrinsic value of the share. The maximum price is the market price. This is shown graphically below. The actual value lies along the dotted line in between the minimum and maximum values.

Fig. 36.2

Slope of Pe depends on the number of shares exchanged.

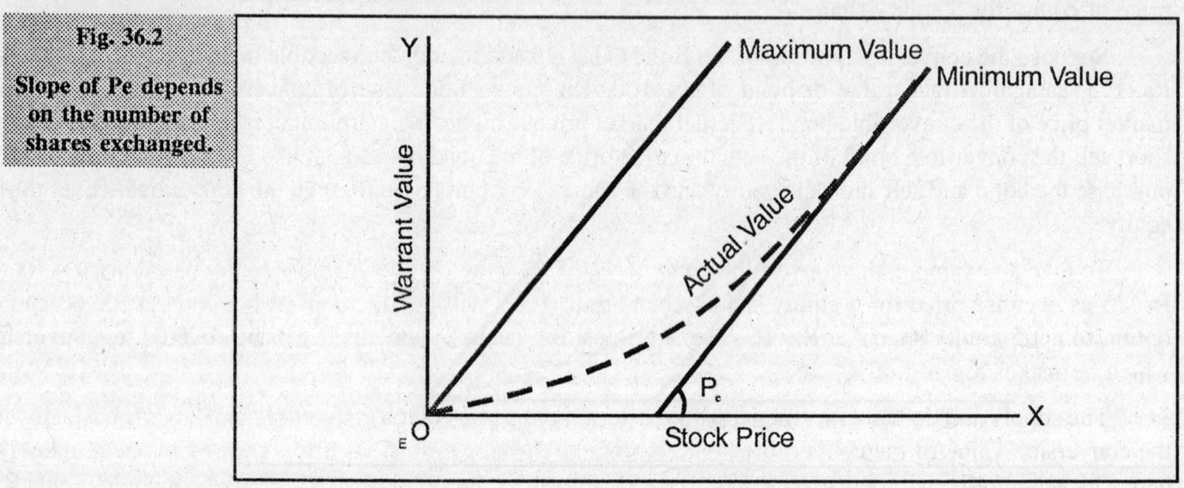

Convertible bond is assumed to be tradeable and has a market value. So is the case with convertible preference shares. It has both investment value and conversion value. Investment value (straight value) is based on the ytm in respect of a bond and dividend on preferred stock, in respect of Convertible Preference Share. Investment value is the face value for bonds; which is the minimum payable to bondholders. The investment value of CPS is $V = \frac{D}{\gamma}$, where D is dividend for preferred stock, and γ is the current yield or appropriate discount rate. For Bonds, we take ytm, instead of γ, for straight value. The conversion value will change with the market price. If the bond can be exchanged for 20 shares, and market price of each is 55, then the conversion value = 55 × 20 = Rs. 1,100.

Investment value = Rs. 1,000

Market Stock price = Rs. 55 and

Market Bond price = Rs. 1,200.

Graphically, the values and market premium for a convertible bond are shown below:

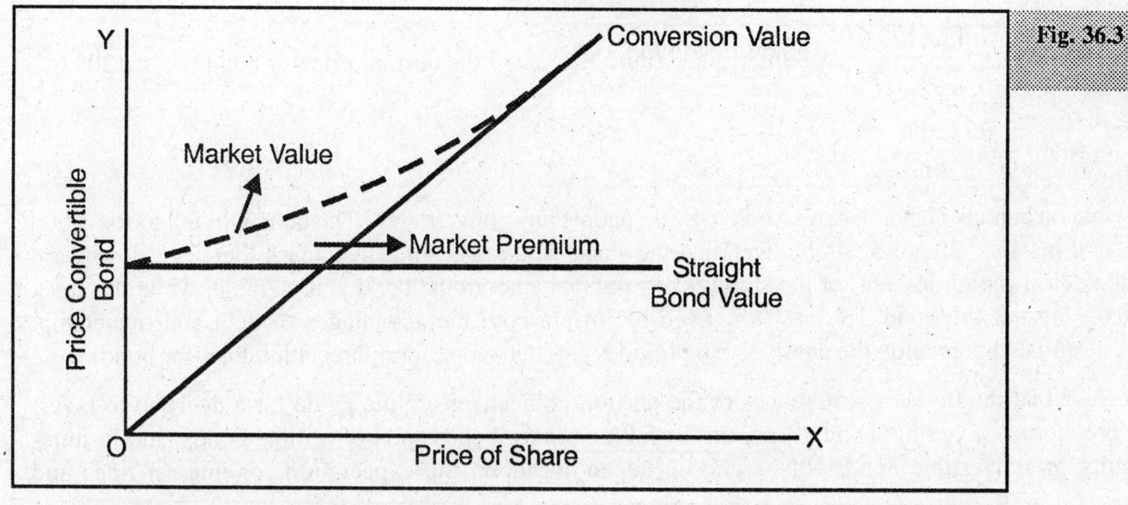

Fig. 36.3

(*i*) Premium over conversion value is

$$= \frac{\text{Bond Price} - \text{Conversion Value}}{\text{Conversion Value}}$$

(*ii*) Premium over Investment value is

$$= \frac{\text{Bond Price} - \text{Investment Value}}{\text{Bond Price}}$$

(*iii*) Conversion parity price of stock

$$= \frac{\text{Bond price}}{\text{No. of shares on conversion}}$$

Examples

Premium over conversion value

$$\text{Rs.} \frac{1200 - 1100}{1100} = \frac{100}{1100} = 9.09\%$$

This suggests that the stock must rise by about 9.09% for the breakeven point to be reached. If stock price is 55, then Rs. 55 + .0909 (55) = Rs. 60

Conversion parity of the stock is also the same, namely,

$$= \frac{1200}{20} = \text{Rs. } 60$$

Premium over Investment value is calculated as,

$$\frac{1200 - 1000}{1200} = 16.67$$

This means that bond can fall in price by 16.67%, if the stock price fell and this provides floor price of bond. Suppose the stock price fell to Rs. 40. The conversion value is Rs. 40 × 20 = Rs. 800 but the bond floor price may remain at Rs. 1000.

In the trading of convertibles, one has to look into the current yields on stock and bonds. Suppose the underlying stock is selling at Rs. 55 and annual dividend is Rs. 1.65, then

Current yield on stock = $\frac{1.65 \times 100}{55}$ = 3%. Interest on Bond is 6% and the current price of bond is Rs. 1200.

Current yield on Bond = $\frac{60 \times 100}{1200}$ = 5%

If the current yield on bond is higher than on stock, why do people buy convertibles? The bond will fall to Rs. 1,000 only and not to Rs. 800 [as 40 × 20 is Rs. 800] even when the stock falls to Rs. 40. This means there is a downward protection for bondholder in capital losses. For the strategy of principal amount the bond is preferable; while the stock can fall to any extent, but not the bond. Besides, a convertible offers both the advantages of debt and ownership. However, if there is a capital appreciation the equity stock provides a better scope for appreciation than for bond.

It will thus be seen that the investor preferences or the portfolio objectives are the guide for a decision to invest in Common Stock, bond or a convertible bond. In periods of falling prices, bonds and convertible bonds, and in times of rising prices equity or convertible bond will be chosen depending upon the expectations of interest rates and market prices.

Brigham's Model on Convertible Bonds[@]

The risk-return features of convertible bonds vary widely. The factors which influence them are the coupon rate until conversion, number of years to convertibility and the expected market discount rate. Bondholder invests in the bond as a hedge against risk for the time being until conversion and appreciation on conversion. The return which the bondholder expects is the discount rate which equates the sum of the annual interest payment till the year of conversion and the terminal conversion value in year (N). The equation for the Bond price if it is convertible is

$$M = \sum_{t=1}^{n} \frac{I}{(1+k)^t} + \frac{Tv}{(1+k)^n}$$

M = Price of bond

Tv = Conversion value if converted

I = Interest received yearly

N = Number of years of holding (t = 1 to n)

K = Discount rate expected

This is graphically explained by Brigham, as shown below:

Fig. 36.4

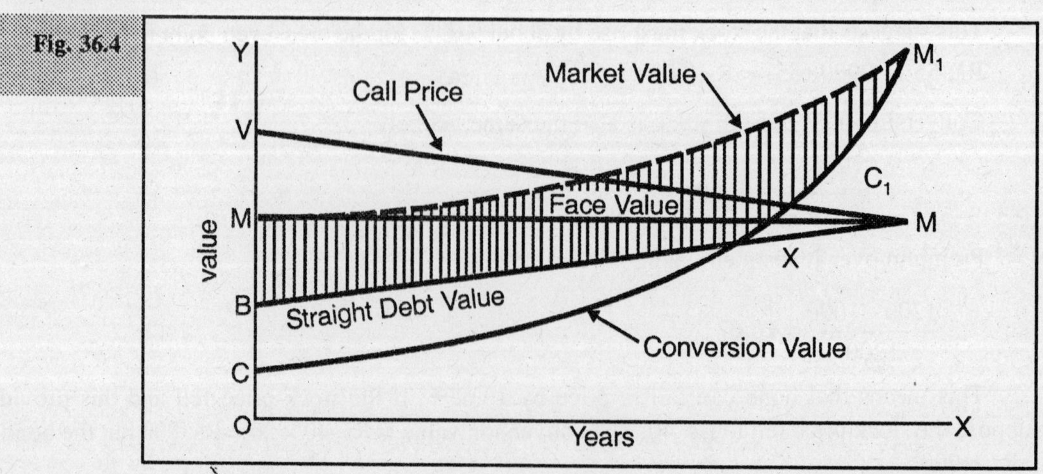

@ Brigham, "An Analysis of Convertible Debentures: Theory and Some Empirical Evidence" —*Journal of Finance*, March, 1966.

Take 12% Convertible Debenture of Tatas — 14% Market Return

MM = Face value = 100

B × M = Straight Debt value

M is Maturity Date

MM_1 Market Price

$C \times C_1$ is conversion value of convertible bond. It is assumed that equity stock price of the corresponding bond is growing at a constant price and $C \times C_1$ rises accordingly every year, until bond is called for conversion — MM_1 is the market price of bond, and this will rise with time in a similar manner as conversion value, $C \times C_1$, but the latter rises faster as time approaches for call or conversion.

Premium is shown by the shaded area say BMM_1 (as shown in the graph).

VM is the call price to be paid if the company redeems before maturity and not converted. VM line falls, as it approaches maturity and joins M, on the final date and disappears. Call price is more than the face value, to give incentive for the bondholder to surrender bonds before maturity and not converted. VM line falls, as it approaches maturity and as maturity approaches, the difference narrows down to zero on the date of maturity. On the call date, market value and conversion value become the same. If the bond is not called, it is paid at maturity or converted into stock. Both these alternatives are not as good as call.

The decline in call premium shows VM is downward sloping.

Premium is shown by the shaded area in the graph, Bx, as straight debt value. The premium on the bond will disappear, if it is to be called or if it is converted. The graph shows that the conversion value goes sharply up, as it approaches the conversion time (M_1).

In practice premium on conversion from bond to equity will offset the lower interest rate offered on convertible bonds and hence they are more attractive than bonds which are not convertible.

It will thus be seen that there is no simple formula for fixation of price for warrants, loyalty coupons and incentives offered by companies, selling debt instruments to public. Some salient features can however, be stated. First, the warrant will entitle the holder to equity shares at a price lower than the market price — allowing a conversion premium. Second, warrant gives an option to the holder to buy the shares or for a specified amount of money. These warrants have only rights and no obligations and will not put the holder to any loss. It has only incentive value and disincentive is not allowed as per the SEBI guidelines.

VALUATION OF OPTIONS

Basically, the value of option is related to the value of the underlying security. The value differs with time before the expiration and at expiration. The value of the stock option has three different zones, as shown below:

(*i*) *Out of the Money:* Where the stock price is below the exercise price.

(*ii*) *At the Money:* Where it is close to or at the exercise price.

(*iii*) *In the Money:* Where the stock price is above the exercise price.

These zones are depicted in the chart below:

Fig. 36.5

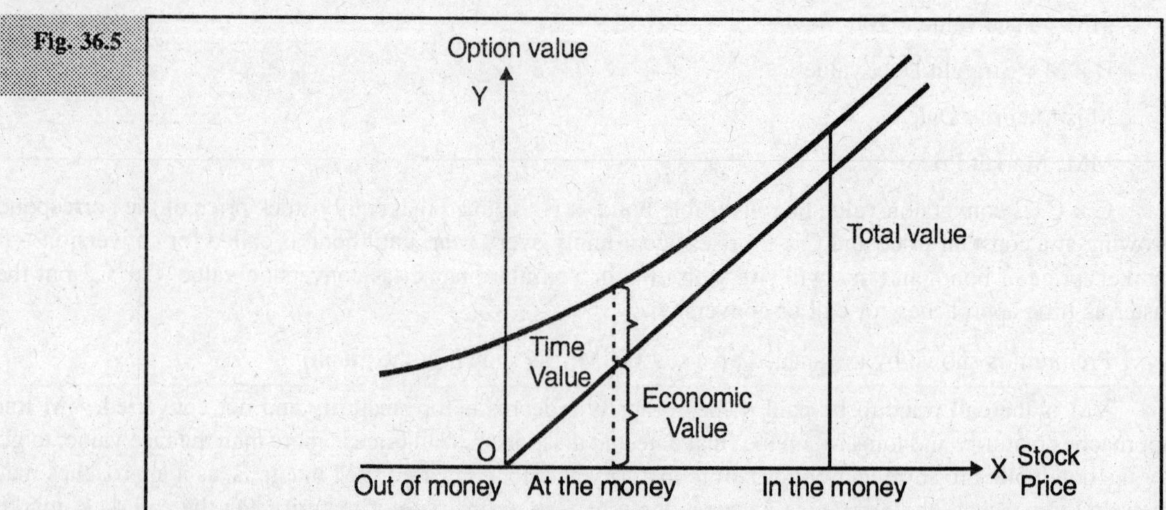

Say the exercise price is Rs. 60. If the stock price is below 60, there is no economic value below the point 'O' in the Fig. 36.5. There is only time value; if stock price starts above Rs. 60 it will have both economic value and time value. As seen from the chart time value is maximum, when the exercise price and stock price are the same but is lower below the exercise price or above it. If the actual price is lower than the exercise price there is less chance of profit on the call. If the actual price is above the exercise price, then there is a chance of profit, and there is less reason to pay a premium over the economic value (intrinsic value).

Factors Affecting the Option Value

There are normally several factors which influence the option value. The more important of them are: (1) expected variance in price or return of the underlying stock, (2) the time to expiration, (3) the level of interest rates, and (4) the dividends and fundamentals of the stock. Leaving aside the fundamentals of the stock and dividends paid, which will generally be reflected in the actual stock price, the influence of other factors are explained in the diagrams below: (Fig. 36.6)

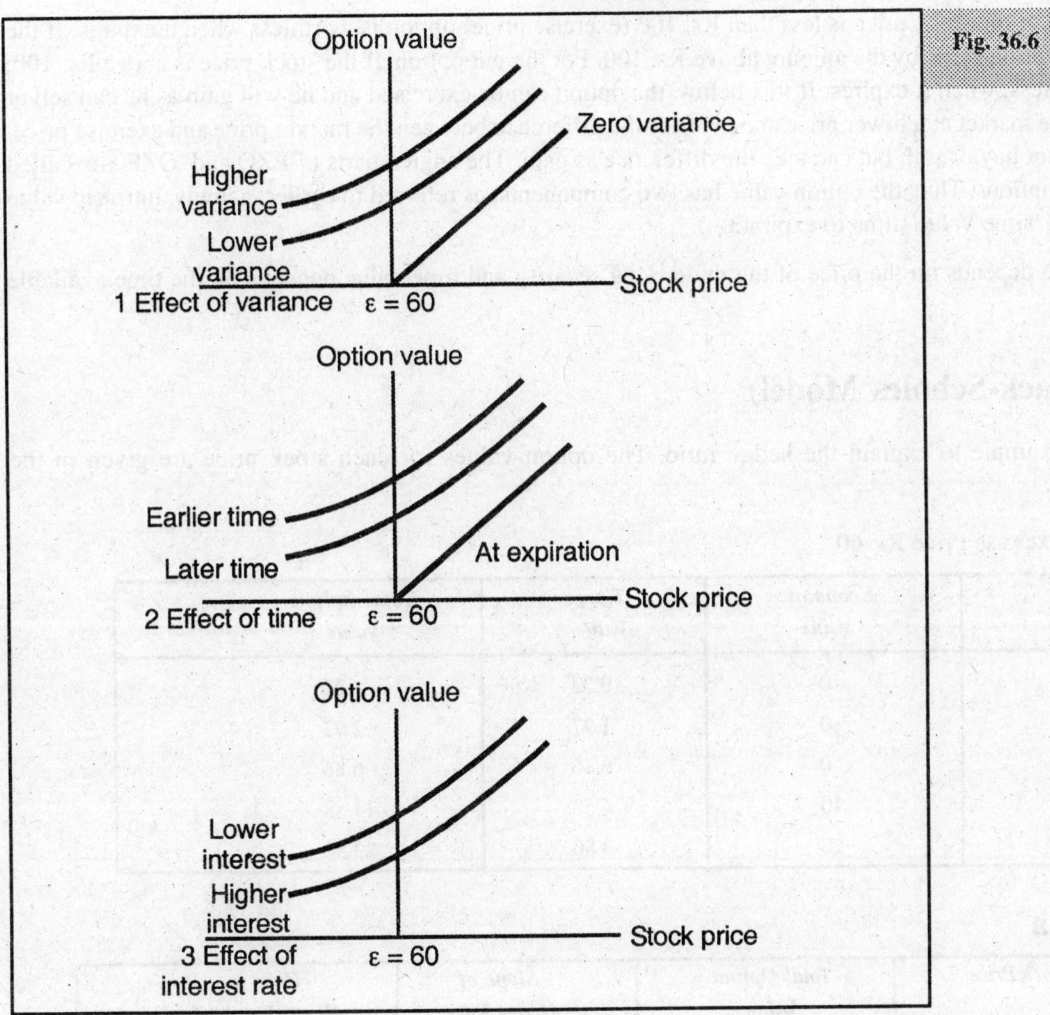

Call and Put Options

A call option is a right to buy and a put option is a right to sell. Their valuations will differ, although the factors referred to above are the same.

The graph below depicts the value of a call and of a put:

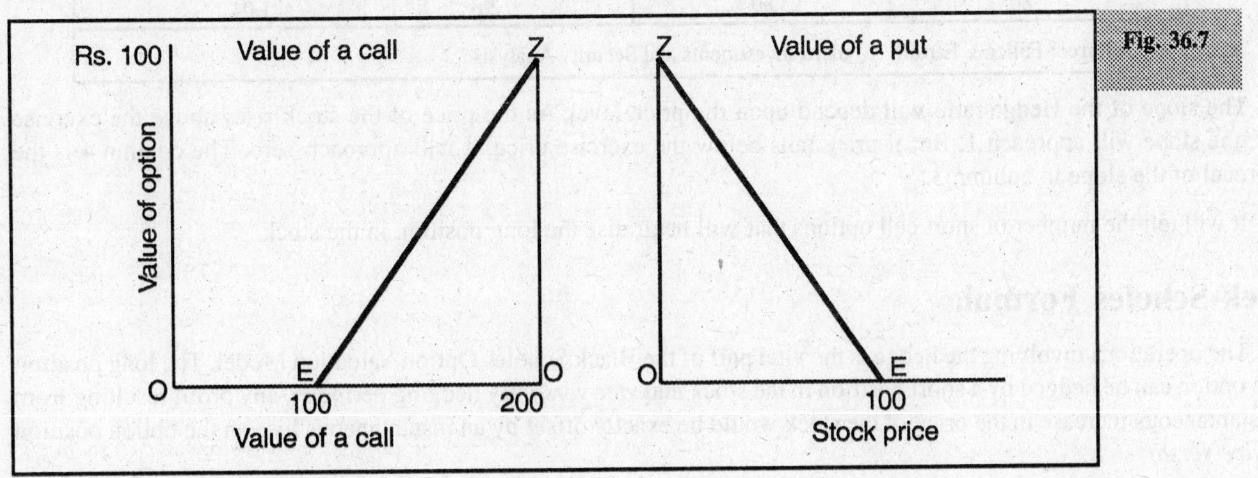

For the call option, if the stock price is less than Rs. 100 (exercise price) option is worthless when it expires. If the price is above, the call option gains by the amount above Rs. 100. For the put option, if the stock price is above Rs. 100, then the option is worthless, when it expires. If it is below, the option can be exercised and he will gain as he can sell at Rs. 100 but buying in the market at a lower price and profit is the difference between the market price and exercise price. In either case he need not buy or sell, but can take the difference as gain. The angled parts of EZO and OZE are called intrinsic values of the options. Thus the option value has two components, as referred to earlier, namely, intrinsic value (or economic value) and Time Value (time to expiration).

The intrinsic value depends on the price of the underlying security and time value depends on the time available before expiry.

Hedge Ratio (Black-Scholes Model)

Take numerical example to explain the hedge ratio. The option values for each stock price are given in the Table below.

Option Value — Exercise Price Rs. 60

Stock Price	*Economic Value*	*Time Value*	*Total Option Value*
Rs. 40	0	0.22	.22
50	0	1.97	1.97
60	0	6.86	6.86
70	10	4.58	14.58
80	20	3.80	23.80

Hedge Ratio Data

Stock Price (1)	*Total Option Value* (2)	*Slope of Hedge Ratio* (3)	*Calls to Neutralise Stock* (4)
40	0.22	0.06	16.67
50	1.97	.32	3.12
60	6.86	.65	1.54
70	14.58	.87	1.15
80	23.80	.96	1.04

Source: Fuller & Farrell. "Modern Investments and Security Analysis."

The slope of the Hedge ratio will depend upon the price level. As the price of the stock rises above the exercise price, the slope will approach 1, But if price falls below the exercise price, it will approach zero. The column 4 is the reciprocal of the slope in column 3.

It will tell the number of short call options that will neutralise the long position in the stock.

Black-Scholes Formula

The operations involving the hedge is the vital part of the Black Scholes Option Valuation Model. The long position in the option can be hedged by a short position in the stock and *vice versa.* By hedging perfectly, any profit resulting from an instantaneous increase in the price of the stock would be exactly offset by an instantaneous loss on the option position and *vice versa.*

Black Scholes formula can be used to hedge the market risk of stock portfolio by proper option strategy. Because we can reach a theoretically riskless position, one can earn a risk free return, by such hedging — that is, the short-term interest rate is the fair value of the option. The option price would adjust to the fair value under equilibrium conditions.

What is Black-Scholes Formula?

If C is the equilibrium value of option, the formula given by Black-Scholes is as follows:

$$C = SN(d_1) - E(e^{-rt}) N(d_2)$$

Where, $$d_1 = \frac{\ln\left(\frac{S}{E}\right) + (rt + 0.5\sigma^2)t}{\sigma\sqrt{t}}$$

$$d_2 = d_1 - \sigma\sqrt{t}$$

and where

S = Current market price of underlying stock

E = Exercise price of the option

r = Risk free rate of return (Continuously compounded)

N (d) = The value of the cumulative normal distribution evaluated at 'd'.

N (d_1) is the hedge ratio or is also called the option's delta for the call option.

t = Time remaining before expiration

σ = Risk of the underlying common stock measured by standard deviation. N (d_1) cumulative density function of d_1 and similar is N (d_2). N (d_1) and N (d_2) denote the probabilities that deviations of less than d_1 and d_2 respectively will occur in a normal distribution that has a mean of 'o' and a standard deviation of 1.

Mathematically 'e' is the base of natural logarithms and is approximately equal to 2.71828. This means that E/e^{RT} is the present value of the exercise price, when a continuous discount rate is used (it is analogous to $E/(1+R)^T$ or $E(e^{-rt})$ used in the formula-the present value of the exercise price, using a discrete discount rate.

The Table on N (d) Values is presented at the end of the chapter.

The quantity $\ln\left(\frac{S}{E}\right)$ is the natural Logarithm of $\frac{S}{E}$

Note: Values of N (d) for various levels of d_1 and d_2 can be had from the Table at the end and a pocket calculator for estimating the fair value of option is necessary to use Black-Scholes Formula.

The B/S Model can be used by reference to Table at the end for values of N (d_1) and N (d_2), with given values of d_1 and d_2. This model is also based on the following assumptions:-

(1) Stock returns are expected to follow a log normal distribution.

(2) There are no costs of transactions and no taxes.

(3) The stock will not pay dividend during the life of the option.

(4) The underlying asset value and the risk free rate are constant during the life of the option.

Implications

Black-Scholes formula is a static analysis. The formula shows that the fair value has the following major inputs:

Common stock price, exercise price, time to maturity, market interest rate and standard deviation of annual price changes. The implications of the formula are:

(1) The higher the price of the underlying stock, the higher is the value of call option.

(2) The longer the time to expiration date (t) the higher is the value of the call option.

(3) The higher the exercise price, the lower the value of call option.

(4) The higher the risk free rate, the higher is the value of call option.

(5) The greater the risk (σ) of the common stock, the higher is the value of the call option.

Black and Scholes: The pricing of options and corporate liabilities. JPE May-June 1973.

Solved Problem (B/S Model)

Given the following values, Calculate the value of call option under the B/S Model:-

$\sigma = .3$, $R_t - .10$, S = Rs. 25 T = 0.3 years and E = Rs. .28

$$D_1 = \frac{\text{In}\left(\frac{25}{28}\right) + \left[.10 + 0.5(0.3)^2\right]0.3}{0.3\sqrt{0.3}}$$

$$= \frac{-0.1133 + (.10 + 0.045)\,0.3}{0.3 \times 0.5477}$$

$$= \frac{-0.1133 + (0.143)\,0.3}{0.16431} = \frac{-0.1133 + 0.0435}{0.16431}$$

$$D_1 = \frac{-0.0698}{0.16431} = -0.425$$

$D_2 = -0.425 - (0.3)\,(0.5477)$

$D_2 = -0.4250 - 0.1643 = -0.5893$

$C_1 = 25\ N\,(-.43) - e^{-10(.3)}\,(28)\ N\,(-0.59)$

From the Table at the end of the chapter the values of N (–.43) and N (–.59) are taken

$C_1 = 25 \times (0.3336) - 0.9704\ (28)\ (0.2776)$

$C_1 = 8.34 - 7.54 = 0.80$

$C_1 =$ Rs. 0.80

Problems

Question 1:

Keys Co. Ltd. has EPS at Rs. 3 with 500,000 shares outstanding. Then the company issued 40,000 shares of 7% convertible preferred shares at Rs. 50. Each preferred share is convertible into 2 shares of equity, which has a market price of Rs. 21 per share.

(*a*) What is the preferred share's conversion value?

(*b*) What is the conversion premium?

(*c*) Assuming the total earnings to remain the same what will be the effect of the issue on primary earnings per share before conversion.

Answer:

(*a*) Conversion value = Conversion ratio x market price per share = 2 × 21 = Rs. 42

(*b*) Conversion premium = $\frac{50}{42} - 1 = 19.05\%$

(*c*) **Effect on primary earnings per share**

With EPS at 3 and total shares outstanding at 5,00,000.

Then 3 × 500,000 = 15,00,000 is total earnings

Less preferred share dividend

Rs. 7% per bond of Rs. 50

Rs. 7 per Rs. 100 and 3½ × 40,000 minus 140,000

(Rs. 3½ per Rs. 50) { 15,00,000 – 1,40,000 = 13,60,000 }

Total Earnings before Conversion = Rs. 13,60,000

No. of shares before Conversion =	500,000
Net Earnings per share before conversion	Rs. 2.72 (13,60,000 ÷ 5,00,000)
Total after tax earnings	15,00,000
No. of shares after conversion	5,80,000

(5,00,000 + 80,000)

Conversion rate is 2 for one and 40,000 shares of preferred stock.

This gives 40,000 × 2 = 80,000. EPS $\frac{15,00,000}{5,80,000} = 2.59$

EPS after conversion = Rs. 2.59.

Question 2:

The current rate of interest on 4 year ZCB of Government of India is 10% and that on 5 year Securities is 9.8%

(*a*) What is the implied forward rate on a one year loan 4 years in the future?

Answer:

Implied forward rate, $\frac{(1.098)^5}{(1.10)^4} - 1$

$= 1.089 - 1 = .089$

which is roughly 9.00%

(*b*) What happens to the forward rate if interest rates decline so that 4 year security yields 8% and 5 year security 8.4%.

Answer:

$$\text{Implied forward rate} = \frac{(1.084)^5}{(1.08)^4} - 1$$

= 1.104 – 1 = 0.104 what is roughly 10%

Question 3:

Goldwan needs to borrow in the bond market three months hence; As he expects the interest rates to rise, he needs hedging. The Company has the option on government bond futures.

(*a*) Should the company buy a put or call option?

(*b*) If the present futures contracts trades at Rs. 100, and a 3 months put option involves, a cost of 1½% based on the strike price. During the three months, interest rates rise and the price government bond went down to Rs. 95. What is the gain or loss on the option per Rs. 1,00,000 contracts?

Answer:

(*a*) To protect against upward movement in interest rates price movements will go down and the Co. should ask for a put option.

(*b*) Gain on option = (1.00 – 0.95) × 100,000 = 5,000

Premium = 1½% × 1,00,000 paid; (minus) 1,500

Net gain Rs. 3,500

Question 4:

Flexico has outstanding warrants with a right to conversion of 2 equity shares at Rs. 24 per share. The data on market price of equity and warrant price are given; the theoretical value of warrant can be estimated by the equation.

NPs – E = theoretical value

where N = no. of shares that can be purchased per every warrant, Ps market price of the Equity share and E is the exercise price of the conversion of warrant into equity.

Observation Numbers

	1	2	3	4	5	6
Market Price	18	20	24	27	32	38
Warrant Price	3	5	8	12	20	29

Applying the above formula, the theoretical values for these observations can be set out as:

	1	2	3	4	5	6
theoretical values	0	0	0	6	16	28
premium of warrant	3	5	8	6	4	1

(Warrant price-minus-theoretical values = premium)

Premium is the highest at 8 when the market price is Rs. 24, which is the same as exercise price and theoretical value is zero. Here there is the greatest leverage and the premium over the theoretical value is the greatest at this point, since volatility is what gives the option value.

Observation 1

Theoretical values 2 × 18 = 36 – 48 (which is the exercise value for 2 shares × Rs. 24).
= negative value or Zero

Observation 2

Theoretical value = NPs – E.

2 × 20 – 48 < 0

Observation 3

2 × 24 – 48 = 0

Observation 4

2 × 27 – 48

54 – 48 = 6

Observation 5

2 × 32 – 48

64 – 48 = 16

Observation 6

2 × 38 – 48

76 – 48 = 28

Premium of warrant = warrant price – Theoretical values

Observatios:

Premium (1) 3 – 0 = 3; (2) 5 – 0 = 5; (3) 8 – 0 = 8

(4) 12 – 6 = 6; (5) 20 – 16 = 4; (6) 29 – 28 = 1

The highest premium is at observation 3 at Rs. 8 as the premium.

Question 5:

Kalyan steel has EPS of Rs. 3 with 5,00,000 shares outstanding, the company issued 40,000 shares of 7% convertible preferred stock at par of Rs. 50. The preferred stock is convertible into two shares of equity for each preferred share. The equity stock has a current market price of Rs. 21 per share. What is the conversion value of preferred stock. What is its conversion premium?

Answer:

Conversion value = conversion ratio × market price per share

Rs. 2 × 21 = Rs. 42

Conversion premium $\frac{50}{42} - 1 = 1.19 - 1 = 19\%$.

Question 6:

Phillips has warrants oustanding which will allow the holder to buy 3 shares of equity for a total of Rs. 60 per warrant. The market price of equity share is Rs. 18 at present. The holders believe the following probabilities about the equity stock six months hence,

Market Price	Rs. 16	18	20	22	24
Probability	15	20	30	20	15

(a) What is the present theoretical value of the warrant?

(b) What is the expected value of stock price 6 months hence from now?

(c) What is the theoretical value, expected of the warrant 6 months hence?

Question 7:

Determine the value of the following call option making use of the Black-Scholes formula given in the Text.

So = Current Market Price = Rs. 95

E = Exercise price = Rs. 105

t = Expiration period to go = 8 months

γ = Riskless rate of interest = 8%

σ = Instantaneous standard deviation of the stock return is 0.6.

Then
$$d_1 = \frac{\text{In}\left(\frac{95}{105}\right) + \left[0.08 + \frac{1}{2}(.36)\right](0.66)}{0.6\sqrt{0.66}}$$

$$d_2 = d_2 - \sigma\sqrt{t}$$

Hint

Calculate

N(d_1) and N(d_2) and plug in the formula for current value of the option.

$$C = SN(d_1) - \frac{E}{e^{rt}} \cdot N(d_2)$$

If the actual value of C is less than the C as calculated above, it is undervalued. Otherwise it is overvalued.

Question 8:

Shanker has a share warrant that can buy 5 shares at an exercise price of Rs. 40 each. At share prices of Rs. 35, 45 and 50, and with respective premiums at 0, 2 and 4, determine the market values of the warrant.

Question 9:

Calculate the floor value of the convertible bond, if the following data are given to you.

Par value	Rs. 1,000
Coupon rate	10%

Maturity period	20 years
YTM of NCB of	8%
Similar nature	
Conversion price	Rs. 40
Market price	Rs. 50

Question 10:

The exercise price of an option stock is Rs. 50 with the market value of Rs. 60 the option contract has an expiration period of 120 days. If Rf (Riskfree rate) is 7%, the variance of return is 0.144. What is the value of the call option under the Black-Scholes Model?

Question 11:

The exercise price of option stock is Rs. 10, which is also the market price. The option contract has an expiration period of 4 years. While the riskless rate of return on the stock was estimated at 9% (continuously compounded) and the expected variance of return on the stock was estimated at 9%. Determine the value of call option under the Black-Scholes Model.

Table

Value of *N(X)* for Given Values of *X* for a Cumulative Normal Distribution with Zero Mean and Unit Variance

X	*0*	*1*	*2*	*3*	*4*	*5*	*6*	*7*	*8*	*9*
-3.	*.0013*	*.0010*	*.0007*	*.0005*	*.0003*	*.0002*	*.0002*	*.0001*	*.0001*	*.0000*
-2.9	.0019	.0018	.0017	.0017	.0016	.0016	.0015	.0015	.0014	.0014
-2.8	.0026	.0025	.0024	.0023	.0023	.0022	.0021	.0021	.0020	.0019
-2.7	.0035	.0034	.0033	0032	.0031	.0030	.0029	.0028	.0027	.0026
-2.6	.0047	.0045	.0044	.0043	.0041	.0040	.0039	.0038	.0037	.0036
-2.5	.0062	.0060	.0059	.0057	.0055	.0054	.0052	.0051	.0049	.0048
-2.4	.0082	.0080	.0078	.0075	.0073	.0071	.0069	.0068	.0066	.0064
-2.3	.0107	.0104	.0102	.0099	.0096	.0094	.0091	.0089	.0087	.0084
-2.2	.0139	.0136	.0132	.0129	.0126	.0122	.0119	.0116	.0113	.0110
-2.1	.0179	.0174	0.170	.0166	.0162	.0158	.0154	.0150	.0146	.0143
-2.0	.0228	.0222	0217	.0212	.0207	.0202	..0197	0192	.0188	.0183
-1.9	.0287	.0281	.0274	.0268	.0262	.0256	.0250	.0244	.0238	.0233
-1.8	0.359	.0352	.0344	0.336	.0329	.0322	.0314	.0307	.0300	.0294
-1.7	.0446	.0436	.0427	.0418	.0409	.0401	0.392	.0384	.0375	.0367
-1.6	.0548	.0537	.0526	.0516	.0505	.0495	.0485	.0475	.0465	.0455
-1.5	.0668	.0655	.0643	.0630	.0618	.0606	.0594	.0582	.0570	.0559
-1.4	.0808	.0793	.0778	.0764	.0749	.0735	.0722	.0708	.0694	.0681
-1.3	.0968	.0951	.0934	.0918	.0901	.0885	.0869	.0853	.0838	.0823
-1.2	.1151	.1131	.1112	.1093	.1075	.1056	.1038	.1020	.1003	.0985
-1.1	.1357	.1335	.1314	.1292	.1271	.1251	.1230	.1210	.1190	.1170
-1.0	1587	.1562	.1539	1515	.1492	.1469	.1446	.1423	.1401	.1379
- .9	.1841	.1814	.1788	.1762	.1736	.1711	.1685	.1660	.1635	.1611
- .8	.2119	.2090	.2061	.2033	.2005	.1977	.1949	.1922	.1894	.1867
- .7	.2420	.2389	.2358	.2327	.2297	.2266	.2236	.2206	.2177	.2148
- .6	.2743	.2709	.2676	.2643	.2611	.2578	.2546	.2514	.2483	.2451
- .5	.3085	.3050	.3015	.2981	.2846	.2912	2877	.2843	.2810	.2776
- .4	.3446	.3409	.3372	.3336	3300	.3264	.3228	.3192	.3156	.3121
- .3	.3821	.3783	.3745	.3707	.3669	.3632	.3594	.3557	.3520	.3483

- .2	.4207	.4168	.4129	.4090	.4052	.4013	.3974	.3936	.3897	.3859
- .1	.4602	.4562	.4522	.4483	.4443	.4404	.4364	.4325	.4286	.4247
- .0	.5000	.4960	.4920	.4880	.4840	4801	.4761	.4721	.4681	.4641
.0	.5000	.5040	.5080	.5120	.5160	.5199	.5239	.5279	.5319	.5359
.1	.5398	.5438	.5478	.5517	.5557	.5596	.5636	.5675	.5714	.5753
.2	.5793	.5832	.5871	.5910	.5948	.5987	.6026	.6064	.6103	.6141
.3	.6179	.6217	.6255	.6293	.6331	.6368	.6406	.6443	.6480	.6517
.4	.6554	.6591	.6628	.6664	.6700	.6736	.6772	.6808	.6844	.6879
.5	6915	.6950	.6985	.7019	.7054	.7088	.7123	.7157	.7190	.7224
.6	.7257	.7291	.7324	.7357	.7389	.7422	.7454	.7486	.7517	.7549
.7	.7580	.7611	.7642	.7673	.7703	.7734	.7764	.7794	.7823	.7852
.8	.7881	.7910	.7939	.7967	.7995	.8023	.8051	.8078	.8106	.8133
.9	8159	.8186	.8212	.8238	.8264	.8289	.8315	.8340	.8365	.8389
1.0	8413	.8438	.8461	.8485	.8508	.8531	.8554	.8577	.8599	.8621
1.1	.8643	.8665	.8686	.8708	.8729	.8749	.8770	.8790	.8810	.8830
1.2	.8849	.8869	.8888	.8907	.8925	.8944	.8962	.8980	.8997	.9015
1.3	.9032	.9049	.9066	.9082	.9099	.9115	.9131	.9147	.9162	.9177
1.4	.9192	.9207	.9222	.9236	.9251	.9265	.9278	.9292	.9306	.9319
1.5	.9332	.9345	.9357	.9370	.9382	.9394	.9406	.9418	.9430	.9441
1.6	.9452	.9463	.9474	.9484	.9495	.9505	.9515	.9525	.9535	.9545
1.7	.9554	.9564	.9573	.9582	.9591	.9599	.9608	.9616	.9625	.9633
1.8	.9641	.9648	.9656	.9664	.9671	.9678	.9686	.9693	.9700	.9706
1.9	.9713	.9719	.9726	.9732	.9738	.9744	.9750	.9756	.9762	.9767
2.0	.9772	.9778	.9783	.9788	.9793	.9798	.9803	.9808	.9812	.9817
2.1	.9821	.9826	.9830	.9834	.9838	.9842	.9846	.9850	.9854	.9857
2.2	.9861	.9864	9868	.9871	.9874	.9878	.9881	.9884	.9887	.9890
2.3	.9893	.9896	.9898	.9901	.9904	.9906	.9909	.9911	.9913	.9916
2.4	.9918	.9920	.9922	.9925	.9927	.9929	.9931	.9932	.9934	.9936
2.5	.9938	.9940	.9941	.9943	.9945	.9946	.9948	.9949	.9951	.9952
2.6	.9953	.9955	.9956	.9957	.9959	.9960	.9961	.9962	.9963	.9964
2.7	.9965	.9966	.9967	.9968	.9969	.9970	.9971	.9972	.9973	.9974
2.8	.9974	.9975	.9976	.9977	.9977	.9978	.9979	.9979	,9980	.9981
2.9	.9981	.9982	.9982	.9983	.9984	.9984	.9985	.9985	.9986	.9986
3.	.9987	.9990	.9993	.9995	.9997	.9998	.9998	.9999	.9999	1.0000

Source: "Theory and Problems of Investments" Shaum's Outline Series. page 214.

PART — VII
Portfolio Theory and Management

Chapter 37: Risk and Return in Portfolio Management

Chapter 38: Capital Asset Pricing Model (CAPM)

Chapter 39: Portfolio Analysis

Chapter 40: Diversification and Techniques of Risk Reduction

Chapter 41: Markowitz Model

Chapter 42: Basics of Portfolio Management in India

Chapter 43: Modern Portfolio Theory

Chapter 44: Portfolio Management: Construction, Revision and Evaluation

Chapter 45: Mutual Funds and Their Schemes

Chapter 46: Disinvestment Management

Chapter 47: Securities Market Report (BSE)

What is the Objective?

The objective of portfolio management is to maximise the return and minimise risk. A portfolio is a basket of investments or assets held by an individual or a corporate body.

What is Risk?

General concepts of risk and uncertainty were already discussed in the earlier chapter. Risk is uncertainty of the income/capital appreciation or loss of both. The two major types of risk are: Systematic or market related risks and unsystematic or company related risks. The systematic risks are the market problems, raw material availability, tax policy or any Government policy, inflation risk, interest rate risk and financial risk. The unsystematic risks are mismanagement, increasing inventory, wrong financial policy, defective marketing, etc.

How to Minimise the Risks?

The company specific risks (unsystematic risks) can be reduced by diversifying into a few companies belonging to various industry groups, asset groups or different types of instruments like equity shares, bonds, debentures etc. Thus, asset classes are bank deposits, company deposits, gold, silver, land, real estate, equity shares etc. Industry groups are tea, sugar, paper, cement, steel, electricity, electronics, computer software etc. Each of them have different risk-return characteristics and investments are to be made, based on individual's risk preferences. The second category of risk (systematic risk) is managed by the use of Beta of different company shares.

What is Beta?

In simple language, Beta is percentage change in the scrip return divided by the percentage change in market return. Here the appreciation in the scrip price relative to the market price index is considered. Leaving aside the mathematical formulae for calculating the Beta over the period of time, one can take readily available betas of well traded companies from Financial Journals like Dalal Street, Căpital Market, ICFAI Journal etc. If Beta is 1, the scrip risk is the same as the market risk. If Beta is greater than 1, the scrip risk is more than the market risk, and if Beta is less than 1, the scrip risk is less than the market risk. The Defensive or risk averse investors should invest in scrips with Beta less than 1. Aggressive risk takers would prefer scrips with Beta greater than 1.

Risk Return Analysis

All investments are risky. The higher the risk taken, the higher is the return. But proper management of risk involves the right choice of investments whose risks are compensating. The total risks of two companies may be different and even lower than the risk of a group of two companies if their risks are offset by each other. Thus, if the risk of Reliance is represented by Beta of 1.90 and of Dr. Reddy's at 0.70 the total of these two is 1.30, on average. But the actual Beta of the group of these two may be less than that due to the fact that covariances of these two may be negative or independent. It may be more than that if there is a strong positive covariance between them.

Degree of Risk and Risk Free Return

Risk on some assets is almost zero or negligible. The examples are Bank deposits, where the maximum return is 6-9%. Similarly, investments in Treasury bills, Government Securities etc., are also risk free or least risky. Their return is 6 to 8%. The riskiness of assets can be represented diagrammatically as follows:

Fig. 37.1

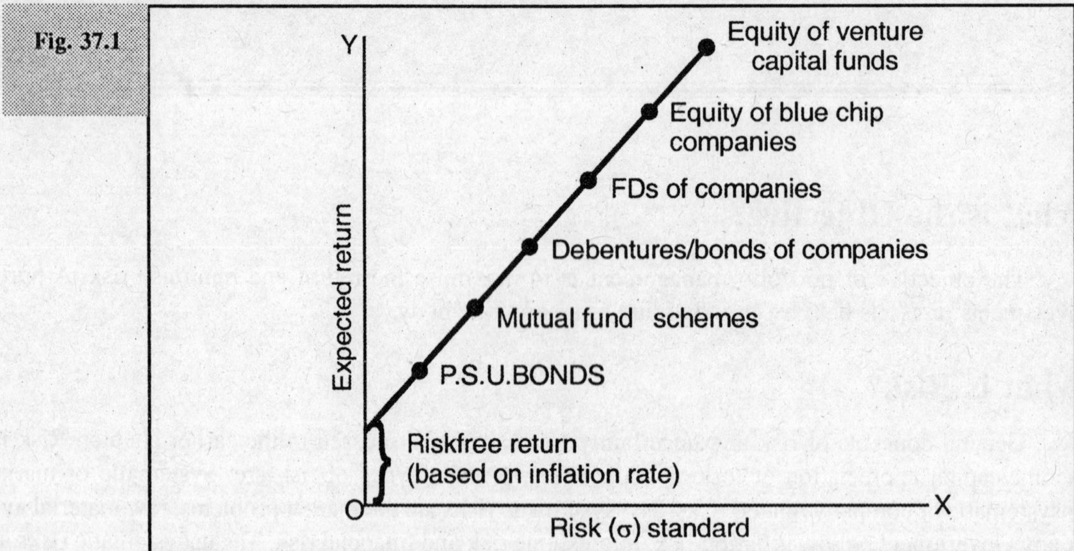

Capital Market Instruments

The main capital market instruments, one can invest and include in his portfolio are as follows:

(a) Equity Shares

(b) Preference Shares

(c) Debentures, Convertible and Non-convertible

(d) Secured Premium Notes

(e) Zero Coupon Bonds

(f) Discount Bonds and Deep Discount Bonds, etc.

Money Market Instruments

The main money market instruments, available for investment include:

1. Treasury Bills
2. Commercial Paper
3. Commercial Bills

4. Certificates of Deposits
5. Participation Certificates
6. Repos
7. Inter-bank Money etc.

The above instruments are discussed in another chapter.

Total household sector savings are about 24% of GDP But their gross savings in financial assets are 13-14% and in net financial assets 10-11% of GDP, which is rather low for development of the economy.

Due to inflation and stagnation in growth of incomes the real savings of the household sector stagnate at around 23-24% of the GDP and for all sectors at around 34-37% of the GDP. The proportion in cash and deposits have increased while those in contractual forms of savings and in shares etc. declined, or stagnated.

The above picture of household portfolio reflects the lack of proper investment expertise and appreciation of portfolio management principles on the one hand and the undue risk aversion of the average household on the other.

WHAT IS A PORTFOLIO?

As the investors acquire different sets of assets of financial nature, such as gold, silver, real estate, buildings, insurance policies, post office certificates, NSC or NSS etc., they are making a provision for future. The risk of each of such investments is to be understood before hand. Normally, the average householder keeps most of his income in cash or bank deposits and assumes that they are safe and least risky. Little does he realise that they also carry a risk with them — the fear of loss or actual loss or theft and loss of real value of these assets through the rise in price or inflation in the economy. Cash carries no interest or income and bank deposits carry a nominal rate of $3^1/_2$% on savings deposits, no interest on current account and a maximum of 9% on term deposits of one year. If the inflation rate is at 8 to 10% as in the Nineties or in 2009 and 2010, then they give negative real returns, which is a loss to the savers. The liquidity on Fixed deposits is poor as one has to wait for the period to maturity or take loan on such amount but at a loss of income due to penal rate. Generally, risk averters invest only in banks, P.O. and UTI and mutual funds. Gold, silver real estate, Nidhis, and chit funds are the other avenues of investment for average Householder, of middle and lower income groups. If the investor desired to have a real rate of return which is substantially higher than the inflation rate he has to invest in relatively more risky areas of investment like shares and debentures of companies or bonds of Government and Semi-Government agencies or deposits with companies and firms. Investment in Chit funds. Nidhis, company deposits, and in private limited companies has the highest risk. But the basic principle is that the higher the risk, the higher is the return and the investor should have a clear perception of the elements of risk and return when he makes investments. Risk Return analysis is thus essential for the investment and portfolio management.

Definition of Portfolio Management

Many times the investors go on acquiring these assets in an *ad-hoc* and unplanned manner and the result is high risk, low return profile which they may face. All such assets would constitute his portfolio and the wise investor not only plans his portfolio as per his risk return profile or preferences but manages his portfolio efficiently so as to secure the highest return for the lowest risk possible at that level of investment. This in short is the art of portfolio management.

Speculative Instinct

Out of available savings, many investors first start with making application for new issues in the capital market. By chance if they get allotment, they are in the market and they accumulate such investments or sell them in the stock market immediately after listing. This is possible if the price quoted after listing is higher than the initial offer price and if the investor is interested in speculation and not investment. If the issue is not appreciating after listing, or if he is a long-term investor, he will keep such investments. In cases where he accumulates the shares of many companies without any plan or design, such investors, if they are not well informed about the market, will end up with a dead weight of paper certificates, without much worth. When they really want money back and if their investments turn out to be trash, they lose their wealth and burn their fingers, particularly in a bearish phase, when prices are on downtrend.

Precautions for Investment

All investors should therefore plan their investments first to provide for their requirements of comfortable life with a house, real estate, physical assets necessary for comforts and insurance for and accident health, life cover and make a provision for a provident fund and pension fund etc., for a future date. They have to take all needed precautions for a comfortable life, before they enter the stock market as it is most risky. But rarely any such plan or design is noticed among investors as they start investment in these markets on the advise of friends, relatives and agents or brokers, without much of premeditation or preparation.

The following chart shows the trade off between risk and return. If you want more return, you take more risk and if no risk is taken, only bank deposits are used.

Fig. 37.2

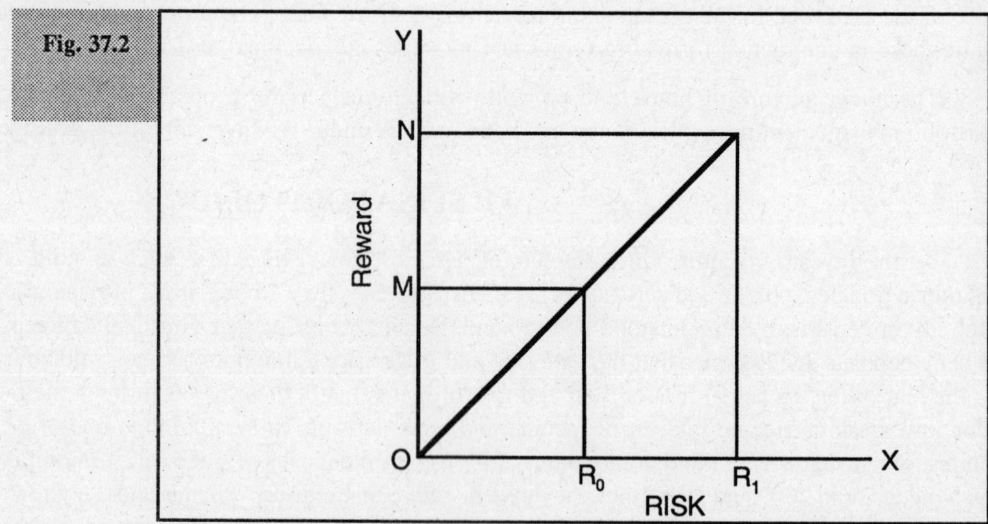

At R_0 risk, the reward is only OM. If we take a higher risk of R_1, the reward will increase to ON. But if reward is desirable, risk is undesirable. Hence, the investor who wants the risk taken to be only Ro, but return to be ON, he has to plan his investments in portfolio. This is what in essence is called Portfolio Management.

Decomposition of Return

The portfolio return is related to risk. There is also a risk free return, which is secured by any investor by keeping his funds in say bank deposits or post office deposits or certificates. Beyond the risk free rate, the excess return depends on many factors like the risk taken, expertise in selectivity or selection, return due to diversification and return for expertise of portfolio Manager.

Fama has presented the decomposition of actual returns into its components. Thus, there is risk free return, excess return, risk premium for taking risk, etc. There is also a return for selecting the proper assets and extra return for the expertise of the portfolio Manager.

An example will make the above statement clear, for which the following values can be taken

Return an Portfolio Rp = 8%

Return on Market Portfolio = 9%

Risk free Rate = 2%

Risk related to SML (Diversification) = 6.5

Composition of the Portfolio Return

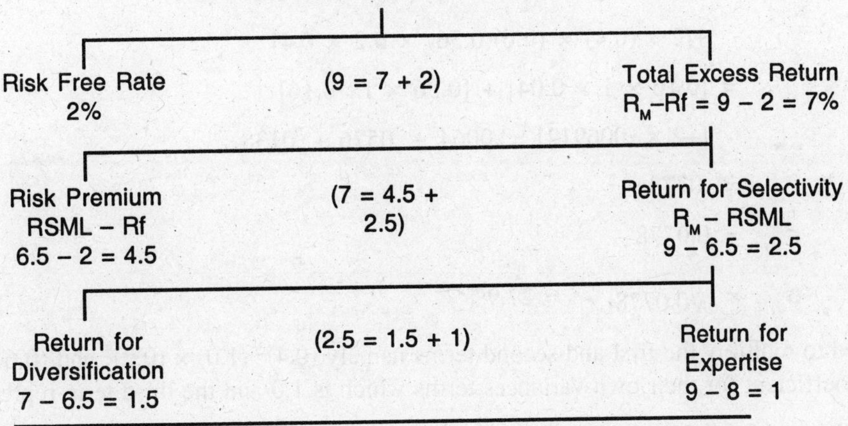

The formula for return is as follows:

$R_i = Rf + (R_M - Rf)\,\beta$, where β is Beta of the company. This can be explained by a problem given below:

Problem

Give Rf = 10% and R_m = 15% were Rf is risk free rate and R_m is the market return and the Expected return and Betas of 4 companies are given below.

Company	*Expected Return*	*Expected Beta*
1	17.0%	1.3
2	14.5%	0.8
3	15.5%	1.1
4	18.0%	1.7
Ri_1 =	10 + (15 – 10) 1.3 =	16.5
Ri_2 =	10 + (15 – 10) 0.8 =	14.0.
Ri_3 =	10 + (15 – 10) 1.1 =	15.5
Ri_4 =	10 + (15 – 10) 1.7 =	18.5

Compared with the Expected return given above those calculated on the basis of calculation of formula for return premium companies 1 and 2 are under valued. Number 3 company is fairly valued and Number 4 Company is overvalued.

The Calculation of Return and risk in a portfolio is explained with the following example.

Example

The equity of Orient and Crompton have expected returns of 15% and 20% and the standard deviations (risk) of 20% and 40%. The coefficient of correlation of these two stocks is 0.36.

Answer: *(a)* What is the expected return and standard deviation of portfolio consisting of 40% of Orient and 60% of Crompton?

(b) What is r and s of the portfolio consisting of 60% of Orient and 40% of the Crompton.

Answer: *(a)* Rp =0.4 (.15) + 0.6 (0.2) =

.06 + 0.12 = 0.18 = 18%.

$$\sigma^2{}_p = [(0.4)^2 \times (1.0) \times (0.2)^2] + [(0.6)^2 \times 1.0 \times (0.4)^2]$$
$$+[2 \times (0.4) \times (0.6)(0.36) \times 0.2 \times 0.4]$$
$$= [0.16 \times 1 \times 0.04] + [0.36 \times 1\times 0.16]$$
$$[+2 \times .006912] = .0064 + .0576 + .0138$$
$$= .0778$$
$$\sigma^2{}_p = 0.0778$$
$$\sigma_p = \sqrt{0.0778} = 27.9\%$$

What is used to multiply the first and second terms namely $(0.4)^2$ $(1.0) \times (0.2)^2$ and $(0.6)^2 \times 1 \times (0.4)^2$ represent. The correlation coefficient for their own variances terms which is 1.0 and the third term represents the covariance.

(b) $R_p = 0.6\,(0.15) + .4 \times (0.2) =$

$$R_p = 0.09 + 0.08 = 0.17 = 17\%$$
$$\sigma^2{}_p = (0.6)^2 \times 1 \times (.2)^2 + (0.4)^2 \times 1 \times (0.4)^2 +$$
$$2(0.6)\,(0.4)\,(0.36) \times (0.2)\,(0.4)$$
$$\sigma^2 = 0.36 \times .04 + 0.16 \times 0.16 + .013824$$
$$= .0144 + 0.0256 + .013824$$
$$= 0.0538$$
$$\sigma = \sqrt{.0538} = 23.2\%.$$

	(r) Return	(s) Standard Deviation (Risk)
Orient	18	27.9
Crompton	17	23.2

Crompton has lesser risk and lesser return.

CHAPTER 38

Capital Asset Pricing Model (CAPM)

The CAPM was developed to explain how risky securities are priced in market and this was attributed to experts like Sharpe and Lintner. Markowitz theory being more theoretical, CAPM aims at a more practical approach to stock valuation.

It is no doubt based on the mean-variance approach to risk for assessment of investment as developed by Markowitz. It explains the behavioural pattern of investors in building up portfolios.

CAPM-Assumptions

The CAPM is based on certain assumptions some of which are common to CAPM and MPT. CAPM is in fact developed as part of MPT (Modern Portfolio Theory). The assumptions are first set out below:

(1) The investor aims at maximising the utility of his wealth, rather than the wealth or return. The difference between them is that individual preferences are taken into account in the utility concept. While some have preference for larger risk who will have increasing marginal utility for wealth, for others, with less preference for risk the incremental wealth will be less attractive if it is attached with more risk. Thus, the preference of investors for risk return will be taken into account in this model.

(2) Investors have similar expectations of Risk and Return. Without these consensus standards, the estimates of mean and variance may lead to different forecasts with the result that the efficient portfolio of each will be different from that of the others. There will be innumerable efficient frontiers, each dependent on the set of preferences of individuals for risk and return. If investors do not have similar expectations, there will be no homogeneity in their conception and no single efficient frontier line will apply to all.

This in turn will imply that the price of an asset, which is the best estimate of the present value of future returns will be different for different investors. This assumption is therefore unrealistic for application in the real world.

(3) Investors make investment decision on a rational basis, depending on their assessment of risk and return. Risk is measured by two factors, mean and variance. In the CAPM we assume that rational investors diversify away their diversifiable risk, namely, unsystematic risk and only systematic risk remains which varies with the Beta of the security. While some use the beta only, as a measure of risk, others use both Beta and variance of returns (total Risk) as the sources of reward or expected return. As these perceptions of risk and reward vary from individual to individual, under CAPM we get a series of efficient frontier lines while in the case of MPT, there will be a single efficient frontier line as the conception of risk and return expectation is assumed to be homogeneous in the latter.

(4) Investors will have free access to all available information at no cost and no loss of time. If the information is not the same for all, no common efficient frontier line can be drawn. Besides even if the information is not available at the same time different conclusions can be drawn regarding expected return and risk and no single price of the capital asset can be conceived.

(5) Investors should have identical time horizons which again is highly unrealistic. Investors have different time horizons and their estimates of stock value will therefore differ, even as the estimated earnings are the same per year. Continuous time models are sometimes used to get over the above difficulty or again one can approximate a single period model as a proxy to multiperiod model on the assumption that returns are the same over time and time has no relevance to expected returns and that expected returns are again independent of the past and current information.

While the above assumptions are common to both CAPM and MPT, some assumptions are specific to CAPM. Thus, there is a risk free asset, which gives risk free return. Investors can borrow and lend unlimited amounts at the same price. This assumption of risk free asset transforms the curved efficient frontier line to a linear one. Risk can be reduced by adding a risk free asset, or borrowing at the risk free rate.

Besides, it is also necessary to assume in CAPM that total asset quantity is fixed and all assets are marketable and divisible. This assumption implies that the liquidity requirement of investors is ignored and there will be no new issues, which are both unrealistic.

After the brief review of the above assumptions we can summarise the requirements for CAPM as follows:

Risk is measured by variance of expected returns. There are two components of Risk — systematic (non-diversifiable) and unsystematic (diversifiable). For diversifiable risk, the investor makes a proper diversification to reduce the risk and for the non-diversifiable portion, he uses the relevant Beta measure to adjust to his requirement or preferences. Due to the possibility of risk free asset and lending and borrowing at the free rate, the investor has two components of the portfolio — risk free assets and the risky market assets. His total return is summation from the above two components.

Under CAPM, the equilibrium situation arises when all frictions, like taxes, divisibility, transaction costs and different risk-free borrowing and lending rates are assumed away. Equilibrium will be brought about by changes in prices due to changes in demand and supply.

CML

Figure below depicts the capital market line with riskless rate of return. Point P is the riskless interest rate. Preferred investments are plotted along the line PMZ, by combination of both risky assets and risk free asset along with the borrowing and lending. The slope of the PMZ is the measure of the reward for Risk taking. P is the risk free return, Em - T is the measure of the risk premium - a return for the risk taking. The reward for waiting is the risk less interest rate, OP, and second reward is the return per unit of risk borne measured by the slope 'α' of the PMZ line. *The internal rate can be considered as price of time and the slope of capital market line as price of the risk.*

Fig. 38.1

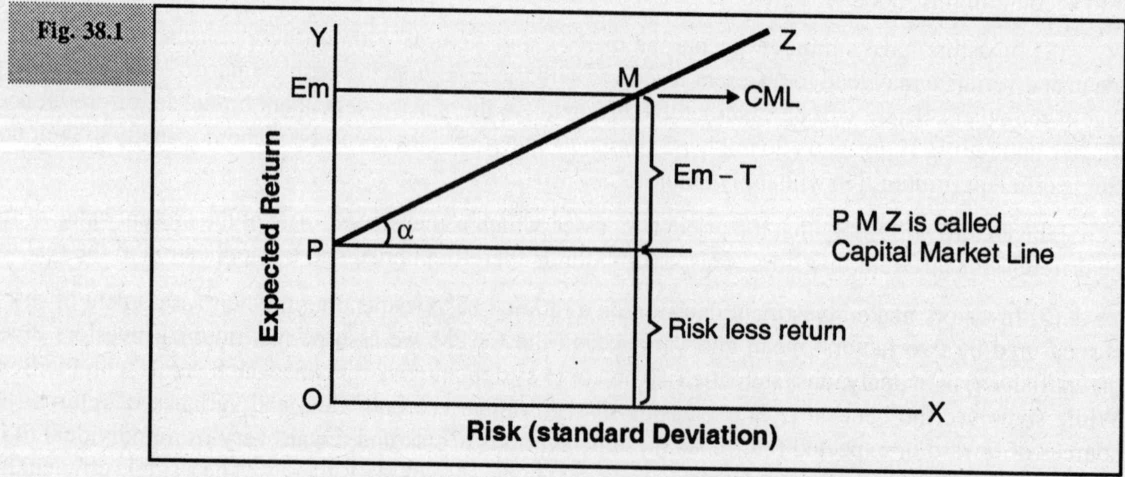

The equation of CML, connecting the risk less asset with the risky portfolio is

$$Re = Rf \frac{RM - Rf}{\sigma m} \sigma e$$ where σm is market risk and σe is portfolio risk.

If the borrowing and lending rates are different, then OQ becomes the borrowing rate and OP will be the lending rate, as shown below. The efficient frontier line with differential borrowing and lending rates will be as shown below:

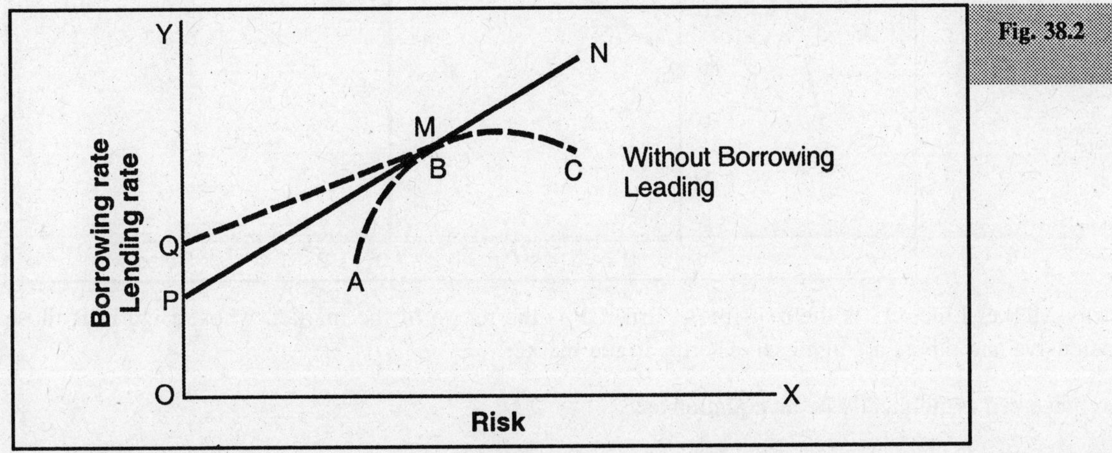

Fig. 38.2

QMN is with the borrowing rate of OQ and PMN is with the lending rate of OP and ABC is the efficiency frontier line without borrowing and lending. The curved line will become linear; if once the riskless asset of borrowing and lending at fixed riskless rate is introduced.

The CML as described above reflects the relationship of total risk and expected return. Total risk includes both systematic and unsystematic risks. It may also include the risk free assets to reduce the total risk. The CAPM has two components of the capital market return, which are reward for waiting or riskless return, and the reward per unit of risk borne as measured by the slope of the CML line.

The investors will have their choice of efficient portfolio somewhere along the line of CML, as all efficient portfolios would be on it. Those which are less efficient will be below the line PMN, in the chart above. The risk free rate can be thought as the price of time and the slope of the capital market line as the Price of Risk.

Security Market Line (SML)

Unlike the CML, which considers the total risk as a measure of variability of returns, SML takes into account only the systematic risk, which is market related and is not possible to reduce or eliminate by diversification. Beta is the measure of risk of a security relative to the whole market, and is used in the SML.

Since the unsystematic risk is already taken care of by diversification in the construction of an efficient portfolio, it is desirable to develop an alternative to CML which will use Beta as the independent variable and can be adopted for use in portfolio management and in purchase of individual securities. Such a line is called Security Market Line, which depicts a linear relationship between expected return and the systematic risk.

The SML curve drawn below shows a positive slope, indicating that the return and risk are positively related. The higher the risk the higher is the return. The Beta of Market portfolio, as represented by the BSE or NSE index is always one. But the company scrip can have Betas higher than 1 or lower than 1. Those with Betas less than 1 are defensive securities and those with Betas above 1 are called aggressive scrips. The graph below shows these types of scrips and the relationship of Beta to expected return.

Fig. 38.3

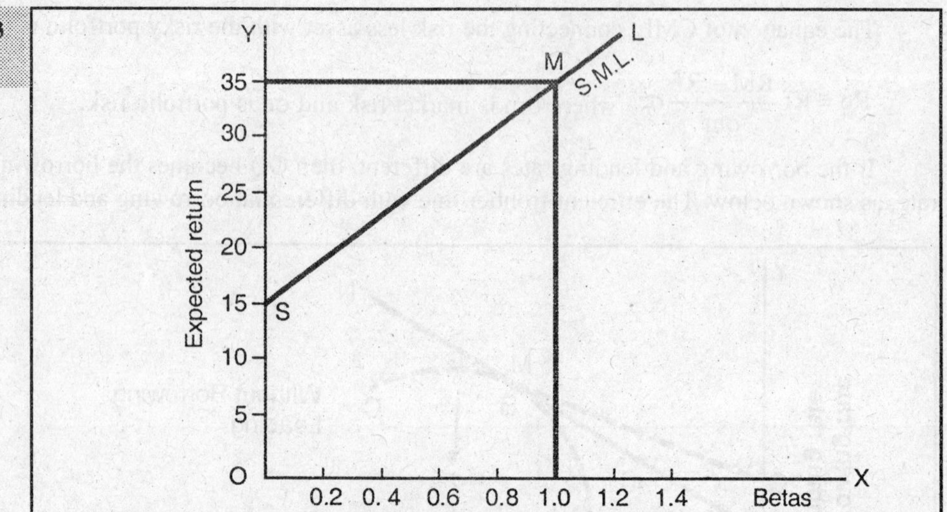

SML is Security Market Line, OS is the risk-free return, OP is the return of the market, whose Beta is 1; those below Beta 1 are defensive and others are aggressive scrips in the market.

SML can be represented symbolically by an equation as:

Ri = Rf + Bi (Rm – Rf)

Ri is the return on the security, i,

Rf is Risk-free return

Rm is Market Return.

Bi is Beta of Scrip i related to Market Risk

If Rf = 10, Rm = 20 Bi = 1.5, which is more risky than the market average, then

Ri = 10 + 1.5 (20 – 10)

= 10 + 15 = 25.0% which is higher than the market return

Suppose the Bi is less risky than the market at 0.75 then

Ri = 10 + 0.75 (20 – 10)

= 10 + 7.5 = 17.5%, which is lower than the market return

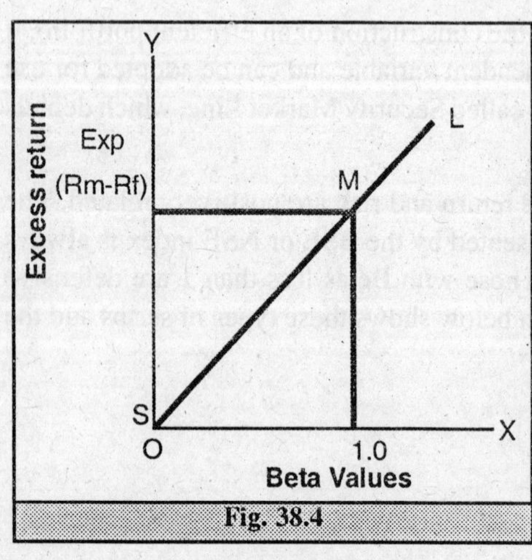

Fig. 38.4

From the above equation, we can estimate the expected return on a security. It is represented as something like a premium or discount on the market return and can be compared. It can be a return on a security as distinguished from a portfolio. If the security is correctly priced it will have Ri = Rf = 0 and SML curve goes through the origin (see chart below) Ri – Rf measures the excess return which varies with the risk taken. Within the chart it is seen that Rm – Rf is excess return if market Beta = 1. The security market line implies that the individual assets and portfolio should be on SML, if they are correctly priced. Beta values should then correctly represent the contribution to the risk of the security to the portfolio. All assets lying above the SML are undervalued and those below the SML are overvalued. If we buy undervalued securities, the returns will be more and *vice versa.* It will thus be seen that SML curve assumes a critical importance in portfolio selection and individual investment decision.

CAPM Analysis

The expected return of a portfolio in equilibrium is equal to risk free rate Rf, plus risk premium which is related to its Beta. Thus, Rp – Rf = risk premium and this is equal to B_{PM} (Rm – Rf) where Rp is expected rate of return and Rf the risk free return.

These symbols are the same as explained above. This leads us to the market model, which relates the expected excess return of the portfolio to the excess return of the market. This is an explanation of the risk premium which gives excess returns. The chart below presents the relation of E [(Rm) – (Rf)], to the E (RP – Rf) viz., in words, excess returns on a portfolio to the portfolio's excess risk over the market risk. This chart presents CAPM in a general form with expected excess market risk related to expected excess return.

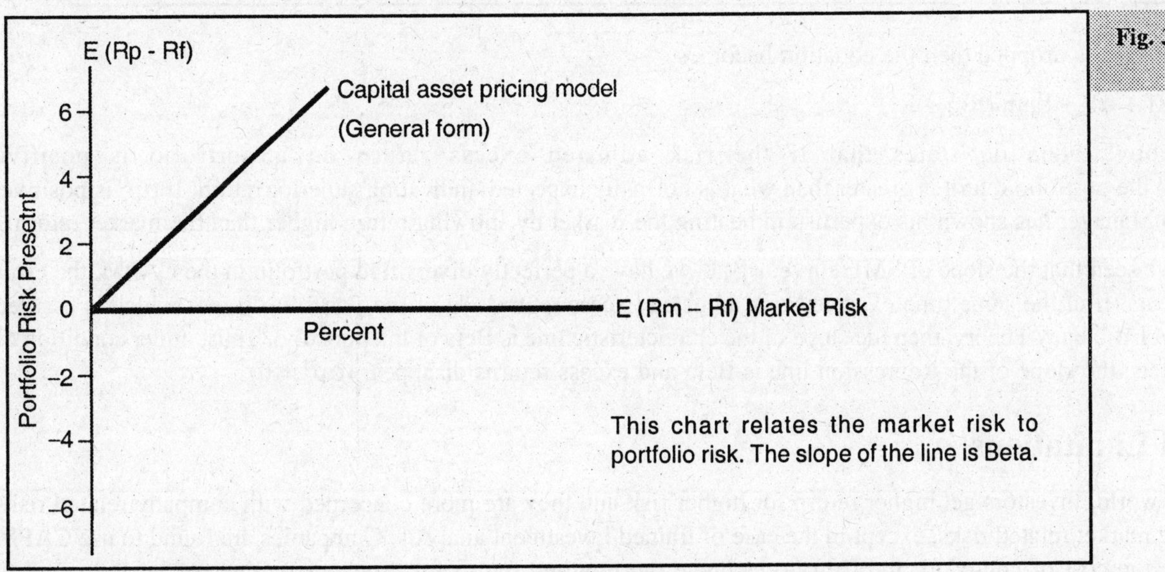

Fig. 38.5

Market Model

Risk Premium form is the one shown above and the equation for this is

RpT = (βpm) × (Rm – Rf)

(Premium for portfolio) ⟶ (Beta) ⟶ (Premium for market)

Beta relates the portfolio premium to market risk premium. If Beta is one they are the same.

Market Model can be presented in the form of a regression equation. Taking the above equation for Risk premium of the portfolio, let us introduce a new concept of risk adjusted excess return which is generated by the expertise of the portfolio Manager, represented by the $\alpha^0 p$. This can be graphically represented as the y-axis intercept for the regression line. $\alpha^0 p$ can be zero, positive or negative, depending on the performance of the portfolio.

When this model is presented in the Risk premium form, the equation is

$$Rp - Rf = \alpha p - Rf\,(1 - \beta pm) + \beta pm\,(Rm - Rf) + rp$$

$$\alpha p^o = \alpha p - Rf\,(1 - \beta pm)$$

As the risk of the portfolio remains unaffected, βpm of the characteristic line remains unchanged but αp changes to αp^o as follows:

$$\alpha p^o = \alpha p - Rf\,(1 - \beta pm)$$

αp^o is risk adjusted excess return

αp is return on portfolio when the market return is zero. In other words, αp represents the excess return of the portfolio, when the market return is equal to riskless rate and rp is the error term or the residual.

αp^o can be the same as αp, when Rf $(1 - \beta pm)$ is zero which happens when βpm is 1; then the excess market return disappears. The above equation now becomes; $Rp - Rf = \alpha p + \beta pm\ (Rm - Rf) + rp$; putting it differently,

$$Rp = \underset{\text{Riskless Return}}{\underline{Rf}} + \underset{\text{Risk Adjusted Excess Return}}{\underline{ap}} + \underset{\text{Systematic Risk Premium}}{\underline{bpm\ (Rm - Rf)}} + \underset{\text{Error Term}}{\underline{rp}}$$

If error term is dropped then the equation becomes

$Rp = Rf + \alpha P + \beta pm\ (Rm - Rf)$

The above equation states that if the risk adjusted excess return on a portfolio is positive $\alpha p^0 > 0$, then the portfolio return is greater than what is normally expected, indicating superior return. If αp^0 is positive, the Portfolio Manager has shown his expertise in beating the market by showing return higher than the market return.

We have seen that the slope of SML curve is β. If we have a perfectly diversified portfolio in the CAPM, the error term disappears. If at the same time expected risk adjusted excess return $\alpha^0 p$ of the portfolio is zero which is assured under Market Efficiency Theory, then the slope of the characteristic line is Beta of the portfolio. Thus, under condition of perfect markets, the slope of the Regression line is Beta and excess returns disappear ($\alpha p^0 = 0$).

Uses and Limitations

In real world, investors get higher return for higher risk and they are more concerned with company related risks than with the market related risks, except in the case of trained investment analysts. Companies are found to use CAPM to determine the cost of equity for the firm, to estimate the required return for divisions or lines of business and to determine the hurdle rates for corporate investments and to evaluate the performance of investment Division in terms of costs and returns. These hurdle rates of return are in general the required rates of return and the corporates assess the past performance of the costs and related returns for each of the Divisions. In the case of public utilities, the CAPM can be used to estimate the costs and rates to be charged to cover the costs. The CAPM is used to regulate the public utilities from the point of view of costs.

Historical return and Betas are used to select the proper risk in investments in the portfolio. CAPM is used to select securities, construct portfolios and evaluate the performance of the portfolio. It is thus a useful tool for investment analysis and portfolio management.

The limitations of the theory are also pointed out by many critics. This theory is unrealistic for any average investor, who goes by the fundamental factors influencing the company, its earnings, dividend and bonus record. Empirical tests of the Model have not proved very useful. The Model is built on *ex-ante* factors while in reality the expectations of the future vary from person to person. Data and analysis is to be based on *ex-post* factors while anticipations of future risk and returns are *ex-ante* and both may not be related. The CAPM is in fact not testable exactly as the exact composition of the market is known and is used in testing. The empirical tests conducted by Richard Roll and others were only tests on samples whether the proxy market portfolio was efficient or not. The use of surrogatives and proxies have not proved the theory as really useful and practical.

CAPM theory is thus a nice theoretical exposition but in actual world, it does not conform to the real world risk-return trends and empirical tests have not given unequivocal support to the theory. It is also found that there are many non-Beta factors influencing the returns. The calculation of Beta is itself of doubtful validity as the historical Betas may not reflect the future risks or returns. In the short-run in particular, projections on the basis of Betas on returns and risk have been found to be unreliable and results contrary to CAPM Theory were noticed. Thus, CAPM is a good theoretical tool but with its own limitations in practical applications.

Capital Asset Pricing Model

The assumptions of CAPM are that the market is in equilibrium and the expected rate of return is equal to the required rate of return for a given level of risk or Beta. CAPM presents a linear relationship between the required rate of return of a security and relates it to market related risk or Beta, which cannot be avoided. The equation for the CAPM Theory is:

$$R_J = Rf + B_J (R_M - Rf)$$

R_J is expected rate of return on security 'J' and Rf is risk free return.

B_J is Beta coefficient — a risk measure for the non-diversifiable part of total Risk. R_M is return on Market Portfolio and R_M – Rf is the excess return for the extra risk.

Limitation of CAPM

It is not realistic in the real world. This assumes that all investors are risk averse and higher the risk, the higher is the return. Investors ignore the transactions cost information costs, brokerage, taxes etc., and make decisions on the basis of single period horizon. The investors are given a choice on the basis of risk-return characteristics of an investment and they can buy at the going rate in the market. There are many buyers and sellers and the market is competitive and free forces of supply and demand determine the prices.

CAPM establishes a measure of risk premium and is measured by $B_J (R_M–Rf)$ Beta coefficient is the non-diversifiable risk of the asset, relative to the risk of the asset.

Suppose Cipla Company has a Beta equal to 1.5 and the risk free rate is say 6%. The required rate of return on the market (R_M) is 15%. Then, adopting the above equation, we have

$$R_J = Rf + (B_J)(R_M - Rf)$$
$$= 6 + 1.5\,(15 - 6)$$
$$= 6 + 13.5 = 19.5\%$$

If the market rate is 15% then the return on Cipla should be 19.5%, because the larger risk on Cipla than on the market.

SML Security Market Line

SML plots the relationship between the Required rate of return R_J and non-diversified risk, Beta, as expressed above in CAPM.

Example

Market Expected Return = 12%

Market Risk Premium (R_M – Rf) = 7

Risk free Return = 5 (Rf)

R_M – Rf = (12 – 5) = 7

If security x has Beta of 1.20

Then $R_J = Rf + B_J (R_M - Rf)$

$= 5 + 1.2\,(7)$

$= 5 + 8.4 = 13.4$ (Aggressive Scrip)

If security y has Beta as 0.80, then it is a defensive scrip. Thus,

$R_J = 5 + 0.8\,(7) =$

$5 + 5.6 = 10.6$

These can be represented as follows:

Fig. 38.6

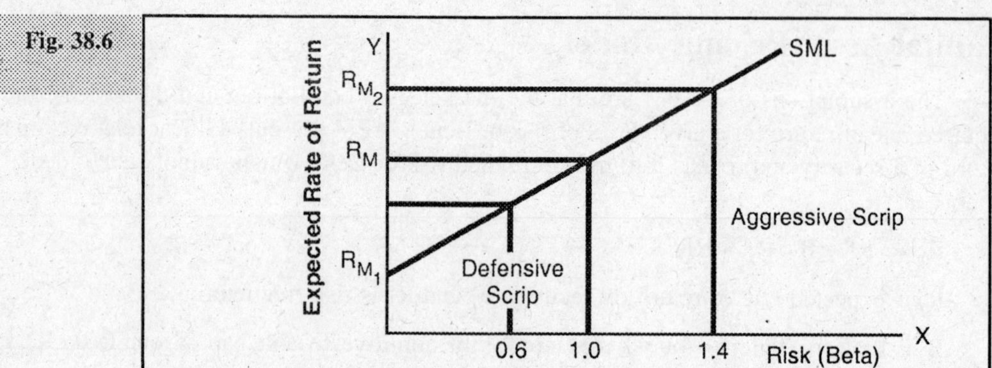

The actual prices of securities may fall above or below the SML. The over-valuation and under-valuation can be seen from the above chart.

When we estimate the expected return after an year, in the absence of historic data on returns and probabilities the following formula which is derived from the basic formula given above is useful.

$$\text{Expected return } R_J = \frac{D_o(1+g)}{P_o} + g$$

Where, D_0 = last paid dividend

P_0 = current market price

g = Growth rate.

If the above return is higher than the equilibrium rate effecting the equilibrium price — a position on the SML — both the stocks, above the SML and below the SML have undergone some changes. The expected rate has to be equated to the required rate of return, when the point of equilibrium is reached on the SML. When the expected return is higher than the required rate, the demand for that security will rise and the price will also rise, bringing down its return to the equilibrium level. If the expected return is lower than the required return the demand will fall leading to a fall in its price, bringing it to the equilibrium level. In the former case, the investors will buy securities and in the letter case, they will sell securities.

Thus, the CAPM is useful to provide insights for the finance Manager to maximise the value of the firm. Following the principle of the higher the risk, the higher is the return, the finance Manager will keep the risk level at the optimum level in performing the investment function or financing function by keeping in mind the return that shareholder expects to take at a given level of risk at the company.

The Finance Manager has to keep in mind the expected returns of the share-holders and the returns he provides should be commensurate with the risk. This risk is reflected in his investment and financing decisions. The SML provides a bench mark reflecting the equilibrium position in the relationship between the risk and return. The risk that is reflected in the non-diversifiable or systematic risk is that the company is exposed to in its operations, financing and investment decisions.

Problems

Q. An investor wants to purchase a Bond with maturity 3 years, coupon rate 11% and par value of 100.

(A) If the investor is requiring YTM 15% of equivalent risk what is the price he should pay?

Ans: $P = \left(\frac{11}{1+0.15}\right) + \frac{11}{(1+0.15)^2} + \frac{111}{(1+015)^3} = 90.9$

(B) If the bond is selling at a price of Rs. 97.59 what is its YTM.

YTM is to be estimated by Trial and error method. Consider 12% as YTM.

Then

Ans: $\frac{11}{(1+0.12)}+\frac{11}{(1+0.12)^2}+\frac{111}{(1+0.12)^3}=97.59$

Hence, YTM is 12%

(C) What is the duration of Bond, if the YTM is 12% and expected return is 10.06%.

Duration	*Value*	*% age Value*	*Weighted Duration*
1 Year	9.82 $=\left(\frac{11}{1.12}\right)$	10.06	0.1006 = 1 X 0.1006
2 Year	8.77 $=\left(\frac{11}{(1.12)^2}\right)$	8.99	0.1798 = 2 X 0.0899
3 Year	79.01 $=\frac{111}{(1.12)^3}$	80.95	2.4285 = 3 X 0.8095
Total	97.60	100.00	2.7089

The duration in the case of value bond of YTM of 12% and expected return 10.06% was shown above. Then the weighted duration of the portfolio is 2.7089.

The Market Model and CAPM may not give similar results as expected excess returns and risk premiums, in the two models are not identical.

Say $\alpha p = 4\%$, $Rf = 6\%$ (riskless return)

β Beta = 2, Rm (expected market return) = 10%.

Expected Risk Premium (Rp – Rf)

Market Model = $\alpha P^{\alpha} + \beta pm\ (Rm - Rf)$

(Rp – Rf) = $4 - 6\ (1 - 2) + 2\ (10 - 6)$

$4 + 6 + 8 = 18\%$

Where, $\alpha P^{\alpha} = \alpha P - Rf\ (1 - \beta m)$

$4 - 6\ (1 - 2) = 10$

CAPM

(Rp – Rf) = $\beta pm\ (Rm - Rf)$

$= 2\ (10 - 6) = 8\%$

$20 - 12 = 8\%$

In the exceptional case when the portfolio is in equilibrium, the expected risk premium of the portfolio **under both** models should be identical. That happens when $\alpha p^0 = 0 = \alpha p - Rf\ (1 - \beta pm)$

Then under Market Model

The excess Premium $= 0 + 2\ (10 - 6)$

$= 2 \times 4 = 8\%$

and under CAPM

$Rp - Rf = 2\ (10 - 6)$

$20 - 12 = 8\%$

Problems

If the risk free rate is 10%, expected return on NSE Index is 18%, standard deviation is 5% (SD). Construct an efficient portfolio to secure 16% return. The efficient portfolio consists of market securities and risk free securities invested in the proportion of W and 1 – W respectively, then

Rp = W (Rm) + (1 – W) Rf

16% = W (18%) + (1 – W) 10%

16 = 18w + 10 – 10W

16 – 10 = 6 = 18W – 10W = 8 W. Thus, 8W = 6

and $W = \frac{6}{8}$ = 75% 1 – W = 25%

Investment in market securities is 75% of the amount and 25% in risk free securities. The portfolio risk in the case is

$$Rp = Rf + \frac{(Rm - Rf)}{\sigma m} \sigma p$$

$$16 = 10 + \frac{18 - 10}{5} \sigma p$$

$$16 - 10 = \frac{8}{5} \sigma p$$

$$6 \times 5 = 8 \sigma p$$

$$\sigma p = \frac{30}{8} = 3.75$$

If now an amount of Rs. 10,000 is to be invested and expected return is 20%, construct a portfolio and calculate its risk

Rp = 20 = W × 18 + (1 – W) 10

20 = 18W + 10 – 10W (viz. 10 + 8W)

10 = 8W

$$W = \frac{10}{8} = 1.25$$

Since it is more than 1, borrow 0.25 or 25% of Rs. 10,000 to invest in market portfolio. Thus own funds are Rs. 10,000 and borrowed funds are Rs. 2,500, with a total of Rs. 12,500.

Risk on the portfolio is calculated as follows:

$$20 = 10 + \left(\frac{18-10}{5}\right) \sigma p = 10 + \frac{8}{5} \sigma p$$

$$20 - 10 = \frac{8}{5} \sigma p$$

$$\sigma p = \frac{10 \times 5}{8} = \frac{50}{8} = 6.25\%$$

Diversification (Random and Naive)

The traditional theory laid down diversification as a technique of selection of securities in a portfolio. This is called "Random diversification" or "Simple diversification," on the basis of straight rule of "two is a better than one." Simple diversification on Random basis was found to be more remunerative by researchers and these number of scrips in a portfolio of individuals is to be around 10 – 15 securities.

Rational basis of why diversification and how to achieve optimal diversification were studied by later researchers, of which Markowitz is reputed to be the pioneer. "Naive diversification" or "Superfluous diversification" may result from random and indiscriminate selection of securities, which does not lead to any reduction of risk. Thus, cycle and tubes are related industries and one invests in those two types of industries which are highly correlated in a positive manner, the risk will be increased by diversification rather than reducing. Naive diversification thus means that diversification in name only which does not reduce the risk. Thus, an investor may have 10 scrips in steel, mini steel and ferrous metals, which will only increase risk. But an investor having 10 scrips spread in cycles, electronics, sugar, steel, auto, etc., will have less risk as these industries are not auto correlated and their risks are independent of each other or even negatively related.

It is thus left to Markowitz and later researchers to show that diversification is a tool to reduce unsystematic risk and how it can be reduced by a study of variances and covariances of securities return, as against the market returns.

Why Diversification?

It is never prudent to put all ones' eggs in one basket, as it may lead to total ruin if the basket itself is broken or lost. The human behaviour is normally risk averse which means that for psychological reasons, he distributes his assets in a variety of risk classes, some in cash, some in bank deposits, insurance, provident fund, pension fund etc. These are all examples of the normal human behaviour of diversifying the asset holdings to reduce risk, provide for contingency and take all precautions against total loss.

(a) Thus, the average investor never puts all his savings in one form or in one security for self-protection and for psychological reasons.

(b) Money kept idle or in some investments which do not give adequate return will be a loss to investor, as he loses the value of money over time. By logic of common sense, investors try to satisfy most of their objectives of savings by putting money in various avenues and that means diversification. The various objectives are income, capital appreciation, safety, marketability, contingency, liquidity and hedge against inflation and for future provision of larger incomes. His choice of investments will cater to these requirements which lead to diversification of investments.

Even without the theoretical basis of covering or reducing the unsystematic diversifiable risk, the investor in the traditional Theory used to adopt some methods of Diversification.

Example on Measurement of Risk

Calculation of Standard Deviation and Variance

As diversification is meant for reduction of risk, its measurement is relevant here.

DCM			Escorts		
Return	Probability	Weighted Average Return	Return	Probability	Weighted Average
8	0.15	1.20	9	0.30	2.70
9	0.20	1.80	10	0.40	4.00
10	0.30	3.00	11	0.30	3.30
11	0.20	2.20			
12	0.15	1.80			
		10%			10%

Average return is the same in both cases but risk is different. DCM has a range of variation from 8% to 12% while the escorts has a variation from 9 to 11, which is less than that in the former.

Calculation of Standard Deviation

Example DCM

Return	Mean	Difference (d)	Square of Deviation (d^2)
8	10	– 2	4
9	10	– 1	1
10	10	0	0
11	10	1	1
12	10	2	4
			$\Sigma D^2 =$ 10

σ = Standard deviation is $\sqrt{\frac{\Sigma d^2}{N}} = \sqrt{\frac{10}{5}} = \sqrt{2}$

σ standard deviation = $\sqrt{2}$ = 1.41

σ^2 = variance is 2

Example Escorts

Return	Mean	Deviation	Square of Deviation
9	10	1	1
10	10	0	0
11	10	1	1
			$Sd^2 = 2$

σ = standard deviation $= \sqrt{\frac{\Sigma d^2}{N}} = \sqrt{\frac{2}{3}} = \sqrt{0.66}$

$\sigma = \sqrt{0.66} = 0.82$

σ^2 = variance = 0.66

Risk on the Escorts is lower in the example, referred to above.

Example of Simple Diversification

Take two securities of TISCO and Reliance

Security	Expected Return	Proportion of Investment
TISCO	20%	25%
Reliance	25%	75%

The return on the portfolio by combining them would be $Rp = W_1R_1 + W_2R_2$. Rs. are returns and W_1 and W_2 are weights of two investments.

Rp = 0.20 (.25) + 0.25 (0.75)

= 5% + 18.75% = 23.75%

Here no consideration is given for risk and covariance of risk among the securities, invested in the portfolio. This can be demonstrated by taking an example of Markowitz diversification.

Markowitz Diversification

Before discussing the Markowitz diversification, what the researches of investors and investment analysts have found is to be set out briefly. Firstly, they found that putting all eggs in one basket is bad and most risky. Secondly, there should be adequate diversification of investment into various securities as that will spread the risk and reduce it; if the number of them say 10 to 15 it is adequate to enjoy the economies of time, scale of operations and expertise utilised by the investor in his analysis.

Reference was already made to Naive diversification, which is a spread of investments into many securities but will not reduce the risk, like buying ten securities all in the shipping industry, which is risky industry in itself. Besides some researchers have found that there is an optimisation process for diversification to reduce the unsystematic or company related risk by choosing such companies which are not closely related or not owned by the same family group in the same industry group. This optimisation process also leads to an investment in 10-15 companies well chosen for differences in their characteristics, nature of the product market, pattern of production etc.

Example

What is the expected return of a portfolio, comprising of the following securities:

Security	Expected Return	% of Fund, Invested
1. DCM	10%	25%
2. Shriram Fibres	15%	25%
3. J.K. Synthetics	20%	50%

$Rp = W_1 R_1 + W_2 R_2 + W_3 R_3$

Rs are expected returns and Ws are weights

$$Rp = (10 \times 0.25) + 15\ (0.25) + 20\ (0.50)$$

$$= 2.5 + 3.75 + 10.0$$

$$= 16.25\%$$

Example

Given the following data on two stocks Tisco and Reliance and their returns, calculate the required measures of expected returns, etc.

Security	Year	Return	Proportion Invested
TISCO	1	10%	40%
	2	16%	
Reliance	1	12%	60%
	2	18%	

$$Rp = \text{Expected Return} = \frac{40}{100} \times \frac{10+16}{2} + \frac{60}{100} \times \frac{12+18}{2}$$

$$= 5.2 + 9.0$$

$$= 14.2\%$$

Calculation of Standard Deviation

$\sigma_r = \sqrt{\frac{X^2}{n}}$ for R stock

RETURN	$(x-\bar{x})$	$(x-\bar{x})^2$
10	− 3	9
16	+ 3	9
26		18

$\bar{x} = \frac{26}{2} = 13$ $\sigma = \sqrt{\frac{18}{2}}$ and $\sqrt{9} = 3$

SD = 3; variance $\sigma^2 = 9$.

$\sigma_s = \sqrt{\frac{X^2}{N}}$ = for S stock

	Return	$(x-\bar{x})$	$(x-\bar{x})^2$
	12	−3	9
	18	+3	9
Total	30	$\Sigma\ (x-\bar{x})$	18

$$\sigma = \sqrt{\frac{\Sigma(X-\bar{X})^2}{N}}$$

$$\sigma^2 = \frac{\Sigma(X-\bar{X})^2}{N}$$

$\bar{x} = \frac{30}{2} = 15$ (S.D.) − $\sigma = \sqrt{\frac{18}{2}} = \sqrt{9} = 3$

variance σ^2 = 9, SD = 3

Calculation of Covariance

Given, σr = 3 σs = 3

Rx = Expected Return on security x

Ry = Expected Return on security y

N = number of observations

Covariance, Cov x. y = $(Rx - R\bar{x})\ (Ry - R\bar{y})$

$$\text{Cov. x. y} = \frac{1}{N}\ (Rx - R\bar{x}) + \frac{1}{N}\ (Ry - R\bar{y})$$

	Return	Expected	Deviation	Product of Deviations
Stock R	10	14.2	– 4.2	4.2 × 2.2
Stock S	12	14.2	2.2	= 9.24
Stock R	16	14.2	+ 1.8	1.8 × 3.8
Stock S	18	14.2	+ 3.8	= 6.84

Cov. = (10 – 14.2) (12 – 14.2) +

$\frac{1}{2}$ (16 – 14.2) (18 – 14.2)

$= \frac{1}{2} \times (-4.2)\ (-2.2) + \frac{1}{2}\ (1.8 \times 3.8)$

$\frac{1}{2} \times 9.24 + \frac{1}{2}\ (6.84)$

= 4.62 + 3.42 = + 8.04

Correlation Coefficient

$$r \times y \quad = \frac{\text{Cov. XY}}{\sigma x \times \sigma y} = \frac{8.04}{3 \times 3}$$

= 0.893

If the coefficient of correlation is high as 0.893, nearer to one, then the degree of risk in the portfolio is also high

SML Example – Security Returns

	Expected Return	Beta	Sd
BSE Index (Market)	.12	1.00	20
Riskless Treasury Bill	.08	0.00	0
Scrip A	.32	1.70	50
Scrip B	.30	1.40	35
Scrip C	.25	1.10	40

Equation for SML is as follows:

Calculate the SML?

Ri = Rf + βi (Rm – Rf)

Scrip A = .08 + 1.70 (.12 – 0.08)

= .08 + .068 = 0.148 = 14.8%

Scrip B = .08 + 1.40 (.12 – .08)

= .08 + 0.056 = .136 = 13.6%

Scrip C = .08 + 1.10 (.12 – 0.08)

= .08 + 0.044 = .124 = 12.4%

CML

All investors have to choose for a combination of two components of the portfolio: (1) Market Risky Portfolio. (2) Riskless Securities. The straight line tangent to the Efficient Frontier Line is called the Capital Market Line. On this line all the efficient portfolios would be lying. The CML chooses the most efficient portfolio and this indicates the market price of risk represented by the formula.

The Return viz., $Rp = Rf + \dfrac{RM - RF}{\sigma m} \sigma p$

The term Rm – Rf/σm is the extra return over the risk free rate by increasing the level of risk (Sd) of the efficient portfolio by one unit.

SML

Taking non-systematic risk as zero for a well diversified portfolio, the only relevant risk is systematic risk measured by Beta. If Beta is zero, it is riskless security. For Market Portfolio, the Beta is one. The straight line called SML is represented by the equation

$Ri = \alpha + b\beta i$ .... Equation 1

if Bi = 0, then the first point of the line is

$Rf = \alpha + b\ (0)$

$Rf = \alpha$

the second point of the line is

$RM = \alpha + b\ (1)$ Where $\beta_M = 1$

As $\alpha = Rf$, $RM - \alpha = b$

then $RM - Rf = b$ .... Equation 2

Combining the above two results, we have the equation of SML

$Ri = Rf + Bi\ (RM - Rf)$

Example

Elecon stock is expected to sell at Rs. 70 a year hence and pay a dividend of Rs. 4 per share. If the Stock's correlation with portfolio is – 0.3

σx 40% σm = 20%, Rf (Risk free Rate) = 5%

$\beta x = \dfrac{\sigma X}{\sigma M}$ x Correlation coefficient

$= \dfrac{40\%}{20\%} \times -.3 = -0.60$

ERp = Rf + Bx Rf

ERp = 5% + (– 0.6 × 5%)

5 – 3 = 2%

Stock price a year hence will be Rs. 70 ($P_1n = 70$ and $D_1 = 4$)

Present selling price $Po = \dfrac{70+4}{1.02}$ = Rs. 72.55

Example [@]

Given the following data, answer the question below:

Category of Assets	*Total Market*	σ	Correlation Matrix *RE*	*E*	*D*	*Total*
RE	Rs. 10, 000 (50%)	20%	1.0	—	—	0.65
E	Rs. 6,000 (30%)	30%	0.3	1.0	—	0.60
D	Rs. 4,000 (20%)	15%	0.3	0.3	1.0	0.30

Portfolio Mix is 50: 30: 20.

What is its S.D.? Following the formula used earlier we have,

$$\sigma^2 = (0.5)^2 (0.20)^2 + (0.3)^2 (.30)^2 + (0.2)^2 (0.15)^2$$
$$+ 2 (0.3) (0.5) (0.3) (.2) (.3)$$
$$+ 2 (0.3) (0.5) (0.2) (.2) (.15)$$
$$+ 2 (0.3) (0.3) (0.2) (.3) (.15)$$
$$= 0.01 + .0081 + 0.0009 + .0054 + .0018 + 0.00162$$

$$\sigma p^2 = .02782$$

$$\sigma = \sqrt{0.02782} = 0.1667$$

$$\sigma = 16.7\%$$

CAPM

Example

If the risk free rate is 8%

Market Risk premium 6%, Market SD is 10%

Calculate the variance of two portfolios —

(1) Risk free investment 30%, Risky Fund 70%.

(2) Diversified portfolio with Beta of 1.5.

Portfolio (1)

$$\sigma_1 = 0.7 (10.0\%) + 0.3 (0) =$$
$$= 7.0 + 0 = 7\%$$

Portfolio (2)

$$\sigma_2^2 = \beta_2^2 \sigma m^2 + 0$$
$$\sigma_2^2 = (1.5)^2 (10)^2 = 2.25 \times 100 = 225$$
$$\sigma_2^2 = 225$$
$$\sigma_2 = \sqrt{225} = 15\%$$

@ Please refer to chapter 42 also.

Example

Indfund has three Investment strategies as given below. Find out the plan with greater risk

Strategy	Investment in % Bonds	Investment in Stocks	Beta of Stocks
A	0	100	1.0
B	20	80	1.0
C	30	70	1.0

Strategy	*Portfolio Beta Calculation*
A	00.0 (0.0) + 1.0 (1.0) = 1.0
B	0.2 (0.0) + 0.8 (1.0) = 0.8
C	0.3 (0.0) + 0.7 (1.0) = 0.7

Strategy A has the largest Risk, as the portfolio Beta is highest at 1.0, as compared to B and C.

Problems

Republic Forge has a beta 1.45, the risk free rate Rf is 10% and r_p expected return on market portfolio is 16%. This company pays a dividend of Rs. 2 a share and expected growth in dividends is 10% per annum.

(a) What is the stock required rate of return according to CAPM?

(b) What is the stock's Market price, assuming the required return?

Answer:

(a) Rp = 10 + 1.45 (16 –10) = 10+8.7 = 18.7%

(b) Following the perpetual Dividend Growth model, we have

$$Po = \frac{D_1}{Rp - g} = \frac{2(1.10)}{(0.187 - 010)} = \left(\frac{2.20}{0.087}\right)$$

$$= \frac{2.20}{0.087} = 25.29$$

The Numerator is the present value of Dividend stream and denominator is the required rate of return or expected rate minus the growth rate of dividend.

Asset Pricing Implication of SML

One of the major assumptions of the CAPM is that the market is in equilibrium and that the expected rate of return is equal to the required rate of return for a given level of market risk or beta. In other words, the SML provide a framework for evaluating whether high-risk stocks are offering returns more or less in proportion to their risk and *vice-versa.*

$$\text{Expected Return} = Dt + \frac{(Pt)\,(Pt - r)}{Pt_1} = \frac{\text{Expected Income}}{\text{Market Purchase Price}}$$

In the absence of historic data, the following formula may be used.

$$\text{Expected Return} = \frac{Do\,(1+g)}{Po} + g$$

Do = Last dividend paid

Po = Current purchase/market price.

g = Growth rate.

To reach equilibrium and their required rate of return points on the SML, both stocks have to go through a temporary price adjustment.

In practice, how does the price of say stock "X" get pushed up to its equilibrium price? Say Investors will be interested in purchasing security "x" if it offers more than proportionate returns in comparison to the risk. This demand will push up the price of x as more of it is purchased and correspondingly bring down the returns. This process will continue till it reaches the equilibrium price and expected returns are the same as required returns.

Equilibrium Price: (SLM)

Problem

Short-term Government securities yield 7% and the expected market return is 12%. Stock X's beta is 0.8, its growth rate is 4% and its last dividend was Rs. 2.0. what would be the stock's equilibrium price?

Answer:

$R_x = R_F + bx\,(R_M - R_F)$ and $P_x = D_o\,(1+g)\;[Rx - g]$

R_x = Rate of return required on stock x

R_F = Risk free rate of interest.

R_m = Return on Market Portfolio.

B_x = Beta co-efficient of stock x.

g = Growth rate of dividend

D_o = Last dividend per share

We are given R_M 12%; $B_x = 0.8$; $D_o = 2.00$; $g = 4\%$: $R_F = 7\%$

$R_x = 7 + 0.8\,(12 - 7) = 7 + 0.8 \times 5 = 7 + 4 = 11\%$

Equilibrium price can be worked out as given below.

$$R_x = \frac{D_o\,(1+g)}{P_o} + g$$

$$11 = \frac{2\,(1+0.4)}{P_o} + 4$$

$$11 = \frac{2.08}{P_o} + 4$$

$$11 - 4 = 7 = \frac{2.08}{P_o}$$

$$P_o = \frac{2.08}{.07} = 29.71$$

Problem

The beta co-efficient of standard company is 1.2. The company is maintaining a 5% rate of growth in earnings or dividends. The last dividend paid was Rs. 2 per share. The risk-free rate of return and the return on market portfolio are 10% and 15% respectively. The current market price of the company is Rs. 14. What will be the equilibrium price per share of standard company?

Answer:

According to CAPM, the expected Rate of Return E(R) is equal to RF + β(R_M – RF)

Given RF = 10%; B = 1.2; RM = 15%.

$$\therefore E(R) = 10 + 1.2\,(15 - 10)$$

$$= 16\%$$

$$E(R) = \frac{D_1\,(1+g)}{P_o} + g$$

$$0.16 = \frac{2\,(1.05)}{P_o} + 0.05$$

$$\frac{2(1.05)}{P_o} = 0.16 - 0.05 = 0.11$$

$$P_o = \frac{2(1.05)}{.11} = \frac{2.10}{.11}$$

$$P_o = \text{Rs. } 19.09$$

Problem: Calculate β_1 and β_2 from the data given:

Year	R_S	R_B	R_M	R_f (TB rate)	y_1 (R_s–Rf)	$(y_1)^2$	y_2 (R_B–Rf)	$(y_2)^2$	x (R_M–Rf)	x^2	xy_1	xy_2
1993	15	10	11	6	9	81	4	16	5	25	45	20
1994	–6	–2	–5	5	–11	121	–7	49	–10	100	110	70
1995	17	13	12	7	10	100	6	36	5	25	50	30
1996	18	9	11	6	12	144	3	9	5	25	60	15
1997	22	11	13	7	15	225	4	16	6	36	90	24
					$\bar{y}_1 = 7$	$\Sigma(y_1)^2 = 671$	$\bar{y}_2 = 2$	$\Sigma(y_2)^2 = 126$	$\bar{x} = 2.2$	$\Sigma(x)^2 = 211$	$\Sigma xy_1 = 355$	$Exy_2 = 159$

From the above Data $\Sigma y_1 = 35$ $\Sigma y_2 = 10$ $\Sigma x = 11$

Systematic Risk = $\beta_1 = \frac{N\Sigma xy - \Sigma x \times \Sigma y}{N\Sigma x^2 - (\Sigma x)^2} = \frac{5 \times 355 - 11 \times 35}{5 \times 211 - 121} = \frac{1755 - 385}{934} = 1.48$

$$\beta_2 = \frac{5 \times 159 - 11 \times 10}{5 \times 211 - 121} = \frac{795 - 110}{1055 - 121} = \frac{685}{934} = 0.73$$

Problem on CAPM

$$V_o = \frac{D_1}{K_c - g}$$

$$D_1 = D_o\ (1 + g)$$

$$D_o\ (1+g)^n = Dn$$

Given the following variables

D_0 = Dividend per share = 3.5%

g = growth rate = 6%

K_C = Required rate of return = 18%

Rf = Risk-free Return = 9%

β = Beta (Systematic risk measure) 1.3

Ri = Rf + b (R_m – Rf)

Where, Rf = 9%, RM = 16% and b = 1.3.

Thus, Ri =9 + 1.3 (16 – 9) = 18.1

Applying the value of Ri as the required rate of return K_C. We have the formula

$$V_1 = \frac{D_1}{K_c - g} \text{ or } \frac{D_o\,(1+g)}{K_c - g}$$

$$= \frac{3.5\,(1+0.06)}{0.18-0.06} = \frac{3.5 \times 1.06}{0.12} = \frac{3.71}{0.12} = 30.92$$

P_1 or V_1 = 30.92

Given P_1 as Rs. 30.92

and given P_o as Rs. 20

$$\text{Return Ri} = \frac{D_1 + (P_1 - P_0)}{P_o} = \frac{3.71 + (30.92 - 20)}{20}$$

$$= \frac{3.71 + 10.92}{20} = \frac{14.63}{20} = 7.3\%$$

Problem on SML

Security	E (R)	β
1	14%	1.20
2	15%	0.75
3	20%	1.50

Given Rf as 9% and R_M = 15%

Calculate the Return on the securities 1 to 3 and compare them with the expected Returns. Security line or SML is given by the formula.

$R_1 = Rf + \beta_1 (Rm - Rf)$

$= 9 + 1.20 (15\text{-}9)$

$= 9 + 7.2 = 16.2\%$

$R_2 = 9 + 0.75 (15\text{-}9)$

$= 9 + 4.5 = 13.5\%$

$R_3 = 9 + 1.5 (15\text{-}9)$

$= 9 + 9 = 18\%$

Security 1 only could secure 16.2% which is higher than the expected return E(R): 14%.

CAPM

Question 1

Given the following Security Market Line $R_i = 0.07 + 0.09\ \beta_i$

What are the returns on the two stocks whose β_s are 1.2 and 0.9.

Question 2

If the CAPM line is as shown below

$R_i = 0.04 + 0.10\ \beta_i$

What is the excess return of the market over the risk free rate and what is the risk free rate?

Question 3

Using the formula for SML, in equilibrium namely.

$R_i = R_f + \beta_i (R_M - RF)$

and Given

$R_1 = 6\%\ \beta_i = 0.5$

$R_2 = 12\%\ \beta_2 = 1.5$

What is the expected return on an asset with a Beta of 2?

PROBLEMS

(1) The following characteristic lines are given for three mutual funds namely Kothari pioneer Templeton and Morgan Stanley.

Kothari pioneer $r_1 = -0.5\% + 1.25\ rm$, $p = 0.8$

Templeton $r_2 = 1.25\% + 0.95\ rm$, $p = 0.75$

Morgan Stanley $r_3 = 0.75\% + 1.35\ rm$, $p = 0.7$

(a) Which fund has the most systematic risk

(b) What percentage of each Fund's risk is systematic and unsystematic.

Answer:

(a) The Fund which has the highest Beta of 1.35 viz., Morgan Stanley has the most systematic Risk.

(b) The percentage of systematic and unsystematic risk in the total risk can be worked by taking the correlation coefficient squared P^2 which gives the systematic risk (p) and 1 – systematic risk is the unsystematic risk.

Kothari pioneer: — Systematic Risk = $(0.8)^2$ = 64%

Unsystematic Risk = 1 – 0.64 = 0.36 or 36%

Templeton :— Systematic Risk = $(0.75)^2$ = 56.25%

Unsystematic Risk = 1 – 0.5625 = 0.44 or 44%

Morgan Stanley: — Systematic Risk = $(0.7)^2$ = 0.49 = 49%

Unsystematic Risk = 1 – 0.49 = 0.51 or 51%

(2) If Risk free Rate (Rf) is 5%, and market return 14% and beta is 1.5 for the security.

(a) determine the expected return for the security.

(b) what happens to expected return if Rm or market return increases to 16%, assuming that other variables do not change.

(c) what happens to expected return if the beta falls to 0.75, assuming that other variables do not change.

Answer:

(a) Ri = Rf + (Rm – Rf)β

= 0.05 + (.14 – .05) 1.5

= 0.05 + 0. 135 = 0. 185 or 18.5%

(b) Ri = 0.05 + (0.16 – 0.05) 1.5

= 0.05 + 0.165 = 0.215 or 21.5%

(c) Ri = 0.05 + (0.14 – 0.05) 0.75 =

= 0.05 + 0.0675 = .1175 = 11.75%.

(3) given Rf = 8% .Rm = 15% and RA = 18%

(a) Find out the Beta for stock A.

(b) What is stock A's return if its Beta falls to 0.75?

Solution:

(a) RA = Rf + (Rm – Rf) β

18 = 8% + (15 – 8) β

18 = 8 + 7 β

7β = 10

β = 1.43

(b) RA = Rf + b (Rm – Rf)

= 8 + 0.75 (15 – 8)

= 8 + 5.25 = 13.25

= 13.25%.

(4) Given Rf = 6%, E(Rm) = 15% and expected returns and expected Betas are as follows.

Stock	*Expected Return*	*Expected Beta*
A	14%	1.20
B	15%	0.75
C	13%	1.50
D	20%	1.60
E	10%	0.80

Which stock is overvalued and which is undervalued, relative to expected return?

Solution:

$E(R_i) = Rf + \beta\,(E(Rm) - Rf)$

$E(R_A) = 6 + 1.20\,(15 - 6) = 6 + 10.8$

$= 16.8\%$ (overvalued)

$E(R_B) = 6 + 0.75\,(15 - 6) = 6 + 6.75$

$= 12.75\%$ (under valued)

$E(R_C) = 6 + 1.50\,(15 - 6) = 6 + 13.5$

$= 19.5\%$ (over valued)

$E(R_D) = 6 + 1.60\,(15 - 6) = 6 + 14.4$

$= 20.4\%$ (over valued)

$E(R_E) = 6 + 0.80\,(15 - 6) = 6 + 7.2$

$= 13.2\%$ (overvalued)

(5) An investment company manages an Equity Fund consisting of five stock, with the following market values and Betas.

Stock	***Market value***		**Betas**
A	Rs.	1,00,000	1.10
B	Rs.	25,000	1.20
C	Rs.	50,000	0.75
D	Rs.	125,000	0.60
E	Rs.	1,65,000	1.30
	Total	465, 000	

If Rf = 7%, E (Rm) = 14%,

What is the portfolio's expected return?

Solution:

Ws are the weights given to five stocks

$$WA = \frac{100,000}{465,000} = 0.22$$

$$WB = \frac{25,000}{465,000} = 0.05$$

$$WC = \frac{50,000}{465,000} = 0.11$$

$$WD = \frac{125,000}{465,000} = 0.27$$

$$WE = \frac{165,000}{465,000} = 0.35$$

Total weight 1.00

Beta of the portfolio = Σ Wi βi

β = 0.22 (1.10) + 0.05 (1.20) + 0.11 (0.75)

+ 0.27 (0.60) + 0.35 (1.30) =

β = 0.242 + 0.060 + 0.0825 + 0.162 + 0.455

β = 1.0015

E (rp) = Rf + (Rm – Rf) β

= 7 + (14 – 7) 1.0015

= 7 + 7.0105 = 14.0105

= 14.01%

Return on Portfolio

Each security in a portfolio cont`ributes returns in the proportion of its investment in security. Thus, the portfolio expected return is the weighted average of the expected returns, from each of the securities, with weights representing the proportionate share of the security in the total investment. Why does an investor has so many securities in his portfolio? If the security "ABC" gives the maximum return why not he invest in that security all his funds and thus maximise return? The answers to this question lie in the investor's perception of risk attached to investments, his objectives of income, safety, appreciation, liquidity and hedge against loss of value of money etc. This pattern of investment in different asset categories, security categories, types of instruments, etc., would all be described under the caption of diversification, which aims at the reduction or even elimination of non-systematic or company related risks and achieve the specific objectives of investors.

Assuming that investor puts his funds in four securities, the holding period return of the portfolio is described in the Table below:

Security	*Proportion of Funds Invested in Each Security*	*Expected Return of Holding Period*	*Contribution of Each Security to Return*
A	30	15%	4.50
B	25	20%	5.00
C	25	25%	6.25
D	20	10%	2.00
	Weights = 100	Weighted return	17.75%

The above describes the simple Calculation of the weighted average return of a portfolio for the Holding period.

Risk on a Portfolio

Risk on a portfolio is different from the risk on individual securities. This Risk is reflected in the variability of the returns from zero to infinity. The expected return depends on the probability of the returns and their weighted contribution to the risk of the portfolio. There are two measures of Risk in this context — one is the absolute deviation and the other standard deviation. These can be explained with following illustrations. The assumed probabilities of each of the returns and the estimation of absolute deviation and standard deviation, based on them are given for illustration:

Event	Probability	Return	Probability X Return	Absolute Deviation	Probability x Absolute Deviation
(1)	(2)	(3)	(4)	(5)	(6)
			(2) × (3)		(5) × (2)
1.	.20	– 10	– 2.00	– 25	+ 5.0
2.	.30	20	+ 6.00	5	+ 1.5
3.	.40	25	+ 10.0	10	+ 4.0
4.	.10	10	+ 1.00	– 5	+ 0.5
	Expected Return		15.00	Average Absolute Deviation	11.0

Column 5 is deviation of the Returns under column 3 from the expected return 15 (Thus, -25 = (– 10 – 15). Column 6 is the result of multiplying deviation under column 5 with the probability in column 2 without considering signs. Thus, one measure of risk is absolute deviations of returns under column 6.

Another measure is the standard deviation and variance

Standard deviation $= \sqrt{\Sigma(x-\overline{x})^2}$

Variance $= \Sigma(x - \overline{x})^2$

The summation of all deviations from the mean and then squared will give the variance. The square root of variance is standard deviation (sd)

x is the expected return on security.

$\overline{x}$ is the mean or the weighted average return. If two Risks are compared, then standard deviations divided by their means are compared. This is the coefficient of variation, namely $\left(\frac{SD}{\overline{X}}\right)$

Example of Standard Deviation

Take a Portfolio XYZ

Possible Outcome	Return	Probability	Weighted Return	Return Deviation from Mean	Weighted Deviation Squared
1	5%	.25	0.0125	–.04	.0004
2	9%	.50	0.0450	.00	.0000
3	13%	.25	0.0325	.04	.0004
		1.00	.090		.0008

Mean $\frac{27}{3} = 9$

Average Expected Return .09 or 9%. (Mean)

The last column of weighted squared deviations are derived by multiplying by the weights of probabilities with squared deviations. Thus, $(.04)^2 = .0016$ and this multiplied by the probability of it 0.25 gives .0004 and so on.

Now, the variance is sum of the weighted squared deviations, namely, .0008

$\sigma^2 = .0008$

SD $\sqrt{.0008} = 0.028$ or 2.8%

When the return of company XYZ is compared with that of company ABC, we have to take into account, their expected return and standard deviation of the return.

Say Company A and B have the following characteristics.

	A	B
Expected Return	0.115 (or 11.5%)	0.09 (or 9%)
Standard Deviation	4.9	2.8

Which company do you prefer? The Company with a higher return of 11.5% has a higher risk than the other company.

Return and standard deviation and variance of portfolios can also be compared in the same manner. Companies can be ranked in the order of return and variance and select into the portfolio those companies with higher returns but with the same level of risk.

Regression Equation

The basic equation for calculating risk can be formulated as a regression equation

Thus, y $= \alpha + B X + E$

Where, y = Return in the security in a given period and X is the market return

α = the intercept where the regression line crosses the y-axis

B = The slope of the regression line

E = Error term containing all residuals

Take the following graph to illustrate the above

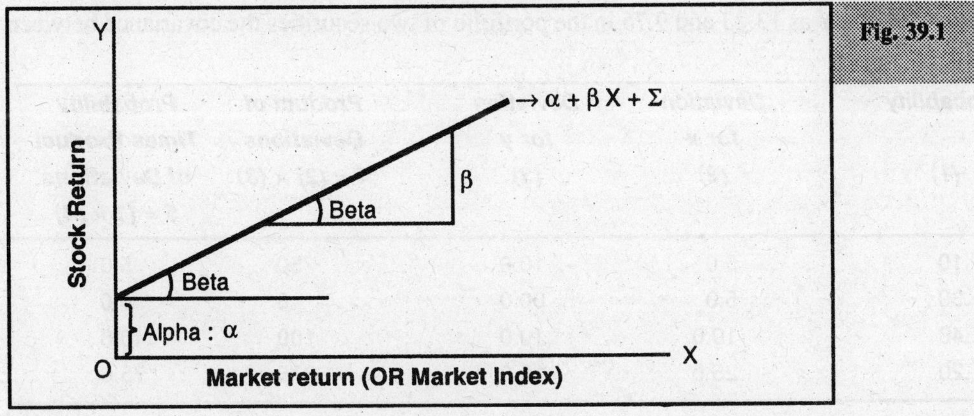

Fig. 39.1

Alpha

α or Alpha is the distance between the horizontal axis and line's intersection with y-axis. It measures the unsystematic risk of the company. If is α positive return, then that scrip will have higher returns. If $\alpha = 0$, then the regression line goes through the origin and its return simply depends on the Beta times the market return.

Beta

β or Beta describes the relationship between the stock's return and the Market index return. This can be positive and negative. It is the percentage change in the price of the stock regressed (or related) to the percentage changes in the market Index. If Beta is 1, a one percentage change in Market index will lead to one percentage change in price of stock. If Beta is zero, stock price is unrelated to the Market index. If the Beta is minus one, it indicates a negative relationship with the Market Index and if the market goes up by a + 1%, the stock price will fall by 1%. Beta measures the systematic risk effectively. On the other hand alpha and Epsilon ($\alpha + \Sigma$) measures the unsystematic risk, which can be reduced by efficient diversification. More details of Beta are discussed elsewhere in the book.

Rho or Correlation Coefficient (covariance)

Rho measures the correlation between two stocks say i and j. If the correlation coefficient is one (+1), an upward movement of one security return is followed by a direct upward movement of the second security. If on the other hand, Rho is –1, the direction of the movement will be opposite as between the stock price and market index. If there is no relation between them, the coefficient of correction can be zero. It can normally vary from – 1 to + 1.

The equation for Rho is

$$P = \frac{\text{Cov (XY)}}{\sigma_x \sigma_y} = \sum_{x=1}^{n} = \frac{Rxi - \overline{R}_i}{\sigma_i} \; \frac{RxJ - \overline{R}_1}{\sigma_J} \; P \times iJ$$

R x i = xth possible return for security i

R x j = xth possible return for security j

$\overline{R}i$ and $\overline{R}j$ are expected returns for i and j

P x i j = Joint probability that Rxi and Rxj occur simultaneously

n = total number of joint observations.

An Example for Covariance and Correlation

Given the standard deviation of X and Y as 13.23 and 9.75 in the portfolio of two securities the covariance between them has to be estimated.

Event	*Probability (1)*	*Deviation for x (2)*	*Deviation for y (3)*	*Product of Deviations 4 = (2) × (3)*	*Probability Times Product of Deviations 5 = (1 × (4)*
1	.10	– 5.0	– 10.0	50	5.0
2	.30	5.0	00.0	0	0.0
3	.40	10.0	10.0	100	40.0
4	.20	– 25.0	– 15.0	375	75.0
				Covariance	120.0

The covariance in the above data is 120

$$r\,x\,y \text{ coefficient of correlation} = \frac{\text{Covariance}}{(\text{SD of x})(\text{SD of y})}$$

$$r\,x\,y \; \frac{120}{13.23 \times 9.75} = \frac{120}{128.99} = 0.93$$

The relationship between coefficient of correction and covariance is expressed by the equation below.

$$r_{xy} = \frac{C_{xy}}{S_x S_y}$$

Where, r_{xy} = Coefficient of correlation

C_{xy} = Covariance between x and y

S_x = Standard deviation of x Returns

S_y = Standard deviation of y Returns

Problem

Calculate the covariance and coefficient of correlation from the following data

Stocks are x and y and their returns and expected returns are given below:

	Return	Expected Return
Stock X	14	18
Stock Y	26	18
Stock X	22	18
Stock Y	10	18

SD First calculate standard deviation σ

X	*Y*	d_x Deviation	d_y Deviation	d_x^2 Squared	d_y^2 Deviations
14	26	– 4	+ 8	16	64
22	10	+ 4	– 8	16	64
Σx 36	Σy 36			32	128

$\overline{X}$ Mean of x = 18, $\overline{Y}$ Mean of y = 18

$$\overline{X} = \frac{36}{2} = 18 \quad \overline{Y} = \frac{36}{2} = 18$$

SD Calculation

$$\delta_X = \sqrt{\frac{32}{2}} = \sqrt{16} = 4$$

$$\delta_Y = \sqrt{\frac{128}{2}} = \sqrt{64} = 8$$

Covariance (CV)

	Return	Expected Return	Difference	Product of Difference
Stock X	14	18	– 4	– 32
Stock Y	26	18	+ 8	
Stock X	22	18	+ 4	– 32
Stock Y	10	18	– 8	

$$CV = \frac{1}{2}(14-18)(26-18) + \frac{1}{2}(22-18)(10-18)$$

$$CV = \frac{1}{2}(-4 \times +8) + \frac{1}{2}(4 \times -8)$$

$$CV = \frac{1}{2}(-32) + \frac{1}{2}(-32) = -16 - 16 = -32$$

Correlation. The formula is

$$r_{xy} = \frac{Cov.XY}{\delta_x \sigma_y}$$

r_{xy} = coefficient of correlation

Cov x y = −32

$\sigma x = 4$ $\sigma y = 8$

$$r_{xy} = \frac{-32}{4 \times 8} = \frac{-32}{32} = -1$$

Correlation coefficient is negative and they are perfectly negatively correlated with a value of 1.

Expected Returns

If we know the ratio in which investments are made in x and y stocks say, that the ratio is 40:60, then investment in X is 40 and investment in y is 60 out of 100

Actual Returns on portfolio are as follows:

In portfolio (1) =

14 and 26 in first year and

the returns are

22 and 10 in second year.

$$\overline{X} = \frac{14+22}{2} = \frac{36}{2} = 18$$

$$\overline{Y} = \frac{26+10}{2} = \frac{36}{2} = 18$$

Expected Return

$R_p = R_1 X_1 + R_2 Y_1$

$R_p = 18\ (.40) + 18\ (.60)$

$= 7.2 + 10.8 = 18$

R_p = Expected Return on the portfolio is 18.

Problem

Given the data below on two companies A & B, calculate the expected return from companies and standard deviation as a risk measure of companies. Which one is better for Return and Risk estimates.

	Company A		Company B	
Outcome	**Expected Return**	**Probability**	**Expected Return**	**Probability**
1	6	0.3	8	0.2
2	10	0.5	14	0.5
3	12	0.2	18	0.3

Solution:

Company A Return (1)	Probability (2)	Weighted Probability Return (3) =(1) × (2)	Company B Return	Probability	Weighted Probability Return
6	0.3	+ 1.8	8	0.2	1.6
10	0.5	+ 5.0	14	0.5	7.0
12	0.2	+ 2.4	18	0.3	5.4
Expected Returns		9.2			14.0

Company A (Expected Return 9.2)

Outcome	Weighted Probable Return	Deviation from Expected Return	Squared Deviations	Weighted Deviations Squared Weighted by Probability
(1)	(2)	(3)	(4)	(5)
1	1.8	9.2–6 = 3.2	10.24	3.072
2	5.0	9.2–10 = –0.8	0.64	0.320
3	2.4	9.2–12 = –2.8	7.84	1.568
			Variance	= 4.960

Expected Return 9.2%

Standard Deviation $\sqrt{4.960} = 2.23$

Company B (Expected Return 14.0)

(1)	(2)	(3)	(4)	(5)
1	1.6	14 – 8 = 6	36	7.2
2	7.0	14 – 14 = 0	0	0
3	5.4	14 – 18=-4	16	4.8
			Variance	= 12.0

Expected Return = 14.0%

Standard Deviation $\sqrt{12} = 3.46$

Risk of Company B is higher, but the return is also higher.

Problem

Given below are the returns on IBM and BSE sensex for a five year period. Calculate Beta, Alpha Residual variance and Correlation:

Year	Return on IBM (Y)	Return on BSE Sensex (X)
1	0.2	0.1
2	0.3	0.2
3	0.5	0.3
4	0.4	0.4
5	0.6	0.5

Solution:

Year	X	Y	XY	X^2	Y^2
1	0.10	0.2	0.02	.01	.04
2	0.20	0.3	0.06	.04	.09
3	0.30	0.5	0.15	.09	.25
4	0.40	0.4	0.16	.16	.16
5	0.50	0.6	0.30	.25	.36
	$\Sigma x = 1.50$	$\Sigma y = 2.0$	$\Sigma xy = 0.69$	$\Sigma X^2 = 0.55$	$\Sigma y^2 = 0.90$

$$\overline{X} = \frac{1.50}{5} = 0.3; \quad \overline{Y} - \frac{2.0}{5} = 0.4$$

Calculation of Beta

β slope of the Regression line is given by

$$\beta = \frac{\eta\Sigma XY - (\Sigma X)(\Sigma y)}{\eta\Sigma X^2 - (\Sigma X)^2} \text{ is the Equation}$$

$$= \frac{(5 \times .69) - (1.5 \times 2.0)}{(5 \times 55) - (1.5)^2} = \frac{3.45 - 3.00}{(2.75) - (2.25)} = \frac{0.45}{0.50}$$

$$\beta = 0.9$$

Calculation of Alpha

The formula is $\alpha = \overline{Y} - \beta\ \overline{x} = 0.4 - (0.9)(0.3)$

$= 0.4 - 0.27 = 0.13$

Formula of Residual Variance

The formula is $e^2 = \dfrac{\Sigma Y^2 - \sigma\Sigma Y - \beta\Sigma XY}{\eta}$

Calculation of Residual Variance

$$e^2 = \frac{\Sigma Y^2 - \sigma \Sigma Y - \beta \Sigma XY}{\eta}$$

$$= \frac{0.9 - 0.13 \times 2.0 - 0.9 \times 0.69}{5}$$

$$= \frac{0.9 - 0.26 - 0.621}{5} = \frac{0.019}{5} = 0.004$$

Method of Calculation of (r)

$$r = \frac{\Sigma XY}{\sqrt{\Sigma X^2 \times \Sigma Y^2}} = \frac{0.69}{\sqrt{0.55 \times .90}} = \frac{0.69}{\sqrt{0.495}}$$

$$= \frac{0.69}{0.703} = 0.982$$

Coefficient of Determination = $r^2 = (0.982)^2 = 0.964$

Variance of IBM

$$\overline{Y} = \frac{\Sigma Y}{\eta} = \frac{2.0}{5} = 0.4$$

Y *Return*	*dy* *Deviation from Mean*		*dy²* *Deviation Squared*
0.2	– .2		.04
0.3	– .1		.01
0.5	+ .1		.01
0.4	0		.0
0.6	+ 2		.04
n =5	Mean = 0.4	Σdy^2	.10

Variance $\sigma^2 = \frac{.10}{5} = .02 = \frac{\Sigma dy^2}{N}$

Standard Deviation $\sqrt{.02} = 0.141 = \sqrt{\text{Variance}}$

Explained systematic variance (.02) X 0.964 = .0193

Unexplained Residual/unsystematic variance =.0007

Total Variance .02

$$\frac{\text{Covariance}}{\sigma x \sigma y} = \sqrt{.02} = .141$$

Variance of BSE Index

Return	dx (deviation)	dx^2
0.10	.20	.04
0.20	.10	.01
0.30	0	0
0.40	.10	.01
0.50	.20	.04
		$\Sigma\, dx^2 = .10$

$$\overline{X} = \frac{\Sigma X}{n} = \frac{1.5}{5} = 0.3$$

$$\text{Variance} = \frac{0.10}{5} = .02$$

$$\sigma = \sqrt{.02} = 0.141$$

$$\text{Coefficient of Correlation} = \frac{\text{Covariance}}{\sigma x \sigma y}$$

Coefficient of correlation can also be worked through the above formula.

Covariance of Returns

Given the following data, calculate the covariance of returns for assets X and Y.

State of the market	Probability of occurance	Annual Returns X	Annual Returns Y
1	0.2	–5%	6%
2	0.4	10	–2
3	0.3	–4	8
4	0.1	7	–9
	1.0		

Expected returns

$$Erx = \sum_{x=1}^{N} Px^{rx}$$

$$Erx = (.2) - (5) + .4\,(10) + .3\,(-4) + .1(7)$$

$$= -1 + 4 - 1.2 + .7 = 2.5\%$$

$$Ery = (.2)6 + 0.4\,(-2) + .3(8) + .1(-9)$$

$$= 1.2 - 0.8 + 2.4 - 0.9$$

$$= 3.6 - 1.7 = 1.9\%$$

Covariance problem can be set in a Tabular form

Prob.	r_x	r_y	$(r_x - Er)$	$(r_y - Er)$		(1 × 4 × 5)
(1)	(2)	(3)	(4)	(5)		= (6)
0.2	–5	6	(– 5 – 2.5) = –7.5	(6 – 1.9) =	4.1	– 6.15
0.4	10	–2	(10 – 2.5) = 7.5	(– 2 – 1.9) =	–3.9	– 11.70
0.3	–4	8	(– 4 – 2.5) = –6.5	(8 – 1.9) =	6.1	– 11.89
0.1	7	–9	(7 – 2.5) = 4.5	(– 9 – 1.9) =	– 10.9	– 4.91
						Cov_{XY} = – 34.65

$$Cov_{xy} = \left(\sum_{1}^{N} r_{xt} - \bar{r}_x\right)\left(r_{yt} - \bar{r}_y\right)$$

Correlation Coefficient

In the above example

Cov. = – 34.65

$$\text{Correlation Coefficient} = r_{xy} = \frac{Cov.xy}{\sigma_x \sigma_y}$$

$$\sigma_x^2 = .2\,(-5 - 2.5)^2 + .4\,(10 - 2.5)^2 + .3\,(-4 - 2.5)^2 + .1\,(7 - 2.5)^2$$

$$\sigma_x^{\ 2} = 11.25 + 22.5 + 12.67 + 2.03$$

$$= 48.45$$

$$\sigma = \sqrt{48.45} = 6.96\%$$

$$\sigma_y^{\ 2} = .2\,(6 - 1.9)^2 + .4\,(-2 - 1.9)^2 +$$

$$.3\,(8 - 1.9)^2 + .1\,(-9 - 1.9)^2$$

$$= 3.362 + 6.084 + 11.163 + 11.881$$

$$= 32.49$$

$$\sigma_y = \sqrt{32.49} = 5.7\%$$

Now,

$$Rxy = \frac{-34.65}{(6.96)\,(5.7)} = -0.87$$

$$= -0.87$$

Correlation Coefficient

The equation for correlation coefficient is

$$\frac{N\Sigma xy - \Sigma x - \Sigma y}{\left\{\left[(N - \Sigma X^2) - (\Sigma X)^2\right]\left[(N\Sigma Y^2) - (\Sigma Y)^2\right]\right\}^{\frac{1}{2}}}$$

Return x	Return y	x^2	y^2	x × y
8	10	64	100	80
−9	−12	81	144	108
14	18	196	324	252
16	20	256	400	320
20	14	400	196	280
Σx = 49	Σy = 50	Σ x² = 997	Σy² = 1164	Σxy = 1040

$$\rho_{xy} = \frac{5(1040)-(49)\times(50)}{\left\{\left[(5)\times(997)-(49)^2\right]\left[(5)(1164)-(50)^2\right]\right\}^{\frac{1}{2}}}$$

$$\rho_{xy} = \frac{5200-2450=2750}{\left\{\left[(4985-2401)\right]\left[(5820-2500)\right]\right\}^{\frac{1}{2}}}$$

$$= \frac{2750}{\sqrt{85,78,880}} = \frac{2750}{2928.973} = 0.9389$$

Covariance of Returns

$$\text{Cov.xy} = \frac{1}{N}\sum_{t=1}^{N}(r_{xi}-r_x)(r_{xi}-r_y)$$

Year	Return x	Return y
1	8	10
2	− 9	− 12
3	14	18
4	16	20
5	20	14

$$\bar{x} = \frac{\sum xi}{N} \qquad \bar{y} = \frac{\sum yi}{N}$$

$$\bar{x} = \frac{49}{5} = 9.8, \quad \bar{y} = \frac{50}{5} = 10$$

$$\text{Cov.xy} = \frac{1}{5} = \left[\begin{array}{l}(8-9.8)(10-10)+(-9-9.8)(-12-10)+\\+(14-9.8)(18-10)+(16-9.8)(20-10)+\\+(20-9.8)(14-10)\end{array}\right]$$

$$= \frac{1}{5}\left[(0+413.6+33.6+62+40.8)\right]$$

$$= \frac{550}{5} = 110.$$

What is Diversification?

Diversification is a technique of reducing the risk involved in investment and in portfolio management. This is a process of conscious selection of assets, instruments and scrips of companies/Government securities, in a manner that the total risks are brought down. This process helps in the reduction of risk, under category of what is known as "Unsystematic Risk" and promotes the optimisation of returns for a given level of risks in portfolio management.

We have seen that in the case of unsystematic risk, the method of lowering the risk is to diversify into a number of companies and a number of industries, for selection of scrips in the portfolio. This diversification may take any of the following forms:

(1) Into different *types of assets,* like gold, real estate, Government securities, corporate securities, etc.

(2) Into different *instruments* or security type bonds, stocks, debentures, Government securities, etc.

(3) Into different *industry lines,* namely, plastics, chemicals, engineering, cement, steel, pharma, I.T., etc.

(4) Into different *scrips of companies,* viz., new companies, growing companies, new product companies etc.

Principles

The principles involved in diversification are as follows:

A single company/industry is more risky than two companies/industries. Two companies in say, steel industry are more risky than one company in Steel, and one in Tyres and Tubes. Two companies, one in steel and the other in chemicals are less risky than two in either steel or chemicals. Similarly, two companies or two industries which are similar in nature of demand or market etc., are more risky than the two in dissimilar industries. Statistically speaking, their variance/covariance should be different. It is proper diversification which involves two or more companies/two or more industries whose fortunes fluctuate independent of one another or in different directions.

Random Diversification

The traditional belief is that diversification involves "not putting all eggs in one basket." This policy involves as many baskets as possible; carried to the extreme it is good to have as many companies as possible, and as many industries as possible in one's portfolio. But this is a misconception as economies of scale operate in the reverse direction (involving diseconomies) with the result that monitoring and review of the portfolio become inefficient, costly and cumbersome and outweigh the benefits of diversification.

There are some accepted methods of effecting diversification:

(1) *Randomness in Selection of Companies and Industries:* The probability of reducing risk is more with a random selection as the statistical error of choosing wrong companies will come down due to randomness of selection which is a statistical technique. This involves placing of companies in any order and picking them up in random manner.

(2) *Optimisation of Selection Process:* Given the amount of money to be invested there is optimum number of companies, where money can be invested. If the number is too small, risk cannot be reduced adequately and if the number is too big, there will be diseconomies and difficulty of supervision, analysis and monitoring will increase risk again. There is thus a optimum number of companies to be chosen for a given amount of investment.

(3) *Adequate Diversification:* Many traditional approaches, emphasise on the need for adequate diversification. This involves as many industries and companies or securities as possible to get the best results. This principle believes in the possibilities of reducing risk to even zero, if there are adequate number of companies and industries. Markowitz emphasised however that what is needed is not only the number of securities to be chosen but the right kind of securities to be chosen. Thus, even if there are a large number of companies they may not reduce risk adequately if they are positively correlated with each other and the market, in which case, they all move in the same direction and many risks will not be reduced and may even increase.

Fig. 40.1

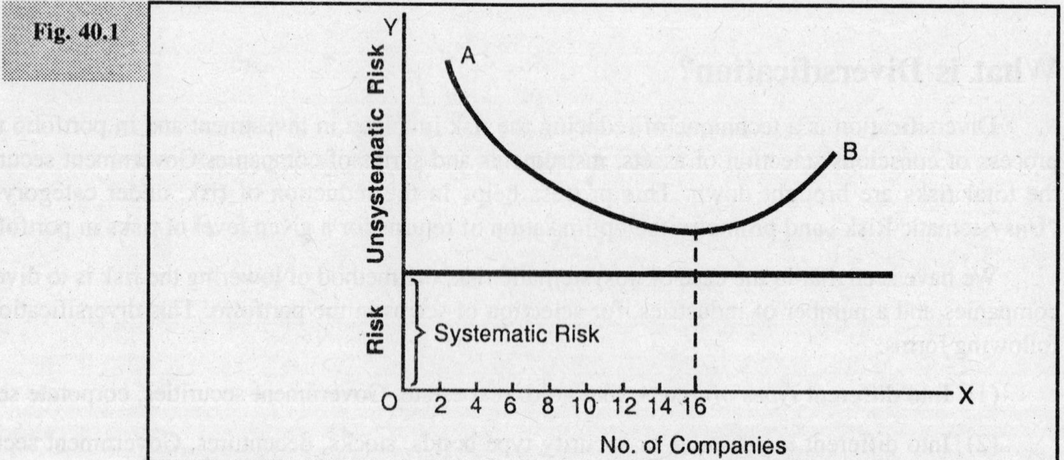

(4) *Markowitz Diversification:* Markowitz emphasised the need for a right number of securities — not too many or too less — and securities which are negatively correlated or not correlated at all. The purpose of diversification is to reduce the unsystematic risk arising out of company's policies and performance. Thus, many of such risks can be reduced by a proper choice of companies and industries. Neither random selection, nor adequate number of securities can guarantee this. One can see from the graph above that for an individual investor a number of around 10-16 companies can secure reduction of risk to an optimum level if they are properly selected as per Markowitz. For Mutual funds or finance companies this number may be higher. The graph shows both systematic and unsystematic risks and the Horizontal line of systematic risk cannot be reduced by diversification, but to a large extent unsystematic risk can be reduced by a right choice of companies and to a limited number. In the graph above, after 16 scrips are accommodated, the curve of unsystenatic risk starts going up.

International Diversification

The benefits of diversifcation are well perceived by Portfolio Managers, that many in developed countries, started investing in Foreign bonds, stocks and other instruments. They found that they can extend diversification principle to foreign stocks, bonds etc., to improve returns for a given risk by adopting proper techniques of diversification.

Why International Diversification?

(1) The size and character of International Equity and bond markets are widely varying that it will increase the scope for larger investment and larger diversification.

(2) The returns in local currencies of some foreign countries are higher than in domestic markets. Thus, for example in Singapore, Malaysia, Taiwan and India the returns in local currencies are higher than in U.S. economy.

(3) The economic trends, business conditions and local profitability and earnings ratios differ widely among countries that the EPS in some developing countries is higher and give opportunity for better diversification and higher returns, through international investments.

(4) International investment is advantageous due to larger investment avenues now open in the first place and secondly due to the imperfect correlation among the international markets. The total risk of a portfolio including the international investment will be lower than with only domestic investment. The degree of volatility, and all risk measures, indicate that these risks vary among the countries and in different degrees and the possibility of covariance, or high correlation will be low.

The frontier of efficiency portfolios can be widened, by inclusion of foreign investments in a portfolio. Thus many International Portfolio Managers prefer to invest in India and so will be the case of Indian Portfolio Managers, if they can diversify into International Investments. There are some directions however which will increase risk in such investments.

Risks in Foreign Investments

(1) Political and social developments may create problems in an unpredictable manner.

(2) Economic and monetary policies may change to their disadvantage. Foreign exchange controls, double taxation, appropriation of foreign assets etc., stand in the way.

(3) Risks of currency fluctuations may pose danger to larger profits depending upon the management in exchange rates. The currency risks are important because the foreign investor when he wants to take home his profits, the desired currency is his local currency, and this has to take into account the exchange rates. The gains or returns out of foreign investments might be offset by opposite and adverse movements in exchange rates. These factors create more risks.

(4) Unforeseen international developments such as wars, political and ideological conflicts etc., might create additional risks.

(5) Foreign information is difficult and foreign accounting and reporting systems differ. All the above factors make the international diversification as desirable provided some active policy of management of portfolio is preferred and even global diversification is achieved. These are factors influencing the global diversification which provide opportunities of risk hedge, due to the diversities in their economies and markets:

Thus, leaving the domestic frontiers, the foreign economies may themselves provide a picture of varying degrees of economic and business fluctuations, high and low inflation rates *vis-a-vis* the GDP growth rates, etc.

Thus, $\frac{P}{E}$ multiple of some markets as in India may be higher than in U.S.A. But the growth rate of India is higher than U.S.A. with the result that potential for growth is higher here. Besides EPS in different countries may vary widely and these have to be studied in terms of domestic EPS. Foreign EPS, adjusted for forward exchange rates, foreign interest rates, inflation rates *vis-a-vis* the GDP growth rates, so that the international investor knows which markets are attractive internationally, and he can pursue a policy of international diversification to secure offsetting of risks — which means that investment risks in Brazil, offsetting investment risks in Germany and yet the returns in total portfolios are higher, when taken back in U.S. dollars. The various markets behave with different degrees of risk/return features such that when the U.S. returns are lower, the companies' total returns may be higher in foreign markets thus reducing the total risk of portfolios including foreign investments.

FFI'S INVESTMENT IN INDIA

FIIs and FFIs were permitted to operate in the Indian capital market since Sept., 1992, in a bid to globalise the markets. Since Jan. 1993, FII investment started in India. By 2005, there were 505 FFIs registered with the RBI/SEBI, operating in India. The cumulative amount of their investment upto March 2001 was more than Rs. 48,802 crores, but after 1996 the inflow slowed down and its impact is felt on the market. The data since 2001 are not comparable to the earlier data. The total FII inflows both Direct and Portfolio investments for the year 2005-06 was US $ 20 billion. In a study published in RBI's Annual Report, 1995-96 it was revealed that BSE Sensex is significantly related ($\gamma = 0.49$) to lagged net investment by FFIs. Such studies are also available in World Bank studies and IMF Studies, which also revealed the significant impact of foreign flows into capital markets of developing countries. They reached a peak in 2007-08 at $ 61.6 billion but declined to $ 21.3 billion in 2008-09.

(*Ref.* Claesseus S. and S. Gooptu, Eds. (1993) "Portfolio Investment in Developing Countries". W.B. Discussion paper No. 228 and Schadler S. and Carkovic M. Eds. (1993) "Resent Experiences with Surges in Capital Inflows," IMF occasional paper No. 108, IMF.)

These flows influence the market through demand pressures, affecting the interest rates and stock prices, money supply, domestic savings and investment activity in the domestic economies.

NRI Investment in India

NRI Investments in India can take any of the following three forms:

(a) Avenues for Personal Investment.

(b) Direct Investment Schemes.

(c) Portfolio Investment Schemes.

(A) Personal Investments Scheme

NRI or Foreign Citizens of Indian origin can acquire any of the following investments in India without RBI's prior permission. These are:

Government Securities, P.O. Savings and National Plan Certificates, UTI units, and their schemes, company deposits Mutual Fund schemes new issues of equity, equity shares, debentures, both on repatriation and non-repatriation purposes, immovable property for residental purpose, India Development Bonds, Housing and Real estate development to the extent of even 100%.

The Investee Company and not NRI has to take prior permission of the RBI in the above cases. Repatriation is permitted if only funds have come from NRE/FCNR accounts and not NRO accounts. The shares of companies, their deposits and debentures and commercial paper are all available for investment on a non-repatriation basis, under this scheme.

(B) Direct Investment Scheme

There are two schemes of 40% and 100% of investment, under this category 40% scheme is for investment in shares and debentures in companies engaged in Industrial and manufacturing activity, Hotels, Hospitals, Shipping Companies, Computer Softwear, oil exploration, etc. There is no ceiling on the amount of remittable dividend, but the investee company has to take the RBI permission in this regard.

100% scheme is for Real Estate Development, Township development, Construction of residential buildings, houses etc., development of roads, building materials, bridges and infrastructure facilities, house finance and Air Taxi operators. They can invest upto 100% in debentures (NCDS), sick industrial undertakings without repatriation. The 100% investment is also permitted for OCBs (overseas corporate bodies with 60% participation of NRIs). They can make investments, in 100% export oriented units, EPZ, and high priority industries with foreign equity participation of 51% with the rest to be left (49%) to NRIs.

Original investment can be repatriated after 3 years from the date of the issue. Actual income or dividends, can be freely repatriable, subject to payment of tax. OCBs are permitted to repatriate after 3 years at 16% net profit and Air Taxi operators only after 5 years and out of accumulated foreign exchange earnings only.

NRIs can invest in High priority industries listed in Annexure II to the latest statement on Industrial Policy. The general guideline is that FIIs, FFIs, etc. can invest in any corporate upto 51% of equity, subject to any changes for permitting their investment upto even 100% of equity, in certain cases as in the development of Real Estate.

(C) Portfolio Investment Scheme

NRIs can freely invest and disinvest without any lock in period in the cases of the investment in Domestic Mutual Funds, without any limit, and in paid up capital and debt capital upto 5% for each individual subject to an overall ceiling of 10% for all NRIs and OCBs, which can be raised upto 30% now if the company passes a Resolution to that effect in the General Body Meeting.

The ADs who have the accounts of NRIs can be used as the medium for portfolio investments on the stock exchanges. RBI's approval is to be secured by the NRI through that particular AD. There is no lock in period and RBI's approval is valid for 5 years. Capital gains and dividends etc., can be repatriated after payment of taxes, if the funds have come through NRE and FCNR accounts.

Sale and Transfer of shares is also permitted by the RBI without prior permission in respect of Govt. securities debentures of corporates, and those on non repatriation basis. However, RBI prior permission is required for transfer to other NRIs, Residents, either by private placement or through any private agency. Those on repatriation basis require permission of the RBI. Rights entitlements and bonus issued are subject to RBI's permission which has to be sought by the company. General permission of RBI is available only for those on non-repatriation basis.

These provisions are subject to constant changes, which are reported in the financial press on a daily basis.

Passive International Investment Strategy

In passive strategy, an International Index fund is the ideal method of investing abroad. Thus, the offshore funds of India, or other International funds of China, Brazil, Mexico, etc., can be used as the index funds, for passive investment. They can alternatively trade in only major world markets, like U.K., Japan, Germany, France, and Switzerland, after a study of their market behaviour. This strategy of investing in balanced portfolio of a large number of countries, with a high degree of diversification may improve the returns on such positions.

Risk in a foreign portfolio in terms of standard deviation of the continuously compounded annualised return is

$V_t = [V_t m^2 + V_c^2 + 2P\, V_c\, V_m]\ ½$

V_c = Exchange Rate risk, V_m is total portfolio risk in local market terms, fully hedged, V_t = total portfolio risk in base currency terms, without currency hedging p = correlation between exchange rate return and portfolio return in local market terms. The above formula indicates that total portfolio risk in foreign markets is lower, if there is a good negative correlation between local currency returns and local market returns in stock market.

The factors influencing such foreign portfolios are: *(i)* Foreign asset local returns, *(ii)* Foreign currency returns, *(iii)* Domestic asset returns, and *(iv)* Correlation Coefficient between these variables.

The return on a fully hedged foreign investment is

$R = Lr + F_p/d$

R = Return an foreign investment fully hedged.

Lr = Local asset returns, F_p/d is the Forward Premium/discount (U.S. Short-term rate and foreign short-term rate).

Active International Investment Strategy

Active strategy is oriented to identifying relatively attractive and unattractive national markets. Such identification is followed by ranking these markets abroad and weightage in one's portfolio is given by such ranking in terms of the attractiveness of the local markets. This identification involves some analytical and predictive powers both in the investment markets and currency markets. The operation of such active strategy is depicted below.

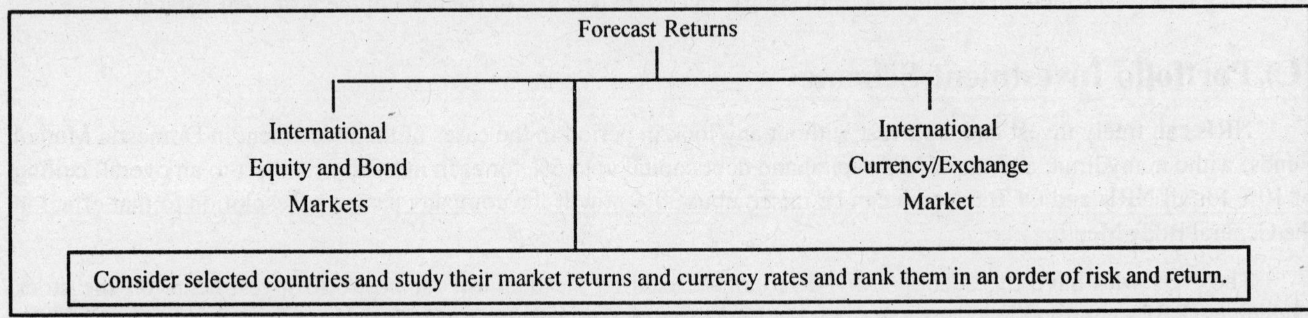

Adjust for hedging of currency rates and Market returns so that an optimum portfolio with higher return and lowest risk is built. International Rating Agencies like Moody's provide country and currency ratings and publish investment grades of countries.

Return Forecasts

An exercise of importance in active Portfolio Management is to forecast the returns in equity market and in currency markets.

If say the foreign equity return is 20% as against 10% of domestic return, foreign investments may look attractive but if that 20% return is lost by adverse currency rate fluctuations or high local tax rates then it is not worthwhile investing abroad.

Example of return forecast Table is given below:

Country	*Currency Forecast Return*	*Equity Market Forecast Return*	*Net Return %*
UK	1.1	18.2	19.3
France	1.0	13.6	14.6
Germany	4.7	13.9	18.6
India	–5.0	20.0	15.0

Equity market returns are high in India but tax rates and currency rate variations create negative return so that investment becomes unattractive in India, as seen from the above Table. In considering various markets the Portfolio Manager takes into account various economic and political factors and not merely equity returns. A few examples are given here

(1) EPS market index and $\frac{P}{E}$ multiple.

(2) Relative growth of the economy and the market. If market earnings growth is higher than the growth rate of GDP it is potentially good market.

(3) If the market capitalisation is low relative to GDP and potentiality of growth of MC is high, such markets are again attractive to foreign investors.

(4) Monthly volatility and annual volatility of prices, should not be very high, for attracting foreign investment.

(5) Liquidity and settlement process in the markets — whether deliveries are prompt and enough scrips are available for delivery at the international standards of T + 3 Delivery.

(6) Good floating stock of companies and wide public holding so as to promote trading in such securities in domestic markets of those countries. The Stock Exchanges have directed in the middle of June 2010 all listed companies to bring up to 25% of public holding of their paid up capital, which may force many promoters to disinvest in favour of the public.

(7) Free and floating currency without current and capital account controls. If the country has only capital account controls but no current account controls, it is partly attractive as in the case of India.

(8) Stable exchange rates or facilities for hedge and cover for forward exchange position are available in these markets.

If the above features are prevailing in a good measure, such countries are worthwhile and attractive for foreign portfolio Management. The breadth of the market in terms of the available number of traded companies and their floating stock are also considered in addition to the expected returns and risks involved in trading in such markets.

International diversification is desirable to improve return and reduce risks. The optimisation process with international diversification is more complicated and active investment strategy will give better returns than passive strategy. Some prior conditions should also be satisfied for optimisation process.

International Investing — Problem

Different countries have different political and currency systems and are in various stages of growth. The inflation rates vary as between the countries. All these factors cause that the security returns and interest rates in different countries are different and that these cause the international coefficients to be lower than the correlation between domestic stocks. Besides correlation matrix as between domestic stocks and international stocks reveal lower correlation which encourage mutlinational investing advantageous for better diversification and greater risk reduction and higher returns on the portfolios involving both domestic stocks and international stocks than in the case of pure domestic asset portfolios.

In international investing, an additional foreign exchange risk has got to be considered by investors. This risk is reflected in the variability of foreign exchange rate, vis-a-vis the domestic currency.

Problem

Exchange rate between US and Germany be 1 DM = $ 0.75 in the beginning of the year and 1 DM = $ 0.90 at the end of the year. Over the year, German equity market return is say 18%, what is the net return to the US investor through his German investment?

The equation is

$$rn = (1 + rd)(1 + rc) - 1$$

where rd is return in equity market and rc is gain/loss in currency market.

$rd = 0.18$

$$\text{and } rc = \frac{0.90}{0.75} - 1 = 1.20 - 1 = 0.20$$

$$\text{Thus, } rn = (1.18)(1.20) - 1$$

$$= 1.416 - 1 = 0.416 \text{ or } 41.6\%$$

This is to be compared with US domestic equity market return of 12%. German returns are not only higher but currency market moved in favour of the US with the result that the US investment in Germany yielded a higher return of 41.6%.

Advantages of Diversification

Advantages of diversification are seen in both returns and risk. Returns can be improved and risks lowered by proper diversification of securities, in those which have negative covariance or are independent. In the chart below, stocks 4, and 5 and portfolio 4 & 5 are having the same expected return of 14% but the standard deviation (σ) of the portfolio 4 & 5 is less than the standard deviation of 4 or 5 alone. By combining 4 and 5 into a portfolio, the investor has reduced the risk without any loss of return.

Take stocks 5 and 6, and a portfolio of 5 & 6. Since the return of any portfolio is the weighted average of individual security returns, the expected return of the portfolio is 12, while that of stock 5 is 14% and of Stock 6 is 10% [average is ½ (14 + 10)] = 12. But the risk or standard deviation of a portfolio is not simply a weighted average of individual securities. Standard deviation, portfolio 5 & 6 plots to the left of a straight line connecting 5 and 6 — which means that there is less risk in the Portfolio than in the weighted average combination (linear line).

Besides, the securities need not be equally weighted as in the above example. If one can design different combinations, he may reach the efficient Frontier line which has least risk for a given return.

Fig. 40.2

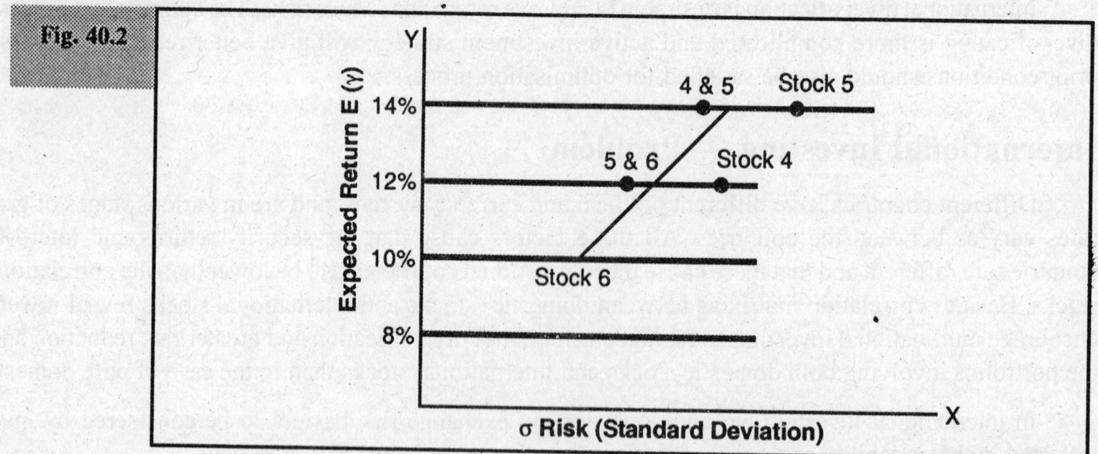

In this chart, as seen above, returns can be improved and risk reduced by diversification. The optimum points of different combinations, giving the least risk for a given level of return will constitute the efficient frontier. Beyond the frontier line, one cannot reduce the risk further, due to diseconomies or difficulties of reducing the risk further. Reduction of risk takes place due to the fact that securities' returns are not perfectly correlated in the portfolio.

Naive Diversification

This refers to the diversification by simply picking stocks at random. This may or may not reduce risk to the optimum level. As the number of stocks in a portfolio is increased randomly, it is possible to reduce the risk upto a point and that too only in respect of the non-systematic risk. The market related systematic risk cannot be reduced by diversification.

Evans & Archers' Study@

Evans & Archer studied the data of 470 NYSE firms during 1958-67 and showed that if the maximum risk of a single stock is 21%, it can be reduced to the extent of approximately 9% and the rest of 12% representing the systematic risk, cannot be diversified away. That is the market risk which the investor has to bear and by using the concept of Beta referred in another Chapter, he can take that much risk, that he can tolerate as per his preference or aversion.

@ J.L. Evans and S.H. Archer, "Diversification and the Reduction of Dispersion — An Empirical Analysis," *Journal of Finance*, (December 1968).

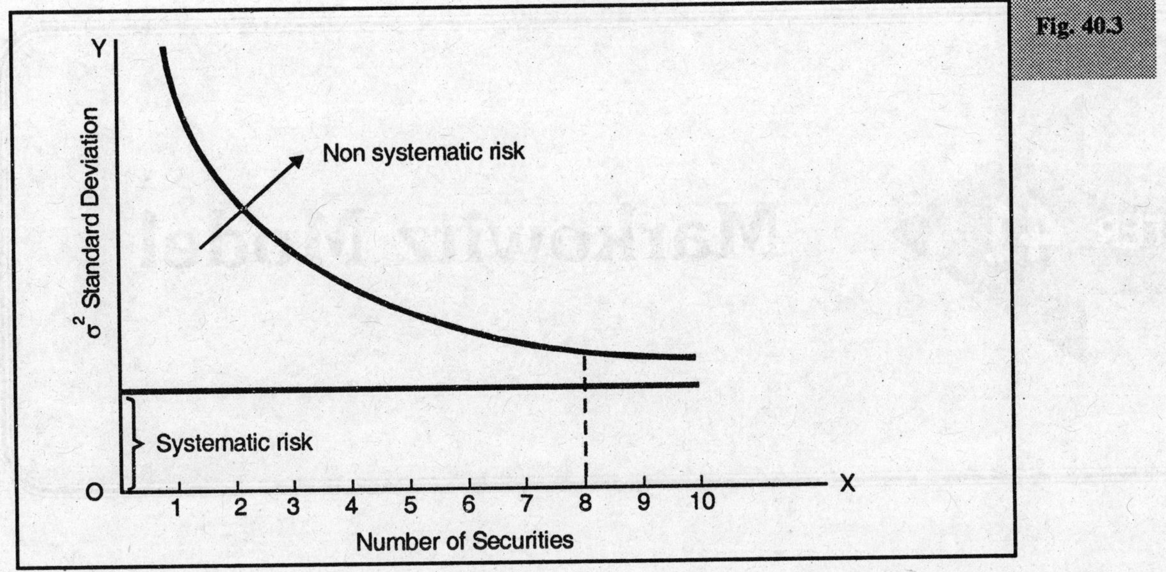

In the above chart the average standard deviation of returns for a single stock was about 21%. When portfolios of two stocks selected were formed, the average standard deviation of this portfolio is about 16%. The average standard deviation (σ) of the portfolio of three stocks was 15% and so on down the line, until, the risk is reduced upto 8 stocks in his study. Most of the diversification benefits were achieved even by the use of 8 stocks portfolio. If all the 470 stocks were grouped together into one portfolio, the standard deviation was 11.6%. Thus, in his study of 470 stocks, the total risk he reduced was only upto about 9% and 12% is the systematic risk or market risk which could not be reduced.

Thus, Evans and Archer study showed the optimum level upto which risk can be lowered and that will lower depending upon stocks chosen and the time period.

CHAPTER 41

Markowitz Model

Harry M. Markowitz is credited with introducing new concepts of risk measurement and their application to the selection of portfolios. He started with the idea of risk aversion of average investors and their desire to maximise the expected return with the least risk. Markowitz model is thus a theoretical framework for analysis of risk and return and their inter-relationships. He used the statistical analysis for measurement of risk and mathematical programming for selection of assets in a portfolio in an efficient manner. His framework led to the concept of efficient portfolios. An efficient portfolio is expected to yield the highest return for a given level of risk or lowest risk for a given level of return.

Markowitz generated a number of portfolios within a given amount of money or wealth and given preferences of investors for risk and return. Individuals vary widely in their risk tolerance and asset preferences. Their means, expenditures and investment requirements vary from individual to individual. Given the preferences, the portfolio selection is not a simple choice of any one security or securities, but a right combination of securities. Markowitz emphasised that quality of a portfolio will be different from the quality of individual assets within it. Thus, the combined risk of two assets taken separately is not the same risk of two assets together. Thus, two securities of TISCO do not have the same risk as one security of TISCO and one of Reliance.

Risk and Reward are two aspects of investment considered by investors. The expected return may vary depending on the assumptions. Risk index is measured by the variance or the distribution around the mean, its range etc., which are in statistical terms called variance and covariance. The qualification of risk and the need for optimisation of return with lowest risk are the contributions of Markowitz. This led to what is called the Modern Portfolio Theory, which emphasises the trade off between risk and return. If the investor wants a higher return, he has to take higher risk. But he prefers a high return but a low risk and hence the need for a trade off.

A portfolio of assets involves the selection of securities. A combination of assets or securities is called a portfolio. Each individual investor puts his wealth in a combination of assets depending on his wealth, income and his preferences. The traditional theory of portfolio postulates that selection of assets should be based on lowest risk, as measured by its standard deviation from the mean of expected returns. The greater the variability of returns, the greater is the risk. Thus, the investor chooses assets with the lowest variability of returns. Taking the return as the appreciation in the share price, if TELCO share price varies from Rs. 338 to Rs. 580 (with variability of 72%) and Colgate from Rs. 218 to Rs. 315 (with a variability of 44%) during a time period, the investor chooses the Colgate as a less risky share.

As against this Traditional Theory that standard deviation measures the variability of return and risk is indicated by the variability, and that the choice depends on the securities with lower variability, the modern Portfolio Theory emphasises the need for maximisation of returns through a combination of securities, whose total variability is lower. The risk of each security is different from that of others and by a proper combination of securities, called diversification, one can arrive at a combination wherein the risk of one is offset partly or fully by that of the other. In other words, the variability of each security and covariance for their returns reflected through their inter-relationships should be taken into account. Thus, as per the Modern Portfolio Theory, expected returns, the variance of these returns and covariance of the returns of the securities within the portfolio are to be considered for the choice of a portfolio. A portfolio is said to be efficient, if it is expected to yield the highest return possible for the lowest risk or a given level of risk. A set of efficient portfolios can be generated by using the above process of combining various securities whose combined risk is lowest for a given level of return for the same amount of investment, that the investor is capable of. The theory of Markowitz, as stated above is based on a number of assumptions.

Assumptions of Markowitz Theory

The Modern Portfolio Theory of Markowitz is based on the following assumptions:

(1) Investors are rational and behave in a manner as to maximise their utility with a given level of income or money.

(2) Investors have free access to fair and correct information on the returns and risk.

(3) The markets are efficient and absorb the information quickly and perfectly.

(4) Investors are risk averse and try to minimise the risk and maximise return.

(5) Investors base decisions on expected returns and variance or standard deviation of these returns from the mean.

(6) Investors prefer higher returns to lower returns for a given level of risk.

A portfolio of assets under the above assumptions is considered efficient if no other asset or portfolio of assets offers a higher expected return with the same or lower risk or lower risk with the same or higher expected return. Diversification of securities is one method by which the above objectives can be secured. The unsystematic and company related risk can be reduced by diversification into various securities and assets whose variability is different and offsetting or put in different words which are negatively correlated or not correlated at all.

Markowitz Diversification

Markowitz postulated that diversification should not only aim at reducing the risk of a security by reducing its variability or standard deviation, but by reducing the covariance or interactive risk of two or more securities in a portfolio. As by combination of different securities, it is theoretically possible to have a range of risk varying from zero to infinity.

Markowitz theory of portfolio diversification attaches importance to standard deviation, to reduce it to zero, if possible, covariance to have as much as possible negative interactive effect among the securities within the portfolio and coefficient of correlation to have – 1 (negative) so that the overall risk of the portfolio as a whole is nil or negligible. Then the securities have to be combined in a manner that standard deviation is zero, as shown in the example below. Possible combinations of securities (1) and (2) are presented below:

Security (1)	*Security (2)*	*S.D.*
80	20	0.8
70	30	0.4
66	34	0.0
20	80	0.8
10	90	0.9

In the example, if $^2/_3$rds are invested in security (1) and $^1/_3$rd in security (2), the coefficient of variation, namely = $\frac{\text{S.D.}}{\text{Mean}}$ is the lowest.

The standard deviation of the portfolio determines the deviation of the returns and correlation coefficient of the inter-relations of securities in the portfolio, invested. The equation is

$$\sigma^2 p = \sum_{t=i}^{N} \sum_{j=1}^{N} x\,i\,x\,j\,rij\,\sigma_i\,\sigma_j.$$

$\sigma^2 p$ = portfolio variance

σp = Standard deviation of portfolio

xi = Proportion of portfolio invested in security i

x_J = proportion of portfolio invested in security J

rij = coefficient of correlation between i and J

σ_i = standard deviation of i

σ_j = standard deviation of J.

N = number of securities

Problem

Given the following example, find out the expected Risk of the portfolio.

Security	*Expected Return*	*Proportion % Invested (X)*	*SD σ*
D.C.M.	10	20	0.2
Escorts	15	20	0.3
TISCO	20	60	0.5

SD (Standard deviation) and coefficient of correlation is

r_{12} = 0.5 (r_1 with respect to r_2)

r_{13} = 0.1 (r_1 with respect to r_3)

r_{23} = – 0.3 (r_2 with respect to r_3)

then

$$\sigma p^2 = x_1^2\,\sigma_1^2 + x_2^2\,\sigma_2^2 + x_3^2\,\sigma_3^2 +$$
$$2\,x_1\,x_2\,r_{12}\,\sigma_1\,\sigma_2$$
$$2\,x_2\,x_3\,r_{23}\,\sigma_2\,\sigma_3$$
$$2\,x_1\,x_3\,r_{13}\,\sigma_1\,\sigma_3$$

Putting the above data into the formula

$$\sigma p^2 = (0.20)^2\,(0.2)^2 + (0.2)^2\,(.30)^2 + (.60)^2\,(0.5)^2$$
$$+ 2\,(.2)\,(.2)\,(.5)\,(.2)\,(.3)$$
$$+ 2\,(.2)\,(.6)\,(-0.3)\,(.3)\,(.5) + 2\,(.2)\,(.6)\,(.1)\,(0.2)\,(0.5)$$
$$= 0.0016 + .0036 + .09 + .0024 - .0108 + .0024$$
$$= 0.1 - .0108 = 0.0892$$

$$\sigma p^2 = .0892$$

$$\sigma p = \sqrt{.0892} = .299 = +.30 \text{ Portfolio Risk}$$

Parameters of Markowitz Diversification

Based on his research, Markowitz has set out guidelines for diversification on the basis of the attitude of investors towards risk and return and on a proper quantification of risk. The investments have different types of risk characteristics, some called systematic and market related risks and the other called unsystematic or company related risks. Markowitz diversification involves a proper number of securities, not too few or not too many which have no correlation or negative correlation. The proper choice of companies, securities, or assets whose return are not correlated and whose risks are mutually offsetting will reduce the overall risk.

For building up the efficient set of portfolio, as laid down by Markowitz, we need to look into these important parameters.

(1) Expected return.

(2) Variability of returns as measured by standard deviation from the mean.

(3) Covariance or variance of one asset return to other asset returns.

In general the higher the expected return, the lower is the standard deviation or variance and lower is the correlation the better will be the security for investor choice. Whatever is the risk of the individual securities in isolation, the total risk of the portfolio of all securities may be lower, if the covariance of their returns is negative or negligible.

Criteria of Dominance

Dominance refers to the superiority of one portfolio over the other. A set can dominate over the other, if with the same return, the risk is lower or with the same risk, the return is higher. Dominance principle involves the trade off between risk and return.

For two security portfolio, minimise the portfolio risk by the equation

$$\sigma p = Wa\,\sigma a^2 + W_b\,\sigma_b^2 + 2\,(W_a\,W_b\,\sigma_a\,\sigma_b\,\sigma ab)$$

$$E\,(Rp) = WaE\,(Ra) + Wb\,E\,(Rb)$$

R refers to returns and E (Rp) is the expected returns. σp is the standard deviation, W refers to the proportion invested in each security σa σb are the standard deviations of a and b securities and σab is the covariance or interrelations of the security returns.

$$\sigma p = \sqrt{\frac{\Sigma X^2}{n}}$$, where Σx^2 is the sum of deviations from the mean squared.

σ^2 is square of standard deviation or called variance.

Covariance is

$$\text{Cov}\;x\;y = \frac{1}{N}\sum_{i}^{N}\left[(Rx - \overline{R}x)\,(Ry - \overline{R}y)\right]$$

The above concepts are used in the calculation of expected returns, mean standard deviation as a measure of risk and covarience as a measure of inter-relations of one security return with another.

Markowitz Model

Risk is discussed here in terms of a portfolio of assets.

As referred to earlier, any investment risk is the variability of return on a stock, assets or a portfolio. It is measured by standard deviation of the return over the Mean for a number of observations.

Types of Risk

I	(Summary)	II
Systematic		Unsystematic
(Market)		(Company Risk)
Examples		*Examples*
Interest Rate Risk		Labour Troubles
Market Risk		Liquidity Problems
Inflation Risk		Raw Materials Risks
Demand and Government Policy		Financial Risks
International Factors		Management Problems

Measurement of Risk (Example)

Standard deviation to be calculated:

Observations: 10% – 5% 20% 35% – 10% = 10% will be their Mean.

Deviation from the Mean	*Square of Deviation*
10 — 10 = 0	0
– 5 — 10 = –15	225
+ 20 — 10 = 10	100
+ 35 — 10 = 25	625
– 10 — 10 = –20	400
Mean = 10	$\Sigma d^2 = 1350$

Standard Deviation (σ_p) $= \sqrt{\left(\frac{\Sigma d^2}{5}\right)} = \sqrt{\frac{1350}{5}} = \sqrt{270} = 16.43$

Scrip Deviation = 16.43

Let Market Deviation be = 10.40

Total Risk $= \frac{16.43}{10.40} = 1.58$

Portfolio Risk

When two or more securities or assets are combined in a portfolio, their covariance or interactive risk is to be considered. Thus, if the returns on two assets move together, their covariance is positive and the risk is more on such portfolio. If on the other hand, the returns move independently or in opposite directions, the covariance is negative and the risk in total will be lower.

Mathematically, the covariance is defined as

$$\text{Cov x Y} = \frac{1}{N}\sum_{t=1}^{N} \left[(Rx - R\overline{x})(Ry - R\overline{y})\right],$$

where Rx is return on security x, Ry return security Y, and $R\overline{x}$ and $R\overline{y}$ are expected returns on them respectively and N is the number of observations.

The coefficient of correlation is another measure designed to indicate the similarity or dissimilarity in the behaviour of two variables. We define the coefficient of correlation of x and y as

$$\gamma\, x\, y = \frac{\text{Cov}\, xy}{\sigma x \times \sigma y} \quad \text{where,}$$

Cov x y is the covariance between x and y and σ_x is the standard deviation of x and σ_y is the standard deviation of y.

Example:

	Return	Expected Return	Variance
I Stock x	7	9	- 2
Stock y	13	9	+ 4
			Product- 2 x 4 = -8
II Stock x	11	9	+ 2
Stock y	5	9	- 4
			Product - 8

Where, N = 2 The covariance equation is as follows:

$$\text{Cov} = \frac{1}{2} \left[(7-9)(13-9) + (11-9)(5-9)\right]$$

$$= \frac{1}{2} (-8) + (-8)] = \frac{-16}{2} = -8$$

The coefficient of correlation can be set out as follows:

$$\gamma\, x\, y = \frac{-8}{(2) \times (4)} = \frac{-8}{8} = -1.0$$

If the coefficient of correlation between two securities is – 1.0, it is perfect negative correlation. If it is + 1.0 it is perfect positive correlation. If the coefficient is '0' then the returns are said to be independent. To sum up, correlation between two securities depend (a) on covariance between them, and (b) the standard deviation of each.

In Markowitz Model, we need to have the inputs of *expected returns,* risk measured by *standard deviation of returns* and the *covariance between the returns* on assets considered.

Portfolio Management (Summary)

(Q) What is Portfolio Management?	(A) Management of Large Investible Funds with a view to maximising return and minimising risk.
(Q) Investments are generally risky—the higher the risk, the higher the return. How to Manage this trade off between Risk and Return?	(A) Efficient portfolios are those with minimum risk for a given expected return. For a planned return, risk can be minimised by using the concept of Beta for Systematic Risk and diversification for Unsystematic Risk.

Two Models Compared

Markowitz Model *Utility Concept*	*Sharpe Model*
Utility of a portfolio is risk adjusted return. It is Equal to portfolio return minus risk penalty. Where Risk Penalty $= \frac{\text{Risk Squared}}{\text{Risk Tolerance}}$ It is portfolio risk, relative to the investor's risk tolerance. The optimal portfolio is one on the efficient frontier that maximises utility. To generate efficient portfolios the Markowitz Model requires — (a) expected return on each asset (b) Standard deviation of returns as a measure of risk of each asset, and (c) the covariance or correlation coefficients as a measure of inter-relationship between the returns on assets considered.	Optimal portfolio is set up by using the single index model of Sharpe. The desirability of any stock is directly related to its excess return to Beta ratio, namely Sharpe Index $= \frac{RJ - RF}{BJ}$ Where, RJ is expected return on the stock, RF is the risk free return, and BJ is the Beta relating the J stock to the market return. Then rank all the stocks in their order of the index value. In Sharpe Model, the return on any stock depends on some constant (α) called Alpha plus coefficient called β (Beta), times the value of a stock Index (I), plus a random component. The equation is $R_j = a_j + b_j I + e_j$ in Sharpe Model.

Sharpe Model Equation was set as, $R_J = \alpha_J + B_J I + e_J$, where,

R_J = Expected return on security J

α_J = Intercept of a straight line or alpha coefficient

β_J = Beta coefficient is the slope of straight line (Regression line)

I = Expected return on Index of the market

e_J = Error term with a mean of zero and standard deviation which is constant.

Alpha (α) is really the value of y in the equation when the value of x is zero. The return on the stock in relation to the return on the market Index, namely, β is a measure of the systematic risk of the market. The error term in the above equation explains the unsystematic risk.

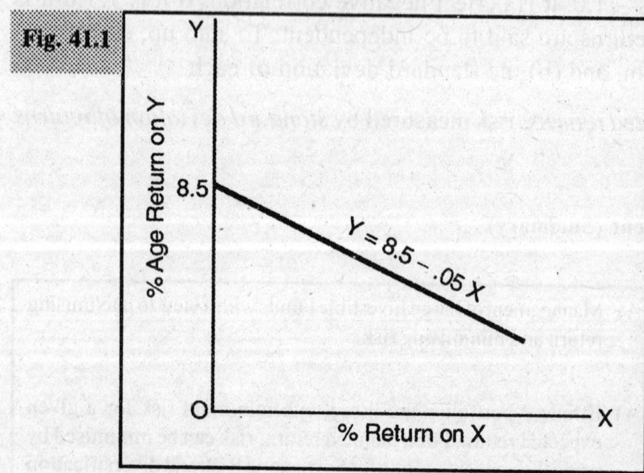

Fig. 41.1

a (α) is measured by making return on y as zero. In the following chart α is 8.5, which is the constant and Beta is .05, calculated for the data, used in the chart. If the return on the Index is say, at 25%, then $R_J = 8.5 - .05\ (25) = 7.25$.

This means that if the market index gives a return of 25%, the security in question will give a return of 7.25% only. Systematic Risk only is used by Sharpe, and it is equal to $\beta^2 \times$ (variance of Index) $= \beta^2 \sigma^2$. Where σ^2 is variance of Index. Unsystematic Risk = Total variance – Systematic Risk plus the error term in his equation.

Sharpe Model (Contd.)
Practical Measurement of Return

Riskless Rate = 6% (Bank rate) or Bank Deposit rate (7 to 9%)

Risk Premium = 5 to 10% depending or the Risk or the Concept of Beta of the security.

$$\beta \text{ Beta } \frac{\text{\% Price Change of a Scrip Returns}}{\text{\% Price Change of the Market Index Return}}$$

Beta is thus a measure of Systematic Risk of the market only and does not represent the unsystematic risk. Market Risk is represented by BSE National Index, in the above formula. In the regression equation given below used by Sharpe, the Unsystematic Risk is represented by the error term, namely, (e), while a or α is the constant slope of the regression line, and Beta (β) is the measure of Systematic Risk.

Example for Regression Equation and calculation of Beta is given below:

$Y = \alpha + \beta X + e$ is the equation

$Y = 0.91 + 0.93X$, where,

$\beta = 0.93$ X = Market Return

Y = Scrip Return

α = Constant = 0.91

Examples of β, calculated

Reliance	—	1.955
ACC	—	0.931
Telco	—	1.153
Tisco	—	1.342
Colgate	—	0.946
Tata Tea	—	0.951

Source : Some Issues of Journal of Chartered Financial Analyst (ICFAI)

On the basis of the above estimates of the stocks Alpha, Beta and expected return and Residual variance (data derived from the above formulas), one can construct a series of efficient portfolios, by using a computer programmer. This will give out the series of corner portfolios and the line connecting them is the Efficient frontier line, in the Sharpe Model.

The chart below represents the corner portfolio sets, indicating the efficient portfolio.@

Efficient corner portfolios

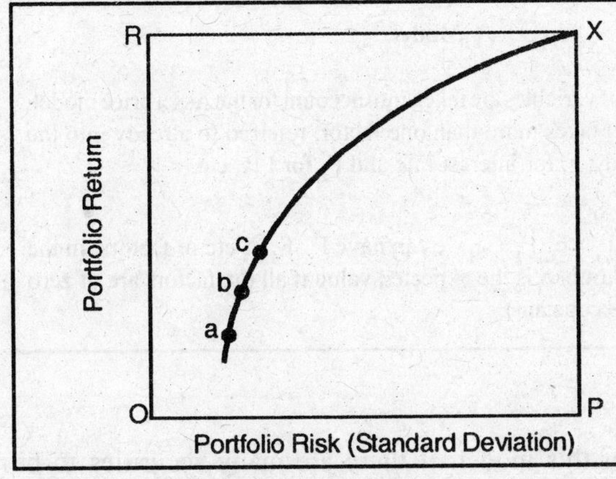

a, b, c... x are the corner portfolios generated from the equations of Sharpe (given below)

Fig. 42.2

Equation for Portfolio Return

$$R_p = \sum_{i=1}^{N} X_i (\alpha_1 + B_i I) - 1$$

This is for calculating the expected return on portfolio where N = total number of stocks, X_i is the proportion devoted to stock, i ; B_i is the Beta on Stock i, I is market index return and is the same for all stocks, estimated.

@ Refer to Chapter 20, of D.E. Fischer & R. J. Gordon, *Security Analysis and Portfolio Management.*

For Portfolio Variance

σ_p^2 = variation of portfolio return

σ_I^2 = expected variance of Index (Market)

e_i^2 = variation in security's return not caused by its relationship to the index

Equation for Portfolio Variance

$$\sigma_p^2 = \left[\left(\sum_{i=1}^{N} X_i \beta_i\right)^2 \sigma_I^2\right] + \left[\sum_{i=1}^{N} X e_i^2\right]$$

ARBITRAGE PRICING THEORY

Introduction

Like the Capital Assets Pricing Model (CAPM), Arbitrage Pricing Theory (APT) is an equilibrium model of asset pricing but assumes that the returns are generated by a factor Model. Its assumption *vis-a-vis* those of CAPM are set out first:

APT	*CAPM*
Investors do not look at expected returns and standard deviations. Based on the law of one price, if the price of an asset is different in different markets, arbitrage brings them to the same price.	Investors look at the expected returns and accompanying risks measured by standard deviation.
Investors prefer higher wealth/returns to lower wealth.	Investors are risk averse and risk-return analysis is necessary.
APT is based on the return generated by factor models.	Investors maximise wealth for a given level of risk.

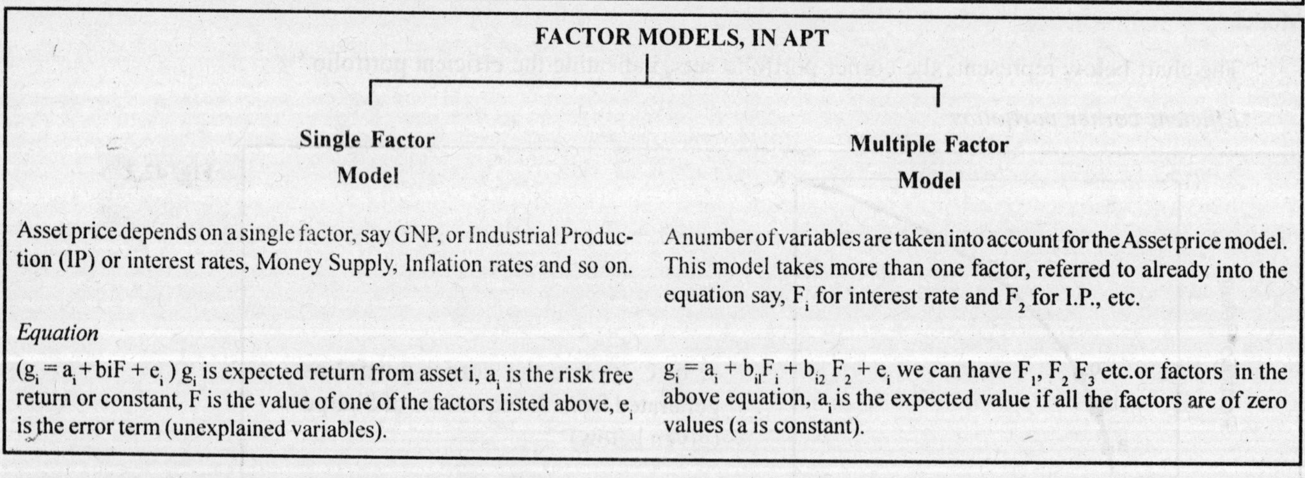

Asset Selection in the Above Model

Investment strategies of many types can also be selected under this model. If there are many securities to be selected, and a fixed amount to be invested, the investor can choose in a manner that he can aim at a zero non-factor risk (e: = 0). This is possible by combining securities to hedge out the sensitivity of a portfolio to all but one factor.

An example will explain this. Let there be three securities A, B and C with the following securities:

Security	*bi1*	*bi2*
A	− 0.40	1.75
B	1.60	− 0.75
C	0.67	− 0.25

If he has Rs. 1,000, he invests Rs. 300 in Security A, Rs. 700 in Security B and nil in Security C, with proportions being 0.3 in A, 0.7 in B and 0 in C.

It will be seen from the equations below that the sensitivity to factors 1, and 2 will be 1.0 and 0 respectively.

$$bp_1 = (-0.40 \times 0.3) + (1.60 \times 0.7) + (0.67 \times 0)$$

$$= (-0.12) + (1.12) + (0) = +1.0$$

$$bp_2 = (1.75 \times 0.3) + (-0.75 \times 0.7) + (-0.25 \times 0)$$

$$= (0.525) + (-0.525) = 0$$

In the above fashion, it would be possible theoretically, although not in practice, to create *"pure factor"* portfolios that are sensitive to only one factor and have insignificant non-factor risk. But in practice, only impure factor portfolios can be created.

Components of Expected Returns

It is convenient to break up the expected return into two parts: *(i)* risk free rate of return, and *(ii)* the rest in the following equation, rf is the risk free return and γ_1 is the expected premium return per unit of sensitivity to the factor 1 for Portfolio$_i$.

$$rp_1 = rf + \lambda_1$$

Similarly, the expected return on pure factor 2 portfolio

$$rp_2 = rf + \lambda_2$$

Thus, the investor by splitting his funds among risk free portfolios and pure factor portfolios, it is possible for him to form a portfolio with almost any sensitivity to each factor. Although theory claims that the non-factor risk can be reduced to zero, it is not possible in real life. Therefore, in practical investment or in portfolio operations, it is better to combine the Capital Asset pricing theory and the APT Model. Most investors prefer, no doubt higher levels of expected return and dislike higher levels of risk. The fact is that there is a trade off between them, which is not considered by the APT Model. Synthesis of CAPM and APT is therefore more realistic.

Beta coefficients can be used to reflect the risk factors and factor sensitivities can also be taken into account to arrive at the expected returns. Thus, if the returns are generated by two factor model, the Beta coefficient of a security will be related to its sensitiveness to the factors and factor Betas can be taken to reflect the different sensitivities of different factors.

Beta coefficient for a security could be obtained by dividing Cov. $(r_i r_m)$ by the variance of the Market Portfolio (σ_M^2)

Thus, $$\beta i = \frac{Cov\,(r_i r_m)}{\sigma_M^2}$$

Security Betas can appear in factor Betas, if we ignore $\frac{Cov\,(r_i r_m)}{\sigma_M^2}$ **in equation below.**

$$\beta i = \left[\frac{Cov\,(F_1 r_M)^1}{s_M^2} \times b_{i1}\right] + \left[\frac{Cov.(F_2 r_M)^1}{\sigma_M^2} \times b_{i2}\right] + \frac{Cov(r_i r_M)}{\sigma_M^2}$$

If the last term becomes zero, as referred to above, then,

$$\beta F_1 = \frac{Cov(F_i r_m)}{\sigma_M^2}$$

$$\beta F_2 = \frac{Cov(F_2 r_M)}{\sigma_M^2}$$

It will be seen that βF_1 and βF_2 are constants as they do not vary from one security to another, the Beta coefficient of a security is a function of its sensitiveness to the pervasive factors. Thus, by taking Betas of securities the question of sensitivity of security return to a factor is taken care of. By this, one can synthesize the APT Model and CAP Model in the empirical work.

Empirical Testing of APT Model

The CAPM as also the practical experience tells us that other things being equal, securities with large *ex-ante* betas will have relatively large expected returns. It does not mean that the actual *ex-post* returns will also be larger. But investment is made on expectation and hence the use of Betas, despite the fact that exact Betas may not really give an indication of actual returns in future.

Beta measurement is itself subject to limitations, as they change widely, with the number of years for which data are taken; the source of data, and the methods of compilation are subject to normal statistical limitations.

Using the actual data on Stock Price Index numbers and security prices of any Stock Exchange, one can compile Betas, the method of which has been explained earlier. Empirical studies done abroad on NYSE data (by Centre for Research in Security Prices (CRSP) at the University of Chicago) showed that the historical Beta values cannot be counted upon to predict the returns precisely. They are useful as some approximations and landmarks to go by.

In months, in which there were excess positive returns, the Beta factors were generally positive in the sense that stocks with historical Betas gave excess returns over the market. In periods when the excess returns were negative, the Beta factor was generally negative, in the sense that stocks with high historical betas, tended to underperform as compared to those with low-historical Betas.

In detailed tests of the original and Zero-beta CAPM, portfolio classes were used to examine the relationship between average returns and historical Betas. The graph below shows the actual relationship for the period 1938 to 1968. The vertical intercept, which corresponds to the zero beta Return, is 0.61% per month, while the average Treasury Bill rate, which corresponds to the risk free rate of interest, was only 0.13% per month. Assuming that Betas are measured relative to a Stock index, they are surrogates for true Betas, and they support the thesis of CAPM to a substantial degree.

Arbitrage Pricing Theory — Problem

Question

$\lambda_1 = 1.8$ — Risk Free Rate $\lambda_0 = 7\%$

$\lambda_2 = 1.25$ — $b_1 = 1.2$

$\lambda_3 = 0.50$ — $b_2 = 1.5$

$b_3 = -0.75$

Equation for APT Model

$$Eri = \lambda_o + \lambda_1 b_1 + \lambda_2 b_2 + \lambda_3 b_3 \ldots$$

$$Eri = 7 + 1.8\,(1.2) + 1.25\,(1.5) + 0.50\,(-0.75)$$

$$= 7 + 2.16 + 1.875 - 0.375 = 10.66$$

Thus, the expected rate of return of the stock is 10.66%

Question

Calculate the equilibrium rate of return for the following three securities

	bi_1	bi_2
A	1.2	1
B	– 0.5	0.75
C	0.75	1.30

Answer

Assume two factor Model as applicable which → $E(r_1) = 4\% + 3\%\ bi_1 + 5\%\ bi_2$

$E(r_A) = 4\% + 3\%\ (1.2) + 5\%\ (+1.0) = 12.60\%$

$E(r_R) = 4\% + 3\%\ (-0.5) + 5\%\ (0.75) = 6.25\%$

$E(r_C) = 4\% + 3\%\ (0.75) + 5\%\ (1.30) = 12.75\%$

In the Graph below, OM is risk free return. Actual CAPM line is shown in the Graph to vary from the Zero Beta line to a substantial extent.

Fig. 42.3

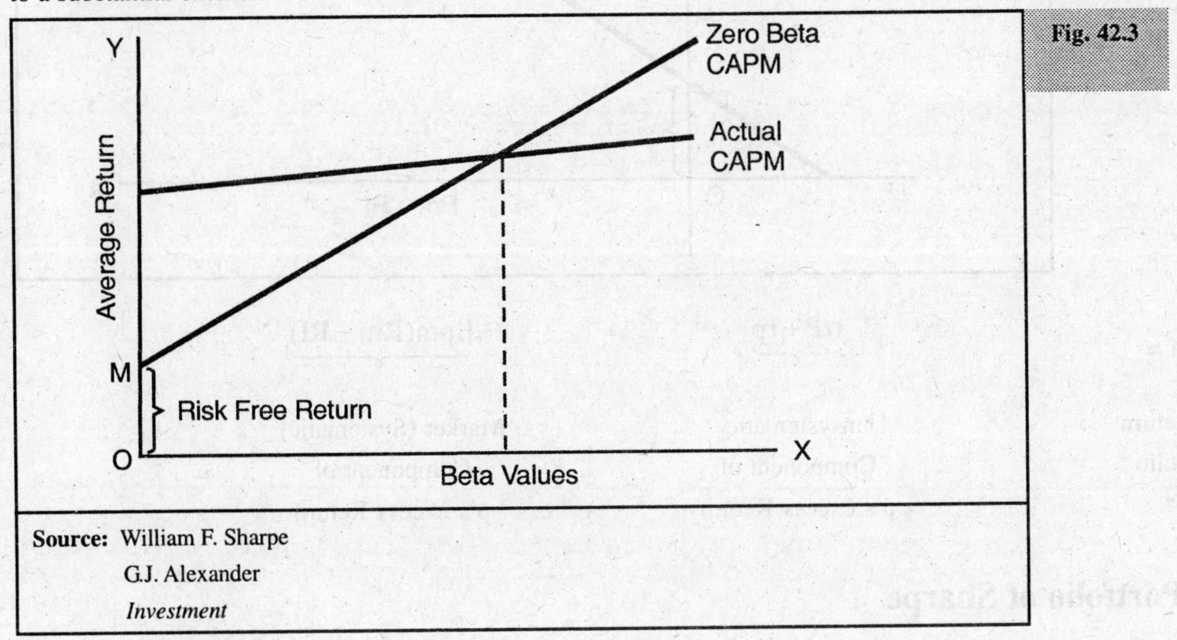

Source: William F. Sharpe
G.J. Alexander
Investment

Sharpe Model

Markowitz Model had serious practical limitations due the rigours involved in compiling the expected returns, standard deviation, variance, covariance of each security to every other security in the portfolio. Sharpe model has simplified this process by relating the return in a security to a single Market index. Firstly, this will theoretically reflect all well traded securities in the market. Secondly, it will reduce and simplify the work involved in compiling elaborate matrices of variances as between individual securities.

If thus the market index is used as a surrogate for other individual securities in the portfolio, the relation of any individual security with the Market index can be represented in a Regression line or characteristic line. This is drawn below, with the excess return on the security on the y-axis and excess return on the Market Portfolio on the x-axis.

The equation of the characteristic line is $Ri - Rf = a + \beta im\ (Rm - Rf) + r_i$

Ri is the holding period return on security i

Rf is the riskless rate of interest

Alpha is the vertical intercept on y-axis representing the return on the security when only unsystematic risk is considered and systematic risk is measured by Beta. ri is the residual component, not captured by the above variables.

Fig. 42.4

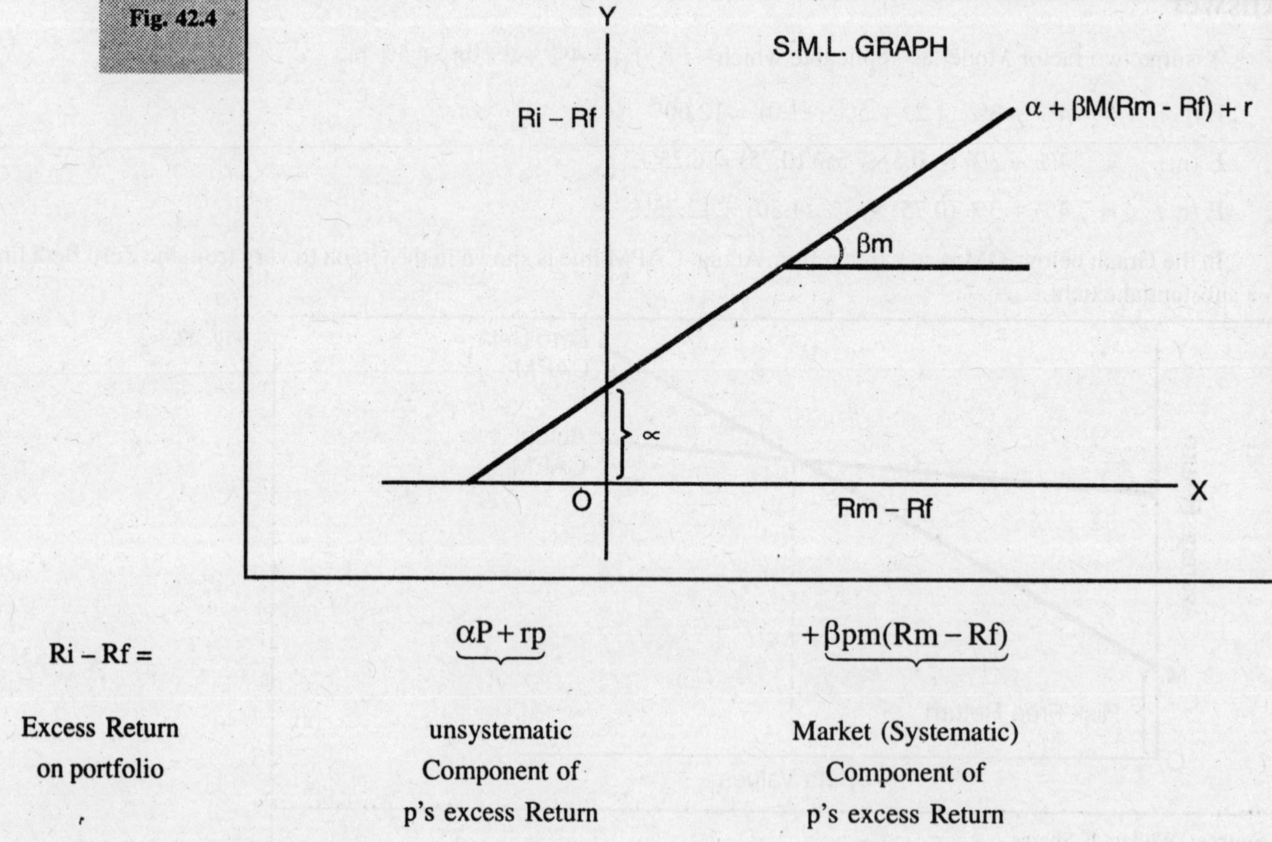

$$Ri - Rf = \underbrace{\alpha P + rp}_{} \underbrace{+ \beta pm(Rm - Rf)}_{}$$

Excess Return on portfolio	unsystematic Component of p's excess Return	Market (Systematic) Component of p's excess Return

Optimal Portfolio of Sharpe

This optimal portfolio of Sharpe is called the Single Index Model. The optimal portfolio is directly related to the Beta. If Ri is expected return on stock i and Rf is Risk free Rate, then the excess return = Ri – Rf

This has to be adjusted to Bi, namely

$\frac{Ri - Rf}{\beta_1}$ which is the equation for ranking Stocks in the order of their return adjusted for risk.

The method involves selecting a cut-off rate for inclusion of securities in a portfolio. For this purpose, excess return to Beta ratio given above has to be calculated for each stock and rank them from highest to lowest. Then only those securities which have $\frac{Ri - Rf}{\beta_1}$, greater than cut-off point, fixed in advance can be selected. The basis for finding the cut-off Rate C_i is as follows:

Basis for Cut-off Rate

For a portfolio of i stocks, Ci is given by cut-off rate

$$\text{Cut-off Rate Ci} = \frac{\sigma m^2 \sum_{t=1}^{J} \frac{(Ri - Rf)\beta_i}{\sigma ei^2}}{1 + \sigma m^2 \sum_{t=1}^{J} \frac{\beta i^2}{\sigma ei^2}}$$

σm^2 = variance in the market Index

σei^2 = variance in the Stock movement in unsystematic Risk.

Ri, Rf Bi have the same meanings as referred to above.

Take an example. Rf = 10, Beta = 1

Expected Return Ri = 15, σei^2 = unsystematic risk is given by 50, then

We have

$$\frac{(Ri-Rf)\beta i}{\sigma ei^2} = \frac{(15-10)1}{50} = \frac{5}{50} = \frac{1}{10}$$

Given σm^2 = market risk = 10.

Then

$$\sigma^2 m \times \frac{\beta i^2}{\sigma e_i^2} = \frac{(1)^2}{50} \times 10 = \frac{1}{5}$$

$$Ci = \frac{\sigma m^2 \dfrac{(Ri-Rf)\beta i}{\sigma e^2 j}}{1+\sigma m^2 \dfrac{bi^2}{\sigma ci^2}} = \frac{10 \times \dfrac{1}{10}}{1+\dfrac{1}{5}}$$

$$Ci = \frac{10(1/10)}{1+(1/5)} = \frac{1}{1.2} = 0.84$$

Example

We have to see that for the optimum Ci that is C*, to be selected, the securities should have excess return to Betas above Ci. Excess return to Beta ratio should be above Ci to be included in the portfolio, to be precise. This C_i is that point which shows the cut-off point between those excess returns to Beta ratios above. The calculation of C requires data, which are shown below:

Rf = Risk free Return = 5%

Security Nos.	*Mean Return Ri*	*Excess Return Ri – Rf*	*Beta Bi*	*Unsystematic Risk* $\sigma e i^2$	*Excess Return to Beta Ratio (Ri-Rf)/Bi*
1	15.0	10.0	1.0	50	10.0
2	17.0	12.0	1.5	40	8.0
3	12.0	7.0	1.0	20	7.0
4	17.0	12.0	2.0	10	6.0
5	11.0	6.0	1.0	40	6.0

Based on the above data, we have to calculate the 'C' values for each security for inclusion in the optimum portfolio. The following Table gives the example:

Security	$\frac{(Ri - Rf)\beta}{\sigma e^2}$	$\frac{\beta i^2}{\sigma e^2}$	$\sum_{i=1}^{J} \frac{(Ri - Rf)}{\sigma e^2}$	$\sum \frac{\beta^2}{\sigma e^2}$	C Value Calculated as shown below
	Excess Return to Beta/Res Var	***Beta Squared/ Res Var***	***Excess Return to Beta/Res var Cumulative***	***Beta Squared/ Resi/var Cumulative***	***Cut-off Rate***
A	0.119	.01525	0.119	.01525	2.22
B	0.109	.01419	0.228	.02944	3.36
C	0.107	.01497	0.336	.04441	4.06

(A) In calculation of C; Rf = 7% Rm = 11% $\sigma m^2 = 26$

$\frac{(Ri - Rf)\beta}{\sigma e^2}$ is 0.119, multiplied by σm^2

so 0.119×26

$$1 + \sigma m^2 \frac{\beta i^2}{\sigma e^2} = 1 + 26\ (.01525)$$

$$\frac{\sigma m^2 \sum \frac{(Ri - Rf)\beta}{\sigma e^2} = 0.119 \times 26}{1 + \sigma m^2 \left(RE \frac{\beta i^2}{\sigma e^2} \right) = 1 + 26(.01525)}$$

$$Ci = \frac{0.119 \times 26}{1 + 26\ (0.1525)} = \frac{3.094}{1.3965} = 2.22$$

$$\text{(B) } Ci = \frac{.228 \times 26}{1 + 26\ (0.2944)} = \frac{5.928}{1.7654} = 3.36$$

$$\text{(C) } Ci = \frac{.336 \times 26}{1 + 26\ (.0444)} = \frac{8.736}{2.1546} = 4.06$$

Res Var = Residual variance σe^2

σm^2 = market variance.

All securities with excess return to Beta ratio above the cut-off rate C*, say 3.0 in the above Table will be chosen in the portfolio. The calculation of cut-off point is also explained. In arriving at the optimal portfolio, the emphasis of Sharpe Model is on Beta and on the Market Index. Sharpe's optimal portfolio would thus consist of those securities only which have excess return to Beta ratio above a cut-off point.

By this method, selection of the portfolio has become easier due to the ranking of the securities in the order of their excess return and applying the yardstick of a required cut-off point for selection of securities. That cut-off point is related to the excess return to Beta rate on the one hand and variance of the market index sm^2 and variance of the stock's movement which is related to the unsystematic risk, namely sei^2.

It is thus seen that Sharpe's Portfolio takes into account both the systematic market related risk and unsystematic risk and residual risk.

Distribution of Investments

Once the choice of securities is made then one has to decide the proportion of his funds to be invested in each security.

The percentage to be invested in each security is

$$Xi^0 = \frac{Zi}{\sum_{J=1}^{N} Z_1}$$

Where,

$$Zi = \frac{\beta i}{\sigma e^2}\left(\frac{Ri - Rf}{\beta i} - C^*\right)$$

The second expression in the bracket will determine the proportion of funds to be invested in each security. The first expression simply scales the weight on each security, so that the total is summing upto 1.

Suppose $= \frac{\beta i}{\sigma ei^2} = \frac{2}{100}$

and $\frac{Ri - Rf}{\beta_1} = 10$ and $C^* = 5$

The value of $Z_i = \frac{2}{100}(10 - 5) = \frac{1}{10} = 0.1$

The proportion to be invested in $Z_1 = 0.1$

On similar lines $= \frac{\beta i}{\sigma ei^2} = \frac{5.65}{100}$

and $\frac{Ri - Rf}{\beta 1} = 8$, then

the value of $Z_2 \frac{5.65}{100}(8 - 5) = \frac{(5.65) X (3)}{100} = \frac{16.95}{100} = 0.1695$

The proportion to be invested in Z_2 is 0.1695

$Z_1 Z_2$ ... etc., should total upto 1; so that whole fund is used.

Question 1:

The return of Flex Stock is related to factors 1 and 2 as given below.

(E) $\overline{R}_J = \lambda_o + 0.6\lambda_1 + 1.3\lambda_2$

Where, 0.6 and 1.3 are sensitivity Coefficients, λ_1 risk premium is 6% and λ_2 is 3% and Risk free return (Rf) $\lambda_o = 7\%$

What is the stock's expected return?

Answer:

$$(E)\overline{R}_J = 0.07 + 0.6 \times (.06) + 1.3\,(0.03)$$
$$= 0.07 \times 0.036 + 0.039 = 0.145$$
$$= 14.5\%$$

Question 2:

The reaction coefficients for two stocks and the market price λ are given below

Factor	λ	b_A	b_B
1	.09	.5	.7
2	–.03	.4	.8
3	.04	1.2	.2

Using APT model and risk free rate at 6% what is the expected return, if two stocks are equally weighted?

Answer:

$$(E)\ \overline{R}_A = 0.06 + .09(.5) - .03(.4) + .04(1.2)$$
$$= .06 + .045 - .012 + .048$$
$$= 0.141 = 14.1\%$$

$$(E)\ \overline{R}_B = .06 + .09(.7) - .03\,(.8) + .04(.2)$$
$$= .06 + .063 - .024 + .008$$
$$= 0.107 = 10.7\%.$$

If they are equally weighted (0.5 and 0.5), Then

$$(E)\ \overline{R}_A = 0.5(14.1) + 0.5\,(10.7)$$
$$= 7.05 + 5.35 = 12.4\%$$
$$= 12.4\%$$

There are two stocks X and Y and three factors. Given the Risk free rate (Rf) at 6% λ_o corresponds to return on risk free asset or the λ in general reflects the market price of risk or expected excess return over the risk free return.

Given the earlier data on reaction coefficients

and if you are investing 1/3rd in X and 2/3rd in Y,

What would be the expected return?

Answer:

$$\Sigma R_x = 1 + b_{1J}\,F_1 + b_{2J}\,F_2 + b_{3J}\,F_3,$$

Using the above equations and ignoring the error term, we have

$$\overline{R}_x = 0.06 + 0.09\,(.5) - .03\,(.4) + .04\,(1.2)$$
$$= 0.06 + .045 - .012 + .048$$
$$= (0.153) - (.012) = 0.141 = (0.153) - (.012) = 0.141$$
$$= 14.1\%$$

$\overline{R}_y = 0.06 + 0.09(7) - .03\,(.8) + .04\,(.2)$

$= 0.06 + .063 - 0.024 + .008$

$= 0.131 - 024 = .107$

$= 10.7\%.$

If we invest in the ratio of 1:2

then $ER_p = 0.333\,(14.1) + 0.666\,(10.7) =$

$= 4.695 + 7.126 = 11.82\%.$

If we invest in the ratio 1:3 in the securities x and y

$ER_p = 0.25\,(14.1) + 0.75\,(10.7) =$

$= 3.525 + 8.025 = 11.55\%$

Problem - 1:

Mr 'X' owns a portfolio with the following characteristics:

Security	*Factor (1) Sensitivity*	*Factor (2) Sensitivity*	*Proportion*	*Expected Return*
A	2.50	1.40	0.30	13%
B	1.60	0.90	0.30	18%
C	0.80	1.00	0.20	10%
D	2.00	1.30	0.20	12%

Assume that the returns are generated by a two factor model. Mr X decides to create an arbitrage Portfolio by increasing the holding of security 'B' by 0.05.

(*i*) What must be the weights of the other three securities in his portfolio?

(*ii*) What is the expected return on the arbitrage portfolio?

Answer: (1) $Xa + Xb + Xc + Xd = O$

(2) $Xa\ ba_1 + Xb\ bb_1 + Xc\ bc_1 + Xd\ bd_1 = O$

(3) $Xa\ ba_2 + Xb\ bb_2 + Xc\ bc_2 + Xd\ bd_2 = O$

$2.5xa + (1.6 \times 0.05) + 0.8 \times Xc + 2 \times d = O$

$1.4\ xa + (0.9 \times 0.05) + 1 \times xc + 1.3 \times d = O$

$Xa = -Xc - Xd - 0.05$ from equation -1

when $Xb = 0.05$

Hint: Calculate Xa, Xc and Xd with Xb given as 0.05.

Problem - 2:

Gopal holds portfolio of two companies A and B with the following details.

	A	*B*
Security Return	10	5
Security Variance	0.0064	0.0016
Investment Proportion	0.5	0.5
Correlation	0.5	

Under the Markowitz Model what is the portfolio return and Portfolio Risk?

Problem - 3:

Following data relates to two securities in the market, i and j.

Security	R_p	σ	P_{iJ}
i	9	7.56	
J	8	3.75	–0.5

Find out the minimum variance portfolio and compute its risk and return.

Problem - 4:

What is optimum portfolio in choosing among the following securities, assuming Rf = 5% and σm^2 = 10% and R_m = 11%.

Security	*Expected Return*	*Beta*	σ^2
A	15	1.0	30
B	12	1.5	20
C	11	2.0	40
D	8	0.8	10
E	9	1.0	20
F	14	1.5	10

CHAPTER 42

Basics of Portfolio Management in India

In India, Portfolio Management is still in its infancy. Barring a few Indian banks, and foreign banks and UTI, no other agency had professional Portfolio Management until 1987. After the setting up of public sector Mutual Funds, since 1987, Professional Portfolio Management, backed by competent research staff became the order of the day. After the success of Mutual Funds in Portfolio Management, a number of brokers and Investment Consultants some of whom are also professionally qualified have become Portfolio Managers. They have managed the funds of clients on both discretionary and non-discretionary basis. It was found that many of them, including Mutual Funds have guaranteed a minimum return or capital appreciation and adopted all kinds of incentives which are now prohibited by SEBI. They resorted to speculative over trading and insider trading, discounts, etc., to achieve their targetted returns to the clients, which are also prohibited by SEBI.

The recent CBI probe into the operations of many market dealers has revealed the unscrupulous practices by banks, dealers and brokers in their Portfolio Operations. The SEBI has then imposed stricter rules, which included their registration, a code of conduct and minimum infrastructure, experience and expertise etc. It is no longer possible for any unemployed youth, or retired person or self-styled consultant to engage in Portfolio Management without the SEBI's licence. The guidelines of SEBI are in the direction of making Portfolio Management a responsible professional service to be rendered by experts in the field.

SOME ASPECTS OF PORTFOLIO MANAGEMENT

Basically Portfolio Management involves:

(A) A proper investment decision-making of what to buy and sell;

(B) Proper money management in terms of investment in a basket of assets so as to satisfy the asset preferences of investors;

(C) Reduce the risk and increase returns.

Investment Strategy

In India, there are a large number of savers, barring the population who are below the poverty line. In a poor country like this, it is surprising that its saving rate is as high as 38% of GDP per annum and investment at 39% of GDP. But the return in the form of output growth is as low as 7 to 8% per annum in the last decade. One may ask why is it that high levels of investment could not generate comparable rates of growth of output? The answer is poor investment strategy, involving high capital output ratios, low productivity of capital and high rates of obsolescence of capital. What is true of the nation at that Macro level is also true at Micro level of individuals and institutions. The use of capital in India is wasteful and inefficient, dispite the fact that India is labour rich and capital poor. Thus, the Portfolio Managers in India lack the expertise and experience, which will enable them to have proper strategy for investment management.

Secondly, the average Indian Household saves around 48% in financial form and 52% in physical form. Of those in financial form, nearly 50% is held in cash and bank deposits, as per the latest RBI data and they have negative real returns or return less than the inflation rates. Besides, a proportion of 30% of financial savings is held in form of Insurance, P.F., Pension Funds etc., while another 5% is in government instruments and Certificates like Post Office Deposits, N.S. Certificates, Public Provident Funds, National Saving Scheme etc. The real returns on Insurance, P.F., etc., are low and many times lower than the average inflation rates. With the removal of many tax concessions for investments in P.O. Savings instruments, Certificates, etc., they also become less attractive to small and medium investors. The only investments, statisfying all their objectives are capital market instruments. These objectives are income, capital appreciation, safety, marketability, Liquidity and hedge against inflation, and investment by average household in shares and debentures is only around 4 to 6% of the total financial savings.

Objectives of Investors: The return on equity investments in the capital market particularly if proper investment strategy is adopted would satisfy the above objectives and the real returns would be higher than any other saving instruments. It is in this context, the art and science of investment and of Portfolio Management became the ***sine-qua-non*** of success.

All investments involve risk taking. However, some risk free investments are available like bank deposits or P.O. Deposits whose returns are called risk free returns of about 4 to 8%. So the returns on more risky investments are higher than that, having risk premium. Risk is variability of return and uncertainty of payment of interest and repayment of principal. Risk is measured by standard deviation of the returns over the mean for a given period. Risk varies directly with return. The higher the risk taken, the higher is the return, under normal market conditions.

Although Indian markets are imperfect and are developing, all the basic principles and theory of portfolio management would apply and these are recapitulated below.

Risk and Beta

Risk is of two components — systematic market related risk and unsystematic risk or company specific risk. The former cannot be eliminated but managed with the help of Beta (β), which is explained as follows:

$$\beta = \frac{\text{\% age change of Scrip return}}{\text{\% age change of Market returns}}$$

If $\beta = 1$, the risk of the company is the same as that of the market and if $\beta > 1$, the company's risk is more than the market risk. If $\beta < 1$, the reverse is the position.

Specific Risk: If risk is company specific risk it can be reduced by diversification into different industries and companies of different types and nature and whose covariances are different and whose performances are disparate.

Types of Risk

Unsystematic Risk	***Systematic Risk***
Company related risks due to higher costs, mismanagement, defective sales or inventory strategy, insolvency, fall in demand and company specific recession, labour problems etc.	Market related risk due to demand problems, interest rates, inflation, raw materials, import and export policy, Tax policy etc., Business Risk, Market Risk, Financial Risk, Interest Rate Risk, Inflation Risk, etc.

Modern Portfolio Theory (MPT): This postulates that public generally are risk averse. In a perfect market, information is free and quickly absorbed by the market. Given the return, risk can be reduced by diversification of investment into a number of Scrips. Each Scrip has its own risk profile. The risks of any two Scrips are different from the risk of a group of two companies together. Thus, if the risk of Reliance (β) is say 1.90 and that of Dr. Reddys is 0.70, the total of these two units is 1.30 as the average. But the actual 'β' may be less at say 1.00, reason being that the covariance of these two may be zero or negative (less than 1).

CAPM & SML: (Capital Asset Pricing Model and Security Market Line) CAPM postulates that in a perfect market, where shares are correctly priced, every security will give a return commensurate with its risk. "β" is a measure of the risk. The market risk is different from the risks of individual Scrips comprising the market. CML relates these to the total risk of the market. But SML refers to the risk, which is undiversifiable market related risk. Total risk is measured by the standard deviation, while the undiversifiable risk is measured by Beta (β). CML, is Capital Market Line and SML is Security Market Line.

Risk premium of portfolio is the excess of the expected portfolio return over the risk free return. Similar is the definition in respect of risk premium of the market, namely, expected Market Return minus Risk Free Return. CML passes through the risk free rate, which represents the true time value of money or the reward for waiting by savers.

Time Value of Money

In portfolio management and investment decision-making, time element and time value of money are very relevant. Savings are automatic or induced. If induced, it requires a return enough to induce them to part with liquidity. Thus, savings and liquidity will be parted by the investors if only their time preference is satisfied by proper return.

Why time preference? Why savers prefer today's return to tomorrow's return? "A bird in hand is worth two in the bush", as the adage goes.

1. More money is to be received after a year, if he has to lend to the user of funds today. He forgoes consumption which has to be compensated.
2. Money lent today can produce something more than before and hence present money is more valuable than money tomorrow. This premium is needed for waiting.
3. Money is losing in value due to rise in prices. Hence, moneylenders lose and borrowers gain in times of inflation. Premium given is to compensate the lenders against loss due to fall in value of money.

Compounding

Future Value Factor (FVF) is $(1 + r)^n$ where (r) is the rate of interest required and (n) is the period of years of waiting.

$Fn = P(1 + r)^n$, or

Future Value = Present Value × (Future Value Factor)

So the return required by savers is related to the waiting period, loss of consumption at present, or liquidity and risk of loss of money or variance of returns.

Discounting

If the future flow of money is known as C_1, C_2, C_3, etc. What is the present value of them and how much is he prepared to pay for them? If he deposits today Rs. 100 he gets Rs. 110 at the end of 1 year and Rs. 121 at the end of 2 years; the interest rate is 10%. This process of finding the present value for future money flows is called discounting. Present value of future amounts is:

$$P = F(n)\,\frac{1}{(1+r)^n}$$

The multiplier $\left(\frac{1}{1+r}\right)^n$ is called PVF or Present Value Factor. We should know the amounts of cash flows (Fn), in the number of years (n) and the required rate of return (r).

Perpetuity

When we receive a fixed sum of money every year upto infinity, it is called perpetuity. Suppose we want to receive Rs. 100 every year for infinity and interest rate is 10%, we have to deposit Rs. 1,000 and the equation is $PV = \frac{a}{r}$ where PV is Present Value of perpetuity, "a" is fixed periodic cash flow and "r" is the rate of interest.

Annuity

Annuity is a constant cash flow for a finite time period of say 5 years (n). Examples of annuity are found in the case of lease rentals, loan repayments, Recurring deposits, etc. More detailed discussion is given on *time element* in a separate chapter.

Application to Portfolio Management

Portfolio Management involves time element and time horizon. The present value of future returns/cash flows by discounting is useful for share valuation and bond valuation. The investment strategy in portfolio construction should have a time horizon, say 3 to 5 years, to produce the desired results of say 20-30% return per annum.

Besides Portfolio Management should also take into account tax benefits and investment incentives. As the returns are taken by investors net of tax payments, and there is always an element of inflation, returns net of taxation and inflation are more relevant to tax paying investors. These are called net real rates of returns, which should be more than other returns. They should encompâss risk free return plus a reasonable risk premium, depending upon the risk taken, on the instruments/assets invested. (Tax factors are discussed in another Chapter). Most of the theoretical inputs necessary for portfolio management are set out briefly here, although they were discussed in detail in other chapters of this book.

Portfolio Construction, Revision and Evaluation

Portfolio Manager has to use all the tools of research like fundamental analysis and technical analysis in addition to Risk-Return analysis to decide on the investment, buying and selling etc. After the design of the Portfolio Strategy, the construction and allocation of funds will lead to the building up of the portfolio. Thereafter the portfolio thus built requires a constant review and revision with the result that operations on it are a continuous process. This is also called Monitoring. Finally, once in a quarter or half year, the portfolio performance is evaluated, for its success by comparing the actual achievements with the targets fixed. This throws light on the efficiency of the investment strategy of Portfolio Manager and helps the revision of portfolio.

MPT and Dominance Concept

The Modern Portfolio Theory (MPT) is based on assumptions of *free and perfect information flow* and the *notion of dominance*. This means that if the market is able to absorb the information, fully and efficiently, price reflects the risks involved given the same return, the investor can choose the scrips with the lowest possible risk. This is possible by diversification into a number of companies of say 10 to 15, which have diverse characteristics of risk. Thus, when any two Scrips behave differently to given changes in the economy and industry and when the co-efficient of correlation between them is less than 1, such scrips can be joined in a portfolio so as to reduce the combined risk of the portfolio.

The notion of dominance tells us that no investor should invest in one company alone and if there are two or more companies with the same risk, then he has to choose the one with higher return and if both have the same return he has to choose the one with lower risk. The investor can reduce the risk by distributing his funds in a diverse variety of companies with varying risks and returns which do not have much auto correlation. Thus, the investor has not only to make proper investment decision of what to buy and when to buy, but has a proper investment strategy through diversification and choice of a proper 'B' for the scrips selected so that the total risk of portfolio is the lowest possible.

Diversification Process

The process of diversification has various phases involving investment into various classes of assets like equity, preference shares, CDs, NCDs, P.S.U. Bonds and Shares, Money market instruments like commercial paper, inter-corporate investments, deposits etc. Within each class of assets, there is further possibility of diversification into various industries, different companies etc. The proportion of funds invested into various classes of assets, instruments, industries and companies, would depend upon the objectives of investor, under portfolio management and his asset preferences, income and asset requirements. The subject is further elaborated in another chapter.

A portfolio with the objective of regular income would invest a larger proportion of funds in bonds, debentures and Fixed Deposits. For such investments, duration of the life of the bond/debenture, quality of the asset as judged by the credit rating and the expected yield are the relevant variables.

Bond market is not well developed in India but debentures, partly or fully convertible into equity are in good demand both from individuals and Mutual Funds. The Portfolio Manager has to use his analytical power and discretion to choose the right debentures with the required duration, yield and quality. The duration and immunisation of expected inflows of funds to the required quantum of funds have to be well planned by the Portfolio Manager. Research and high degree of analytical power in investment management and bond portfolio management are necessary.

The bond investments are thus equally challenging as equity investments and more so in respect of money market instruments. All these facts bring out clearly the needed analytical powers and expertise of Portfolio Manager. Bond market is discussed in a separate chapter elaborately.

Besides all the above concepts are already dealt with in earlier chapters.

SEBI Guidelines for Portfolio Managers

It will thus be seen that Portfolio Management is an art and requires a high degree of expertise. The merchant banker has been authorised to do Portfolio Management Services, if they belong to Categories I and II as licensed by the SEBI. This classification of merchant bankers was dropped in 1996 and only the category I merchant bankers is allowed to operate in India. Others who want to provide such services should have a minimum networth of Rs. 50 lakhs and expertise, as laid down or changed from time-to-time by the SEBI and would have to register with the SEBI. The SEBI have set out the guidelines in this regard, in which the relations of the client *vis-a-vis* the Portfolio Manager and the respective rights and duties of both have been set out. The code of conduct for Portfolio Managers has been laid down by the SEBI. The job of Portfolio Manager in managing the client's funds, either on discretionary or non-discretionary basis has thus become challenging and difficult due to the multitude of obligations laid on his shoulders by the SEBI, in respect of his operations, accounts, audit etc.

It is thus clear that Portfolio Management has become, a complex and responsible job which requires an in-depth training and expertise. It is in this context that the regulations of SEBI on Portfolio Management become necessary so that the minimum qualifications and experience are also ensured for those who are registered with SEBI. Nobody can do Portfolio Management without SEBI registration and licence.

The SEBI has given permission to Merchant Bankers to do Portfolio Management. As per the guidelines of September, 1991 a separate category of Portfolio Managers is also licensed by SEBI for which guidelines were given in January 1993. A code of conduct was also laid down for this category, as is the case with all categories of capital market players and intermediaries.

Portfolio Management Service

As per the SEBI norms, it refers to professional services rendered for management of Portfolio of others, namely, clients or customers with the help of experts in Investment Advisory Services. The latter involves the advice regarding the worthwhileness of any particular investment or advice of what to buy and sell. Investment management on the other hand involves continuing relationship with client to manage investments with or without discretion for the client as per his requirements.

Who can be a Portfolio Manager?

Only those who are registered and pay the required licence fee are eligible to operate as Portfolio Managers. An applicant for this purpose should have necessary infrastructure with professionally qualified persons and with a minimum of two persons with experience in this business and a minimum networth of Rs. 50 lakhs. The Certificate once granted is valid for three years. Fees payable for registration were Rs. 2.5 lakhs every year for two years and Rs. 1 lakh for the third year. From the fourth year onwards, renewal fees per annum are Rs. 75,000. These fees are subject to change by the SEBI.

The SEBI has imposed a number of obligations and a code of conduct on them. The Portfolio Manager should have a high standard of integrity, honesty and should not have been convicted of any economic offence or moral turpitude. He should not resort to rigging up of prices, insider trading or creating false markets, etc. Their books of accounts, are subject to inspection and audit by SEBI. The observance of the code of conduct and guidelines given by the SEBI are subject to inspection and penalties for violation are imposed. The Manager has to submit periodical returns and documents as may be required by the SEBI from time-to-time.

Method of Operation

The Professional Portfolio Manager can be approached by any individual or organisation with a minimum amount of investible funds of Rs. 1 lakh or Rs. 2 lakhs. If the Manager is willing to accept him as his client, a contract is entered into for management of his funds either on discretionary basis or non-discretionary basis, specifying the objectives, risk to be tolerated, composition of assets/securities in the Portfolio and their relative proportion, fees payable and time period of management, as per the preference of the client etc. The client's data base is collected, namely, his available income and assets, his needs, his risk preferences, his choice for income or growth or both and host of personal details of the client so as to enable the Manager to design a Proper Investment Strategy for him.

SEBI Norms

SEBI has prohibited the Portfolio Manager to assume any risk on behalf of the client. Portfolio Manager cannot also assure any fixed return to the client. The investments made or advised by him are subject to risk which the client has to bear. The investment consultancy and management has to be charged at rates which are fixed at the beginning and transparent as per the contract. No sharing of profits or discounts or cash incentives to client are permitted.

The Portfolio Manager is prohibited to do lending, badla financing and bills discounting as per SEBI norms. He cannot put the clients' funds in any investment, not permitted by the contract, entered into with the client. Normally, investments can be made in both capital market and money market instruments.

Client's money has to be kept in a separate account with the public sector bank and cannot be mixed up with his own funds or investments. All the deals done for a client's account are to be entered in his name and Contract Notes, Bills etc. are all passed in his name. A separate ledger account is maintained for all purchases/sales on client's behalf, which should be done at the market price. Final settlement and termination of contract is as per the contract and for the time period agreed upon. Notice of termination of contract is also as per the contract. During the period of contract, Portfolio Manager is only acting on a contractual basis and on a fiduciary basis. No contract for less than a year is permitted by the SEBI.

Investment Advisors and Investment Consultancy firms are also put on par with portfolio managers. They are also subject to regulation and licensing by the SEBI. No intermediary of any kind in the capital and stock market can operate without prior consent and registration by SEBI.

What is Modern Portfolio Theory (MPT)

MPT Postulates that savers are generally risk averse and try to reduce risk by all possible methods. The markets are perfect and absorb all information perfectly and returns are the same whenever you enter the market. The principle of Dominance is applied to select a portfolio on the frontier line.

MPT depends on the concepts of diversification and use of Beta for reducing the risk and the concept of Dominance for selection of a Portfolio with least risk, with returns being given. These concepts are explained below:

Basis of Modern Portfolio Theory

The Tripod on which the MPT depends comprises the following concepts:

A. Diversification-Investment in more than one Security, Asset, Industry etc. with a view to reduce risks

Diversification — An Example:

Expected Return of X = 20%

Expected Return of Y = 30%

Risk (σ) of Security X = 10%

Risk (σ) of Security Y = 16%

Coefficient of correlation, between X and Y can have three Scenarios –1, 0.5 or +1. Corresponding Graph looks as follows:

Investment in X 40% and in Y = 60%.

Return on Portfolio = (20 × 0.4 + 30 × 0.6) = 26%

Risk on Portfolio, which is normal average risk (10 × 0.4 + 16 × 0.6) = 13.6%

If diversification has to give an advantage, the coefficient of correlation is to be considered. If the average risk of Portfolio has to be less than 13.6%, the Co-efficient of Correlation of these returns of X and Y has to be less than 1.0. If the Coefficient is + 1.0, the return moves along the straight line AB. Suppose it is – 1.0, then the risk can be reduced to zero, because the risk of the one can be perfectly offset by that on the other. If it is 0.5 (or anything between + 1.0 and –1.0) then the diversification can reduce the risk on the Portfolio and the return will move along the Curve. This is explained easily by graphical method rather than mathematical method. If you are on the Curve AB rather than straight line AB you can improve return without increasing the risk, at say point Q from Q to P at the same level of risk.

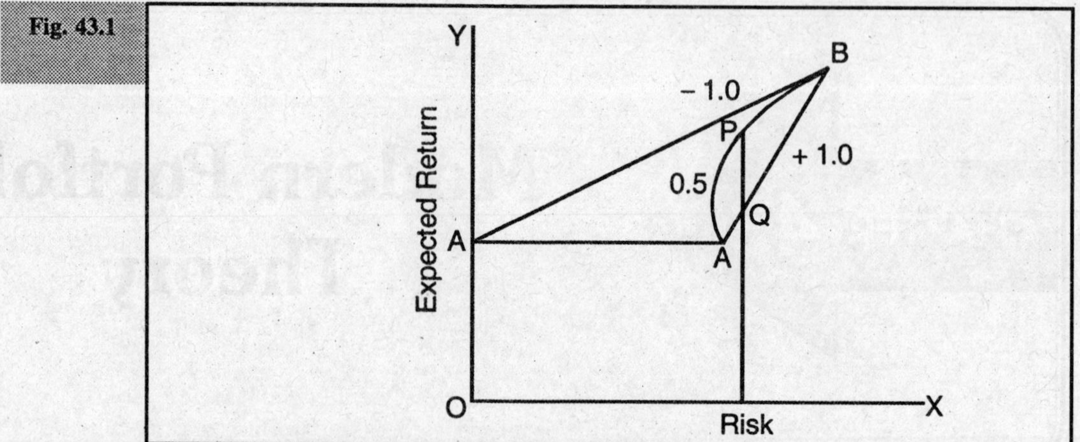

B. Cap Theory and Concept of Dominance (Capital assets pricing model)

Risk and return have a relationship. If you want to increase the return you should also be prepared to accept higher risk. You are entitled to various combinations of assets in your Portfolio. These combinations are called opportunity set — a set of all possible Portfolios given the constraint of money available for investment. The upper boundary of the opportunity set is called the efficient frontier because by so moving, you are improving the return for the same level of risk as shown in Fig. 43.2. You move from Point Q to Point P, both of which are within the opportunity set but by such move you improve the return and this proves to be more efficient. The Portfolio Manager has to do this by constantly analysing the company's performance/returns *vis-a-vis* the risk.

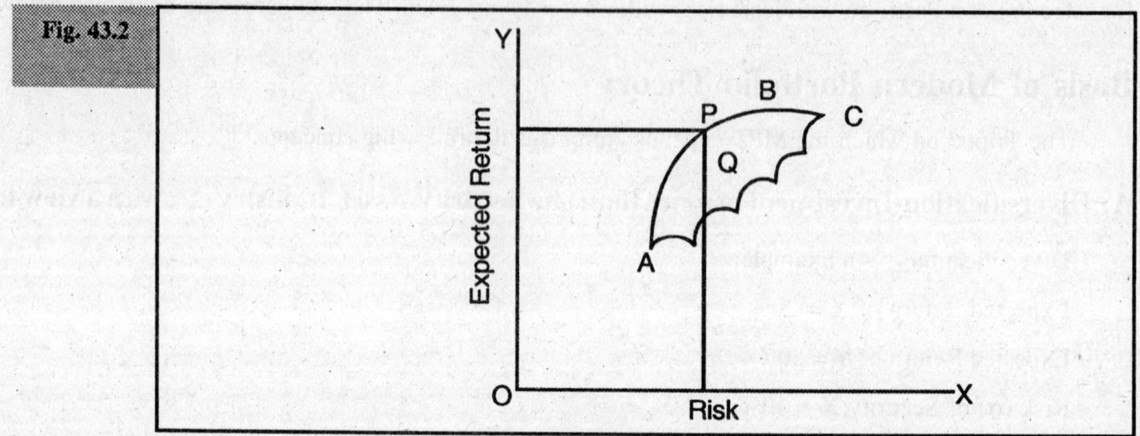

Dominance Concept

The Portfolio Manager has the opportunity to include risk-free assets in his Portfolio like a government bond or bank deposit. If he includes such risk free asset, he lowers the risk of the total Portfolio and moves from point V to point P by lowering the risk from 20% to 15% but by corresponding lowering of the expected return also. (Fig. 43.3)

More importantly he will move on to a new efficient frontier point say from P to M. M will have the same risk as V but with a substantially higher return, say 35%. This shows that equities can be combined with bonds or other riskless assets and the concept of dominance will apply and he moves to an optimum point on the efficient frontier line (C – D).

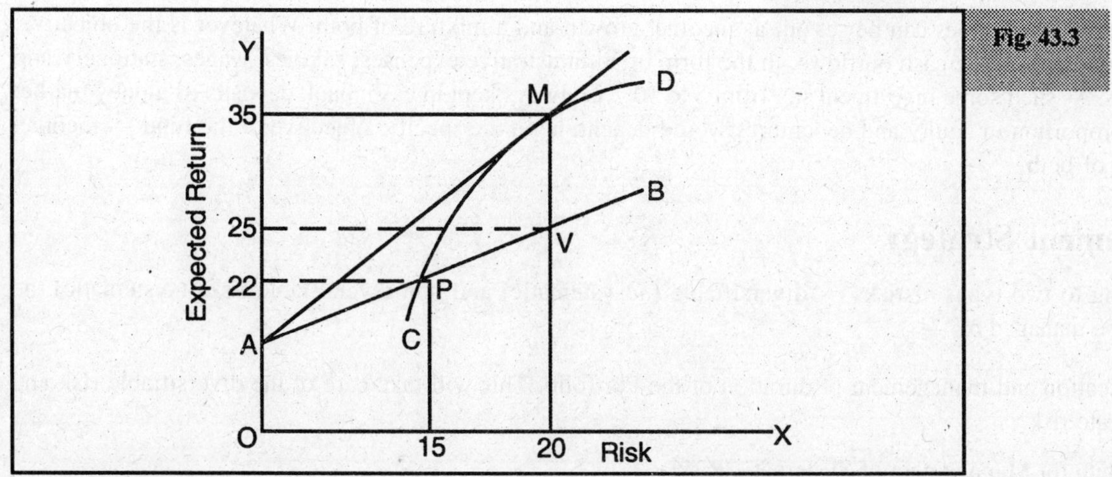

Fig. 43.3

C. Role of Beta

According to CAPM, the market related risk and not total risk is relevant. This systematic risk can be reduced by using Betas. It is a measure of sensitivity of the return of one asset to the market return.

Every asset will have a total return comprising two components.

(a) Risk free return — a return for mere waiting or loss of liquidity for the period of investment.

(b) Risk premium, which is return for risk taking and varies from asset to asset, depending upon the degree of Risk taken.

Modern Portfolio Theory postulates the following axioms:

1. Diversification reduces the total risk but applicable only to company specific unsystematic risk.
2. CAPM states that where shares are correctly priced every security is expected to earn returns commensurate with the risk it carries.
3. The riskiness of a security is to be seen in the context of Portfolio or market related risk, but not in isolation.
4. The importance of Beta is for managing non-diversifiable part of risk.

Portfolio Investment Strategy

Different assets have different risk characteristics; some of them are also risk free assets like cash and bank deposits. Among the Capital Market Instruments equities are most risky, followed by debentures which are less risky and then public sector bonds or government securities which are least risky. There are also money market instruments like commercial bills, treasury bills etc., which are of short duration and less risky. Thus, the risk characteristics vary from asset class to asset class.

The following major asset classes are used for Portfolios by Mutual Funds and Professional Fund Managers.

(a) Equities (variable income instruments)

(b) Debentures, Bonds etc. (Fixed income instruments)

(c) Cash and Money Market Instruments. (Short Duration Instruments)

Asset Allocation

Investor's data base is the starting point for designing an investment strategy. Does he want a regular income? How regular, monthly or yearly? Does he want regular cash inflows to meet the liabilities as they fall due for repayments? What is his asset-liabilities mix or inflow-outflow pattern? Does he want only capital appreciation or a mixture of both income and capital appreciation?

Broadly investor's objectives can be set out as income, growth and a mixture of both. Whatever is the objective, every investor of funds has some cash outflows, in the form of administrative expenses, salaries, wages, stationery and incidental expenses. As such some investment say from 5 to 10% is always kept in cash, bank deposits or money market instruments. The proportion in equity and debentures would depend upon the specific objective of the fund — income, growth or mixture of both.

Risk Management Strategy

Corresponding to two types of risks — diversifiable (unsystematic) and non-diversifiable risks (systematic) the portfolio risk can be managed by —

(a) Diversification and management of duration of the Portfolio. This will take care of the diversifiable risk and interest rate risk.

(b) Use of Beta for Management of Systematic Risk.

Duration

The concept of duration can be explained by taking the life or maturity period of the asset class. If the bond has zero coupon rate, its duration is the same as its maturity. But the duration of equity is infinity, but represented by $\frac{MP}{EPS}$ or $\frac{MP}{DPS}$ where EPS is Earnings Per Share and DPS is Dividend Per Share. The average Market price is P and EPS is related by what is called the market P/E Ratio; representing the above equation, the market $\frac{P}{E}$ has its duration as 20-25 at present. The duration of bonds or debentures is the life to maturity and the duration of cash and money market instrument is zero. Theoretical discussion on duration was given in a separate chapter.

EX: The duration can be made about 5 years by adopting the following investment pattern explained in a crude manner:

15% in Equity (25 years) 0.15 × 25	= 3.75
60% in Bonds/Debentures (3 year maturity) 0.6 × 3	= 1.8
25% in Money Market Instruments 0.25 × 0	= 0
Total Duration	5.55

For the elaboration of this concept, reference may be made to chapter on Bonds. (Chapter - 35)

Beta

Management of Beta is done as follows:

Beta on equity shares varies from company to company. Calculate the Betas and take the average Beta, for selected Scrips in the Portfolio. If investor wants the market risk and market return, then the Beta of the Portfolio should be 1. If the actual shares in the Portfolio give a Beta of 1.2, then an investment of 80% in equities gives the Portfolio Beta as 1.2 × 0.8 = 0.96 and the rest of the 20% is invested in bonds and money market instruments.

If the investor is risk taking then the Portfolio should be aggressive with Beta of more than 1. If on the other hand he is risk averse, the Portfolio Beta should be less than 1 and it is a defensive Portfolio. Thus, the investment strategy should be decided after laying down first the allocation of funds to different asset classes in the form of proportions and then the selection of instruments and Scrips would be decided within each asset class, based on their fundamentals. The Table 43.1 compares the Beta with the Volatility of selected scrips.

Table 43.1 Beta and Volatility

Names of the Company	*Betas*	*Price Volatility*	*EPS*	*Price/Rs.*
20th Century	1.519	12.6 Times	7.49	85
Apollo	1.6130	14.2 " "	11.86	137
Essar Ship	1.448	8.4 " "	2.82	41
Hotel Leela	1.525	6.1 " "	0.62	34
I.T.C.	1.430	9.2 " "	9.88	485
J.K. Synthetics	1.616	6.9 " "	0.71	23
Nagarjuna Finance	1.430	23.3 " "	6.04	19
Reliance	1.778	5.34 " "	10.73	193
Thomas Cook	1.999	14.6 " "	24.01	900
Hindustan Lever	0.859	3.8 Times	7.03	375
Bajaj Auto	0.729	3.5 " "	11.89	240
Boots Pharmaceuticals	0.604	4.8 " "	6.79	217
Punjab Alkalies	0.502	6.6 " "	10.14	99
Spartek Ceramics	0.243	4.4 " "	5.67	87
Vindhya Tele Links	0.477	5.4 " "	9.05	202

It will be seen from the Table that Betas vary with the time periods of study; high Betas based on historical data do not reflect the high price volatility and there is no guarantee that high Betas go with high return and low Betas go with low returns. Table 43.1 presents the data on selected companies with Betas, price volatility (High/low ratios) Earnings Per Share (EPS) and actual market price-all data of 1993 only. It is seen from the Table that historical Betas are not correlated with either price volatility or earnings per share. The date of the data (1993) is immaterial as conclusions are valid at all times. Only in some cases, high Betas went with high prices

Target Return

The basic principle in the market, is that the higher the risk taken, the higher is the return. An investor who wants only risk free return can have all his funds invested in Government bonds and bank deposits which will yield only risk free return of around 6 to 8%. But if the investor wants to have a higher return and takes risk accordingly, then risk premium will be available to him. Assuming the riskless return as 7% if he wants a return of 20%, then the risk premium should be 13%. The portfolio Manager has to invest the majority of his funds in equities with a Beta, of more than 1. If the market return is 20% then with a Beta of 1.3, he will get 26%, which is the target return.

Borrowing for Investment

Equities are most risky and have long duration and their Betas are high. Bonds have negligible Beta and moderate duration while Money Market instruments have negligible or zero duration. The range of Beta and duration can be widened by borrowing for investment. If a fund manager with Rs. 1 lakh borrows another Rs. 1 lakh and invests Rs. 2 lakhs, in equity Portfolio, even with a Beta of 1.00, his overall Portfolio Beta is actually 2.00 because his Portfolio is Rs. 1 lakh and his equity Portfolio is Rs. 2 lakhs (which is 200% of his own Portfolio). This gives almost double the returns expected and even after paying the interest component on borrowed funds, he enjoys the leverage and improves his networth.

Problems

Question 1

If the returns on stocks A and B are as follows:

Calculate the average rate of return for each stock during the given period.

If A and B are held at 50:50 ratio in a portfolio, what is the portfolio return.

Year	*A's return*	*B's return*
1984	−12.24	−5.0
1985	23.67	19.55
1986	35.45	44.09
1987	5.82	1.20
1988	28.30	21.16
	81.0	81.0

$$\overline{A} = \frac{81}{5} = 16.2;\ \overline{B} = \frac{81}{5} = 16.2$$

$$\sigma_A = \sqrt{\sum_{1}^{n} \frac{Kt - KAve}{n-1}}$$

	DEVIATION		*DEVIATION SQUARED*		
1984	(−12.24−16.2)	=	$(-28.44)^2$	=	808.83
1985	(23.67−16.2)	=	$(7.47)^2$	=	55.80
1996	(35.45−16.2)	=	$(19.25)^2$	=	370.56
1997	(5.82− 16.2)	=	$(-10.38)^2$	=	107.74
1988	(28.30−16.2)	=	$(12.1)^2$	=	146.41

$$\frac{1489.34}{4} = 372.33$$

$\sigma_A = \sqrt{372.33}$

$\sigma_A = 19.30\%$

working is not shown here in the case of σ_B

For the portfolio stock A and B are combined in the ratio of 50 : 50

Portfolio Return Equation (A and B) is

1984; (0.5) Ar + (0.5) Br.

R_P = (−12.24) 0.5 + (−5.0) (0.5) = − 8.62

1985; (+23.67) 0.5 + (19.55) 0.5 = 21.61

1986; (+35.45) 0.5 + (44.09) 0.5 = 39.77

1987; (5.82) 0.5 + (1.2) 0.5 = 3.51

1988; (28.30) 0.5 + (21.16) 0.5 = 24.73

Portfolio Return ($\overline{R}_P$) $= \frac{81.0}{5} = 16.20$

Portfolio Risk = Standard Deviation of Portfolio

(1) $(-8.62 - 16.2)^2 = (-24.82)^2 \quad = 616.03 \; (R_P - \bar{R}_P)$

(2) $(21.61 - 16.2) = (5.41)^2 \quad = 29.27$

(3) $(39.77 - 16.2) = (23.57)^2 \quad = 555.54$

(4) $(3.51 - 16.2) = (-12.69)^2 \quad = 161.04$

(5) $(24.73 - 16.2) = (8.53)^2 \quad = 72.76$

$$\sigma^2 = \frac{1{,}434.64}{4} = 358.66$$

$\sigma = \sqrt{358.66}$

$\sigma =$ 18.9% Portfolio Risk

The formula for covariance is as follows:

$$= \frac{1}{N} \Sigma\, (R_{1J} - \bar{R}_1)\, (R_{2J} - \bar{R}_2)$$

Calculate the covariance between the A and B Stocks, given above?

Question 2

Stocks A and B showed the following returns for two years.

Year	Stock A	Stock B
1997	10%	12%
1998	16%	18%

(a) What is the expected return on a portfolio made up of 50% of A and 50% of B Stock and what is the portfolio risk?

(b) What is the standard deviation of each stock?

(c) What is the covariance of stock A and B?

(d) Determine the coefficient of correlation of stocks A and B.

CHAPTER 44

Portfolio Management: Construction, Revision and Evaluation

The portfolio theory is the basis of portfolio management and relates to the efficient portfolio investment in financial and physical assets, including shares and debentures of companies. A portfolio of an individual or a corporate unit is the holding of securities and investment in financial assets. These holdings are the result of individual preferences and decisions of the holders regarding risk and return and a host of other considerations.

Fact Sheet — Clients' Data Base

The following preferences of the investor are to be noted first in investment decisions. These will constitute the data base of the investor or client.

(1) Income and savings decisions — how much income can be saved for contingencies and the present position of wealth, income and savings of the investor.

(2) Asset preferences profile — preference for riskless assets like bank deposits or for risky stock market investment:

(a) the degree of risk the investor is capable of taking and willing to take;

(b) the risk aversion and preference for safety and certainty;

(c) requirements of regular income;

(d) objective of capital appreciation;

(e) objective of speculative gains; etc.

(3) Investor's objectives, constraints and financial commitments.

(4) Tax brackets into which the investor falls and his preference for planning the tax liability.

(5) Time horizon in which investment should fructify or results expected.

These and other factors constitute the "Fact Sheet" of the investor on the basis of which the individual portfolio is to be structured, constructed and managed.

The motives for saving are varied depending on the individuals. For example, provision for insurance, contingencies, contribution of PF, pension funds, etc., which are mostly contractual obligations, provision for future income, etc., are some of the motives. Some of the savers are influenced by interest return or stable income while others are by speculative gains or get-rich-quick motive.

Objectives of Investors

The investors' objectives are to be specified in the first place. The objective may be income, capital appreciation or a future provision for contingencies such as marriage, death, birth, etc. Provision for retirement and accident could be covered by contractual obligations like insurance and contributions to PF and pension funds. A certain amount of savings has to be kept as cash with themselves or in deposit with banks or post offices to facilitate daily transactions for purchase and sale. While cash earns no interest, savings deposit with banks, co-operatives and POs would earn 3 ½% on savings accounts. But when inflation is prevalent in the economy at an average rate of 4-6%, this return of 3.5% will provide only a net negative return to the savers. So the amounts kept in the form of cash and deposit with banks, etc., should normally be the bare minimum. The rest of the amount has to be spread in various investment avenues, earning higher returns than the normal inflation rate of 4 to 6%. These investment avenues are discussed in a separate chapter.

Motives for Investment

The investor has to set out his priorities of investment keeping the following motives in mind. All investors would like to have:

1. Capital appreciation.
2. Income.
3. Liquidity or marketability.
4. Safety or security.
5. Hedge against inflation.
6. A method of tax planning.

The investor gets his income from the dividend or yield or interest. There will be capital appreciation also in the case of equities. The liquidity and safety of an investment will depend upon the marketability and the credit rating of the borrower, namely, the company or the issuer of securities. These characteristics vary between assets and securities. An investor is also concerned in having a tax plan to reduce his tax commitments so as to maximise the take home income. For this purpose, investor should specify his income bracket, his liabilities and his preference for tax planning etc. The investment avenues have certain characteristics of risk and return and also of some tax concessions attached to them. These tax provisions as such can influence the investors in a very big way as these provisions will alter the risk return scenario of investment alternatives. It is, therefore, necessary that all these avenues should be assessed in terms of yields, capital appreciation, liquidity, safety and tax implications. The investment strategy should be based on the above objectives after a thorough study of the goals of the investor, in the background of characteristics of the investment avenues.

Tax Provisions

It is apt to start with the tax-exempt incomes of the securities in which investment can be made. The incomes by way of interest on PSU bonds, N.S. certificates, securities of the Central Government and those deposits specified by the Central Government like RBI Relief Bonds are exempted from income tax subject to certain limits or conditions. The P.O. deposits, certificates and other claims operated by the POs are exempted along with others from income-tax up to a limit. This limit is inclusive of a sub-limit for UTI income distribution. This exemption is, however, not applicable to Indira Vikas Patra, Kisan Vikas Patra and NSC VIII Issue. Deposits in PPF and NSS are exempted from taxes in the year of deposit and subject to some limits in the year of withdrawal except in the case of NSS, which is, however, taxable in the year of withdrawal. PPF is the best method of tax saving upto a limit. All these exemptions are replaced by one lumpsum limit of Rs. one lakh in specified assets under Section 80C in 2005-06.

Under the category of insurance, in addition to LIC policies, the ULIP (of UTI) enjoys popularity due to the tax shelters:

- Wealth tax exemption for all investments in shares and debentures along with other eligible investments.
- Income-tax exemption up to Rs. 12,000 aggregate income from bank deposits, shares, P.O. deposits, Mutual Funds and other specified categorics of investment.

All dividend incomes from companies and M.Fs in the hands of investors are free from income tax from 1997-98 onwards, but have become taxable in the hands of investors in 2002-03.

Capital Gains

Capital gains refer to profits earned on the transfer of capital assets, sale or exchange, etc. These gains are long-term gains, if they are held for more than 36 months for all assets except shares of a company for which this period is 12 months. Long-term capital gains are taxable at a lower rate of 20% to residents. Under Sections 54E and 54F of the Income-tax Act, the long-term capital gains are exempt, if these funds are invested in Central Government securities, UTI and CGI Schemes and other specified bonds of semi-government bodies. In the year 2000-01, this exemption is extended only to investments in bonds of NABARD and NHAI and Infrastructure Bonds.

Income from interest on debentures and on company deposits is tax deductible at source, if it exceeds Rs. 2,500 p.a. The exemption available from income tax for NSS deposits up to Rs. 40,000 per year was since withdrawn in 1992-93. Tax exemption is also available in respect of income from government securities, semi-government bonds, bank deposits, income from mutual funds, etc., upto a limit. In the budget for 1990-91, a new scheme called Equity linked Saving Scheme was announced by the government under Section 88A of Income Tax Act to provide a tax rebate of 20% of the investment made in the eligible assets and new issues, or eligible M.F. Scheme. This was extended upto a limit of total investment of Rs. 70,000 p.a. in 1996-97, in respect of investments in selected avenues such as Insurance, P.F., PPF, NSS and Infrastructure bonds, etc.

Details of tax provisions are discussed in a separate chapter, and they are variable from year to year.

Portfolio Construction[1]

Portfolio construction refers to the allocation of funds among a variety of financial assets open for investment. Portfolio theory concerns itself with the principles governing such allocation. The objective of the theory is to elaborate the principles in which the risk can be minimised, subject to a desired level of return on the portfolio or maximise the return, subject to the constraint of a tolerable level of risk.

Thus, the basic objective of portfolio management is to maximise yield and minimise risk. The other ancillary objectives are as per the needs of investors, namely:

1. Regular income or stable return;
2. Appreciation of capital;
3. Marketability and liquidity;
4. Safety of investment; and
5. Minimising of tax liability.

In pursuit of these objectives, the portfolio manager has to set out all the various alternative investments along with their projected return and risk and choose investments which satisfy the requirements of the individual investor and cater to his preferences. The manager has to keep a list of such investment avenues along with the return-risk profile, tax implications, yields and other return such as convertible options, bonus, rights, etc. A ready reckoner giving out the analysis of the risks involved in each investment and the corresponding returns should be kept.

Risk-Return Analysis

All investments have some risks. Investment in shares of companies has larger risks or uncertainty. These risks arise out of variability of returns or yields and uncertainty of appreciation or depreciation of share prices, loss of liquidity etc. The risk over time can be represented by the variance of the returns, while the return over time is capital appreciation plus payout, divided by the purchase price of the share.

Normally, the higher the risk that the investor takes, the higher is the return. There is, however, a riskless return on capital of about 6%, which is the bank rate charged by the RBI or long-term yield on Government securities at around 7%-8%. This riskless return refers to lack of variability of return and no uncertainty in the repayment of capital. But other risks such as loss of liquidity due to parting with money etc., may, however, remain but are rewarded by the total return on the capital. The risk free return and variable return are shown in the adjacent Fig. 44.1

1. Refer to Graham and Dodd, *Security Analysis.*

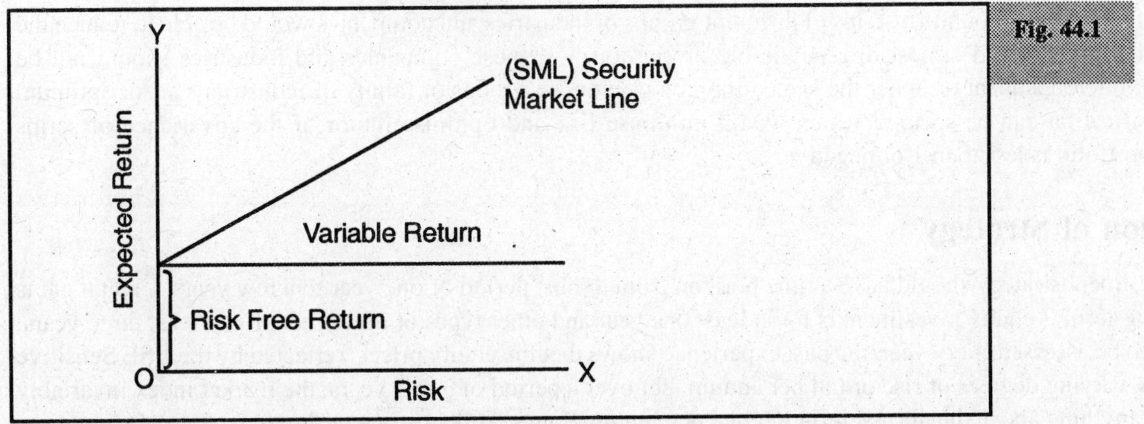

Fig. 44.1

The risk-return relationship can be represented in a diagrammatic form as in Fig. 44.2 below[2].

Risk-return is subject to variation and the objective of the portfolio manager is to reduce that variability and thus reduce the risk by choosing an appropriate portfolio.

There are two types of risks, namely, *(a)* Market risk or systematic risk, and *(b)* Company risk or unsystematic risk.

The unsystematic risk can be reduced by diversifying the portfolio of scrips up to an optimum level of about 15 shares. These scrips should be so chosen that the risks on each of them are diverse and their variability of return is also different. By investing in such a diverse set of scrips, the total risk can be reduced as some of them may have positive and others negative covariance and they may vary in the degree of risk as well. The risk that can be reduced is called unsystematic risk and these risks are represented diagrammatically in Fig. 44.2 here. The details are discussed in an earlier Chapter.

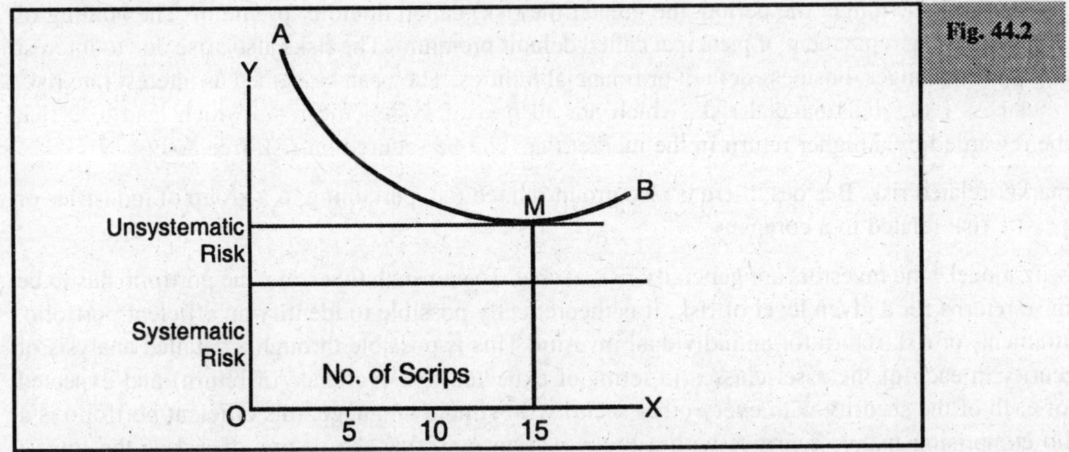

Fig. 44.2

The unsystematic risk can be lowered by diversifying into a basket of scrips. Thus, at the level of 15 scrips in the diagram, the lowest level of risk is obtained at the point M on the AB curve representing the unsystematic risk of the investor. Thus, a degree of diversification of investment is a necessary prerequisite of portfolio management and for reducing the risk. But beyond the point M, the portfolio becomes unmanageable and diseconomies operate as to increase risk rather than reduce it. Some residual unsystematic risk may still remain after diversification also.

In the management of a portfolio, the problem of risk management is vital. Given the individual preference of portfolio holders, the portfolio is to be constructed in such a manner that it is exposed to the minimum risks which the owner can carry, subject to which the returns are to be maximised. Although the market-related risks cannot be reduced, the company-related risks can be eliminated through a proper diversification. As shown in the above diagram, a proper

2. Cohen, Zinbarg and Zeilkel, *Managing Ingestment Portfolios*, (Ed.) H. Maginn and D.L. Tuttle, *Investment Analysis and Portfolio Management.*

portfolio diversification into around 15 scrips of different groups of industries and companies would be able to reduce the company-related risks involved almost to a negligible proportion. But these companies and industries should not be unduly related or interdependent or under the same umbrella of industry groups or family of industrialists. An optimum degree of diversification can be secured which would minimise risk and optimise return, if the covariance of scrips included in the portfolio is less than 1 or negative.

Time Horizon of Strategy

Every investment strategy should have a time horizon from a short period of one year to a few years. Capital gains is considered long-term if equity investment is for at least one year and other types of investment for at least three years. If investment is to be assessed every year, the past experience shows that the equity prices, reflected by the BSE Sensitive Index, may show varying degrees of rise or fall per annum, but over a period of 3 to 5 years, the market index invariably showed a rise of anything above the normal inflation rate per annum. So investment strategy should be for a medium time period of 3 to 5 years.

Portfolio management encompasses three major categories of activities:

1. Asset allocation — type of assets to be chosen among fixed income securities of the government or private corporate units, preferred stock debentures or equities, etc., of various groups of industries.
2. Review and shifts as between classes of assets to take advantage of risk-return characteristics, or changes in them.
3. Security selection within each asset class such as choosing a higher growth type of companies (blue chips).

Types of Risk

The risk is measured statistically by the degree of variance or standard deviation of returns. There is also a risk involved in time period of holding (the longer the period, the greater the risk) called liquidity premium. The holding of security is subject to the default risk in repayment of principal called default premium. The risks also arise due to interest rate variability, purchasing power changes, business default or financial failures. They can be named as interest rate risk, purchasing power risk, business risk, and financial risk, which are all part of systematic risks which lead to a risk premium. These are to be rewarded by a higher return in the market than can be secured on risk-free assets.

The above is the market-related risk. Besides, there is also group-related risk pertaining to a group of industries or firms. There is also a specific risk related to a company.

As per the Markowitz model,[3] the investors are generally risk-averse. To suit such investors, the portfolio has to be so designed as to maximise returns for a given level of risk. It is theoretically possible to identify an efficient portfolio, which satisfies the requirements of risk-return for an individual investor. This is possible through a detailed analysis of information on each security in each of the asset classes in terms of expected risk (variance of return) and expected return, and covariance of each of the security with every other security. In simple language, this efficient portfolio is a well-diversified portfolio comprising many securities with a low covariance so that the degree of risk is the lowest possible. Companies under different industry groups and different family managements and with different characteristics are to be chosen in that portfolio.

Efficient Portfolio

To construct an efficient portfolio, we have to conceptualise various combinations of investments in a basket and designate them as portfolios 1 to n. Then the expected returns from these portfolios are to be worked out. The risk on these portfolios is to be estimated by measuring the standard deviation of different portfolio returns. To reduce the risk, investors have to diversify into a number of securities whose risk-return profiles vary.

3. H. M. Markowitz, *Portfolio Selection: Efficient Diversification of Investments*, (John Wiley, 1959).

Thus, portfolios carry returns to compensate for interest risk (risk-free return) + a premium for purchasing power risk, market risk, business risk and financial risk. Some risks constitute unsystematic risks, which can be reduced or eliminated by diversification. Thus for each individual security and for a combination of securities represented by the basket in the BSE Sensitive Index or National Index, the expected returns and standard deviations can be worked out. The expected return has to be weighted by the probable chance of getting the return through proper weights and the weighted average return should be worked out. The standard deviation around the expected return can also be worked out as shown below:

Return in Per Cent	*Chance of Getting Return*	*Expected Return in Per Cent*	*Standard Deviation about Expected Return in Per Cent*	
10	0.20	$10 \times 0.20 =$ (2.0)	$(10 - 13.4)^2 \times 0.20$ +	= 2.31+
12	0.30	$12 \times 0.30 =$ (3.6)	$(12 - 13.4)^2 \times 0.30$ +	= 0.59+
15	0.40	$15 \times 0.40 =$ (6.0)	$(15 - 13.4)^2 \times 0.40$ +	= 2.56+
18	0.10	$18 \times 0.10 =$ (1.8)	$(18 - 13.4)^2 \times 0.10$	= 2.12
	1.00	(Wt. average 13.4)	$\sigma = \sqrt{7.58} = 2.7$	7.58 = Variance = σ^2

The standard deviation signifies that, on an average, each possible return is 2.7% away from the expected return of 13.4%. The deviation of 2.7% could be on either side of the expected return. This is the risk measure of a portfolio, which is already explained in an earlier chapter.

The efficient portfolio can be estimated by presenting the various portfolios in terms of expected return and standard deviations as shown in the following table:

Portfolio No.	*Expected Return in Per Cent*	*(Risk) Standard Deviation*
1	5	1
2	7	2
3	8	3
4	10	5
5	11	5
6	12	5
7	12	7
8	14	10
9	18	12

If we compare portfolio Nos. 4 and 5, we see that for the same standard deviation of 5, portfolio No. 5 gives an expected return of 11% higher than that on No. 4, thereby making it an efficient portfolio. If we compare portfolio Nos. 6 and 7, we see that with the same return of 12% in both the portfolios, standard deviation is lower in portfolio No. 6. Thus, portfolio No. 6 is an efficient portfolio.

These points can be depicted as in Fig. below. The expected return is shown on the Y-axis and standard deviation measuring risk on the X-axis. The points connecting the expected return with its standard deviation can be shown as AB graph, constituting the feasible opportunity set. The outermost point on this graph is the most efficient portfolio, say, M on the AB graph while the AB graph is called the efficient frontier. M is the most efficient combination for the individual under consideration (Ref. *Investment Management* by Simha, Hemlata and Balakrishnan).

The individual investor is generally risk-averse according to the well-known author Markowitz. His objectives are influenced by the stage of life, his financial circumstances and psychological makeup. A young investor may have, for example, a higher level of tolerance of risk than a retired person or a middleaged person. The latter prefers a larger income with less risk. There is a trade-off between risk and return.

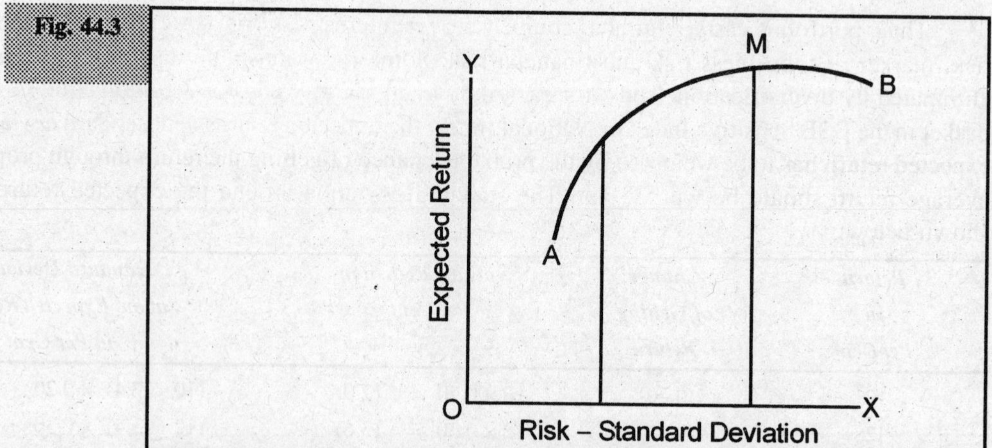

According to the capital pricing model, efficient frontier is defined as a risk-return trade-off curve. It is efficient because it provides the maximum return at a given level of risk of the investor. The investor's capacity to take risk sets the point of optimum efficiency on this curve, which is the best for him. Diversification of securities and assets in the portfolio reduces the risk, provided their covariance is low and they are dissimilar in nature.

The total risk is measured by the standard deviation of the return, and market risk by the concept of Beta. Beta reflects that part of a portfolio's return and variation in returns which is attributable to the overall movement of the market rather than to any unique characteristic of the Company.

The efficient frontier of Markowitz and the use of Beta can be graphically represented as in Figs. 44.4 and 44.5. AB is the capital market line, representing the market possibilities of risk and return (given by the BSE Index). On the same graph, the efficient frontier curve is drawn as EF. At point M, for the given risk of OR, the return is maximised for the investor at OC.

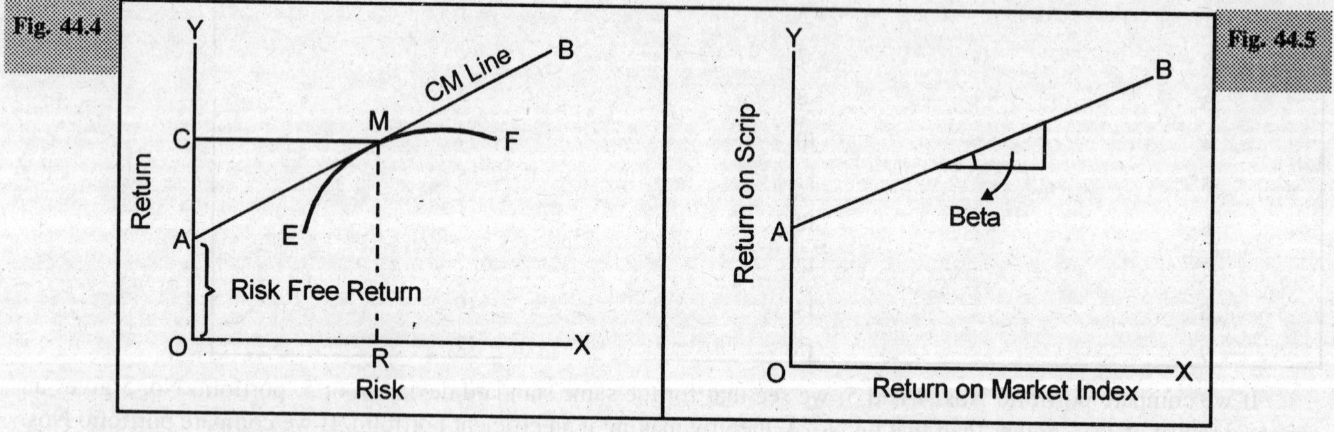

In actual practice, β can be derived by the formula: Price of Scrip A (% age)/÷ or divided by Prices of scrips included in BSE Index (% age) — the relation of the individual scrip to that of the basket of scrips as represented by the BSE Index. If Beta is 1 (slope is 45^0), then, on an average, one percentage return on the market basket will be associated with a one percentage return on the individual scrip. If Beta is greater than one it will give a larger return than the average market return. These high Beta scrips are very volatile and risk is also high. On the other hand, if Beta is less than 1 (called defensive scrips), the risk is low and the return is also lower than the market return. Depending on the investor's choice, the Beta is to be selected and scrips with such Beta should be held in the portfolio Fig. 44.5 depicts Beta as the angle made by the line of regression between market return and the individual scrip return.

Market Efficiency Theorem[4]

Since the behaviour of the market is outside the control of the investor, he can only reduce the specific component of risk by choosing the individual scrips with proper Betas to achieve the result of diversification and lower the risk. The comparative risks of alternative well-diversified portfolios can be measured by their Betas. If the markets are efficient, the performance of any portfolio would average out to that of the performance of the market and nobody can out perform the market.

In the real world, there are three different levels of efficiency of the stock market, namely, the weak form, the semi-strong form and the strong form. These concepts are useful in portfolio management for investors, and are discussed in details in an earlier chapter.

In the weak form, the successive changes in stock prices are independent of each other and the historical market data are already embodied in the existing price.

In the semi-strong form, stock prices adjust rapidly to all new public information, both market and non-market data, and action taken after the event will produce no more than random results.

In the strong form, stock prices fully reflect not only public information but privately-held information which may later become public.

If, in the real world, the market efficiency is of a strong form, then the performance of any basket of scrips in any portfolio is as good as any other and no individual investor can out perform the market. If however, the market efficiency is of a weak form, there is scope for selection of a portfolio which is optimal for the investor in terms of risk and return and yet out perform the market by a proper choice of aggressive scrips with Betas suitable for the purpose.

Diversification

Risk in a portfolio can be reduced by a proper diversification into a number of scrips. The companies chosen should not be too many or too few but of an optimum size as to be efficiently manageable. The economies of scale in management apply to this analysis. It will be seen from Fig. 44.6 that the higher the risk, higher is the return in the normal process. The risk-return relationship is shown in the graph.

Depending upon the investor's preferences and his income requirements, the strategy of investment should be at A, B or C respectively. Assuming that he takes some risk at B or C, this risk can be reduced so far as it concerns the specific company risk, but the market risk is outside the control of the portfolio manager. The risk can be reduced by a proper diversification of scrips invested. It is also possible to have a combination of A, B and C positions in a portfolio so as to have a diversified risk-return pattern.

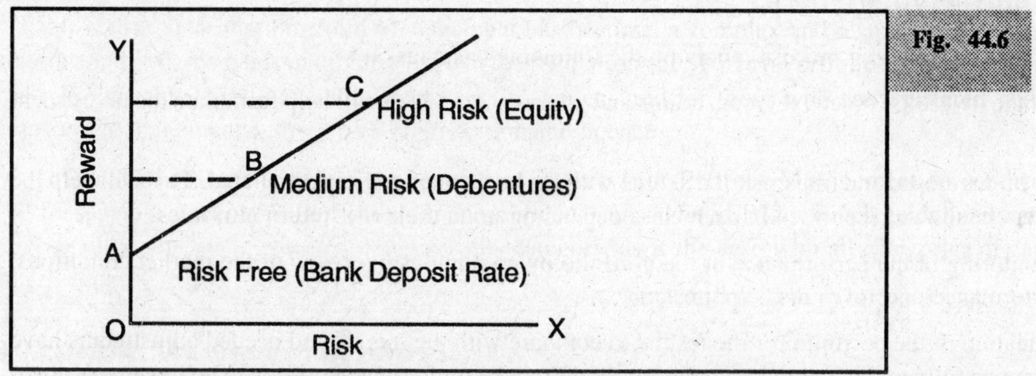

Fig. 44.6

In order that this diversification secures the results in an optimal manner, the number of scrips chosen should be limited to 12-15. As Fig. 44.7 shows, the risk is first reduced as the number of companies is increased but after a point, the risk again increases due to the operation of diseconomies of scale. The risk can be lowered from OM to ON by increasing the number of companies from 5 to 15, after which risk cannot be lowered as the curve AB representing the unsystematic risk starts going up again.

4. D. C. Fischer & R. J. Jordan: *Security Analysis and Portfolio Management*, Chapter 1, 18 and 19.

Fig. 44.7

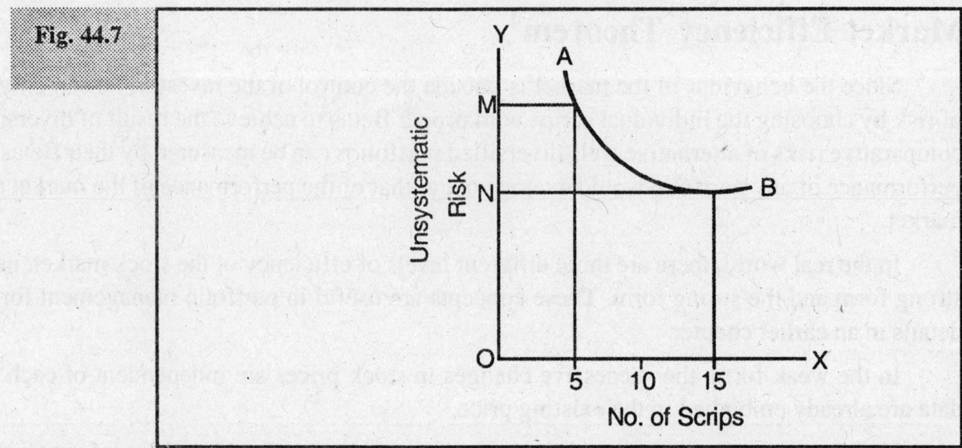

The optimum number of companies should be such that they are of divergent qualities in terms of performance, product lines, management, marketing, etc. Such a diversification only can secure reduction of risk and maximisation of returns. In this process, a proper selection of scrips with Betas of aggressive nature (B > 1) and some with defensive nature (B < 1) should be chosen, depending upon the individual preferences of the investor. In the selection of these companies, all the processes explained above under portfolio management should be followed and after analysis and assessment, investment should be made.

Portfolio Management

Portfolio management is a process encompassing many activities of investment in assets and securities. It is a dynamic and flexible concept and involves continuous and systematic analysis, judgement and operations. The objective of this service is to help the novices and uninitiated investors with the expertise of professionals in portfolio management. Firstly, it involves construction of a portfolio based upon the fact sheet of the investor giving out his objectives, constraints, preferences for risk and return and his tax liability. Secondly, the portfolio is reviewed and adjusted from time-to-time in tune with the market conditions. The adjustment is done through changes in the weighting pattern of the securities and asset classes in the portfolio. Changes in the composition of portfolio will have to be done if there are any changes in the conditions and preferences of investors, due to factors beyond his control. The shifting of assets and securities will take advantage of changes in market conditions and in prices of the securities and assets in the portfolio. Thirdly, the evaluation of portfolio performance is to be done by the manager in terms of targets set for risk and return and changes in the portfolio are to be affected to meet the changing conditions.

Elements of Portfolio Management

Portfolio management is an on-going process involving the following basic tasks:

(1) Identification of the investors' objectives, constraints and preferences, which will help formulate the investment policy.

(2) Strategies are to be developed and implemented in tune with the investment policy formulated. This will help the selection of asset classes and securities in each class depending upon their risk-return attributes.

(3) Review and monitoring of the performance of the portfolio by continuous overview of the market conditions, companies' performance and investors' circumstances.

(4) Finally, the evaluation of the portfolio for the results to compare with the targets and needed adjustments have to be made in the portfolio to the emerging conditions and to make up for any shortfalls in achievement *vis-a-vis* targets.

The collection of data on the investors' preferences, objectives, etc., is the foundation of portfolio management. This gives an idea of channels of investment in terms of asset classes to be selected and securities to be chosen based upon the liquidity requirements, time horizon, taxes, asset preferences of investors, etc. These are the building blocks for construction of a portfolio.

According to these objectives and constraints, the investment policy can be formulated. This policy will lay down the weights to be given to different asset classes of investment such as equity shares, preference shares, debentures, company deposits, etc., and the proportion of funds to be invested in each class and selection of assets and securities in each class are made on this basis. The next stage is to formulate the investment strategy for a time horizon for income and capital appreciation and for a level of risk tolerance. The investment strategies developed by the portfolio managers have to be correlated with their expectation of the capital market and the individual sectors of industry. Then a particular combination of assets is chosen on the basis of investment strategy and manager's expectations of the market.

Execution of Strategy

The next stage, namely, implementation and execution of this investment process, is the most critical process in the portfolio management. Here the research, analysis and the judgement of the manager are very essential inputs in the process. His initiative, innovation and judgement would be the basis of his success in management. The performance of the portfolio is evaluated and adjustments are made in the portfolio composition from time-to-time. This is called monitoring and restructuring of portfolios for improving the performance to make it optimal and efficient. The changes in investor's conditions and in the market conditions and in industry performance are taken into account in the portfolio adjustments.

The porfolio thus constructed may relate to the needs of a given level of income, a provision for contingencies and a preference for fixed income, etc.,. of the investor. Some investors would prefer assets like real estate, gold, debentures or bonds giving a fixed income while a few would prefer riskless investments in PSU bonds — short-term or long-term government securities, etc. Certain risk-takers may prefer investment in high-yielding growth stocks and venture equities.

Monitoring

Monitoring of these portfolios is a continuous upgrading and changes in asset composition to take advantage of the changes in market conditions and economic and industry performance. Portfolio monitoring is a continuous on-going assessment of the current portfolio to the goals, changes in investors' preferences, capital market conditions and expectations. The monitoring requires a periodic meeting with investors to know the changes in the conditions, continuous review of the investment policy relative to investors' preferences.

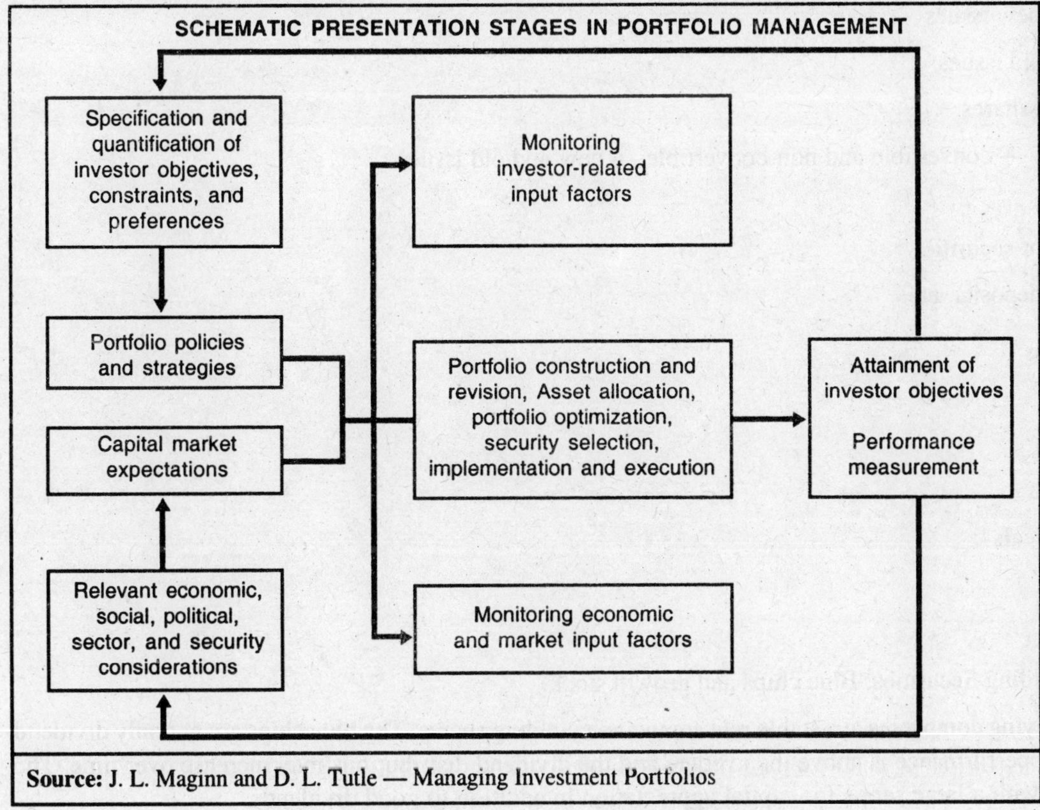

Fig. 44.8

Schematic Presentation of Stages in Portfolio Management.

Source: J. L. Maginn and D. L. Tutle — Managing Investment Portfolios

The current investment strategy reflects the capital market conditions and expectations and any changes in them will bring out the changes in optimal conditions in the portfolio. The portfolio is thus subjected to the ongoing review and assessment to change the composition of the portfolio in tune with the changing conditions in the market and of the investor.

To give specific examples, if market conditions change and the prospects of the cement industry are likely to be better in the coming year, as judged by the Government policy changes *vis-a-vis* the steel industry, then the investor preferences can be better satisfied by shifting from steel shares to cement shares. Besides, within the cement industry, a manager may shift from a poorly performing company like Orient Cement to a better performing company like India Cement. Similarly, changes can take place as between different asset classes such as moving from debentures to equities and *vice versa* or from income stocks to growth stocks, etc.

Thus, portfolio changes can be brought about by the changes in market expectations and from the quarterly, half-yearly results or yearly results of the companies, industry and economy. These adjustments of the portfolio may also be initiated due to changes in the managers' expectations of the company and market or asset classes. Certain changes in asset classes may have a time limit as a critical input. Thus, purchases and sales of equity shares on the stock market are to be well-timed based upon the assessment of the market technical position. This requires technical analysis in addition to fundamental analysis. In fact, any shift of the investment from one type of asset to another requires a careful analysis of time, risk-return and host of other factors.

An important characteristic of the portfolio is risk reduction, which can be achieved by a diversification of the portfolio into the various asset classes and securities within the asset class. Changes in security prices or market expectations of the manager may have necessitated changes in the asset composition. The efficient frontier in terms of modern portfolio theory may itself change the composition of the portfolio due to the change in the Beta value in the longer time horizon. The composition has to be changed to bring portfolio back to the optimal conditions and back to the efficient frontier line.

The investment alternatives for portfolio management are set out below:

1. Asset Classes:
   - *(a)* Equity — new issues
   - *(b)* Equity — old issues
   - *(c)* Preference shares
   - *(d)* Debentures — convertible and non-convertible — new and old issues
   - *(e)* PSU Bonds
   - *(f)* Government securities
   - *(g)* Company deposits, etc.
2. Industry Groups:
   - *(a)* Textiles
   - *(b)* Cement
   - *(c)* Aluminium
   - *(d)* Petrochemicals
   - *(e)* Fertilizers
   - *(f)* Paper, etc.
3. High Income Yielding Securities; Blue chips and growth stock.

Regular dividend paying companies at a stable rate are income yielding shares. The blue chips are not only dividend paying regularly but their performance is above the average and the dividend distributions may increase over time. The growth stocks are shares with a large scope for capital appreciation in addition to good dividends.

4. Companies with export orientation and those with only domestic demand.
5. Companies based on location as those in the west, south, east and north of India.
6. Type of management, *viz.*, family type, professional type, etc.

Building of the Portfolio

The portfolio construction, as referred to earlier, is made on the basis of the investment strategy, set out for each investor. Through choice of asset classes, instruments of investments and the specific scrips, say of bonds or equities of different risks and return characteristics, the choice of tax characteristics, risk level and other features of investments, are decided upon. The construction of Portfolio and other elements in the portfolio management are already set out in Fig. 44.8.

Portfolio Revision

After fixing the target Beta and duration of the portfolio, the investment activity starts with the selection of Scrips and Bonds, etc. But the portfolio once constructed undergoes changes due to changes in market prices and a reassessment of companies and the portfolio Beta and the proportion in each asset class will change to bring back the portfolio to the targetted level of Beta and duration; portfolio revision will take place and composition of portfolio will change. A change in interest rate will also affect the portfolio through change in duration. Constant market changes necessitate readjustment of portfolio leading to purchases and sales of equities, bonds etc., which in turn will result in change in Beta and duration.

Thus, any portfolio requires constant monitoring and revision. Operations on a portfolio will thus take place on a daily basis, keeping in mind, the targetted Beta, duration and return. Changes in investor's financial status, his preferences and market conditions, will also require changes in portfolio composition.

The next stage is performance evaluation which is referred to later. Before we discuss evaluation, it is necessary to set out some theoretical tools like security analysis, Markowitz model, risk-return evaluation etc. These are referred to below, briefly, although they were set out in detail, in earlier Chapters.

SECURITY PRICING AND PORTFOLIO MANAGEMENT

Portfolio Management is based upon Security Analysis, which is an Analysis of Share prices.

(1) Analysis at Macro Level of Market (2) Analysis at Micro Level of Company

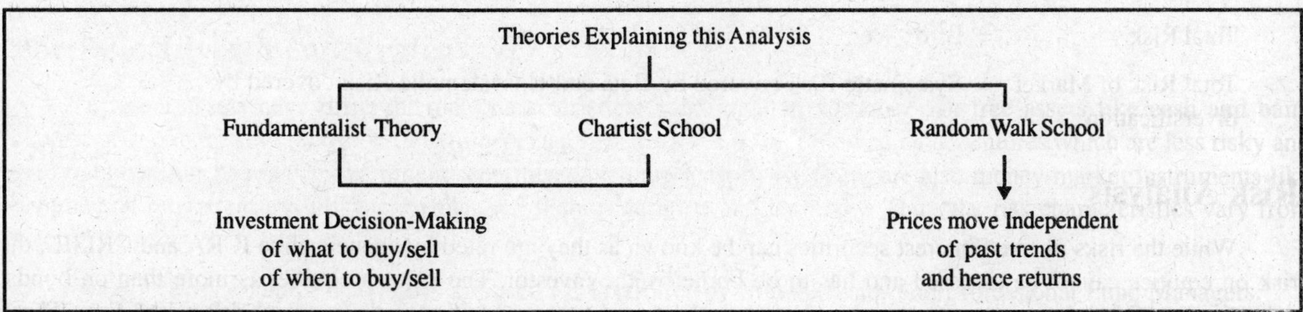

Markowitz Model of Portfolio Theory

This Portfolio Model is based on the exposure to market risk and the degree of diversification of the portfolio. The Beta of the portfolio provides a measure of exposure to market risk and the coefficient of determination, namely, R^2 provides a measure of diversification.

Cross sectional measures are used for risk estimates for individual holdings, that comprise the portfolio. The individual Scrips in the portfolio have their own Betas, which are weighted by the proportion of the funds invested in each. The Table below gives an example:

Company	Proportion of Portfolio	Betas of Scrips	Weighted Values
Scrip A	.11	1.65	.18
Scrip B	.11	1.40	.15
Scrip C	.17	1.25	.21
Scrip D	.23	1.05	.24
Scrip E	.38	0.85	.32
	1.00		1.10

Depending on the risk preference of the investor, weights can be changed to get the desired portfolio Beta to less than 1.1 or more than 1.1 (got in the above Table).

In the same way, the portfolio R^2 or R can be calculated and compared with the market return and its R^2 or R. The standard deviation for the portfolio can be compared with that of the Market Index return and its R to ensure that its R is suitable to the investor's risk preferences.

William Sharpe has suggested a new model. Instead of comparing the risk of each Scrip to every other Scrip, it can be compared with market risk, which leads to the comparison of market return to Scrip Return. He takes into account only the systematic Risk on the Portfolio (β).

$Ri = \alpha + \beta I + e$

α is the intercept of the straight line.

β is slope of the straight line or β co-efficeient.

I is expected return on Market Index, and e is the Random component.

The Sharpe Index method has given us two components of Risk.

Systematic Risk = $\beta^2 \times$ Variance of Index.

= $\beta^2 \sigma^2$

Unsystematic Risk = Total Variance of a Portfolio

Security Risk – Systematic Risk = e^2

Total Risk = $\beta^2 \sigma^2 + e^2$

Total Risk of Market = Systematic Risk covered by Beta and Unsystematic Risk covered by diversification.

Risk Analysis

While the risks of fixed interest securities can be known as they are rated by agencies like ICRA and CRISIL, the risk on equities cannot be assessed and has to be borne by the investor. The risk on equities is more than on bonds, debentures or fixed deposits and not amenable to scientific measurement as that is the residual risk of the firm. These risks may be due to inflation, interest rate changes, financial risk, business risk, market risk, liquidity risks, and other risks. Some of them relate to the market and economy and hence not controllable while the others are company specific in nature, which can be controlled and reduced by diversification. Thus, investment in more than one company and industry is necessary for reducing risks. Investment in too many companies, may not be desirable but investment in two companies in steel industry is not having the same risks as investment in one Steel Company and one drug company. Risk concepts and related aspects are dealt with already in another chapter.

EVALUATION OF PORTFOLIO PERFORMANCE

Investment analysts and Portfolio Managers continuously monitor and evaluate the results of their performance. The revision of portfolio investments is conducted on the basis of such monitoring and evaluation. The ability of Managers to out perform the market depends on their expertise and experience. The basic features of good Portfolio Managers are their ability to perceive the market trends correctly and make correct expectations and estimates regarding risk, returns, ability to make proper diversification, to reduce the company related risk and use proper Beta estimates for selection of securities to reduce the systematic risk. In such case, it is possible for an expert Portfolio Manager to show superior performance over the market. This performance also depends on the timing of investments and superior investment analysis and security selection. He has to have the acumen to select the under valued shares under each risk class, for which a high degree of equity research is needed.

The two major factors which influence his performance are the return achieved and the level of risk that the portfolio is exposed to. The Manager has to make proper diversification into different industries, asset classes and instruments so as to reduce the unsystematic risk to the minimum for a given level of return. The market related risk has to be managed by a proper selection of Beta for the securities.

Criteria for Evaluation of Portfolio

Portfolio managers and investors who manage their own portfolios, continuously monitor and review the performance of the portfolio. The evaluation of each portfolio, followed by revision and reconstruction are all steps in the portfolio Management.

Managers and Analysts wish to know how well they performed in their investment strategies in terms of return *per unit of risk*, both in absolute terms and relative terms relative to overall market performance. They have to assess the extent to which the objectives aimed at are being achieved say in terms of income, capital appreciation, risk and returns, etc.

In this context, evaluation has to take into account whether the portfolio secured above average returns, average or below average, as compared to the market return. The ability to diversify with a view to reduce and even eliminate all unsystematic risk and expertise in managing the systematic risk related to the market by use of appropriate risk measures, namely, Betas are needed. Selection of proper securities is thus the first requirement.

Superior timing and superior stock selection may result in above average return. Diversification in terms of Markowitz model or Sharpe's Single Index Model will reduce the market related risk and maximise the returns for a given level of risk. Market returns being related positively to risk, evaluation has to take into account:

(1) Rate of returns, or excess return over risk free rate.

(2) Level of Risk both Systematic (Beta) and Unsystematic and residual risks through proper diversification.

Under the Traditional theory, the evaluation is only in terms of the rate of return, particularly in comparison with other assets of the same risk class. The theory of Markowitz and Modern Portfolio Theory have opened up the avenue for selecting and evaluating the portfolios on the basis of risk adjusted return. Modern portfolio theory has postulated that the portfolio selection and evaluation should be on the basis of both Risk and Return and the objective should be to optimise the return for a given level of risk or to minimise the risk for a given level of return. Due to uneven fluctuations of returns and high degree of variability of returns, risk adjusted returns become the basis for evaluation. This is possible due to later developments involving the quantification of risk by the statistical measures of S.D., variance and covariance of returns of securities in a portfolio.

There was no composite index, which measures both return and risk under the Traditional Theory. In Modern Portfolio Theory it became necessary to develop some composite measures of both return and risk in portfolio performance, as the objective now is maximisation of return and minimisation of risk. Because of the trade-off between them, simple maximisation of returns or single goal of minimisation or risk will be defeating the objectives of Modern Portfolio Management.

It was in this context that later researches have tried to evolve a composite index to measure risk based returns taking into account the different components of risk, *viz.*, systematic, unsystematic and residual risk. The credit for evolving these criteria goes to Sharpe, Treynor and Jensen.

Example of Sharpe's Measure

Sharpe's measure is $ST = \dfrac{Rt - Rf}{\sigma_t}$

Where ST is Sharpe index when, Rt is average return on portfolio, Rf is risk free return, σ_t is the total risk of the portfolio.

It measures total risk by standard deviation. Reward is in the numerator as risk premium. Total risk is in the denominator as standard deviation of its return. We get a measure of portfolio's total risk and variability of returns in relation to the risk premium which is the product of the portfolio Manager's expertise.

The method adopted by Sharpe is to rank all portfolios on the basis of evaluation measure ST. If one portfolio has more ST than another, the first one is better performer as per the Sharpe's measure. Take the following example:

Portfolio	*Average Return*	*S.D.*	*Average Rf (Risk Free Rate)*
A	20%	4%	10%
B	24%	8%	10%

By applying the above formula, we have

For A portfolio

$$St_A = \frac{0.20 - 10}{.04} = \frac{.10}{.04} = 2.50$$

For B portfolio

$$St_B \frac{0.24 - .10}{.08} = \frac{.14}{.08} = 1.75$$

As the first one is ranked higher at 2.5% more than the second 1.75, the first is a better performer. This is shown graphically as follows:

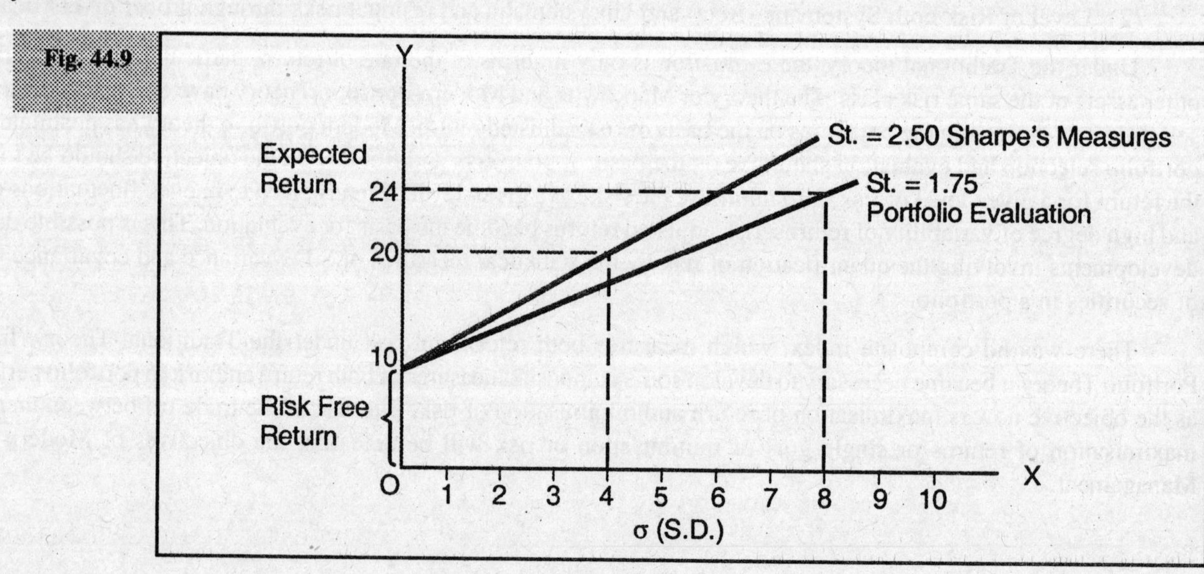

Fig. 44.9

Treynor's Measure

In Treynor's measure, the risk measure of standard deviation, namely, total risk of the portfolio is replaced by market risk, measured by Beta, which is not diversifiable. The equation can be set out as:

$$T_n = \frac{R_n - Rf}{\beta_n}$$

T_n = Treynor's measure of evaluation

R_n = Return on the portfolio, Rf = Risk free rate, β_n is Beta of the portfolio as a measure of systematic risk.

Treynor based his formula on the concept of characteristic line. This line is the least squares regression line relating the return to the risk and Beta is the slope of the line. The regression line takes the form of

$R_p = \alpha + \beta x + e$

R_p is the return of portfolio,

α is the intercept reflecting the risk free return

β is the slope of the line and is the market return and e is the error term.

Thus, concept can be graphically represented as follows:

Based on this characteristic line Treynor formula is

$$T_n = \frac{R_n - Rf}{\beta_n}$$

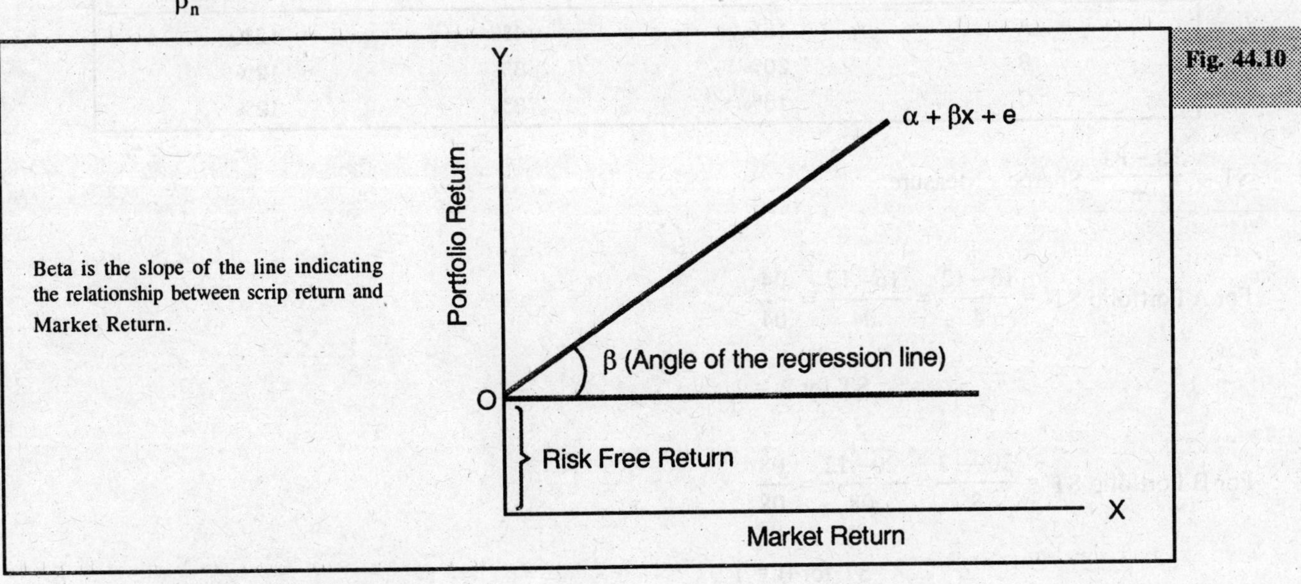

Fig. 44.10

Take a Problem as an example

Portfolio	*Return*	B_n	R_f
A	20	0.5	10
B	24	1.0	10

For A, $T_{nA} \frac{.20-.10}{0.5} = \frac{.10}{.5} = 0.2$

For B, $T_{nB} \dfrac{.24-.10}{1.0} = 0.14$

Portfolio 'A' performs better than Portfolio B as $T_{nA} > T_{nB}$.

The numerator in Treynor's formula is the reward, measured by risk premium or excess returns and denominator is volatility as measured by Beta coefficient.

The difference between Sharpe measure and Treynor measure is the following:

Sharpe takes the total risk of portfolio into account while Treynor considers only systematic risk as relevant to performance. Total risk consists of both systematic and unsystematic risk, while the latter is amenable to reduction by management of proper diversification, the former cannot be eliminated but borne by the investor. The higher this market

elements of risk in both the portfolio measurements is the systematic variance. The ranking of portfolios on the basis of both the measures therefore should give identical results. But it is possible that these two measures in practice give varying results due to differences in the investment strategies and diversification techniques.

Problems

Example on Evaluation of Portfolio Performance

The Measure of Sharpe's performance evaluation may be calculated from the following data:

Three Portfolios of the Securities

Portfolios	*Return*	*Standard Deviation*	*Riskless Rate of Return*
A	16%	4%	12%
B	20%	8%	12%
C	18%	3%	12%

$ST = \dfrac{Ri - Rf}{\sigma i}$ Sharpe's Measure

For A Portfolio $ST = \dfrac{16-12}{4} = \dfrac{.16-.12}{.04} = \dfrac{.04}{.04}$

ST for A = 1

For B Portfolio $ST = \dfrac{20-12}{8} = \dfrac{.20-.12}{.08} = \dfrac{.08}{.08}$

ST for B = 1

A & B both have the same measure and are equally attractive in performance. But take the case of portfolio 'C'.

For Portfolio ST $\dfrac{18-12}{3} = \dfrac{.18-.12}{.03} = \dfrac{.06}{.03} = 2.0$

ST for C = 2.0

'C' ranked better than A and B, as it has a higher performance index according to the Sharpe's model and his performance evaluation formula.

EVALUATION PROBLEM

Comparison

Problem

Portfolio	Return	Sd.	Riskless Rate	Beta
A	6.00	15.24	3.0	1.00
B	3.30	4.92	3.0	2.85

Compare Treynor's Index with Sharpe's Index

Treynor's Index	Sharpe's Index
$T_n = \dfrac{m - r^o}{\beta n}$	$S_t = \dfrac{rt - rf}{sd}$
For A	
$T_n = \dfrac{6 - 3.0}{1.00} = 3$	$S_t = \dfrac{6 - 3.0}{15.24} = \dfrac{3.0}{15.24}$
$T_n = 3.00$	$St = 0.19$
For B	
$\dfrac{3.30 - 3.0}{2.85} = \dfrac{0.30}{2.85}$	$S_t \dfrac{3.30 - 3.0}{4.92} =$
$T_n = 0.1$	$S_t = \dfrac{0.30}{4.92} = 0.06$

A comparison of the two measures, namely, Treynor's and Sharpe's performance Evaluation, is made in the above example.

Conclusion: By Treynor's measure the portfolio 'A' is better as it has a higher rank of 3.00 than that of B (0.1). By Sharpe index measure also, the same conclusion is arrived, namely, Portfolio A is better than 'B' as the former got a rank higher than the latter.

Jensen's Measure

Jensen's measure of the performance of portfolio is different from that of Sharpe and Treynor in that the latter provides a measure of ranking the relative performance of various portfolios on a risk adjusted basis while the former gives a measure of absolute performance on a risk adjusted basis. This standard, based on CAPM, measures the portfolio Manager's predictive ability to achieve higher return than expected for the given riskiness.

Jensen's Model

$$R_{Jt} - R_{ft} = \alpha_J + \beta_J (R_{Mt} - R_{ft})$$

R_{Jt} = Average return on portfolio J for period 't'

R_{ft} = Risk free rate of return for period 't'

α_j = Intercept of the Graph, measuring the forecasting ability of the Manager

β_J = Systematic risk measure

Rmt = Average return on the Market Portfolio for period t.

It is possible that $\alpha_J = 0$, which is neutral performance or the same as that of market.

$\alpha_J > 0$, it is superior performance over the market

$\alpha_J < 0$ it is inferior performance

The Jensen's approach can be illustrated by an example.

The data on portfolio results, Beta of the portfolios and Market Index results are set out as follows:

Portfolio	Return on Portfolio	Portfolio Beta
1	18%	1.2
2	15%	0.8
3	21%	1.5
Market Index	16%	1.00

Market Beta 1.0 and Risk free Rate 10%

The return of 3 portfolios on the basis of CAPM are as follows:

$R_p = R_F + (R_{M1} - R_F)\ \beta$ where $R_M = 16$.

(1) Portfolio I = 10 + (16 – 10) × 1.2 = 17.2%

(2) Portfolio II = 10 + (16 – 10) × 0.8 = 14.8%

(3) Portfolio III = 10 + (16 – 10) 1.5 = 19.0%

Actual *vs* Estimate; Portfolio I = 18 – 17.2 = 0.8%

Portfolio II = 15 – 14.8 = 0.2%

Portfolio III = 21 – 19.0 = 2.0%

The above data show that the best managed Portfolio, as per Jensen's approach is that of Portfolio III, which has out performed the market and gave 2% return above that would have been got under CAPM for the given level of risk. While the actual return of portfolio 'P' is what is achieved, it may be above the vertical distance from the required return as judged by the market return.

The Jensen and Fama net selectivity measures may give opposite or different results. This is due to the use of total risk in one case and the systematic risk on the other. In both cases the actual Portfolio return is compared and evaluated as excess over the market return or required return for a given level of risk.

Evaluation Criteria for Portfolios

Treynor and Sharpe Index models provide measures for ranking the ***relative*** performances of various portfolios on a risk adjusted basis. But Jensen has constructed a measure of ***absolute*** performance on a risk adjusted basis.

A simplified version of his basic Model is given by:

$R_{Jt} - R_{Ft} = a_J + b_J\ (R_{Mt} - R_{Ft})$

R_{Jt} = Average return on portfolio for period t

R_{Ft} = Riskless rate of return for period t

a_J = Intercept that measures the forecasting ability of the Manager

b_J = A measure of systematic risk

R_{Mt} = Average return on market for period t

Graphical Representation of Jensen's Measure is given below. For Sharpe and Treynor, the intercept of the line is at the origin but in the case of Jensen, it can be at any point, including the origin.

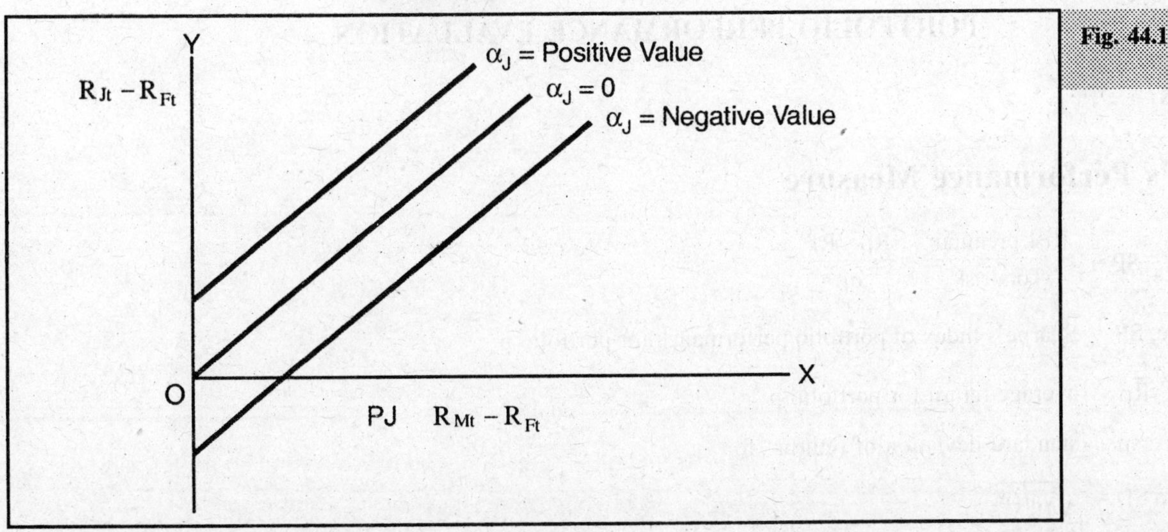

Fig. 44.11

If α, is positive it indicates superior performance; if α, is negative it indicates inferior performance and α_0 is neutral performance — something similar to market average.

As compared to the normal evaluation of a portfolio as against the market portfolio in relative terms by Treynor and Sharpe, the Jensen's approach is more general and absolute in measure.

Thus, Sharpe's measure ST is set out as $ST = \frac{rt - r^o}{\sigma_t^2}$, where rt is the average return on portfolio t and r^o is the riskless return and σ_t^2 is variance (risk measure) of the returns on portfolio. Here σ^2 takes the total risk while the same in formula of Treynor takes Beta, and Beta (β) is a measure of systematic risk and not total risk.

Treynor's measure is also set out as:

$Tn = \frac{r_n - r}{\beta_n}$, where r_n and r have the same meanings as under Sharpe's formula.

The graphical presentation of both is given above:

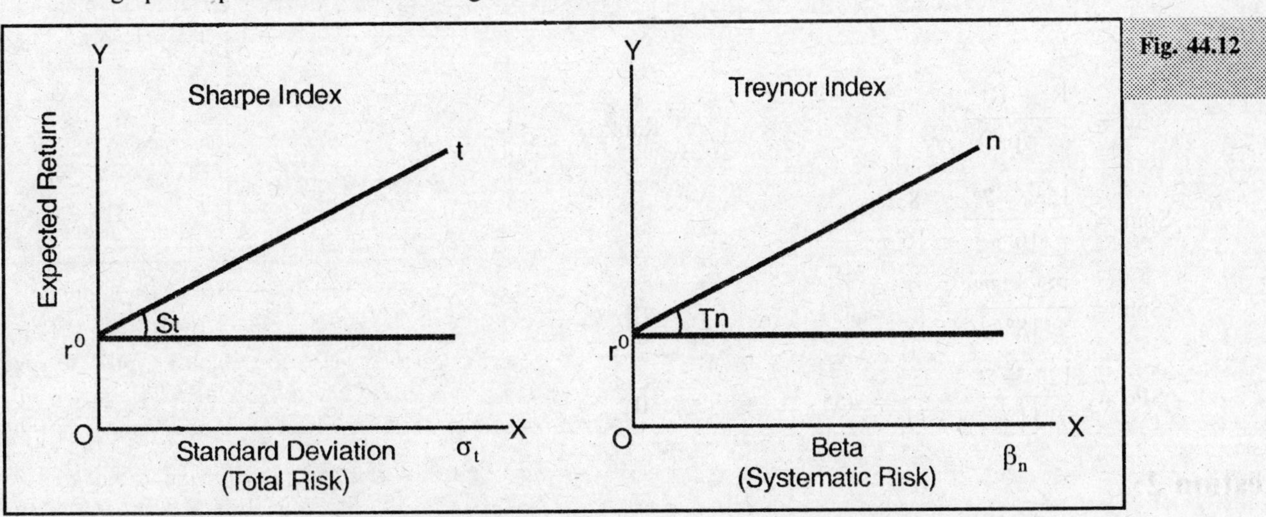

Fig. 44.12

The graphs are self-explanatory. While Sharpe Index used standard deviation, Treynor used Beta, the measure of systematic risk.

In the case of Sharpe model, the standard deviation measuring total risk (σ) is used. In Treynor model, only systematic risk which is market related and can not be diversified is used. Their results will be different and need not be similar or identical.

PORTFOLIO PERFORMANCE EVALUATION

Problems

I Sharpe's Performance Measure

$$SP = \frac{\text{Risk premium}}{\text{Total risk}} = \frac{\overline{Rp} - Rf}{\sigma p}$$

Where, SP = Sharpe's Index of portfolio performance for portfolio p

$\overline{Rp}$ = average return for portfolio p

sp = standard deviation of returns for

portfolio SD = $\sqrt{var(r)}$

Rf= Riskless rate of interest, $\left(\sqrt{Var(R)} = O\right)$

Question 1:

The rate of return and risk for three growth-oriented firms were calculated over the most recent 5 years and are listed below:

Growth Firm	*Return*	*Risk (s)*
M	15%	16%
N	13	18
O	12	11

Rank each firm by Sharpe's index of portfolio performance if the risk free rate is 7 per cent.

Answer:

Rf = 7

$$Sp = \frac{\overline{R}_p - Rf}{\sigma p} \qquad \text{Rank}$$

$$Spm = \frac{15\% - 7\%}{16\%} = \frac{8}{16} = .5 \qquad \text{I}$$

$$Spn = \frac{13\% - 7\%}{18\%} = \frac{6}{18} = .333 \qquad \text{III}$$

$$SPo = \frac{12\% - 7\%}{11\%} = \frac{5}{11} = .455 \qquad \text{II}$$

Question 2:

Consider the three investments below assuming that Government Treasury bills yielded a constant rate of 7%. Calculate the risk adjusted performance of each of the investment funds using the Sharpe's measures?

Year	A	Deviation	B	Deviation	C	Deviation
1993	+5	+2.4	+4	0.8	+6	+2
1994	+0	−2.6	+1	2.2	−1	−5
1995	−5	−7.6	−4	−7.2	−10	−14
1966	+8	+5.4	+10	+6.8	+18	+14
1997	+5	+2.4	+5	+1.8	+7	+3

$(\overline{R})\ \frac{13}{5} = 2.6;\quad \frac{16}{5} = 3.2;\quad \frac{20}{5} = 4$

(Deviation)² A	(Deviation)² B	(Deviation)² C
5.76	0.64	4
6.76	4.84	25
57.6	51.84	196
29.16	46.24	196
5.76	3.24	9
$\sigma^2 p$ = 105.04	106.80	430
σp = 10.24	10.33	20.7

Rank

$$SP_A = \frac{\overline{R}p - R_f}{sp} = \frac{2.6-7}{10.24} = \frac{-4.4}{10.24} = -0.43 \qquad \text{III}$$

$$SP_B = \frac{3.2-7}{10.33} = \frac{-3.8}{10.33} = -0.37 \qquad \text{II}$$

$$SP_C = \frac{4-7}{20.7} = \frac{-3}{20.7} = -0.14 \qquad \text{I}$$

The ranks are as shown above:

Treynor's Measure

$$T_p = \frac{\text{Risk premium}}{\text{Portfolios beta coefficient}} = \frac{Rp - R_f}{bp}$$

T_p = Treynor's index of performance for portfolio.

Rp = the average return for portfolio.

R = the risk free rate of interest. Var (R) = 0

bp = the beta for the portfolio.

Problem

Rank the three Firms with the Treynor performance Index; given the following data

Growth Firm	Return	Risk	Beta	Risk Free Rate
M	15%	16%	1.15	7%
N	13%	18%	1.25	7%
O	12%	11%	0.90	7%

Answer:

$$Tp = \frac{\overline{R}p - Rf}{bp}$$

Rank

$$Tp_M = \frac{15-7}{1.15} = \frac{8}{1.15} = 6.96$$ I

$$Tp_N = \frac{13-7}{1.25} = \frac{6}{1.25} = 4.8$$ III

$$Tp_O = \frac{12-7}{0.9} = \frac{5}{0.9} = 5.55$$ II

Jensen's Performance Measure: (JP)

$$Jp = \frac{\text{Alpha}}{\text{BETA}}$$

Jensen's Alpha and the Beta Coefficients for four stocks are given below:

Stocks	*Alpha*	*Beta*
M	1.0	.9
N	1.25	1.25
O	1.07	1.15
P	1.15	0.85

Answer:

Rank

$$Jp_M = \frac{1}{.9} = 1.11$$ II

$$JP_n = \frac{1.25}{1.25} = 1$$ III

$$Jp_o = \frac{1.07}{1.15} = 0.93$$ IV

$$Jp_p = \frac{1.15}{.85} = 1.35$$ I

Question 1

Determine the Treynor's and Jensen's measures of portfolio performance from the following information.

Average rate of return on market portfolio = 18%

Average rate of return on this portfolio = 19%

Average risk free return = 12%

Standard deviation of this portfolio = 14%

Beta of portfolio, under consideration = 0.95.

Question 2

From the following data on returns and risks of portfolios A to E calculate the Sharpe measure and Treynor measure of portfolio performance, if Rf is 3%.

Portfolio	Expost Return	σ_t	Beta
A	7	3	0.4
B	10	8	1.0
C	13	6	1.1
D	15	13	1.2
E	18	15	1.4

Question 3

Given the following information on two Mutual funds Tatas, Birlas and the Market Index Portfolio, rank the performance of these from the available measures of Treynor and Sharpe?

	Tatas	Birlas	Market
Rp.	16	12	15.7
σp	13	9	13.0
β_p	0.83	0.66	1.0
and Rf (Risk free rate) = 6.2%.			

Returns and Performance Evaluation — Problems

(A) Arithmetic and geometric Mean of returns

Question 4

Zerox Co. posted the following returns in four years, find out the arithmetic and geometric mean rates of return for the company.

Answer:

	Returns (in %)
1995	9
1996	7
1997	–5
1998	14

$$\text{Arithmetic mean} = \frac{9+7-5+14}{4} = \frac{25}{4} = 6.25\%$$

Geometric Mean

$$= \left[\sqrt[4]{(1.09)\,(1.07)\,((0.95)\,(1.14)}\right] - 1$$

$$= \sqrt[4]{1.263} - n = 1.060 - 1 = 6.0\%$$

(B) Sharpe's Performance Measure

Question 5

The following portfolios have performed over the last 3 years as follows. Rank them in order of poor to the best portfolio as per Sharpe's measure:

	Return	S. D. (σ)	Risk Free Rate
X Fund	12	11	7
Y Fund	15	16	7
Z Fund	13	18	7

Answer:

$$Sp = \frac{rp - R}{\sigma}$$ where is the $r\ p$ is the portfolio return, R is Risk Free rate and σp is S.D.

$$Sx - \frac{.12-.07}{.11} = \frac{0.5}{0.11} = 0.45 \quad \text{IInd}$$

$$Sy = \frac{.15-.07}{.16} = \frac{0.8}{0.16} = 0.50 \quad \text{IIIrd}$$

$$Sz = \frac{.13-.07}{.18} = \frac{0.6}{0.18} = 0.33 \quad \text{Ist}$$

(C) Treynor's Performance Measure

Question 6

Given the following data, rank the three funds in the order of their performance.

	Return	Beta	Risk Free Rate
X	17	1.5	7
Y	15	1.2	7
Z	8	0.9	7

Answer:

$$Tp = \frac{rp - R}{\beta p}$$

$$Tx = \frac{0.17-.07}{1.5} = \frac{0.10}{1.5} = 0.066 = 6.6\%$$

$$Ty = \frac{0.15-0.07}{1.2} = \frac{0.08}{1.2} = 0.066 = 6.6\%$$

$$Tz = \frac{0.08-0.07}{0.9} = \frac{.01}{0.9} = 0.011 = 1.1\%$$

x and y funds rank equally and z comes last

(D) Jensen's Performance Measures

Question 7

Given the Alpha and Beta values of the X, Y and Z companies, rank them in the order of Jensen's Performace Measure:

	Alpha	Beta
X	1.25	1.50
Y	1.07	1.15
Z	1.15	0.85

$Jx = \frac{\text{Alpha}}{\text{Beta}} = \frac{1.25}{1.50} = 0.83$ IIIrd

$Jy = \frac{1.07}{1.15} = 0.93$ IInd

$Jz = \frac{1.15}{0.85} = 1.35$ Ist

(E) Calculation of Alpha and Beta

Question 8

Given the following data, calculate α and β coefficient for the 5 year period.

Year	Ind Ratna (r1)	B.S.E. Sensex (rm)	T. B rate (Rf)
1	15	12	8
2	11	9	6
3	13	10	7
4	– 5	– 4	9
5	7	5	5

Answer:

$\overline{y} = A + b\overline{x}$

we have to calculate α and β, in the formula

$\alpha = \overline{y} + \beta\overline{x}$

$$\beta = \frac{N\sum xy - \sum x \sum y}{N\sum x^2 - (\sum x)^2}$$

Year	r_1	rm	Rf	x = (rm – Rf)	y (ri – Rf)	xy	X^2
1	15	12	8	4	7	28	16
2	11	9	6	3	5	15	9
3	13	10	7	3	6	18	9
4	– 5	–4	9	– 13	– 14	182	169
5	7	5	5	0	2	0	0
			$\Sigma x = -3$	$\Sigma Y = 6$	$\Sigma xy = 243$	$\Sigma x^2 = 203$	

$$\left\{\bar{y} = \frac{6}{5} = 1.2;\ \bar{x} = \frac{-3}{5} = 0.6\right\}$$

$$\beta = \frac{5 \times 243 - (-3)(6)}{5 \times 203 - (-3)^2} = \frac{1215 + 18}{1015 - 9}$$

$$\beta = \frac{1233}{1006} = 1.226$$

$$\alpha = \bar{y} - \beta\bar{x} = 1.2 - 1.226 \times (-0.6)$$

$$= 1.2 + 0.73 = 1.93$$

TAKE HOME PROBLEMS

I. Given the following data, calculate the Sharpe Index, Treynor's index and Jensen's index of performance and explain their implication.

Fund	Mean Return	Beta	S.D.	Mean Market Return
XYZ	0.13	1.00	15%	0.12
ABC	0.18	2.00	19%	

Risk free rate is 8%

II. Given the following information calculate the Treynor's and Jensen's measure of portfolio performance?

Average rate of return on Portfolio 19%

Average rate of return on Market 18%

Risk Free Rate = 12%

S. D. of Portfolio Return = 14

Beta of Portfolio = 0.95

Beta of Market = 1.00

Note: For more Problems and Solutions in any chapter Refer to "Theory and Problems of Investments" — By J.C. Francis & R.W. Taylor.

CHAPTER 45 Mutual Funds and their Schemes

Introduction

In India, the only mutual fund operating for a long time since 1964 was the UTI. It is an open-ended mutual fund, whose units can be sold and repurchased at any time. It is in the public sector, enjoying a monopoly position and some unique tax benefits such as exemption from income-tax of its entire income. Although the UTI has operated a number of schemes linked to insurance and gifts, and some tax benefits, income declared by it to unit holders is not subject to any tax deduction at source and is exempt from income tax. Since 1995-96, there was a TDS, if the annual income is more than Rs. 10,000, which was removed in 1999-2000.

Mutual Funds have been set up since 1987 by the public sector banks following an Amendment to the Banking Regulation Act in 1983, which empowered the RBI to permit the banks to carry on non-banking business such as leasing, mutual funds, etc. under Section 6 of this Act. Since then, the SBI, Canara Bank, Punjab National Bank and some other nationalised banks have set up their own mutual funds. The business of mutual funds has caught the imagination of the financial community and has grown at a rapid pace in India. These funds cater mainly to individual investors and small savers. It was thrown open to private sector and foreign sector in 1992-93. During 1996 to 2002, this Mutual Fund business was in a bad shape due to depressed conditions in the capital market. As the UTI and MFs are mobilisers of funds for investment in stocks and shares in the capital market, they become part of this book dealing with investment and Investment Management.

Definition

Mutual funds are associations or trusts of public members who wish to make investments in the financial instruments or assets of the business sector or corporate sector for the mutual benefit of its members. The fund collects the moneys of these members from their savings and invests them in a diversified portfolio of financial assets with a view to reduce risks and to maximise their income and capital appreciation for distribution to its members on a pro-rata basis. They enjoy collectively the benefits of expertise in investment by specialists in the trust, economies of scale which no single individual by himself could enjoy. Mutual fund is thus a concept of mutual help of subscribers for portfolio investment and management of these investments by experts in the field. These funds are set up under the Indian Trusts Act. UTI is governed by its own Act.

Types of Funds

These funds are of various types and set up for various purposes and objectives. Some are close-ended with contributions from members collected during a definite time-frame of a few days to a few months. Thus, the issue of CanGrowth was kept open for only a few days, while the LIC Mutual Fund (viz., Dhanaraksha) was kept open for a few months. The life of the Fund, which is close-ended, may also be for a specific period of 3 to 7 years after which the income and profits in the form of capital appreciation etc. are all distributed back to the members after deduction of expenses of the Funds by its Trustees. Some of the mutual funds are open-ended like the UTI Scheme of 1964 under which units are purchased and sold throughout the year and a member can enter the scheme any time or walk out of it also any time. These are perpetual schemes without an end, each individual member enjoying the benefits of expert investment in the form of income and growth during the period of his stay with the UTI.

Further, the funds can be classified into three types by objectives, namely, those for income alone, for growth alone (capital appreciation) and for both. The income funds aim at the maximisation of income without pursuing the growth objectives, while the growth funds specialise in securing capital appreciation, irrespective of income. But Income and Growth Funds aim at both and in a judicious mix.

These funds can also be classified into various types based on the pattern of their investments. Some funds may invest in debentures alone or fixed interest securities like the Government Bonds and Treasury Bills. Others may invest in variable dividend securities like equities and bonds of companies. There may be a few who invest only in government and semi-government bonds called gilt funds. In advanced countries there are funds specialising in this manner and in fact some funds are set up only for investment in real estate. In countries like the USA and the UK, where the mutual fund business has grown vastly, there are thousands of such funds, some of them being quoted and traded on the stock exchanges as well. In these countries, mutual funds are well regulated but permitted to be set up in the private sector. Besides, the funds business has just been initiated by breaking the monopoly of the UTI for the first time in 1987 but even so, the permission to set up mutual funds in India was granted only to public sector agencies until 1992. The policy has been liberalised since, to permit private sector also to set up Mutual Funds. There were only 5 Mutual Funds in the year of begining *i.e.* 1993-94. There are at present about 28 private mutual sector funds operating in India and 4 in public sector mutual funds in addition to UTI.

Unit Trust of India

The UTI was created with the aim of tapping the savings of the small man and to deploy the funds for productive purposes, offering an attractive return and growth to the investors while minimising the risk element for individual investors.

Being the first of its kind and that too in the public sector, the UTI has been vested with both management and trusteeship functions in one body which is the Board of Trustees. The Unit Trust of India Act, 1963, under which UTI was constituted, did not initially permit it to take up activities other than dealing in "units" defined under the Act, investment and dealing in securities and other business arising out of the formulation of any unit scheme. These restrictions have now been removed and the UTI has been permitted to take up such other activities as direct lending of funds, bill rediscounting, leasing, financing of housing projects, and hire-purchase financing and to set up subsidiaries for many financial services and banking.

The growth in the business of UTI, especially during the eighties, has been spectacular. The gross sales of units (under all schemes) which has amounted to Rs. 10 crores in the first year, i.e., in 1964-65, recorded a rapid growth, especially since 1982-83 and rose to Rs. 3,701 crores in 1988-9, and further to Rs. 4,122 crores in 1990-91. UTI along with all its funds have a total investible funds of about Rs. 70,000 crores, at end March 2002, when it was split up into two units UTI-I and UTI-II.

UTI Schemes for Resident Indians

The UTI offers a variety of investment schemes (funds) to the investing public. As in March 2002, It had, in all, six open-ended investment schemes, *viz.*, Unit Scheme 1964, Unit Scheme 1971 (Unit-Linked Insurance Plan), Unit Scheme for Charitable and Religious Trusts and Registered Societies 1981, Capital Gains Unit Scheme 1983, Children's Gift Growth Fund Unit Scheme 1986 and Parents' Gift and Growth Fund Unit Scheme 1987, catering to the various sections of society. A special mention needs to be made here of the more popular amongst the open-ended schemes, viz., those of 1964, 1971 and 1983. The US 64 of UTI was involved in a scam in 2000-01 due to gross mismanagement. UTI has lost the confidence of investors and was in for liquidity problems.

Of the close-ended schemes, a majority are Monthly Income Schemes, specifically aimed at the retired and aged investors, giving the latter an assured level of income with a total safety of capital. Among the close-ended ones, the Monthly Income Schemes with Extra Bonus and Growth benefits seem to be more popular with the investors.

For domestic investors, the UTI introduced a growth-oriented mutual fund known as "Mastershares" in September 1986. The scheme was very popular, attracting funds of Rs. 1.58 billion against the original target of Rs. 500 million. The NAV of master-shares has moved up and down many times since then, but is even quoted below par value of Rs. 10, many times before its closure.

Offshore Funds

The Unit Trust of India took the initiative of entering the international arena by launching the close-ended 'India Fund', in 1986, providing an opportunity for non-resident Indians and other foreign individuals and institutions to make portfolio investments in the Indian capital market. The fund is quoted on the London Stock Exchange.

This was followed in July 1988 by the 'India Growth Fund', also close-ended, and quoted on the New York Exchange. The issue price for the fund is $10 and the NAV and the current quotations are substantially higher. The initial subscriptions to the two funds were limited to £128 million $60 million, respectively. There are presently more than six offshore funds set up since 1984, by the UTI whose market value has crossed 1 billion by end January 2000. There are of course many other offshore funds, set up by SBI, IDBI and other public sector units.

SBI Mutual Fund

The SBI Markets Limited, SBI's merchant banking and leasing arm, floated the SBI Mutual Fund (SBIMF) as manager and trustee in 1987. The SBIMF has so far developed many schemes for the benefit of the domestic investing public: Magnum Regular Income Scheme (MRIS), 1987, Magnum Tax Saving Scheme (MTSS) 1988-89, Magnum Regular Income Scheme (MRIS) 1989 and Magnum Monthly Income Scheme (MMIS) 1989 (MTSS) 1990, (MRIS) 1990 etc. The last mentioned scheme was kept open for more than a month. All the four schemes are basically income-oriented in nature, although an element of capital appreciation is built into them. As the name itself suggests, MTSS 1988-89 provided for a tax rebate of 50% of the amount invested therein under Section 80 CC of the Income Tax Act, 1961, subject to a maximum of Rs. 20,000, inclusive of other investments eligible under this Section.[@] Similarly, the two MRIS conferred on investors a rebate on income up to Rs. 12,000 under Section 80L of the Income-tax Act, 1961. The first three close-ended funds launched by SBIMF in the span of a year and a quarter enabled it to mobilise funds to the tune of Rs. 2.47 billion and created investible resources of about Rs. 2.60 billion by March 1989. There are a number of other Schemes floated by the SBI cap later on.

India Magnum Fund N.V.

Although a relatively new entrant in the mutual fund industry, the SBI Mutual Fund has made remarkable strides in a short span of time. The government has approved the State Bank of India's proposal to launch an off-shore Mutual Fund named "Indian Magnum Fund N.V." This close-ended fund, constituted in Netherlands Antilles, is managed by the SBI Capital Markets Limited, in association with Morgan Stanley Asset Management, New York, a well-known international investment management institution. The targeted amount of mobilisation is US$ 100 million and the duration of the fund is 25 years. It garnered $ 157 million by end-October, 1989, when it was closed.

Other Funds

Another public sector bank to enter the mutual fund field is Canara Bank who, through its subsidiary Canbank Financial Services Limited, has created the Canbank Mutual Fund (CMF). The Canbank Mutual Fund has launched many schemes so far, viz., "Canshare", a growth-oriented fund with no guaranteed fixed return and "Canstock", a purely income-oriented fund on the lines of SBIMF's Magnum 1. Both these close-ended funds have fared well in the market and

@ All the tax exemptions for mutual funds are replaced by one, *viz.*, 20% rebate for an investment of Rs. 10,000 in equity linked schemes, which was also scrapped in 2005-06 Budget proposals.

have declared handsome return to the investors. To cater to the demands of the corporate sector, the CMF floated two other pure money market funds — Cancigo and Cangilt — which are purely liquid funds created to attract the surplus funds of the corporate sector. Other funds called "CanGrowth" and "CanStar" were floated in 1989, for the public investors and a host of other schemes were floated later on.

Close on the heels of these mutual fund companies, the Life Insurance Corporation of India (LIC) has also constituted its own mutual fund named "LIC Mutual Fund" (LICMF). The fund was launched, on June 19, 1989, and many products have been offered for investment. The three schemes opened first for investment are: *(i)* "Dhanashree" close-ended income and growth-oriented scheme, open till October 31, 1989, of units with a face value of Rs. 10 each and a minimum number of units 100, with a guaranteed rate of return of 11% p.a.; *(ii)* "Dhanaraksha" — open-ended recurring investment scheme, the maximum amount of investment under which is Rs. 60,000 (spread over a period of 10 or 15 years), and which offers life and accident cover; *(iii)* "Dhanavriddhi" — an open-ended fixed investment scheme with investment spread over 7 years to 10 years, the starting insurance cover being equal to the amount invested, subject to a maximum of Rs. 40,000. All these schemes of the LICMF are similar to the schemes offered by other mutual funds, with the additional benefit of life and accident insurance cover in the case of "Dhanraksha" and "Dhanavriddhi."

While several mutual funds as above are already in operation, other commercial banks like the Indian Bank, Central Bank of India, Punjab National Bank of Baroda and Bank of India and financial institutions like the General Insurance Corporation of India, have either singly or jointly, taken steps to set up their own mutual funds and their schemes were also in operation. Early in 1992, the Government Policy was changed to allow private sector mutual funds also to operate on equal terms with public sector mutual funds.

Overall Progress in India

The Mutual Fund movement gained momentum in India only since 1987, UTI being the only institution in the field till then. Its performance as well as the response received by the schemes floated SBIMF and CMF — the two initial entrants — in recent years should certainly make one optimistic about the future of this movement. GIC and LIC Mutual Funds are also reportedly evoking good response from the investing public. These developments and the entry of other commercial banks and private corporate sector have shown good potentiality for their growth in India. There are about 467 M.F. Schemes in operation as in March 2005. The MF schemes are now more transparent and data on their investments and their NAV are published regularly by the AMFI.

Investment Policy

The investment policy of the fund would depend on the objectives of the fund, namely, income, growth or both. Normally, one-third of the funds is used for investment in the money market and government bond market where the liquidity is good. Of the rest, the bulk of the amount would be invested in fixed interest securities like debentures (CD or NCD etc.) or fixed deposits with companies, if the objective of the fund is income. If, on the other hand, the objective is growth, the bulk of the investment would be in equities and new issues. The relative proportions would depend on the importance of the objectives of income and growth. Only a small proportion of the funds would be kept as bank deposits or Treasury Bills or in money market for conversion into ready cash.

Steps to Popularise Mutual Funds

One of the major shortcomings of the existing funds appears to be that a significant share of the funds mobilised comes from the corporate sector. Fiscal reliefs available to the corporate sector on dividends from mutual funds have been encouraging corporate investment in such funds. There is obviously a lot to be done to attract the individual investor. Commercial banks with their vast network of branches and close relationship with the household sector are, of course, very well-placed to fulfil this function. The UTI is also geared to cater more to the individual investors. UTI was restructured in 2002 with FIs as sponsoring agencies, with no past liabilities attached to them and the Government getting out of it. The UTI would not resort to schemes with guaranteed incomes. All the future schemes would be NAV based.

With a view to making the mutual fund schemes more popular with the small investors, the Government of India has permitted various tax concessions to the investors. The Equity Linked Savings Scheme (ELSS) implemented by the Mutual Funds, is a further step in this direction. Investment in this scheme will have the benefit of tax concession. The LIC and GIC have additional benefits of insurance cover to a certain extent. Now, the income from investment in the UTI and other funds is treated on equal terms for tax purposes. A uniform treatment to all the mutual funds and even to venture capital funds is given so that there is a level playing field for all and performance comparisons are meaningful.

Response of NRIs

The response of Non-Resident Indians to the mutual fund movement in India has been so far rather lukewarm, though the off-shore funds launched by the UTI and SBI have been well-received by them. The sale of units to NRIs, represented less than 10% of the total sales of UTI. The outstanding amount in NRI unit-holders' accounts is also relatively small.

For All MFs Common Rules

While the RBI guidelines for mutual funds set up by banks are welcome, banks which have floated mutual funds want that the regulatory framework for operating such funds should be common for all agencies wishing to float such funds and that there should be no discrimination between the different government agencies. SEBI has also started regulating mutual funds registered with RBI. The guidelines issued by SEBI in 1992 are set out in Annexure II, while those of RBI are in Annexure I.

The banks are given permission for their mutual funds, set up by them to underwrite public issues just as the Unit Trust or insurance companies. They also are permitted to participate in the inter-bank call money market since 1990.

Since bank mutual funds are to be constituted as trusts, it was felt that these funds should be treated as trustee securities and entitled to all the tax benefits available to such securities. In such case, the income on such funds are totally tax-free as in the case of UTI.[@]

All incomes of Mutual funds have now been exempt from taxation as in the case of UTI. Recently, mutual funds have been permitted to operate in the money market and the RBI has announced its willingness to permit banks to set up money market mutual funds, in 1995.

Advantages of Mutual Funds

Mutual funds increase the mobilisation of investible funds of the community by pooling the resources of a large number of small savers for corporate investment. Mutual Funds reduce the risk of shareholding for the holder, by evolving schemes, suitable to the preferences of the saver looking for either income or capital gains. The mutual funds develop the expertise by setting up a professionally-managed structure which would look after the needs of the investing public for gainful and low-risk investment.

Some mutual funds are also area specific to an objective or purpose specific e.g., Japan Fund, India Fund etc., which necessarily provide access to foreign investors into domestic securities of particular economies.

The mutual funds can promote the investment habit of the rural and semi-urban areas and increase the proportion of investing public and of the shareholding population in India.

Structure and Growth of M.F. Industry

The MF industry in India started in 1964 with the Unit Trust of India (UTI). It has mobilised the savings of the public for investment in the stock and capital markets. The resources mobilized by it in 1970-71 was only Rs.18 crores which grew to Rs.4,548 crores by 1999-2000. After that, there are more repayments than inflows due to investment mismanagement by UTI., due to which the UTI was split into two units — one in the public sector taken over by the Government and the other in the private sector regulated by the SEBI.

@ A mutual fund is exempted from tax payment under Section 10 (23D), provided it distributes 90% of its profits.

This industry was thrown open to the Public sector banks and the Financial institutions by an amendment to the BR ACT in 1983. In the nineties, there were nine such public sector mutual funds, run by banks and LIC, GIC and IDBI. They also ran into difficulties and by 2005-06, there were only 4 such MFs excluding the UTI. When they started operations in 1987-88, they raised Rs.250 crores which increased to Rs.14,947 crores by 2006-07. The net resources mobilised by them in 2007-08 was Rs. 20,497 crore, which declined to Rs. 5,721 crore in 2008-09 (SEBI data). The reasons for such fatalities are the bearish market conditions and lack of the needed expertise among the public sector human resources.

This industry was thrown open later in 1992-93 to private and foreign sectors and a number of companies jointly or singly with the foreign counterparts, have started operations and they proved their efficiency much more than the other agencies existing in the industry. At one time, there were 37 such agencies doing business as MFs which came down to 22 private sector agencies by 2006-07. They started operations in 1993 when they mobilized the resources from the public of about Rs.1,559 crores which went up to Rs. 42,977 crores by 2005-06. The performance of the private sector was far superior in terms of raising resources and in management of the investment funds. Their share in the total mobilization of resources was raised from nil in 1992-93 to about 80 to 90% of the total mobilization, during 2005 to 2007.

In 2007, the MF industry in India was ranked as the 24th in the world with $88 billion assets. This was an improvement due to the booming economy, and shinning financial markets in India in the recent past with a growth rate of 7% to 9% in GDP. The U.S. stands first in the world MF industry followed by Luxembourg and France. India's performance is not rated well, despite all bullish factors in the economy due to Government policies, tax structure and risk aversion of the average Indian. There is large potential for growth of this industry in India, which may hopefully be realized by the entry of Pension funds into the capital markets by the passage of the pending bill called the Pension Bill now in the Parliament.

Regulation of Mutual Funds

Leaving aside UTI, which has been existing since 1964, two Financial Institutions, namely, LIC and GIC has set up their Mutual Funds in 1989 and 1990 respectively. Since 1987, starting with SBI, a number of Public Sector banks have set up Mutual Funds, which have been regulated by the RBI. The Mutual Funds of LIC and GIC were regulated by the Investment Division of Ministry of Finance.

After SEBI got legal status in 1992, all Mutual Funds have been brought under its supervision, except the Money Market Mutual Funds and offshore Mutual Funds, which are also bound by the guidelines of RBI, and Ministry of Finance. Nearly Rs. 60,000 crores were collected by UTI and an estimated Rs. 30,000 crores by various Mutual Funds set up since 1987, as contributions of savings from investors. The Mutual Fund movement has got a startling momentum by 1990-91 but there was a setback to this in 1992, following the securities scam in which a number of banks and Mutual funds were involved in Financial irregularities. Since then, the SEBI has tightened its regulations.

The new guidelines were laid down in respect of Mutual Funds for authorisation and licensing of all Mutual Funds and each of their individual Schemes. As visualised by the Government Policy, not only public sector, but private sector and joint sector mutual funds are now permitted and licensed by the SEBI. All mutual funds including bank sponsored MMMFs and many schemes of UTI are brought under the regulation of SEBI and Securities Appellate Authority.

The legal structure and organisation of Mutual Funds as laid down by SEBI guidelines is as follows: (see next page)

Authorisation of Existing Mutual Funds

Licensing and authorisation of existing mutual funds was initiated by the SEBI, along with the licensing of Merchant Bankers, even before the SEBI has got legal status in April 1992. As mutual funds were set up by public sector banks, they were authorised by the RBI and each of their schemes were to be approved by the latter. But gradually SEBI took over the responsibility of authorising and supervising them except in the case of pure Money Market Mutual Funds or the off-shore Mutual Funds which are governed by the regulations of RBI and Ministry of Finance.

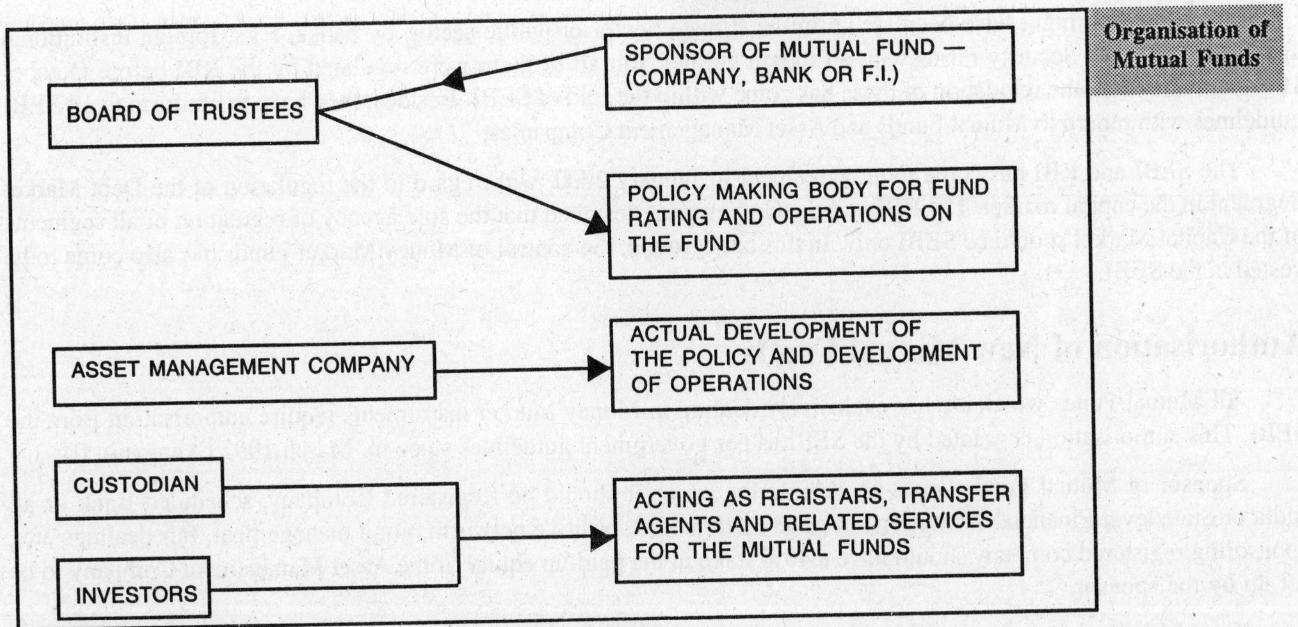

Money Market Mutual Funds (MMMFs)

The MMMFs can be set up by scheduled Commercial Banks and FIs, or companies as defined under Section 4A of Companies Act. The limit for these Funds set up by banks is at 2% of the sponsoring bank's fortnightly average aggregate deposits. They are intended to operate only in money market instruments like commercial paper and as they should encourage individual participation in these funds, only individuals and NRIs can subscribe to the Schemes of MMMFs. It was extended to companies also later. The minimum locking period was 30 days but was reduced to 15 days in 1998 and no minimum return should be guaranteed. The bank's reserve requirements will not apply to these funds, as per the Guidelines. During 2000, these funds were brought under the sole supervision of SEBI. They are to be separate entities as Trusts. They are given some further concessions like cheque writing facility under the Monetary Policy Statement for 1999-2000 for gilt Funds and Liquid Income Schemes. Later on, the RBI has also allowed the Private Sector to set up MMMFs. RBI guidelines for MMMFs are set out in Annexure - III.

MMMF's Regulation

It was decided in October 1999 that RBI will cease to regulate the Money Market Mutual Funds and that SEBI will take over the regulation from them like other Capital Market Mutual Funds. MMMFs, registered with RBI will have to seek SEBI registration from October 1999. The banks and Public Financial institutions, which floated MMMFs were asked not to offer Money Market deposit accounts. If the banks want to operate MMMFs, they have to set up asset Management Company with an investment of Rs. 10 crores. Besides they have to follow the Trust Structure, necessary for setting up of Mutual Funds, as per the SEBI guidelines.

This change was necessitated to bring all the MMMFs on par with Liquid Funds, floated by regular Mutual Funds. They will no longer be required to observe a lock in period of 15 days, as hitherto, under the RBI guidelines, uniformly all Mutual Funds are brought under a single window control of the SEBI. The deposits of banks are insulated from the deposit accounts of MMMFs which separates banking business from the Mutual Fund business.

The banks will have to set up separate outfits of a Mutual Fund and observe all the SEBI guidelines, if they want to operate any schemes of Money Market Mutual Funds. They have also to take prior permission of RBI before approaching SEBI. This is a healthy development in many ways, as the SEBI can now regulate on an even level all the Mutual Funds, whether they are operating in the Money Market or capital market. Secondly, banks will have to separate their money market mutual fund business and follow the regular mutual fund route to operate any schemes of deposit accounts for money market operations. Control will also be strengthened and the growth of MMMF business will be on healthier grounds.

It has been decided to allow cheque writing facility to gilt funds and to those liquid funds' Income schemes of Mutual Funds, which predominantly invest in Money Market instruments upto not less than 80% of their corpus, subject to the same safeguards, as prescribed for MMMFs. The RBI was expected to issue operating guidelines in this regard.

The MMMFs might have been set up in the Private Sector or public sector, by banks, F.I.s, foreign institutional agencies or Foreign Security Firms with an Indian partner. But all of them were regulated by the RBI before October 1999. But after that, the regulation of these has come within the fold of SEBI. Besides, they have to conform to all SEBI guidelines with regard to Mutual Funds and Asset Management Companies.

The SEBI and RBI has come to an agreement in January 2000, with regard to the regulation of the Debt Market Segment in the capital market. The RBI and the Government designed that the sole agency of regulation of all segments of the Capital Market should be SEBI only. In this background, the control of Money Market Funds has also come to be vested in the SEBI.

Authorisation of New Mutual Funds

All Mutual Funds which are not exclusively dealing in Money Market instruments require authorisation from the SEBI. This authorisation is granted by the SEBI as per government guidelines since in March 1992 (Annexure II).

Sponsor of Mutual Fund should be eligible for which it should be Registered Company, scheduled Bank or all India or State level Financial Institutions of good track record, positive networth, good management, fair dealings etc., sponsoring registered company should have a 40% stake in the paid-up equity of the Asset Management Company to be set up by the sponsor.

The AMC should be a private or public limited company either listed or not. The AMC may be a new or an existing company, carrying on the business of merchant banking, venture capital, leasing or any other financial services. If the sponsoring company is having a stake of 40% of its net worth as required, the rest can be brought in by public issue, NRIs or foreign equity participation as permitted by the RBI. The AMC should not invest funds in any company under any of its schemes managed by it for which it has provided any financial service. The SEBI should approve the Memorandum and Articles of Association of the AMC. The AMC itself will be approved by the SEBI based on the MAA (Memorandum and Articles of Association), its business lines and subject to the restrictions on its business imposed under the guidelines.

The guidelines lay down the authorisation process subject to the following conditions:

(A) Sponsors to be eligible should be a Private or Public Limited Company, bank or F.I. The sponsoring agency should set up a Trustee.

(B) Trustee should be eligible and the Trust Deed should have the approval of SEBI. Eligibility of trustee depends on the composition of the Board of Trustees, their earlier experience and expertise, professional qualifications, etc., of each of the members of the Board, their past track record and organisation and management of Trustee Company and subject to the SEBI's approval of MAA. The Trust Board would lay down the policy.

The SEBI while granting the authorisation for the setting up of a Mutual Fund, would also approve the AMC and Custodian as part of the package. The Custodian should be different from the AMC which would manage the Fund. The Sponsor and Trustee Companies cannot act as Custodian. If the sponsor has a custodian division, it can act for other Mutual Funds not set up by the sponsor. There should be no areas of conflict between the interest of Mutual Funds, for which a custodian is rendering services. The investment criteria, expenses and income distribution etc. are all controlled by SEBI, through their guidelines, given in the Appendix.

The approval of any agency as Custodian would depend upon its track record, experience, quality of service transparency and computerisation and other infrastructual facilities. The SEBI, may stipulate any conditions for the Custodian to act for the mutual fund in question or for one or more Mutual Funds.

Every scheme of Mutual Fund as much as the Mutual Fund should be approved by the SEBI. Every Mutual Fund should have designated a compliance officer who would deal with SEBI and is responsible for compliance with SEBI guidelines and conditions.

All applications for such approvals should be in specified forms either for authorisation of Mutual Fund or any of its schemes. It will thus be seen that the authorisation of Mutual Fund would involve approval of the sponsor, the trustee, AMC and the Custodian all together, who are responsible for the management of Public Funds.

Mutual Funds Present Status

Many private sector mutual funds have entered the fray but the performance was far from satisfactory with the market price of many schemes quoting below the NAV. This NAV is calculated by dividing the market value of all investments + Accrued income and Receivables + other assets minus liabilities and accrued expenses except unit capital and Reserves by the number of units outstanding. Valuation norms for calculation of NAV are laid down by SEBI. Mutual funds have to deduct tax at source, if they pay a dividend above Rs. 10,000 P.A. at a rate of 15% for individuals and 20% for companies. These tax provisions frequently changed from year to year. The performance of private sector, however, improved and surpassed that of public sector MFs, since 1999.

Mutual funds can incur initial expenses of 6% of total funds raised and 3% every year. They have to pay 90% of their net income as dividend to unit holders.

Mutual funds are now permitted to invest upto 100% of mobilised funds in money market instruments for six months from their subscription and again revert back to 100% in these instruments six months before redemption. The details of these investment and accounting guidelines are in Annexure I and II.

In March 2009, there were about 32 Mutual Funds, of which there are about 28 Mutual Funds in private sector. There are always fresh funds coming in and some funds closed due to redemption while there are some under repurchase facilities, as in the case of open ended funds. Close ended funds should normally be listed on stock exchanges, except when there is a repurchase provision.

In 2005 the mutual funds were able to invest in exchange traded funds of major world indices. The ceiling of aggregate investments by mutual funds in overseas investments was kept at 10% of the Mutual Funds.

The face value of mutual fund units is normally Rs. 10, but sometimes Rs. 100. For those listed and traded, there is a market price, which is different from Net Asset value. As the return for the long-term investors is more, than the total return on investment by the total funds' investment performance, since launch, the investor's annual return on such schemes may not be higher than 13-15%. But some schemes have done relatively well such as Master Share and some relatively poor such as Master Gain. But by 2002, Master share was quoted below par as in the case of many Mutual Fund Schemes. U.S. 64 of UTI was almost dismantled and has undergone many changes, UTI had to be rescued by the government and sponsors.

The SEBI has set up a committee on Mutual funds late in 1995 and its recommendations were available in 1996. These relate to standardisation of NAV, calculation, exemption from listing for some schemes, management remuneration to AMCs, accounting practices, fixation of a band of 7% between purchase and repurchase prices and standardisation of such practices, etc. These aim at healthy growth of mutual fund business in India. Early in 1998, the AMCs have been asked by SEBI to double their Networth from Rs. 5 crores to Rs. 10 crores. SEBI (Mutual Fund) Regulations were amended to permit MFs to trade in derivatives and trading/investments in Foreign Markets for portfolio balancing. SEBI laid guidelines for valuation of unlisted companies and for treatment of non-performing assets by MFs. They can invest upto 10% of their funds in foreign listed companies.

Taxation and M.Fs

So far as the MF is concerned, under section 10 (23D) of the Act, any income received by the MF is exempt from tax. Under Section 115 R, income distributed to a unit holder or investor of the Mutual Fund shall be charged to tax at a flat rate of 10% plus surcharge if any, payable by the MF. But for funds, investing more than 50% in equity or equity related instruments the dividend distributed by MF is exempted from the above (10% plus surcharge) for three years from April 1, 1999.

The steep increase in tax rate on the income distribution by Mutual Funds from 11 to 22% in respect of debt oriented schemes and the withdrawal of the benefits under Sections 54 EA, & EB to Mutual Funds are likely to have a negative impact on mutual fund industry, from 2000-01. From 2002-03 income distributed by MFs and in the hands of investors has become taxable; but was withdrawn later.

SEBI has been notifying from time to time regulations governing the Mutual Funds their operations, their advertisement, meeting of Trustees etc. with a view to better disclosure, investor protection and better services. For example, it is notified that any delay in repayment of moneys under schemes, which have matured by Mutual Funds is subject to penal interest rate.

So far as the unit holders are concerned, no tax is deducted at source and under Section 10 (33) of the I.T. Act, any income received by them will be exempt from income tax in their hands. Any capital gain of a long-term nature (if the same is held by investor for more than 12 months) will be subject to the following rates of tax.

Resident Individual & HUF—	10% plus surcharge
Partnership Firms/Indian Companies	20% plus surcharge
Non-resident Indians	20% plus surcharge
For FFIs/OCB/FIIs,etc.	10% (under Section 115 AB)

Any capital gains of a short-term nature, if the units of MF are held for less than 12 month should be added to the income of the unit holder and taxed at the following rates, which are maximum rates

Resident Individual & HUF—	30% plus surcharge of 3%
Partnership Firms/Indian Companies	30% plus surcharge
Non-resident Indians	30% (No surcharge)
F.F.I.s.	30% (No surcharge)
Foreign Companies	30% plus surcharge of 2.5%

For residents, there is no tax deduction at source, as per the Act and the Regulations under the Act. For Non-residents, the TDS on capital gains of short-term nature is 30% and of long-term nature at 20%. For Foreign Companies, the TDS on Capital gains of short-term nature is at 30% and of long-term nature at 20%. The only exemption from TDS or taxation of capital gains is in respect of Tax saving equity linked schemes of M.Fs. Capital gains of long term nature was exempt from tax under the Budget for 2003-04. The later Budgets have given more tax concessions and investment avenues abroad for their better performance.

Wealth Tax

The units of MFs. are not treated as wealth and hence no wealth tax is payable.

Gift Tax

The units of any value can be gifted without attracting gift tax by both the donor and the donee. The Gift Tax Act 1958 was repealed in October 1998, whereby no gift tax is now payable.

Saga of Fortunes of MFs

In 1964 and upto 1987-88 UTI strode the scheme like a colossus, alone in the field as a single public sector Mutual Fund. By 1990-91, there were 5 public sector mutual funds already set up, controlling a market share of mutual fund business of 10% in the country. By 1993-94, the private and foreign sector mutual funds started their foray into this business. The International names, Morgan Stanley, Tanners, Jardine Fleming, Merril Lynch, Prudential etc. have appeared on the scene of Mutual Funds.

As on March end 2009, there were 4 public sector mutual funds and about 28 private sector mutual funds, in addition to U.T.I. There was a large scale erosion in the market value of investments by U.T.I., due to their mismanagement and Scams. Net resources mobilised by UTI fell from a peak of Rs. 11,057 crores in 1992-93 to a net outflow of Rs. 6,314 crores in 1995-96. The net amount mobilised from public picked up again from a low of Rs. 170 crores in 1998-99 to Rs. 1999 crores in 2000-01. The Table 37.1 presents a picture of resource mobilisation by all mutual Funds over the last decade.

Table: Net Resource Mobilisation by MFs

(in Rs. crores)

Year	UTI	Public Sector MFs	Private Sector MFs	Total
1990-91	4553	2956	—	7,509
1993-94@	9297	385	1560	11,243
	(82.7)	(3.4)	(13.9)	(100)
2000-01	1999	1623	9,717	13,339
	(15.0)	(12.2)	(72.8)	(100)
2001-02	-7284	1330	13977	8,023
	(–90.8)	(16.5)	(174.2)	(100)
2003-04	1050	3762	42,873	47,684
	(2.2)	(7.9)	(89)	(100)
2006-07	7326	7258	76687	91,271
	(8.1%)	(7.9%)	(84.0)	(100)
2007-08	10678	9964	163356	183998
	(5.8)	(5.4)	(88.8)	(100)
2008-09	–4112	10447	–28685	–22355

@ Private sector mutual Funds were permitted from 1993 only. Figures in brackets are percentages to total.

It will be seen from the above Table that the share of UTI fell from a high of 82.7% in 1993-94 to a low of 6% in 2007-08, while the share of private sector mutual Funds rose from 13.9% in 1993-94 to 89% in 2008-09. The Association of Mutual Funds (AMFI) publishes these data regularly. The AMFI is also reported to have arranged for preparing an Index on mutual Funds performance, based on their schemes. Rating of mutual Funds is also proposed.

UTI whose share was 95% of the market in 1995-96, declined to 60% in 1998-99 and further to 15% in 2000-01. There are now about 30 AMCs with an asset base of Rs. 9 lakh crores in May 2010. As at end Nov.1999, total Investment funds of all Mutual Funds were Rs. 9205 crores which rose to Rs. 100,594 crores by March 2002, and Rs. 4,17,299 crores by March 2009.

The trend in the industry, as in general, was towards financial strengthening, mergers, takeovers etc. The weaker ones are either closed or taken over during the recent years. Equity Funds started looking up and showed better performance in 1999, while debt funds were popular between 1996 to 1998. That was the worst period for equity funds as stock and primary markets were in doldrums. The years 1999 and 2000 saw again the revival of equity Cult and hey days for Mutual Funds to thrive, as Stock and Capital markets turned bullish and economy turned into a recovery phase.

The minimum paid up capital of AMC was raised to Rs. 10 crores, but many foreign AMCs were set up more recently with 5 to 10 times the minimum required. An asset base of Rs. 500-700 crores was felt necessary for an AMC to break even. Many public sector mutual funds like those of Bank of India, Bank of Baroda, Canbank GIC etc., have had difficult times. The process of mergers and restructuring helped some to revive. But the private and foreign mutual funds, have fared better than public sector Mutual Funds.

The tax sops in 1999-2000 Budget have helped the mutual funds. The revival of stock markets and low interest rates and economic recovery have boosted the equity sentiment. But it was temporary and equity markets were depressed in 2000 to 2002 and so were the Mutual Funds. There was a boom and recovery from 2004 onwards, when the MFs have also fared better.

The asset base of Mutual Funds has increased by 5 times over the decade. The annual growth rate is about 30%. Total assets by MFs stood at Rs. 7.68 lakh crores as at the end April 2010. The trend to merger and takeover has helped the private sector mutual funds, while restructuring and financial strengthening has aided the public sector mutual funds. The competition to the public sector from the private sector was a healthy trend to boost the industry. The year 1999 saw the turning point in the mutual Fund industry and the new millennium was ready for a take off in this industry. Investor education, change in the stock market sentiment and new distribution channels like banking on internet, Demat form of shareholding have all helped the industry.

Stock Lending by Mutual Funds

The Mutual Funds have approached the SEBI approved intermediaries to enter into agreements to operate stock lending scheme. The Mutual Funds which showed interest in equity lending are the Canbank, Reliance, Kothari and Alliance Capital. They want to earn additional income by activising their idle core investments in their custody for badla lending of securities. This type of lending has risks associated with it namely reinvestment risk and potential asset-liability mismatch.

Lending increases portfolio returns on the stocks lent. But potential losses may be there due to over exposure to low credit quality clients. Lending Securities to such clients is a real risk. When the M.F. lends securities, they are transferred into the name of the intermediary or the borrowing broker, while all corporate benefits continue to accrue to the M.F. Thus the MF benefits from two streams of income — one received for lending securities and another for reinvesting the cash proceeds so received. As against these benefits, the MF will have to face liquidity risk, reinvestment risk and expose the funds to the credit and interest rate risks arising out of stock lending and consequential inflow of cash. There are cases when lending institutions have lost their funds, as in the case of Harris Trust & Savings Bank, and Mellon Bank in the U.S.A.

Latest Trends

The performance of mutual Funds and the investor confidence in them have received a setback since 1996, particularly due to poor performance of U.T.I. and many scams involving UTI and banks. The nexus between banks and brokers has struck a blow to the stock and capital markets and led to a negative resource mobilisation during 1995-97 by all mutual Funds, mainly due to the U.T.I. Since then, the performance of all public sector mutual funds showed a marked deterioration, while the performance of private sector mutual funds revealed a relatively better performance. The main depressing factor was the poor stock market conditions, following scams and poor asset management in UTI and public sector mutual funds, particularly during 1997-2001.

The U.S. 64 of UTI which was the Pioneering Scheme of UTI was in deep trouble and recorded a massive loss of market value of assets. Three committees, namely those of Deepak Parekh, Malegam and Tarapore have made drastic recommendations for privatisation and for restructuring of U.T.I., during 1998-2001. The Government have accepted these recommendations and a scheme of protecting investor interests and of bringing UTI under the surveillance of SEBI like other Mutual Funds by change of UTI Act or its repeal has been formally announced by the Government, early in 2002. UTI will now have a Trust, Sponsors and AMCs like other mutual Funds in India under SEBI governance.

UTI Act of 1963 was replaced in October 2002 and UTI was restructured into two organisations UTI-I and UTI-II. UTI-I encompasses U.S. 64 scheme and other assured return schemes to be continued as they are. UTI-II has all the other NAV based schemes to be run on professional lines under the supervision of SEBI.

The SEBI regulations of mutual Funds were liberalised and streamlined from time to time. Mutual Funds were allowed to invest in mortgage backed securities of investment grade and above which would help housing finance since April 2000. Open ended Funds can now invest upto 5% of their net asset value in equity instruments of unlisted companies. Investment limit in such equities was kept unchanged at 10% for close ended funds. The maximum limit for investment in respect of open ended funds was raised from 5% to 10% of NAV in listed companies, in June 2000. The SEBI has also banned mutual Funds from making schemes with assured returns or make any claims on the basis of their past performance.

The norms relating to code of conduct of M.F.s, criteria for classification of NPAs and their disclosures, treatment of income accrued or NPAs and provisions to be made, disclosure of NPAs in half-yearly portfolio reports were streamlined. The period of initial offer of a scheme and despatch of certificates, standardisation of format, treatment of unclaimed deposits and the standards of trading by the employees were tightened. Disclosure and transparency standards relating to the Asset Management Companies (AMC's) were also made stricter. The SEBI was given draconian powers of search and seizure and imposition of high penalties on listed companies and the broker firms.

The UTI's structural reorganisation took place in February 2003 with its splitting up into two identities namely UTI-I and UTI-II. The UTI-I has taken over all fixed income schemes like *U.S.* 64 and UTI-II have all NAV based schemes. The UTI-II is sponsored by FIs like LIC, SBI etc. and becomes independent of Govt., but run by Private sector professional AMCs and like other mutual Funds comes under SEBI guidelines and supervision and regulation of SEBI. The UTI-I, however, continues to be under Govt. control and responsibility.

U.S. 64 scheme which suspended sale and repurchases in June 2002, following the revalation of many irregularities and scams and was wound up in its original form in May 2003, with the Government bearing its liabilities and losses. It took a new form of (UTI-II) NAV based scheme with only sales from June 2003 and no repurchases. It is quoted and listed on the Stock exchanges on the basis of its market determined NAV. Trading takes place and liquidity is imparted to the units by sale in the market.

EVALUATION OF THE PERFORMANCE OF THE MFS

The evaluation of the performance of the MFs can be graded in two respects — one in respect of the funds mobilization from the public and second in respect of the portfolio performance of funds deployed by the MFs. More important than these two aspects is the contribution of the MFs to the growth of the economy through the deployment of funds in financial markets.

The resource mobilization as seen in the data given above in the chapter is no doubt good but if it is due to large funds contributed by the corporates and not direct from the individual savers, it is no achievement. In the absence of the data of details and breakdowns, it is difficult to arrive any worthwhile conclusion in this respect. Besides, there is no consistent growth of funds mobilized by the MFs, as there are variations from year to year and in some years the resource mobilized was also poor due to depressed market conditions and poor performance of the MFs themselves. If there is good mobilization in the last few years, it was due to private sector MFs and booming market conditions. In the year of 2007-08 of the total net mobilization of Rs. 1,83,998 crores, about Rs. 1,63,356 crores was due to private sector MFs. The first conclusion is therefore that Funds mobilization *prima facie* was poor but for the private sector MFs.

The MF contribution to the growth of the stock and capital markets is however very substantial, next only to the FFIs and FIIs. About Rs. 5.05 lakh crores of funds were the assets of the MFs which are deployed in the markets as assets as at end March 2008. These funds are used for the portfolio management for and on behalf of the public, which leads to the growth of the corporate sector and through them of the economy. The BSE market capitalization has grown by 17%, while the growth of the economy in 2006-07 was by 9%. The BSE Sensex has grown by 16% in 2006-07 on top of a rise of 74% in the preceding year — a total of 90% in two years. But the returns given by the MFs to the public was much less than this. This shows that the MFs in India could not outperform the market return, as expected in theory. If some of the funds could do it, they are only the foreign controlled and managed MFs in India.

Following from the above analysis, it was also clear that the portfolio management by MFs was far from satisfactory except for a few foreign controlled and managed MFs. The reason for this state of affairs is that the expertise and experience in this line by the personnel handling in the AMCs has been far from satisfactory. This conclusion is buttressed by the fact that the weak are weeded out during the last few years. In the public sector, UTI has the distinction of mismanagement of funds under the US 64 during 1999-2001, necessitating the Government interference in the UTI affairs and splitting the UTI into two units — one taken over by the Government and other privatized to be controlled by the professionals in the FIs. Of the nine public sector MFs originally set up, five were wound up or merged with others. Of the 45 private sector MFs functioning at one time, there are only 28 functioning as in March 2009, showing the woefully high mortality rate among the MFs. The reason was their poor performance leading to lack of viability and inadequate public support to them. The above facts clearly evidence the truth of lack of expertise among the AMCs doing the portfolio management for MFs. But the MFs have good potential.

ANNEXURE I

RBI GUIDELINES ON MUTUAL FUNDS

Some of the commercial banks in the public sector have set up mutual funds and a few others are in the process of setting them up. On an examination of the operations of the mutual funds already functioning, it was considered necessary to issue guidelines on certain important aspects, as indicated below, with a view to their orderly functioning and in the interest of ensuring investor confidence.

Constitution and Management

(i) Every "mutual fund" shall be constituted as a Trust under the Indian Trust Act and the sponsoring bank should appoint a Board of Trustees to manage it. The Board of Trustees should have at least two outside trustees, i.e., those who are not connected with the sponsoring bank and who are persons of ability and integrity and have the proven capacity in dealing with problems relating to investment and investor protection. The overall superintendence, direction, control and management of the affairs and business, of the funds should vest in the Board of Trustees.

(ii) The day-to-day management of the schemes under the fund, as may be delegated by the Board of Trustees, should be looked after by a full-time Executive Trustee who should not be concurrently discharging any other responsibility in the convened bank. If the management of the mutual fund has been assigned to the bank's subsidiary, the full time executive trustee should not be holding any other position.

(iii) An "arm's length" relationship should be maintained between the sponsor bank and the Board of Trustees who manage the mutual fund and care should be taken that in putting through the transactions, there is no clash of interest between the sponsor bank and the beneficiaries under the schemes of its mutual fund. In case the management of mutual fund has been entrusted to a subsidiary of the bank, similar care should be exercised by the latter to avoid any clash of interest between itself and the beneficiaries under the scheme of the mutual fund.

(iv) *(a)* The sponsor bank's contribution to the corpus of the fund should be a minimum of Rs. 25 lakhs or such higher amount as may be specified by the Reserve Bank. The corpus may be converted at a later date into subscription to any of the schemes of the fund with the approval of the Board of Trustees of the fund. No additional contribution should be made by the sponsor bank to the corpus without the prior approval of the Reserve Bank.

(b) In addition to the contribution to the corpus, the sponsor bank should contribute and maintain in each of the fund's schemes by way of its stake an amount equivalent to 1 per cent of the total amount outstanding. This stipulation will not however, apply to special schemes wherein the sponsor bank cannot participate.

(v) Banks should obtain the Reserve Bank's prior approval before announcing any scheme of a mutual fund, irrespective of whether it is identical or not to any of the earlier schemes approved by the Reserve Bank.

Investment Objectives and Policies

(vi) The investment objectives and policies of the mutual fund should be laid down in the trust deed and every scheme to be launched by the fund must be in accord with such broad objectives and policies and the rules and regulations framed in conditions therewith.

(vii) While inviting subscription from the public, the mutual fund should make statement of the investment objectives of the fund and its investment policies, besides the terms and conditions of the scheme.

(viii) The subscription amounts collected by mutual funds are primarily intended to be channelised into the capital market instruments like government and other trustee securities, share/debentures of public limited companies, bonds of public sector undertakings, etc. and except for the extent indicated in (ix) below, the mutual funds should not undertake direct or indirect lending, portfolio/funds management, underwriting, bills discounting, money market operations, etc., which are essentially banking/merchant banking functions.

(ix) There is, however, no objection to the mutual funds investing the amounts initially collected for a scheme in the money market instruments, rediscounting of bills, or bank deposits for periods not exceeding six months. The mutual funds may also invest their temporary surplus fund in similar instruments up to not more than 25 per cent of their total investible funds. Such short-term/ temporary investments can, however, be made only if they are permissible under the Charter of the Fund.

(x) The mutual funds should invariably take delivery of scrips purchased and, in the case of scrips sold, give delivery thereof to the purchaser. The scrips purchased should be transferred in the fund's name.

(xi) In no event should a mutual fund make short sale/purchase of securities or carry over the transactions from one settlement period to the next settlement period.

(xii) The mutual funds should not make investments in any other unit trust, mutual fund of similar collective investment schemes. The funds should not also invest in the shares, etc. of investment companies/corporations.

Prudential Exposure Ceiling Limits

(xiii) From the point of view of spreading the risk, it is necessary that the portfolio of a fund is diversified. A mutual fund should follow the following prudential guidelines in this regard:

(a) It should not hold, under any one scheme, more than 5 per cent of issued share capital or debenture stock of any company. In case more than one scheme is operated by a fund, such holdings in respect of all its schemes put together should not exceed 15 per cent of the paid-up capital or debenture stock of a company.

(b) The total amount invested by a fund from any of its schemes in the shares, debentures etc. of any specific industry (such as cotton textiles, tea, tyres, etc.) should not exceed 15 per cent of a scheme's fund. This provision will not, however, apply to a scheme which has been floated for investment in one or more specified industries, and a declaration has been made to that effect.

Pricing Policy

(xiv) The maximum spread between the purchase and selling prices of units/shares of any scheme should not be more than 5%.

Income Distribution

(xv) The total cost of managing any scheme under a fund, including management fees and other administrative costs, should be kept within 5 per cent of the total income of the scheme.

(xvi) Income distribution by way of dividend or capitalisation of gains should not be made on the basis of revaluation of the stock holdings or unrealised capital appreciation.

(xvii) Depreciation on investments held and provision for bad or doubtful debts, if any, have to be provided for to the satisfaction of auditors before declaring any dividend. Further, a fund should also create a dividend equalisation fund for each scheme by appropriating a part of its surplus income.

Statement of Accounts and Disclosure

(xviii) A mutual fund should maintain separate accounts of each scheme launched by it, segregating the assets under each scheme. No switching of assets between the schemes should take place, except with the prior approval of the Board of Trustees and at the prevailing market rates.

(xix) The Board of Trustees of mutual funds should prepare an annual statement of accounts in respect of each of the schemes which should contain, *inter alia,* statements of assets and liabilities and income and expenditure accounts duly audited by qualified auditors. Further, an abridged version of the annual account together with the reports of auditors and the Board of Trustees, should be published for the information of subscribers to the concerned scheme.

(xx) The Board of Trustees of mutual funds should disclose the net asset value of each of the schemes and the method of valuation for the benefit of the concerned subscribers.

(xxi) Sponsor banks should furnish to the Reserve Bank duplicate, the following reports on a regular basis:

(a) A half-yearly report indicating the performance of the mutual fund as a whole as well as each scheme.

(b) Audited annul statement of accounts, together with the reports of auditors and the report of the board of trustees.

(c) Scheme-wise details of investment portfolio of the funds, value of such investments, changes in the portfolio since the previous annual report and industry-wise exposure.

SEBI

The following are the guidelines for mutual fund:

Mutual funds have become a major vehicle for mobolisation of savings particularly from the small and household sectors for investment in the stock market. In view of their growing importance in the capital market, their expanding investor base and the decision to allow mutual funds to be set up in the joint and private sectors it has become necessary to evolve a comprehensive set of prudential guidelines for the all-round development and regulation of mutual funds and for ensuring investor protection. These guidelines are laid down below.

Scope

These guidelines shall be applicable to all mutual funds which invest primiarily in the capital market and also partly in money market instruments subject to the following:

(a) Money market mutual funds that would invest exclusively in money market instruments would be regulated by the Reserve Bank of India on the basis of specified guidelines to be laid down by the RBI. However, money market schemes of other mutual funds would be regulated by the Securities and Exchange Board of India. These regulations will be in conformity with the guidelines to be issued by the Reserve Bank for money market mutual funds investing exclusively in money market instruments.

(b) Offshore funds which have non-residential investors and are regulated by the provisions of the countries where these are registered shall be outside the purview of these guidelines. These funds shall continue to be governed by the rules and procedures laid down for the purpose of approving and monitoring their performance by the department of economic affairs, ministry of finance and the government's/RBI's directives on this subject.

(c) Mutual funds with special characteristics, e.g., funds dealing with assets other than securities may be specifically exempted by the government from the purview of these guidelines.

Existing mutual funds should conform to these guidelines within a period of 6 months from the data of issue of these guidelines.

Establishment

Mutual funds shall be authorised for business by the Securities and Exchange Board of India (SEBI).

Mutual funds shall be sponsored by the registered companies with a sound track record, general reputation and fairness in all their business transactions.

Mutual funds shall be established in the form of trusts under the Indian Trusts Act. The sponsoring institution will be free to work out the details regarding the constitution of the Trust.

The Trust shall then be authorised to float one or several different schemes under which units shall be issued to the investors.

Mutual funds shall be operated only by separately established Asset Management Companies.

Asset Management Company (AMC)

Authorisation for Business

AMC shall be authorised for business by SEBI on the basis of the following criteria:

(a) AMCs which are already existing should have a sound track record, general reputation and fairness in all their business transactions.

(b) The directors of AMCs should be persons of high repute and standing having at least 10 years of professional experience in the relevant field such as portfolio management, investment analyis, financial administration, etc.

(c) At least 50% of the board of AMC should be independent directors not connected with the sponsoring organisation.

(d) The AMC should at all times have a minimum net worth of Rs. 5 crores.

SEBI shall approve the memorandum and articles of association of the AMC.

The name of the directors and any subsequent changes must be intimated to SEBI.

SEBI may lay down additional selection criteria or change them from time to time for regulating the expansion of mutual funds in the larger interest of mutual funds industry and healthy growth of capital market.

Except in the case of bank sponsored AMCs where the prior concurrence of RBI would be required, SEBI may withdraw the authorisation granted to any AMC if it is found to be not serving the best interests of investors or of mutual funds industry or of capital market. The board of trustees, of a mutual fund in such cases, should reappoint another AMC or liquidate the mutual fund as may be necessary with 3 months of withdrawal of authorisation of the existing AMC and distribute the proceeds to unit holders.

Restrictions on Business Activities

AMC should not be allowed to act as the trustee of a Unit Trust. In other words, the AMC and the trustee should be two separate legal entities.

AMC should not be permitted to undertake any other business activity than management of mutual funds, and such other activities as financial services constantly, exchange of research and analysis on commercial basis as long as these are not in conflict with the fund management activity itself.

An AMC or its affiliate acting for a fund cannot act the AMC for any other funds. For this purpose, a company is considered as an affiliate if it is a company:

(a) Which directly or indirectly, and by itself, or in combination with other persons exercises a significant control over the AMC.

(b) Over which the AMC directly or indirectly, and by itself or in combination with other persons exercises a significant control.

(c) Over which significant control is exercised directly or indirectly by person or persons or the persons or the relatives of such persons whether by themselves or in combination, as are the same person or persons or the relatives of such person or persons whether by themselves or in combination who exercise significant control over the AMC.

(d) In which any director, officer or employee of the AMC is a director, officer or employee.

(e) Without prejudice to the generality of the above restriction, significant control shall be deemed to exist.

(i) In relation to company, where any person or combination of persons directly or indirectly own, control or hold with power to vote 3 per cent or more of the voting shares of such company.

(ii) In between two companies if the same person or combination of persons directly or indirectly own, control or hold with power to vote 3 per cent or more of the voting shares of each of the two companies.

No person should be a Director of more than one AMC.

No person who is a Director of an AMC should hold the position of a Trustee, or Director in a Trust company, of funds operated by the same AMC.

No person should be a Director/Trustee in more than one Trust Company/Board of Trustees.

Trustees and Trust Companies

Trusteeship functions should be carried out by separately established Trust Companies. Until such companies are formed, existing debenture-trustees, banks and financial institutions may be allowed to act as mutual fund trustees, or a separate Board of Trustees consisting of individuals of sufficient repute and experience may act as mutual fund trustees.

At least 50 per cent of the Board of Trustees shall be independent outside members. They shall not have any affiliation with the sponsoring institution or any of its subsidiaries.

The Trust Company and/or the composition of the Board of Trustees including the eligibility of each member should be intimated to SEBI.

The Trustees should have the responsibility to ensure that managers comply with the Guidelines and report periodically to the investors in the fund that this is the case. This should entail, *inter alia,* the following checks:

* that investments are of the permitted kind and within set limits;
* that the fund's assets are duly protected;
* that transaction in units are properly executed by the manager which may include spot checks on;
* pricing of units;
* payments into and out of the fund;
* internal controls (e.g., for capital adequacy);
* that income due to the fund is properly accounted for;

* that all expenses and charge to the fund are as permitted;
* that distributions from the fund are properly made.

In order to effect these checks the Trustees should have the right to obtain from the AMC all information concerning the operations of the Trust.

The AMC should submit a quarterly report of the functioning of the mutual funds to the Trustees. The Trustees in turn should submit a six-monthly report to the SEBI, and an annul report to the investors in the funds.

Trust Deeds

The sponsor should submit the trust deed to SEBI for prior approval.

The trust deed should include all safeguards considered to be essential for investor protection.

Custodian

The mutual funds shall use the services of a custodian registered with SEBI.

It should be ensured that the custodian should be totally delinked from the AMC.

Each authorised unit trust should be allowed to float different schemes as long as the Asset Management Company concerned meets the required capital adequacy criteria and whose authorisation has not been withdrawn by SEBI for any reason, whatsoever.

Each scheme floated by a mutual fund should have prior registration with SEBI. The asset management company should prepare a prospectus/letter of offer for each scheme and should get it vetted by SEBI before inviting public participation. SEBI shall decide each proposal within 30 days of its receipt, failing which, the scheme may be floated by the fund presuming SEBI's clearance.

Mutual funds should be allowed to start and operate both closed-end and open-end schemes.

The closed-end schemes shall be considered for approval as per the receipt, failing which, the scheme may be floated by the fund presuming SEBI's clearance.

Mutual funds should be allowed to start and operate both closed-end and open-end schemes.

The closed-end schemes shall be considered for approval as per the procedures applicable to capital issues by companies.

For each close-end schemes shall be considered for approval as per the procedures applicable to capital issues by companies.

For each closed-end scheme, the mutual fund should be required to raise atleast Rs. 20 crores and for each open-end scheme, at least Rs. 50 crores. The entire subscription should be refunded to the investors, (a) the minimum amount of Rs. 20 crores or 60% of the targeted amount, whichever is higher, is not raised for a closed-end scheme, or (b) the minimum amount of Rs. 50 crores of 60% of the targeted amount, whichever is higher, is not raised for an open-end scheme.

Mutual funds should not be permitted to keep close-end schemes open for subscription for more than 45 days. For open-end schemes, the first 45 days of the subscription period should be considered for determining the target figure or minimum size.

Mutual funds should provide continuous liquidity. Closed-end schemes should be listed on exchanges. For open-end schemes, mutual funds shall sell and repurchase units at pre-determined prices based on net asset value and such prices should be published at least once in a week.

Each scheme under the same management should have a clearly identified and responsible fund manager.

Investment Limitations

Mutual funds will be allowed to invest only in transferable securities either in the money market or in the capital market, including any privately-placed debentures or securitised debt.

(a) Privately place debentures, securitised debt and other unquoted debt instruments holdings shall not exceed 10% in case of growth funds, and 40% in case of income funds.

(b) All debt instruments must have been rated as investment grade by an approved credit rated, the specific approval of the board of AMC should be taken to become eligible for holding in the portfolio.

Mutual funds should not be allowed to give term loans for any purpose.

No individual scheme of the mutual fund should invest more than five per cent of its corpus in any one company's shares.

No mutual fund under all its schemes should own more than five per cent of any company's paid-up capital carrying voting rights.

No mutual fund under all its schemes taken together should invest more than 10% of its funds in the shares or debentures or other securities of a single company.

No mutual fund under all its schemes taken together should invest more than 15% of its funds in the shares and debentures of any specific industry (such as cotton textile, tea, tyres etc). This provision will not, however, apply to a scheme which has been floated for investments in one or more specified industries and a declaration to that effect has been made in the offer letter.

No scheme should invest in or lend to another scheme under the same AMC.

Mutual funds must take delivery of scrips purchased and give delivery in the case of scrips sold and in no case shall engage in short selling or carry-forward transactions or badla finance. The scrips purchased should be transferred to the fund's name and scheme also.

Transfers from one scheme to another in the same mutual fund should be allowed only if,

(a) such transfers are done at the prevailing market price for quoted instruments on spot basis,

(b) the securities so transferred would be in accordance with the investment objective of the transferee scheme,

(c) transfer of unquoted instruments should be done only with specific approval of the board of trustees,

(d) the registration and accounting of the transaction is completed and is ratified in the next meeting of the board of trustees.

Winding up

Each closed-end scheme should have a duration fixed in a number of years, at the end of which, it should be wound up or extended with the permission of SEBI.

An open-end scheme shall be wound up if the total number of units outstanding after repurchases at a point of time falls below 50% of the originally issued number of units.

Expenses

The asset management company may charge the mutual fund with investment management and advisory fees which should have been disclosed fully in the prospectus subject to the following ceiling:

(a) 1.25% of the weekly average net assets outstanding in the current year for the scheme concerned as long as the net assets do not exceed Rs. 100 crores, and

(b) 1% of the excess amount over Rs. 100 crores, where net assets so calculated exceed Rs. 100 crores.

In addition, the asset management company may charge the mutual fund with the following expenses:

(a) mutual issue costs of sponsoring the fund and its schemes.

(b) recurring expenses including, *(i)* marketing and selling expenses including agent's commission, if any *(ii)* brokerage and transaction cost *(iii)* registrar services for transfer of shares sold or redeemed.

The asset management company, should be expected to meet all its expenses and responsible to provide the following:

(a) office space, supplies and personnel including analysts and portfolio managers,

(b) regulatory compliance and reporting services,

(c) preparation and distribution of the fund's prospectus, annual and periodic reports and other investor communications,

(d) advertising and other sales material,

(e) according services and preparation of tax returns,

(f) insurance coverage and other services.

The fees payable to the trustees shall be charged to the mutual funds.

The fees payable to the custodian for safekeeping of fund assets and related matter shall be charged to the mutual fund.

The initial issue expenses should not exceed 6% of the funds raised under each scheme.

In any case, the total of all the expenses charged to the fund except the initial issue expenses should not exceed 3% of the weekly average net assets outstanding during the current year and the same shall be disclosed through advertisements, accounts, etc.

All expenses should be clearly identified and appropriately attributed to the individual schemes.

Income Distribution

All mutual funds must distribute a minimum of 90 per cent of their profits in any given year.

Rights of the Parties

The asset management company can be changed by either the trustee company board or by 75% of investors in the fund.

If a change in the asset management company is recommended by the trustee company/board, it should be subject to scrutiny and approval of SEBI.

If the sponsor of a mutual funds recommends change of the trustee, it should be subject to the scrutiny and approval of SEBI.

SEBI should have the right to review a mutual funds's role in takeovers.

Accounting Requirements

Mutual funds should be required to segregate their earnings as current income, short-term capital gains and long-term capital gains.

Accounting for all the schemes should be required to be done for the same year ending.

For all quoted instruments, mutual funds must calculate weekly NAV at the last available closing market prices. For unquoted investments, the valuation may be done once weekly either at cost or by any other method authorised by SEBI. For investments considered doubtful, the directors' best estimate may be accepted, subject to the auditors' certificate of reasonability.

Disclosure and Reporting

SEBI will have the right to call for any information regarding the operations of the mutual funds any of its schemes from the mutual fund, asset management company, custodian, sponsor or any other person associated with the mutual fund.

SEBI will require from every mutual fund at least the following periodic reports, in addition to any other it may see fit:

(a) Copies of the duly audited annual statements of account including the balance sheet and the profit and loss account for the fund and for each scheme, once a year.

(b) Six-monthly unaudited accounts as above.

(c) A statement of movements in net assets for each of the schemes of the funds, every quarter.

(d) A portfolio statement, including changes from the previous periods, for each scheme, every quarter.

SEBI shall also lay down the accounting policies to be complied with by all mutual funds and the format and contents of the financial statements and other reports.

SEBI shall require all mutual funds to adopt a written code of ethics designed to deal with the potential conflicts of interest that may arise from transitions by the affiliated persons or companies. SEBI shall require a quarterly report from the interested persons or companies, disclosing all reportable transactions as determined by SEBI in a format prescribed by SEBI.

SEBI shall lay down a common advertising code for all mutual funds to comply with.

All mutual funds will be expected to submit to SEBI the texts of the marketing literature and advertisements issued to the investors.

The marketing and publicity brochures for each scheme shall properly disclose the investment objectives, the method and periodicity of valuation of investment, the exact method and periodicity of sales and purchases and other details considered by SEBI to be essential for investors.

SEBI can, after due investigation, impose penalties on mutual funds for violating the guidelines as may be necessary. However, for cases of penalties of suspension or deauthorisation of mutual fund entities, prior concurrence of RBI and the government shall be taken.

Appeals against decisions of SEBI lie to the Department of Economic Affairs, Ministry of Finance.

The SEBI has recently allowed the Mutual Funds to invest 100% of funds raised in Money Market upto 6 months and thereafter later 30% of funds for 6 months to one year and only 25% in Money Market and again 100% of funds in Money Market, 6 months prior to repayment to investors.

ANNEXURE III

SCHEME FOR MONEY MARKET MUTUAL FUNDS — GUIDELINES (RBI)

Please refer to our circular DBOD No. 13/24.01.013/91-92 dated 29 April 1992 wherein a scheme of Money Market Mutual Funds (MMMFs) was introduced by the Reserve Bank of India. In this connection we invite your attention to the Governor's circular No. CPC. BC.148/ 07.01.279/95-96 dated November 23, 1995, wherein with a view to providing greater liquidity and depth to the money market and in order to make the scheme more flexible and attractive to banks and financial institutions certain modifications to the existing scheme have been introduced. The salient features of the scheme as modified are indicated below:

1. Eligibility to set up MMMFs

MMMFs can now be set up by scheduled commercial banks and public financial institutions as defined under Section 4A of the Companies Act, 1956 or through their existing Mutual Fund/Subsidiaries engaged in Funds Management as well as mutual funds set up in the private sector. Private sector mutual funds can set up MMMFs with the prior approval of Reserve Bank of India, subject to other extent terms and conditions stipulated under the Scheme and should also get Securities & Exchange Board of India (SEBI) clearance to ensure that there is no infringment of SEBI guidelines on money market investments for amount/duration.

2. Structure of MMMFs

(i) MMMFs can be set up departmentally in the form of a division/department of the banks/financial institutions/mutal funds/subsidiaries i.e., "in house" MMMFs wherein the assets and liabilities of such MMMFs would form part of the eligible institutions' balance sheet or as separate entity, i.e., as a"Trust."

(ii) MMMFs can be operated either as Money Market Deposit Accounts (MMDAS) or Money Market Mutual Funds (MMMFs). MMDAs schemes could be operated either by issuing Deposit receipt or through issue of Pass Book without cheque book facility. MMMFs could float both open-ended and close-ended schemes.

(iii) Where MMMFs are set up as a Trust, a Board of Trustees should be appointed by the sponsoring institution to manage it. The day-to-day management of the schemes under the Fund is set up as a Trust, should be looked after by a full time Executive Trustee or a separate Fund Manager if set up as a Division of bank/financial institution/mutual fund/subsidiary.

(iv) Banks and public financial institutions are free to formulate special schemes as per their requirements subject to the guidelines stipulated by the Reserve Bank of India. MMMFs should foward the details of the scheme together with copies of offer letter, application form etc. to the Reserve Bank of India at least one month before announcing the launching of any scheme.

3. Size of MMMFs

The minimum size of a MMMF of Rs. 50 crores stipulated in our circular of April 29, 1992 is withdrawn. Likewise, the prescription of a ceiling for raising resources under various schemes by MMMFs set up by banks/financial institutions/mutual funds/subsidiaries is also withdrawn.

4. Who can Subscribe

As MMMFs are primarily intended to be a vehicle for individual investors to participate in the money market, the units/shares of MMMFs can be issued only to individuals. Individual Non-Resident Indians (NRIs) may also subscribe to shares/units of MMMFs. The dividend/income on such subscriptions will be allowed to be repatriated. The principal amount of subscription will, however, not be allowed to be repatriated abroad. The corporates are also allowed to invest in them, later on.

5. Minimum Size of Investment by a Single Investor

MMMFs would be free to determine the minimum size of investment by a single investor.

6. Investment Objectives and Policies

The investment objectives and policies of MMMFs should be laid down by the sponsor bank/institution or concerned mutual fund and every scheme to be launched by the MMMFs should be in accord with such broad objectives and policies and the rules and regulations framed in this regard. While inviting the subscription from the public, MMMFs should make a clear statement of investment objectives of the MMMFs and the investment policies besides the terms and conditions of the scheme. MMMFs should not give any guarantee or indication as to the rate of return on investments while announcing any scheme.

7. Investments by MMMFs

(i) The resources mobilised by MMMFs should be invested exclusively in the following money market instruments, namely:

(a) Treasury bills and dated government securities having an unexpired maturity upto 1 year,

(b) call/notice money,

(c) commercial paper,

(d) commercial bills arising out of genuine trade/commercial transactions and accepted/It has been decided that the limits on investments in individual instruments stipulated in our circular of April 29, 1992 should be withdrawn and MMMFs are now free to determine the extent of their investments in each instrument as indicated below:

Limit (per cent of resources of MMMFs)

Instruments	*Existing*	*Revised*
(a) Treasury Bills and dated Government Securities having an unexpired maturity upto 1 year	Minimum 25 per cent	Maximum limit withdrawn.
(b) Call/Notice Money	Maximum 30 per cent	Maximum limit withdrawn.
(c) Commercial Paper	Maximum 15 per cent. The exposure to commercial paper issued by an individual more than 3 per cent of the resources of the MMMF	The exposure to commercial paper issued by an individual company should, however, not be more than 3 per cent of the resources of the MMMF as a prudential requirement.
(d) Commercial Bills arising out of genuine trade/commercial transactions and accepted/co-accepted by banks	Maximum 20 per cent	Maximum limit withdrawn.
(e) Certificate of Deposit	No Limit	No limit.

The investments should be made in accordance with the prudential guidelines which may be issued by the Reserve Bank of India from time to time. MMMFs shall not deploy their funds in capital market instruments so that their investments are not exposed to undue risk.

(ii) Switching of assets between schemes should be at market rate and based on conscious investment decision; and

(iii) Borrowing and lending between schemes of the MMMFs as also between the MMMFs and the sponsoring institutions are prohibited.

8. Delivery of Instruments

MMMFs should invariably take delivery of money market instruments purchased and give delivery of the instruments sold.

9. Reserve Requirements

In the case of MMMFs set up by banks, the resources mobilised by them would not be considered as part of their net demand and time liabilities and as such these resources would be free from any reserve requirements.

10. Minimum Lock-in-period and Repurchase

The minimum lock-in-period for investments in MMMFs would be 45 days (reduced to 30 days later). The MMMFs would be free to offer repurchase facilities to the investors subject to the minimum lock-in-period. The details of the repurchase facility including the procedures should be made clear in the offer document.

11. Insurance Cover

The funds invested in MMMFs will not have insurance cover from the Deposit Insurance and Credit Guarantee Corporation of India. This aspect must be clearly brought out in the offer documents by MMMFs.

12. Stamp Duty

The shares/units issued by MMMFs would be subject to stamp duty. Similarly, transfer of units of MMMFs after holding for a lock-in-period of 46 days would be subject to stamp duty.

13. Format of Certificates of MMMFs

The units of MMMFs should be issued in the form of a certificate indicating the number of units purchased by the investor.

14. Application Form

MMMFs may devise suitable appplication form the subscribing to their schemes.

15. Security Aspect

Since units are freely transferable, due care must be exercised by the MMMF in the matter of printing/safe custody of the instrument. They should be signed by two or more authorised signatories.

16. Regulation of MMMFs

The setting up of MMMFs would require prior authorisation of Reserve Bank of India. Furthermore, MMMFs set up by banks, their subsidiaries and public financial institutions would be required to comply with the guidelines and directives that may be issued by the Reserve Bank of India from time to time. The private sector MMMFs would need clearance of SEBI; the approval of Reserve Bank of India would be necessary to enable them to operate in the money market.

The Reserve Bank of India shall have the powers in the interest of banking policy and public interest, to issue directions, call for any information, inspect the books and accounts of the MMMFs; any inspection of private sector MMMFs would be undertaken by SEBI.

17. Accounting

The accounts of MMMFs should be kept distinct and separate from those of the parent institutions. In the case of "In-house" MMMFs, it should be ensured that there is no conflict of interest between MMMFs and their parent organisation. The transfer of assets between MMMF and the sponsoring institution should be at market rate and should be subject to the approval of the sponsoring institution's Board.

18. Statement of Accounts and Disclosure

MMMFs should maintain separate account of each scheme launched by it segregating the assets under each scheme. MMMFs should prepare an annual statement of accounts in respect of each of their schemes which should contain, *inter alia*, statements of assets and liabilities and income and expenditure account duly audited by qualified auditors, other than the auditors of the parent organisation. An abridged version of the annual accounts together with the reports of the auditors should be published for the information of subscribers to the concerned scheme.

19. Management of MMMFs

"In-house" MMMFs should take adequate and effective measures to ensure that management, accounting and custody of their asset should be kept distinct and separate from those relating to the bank/financial institution/subsidiary/mutual fund.

20. Net Asset Value

MMMFs should calculate Net Asset Value (NAV) of each scheme and disclose the NAVs periodically for the benefit of the investors. To start with, MMMFs may determine and disclose NAV once in a week. Thereafter, NAV may be determined twice in a week or even daily. The method to be followed for calculation of NAV should be disclosed in the offer letter of each scheme.

21. Expenses

The total expenses of the Fund including pre-issue expenses, trusteeship fees/management fees, etc. should be kept at reasonable levels and should be disclosed fully in the Fund's Annual Reports/balance sheets.

22. Furnishing Reports to Reserve Bank of India

The sponsor bank/financial institution/subsidiary/mutual fund should furnish to Reserve Bank of India, in duplicate, the following reports on a regular basis.

(*a*) quarterly report indicating the performance of the MMMF as a whole and each scheme thereof.

(*b*) scheme annual statement of accounts, together with the reports of the Auditors.

(*c*) scheme-wise details of inverstment portfolio of the Funds, value of such investments, changes in the portfolio since the annual report and asset-wise exposure.

(*d*) specific information on investments in certain segments of the money market as may be called for by the Reserve Bank of India.

23. Banks/Financial institutions/Mutual funds/subsidiaries desirous of setting up MMMFs may forward their applications to the Chief General Manager, Department of Banking Operations & Development, Reserve Bank of India, Central Office, Centre 1, World Trade Centre, Cuffe Parade, Colaba, Mumbai-400 005, together with other supporting particulars/ documents such as details of proposed constitution and organisational structure, draft Trust Deed (wherever applicable), details of scheme/s, etc.

24. Detailed operating procedures for private sector mutual funds are being worked out by the Reserve Bank and the Securities & Exchange Board of India.

Introduction

Investment and Disinvestment are two sides of the same coin. When we deal with investment management, it automatically encompasses, disinvestment also, as what is investment for one is disinvestment for another, particularly in the secondary market. In portfolio management, investment and disinvestment go together as the portfolio is changed form time-to-time depending on the changes in the needs and preferences of the investor and following the changes in market conditions and information flows. If an investment decision is made based on some criteria, it follows that decision can be reversed leading to disinvestment, if the criteria is not satisfied. If thus investment and disinvestment go together, why do we need a separate treatment for disinvestment?

If investment is an art and science, the more so is the Disinvestment Process. In certain conditions of Prolonged bearishness in the stock market, depressed conditions in the primary market or disturbed crisis situations due to excess liquidity or liquidity crunch in money market and call money segment, etc., disinvestment becomes a major problem leading to liquidity crisis and insolvency and even defaults. If investment is an important activity, the disinvestment is more so as trading in any market involves both investment and disinvestment. Days were there, when banks and financial institutions used to make only investments in money market instruments and gilt-edged securities and rarely did they make any disinvestment. The majority of individual investors are reported to have been holding their investments for life time or twenty to thirty years, as per some surverys. The Indian investors, banks, financial institutions etc., have been used to make only investments and the art of disinvestment and trading for booking profits and gains or to take any advantage of any changes in yields, interest rates and price appreciation etc., has not developed well in India as it needs some expertise and experience.

What is Disinvestment?

Investment refers to conversion of money or cash into securities, stocks, debentures, bonds or any other claims on money. On the same lines, disinvestment involves the conversion of money claims or securities into money or cash. Here money is used in the sense of coins, currency and credit instruments like cheques, MT, TT, DD etc., which are payable to drawee or holder in due course and on demand. If these instruments have a usance period and a fixed maturity date, they are credit instruments like Bills of Exchange, Treasury bills, Commercial and trade bills which are all short-term claims on money. Disinvestment relates to those instruments as well. If the claims are of long-term nature, like shares, bonds and debentures etc., they are part of the capital market and investment and disinvestment criteria are slightly different in them in terms of risks and return in addition to differences in duration and maturity, from investments in other markets. Disinvestment may also refer to sale, transfer and disposition of any investments. As investments are risky, so also the disinvestments. In that sense, disinvestment management is also an art and science in operations. In fact, trading in securities and money market instruments involves both, Investment and Disinvestment. As in the case of investment decisions in portfolio management, the disinvestments are to be based on rational and scientific grounds. The liquidity conditions in the market and, changes in information flows and many other factors influence the disinvestment decisions.

Risks and return are to be weighed and the costs of information and transaction costs, etc., are to be considered and alternative opportunities lost due to disinvestment are to be assessed and a decision to disinvest has thus to be taken on many rational grounds, which are part of this management science.

Why Disinvestment?

Some of the reasons why disinvestment takes place are listed below:

(1) Mergers and acquisitions of companies by which shareholders are sometimes adversely affected due to dilution of equity.

(2) Government Policy Changes affecting the economy in general, fiscal and monetary policies influencing the company or industry in question.

(3) Tax changes or tax rate adjustments, which adversely affect the company.

(4) Dividends and Earnings data and deteriorating fundamentals of the company.

(5) Timing as determined by the technical analysis and chartist method of locating trend reversals and sell signals for the purpose of disinvestment.

(6) Disinvestment is part of the investment process and as investment is a part of the portfolio management, so is the disinvestment process. They are two blades of the same scissors.

(7) Due to changing market conditions, some companies become potentially sick or show symptoms of maturity and stagnancy which are to be disinvested as early as possible.

(8) Disinvestment is also needed for good companies for profit-making and booking capital gains or capital losses. In the case of banks and financial institutions dealing in Gilt-edged securities, P.S.U. bonds and semi-Government, and trustee securities, the process of investment and disinvestment is a regular feature for adjustment in SLR. or CRR position and for responding to changes in yields and duration.

(9) Disinvestment is needed to take advantage of changes in interest rates, yields, capital appreciation or depreciation or avoidance of capital losses, changes in duration of the portfolio and a host of other reasons, in the Bond management strategies.

(10) In many cases as the case of individuals and mutual funds, disinvestment takes place to meet the transaction or repurchase needs or to adhere to any guidelines of SEBI or the RBI.

Role of Disinvestment

Disinvestment is equally important as investment in Portfolio Management for many reasons. In some situations, disinvestment becomes unavoidable due to unexpected changes in the market conditions, fall in share prices, likely changes in Government policies or problems of the company leading to its sickness, fall in sales and profits etc.

Disinvestment will also become necessary for fundamental factors and technical factors. On the basis of the study of fundamentals, a number of companies in one's own portfolio are likely to show stagnant growth or no growth, reduced profits, lower P/E ratio, losses resulting in wiping out 1/4th to ½ of the networth of the company. If the investor perceives such impending developments he has to disinvest such securities. If for example even bigwigs like ITC and Shaw Wallace were involved in abnoxious scams involving millions of foreign exchange drain from the country, many investors sold off their shares of these companies. When Sandoz and Hind Ciba agreed to merge the Sandoz shareholders were unhappy with the terms of conversion of shares of Hind Ciba, many were prepared to dispose off their shares. In more recent years GTB and Satyam Computers were involved in huge scams. The investors got scared and had to disinvest and suffered losses in the process. Yet another reason could be Government Policy changes. Due to continued drift in infrastructure industries, of particularly electricity and crude, the fear of rise in oil prices had led to a crash in Auto and cement shares in December 1996. The impending slow down in the economic activity may lead to continued bearish phase in the market, when disinvestment may be planned by some investors particularly in industries depending on the infrastructural facilities.

Even in B_1 Group of cash shares on BSE, many companies were quoting below par many times due to poor fundamentals. In 1999, the BSE has created a separate category of 'Z' group to comprise of such companies which are violating the listing requirements and ignoring investor complaints and their interests. Since June 1996 the BSE sensex fell to a three year low of 2713 on December 3,1996 from a three year high of 4643 reached an Sept. 12, 1994. On June 17, 1996 the sensex was 4131 and fell to close at 2795 on Dec. 3, 1996 — a fall of 33% in five months. In such a scenario of continued bearishness, disinvestment becomes a problem and investor loses heavily on any such disinvestment. In all these situations disinvestment requires more expertise than investment itself.

Disinvestment Under Adverse Conditions

Disinvestment becomes impossible when the security prices are quoting well below the purchase prices. This is true of the majority of the newly listed companies also. It is understood that out of 2601 new issues listed between January 1, 1994 and July 12, 1996, 2505 issues (96% of new issues) were quoted below issue prices leading to erosion in the value of investment. Some 75 companies in B_1 Group on BSE have reached new lows with 14 of them quoting below par value of Rs. 10.

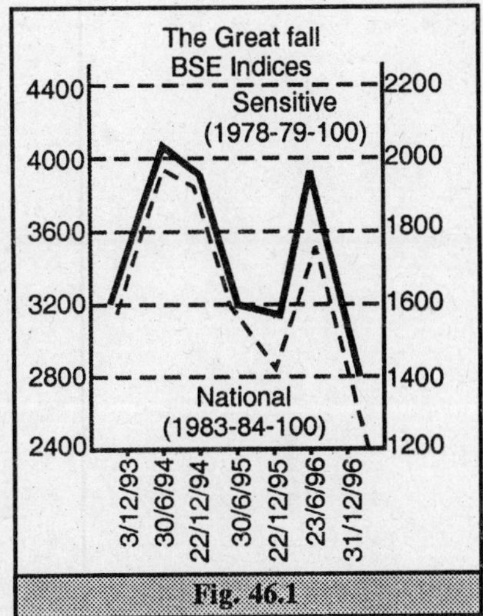

Fig. 46.1

Out of 55 listed schemes of Mutual Funds on BSE as many as 43 were quoting at prices lesser than the NAV. Most of the investors of mutual funds would thus find it difficult to make any disinvestment, as they will lose heavily on any sales. Money is tied down in such apparently illiquid investments. In effect the liquidity is not possible, although in theory, the liquidity is provided by a quotation. In such a scenario also, disinvestment is a critical problem.

BSE Sensex had reached a peak of 4643 in Sept. 1994 and then fell into a continued bearish phase to reach a low of around 3038 in December 1995 — a fall of 35% or so, but went up again to around 3367 at end March 1996 before falling to a three year lower of 2713 by mid December 1996 — a fall of 20%. These ups and downs are seen in the attached chart for the period 1993 to 1996. With the fall in prices values have also fallen. Thus, the annual turnover was Rs. 84,536 crores in 1993-94 and fell to Rs. 50,064 crores in 1995-96 but rose again to Rs. 124,284 crores in 1996-97. During the month of December 1996, when the sensex reached a three year low, the daily turnover was only Rs. 400 crores a day; as against an earlier peak of Rs. 1500-2000 crores a day on BSE. The low of 1998 was 2,951 on June 22 as against a high of 4,605 on August 6, 1997.

The three year low of B.S.E. Sensex was 2741 reached on October 23,1998. At end March 1999, the sensex reached 3739, as compared to 3893 at end March 1998 a fall of 3.9% over the year 1998-99. There was a recovery from October 1999 and zoomed to reach a new all time peak of 6150 on Feb. 14, 2000. As compared with the low of 2742 reached on Nov. 30, 1999, the Sensex showed a rise of 124%, as on Feb. 14, 2000. There was unprecedented volitility in the market with prices making movements on either way such that the SEBI has intervened in the market by imposing special volitility margins on selected scrips from January 2000 onwards.

The value of trade and price increase both on NSE and OTCEI have similarly declined for prolonged periods. Such depressed state of the markets create problems for disinvestment. In the OTCEI for example volume of trade fell from Rs. 365 crores in 1994-95 to Rs. 107 crores in 1996-97, bulk of the fall being in listed equity shares. On NSE; the number of listed companies stood at 785 and permitted securities at 320 as at end March 2001, with an annual turnover of Rs. 13.4 lakh crores in 2000-01 which was one and half times that of the BSE.

Recent Price Trends

In the lastest period of 2004 to 2009, there were boom conditions with the BSE sensex rising from a low of 5,022 in August 2004 to 6,493 at end March 2005 and thereafter with occasional reactions, it reached 13,072 at end March 2007, and 15,700 in July 2007. Over the ten year period of 1997 to 2007, there was a sharp rise of 3½ times in the BSE sensex. The Graph on next page shows these trends over the decade 1997 to 2009.

It will be seen from the Table that steep rise took place between 2003 to 2008, due to strong economic fundamentals, and larger forcigh inflows into the Indian markets. After March 2008, the trend is that of a steeper rise to 15,838 by end March 2008 but Fell to 8,995 by March 2009. There were frequent reactions to the uptrends during 2005 to 2009. Before 2003, there was a flattening of the index which moved in a narrow grade of 3,000 to 5,000, due to uncertain economic and political conditions and slower growth of the GDP and lower FII inflows into with the country (the trend is shown in the Graph and The Table on next page). There was a steep fall in 2009 due to global recession and outflow (net) of FII funds from Indian markets.

Data used for Drawing the graph

Table
SENSEX DATA

Years on X Axis Month of March	BSE Sensex on Y Axis (Monthly averages)
1997	3,762
1998	3,817
1999	3,689
2000	5,262
2001	3,808
2002	3,581
2003	3,156
2004	5,613
2005	6,679
2006	10,857
2007	12,858
2008	15,838
2009	8,995

Source: RBI Monthly Bulletins

Fig. 46.2

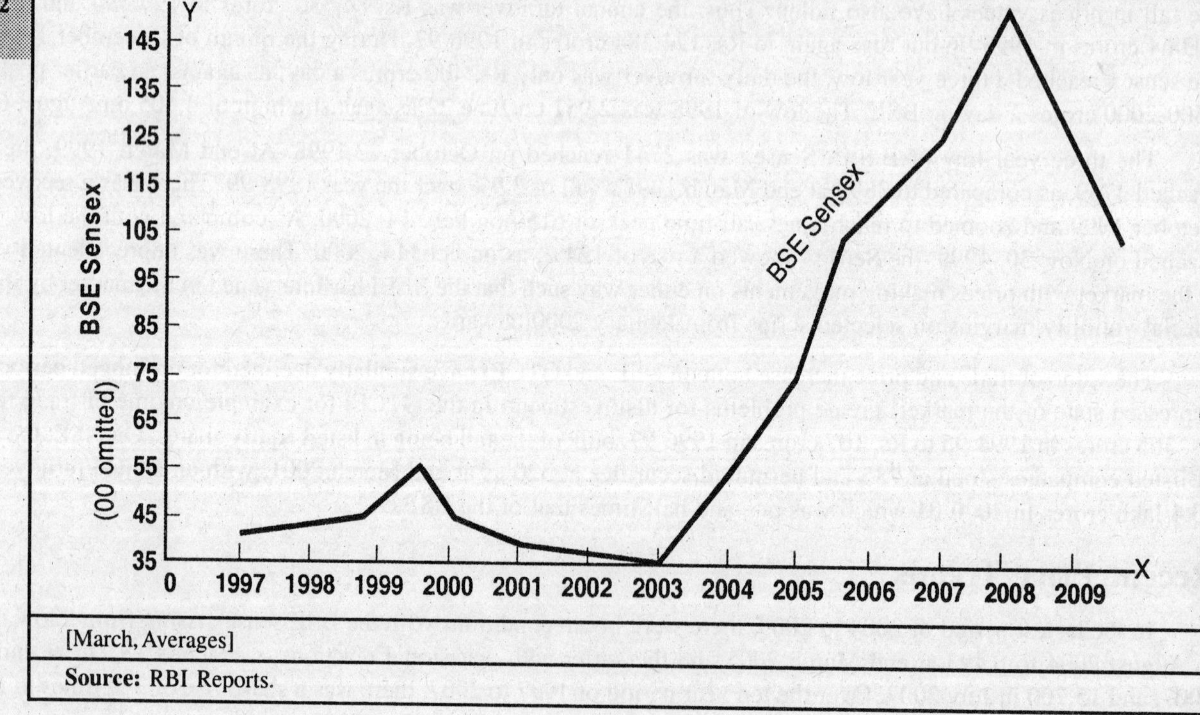

[March, Averages]

Source: RBI Reports.

The long-term trends in BSE share price indices are seen in the following Table:

End March Data	*1990*	*1995*	*1996*	*2000*	*2004*	*2005*	*2006*	*2007*	*2008*	*2009*
BSE Sensex	781	3,261	3,367	5,001	5,591	6,493	11,280	13,072	15,644	9,709
Percentage Change	+15.4%	−13.8%	+3.2%	33.7	83.4	16.1	73.7	16.0	19.6	−38%

New Issue Trends

(Rs. Crores)

	1992-93	1995-96	1996-97	1998-99	2000-01	2003-04	2004-05	2005-06	2006-07	2007-08	2008-09
Public Issue	6,059	10,529	7,781	2,602	4,416	2,822	9,866	16,938	28,172	47,477	2,674
Rights Issue	12,627	5,843	2,663	2,411	533	853	3,616	4,216	27,175	9,371	11,997
Total	18,686,	16,372	10,424	5,013	4,949	3,675	13,482	21,154	29,756	56,848	14,671

The depressed primary market conditions are clearly seen from 1995-96 to 2000-01, and these have repercussions on the secondary market as well. There were depressed conditions in both the Primary market and Secondary market again in 2009, as can be seen from the above tables. The Granger's causality tests showed that in India there are inter connections between the primary markets and secondary markets and causality runs both ways. If an investor wants to disinvest in primary market there is no way for him except for the shares to be listed on the secondary market. If the secondary market is depressed, funds are tied down in the market and creates illiquidity among investors, which in turn makes the primary market stagnant and depressed. Thus, both the wings of the capital market and the institutional agencies in the capital market find it difficult to disinvest and get out of the markets, in such situations.

Disinvestment Motivated by Market Conditions

The primary market conditions are depicted earlier over a period of ten years both in respect of public issues and rights issues. At the boom times of the market, namely, 1993-94 and 1994-95 either public issues or rights are both received well by the investors, when the stock market conditions were also good, but not so during 1995 to 2001. The markets picked up during 2003 to 2007.

The principles of disinvestment in any market are the basic tenets which are set at below:

Trading/Investment

(a) Buy low and sell high. Buy lower and sell only when the purchase price plus some gain is available; when the market is declining, buy lowest and sell atleast to cover the purchase price.

(b) When trading, a margin of 10% gain or loss or stop loss order can be set at 10% to get into disinvestment.

(c) In a Portfolio of shares, sell only overpriced shares whose fundamentals have weakened and bottomlines are expected to decline.

(d) Sell, to start with, cats and dogs of companies in the Portfolio even when no Profit can be booked. Short-term losses can be booked to show against short-term gains for tax purposes.

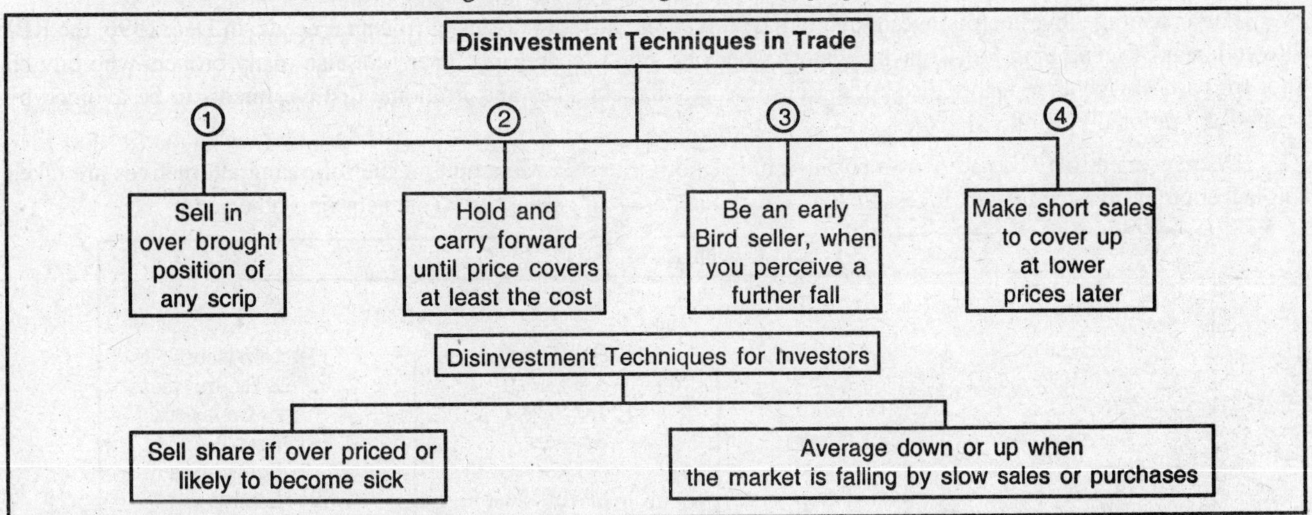

Normal Principles of Disinvestment are:

Buy	: Under priced shares, Growth shares, new product and promising Companies.
Sell	: Over priced shares, stagnant and decadent Companies or those expected to show declining bottom lines.
Hold	: When Companies are good, and promising, but market conditions are bad or the Company's share price is moving in a narrow grove.
Average up	: When the market is going up sell in small quantities to average up the sale price.
Average down	: When the market is going down, buy in small quantities, and sell when there is technical recovery or when there is buying support at around the settlement time.

Follow the Contrary Position: When there are over bought conditions in some scrips, then follow the principle of short sale and when there are many sellers in a scrip buy and carry forward without taking delivery.

Taking delivery and giving delivery are necessary for mutual funds and some Trust funds, LIC, GIC, etc., but for the companies, individuals and institutional agencies, taking and giving delivery can be avoided in trading for disinvestment.

Types of Disinvestment

Disinvestment, as referred to earlier, is as necessary as investment. In review and revision of portfolio management, ***disinvestment*** is an accepted method of adjustment of the portfolio to the preferences of investors, changes in market conditions and fresh information flows forthcoming from time-to-time. In the equity market, some scrips lose their charm due to poor financial performance and changes in market demand, financial mismanagement, when disinvestment in those shares become necessary. In the bond market, any needed changes in duration of the Portfolio, changes in interest rates and expectations of yield changes and monetary and credit policy changes will influence disinvestment decisions. Government bonds of low yields are switched for high yields. In times of expected rise in interest rates or yields, Portfolio Manager may switch from short-term bonds to long-term bonds and *vice versa.* The risk of change in interest rates is higher, the higher the maturity period and lower the Coupon Rate. The long maturity bonds suffer capital losses for rise in yields and in times of rising interest rates and yields, the capital losses on long bonds have to be offset by reinvestment of interest at higher yields. The adjustments of maturities, duration, swifts as between different bonds, with varying coupon rates are all part of the bond management strategies.

Similarly, in times of depressed equity markets, the Treasury Manager may shift investments from equity to bond market, particularly when interest rates are rising as in 1996. When both bonds and equity markets are bearish, as in 1997-98 the investor may shift from capital market to other markets like commodities, futures, gold, silver and real estate, etc.

For an average investor, disinvestment may be forced on him for reasons of financial needs. In Dec. 1996, the RBI allowed banks to lend upto Rs. 10 lakhs against securities, bonds shares etc. There are also many brokers who buy on spot for cash payments at heavy discounts. But these are distress sales and irrational disinvestments to be avoided by trained and rational Portfolio Managers.

Disinvestment may be for investment in better opportunities. For example, if the following alternatives are taken into account an investor may disinvest in one or two categories of assets for investment into others.

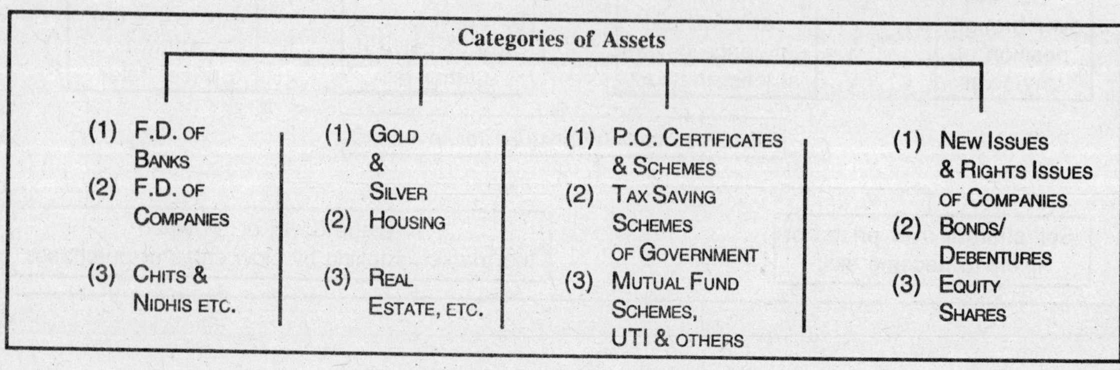

Assume that the investor has 13% coupon bonds of Government and 16.5% Bonds of ICICI. Suddenly the Gold prices fell to a new low and he is bullish on gold in 1997. He will disinvest in bonds and prefer to buy gold at lower prices of $ 360 per fine once as against a peak of $ 384, two months ago. See the accompanying Chart (Fig 46.3). In March 1999, monthly average gold price was $ 286 per five ounce, which was a very steeper fall than in equities during the same period (Oct. 97 to March 99).

Factors Influencing Disinvestment

Disinvestment takes place as an offshoot of the following financial activity in the markets.

(1) Trading and speculative gains by short-term investors lead to disinvestment in the stock market.

(2) Booking Profits, both short-term and long-term due to capital appreciation in the markets.

(3) Avoiding possible losses by disinvestment in potentially non-viable and sick units, through research based fundamental Analysis.

(4) Taking advantage of interest rate changes or changes in expected yields.

(5) Adjustment of the portfolio of investments through continuous investment and disinvestment activity and shifting from low yielding to high yielding instruments and from low priority activity to high priority activity and from less profitable activity to more profitable activity.

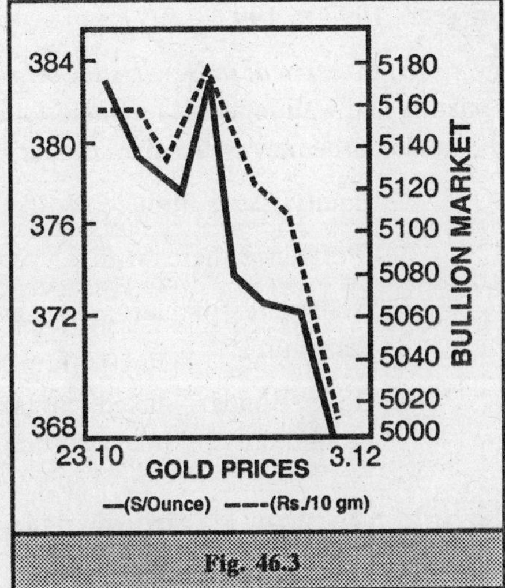

Fig. 46.3

(6) To cater to changing market conditions and changing investor preferences and their perceptions of future returns from different instruments and assets.

(7) To take advantage of potential gains from various sub-markets such as from equities to bonds and *vice versa*, or from money market to capital market or from one sub-market like ICD to Bill discounting or from one market to another like shifting from capital market to gold market or commodities markets etc.

(8) Disinvestment for reasons of financial hardships and urgent need for cash leading to distress sales.

ROLE OF FUNDAMENTAL FACTORS

How to make Disinvestment Decision?

Disinvestment decision of a person depends on his preferences, income, wealth and his likes and dislikes. For example, a retired person requires regular income, safety of his funds, much more than the speculative gains or appreciation. On the other hand, a young working Executive who has regular monthly income invests for capital appreciation. A businessman may invest for tax planning purposes. Thus, the objectives of investors would be different for different persons and one has to be clear of his objective before one makes a decision for disinvestment.

Objectives

Normally, the objectives of an average investor are: income, safety of funds, liquidity or marketability and capital appreciation. Disinvestment may aim at liquidity or safety or for just booking profits.

Investment Avenues

The alternative investment avenues for the investor are to be considered first, so as to satisfy the above objectives of investors. The following categories of investments are open to investors as avenues for investment and disinvestment.

(a) Investment in Bank Deposits — Savings and Fixed Deposits: This is the most common form of investment for an average Indian and nearly 50% of funds in financial saving of household sector are used in this form. These are least risky but the return is also low. One may shift funds from here to bonds or Company deposits for higher return.

(b) Investment in P.O. Deposits, National Savings Certificates and other Postal Savings Schemes: Many people in villages and semi-urban areas are investors in these schemes due to lower risk of loss of money and greater security of funds. But returns are also lower than in Stocks and Shares, which may lead to disinvestment. Some may shift to chit funds or Nidhis. Interest rates savings media were reduced in Jan. 2000 to 2003.

(c) Investment in Mutual Fund Schemes or UTI Schemes: These are less risky than direct investment in stocks and shares as these enjoy the expert management by the Portfolio Manager or Professional experts. They also have the advantage of a diversified portfolio involving the reduction of risk and economies of scale reducing the cost of investment. But at times when mutual funds show poor returns, one may disinvest in them for better return elsewhere, as in the case of years 1997 to 1999.

(d) Investment in New Issues Market: A new entrant in the Stock Market should preferably invest in New Issues of existing and well reputed companies either in equity or debentures. Incidentally the instruments in which investment can be made in the new issues market are:

1. Equity issues through prospectus or rights renounced by existing shareholders.
2. Preference shares with a fixed dividend either convertible, into equity or not.
3. Debentures of various categories — convertible fully, convertible partly, convertible and non-convertible debentures.
4. P.S.U. Bonds — taxable or tax-free with fixed interest rates. If investment is made in Primary market, it has to be sold only in Stock Market.

Stock Market Disinvestment

As far as the stock market is concerned, investment and disinvestment in shares is most risky as the likelihood of fall or rise in prices is uncertain. But the returns may also be high commensurate with risk. A host of imponderable factors operate in the stock market and a genuine investor has to do the following things:

1. Study the Balance Sheet of the company and analyse the prospects of rise in Gross block, sales and profits.
2. Analyse the Market Price in terms of book value and profit earning capacity (or P/E ratio) and use them to know whether the share is overvalued or undervalued.
3. Study the expansion plans or tax savings plans and analyse the company's financial strength, profitability, bonus and dividend paying strength, through the mechanism of financial ratios.
4. Study whether the management is professional and good and whether other accounting practices are dependable and consistent. The company becomes attractive to buy if the financial ratios support the view that the fundamentals are strong and the shares are worth buying.
5. Lastly, if the price of the share is overvalued on the basis of the projected earnings for the coming half year or one year and its P/E ratio is higher than the industry average, then it is worth selling. For assessing the undervaluation and overvaluation, analyst and his analytical power count for this purpose.

Fundamental Analysis

What ratios one should look into for Balance Sheet Analysis of a company for making a disinvestment decision? Any decision in this regard is to be based on a study of fundamental factors of the company and the intrinsic worth of the shares.

There is no single ratio which will explain the share price performance of a company. The whole Balance Sheet has to be analysed including the footnotes for knowing the strength of a company and its share price performance. For a casual investor who has no professional background and no time for analysing the whole Balance Sheet, he should however look into the Balance Sheet of the company and analyse the data for five or more years in respect of the following variables:

1. *Efficiency in the Use of Capital:* Examine the ratio of equity to Gross block or to capital employed (equity + preference capital + reserves + long-term debt capital). This will indicate how efficient the company is in capital use, and if inefficiency is apparent, it is a fit case for disinvestment.

2. *Leverage Ratio:* Examine how equity holders benefit by borrowed capital through the debt-equity ratio. The leverage is provided by debt capital to the equity-holders. If debt is very large and earnings potential is declining, it is a high risk company to be disinvested.

3. *Turnover Ratio:* This is the ratio of sales to the equity capital explaining how equity capital is used for improving sales. If sales are not rising and unutilised capacity is growing, it may grow sick anytime.

4. *Profitability Ratio:* Examine how sales would improve the profits through a study of the ratio of Gross Profits to Sales — G.P. Morgan relates the G.P. divided by sales turnover or net profits to the profitability of operations.

5. *Shareholders' Return:* The ratio of net profits to equity will indicate the return to shareholder. But as all earnings either paid as dividend or ploughed back into reserves as depreciation or any other reserves, are belonging to the shareholders only PBDT Profits Before Depreciation and Taxes (Gross profits-minus interest) are the total earnings for equityholders, of which a part is paid as taxes, a part as dividends to shareholders and the rest is ploughed into reserves for use by the company. All earnings should therefore be considered for profitability.

6. *Dividend Policy:* As the shareholders are interested in a regular dividend distributed to them, dividend paid divided by the total net profit will indicate the dividend policy of the company. A company which is not earning good profits or dividend is skipped for two or more years, it is a Company likely to be sick and can be disinvested.

7. *Book Value:* As the share price is an indication of the company's networth and its intrinsic value, the book value is one of the measures of share price and is calculated as the networth divided by number of equity shares. If the book value is eroded by 50% due to losses over years, that Company should be disinvested immediately.

8. *Earnings Per Share (EPS):* The net profits divided by the number of equity shares of the company give the earnings per share (PBDT divided by the number of equity shares). This will represent company's earning capacity for equityholders. If EPS is declining over a couple of years, it is a fit case for disinvestment.

9. *P/E Ratio:* Market price divided by the Earnings Per Share (EPS) would indicate the multiple by which the price discounts the earnings per share of the company; a low P/E ratio relative to other companies in the same industry would indicate that price is attractive for a buy provided other financial parameters of the company are also good. But if the company is not earning good profits every year, has no expansion plans and is skipping dividends then that company has to be disinvested.

10. *Expansion Plans:* If the company has no expansion plans, it will not grow and so is the sales. The company will have no potential to realise higher sales. and higher profits in the coming years. If on the other hand the growth of gross block and growth of sales are both high and profit margins are low, then the efficiency is poor and profit margins would not improve if efficiency is low and then the company is likely to be in red. Such company's share will be low priced at present but it is better to get out of such companies.

More details are set out in the chapter of Fundamental Analysis.

FIIs and the Art of Contrariness

Most institutional investors and traders do not have long-term view of gains. Investment bankers and FIIs have started taking a short-term view of the market. Their purchases and sales have a major impact on the price trends in India. Studies made by CMIE, RBI and other Research bodies have shown that FII investment is the major cause of instability in the market prices. So one of the principles of disinvestment is to follow contrary view to that of FIIs. If there is a net selling by FIIs, keep off the market, if you cannot buy. When FIIs have turned buyers, sell the investments that you would like to disinvest. Besides, it is necessary for all traders and institutional investors to keep a tap on what FIIs feel and what they write about various companies in their portfolios. As FIIs have turned out to be major players in the Indian markets, their views and statements expressed orally or in press have found to have some influence on the market which the traders and operators in the market have to keep a pulse on.

Disinvestment Through study of Indicators is recommended. Although the markets may be depressed and caught in a bear hug, there are times when there will be technical corrections rallies and short upward movements. The traders in need of disinvestment have to keep a continuous watch on the price chart, moving Average chart and ROC chart. The price and rate of price changes indicate the deceleration and acceleration of the price trends and volumes and rates of change of volumes support the trends or indicate to likely reversals albeit short, even for a day, may be taken advantage by the traders for disinvestment. These technical factors are discussed in detail later.

FII Investments in India

According to a study of SEBI, released late in December 1996, FII investments have not slowed down and that they are not the cause of the present depressed conditions in the market. The fact which that study missed is that the reasons for bearishness are domestic factors of sluggish economic growth and industrial progress, slow down in the pace of infrastructural production, and unfriendly policy measures of the Government etc.

The cumulative FII investment from November 1992, when they were first permitted to enter into Indian capital market upto end 2001, was a total of about Rs. 55,000 crores. The study revealed that the months in which there were large net investments were also the months when the markets were buoyant (Nov. 1993 to June 1994, June 1995 to September 1995 and January 1996 to July 1996). These upswings in investments were followed by very low net investments, thereafter, presumably due to many depressing factors. It was found that their net investment was negative in 1998-99 and again in 2008-09. What happened was that their net investments were bunched in a few months in a year when the markets were also bullish. Months with large net investments were followed by very low investments in other months. Being large holders of funds, their entry and exit in the market had a significant effect on the ups and downs in the market sentiment and in price fluctuations, which any investor has to watch out for disinvestment. The Role FIIs in the market is to be watched for disinvestment.

The Table below on the Data on Net FII Investment shows that there was decline in the amounts during 1997 to March 1999 and thereafter particularly from Nov. 1999, there was a pick up in their net investments. From October 1999, the secondary market also started picking up due to improved sentiment following the news of improved fundamentals of the economy, establishment of a stable Government at the centre after the general elections in October 1999 and change in Government policies.

Table

Net FII Portfolio Investment

(in Rs. crores)

Year	*Amount*
1996-97	11,758
1497-98	6,696
1998-99	–257
1999-2000	13,112
2000-01	12,609
2001-02	9,639
2002-03	4,738
2003-04	52,279
2004-05	41,854
2005-06	55,357
2006-07	31,630
2007-08	1,18,348
2008-09	–64,206

Source: RBI: Balance of Payment Data

FII investments peaked off in 1996-97 and after declining for the next two years picked up again in 1999-2000 and reached a new peak in 2000 at Rs. 13,112 crores. The rise was sharp during 2003 to 2006. There was a fall in 2006-07 and again in 2008-09, when the markets were depressed.

Role of Technical Factors

Technical analysis of the market is the best way to keep informed of the likely trend reversals. If Advance-Decline lines are showing a trend and also a possible reversal, all the other market indicators have to be watched, namely, price indices, FII purchases and sales, volume turnover in A group and B_1 and B_2 together for reflecting the speculative and investment trends, daily high-low positions for the shares to be disinvested, spread or volatility of price movements and scrupulously follow the daily price charts, moving average price lines and look out for single point and double point sale signals for confirmed price reversal indicators to make disinvestments. The chart given in next page depicts the price and volume relationship of a scrip for illustration.

The charts give the price and trend lines for a close study. The chart provides an example for giving buy and sell signals through the moving average price charts. These signals can be checked up by a number of other indicators like ROC or oscillators. RSI and MACD etc. The example of a company scrip studied is Rasi Cement, whose daily price chart and moving average price trends are studied to give signals for disinvestment also.

Although there are standard methods of disinvestment by study of fundamentals and weeding out those potentially sick and those with declining bottom lines and deteriorating fundamentals, those are to be accepted as a first step. Once companies to be disinvested are located, it may not be possible to disinvest due to market conditions. Here comes the second step of study of technicals for locating the proper timing.

Timing of Disinvestment (Through Technical Analysis)

Unless the disinvestment is a distress sale, it has to be well timed to reap the optimum gain. Such timing can be sought from research analysis of the market Trends called the Technical Analysis. Reference was made in an earlier chapter to the Chartist method, moving average method and diagnosis of reversal trends for getting the sell signals. Some more important tools are referred to:

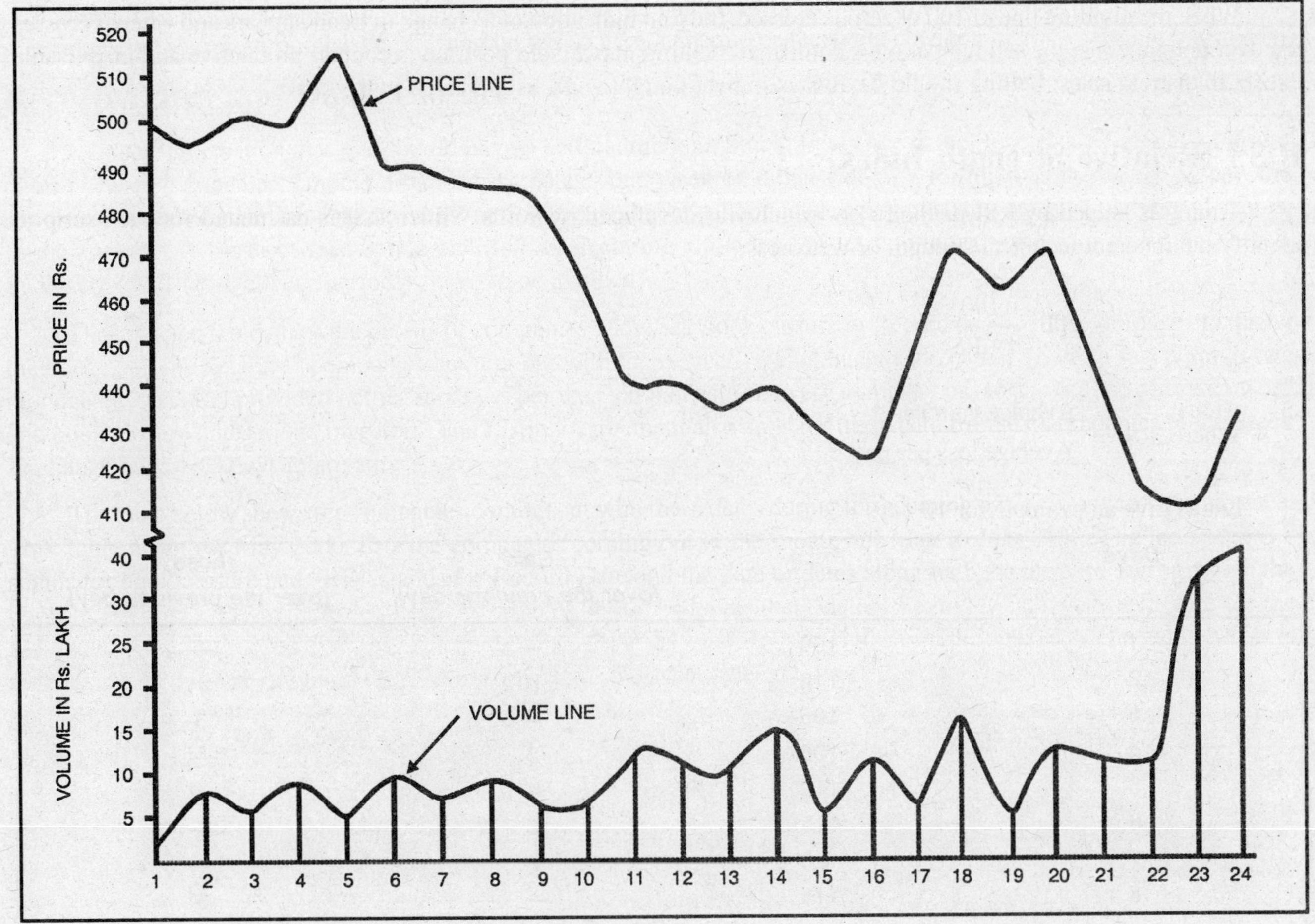

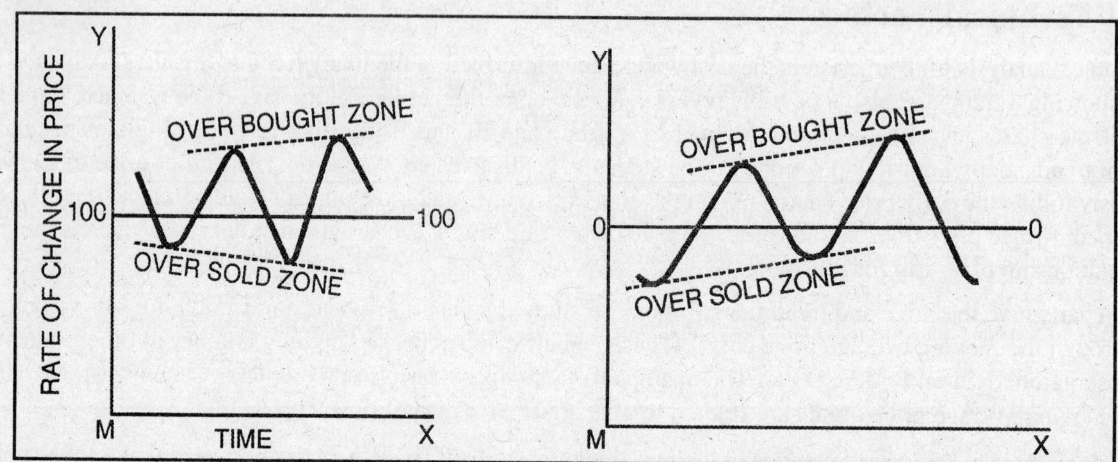

ROC or oscillators. It is an important indicator for identifying the trend reversal and knowing the overbought position or oversold position in a scrip.

Rates of change in prices or oscillators can be calculated for daily closing prices or weekly or monthly or any period of days. Suppose we have chosen 5 days oscillators to coincide with the trading period. The first day closing quotation is say Rs. 150 and after 5 days the closing quotation is Rs. 165 which is 110% of the price five days ago. Suppose the price fell on the next day to Rs. 135 it is 82% of the price (165). Thus, these changes can be expressed on either side of 100 or in terms of positive and negative changes over the period. In the first case, the chart shows movements below and above 100 and in the second case, the movements are positive or negative changes shown relative to the zero line.

When the dividing line of 100 or zero is crossed, the first indication of a change in trend appears and when it crosses the over bought zone, the sell indication is confirmed. Selling in oversold position is counter productive and inadvisable except in distress sales. Selling should be always in over bought zone, as indicated in the chart.

R.S.I (Relative Strength Index)

Timing is helped by RSI method also, which was developed by Wells Wilder. RSI is calculated for each scrip to identify the inherent technical strength or weakness.

$$\text{RSI} = 100 - \frac{100}{1+\text{RS.}}$$

$$\text{Where, RS} = \frac{\text{Average gain per day}}{\text{Average loss per day}}$$

Let us give an example for 10 days RSI

Days	*Price*	*Gain (over the previous day)*	*Loss (over the previous day)*
1	100	—	—
2	110	10	
3	105	—	5
4	108	3	—
5	112	4	—
6	115	3	—
7	120	5	—
8	115	—	5

9	110	—	5
10	95	—	5
10 days' average		$\frac{25}{10}$	$\frac{20}{10}$
Gain / Loss		2.5	2.0

$$Rs = \frac{2.5}{2.0} = 1.25$$

$$RSI = 100 - \left(\frac{100}{1+1.25}\right) = 100 — 44.4 = 55.6$$

The subsequent observations should be used to compile a series of RSI data.

After calculating such data for a number of days, a graph as shown below can be drawn representing the data on RSI. The Graph foretells a rise or a fall and time for disinvestment. One can develop his own skill in tracing turning signals, for both purchases and sales based on the reversal trend.

In daily movement of prices, there will be both rise and falls. If we take closing prices and compare them, sometimes each successive top will be higher than the previous top and at a point when next peak is lower than the previous one, the first sign of change of trend or sell signal is registered. In the above chart, for example there are three peaks each rising above the previous one (A, B, and C) and afterwards if the peak is lower than C and even B, we have sell signals for disinvestment. One should always sell scrips which are in overbought zones and even selling short will pay-off on some occasions.

The disinvestment decisions have to be taken with extreme care to make the optimum profit. As it is not possible for many to capture the exact peak, the prudent investor will sell around 5 to 10% on either side of the peak, as a rule of the Thumb. On continuous study of these charts, one can develop the needed expertise for correct timing of investment and disinvestment decisions.

On a study of RSI chart with that of the daily price chart, one can see either divergence or convergence of their trends. If the share price is moving up when RSI is falling and *vice versa* they are examples of divergence, which indicate the likely turning points in the trend of share prices for the purpose of disinvestment, if divergence occurs in the over bought zone, then sell signal may be indicated. The Resistance and support lines are easily discernible by a study of these charts over a long period of time, in the RSI lines as in the daily price charts. Break outs, and reversals should be noticed in the overbought zone when disinvestment can be made.

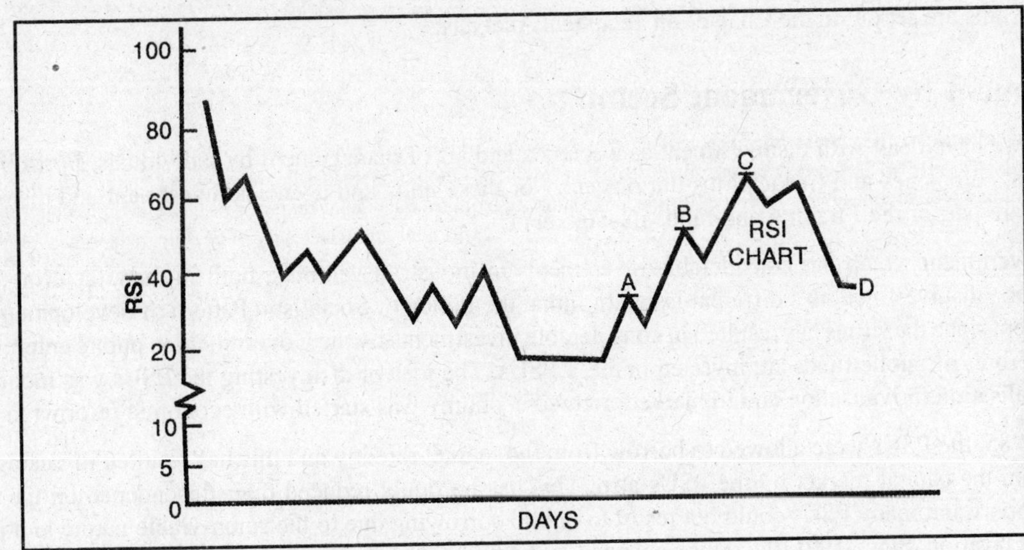

Moving Average Convergence and Divergence (MACD)

MACD is another indicator used for disinvestment and investment process. It measures the convergence and divergence between two exponential or simple moving averages. Two series of closing price data-one for short-term moving average of say 12 day and the other for 26 days of long-term moving average are to be calculated. The MACD should reflect the absolute differences between these two moving averages. With differences shown the Y-axis and days represented on the X-axis the chart can be drawn with a MACD line oscillating across the zero line.

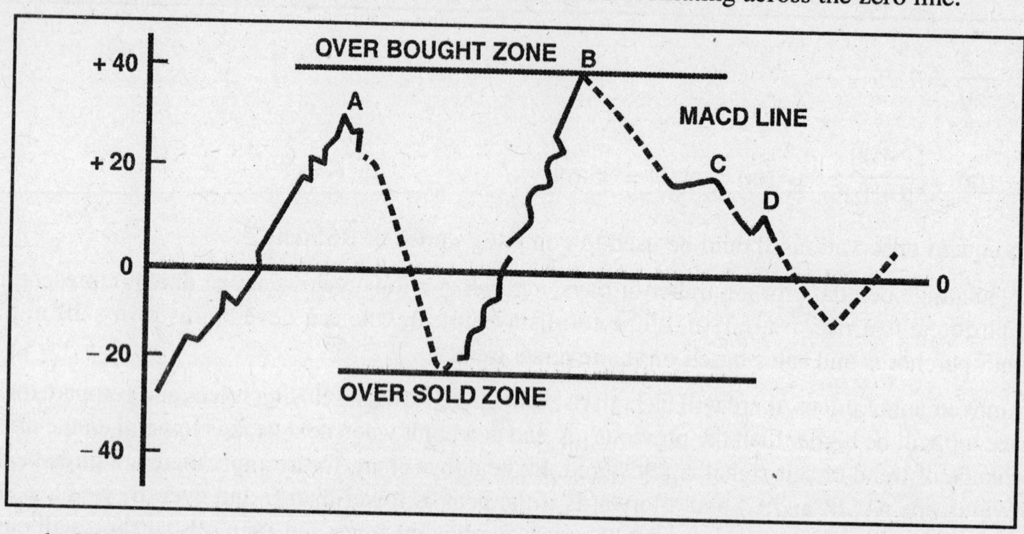

As long as the MACD line moves above the zero line but likely to cross it, we have to select a point for disinvestment. Care has to be taken to see that some false signals are not pursued, but disinvestment may be based on some confirmation of likely trend to cross the zero line from above. This means that the short-term moving average is above the longer one, and the MACD is positive and in the opposite case, it is negative and falls below the zero line. This is seen from the above chart of MACD.

One can see many sell signals in the above chart, namely, A, B, C and D but after D the line started falling continuously and crossed the zero line and thus the point of 'D' is the last chance for disinvestment with advantage. If the market is in the overbought zone one can sell but not in the coversold zone. A daily chart prices will first give preliminary indications, which are to be confirmed by the oscillators or the MACD lines referred to in this chapter. Even with confirmation, one cannot be certain that the disinvestment has taken place at the right time. Experimentation, and research through simulation are the only guides to expertise and experience in the field of technical analysis to act as an aid for disinvestment management.

More details are set out in the Chapter on Technical Analysis.

Disinvestment by Government Sector

So far, we have dealt with disinvestment as a science and art of management by individuals, Portfolio Managers, Mutual Funds, companies and financial institutions etc. For these units and agencies investment and disinvestment go together and are part of their trading and funds management.

For Government which has considerable investments in industrial ventures, both in manufacturing, trading and services sectors, disinvestment is a different issue. In India, the Policy of Socialistic Pattern of development pursued by the Government since the fifties has resulted in considerable investments by the Government in public enterprises. Nearly Rs. 2.3 lakh crores of public funds are invested in these PSUs. The idea of disinvesting the PSUs was mooted when the trend to globalisation, privatisation and to market oriented economy was started with economic reforms in 1991-92.

Since 1985, the PSUs were allowed to borrow from the market directly and this has resulted in raising large sums of money from the capital market by the PSUs also. This has no doubt reduced their dependence on the government budgetary support, but many PSUs could not resort to public borrowing due to their non-viable nature and poor state of their financial position. Since 1991, the policy changed in the direction of privatisation and deregulation.

The public borrowing by PSUs continued through issue of Tax free and Taxable bonds. Total borrowing of this type stood at Rs. 15,588 crores in 2000-01. Tax free bonds were discontinued since the year 2003-04. Taxable bonds worth Rs. 12,840 crores were issued in the year 2008-09 as against the peak amount of Rs. 15,969 crores in 2000-01.

In 1993-94, the net disinvestment was a negative figure of Rs. 48 crores and the disinvestment figures since 1994 have substantially improved, until 1996, when again the disinvestment fell to a disappointing low of only Rs. 1,397 crores as against the Budget provision of Rs. 7,000 crores, for 1995-96.

The disinvestment process by the government was started in 1991-92 after the economic reforms were initiated in July 1991. During 1992, 1993 and 1994, there was a moderate disinvestment by the PSUs. But there was a setback to this process later due to poor investment climate in the economy and the continued bearish conditions in the market during 1995-96.

The process initiated in 1991-92 met with massive criticism about the mechanics of disinvestment on the one hand, that is through the route of mutual funds and public financial institutions, and secondly, on the ground of higher premiums charged on these disinvested shares. Thus, after they were listed as in the case of SAIL, BHEL, IPCL, etc., the prices fell in the market reflecting the higher premiums charged by the FIs and Mutual Funds, when they were disinvested. There must be some miscalculations of the intrinsic worth of the disinvested shares and of the investors perception of their worth. There was also utter disregard of market perceptions. Thirdly, some of these PSUs have under-performed as compared with the expectations of the investors and the rating given to the management efficiency and financial fundamentals came for serious doubts and criticism.

Subsequent disinvestment process met with some resistance from the investors as a result. The disinvestment of profit making PSUs picked up again in 2001-02, to be followed more vigorously in later years.

Problems of PSU Disinvestment

As referred to earlier, disinvestment became a problem to the government due to poor or non-viable financial position and fundamentals of many PSUs. Besides, PSU disinvestment has met with some difficulties during 1995-96 due to highly depressed market conditions and investor resistance to equity. The Budget for 1996-97 has provided for disinvestment of Rs. 5,000 crores by the PSUs as against only Rs. 380 crores were actually raised. Yearwise details of disinvestment by government in equity holdings of PSUs are as follows:

TABLE

Disinvestment Data

		Disinvestment (in Rs. Crores)
1994-95	Accounts	5,078
1995-96	Accounts	1,397
1996-97	Accounts	380
1997-98	Accounts	912
2000-01	Accounts	2,125
2001-02	Accounts	3,646
2002-03	Accounts	3,151
2003-04	Accounts	16,953
2004-05	Accounts	4,424
2005-06	Accounts	1,581
2006-07	Accounts	534
2007-08	Accounts	38,795
2008-09	Accounts	2,567

Source: RBI Handbook of Statistics.

During 1994-95, the disinvestment process was fairly successful, having raised Rs. 5,078 crores mostly due to sales to FIs, MFs, etc., but in 1995-96, as against the Budget provision of Rs. 7,000 crores, only Rs. 362 crores were raised excluding Bonus Shares, for reasons explained earlier. The Budget for 1996-97 has again provided for a larger amount of Rs. 5,000 crores, which did not materialise due to continued bearish phase, in both the primary and secondary markets during the whole year 1996, particularly since July 1996. In 1999-2000, the actual realisation of disinvestment proceeds worked out to only Rs. 1,000 crores. In Union Budget the target for disinvestment was put at Rs. 12,000 crores for 2001-02, against which Rs. 3,646 crores were raised. In April 2007 the Govt. disinvested its share in Maruti and realised Rs. 2,360 crores, as reported in Financial Press.

A disinvestment commission was set up in 1996 to lay down guidelines for disinvestment of PSUs, under the chairmanship of Mr. G.V. Ramakrishna. It was reported that this commission has engaged the services of three Indian Credit Rating agencies to study 40 PSUs referred to them for possible disinvestment. The allotted PSUs were studied by the respective credit rating agencies for their future profitability, technology levels, share value and other relevant details. Their reports were released to the commission. A separate Dept. of Disinvestment was created by the Government to establish a systemic policy approach and hasten the process of Disinvestments in 1999.

A National Investment Fund (NIF) was set up after 2004 and all the proceeds of disinvestment of central P.S.U. are required to be routed through and into it, which is maintained outside the consolidated fund of India. The income from the fund has to be used for infrastructure, and for reviving the revivable PSUs.

NAVARATNAS

Among this list of companies, there are a good number of profitable giant PSUs like BHEL, IPCL, SAIL, ONGC, OIL, Air India, ITI, BEML etc., for disinvestment. Of these nine were identified as Navaratnas to be eligible for a quick pace of disinvestment. Although there was some proposal that the World Bank would fund through a grant, the Commission on disinvestment to help its process of privatisation and for undertaking disinvestment successfully, there has been no receipt of such funds so far.

The immediate cause of anxiety for the government is the continued bearish phase of the market which will make it impossible for the government to disinvest the PSUs successfully. There has been criticism in the past on the disinvestment process by the government followed earlier to which a reference was made already. Bids were called from FIs, MFs and UTI etc., for contribution to the proposed amounts of equity issue to be disinvested. Reportedly, merchant bankers were also not involved and no underwriting was resorted to. The public offer was also made in some cases for parts of the amount disinvested. As the experience has shown, many such PSU shares were quoted below the issue price, after they were listed, with the result that public investors were scared of investing in PSU shares, even when they are profit-making. The premium charged by them may be high or the expectations of investors were too high and they are disappointed. The normal process of such disinvestment in foreign countries is to entrust such jobs to well established security firms and merchant banks to buy wholesale and retail them later to public at very realistic prices in good market conditions. That seems to be one of the ways to be followed in India too. Right pricing and right timing are equally important. For right pricing, credit rating and a study of the strength of fundamentals is necessary. Evaluation of the NAV and auditor's reports on the possible price range, in which one should sell are also necessary. These and other aspects were dealt with in the Reports of the Disinvestment Commission and their recommendations are under active consideration and implementation by the government. But disinvestment by the Government of PSUs has come to stay. The disinvestment process slowed down since 2004 due to the opposition of the leftist parties for disinvestment of profit making companies. There will be no takers for loss making PSUs anyway. Some state government have also disinvested in their P.S.Us., as per the data on state government finances.

During 2009-10. The government raised Rs. 25,000 crores from disinvestment in Oil India, NMDC, REC and NTPC. During 2010-11, some major PSUs, which will be divested are SAIL, Coal India, Hindustan Copper and Engineers India, which will realise some Rs. 40,000 crores, as targeted by the Govt. The Govt. have decided to divest in about 35 PSUs in the next 5 years and any PSU with Govt. stake of more than 90% will be eligible to be divested and if they are not listed, they will be first listed on the stock exchanges.

Central Public Sector Undertakings

As at end 1999, there were 236 operating PSEs, of which 134 were profit making and 102 were non-profit making. The gross profit as a percentage of capital employed was 16% in 1997-98. This gross profit does not tell the net return to the government, which is 7.7 per cent for all PSEs, on the capital invested by the Government. Their borrowing cost on an average was higher at 12 per cent. The gap is met from the Budget revenues which is a drain on the public exchequer.

The disinvestment process was slow due to delays in administrative decision making red tape, and political difficulties in implementation and due to bad market conditions. Towards the end of 1999, the Government have set up a separate Department of Disinvestment and Disinvestment Commission was reconstituted in July 2001.

DIVESTMENT METHODS OF GOVERNMENT

To achieve the targets of disinvestment, the Government have decided on three possible methods, namely the SPV or special purpose vehicle, the Trust Route and the Warehousing method.

The SPV method and Trust methods involve of the setting up of a separate body to which the Government would pass on its holding and which in turn arranges for divestment. The main difference between SPV and Trust methods is that the Trust method provides for a mechanism of checks in the absence of parliamentary audit, while the SPV method lacks this mechanism.

Under the warehousing method, there are three models — namely a buy back arrangement with the Government on outright sale to FIs and a Trust market making by the FIs for the Government holdings. In all these cases, FIs and mainly public FIs will have to bear the burden. The Government have to negotiate with the FIs, in respect of the most suitable method for each of these models.

The buy back arrangement is flexible in that the FI can buy the stock from the Government to ultimately pass them on to the public. If there is any fall in prices, the government would buy back at the original sale price. This flexibility is not there in the other methods of warehousing. In the case of out right sale to FIs it is good for the government to close the deal leaving the FIs to book profits or losses in their sale to public. But it would appear as if FIs are forced by the government, as they are also public bodies owned fully or partly.

OPEN BIDDING PROCESS OF DIVESTMENT

The objective of open bidding process in its transparency in resources raised by the Government by selling its stake. This is not the same as the adoption of strategic partner route as recommended by the Nitesh Sangupta Committee. The Finance Ministry under pressure to raise resources is attempting to sell a singificant stake Bharat Petroleum Corporation and IBP on the lines of the sale of the stake in IPCL, which attracted bids from major players in oil sector like SOROS Group, Mitsubishi and Reliance Industries.

A Proposal on Mutual Fund Route

In December 1999, the FIs and banks have planned to set up an Asset Management Company and Mutual Fund owned by them by putting in their own funds to the extent of Rs. 4,000 crores. All major Public Sector FIs, LIC, GIC, UTI, SBI and a few other public sector banks will put in funds. The AMC will buy at the market going rates the offered stock held by the Government in the major oil, Telecom and I.T. Public Sector undertakings. There will be about a dozen companies which are profit making.

The AMC will hold them and disinvest as and when the market can absorb. It is estimated that the capacity to absorb by the market in 1999-2000 may not be more than Rs. 2,000 crores, and any public issue route may not absorb all the divestment planned by the Government.

The planned Mutual Fund is likely to be managed by the UTI, as it has got enough experience in this line. The mutual fund route is preferred, as warehousing route may not really help the Government. Direct issue at home or abroad may not fetch the required money.

Banks' Divestment Scheme

The Government have planned to divest some 5 public sector banks in 1999-2000. It would sell its equity stake in the following profit making banks, namely PNB, Allahabad Bank, Andhra Bank, I.O.B. and Punjab and Sind Bank under the existing policy, which was done through Initial Public Offers (IPOs) to the public for subscription, before 2004, when the policy was changed.

In all the above banks, the Government held 100% of equity. The respective proportions of equity held in these banks are as follows, as on March 2006.

A. B. 51.5%

Allahabad Bank 55.23%

I.O.B. — 61.24%

P.N.B. — 57.79%

U.B.I. — 55.43%

The bouyant response to the Syndicate Bank issue in 1999 has prompted the Government to clear the public issues of these banks. Besides there was over subscription many times in respect of IPOs by Syndicate Bank. The bank offerings have in general done well as in the case of Corporation Bank, even when the market conditions were bad. Denationalisation and privatisation is part of the agenda of banking reforms, which the government has been pursuing.

The bank privatisation is planned to bring down in stages in the Government holdings near to the level of 33% of total equity. Bank shares seem to have a good demand in the market as perceived by merchant bankers and market operators. Many profit making banks like A.B, Indian Bank, etc., have raised fresh capital from the market, which was used to reduce the government holding in the respective banks.

Some of the public sector banks will be further capitalised as they have inadequate capital adequacy as in the case of Central Bank, IDBI Bank, UCO Bank, etc., whereby, they can be revitalised and pay larger dividends to the government.

Securities Market Report (BSE)

Securities Markets and Investment

This book on Investment and Securities Markets in India is closely connected to the Stock Markets, as securities are listed and traded on the stock markets and Investments are made in these securities listed on the stock markets, which are all dealt with in this book. The relevance of the stock market reports to the subject matter under consideration of this book is clear from this.

This chapter deals with the interpretation and analysis of the daily stock market reports, with particular relevance to the BSE. The BSE information is supplemented with that of the NSE wherever it is possible. The BSE is chosen for two reasons: One, it has a hoary antiquity and a tradition of all possible trades, including the BADLA which has been replaced by the Derivatives trading. Second, it has the largest number of listed securities which are about three times larger than that on the NSE, and it has a larger market capitalization and its sensex as the index number of industrial securities is well known all over the world markets.

Objects

The object of this chapter is to familiarise the reader with the jargon used in the Daily Stock Market Reports. An analysis of the daily reports and interpretation of these data and information in the Reports is necessary kit of the security market Analyst. It is therefore relevant for all Finance students to know the technique of analysis of the Daily Market Reports. Although the analysis as at a point of time its relevance for all times remains with only minor changes.

In India there are 23 Stock Exchanges including the Interconnected Stock Exchange which started operating in 1998. Of these, only two BSE ad NSE, account for 70 to 80% of the total volume of trade in India. Of these two, only BSE has the hoary antiquity, width and depth of the market for equities with the largest number of scrips and a wide range of companies listed on it. Besides as the daily reports of B.S.E. are more detailed and varied, an attempt is made to analyse the BSE Reports supplementing it with NSE Reports, wherever necessary. Infact the BSE Reports for equity trading are more elaborate, while NSE Reports for wholesale debt segment encompassing gilt edged Market and Money market are more relevant but brief. BSE Reports are thus taken for indepth analysis in this chapter and these Reports as published in Economic Times are taken as the basis for our analysis. As it is only for illustration, the date of the data is not material.

Global Comparison

With the operation of FIIs in India and given the role of FFIs in the capital market operations in India and with Indian Companies getting listed NASDAQ and other foreign stock Exchanges, in addition to the already existing trading abroad of our GDRs, and ADRs, Indian markets are getting increasingly globalised. Many I.T. companies like INFOSYS and Satyam are traded in the U.S. and the sentiment of trade there is getting reflected on Dalal street as well. This trend to globalisation of Indian stock markets is evident particularly since the New Economy Stock got prominence in the new millennium from the year 2000. The BSE Reporting is thus getting increasing attention the world over and has thus become necessary to attempt here an analysis of its coverage and sophistication.

Overview of BSE Market Report

The Stock Exchange, Mumbai has the largest number of listed companies of more than 5000 on its trading list. But the number of traded scrips on any day varies form 2000 to 3000. These scrips have been put under four categories, namely 'A', B_1, B_2, and Z groups. There is another group "others" which include "T", "S" and "TS" categories. 'T' is trade to trade group of cash delivery "S" refers to those traded in the INDONEXT of BSE providing platform for nation wide-trading and "TS" includes those trade to trade deals in 'S' category.

There are about 140 companies in 'A' group as on 10th May, 2010 of which 104 were covered for Badla Report in May 2000 after which Badla lost its significance. These scrips in the forward list are having the carry forward facility. As at end March 2009, there were slightly more than 200 scrips in 'A' Group BSE, out of a total of about 5000 listed companies. B_1 and B_2 groups including the 'Z' group cover the rest of the scrips, which are traded roughly on any day. 'Z' group shares are quoted separately and are not included in B_1 and B_2 groups. Besides, scrips kept in depository form are quoted separately as those of Depository stocks. Similarly those in compulsory Rolling settlement system are quoted in a separate format. With the introduction Compulsory Rolling settlement, the importance of Badla has gone. Even the 'Z' Category is now included under "others."

The debt trading was minimal on BSE and it is mostly concentrated on NSE . Besides, BSE also puts out daily a list of stocks with high volumes of trade and low prices, used mostly for speculation. At the other end, a list of high fliers in speculation involving a rise or fall in prices between 8% to 12%, hitting the circuit band at bottom or top is also published daily. The net long purchase positions and net short sale positions in all the scrips available for carry forward can be got daily in the published data. There is a list of selected toppers in turnover on the B.S.E. There is also a Table of scrips with rising prices and falling prices over the last five trading days under the Head of Gainers and Losers. Bulk deals, insider trading stocks, new highs and new lows, etc., are all published by the E.T., B.S., B.L, etc. As in May 2010, the Daily reports consist of A Group (specified) and "others" which inlude B_1 B_2 and Z etc. Besides there is a section of futures and options whose quotes are published in the daily financial press.

Globalisation Trend

The episodes of activity during the first half of the year 2000 bear evidence of good correlation between BSE and Nasdaq sentiment and volatility trends. The fears of U.S. Economy and Fed have been felt on Nasdaq as much as on BSE. The opening up of the economy and of its markets has its impact on the Indian financial markets, whether it is capital market, Money market or Forex market.

The Table below presents the data on correlation between the volatility on Nasdaq and that on the Asian markets. The normal daily performance of volatility since 1993 was generally having lower correlation in India relative to other Asian markets like China, Hong Kong, Singapore, Taiwan etc. But this correlation increased after episodes of wild swings such as those with 3 to 5% daily rise or fall on the Nasdaq. This would mean that even Indian markets can have tailspins, based on the volatility of world markets. The Nasdaq of U.S.A. is now collaborating with London and Tokyo markets of similar nature and common Listing and trading for 24 hours in a day in many scrips will be the order of the day in the coming years.

In the above context, the BSE Report should be analysed first for any global links or reflection of global trends. The chart below should be the basis of evidence of interlinkages between Indian markets and foreign markets. In particular, NASDAQ of U.S.A. Dow Jones of New York Stock Exchange FTSE index of London Stock Exchange, NIKKEI of Tokyo Stock Exchange and Hang Seng Index of Hong Kong Stock Exchange should be examined after Juxtaposing them with BSE and NSE Indices of India. The adjacent Table on Stock Market Price Indices for one day (May 8th 2000) bears out the trends on the BSE in comparison with Skindia GDR Index (reflecting the performance of our companies Abroad) and Dow Jones of New York, FTSE of London etc. Thus, the BSE Sensex fell on that day by 230 points and Nikkei average by 239 points and Hang Seng by 367 points.

Table 47.1 Volatility and Correlation

Correlation with Nasdaq	Normal daily performance Since' 93	Only for the days when Nasdaq rose/fell by over				
		1%	2%	3%	4%	5%
China	23.1	31.9	39.3	52.2	60.1	63.5
Hong Kong	33.2	46.1	54.8	63.2	63.1	70.3
India	10.5	16.5	27.6	33.8	38.8	45.1
Indonesia	21.5	30.4	41.3	48.4	63.2	68.4
Korea	21.5	29.6	37.4	50.2	66.7	64.9
Malaysia	22.7	31.7	41.7	53.6	61.8	70.4
Philippines	23.6	36.3	48.5	55.8	59.0	52.0
Singapore	26.7	39.0	48.2	54.4	59.4	68.1
Taiwan	13.4	21.1	28.3	29.1	39.2	40.3
Thailand	17.2	26.4	32.8	36.8	50.1	62.4

During normal times correlation between Nasdaq and Asian markets, including India, was quite low. However correlation rises significantly after episodes of wild swings.

Note: For Asian markets, performance is taken for the day following the Nasdaq performance day. Performance is based on local currency indices. ET, May 9, 2000.

Source: CLSA

The fall was almost universal; despite strong fundamentals of our companies the sentiment was bearish on that day. The Skindia GDR however showed a mild upswing indicating that the underlying investor interest abroad in our companies may be different from that of Indian Investors and Foreign investors in India. But Nasdaq sentiment was weak due to fears of the outcome of the forthcoming U.S. Federal Reserve meeting (slated for the third week of May). The BSE as also Nasdaq was hit by rumours and the strong currents of FII operations. The daily press now reports the quotations of Nasdaq, Dow Jones. FTSE, Nikkei, DAX, CAC, SPTSX, AS30, etc., under the caption of Developed Markets. As in 2010, some of these indices are not published on a daily basis, in the E.T.

As on May 8, 2000

Table 47.2 Stock Markets - Price Indices

The et Share Indices		
Mindex	4187.29	(-333.04)
Lifex	1358.78	(-16)
Brandex	1076.56	(-56.13)
Other Indices		
BSE Sensitive	4463.40	(-230.48)
National	2265.84	(-123.29)
BSE 200	483.76	(-25.65)
S&P CNX Nifty	1365.05	(-57.35)
S&P CNX Defty ($)	N.A.	
CNX Nifty Jr.	2681.45	(-98.40)
S&P CNX 500	1018.75	(-47.27)
CNX MIDCAP 200	N.A.	
Skindia GDR	1004.89*	(+13.70)
Dow Jones	10523.38*	(-54.48)
Nasdaq	3727.23	(-89.59)
FTSE	6195.60	(-43.20)
Nikkei	18199.96	(-239.40)
Hang Seng	14901	(-367.64)

Note: Figures in brackets are absolute changes over previous day. As there are for illustration the date of the data does not matter.

Source: ET, May 9, 2000.

If will be of interest to note that on the previous trading day namely May 5 (Friday) speculative buying by FII led the upswing by 3% from 4554 to 4694 showing a net gain of 140 points. On Monday May 8, 2000 speculative profit taking led to sales by FIIs which resulted in a fall in sensex by 5% from 4694 to 4464 — a loss of 230 points on one day. On both these days, some share prices have hit the circuit breakers. The present level of circuit breaking is 8% to 12% in both directions. This means that if the price of any scrip rises or falls by 12%, trading in that scrip is stopped for some time as per the prevailing SEBI guidelines. This is in the nature of trading restriction, comparable to high margins. Infact the SEBI has already imposed volatility margins on highly speculative scrips. On top of volatility margins, the circuit breakers act as a check on undue speculative upswing or downswing on the scrip price. Thus the off loading of Infosys and Wipro shares by FIIs led to their prices hitting the circuit break limit of 12% floor, on May 8th. On the other hand a number of I.T. scrips such as Digital, Global Tele. Satyam, HCL, Infosys have hit the ceiling limit of circuit breakers at 12% on the upswing, on May 5th (The previous trading day.)

Daily Report Analysis

The Text of the Report for one day namely May 8th is reproduced below from E.T. The fall of 5% in sensex on that day was due to FII selling, as seen earlier. Secondly, most of the speculative attacks were on the I.T. stocks and New Economy stocks, like HLL, Zee etc.

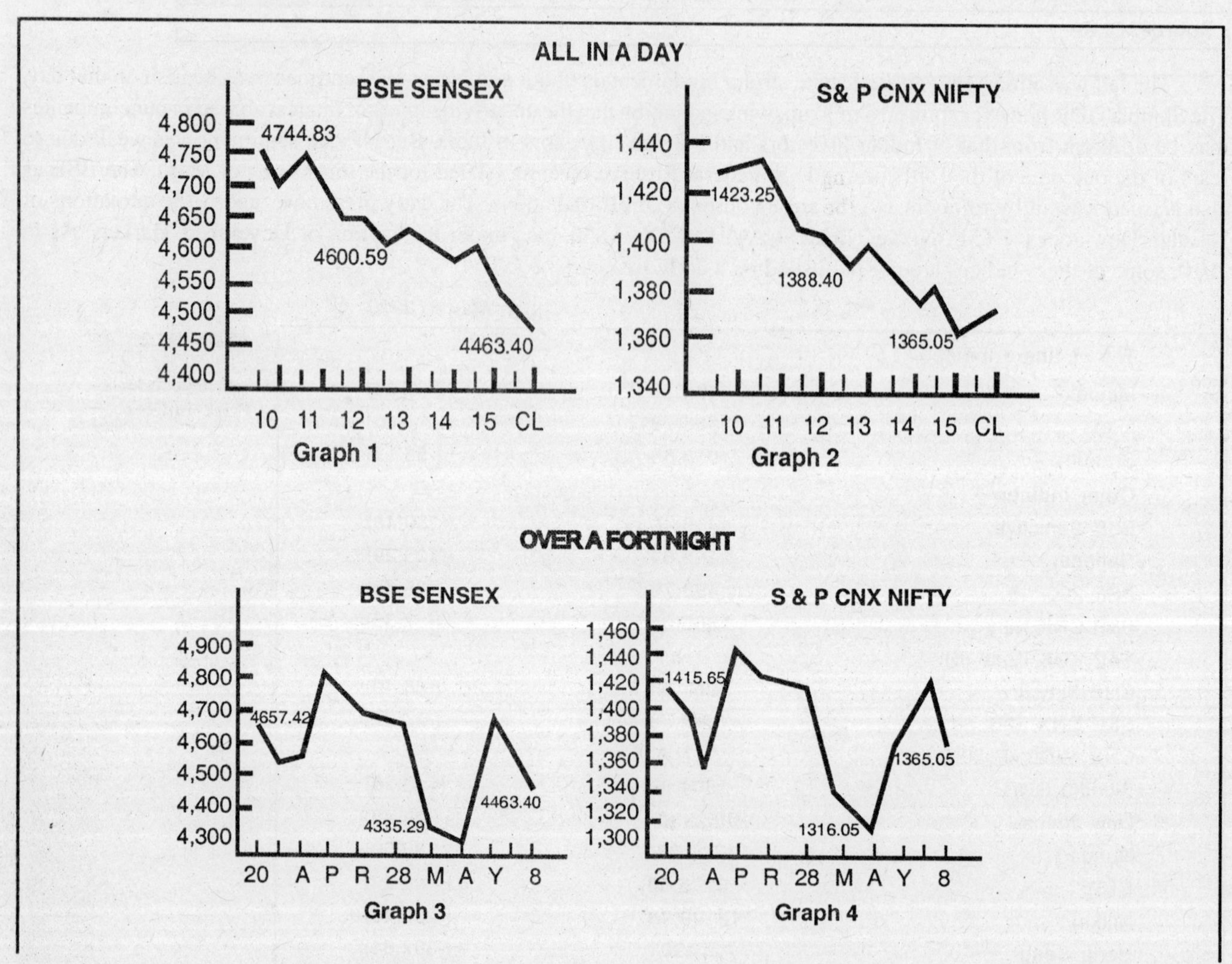

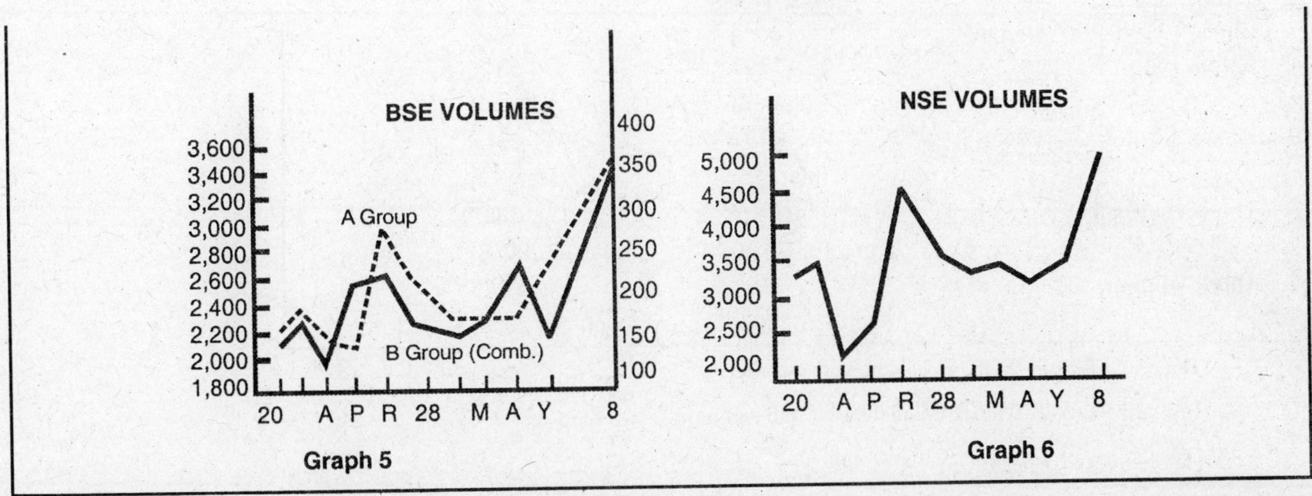

Daily reports in the press contain the details of prices, volume of trade, highs, lows etc. The stock prices included in major indexes; their capitalisation and weightage changes etc. are given separately. The details of prices are given under various heads of Rolling Stocks, Technology stocks, Pharma stocks, etc., and in groups of A, and "Others."

The above extract provides a bird's eye view of trading from 10 am to 4 pm on one day in the form of Graphs (1) and (2) on BSE sensex and NSE Index (S&P CNX Nifty). Sensex fell from 4744 to 4463 during the trading day, while the NSE Nifty dropped form 1423 to 1365. The next two graphs (3) and (4) give an overview of a fortnight trading from April 20 to May 8th, both on the BSE and NSE. These two charts clearly bring out the sea saw movements and volatile upswings and down swings in the Index. The next two graphs (5) and (6) give the volumes of trade in value terms. (Rs. crores). The volumes an BSE include both A' and B group separately while the volumes on the NSE are generally higher.

The NSE although started trading only in 1994, picked up volumes very fast and is now leading even the B.S.E in this respect. The reasons are not far to seek, as its members are high networth companies, FFIs, FIIs, Indian FIs, banks and mutual funds and listed companies traded are again the top rated and well traded high net worth companies. The listed companies on the NSE are only about one-fourth of the listed companies on the BSE and market capitalisation on BSE is about 90% of all India market capitalisation. But the trade turnover on NSE is higher than on the BSE and both NSE and BSE together account for about 70 to 80% of all India trade turnover. Nearly more than 10,600 companies were listed at various stock Exchanges in India at one time of which about 5,000 companies are listed on BSE and about 15000 companies on NSE now in 2010. Almost all companies of good networth of above Rs. 10 crores are now listed on both NSE and BSE.

PRICE INDEX SNAPSHOTS OF THE MARKET

The data on BSE Sensex and NSE Nifty are presented in the accompanying table to give a micro picture of a day's performance in the back ground of broad time frame of three year High and low. If the data are to be reframed, the day's high and low are to be seen in the background of one year High and low and three year High and Low. As the Table 47.3 shows the extent of the range is narrowing down over period.

Table 47.3

Snapshot of Markets for March 2010

	Sensex	*Nifty*
Previous Close (Friday, March 12, 2010)	17,167	5133
Open	17172	5131
High	17245	5158
Low	17127	5122
Close	17166	5137

Change Over previous close	–1.3	+3.6
52-Wk High	17790 (Jan. 6)	5311 (Jan. 6)
52-WK Low	8481 (Mar. 13)	2617 (Mar. 13)
Three year-high	21207 (Jan., 10, 2008)	6357 (Jan. 8, 2008)
Three year-low	7697 (Oct. 27, 2008)	2253 (Oct. 27, 2008)

— Three year Range - 2.76 times (More than two times)

— One year Range 2.10 times (More than one and half times)

— Day's Range of variation 1% to 3% only.

This is as it should be, in view of the time gaps involved. Today's price is better than that three years ago and one year ago, if the lows are compared but not so if the highs are compared which means that the market has potential for improvement to reach a higher level in the days to come, if the underlying trend continues. The picture is as follows.

	Lows	Highs
Three years Data	7691	21207
One year Data	8481	17790
Day's Data	17127	17245

The underlying long term trend is bullish but the intermediate trend is reactionary and the day's picture is bearish by comparing the open and close and high and low for the day with a net loss of one point. Similar upswings and downswings were noticed in the more recent episodes of September to November 2005 and in 2009-10. All the above data are kept for illustration as the dates of the episodes are not relevant for principles.

The analysis of a Day's Report has thus to be made in the background of intermediate and long term trends. Different investors have different perceptions of time horizon on investment — day to day gain, medium term gain and long-term appreciation have to be kept in mind.

Trade Turnover

Next to price index, the most important indicator to be looked into in the Security Market Reports is the volume of trade. The Trade Turnover has two aspects namely value and volume. The value of trade is the total of purchases and sales in terms of crores of rupees. The volume of trade is represented by number of shares in lakhs, irrespective of the face value or market value of share.

Table 47.4

Turnover on BSE (6 to 12 th May 2008)

	12/5	9/5	8/5	7/5	6/5
BSE					
Turnover (Rs. Cr.)	6008	6595	5966	6622	6742
Share Trd. (Lakh)	3774	4041	3658	4093	3697
No. of Trades (Lakh)	25.42	25.20	23.88	25.39	24.21

On both the counts, the data on BSE are presented in the accompanying Table from 6/5/2008 to 12/5/2008 for a period of 5 days of trading. This will give an idea whether the volume is increasing, or decreasing or fluctuating in a range of limits. The Table presented earlier shows that broadly the value of turnover is increasing while the volume in terms of number of shares is fluctuating with in a narrow range. This would mean that although sentiment is weak, an undercurrent of firmness is visible in that the economic fundamentals of the corporate sector are continuing to be strong. Although the data relate to 2008 this is kept here to show the fluctuating nature of turnover and trade volume.

Table 47.5

Up and Down on BSE of Daily Traded Scrips

(as on 12th March, 2010)				*(No. of traded scrips)*	
	'A'	**'B'**	**'S'**	**Others**	**Total**
Advances	69	666	145	151	1031
Declines	127	1211	296	213	1847
Unchanged	2	57	9	18	86
Total	198	1934	450	382	2964

'*S*' Group relates to those on cash versus delivery.

Advance/Decline Line

The underlying trend can also be seen by the accompanying table on "up and down on BSE" Table 47.5. The number of Advancing and Declining Scrips and those unchanged are presented on the basis of category wise scrips namely 'A' group B and S groups. The fact that declines are more in the "A" group indicates that larger number of speculative scrips are being offered for sale and selling pressure is more. But the fact that there are larger number of declines in 'B' group - investment type-reflects that sentiment underlying in the market is also bearish. Out of scrips quoted and traded on that day (March 12, 2010), leaving aside 86 scrips which have not recorded any change in prices, 1031 scrips recorded upward movement, while 1847 scrips recorded declines.

(in Rs Crores)

Table 47.6

FII Activity

	Equity			*Debt*		
Date	*Buy*	*Sell*	*Net*	*Buy*	*Sell*	*Net*
11/3	2303	1856	447	1328	193	1135
10/3	2717	2299	418	505	604	-99
9/3	3730	1960	1770	1682	1096	586
8/3	4461	2202	2260	179	364	-186
5/3	3463	1583	1879	276	200	77
Tot Mar	26012	15998	10014	7487	4054	3433
Total 2010	**126176**	**115185**	**10991**	**37351**	**22904**	**14448**

ET. March 13, 2010

MF Activity

	Equity			*Debt*		
Date	*Buy*	*Sell*	*Net*	*Buy*	*Sell*	*Net*
9/3	719	633	27	2856	1638	1217
8/3	797	998	-201	2957	1055	-1903
5/3	594	1121	-527	4230	2065	2164
4/3	503	854	-351	1907	936	971
Tot Mar	4097	5186	-1150	15646	9000	6646
Total 2010	**32331**	**35436**	**-3159**	**133041**	**86022**	**47019**

ET. March 13, 2010

Now FII and MF activities are presented under two heads namely Equity and Debt. Minus sign indicates net sales, which reflects the bearish market.

Role of Institutional Agencies

In Daily reports, as much as in the longer time horizons, both investment and speculative activity have to be captured in Daily Reports as they leave their own impact on the market. This impact is seen both in price and volume of trade and they are inter linked. The price and volume trends and their interpretation were discussed in the chapter on Technical analysis. So far as the daily reports are concerned, technicals, play a greater role than fundamentals as the temporary demand and supply factors are tossed from pillar to post by sentiment, expectations and psychological factors.

It may be noted that market moved from bearishness to bullishness on a daily basis and was highly volatile during January to March 2010. These days are classical examples of the role of sentiment on the market. The fundamentals of the economy are good. The intrinsic factors in the I.T. sector, which is subject to speculative onslaughts are sound and the rumours regarding Infosys and wipro were found to be unbased, and these scrips alongwith some other New Economy scrips were found to touch the circuit breakers both at the ceiling and floor (12% on either side which was infact wider than the 8% limit which was fixed earlier). This limit was further raised to 16% in June 2000. The same was the story of January 2009, when Satyam Comp. Scam was unveiled, due to factors disscussed in an earlier chapter.

The above sentimental factors which play havoc on the market are aided by the institutional players in the market who have the muscles of money power. These major institutional players on the BSE are the FIIs, FIs and Mutual Funds. The data on their daily purchases and sales are published by the SEBI on a daily basis. It is obligatory as per the SEBI guidelines, that these agencies report their trade details to SEBI and Stock Exchanges. Accordingly these data can be had form the daily Reports in the financial press. But these data come with a time lag of one or two days.

As the above Tables show, bulk of the funds are pumped in and out by FIIs, involving a total of purchases and sales of about Rs. 3,000 to 5,000 crores on a day. If their purchases are more than sales involving a net long position, the market may turn out to be bullish and if net sales are more involving a short position, the market may turn bearish. The fact that short position is more risky and more speculative is a known fact and that is one of the reasons why SEBI has prohibited payment of Badla to naked short sellers from May 2000. They have no owned or borrowed shares in those scrips, but yet they sell the shares meant for carry forward, in the hope of covering them later when the prices fall. They are typical bears and if they are lucky and if prices fall, they gain by differences in prices. But SEBI does not want to encourage them with the Badla incentive also and hence prohibited the payment of Badla to them, irrespective of whether they gain or lose.

The activity of Mutual Funds and their purchases and sales involving Rs. 3000 to 4000 crores is another major factor, influencing the market sentiment. Their total volume of trade and their net position indicate whether there is in market over bought or over sold position. In fact as per SEBI guidelines Mutual Funds can not speculate but give delivery and take delivery and cannot participate in the badla activity. Even so, their sheer volume of trade has some influence on the market. But bulk of their activity is concentrated in the debt market as they need fixed income returns.

As judged by their trading activity over the trading cycle of 5 days, the mood of the market can be explained. The market was gaining and optimistic in sentiment culminating in euphoria of a quantum Jump on 5th and 8th March 2010. But these gains were mostly wiped out by the violent attack of the bears on the next day. This type of swings of bullish and bearish nature accentuate the volatility of the market and the FII activity and Mutual Fund purchases and sales reflect these moods and in fact accentuated or attenuated by their activities. They are also therefore considered as one of the main indicators of the market as reported in the press.

Trading Cycle

BSE also publishes its settlement programme, for all groups of scrips namely A, B_1, B_2 & "others". The settlement is after 5 days of trading with a trading cycle of Monday to Friday week. The attached extract gives the illustration in this regard.

The settlement numbers based on a fixed pattern of weekly settlements of Monday to Friday are published in advance of many settlements at a time. Their pay in and payout dates are also indicated in this print out. For each trading cycle there will be no delivery period and pay-in and pay-out days. SEBI has directed that all Stock Exchanges should have uniform trading cycle and clearing system. We have shifted from T + 14 to T + 3 day settlement and some to T + 1 settlement.

Table 47.7

BSE Settlement Programme

Sett No.	Trading Day	No-Delivery Period Demat Physical	Pay-In/ Pay-out
DR-233	11/03	08/03/2010-25/03/2010	15/03/2010
DR-234	12/03	10/03/2010-27/03/2010	17/03/2010
DR-235	15/03	11/03/2010-28/03/2010	18/03/2010
DR-236	16/03	11/03/2010-28/03/2010	18/03/2010
DR-237	17/03	12/03/2010-29/03/2010	19/03/2010
DR-238	18/03	15/03/2010-01/04/2010	22/03/2010
DR-239	19/03	16/03/2010-02/04/2010	23/03/2010
DR-240	22/03	18/03/2010-04/04/2010	25/03/2010
DR-241	23/03	19/03/2010-05/04/2010	26/03/2010
DR-242	25/03	22/03/2010-08/04/2010	29/03/2010
DR-243	26/03	23/03/2010-09/04/2010	30/03/2010
DR-244	29/03	24/03/2010-10/04/2010	31/03/2010
DR-001	30/03	29/03/2010-15/04/2010	05/04/2010
DR-002	31/03	30/03/2010-16/04/2010	06/04/2010

March 2010 Data

The investor with this information of pay in and payout will know in advance when he is expected to give shares for sale or receive shares on purchase and when he has to give a cheque or receive a cheque.

Record Dates and Book Closure

Another information that one should have when trading on a Stock Exchange is the Record dates or Book closure dates of listed companies. On and around these dates - one week on either side or a fortnight as the case may be - the scrips in this regard enter into "no delivery" period and the buyer cannot get delivery of shares nor give delivery of shares, as the books of Register of members are closed for declaring a dividend or for entitlement of Bonus or Rights shares. Such scrips on "No-Delivery periods", have to be avoided.

The attached table gives the details of companies with their book closure or Record dates and the purpose of closing the books. All the details of companies coming out with the respective announcements in a period of a fort night to two months are generally provided in this Table. As per the Companies Act, every company has to give notice of these record and book closure dates to the investors. The Listing Agreement also calls for these data from the companies to the Stock Exchange atleast 42 days in advance.

The table below shows the companies coming out with these dates during forthcoming one or two months in advance. This Table given for May 2000, lists the companies coming out in the months of May to July 2000. The letters "B.C." stands for book closure and "RD" stands for Record Date and the date or dates along with the purpose during which the books are closed are also indicated here. A fortnight before and after these dates, the investors have to take care for the No- delivery period for those scrips. The quotations will be Ex-dividend Ex-rights or Ex-Bonus, etc. The Table below is for illustration purpose only and the date of the Table is not very relevant.

Table 47.8
Book Closures and Record Dates

Company	B.C. R.D.	Book-Closure Record-Date	Purpose
Advanced Mic	BC	27/05	8% Dividend
Besco	RD	16/05	12.5% Interim Div.
Ceeta Ind.	BC	38/05-05/06	AGM
Charminar Gr	BC	28/06-30/06	AGM
Deltron	BC	16/05-24/05	AGM
Dig-Equip	BC	07/07-21/07 Div. (Rev)	AGM/15%
Gemeni Commun.	BC	01/07-18/07	AGM
Georg Fische	RD	25/05	Interim Dividend
Global Tele	BC	23/06-07/07	AGM & Dividend
Guj. Vit. Phar	RD	27/05	5% Interim Div.
Himat Seide	RD	12/05 & 30% Ist Interim Dividend (2000-01)	30% 2nd Int. Div.
Hindoo. Spin.	BC	20/06-28/06	AGM
Intern. Combust	RD	20/06	15% Int. on NCDs
Northern Proj.	BC	21/06-30/06	AGM
OK Play	BC	14/06-20/06	AGM
Orient. Bank	BC	05-17/05	35% Dividend
Paper Products	RD	27/06	14% Int. on PCDs
Paper Products	RD	26/09	14% Int. on PCDs
Paper Products	RD	27/12	14% Int. on PCDs
Paper Products	RD	27/03/2001	14% Int. on PCDs
Pennar Prof.	BC	22/06-28/06	AGM
Pidilite Ind	BC	27/06-03/07	Bonus/Final Div.
Reliance Inds.	BC	25/09-30/09	18% Int. on FCDs
Reliance Inds.	BC	23/12-30/12	18% Int. on FCDs
Reliance Inds.	BC	24/03/01-31/03/01	18% Int. on NCDs
Reliance Inds.	BC	24/06-30/06	18% Int. on FCDs
Reliance Inds.	BC	23/10-31/10	14.5% Int. on NCDs
Rosell Ind.	BC	21/06-28/06	AGM
Shri.MM. Soft	BC	30/05-31/05	10% Dividend
Tata Chem	BC	09/08-24/08	Final Dividend
Tea Time Ltd.,	BC	21/06-30/06	AGM
Usha Beltron	BC	20/07-26/07	AGM

Circuit Band Hitters

The Scrips which have hit the circuit breakers or the band of price limits of 8 to 12% on either side are also published both by the BSE and NSE. The price data of today's close, previous close and percentage change involved in each of the selected scrips are also presented in their daily Reports. The scrips which break the circuits are of two categories namely the Day's Best and Day's worst, indicating upswing and downswing scrips respectively. The investors will come to know from the data, the scrips in which speculation is more or less concentrated on that day.

Along with this data, the first selected turnover toppers in group A, B_1 and B_2 of the BSE and NSE are listed along with the number of shares traded and gross value of trades and number of trades. From these data, one can know how many toppers have hit the circuit breakers, what is the average value of the trade and the proportion of shares traded to the outstanding shares of each of these companies.

Speculative Positions

Badla and carry forward is allowed in about 150 scrips falling in A group on the B.S.E. The data on their daily net *short* position and *long* positions and the volume (number of shares) and value (Rs. Crores) in respect of each other these scrips were also published. The short positions are net sales made without the intention of giving delivery of shares and long positions are net purchases made without the intention of taking delivery of shares. Each broker's net short sales and net long purchases are added to arrive at the total net short positions and net long positions held by all members in each of the scrips, allowed to be carried forward. The data published daily when Badla was in operation were those of total net short sales and net long purchases both in terms of number of shares involved and their values in rupees.

The interpretation of these data is easy once the reader knows the mechanics of badla trading, speculative trade and investment trade and the role of volumes and price etc. which are set out in other chapters of this book. One can identify the scrips subject to high speculation, whether the net sales position is more than the net purchase position, leading to backwardation charges and what is the technical position in each of the scrips and in the total market as a whole etc. A shrewd Analyst can also know the likely trend in each of the scrips during the settlement period, based on the net accumulated purchases or sales outstanding which have to be squared up or unwind the position or carry forward by the last day of the trading cycle for each settlement.

Short sales positions are those of bears while long purchase positions are those of Bulls and the relative strengths of bulls and bears are known from these data. If any of the bulls or bears are weak and the market is going against them they may turn out to be defaulters and the Trade settlement Guarantee fund has to be used to salvage the market at that time.

The Badla data are no longer published or used as the Rolling Settlement System has replaced Badla and Badla data is no longer relevant.

Surveillance System

The Stock Exchange Surveillance system and their trading control system aim at imposing margins, operate the circuit breakers, impose limits on brokers in respect of any scrips or total for all scrips and convert trade in any scrip to a Rolling settlement basis or for spot trading and cash delivery etc would all be based on the analysis of the above data on trade turnover and price movements during the trading time of 10 AM to 4 PM on any day. These data are also used by SEBI and Research groups for Investment Analysis. The trading time has been changed to 9 AM to 4 PM, intstead of 10 AM to 4 PM in January 2010.

Index Details

BSE also gives out daily the sensex data along with prices performance of each of the scrips included in the Index (30 in number), their market capitalisation and the Day's weightage of each of these scrips in the total Index. Market capitalisation is derived by multiplying the number of outstanding shares in each of the companies by their day's closing price. The proforma used is as follows:

Company's name, Day's closing price; previous trading day close' percentage change in price for the day, Market capitalisation of that scrip, Day's weightage of each of these scrips in the Index; and the percentage change in weightage.

Similar data with respect Sensex which includes 30 actively traded scrips on the BSE and NSE, are also presented in a similar fashion giving out their market capitalisation and changes in it. The NSE scrip prices are also similarly presented for S & P CNX Nifty giving out the price and market capitalisation data in respect of the 50 most actively traded scrips included in the Nifty. Barring the minor details of small changes, the trends arrived at in respect of price, market capitalisation and its weightage in the total index etc. are almost the same in all these Indices.

BSE Stock Tables

The table below on BSE/NSE scrips gives an extract specimen of Market trade Quotes on May 10, 2000 for illustration.

SE Forward/NSE

BSE Code, Co., Priqs. [Vol., Value. Rs.OOOs. Trades]	*P/E*	*2-WkH/L*
[410] *ACC* (123) 123, 128, 95,115, *50L*, 126.95 *[2345735,290013.05,9300]*		303/116
(122. 95) 121, *10*, 128.95, *115.60,126.55 [2746078,338126,23,12207]*		*298/116L*
[2] ABB Ltd. (171.95) 170,172, 168.25, 171.25 [13447,2294.64,192]	19.1	500/153
(169.95) 169, *173.50*, 167.75, *169.90 [19330, 3280.69*, 244}	18.9	503/146
[8] Amara Raja B (81) 80.10,82,80,81.30 [9285, 751.46,93]	2.5*	344/74
(80.70) 80.90, 81.30, 78.50, 80.30 {13615, 1091.83, 147]	2.4	364/73
[877] Apollo Tyre (94)94.05, 92, 92.40 [25868, 2400.87, 240]	5.7*	267/43
(94.75) 92.50, 94,91.25,91.80 [45952,4235.30,363]	5.7	26/41
[32129] Aptech Ltd. (813) 781,836,770,835 [18254, 14760.58,895]	*40.9*	1540/315
(809.25) 77,833.90,770, 829.30 [27357, 22114.06, 1062]	*40.6*	1547/311
(101) Arvind Mills (10.30) 10.30, 10.70, 10.45 [39612,414.72, 131]	-	47/10
(10.45) 10.50, 10.60, 10.05, 10.50 [78132, 812.75, 245]		*4710L*
[477] Ashok Leyl (68.35) 68,67.50,69.85 [36872,2524.51,247]	*10.6**	159/34
(68.95) *67.15,69.50,67.15,69.25 [4462,3064,24,309]*	*10.5*	161/34
[820] Asian Paint (397.50) 390.50, 399.50, 396 [1584, 628.11, 55]	17.3*	501/221
(393.10) 392.05,400,390,395,15 [3731, 1471.13,69]	17.3	530/217
/26991] Atlas Copeo (124) *118.05L*, 124.25, 121.75 *[704,86.16,16]*	12.9	279/118
(123) *11320*, 124, *113.20, 120.60 [749,90.16,14]*	128	*281/113L*
(490) Bajaj AutO!(350.25) 349~ 352, 347.95, 351 [67814,23735.04,532]	6.8*	625/257
(350) *346..W*, 352.40, 346.10,350.45 [41225, 14430,94,344]	6.8	6291260
[120] Ballarpur In (61.50) 61, 58, 60.95 [44511,2646.69,290]	8.7	93/27
(61.55) 60.60, 61.70, 57.05, 60.15 [43894,2620.99,272]	8.6	96/27
[32134] Bank ofBaro (38.30) 38.30, 38.75, *37.75L*, *38.50 [39665*, 1519.96, 162]	*5.0*	88/38
(38.25) 38.15, 39; 25, 37.60, 38.75 [68906,2642.53,320]	*5.0*	88/37
[32149] Bank ofInd. (14.15) 14,14.15,13.90,14 [30595,427.95,87]	4.2	26/14
(14.05) 14, 14.25,13.85, *14.05* [54185, 759.71, 166]	4.2	*26/14L*
[42] BASF India (91) 90.10,91.75,90,90.50 [3895,352.48,55]	*11.0**	244/83
(90.95) 90,92, 88.50, 90.95 [4544,411.72,69]	11.1	252/84
[43] Bata India (80) 80.05,78.05, 79.20 [11904,944.34,151]	13.4	242/76
(80.65) 81.80, 81.80, 79.15, 80.45 [20677, 1654.99,267]	13.6	245/76
[44] Bausch & Lomb (42.30) 42.25,40.50,42.50 [12634, 526.29,97]	15.7*	188/38
(42.10) 42,43,41,42.15 [32744, 1368.43,212]	15.6	189/40
[493] Bharat Forge (184) 182.05,186, 180, 184 [7251, 1325.19, 124]	*11.0**	366/64
(184.05) 188,198.50,182,186.30 [16817, 3098.67, 194]	11.1	382/64
[547] Bharat Petro (157) 156.95,161,153.05, 160.10 [33671,5313.00,463]	32*	450/146
(156.20) 154.50, 160, 151.30, 158.95 [48607,7647,7647.17,517]	3.2	452/149
[103] BHEL (111.60) 111,112,40, 108,112 [555352,61409.76,2820]	4.3	350/82
(111.60) 110.15, 112.90, 108.10, 112.05 [558646,61885.30,3542]	4.3	394/83
[20] \ Born Dyeing (51) 50,52,49,51 [5438,2744.03,341]	*6.0**	80/33
(51.20) 51.50,51.75,49,55,51.35 [63533,3198.74,289]	6.1	82/33
[74] BPL Limited (153) 152.50, 155, 148.10, 154.05 [109655, 16573.65, 1118]	3.9*	636/140
(153.20) 150.10,154.60,148.10,152.80 [110351, 16659.73, 1143]	3.9	637/145
[825] Britania Ind (601) 600,570,598 [4858,2854.28, 123]	35.7*	1206/449
(590.40) 579,595,565, 589.80 [9058,5283.58,232]	35.3	1520/462

[390] BSES Ltd. (255.50) 254, 271, 251.10, 269+ [1070256,282605.89,6197]	12.4*	392/139
. (257.75) 255.25, 272.45, 254,10,269.10 [933001, 248056, 76,5274]	12.4	385/140
[76] Burrough Wel (314.70) 310,312,301,308.35 [3016. 931.86. 126]	9.6	800/290
(311.60) 305,310.60, 300.50, 309.20 [4037, 1243.21, 130]	9.7	810/291
[793] Cadbury (1) (822.60) 807, g1,O, 836.50 [2338, 1921.07,68]	54.2	1060/605
(823.55) 815,855,800.05,846,05 [2419,2011.23, 112]		
ET May 10th, 2000		

The first figure in brackets given in the attached Extract is the BSE Stock code. This is followed by the company's stock name like ACC or ABB Ltd. etc., then followed by previous day's closing price in brackets. The next four figures are to-day's opening, High, Low and closing.

The prices of today are followed in brackets by the volume of traded shares, Net traded value and the number of trades in that order.

The next line gives in italics the corresponding price on NSE for the same scrip. Then there is separate row for $P/_E$ Ratio, followed by the last row with the 52 week High and Low of the scrip. $P/_E$ is the ratio of the stock closing price to the Earnings per share (EPS). Here EPS is defined as the company's net profits in the last two half years, or 12 months or the last four quarters, (depending upon the availability of data) divided by the total number of outstanding shares. In case any company's name is under lined, that means that its closing price falls below the last offer price which is the price that the company has last offered its shares to the new or existing shareholders through public offer, rights issue or private placement.

In the event a scrip is quoting at a new high or new low, the entire line is shown in bold type with 'H' or 'L' next to the price. A significant change in price (3% rise or fall of 'A' group scrips or 15% change in the case of cash shares) is shown in BSE scrips with a Bold Type + or — after the figures depending upon whether it is rise or fall.

Main Indicators

Economic times gives regularly the data on major Indices and other Indices as shown below. The Tables provide the data on Index of today's prices (closing) as against the closings of the previous trading day and the percentage change over the day. These data relate to May 9, published in E.T. on May 10, 2000, presented here for illustration.

The prices of today are followed in brackets by the volume of traded shares, Net traded value and the number of trades in that order.

Table 47.9

May 2000 Data

Major Indices				Other Indices			
Index	***Today's***	***Previous***	***Chg.***	***Index***	***Today's***	***Previous***	***Chg.***
ET Mindex	4371.39	4187.29	184.10	BSE-500	1502.37	1468.05	34.32
ET Lifex	1354.43	1358.78	-4.35	BSE-100	2321.61	2265.84	55.77
ET Brandex	1103.06	1076.56	26.50	BSE-200	495.53	486.76	8.57
				Skindia GDR	956.30	1004.89	-48.59
BSE Sensex	4578.49	4463.40	115.09	DSE	916.89	905.61	11.28
S&P CNX Nifty	1378.55	1365.05	13.50	CSE	1979.63	1969.96	9.67
S&P CNX 500	1040.31	1018.75	21.56	MSE	5167.59	5074.11	93.48

ET MAY 10TH, 2000

Among the major Indices, the three Indices of ET and BSE sensex BSE 100 BSE 200 and BSE 500 are given alongwith S&PCNX Nifty, S&P CNX 500, Skindia GDR, DSE, CSE and MSE Indices. The last three namely DSE, CSE and MSE Indices belong to the three major stock Exchanges of Delhi, Kolkata and Chennai. The Skindia GDR traces out the prices of Indian Companies' GDRs traded and quoted abroad. This index shows a fall of 48 points on May 9, 2000, while the other Indices have all shown a rise barring the ET Lifex. (Table 47.9)

The fall in skindia GDR Index only shows that the foreign investors are guided by a separate set of factors. Infact this index showed a rise on May 8 when all other Indices showed a steep fall. On May 9, 2000, the declines were lower at 638 while the number of advances was higher at 688. The value of turnover was however lower in May 9, as compared to May 8. The uptrend in prices was around 2.6% - (a gain of 115 points in the Sensex) on May 9, as against a fall of nearly 5% on May 8, 2000. In 2010, the ET indices, SEP CNX 500, etc., are not published in the daily E.T. paper, but only BSE sensex x and NSE NIFTY are published daily.

Face Value

The face value of scrips varied from Rs. one to hundred and SEBI has allowed listed companies to have any face value dropping the fixed face value system of Rs. 10 in 1999. Some companies have shares of Rs. 1, Rs 2, Rs. 4, Rs. 5 Rs. 20, Rs. 50 and Rs. 100, while a vast majority continued to have Rs. 10 as face value. Such changes in face value are indicated by suitable asterix. Scrips having quotes below the face value are not shown and included in New Highs and New lows. An Astertix against $P/_E$ ratio indicates, that the Earnings data relate to the last four quarters.

Market Macro Indicators

The BSE also gives the $P/_E$ ratio jointly for all the sensex companies on a daily basis as also for the National Index (100). On similar lines, the ratio of market price to book value for all sensex companies together is also provided in the BSE. These aggregate $P/_E$ ratios and price to book value ratios in respect of BSE sensitive series (30) and BSE National Series (100) are useful as bench marks indicative of the market performance relative to the corporate fundamentals, as reflected in EPS and Book value etc.

As important Indicators of BSE, the RBI published the following data in its Annual Reports. For the selected years, the data in respect of BSE activity are presented here. Similar data for NSE are also published by the RBI.

Table 47.10

	1998-99	1997-98	2000-01	2001-02	2006-07	2008-09
(1) BSE Sensex (Average)	3294.78	3812.86	4269	3332	12277	12366
(2) Price Earnings Ratio (relating to sensex)	12.86	14.51	23.9	16.6	20.3	13.7
(3) Price-Book value Ratio (relating to sensex)	2.26	2.73	3.6	2.4	5.1	2.7
(4) Yield percent per annum	1.82	1.53	1.3	2.0	1.3	1.8
(5) Turnover (Rs. crores) (cash)	3,11, 999	2,07, 845	10,00,031	3,07,292	9,56,185	1,100,074
(6) Market capitalisation (Rs. crores) at end March	5,42, 942	5,60, 325	5,71,563	6,12,224	35,45,041	30,86,076

Source: RBI– Annual Reports

Badla Statistics

Reference was made earlier to carry forward business permitted in about 150 scrips in 'A' group on a weekly basis on the BSE until 2001. Net outstanding short sales and net long purchases were permitted to be carried forward on the settlement day once in a week on the last trading day. For the purpose of carry forward, the stock Exchange fixes the clearing rate which is almost the same as the closing rate on the last trading day for each of the scrips. The data shows the closing price on the last trading day and clearing rate fixed for carry forward. The badla rate, High and low and weighted average badla rate in Rs. for each of the scrips were also published. Total outstanding quantity, net outstanding quantity carry forward purchase and sale quantities and net outstanding *value* of scrips carried forward are all presented. Net outstanding position, scripwise can be seen, as also overall position from the published data. The larger the net outstandings, the better is supposed to be interest in a given scrip. Badla rate will depend partly on the cost of funds borrowed from the money market. More importantly it also depends on the net technical position in the market. If funds are available cheaply, there will be lower badla rates and larger carry forward and better sentiment. Liquidity flow is the basis for this. Badla rates also depended on the many market conditions. This discussion of Badla is only for historical record and has no application to the present day practices.

Generally, as it is easy to borrow funds than borrowing scrips, net outstanding purchases will be more than net outstanding sales in any scrip. If in any scrip, the net outstanding position is small as in the case of ABB Ltd, Arvind Mills and Asian paints, it must be due to lack of interest in the scrip and badla rates for these scrips will be high as few badla financiers are interested in them. The supply will be less relative to demand for them for badla finance. But in respect of popular scrips like ACC Appollo Tyres etc., the badla rates will be relatively low; long positions are high relatively both in the volume and value and the companies are fundamentally good to hold.

The higher Badla rate 52 paise in respect of Bajaj Auto is due to its high price of Rs. 350/=. High priced scrips will attract higher badla rates. Satyam computer which has a high price of about Rs. 3275 per share (not seen in the Table), the badla rate is as high as Rs. 33.52. Similar is the case of wipro at a rate of Rs. 32.30. The exception is the case of Hindustan Lever (HLL not shown in the Table) where the badla rate is low at Rs. 3.14 for a share price of Rs. 2540, due to the fact that there was a lower number of shares to be carried forward, decline in long positions and rise in short positions. If there are short positions to be used for offsetting long positions there will be lower badla rates for such scrips.

It will thus be seen that there are a wide variety of factors which influence Badla rates and that these are not expressed in percentage per annum, but in terms of Rupees and paise per share for a fortnight or three weeks, after which the positions will be reversed again. Badla if borrowed in money terms for long positions or borrowed in terms of shares for short position are for periods of 15 to 20 days for each settlement. Borrowing shares for carry forward is part of the Badla business which NSE arranges under what is called Automatic Lending and Borrowing scheme (ALBS).

Just as Badla rates are difficult to interpret in terms of any one specific variable, Badla statistics is also a complicated set of data, amenable to various interpretations. Clearing rates for each settlement as compared to earlier settlements is one factor which has to be examined to interpret the trend. Secondly, the relative purchase and sale positions are another factor to be looked into. Thirdly whether net purchase position is growing or declining, how much is the short sale position in the same scrip and whether the short sales are growing and accumulating will be the additional questions to be answered. For these factors to be examined, the Analyst has to keep track of the Badla positions in each of the scrips in all the settlements in a continuous fashion and study them.

Some questions which an insider only can understand and the Stock Exchange authorities will know relate to the number of short sellers, the quantity of short sales in each scrip and whether they are naked short sales or covered etc. Similarly what are the net long purchase positions, whether they are cumulatively growing or declining for each of the members involved and any set of members, who are cornering these positions or acting in collusion to manipulate the prices and what is the level of long purchases that each member has got and for how many days that position is carried forward etc., are the other relevant questions to be investigated by the stock exchange Authorities and the SEBI.

If the market has to be sound, there should be both long purchases and short sales and no member or a group of members should accumulate any position, so as to adversely affect the net balance in the market. Besides and more importantly the concerned members involved in carry over position should be financially sound and viable. There should be no undue accumulation or liquidation of position all of a sudden. Generally market players know the other players in the market and their financial soundness. Financially weak members have to be avoided in this game, so as to avoid defaults and difficulties in payments. Shrewd players play safe here.

All the above information will be available with the Stock Exchange authorities and the major players in the Badla trade may know the answers to many of the above questions. But the general reader or ordinary investor will not be able to understand the inside position from the published data. For a shrewd analyst who has been on the Job for long, the likely trends in the performance of scrip prices and the technical position in the market etc. can be understood and forecasted through charts and moving Average methods in technical analysis. The technical position reflecting the daily demand and supply factors, prices and volume etc. depend on the prevailing long and short positions in each of the scrips and net outstanding position and floating stocks in the scrip and the members' position in the scrip and their financial backing etc. The Analyst should have a grasp of all these factors.

Badla trading was replaced by Compulosry Rolling Settlement System in most of the stocks during June - December 2001. Then the Badla data was stopped from publication. These have now only historical importance.

Table 47.11

BSE Badla Statistics For May 6, 2000 — Illustration

Sr. No.	Scrip	Closing Rate	Clearing Rate (Rs)	Badla Rate High	Badla Rate Low	Weighted Average Badla (Rs.)	Total Outstanding Quantity	Carry Forward Net Purchase	Carry Forward Net Sale	Net Outstanding Qty. (000)	Net Outstanding Value (Rs. Lakhs)
1.	ACC	124	125	1	0.06	0.17	2941463	2756323	54078	2706176	3387.59
2.	Abb Ltd.	168	169	0.35	0	0.26	238179	227520	2282	226780	383.85
3.	Amara Raja B	83	83	0.6	0.05	0.13	167969	153489	25540	152667	126.92
4.	Apollo Tyres	97	97	0.2	0.05	0.15	740920	717436	28625	675986	656.75
5.	Arvind Mills	10	10	0.02	0	0.01	1617657	1516752	7900	1599457	160.2
6.	Asian Paints	405	405	0.9	0	0.63	15851	14725	3374	14652	59.44
7.	Atlas Copco	121	121	0.34	–3.5	0.16	49164	38765	5717	47466	57.51
8.	Bajaj Auto	350	350	0.87	0.23	0.52	1150401	1110971	68524	1037348	3636.1
9.	Ballarpur In	56	57	0.11	0.02	0.07	1231035	1223658	17336	1328554	758.29
10.	Basf	91	91	0.2	0.01	0.14	311241	302291	1553	297052	270.75

Note: The date of data does not matter as it is for illustration and importance of Badla has now gone. These data were available upto 2000-2001. only.

Derivatives Trading

In the month of June 2000, both BSE and NSE started trading in Index Derivatives with three types of contracts, for futures namely one month, two months and three months. The trade data in this Section are published on a daily basis with information on Open, High, Low, Close, number of contracts, number of trades, value in Rs. and outstanding position in the market.

Under the futures head, the data on sensex futures, Nifty futures, equity futures on BSE and NSE which are traded currently are given now separately in the Daily press. Similarly under the head of options, sensex options, Nifty options and equity options on BSE and NSE are published in the daily press showing call options and put options separately. The data on futures presented include open with high, low, close, traded quantity and value, number of contracts etc., in respect of Futures. Similarly, under the head of options, both call and put options, the data furnished in the press include price, premium open, high, low, close, type of contract price, etc., number of contracts along with open interest and expiry dates, etc.

TRADING PATTERNS IN THE MARKETS

Since the last one and half decades, when the economic and financial reforms were started, there were major changes in the trading pattern on the stock and capital markets. The trading cycle, settlement and clearance were brought down in time taken due to demat form of trading, electronic clearance and settlement, etc. We have moved from T+14 settlement cycle to T+3 and in some cases to T+1 also. Badla trading was replaced by rolling settlement system and Automatic Borrowing and lending system substituted the Badla lending and borrowing of shares and naked short selling was banned which made the trading system more healthy and less time consuming.

Although there were 23 stock exchanges, nearly 80% of the volume of trading was concentrated in BSE and NSE. Of these, trading turnover in the NSE was more than in the BSE because of the larger volume of trade taking place and high networth companies traded and high networth members trading on the NSE. There was also a larger concentration of FFIs and FIIs and Indian FIs and MFs trading on the NSE, due to quicker systems and procedures prevailing there. On the other hand, the market capitalization was higher on the BSE due to larger number of companies listed there and their higher networth. The BSE has a hoary antiquity of trading and a credible system of settlement and clearance.

The importance of equity markets has grown vastly in the recent past and market, capitalization of the stock reached a level equivalent to that of GDP at current prices. When in January 2008, the sensex surpassed the level of 20,000, the market capitalization was much more than the GDP in India which compares very well with the advanced markets of Japan and the USA.

Another development is fastest growth of the Futures and Options markets, although they were started only in 2001 to 2003 in India. During 2007–08, for example, the turnover in the cash maket was about Rs. 35 lakh crores on the NSE, while the same in F&O segment, it was Rs. 131 lakh crores which was four times the turnover in the cash market. Besides, this is more so on the NSE, due to active participation of the foreign institutions and foreign investors there. In 2006-07, the turnover in the cash market was Rs. 19 lakh crores, but that in the derivative market had gone up to Rs. 74 lakh crores. This has declined relatively in 2008-09 due to bear phase in the market, following the global recession.

From the above discussion on the trading patterns on the stock exchanges, two prominent features are discernible. Firstly, the NSE has overtaken the BSE in the volume of trading and the value of trading in cash segment itself, although it was set only in 1994 as against the BSE which has a hoary antiquity of 150 years. Secondly, the turnover in the derivative segment is growing faster than in cash segment in general. But this is particularly visible on the NSE although they were started only decade ago in 2001. The Indian financial markets have now come of age and comparable to their Western counterparts in most aspects.